PQ 4-30-87

The Blackwell Encyclopaedia of
Political Thought

The Blackwell Encyclopaedia of
Political Thought

Edited by
David Miller

Advisory Editors
Janet Coleman
William Connolly
Alan Ryan

Blackwell Reference

First published 1987

Basil Blackwell Ltd
108 Cowley Road, Oxford, OX4 1JF, UK

Basil Blackwell Inc.
432 Park Avenue South, Suite 1503
New York, NY 10016, USA

British Library Cataloguing in Publication Data

The Blackwell encyclopaedia of political thought.
1. Political science — Dictionaries
I. Miller, David, *1946–*
320'.03'21   JA61

ISBN 0-631-14011-5

Library of Congress Cataloging in Publication Data

The Blackwell encyclopaedia of political thought.
Bibliography: p.
Includes index.
1. Political science — Dictionaries. I. Miller,
David (David Leslie)
JA61.B57   1987   320'.03'21   86-29972
ISBN 0-631-14011-5

Typeset in 9½ on 11pt Linotron Ehrhardt
by Oxford Publishing Services, Oxford
Printed in Great Britain by Butler and Tanner Ltd, Frome, Somerset

Contents

Preface

This *Encyclopaedia* provides the student (whether professional or amateur) of political thought with a reliable guide to the major ideas and doctrines that influence the contemporary world; it outlines the thought of leading political theorists, past and present, and considers the ways in which thinking about politics has evolved historically. We have confined our attention largely to the western tradition of political thought – although we have included survey articles on Chinese, Hindu and Islamic political thought which we hope will introduce the reader to these non-western traditions, we make no claim to comprehensive coverage. We have included the thought of philosophers, historians, lawyers, economists and sociologists only when they have made some direct contribution to political debate. In order to keep entries on individual thinkers within reasonable bounds, we have made extensive use of survey articles to cover major episodes in political thought (e.g. the Greeks, the Renaissance) and major traditions (e.g. liberalism, Marxism); minor figures falling within the scope of such articles are given two or three lines and cross-referenced. Finally, we have not attempted to deal comprehensively with the specialist literature of modern political institutions, this being the purpose of a forthcoming companion volume, *The Blackwell Encyclopaedia of Political Institutions*.

Writing about political ideas is in a small way itself a political activity. Our policy has been to select the best contributor for each topic regardless of academic or political allegiance, and to place no restrictions on choice of approach. We believe that the outcome is a collection of articles that are authoritative without being dull or stereotyped. But the attentive reader will soon become aware that few political ideas can be given a simple, straightforward definition; nor can there be uncontroversial readings of the works of political thinkers. This is uncomfortable terrain for those who believe that to every question there is one right answer. If, besides being informative, we have succeeded in communicating something of the open-endedness of political thinking in the articles that follow, we shall feel doubly pleased.

DLM
JC
WEC
AR

October 1986

Contributors

Aziz Al-Azmeh   **AA**
University of Exeter

Julia Annas   **JEA**
St Hugh's College, Oxford

Peter D. Anthony   **PDA**
University College, Cardiff

Shlomo Avineri   **SA**
Hebrew University of Jerusalem

Terence Ball   **TB**
University of Minnesota

Benjamin R. Barber   **BRB**
Rutgers University

Rodney Barker   **RB**
University of London

Jonathan Barnes   **JB**
Balliol College, Oxford

Brian Barry   **BMB**
California Institute of Technology

David Beetham   **DB**
University of Leeds

Ronald Beiner   **RSB**
University of Toronto

Richard Bellamy   **RPB**
Nuffield College, Oxford

Antony Black   **AB**
University of Dundee

Anthony Brewer   **AAB**
University of Bristol

Alison Brown   **ABr**
University of London

J. H. Burns   **JHB**
University of London

J. Burrow   **JWB**
University of Sussex

Margaret Canovan   **MEC**
University of Keele

April Carter   **AFC**
Banbury, Oxon.

Terrell Carver   **TC**
University of Bristol

Alan Cawson   **AC**
University of Sussex

Janet Coleman   **JC**
University of Exeter

William E. Connolly   **WEC**
The Johns Hopkins University

Diana Coole   **DHC**
University of Leeds

James Cotton   **JSC**
University of Newcastle upon Tyne

Maurice Cranston   **MC**
University of London

Michael H. Crawford **MHC**
Christ's College, Cambridge

Alfonso J. Damico **AJD**
University of Florida

Mark Davie **MD**
University of Liverpool

R. W. Davies **RWD**
University of Birmingham

Graeme Duncan **GCD**
University of Queensland

Robert Eccleshall **RRE**
Queen's University of Belfast

Daniel Eilon **DE**
University of Warwick

Jean Bethke Elshtain **JBE**
University of Massachusetts

Joseph V. Femia **JVF**
University of Liverpool

Moses Finley **MIF**

Murray Forsyth **MGF**
University of Leicester

Elizabeth Fox-Genovese **EF-G**
Emory University

Michael S. Freeden **MSF**
Mansfield College, Oxford

R. G. Frey **RGF**
Bowling Green State University, Ohio

Richard B. Friedman **RBF**
State University of New York at Buffalo

Ruth Gavison **RG**
Hebrew University of Jerusalem

Irene L. Gendzier **ILG**
Boston University

Norman Geras **NG**
University of Manchester

Alan Gewirth **AG**
University of Chicago

Alan H. Goldman **AHG**
University of Miami

Jack A. Goldstone **JAG**
Northwestern University, Illinois

Barbara Goodwin **BG**
Brunel University

David Gordon **DG**
Institute of Humane Studies, Menlo Park, California

John G. Gunnell **JGG**
State University of New York at Albany

Amy Gutmann **AGu**
Princeton University

Peter Halfpenny **PH**
University of Manchester

John A. Hall **JAH**
University of Southampton

Joseph Hamburger **JH**
Yale University

Iain Hampsher-Monk **IWH-M**
University of Exeter

Neil Harding **NH**
University College of Swansea

Christopher Harvie **CTH**
University of Tübingen

Roger Hausheer **RNH**
University of Bradford

Jack E. S. Hayward **JESH**
University of Hull

Arnold Heertje **AH**
University of Amsterdam

Harro Höpfl **HMH**
University of Lancaster

Thomas A. Horne **TAH**
University of Tulsa

John Horton **JPH**
University of York

S. L. Jenkinson **SLJ**
Polytechnic of North London

James Turner Johnson   **JTJ**
Rutgers University

Peter Jones **PJ**
University of Newcastle upon Tyne

Eugene Kamenka **EK**
Australian National University

David Kettler· **DK**
Trent University, Ontario

Jerome B. King **JBK**
University of Massachusetts

Preston King **PK**
University of Lancaster

Baruch Knei-Paz **BK**
Hebrew University of Jerusalem

Isaac Kramnick **IK**
Cornell University

Nicola Lacey **NML**
New College, Oxford

A. Laurence Le Quesne   **ALLeQ**
Shrewsbury

Jack Lively **JL**
University of Warwick

Steven Lukes **SL**
Balliol College, Oxford

Neil MacCormick   **NMacC**
University of Edinburgh

Don Markwell **DJM**
Merton College, Oxford

Geoffrey Marshall   **GM**
The Queen's College, Oxford

Roger D. Masters **RDM**
Dartmouth College, New Hampshire

David McLellan **DTMcL**
University of Kent at Canterbury

Robert J. McShea **RJMcS**
Boston University

Wilson C. McWilliams   **WCMcW**
Rutgers University

Keith Middlemas **KM**
University of Sussex

David Miller **DLM**
Nuffield College, Oxford

Robin Milner-Gulland   **RRM-G**
University of Sussex

Cary J. Nederman   **CJN**
University of Canterbury, NZ

Robert Nisbet **RN**
Columbia University

Noel O'Sullivan   **NO'S**
University of Hull

William Outhwaite   **WO**
University of Sussex

Thomas L. Pangle   **TLP**
University of Toronto

Bhikhu C. Parekh   **BCP**
University of Hull

David Parker **DP**
University of Leeds

Geraint Parry   **GP**
University of Manchester

Mark Philp **MP**
Oriel College, Oxford

Hanna Fenichel Pitkin   **HFP**
University of California, Berkeley

Raymond Plant   **RP**
University of Southampton

Leon Pompa **LP**
University of Birmingham

David Paul Rebovich   **DPR**
Rider College, New Jersey

Andrew Reeve   **AWR**
University of Warwick

Melvin Richter   **MR**
City University of New York

CONTRIBUTORS

Patrick Riley **PR**
University of Wisconsin

Alan Ritter **AIR**
University of Connecticut

John C. Robertson **JCR**
St Hugh's College, Oxford

F. Rosen **FR**
University of London

Nancy L. Rosenblum **NLR**
Brown University

Alan Ryan **AR**
New College, Oxford

Lyman Tower Sargent **LTS**
University of Missouri, St Louis

David Lewis Schaefer **DLS**
College of the Holy Cross, Massachusetts

Gordon J. Schochet **GJS**
Rutgers University

Morton Schoolman **MS**
State University of New York at Albany

R. Andrew Sharp **RAS**
University of Auckland

Jeremy Shearmur **JS**
*Centre for Policy Studies, London and
    University of Manchester*

Garrett W. Sheldon **GS**
University of Virginia

L. A. Siedentop **LAS**
Keble College, Oxford

G. W. Smith **GWS**
University of Lancaster

John Stanley **JLS**
University of California, Riverside

Peter G. Stein **PGS**
Queens' College, Cambridge

Hillel Steiner **HS**
University of Manchester

Zeev Sternhell **ZS**
Hebrew University of Jerusalem

Tracy B. Strong **TBS**
University of California, San Diego

Barbara Taylor **BGT**
Bulmershe College of Higher Education

Keith Taylor **KT**
Coventry (Lanchester) Polytechnic

Richard Tuck **RFT**
Jesus College, Cambridge

James Tully **JT**
McGill University

Ursula Vögel **UV**
University of Manchester

Jeremy Waldron **JJW**
*University of Edinburgh and University of
    California, Berkeley*

Albert Weale **APW**
University of East Anglia

Stephen K. White **SKW**
*Virginia Polytechnic Institute and State
    University*

Beryl Williams **BW**
University of Sussex

Donald Winch **DNW**
University of Sussex

Markus H. Wörner **MHW**
Free University, Berlin

Anthony Wright **AWW**
University of Birmingham

John Zvesper **JZ**
University of East Anglia

Editorial Notes

1   It is important to make full use of the cross-referencing system. In each entry capitals are used to indicate other entries where fuller information can be found. Consult the index for a complete list of references to a particular topic or person.

2   Each entry is followed by a reading list that includes modern English language editions (where these exist) of the texts referred to in the entry, as well as relevant secondary literature. Material that is especially suitable for further reading is indicated by a dagger (†).

3   When a particular text is discussed in an entry the date of first publication is given in brackets. (Occasionally, in cases where the text remained unpublished for a long period, the date given is the date of composition.) Texts given in the reading list but not otherwise mentioned have the original date (if this differs from that of the edition cited) in brackets after the title.

4   Sources of quotations are normally indicated simply by author's name and a page number; full details are given in the reading list. If two or more works by the same author appear in the list a short title is used to avoid ambiguity.

A

absolutism The term now has no precise meaning. It is loosely applied to governments exercising power without representative institutions or constitutional restraints. Though often used today as a synonym for tyranny or despotism 'absolutism' is usually applied to early modern states. As a member of a family of regime types it was joined in the nineteenth century by Bonapartism or Caesarism; and in the twentieth, by totalitarianism. All regime types in this family have generated analogous discussions about the questions of whether absolute or total power was ever in fact attained, or is in principle attainable. (See also DESPOTISM and TOTALITARIANISM.)

The term first appeared in French in about 1796 and in English and German in about 1830. Like 'enlightened despotism' it was a neologism coined by historians after the disappearance of the phenomenon it was meant to designate. During the nineteenth century it was for the most part used pejoratively. It is still used by historians of political theory, and by those concerned with the emergence of states from the sixteenth to the eighteenth centuries. On the one side absolutism figures in discussions of sovereignty, constitutionalism, rights, resistance, and property; on the other it figures in historiographical disputes among non-Marxist and Marxist historians about the dating, functions, and class or social basis of the period once described as the age of absolutism (1648–1789). Some non-Marxist historians regard absolutism as a contested concept better rendered as absolute monarchy.

Historians of political and legal thought have learned to exercise caution when treating both the disputes occasioned by more centralized and efficient monarchies and the theories used to legitimate or to assail them. At issue is the meaning of the language used by early modern theorists and the degree of actual unrestrained power attained in the practices of the regimes they designated. The most prominent advocates of absolutism among political theorists were BODIN and Bossuet in France, HOBBES and FILMER in England. In discussing the contested concepts used by and about them, Daly has proposed that analysts ask the following questions about uses of the words absolute and absolutism in the seventeenth-century political vocabulary:

[W]hat does the user mean? In what part of the century is he speaking? What party, or faction does he belong to? . . . [Is he saying] That the king has no superior? Or is not elected? Or cannot be resisted? Does 'absolute' refer to the king's power to occupy the throne, or to the extent of power the throne gives him? Does it refer to a particular legal right or to the form of government? Does it denote a monarch's right to raise taxes and make law without consent? (pp. 249–50)

Jean Bodin was the most important theorist of SOVEREIGNTY. The disorders of his time in France led him to assume the need to concentrate authority in a centralized state. Political and social stability, he held, required that in every state there be a supreme or sovereign authority, unlimited in its jurisdiction and perpetual in its exercise of power. Sovereignty did not imply for Bodin unlimited power over the persons and property of subjects. The sovereign was subject to limitations imposed by natural law and fundamental customary law (e.g. consent to taxation). But neither natural nor customary law might be enforced by the

1

community; legally, a sovereign could not be resisted or deposed. Sovereignty is absolute and indivisible. Either the prince of an independent state is absolute, or else he is subject to some other power such as the estates, which is then sovereign.

A more theological version of absolutist theory was that of Bishop Bossuet, a contemporary of Louis XIV. Bossuet combined traditional scriptural and metaphorical concepts with newer juridical and Hobbesian arguments. Applying a mode of thought long familiar in France, Bossuet treated the king as placed by God in a position to advance the public interest, as well as to protect humble subjects from local tyrants. Such functions require a powerful central authority. Bossuet went on to claim for the king in the state the same position as that held by God in the universe. A Hobbesian argument was added by Bossuet when he claimed that everyone in the state gains security by surrendering to the sovereign all individual rights. The monarchy, like God, is both constitutive and directive; it alone preserves the people from anarchy. Bossuet multiplied moral injunctions to the king: he should rule in ways at once beneficent and disinterested; he should follow established law; he should remember that God will judge him.

Although 'absolutism' was a nineteenth-century coinage in English, the term absolute was hotly disputed in sixteenth- and seventeenth-century political and legal discussions of absolute monarchy. In Tudor England Sir Thomas Smith could use the word absolute in both pejorative and laudatory senses. He blamed Louis XI for changing France from a 'lawful and regular raigne' to 'absolute and tyrannical power and government'. But Smith proudly ascribed to Parliament 'the most high and absolute power of the realm of Englande' (see Daly, pp. 228–9).

Ambiguities in Tudor political uses of 'absolute' gave way in the seventeenth century to sharply focused disagreements during the Civil War and after. Parliamentary writers equated absolute power with tyranny or oriental despotism. They refused to allow that the king had any absolute right to obedience.

Samuel Rutherford wrote that 'an absolute unlimited monarchy . . . is the worst form of government' (see Daly, p. 237).

Although Civil War royalist writers agreed about the powers of the king they did not all concur in describing these powers as absolute. Some who held that England was a monarchy limited by law denied that the king had arbitrary power to legislate at his 'will and pleasure'. Even Henry Ferne, when arguing for complete and passive obedience, denied that non-resistance implied absolute monarchy: 'It is not the denial of resistance that makes a monarch absolute, but the denial of a law to bound his will'. Other royalist theorists, after the Restoration, argued that the king's powers were absolute in the sense that they could not be limited by law.

The two best-known theorists to argue that the king's powers were both absolute and arbitrary were Hobbes and Filmer, both of whom applied Bodin's theory of sovereignty to England. Hobbes ascribed exclusive, unlimited, and irresistible power to the 'absolute sovereign', whether king or assembly. He also tried to remove the distinction between limited and absolute monarchy by denying that tyranny meant anything more than monarchy disliked.

Hobbes's theory of sovereignty was shared by Sir Robert Filmer, who almost alone among royalists went on to describe the monarchy as arbitrary in the sense that the king could do whatever he wished. This went beyond denying that any legal limitation could be placed upon the sovereign, or the positive assertion that the king could exercise powers belonging to him. Filmer, like Hobbes, denied that tyranny was a meaningful term. Filmer also identified the powers of kings with those of fathers as being alike natural and bestowed by God.

These positions offered opportunities to Filmer's Whig critics. LOCKE attacked Filmer's identification of absolute with arbitrary monarchy as incompatible with civil society and as no form of civil government. While found among orientals, such as the Turks, such rule was despotic. Englishmen could not accept what Filmer advocated, described by Locke as:

a Divine unalterable Right of Sovereignty, whereby a Father or Prince hath an Absolute, Arbitrary, Unlimited, and Unlimitable Power, over the Lives,

Liberties, and Estates of his Children and Subjects; so that he may take or alienate their Estates, sell, castrate, or use their Persons as he pleases, they being all his Slaves, and he Lord or Proprietor of everything, and his unbounded Will their Law (Locke, *First Treatise*, §9).

After 1689, the term absolute rule became emptied of any practical, political significance in England. The same was not true in North America, where, equated with absolute tyranny and absolute despotism, it appeared in the Declaration of Independence.

Today absolutism is mainly a subject of debate among historians. Marxists continue to search for the class basis of absolutist states. Among non-Marxist historians there has emerged a consensus that the absolutist monarchies of Europe never succeeded in freeing themselves from restraints on the effective exercise of their power by traditional practices, combinations of social forces, and the laws or institutions inherited from the past (see Durand and Vierhaus). Nowhere was complete freedom of action attained, not even in France under Louis XIV whose reign is often used as the model or embodiment of absolutism. At the time when absolute sovereign power was exalted by political theorists as never before, those older orders and estates that were losing power nevertheless succeeded in preventing the victory of absolutism. What remains to be explained about this outcome is the significance of those theorists who criticized or provided alternatives to the political theory of absolutism.

MR

Reading
Bodin, J.: *The Six Books of a Commonweal* (1576), trans. R. Knolles, ed. K.D. McRae. Cambridge, Mass.: Harvard University Press, 1962.
†Daly, J.: The idea of absolute monarchy in seventeenth-century England. *Historical Journal* 21 (1978) 227–50.
†Durand, G.: What is absolutism? In *Louis XIV and Absolutism*, ed. R. Hutton. Columbus, Ohio: Columbia University Press, 1976.
Filmer, R.: *Patriarcha and other political works* (1647–52), ed. and intro. P. Laslett. Oxford: Blackwell, 1949.
†Franklin, J.: *Jean Bodin and the Rise of Absolutist Theory in France*. Cambridge: Cambridge University Press, 1973.
Hobbes, T.: *Leviathan* (1651), ed. C.B. Macpherson. Harmondsworth: Penguin, 1968.
Keohane, N.: *Philosophy of the State in France*. Princeton, NJ: Princeton University Press, 1980.
Locke, J.: *Two Treatises of Government* (1689), ed. P. Laslett. New York: Mentor, 1965.
Rowen, H.H.: Louis XIV and absolutism. In *Louis XIV and the Craft of Rulership*, ed. J.C. Rule, Columbus, Ohio: Ohio State University Press, 1969.
†Vierhaus, R.: Absolutism. In *Marxism, Communism and Western Society*, vol. I. New York: Herder & Herder, 1972.

Acton, John Emerich Dalberg, 1st Baron (1834–1902) British historian. Acton was born into a Shropshire Catholic gentry family with strong Bavarian and Neapolitan connections, and succeeded to the family baronetcy at the age of three. On account of his religion, he did not go to an English university but studied in Munich under the historian Düllinger. Acton moved in high social and political circles; he was the stepson of the foreign secretary Lord Granville and an intimate of Gladstone, and became a lord-in-waiting to Queen Victoria. He served as Whig MP for Carlow (1859–68) and was raised to the peerage in 1869. He was in Rome for the Second Vatican Council and was a leading opponent of the declaration of Papal Infallibility in 1870. He owned and edited the Catholic journal *The Rambler* (later *The Home and Foreign Review*). In 1895 he was appointed to the Regius chair of history at Cambridge, which he occupied until his death. The chief monument of this last period of life is his work for the *Cambridge Modern History*. For most of his life Acton worked as a scholar of private means, independent of academic institutions. His projected History of Liberty was never written, and his published work consists essentially of lectures and articles. As a historian he is remembered for his concept of the historian's role as that of impartial judge and moral censor.

Acton's political ideas derive chiefly from the Whig tradition, most notably from BURKE, supplemented by the influence exercised on him, as on many intellectual liberals of his generation, by TOCQUEVILLE. Acton was a strong opponent of the concept of unlimited popular sovereignty, which he traced to Rousseau and the French Revolution and which he saw as absolutist and tyrannical. He has been regarded by some as a prophet and critic of

TOTALITARIANISM. His own allegiance was given to the notion that liberty was secured by countervailing powers, in a manner which represented an extension of English Whig notions of constitutional balance. He was only rather idiosyncratically related to the English Whig tradition, however. He saw the Catholic church in the past as the guardian of liberty, through its assertion of the superior claims of spiritual interests, which he tended to identify with the supremacy of conscience, and through its function as a buffer against the unlimited sovereign power of the secular state.

Acton also celebrated the right to freedom of conscience asserted in the Puritan tradition, especially as manifested in the American Revolution. In modern times he saw liberty as endangered by what he considered to be the rival doctrine of equality, with its tendency to erode independent centres of power and to promote the authority of the state. He was at the same time a strong critic of the authoritarian tendencies of nationalism when embodied in the centralized nation-state. Chiefly through the work of his pupil J. N. Figgis, Acton had some influence on the doctrines of political PLURALISM which were emerging during the early years of the twentieth century. Acton's own writing tends to be diffuse and not always easy to interpret, being rich and allusive rather than precise and systematic.   JWB

Reading

Acton, Lord: *Essays on Freedom and Power*, ed. G. Himmelfarb. London: Meridian, 1956.

———: *Essays on Church and State*, ed. D. Woodruff. London: Hollis, 1952.

†Himmelfarb, G.: *Lord Acton: a study in conscience and politics*. London: Routledge, 1952.

†Matthew, D.: *Lord Acton and his Times*. London: Eyre & Spottiswoode, 1968.

Adams, John (1735–1826)   American statesman and political philosopher; president of the United States, 1797–1801. Although Adams was a leader of the Federalist movement (which projected and established the American Constitution of 1787), his recognition of the irrational element of political psychology led him into profound disagreement with the more orthodox Federalism of HAMILTON and MADISON. These disagreements are already visible in his *Thoughts on Government*, a revolutionary pamphlet published in 1776, but they are clearest in his *Defence of the Constitutions of Government of the United States* (1787) and *Discourses of Davila* (1791). His contemporaries' concern with constructing political solutions to conflicts arising out of selfish economic motivations appeared somewhat superficial to Adams. The fundamental human motivation, he thought, was not economic self-interest but 'the passion for distinction'. This passion made men social creatures, although not particularly benevolent ones. The search for esteem could take the form of a desire for fame (hence 'your patriots and heroes, and most of the great benefactors to mankind'), but this drive for approbation was also expressed in economic ambition (*Works*, VI, pp. 232–63). Whatever form the passion took, it remained insatiable and irrational. Therefore it could not be relied upon to produce good government by means of representative schemes such as the one defended by Hamilton and Madison in *The Federalist*, or Jefferson's 'natural aristocracy', for there was no way to ensure that the people would defer to the truly talented and virtuous rather than to the merely rich or well-born (*Works*, VI, pp. 249–50; *Adams-Jefferson Letters*, II, pp. 397–402).

All Federalist thinking had retreated in the 1780s from the republican idealism of 1776. Adams's disillusionment with revolutionary republicanism was simply more profound and more comprehensive. Given his political psychology, a loss of faith in the republican virtue of the American people dictated a return to the idea of a mixed regime. Adams defended the constitutions of the individual states only in so far as they embodied this idea. He interpreted the bicameral legislatures of the states as devices to contain and to balance the aristocratic, socially successful class and the democratic, socially aspiring class. Since neither class sought the public interest, and since the balance between the two was not automatic, a good constitution also had to include an executive (a monarch) powerful enough to mediate between the aristocracy and the democracy. Adams interpreted the Constitution of 1787 in the same terms. He did not recommend hereditary monarchy and aristocracy (although he thought that these would probably come to America in time), but he insistently interpreted the articulation of American governments in terms of the social hierarchy produced by irrational deference. This made his political thought extremely unpopular. Americans were not prepared to be quite so realistic, and they were still firmly republican. Adams was therefore an isolated thinker, who is often studied as an illuminating contrast to his more influential contemporaries.

JZ

Reading

Adams, C.F. ed.: *The Works of John Adams*. 10 vols. Boston, Mass.: Little, Brown, 1850–6.

†Cappon, L.J. ed.: *The Adams-Jefferson Letters*. 2 vols. Chapel Hill, NC: University of North Carolina Press, 1959.

Howe, J.R. Jr: *The Changing Political Thought of John Adams*. Princeton, NJ: Princeton University Press, 1966.

Paynter, J.: John Adams: on the principles of political science. *Political Science Reviewer* 6 (1976) 35–72.

Wood, G.S.: *The Creation of the American Republic*. Chapel Hill, NC: University of North Carolina Press, 1969.

Zvesper, J.: *Political Philosophy and Rhetoric: a Study of the Origins of American Party Politics*. Cambridge: Cambridge University Press, 1977.

Adorno, Theodor (1903–1969) German philosopher. A leading member of the Frankfurt School, interested chiefly in philosophy and cultural criticism. See CRITICAL THEORY.

Alembert, Jean le Rond d' (1717–1783) French philosopher. D'Alembert, who won early fame as a mathematician and geometer, was the most strictly rationalistic of the eighteenth-century *philosophes*, the true bearer of Descartes's message of the importance of 'clear and distinct ideas'. His views on politics and society reflect his demand for order in all things. He agreed with VOLTAIRE about the desirability of royal absolutism, not from any sentimental attachment to monarchy but because he thought it offered the best prospect of systematic rule. D'Alembert further believed, with PLATO, that rational government would be best secured if the most rational men, namely philosophers like himself, were put in

charge of the king's government. He did rather less theorizing about politics than other *Encyclopédistes*, but took more action to put his ideas into effect, for d'Alembert occupied a privileged position in the scientific establishment of France, and he used it to promote like-minded intellectuals to key positions in the kingdom (see FRENCH ENLIGHTENMENT).

He was a man of frail physique, having started life as an orphan abandoned on the steps of the church of St Jean le Rond in Paris. Although he was later claimed by his natural father, and given a good education, he did not grow to full stature and was considered by such friends as DIDEROT and ROUSSEAU to be excessively discreet, if not pusillanimous, in his dealings with authority. D'Alembert, on his side, mistrusted the imagination and spiritual fire which prompted Rousseau and Diderot to their brave deeds; he saw no advantage to be gained from defiance of the censorship.

Even so, d'Alembert did not respond as did some other *philosophes* to the advances of such powerful foreign monarchs as Frederick of Prussia or Catherine of Russia, both of whom tried to enlist him in their service. He respected their rank, but had no illusions about their intelligence. Moreover, d'Alembert had a sincere attachment to the principle of liberty, and could never share the hope that such enlightened despots as Frederick might be made to serve the interests of freedom.

He was noted for his personal loyalty; until middle age he continued to live with his foster mother, then he moved in with his platonic mistress, Julie de l'Espinasse, and in his writings he urged all French intellectuals to work and stick together, instead of destroying their influence by internecine fighting. He had an exalted conception of the 'republic of letters', which contrasted oddly with his cold view of any other kind of republic. He detested priests; but he looked forward to a world where intellectuals acted as secular priests in society as well as administrators in the state.

MC

Reading

Alembert, J. d': *Oeuvres de d'Alembert*, ed. J.F. Bastien. Paris, 1803.

†Grimsley, R.: *Jean d'Alembert*. Oxford: Clarendon Press, 1963.

ALIENATION

Pappas, J.N.: *Voltaire and d'Alembert*. Bloomington, Ind.: Indiana University Press, 1962.

alienation A central concept in modern social and political theory, in theology, and in sociology and psychology. Most simply stated, alienation refers to the condition of separation or estrangement. The term derives from the Latin verb *alienare*, to separate, remove or take away. Alienation originally referred to the transfer of one person's property to another but gradually it acquired a wider range of reference and came to be associated with the removability or irremovability of such non-material possessions as rights and liberties and with the features or properties which we are said to share by virtue of being citizens or human beings. Hence, in eighteenth-century usage, an 'inalienable right' was one that could not be alienated, i.e. traded, transferred, sold, or otherwise parted with in such a way as to deprive one's heirs. These earlier meanings survive today in the language of the law, in which property (and affections) are still said to be 'alienable'. This is not, however, the sense in which the term has come to be used in modern social theory. In the last two centuries alienation has acquired still other meanings, several of which will be discussed below. The popularity and currency of these modern meanings is a relatively recent development. The 1930 *Encyclopaedia of the Social Sciences*, for example, contains an article on 'Alienation of property' – that is, on alienation in its older legal sense – but none on alienation in any of its more modern philosophical, psychological, and sociological senses. By contrast its successor, the *International Encyclopedia of the Social Sciences*, includes a lengthy entry on alienation (see Lichtheim).

If anything, alienation has in recent years suffered from a surfeit of meaning. For some it is an analytical concept in sociology, for others a synonym for vague feelings of *angst* or even *ennui*, and for yet others a central concept in critical theory. So diverse and varied have these meanings become that some contemporary commentators have suggested that the term has become virtually meaningless, a 'fetish word' for which 'people seem to delight in finding ever different uses'. 'Using the term "alienation" without explaining any further what one has in mind communicates little more today than does tapping one's glass with one's spoon at a banquet; neither does much more than attract attention' (Schacht, pp. 244–5). Some critics have even suggested that the term be abandoned altogether.

Such a proposal is both extreme and unnecessary. For while it is true that quite different accounts of alienation are offered by Christian theologians, by Hegel and Marx, and by modern existentialists, psychologists, and sociologists, these can be compared, contrasted, and assessed according to the ways in which each answers the following questions: Who, exactly, is said to be separated from what (or whom)? What is the occasion or cause of this separation? What is the result or outcome of this condition of estrangement? Is this condition a good thing, a bad thing, or neither? Is its occurrence inevitable, or is it avoidable? Can the condition of alienation be corrected or overcome? By what means might this condition be overcome? Assuming that alienation can be overcome, what would non-alienated existence look like? Different accounts of alienation supply quite different answers to these questions.

In its traditional Christian-theological version, for example, alienation refers to man's estrangement from God. Brought about and maintained by sin, such separation results in human unhappiness and a longing for oneness with God. Although undesirable, this condition is, for human beings, an inevitable one. It can, however, be overcome by begging God's forgiveness and accepting Christ as one's saviour. What such non-alienated existence would look like, no one can say with any certainty, since no human is capable of attaining such bliss or oneness in this life. There are, of course, many sectarian variations upon these themes.

In its numerous non-theological versions alienation refers to man's estrangement from himself, from other human beings, and/or from certain human potentials. Two of the more important and influential accounts are offered by HEGEL and MARX.

According to Hegel's account, consciousness or spirit (*Geist*) develops into ever-higher forms through successive separations or 'alienations'. Human history is nothing less than the story of spirit's self-development through separation or self-estrangement. This spiritual odyssey, unfolding through time and largely independent of individual intentions or purposes, can in some respects be compared with the spiritual or psychological development of individual human beings. An infant, for example, is incapable of distinguishing itself from its mother. Gradually, and without conscious intent, the infant becomes aware of itself as a separate creature with wants and needs distinguishable from those of its parents. This transition from infancy to childhood is the first of several 'alienations' through which the individual develops his or her own distinctive personality. As with individual biography, so too with human history: the human species develops its distinctive characteristics through successive self-estrangements, each expressed, encapsulated, and articulated (by those few who are philosophers) in sequential stages of historical development. The history of philosophy is therefore, for Hegel, an account of these articulations, which can in effect be read as interim reports on the progress of the spirit's self-unfolding in human history. Repeatedly separating itself from its earlier manifestations, spirit constantly outgrows itself in ways that it did not, and indeed could not, foresee. Such separation or alienation is, according to Hegel, a necessary feature of history and human progress.

Marx also views alienation in historical terms. According to him, alienation (*Entfremdung*) assumes different forms and meanings in different historical epochs. In capitalist society members of the working class are alienated in four interrelated senses. First, the labourer is estranged from the product of his labour – because he is forced to sell his labour-power he does not own what he produces; his product accordingly assumes an 'alien' aspect. Second, since the labourer cannot recognize his labour as an expression or embodiment of his human power of creative transformation, he is estranged from the process of production, i.e. from the activity of labouring itself. Third, the labourer in capitalist society is estranged from those powers or

potentialities that are distinct to his 'species-being', particularly that of freely creating and enjoying beautiful things. And fourth, the capitalist system of production, with its competitive ethos and its division of labour, estranges each labourer from his fellows. Marx answers the previously posed questions in this way: The proletarian is estranged from his product, from the process of production itself, from his full human potential, and from his fellow workers. This four-fold estrangement is brought about by the conditions of capitalist production. The result is that the labourer becomes a deformed shell of a human being. This condition can be overcome only by the revolutionary overthrow of the capitalist system. Finally free to express and embody their many-sided human potentialities, unalienated men and women would cease to lead fragmented lives, discovering fulfilment in their labour and wholeness in their existence.

Although especially evident in his early writings, this 'humanist' aspect of Marx's thinking was not altogether absent from his later work. Not published until 1932, nor translated into English until the late 1950s, Marx's early writings – the so-called Paris Manuscripts of 1844 – had a profound effect on many European and Anglo-American thinkers in the period following the second world war. Marx's account of alienation appeared to them to be a weapon well suited to anyone critical of capitalism but equally disillusioned with communism as it had developed in the Soviet Union and in Eastern Europe. The concept of alienation accordingly became a cornerstone of 'critical' or 'humanist' Marxism in the West.

The theme of alienation, if not often the word, figures prominently in the literary and philosophical reflections of post-war writers such as Jean-Paul SARTRE, Albert CAMUS, and others often referred to (rightly or wrongly) as 'existentialists' (see EXISTENTIALISM). For many existentialists estrangement – from others and even from oneself – is not a condition confined to the present day but is an ineliminable feature of human existence. Every human being lives and dies alone, a stranger to himself no less than to others. The theme of alienation or estrangement looms large in Sartre's *Roads to Freedom* (1945), in Camus's *The Stranger* (1942), and in Colin Wilson's *The Outsider*

(1956). For these writers, as for Hegel, such estrangement is the emblem of and the price we pay for human freedom. Unlike Hegel and Marx, however, they held out no hope for the eventual historical conquest of this feature of the human condition. We are, in Sartre's famous phrase, condemned to freedom. To believe in, or to hope for, emancipation from this condition is to be guilty of 'bad faith'.

Although arguably the most important and influential, the Hegelian, Marxian, and existentialist accounts of alienation are by no means the only ones to have gained some currency in recent years. Other versions of alienation are to be found in the writings of thinkers as different as Karl Jaspers, Gabriel Marcel, Martin HEIDEGGER, and Erich Fromm, and in numerous sociological and psychological analyses. Possibly because of too careless and too frequent use in popular parlance – particularly during the 1960s and 1970s – the term alienation appears to have fallen from favour and to have lost some of its critical edge and analytical power.   TB

Reading

Feuer, L.: What is alienation? The career of a concept. *New Politics* 1 (Spring 1962) 116–34.

Fromm, E.: *The Sane Society*. New York: Fawcett, 1955.

Hegel, G.W.F.: *Phenomenology of Spirit*, trans. A.V. Miller. Oxford: Clarendon Press, 1977.

Lichtheim, G.: Alienation. In *International Encyclopedia of the Social Sciences*, ed. David L. Sills, vol. I, pp. 264–8. New York: Macmillan/Free Press, 1968.

Lukes, Steven: Alienation and anomie. In *Philosophy, Politics and Society*, 3rd ser., ed. P. Laslett and W.G. Runciman. Oxford: Blackwell, 1967.

Marx, K.: Estranged labour. In *The Economic and Philosophic Manuscripts of 1844*. New York: International Publishers, 1964.

Ollman, B.: *Alienation: Marx's Conception of Man in Capitalist Society*. Cambridge: Cambridge University Press, 1977.

Pappenheim, F.: *The Alienation of Modern Man*. New York: Monthly Review Press, 1959.

†Schacht, R.: *Alienation*. New York: Doubleday Anchor, 1970.

Althusius (Althaus), Johannes (d. 1638) German jurist and political philosopher. Since his rediscovery by Gierke in the 1870s Althusius has been regarded as an important theorist of consent, contract, federalism and corporatism. A Calvinist, he became doctor of civil and ecclesiastical law at Basle (1586), married in 1595, and studied theology at Heidelberg. In 1604 he became syndic (legal secretary) of Emden, where he spent the rest of his life; this small Calvinist town, supported by the nearby Dutch, was in conflict with the local Lutheran count. Althusius's political sympathies lay with quasi-independent towns and Estates General. His *Politica Methodice Digesta* (*Systematic Analysis of Politics*) was first published in 1603, and an expanded version in 1610.

Althusius's distinctive view of society and politics rests on his quite original drawing together of biblical, neo-Calvinist and Aristotelian ideas, and the ethos of the German guild-towns. Politics is based on *consociatio* (association, alliance, relationship), and consists of *communicatio* (sharing, exchange) of material goods, friendship and law. There are five types of association: family, college or guild, city, province, and kingdom or empire (*universalis consociatio*). Each is characterized by special ties both of affection and of contract. There is no boundary between economy, society and polity; the commonwealth or state (*respublica*) is based on mutual need, which leads to mutual aid, division of labour and commercial intercourse, which in turn lead to friendship and mutual concord. In his numerous chapters on the commonwealth, Althusius discusses at length law and its execution, economic policy, 'the nature and affection of the people' (pp. 203–5) and moral ties between rulers and people. Family and college are private associations, city, province and kingdom are public; only the family is 'natural'. While the kingdom is unique in possessing sovereignty (*maiestas*), the other associations also possess in effect inalienable rights, since each meets certain human needs in a particular way, their legitimacy being grounded in consent. As in HEGEL, they exist as separate levels of socio-political organization between the individual and the overall state: cities being made up not of individuals but of families, households and colleges, and kingdoms of cities and provinces.

Althusius's constitutional prescriptions for

the kingdom involved a confederal, quasi-democratic interpretation of the German Empire, allowing cities and provinces considerable autonomy, and imposing parliamentary, constitutional limits on the prince. Sovereignty belongs collectively to the constituent cities and provinces, 'to the whole body of the association of the kingdom' (pp. 91–2). Kingship is based upon a mutually agreed constitution (e.g. the Golden Bull): 'the fundamental law is nothing other than certain pacts, under which several cities and provinces have come together . . . with common labour, counsel and aid' (p. 169). The people, i.e. these corporate members, enter into a contractual relationship with 'the supreme magistrate' 'as to the form and method of subjection' (p. 160); their power is greater than the prince's. Every actual state has a mixed form of government, comprising assemblies, intermediate magistrates and a prince. 'Ephors', e.g. the German electoral princes, have reserve emergency powers, including the election of a king and the removal of a tyrant.

AB

Reading

Althusius, J.: *Politica Methodice Digesta*, intro. C.J. Friedrich. Cambridge, Mass.: Harvard University Press, 1932.

———: *The Politics of Johannes Althusius*, trans. and abbr. F.S. Carney. London: Eyre & Spottiswoode, 1965.

†Black, A.: *Guilds and Civil Society in European Political Thought from the Twelfth Century to the Present*, pp. 131–42. London: Methuen, 1984.

Gierke, O.: *Johannes Althusius und die Entwicklung der naturrechtlichen Staatstheorien* (1880); *The Development of Political Theory*, trans. B. Freyd. London and New York: Allen & Unwin, 1939, new edn. 1966.

Mesnard, P.: *L'essor de la philosophie politique au XVIe siècle*, 567–616. Paris, 1936.

Althusser, Louis (1918–) French Marxist philosopher. A series of essays he wrote during the 1960s gained Althusser an international readership and left a noticeable mark, in particular, on the development of Anglophone Marxist culture. This influence was due in large measure to his insistence on the scientific character of MARX's mature theory, in face of a growing tendency at the time to highlight the ethical and humanist, and the Hegelian, strands within that thinker's work (see MARXISM).

Althusser argued that between the avowed humanism of Marx's early writings, centred on the notion of ALIENATION, and the concepts of historical materialism elaborated and refined by him from 1845 onwards, there was an 'epistemological break': in other words, a radical, qualitative difference, separating the emergent materialist science of history from the ideology which had preceded it. Despite some apparent continuities of detail, each had its own distinct 'problematic' – Althusser's term for its underlying theoretical structure. The very terms in which he made this argument, the 'problematic' and related concepts, were said to derive from a new philosophy Marx had inaugurated together with his scientific theory of history. This philosophy, in essence a theory of knowledge, was profoundly anti-empiricist, representing knowledge not as a relation between perceiving subject and external object but rather as a type of production, or 'practice', in which theoretical means of production are brought to bear on theoretical raw materials to produce a theoretical product – the whole process taking place, in Althusser's words, 'entirely in thought'. This conception of practice was not confined to knowledge or science. All levels of social reality – the economic, the political, ideology – were said to be similarly structured, with their own type of raw materials, means of production, and products. The social whole was the combination of these distinct practices, a complex structure of layers and levels, 'overdetermined' because of the plurality of causes effective within it, the economy being determinant only 'in the last instance'. It was the causality of this global structure and its constituent regional structures that was operative in history, undermining the pretensions of the human subject to any genuine agency in the process. Marxism, Althusser claimed, was in fact 'a theoretical anti-humanism'. It denied the existence of a universal human nature or essence.

Althusser's work provided a healthy corrective to notions then prevalent within Marxist discussion. If Marx's ideas have a deep or enduring importance, this is due – not only, perhaps, but at least – to their theoretical, or cognitive, content, the intellectual purchase they have been able to give on the history of humankind. Between the themes of his early writings and full-grown historical materialism there lies, unquestionably, a series of significant changes, mutations, innovations. At the same time, in pressing this claim Althusser was guilty of much pretension and posturing. Some of his attributions, reflecting the latest in French fashions, were alien to Marx's thought; much of what he excluded, human nature for example, was there plain as day. Equally, for all his emphasis on the materialist character of Marxist theory, the philosophy of practice he elaborated bore many of the marks of a speculative and idealist metaphysic.　　　NG

Reading

Althusser, L.: *For Marx*. London: Allen Lane, 1969.
—— and Balibar, E.: *Reading Capital*. London: New Left, 1970.
Anderson, P.: *Arguments within English Marxism*. London: New Left/Verso, 1980.
†Geras, N.: Althusser's Marxism: an assessment. In *Western Marxism: a Critical Reader*, ed. New Left Review. London: New Left/Verso, 1977.
†Glucksmann, A.: A ventriloquist structuralism. In *Western Marxism: a Critical Reader*.
Thompson, E.P.: *The Poverty of Theory*. London: Merlin, 1978.

Anabaptists　　Radical Protestants whose movement originated in sixteenth-century Switzerland. The name literally means 'rebaptizers' from their belief in adult baptism. Their fundamentalist outlook led them to see the church as a voluntary association, radically separate from civil government. The Anabaptists acquired political notoriety when they gained control of the city of Münster in 1534 and instituted a short-lived communist theocracy. See REFORMATION POLITICAL THOUGHT.
　　　DLM

Reading

Cohn, N.: *The Pursuit of the Millennium*, ch. 13. London: Paladin, 1970.

anarchism　　The core of anarchism is the doctrine that society can and should be organized without the coercive authority of the state.

Although it is possible to find anarchist tendencies in the thought of many individuals stretching back to antiquity, the first political theorist to argue unequivocally for a stateless society was GODWIN in a book published in 1793; the first to call himself an anarchist was PROUDHON. Anarchism as an ideology had its greatest influence in the late nineteenth and early twentieth centuries, when revolutionary movements of this persuasion emerged in a number of western countries. More recently its impact has weakened, although numbers of individuals continue to think of themselves as anarchists, and sporadically impinge on the political scene.

Anarchist thinkers by no means form a homogeneous group, and at times they may seem to be held together only by their recognition of a common enemy, the state. They differ most overtly about the economic arrangements that should prevail in a stateless society: on this question anarchists form a spectrum, ranging from defenders of private property and free competition in the market, to advocates of complete common ownership, co-operative labour and distribution according to need. These differences, which will be analysed in greater depth below, reflect divergences of view on more fundamental questions, such as the meaning of JUSTICE and FREEDOM, and the possibilities of HUMAN NATURE.

All anarchists agree, however, on the need to dispense with compulsory forms of AUTHORITY, of which the state is merely the highest development. They do not necessarily object to authority of every kind: most anarchists would recognize the authority of experts – scientists or doctors, for instance – in their own fields, and many would recognize the moral authority of collective decisions taken in a genuinely democratic manner. Their criticisms are directed at authority assumed by people with no special claim to it; at authority that stretches beyond particular areas of expertise to embrace the whole of human existence; and, above all, at authority that enforces its commands coercively. The state is plainly guilty on all three counts; the anarchist critique extends, however, to other hierarchical forms of authority – to churches, to armies, to enterprises run by capitalist bosses, and, in more recent times, to impersonal bureaucracies. All these institutions are denounced for coercing their victims, and for exploiting them by extracting money or services by threat and indoctrination.

Anarchists reject two popular justifications of the state: that it performs useful social functions, and that its authority is legitimized by the CONSENT of its subjects. For anarchists, many of the tasks carried out by the state are necessary only for the state's own benefit: it undertakes national defence, for instance, but what it is really doing is defending its own sovereignty against other states. Other functions, such as personal protection, would in the absence of the state be carried out privately or by local communities. As for the idea of consent, anarchists ask when consent is supposed to have been given, and what happens to individuals who now try to withdraw it. They reject the view that elections are a genuine means of agreeing to be governed, seeing them instead as occasions when the populace is tricked into supporting one or other member of the ruling class.

Anarchism looks forward to a society in which personal freedom is at a maximum; in which material goods are fairly distributed; and in which common tasks are carried out by voluntary agreement. But there are major differences of opinion as to how these desirable aims may be achieved. Four main currents in anarchist thought may be distinguished: individualism, mutualism, collectivism and communism.

Individualism

Individualists take the sovereign individual as their starting point. Each person has an inviolable sphere of action upon which no one else must intrude, and social relationships are formed primarily through exchange and contract. The German nihilist Max Stirner (see YOUNG HEGELIANS) is often regarded as the originator of this school, but Stirner's uncompromising egoism – the individual, he believed, should always act exactly as he pleases, taking no notice of God, state, or moral rules – left little room for any constructive proposals. More typical of individualism were the nineteenth-century American anarchists Josiah Warren, Lysander Spooner and Benjamin Tucker.

Warren advocated a system of 'equitable commerce' whereby each producer, working either alone or in association, would exchange goods on the basis of the labour time embodied in them, using a system of labour notes. He set up 'Time Stores' to demonstrate the viability of his system, and also founded several experimental communities based on individual proprietorship and exchanges of labour. Tucker developed the theory of individualism more fully in a series of magazine articles collected as *Instead of a Book* (1893). His basic principle was that each person should enjoy the maximum liberty compatible with an equal liberty for others, implying in particular unlimited rights to acquire and dispose of goods in the market. Tucker attacked all state-created monopolies, especially monopolies in land and money. Without the state, he argued, each person could exercise his right to protect his own freedom, if necessary using the services of a private protective association. Spooner was located more firmly in the tradition of natural law, and is celebrated mainly for his withering attack on the US constitution, in the course of which he exposed the weaknesses of the contractual theory of the state.

Individualist anarchism has recently been revived, and now forms part of the broader movement known as LIBERTARIANISM. But while the earlier individualists thought that a society of equal freedom would radically modify capitalism (Tucker, for instance, regarded himself as a socialist), their modern descendants celebrate that system, and often describe themselves as 'anarcho-capitalists', a phrase that attracts vitriolic condemnation from anarchists of other persuasions.

Mutualism

Mutualism can be seen as a mid-point between individualist and collectivist versions of anarchy. The term was adopted by PROUDHON and his followers for their economic system, which in Proudhon's eyes reconciled property and communism. His principle was that each person might possess his means of production (tools, land, etc.) either singly or collectively, but should only be rewarded for his labour, thus eliminating profit and rent and ensuring a high degree of equality. Exchange was to occur through an ethical form of bargaining in which each party sought only an equivalent for what they were offering. Integral to this scheme was the establishment of a mutual credit bank which would lend to producers at a minimal rate of interest, covering only its costs of administration. Despite the practical failures of Proudhon's experiments along these lines, his French disciples played an influential role in the early years of the First International, before being outflanked by the collectivists.

Collectivism

Collectivism became the dominant strand in the anarchist movement under the influence of BAKUNIN. Abandoning Proudhon's tenderness towards the smallholding peasant and the artisan, the collectivists looked forward to a future in which organized labour had expropriated capital, each group of workers managing their own means of production. The distribution of the proceeds would be a matter for collective decision, but it was generally assumed that rewards would be proportional to labour, at least for the foreseeable future. The collectivists opposed what they saw as the authoritarian COMMUNISM of MARX and his followers.

Communism

The assumption that communism could only be imposed by an authoritarian state was challenged by the next generation of anarchists, particularly Malatesta, Elisée Reclus and KROPOTKIN. They argued instead that natural human solidarity would lead to the obliteration of all property distinctions. In an anarchist society each person would make use of common resources according to need. Productive work would be organized on the supply side by voluntary associations of workers and on the demand side by local communes, whose task it would be to identify the needs of the people living in their area. Communes would federate to co-ordinate projects such as road and railway systems that crossed their boundaries.

Communist anarchism rests on a view of human nature that is diametrically opposed to the egoism of Stirner and the individualists. It presupposes that people will work without material incentives and that, in the absence of private property, the problem of crime will so far diminish that offenders can be dealt with informally, without recourse to the coercive apparatus of law. Many would therefore see it as a form of UTOPIANISM. Anarchists of this persuasion would say in their defence that no human society could survive unless people were already co-operative and altruistic to a substantial degree.

Since the 1880s most anarchists have regarded communism as the highest form of social organization. They have attacked private ownership along with political authority as an inherently exploitative practice. At the same time they have been aware of the need to reconcile communal property with the basic anarchist commitment to freedom. They have stressed, therefore, that a communist system must be adopted voluntarily rather than imposed by force, and many have accepted collectivism as a viable transitional arrangment until people feel sufficient solidarity to dispense with property distinctions entirely. Individualists, on the other hand, use the issue of freedom as their springboard from which to assault communist proposals.

Anarchism and Marxism

The mainstream anarchist vision of future society closely resembles that of Marx and MARXISM, yet anarchists and Marxists have been at war in the socialist movement ever since Marx delivered his attack on Proudhon in *The Poverty of Philosophy* (1846). This rivalry reached its peak during the short-lived First International, when Marx's supporters fought with Bakunin's for control of that organization, a conflict which ended in the break-up of the International in 1872.

The immediate issue was whether the path forward to socialism (and eventually communism) lay through the destruction of the state, as the anarchists believed, or through the creation of a workers' state (or proletarian dictatorship), as the Marxists believed. For the anarchists, any political body, even one staffed exclusively by proletarians, would take on the universal characteristics of the state and inevitably become a new source of privilege and oppression. A socialist state, whose powers would extend to the organization of economic life, was likely to be the most oppressive of all; it would, in Bakunin's words, 'be nothing but a barracks: a regime, where regimented working men and women will sleep, wake, work, and live to the beat of a drum; where the shrewd and educated will be granted government privileges . . . ' (*Bakunin on Anarchy*, p. 284).

Behind this political division lay differences in general outlook. The anarchists found Marx's idca of a social science, in which historical epochs succeeded one another according to economic laws, excessively deterministic. It underestimated the power of revolutionary ideas and the 'spirit of revolt'. Moreover, although the anarchists acknowledged that a dominant economic class would always strongly influence the activities of the state, they saw political power as having independent roots, and its own internal dynamics. Finally, they did not share the Marxists' faith in the revolutionary potential of the urban working class; when they appealed for support to the 'proletariat', they had in mind a more heterogeneous mass comprising peasants, artisans and down-and-outs, as well as urban workers. They placed their trust primarily in those who had nothing to lose by a revolutionary upheaval.

Revolutionary change
Given their general attitude to the state, the anarchists were naturally opposed to all attempts to reform society by parliamentary means, as well as to attempts to overthrow the existing regime and replace it with a new political body. They studiously abstained from participating in elections or conventional politics of any sort. Most of them continued nonetheless to think in terms of a revolutionary transformation of society. For men like Bakunin, Malatesta and Kropotkin this meant a mass revolt against existing forms of authority and economic institutions, leading to the spontaneous construction, on a local basis, of new forms of organization. There was no room here for political leadership in the usual sense. The role of anarchist intellectuals was to be primarily an educative one: they had to stir up the spirit of revolt by pointing out injustices, and implant anti-authoritarian ideals in the masses. Education by the written and spoken word proved, however, to be a frustratingly slow business, and so there was born the idea of 'propaganda by the deed'. As first interpreted

by Malatesta (who attempted to put it into practice) this meant displaying anarchism in action, through fostering local rebellions which would serve as a model and a stimulus to the masses elsewhere. Later, in the 1880s and 1890s, it came to mean individual acts of terror, for example the assassination of political leaders or prominent industrialists. This was the period in which the popular image of anarchists as ruthless men with bombs under their coats became fixed in the public mind. Neither version of propaganda by the deed bore any fruits: local insurrections were invariably suppressed by the police or the army, and terrorist activities merely created a climate of opinion in which perfectly innocent anarchists would be thrown into gaol.

The most hopeful revolutionary strategy sprang from an alliance between anarchism and SYNDICALISM. Anarcho-syndicalists looked to the trade union movement both as a means of organizing the proletariat for revolution, and as a scaffold around which the new society could be built. Anarchists played a prominent role in the French syndicalist organization, the CGT (Confédération Générale du Travail), before 1914, and after the war in its Spanish equivalent, the CNT (Confederación Nacional de Trabajo). It was in Spain that the anarcho-syndicalist idea had its greatest opportunity, on the outbreak of the civil war in 1936. The anarchists proved to be an effective revolutionary force, and many factories and villages were collectivized, generally with some success. It was not, however, possible to implement libertarian communist ideals on a full scale under the conditions prevailing in Spain. Eventually the anarchists succumbed to pressure from their republican allies and abandoned many of their revolutionary gains in the interests of winning the war.

The idea of revolution has not been endorsed by all anarchists. Individualists have been suspicious of the threat to freedom that revolutionary organization poses, and other anarchists have argued that the transformation of human relationships that anarchy requires can only come about through a long period of education; revolutions can destroy, but they cannot of themselves rebuild the society of future.

13

The significance of anarchism

Anarchism can be assessed from two points of view: as a self-contained ideology, and as a fertilizer of other political traditions. Seen in the first way, it can only be written off as a failure. It has never attracted large numbers of adherents, and its influence on the course of world history has usually been nugatory. Nor is this surprising. The anarchist idea of a society organized without central authority seems to run directly counter to the experience of all advanced societies, where industrialization has gone hand in hand with an enhancement of the state's role. Anarchism as a complete package requires a massive leap of faith.

As a source of critical ideas for other ideologies and movements, however, it can claim greater success. It has been a constant presence in the socialist tradition, helping to counterbalance the centralist and statist outlook of many socialists. It has encouraged liberals to overcome their inconsistencies and hypocrisies over matters such as freedom of speech. It has contributed to the growth of FEMINISM; the anarchist ideal of human relationships free from coercion and exploitation has been extended to the relationship between men and women (for instance by Emma Goldman, a Russian-born anarchist prominent in the US early in this century). The strand in anarchist thought (deriving particularly from TOLSTOY) that opposes all violence on principle has often underlain PACIFISM. More recently the radical wing of the environmental movement has absorbed anarchist ideas, and anarchists have even been prominent in the campaign for ANIMAL RIGHTS. These apparently disparate influences are connected by two main ideas: opposition to all relations of power, no matter how persuasively camouflaged, and belief in direct action, instead of conventional political methods, as a means of combating them. These ideas, rather than elaborate blueprints for social reconstruction, seem likely to form the lasting contribution of anarchism to political thought.

DLM

Reading
(See also under BAKUNIN, GODWIN, KROPOTKIN, PROUDHON and TOLSTOY.)
Bakunin, M.: *Bakunin on Anarchy*, ed. S. Dolgoff. New York: Vintage, 1972.

Bookchin, M.: *Post-scarcity Anarchism*. London: Wildwood House, 1974.

†Carter, A.: *The Political Theory of Anarchism*. London: Routledge & Kegan Paul, 1971.

†Joll, J.: *The Anarchists*, 2nd edn. London: Methuen, 1979.

Krimerman, L.I. and Perry, L. eds.: *Patterns of Anarchy*. New York: Anchor, 1966.

Malatesta, E.: *Errico Malatesta: his Life and Ideas*, ed. V. Richards. London: Freedom, 1965.

†Miller, D.: *Anarchism*. London: Dent, 1984.

Rocker, R.: *Anarcho-syndicalism*. London: Secker & Warburg, 1938.

Taylor, M.: *Community, Anarchy and Liberty*. Cambridge: Cambridge University Press, 1982.

Tucker, B.R.: *Instead of a Book*. New York: B.R. Tucker, 1893.

Warren, J.: *Equitable Commerce*. New York: Fowlers & Wells, 1852.

†Woodcock, G.: *Anarchism*. Harmondsworth: Penguin, 1963.

ancient constitution A widely used idea in European political thought between the sixteenth and eighteenth centuries, employed chiefly to counter claims to royal ABSOLUTISM. The idea of an ancient constitution encapsulates the claim that the king's powers were derived from, and therefore limited by, a fundamental constitution whose enactment was now lost in the mists of history. Its provisions could, however, be seen in the common law, which accordingly circumscribed the king's exercise of his prerogative. In England the ancient constitution was frequently traced to the Anglo-Saxon period and counterposed to the 'Norman Yoke' which William I and his successors had placed on the necks of the people.   DLM

Reading
Pocock, J.G.A.: *The Ancient Constitution and the Feudal Law*. Cambridge: Cambridge University Press, 1957.

animal rights A concept signifying concern with human treatment of non-human animals. The moral and political issues raised by animals have been approached in terms of many different philosophic assumptions and meta-physical beliefs from the beginning of recorded thought – from the Greek myths, Platonic and neo-Platonic philosophy and Judaeo-Christianity, through the Renaissance humanists, a cluster of Enlightenment philosophers and rationalists (Kant, Descartes), Jeremy Bentham and other nineteenth-century utilitarians, up to the present day when animal liberation, welfare, rights and protection are the shared as well as competing concern of anthropological and ethical understandings.

Fundamental questions asked by those involved in debates concerning animals and their moral status include: What is the justification for human dominance over other creatures? On what grounds can humans justify killing, eating, inflicting pain upon and restricting the freedom of movement of non-humans? If animals are given no moral weight but are regarded as means to be deployed towards human ends, are we not logically compelled to diminish the moral worth of humans who do not meet various standards of rationality and autonomy, including the mentally incompetent, the permanently disabled, and the senile? On what moral basis do we defend the view that the lives of animals are of less intrinsic worth than those of human beings? Can we attribute 'rights' to animals and, if so, how? Do animals constitute an oppressed and exploited group, and under what set of assumptions can this case be made?

Although many of the terms ('rights', 'liberation', 'oppression') of the modern debate over human use and abuse of animals were unfamiliar to the ancients, a core set of considerations, embedded in the questions above, appear through the centuries. The historian Plutarch and the neo-Platonic philosopher Porphyry both insisted that human excellence, *arete* or 'acting well', required a refusal to inflict unnecessary suffering on any other creature, human or non-human. On these grounds Plutarch and Porphyry were philosophic vegetarians whose convictions concerning the moral status of animals precluded human killing and eating of them. They saw vegetarianism as central to an overall world view, expounded in Plutarch's treatise 'Of Eating the Flesh' in his *Moralia* and in Porphyry's *De abstinentia*.

The rationalist tradition, including two of its key exponents, Descartes and KANT, has been dismissive of the moral worth of animals.

Descartes's view is most extreme, holding that animals are without consciousness of any sort and are merely mobile machines. Postulating an absolute chasm between mind and matter, and locating animals wholly in the sphere of matter, Descartes places them beyond the bounds of moral and rational concern. Kant, working within a different rationalist framework, claims that animals are not conscious of themselves but are merely a means to man's end. Placing problems of suffering, emotion, and feeling outside the realm of philosophic concern, the rationalists dismissed the question whether or not animals feel pain or, indeed, have feelings of any kind. Philosophical indifference did not obliterate all popular feeling, however, and the first law against cruelty to animals was passed in the colony of Massachusetts in 1641. This prohibited 'tyranny or cruelty towards any brute creatures which are usually kept for the use of man'.

Despite powerful rationalist dismissals, many Enlightenment humanitarians did care about animals. From the eighteenth century onwards, individual philosophers and groups of concerned persons banded together to mitigate extreme cruelty towards animals. Starting from a utilitarian standpoint, several late eighteenth- and nineteenth-century thinkers put the question of animals back on the ethical agenda (see UTILITARIANISM). Worthy of particular note were Jeremy BENTHAM, 'The question is not, Can they *reason*? nor Can they *talk*? but Can they *suffer*?' (*Introduction to the Principles of Morals and Legislation*, 1789) and Henry Salt whose *Animals' Rights considered in relation to Social Progress* first appeared in 1892. Salt's case on behalf of animals was unflinching. He attacked any and all practices which inflicted cruelty upon sentient beings. Salt's earlier work, *A Plea for Vegetarianism*, exerted a deep influence on such influential proponents of vegetarianism as George Bernard Shaw and GANDHI. Societies for the prevention of cruelty to animals arose during the nineteenth century, attracting thousands of members, and influencing the course of social change and political legislation.

The contemporary rise of a vocal and diverse movement against animal suffering, as well as a return to robust philosophic debates concerning animals, has strong historic antecedents.

Current philosophers, most prominently Peter Singer and Tom Regan, insist on rational grounds that non-human animals have rights and are oppressed (see Singer and Regan). Points of dispute between defenders of animal rights and welfare and their opponents include animal experimentation and factory farming. Although anti-vivisection leagues are of long standing, the use of enormous numbers of animals in a variety of experimental situations (currently estimated at 60–100 million in the United States yearly) was less widely known before it was raised by animal rights advocates. Similarly, although particular acts of brutality against individual animals by their domestic keepers have always been an issue, the comparatively recent transformation of farms into streamlined financial concerns has meant that hundreds of millions of factory farm animals are now denied such elementary freedom as space in which to move.

A notable feature of the modern animal liberation movement is the extent to which philosophic argument and practical action are linked. Perhaps more visibly than in any other contemporary social and political force, animal advocates justify their actions on philosophic grounds full of powerful ethical imperatives.

JBE

Reading

Dombrowski, D.A.: *The Philosophy of Vegetarianism*. Amherst, Mass.: University of Massachusetts Press, 1984.

Frey, R.G.: *Interests and Rights: the Case against Animals*. Oxford: Oxford University Press, 1980.

Magel, C.R.: *A Bibliography on Animal Matters and Related Matters*. Boston, Mass.: University Press of America, 1981.

Mason, J. and Singer, P.: *Animal Factories*. New York: Crown, 1980.

†Midgley, M.: *Animals and Why They Matter*. New York: Penguin, 1983.

Regan, T.: *The Case for Animal Rights*. Berkeley, Calif.: University of California Press, 1983.

Rowan, A.N.: *Of Mice, Models and Men: a Critical Evaluation of Animal Research*. Albany, NY: SUNY Press, 1984.

†Singer, P.: *Animal Liberation: a New Ethics for our Treatment of Animals*. New York: Avon, 1965.

Turner, J.: *Reckoning with the Beast: Animals, Pain, and Humanity in the Victorian Mind*. Baltimore: The Johns Hopkins University Press, 1980.

anomie   The ancient notion of lawlessness incorporated into modern sociology by DURK-HEIM, who defined it as a lack of constraining rules to curb and channel individuals' desires – a social condition that was psychologically harmful (leading in the extreme to suicide), and socially disintegrative. It was, Durkheim thought, inherent in modern societies – in marriage (with the breakdown in matrimonial regulation) and in economic life, which had lost an established and accepted normative framework. Robert Merton adapted the notion to a different purpose, defining it as a disjunction between cultural norms and people's socially structured capacities to live by them.

SL

Reading

Durkheim, E.: *Suicide: a Study in Sociology* (1897), trans. J.A. Spaulding and G. Simpson. Glencoe, Ill.: Free Press of Glencoe, 1951.

Merton, R.K.: *Social Theory and Social Structure*. Glencoe, Ill.: Free Press of Glencoe, 1957.

Aquinas, Thomas (1224–1274)   Theologian and philosopher. Born near Naples, of a noble and powerful Southern Italian family, Aquinas joined the newly formed Dominican order against the wishes of his family. As a friar he was sent to study in Paris under Albert the Great whom he later followed to Cologne. Back in Paris, then at the papal court in Rome, and lastly in Paris again, he took part in the major philosophical and theological controversies of the day. He fought the decisive battle which admitted the works of ARISTOTLE into the university curriculum. He was of the first generation to benefit from William of Moerbeke's Latin translation of Artistotle's *Politics* which had not been available in the West since antiquity.

Aquinas was very familiar with the political conditions of his time, although his approach to politics was firstly theoretical. He attempted to harmonize the rational insights of the classical world with revealed Christian truths. But he also wrote to justify the role of his Dominican order in the church hierarchy and as such was engaged in the debate between mendicant and secular clergy at the University of Paris. The latter, jealous of privileges granted by the papacy to Franciscans and Dominicans in the university structure, tried to oust mendicants from the corporation of university masters but without success.

Aquinas is primarily known as the author of perhaps the greatest synthesis of medieval Catholic theology and philosophy, the *Summa theologiae* (1266–73). He also wrote commentaries on Aristotle's *Politics* and *Ethics*, as well as Book I of a 'mirror for princes' known as the *De regimine principum*. As part of his duties as a bachelor of theology he also commented on *The Sentences* of Peter Lombard, the standard theological handbook of the day, and he wrote a *Summa contra gentiles* and a work on *The Government of Jews*.

Aquinas's political ideas are scattered throughout his works, and his views are presented in the then standard scholastic format of question, presentation of opposing views, and conclusion. His aim was to provide a complete system of Catholic faith, morality, reason and practice, as these were understood by medieval Christianity. This was to be founded not only on current practice but also on the authority of the Bible and on the philosophy of Christian Fathers such as AUGUSTINE, Jerome and Chrysostom, as well as on the traditions of ROMAN and CANON LAW. Aquinas reinterpreted the dominant Augustinian interpretation of history and politics by concluding that the state *had* positive value in and of itself, not only in securing peace but as an expression of God's providence and will for mankind. He championed a programme of a society imbued with Christian ideals, for the State was natural rather than a consequence of Adam's sin. Man fulfilled himself in two ways: as a good citizen and as a Christian seeking salvation. Aquinas is therefore seen as reconciling pagan Aristotelianism and Christianity. Grace, he said, does not destroy nature but perfects it.

Politics for Aquinas implies a moral responsibility, the deliberate guiding by man's reason of his will in all social actions. Political prudence deals with the correct choice of means to a moral end, the common good of the community or state. Men are naturally endowed by God with a capacity to know the good and, although prone to error, are capable of pursuing the good. Reason was not impaired by the Fall; the will of man, however, was so impaired. Man

can know the good by himself, but he also knows that he requires supernatural aid for salvation. In the realm of reason, i.e. that of politics, man can, however, do the good; human values and truths are not obliterated by the revelation of higher ones, and natural reasoning is dignified by being involved in building up a near-perfect civilization through the recognition of a natural sphere of rational and ethical values, universally applicable to all men, Christians and pagans alike. This rationally known standard of justice is embodied in the law of nature (see LAW).

The *Summa theologiae* (henceforward *ST*) contains a *tractatus de legibus* in which Aquinas considers (1) the eternal law; (2) the divine law; (3) the law of nature; and (4) human positive law.

(1) The eternal law is the wisdom of God as governor of all actions and movements of the created cosmos. This eternal law serves as an exemplar of law directing the actions of the created universe; from this exemplar derive all other, more limited forms of law. As the eternal law is the plan of government in God, then all laws, so far as they accord with right reason, derive from this law (*ST* I II Q. 93 art. 3 concl.).

(2) The divine law as set forth in Scripture, such as the commandments, serves as additional guidance when added to those precepts of the natural law known by all rational men.

(3) Men share a natural inclination to good with all of creation: they seek self-preservation automatically. They also have more specific inclinations in common with animals: the sexual instinct and the rearing of offspring, for example. Most important and unique to men is their natural inclination to know the truth about God and to live in society. Men are therefore social and political animals, as well as being naturally religious. The natural law applies to them alone as conscious, rational, moral, social creatures, teaching them to avoid ignorance and not to give offence to or harm others with whom they must associate. There is, then, one standard of truth and rightness for all men and it is naturally and equally known by all. But when it comes to the particular conclusions

17

drawn from such eternal moral principles, although the standard of truth remains fixed the specific circumstances of its application vary. As history changes, the secondary precepts or conclusions drawn from immutable moral first principles also change in particular cases. The natural law is not altered but added to.

(4) Men's natural inclination to virtuous action could, by a certain education in discipline, be converted into virtuous habitual behaviour. Positive law acts in such an educational manner, preventing men from doing evil in order to provide a peaceful life for the community. It was therefore necessary to enact positive, rational, human laws.

Human law as positive enactment only has the quality of law in so far as it proceeds according to reason. This means that a prince is subject, voluntarily, to reason and to the natural law, as is any man. If, therefore, the positive law enacted by a sovereign is at variance with natural law and reason, it is no longer legal but a corruption of law (ST I II Q. 95 art. 2 concl.). The validity of law depends on its being just, i.e. reasonable. While the natural law establishes that its transgressors shall be punished, it is the positive human law which determines the specific penalty. And positive law is further divided into the law of nations (e.g. general norms governing buying and selling and other activities necessary to social intercourse in all countries) and civil law (which comprises particular applications of the natural law to local conditions).

All human law must be directed to the common welfare of the city or state. Human law is promulgated by the ruler of the community according to the particular political regime. Aquinas is most in favour of a monarchy, but one which has the character of a mixed government that is constituted by and takes advice from the nobility, and reflects the opinions of the wise, the wealthy, and the entire people. The law of this state achieves the common sanction of nobles and people. The best ordering of power in a city or kingdom is obtained when there is one virtuous commanding head but where those under him participate in the election of those who rule (ST I II Q. 105 art. 1).

In his earlier works Aquinas argued that irrational laws established by self-seeking tyrants rather than community-minded sovereigns are not obligatory and the overthrow of such government is praiseworthy, and is not sedition. But he added in the *Summa* that if the disorder and scandal resulting from the toppling of a tyrant by the community is likely to lead to even *greater* harm and disturbance than already exists, overthrowing the government is not advisable. There is never a private right to depose or kill tyrants; such action must only be that of a public authority.

Although Aquinas seems to sketch an autonomous realm of nature and reason in which secular politics operates, he also argues that the natural and temporal realm of power is ultimately subject to the spiritual. He places the common interest of the faithful and their spiritual well-being within the province of the church as educator, promoting the life of virtue, and therefore arguing for a harmony of the two jurisdictions, CHURCH AND STATE, in the Christian polity. Earthly felicity must be promoted so that it leads to happiness in heaven.

He sees that the possession of material things is natural to men, therefore private PROPERTY is permissible. The division of the community into spheres of private property is utilitarian, for peace and commerce, and results from *human agreement* enshrined in positive law. But beyond the satisfaction of limited needs and a modest profit, the superabundance possessed is owed, by natural right, to the poor and is to be used for the common welfare. It is left to individuals to make provision for the poor from their own wealth, except in cases of urgent necessity where a starving person may take what legally belongs to another and not be considered to have obtained such through robbery. Private property is circumscribed by prior natural necessity and morality. Excessive profit-seeking for gain is condemned, although trading and a moderate profit for the upkeep of one's household or for maintenance of the poor or for the welfare of the community is acceptable. Usury is never permissible, since money merely facilitates exchange and its use lies in its consumption or expenditure.

Aquinas was initially an exceedingly highly respected Dominican theologian among other luminaries of the scholastic age. But he came to be, especially in the nineteenth century, the voice of Catholic orthodoxy. He was sanctified in the fourteenth century. His theory of the state helped to put European political thought on a new plane where secular rulers exercised prudential rationality and autonomy. Not only do men need states but states serve men as the first, moral, natural step on the road to eternal felicity.   JC

Reading
Aquinas, T.: *Summa theologiae*, ed. T. Gilby. 60 vols. London: Blackfriars, 1963–81.
†Black, A.: St Thomas Aquinas: the state and morality. In *Political Thought from Plato to NATO*. London: BBC publications, 1984.
†D'Entrèves, A.P. ed.: *Aquinas: Selected Political Writings*. Oxford: Blackwell, 1948.
O'Connor, D.J.: *Aquinas and Natural Law*. London: Macmillan, 1967.
Weisheipl, J.: *Friar Thomas D'Aquino: his Life, Thought and Works*. Oxford: Blackwell, 1974.

Arendt, Hannah (1906–1975) Political thinker and analyst of totalitarianism. Born in Königsberg of a Jewish family, Arendt spent her youth studying philosophy with the EXISTENTIALIST thinkers Heidegger and Jaspers. She was alerted to politics by the rise of Nazism, which forced her to flee Germany; eventually she escaped, via France, to the USA, where she published her major works in English.

Both in manner and in content Arendt's writings are highly idiosyncratic, standing outside familiar classifications. She described her approach as 'thinking without banisters', trying to understand the meaning of political experience rather than to amass knowledge or prove theories. While she owed a good deal to HEIDEGGER's existentialist phenomenology and his assimilation of philosophy and poetry, her political concerns and opinions were very much her own. The only established political viewpoint with which she could plausibly be linked is the half-forgotten tradition of REPUBLICANISM which inspired Machiavelli, the Founding Fathers and Tocqueville. All modern schools of political thinking seemed to her to have abandoned authentically political values in favour of social ones.

Arendt first made her name with the publication in 1951 of *The Origins of Totalitarianism*, in which she maintained that Nazism and Stalinism between them constituted a new and specifically modern form of government which should not be confused with traditional forms of oppression. TOTALITARIANISM aims at total domination within and world conquest without; its salient features are ideology and terror – terror (seen in its most extreme form in the Nazi extermination camps) used not to deal with opponents but to put into practice an ideology that proclaims the 'laws' of history. Arendt attempted to identify the elements in recent European experience which had made totalitarianism possible: the specific political and social position of the Jews, which had given antisemitism a new force; imperialism, which generated racist movements and world-wide expansion of power; and the dissolution of European society into uprooted masses, so lonely and disoriented that they could be mobilized behind ideologies.

The book is particularly notable for the vividness with which it evokes the experience of totalitarianism, in which respect it contrasts sharply with more academic treatments of the subject. It has, however, been criticized on many grounds, from Arendt's equation of Nazism with Stalinism to her reliance on literary evidence in tracing their antecedents, and ever since its publication it has been highly controversial. There was even more controversy, especially within the Jewish community, when Arendt returned to the subject in *Eichmann in Jerusalem* (1963), a book prompted by the trial of a prominent Nazi. Subtitled 'A report on the banality of evil', the book maintained that Eichmann's crimes proceeded less from deliberate wickedness than from sheer bureaucratic mindlessness, an inability to think about the significance of his actions.

The attempt to 'think what we are doing', to confront experience without misleading presuppositions, was the purpose of her most ambitious and systematic philosophical work, *The Human Condition* (1958). In this she examines the modes of human activity and the conditions under which they take place, challenging modern presuppositions by arguing that there is an intrinsic hierarchy among activities. Within this ranking, Labour, the routine behaviour which ministers to the material life and comfort of the human species, has the lowest place. Above Labour stands Work, the activity of the craftsman or artist who creates the lasting objects that make up the human world and provide a home for human beings on earth; but above Work stands Action, the public interaction between equals which is the stuff of politics.

Arendt's discussion draws attention to the 'plurality' of human beings, to the fact that Action goes on among others who are unique and have different standpoints from which to view the common world. She also stresses 'natality' (in contrast to the standard existentialist preoccupation with mortality) – new human beings are constantly entering this common world, each free to begin something new. Politics has a special significance, because only in action can individuals disclose their uniqueness: only there can they experience freedom and bestow meaning upon human life. In addition to celebrating politics, however, she also draws attention to its extreme fluidity: the power which can be generated when free individuals act together in public, and the difficulty of institutionalizing and making permanent such spaces for action. Contrasting modern states with the Greek *polis*, in which political freedom was understood and enjoyed by the citizens, Arendt argues that the proper worth of human activities has been obscured by a number of historical developments. The contrast between public and private life has been lost in the rise of 'society', i.e. the nation-wide organization of individuals' private interests. Economic and scientific changes and introspective philosophy have between them deprived people of the experience of inhabiting a stable human world and, as a result of being 'worldless', modern men have increasingly exaggerated the value of sheer survival.

Another major work, *On Revolution* (1963), reflects upon the problems of trying to found a free political system. In a controversial analysis Arendt contrasts the American Revolution, which succeeded in establishing a free constitution, with the French Revolution, which degenerated into violence and tyranny. In France, she claims, the political problem of creating a permanent space for free action was pushed aside by the social problem of mass poverty. The revolutionaries themselves were misled into terror by their 'pity' for the poor (which Arendt distinguishes from 'compassion' and 'solidarity' with their suffering). Even in America, however, the legacy of the revolution was ambiguous. The constitution left most citizens outside the political arena, with the result that they rapidly lost all public spirit and came to see politics merely as a means to private happiness. In opposition to the universal modern assumption that the point of all politics must be to improve the standard of living, Arendt reasserts what she calls the 'lost treasure' of the revolutionary tradition, experienced in successive revolutions but then forgotten – namely the 'public happiness' of engaging in free political action among one's fellows. The true point of revolution, she claims, is to engage in such action and found a new body politic to perpetuate it. Recalling the spontaneous emergence of face-to-face citizens' councils in many revolutions, she suggests that a system based upon a federation of such councils would be preferable to representative democracy.

It was not Arendt's purpose, however, to propose solutions to the problems she identified. In modern times, she believed, the historic underpinnings of political systems had disappeared with the decline of the 'Roman trinity' of religion, tradition and authority, with the result that we are confronted anew by the elementary problems of human living-together. In a sense, this means that the future is open, and indeed Arendt continually stresses the human capacity to initiate new things. However, her emphasis upon the freedom of individuals to take political action was accompanied by a vivid sense of the unpredictability of such action and of its tendency, given the interactions between plural individuals, to produce unintended and uncontrollable results. She therefore ruled out any notion that the function of political philosophy is to draw up a blueprint for future realization.

Although Arendt's ideas have considerable internal coherence she deliberately refrained from system-building, emphasizing the provisional character of thinking; this (unlike 'cognition' of the scientific type) resembles Penelope's weaving in continually undoing the work it has accomplished. In her last work, the unfinished and posthumously published *Life of the Mind* (1978), Arendt turned her reflections upon the experience of mental life itself in two volumes, *Thinking* and *Willing*, which were to have been completed by another on *Judging*.

Just as Arendt cannot be assigned to any pre-existing party, neither did she establish any school of thought, and it is as yet too early to judge her significance for political philosophy. Her critics point to the undeniable arbitrariness of her assertions as a reason for not taking her seriously, while her admirers maintain that her originality and her talent for recognizing and describing neglected political experience place her among the most important thinkers of our time.   MEC

Reading

†Arendt, H.: *The Origins of Totalitarianism*. New York: Harcourt Brace, 1951.

†————: *The Human Condition*. Chicago: University of Chicago Press, 1958.

————: *On Revolution*. New York: Viking, 1963.

————: *Eichmann in Jerusalem*. New York: Viking, 1963.

————: *Between Past and Future*. New York: Viking, 1968.

————: *Men in Dark Times*. New York: Harcourt Brace World, 1968.

————: *On Violence*. Harmondsworth: Penguin, 1969.

————: *Crises of the Republic*. New York: Harcourt Brace Jovanovich, 1972.

————: *The Life of the Mind*. New York: Harcourt Brace Jovanovich, 1978.

†Canovan, M.: *The Political Thought of Hannah Arendt*. London: Dent, 1974; Methuen, 1977.

†Kateb, G.: *Hannah Arendt: Politics, Conscience, Evil*. Oxford: Martin Robertson, 1984.

†Parekh, B.: *Hannah Arendt and the Search for a New Political Philosophy*. London: Macmillan, 1981.

Young-Bruehl, E.: *Hannah Arendt: for Love of the World*. New Haven, Conn.: Yale University Press, 1982.

Aristotle (384–322 BC) Greek philosopher. Aristotle was born in Stagira, in northern Greece. His mother was rich. His father was physician to the King of Macedon. In 367 he removed to Athens and associated himself with PLATO's Academy, where he remained until Plato's death in 347. After some years in the eastern Aegean he was invited to the Macedonian court at Pella as tutor to the young Alexander the Great. Eight years later, in 335, he returned to Athens and founded his own school of philosophy. On Alexander's death in 322 anti-Macedonian sentiments swept Athens. Aristotle prudently left the city. He died a few months later.

His was a ubiquitous genius, and the list of his writings is daunting in length and variety. He wrote much on topics in political science. The most remarkable of these works is the set of *Constitutions* (histories and descriptive analyses of the political institutions of more than 150 Greek states) of which only the *Constitution of the Athenians* survives; the most celebrated is the *Politics*.

The eight books into which the *Politics* is divided fall into three groups: Books I-III discuss the STATE – its origins, its nature, its principal varieties – in relatively abstract terms; Books IV-VI contain detailed accounts of the different sorts of 'constitutions'; Books VII-VIII form the opening fragment of a lost or unfinished essay on the Ideal State. The three parts do not – and were not intended to – form a unified whole. Nor are they always polished. The *Politics* is not a definitive textbook on political theory.

Political science is concerned with the state or *polis*. Aristotle's approach to the subject is a self-conscious mixture of the theoretical, the empirical and the normative. He analyses and refines the concepts with which political thought must operate. He applies these concepts to the historical evidence amassed in his *Constitutions*. He condemns certain political institutions and he commends others. The *Politics* is analytical, descriptive and (in intent at least) practical.

Aristotle begins by arguing that the state is a *natural* entity [I, i]. The intrusion of nature is not casual: it pervades the whole of Aristotle's political thought. Humans – like bees or elephants – naturally congregate: individuals join in households, households band into villages, villages coalesce into states. The emergence of the state is the culmination of a natural process. (Aristotle explicitly rejects the view that the state's authority rests on any 'social contract' [1280a25 ff].) And the state is the perfect form of human community; for we are *by nature* 'political animals' [1253a2] in that we

21

cannot flourish, or live 'the good life', unless we are citizens of a state. We possess certain capacities, notably the capacity to reason on matters of justice and injustice, which can only be fully exercised in the context of a state and which must be exercised if we are to flourish. For Aristotle humans, unlike bees, are political rather than social creatures: social co-operation requires political organization. Anarchism is unnatural.

States are self-sufficient in the sense that citizens will find everything they need for the good life within the boundaries of the state. Households and villages are clearly not self-sufficient in this way. Nation-states are self-sufficient, but within them the good life is impossible [1326a27 ff]: you cannot have a state consisting of 100,000 citizens any more than you can have a ship that is five miles long. (Every modern state – with the possible exception of San Marino – is unnatural.)

A state is a community of citizens, and a citizen is someone who is eligible for political office [III, i] (see CITIZENSHIP). (Aristotle construes the word office very broadly: to serve on a jury is to hold an office.) But there are many different forms of state, the differences being determined by the different types of 'constitution' (politeia) or ways of ordering and allocating offices. Aristotle devotes much space to a taxonomy of constitutions. He begins with a simple system [III, iv]. A state may be governed either (1) by a single ruler, or (2) by a small group, or (3) by a large group; and the rulers may rule either (a) in the interests of all or (b) in their own interests. We thus get six basic constitutions, three 'correct' and three 'deviant': (1a) kingship, (2a) aristocracy, (3a) constitutional government, (1b) tyranny, (2b) oligarchy, (3b) democracy. This scheme is neat but crude; later [IV and VI] Aristotle introduces subclassifications, and in the end he prefers to characterize features of constitutions rather than constitutions themselves as aristocratic, democratic, and so on [1317b17 ff]. For there are numerous offices in any state [VI, v], and a single constitution may, for example, embrace democratic features (if all citizens are eligible for jury service) and also kingly features (if the military forces are in the hands of one man).

Aristotle is greatly concerned with the conditions under which states, whether correct or deviant, may enjoy stability. He holds that the underlying cause of political strife (stasis), and hence of revolution, is inequality [1301b26 ff]. For although any number of trivial things – a lover's tiff, for example – may precipitate stasis [V, ii], the revolutionaries are themselves always struggling for EQUALITY and justice. Equality means different things to different men [1301b29], and it is not a purely economic notion; but the main element in stasis is money: revolutions generally occur when the poor rise against the rich. The statesman, whatever his political colour, is offered advice on how to produce equality or its appearance and on how to restrain or divert the passions of the unequal. Aristotle does not regard all political change as bad [1268b25 ff]; but he does regard it as the primary duty of a statesman to preserve the constitution of his state.

These considerations explain Aristotle's praise of a 'middle' or 'mixed' constitution. For the best sort of state turns out to have a form of constitutional government in which all citizens have access to at least some offices, whereby they 'rule and are ruled by turns' [IV, ix]. Kingship may be best under certain conceivable conditions [III, xi]; but in practice we should prefer a constitution which blends democratic and oligarchic features, and in which the 'middle class' is in control. For if the 'middle' class, those who are neither rich nor poor, are sufficiently numerous to hold the balance of power, then the state will enjoy the greatest stability [1297a6 ff]. Moreover, collective decisions are most likely to be good decisions [III, vi]: just as a feast to which each guest brings a special dish of his own will probably be better than one victualled by a single host, so a collective decision will probably be better than one made by a single individual. Each member of the collectivity will have his own speciality and the collective judgment will amalgamate the various individual expertises. This may seem an optimistic assessment: why should we not suppose that individual expertise will be submerged in general incompetence? And in fact Aristotle admits that collective decisions will be best only in special circumstances [1281b15 ff].

The constitution provides the formal framework within which the ideal citizen rules and is ruled. What will be the substance of the state? The unfinished nature of Books VII-VIII means that we can only give a partial answer to this question. Aristotle says something about the size of the state [VII, iv], about its geography [VII, v] and material physiognomy [VII, x-xi], and about its national character – the citizens should be both spirited and intelligent, as Greeks typically are and foreigners typically are not [VII, vi]. He also discusses international relations: the state must have the ability to defend itself against military attack, but it will not nurture imperial ambitions or embark upon aggressive warfare [VII, ii]; for it is in conditions of peace that men live the good life, and an imperialist policy would enlarge and hence destroy the state. Nor, being self-sufficient, will the state indulge in extensive commercial or cultural trading [1327a27 ff].

The citizens will undertake the various political offices, and in their youth they will do military service. They will also be the sole private landowners [1329b36 ff]. (Aristotle argues strongly against the sort of communism which Plato had recommended [II, ii]: he holds that property should be *owned* privately but *used* in common – that is to say, property owners are to exhibit the friendly virtue of generosity [1330a1].) The citizens are the only genuine parts of the state, but the population will also include numerous non-citizens – children, women, slaves, resident aliens, and the like – on whom the citizens will depend. For the citizens themselves will not labour: agricultural and industrial production will be in the hands of vassals or (better) of slaves.

For some men are 'natural' slaves [I, ii]. There are humans who lack certain rational powers: they can follow orders and even advice but they cannot initiate practical deliberation for themselves, since they have no 'deliberative' faculty [1260a12]. It is in the interest of such people to be slaves, and it is natural and right that they should be enslaved [1255a1 ff]. In his own day Aristotle's account of slavery was not uncontroversial, and his argument for it is peculiarly frail. For even if some people do entirely lack the power to deliberate, it hardly follows that they should be enslaved or treated as mere 'living possessions' [1253b32].

Women, too, are intellectually deprived: although they possess a deliberative faculty, it is not 'sovereign', being too readily overcome by passion [1260a13]. Aristotle allows that women, who form half the free population, should be given an education [1260b13 ff], and their position within the household economy is important; but he never considers that they should count as citizens or be given any political rights.

The state will regulate marriages and births [VII, xiv]; and, most necessarily, it will determine the training and education of infants, children and young men. For it must supervise all education [VIII, i], and all citizens must have the same education [VII, xiii]. Much of Book VIII is given to a disquisition on musical education: should children learn music, and if so why? what kinds of music should they learn? should they become performers or listeners? if performers, what instruments should they learn? and so on.

The detailed concern with musical education expresses vividly an essential characteristic of Aristotle's political thought. He was an authoritarian. His state will determine whether and when I may play the flute [1341a17 ff]. It will impose a strict censorship on the arts [1336b12 ff]. State officials will decide what stories may be read to children [1336a28 ff]. This is not a superficial phenomenon: it has its roots deep in Aristotle's political thought.

First, the state exists for the sake of the good life – its goal or end *(telos)* is the well-being of its citizens. It is very easy to infer from this that the government should legislate for the good life, and that all citizens should have their well-being underwritten by state action [1325a5 ff]. (The inference is fallacious. To say that the end of the state is the good life is simply to say that humans can only or best flourish within the context of a state. Nothing whatever follows about the proper scope and role of government in promoting the good life.) Second, men, being political animals, are defined in terms of the state: they are thus *parts* of the state [1253a19 ff], and they belong to the State [1337a27 ff]. The citizen's private interests are subordinate to the public good. Again, it does not follow that the legislator is entitled to determine any of the citizen's activities. Again, it is easy to think that it *does* follow.

Aristotle's citizens are, of course, free men. But their FREEDOM is not the democratic ideal of 'doing whatever you want' [1317a40 ff]. This is an ideal for which Aristotle has no sympathy. Aristotelian freedom is simply the opposite of slavery: citizens are not slaves, they are not owned (not even by the state), they are free. Is the good life compatible with such an etiolated freedom? The brief sketches of human felicity in the *Politics* refer explicitly to the longer accounts in Aristotle's *Ethics*. But in both the *Eudemian* and the *Nicomachean Ethics* Aristotle insists that the good man must be autonomous, that he must choose his own actions and act on his choices. It is not clear how far this generous notion is consistent with the authoritarianism of the *Politics*.

Aristotle's political philosophy is in parts abhorrent, in parts bizarre. It is, moreover, in certain parts surprising. He lived through a period of profound political change during which the traditional small city-states, jealous of their autonomy and confederating only in time of crisis, gradually capitulated to the expanding empire of Macedonia. Aristotle had strong ties with the Macedonian court. In addition, he was in effect a stateless person: for most of his life he was a resident alien or 'metic', with no right to participate in the political life of the states in which he lived. A metic himself, he insists that the best life for man is that of the citizen. A familiar of kings, he regards monarchy as undesirable. A witness to the growth of Macedonian power, he condemns empire as a degenerate form of political association. If Aristotle's political theory was moulded – and also limited – by the historical conditions of his age, it was not crudely determined by his own political circumstances.

The empirical and historical studies included in the *Politics* mean that it is still a central text for students of ancient history. The analytical and theoretical work, particularly in connection with the constitutions, makes the *Politics* a classic of political theory. But it is, paradoxically, the alien nature of much of Aristotle's thought which ensures that the *Politics* remains a fascinating and a living text.   JB

References

All references in square brackets are to Aristotle's *Politics*. Roman numerals in upper and lower case give book and chapter numbers (e.g. IV, iii refers to chapter 3 of the fourth book of the *Politics*); where more precise reference is required, the standard 'Bekker system' (found in the margins of most translations and texts, and used by all scholars) is employed.

Reading

Aristotle: *The Complete Works*, ed. J. Barnes; includes *The Politics*, trans. B. Jowett. Princeton, NJ: Princeton University Press, 1984.

———: *The Politics*, ed. E. Barker, 2nd. edn. Oxford: Clarendon Press, 1948.

†Barnes, J.: *Aristotle*. Oxford: Oxford University Press, 1982.

———, Schofield, M. and Sorabji, R. eds: *Articles on Aristotle: 3 – Ethics and Politics*. London: Duckworth, 1977.

Fritz, K. von and Kapp, E.: *Aristotle's Constitution of Athens*. New York: Hafner, 1950.

†Mulgan, R.G.: *Aristotle's Political Theory*. Oxford: Oxford University Press, 1977.

Robinson, R.: *Aristotle's Politics, Books III and IV*. Oxford: Clarendon Press, 1962.

Steinmetz, P. ed.: *Schriften zu den Politika des Aristoteles*. Hildesheim: Olms, 1973.

Augustine of Hippo (354–430) Bishop and theologian. Born in what is now Algeria, Augustine trained in classical Latin rhetoric, first in North Africa and then in Rome, where he became professor of rhetoric. After meeting Ambrose, the classically erudite Bishop of Milan, Augustine was turned away from his earlier attraction to the dualist religion, Manicheeism, studied neo-Platonic philosophy through Latin translations, and experienced an emotional conversion to Christianity (386).

Earlier in the fourth century the Emperor Constantine had become Christian and by the 380s Christianity was adopted as the official Roman religion. Not only was the persecution of Christians at an end but the Christian conversion of imperial Rome meant that the divine will was now seen as established in the civil heart of governmental decision-making, the state supporting the development of the institutional church. The church, especially in North Africa (to which Augustine returned and where he was to become the Bishop of Hippo), was to find itself increasingly implicated in legal and political activities. Through his numerous theological writings Augustine became one of the major architects of Latin Christian political theory in a declining Roman civilization. In 410 the 'eternal' city of Rome was sacked by the barbarian Alaric and his Goths, and Augustine began his *City of God* (413–25). Here he developed an answer to hostile attacks on Christianity, attacks which blamed the fall of Rome on Christian indifference to the survival of the state. In instalments, Augustine developed his most influential doctrines: of history, of grace and predestination, of free will, of a true republic, of the duties of Christians to the state, of the just war, of the relation of the institutional church to secular government, and of the relationship between Christians who are members of the city of God on earth and those men who are members of the city of man. The theme of the two cities, of God and of man, guided political theorizing throughout the next 800 years of the Middle Ages and beyond (see CHURCH AND STATE). A prolific author and a fine rhetorician, Augustine made his *City of God* the summa in which all the strands of his political theory are brought together in encyclopaedic fashion, a mixture of neo-Platonic philosophy, Christian doctrine, biblical history, and contemporary responses to problems in church and state on the eve of Rome's fall.

Augustine argued that a man's true end lies beyond history. Human history is depicted as a sine curve of good and bad events whose ultimate meaning is inscrutable to man, but mapped out by God. As a flux of outward events history hides within it a drama of sin and redemption, to be resolved only after historical time. No earthly state, as a consequence, can eternally ensure security from internal and external attack. The classical political traditions of Greece and Rome were wrong and arrogant in arguing that man's fulfilment came with citizenship in a rational and just state. This could not be achieved. Nonetheless, Augustine believed government to be ordained by God, even though human history appears to be no more than a catalogue of disastrous wars attempting to secure a short-lived peace. The classical tradition's belief in the rationality of man and in his capacity for rational and just self-government was naive. Because of Adam's

sin man is forever a victim of irrational self-love and of lack of self-knowledge and self-control. Government is instituted with divine sanction in order to preserve a relative worldly peace and not as a means of human fulfilment. Indeed, governments could exist without justice but they were to be considered no more than large-scale bands of robbers, securing peace through arbitrary domination and coercion. In a good Christian state a proper concern for justice must include God, but even this state could never be man's true home.

Augustine did not argue for the establishment of a theocracy in the world. Instead he described the sacramental role of priests working hand in hand with good government to counteract what he saw as man's corrupted nature, corrupted beyond any hope of rational self-amelioration. Augustine argued that the whole human race fell in Adam, the transmission of this sin being bound up in the concupiscent sexual impulse. Man, as a consequence, was incapable of any act of pure good will. Although men are naturally social, they are responsible for making wrong choices; but when they choose well, they do so only with divine aid through unmerited grace. Strict justice would consign all men to hell. But faith in God's mercy allowed Augustine to interpret the Bible as indicating that God had chosen a minority of souls for salvation through an inscrutable decree of predestination superior to any merit or any act historical man may perform. Augustine developed this doctrine of grace in his debate with the British monk Pelagius. His doctrine of free will pursued the issue further. Although God foreknew Satan's fall through pride and Adam's sin through disobedience, their individual freedoms to take these evil decisions were not hindered by God's knowledge, so that Adam's sin was not predetermined but only foreknown by God. Moral evil in the world is a conscious decision to misuse free will. But human history and society will always betray uncontrollable elements of pride and concupiscence. Hence the need for government, even tyrannical government, against which there are no appeals, for all tribulations are deserved.

Governments are divinely instituted as means of keeping order and civil peace. In examining CICERO's republican theory of government, Augustine argued that a just commonwealth must constitute a rational multitude united by a common love of God rather than a common love of material well-being of the social order. Cicero's Rome united people materially rather than spiritually. For Augustine, a true state is therefore a true church but its unity will only be realized after history. The actual institutional church includes the chaff as well as the wheat. No truly good commonwealth or church has existed or will exist in time. We do not have a clerical definition of the state, implying a theological hierarchy in control of moral issues in society. Augustine does, however, argue that the secular state is a moral entity and that states can choose to do what is morally right as well as what is morally wrong; since actual states will always include evil, self-regarding wills, the state must step in as public executioner. Those Christians called to secular power must indeed assume their responsibilities to keep order and civil peace, knowing nonetheless that their knowledge of any case is fallible and that they may well have to take decisions in which they have tragically misjudged the situation. Instead of arguing for Christian pacifism, Augustine argues the reverse, that Christians have duties to the state; they must serve in public office and may be called upon to fight a JUST WAR. Because civil societies can be perverted by evil faithless men, a state can justly decide to wage a war, seeing itself as tragically required to fight the greater injustice of the opposing side. Augustine does not condemn defence, but he is not to be understood as supporting an animus of revenge. A just war is fought to secure a just peace, but no earthly state is entirely just and therefore there is no possibility of a Christian utopia being realized in history.

The *City of God* begins as an apologetic defence of Christianity, debating whether the calamity of Alaric's sack of Rome occurred because Rome had forgotten her ancient pagan ways. It proceeds to construct a theory of society and history by means of the story of the origin of the city of God and the city of men. In Books XV-XVIII Augustine traces the origin of the two cities, and in Books XIX-XXII he relates the consummation of the two cities in eternity.

Much of his exposition resulted from his confrontation with the heretical Donatist sect in North Africa.

Augustine distinguishes the social life for man that is divinely ordained and natural from the values of Roman social life where worldly honour and self-assertive patriotism exalt love of self over all else. The sack of Rome was not a supreme crisis in human history; mankind's true crises occurred in Eden and at Calvary. Since the Fall there have always been two cities in history, distinguished by their respective loyalties, one to self, the other to God. One city served the rebel angels, the other those loyal to God. These cities are inextricably mixed in history. The seeking of peace and social good in an organized city typified for Augustine the quest of all civilizations. But the tension between Cain, the founder of a city, and Abel, the sojourner awaiting citizenship beyond history, is ever present. All men have always desired to share peace, resolve tensions, and control discordances in social life, but members of the city of men regard earthly political peace and material wealth as sufficient. This, however, is a transient city. Some men know that their true home is in heaven and that they are like pilgrims in the city of men. They live according to the customs of the land, pursue common business, serve the state when called, but ultimately they are users rather than lovers of this world. They are obliged by divinely instituted government to play their part but realize that their ultimate citizenship in the city of God after history is given gratuitously by God and can never be merited by earthly works. Because men are uncertain of membership in the transcendent city of God, the true church can never be realized in a coherent society on earth. The two cities merely progress through history in confused fashion, and only at the Last Judgment will membership in the eternal city be resolved. The church militant in history is no more free of perils than is the secular state; it serves sacramental functions as a dispenser of grace without which men can do no good. Baptism and communion do not secure salvation but they are a *sine qua non*, so that the heterodox and the pagans are excluded from transcendent hope. The sacramental church, according to Augustine, despite its faults must be universal. But the city of God is not the visible church. It is the invisible, non-cohesive communion of saints who will be united as the body of the elect after history. The visible church, however, must serve the invisible and it must be universal, world-wide, and opposed to exclusionist, particularist, and nationalist tendencies. This idea would be heartily taken up in the Middle Ages by papal theories intent on making institutionally concrete (and on an international level) Augustine's more other-worldly emphasis.

Augustine's universalist language inspired later ages to develop a doctrine of the church as a perfect society with powers necessary to any self-sufficient community regarding property and governance. Implying in principle that there was no salvation outside the church, Augustine inspired the medieval development of papal monarchy. As the church in the Latin West became to conquering barbarians the symbol and source of Roman culture and organization, it assumed, even in the fifth century, aspects of a plenitude of power that would develop into the medieval ideology of a strong papacy, so central to the thirteenth- and fourteenth-century political debate concerning the respective *dominium* and jurisdiction of church and state (see MEDIEVAL POLITICAL THOUGHT). Although Augustine did not think civil and ecclesiastical authorities were distinct co-ordinating powers occupied with governing men, his words were interpreted to justify a two-swords theory of world rule, spiritual and temporal, pope and emperor. It is also doubtful whether he intended to subjugate state to church, for the state, as he saw it, was not the secular arm of the church, but a distinct institution that was to be advised by the church. This was converted in the Middle Ages into the theory and practice of a theocratic state controlling law for spiritual ends. At the heart of the papal theory of power was an interpretation of Augustine's theory of true governance and *dominium* founded on grace.

Augustine's model of man as entirely dependent on God's grace to commit worthy acts would be adopted and rejected in turn as future medieval generations attempted to reconcile his negative views on the necessity of the state with the more positive and optimistic ones of

ARISTOTLE, reinterpreted for the Latin Christian West by Thomas AQUINAS in the thirteenth century. Augustinianism would be revived by Luther and the sixteenth-century Reformation (see REFORMATION POLITICAL THOUGHT). JC

Reading

Augustine, St: *The City of God*, ed. D. Knowles, trans. H. Bettenson. Harmondsworth: Penguin, 1972.

†Brown, P.: *Augustine of Hippo: a Biography*. London: Faber & Faber, 1967.

†Coleman, J.: Augustine. In *Political Thought from Plato to NATO*. London: BBC publications, 1984.

Markus, R.A.: *Saeculum: History and Society in the Theology of St Augustine*. Cambridge: Cambridge University Press, 1970.

Marrou, H.I.: *St Augustine and his Influence through the Ages*. New York: Harper Torch, 1957.

Martin, R.: The two cities of Augustine's political philosophy. *Journal of the History of Ideas* 33 (1972).

Austin, John (1790–1859) English jurist and legal philosopher. Born into a well-to-do middle class background, Austin became an army officer (1806–12), barrister (1818–26), professor of jurisprudence at London University (1826–32), and (1834) lecturer in jurisprudence at the Inner Temple. He spent some years in public service, and in 1820 married Sarah Taylor who was a source of inspiration to him; they lived in France and Germany until the 'Year of Revolutions' of 1848, then in Weybridge until his death.

Austin is the chief spokesman and exponent of English analytical legal positivism in the specific version now known as (and much criticized as being) 'the command theory of law' (see LAW). His chief and most influential work, *The Province of Jurisprudence Determined* (1832), was developed from the introductory section of the lecture course which he presented in his capacity as first professor of jurisprudence in London. As a lecturer Austin was so unsuccessful in holding an audience that he resigned the chair in 1832; his Inner Temple lectureship of 1834 was no more successful. The book, however, had a different fate, being surely the most widely read, cited and criticized text of legal theory in English, far outstripping the legal writings of BENTHAM which were its model, and even more so works of the German Pandectist school such as those which Austin studied in Germany, 1826–8, while preparing to discharge professorial duties. A crippling literary perfectionism prevented Austin's publication of any other work save a few political pamphlets, and not until after his death was Mrs Austin able to see into print the full *Lectures on the Philosophy of Positive Law* (1861), which presented a thorough analysis of all the main concepts and institutions of law in the spirit of the *Province*'s definition.

That definition is strictly positivist in separating entirely the existence of a law from its merit or demerit as such. It is voluntarist in restricting laws properly so called to the commands (acts of will) issued by superiors to inferiors under the threat of some sanction in the event of disobedience. Commands which are laws have, as such, to be general, and have to emanate from an ultimate superior or sovereign (see SOVEREIGNTY). A sovereign is a commander whose general commands are habitually obeyed by the bulk of a reasonably numerous population which in turn has no habit of obedience to any other human individual or group. (Sovereigns can be either individuals or, as in Britain or the USA, collectivities of persons.)

The state in this view is simply another term for the sovereign; or, in a different usage it is, as an independent political society, the corporate entity comprising sovereign and subjects taken together. Where sovereigns are collective bodies, they of course have to be defined in constitutional provisions. But constitutions of this sort cannot be 'laws' in their ultimate provisions, since of necessity they are not commanded by sovereigns. Hence constitutional law in its highest reaches is reclassified as positive morality only – and so too is law among sovereigns or states, public international law. These theses, and corollaries as to the legal illimitability of sovereign power and absence of strict rights against sovereigns, have been much criticized. Later positivism (e.g. H. L. A. Hart's) has dropped the voluntarist thesis of laws as commands, restoring customary social norms to the category law, and focusing on facultative as well as imperative aspects of law.

Austin's political philosophy is utilitarian, though more clearly rule-utilitarian than Bentham's (see UTILITARIANISM). A devout Unitarian, he believed in divine law as that which is laid down by a utilitarian as well as unitarian deity. Utility and divine law are the supreme tests of a positive law's merit or demerit; they are not however the criteria of its existence.

NMacC

Reading

Austin, J.: *The Province of Jurisprudence Determined and Uses of the Study of Jurisprudence*, ed. H.L.A. Hart. London: Weidenfeld & Nicolson, 1954.

———: *Lectures on the Philosophy of Positive Law*, ed. S. Austin. London: John Murray, 1863.

†Morison, W.L.: *John Austin*. London: Edward Arnold, 1982. [Contains an extensive bibliography.]

authority In politics and law, authority is now commonly understood as the right to perform some action, including the right to make laws and all lesser rights involved in ruling; it should be distinguished from POWER understood as the ability to compel obedience. This conception of authority has long been the subject of intense and ceaseless dispute: it swiftly evokes the problem of POLITICAL OBLIGATION on one side and problems about the liberty, rights, and autonomy of the individual on the other. But this is not the only meaning that the multifaceted notion of authority bears, even in political matters, and an analysis of the relationship between persons that it involves must be central to any thorough attempt to understand it.

To begin with, two approaches to the interpretation of the authority relation should be distinguished. First, there is the broad and elastic approach, prevalent in the contemporary social sciences, in which authority is used to refer to any system of power or social control that is regarded as legitimate by those involved in it. Here the point of calling an arrangement authoritative is not to focus attention on a distinctive mode of ruling and being ruled, but to indicate that a particular type of attitude exists among a people regarding the mode of subordination to which they are subject, whatever it happens to be. From this perspective, authority may be construed as a universal phenomenon, coextensive with organized society and encompassing radically different types of relationships. The most influential version of this approach remains that of Max WEBER, who devised his widely-used typology of charismatic, traditional, and legal-rational authority systems as an exhaustive classification of 'systems of domination'.

Second and by contrast there is the more focused approach to authority that has figured in western legal and political philosophy, especially in theories concerned with the emergence and singular character of the modern state. Here the notion of authority has been employed to define the specific nature of a perhaps novel relationship between ruler and ruled, and to disentangle it from other relationships with which it tends to get confused. This approach is epitomized in a well-known statement by Hannah ARENDT: 'If authority is to be defined at all, it must be in contradistinction to both coercion by force and persuasion by argument.'

The specific character of this interpretation of authority can be brought out by considering the actual use of the language of authority in human affairs. The word 'authority' and its cognates, 'author', 'authentic', 'authoritative', 'authorize', etc. have a complex history in the western world, going back to the ancient Roman *auctor* and *auctoritas*; it gradually came to be used in a wide array of activities and transactions besides politics and law, including religion, education, family matters, and now indeed in almost any joint enterprise; wherever this language has been appropriated it has served to assert or to deny a distinctive type of demand on the conduct or belief of others. Many different forms of expression are said to be authoritative: creeds, doctrines, opinions, testaments, and books (such as the Bible) where the response called for is conceived as belief, faith, or trust, as well as laws, constitutions, judicial decisions, commands, and other prescriptions intended to regulate conduct. So in turn authority has been imputed to *persona* of all sorts: lawgivers, lawmakers and founders, judges and officials, parents and teachers, experts, intellectuals, priests, prophets, and other intermediaries. These various authors are said to be vested with authority, to have or to exercise it, to be in authority or to be authorities on some matter, to act or to speak with authority; and the authority they claim or possess is said to be recognized,

granted, denied, challenged, obeyed, evaded, flouted, or lost.

The intricacy of this discourse is obvious, and a full-scale account of authority would need to examine the many significant differences and similarities discernible in this array. Still it may be suggested that there is an underlying theme, and one of the advantages of concentrating on the language of authority is to remind us that what we are dealing with is a special communicative relationship between a speaker, his utterance, a listener, and his response. A rough definition may be ventured as follows. Words are taken to be authoritative by a listener when he recognizes that the claim they make to be heeded is not conditional on his own personal examination and assessment of the reasons or arguments on which they rest, but rather on the consideration that they come from a particular speaker who, because of some identifying characteristic that sets him apart from others, is acknowledged to be entitled to receive this special response.

Authority, then, is a relational concept. The meaning of 'the authority of scriptures', 'the authority of the church', 'parental authority', 'congressional authority', etc., is to be brought out by reference to the specific nexus that obtains between the four elements: author, utterance, auditor, response. Further, this communicative relation is a distinct relation: it is distinct from coercive relations of all sorts because the claim made to adherence depends on the antecedent authentication of the speaker, not on his consequential power to produce unwanted effects; and it is distinct from relations of persuasion and advice because the claim is not dependent on arguments designed to elicit agreement from the auditor on the desirability of what is required of him.

The concept of authority has a basic structure. A system of political authority can exist only if those who fall within its jurisdiction desist from making compliance dependent on their own judgment of the desirability of what the law prescribes. To borrow from the illuminating analysis by Joseph Raz, an authoritative act of government is an 'exclusionary reason' for action. Where ruling takes the form of authoritative utterance, it becomes possible to govern without obtaining first-order agreement on the particular merits of what the laws require.

The literature on authority reveals, however, widely disparate and often systematically ambiguous formulations of precisely what this element of authoritative submission allows and disallows. For some, it requires merely giving up the right to act on one's judgment and accordingly is compatible with disapproval of what is prescribed; here authority permits 'assent without credence' and this understanding of authority was for SPINOZA one key to the reconciliation of political allegiance with the freedom to philosophize to which his *Theologico-political Treatise* (1670) was devoted. But for others (COMTE, for example), authority requires the abandonment of 'critical thought' in favour of belief in or identification with the deliverances of authority, so that the type of commitment demanded by authority makes the very existence of 'negative philosophy' an illicit activity within society. In fact, however, much writing on authority does not present the alternatives as sharply as the preceding remarks suggest; ironically even the very literature preoccupied with the issue of the compatibility of authority and autonomy appears to have forgotten or obfuscated what is at stake in the question of political commitment.

Again, an authoritative arrangement can exist only when there is some public and accepted criterion of authentication or 'rule of recognition' for identifying those persons who are entitled to positions of authority. However it is widely felt that a decision taken by the occupant of an office in accordance with established constitutional procedures cannot suffice to provide an exclusionary reason for action unless that person is also an authority on the subject-matter of his decisions, or his decisions can be trusted to reflect the shared values of the community. Intellectual authority thus becomes the prototype model of political authority, and writers often build up their case for a particular account of political authority by appealing to examples of 'expert authority' or 'epistemic authority', so committing themselves to the view that political authority must be grounded on superior knowledge, insight, or experience, or restricted access to a truth about the way society should be organized. This approach has in turn led many writers on authority to denounce formal-legal conceptions of authority as 'deformed', as in Gadamer's onslaught against Spinoza and the 'Enlightenment' for failing to appreciate that 'the authority of persons is based ultimately . . . on recognition and knowledge – knowledge, namely, that the other is superior to oneself in judgment and insight and that for this reason his judgment takes precedence, i.e., it has priority over one's own' (*Truth and Method*, p. 248). The same assumption can also be discerned behind the contention that the very idea of authority must have vanished from the modern world, because the epistemological assumptions supposedly required by any genuine system of political authority have been discredited by modern scepticism.

The difficulty throughout is that the concept of authority, although it possesses certain basic features, cannot be stabilized; it varies according to its place in the context of some theory or ideology concerned with larger questions of human destiny and human nature. So, for example, the question of the character of the commitment that may be properly demanded by political authority turns on the question of the ground on which authority is conceived to rest by those who accept it as legitimate. Where political authority is taken to be based on superior knowledge or restricted access to a truth, it is impossible for a person to acquiesce in authority and yet to conceive himself as capable of and warranted in forming a judgment on an equal footing with the bearer of authority. But where authority is dissociated from truth-claims and is grounded on authorization by those who are to be subject to it there is no incompatibility in principle between the acceptance of authority and the formation of independent judgment. From this standpoint it is arguable that the fundamental turning-point in the history of our understanding of authority took place with the reformulations of philosophers like HOBBES and Spinoza who, under conditions of political-religious crisis, came to construe authority as a human artifice to be recognized as such by all implicated in it. But deep dissatisfaction with political philosophy of this sort has always been a feature of the political and intellectual scene, and under various doctrinal pressures, the boundaries of the concept of authority have turned out to be elastic after all, thus opening out on to Max Weber's project even within the 'modern' world. RBF

Reading

Arendt, H.: What is authority? In *Between Past and Future*. Cleveland and New York: Viking, 1968.

†Flathman, R.: *The Practice of Political Authority: Authority and the Authoritative*. Chicago: University of Chicago Press, 1980.

†Friedrich, C.J. ed.: *Nomos I: Authority*. Cambridge, Mass.: Harvard University Press, 1958.

Gadamer, H.-G.: *Truth and Method*. New York: Continuum, 1982.

Hobbes, T.: *Leviathan* (1651), ed. C.B. Macpherson. Harmondsworth: Penguin, 1968.

Oakeshott, M.: *On Human Conduct*. London: Clarendon Press, 1975.

Raz, J.: *The Authority of Law*. Oxford: Clarendon Press, 1979.

Spinoza, B.: *Theologico-political Treatise* (1670). In *The Chief Works of Benedict de Spinoza*, vol. I, ed. R.H.M. Elwes. New York: Dover, 1951.

†Watt, E.D.: *Authority*. London: Croom Helm, 1982.

Weber, M.: *The Theory of Social and Economic Organization* (1922), trans. A.R. Henderson and T. Parsons. New York: Macmillan, 1947.

Wolff, R.P.: *In Defense of Anarchism*. New York: Harper & Row, 1970.

autonomy   Literally meaning 'self-rule', autonomy is ascribed in popular political parlance to self-governing states, or to institutions or groups within states that enjoy a substantial degree of independence and initiative. In political thought the term is often now used to refer to an aspect of personal FREEDOM. Autonomous individuals are those whose ends and purposes are authentically chosen, as opposed to those who allow themselves to be conditioned by external forces. But, as with positive senses of freedom generally, the criteria of authentic choice may be specified in different ways, and so it may be a matter of dispute which persons should be counted as autonomous. DLM

Reading

Young, R.: *Personal Autonomy: Beyond Negative and Positive Liberty*. London and Sydney: Croom Helm, 1986.

B

Babeuf, François Noël (Gracchus) (1760–1797) French revolutionary. Babeuf extended the radical principles of the Revolution to a demand for social equality, arguing for community of land and goods. See COMMUNISM.

Bacon, Francis, Lord Verulam (1561–1626) British statesman and philosopher. Bacon spent more of his life in the practice of the political arts than in reflection upon them. The nephew of Lord Burghley, he was both the confidant of the Earl of Essex and in the end the man who had to draw up Essex's indictment for treason. Even by the standards of Tudor and Jacobean England, Bacon's career was a stormy one, involving a long-drawn-out struggle with Sir Edward COKE on his way to the lord chancellorship, and a sudden dismissal from high office under impeachment for bribery. Noted in his own day as the author of shrewd memoranda on matters of immediate moment, his historical reputation rests on his philosophy of science and on his unfinished sketches of a scientific utopia.

At his aphoristic best in his *Essays* (1625), Bacon is at his most serious in *The Advancement of Learning* (1605) and in his utopian sketch for the *New Atlantis* (1627). Bacon was hostile to the excesses of scholasticism and to theorists who looked only for evidence to support their own preconceptions; he was an uncompromising empiricist who took the first steps towards elaborating an inductive logic. Nor was induction a matter of simply piling up supporting evidence; we could only be confident of a generalization if we had looked for contrary evidence, too. But the advancement of science was not just a matter of good method; it needed political support. In *New Atlantis* the College of the Six Days' Works was an embryonic Royal Society – whose founders were indeed stimulated by Bacon – which would support invention and discovery. The political background to all this is only implicit, but it appears to be an enlightened theocracy – although in the *Essays* he writes as a disciple of the republican Machiavelli.

Bacon combines themes from PLATO and the ENLIGHTENMENT, and stands at the junction between Christian Europe and the secular, scientific world which replaced it. AR

Reading
Bacon, F.: *The Advancement of Learning* and *New Atlantis*, ed. A. Johnston. Oxford: Oxford University Press, 1974.

———: *Essays*, ed. J. Pitcher. Harmondsworth: Penguin, 1985.

†Manuel, F. and Manuel, F.: *Utopian Thought in the Western World*. Cambridge, Mass.: Belknap, 1979.

†Quinton, A.: *Bacon*. Oxford: Oxford University Press, 1980.

Bagehot, Walter (1826–1877) British journalist and political and constitutional theorist. Bagehot was born into a Unitarian banking family in the west of England and educated at University College, London, afterwards returning to Somerset to help in running the family bank. Later he became editor first of the *National Review* and then, from 1860 to his death, of *The Economist*. He wrote copiously for the periodical journals of the time and his best known works, *The English Constitution* (1865) and *Physics and Politics* (1867), both appeared originally as series of articles. A polymath, he wrote perceptively and entertainingly on literary, political, historical and economic subjects, with a literary manner which was genial, tolerant and conversational; his stance was that of a shrewd, pragmatic man of the world who understood business and the stolid English national character but who nevertheless understood the importance, in the long run, of original speculative ideas.

Bagehot's political position was that of an unillusioned conservative liberal who valued intelligence and believed in progress but who knew that intelligence needed to be complemented by realism and the ability to work with the prejudices and limitations of average mankind, and that progress was therefore necessarily slow. It was a view which readily found justification in the gradualist notions of 'social evolution' which were becoming established in his time and of which, in *Physics and Politics*, he became a leading exponent. Bagehot was also a strong believer in another popular notion of the period, the importance of 'national character' in politics; he saw the English as predominantly sluggish and in need of ideas to save them from stagnation, the French as too volatile and lacking the stability of habit – what he provocatively called 'stupidity' – necessary to self-government. His earliest articles were written from Paris in 1852 on the coup d'état which established the Second Empire; Bagehot took the line, unpopular with liberals, that the circumstances justified strong measures, though he later became a critic of Napoleon III's regime.

In *The English Constitution* Bagehot set out to attack what he presented as the orthodox view of the division of powers between executive and legislature. In fact this view was already old-fashioned and Bagehot's revision was not quite as original as he claimed, but it was he who gave definitive form to the new orthodoxy. He argued that executive and legislature were closely linked by the Cabinet, which was essentially a committee of the House of Commons. The new interpretation that Bagehot proposed was a distinction between the 'efficient' and 'dignified' parts of the constitution. The efficient part was the House of Commons with the Cabinet as its executive arm, the monarchy and the House of Lords chiefly belonged to the dignified part; the function of the former was to conduct business, that of the latter to provide stability by the impression it made on the popular mind.

In *Physics and Politics* Bagehot tried to adapt modern biological theories, notably the Darwinian struggle for existence and physiological explanations of habitual and reflex behaviour, to an account of human history significantly derived from Henry MAINE and from George Grote's *History of Greece* (see SOCIAL DARWINISM). Bagehot argued that progress required both stability and innovation. Stability was produced chiefly by the powerful influences of imitation and habit, which co-ordinated social behavior in a 'cake of custom', but the struggle for existence between societies also attached advantages to some kinds of innovation. A balance between the two was the ideal, and in the latest stage of human history, 'the age of discussion', innovation, instead of being accidental, becomes the subject of rational scrutiny. Liberal constitutionalism is therefore presented as the latest stage of historical development and the best guarantee of continued orderly progress.   JWB

Reading

Bagehot, W.: *Collected Works*, ed. N. St John-Stevas. London: The Economist, 1965. [Vol. V contains *The English Constitution*, vol. VII *Physics and Politics*.]

————: *The English Constitution*. London: Collins, 1963.

————: *Physics and Politics*. Boston, Mass.: Beacon, 1956.

Buchan, A.: *The Spare Chancellor: the life of Walter Bagehot*. London: Chatto & Windus, 1959.

†St John-Stevas, N.: *Walter Bagehot: a study of his life and thought, together with a selection from his writings*. London: Eyre & Spottiswoode, 1959.

Bakunin, Michael (1814–1876) Russian anarchist. Bakunin was influenced in his early years by HEGEL, but on visiting Germany during 1839–41 he absorbed the more radical ideas of the YOUNG HEGELIANS. During the next two decades he was chiefly involved in propagating the cause of Slav nationalism. Imprisoned by the tsar from 1851 to 1857, he returned to Western Europe in the 1860s, and passed the remainder of his life as an agitator and propagandist for ANARCHISM. Famous for his intrigues and the secret societies that he was continually forming and dissolving, Bakunin struggled with MARX for control of the First International between 1869 and 1872.

Bakunin's mature thought is expressly and vehemently anti-political. All political theorists, in his view, took original sin as their starting point. Beginning with variants of the proposition that man was inherently flawed by egoism they had unanimously concluded that a portion of his liberty had to be yielded to the state that alone could act as a curb to his vicious nature. In this respect the necessity of the state is notionally tied to the central proposition of all religions; historically too, Bakunin contended, the rise and perfection of the state coincided with that of religion. The two co-existed in his view in a 'symbiotic' functional relationship. Both claimed and granted to each other exclusive jurisdiction in their respective spheres, both fed on and conspired to maintain public ignorance and superstition in order to bolster their own authority and to convince man of his own impotence in managing his spiritual or social affairs. All authority partook of the nature of religious authority in so far as it created a mysterious and impenetrable world accessible only to its licensed interpreters and in so far as it conspired to sustain in men the presumption of their own wickedness. Throughout his turbulent life Bakunin was an implacable atheist and anti-statist.

Man, in Bakunin's view, was a notionally sociable being possessed of an instinct for freedom through self-activity within a community of equals. God and the state, ignorance, superstition and the presumption of impotence were the declared enemies of human liberation. They could be combated through the penetration of natural laws, uncovered by positive science, down to the popular masses. If science was to be the solvent of religion, rebellion was to dissolve the habit of obedience. The 'sacred instinct of revolt', as Bakunin termed it, was the essential attribute of man, dulled but never totally extinguished in proportion to the development of civilization. Those least touched by, or most marginal to, the development of capitalist civilization were therefore most likely to begin the process of revolutionary destruction. The positive re-appropriation of man's powers and potentials (or liberty proper) could only be effected through the free association of individuals in pursuit of common purposes within a federation of free communes. But no man could be free, in Bakunin's view, so long as he remained economically dependent upon another. The compulsion of the wage-relation and the hierarchical pattern of authority within the productive process replicated the patterns of domination and subordination within the legal and political structures. Freedom demanded therefore that all should be afforded the material wherewithal of economic independence. It followed that property rights would have to inhere in the community. Consistent anarchism was, in Bakunin's conception, necessarily socialist.

Bakunin's thought refined itself principally in opposition to that of Marx, and libertarian socialists continue to esteem him for his prophetic critique of the likely consequences of the Marxist dictatorship of the proletariat (see ANARCHISM). Bakunin was not, however, a systematic thinker either in his mode of composition (he never completed any of his more substantial writings) or in the consistency and coherence of his standpoints. He was indeed proud of his eclecticism and within his thought there was an uneasy blend of materialism and romanticism, hymns to spontaneity and preoccupation with conspiratorial organization, internationalism and Germanophobia. Like his mentor PROUDHON, he was suspicious of the narrow schemata of pedants. The ambiguities in his thought have nourished the claims of the most diverse contemporary commentators and groups to appropriate him as a harbinger of their causes.   NH

Reading
Bakunin, M.: *Oeuvres*, tomes I–VI. Paris: Stock, 1912–13.
———: *Izbranniye Sochineniya*, tomes I–V. Petersburg: Golos Truda, 1920–2.
———: *Archives Bakounine*, tomes I–VII. Leiden: Brill, 1961–81.
———: *Selected Writings*, ed. A. Lehning. London: Cape, 1973.
———: *Bakunin on Anarchy*, ed. S. Dolgoff. London: Allen & Unwin, 1973.
†Carr, E.H.: *Michael Bakunin*. London: Macmillan, 1937.
†Kelly, A.: *Michael Bakunin*. Oxford: Clarendon Press, 1982.

Masters, A.: *Bakunin: the Father of Anarchism*. New York: Saturday Review Press, 1974.

Venturi, F.: *Roots of Revolution*. London: Weidenfeld & Nicolson, 1960.

Barrès, Maurice (1862–1923) French writer and politician. Barrès was the most important theoretician of radical NATIONALISM at the turn of the century, extremely influential in the literary and political worlds. He was elected as a Boulangist Deputy on a nationalist and anti-semitic platform in 1889. In 1906 he was both elected Deputy for Paris, a position he retained until his death, and became a member of the *Académie française*. A pioneer of the French political novel, he expounded his theory of nationalism in his major works: *Les Déracinés* (1897), *L'Appel au soldat* (1900), *Leurs Figures* (1902) and *Scènes et doctrines du nationalisme* (1902).

The point of departure of Barrèsian nationalism is the need to provide the country, regarded as 'disunited and decerebrated' – that is to say, threatened with death and disintegration – with the means of salvation. Barrès believed that if the country was to be preserved from decadence the French collectivity had to be re-endowed with a soul, an identity and a desire to live and to struggle; he consequently elaborated a theory of tribal nationalism on a basis of SOCIAL DARWINISM, romanticism and biological determinism. Barrès held that the old theory consecrated by the French Revolution of a collectivity consisting of an aggregate of individuals was replaced by a theory of organic solidarity expressed in a cult of the Land and the Dead, the equivalent of the German notion of Blood and Soil. He regarded the nation as an organism comparable to an animate being or a tree, and nationalism as a system of ethics, of criteria of behaviour dictated by the general interest regardless of the will of the individual. Barrès conceived a kind of relativity which enabled him to deny the validity of moral absolutes: truth, justice and law, he believed, existed only in relation to the needs of the collectivity.

His physiological determinism, his view of man as a mechanism determined by his membership of a collectivity, were contributory elements in his vision of a closed society. A violent anti-rationalism and belief in the primacy of the unconscious over reason completed this new nationalist ideology. But the salvation of the nation also required a deep political reform. It implied a permanent struggle against LIBERALISM, DEMOCRACY, MARXISM and the creation of a strong, authoritarian regime.

This cult of deep and mysterious forces necessarily entailed, as its natural corollary, a violent anti-intellectualism. Barrès gave a lengthy condemnation of the critical spirit and its products, setting against them instinct, intuitive and irrational sentiment, emotion and enthusiasm, the deep forces which determine human behaviour and constitute the reality and the truth of things as well as their beauty. Rationalism, he maintained, is the product of the 'uprooted': it blunts sensitivity, deadens instinct and can only nullify the motive forces of national activity. It followed that, in order to preserve the nation, one had to address oneself to the people. Barrès exalted the primitive force, the vigour and vitality to be found in the people, who had not been contaminated by the rationalist and individualistic poison.

Since it was the mass which was truly the nation and since the primary aim of politics is to assure the integrity and power of the nation, nationalism, Barrès believed, could not allow the social question to remain unsolved. Barrès was one of the first national socialists, one of the most prominent exponents of modern anti-semitism, and one of the first to lay the intellectual bases of FASCISM. ZS

Reading

Barrès, M.: *L'Oeuvre de Maurice Barrès*. 20 vols. Paris: Club de l'Honnête Homme, 1965–8.

Doty, C.S.: *From Cultural Rebellion to Counterrevolution: the Politics of Maurice Barrès*. Athens: Ohio University Press, 1976.

Madaule, J.: *Le Nationalisme de Barrès*. Marseilles: Sagittaire, 1943.

†Sternhell, Z.: *Maurice Barrès et le nationalisme français*. Paris: Armand Colin, 1972; pbk Brussels: Complexe, 1985.

————: *La Droite révolutionnaire: les origines françaises du fascisme*. Paris: Seuil, 1978; pbk 1984.

Touchard, J.: Le nationalisme de Barrès. In *Maurice Barrès: actes du colloque*. Nancy: Université de Nancy, 1963.

Bayle, Pierre (1647–1706) Philosopher and

man of letters. Bayle was born at Carla in the French Pyrenees. Though a member of the minority Huguenot community and the son of a pastor, his education owed as much to the classics and humanities as it did to Calvinist theology. Completing his studies at Geneva, Bayle taught philosophy at the Protestant Academy of Sedan until it was closed by the French authorities in 1682. He then sought refuge in the Netherlands where a post was created for him in Rotterdam as professor of philosophy and history. Freed from the censorship of his homeland Bayle found in exile a second vocation as journalist and essayist.

In 1682 Bayle published his *Lettre sur la comète*, and his *Critique générale de l'histoire du calvinisme de M. Maimbourg*. The year 1686 saw two more polemical works: *Ce que c'est que la France toute catholique sous le règne de Louis le Grand*, and *Commentaire philosophique sur ces paroles de Jesus Christ 'Contrain-les d'entrer'*. In 1684 Bayle founded an international monthly review of books entitled *Nouvelles de la République des lettres* committed to the free promotion of ideas across frontiers, whether scientific, medical, or theological. This ran for three years. When, in 1692, he was commissioned to write his *Dictionnaire historique et critique*, Bayle was able to make a living entirely from his pen.

Bayle's contribution to political thought lies mainly in exposure of controversy among philosophers and theologians, in his advocacy of the freedom to do so, and in his proposals for subordinating clerical dogmatism to an enlightened civil control. He supported the absolute sovereignty of the civil ruler but rejected the doctrine popularized by HOBBES that a single national church was essential for maintaining public order. The ruler's proper commitment was to religious impartiality, not to any doctrine of religious uniformity (see TOLERATION).

Bayle's views are often misinterpreted by commentators; to many eighteenth-century reformers, they implied mere toleration – not necessarily the right to individual free thought. In fact, Bayle's heterodoxy anticipates many tenets of modern liberal theory: freedom of scientific enquiry, an uncensored press, the freedom to teach new ideas, and above all the notion that the good society is one that does not impede constructive criticisms of its own institutions.   SLJ

Reading

Bayle, P.: *Oeuvres diverses*. The Hague, 1737.
——: *Dictionnaire historique et critique* (1696). Rotterdam, 1740.
†Dodge, G.H.: *The Political Theory of the Huguenots of the Dispersion*. New York: Columbia University Press, 1947.
Jenkinson, S.L.: *The political thought of Pierre Bayle 1680–1690*. (University of Sheffield, thesis, typescript, 1975.)
†Labrousse, E.: *Bayle*, trans. D. Potts. Oxford and New York: Oxford University Press, 1983.
——: *Pierre Bayle*. 2 vols. The Hague: Martinus Nijhoff, 1963–4.
Plamenatz, J.P.: *Man and Society*. London: Longman, 1977.
Popkin, R.: *History of Scepticism from Erasmus to Spinoza*. Berkeley: University of California Press, 1975.
Rex, W.E.: *Essays on Pierre Bayle and Religious Controversy*. The Hague: Martinus Nijhoff, 1965.

Beccaria, Cesare Bonesana (1738–1794) Italian criminologist, economist and man of letters. Born in Milan of a well-to-do Pavian noble family, and with an idle and aristocratic temperament, Beccaria was inspired with the ideas of the ENLIGHTENMENT by Pietro and Alessandro Verri, the main founders of the Lombard reformist movement. Together they founded the Accademia dei Pugni (Academy of Fists) (1762) and collaborated on the Milanese review *Il Caffè* (1764–6). Through Alessandro, an official at the Milan prison, and the promptings of Pietro, Beccaria came to write the group's chief work, *Dei delitti e delle pene* (On Crimes and Punishments) (1764). It quickly became a classic of Enlightenment culture. Translated into French (1766) and English (1767), it earned the praise of VOLTAIRE, DIDEROT, BLACKSTONE, BENTHAM, JEFFERSON, and Catherine the Great, among others, thereby influencing the movement for penal reform, particularly the abolition of the death penalty and torture. In 1768 Beccaria was given a personal chair in 'cameralist science' in the Palatine School of Milan. His lectures of 1769–70, published posthumously as *Elements of Political Economy* (1894), have led some to hail him as the Italian Adam SMITH, on account of the similarity of their views on the division of labour and the determination of wages. He was, however, closer to the doctrines of the physiocrats in most of his economic theories (see PHYSIOCRACY). He was a devotee of ROUSSEAU, and his letters are full of the proto-Romanticism of *La Nouvelle Héloïse*, an influence which broadened his application of utilitarianism to include an appreciation of the depth and nature of individual feeling.

Beccaria's principal work is undoubtedly *Dei delitti e delle pene*. Its success derives from its fusing of the various strands of the Enlightenment, represented by his favourite authors MONTESQUIEU, HELVÉTIUS and Rousseau. The famous preface became a manifesto of the movement, combining as it did the desire for a science of society with a concern to improve the well-being of humankind. Beccaria started from a contractarian theory of the origins of society, arguing that the individual sacrifices to the political community only so much of his liberty as 'suffices to induce others to defend it' (p. 13). Developing earlier formulations of Helvétius and Pietro Verri, he expressed this goal in utilitarian terms as securing 'the maximum happiness divided among the greatest number' (p. 9) (see UTILITARIANISM). Nevertheless, the contractual foundation of society gives the individual rights against the use of simply any method to produce the greatest aggregate happiness, so Beccaria cannot be deemed a utilitarian in the classic Benthamite sense, for '[t]here is no freedom if the laws permit that in certain circumstances a man ceases to be a "person" and becomes a "thing"' (p. 50). He summed up this requirement in the general theorem: 'That a punishment may not be an act of violence . . . against a private member of society, it should be public, immediate, and necessary, the least possible in the case given, proportioned to the crime and determined by the laws' (p. 104). This led him to condemn most of the contemporary practices of torture, mutilation and capital punishment and to call for a more humane system of imprisonment. He did not, however, consider PUNISHMENT as a means of reforming the criminal, merely as a deterrent.

RPB

Reading

Beccaria, C.: *Opere*, ed. S. Romagnoli. 2 vols. Florence: Sansoni, 1958.

———: *Dei delitte e delle pene. Con una raccolta di lettere e documenti relativi alla nascita dell'opera e alla sua fortuna nell'Europa del Settecento*, ed. F. Venturi. Turin: Einaudi, 1965.

———: *On Crimes and Punishments*, trans. H. Paolucci. Indianapolis: Bobbs-Merrill, 1963.

†Venturi, F.: Cesare Beccaria and penal reform. In *Italy and the Enlightenment*, ed. S.J. Woolf. London: Longman, 1972.

———: *Settecento riformatore: da Muratori a Beccaria*, pp. 645–797. Turin: Einaudi, 1969.

behaviouralism The view that political behaviour can and should be studied scientifically, in particular through the use of quantitative methods, with the object of creating a political science based entirely on empirical data. See POLITICAL THEORY AND POLITICAL SCIENCE.

Bellamy, Edward (1850–1898) American journalist and socialist. Author of the utopian novel *Looking Backward* (1888). See UTOPIANISM.

Bentham, Jeremy (1748–1832) British utilitarian philosopher, jurist, and reformer. Bentham has been an important and influential figure in the development of modern political thought. His writings have become classic texts in philosophy, government, law, social administration and economics, and few subsequent writers have been able to ignore the theories and arguments which he developed throughout his long life. In method, he introduced a system of logical analysis and attention to detail which had not been attempted since Aristotle, and he was able to transform the way in which these subjects were studied. With these theoretical preoccupations he combined a practical bent which led him not only to attempt to apply his ideas to numerous projects, but also to his important role as an advocate of – ultimately radical – reform. His ideas formed the basis of PHILOSOPHIC RADICALISM, and few deny that he had considerable influence on the great reforms of the Victorian period.

Apart from this practical, reforming side, to which he gave much of his time, as with the Panopticon scheme for a model prison, Bentham's major achievement was to transform the way in which philosophical and political ideas were conceived and expressed. The distance in method and substance between Montesquieu, Hume and Blackstone on the one hand and Bentham on the other was far greater than that between Bentham and political thought in the twentieth century, and that great distance was created largely by Bentham himself. In spite of his importance, Bentham's ideas have, until recently, been studied mostly through others: e.g., the jurisprudence through John AUSTIN, the theory of democracy through James MILL and the utilitarian philosophy through John Stuart MILL (see UTILITARIANISM). This tendency has been partly due to the difficulties of Bentham's style which have deterred all but determined scholars, the fact that he seldom prepared his writings for publication, and the disadvantage that the only well-known edition of his writings has been the inadequate and incomplete *Works of Jeremy Bentham* (1838–43), edited by his literary executor, John Bowring. The new edition of the *Collected Works* (1968–in progress), which will publish in approximately sixty-five volumes Bentham's main works and correspondence, should provide a new perspective for estimating the scale of his achievement.

Bentham's youth, though not so well known as that of John Stuart Mill, must have been equally difficult. His considerable gifts were recognized at an early age by his father; he entered Westminster School at the age of seven and went on to Queen's College, Oxford at twelve. He was destined for a legal career, but although he was admitted to the Bar he frustrated his father's ambitions in not practising law.

By the mid–1770s, Bentham was engaged in two major projects. The first was a study of penal law and especially an analysis of offences and punishments. From this material, he eventually published his best-known work, *An Introduction to the Principles of Morals and Legislation* (printed in 1780 and published in 1789), which was intended to introduce a comprehensive penal code. As sequels to the

Introduction he wrote two works: *Of Laws in General* (first published in 1945 as *The Limits of Jurisprudence Defined*) and *Indirect Legislation* (first published by Dumont in the *Traités de législation, civile et pénale* (1802) and in English in the Bowring edition). These three works constitute major parts of Bentham's early jurisprudence, and though the actual study of penal law was not completed, parts of it were published in the *Traités* and in the *Théorie des peines et des récompenses* (1811), both of which were edited by Dumont (see PUNISHMENT).

Bentham's second project was his extensive critique of BLACKSTONE's *Commentaries on the Laws of England* which was incomplete and not published until 1928, but from this material he published anonymously his first major work, *A Fragment on Government* (1776). The *Fragment* discussed critically a brief passage in Blackstone which dealt with the English constitution in Lockeian terms and examined such notions as the state of nature, social contract, consent, sovereignty, and the mixed constitution (see LOCKE). Bentham's object was largely critical, and although he did not develop an alternative political theory to that of Blackstone, he called into question the Lockeian concepts which had become widely accepted in his day. In addition to these works, he began to take up economic issues, on which his first published work was *Defence of Usury* (1787), a critique of Adam SMITH's discussion of usury in the *Wealth of Nations*.

On the eve of the French Revolution Bentham had established a modest reputation. Through his friendship with Lord Lansdowne, he had made contact with *philosophes* in France, and eventually he developed a friendship with Étienne Dumont, the Swiss writer and reformer whose French versions of his works (especially the *Traités*) were to make him famous throughout the world. Although he was not part of the reform movement in England, Bentham wrote several manuscripts in support of democratic institutions in France. His *Draught of a New Plan for the Organization of the Judicial Establishment of France* (1790), a work designed to reform the French judicial system, led to his being made an honorary citizen of France in 1792. Like many of those initially sympathetic to the Revolution, Bentham soon turned against its excesses. He was also opposed to the revolutionary rhetoric of the French, and especially to the concepts used in the *Declaration of rights*. Natural RIGHTS, he wrote in *Anarchical Fallacies*, were 'simple nonsense' and 'natural and imprescriptible rights' were 'nonsense upon stilts' (*Works*, ed. Bowring, II. p. 501). Bentham believed that liberty could be secured only where rights were established through a legal system. After his 'conversion' to radicalism he would also argue that a system of representative democracy and open government was necessary to secure these legal rights.

Bentham's 'conversion' took place during the years 1809–10, though he did not write publicly in favour of universal suffrage, the secret ballot, and annual parliaments until 1817 with the publication of the *Plan of Parliamentary Reform*. Before 1809, with the exception of the essays written at the time of the French Revolution, Bentham displayed an indifference to political and constitutional issues but a number of factors, such as the influence of James Mill, the failure of the Panopticon, his abiding belief in reform and especially the reform of the legal system, contacts developed with various reformers, and the establishment of the liberal regime in Spain, seem to have led to a fundamental shift in his political thought. This shift culminated in the massive, unfinished *Constitutional Code* (1822–), in which he developed at great length and in considerable detail his utopian vision of a constitutional democracy and his sharp critique of existing political systems. Nevertheless, he did not become wholly absorbed either in constitutional or political issues. His writings at this time spanned an enormous range of subjects including education, logic and language, rhetoric, religion, as well as numerous works on specific legal themes such as evidence, judicial organization, property registration, public economy and other such subjects.

By the 1820s, with many of his works in print and the volumes edited by Dumont widely circulated, Bentham's reputation in Europe and Latin America, as well as in Britain, was established. His correspondence was enormous, and a steady stream of politicians, adventurers, and scholars visited his London home at Queen's Square Place. A number of his works were edited by others: the *Rationale of Judicial Evidence* (1827) by John Stuart Mill, the *Book of Fallacies* (1824) by Peregrine Bingham, *Not Paul but Jesus* (1823) by Francis Place, and the *Analysis of the Influence of Natural Religion* (1822) by George Grote. The *Westminster Review*, edited by John Bowring and financed by Bentham, was founded in 1824 and established philosophic radicalism as an alternative to the Whig doctrines espoused by the *Edinburgh Review*. Bentham also campaigned at this time for both legal and parliamentary reform in England. Nevertheless, his main intellectual preoccupation during the 1820s, though he was already in his seventies, was his renewed attempt to construct a *Pannomion* (complete code of laws) which would include civil, penal, procedure and constitutional codes. In contrast to his earlier attempts at codification, the *Constitutional Code* was given pride of place and it was here that Bentham's mature political theory was developed. The work was legal rather than philosophical in form, but the philosophical examination of such subjects as liberty, equality, rights, obligation, and sovereignty can be abstracted from other works which he wrote at the time. The *Constitutional Code* itself dealt with problems of organization and structure and contained remarkable discussions, for example, of how the armed forces might be organized so as not to threaten the institutions of representative democracy, of the conditions for establishing open government, of the means by which corruption by officials might be reduced without depriving them of the power necessary to perform their duties, and of how the judiciary might be organized so as to provide easy and inexpensive access to the judicial system for all members of society.

In his political thought Bentham made three important contributions to the development of LIBERALISM. Firstly, he used ideas he inherited from Locke, Hume, Montesquieu and Helvétius to mount a thorough attack on the received Lockeian doctrine. After Bentham, the most vital strand in liberal thought was based on utilitarian principles. Secondly, in the 1820s he provided a new approach to constitutional theory which advanced the precepts and absorbed the criticisms of the great period of constitutional thought and practice around the time of the American and French revolutions. Bentham gave to this existing theory not only new foundations but also a new emphasis on administrative and judicial organization and on the responsible exercise of power. Finally, by conceiving the ends of legislation to include security, subsistence, abundance and equality, and by envisaging political structures to advance these ends, Bentham foresaw the needs and aspirations of the modern democratic state. He left this legacy to John Stuart Mill who, though not so enthusiastic about democracy as Bentham, adopted many of his concepts and categories.   FR

Reading

Bentham, J.: *The Collected Works of Jeremy Bentham*, ed. J.H. Burns, J.R. Dinwiddy and F. Rosen. London: Athlone Press; Oxford: Clarendon Press, 1968–; especially: *An Introduction to the Principles of Morals and Legislation*, ed. J.H. Burns and H.L.A. Hart. London: Athlone Press, 1970; *A Comment on the Commentaries* and *A Fragment on Government*, ed. J.H. Burns and H.L.A. Hart. London: Athlone Press, 1977; *Of Laws in General*, ed. H.L.A. Hart. London: Athlone Press, 1970; *Constitutional Code*, I, ed. F. Rosen and J.H. Burns. Oxford: Clarendon Press, 1983.

————: *The Works of Jeremy Bentham*, ed. J. Bowring. Edinburgh: William Tait, 1838–43.

Dinwiddy, J.R.: Bentham's transition to political radicalism, 1809–10. *Journal of the History of Ideas* 26 (1975) 683–700.

Halévy, E.: *La Formation du radicalisme philosophique*. 3 vols. Paris: Félix Alcan, 1901–4; trans. M. Morris: *The Growth of Philosophic Radicalism*. London: Faber & Faber, 1928.

†Harrison, R.: *Bentham*. London: Routledge & Kegan Paul, 1983.

†Hart, H.L.A.: *Essays on Bentham, Jurisprudence and Political Theory*. Oxford: Clarendon Press, 1982.

†Hume, L.J.: *Bentham and Bureaucracy*. Cambridge: Cambridge University Press, 1981.

†Rosen, F.: *Jeremy Bentham and Representative Democracy: a Study of the Constitutional Code*. Oxford: Clarendon Press, 1983.

Bernstein, Edward (1850–1932) German socialist theoretician. The son of a Berlin railway engineer, Bernstein joined the German Social Democratic Party in 1872 and soon became one of its leading journalists. The anti-socialist laws compelled him to emigrate to England where he was strongly influenced by the Fabians. On returning to Germany Bernstein became one of the leading advocates of REVISIONISM which aroused all the more heated controversy as Bernstein was seen (together with KAUTSKY) as the heir of MARX and ENGELS. As a Reichstag deputy, Bernstein opposed the 1914–18 war and left the Social Democratic Party. Although he returned later to both the party and the Reichstag, his influence towards the end of his life was much diminished.

In his earlier writings Bernstein was concerned, as he saw it, to bring Marx's ideas up to date in the light of contemporary social developments. Summarizing his views, he wrote: 'Peasants do not sink; middle class does not disappear; crises do not grow even larger; misery and serfdom do not increase.' From a close observation of recent trends and statistics, Bernstein claimed that capitalism was stabilizing itself through the creation of cartels and monopolies. But while control was being concentrated institutions such as joint stock companies were spreading ownership ever more widely. At the same time real wages were rising and the middle class was expanding. The political and intellectual corollary of this was that socialism could be seen as the successor to liberalism: capitalism had shown itself to be sufficiently adaptable for there to be hope of its gradual transformation into socialism, which was seen as the more or less peaceful inheritor of a fully developed capitalism. Bernstein had an extremely empirical bent to his thought – largely on account of his rejection of Hegel and any dialectical approach. The very barrenness of his positivist views led him to seek a separate moral basis for his socialism which he found in the philosophy of KANT, then undergoing a revival. Bernstein's favourite maxim was that the movement was everything and the goal nothing. His strength lay in the detailed observation of contemporary trends and his strong moral sense. But at the same time he was an extremely eclectic thinker and incapable of interpreting his observations in the light of any coherent and systematic theory. (See also SOCIAL DEMOCRACY.)   DTMcL

Reading
†Bernstein, E.: *Evolutionary Socialism* (1898). New York: Schocken, 1961.
Gay, P.: *The Dilemma of Democratic Socialism*. New York: Schocken, 1962.
McLellan, D.: *Marxism after Marx*, ch. 2. London: Macmillan, 1980.

Blackstone, William (1723–1780) English jurist and judge. Blackstone is justly famed for his great institutional work on the common law of England, hugely influential in England, in all the common law territories of the Empire, and not least in the United States whose independence from Great Britain entailed no abrogation of common law, but a great need for some lucid and compact statement of it. Blackstone's *Commentaries on the Laws of England* (4 vols, 1765–9) emerged from lectures he delivered in Oxford University, first as a Fellow of All Souls (elected 1743, in residence and lecturing from 1753) and then as first Vinerian Professor of English Law (1758–66). He had been educated at Charterhouse and Pembroke College, Oxford (from 1738), and was called to the bar in 1746, where his practice never greatly flourished.

After his main teaching period, he was a member of Parliament in the Tory interest from 1761, giving voice and vote rather uncritically to the government's concerns (and, ironically, opposing the claims of the American colonists). He became a judge in 1770, serving in the Common Pleas with a brief interlude in King's Bench; but his health and his judicial performance were somewhat indifferent, and he died in 1780 at the age of fifty-seven.

By the late eighteenth century, England had become almost alone in Western Europe (and contrasting sharply even with Scotland, as Blackstone would have well known even without Lord Mansfield telling him) in having no comprehensive articulate institutional statement of its modern laws. Blackstone's lectures, lucid in content if not eloquent in delivery, and later his polished and elegant *Commentaries*, remedied this. After the introduction, where he sets out a rationalist version of natural law theory similar to that of GROTIUS and purports to ground English law therein, he proceeds to expound the law of (or 'rights of') persons in Book I; then in Book II the law of property or 'rights of things'; in Book III 'private wrongs' (torts) and their remedies; and finally in Book IV 'public wrongs' or criminal law, a humane and far from uncritical account of the still barbarously punitive law of crimes in England.

At the level of legal and political theory Blackstone adds little to the traditions on which he draws. But in terms of political and constitutional history he expresses with particular clarity the Old Whig perception of the eighteenth-century constitutional order achieved in the Revolution of 1688 (and consolidated in the Union of 1707). Nor should the importance or influence of his doctrinal systematization of English law ever be overlooked.

The complacency of Blackstone's general view of the British constitution and the English law, and the lack of philosophical rigour in his jusnaturalism, inspired the wrath of at least one of the auditors of his lectures. Hence sprang Jeremy BENTHAM's blistering critique of Blackstonian jurisprudence in *A Fragment on Government* (1776) and *A Comment on the Commentaries* (unfinished, published 1928). Natural law theory and conservative constitutionalism were the spurs to positivist jurisprudence and radical utilitarianism. Yet legal reform presupposed understanding of law, and Blackstone had wrought better to that end than Bentham ever allowed.   NMacC

Reading
Bentham, J.: *A Comment on the Commentaries* and *A Fragment on Government*, ed. J.H. Burns and H.L.A. Hart. London: Athlone Press, 1977.
Blackstone, W.: *Commentaries on the Laws of England*. Facsimile edn. Chicago: Chicago University Press, 1979.
Boorstin, D.: *The Mysterious Science of the Law*. Cambridge, Mass.: Harvard University Press, 1941.
†Jones, G.: *The Sovereignty of the Law: Selections from Blackstone's Commentaries*. London: Macmillan, 1973.
Milsom, S.F.C.: *The Nature of Blackstone's Achievement*. London: The Selden Society, 1981.

Blanc, Louis (1811–1882) French socialist. In *The Organization of Labour* (1839) Blanc outlined a scheme for state-funded 'national workshops' to be run by associations of workers. See SOCIALISM.

Blanqui, Louis-Auguste (1805–1881) French communist and revolutionary. Primarily an active revolutionary, Blanqui was also a theorist of revolutionary strategy. Most of his writing was done in prison (he spent forty years behind bars), and was not produced in any systematic form. Much of it has been lost, so students of his thought encounter some difficulty in getting a clear overall picture of what he had to say.

Blanqui's chief contribution was undoubtedly a theory of the revolutionary seizure of power, emphasizing the need for a swift coup d'état carried out by a small vanguard of dedicated conspirators who would subsequently consolidate power by dictatorial methods. The revolutionary overthrow of bourgeois liberalism was seen as an immediate possibility once the vanguard had been established. Furthermore Blanqui reserved an important role within this elite for individual agitators drawn from the bourgeoisie itself. This strategy achieved little success for Blanqui and his followers during his lifetime, but it served as an important link between the Jacobin tradition of direct action (in the 1789 French Revolution) and the Russian Bolshevik tradition inspired by Lenin.

Blanqui's view of post-revolutionary society has often been seen as somewhat utopian. He placed a great deal of emphasis on the importance of beliefs and ideas in shaping social organization, and he seems to have regarded education as the chief agent of social transformation. Under COMMUNISM state power would not diminish, but would be used to create an association of workers living in conditions of equality.

Blanquists played a significant role in the Paris Commune of 1871, and continued to exert some influence on the French left into the early twentieth century.   KT

Reading

†Bernstein, S.: *Auguste Blanqui and the Art of Insurrection.* London: Lawrence & Wishart, 1971.

Blanqui, L-A.: *Textes choisis*, ed. V. P. Volguine. Paris: Éditions Sociales, 1955.

†Spitzer, A.: *The Revolutionary Theories of Louis-Auguste Blanqui.* New York: Columbia University Press, 1957.

Bloch, Ernst (1885–1977) German philosopher. A critical Marxist, Bloch emphasized the utopian element in Marxist thought (see UTOPIANISM). His major work was *Das Prinzip Hoffnung*, 1954–9 (*The Principle of Hope.* Oxford: Blackwell, 1986).

Bodin, Jean (1529/30–1596) French philosopher and political writer. A native of Angers, Bodin studied law at his home university before moving to Toulouse where he branched out into history, metaphysics, mathematics and astronomy in addition to acquiring a competence in several languages. Plans for a legal career gave way to his interest in politics which brought him into court circles and the service of the Duc d'Alençon, younger brother of the future Henry III. Forfeiting the king's favour in 1577 because of his opposition to any further alienation of the domain and the pursuit of the war against the Huguenots, Bodin retired to Laon where, by virtue of his marriage to Françoise Trouilliart, he acquired the office of *procureur du roi*. In his later years he espoused the cause of the Catholic League, a particularly bizarre decision given both his earlier attitudes and his increasingly marked Judaism. Bodin probably feared the loss of his office, and the episode serves as a pointed reminder that practically his entire adult life was passed amid the turmoil of civil and religious strife.

Not surprisingly, his extensive writings reflect both a desire for the restoration of the integrity of the body politic and a deeply religious search for personal reassurance. They reveal on the one hand a humanist scholar drawing inspiration from classical, historical and legal sources and on the other a deep, at times mystical, preoccupation with an imaginary universe resting on a fusion of Thomist, Judaistic and neo-Platonic concepts. If his first major work was a precocious analysis of the causes of the alarming price inflation of the sixteenth century his last published work, which dealt with witchcraft, showed how firmly he shared the popular conception of a world inhabited by both good and evil spirits. Even the analysis of the STATE and CIVIL SOCIETY contained in *Les six livres de la république* (The Six Books of a Commonweal) of 1576, on which Bodin's stature as a political theorist rests, cannot be fully understood if it is removed from the context of the metaphysical universe in which it is set.

This work is celebrated for its definition of SOVEREIGNTY as the untrammelled and undivided power to make general laws. Without such power a state cannot properly be held to exist and it is the locus of this supreme legislative power which determines whether the state acquires a monarchical, aristocratic or democratic character. This definition excluded mixed states of the Aristotelian type. It also marked a significant departure from the traditional emphasis on the king as judge and the attendant idea that his *raison d'être* was the administration of justice. Sovereignty did not in Bodin's view depend on whether laws were just or not but on the power to make them. Moreover, as he allowed subjects no right of either consent or resistance to the laws of the sovereign power, he is generally held to have provided one of the essential ideological underpinnings of the monarchical ABSOLUTISM which culminated in the reign of Louis XIV. Bodin certainly gave impetus to the formulation of the secular and utilitarian concept of sovereignty which is familiar today.

While recognizing that Bodin's idea of sovereignty has proved the most enduring and pervasive of his ideas, it should be remembered that the *Six Books* were not a treatise on sovereignty but a description and defence of a Commonweal. This Bodin defines at the outset as a 'lawful government of many families and of that which unto them belongeth, with a puissant sovereignty'. The emphasis on '*lawful* government' has a significance of its own and cannot be treated simply as an aspect of the discussion of sovereignty. On the contrary, central to Bodin's analysis is an explicit and crucial distinction between the form of the state which is determined by the locus of sovereignty and the form of government: a monarchical state can assume a tyrannical, lordly or just form, an aristocracy might be administered in a popular fashion, while a democratic state could employ aristocratic methods.

Bodin felt that the best model of government was that represented by the French type which he described as a 'just monarchy'. For, in this system, the absolute power of the monarch was moderated by the need to recognize the force of natural and divine law. Just as God was the all-powerful ruler of the universe, so was the king all-powerful in his sphere; but like God, of whom he was the image, he was expected to temper power with justice. Although the king had the right to make laws without consent, to overrule custom, and even to ignore existing laws, he should not, Bodin emphasizes, use such rights without due care and consideration for the welfare of his subjects. If changes were necessary he should 'imitate and follow the great God of nature who in all things proceedeth easily and little by little'. In practice this meant recognizing the role of those people and institutions which shared in the process of government. Not only did Bodin feel that the king ought to consult his counsellors even on minor matters, he also insisted that the 'just monarchy hath not any more assured foundation or stay than the Estates of the people, Communities, Corporations and Colleges'. A 'Commonweal can no more maintain itself without a Senate than the body itself without a Soul or a man without reason . . . '. Though Bodin despised the capacity of the common people for self-government he was equally aware that tyrants only disturb the natural order by generating fear, hatred and dissidence. Indeed the 'chief end of all Commonweals is to flourish in piety, justice, valour, honour and virtue'.

Though a Commonweal cannot subsist without 'those ordinary actions which concern the preservation of people's welfare, as the administration and execution of justice, the providing of victuals' and so forth, these constitute only the 'beginnings of a Commonweal'; once a man has satisfied his basic material needs he is able to live more virtuously and begin to consider first the 'mutations, risings and downfalls of Commonweals' and then the beauty and harmony of the natural order. Finally, through the development of the intellectual virtues – Wisdom, Knowledge and Religion – the Commonweal can achieve its ultimate goal which is to bring men to the 'divine contemplation of the fairest and most excellent object that can be thought or imagined'. Bodin's Commonweal is, in fact, part of a highly traditional religious teleology;

its purpose is to enable men to live in harmony with the laws of nature and to comprehend the divine causality which underpins the entire cosmos. Conversely, comprehension of this Divinity equips men to organize the Common-weal on a basis that, precisely because it reflects and contributes to the universal harmony, will enable it to endure. To sustain this position Bodin used conventional chain-of-being imagery. Man, part mortal and part immortal, finds his natural place betwixt the beasts and the angels. Civil society itself is composed of the traditional three estates – clerics, warriors and the common people – each with their specific functions and qualities; in this well-ordered Commonweal can be seen a reflection of man's own nature, with understanding holding 'the chief place, reason the next, the angry power desirous of revenge the third and brutish lust and desire the last'. Order is preserved by a carefully contrived balance of contrary forces in which the extremes of each element of the universal chain-of-being are linked by interme-diate degrees one to another. Similarly, the best form of justice is one which combines recogni-tion of the natural inequality of men with the notion of equity, thereby uniting contrary principles and creating, as with music, harmony out of potential discord.   DP

Reading

Bodin, J.: *Method for the Easy Comprehension of History* (1566), trans. B. Reynolds. New York: Columbia University Press, 1945.

————: *The Six Books of a Commonweal*, trans. R. Knolles, ed. K.D. McRae. Cambridge, Mass.: Harvard University Press, 1962.

————: *Colloquium of the Seven about Secrets of the Sublime* (1841), trans. M.L.D. Kuntz. Princeton, NJ: Princeton University Press, 1975.

Denzer, H. ed.: *Jean Bodin*. Munich: C.H. Beck, 1954.

†Franklin, J.: *Jean Bodin and the Rise of Absolutist Theory*. Cambridge: Cambridge University Press, 1973.

†King, P.: *The Ideology of Order: a Comparative Analysis of Jean Bodin and Thomas Hobbes*. London: Allen & Unwin, 1974.

Lewis, J.U.: Jean Bodin's 'Logic of Sovereignty'. *Political Studies*, 16 (1968) 202–22.

†Parker, D.: Law, society and the state in the thought of Jean Bodin. *History of Political Thought* 2 (1981), 253–85.

Rose, P.L.: *Bodin and the Great God of Nature. The Moral and Religious Universe of a Judaiser*. Geneva: Droz, 1980.

Bolingbroke, Henry St John, 1st Viscount (1678–1751) British statesman, historian, phil-osopher, and political pamphleteer. As Tory secretary of state for Queen Anne, Bolingbroke negotiated the Treaty of Utrecht, bringing peace to England and Louis XIV's France. Failing to become first minister in 1714, Bolingbroke left politics and settled in France where he remained for ten years. While there, and after a brief period in the service of the Stuart Pretender, Bolingbroke turned to histo-rical and philosophical studies. When he returned to England in 1725, he assumed the intellectual and political leadership of the Tory opposition to Robert Walpole's long ministry. For nearly twenty years, Bolingbroke attacked Walpole's administration through his journal *The Craftsman* and in a series of political and historical tracts that included his *Remarks upon the History of England* (1730), *Dissertation upon Parties* (1734), and *The Idea of a Patriot King* (1739).

In his opposition to Walpole, and to Wal-pole's 'court' faction, Bolingbroke provided the core of the 'country ideology' in its eighteenth-century form. By associating corruption with social and political themes he made it a central concept in the language of eighteenth-century Anglo-American politics. Much richer than simple venality or fraud, corruption is enve-loped by a Machiavellian republican image of historical change: corruption is the absence of civic virtue (see REPUBLICANISM). Corrupt man is preoccupied with self and oblivious to the public good. Such failures of moral personality, such degeneration from the fundamental commitment to public life fuel the decline of states and can be remedied only through periodic revitalization by returning to the original and pristine commitment to civic virtue. Calls for such renewals form the response to corruption, and this is what Bolingbroke urged in his plea for a Patriot King.

Bolingbroke's achievement was to appro-priate this republican and Machiavellian lan-guage for the social and economic tensions developing in Augustan England over the rise of government credit, public debt, and central banking, as well as for political issues, such as Walpole's control of Parliament through patronage or concern over standing armies. Themes of independence and dependence, so critical to the republican tradition (the former essential to any commitment to the public good), were turned by Bolingbroke into a social map of independent country proprietors opposing placemen and stock jobbers and a political map of a free Parliament opposing a despotic court. In addition, Bolingbroke stamped this eighteenth-century republican-country tradition with its socially conservative and nostalgic quality, opposed not only to commerce but also to social equality.   IK

Reading

Bolingbroke, H. St J.: *Political Writings*, ed. I. Kramnick. Arlington Heights, Ill.: Harlan Davidson, 1970.

————: *Historical Writings*, ed. I. Kramnick. Chicago: University of Chicago Press, 1972.

————: *The Idea of a Patriot King*, ed. S.W. Jackman. Indianapolis: Bobbs-Merrill, 1965.

†Dickinson, H.T.: *Bolingbroke*. London: Constable, 1970.

Hart, J.: *Viscount Bolingbroke: Tory Humanist*. London: Routledge & Kegan Paul, 1965.

Jackson, S.W.: *Man of Mercury*. London: Pall Mall, 1965.

†Kramnick, I.: *Bolingbroke and his Circle*. Cambridge, Mass.: Harvard University Press, 1968.

bolshevism A version of Marxism associated with the Bolshevik Party, formed in 1903 after a split in the Russian Social Democratic Labour Party, and especially with LENIN. It emphasized the importance of a tightly-knit 'vanguard' party as an agency for instilling revolutionary consciousness in the proletariat. See SOVIET COMMUNISM.

Bonald, Louis Gabriel de (1754–1840) French conservative. Bonald was one of a small group of writers whose opposition to the Revolution led them into fundamental criticism of the ideas of the ENLIGHTENMENT, which they held responsible for the subversion of the *ancien régime*. Because they believed that aristocratic institutions corresponded uniquely to the Christian revelation about God and man,

and traced most characteristics of Enlightenment thought to its materialism and hostility to theism, these writers have been given the inelegant title 'theocrats'. Yet if the eloquent and imaginative Joseph de MAISTRE was the St Augustine of the Counter-Revolution, Louis de Bonald should be seen as its Thomas Aquinas.

Bonald was born into a family of provincial nobility at Millau, and after studying at the Oratorians College in Paris he became an officer in the Royal Guard. However, he soon returned to Millau, married, and became mayor, which stimulated a lifelong interest in the role of the commune in a properly organized society. Bonald seems to have welcomed the Revolution at first, but in 1791 he joined the emigré army in Germany. After a period of intense study Bonald published anonymously, in 1796 at Constance, his *Théorie du pouvoir politique et réligieux dans la société civile*. . . . Then he returned secretly to France, where Napoleon's favour allowed him to remain. Within a few years Bonald published his *Essai analytique sur les lois naturelles de l'ordre social* (1800), *Du divorce considéré au XIXᵉ siècle* (1801) and *Législation primitive* (1802). These works brought him to the attention of Fontanes and Chateaubriand, and in 1808 he was offered a post on the council of the University. After the Restoration he was elected deputy for the Aveyron, and took a leading part in the *chambre introuvable* which, among other things, abolished divorce. Bonald became a minister in 1822 and a peer in 1823, presiding briefly over censorship during the ultra-royalist ascendancy. *Ultras* looked upon him as their chief ideological spokesman. Bonald's last work was published in 1827. The July Revolution of 1830 led him to withdraw from public life, though he lived until 1840.

Bonald's writings are symmetrical to a fault and deductive in form, while his prose style, too often dismissed as ponderous, has a somewhat archaic purity. Taking up eighteenth-century discussions about the origins of language, to which Condillac and ROUSSEAU had contributed, Bonald insisted on the priority of language to thought ('l'homme pense sa parole avant de parler sa pensée') and inferred from that premise the divine institution of language. The sense in which language and, *a fortiori*, social institutions, are necessary preconditions of individual thought and action provided Bonald with a base from which to attack the INDIVIDUALISM of eighteenth-century philosophy and political theory. The imagery he relied upon to depict the eighteenth-century conception of society – a pile of sand or collection of atoms – was to have a profound influence on nineteenth-century sociological argument (of both conservative and liberal cast). The ultimate source of social atomization, Bonald insisted, was religious disunity or Protestantism. Social unity could only be restored by shared, authoritative beliefs underpinning intermediate institutions such as the family, rural commune and local gentry.

Bonald contrasted the sinister effects of urban life on family structure and attitudes towards authority with the patriarchal attitudes of a somewhat idealized rural community, arguing that only communities where the gentry exercised their proper role could prevent legitimate government from degenerating into despotism. Bonald combined themes from the eighteenth-century aristocratic reaction to growing royal power with a new quasi-mystical cult of royal authority (relying on the concept of 'sovereignty' less than Maistre). It was an uneasy combination which Bonald's passion for logic – in particular, triadic relations – did not entirely conceal. The crux of his position remained the dubious stipulation that society properly so-called is only possible on an aristocratic model. LAS

Reading

Bonald, L.G. de: *Oeuvres complètes de M. de Bonald*. Paris: J.-P. Migne, 1859.

†Godechot, J.: *The Counter-Revolution: Doctrine and Action 1789–1804*. London: Routledge & Kegan Paul, 1972.

†Nisbet, R.: De Bonald and the concept of the social group. *Journal of the History of Ideas* 5 (1944) 315–31.

———: Conservatism and sociology. *American Journal of Sociology* 58 (1952) 167–75.

Spaemann, R.: *Der Ursprung der Soziologie aus dem Geist der Restauration: Studien über L.G.A. de Bonald*. Munich: Käsel, 1959.

Bosanquet, Bernard (1848–1923) English philosopher, political theorist and philanthropist. Bosanquet was educated at Balliol College, Oxford, where he came under the influence of T. H. GREEN's IDEALISM. He taught at Oxford from 1871 to 1881, when an inheritance enabled him to leave and devote himself to scholarship and social work, returning only briefly to academia as professor of moral philosophy at the University of St Andrews, from 1903 to 1908. He wrote on a variety of topics, principally aesthetics, logic, metaphysics and social philosophy, approaching all of them from an idealist standpoint. His interest in the last was particularly strong. He became an activist in the London Ethical Society, establishing a School of Ethics and Social Philosophy in 1897, which was incorporated into the London School of Economics in 1902. With his wife Helen he worked for the Charity Organization Society and spoke on its behalf to the Royal Commission on the Poor Law of 1909.

Bosanquet's principal work of political theory is *The Philosophical Theory of the State* (1899). Thanks to L. T. HOBHOUSE's trenchant criticism, this book has gained a reputation as a defence of the authoritarian state: a Platonized version of Hegel, which renders the individual totally subordinate to a putative general will of society. However, this account creates a paradox, since Bosanquet followed the view of the Charity Organization Society, to whose secretary the book is dedicated, in maintaining that state interference undermined individual morality and freedom. This apparent contradiction stems from an ambiguity in Bosanquet's account of POLITICAL OBLIGATION. Supplementing Green's theory with notions drawn from social psychology, Bosanquet claimed that the real will of the individual, that which realizes his potential, can only be achieved in co-operation with others within the state. All human aspirations for a better life involve freeing ourselves from the constraints of transient, purely biologically determined, wants and desires, and are expressive of a good will common to us all (pp. 128–30, 139–44). The good will cannot be realized by any one individual, for no single person can attain the achievements of mankind as a whole, nor even fulfil his or her own capacities without the support and forbearance of others. Our moral and political duty, therefore, is to respect and maintain the complex of goods necessary for all members of society to realize themselves (p. 190). However, the state's role is primarily negative: to 'hinder hindrances' to the individual's acquisition of moral character through effort (p. 178). Since moral improvement derives from a willed overcoming of material obstacles, self-help should be encouraged whenever possible. As Bosanquet believed that poverty resulted principally from a lack of moral will-power on the part of the poor themselves, he argued that inspiring self-improvement and social co-operation were better remedies than state subsidies – a requirement met by the Poor Law system of workhouses and judicious charity to the 'deserving poor'. State education, in contrast, helped a pre-existing desire for betterment, and was a common good necessary for human fulfilment (pp. 185–6). This different interpretation of social processes led Bosanquet to draw fewer collectivist conclusions from idealist premises than did many of Green's other followers.   RPB

Reading

Bosanquet, B.: *The Value and Destiny of the Individual.* London: Macmillan, 1913.
——: *The Philosophical Theory of the State*, 3rd edn. London: Macmillan, 1920.
—— ed.: *Aspects of the Social Problem.* London: Macmillan, 1895.
†Collini, S.: Hobhouse, Bosanquet and the state: philosophical idealism and political argument in England 1880–1918. *Past and Present* 70–3 (1976) 86–111.
Hobhouse, L.T.: *The Metaphysical Theory of the State: a Criticism.* London: Macmillan, 1918.
†Milne, A.J.H.: *The Social Philosophy of English Idealism*, ch. 7. London: Allen & Unwin, 1962.

bourgeoisie The Marxist term for the class of capitalists, often extended to include professional and managerial groups linked by direct economic interest or social connection to the owners of capital. See CLASS, MARXISM.

Bracton, Henry de (d. 1268) English jurist at the court of King Henry III, Bracton is traditionally credited with authorship of *De legibus et consuetudinibus angliae* (1239?), one of the seminal works of the English legal and political tradition. Though he may have shared its composition with others, his name can still safely be associated with its design and construction.

The political theory of *De legibus* is built on the doctrine of personal monarchic government. The king's *potestas* (power) is co-extensive with the royal *voluntas* (will). The authority of the king is therefore fixed by his characteristic moral disposition towards virtue and justice.

De legibus specified that the royal *voluntas* is primarily concerned with adjudication rather than with legislation. Laws are promulgated through a co-operative process; the king merely assents to those statutes which have received approval from the magnates and community of the realm. In addition Bracton acknowledged that local custom may also have the force of law. Hence the law of the land is not dictated by the king's pleasure but is truly 'common'. The king's jurisdiction, therefore, pertains wholly to the enforcement of law through judicial judgment and coercive punishment. Bracton takes the crucial feature of royal power to be the performance of justice ('render to each that which is his') in conjunction with the penalizing of offenders against justice by means of the 'material sword'.

In the conduct of this role Bracton likens the king to God. The divine will is both the ultimate source of all justice and the final avenger of all transgressions. Since the ruler's will is characterized by analogous tasks, the royal office is an imitation (albeit earthly and imperfect) of the Supreme Will. Therefore *De legibus* recurrently depicts the king as the 'minister' or 'vicar' of God.

Although Bracton's king has neither peer nor superior, he is unable to hear all cases and enforce all laws by himself. The crown must delegate some rights and prerogatives to men of lesser station. This is accomplished by two distinct types of grants: those which the monarch controls directly through commissions to magistrates who exercise their powers in the royal name and those which are assigned as 'privileges' to the nobility with whom the king associates himself in governing the realm.

De legibus specifies that the king is ultimately responsible for regulating and protecting against abuses of both forms of delegated authority. How is it to be ensured that the king himself will uphold the law and judge in accordance with it? Following the juristic and philosophical conventions of his day, Bracton maintains that the characteristic moral orientation of the king's *voluntas* towards goodness entails a stable disposition to obey all just legislation. In this sense the king is 'under God and the law, but not under men', because he 'bridles' himself through the self-imposed restraint of his own will.

Bracton may also have believed, however, that inferiors must occasionally restrain their royal superior, at least if we are to accept as genuine a currently disputed *addicio* to the text of *De legibus* in which it is proclaimed that the *curia* (barons and earls) of the king ought to 'bridle' him when he commits an injustice. The barons and earls may so 'bridle' the monarch because they are his 'partners' in governing the realm, and 'he who has a partner has a master'. *De legibus* thereby provides an early and influential theory of the institutional limitation of royal prerogative. Although the *addicio* is probably inconsistent with the main tenets of *De legibus*, it was taken by late medieval and early modern admirers of Bracton to be an integral part of his argument.   CJN

Reading

Bracton, Henry de: *De legibus et consuetudinibus angliae*, ed. G.E. Woodbine, rev. and trans. S.E. Thorne. 4 vols. Cambridge, Mass.: Harvard University Press, 1968–77.

†Hanson, D.W.: *From Kingdom to Commonwealth*. Cambridge, Mass.: Harvard University Press, 1970.

Kantorowicz, E.H.: *The King's Two Bodies*. Princeton, NJ: Princeton University Press, 1957.

McIlwain, C.H.: *Constitutionalism: Ancient and Modern*. Ithaca, NY: Cornell University Press, 1958.

Maitland, F.W. ed.: *Bracton's Note Book* (1887); repr. Littleton, Col.: Rothman, 1983.

†Nederman, C.J.: Bracton on kingship revisited. *History of Political Thought* 5 (1984) 63–77.

Richardson, H.G.: *Bracton: the Problem of his Text*. London: The Selden Society, 1965.

Buber, Martin (1878–1965) German philosopher and Jewish theologian, involved from an early age with the Zionist movement. His main work of social theory was *Paths in Utopia* (1949), an exploration of the decentralist, communitarian tradition in socialist thought. See UTOPIANISM.

Bukharin, Nikolai Ivanovich (1888–1938) Russian Marxist and economist who contributed to the theory of IMPERIALISM. After the Revolution, he helped develop the theory of 'socialism in one country', before falling out of favour with Stalin. See SOVIET COMMUNISM.

bureaucracy This term has a number of different meanings. It can mean a system of administration carried out on a continuous basis according to set rules by trained professionals. It can also mean a system of government in which the leading executive positions are filled by professional administrators, rather than by elected representatives. It can denote the corps of professional administrators as a distinctive social group, or it can be used in a derogatory manner, to indicate the characteristic vices of such administration: 'red tape', unresponsiveness, delay, etc.

The second of these meanings was most common among nineteenth-century writers who contrasted bureaucracy ('rule by the bureau') with systems of representative government. It was Max WEBER who was responsible for establishing the first meaning as the standard one in twentieth-century social science. He noted that administration by professional experts was becoming increasingly prevalent in all political systems, of whatever type, and indeed in all organizations where complex and large-scale administrative tasks were undertaken: business enterprises, trade unions, political parties, and so on. He defined bureaucracy as a system of administration embodying the following characteristics: hierarchy (each official has a clearly defined competence and is answerable to a superior); impersonality (the work is conducted according to set rules, without arbitrariness or favouritism, and a written record is kept of every transaction); continuity (the office constitutes a full-time salaried occupation, with security of tenure and the prospect of regular advancement); expertise (officials are selected on merit, are trained for their function, and control access to the knowledge stored in the files). These characteristics, Weber argued, together maximize administrative efficiency, and make bureaucracy inescapable for complex industrial societies.

Though not everyone would agree with Weber's conclusion, his definition of bureaucracy has the great merit of clarity, and most subsequent writers have taken his analysis as their starting point for exploring the problems bureaucracy raises. These problems can be usefully distinguished according to disciplinary focus. In the sphere of administrative or organizational theory a central question has been whether the characteristics Weber identified as intrinsic to bureaucracy do in fact maximize administrative efficiency. A strict hierarchy can reduce the flow of ideas and information upwards; adherence to rules can induce inflexibility; tenured positions of privilege can foster conservatism. Further, studies of administrative systems in practice suggest that they operate through networks of personal relations, and that these facilitate smooth running rather than obstruct it. In general it can be questioned whether a single administrative model is appropriate to all organizations, industrial as well as governmental, or to all environments, stable as well as rapidly changing; or whether a single concept of efficiency can embrace the very different purposes of modern organizations. For example, a broad area of individual discretion may be appropriate within an economic enterprise whose performance is assessed only by the most general criterion of profitability. A government welfare office, on the other hand, being publicly answerable for the uniform treatment of all citizens, has to be much more tightly rule-governed and allow minimum discretion to its officials.

Sociological theory has been interested in bureaucracy as a social category, representative of the new middle class, and distinct from both capital and labour. Its position of social power and privilege derives from the possession of scarce skills and educational qualifications, and from its authority position within an organizational hierarchy. Disagreement exists about the relation between this group and capital itself. Theorists of the 'managerial revolution' argue that knowledge and organization are increasingly replacing capital as the leading social force of advanced industrial societies, and that there is a corresponding convergence between the social structures of East and West,

despite their differences of economic ownership. Opponents of this position contend that in Western societies bureaucracy in both state and economy is aligned with the still dominant power of capital, whether through personal background and interests, social function, or structural determination. There is agreement, however, that bureaucracy comprises the leading social force in societies of the Soviet type, though it is disputed whether it constitutes a class or merely a social stratum. Against the former thesis are the limitations on personal appropriation by officials, and on the transmission of their privileges to their offspring. Against the latter is their collective monopoly, via the centralized party structure, over the process of extraction and disposal of the surplus product. The dispute is not just a conceptual one of how CLASS is to be defined, but a practical one of what kind of political process is required to remove the bureaucracy from its position of social pre-eminence.

In the field of political economy, orthodox economic theory posits a fundamental contrast between the principles of bureaucracy and the principles of the market. The latter represents the sphere of competition, dynamism and freedom of choice, where the former represents monopoly, stagnation and compulsion. On this view a society will be dynamic to the extent that its production is organized according to market principles, with the necessary role of bureaucracy in social welfare being kept to a minimum. At the opposite pole, Marxists explain the huge expansion of bureaucracy under capitalism as itself the result of the market: its inherent tendencies towards monopoly, and its creation of insecurity and deprivation, must be remedied by massive state provision, while its attendant class conflict can only be contained by an extensive apparatus of coercion. On the Marxist view, the hierarchy, secrecy and social privilege characteristic of bureaucracy derive from its class-coercive function, whether under capitalism, or in non-capitalist societies undergoing a state-induced process of primitive accumulation. Marxists tend to be less specific about what alternative form of administration might replace bureaucracy in an advanced socialist society.

Within political theory the main problem

discussed is the threat posed by bureaucracy to the democratic principles of open and accountable government. Their control of official knowledge and their permanence give professional administrators the power to frustrate or manipulate the politicians who supposedly determine policy. Theories of DEMOCRACY can be distinguished according to the strategies they propose for overcoming this problem of bureaucratic power. Elitist-oriented theories stress the role of political leadership and advocate measures designed to secure political control of the bureaucracy, such as the political appointment of top civil servants, or the creation of political advisers to ministers. Theorists of open government advocate public access to government documents on the principle that ministers as well as administrators have a vested interest in secrecy. More participatory theorists look to popular involvement in scrutinizing and influencing administration at the local level, on the grounds that the character of policy cannot be separated from the manner of its execution. These positions are not mutually exclusive. Together they suggest that the requirements of a democratic system of administration cannot be simply derived from a general model of bureaucracy.

In conclusion, most writers since Weber have seen the necessity for some variation from his strict bureaucratic model, depending on the context within which an administrative system operates, and the purposes which it serves. However, there is a danger of exaggerating the deficiencies of bureaucracy by making it responsible for ills of which it is as much the expression as the cause. And the presence of systematic favouritism, arbitrariness, or unpredictability in government indicates that a society can suffer from too little bureaucracy (in the properly Weberian sense of rule-bound, impersonal administration) as well as from too much. Bureaucracy is an ambivalent phenomenon, rather than wholly bad.   DB

Reading
†Albrow, M.: *Bureaucracy*. London: Macmillan, 1970.
†Blau, P.M. and Meyer, M.W.: *Bureaucracy in Modern Society*. New York: Random House, 1971.
Djilas, M.: *The New Class*. London: Thames & Hudson, 1957.
†Kamenka, E. and Krygier, M.: *Bureaucracy*. London: Edward Arnold, 1979.
Kellner, P. and Crowther-Hunt, N.: *The Civil Servants*. London: Macdonald Futura, 1980.
Lindblom, C.E.: *Politics and Markets*. New York: Basic, 1977.
Page, E.C.: *Political Authority and Bureaucratic Power*. Brighton: Wheatsheaf, 1985.
Rizzi, B.: *The Bureaucratization of the World*. London: Tavistock, 1985.
Weber, M.: *Economy and Society* III, ed. G. Roth and C. Wittich, trans. E. Fischoff *et al.* New York: Bedminster, 1968.

Burke, Edmund (1729–1797)   British statesman and political theorist of conservatism. Born in Dublin, Burke was educated at Trinity College Dublin (1743–8), and then went to London to read law. He soon gave this up, intending to make a literary career for himself, moving in the artistic circle of Johnson, Goldsmith, Reynolds and Garrick and becoming founding editor of the *Annual Review*. His first published works belong to this period: the satirical *Vindication of Natural Society* (1756) and *A Philosophical Enquiry into the Origin of Our Ideas of the Sublime and the Beautiful* (1757).

Shortly after this Burke began to neglect literature for politics and he served in the office of Lord Halifax, Lord Lieutenant of Ireland, from 1761 to 1764. His enduring and significant political connection was not made until 1765 when he was invited by the incoming prime minister, Lord Rockingham, to become his private secretary. Burke soon established himself as the major spokesman and pamphleteer of the Rockingham Whigs, on whose behalf many of his writings were undertaken. The two major pamphlets of this period are the *Observations on a late Publication Intituled* [sic] *'The Present State of the Nation'* (1769) and a year later the more famous *Thoughts on the Causes of the Present Discontents*. Much of them is devoted to a justification of party – still a potentially unpatriotic notion in the eighteenth century.

From 1770 until the American Revolution Burke also acted as an agent in Parliament for the colony of New York, and in a series of famous speeches and letters he tried to persuade Parliament and his constituents to moderate their attitude and demands in the hope of saving the colonial relationship. In

1774, having hitherto represented the pocket borough of Wendover, Burke was elected for Bristol. His speech at the close of the poll is a famous articulation of the view that the proper relationship between an MP and his constituents is one of REPRESENTATION, not delegation. Burke was, however, rejected by Bristol at the next election – it might be said for heeding his own advice too well. From 1780 to his retirement in 1794 he sat for Malton, a borough in the gift of the Rockinghams.

In 1782 and 1783 Burke briefly held his only periods of office, as Paymaster-General both in Rockingham's ministry, and subsequently in the Fox-North coalition. Two more causes undertaken by Burke at this time were the reformation of the Crown's finances and the regulation of British rule in India, then in the hands of the East India Company. The nine-year-long unsuccessful impeachment of Warren Hastings, the returned governor of Bengal, was considered by many to mark the end of Burke's career. But his critical response to the French Revolution produced the pamphlets by which his posthumous reputation was transformed from that of a thoughtful writer on matters relating to the British Constitution to that of the acknowledged major exponent of the conservative reaction to the French Revolution. *Reflections on the Revolution in France* (1790) shocked many Whig colleagues, who, while uncertain themselves what to make of events in France, were astonished at Burke's apparent apostasy from a lifetime's commitment to reform. He defended his position in his *Appeal from the New to the Old Whigs* (1791), and developed his critique of revolution further in his *Thoughts on French Affairs* (1791) and the four *Letters on a Regicide Peace* (1796–7).

Burke's view of politics is dominated by a historical perspective. He saw the state as the result of a process of historical growth which he often likened to that undergone by living organisms. Similarly incapable of surviving dissection, the state was also greater and more complex than any of the parts which made it up. He saw the ensemble of relationships comprising society as ultimately dependent on the habitual responses of the individuals composing it. These responses are the manners, customs, and rules, expressed and unexpressed, into which we are socialized, strikingly defended by Burke as 'prejudice', and in his view much more reliable when they are habits than when they are self-consciously followed rules or moral doctrines: 'Prejudice', he wrote, 'renders a man's virtue his habit.' The congruency of this ensemble is, for Burke, a result of piecemeal accommodation by past generations gradually melding the whole together. Although Burke thought this true of all societies inasmuch as they managed to perpetuate themselves over time, it was, he thought, particularly true of the English constitution, largely as a result of the dominance of the idea of precedent in common law. In contrast to earlier, and more historically naive Whigs, who subscribed to the myth of a virtually unchanging ANCIENT CONSTITUTION in accordance with which reformations such as that of 1688 must occasionally be carried out, Burke came to see the constitution as the result of a gradual and unwitting development over time. One important consequence of this was that society was not properly subject to rational scrutiny, since the 'fit' between institutions, customs and practices would not conform to any known or discoverable general rules.

This view of the limitations of individuals' rational capacity to analyse society exemplifies one of Burke's most famous targets: abstraction or rationalism in political thought. In particular he deprecated the direct application to civil society of criticisms drawn from theories of natural rights or of the state of nature, as argued by many SOCIAL CONTRACT theorists. He pointed out the folly of applying to civilized society 'rights which do not so much as suppose its existence'. The 'social contract', if it could be said to exist at all, certainly marked the surrender of natural rights; but instead of dispensing with the notion, as had HUME, Burke characteristically converted it from a radical into a powerfully conservative image:

Society is indeed a contract . . . but it is not a partnership in things . . . of a temporary and perishable nature. It is a partnership in all science, a partnership in all art; a partnership in every virtue, and in all perfection . . . . As the ends of such a partnership cannot be obtained in many generations, it becomes a partnership between . . . those who are living, those who are dead, and those who are yet to be born (*Reflections*, pp. 194–5)

Burke generally ridiculed the prevailing vogue for using an idealized primitive 'nature' as a criterion of moral or political excellence; once again he subverted the radical argument by insisting that 'art is man's nature', and nature otherwise was to be identified with the primitive, the chaotic, and the sublimely terrible, over which civilization created a decent, if frail, veneer. The maintenance of this civility Burke saw as vulnerable to abstract analysis and to rationally arrived at schemes of reform, however well meant. It was circumstance, he argued, that gives the character to rules and principles, which cannot therefore be judged good or bad in the abstract but only as they operate within particular societies. Whereas functioning constitutions are the product of many minds over time, theories of government, even those which attempt merely to describe constitutions, are the product of a single, limited intelligence; and, thought Burke, 'the individual is foolish but the species is wise'. Such pessimism concerning our ability rationally to comprehend the operation of society must, Burke argued, lead to a presumption in favour of the status quo, and a rejection of speculative and systematic schemes of reform.

Burke's conservatism therefore rests on a philosophically grounded scepticism concerning the possibilities of discovering the historical processes by which societies develop. It is not concerned, as are some other forms of CONSERVATISM, to identify an ideal in the past, or even the present, to which we must constantly return. Indeed his contemporary reputation was as a reformer. 'We must reform', he argued, 'in order to preserve'; and again: 'a society without the means of reformation is a society without the means of preservation.' However, for Burke, reform must always be undertaken to alleviate a clear and present evil, and be limited to that end; it should not be directed at bringing society into conformity with rationally inspired standards.

These arguments came to a head in Burke's writings against the French Revolution, an event he viewed as inspired by precisely the kind of abstract theories he detested. He compared the French unfavourably with the British in 1688 who had changed their personnel but kept their institutions, while the French although keeping their king (which was still the case when he wrote) were destroying the institutions which supported him.

Burke's sensitivity to the interrelatedness of culture and institutions led him, despite his fundamental scepticism, to defend specific institutional supports for the beliefs and practices of a society which was to conduct its politics conservatively. In particular, while advocating religious toleration he strongly supported an established church, and though himself a commoner he could not envisage a stable society without a landed aristocracy. Only the wealth sufficient to support leisure could, he thought, provide the cultural continuity on which society depended, and only landed, inherited wealth could guarantee individuals with an interest in its perpetuation.

At the more parochial level of the British constitution Burke is famous for his defence of the independence of Parliament. This forms an important strand in the Whig notion of 'custodial politics': the responsibility of those born or (more rarely) chosen to exercise the trust on behalf of the community. The defence of Parliament focused on a number of issues, notably his advocacy of party politics based on shared political principles, and on his rejection of constituency delegation of MPs. The former may be seen as a way of concerting policies whilst protecting the independence of MPs from the influence of government patronage, a preoccupation of eighteenth-century opposition thinkers, while the latter protected them from direct control by their constituencies, some of which were becoming politically aware of national issues at this time.

Burke's defence of party has suffered more than most of his work from his association with the Rockingham Whigs, for whom it could be seen as a convenient doctrine. It seems unlikely, as was once thought, that Burke anticipated the two- or even three-party system with the opposition as a permanent alternative government, but rather saw party as a device to be deployed at times of danger to the constitution: 'when bad men combine the good must associate'.

Burke's defence of the American revolutionaries is sometimes seen as surprising in view of his later attack on the French. However, Burke saw the Americans' claims as based on the traditional and positive rights of Englishmen to reject taxation without representation, and not, as was to be the case with the French, rooted in abstractions such as the 'natural rights of men'. Where he found Americans having recourse to speculative political arguments, he roundly deprecated it as the consequence of their misgovernment.

Burke's reputation reached its zenith in the nineteenth century, but he has continued to provide inspiration for conservatives well into the second half of the twentieth. A wide range of interpretative literature characterizes him in various ways, from a kind of intuitive and conservative utilitarian, through a proto-romantic to an essentially legalistic thinker. Since the second world war the legalistic school has dominated, though some historians continue to try to formulate a theoretically respectable 'pragmatic' Burke.

Burke's use of legal terminology is everywhere abundant, but whether he should be seen predominantly in the common or natural law tradition is unclear, as is the particular historical twist that he gives to both these patterns of thought. Future work on Burke by historians of political thought may well involve reassessing his relationship with the SCOTTISH ENLIGHTENMENT school, notably SMITH and Hume, on whom much work has recently been done. Scholars approaching Burke from literary fields have focused on his style rather than on the substance of the arguments he uses. A satisfactory interpretative synthesis may well result from viewing Burke as primarily a rhetorician, who drew eclectically on the full range of arguments congenial to his audience.

IWH-M

Reading

Boulton, T.J.: *The Language of Politics in the Age of Wilkes and Burke*. London: Routledge & Kegan Paul; Toronto: University of Toronto Press, 1963.

Burke, E.: *Reflections on the Revolution in France*, ed. C. C. O'Brien. Harmondsworth: Penguin, 1968.

———: *Edmund Burke on Government, Politics and Society*, selected and ed. B.W. Hill. London: Fontana, 1975.

———: *The Political Philosophy of Edmund Burke*, selected and introd. I. Hampsher-Monk. London: Longman, 1986.

———: *Writings and Speeches of Edmund Burke*, ed. P. Langford. Oxford: Oxford University Press, 1981-.

†Cobban, A.: *Edmund Burke and the Revolt against the Eighteenth Century*. London: Allen & Unwin, 1973.

Dreyer, F.A.: *Burke's Politics: A Study in Whig Orthodoxy*. Waterloo, Ont.: Laurier University Press, 1979.

†Freeman, M.: *Burke and the Critique of Political Radicalism*. Oxford: Blackwell, 1980.

†Macpherson, C.B.: *Burke*. Oxford: Oxford University Press, 1982.

Mahoney, T.H.D.: *Edmund Burke and Ireland*. Cambridge, Mass.: Harvard University Press, 1960.

†O'Gorman, F.: *Edmund Burke: His Political Philosophy*. London: Allen & Unwin, 1973.

Pocock, J.G.A.: Burke and the Ancient Constitution: a problem in the history of ideas. *Historical Journal* 3 (1960) 125–43.

†Stanlis, P.J.: *Edmund Burke and the Natural Law*. Ann Arbor: University of Michigan Press, 1965.

C

Cabet, Étienne (1788–1856) French socialist. Advocated a regimented form of communism in his utopian novel *Voyage en Icarie* (1840), and attempted to implement it (with limited success) at an Icarian colony in Illinois, USA. See COMMUNISM.

Calhoun, John Caldwell (1782–1850) American statesman. Calhoun served as representative (1810–17) and senator (1832–44, 1845–50) for South Carolina; he was secretary of war (1817–25), secretary of state (1844–5) and vice-president of the United States (1825–32). He wrote *A Disquisition on Government* and *A Discourse on the Constitution and Government of the United States*, both published after his death, as well as numerous addresses and letters.

Originally a militant nationalist, notably among the 'war hawks' at the time of the war of 1812, Calhoun became more and more identified with the defence of the South, slavery, and the rights of the states within the federal union.

In his *Disquisition*, Calhoun rejected the doctrine of natural rights, contending that human beings are not born free and equal, but in a 'social and political state', subject to authority. Calhoun's theory, however, rests on individualistic premises: self-preservation is 'the all-pervading and essential law of the animated universe' and 'direct or individual affections are stronger than . . . sympathetic or social feelings'. In fact, Calhoun saw a danger in sociability; he defended inequality as a necessary spur to effort, anticipating SOCIAL DARWINISM by arguing that competition for rank provides the 'greatest impulse' to human progress. Freedom is the natural human goal,

but it is a 'reward to be earned', not an original right.

These arguments obviously did not apply to slavery: slaves were excluded from competition and could not 'earn' freedom. Calhoun's most basic justification of slavery derived from the 'scientific' case for racial inequality. He also contended, however, that slavery moderates class conflict (because slave owners must care for their 'capital') and thereby promotes social stability.

Like most Southern theorists Calhoun contended that the states, originally sovereign, had created the Union and, since sovereignty cannot be divided, retained their sovereign right of secession. He went beyond this legal case, however, to develop a more distinctive and theoretical argument. Following MADISON in *The Federalist* (no. 10), Calhoun maintained that the chief danger to republican government is the possibility that power will fall into the hands of some narrow party or faction. Public spirit is no adequate protection against this, given the priority of individual feelings and private interests. It is necessary to design institutions which make it impossible for government to suppress any major interest in society. Madison had considered that the diversity of interests in the federal union, combined with majority rule, would achieve this result. Calhoun found this argument inadequate, and with it the federal constitution.

Following the precedent of Timothy Ford's theory of the 'dual contract' (1794), Calhoun insisted that 'interests as well as number' must be considered in the definition of a majority. A majority must be 'concurrent', made up of majorities within each interest, so that each major interest has a veto on policy. In this way no interest will be either so excluded or so damaged as to find political association intolerable. Concurrent majority, Calhoun held, would make possible the preservation of the union.

Yet the paralysing conservatism resulting from concurrent majority rule would be likely to infuriate numerical majorities, creating a new threat to political order. Calhoun's mechanical solution also ignored the conflict of first principles in the American republic. As LINCOLN recognized, the old union could not endure 'half slave and half free'. WCMcW

Reading

Calhoun, J.C.: *A Disquisition on Government*, with selections from the *Discourse*, ed. C. Gordon Post. Indianapolis: Bobbs-Merrill, 1953.

†Gabriel, R.H.: *The Course of American Democratic Thought*, pp. 103–11. New York: Ronald, 1940.

†Hartz, L.: *The Liberal Tradition in America*, pp. 145–77. New York: Harcourt Brace, 1955.

†Jenkins, W.S.: *Pro-Slavery Thought in the Old South*. Chapel Hill, NC: University of North Carolina Press, 1935.

†Parrington, V.L.: *Main Currents in American Thought*, vol. II, pp. 69–82. New York: Harcourt Brace, 1958.

†Wiltse, C.: *A Life of John C. Calhoun*. 3 vols. Indianapolis: Bobbs-Merrill, 1944–51.

Calvin, Jean (1509–1564) French theologian and reformer, Genevan citizen from 1559. His work as church-reformer of Geneva, theologian, scripture-commentator and polemicist made him the leading authority for Reformed churches in France, the Netherlands, Britain, and parts of Central Europe.

In its first version (1536) Calvin's theological masterpiece, the *Institution of Christian Religion*, was largely a systematization of Lutheran theological themes, and it was caught in the same political difficulties. It concentrated on justification by faith and not by works, the contrast between the freedom of the Christian and Romanist 'tyranny', and the paradigmatic status of the 'invisible' church. Precisely these doctrines however, as LUTHER had already learned, underwrote sectarian tendencies *within* evangelical churches: to the evangelical radical, actual churches are never sufficiently

free or reformed. Sectarians, furthermore, threatened not only evangelical churches: the 'Radical Reformation' also denied the authority of secular government over the Elect, and an Anabaptist attempt to establish a millenial 'Kingdom of Christ' at Münster had only recently been crushed. To such disruptive inferences from evangelical theology and the resultant discredit to the Reformation as a whole, Calvin (like Luther) responded with a particularly strict doctrine of obedience: secular government is instituted by God for Christians, magistrates are his vice-regents, and Christian private citizens are not even permitted to discuss the best form of government. This is the only part of the book devoted to politics; ecclesiastical politics were scarcely mentioned. But this doctrine merely legitimated the control of 'evangelical' rulers over churches that the first generation of Reformers had already found indefensible, albeit irremediable (see REFORMATION POLITICAL THOUGHT).

German Protestants in the 1530s were engaged in armed resistance against their emperor, their lawful overlord, and Calvin also needed to consider the needs of his coreligionists in France, whose monarchs outlawed the Reformation. The doctrine of 'passive obedience', according to which resistance to rulers may not take armed or organized form, therefore required qualification. Calvin accordingly, again like Luther, attempted to restrict the jurisdiction of secular government to the maintenance of an 'outward' peace and a merely civil justice; beyond this it has no right to the obedience of Christians. And while Christians who are *private* persons may never resist 'tyranny' by violent or illegal means, Calvin, like Luther's followers, conceded that the laws of some commonwealths provide for 'popular (Lutherans have said 'lesser') magistrates', empowered to offer 'resistance to tyranny', and cited Spartan ephors, Roman tribunes and 'perhaps' the 'chief assemblies' (that is, Estates General, Parliaments, etc.) of the European polities as examples.

This version of Calvin's political doctrine was reached before he had any practical experience of ecclesiastical politics. Having taken charge of the church of Geneva shortly after the publication of the first *Institution*, his expulsion by its government and exile at Strasbourg in 1538 (where he was minister of the French congregation and had the counsel of Martin Bucer, the Reformer of Strasbourg) his recall to Geneva in 1541, his experience of the international politics of the Reformation, and his more mature reflection about scripture, all served to redirect Calvin's thinking to the needs of 'visible' churches, and to identify more clearly the threat posed to their integrity by supposedly 'godly' rulers. His insights, first formulated in draft constitutions and confessions of faith for the Genevan church, were subsequently incorporated into his many volumes of scripture commentaries and into successive editions of the much revised, recast and translated *Institution*. The last edition (1559/60) explicitly identified 'flatterers of princes' as well as sectarians as the main threats to 'purity of doctrine'.

In its later formulation, Calvin's theology envisages a 'Christian commonwealth' (not a Lutheran conception), of which both spiritual and civil governments are essential and equal components, independently authorized by God to co-operate in the establishment of a 'godly discipline'. In the final edition of the *Institution*, one entire book out of the four is devoted to the (visible) church and 'civil administration' jointly. 'Godly discipline' replaces 'Christian liberty' (a doctrine Calvin came to regard as positively inviting misunderstanding) as the *leitmotif* of Calvin's thought. 'Godly discipline' is conceived as essentially a training in righteous conduct: punishment and repression are merely subsidiary aspects of it. True righteousness is a gift of God alone but it is conducive to a striving towards religious and moral perfection in this life. And God has appointed the 'two-fold government' to assist Christians in this striving: they need both governments equally. In Calvin's conception of the Christian life the willing and zealous performance of spiritual and civil duties comes to be the keynote; these duties have as their aim the 'building up' of the church, and thus zeal for true religion loses its sectarian connotation.

A godly polity, then, is both a civil and a spiritual collectivity. In this context the earlier attempt at a jurisdictional distinction between the arms of its 'two-fold' government has little place, any more than it had in the ecclesiastical order Calvin established at Geneva. The *Institution* in fact always specifically instances the defence and furtherance of true religion as one of the ends of civil government. The whole point of the 'two-fold government' of the godly polity is to harmonize religious and civil commitments and (if necessary) punishments for and deterrents against derelictions of duty. What remains vital is that the personnel and the means employed by the respective governments should remain distinct, so that each controls and spurs on the other. The secular 'magistracy' – Calvin favoured the republican word, as compared to Luther's equation of secular authority with 'princes' – uses the sword; the church only uses persuasion, with excommunication as the last resort. But both make their contribution in their distinctive ways to a good order which is at once religious and civil. Some division of labour is of course proper and prudent: it is not for the clerical college to conduct foreign policy or to administer the ordinary workings of the criminal and civil law, any more than magistrates are called upon to preach, though Genevan magistrates were much given to sententiousness. (See also CHURCH AND STATE.)

If one authority is by rights superior to the other it ought to be spiritual government (i.e. the clergy). From his training as a classics scholar and lawyer Calvin always retained a profound respect for the moral and political wisdom of the (pagan) Ancients. But whenever any matter became controversial, Calvin always seemed to prefer Revelation to unaided Reason as the means of recognizing the will of God, with the clergy as its authorized interpreter. However, Calvin did not intend clerical domination of the polity: his ideal is one of co-operation, on more or less equal terms, of the twin 'administrators' of the divine will. He spared no theological or practical effort to re-establish the prestige of the 'evangelical' clergy, and thus to ensure that their co-operation with temporal 'governors' did not degenerate into subservience.

It is therefore not the Romanist distinction between clergy and laity that is incompatible with the Gospel. Calvin insisted also that the task of the clergy is indeed to 'govern' the laity, however much such language grated on evangelicals, nurtured in anti-clericalism. What a well-ordered reformed church requires, in Calvin's view, is a highly trained, self-policing and self-animating elite of spiritual governors. Luther's 'priesthood of all believers' has no place in his thought. What is unscriptural and intolerable is the Romanist confusion of coercive and spiritual power, and the absolute monarchy of the papacy. (Calvin eventually came to see any absolute monarchy anywhere as incompatible with God's monarchy.) On Calvin's interpretation, scripture authorizes a collegial ministry, perhaps with an admixture of congregational participation in their appointment and supervision. He fully acknowledged the similarity between the form of church government he was here commending on scriptural grounds, and the 'mixed' (or limited) form of secular government, composed of elements of monarchy, aristocracy and democracy, the prudential advantages of which had been asserted by philosophers. Indeed, he introduced a guarded but unmistakable expression of preference for a pure or modified aristocratic form of civil government into editions of the *Institution* from 1543 onwards, giving prudential grounds which obviously also had weight in his ecclesiastical reflections; namely that such an arrangement fettered the licence and exorbitance to which every individual is naturally prone, without abolishing a moderate liberty.

Calvin thus conceived of the polity as a telocracy, an association with an overriding purpose, in which all the associates are obliged to participate. It is not surprising, therefore, that he identified 'heresy' and dissent as peculiarly dangerous to both the civil and the ecclesiastical polity, and conversely that he should have been indulgent, as far as circumstances in his judgment permitted, towards arrangements which would render the participation of citizens/church-members more voluntary, including envisaging a role for them in the selection of both ministers and magistrates. The tension between 'godly discipline' and voluntary allegiance and participation is one which is permanent in the Calvinist tradition.

HMH

Reading

Calvin, J.: *Institution of Christian Religion*, vols XX and XXI, ed. J.T. McNeill, trans. F.L. Battles. Library of Christian Classics. Philadelphia: Westminster Press, 1960.

Dillenberger, J. ed.: *John Calvin: selections from his writings*. Missoula: Scholars Press, 1975.

Chenevière, M.E.: *La Pensée politique de Calvin*. Geneva: Slatkine, 1970.

†Höpfl, H.: *The Christian Polity of John Calvin*. Cambridge: Cambridge University Press, 1982.

Monter, E.W.: *Calvin's Geneva*. London and New York: Wiley, 1967.

Parker, T.H.L.: *John Calvin: a biography*. Philadelphia: Westminster Press, 1975.

†Wendel, F.: *Calvin: the Origins and Development of his Religious Thought*. London: Collins, 1963.

Wolin, S.S.: *Politics and Vision*, ch. 6. Boston: Little, Brown, 1960.

Campanella, Tommaso (1568–1639) Italian philosopher and scholar. Author of *The City of the Sun* (1602), a utopian work which describes an ideal commonwealth without private property. See UTOPIANISM.

Camus, Albert (1913–1960) French Algerian novelist and political thinker. Of working-class origins, he won a scholarship to the *lycée* in Algiers, and came under the influence of his philosophy teacher, Jean Grenier, an exponent of the EXISTENTIALISM which was just coming into fashion in France. Camus, prevented by tuberculosis from following Grenier into the academic profession, turned to literary activity, winning early fame as a 'philosophical novelist'. He developed in fiction and other forms of imaginative literature a form of existentialism which repudiated the puritan elements so marked in such theorists as Kierkegaard, HEIDEGGER and SARTRE, fusing his existentialism instead with hedonistic elements derived from Hellenistic paganism. Together with the central doctrine concerning *l'absurdité*, or irrationality of a universe without God or any absolute moral law, Camus advanced what he considered Southern or Mediterranean ideals of warmth and happiness against the cold and deadly ideologies of the North.

His distinctive form of existentialist ethics yielded in turn a distinctive form of existentialist politics. In one of his early essays, *Lettre à un ami allemand* (1943), he reproaches his German friend for having proceeded from the justifiable assertion that the universe is irrational to the conclusion that he should support the manifestly irrational politics of Hitler. Camus argues that it is better to respond to the irrationality of the universe by creating an order for humanity in the form of justice. Since the existentialist criterion for authenticity in morals is action, not words, Camus completed his argument by engaging first in political journalism in Algiers and, after the defeat of France in 1940, by taking up arms in the Resistance movement.

Camus's novel *L'Étranger* (The Outsider) (1942), appearing during the Occupation, was acclaimed by Sartre, and the author was hailed in Paris after the Liberation as both an outstanding novelist and a Resistance hero. But Camus soon distanced himself from the 'Northern' existentialists, who became increasingly pro-Soviet and pro-Marxist, despite the vast theoretical gulf which divided existentialism from Marxism. Camus accused Sartre, MERLEAU-PONTY, Simone de Beauvoir and their associates of surrendering to the emotional appeal of violence and ideological extremism. He countered their arguments with an appeal to the 'Mediterranean' wisdom of moderation, or *la mesure*, and patience. In an essay *Le Mythe de Sisyphe* (The Myth of Sisyphus) (1942) he depicts his hero Sisyphus doing the same thing over and over again, but nevertheless experiencing happiness.

His most substantial contribution to political theory is *L'Homme révolté* (The Rebel) (1951), in which he claims that the true rebel is not the revolutionary, the man who itches to overthrow the existing order and usher in a new world, but the man who resists injustices by means well calculated to make things better for living men, and not make them worse. The book is a sustained plea for 'piecemeal social engineering' or liberal social democracy of a kind, it must be said, more familiar in Great Britain and Scandinavia than in any 'Mediterranean' country.

By the time of his death in 1960 at the age of 46 Camus had been totally repudiated by the left-wing establishment in Paris, not only because of his anti-communism but because of his refusal, as a French-Algerian, to support the cause of the FLN, the Algerian Liberation Front. Camus continued to advocate reconciliation between the races in Algeria long after extremism had destroyed any real hope of such policies succeeding. At the same time, he alienated the Right by withdrawing from a UNESCO committee as a protest against the admission of Franco's Spain. His times were singularly unresponsive to the appeal of *la mesure*.   MC

Reading

Camus, A.: *The Outsider*, trans. S. Gilbert. London: Hamish Hamilton, 1946.

———: *The Rebel*, trans. A. Bower. London: Hamish Hamilton, 1953.

———: *Resistance, Rebellion and Death*, trans. J. O'Brien. London: Hamish Hamilton, 1961.

———: *Carnets, 1942–1951*, trans. P. Thody London: Hamish Hamilton, 1966.

†Cruikshank, J.: *Albert Camus and the Literature of Revolt*. London: Oxford University Press, 1959.

†Thody, P.: *Albert Camus 1913–1960*. London: Hamish Hamilton, 1961.

canon law   The formal rules of a Christian church: canon law affected political thought in Latin Christendom, chiefly from *c.*1100 to *c.*1500. The canons of the church deal with personal morality, church discipline, administration of the sacraments, the status and powers of clergy. In the Eastern and the Protestant churches, canon law did not acquire the importance it had in the Roman Catholic Church during the European Middle Ages. This was due to the extension, centralization and elaboration of clerical authority over laymen, including secular rulers. Medieval Latin canon law consisted of rulings by earlier councils, important papal decrees and selected *dicta* by church fathers. These were sorted out, clarified, arranged and codified, leading to Gratian's *Decretum* (*c.*1140), which attempted to reconcile contradictions. Western canon law was conceived as a universal, systematic code, parallel to the civil law of ancient Rome (although, as Maitland noted, its jurisprudence was vastly inferior). Meanwhile the hyperactive papacy issued a stream of judgments and decrees, many of which were deemed worthy to enter further authoritative compilations, the *Books of Decretals* (1234 onwards). These were applied in church courts, and considerable influence on developing secular codes was exercised by their principles, and by learned clerical jurists who used biblical, patristic and canonical precepts to impart a higher and often innovative sense of justice to traditional legal practice, for example in the twelfth-century English reforms. The very ideas of universal moral laws systematically to be applied to law and judicial process, and of legislative change and rationalization, owed much to canon law (see Berman).

Canon law became influential partly through what it actually said about political questions, but also by providing, in the ecclesiastical constitution, a model for the developing secular polities. Its importance for political thought was due to outstanding works by canonist commentators, notably Huguccio (d. 1210), Innocent IV (d. 1254), Hostiensis (d. 1271), Zabarella (c. 1335–1417) and Tudeschi (Panormitanus: 1386–1445). Far ahead of contemporary civilians and publicists, they articulated the premises and constitutional details of monarchy, election, corporate personality and consent. While speaking primarily of the church, they drew arguments from natural law, and still more from Roman civil law, and from secular experience, so that a great deal of what they said had general meaning, and, consequently, implications for secular polities. Their arguments were imported wholesale into secular political thought. (See also MEDIEVAL POLITICAL THOUGHT).

Canonists argued that clergy had precedence over secular powers, the pope over the emperor: the former could, on religious or moral grounds, dictate to, sanction and depose the latter. Secular authority is justified by its purpose, and by its being seen to achieve that purpose (see Ullmann, Medieval Papalism). This led, in response, to precocious articulation of rationalistic foundations for the secular state. Secondly, canonists spelled out the implications of sovereignty (suprema potestas) as applied to the pope: the papacy is the court of final appeal, source of legislation, overseer of church government, yet the individual pope may err and be deposed by a council. BODIN admitted his debt to the canonist notion of sovereignty. The canonists have been particularly renowned for

their doctrine of corporations (see Gierke, pp. 238–351); these customarily included towns and 'colleges' (i.e. craft-guilds, voluntary religious bodies, friendly societies), but the canonists were primarily concerned with local and collegiate churches, diocesan chapters and monastic communities. These, they argued, were a distinctive category of social and legal entity in that, without being states or political communities, they had corporate rights, duties and possessions, which belonged to the group as a whole, not to its individual members. Hence decision-making here must be collective. The rulers of such bodies were elected by them and could, in the nature of the corporation, do certain things only by common consent. Whereas civilian lawyers prescribed majority rule, canonists tended to favour 'the greater and saner part' (maior et sanior pars), giving a minority ground for appeal (see Tierney, Foundations, p. 223).

Innocent IV, arguing against severe collective punishments, insisted that a corporation exists only 'by fiction of law'; on the other hand, he gave carte blanche to the self-formation of the craft-guilds. It is probably, therefore, wrong to say (as Gierke and Ullmann did) that this 'fiction-theory' was an instrument of monarchical or state sovereignty. Some fourteenth-century canonists said that the pope was virtually absolute monarch; but the Great Schism (1378) led them to emphasize limits on papal power. Zabarella and Tudeschi used corporation theory to argue that the pope must govern by consent and has less authority than 'the whole corporation of the church', which may express itself through a general council. The canonists were a major source for CONCILIARISM (see Tierney, Foundations, pp. 220–37), and so indirectly for parliamentary constitutionalism (see Tierney, Religion).   AB

Reading

Berman, J.H.: Law and Revolution: the Formation of the Western Legal Tradition. Cambridge, Mass. and London: Harvard University Press, 1983.

Gierke, O. von.: Das deutsches Genossenschafisrecht, vol. III. Berlin, 1881.

Tierney, B.: Foundations of Conciliar Theory: the Contribution of the Medieval Canonists from Gratian to the Great Schism. Cambridge: Cambridge University Press, 1955.

†————: *Religion, Law and the Growth of Consti-tutional Thought 1150–1650*. Cambridge: Cambridge University Press, 1982.

Ullmann, W.: *Medieval Papalism: the Political Theories of the Medieval Canonists*. London: Methuen, 1949.

————: *Law and Politics in the Middle Ages: Introduction to the Sources of Medieval Political Ideas*. London: Hodder & Stoughton, 1975.

capitalism An economic system composed primarily of privately owned enterprises competing in a free market. Capitalism has been defended by political thinkers on a number of grounds: it is economically efficient; it confers freedom, both directly through the scope it provides for economic initiative and indirectly through its well-confirmed association with liberal political institutions; it makes individuals responsible for their own fate, thereby encouraging self-reliance; and it provides an outlet for personal ambitions that might otherwise prove politically disruptive. For examples of such defences, see CLASSICAL POLITICAL ECONOMY, LIBERTARIANISM, SMITH and HAYEK. Capitalism has been forcefully attacked by advocates of SOCIALISM, and especially by MARX and his followers (see MARXISM), the latter maintaining that capitalism necessarily involves the ALIENATION and EXPLOITATION of the working class, and that, far from being economically efficient, the system will fall victim to ever-worsening economic crises. A more moderate response is to be found in SOCIAL DEMOCRACY, which tries to mitigate the evils of unrestricted capitalism by selective state intervention.

Capitalism should not be confused with the market economy itself. It presupposes a separation between those who work in enterprises and those who own them, which distinguishes it both from peasant economies and from forms of socialism based on co-operative ownership. A more difficult issue to settle is the degree of state intervention which can occur in an economy before we should cease to describe it as capitalist. Neologisms such as STATE CAPITALISM have been coined to deal with this problem.   DLM

Reading
Hirschman, A.O.: *The Passions and the Interests: political arguments for capitalism before its triumph*. Princeton, NJ: Princeton University Press, 1977.

Schumpeter, J.: *Capitalism, Socialism and Democracy*, pt 2, 5th edn. London: Allen & Unwin, 1976.

Carlyle, Thomas (1795–1881) British historian and social critic. The son of a stonemason and farmer in Dumfriesshire, Carlyle was educated at the local grammar school and at Edinburgh University. Abandoning his original intention of becoming a minister in the Presbyterian Church, he earned a precarious living with private tutorships and by contributing articles to the *Edinburgh Review* and other periodicals until 1834, when he and his wife moved south to London where he spent the rest of his life. His first book, *Sartor Resartus* (1833) – an idiosyncratic combination of spiritual autobiography and wide-ranging philosophical disquisition – made little impression, but his reputation was established by his history of *The French Revolution* (1837). He followed this with a series of works of history and social criticism, of which the most important are *Heroes and Hero-worship* (1840), *Past and Present* (1843), *Letters and Speeches of Oliver Cromwell* (1845), *Latter-Day Pamphlets* (1850), and the *History of Frederick the Great* (1858–65).

Although an extremely acute social critic, Carlyle was uninterested in political theory as such, and contemptuous and dismissive in his attitude to contemporary political issues. His writings nevertheless repeatedly imply political attitudes and pass political judgments, and these can broadly be seen as crystallizing about three central points: an emphasis on an overriding divine justice as the only final determinant of the success of human actions, its mediation through the instinctual moral unity of a society (making popular revolution the ultimate sanction against a corrupt political leadership), and the need for paternal and charismatic leadership ('Hero-Worship') to bring the instincts of the many to a focus and give them practical effect.

These ideas are broadly akin to the organic tradition of Romantic political thought (see ROMANTICISM), but Carlyle's radicalism distinguishes him from the Burkean conservatism which was the dominant British form of this tradition. Carlyle always described himself as a radical – his radicalism is especially evident in his earlier writings and pre-eminently in *The*

French Revolution, in which his sympathy for the revolutionary cause is unconcealed – but he was never a democrat. Regarding representative institutions as sterile arrangements of mere political machinery, in his later years he came increasingly to admire authoritarian forms of government – 'despotism is essential in most enterprises' (*Past and Present*) – as exemplified by Oliver Cromwell and Frederick the Great. The criterion of the worth of a society comes increasingly to be identified with its ability to recognize its true 'heroes' and to submit to their inspired leadership, while the 'heroes' themselves becomes increasingly absolutist and decreasingly charismatic figures.

Carlyle's notion of the heroic leader as the representative and emanation of his people has led to his sometimes being regarded as a precursor of twentieth-century fascism, but the identification is misleading in view of the strong religious framework of his ideas, the complete absence of the totalitarian element and his comparative lack of interest in nationalism. A maverick political romantic, he produced no body of political ideas coherent enough to attract disciples, and his main significance lies in other fields. ALLeQ

Reading

Brinton, C.: *English Political Thought in the Nineteenth Century*. New York: Harper Torchbooks, 1962.

†Campbell, I.: *Thomas Carlyle*. London: Hamish Hamilton, 1974.

Carlyle, T.: *Works*, ed. H.D. Traill. London: Centenary Edition, 1896–8.

——: *Selected Writings*, ed. and intro. A. Shelston. Harmondsworth: Penguin, 1971.

Cassirer, E.: *The Myth of the State*. New Haven: Yale University Press, 1946.

Kaplan, F.: *Thomas Carlyle*. Cambridge and New York: Cambridge University Press, 1983.

Lehman, B.H.: *Carlyle's Theory of the Hero*. Durham, NC: Duke University Press, 1928.

†Le Quesne, A.L.: *Thomas Carlyle*. London and Toronto: Oxford University Press, 1982.

Lippincott, B.E.: *Victorian Critics of Democracy*. Minneapolis: University of Minnesota Press, 1938.

Chamberlain, Houston Stewart (1855–1927) British-born propagandist naturalized in Germany. Gave a racist analysis of European history in *The Foundations of the Nineteenth Century* (1911), arguing for Aryan superiority. See RACISM.

checks and balances In England the idea that free government was preserved by the balancing and checking of one part of the government by another was expressed by many writers, such as BOLINGBROKE and BLACKSTONE. King, Lords and Commons, as the three estates of the realm, were seen as representing different principles (monarchical, oligarchical and popular) whose juxtaposition might preserve the balance of the constitution and the liberties of the subject (a thesis contested by Jeremy BENTHAM). The common law and the idea of natural justice were also seen as limitations on unchecked executive power. These ideas seem to have exercised an important influence on American constitutional doctrine when combined with the rather different ideas of functional separation of the branches of government, drawn from MONTESQUIEU. (See also SEPARATION OF POWERS.) GM

Reading

Barker, E.: *Essays on Government*, ch. 5. Oxford: Clarendon Press, 1945.

Bentham, J.: *A Fragment on Government*. In *A Comment on the Commentaries* and *A Fragment on Government*, ed. J.H. Burns and H.L.A. Hart. London: Athlone, 1977.

†McIlwain, C.H.: *Constitutionalism and the Changing World*. Cambridge: Cambridge University Press, 1939.

Chinese political thought Despite the long dominance of a Confucian orthodoxy, Chinese political thought rivals that of Europe in richness and diversity. For purposes of periodization it may be divided in the following manner. During the Shang and Chou dynasties (*c.*1766 to 1122 BC, and from 1122 BC) which ruled the lower Yellow River basin, though there was as yet no political thought, a distinctive political tradition developed. From the beginning of the disintegration of the Chou dynasty (after 770 BC) into a collection of warring states down to the unification of those areas which are still the core of ethnic China by the Ch'in dynasty (221 BC), a great efflorescence of theorizing on government occurred.

This was the 'hundred schools' period still referred to by contemporary Chinese as a model of free and lively discourse (thus Mao's saying: 'let a hundred flowers bloom, let a hundred schools of thought contend'). The most important of these schools were Confucianism, Legalism, and Taoism. After the short-lived Ch'in dynasty, China was ruled by a succession of dynasties (from 206 BC) more or less committed to Confucianism, though with some interludes in which Taoism and Buddhism for a time captured the fashion at court. This period may be referred to as that of official Confucianism, though this was a syncretic and evolving doctrine far removed from the views of its founder. Undergoing a philosophical refoundation during the eleventh and twelfth centuries (the neo-Confucian revival), Confucianism remained the creed of the empire until the extinction of the last dynasty (in 1911), though its influence lives on in China as well as in the East Asian cultural area.

The first texts in Chinese political thought were long associated with the Chou dynasty, though subsequent scholarship has established that some parts of them are later fabrications. These 'classics' are compilations of poems, historical and court records, and writings on divination, and it has been the traditional view that they incorporated the written remains of a golden age of civilization. The most cryptic and elusive sayings were invested with a heavy burden of meaning and generated lengthy commentaries accordingly. Of particular significance are two political traditions identified by these commentators. The first concerns 'the mandate of heaven', being the notion that the ruling house is entrusted with the governance of the empire provided its rule is virtuous and beneficent, but forfeits the right to rule if the ruler becomes corrupt or disasters afflict the population. The second concerns the exemplary moral behaviour of certain of the early sage rulers, one of whom passed over his own son in order to select a commoner of surpassing virtue to be his successor.

The first political thinker (leaving aside the legalist Kuan Tzu, d. 645 BC, whose writings are notoriously corrupt) was Confucius (K'ung Fu-tzu, 551–479 BC). Although the writing and transmission of other texts was attributed to him in ancient times, his views may most reliably be sought in the *Analects*. Later traditions ascribed to him the status of a great official and even the possession of supernatural powers, but it is clear from contemporary evidence that he was a travelling scholar and teacher of very modest means who was never greatly successful in catching the ear of the powerful despite holding minor office for a period in his native state. Confucius's stated intention was to revive the rites, ceremonies and usages of the languishing Chou dynasty, but his proposals for dealing with the disorder and evil of his times contain notable innovations. The Confucian ideal is rule by moral example rather than by military supremacy or according to hereditary succession. The ruler should so order his person and household that all men shall wish to be his subjects, and no laws will be required to control their conduct. The advisers and officers of the ruler's government should be men of genuine merit ('gentlemen') as revealed by their learning and scholarly accomplishments. Confucius believes that those adept at the scholarly arts will take 'benevolence' (the chief Confucian virtue) as the standard for their conduct and will accordingly work for the welfare of the common people whose labour is the only source of real wealth. Confucius makes no distinction between familial and political authority, regarding the society as an extension of the ruler's household and the well-ordered family as the foundation of the state.

In carrying on many of the aristocratic traditions and values of Chou civilization Confucius effected in them a considerable transformation. He accepted without question the need for social hierarchy and a division of labour (between peasantry and literati), but he thought most men capable of some improvement through learning and did not himself withhold instruction from those who presented even the meanest offering, provided they showed application. He emphasized the many duties of the ruler to his subjects, and of the men of learning to service for the state, and their obligation to offer advice based upon their knowledge of the requirements of benevolence even if this advice was unwelcome. And apart from some references to a (non-anthropomorphic) 'heaven' as the source of virtue and the arbiter of fate, the underpinnings of Confucius's theory are secular rather than spiritual, the correct observation of political rites and ceremonies being accorded something of a religious dimension.

Confucians later developed this theory in strikingly different ways. Mencius (Meng Tzu, c.372–289 BC), a scholar very influential in his day, whose works came to be second in authority only to those of his master in later times, chose to dwell on the Confucian view of the sources of virtue. In a theory likened to western moral intuitionism Mencius held that the 'original heart' of each man (itself a reflection of the cosmic order) contained the embryonic stirrings of the four virtues, the development of which depended upon a favourable environment, and particularly an appropriate education. He was sharply critical of the reliance upon force by the overlords of the time, calling for kingly government in the interests of the people and going so far as to justify tyrannicide. Hsün Tzu (c.298–238 BC), who was an official as well as a teacher, advanced an opposed interpretation of the Confucian inheritance. He saw appetite as the most salient aspect of human nature ('things few, desires many'), though he also affirmed the universal human capacity for learning and culture. Of a Hobbesian turn of mind (he was also insistent upon the need for clear and consistent naming as the only foundation for proper reasoning) and writing at a time of almost incessant warfare, he looked to the civilization and its rites and ceremonies as the only source of order. Men must learn virtue therefrom, the members of each generation requiring an arduous schooling lest they remain mere creatures of appetite. For the oversight of such a task a kingly government dominated by Confucian advisers was crucial. Whereas Mencius was of a mystical turn of mind Hsün Tzu was a rationalist. 'Heaven' he reduced to the workings of nature, and declared that as nature was indifferent to human strivings men were themselves the makers of their fate.

Legalism (or the 'school of method'), the chief rival of Confucianism, did not stem from the writings of a single theorist, but is rather an amalgam of diverse elements given a philosophical gloss by the last great Legalist theorist,

Han Fei Tzu (c.280–233 BC). The earliest Legalists (setting aside Kuan Tzu, d. 645 BC) were Shang Yang (d. 338 BC) and Shen Pu-hai (c. 400–337 BC). The former succeeded by his policies in raising the most westerly of the warring states, Ch'in, to a pinnacle of efficiency and power, thus laying the foundation for the unification of China under Ch'in aegis in the following century. Shang Yang's intention was to organize the state as an efficient instrument of war. Hereditary office holders were to be replaced by able administrators who would take the will of the prince as law, and agriculture and handicrafts were to be encouraged at the expense of merchant activity and idle consumption. Contending doctrines were to be rooted out in favour of the common people taking the magistrates as their teachers, and the population was to be organized such that each group was responsible for the conduct of its members. A contemporary of Shang Yang, Shen Pu-hai served for some years as chancellor of the small state of Han. Although his writings now exist only as fragments it is clear that he devoted much attention to administrative technique and the methods of rule. His recommendations to the ruler advise an approach to his duties which has much in common with the Taoist cultivation of non-attachment as the path to sagehood. The ruler is as the hub of a wheel, unmoving while the ministers and officials, the spokes, are in unceasing rotation. His will is crucial if government is to be possible yet he remains the master of the situation by refraining from indicating his preferences in advance of his decision and avoiding involvement in the framing of actual policy.

These and other elements are drawn together in the writings of Han Fei Tzu, along with Hsün Tzu perhaps the most rewarding of Chinese political theorists for the western reader. Han Fei Tzu, having studied under Hsün Tzu in his youth, takes over something of the latter's estimate of human nature and its malleability though he severs it from the Confucian belief in benevolence. He advances the view that the standards of the private man and those of the state are at variance, and that the ruler should exercise perfect liberty in the use of the 'two handles' (rewards and punishments) to ensure that the standards of the state will prevail, as only these will produce order. In developing in a sophisticated and philosophical manner the original Legalist notion that the state should be organized such that the will of the prince should be the law, Han Fei Tzu touches on a problem found much later in western thinking of this genre. The administration of the state should be as ordered, as predictable, and as free from personal caprice as possible – 'the law no more makes exceptions for men of high station than the plumb line bends to accommodate a crooked place in the wood' – thus establishing constraints which would also apply to the ruler.

The political theory of Taoism (not to be confused with the religion of that name which developed later) is the most difficult to elucidate. The earliest chapters of the writings attributed to Chuang Tzu (written about the fourth century BC) advise the aspiring sage to withdraw from the world. Man's strivings are all in vain in an indifferent universe; the wise man therefore cultivates simplicity and uselessness and comes to comprehend thereby the absurdity of human existence. In the writings ascribed to Lao Tzu (which were written by about the middle of the third century BC) this advice can also be found, as can a poetic and subtle elaboration of its metaphysical basis. The *tao* or 'way' (a term used by the Confucians, but in a different sense) is all encompassing, and being potentially without limit is beyond human comprehension. It is also 'unkind' as its movement proceeds unchecked by and unconscious of the activity of man. Accordingly the sage finds enlightenment in inaction. But in an argument reminiscent of the advice of some Legalist writers to the ruler (and here it should be noted that later commentators found a philosophical affinity between Taoism and Legalism) Lao Tzu also maintains that it is precisely the Taoist sage, with the calmness of mind that comes from a lack of attachment to the transient things of the human world, who would make the ideal ruler. He then elaborates a vision of rural simplicity in which the old practices are followed and the clever are prevented from playing any role, inaction being also the supreme political wisdom.

Apart from these three major schools others deserve mention. Mo Tzu (*c.*479–390 BC), in his time a great rival of Confucius, was the founder of a military order devoted to countering aggressive warfare. Arguing that the Confucians in encouraging filial piety founded their political philosophy upon partiality, which was the root cause of all conflict, he developed a theory based on universal and equal regard (or love) for all men. He was also critical of Confucius for wasting time and resources on elaborate ceremonies and mourning rites, maintaining instead that every policy adopted by the state should be directly addressed to the needs of the common people. How he expected to identify and effect such policies is not clear from his extant writings. On the one hand he put forward a populist epistemology – what is true can be seen, in part, from what the people believe – but, on the other, he was also a strict advocate of the notion of 'identification with the superior' to ensure that all in the state were obedient to a single direction. Later followers of Mo Tzu, who constituted themselves into a quasi-religious sect, developed a system of logic not inferior to that of the Greeks, but Mo Tzu's influence thereafter declined and his writings were neglected until recent times. China in this period was also host to the 'school of names', a diverse collection of sophists and logicians who debated problems of existence, relativity, causation and other such philosophical issues (Hui Shih, *c.*380–305 BC, stating Zeno's paradox of motion, and Kung-sun Lung writing at the same time on the problem of particulars and universals). Although they did have some impact on political thought, several of their number also holding political office, their role cannot be compared to that of the Sophists of classical Greece. The sophistication of Chinese writing on the politics and strategy of the warfare that was endemic at the time should also be noted. The treatise traditionally ascribed to Sun Tzu (perhaps to be identified with Sun Pin, who lived in the fourth century BC, or his putative ancestor Sun Wu, of the preceding century), apart from being a masterwork of strategy, explicitly develops the connection between politics and war and contains a chapter on the techniques of subversion worthy of the twentieth century. Finally, numerous metaphysical schools (including the *yin-yang*, and five elements schools) flourished, though their impact on political thought was not as yet direct.

When Ch'in unified ethnic China in 221 BC its rulers did so under the banner of Legalism. The short and oppressive reign of the house of Ch'in (the emperor advised by, among others, Li Ssu, fellow student with Han Fei Tzu of Hsün Tzu) laid the foundation for the bad press Legalism has enjoyed in China ever since, though in recent times Mao Zedong sought to improve the reputation of the school by comparing the exploits of the Ch'in emperor with his own achievements. When the Han dynasty (a name to become eponymous with the Chinese people) chose to proclaim (in 141 BC) a single school as that to be identified with the empire they chose Confucianism; but this was a Confucianism transformed almost beyond recognition by the syncretic approach of the school's proponents, and the practical exigencies of ruling a vast and populous domain.

The Han Confucians, of whom Tung Chung-shu (c.179–104 BC) was the most influential, tried to amalgamate Confucian political and moral philosophy with the metaphysical and cosmological speculation of the *yin-yang* and five elements schools, and the exponents of the divination notions found in the *Book of Changes* (*I Ching*). Tung Chung-shu conceived of the universe as an organic entity in which *yin* (representative of all that is dark, submissive, female) and *yang* (representative of all that is bright, aggressive, male) and derivatively the five elements (water, fire, wood, metal, earth) are in constant movement according to a pre-determined order. This movement produces the seasons, life, and man. Man is both the noblest of living beings and also a microcosm of the universe; his nature (which is the source of the virtues, including benevolence) is admixed with feeling or emotions just as in the universe *yang* intermingles with *yin*. To develop his nature (for few can do this unaided) and thereby cause benevolence to become manifest and emotion regulated, man needs culture which it is the responsibility of the kingly ruler to provide. Thus Tung Chung-shu has grafted certain Confucian political and ethical notions upon an entirely different metaphysics. His theory contains other elements, including a philosophy of history in which dynasties

succeed one another according both to the mandate of heaven and also to a predetermined cycle of colours and cardinal positions; he also advanced the view that portents and natural disasters were an indication that the ruler had acted such that the correct order and pattern had been violated, a transgression for which sacrifices and amends would be required. Han Confucianism was also eclectic in its incorporation of many Legalist practices in the administration of the empire. These were often openly acknowledged, as in the 'Discourses on Salt and Iron' (81 BC) which is the record of a dialogue between the Legalist-inclined defenders of the government's record particularly on military and administrative spending, and their critics who make consistent appeal to the Confucian value of frugality and the importance to the state of ethical standards rather than the costly machinery of bureaucratic compulsion. This lively and readable work is reminiscent of nothing so much as a contemporary argument between socialists and free marketeers. Worthy of note also in this period is the appearance of the first great Chinese history, written by Ssu-ma Ch'ien (c.145–90 BC).

For a time during the early centuries AD much intellectual interest was focused upon Taoism, but thereafter Buddhism began to exert a major attraction upon the Chinese intellect, reaching the height of its philosophical, religious, and political influence during the T'ang dynasty (AD 618–906). It was to counter what some then saw as a foreign creed, as well as to confront the philosophical issues (and particularly the problem of existence) raised in Buddhist metaphysics, that a body of scholars began what has come to be known as the neo-Confucian revival. Beginning in the Sung dynasty (960–1279) the influence of neo-Confucianism spread, even despite the Mongol invasions, so that by the beginning of the Ming dynasty (1368–1644) it became the philosophical orthodoxy. By this time the Chinese system of government rested upon the regular selection of a bureaucracy through examinations in the Confucian arts and writings, and the extensive use of printing had widely disseminated the works of Confucius and his latter-day interpreters throughout the empire (and to Korea, Japan and Vietnam). The neo-Confucians and their students were as much administrators and men of affairs as scholars, and their arguments often had practical implications for government policy, and sometimes painful consequences for themselves.

Although neo-Confucianism was a broad movement embracing many varieties of argument, Chu Hsi (1130–1200) came to be acknowledged by the fourteenth century as its leading exponent. The metaphysical foundation of Chu Hsi's political philosophy resembles that of western neo-Platonism. Every existent thing is the material instantiation of a particular and inflexible principle or standard: the universe is therefore composed of that which is 'in shapes' or matter (ch'i), and that which is 'above shapes' or principle (li). The summation of all the principles in the universe is the Supreme Ultimate (t'ai chi), and as Chu Hsi's philosophy is (following Han Confucianism) a philosophy of organism so the Supreme Ultimate is immanent in each thing. The principle of a thing is, as in Platonism, perfect, but in being clothed in material form the possibility of imperfection and thus evil arises. In order to avoid evil and move towards the perfection that is their unique principle, men (and particularly the scholar-literati) must pursue mental cultivation, endeavouring to understand principles, and thereby their summation, by 'the investigation of things'. Here Chu Hsi had in mind not so much an empirical investigation of the material world as a leap of intuitive insight akin to the 'sudden enlightenment' of Ch'an (Zen) Buddhism, except of course that what was to be apprehended was the pattern of an existent cosmic order rather than its fundamental unreality. New force was given to the Confucian direction to 'rectify oneself and restore the rites'. Having sought the Supreme Ultimate in himself the scholar had an overriding duty to reform the human world according to the principles of which he now had knowledge. Far from Confucianism being, as in Max Weber's view, a comfortable and conformist creed, it imposed a heavy twofold burden or sense of predicament upon its exponents.

Chu Hsi's ideas were sufficiently dominant to be described as an orthodoxy, but other scholars did develop contrary interpretations of the Confucian tradition, most notably Wang Yang-ming (1472–1529) who maintained the identity of the mind and the principle of things (li). Thereafter Confucianism had its critics, and philological inquiry undermined some of the traditional views as to the composition of the early texts, but it remained a living force down to the end of the nineteenth century. The great radical and moving spirit of the 1898 reform movement, K'ang Yü-wei (1858–1927), based his policies (which if implemented would have destroyed much of the traditional structure of the empire) on his interpretation of Confucius as a reformer, and a thoroughgoing re-evaluation of Confucius was only initiated during the intellectual ferment that accompanied the May Fourth Movement of 1919.

Modern Chinese political thought reflected the influences of almost every variety of western political theory that found its way into translation. The doctrine of nationalism, conforming in some respects to the Chinese view of their identity, had many adherents, including Sun Yat-sen (1866–1925). But even Chinese Marxism (see MAO ZEDONG) continued to incorporate many Confucian preoccupations.   JSC

Reading

†Ames, R.T.: *The Art of Rulership: a study in ancient Chinese political thought.* Honolulu: University of Hawaii Press, 1983.

Chan, Wing-tsit, ed.: *A Source Book in Chinese Philosophy.* Princeton, NJ: Princeton University Press, 1963.

————: *Reflections on Things at Hand: the Neo-Confucian anthology compiled by Chu Hsi and Lü Tsu-Ch'ien.* New York: Columbia University Press, 1967.

Confucius: *The Analects*, trans. D.C. Lau. Harmondsworth: Penguin, 1979.

†Creel, H.G.: *Confucius and the Chinese Way.* New York: Harper & Row, 1960.

————: *Shen Pu-hai: a Chinese political philosopher of the fourth century BC.* Chicago: University of Chicago Press, 1974.

de Bary, W.T.: *Neo-Confucian Orthodoxy and the Learning of the Mind-and-Heart.* New York: Columbia University Press, 1981.

Fung Yu-lan: *A Short History of Chinese Philosophy.* New York: Collier-Macmillan, 1948.

†Hsiao, Kung-chuan: *A History of Chinese Political Thought, vol. I: From the Beginnings to the Sixth Century AD.* Princeton, NJ: Princeton University Press, 1979.

Lao Tzu: *Tao Te Ching*, trans. D.C. Lau. Harmondsworth: Penguin, 1963.

Levenson, J.R.: *Confucian China and its Modern Fate: a trilogy*. Berkeley: University of California Press, 1958–65.

Mencius: *Mencius*, trans. D.C. Lau. Harmondsworth: Penguin, 1970.

Metzger, T.A.: *Escape from Predicament: Neo-Confucianism and China's Evolving Political Culture*. New York: Columbia University Press, 1977.

†Rubin, V.A.: *Individual and State in Ancient China: essays on four Chinese philosophers*. New York: Columbia University Press, 1976.

Watson, B. trans.: *Basic Writings of Mo Tzu, Hsün Tzu, and Han Fei Tzu*. New York: Columbia University Press, 1967.

church and state   The relation between church and state may be seen as an institutional phenomenon, but also, and more fundamentally, as the rapport that exists within the human species between the spiritual or inner life and the social and collective life. Modern theologians tend to agree that religion can be explicable in both the mystical and the scientific modes of expression. Scientists such as the late Alastair Hardy have also attempted to account for the spiritual dimension of human beings in terms that do not need to conflict with scientific hypotheses such as the theory of evolution. Among the modern pioneers of the phenomenon of spirituality and its reflection in organized religion, including religion's impact on law, morality and society, are William James in *Varieties of Religious Experience* (1902), E. D. Starbuck in *The Psychology of Religion* (1899), and Émile DURKHEIM in *Elementary Forms of Religious Life* (1911).

Anthropologists who study primitive peoples conclude with a similar certainty that where there is a human community there will be some form of expressed conviction that there are inner and higher forms of experience which, when shared, link members of a given community in a social relationship.

Hardy, writing as a biologist, suggests that we should associate consciousness with the development of speech. The growing child comes at a certain stage to be aware of his or her Self. This in turn gives rise to an intuitive sense of an Other who is aware of him or her and can offer advice, when the need arises to face choices between alternatives. Likewise in the public domain the need of the lawmaker to seek counsel from a wiser authority is reflected in the relations that develop between ruler and oracle, king and priest, state and church.

In modern times ideologies such as fascism, communism or Maoism – claiming to say little about the spiritual Self – can serve as a form of national religion. A distinction should be made therefore between religion when it serves the state, religion when it serves the individual, and religion when it serves both. Some of the great religions, including Judaism, Christianity and Islam, fall into the last category. Religion 'makes man do the biggest things he is capable of' in the judgment of the anthropologist Malinowski, by which he meant that religion, because it makes individuals feel that they have access to a higher source of help, encouragement and strength, also enables groups to unite and to work for common purposes. Social cohesion is strengthened within groups which share and transmit common beliefs and rituals, and this is reinforced by the growth of a body of religious teachers who can rarely avoid making an impact on a community's social and political institutions.

In practice, references to 'church and state' tend to denote the relationships that exist between the Christian religion and governments. The concept has a long history and a unique importance in the political thought developed under Christianity in the western world. The distinction between church and state was not a pronounced feature of pre-Christian civilization. On the contrary, until the adoption of Christianity by the Roman Empire in the fourth century, the secular rulers, including the Roman emperors, were accorded a supreme religious function. The ruler might be seen as the representative of the people to the gods, or he might himself be regarded as divine. In the ancient civilizations of China, Egypt, Babylonia, Assyria, Persia, and South and Central America, the combination of priest and ruler seems to have been a consistent feature.

Judaism offers the first example of a society which, in the face of submission to a conqueror (Jerusalem fell in 586 BC), insisted on retaining a religious identity separate from its rulers. Christianity, as an offshoot of Judaism and also subject to the Roman Empire, found no difficulty in conceiving similarly of its own religious fellowship. The words of the Gospel that were used to express this differentiated loyalty were (Matt. 22:21): 'Render therefore to Caesar the things that are Caesar's and to God the things that are God's.' Persecution of Christians followed precisely because the imperial authorities feared those who refused to worship the divinity of the state in favour of a non-nationalistic and higher divinity which lacked geographical (and cultural) boundaries. The word *ecclesia* which the Greeks gave to their legislative meetings was used by Christians to describe their religious meetings. For the Christians *ecclesia* was a translation from the Hebrew *gahal*, which had a specifically religious significance implying the spiritual fellowship of the Chosen People.

Within the Roman Empire, Christianity spread rapidly. Its leaders sought acceptance of their claim that their religion, though inwardly transforming, in no way affected their political loyalties, to which they would testify with martyrdom rather than violent rebellion. Even after Constantine (306–37) had embraced the Christian faith, and after Christianity had been declared first a legal religion (313) and then the official religion, the Fathers of the Church – such as AUGUSTINE (354–430) and Pope Gelasius I (492–7) – continued to affirm the *duality* of civil and religious authority. That these two powers should be balanced within the state remained a key tenet of Christian thought, though one subject to a wide range of interpretations.

With the rise of a Christian church within a Christian empire began a unique era in political thought and organization. In spite of the decline of the Roman Empire, the institution of the Roman church was to last from the Council of Nicaea, presided over by Emperor Constantine in 325, until Luther unleashed the Protestant Reformation in 1518 – more than a thousand years later. It included for many centuries the Eastern Empire centred on Constantinople, until the great Schism of 1054.

It can be misleading to say that the political theory promoted by the apologists for this political system was a theory of church *and* state. Christian writers believed that the church hierarchy and the imperial or civil hierarchy were sharers of power in a jointly directed Christian condominium. The Anglican historian John Neville Figgis has clarified this potential misinterpretation by the twentieth-century student, when he observes that in the Middle Ages 'the Church was not *a* State, it was *the* State; the state or rather the civil authority (for a separate society was not recognized) was merely the police department of the Church' (*Political Thought*, p. 5).

Historians of political thought often retain the Latin vocabulary of the Christian writers themselves as a way of stressing that to translate can be to mislead. By *sacerdotium* is meant both the institution of the church and also its higher, or longer term, moral responsibility. By *imperium*, or *regnum* (according to whether one is referring to an empire or a kingdom), is meant both the institution of the civil authority and its particular functions, which were to keep order within and protect society generally from external forces bent perhaps on its destruction. The two powers in partnership convey the sense of how Christian theorists conceived the nature of good government. Because modern political thought does not use the same imagery we are prone to misunderstand Christian theory. Sometimes their vision was referred to by use of the metaphor of the Two Swords expounded as early as 494 by Pope Gelasius I. The right balance had to be struck, according to time and place, between the exigencies of this world and the imperatives of the next. Theoretically, the symbolism represented the Christian preoccupation with the inner life, and the quest for its fulfilment, a consideration that called for an intertwining of society's moral concerns and its agency of physical law enforcement.

By the end of the fourth century, the church was using the secular arm of *imperium* to bring pagans and Christian sectarians into the organized church. Augustine, Bishop of Hippo, was and remains the giant of Christian political thought. In his defence of Christianity, *The City of God* (413–25), he merged the Roman legal scholarship in which he had received his initial training and Christian theology to which he had been converted, to provide the definitive justification of the Christian Republic. Augustine distinguished between the worldly state and the city of God; others interpreted him as identifying the city of God with the church. Hence the church was supreme over all the nations of the earth. This was in later centuries accepted everywhere in the West. Thus it was that the church of the Middle Ages came to regard itself through its hierarchy and ecumenical councils as a divinely inspired authority: moral, intellectual, and political.

Once the Roman Empire had receded and its power had been taken back by its former subject peoples, the church became the main repository of educated thought and opinion at every level of society (see MEDIEVAL POLITICAL THOUGHT). Inevitably, ecclesiastics penetrated the administration of the kingdoms and other feudal entities. Often they were the only competent administrators available to carry out secular commissions. By the same token, entry into the church was an important avenue of social advancement. The use of Latin as the *lingua franca* of Christendom and the pivotal position of the church in determining who might acquire competence in its use provide both an indicator and an explanation of the power which the church was to acquire.

Emperor Charlemagne (800–14), however, challenged the authority of the *sacerdotium*. He claimed the status of direct appointment by God, without need of endorsement by the pope. He appointed bishops by his, rather than papal, authority and required these bishops to take on the sorts of duties that were demanded of secular vassals. Churchmen themselves were confronted by circumstances in which they might choose whether to support the secular ruler within whose territory they were located geographically, or the authority of the pontiff, who claimed their spiritual allegiance.

The accession to the papal throne in 1073 of Gregory VII swung the pendulum the other way. Specifically, Gregory prohibited the lay investiture of bishops (see INVESTITURE CONTROVERSY). His ruling was immediately challenged by Emperor Henry IV with an attempt to secure the deposition of the pope, who in turn responded by excommunicating the emperor, absolving the emperor's vassals from their feudal oaths of loyalty.

The notable feature is that though the antagonists and the political commentators disagreed over the issues, and over the extent to which the parties were exceeding their powers,

the doctrine of the two powers as such was never questioned. Like the modern constitutional beliefs in CHECKS AND BALANCES or the 'swing of the pendulum' in the two-party system, the notion that there *should* be two swords was accepted, and provided the framework for debate.

From the eleventh century, there was a slow trend in Europe towards the strengthening of the feudal states, and the development within them of independent elites. Trained in both civil and canon law, they drew confidence from their classical and humanistic studies to challenge the papal claims to pronounce in the sphere of temporal jurisdiction.

The intermeshing of the powers of the *regnum* and the powers of the *sacerdotium* in any given European society remained unchanged for ordinary subjects. There was additionally a complicated relationship between the local ecclesiastical authorities and the 'central' emissaries of the pope in Rome. The setting up of the Inquisition illustrates this. Departures from ecclesiastically sanctioned orthodoxy brought about in the twelfth century the notion that the matter needed a certain uniformity of approach. Pope Gregory IX, in 1233, therefore commissioned orders of friars to travel from place to place to investigate those who were thought to be deviant or heretical. If found guilty, they would then be punished by the local, secular authorities. Horror of the activities of the Inquisition among contemporary critics seems to have been evoked as much by the consideration that the inquisitors were not locally directed as by the nature of their policies.

Only by slow degrees did Christian subjects lose their sense of a dual allegiance, and then civil rulers found, by the same token, that they could keep power without having to defer to papal authority. Thus when Henry VIII of England, by his Act of Supremacy of 1534, established a state church, he was giving formal expression to a changed balance of power between civil and ecclesiastical authority that already existed in practice.

The sensational subject matter of some of the disputes between *regnum* and *sacerdotium* – especially those which led to the casting down of the mighty from on high – attracted more attention than the finely poised balance of power within feudal Christendom which gave rise to them. From the point of view of political theory, there was an astonishing energy and vitality within this complex system of checks and balances which ensured that abuse of power – to which rulers are always susceptible – was subject to a non-violent form of public challenge in the widest possible international context. As we shall see, it was the church's claim to exercise *infallible* judgment rather than its duty to exert moral leadership that was to be contested. In the challenge to papal infallibility many forces were united: theological, scientific, and philosophical movements, and above all the political ambitions of secular rulers wishing to assert national autonomy.

The Protestant Reformation marks the period in which the doctrine of the Two Swords was replaced by the doctrine of the Sovereign State (see REFORMATION POLITICAL THOUGHT). Acknowledging the absolute, secular sovereignty of the ruler was initially seen as an expedient, a means of bringing to a halt the shocking carnage unexpectedly released by the clashes between orthodox theologians and their zealous critics. Faced in 1520 with LUTHER's provocative attack on conventional theology – on grace, on free interpretation of Holy Writ, on clerical celibacy, on the sale of indulgences, and on payment of taxes – the papal authorities, presuming their ability to call on the secular arm of the emperor to bring Luther in person to Rome, found themselves resisted. Luther could command unexpected support, including the protection of his Prince. In other parts of Christendom, such as France, England and the Low Countries, demands for theological reform spread rapidly, and attempts to suppress them brought not a return to orthodoxy, but even greater civil discord.

Given that no military party could prevail, various truces reflected the desire for peace. But there was no clear theory to match the practice. A slow change in thinking seems to have come about between the Peace of Augsburg in 1555 and the Peace of Westphalia in 1648. The compromise that was never expected to become a theory was contained in the formula *cuius regio eius religio* – 'to each prince his own religion'. The practical consequences entailed were, first, that religious doctrine and organization should, for the time being, accord with the religion of the secular ruler. Second, there should be no intervention by one sovereign state in the religious affairs of another.

Two unanswered questions about church and state were implicit in these practical rules. The first centred on the meaning and application of 'sovereign' (see SOVEREIGNTY). This superficially legal question was addressed by the French jurist Jean BODIN. How should the civil authority in sixteenth-century Europe distinguish between a sovereign state and a state that was merely a vassal state? Bodin judged that the sovereign state could be identified by certain marks which included *inter alia* the powers to make law and to be subject to none made by another, to appoint magistrates, prefects and military commanders, to make war, and to be the highest body of appeal. Other attributes of the sovereign state should include the sole power of taxation, the right to determine what language was to be used, and the power to collect the revenues from vacant bishoprics. In short, to be acknowledged as a 'sovereign' state held consequences important for the physical security of political communities, including the right to be exempt from religious persecution.

The second question concerned the moral justification of secular sovereignty. Could a Christian justify a state at all in which a secular sovereign rather than a religious leader decided what was right or wrong? This was the issue that caused the greatest difficulty for the Reformers. Luther and Zwingli decided affirmatively, but on condition that religious leaders like the Prophets of the Old Testament were closely consulted. CALVIN held a more theocratic view whereby the leaders of the church community decided matters of religious doctrine, reinforcing it by admonition and punishment where necessary. In short, rationalist and humanist critics of the orthodox church might well expect more enlightenment to come from laymen than from either orthodox or reforming theologians.

Thomas HOBBES provided the most original and coherent theory of the secular, sovereign state in his classic work, *Leviathan* (1651). He wrote not only as a philosopher and classical scholar but also as a Protestant with an intense commitment to the English Reformation. He made a clear distinction between religion when it serves the inner life and religion when it serves the state, believing that Christianity in essence should do the former, but that under a reformed Christian Commonwealth it might do both. Hobbes was passionately antagonistic towards the authoritarianism of the Roman Curia which he judged to have defined Christian doctrine falsely, contrary to truth and reason, to promote its own worldly power.

The foundation of all states, in Hobbes's theory, lay in the maintenance of public order. Only when order had been retrieved from chaos was public morality possible, allowing individuals to engage in collective activities, including religious worship. Christians in the contemporary world, as in the pre-Christian Roman era, were required 'to render to Caesar what is Caesar's', and Caesar was the sovereign who could keep order not the sovereign who was sanctioned by a prophet – who might be true or false – to promote a particular doctrine or ritual. To believers in the false political authority claimed by the pope, Hobbes offered the counsel that they had been grotesquely deceived. Christian individuals should interpet Holy Writ for themselves, not rely on the interpretations of others.

Among writing on church and state, *Leviathan* marks an utter break with the Augustinian and medieval tradition. Not only does Hobbes refuse altogether the metaphor of the Two Swords, he substitutes for it the mighty Leviathan – the secular ruler who holds in one hand the weapon of the sovereign state and in the other the pastoral crook of the national church.

The nation-state's independence from external religious authority was thus confirmed by the doctrine of sovereignty. What had still to be determined was the place within the state of organized religion. There were many possible relationships, ranging from the church as a constitutionally established branch of the national administration to the church as one of a myriad of groups of co-religionaries, united in pursuit of inncr spirituality according to thcir own doctrines.

To most minds of the seventeenth and eighteenth centuries an established church reflected the proper relationship between the post-Reformation church and government. Its task was to provide a uniform ceremony for public occasions, and to teach – not dogma or irrational or superstitious doctrine, but the use of Reason itself. Hobbes stated that the pastor's teaching should be conveyed by means not of 'power over the consciences of men' but through 'wisdom, humility, clearness of doctrine, and sincerity of conversation, and not by suppression of the natural sciences, and the morality of natural reason' (p. 711). A national civic church was supported by other Protestants, including GROTIUS, SPINOZA, and, much later COLERIDGE, who would have transformed the Established Church into a national agency for education and culture.

By contrast, those who saw Christianity being concerned first and foremost with the individual's inner holiness – especially the Puritan sects – dissociated Christianity from the state. Their path was towards voluntarism, fundamentalism, and the free interpretation of the Scriptures. John LOCKE, whose writings on the subject included *The Reasonableness of Christianity* (1696) and *Letters on Toleration* (1689, 1690, 1692), hoped for a reconciliation of these extremes. He supported a Broad or Latitudinarian Church of England as well as legal toleration for the Dissenters who could not accommodate themselves within even a Latitudinarian formula.

In modern times, the plural or heterodox state has become the positive, alternative model to mere TOLERATION. Pierre BAYLE proposed it in the 1680s, but even the French Huguenots, who would have gained freedom from persecution thereby, tended to agree that disunity in religion was unseemly in a nation. The United States Bill of Rights (1791) seems to have been the first constitutional recognition that pluralism in religion might be positively justifiable in its own right; it asserts firmly that *no* law concerning 'the establishment of a religion' or 'prohibiting the free exercise thereof' should be made by Congress (see Brownlie, p. 11), and thereby provides a working example of a secular administration presiding over a religiously plural society.

The toleration of sects by an established church led, as the orthodox theologians feared and predicted, in the long run to a separation of

71

church and state, and the disestablishment in many countries, such as France, of formerly established churches. From being conceived of first as a partner with government, then as an agency of administration, some churches now see themselves as a voluntary group in society whose political role – if any – is that of moral educator and pressure group. How this development should be evaluated depends on the extent to which it is thought that Christianity, in its essence, serves society or the individual's inner life. The range of positions on the continuum between these poles is of immense importance for political analysis.   SLJ

Reading

Church and State: Report of the Archbishops' Commission. London: Church Information Office, 1970.

Brownlie, I. ed.: *Basic Documents on Human Rights.* Oxford: Clarendon Press, 1971.

Figgis, J.N.: *Churches in the Modern State.* London: Longmans, 1913.

————: *Political Thought from Gerson to Grotius 1414–1625.* New York: Harper Torchbooks, 1960.

Hardy, A.: *The Spiritual Nature of Man.* Oxford: Clarendon Press, 1979.

Hobbes, T.: *Leviathan,* ed. C.B. Macpherson. Harmondsworth: Penguin, 1968.

Jordan, W.K.: *The Development of Religious Toleration in England.* 4 vols. London: Allen & Unwin, 1932–40.

Kaman, H.: *The Rise of Toleration.* London: Weidenfeld & Nicolson, 1968.

Malinowski, B.: *The Foundation of Faith and Morals.* London: Oxford University Press, 1936.

†Moyser, G. ed.: *Church and Politics Today.* Edinburgh: Clark, 1985.

Nicholls, D.: *The Pluralist State.* London: Macmillan, 1975.

Sabine, G.H. and Thorson, T.L.: *A History of Political Theory,* 4th edn. London: Holt, Rinehart & Winston, 1981.

†Sturzo, L.: *Church and State.* 2 vols. Harmondsworth: Penguin, 1962.

Troeltsch, E.: *The Social Teaching of the Christian Churches.* 2 vols. London: Allen & Unwin, 1931.

Cicero, Marcus Tullius (106–43 BC) Roman orator and man of letters. Cicero was born into a wealthy family of Arpinum, an Italian town some 100 km south-east of Rome, which had acquired full Roman citizenship in the early second century BC. Members of Cicero's family had held office in Arpinum and his immediate ancestors were on terms of intimacy with members of the elite in Rome. In the generation before that of Cicero, another citizen of Arpinum, Gaius Marius, had entered politics in Rome and by virtue of his possession of outstanding military talent in a period of crisis achieved the unique distinction of holding the consulship seven times.

Cicero was given the best education which money could buy, much of it at the hands of men of learning from the Greek world. There is no doubt that he was determined from an early age to seek office in Rome. Although he saw action as a junior officer in the Roman army in the war against the Italian allies in revolt in 89, Cicero decided to seek power by the exercise of his talent as an orator. The skill of two great orators of the first century, M. Antonius and L. Licinius Crassus, whom Cicero heard on a number of occasions, presumably influenced him in this direction.

Cicero began his career as an advocate in the law-courts at the end of the eighties. To a slightly earlier period belongs a short treatise on oratorical method. The speeches and the treatise reveal a generally conservative attitude to the organization of the Roman state, but show no trace of a theoretical interest in analysis or explanation. Cicero's skill, regularly and successfully deployed for the defence – he once acted as prosecutor, against C. Verres in 70 BC – rapidly brought him friends and influence. He progressed rapidly through the hierarchy of offices and came to the consulship at the earliest legal age in 63 BC, without ever commanding an army or governing a province.

As consul he felt obliged to condemn to death without trial some of those involved in the conspiracy of Catiline, and in 58 BC he was exiled briefly for this misdemeanour. He had never been as important as he wished to believe and he was now largely marginal to the course of Roman politics and the progress of the Roman revolution. This marginal position both allowed him and perhaps impelled him to reflect on the political organization of the Roman state.

During and maybe before his consulship he had formulated the view that concord between the various orders of the Roman state was the key to its salvation. This view was no doubt correct, but it was hardly a programme for political action.

In a speech delivered on behalf of one P. Sestius in 56 Cicero attempted to find a way of side-stepping the division in the Roman state between *optimates* and *populares*. The former held that the state should be governed by its elite, with only limited control by the sovereign people, the latter that the people should play an active role and should also derive substantial tangible benefits from the Roman possession of an empire. Cicero's argument was that all who had the welfare of the state at heart were in fact *optimates*. Again, the idea was not such as seriously to influence Roman politics.

In fact, Cicero's career as a political thinker is largely detached from his career as a politician. Although, as we shall see, his own experience informs his writings, these are largely an attempt to advocate a Rome as it was believed to have existed in the second century BC and represent a completely different approach from the prescriptions of his consulship and the *Pro Sestio*, which were at least attempts to respond directly to existing situations.

The *De re publica* was begun in 54 and finished in 52; probably Cicero then began to write the *De legibus* which may well may have been in his mind all along. (We do not know when the *De legibus* was finished.) In other words, the relationship between the two works is quite different from that between the *Republic* and the *Laws* of PLATO. In another respect however the debt to Plato is considerable. The *De re publica* is a general account of the principal elements in the Roman state and their proper relationship to each other. Influenced by Stoic philosophy Cicero provides an important definition of Natural Law which influenced later political thought (see LAW). The principal oddity of the work is that although Cicero accepts the traditional institutions of the Roman state – assemblies, senate, magistrates – he also holds that the whole should be in some way under the guidance of one man. Precisely how guided democracy is to work Cicero does not explain (this portion of the text on the *rector reipublicae* has not survived). More interesting is the fact that although Cicero regards the Roman constitution as a mixed one, as others had before him (see POLYBIUS), he does not regard it

as important to analyse the relationship between assemblies, senate and magistrates. He is far more concerned with how to hold the balance between the many and the few and to ensure the dominance of the latter. Here the influence of Plato is particularly clear.

One is driven to the conclusion that, in general terms, Cicero inferred from the politics of his own day that the people were out of control and that they could not be controlled within the free play of Republican institutions. The only solution was some form of guidance. This general approach seems much more important that the fact than in 52 Pompey was briefly sole consul and arbiter of the fortunes of Rome.

The *De legibus* contains a series of rules for the conduct of sacred and secular affairs and a prolonged commentary in both cases. Although Cicero claims to be recommending a Roman state as he supposed it to have existed in the middle of the second century BC, he in fact admits a number of detailed measures which were only true of Rome in the very late Republic, such as automatic recruitment to the senate of those who had held the office of quaestor.

It may be thought that Cicero's advocacy of the existence of a single guide and mentor for his ideal state is one of the foundations of the Principate (see ROMAN POLITICAL THOUGHT). But what Augustus set out from the beginning to create was an absolute (if disguised) monarchy, for which indeed Cicero unwittingly furnished a constitutional device, in the shape of the powers he had granted to Brutus and Cassius in 43 BC.

It was left to the great Christian writer of the Late Empire, Saint AUGUSTINE, to turn the *De re publica* to account in expounding the proper governance of the City of God.   MHC

Reading

Cicero: *De re publica* and *De legibus*, trans. Keyes. London: Heinemann, 1951.

†Douglas, A.E.: *Cicero*. Oxford: Clarendon Press, 1968.

Michel, A.: *Rhétorique et philosophie chez Cicéron*. Paris: Presses Universitaires de France, 1960.

Millar, F.G.B.: State and subject: the impact of monarchy. In *Caesar Augustus. Seven Aspects*, ed. F.G.B. Millar and C. Segal: Oxford: Clarendon Press, 1984.

†Rawson, E.: *Cicero*. London: Allen Lane, 1975.
————: *Intellectual Life in the Late Roman Republic*, ch. 19. London: Duckworth, 1985.

citizenship A pressing practical concern to Greek city states, and therefore a pressing concern to classical political theorists. Small states plagued by internal strife between rich and poor and incessant wars with their neighbours sought the recipe for social peace: was it safer to keep power in a few hands or to spread it more widely; was it safer to make it difficult or easy for foreigners to acquire citizenship? Having seen Athens ruled by the murderous government of the Thirty Tyrants and by a fickle democracy which had sentenced his master SOCRATES to death, PLATO tried to bypass such questions with his recipe for the absolute authority of Guardians or 'philosopher-kings'. But ARISTOTLE restored the problem of citizenship to the centre of the discussion.

Political authority was distinctive because it was the authority of office-holders exercised over citizens, according to constitutional rules. It was therefore conventional, limited, and most unlike the natural authority of husbands over wives or the absolute authority of masters over slaves. Citizens were equals under the law, even if one was wealthier than another, or one or other held office for the moment. On the whole, it was wise to spread citizenship widely, so long as those who were enfranchised were reasonably well off and not tempted to employ their political power to rob the wealthy.

But citizenship was impossible for anyone without sufficient leisure to understand political issues, for anyone whose occupation was mechanical and limited, and for women, whose proper place was in the home and not in the *agora*. Citizenship was impossible in Persia and in cold northern climes, because politics was impossible there: excessive heat made men supine and ready for despotism, excessive cold meant that they were confined to bare survival. Nor could a state contain very many citizens before ceasing to be a state; beyond some ten thousand they would be too many to know and feel friendship for one another.

Aristotle's discussion of citizenship assumed that the crucial problem was securing stable government under law; it assumed that men naturally wanted to hold political office, and set out to discover what sort of people could compete for office without civil strife. Life in the *polis* was the highest this-worldly good for man, and the excellence of the good citizen was part of the highest human excellence. The breakdown of the Greek city-state, the rise of the Hellenistic and Roman empires, and the intellectual ascendancy of Christianity turned the philosopher's gaze inwards, or towards the next life. Men were citizens of the whole world, or of the city of God, but earthly citizenship was not an essential part of the good life.

The revival of the classical argument cannot be dated precisely. But what was revived in Renaissance Europe was less Aristotelian than Roman. The citizens of Rome were the heroes of MACHIAVELLI's reflections on the history of the Roman Republic, for it was their *virtú* which secured Rome's greatness. Contrasting the instability and vulnerability of Florence with the power and stability of Rome, Machiavelli asked how Rome preserved her freedom for so long, and the *virtú* of her citizens was a large part of the answer. Rome's freedom had two aspects, her invulnerability to attack by other states, and the absence of internal tyranny by any individual or class. What citizen *virtú* contributed was self-discipline, patriotism, simple piety and a willingness to forgo private gain for the sake of the public good (see REPUBLICANISM).

Although Hobbes denounced and Locke ignored the ideals of classical republicanism, the problems of citizen virtue preoccupied publicists and controversialists from the sixteenth to the nineteenth centuries. It was a 'backward-looking' preoccupation in the sense that it took the Roman republic as its political ideal; and in spite of the lesson of Bernard MANDEVILLE's *Fable of the Bees* (1714) that 'private vices' brought 'public benefits', its proponents were slow to come to terms with the positive virtues of the commercial and individualistic society coming into existence in Western Europe. Indeed, as late as 1762, ROUSSEAU's *Social Contract* was avowedly hostile to the complexity, luxury and individualism of the eighteenth century and looked to Sparta and Rome for its political ideals.

It was not the ancients' warlike qualities that

Rousseau admired, but the simplicity of their lives, their unswerving public spirit and their fitness for self-government. Whether he thought it possible to turn eighteenth-century Frenchmen into Roman citizens is debatable, but by 1800 it was widely acknowledged that the task was impossible. Eighteen years later Benjamin CONSTANT's *Essai sur la liberté des anciens comparée à celle des modernes* drew the moral from the French Revolution's failure to recreate republican virtue: ancient citizenship and ancient liberty were political and participatory, demanded austerity and simplicity, and were to be had only in small, warlike states; modern FREEDOM was the freedom of the private person rather than the citizen, and was freedom from politics as much as freedom in politics. Modern man had lost something, but he had gained much – for example prosperity, individuality and peace.

The rebirth of discussions of citizenship was not long in coming. The slow but steady widening of the franchise in the nineteenth century meant that formal citizenship was extended to men who were economically 'dependent', that is, employed by others. The question was whether their citizenship could be made more than merely formal. MARX, who regarded the distinction between political and economic life, or between private and public life, as an aspect of the alienation of a class-divided society, looked forward to socialist forms of industrial and social self-government which would reconcile the Greek ideal of civic participation with the modern concern for individuality and economic well-being.

This ideal presupposed revolutionary change, but the neo-Hegelians and their successors looked for reforms which would close the gap between the ideals of universal citizenship and the realities of widespread poverty and dependence. A similar impulse lay behind DURKHEIM's *Professional Ethics and Civic Morals*. In essence, the problem was seen as that of reducing class divisions and integrating the ordinary person in the government of all aspects of his or her society. This has generally been thought to demand two kinds of state-sponsored change, one in the direction of creating a welfare state, the other in the

direction of extending industrial self-government. An essay by T. H. Marshall, 'Citizenship and Social Class,' is the best-known attempt to link the welfare state's attack on poverty with the ideal of 'full citizenship' for all.   AR

Reading

†Aristotle: *The Politics*, ed. E. Barker, 2nd edn. Oxford: Clarendon Press, 1948.

Durkheim, E.: *Professional Ethics and Civic Morals*, trans. C. Brookfield. London: Routledge & Kegan Paul, 1957.

Holmes, S.: *Benjamin Constant and the Making of Modern Liberalism*. New Haven, Conn.: Yale University Press, 1984.

†Machiavelli, N.: *The Discourses*, ed. B. Crick. Harmondsworth: Penguin, 1970.

Marshall, T.H.: Citizenship and Social Class. In *Sociology at the Crossroads, and other essays*. London: Heinemann, 1963.

Pocock, J.G.A.: *Virtue, Commerce and History*. Cambridge: Cambridge University Press, 1985.

†Rousseau, J.-J.: *The Social Contract*, trans. M. Cranston. Harmondsworth: Penguin, 1968.

civil disobedience Usually taken to mean deliberately disobeying a law for reasons of religious, moral, or political principle; in its strictest sense civil disobedience implies breaking a law which is in itself unjust, but the term is also used to denote protests which involve breaking the law as a byproduct of opposing a particular policy, or of pressing for political reform.

The American writer Henry David THOREAU coined the term 'civil disobedience', which was the title given to an essay he wrote in 1848 to explain why he had for several years refused to pay taxes to the state of Massachusetts, and had eventually spent a night in gaol. He had taken this action to protest against two policies of the United States government: the war against Mexico and the continuation of slavery in the South. Thoreau asserts the need for people to act to resist injustice when their own government is perpetrating the injustice: voting alone is not enough. The duty of civil disobedience is implicitly contrasted with the duty of civil obedience, the duty to obey the law often posited by political philosophers.

The theory and practice of civil disobedience were refined nearly a century later by GANDHI in the context of his development of a philosophy of nonviolence and nonviolent struggle. A well-known example of civil disobedience is the march he led to the sea in 1932 to defy the ban imposed by the British colonial regime on the making of salt by Indians. Gandhi argued that civil disobedience was based on a profound respect for the law in general; that those undertaking it should always do so nonviolently, that they should do so publicly, and that they should show their willingness to accept the full penalties entailed in breaking the law. He also believed that civil disobedience should only be undertaken when efforts at persuasion and petition had been tried and failed. Gandhi differed from Thoreau in laying stress on strict nonviolence, on a general duty of civil obedience, and on the need to try all forms of constitutional political action first; Thoreau's own position was more individualistic and more anti-government in tone.

It is Gandhi's conception that has usually been accepted in recent discussions of civil disobedience. John RAWLS, for example, defines civil disobedience as a 'public, nonviolent, conscientious yet political act contrary to law usually done with the aim of bringing about a change in the law or policies of the government' (*A Theory of Justice* p. 364).

Justifications of civil disobedience tend to appeal to a higher moral law than the laws of any particular government, and to the need to resist absolutely a flagrant breach of HUMAN RIGHTS. Both arguments can be found in Thoreau. In addition appeal is often made to a higher national or INTERNATIONAL LAW. Civil Rights protesters in the Deep South of the USA in the period 1955–63 could appeal to the principles of the American Constitution when breaking local laws that imposed racial segregation. Demonstrators against nuclear weapons or the Vietnam war have sometimes claimed they are upholding international law. A further argument sometimes used to justify civil disobedience is that the urgency of the danger to human life cannot be met adequately by the normal democratic and electoral processes – this was a point made by Bertrand RUSSELL as a reason for civil disobedience against nuclear weapons.

One of the questions central to civil disobedience, but often not resolved by movements which resort to it, is whether its purpose is primarily persuasive or coercive. If the demonstrators' aim is to dramatize their opposition to a policy and to show the strength of their conviction by their willingness to suffer for their beliefs, they may change the minds of some of their opponents or fellow citizens. This persuasive use of civil disobedience may hasten the negotiated settlement of a conflict or political reform. If on the other hand civil disobedience is designed to fill the gaols or to make a policy impossible to implement, then demonstrators are putting direct pressure on the resources of government or seeking immediate victory. In practice the division between the two is not clear-cut, and may simply depend on the numbers involved, but tactics of civil disobedience can stress persuasion or direct effectiveness. For example peace demonstrators who publicly trespass on a military base and invite arrest are emphasizing their opposition to the purpose of the base, but demonstrators who seek to block actual operations at the base appear to be aiming at its total immobilization.

Civil disobedience occupies a middle ground between constitutional forms of political action on the one hand and rebellion or revolution on the other. It may be seen as an extreme, but in certain circumstances acceptable, form of protest within a spectrum of political methods used in constitutional and democratic states. It is easier to argue for this position if the purpose of civil disobedience is persuasive and if it is conducted in a strictly nonviolent and public way. Civil disobedience may however be the precursor to a movement of total resistance to the existing regime, or lead on to violent forms of protest or rebellion. Whilst it is widely accepted that total resistance is justifiable against a dictatorship, a foreign occupation or a fundamentally unjust regime, normally it is condemned if it occurs within a regime which respects the rights of its citizens and in which the government can be influenced or changed from below. In any particular case, however, those for and against civil disobedience may also disagree about how far the government does respect rights and liberties, or about the extent of genuine democracy.

Civil disobedience has become a more common and a more widely accepted form of protest in the West in the period since the 1950s. But there are still many people who doubt whether it is ever justifiable to break the law when other forms of protest and pressure are available which are legal. They fear the illegality will spread and that a political climate may be created that undermines respect for democratic procedures. It is a debate that is unlikely to be fully resolved. AFC

Reading

†Bedau, H.A. ed.: *Civil Disobedience: Theory and Practice*. Indianapolis: Bobbs-Merrill, 1979.

Gandhi, M.K.: *Non-violent Resistance* (1951). New York: Schocken, 1961.

Rawls, J.: *A Theory of Justice*, ch. 6. Cambridge, Mass.: Harvard University Press, 1971; Oxford: Oxford University Press, 1972.

†Singer, P.: *Democracy and Disobedience*. Oxford: Clarendon Press, 1973.

Thoreau, Henry D.: Civil disobedience. In Bedau ed.

Walzer, M.: *Obligations: Essays on Disobedience, War and Citizenship*. Cambridge, Mass.: Harvard University Press, 1970.

civil liberties Freedoms which either are, or ought to be, protected by law; leading examples include the freedoms of speech, movement and association. They form an important subclass of HUMAN RIGHTS, though whether they are more or less important than other such rights (notably rights to various material benefits) is much disputed. The defence of civil liberties is a major preoccupation of LIBERALISM.

civil society (1) Originally, a generic term for society and state, synonymous with 'political society'. (2) More recently, social and economic arrangements, codes, institutions apart from the state.

(1) Civil society (from the Latin *civilis societas*) entered European usage *c.*1400 with a nexus of meanings given to it by CICERO in the first century BC. It referred not only to individual states but to the condition of living in a civilized political community sufficiently advanced to include cities, having its own legal code (*ius civile*), and with undertones of civility and urbanity (barbarians and pre-urban cultures

were not civil societies), of civic partnership – living and being ruled according to civil laws – and of the refinements of 'civil life' and 'the commercial arts' (see Adam Ferguson, *Essay on the History of Civil Society*, 1767). In contractarian political thought, and in the writings of LOCKE especially, 'political or civil society' was contrasted with paternal authority and the STATE OF NATURE. The implication was that a money economy, ready exchange in something like a free market, technological development affording comfort and decency to civilized and intelligent persons, and a law-abiding political order comprised a satisfactory and progressive state of human affairs.

(2) HEGEL and MARX inverted this implicit moral judgment. Civil society (*bürgerliche Gesellschaft*) meant the state of human development so far reached by advanced peoples, but it was self-seeking and avaricious, lacking the warmth and moral cohesion of primitive society. It now referred to an economic and social order moving according to its own principles, independently of the ethical demands of law and political association. Marx held that under civil society law really benefited only the privileged 'bourgeoisie'. Nevertheless, the term *bürgerliche Gesellschaft* could also be applied to pre-capitalist societies, and it is unfortunate that it has sometimes been translated back into English as 'bourgeois society', sometimes as 'civil society'. For writers in the traditions of Hegel and Marx civil society has come to mean the social, economic and ethical arrangements of modern, western, industrial-capitalist society considered apart from the state. In general usage today civil society lacks moral overtones, and refers to the non-political aspects of the contemporary social order so that, for example, it can be debated whether there is congruence or dissonance between civil society and the state. AB

Reading

†Black, A.: *Guilds and Civil Society in European Political Thought from the Twelfth Century to the Present*. London: Methuen, 1984.

Ferguson, A.: *An Essay on the History of Civil Society*, ed. D. Forbes. Edinburgh: Edinburgh University Press, 1966.

class Social class is a concept which describes

the divisions in a society. Three areas or 'levels' of social life can be identified:

(1) what we may call the economic structure, consisting of sets of relations in the sphere of the production and exchange of goods and services – social relations that are independent of and external to individuals' wills and that define 'empty' positions that they fill;
(2) the intersubjective or meaningful level of social consciousness, the 'world from within' of lived experience that comprises how individuals see themselves and one another;
(3) the level of action, both individual and collective, in various spheres of life, encompassing individuals' behaviour as private persons, consumers, workers, citizens, their lifestyle and voting behaviour, and how they organize, industrially and politically.

Briefly, we may say that classes exist in a given society to the extent that there are significant links between these three levels of social life: if economically determined positions correlate significantly with people's lived experience and consciousness, and if both of these have a significant bearing on how they behave as consumers, workers or citizens – on how they live, the organizations they join, the parties they support, and so on.

To see this, we may construct the following thought experiment. Imagine a society in which no such links obtain. People's occupations or market positions, say, have absolutely no bearing on their self-understanding or interpretation of their social world (which is defined in quite other ways – in terms of kinship, perhaps, or religion) and neither has any relation to their individual or collective actions, which are quite unpredictable on the basis of either. Could classes really be said to exist in such a society?

Theories of class can be thought of as ranged along a continuum whose poles can be neatly seen as occupied by the classical positions of MARX and WEBER respectively. At the former end the picture is very tightly and narrowly drawn. Not only are the links between levels rather tight; they are unidirectional, the causal flow going from economic structure through consciousness to action. Over time the 'two great classes directly facing

each other, bourgeoisie and proletariat' (*Communist Manifesto*, §1), defined by how they stand to the relations of production, gradually consolidate under capitalism, absorbing other classes within them, developing class consciousness and industrial and political organizations, and in due course fight out a revolutionary conflict that can only end in the overthrow of capitalism itself. But the picture is narrow as well as tight. At each level the focus is confined: at the first, to relations of production (more specifically, ownership of the means of production); at the second, to the worlds of work and politics; and at the third, to industrial and political action.

By contrast, Weber's picture is more broadly defined. The links between levels are looser and the causal flow can go in various directions: from economic position to consciousness and action, but also, for instance, from shared status and religious belief to economic structure (furnishing a basis for the securing of economic advantage) or to political organization. Moreover, and in consequence, there is no overall story of a development through time from class structure through class consciousness to class action, nor any underlying theory of 'class interests' that could explain such a development: the historical possibilities are far more open and indeterminate. The focus at each level is also much broader: at the structural level, it encompasses not only productive relations but also the sphere of 'circulation' and 'market positions' (though Weber, like Marx, did think that the possession or non-possession of property was basic to all class situations); and at the levels of consciousness and action, it encompasses ethnicity, religion, status, etc., and the spheres of consumption and distribution as well as work and politics.

Which is the more promising theoretical position partly depends upon one's criterion of what counts as a good theory. Judged as a coherent theoretical scheme that risks much and, if true, would have considerable explanatory and predictive power, Marx's theory wins hands down. Judged as a framework for analysing contemporary societies that risks much less by leaving more connections and developmental possibilities open, Weber's theory scores more highly on grounds of descriptive adequacy. Contemporary class theory is still drawn to one or other of these poles, or else to the task of reconciling them, the neo-Marxists seeking to account for the 'relative autonomy' of consciousness and politics, the neo-Weberians seeking underlying principles that could explain the diverse forms of subordination and inequality.

Underpinning class relations Marxists see EXPLOITATION (the superordinate expropriating surplus value from the labour of the subordinate), while the Weberians see POWER (restricting access to resources and opportunities through 'social closure'). For both, however, class relations are asymmetrical and antagonistic, involving conflicting interests, where some win and others lose. Other more harmonistic pictures of class have been historically significant, from Adam SMITH to recent American functionalist theories of stratification. But this is not the predominant view today. Neo-Marxists have argued about where the class boundaries lie, how to deal with 'intermediate' classes, and, most recently, how to conceptualize exploitation more generally, generating different class systems from the exploitation of different kinds of productive assets. Neo-Weberians, defining class (at level 3) by its modes of collective action, have sought to show how rights to productive resources, credentials, party membership, lineage, etc., can all be distinct bases for social closure in the struggle for distributive advantage. But the Marx-Weber continuum still dominates the debate.   SL

Reading

Bauman, Z.: *Memories of Class: the Pre-History and After-Life of Class*. London: Routledge & Kegan Paul, 1982.

Carchedi, G.: *On the Economic Identification of Social Classes*. London: Routledge & Kegan Paul, 1977.

Dahrendorf, R.: *Class and Class Conflict in an Industrial Society*. London: Routledge & Kegan Paul, 1959.

†Giddens, A.: *The Class Structure of the Advanced Societies*. London: Hutchinson, 1973.

—— and Held, D.: *Classes, Power and Conflict*. London: Macmillan, 1982.

Marshall, T.H.: *Sociology at the Crossroads, and other essays*. London: Heinemann, 1963.

Marx, K. and Engels, F.: *The Communist Manifesto* (1848). In *Selected Works*. Moscow: Foreign Languages Publishing House, 1962.

†Ossowski, S.: *Class Structure in the Social Consciousness*. London: Routledge & Kegan Paul, 1963.

Parkin, F.: *Marxism and Class Theory: a Bourgeois Critique*. London: Tavistock, 1979.

Poulantzas, N.: *Classes in Contemporary Capitalism*. London: New Left, 1975.

Roemer, J.: *A General Theory of Exploitation and Class*. Cambridge, Mass.: Harvard University Press, 1982.

Weber, M.: Class, status, party. In *From Max Weber: Essays in Sociology*, trans. and ed. H.H. Gerth and C. Wright Mills. London: Routledge & Kegan Paul, 1948.

†Wright, E.O.: *Classes*. London: Verso, 1985.

classical political economy A tradition of economic analysis that flourished especially in England from the end of the eighteenth to the middle of the nineteenth century, the period of the Industrial Revolution. Though important contributions to this tradition can be found in the earlier work of Richard Cantillon and David HUME, Adam SMITH's *An Inquiry into the Nature and Causes of the Wealth of Nations* (1776) is usually taken to mark its beginning. Among its most noteworthy practitioners were Malthus, Ricardo, Senior, McCulloch, James MILL, J. S. MILL and the French economist Say. Particularly important to disseminating its ideas were the Political Economy Club, founded in 1821, and the *Edinburgh Review*. The economic thought of Karl MARX may also be understood as part of the classical tradition.

The origins of classical political economy lie in Smith's attack on MERCANTILISM and in his argument for 'the system of natural liberty'. He criticized mercantilist regulations because they closed foreign markets, kept the division of labour from being fully utilized, and thus inhibited economic growth. Growth also depended on the proportion of productive to unproductive labour, a distinction Smith made between labour that produced goods that were tangible and labour that was used up in the performance of personal services. Frugality diminished the amount spent on personal services and increased the capital available to employ people in the division of labour. With the accumulation of capital in a growing economy Smith believed that the wages of labour would be bid up, a process he and other classical economists approved because they saw high wages as incentives to industriousness.

In Smith and the classical tradition, the economic problem was identified with the struggle to produce wealth from nature. In this struggle the efficiency of labour was the crucial variable. Thus the labour theory of value, the theory that only labour conferred value on goods and (in large part) explained relative prices, was central to the intellectual apparatus of the classical economists.

Classical political economy must be distinguished from neo-classical economics or the marginal revolution associated with the work of Jevons in the 1870s. While neo-classicists are concerned with the most efficient allocation of given, scarce resources between competing consumer preferences, the classical economists were most interested in expanding resources and in allocating them to stimulate further growth. A comparison of classical and neo-classical economic thought brings out the generally empirical and policy orientation of the classicists. Classical political economy has aptly been called 'a statesman's guide to economic growth' (O'Brien, p. 34).

The advice given to statesmen by these economists was usually to end government regulation. Smith's criticism of apprenticeship rules, monopolies, tariffs, duties, and other restrictions had an influence on classical political economy in the form of a tendency towards *laissez-faire*. In the New Poor Law of 1834, the budget of 1845 which removed duties on over four hundred items, and the repeal of the Corn Laws in 1846, the theoretical arguments of classical political economy had important policy consequences. The generally anti-paternalist attitude of these economists is illustrated by Ricardo's advocacy in Parliament of religious toleration, freedom of the press, and parliamentary reform. The values of classical political economy are, then, closely associated with those of the western liberal tradition – individualism, tolerance, and limited government (see LIBERALISM).

But classical political economy did not endorse *laissez-faire* dogmatically. These economists were primarily utilitarians rather than upholders of natural rights, and were ready when the public good would be served to use the power of government. As McCulloch wrote, 'The principle of *laissez-faire* may be safely trusted to in some things, but in many more it is wholly inapplicable; and to appeal to it on all occasions savours more of the policy of a parrot than of a statesman or a philosopher' (see O'Brien, p. 272). The government activities that one or the other of these economists championed include protection for new industries, child labour laws, aid to disabled and aged workers, public education, and measures to improve public health. Even in Malthus's famous attack on the old Poor Law and Ricardo's campaign against the Corn Laws it was understood that, to minimize suffering, abolition should occur gradually. Considering their long list of (often divergent) policy recommendations it becomes clear why some commentators describe them as, above all, reformers.

Economic growth continued to be the central concern of classical political economy after Smith, though the emphasis shifted away from Smith's moderate optimism toward the more intractable impediments to growth. Most famous among these more pessimistic appraisals is that of Thomas Malthus (1766–1834), who was appointed to the first university chair in political economy in 1804. Malthus wrote his *Essay on the Principles of Population* (1798) against the idea that human misery was the result of institutions, particularly private property. Malthus attempted to demonstrate that the constant tendency of population to increase geometrically put pressure on the earth's agricultural resources, which could be increased only at an arithmetic rate. Because of this disproportion, population increase was held in check either by forces that acted on the birth rate (such as birth control, called a preventive check) or on the death rate (such as infant mortality, called a positive check). His characterization of these inevitable checks as the result of vice or misery was his answer to optimism. In his second edition (1803) he softened this harsh conclusion by including as a preventive check moral restraint (meaning later marriages), which he admitted did not fall under vice or misery.

Malthus's theory implied that the condition of the working class tended toward subsistence, since the effects of higher wages were soon wiped out by an increase in population, and that government relief was self-defeating. Poor laws, he argued, 'increase population without increasing the food for its support' (p. 97). Malthus underestimated the ability of people to limit their families in order to increase their standard of living, and the ability of agricultural improvements to increase food production. Both of these points were raised against him by Senior and McCulloch. But Malthus never abandoned the possibility of finding reforms to assist the labouring class. He suggested that agriculture ought to be encouraged in preference to manufacturing so that more food was produced, and that public education should be provided to enhance the ability of the poor to engage in moral restraint.

Malthus had another reservation about the possibility of uninterrupted growth and, because of it, became embroiled in the 'glut controversy'. Primarily in his *Principles of Political Economy* (1820) he questioned the belief that saving and investment were always beneficial. Malthus maintained that it was possible for savings to result in the production of more goods than could be consumed and that such a glut would be followed by a depression. He doubted that the purchasing power of the labouring classes would automatically increase as quickly as the ability of society to invest and produce. In effect, Malthus thought a level of investment that would guarantee full employment could not be maintained and that a level that could be maintained would not result in full employment. His awareness of the need for a balance between investment and consumption or demand led him to advocate public works projects and to view favourably luxury spending and the employment of servants, particularly by landlords.

After Smith, the most important of the classical political economists was David Ricardo (1772–1823). Ricardo made a fortune in the stock market, retired from business to become a country gentleman, and was elected to Parliament in 1819. His major work, *The Principles of Political Economy and Taxation* (1817), introduced to economic analysis the power and difficulties of reasoning deductively from the fewest possible assumptions.

It was a common assumption among the economists of this period that over a period of time the return to investment would decline to a level too low to sustain continued growth. The result was called a stationary state. The spectre of such a state was used by Ricardo in his famous criticism of the Corn Laws. These laws created barriers to the importation of inexpensive corn and guaranteed a high price for British corn. Ricardo tried to show that unless cheap agricultural products were allowed into England the stationary state would soon result. To make his point, Ricardo relied upon the principle of diminishing returns from land. To feed an increasing population, land of less and less fertility would have to be brought under cultivation. As a consequence constant investments of capital and labour applied to land would return a decreasing output. It was Ricardo's purpose to lay bare the consequences of this for the distribution of rents, profits and wages to the three classes of society – landlords, manufacturers and labourers. Since the recourse to less fertile land increased the value of more fertile agricultural land, tenant farmers in their competition for the best land bid up the rents that went to landlords. Farming increasingly less fertile land also increased the cost of agricultural products and resulted in higher money wages, since labourers had to earn more to purchase their subsistence. Because wages and profits are paid from the fund that remains after rents have been subtracted, higher wages meant lower agriculture profits. And since a competitive economy can have only one rate of profit, lower profits in agriculture meant that profits in all other areas also declined. Limiting the importation of inexpensive corn into England required England to grow more itself, to cultivate land of decreasing fertility, and therefore to suffer a decline in profit rates.

Ricardo's concern with international trade led him to formulate the theory of comparative advantage. Here he demonstrated the benefits of free trade in a way superior to Smith and in so doing stressed the advantages to England of concentrating on manufacturing. Ricardo's theory was also an attack on landlords (regarded by him as unproductive) who benefited from the high price of British corn. Ricardo's conclusion that the interest of the landlord is always opposed to the interest of every other class of society was an extraordinary statement in a country that had always thought of the land-owner as representing the permanent interests of the nation. Not surprisingly, Ricardo rejected Malthus's glut theory with its defence of landlords' luxury spending. He relied upon Say's Law, the idea that the demand for goods increases at the same rate as their production, to show that a glut was impossible. Full employment, according to Ricardo, is the normal equilibrium for a competitive economy.

The last great work of classical political economy was J. S. MILL's *Principles of Political Economy* (1848), 'the undisputed bible of economists' through the second half of the nineteenth century. While it contained real advances in the analysis of such topics as international trade, interest, and economies of scale, Mill's *Principles* is most famous for the distinction he made between production, which he maintained is determined by the laws of nature, and distribution, which depends upon institutions that are subject to some degree of human control. By making this distinction, Mill found room in the science of classical political economy for the economic reorganization and moral reforms that were his deepest concerns.

Chief among the reforms he advocated was the education of the working classes and the need for family planning. Mill also found a role for unions in improving the conditions of workers. At first, his defence was the usual one that unions kept employers from agreeing among themselves to pay less than the market wage. In later years Mill's consideration of this issue led him to disavow the wage fund theory, the idea that the amount of total wages that could be paid to workers was fixed by the past performance of the economy. In popular debates especially, this idea was used to show that an increase in the wages of one group of workers could only occur at the expense of another group of workers. Mill's recantation of the wage fund theory meant that unions could be seen as obtaining wage increases by forcing employers to divert to workers capital that might have been saved or consumed by owners. His concern for labour also led him to argue that if the introduction of new machinery hurt the working class, government must find a way to moderate the process of mechanization. Even

more characteristic of Mill were his proposals to support peasant proprietors and worker-owned enterprises, and his reappraisal of the stationary state. For if that state meant that 'while no one is poor, no one desires to be richer' Mill thought it signalled the end of man's struggle against nature and held out the possibility of great moral improvement. In Mill's general suspicion of government but willingness to recognize the exceptions that justified its activity, and in his concern for the prosperity of labourers but insistence that reforms be consistent with the science of economics, he perfectly represented classical political economy.   TAH

Reading
†Coats, A.W. ed.: *The Classical Economists and Economic Policy*. London: Methuen, 1971.
Malthus, T.: *An Essay on the Principle of Population*, ed. A. Flew. Harmondsworth: Penguin, 1971.
Mill, J.S.: *Principles of Political Economy*, ed. J.M. Robson. Toronto: University of Toronto Press, 1965.
†O'Brien, D.P.: *The Classical Economists*. London: Oxford University Press, 1975.
Ricardo, D.: *The Principles of Political Economy and Taxation*. In *The Works of David Ricardo*, vol. I, ed. P. Sraffa. Cambridge: Cambridge University Press, 1951.
Schumpeter, J.A.: *History of Economic Analysis*. New York: Oxford University Press, 1975.
Smith, A.: *An Inquiry into the Nature and Causes of the Wealth of Nations*. Oxford: Clarendon Press, 1976.
†Winch, D.: The emergence of economics as a science. In *The Fontana Economic History of Europe*, vol. 3: *the Industrial Revolution*, ed. Carlo Cipolla. London: Collins/Fontana, 1973.

Coke, Sir Edward (1552–1634)   English lawyer and legal writer. Coke held office as solicitor-general, attorney-general and chief justice but was dismissed from this last position by James I in 1616. Such a career was inevitably accompanied by both personal rivalries and constitutional wrangles; it was Francis BACON, Coke's chief competitor for office and advancement, who drew up the document detailing Coke's 'innovation into the law' upon which James acted.

Coke produced two sets of volumes concer-ned with the nature of law and with the interpretations of laws. The *Institutes of the Laws of England* (1628–44) was a four-volume study, the first of which was devoted to a lengthy commentary on an earlier legal treatise, Littleton's *Tenures*. The second was also concerned with property, or *meum* and *teum*, while the third explained pleas of the crown, or crime, and the fourth dealt with the organization of the judicial system and attempted to explain the various jurisdictions. At a time when the king's prerogative powers were disputed, these were contentious political issues. The other set of thirteen volumes, two of which were posthumously published, were *Reports* of cases (1600–59). Coke himself claimed that the *Reports* 'related the opinion and judgment of others', while the *Institutes* were concerned with his own; but some doubt has been expressed about this, and in particular over the accuracy and objectivity of the *Reports*.

These volumes are of immense interest to legal historians; they came to be regarded as a major authority on the law, not least because later lawyers were disinclined to repeat Coke's work on the medieval precedents. Political theorists have been particularly concerned with two aspects of Coke's doctrines, namely his account of the nature of common law and the possibility that he displayed a systematic bias in his judgments or reports of cases which, for the reason given above, influenced the development of law.

Coke's account of the nature of common law insisted that custom and precedent, as well as parliamentary enactment, are its sources. He supposed the existence of fundamental law, with which no judgment is to conflict, represented in particular by Magna Carta. He also claimed that the law is 'an artificial perfection of reason' brought about by the refinements of a succession of 'grave and learned men', a perfection to which no individual's natural reason could aspire (*Institutes*, vol. I, 6th edn 1670). This was not an argument James found appealing; HOBBES attacked it in his *Dialogue of the Common Laws* (1681), rejecting in particular the argument that the supremacy of the common law limited the claims of the monarch. Strikingly similar arguments about the relation between the reason embodied in an institution and an individual's natural reason were used by BURKE in the eighteenth century to argue for conservative conclusions, while a dictum attributed to Coke that we should live under a 'government of laws not men' was invoked during the American Watergate scandal of 1977.

Since Coke's writings were subsequently regarded as authoritative, any inaccuracy or bias in his judgments or *Reports* would be very significant. Some historians have detected a bias in favour of economic liberalism, or the freedom of property owners, but the evidence is contested, and in many cases there is little or nothing with which Coke's account may be compared. It is further disputed whether the bias in question should be attributed to Coke in particular or to the judges in general.   AWR

Reading
Bacon, Francis: Innovation into the laws and government. In Bowen.

Bowen, C.D.: *The Lion and the Throne*. London: Hamish Hamilton, 1957.

Coke, Sir Edward: *Institutes of the Laws of England*. 4 vols. London, 1797.

———: *Reports* 13 vols. London, 1777.

†Hill, C.: *Intellectual Origins of the English Revolution*. London: Panther, 1972.

Hobbes, T.: *Dialogue of the Common Laws*, ed. J. Cropsey. London and Chicago: University of Chicago Press, 1969.

Malament, B.: The 'economic liberalism' of Sir Edward Coke. In *Yale Law Journal* 76 (1966–7) 1321–57.

Pocock, J.G.A.: *The Ancient Constitution and the Feudal Law*. Cambridge: Cambridge University Press, 1957.

Wagner, D. O.: Coke and the rise of economic liberalism. *Economic History Review* 6 (1935) 30–44.

Cole, G. D. H. (1889–1959)   British social theorist. See GUILD SOCIALISM.

Coleridge, Samuel Taylor (1772–1834) English poet and thinker. Although he is now most celebrated as a poet and literary critic, Coleridge devoted rather more of his life to philosophy, theology and political thought. His developed political philosophy was rooted in an IDEALISM which drew upon German philosophers such as KANT, FICHTE and Schelling, and also upon Platonism and Christian theology. He is arguably the foremost English conservative thinker of the nineteenth century.

As a young man Coleridge's sympathies were with the radicals. He welcomed the French

Revolution, satirized the British constitution and bitterly attacked the doctrines and institutions of the Anglican Church. He shared with GODWIN the belief that evil was a product of social institutions, especially private property. For a while he and Southey planned to establish a 'pantisocracy' in America: an egalitarian community whose perfect social environment would yield perfect individuals. However, he fought shy of advocating violent revolution at home and, in his political lectures (1795) and his journal *The Watchman* (1796), placed greater emphasis upon moral and religious education than upon institutional change as a means of achieving reform.

Coleridge soon began to have doubts about the French and became increasingly gloomy about the prospects for political reform. By 1798 he was ready to declare that he was 'no Whig, no Reformer, no Republican' and the articles that he wrote for the *Morning Post* between 1798 and 1803 evince a qualified resignation to the existing social and political order.

Coleridge's mature political writings – *The Friend* (1809–10), his articles in the *Courier* (1804–18) and his two *Lay Sermons* (1816 and 1817) – ranged over a variety of themes, including the relation of morals and politics, criticism of the ideas of HOBBES and ROUSSEAU, and the Bible as the best guide for the statesman. These essays are perhaps most notable for their social criticism, exemplifying the romantic reaction against the Industrial Revolution. Coleridge was deeply critical of the undue influence of commercial values, of the ideas of the classical economists, of the lack of regulation of manufacturers, and of the plight of the poor. He particularly deprecated the adoption of commercial values in agriculture, arguing that the upper classes should treat their lands not as an economic resource to be exploited for personal gain but as a trust carrying social responsibilities.

Coleridge's most important and influential political work was his last: *On the Constitution of Church and State according to the Idea of each* (1830). There he elaborated a comprehensive political theory grounded in his Idealist philosophy. Fundamental to that philosophy was a distinction between reason and understanding.

The understanding as a form of knowing was tied to sense-experience. Reason, by contrast, was the source of our knowledge of those 'supersensual truths' which Coleridge designated 'Ideas'. Much false philosophy – such as empiricism and UTILITARIANISM – resulted, he believed, from attempts to comprehend through the understanding matters which were truly intelligible only to reason. In particular, the ultimate ends of human conduct, both moral and political, were discernible as Ideas of reason. He believed that these Ideas inhabited men's thoughts and guided their conduct, although often unconsciously. Hence his belief that institutions frequently embodied, albeit imperfectly, the Ideas by which they were to be judged.

For Coleridge, a political system should ideally be made up of opposing but duly balanced and interdependent forces. The state should embody the two forces of permanence and progression, an idea realized in the British Parliament by the dominance of the landed classes in the Lords and of the commercial and professional classes in the Commons. These needed to be underpinned by a moral culture fostered and disseminated by a National Church or 'clerisy'. Coleridge's National Church was not a church in any ordinary sense but comprised all the learned of the nation who, by developing and diffusing knowledge, cultivated the 'humanity' of the population and equipped them to be citizens. Church and state together constituted the 'organized' powers of the body politic, which were counterposed to 'free and permeative' influences such as the press and public opinion, and these, in turn, as 'actual' powers were set against the 'potential' powers of the body politic.

Coleridge's political idealism has been dismissed as no more than a metaphysical garb thrown around the established institutions of his day. The criticism is not without force but belies the original and interpretive elements in his political thought. His conception of the clerisy and its social role proved particularly influential, not least for J. S. MILL.　　PJ

Reading
†Calleo, D.P.: *Coleridge and the Idea of the Modern State*. New Haven and London: Yale University Press, 1966.

Coburn, K. ed.: *The Collected Works of Samuel Taylor Coleridge.* 16 vols. London: Routledge & Kegan Paul; Princeton, NJ: Princeton University Press, 1969– .

———: *The Notebooks of Samuel Taylor Coleridge.* 5 vols. London: Routledge & Kegan Paul, 1957– .

†Colmer, J.: *Coleridge, Critic of Society.* Oxford: Clarendon Press, 1959.

———: Coleridge and politics. In *S.T. Coleridge,* ed. R.L. Brett. London: Bell, 1971.

Griggs, E.L. ed.: *Collected Letters of Samuel Taylor Coleridge.* 6 vols. Oxford: Clarendon Press, 1956–71.

Leavis, F.R. ed.: *Mill on Bentham and Coleridge.* London: Chatto & Windus, 1971.

Woodring, C.R.: *Politics in the Poetry of Coleridge.* Madison: University of Wisconsin Press, 1961.

collectivism The pursuit of goals by common action, usually, though not necessarily, at the level of the nation as the largest collectivity, and through the agency of the state. The term is sometimes used as a synonym for SOCIALISM. It is not normally employed as a term of self-description and hence is not used with the analytical or prescriptive intention associated with the term INDIVIDUALISM with which it has frequently been contrasted.   RB

Collingwood, Robin George (1889–1943) English idealist philosopher and historian. Born in Coniston, Lancashire, Collingwood was a fellow of Pembroke College, Oxford, from 1912 and Waynflete professor of metaphysical philosophy 1935–41. He is chiefly known for his contributions to the philosophy of the social sciences and aesthetics, and as a historian of ancient Britain; only the first will be examined here.

Collingwood was influenced by the contemporary Italian idealists CROCE and, particularly, Gentile to believe 'all history is the history of thought' (see IDEALISM). He distinguishes human actions, which can be known from the 'inside' in the thoughts of the agent, from natural events, which can be understood only in terms of their 'outside' or external manifestations. Human acts must be explained in terms of the motives and intentions of the individual actor. Causal and law-like explanations are only appropriate for the regular and predictable events of nature. Since human beings are self-defining animals it is impossible to assume a constant frame of reference and meaning for human affairs analogous to the concepts of natural science. It is necessary to 'relive' the thoughts of others in order to comprehend the meaning of their acts. However, Collingwood does not draw subjectivist or relativist conclusions from this thesis. Underlying his argument is an historicist assumption of the continuity and progress of human thought. The self-development of the individual thinker must parallel that of the history of thought to produce a systematic philosophy which includes within it all that has gone before (see HISTORICISM). Civilization is the process of becoming, linking the thought of the past to the present. Thus all present thought implicitly continues and criticizes the thought of the past.

Collingwood's only complete outline of his philosophy was in *Speculum Mentis* (1924), in which he describes five 'forms of experience' – art, religion, science, history and philosophy – which constitute an ascending order of truth in which each phase develops to the point where through its inadequacy it generates its successor. This was further refined in later works as a dialectical process involving different stages in the development of knowledge both within history and within the individual. In these works philosophy is resolved into history, for no philosophy is without the 'absolute presuppositions' which belong to thought at any particular time (*Essay on Metaphysics*, p. 55).

The second world war appears to have qualified Collingwood's faith in the progress of western civilization. The *New Leviathan* (1942) attempts to bring the 'classical politics' of Hobbes up to date. There are three types of ethics which, in ascending order of rationality, are utility, right and duty. The first involves ends-means justification, the second consists in following a rule, and the third implies a self-conscious act of will. Politics is a dialectical progress from a state of nature (savagery) to a social community (civility), in which the individual's will is inseparable from the social will. The western political tradition represents this civilizing 'process of approximation to an ideal state' but is periodically subject to barbarism. Nazism was one such resurgence of barbarism, an attempt to return to the pre-social state of *bellum omnium contra omnes.* '*Being civilized*', on the other hand, 'means living, so far as possible, dialectically, that is, in constant endeavour to convert every occasion of non-agreement into an occasion of agreement' (*New Leviathan*, 39.15). History is a Manichaean struggle between these two tendencies, although civility is ultimately, if never completely, victorious over barbarity.   RPB

Reading

Collingwood, R.G.: *Speculum Mentis*. Oxford: Clarendon Press, 1924.

——: *Essay on Philosophical Method*. Oxford: Clarendon Press, 1933.

——: *An Autobiography*. Oxford: Clarendon Press, 1939.

——: *Essay on Metaphysics*. Oxford: Clarendon Press, 1940.

——: *New Leviathan*. Oxford: Clarendon Press, 1942.

——: *The Idea of History*. Oxford: Clarendon Press, 1946.

——: *Essays in the Philosophy of History*, ed. William Debbins. Austin: University of Texas Press, 1965.

†Krausz, M. ed.: *Critical Essays on the Philosophy of R.G. Collingwood*. Oxford: Clarendon Press, 1972.

†Mink, L.O.: *Mind, History and Dialectic*. Bloomington: University of Indiana Press, 1969.

Strauss, L.: On Collingwood's philosophy of history. *Review of Metaphysics* 5 (1952) 559–86.

communism The concept of communism pre-dates Marx by more than two thousand years. In PLATO's *Republic* private property is prohibited to the ruling Guardians. Plato's reason for forbidding property, and even that possessive relationship, marriage, was that rulers could not take disinterested decisions if they had vested interests. Early Christians practised community of possessions ('primitive Christianity'), not only because they lived in enclaves, under constant threat, but also because Christ's own teachings enjoined them to abjure possessions. Although this phase of Christianity was short-lived, the idea of community of possession re-emerged in medieval monasteries, where personal poverty was the first vow. The reasons were similar to Plato's: monks and nuns could not properly dedicate themselves to God's service while encumbered by worldly goods and cares. Furthermore the ownership of necessities and other resources by the monastery ensured a closer binding of individual members to the community and prevented individual independence and rivalry. (The vow of chastity likewise prevented sexual distraction and competition.) The abolition of private possession has two grounds: the purifying of the individual from material concerns, and the greater social cohesion of the community, best promoted by eliminating economic independence and conflict.

The case for community of possessions was again advanced in the sixteenth century in MORE's *Utopia* (1516), and in the seventeenth by certain LEVELLERS who, quoting the Bible, stressed God's intention that men should enjoy the world in common. In the eighteenth century the Abbé Mably, who thought that property had come about with the Fall, proposed ascetic communism as a cure for luxurious living and aggression; he attacked entrepreneurs and bankers especially. The Enlightenment thinker Morelly also advocated agrarian communism, based on small communes, where sumptuary laws would operate to prevent variety even in dress, and to prevent the development of inequality. (Similar proposals were made by ROUSSEAU.) There was to be no private ownership except of daily necessities and the tools of one's trade. Everyone was kept by, and employed by, the community, and there was a strict obligation to work. The French revolutionary Babeuf followed Morelly and Rousseau, stressing the fundamental equality of individuals in his *Manifesto of the Equals* (1796): 'Since all have the same needs and the same faculties let them henceforth have the same education and the same diet' (p. 79). Ownership and inequality were the source of all evil in society. Babeuf also championed agrarian communism, achieved through revolution. Property would be held by the community; all would be obliged to work. The goal of work was abundance, but life would be modest and frugal.

The French sociologist DURKHEIM argued that these communists, with whom he bracketed Rousseau, were seeking a moral solution to egoism, indulgence and other vices – hence the emphasis on asceticism. They questioned the moral propriety of ownership rather than its social expediency. He contrasted the early communists, who looked back to pre-industrial society – and often, politically, to the classical republics – with socialists such as SAINT-SIMON who were forward-looking realists (see Durkheim, chs 2, 3). Of course eighteenth-century French communists had not experienced industrialism, so their advocacy of agrarian communism is unsurprising. However, agricultural society is inherently more consonant with the principle of absolute equality than industrial society, where the division of labour inevitably produces differences of status, function and income. Early communists, including More, also saw hard work as the key to solving scarcity problems; this simple equation is more applicable to an agricultural economy than to an industrialized society.

Nineteenth-century communists adapted the doctrine to the industrial era. Cabet, extolling equality and 'fraternal communism', proposed large factories and the extensive use of machinery, as well as communalization of land. Communism must extend to the new nation-states, not just to small communes. Cabet considered Christianity an anti-property doctrine and his communist utopia, Icaria, was based on 'true' Christianity. The most subtle and penetrating theory of communism was provided by MARX. He castigated the 'crude and unthinking communism' of those like Cabet, which merely extended the ownership principle to everyone ('general private property'). Crude communism was the realization of 'universal envy'. True communism, by contrast, was the positive abolition of the property principle, which would end human self-alienation and create a real, moral relationship between individuals and between man and nature. The institution of property makes us unable to enjoy an object unless we possess it – and so thwarts our desires. Under true communism, *communal* enjoyment will be possible (see 'Private Property and Communism', pp. 145–57). Communist production is a co-operative activity and there is no distinction, finally, between physical and mental labour: individuals can enjoy both without undue specialization. It is questionable whether the self-fulfilment and abolition of the division of labour which Marx describes in his early

writings could be achieved in a communist society which, elsewhere, he describes as industrial, given the tendency of industrialization to produce bureaucracy and specialization. Many anarchists contemporary with Marx also advocated communal ownership (KROPOTKIN called his system 'anarcho-communism') but they feared the centralization which Marx's communism seemed to entail, which would threaten individual freedom. In the event, their fears about state communism were proved right (see ANARCHISM).

'Communism' connotes both *sharing* and *community*. Ideal communism would not merely herald the end of private wealth and private ownership of productive assets – as capitalist critics fear – but also a different way of life, based on co-operation and community solidarity. The similarity to the Christian ideal, emphasized by many pre-Marxist communists, is striking. The keywords 'equality' and 'fraternity' characterize communism. However, central to communism there is also an ideal of liberty. This differs from the individualistic concept prevalent in the liberal West. The logic of communism suggests that freedom – freedom from oppression, want and exploitation – must be achieved simultaneously for everybody, by destroying structures which militate against the freedom of the many while buttressing the privileges of the few. Freedom under communism would characterize the community as much as its individual members. As BAKUNIN said, 'the freedom of all is essential to *my* freedom'. Essentially, communism means holding everything, including freedom, in common. The principle is less one of equal distribution than one of equal co-ownership of material and other resources. Personal possessions are not necessarily condemned; past thinkers advocated asceticism and minimal consumption, but communists today certainly countenance enjoyment of consumer goods. There is however an unresolved dilemma: should ownership be entirely abolished to end conflict and oppression and to nurture fraternity, homogeneity of interests and inter-dependence, or does communism mean extending the rights and benefits of ownership equally to all, thereby validating the urge for possession? The communist ideal has always been advanced as an antidote to egoism, especially egoism made concrete in ownership; however, examples of ideal communism in action are rare. Perhaps it has only been realized in religious communities, in some secular communes, and among the few 'primitive' peoples remaining in the world, where sharing is a way of life. It does not seem to have been realized in communist countries. (See also SOVIET COMMUNISM.)   BG

Reading

Babeuf, G.: *Manifesto of the Equals*, trans. S. Lukes. *The Good Society* ed, A. Arblaster and S. Lukes. London: Methuen, 1971.

Beer, M.:*A History of British Socialism*, vol. I. London: Allen & Unwin, 1953.

Corcoran, P. ed.: *Before Marx: Socialism and Communism in France, 1830–48*. London: Macmillan, 1983.

Durkheim, E.: *Socialism and Saint-Simon*, trans. C. Sattler, ed. A.W. Gouldner. Yellow Springs, Ohio: Antioch, 1958; London: Routledge & Kegan Paul, 1959.

†Gray, A.: *The Socialist Tradition: Moses to Lenin*. London: Longmans Green, 1946.

†Marx, K.: Private Property and Communism (1844). In *Karl Marx: Early Texts*, trans. D. McLellan. Oxford: Blackwell, 1972.

————: *Critique of the Gotha Programme* (1875). In *Marx and Engels: Basic Writings on Politics and Philosophy*, ed. L.S. Feuer. New York: Anchor, 1959.

Marx, K. and Engels, F.: *The German Ideology* (1845–6) and *The Communist Manifesto* (1848). In *Selected Works*, vols I-III. Moscow: Progress Publishers, 1969.

community   It has been said that 'community' has a high level of use but a low level of meaning, and it is certainly one of the most pervasive, yet indefinite, terms of political discourse. On the one hand it appears to identify particular forms of social interaction, though what these are has been a matter of dispute; on the other hand its use is usually meant to imply something positive and valuable about the social relations thus defined, though across the political spectrum there is disagreement as to where its value resides. Both the left and the traditional or romantic right set great store by community, but the social conditions and the quality of the relationships which are thought to embody it are very different in each perspective. Liberals, on the other hand, while recognizing the beguiling power of the appeal to community, have never really known how to incorporate a rich sense of community into liberal theory, because LIBERALISM's commitment to individual freedom seems to cut across communitarian assumptions. These complexities have not led to any decline in the use made of the notion community, particularly as a legitimizing device in social policy and welfare contexts in which, it seems, the emotional power of the appeal to community is used to set policy preferences in a favourable evaluative light with the minimum of empirical content. There are therefore both empirical and ideological disputes about the nature of community and, as will be seen, these disputes are interlinked.

Given these complexities, it is difficult to bring order to these disputes, but there are a number of models which can be employed to clarify the discussion. The first model links community with location, and this certainly has a very strong historical basis. The German language, for example, has two words for community, *Gemeinde* and *Gemeinschaft*, the former referring explicitly to the local community, the latter having a rather broader meaning. The two uses were originally closely linked: in medieval times *Gemeinde* referred to the totality of citizens owning equal rights to land and hence locality was synonymous with community. *Gemeinschaft* has a wider sense now referring to the quality of the relationships between people in a particular place. In this sense locality is not a sufficient condition of community because the appropriate quality of relations may not exist in a particular locality. A good deal of subsequent debate about community has been over what specifically are the qualities of relationship which define community, and whether or not these qualities presuppose the physical proximity of the people in question.

One of the most important and frequently cited attempts to identify the qualities characteristic of community is to be found in Ferdinand Tönnies's *Gemeinschaft und Gesellschaft* (Community and Association) (1887) in which it is argued that the empirical qualities that define a community are given by its origin. Whereas associations of various sorts can be self-consciously built, instituted or contracted into, a true community is organic, based upon blood, kinship, shared habitat and locality, and a set of common attitudes, experiences, feelings and dispositions. Community is something which one is born into and grows within. Tied as it is ιο kinship and necessarily shared locality, community cannot be resurrected or rebuilt, its passage can be noted or mourned but it cannot be reinstated. Community is emphatically not a matter of individuals coming together to advance their specific interests; indeed in Tönnies's view individuals only come to develop an idea of interests because they have been born into a specific community. Unlike society or association, community is therefore a matter of birth, status, habit and disposition as opposed to contract and interest. While locality is a necessary condition for the emergence of these qualities, it is not sufficient, for they require a habitat of a special sort – the pre-industrial village community would be the most obvious example here.

An alternative attempt to define the qualities which characterize community is to be found in MacIver's *Community* (1917) which focuses upon the communality of interests. This conception of community has its roots in ROUSSEAU's distinction between the GENERAL WILL and the Will of All. Community of interest, as MacIver sees it, is not the aggregate of individual private interests, but is rather dependent on the existence of a group, which in his view can be as large as a nation. Unlike Tönnies, MacIver accepts the idea that community can be created by will, but it has to be a will of a particular sort, namely for a common good, or a set of interests which a group has in common. Because community is a matter of the empirical extent of common interests, it is a matter of degree, and elements of both *Gemeinschaft* and association may be found in present-day societies.

The third model is much more restricted in scope and, in opposition to Tönnies, allows for partial communities based upon the coming together of individuals with specific private interests. Whereas in MacIver's view if something is a community it must be based upon common interests, a direct concern with the welfare and status of others, the present view tends to take the interests in question as

private and restricted. Typically these interests will be related to the division of labour – hence there can be communities based upon private interests which may not be directly tied to a shared locality or physical proximity, although there will have to be shared experiences on which the linking of interests can be based. Hence, on this view, trades unions and professional and occupational groups may in certain circumstances be seen as embodying a sense of community. This model is clearly at the opposite extreme to that of MacIver, stressing as it does individual interests and community as a specific device for enhancing and extending these interests.

In all these cases physical location is not a sufficient condition for the existence of a community. For MacIver and Tönnies it is a necessary condition, but all are agreed that it is something about the quality of the relationships that makes a social grouping into a community. While the partial community theorist does not see physical location as absolutely necessary, it is clear from the examples offered, e.g. occupational communities, that in a broad sense a shared habitat is necessary; for instance a shared background to work or a profession, although this may have a widely differentiated geographical spread which may cross national boundaries.

It has been argued that disputes about the empirical qualities which communitarian relationships must possess could be bypassed by requiring, as a minimum definition, that they must embody a sense of solidarity and give individuals a sense of significance. Nevertheless, it is not at all clear that this is much of an advance. Even if the definition were to be accepted, and it might not be because for example it might make a family unit into a community, it still needs to be made more specific. What sorts of relationship give this sense of solidarity and significance? For Tönnies only ties of locally mediated identities of blood, kinship, race, disposition; for MacIver the development of common interests; for the theorist of partial community an identity of private interest. In this sense, therefore, while solidarity and significance may define the *concept* of community these features when interpreted will yield different *conceptions* of community.

Given that there are disputes about the qualities of relationships which define a community, it is not surprising that these correlate to some degree with ideological differences. On the whole traditional CONSER-VATISM would favour something like Tönnies's account of community with its emphasis upon rootedness, natural identities and organic relations between individuals – a community of naturally-related persons as opposed to an instrumental association based upon a contract for the furtherance of interests. In extreme forms this conception of community can become threatening, as in the Nazis' use of the idea of *Volksgemeinschaft*, or the community of the racial people, which depended heavily upon ideas of blood relationships and the rootedness of the organically given soil and landscape (see RACISM). The socialist, on the other hand, will typically endorse an idea of community such as that developed by MacIver from Rousseau, but will see the commonality of interest which it requires as emerging only in the socialist society of the future (see SOCIALISM). Capitalist society, in this view, because of its competitive nature and the private ownership of the means of production which provide the pervasive background against which interests are articulated, is incapable of generating the types of other-directed common interests which community requires. In addition the more traditional communities conforming to the Tönnies model by their very parochialism make the achievement of a genuine common interest, which will require the abolition of class relationships, more difficult to obtain. The close relationship which people feel to traditional communities may inhibit the development of class consciousness, which according to MARX is a necessary precursor of a socialist revolution and a classless society. In addition, for the Marxist, traditional communities embody a high degree of false consciousness about the nature of their constitutive relationships. Finally the liberal or social democrat, committed to a central place in political and social life for individualism and private interest, will typically favour the partial community approach. Whereas Tönnies saw an individual as part of a total community within which his or her whole life was to be lived, the liberal sees human nature as too complex to be satisfied by one sort of social order, however rich the quality of its relationships. Individuals have the right to choose the communities of which they wish to be a part, and the good society does not itself embody communal elements so much as provide the environment in which partial communities of all sorts may find a place. (See also LIBERALISM.)   RP

Reading

Hiskes, R.P.: *Community Without Coercion*. London and Toronto: Associated University Press, 1982.

König, R.: *The Community*, trans. E. Fitzgerald. London: Routledge & Kegan Paul, 1968.

MacIver, R.M.: *Community: a Sociological Study*. London: Macmillan, 1917.

†Nisbet, R.: *The Sociological Tradition*. London: Heinemann, 1967.

†Plant, R.: *Community and Ideology*. London: Routledge & Kegan Paul, 1974.

———, Lesser, H. and Taylor-Gooby, P.: *Political Philosophy and Social Welfare*. London: Routledge & Kegan Paul, 1981.

Tönnies, F.: *Community and Association*, trans. C.P. Loomis. New York: Harper & Row, 1963.

Comte, Isidore Auguste Marie François Xavier (1798–1857) French political philosopher and pioneer sociologist. Comte came from a Catholic and royalist background against which he initially reacted, although he later looked back with undisguised nostalgia to the 'Catholic-feudal' medieval synthesis. He was influenced for life by his studies at the École Polytechnique, where he acquired an unbounded confidence in the methods of the natural sciences and became imbued with the rationalist spirit of the *Encyclopédie*. Sent down from the École as a ringleader of a revolt against authority, Comte ironically spent much of his life there from 1832 teaching mathematics in a subordinate position. The other great formative influence on his life was SAINT-SIMON, whose secretary and collaborator he was from 1817 until their split in 1824. So close was their intellectual association during these years that it is hard to separate what was due to each of them. While Comte gave systematic expression to Saint-Simon's scientism, he went much further in developing the particular brand of scientism known as POSITIVISM. Nevertheless, Saint-Simon imparted to Comte a belief that the post-revolutionary reorganization of society could not be based simply upon scientists and scientific knowledge (what Comte called the 'spiritual power') but had to be supplemented by industrialists and industrial development (the function of the 'temporal power').

In the early 1820s Comte formulated in seminal essays the ideas that foreshadowed in a particularly forceful way what he was to expound more laboriously for the rest of his life. In conjunction with a propensity to manic overwork and depressive aftermath, two women played an important part in his life. In 1825 he married a former prostitute, and his serious nervous breakdown of 1826 was caused by a combination of intellectual over-exertion and his wife returning to prostitution as a source of family income (see Gouhier, *La Vie d'Auguste Comte*, pp. 116, 119, 151 and ch. 7). In 1844, after completing his *Cours de philosophie positive* and before embarking on the *Système de politique positive*, his meeting with Clotilde de Vaux exacerbated his religious predilections. The spiritual power he had learnt from de MAISTRE to esteem in his youth now came to the fore, so that scientists no longer so much replaced the priesthood as became the priesthood. However, all the essential ideas of 'positive politics', including the very title, were sketched out thirty years before in what Hayek (p. 193) has called 'one of the most pregnant tracts of the nineteenth century'.

Comte's scientistic attempt to eliminate politics as traditionally conceived in favour of a meritocratic and technocratic management of public affairs clearly emerged in his essay, 'A brief appraisal of modern history' (1820). He was still close to Saint-Simon when he argued that the scientific, industrial and political revolutions had paved the way for a new social system in which 'the people do not require to be governed (i.e. commanded). It is sufficient for the maintenance of order that the affairs of common interest should be regulated' (Early Essays, p. 102). The new industrial society was to be organized jointly by those possessing scientific skills and the bankers and industrialists who controlled the resources necessary to create wealth. Comte compared the coercive, pre-positive past with the social partnership characteristic of the future order. 'The military leaders *commanded*; the industrial leaders only *direct*. In the first case the people were subject, in the second they are *partners* ... from the humblest workman to the richest manufacturer and the ablest engineer' (Early Essays, p. 104). However, Comte made it clear that there was to be no democracy; the people were to play only a 'passive' and 'subordinate' role in matters of decision. To those who feared that he was advocating a 'despotism founded on science', Comte replied that the results of science were by their nature provisional and verifiable, so that science could not be the basis for oppression. He attempted to take the sting out of the power he attributed to scientists by making their decisions not the result of arbitrary will but the necessary result of what the facts 'dictated'.

What Comte rightly regarded as his 'fundamental opuscule' of 1822, which had three successive titles – 'System of positive politics' in 1824 and 'Plan of the scientific operations necessary for the reorganization of society' in 1854 – was intended to serve the function of d'Alembert's preliminary discourse to the *Encyclopédie*. This extended essay lives up to Hayek's claim that what was envisaged was *The Counter-Revolution of Science*. Comte argued that it was impossible to turn the clock back to the monarchical-military-theological past that constituted the feudal, pre-revolutionary order. Nor could the unscientific sovereignty either of individual reason in matters of the mind or of the people in political decisions provide a secure basis for a reorganized society. Nothing was more ridiculous than the successive attempts of constitutional lawyers to construct stable institutions on the foundations of the revolutionary principles that had destroyed the old order. Comte asserted that 'scientific men ought in our day to elevate politics to the rank of a science of observation' (Early Essays, p. 134). He went on to base what in the early 1820s he called 'political science' – subsequently dubbed 'social physics' and in 1838 christened 'sociology' – upon a law of historical development, the historicist 'law of the three stages'. This 'invariable law based upon the nature of things' (Early Essays, p. 141) – in which he was anticipated by Turgot but inspired by Condorcet – has become Comte's principal claim to enduring fame. Humanity was progressing from the theological state of monarchy through the metaphysical state of democracy to the positive state of scientism and industrialism. As well as having the capacity to avert or mitigate violent revolutions, Comte claimed 'the superiority of the positive polity . . . consists in the fact that the positive system *discovers*, whereas other systems *invent*' (Early Essays, p. 153). Authority had to be based not on force or wealth but on the scientifically observed facts, which required the re-establishment of a 'spiritual power'.

In the last of the three seminal essays finished just before his nervous breakdown of 1826, Comte described the way in which he believed post-revolutionary opinion could be governed. Concerned to recapture the Europe-wide, medieval moral communion, of which de Maistre's *Du Pape* had provided the most penetrating and systematic statement, Comte was clear that though the great reactionary had offered a powerful antidote to subversive liberalism he was incapable of restoring what the historical process had destroyed for ever. Only a political science possessing the dynamism of the French Revolution and the authority of Roman Catholicism could restore social consensus without recourse to crude coercion. Unity through a modern community of doctrine – what Huxley called 'Catholicism minus Christianity' – would counteract the tendency towards class conflict that a narrowly economic division of labour would promote between employers and workers. The scientistic spiritual power would have the task of preventing the despotism of the richest replacing that of the strongest, by regulating economic forces in the general interest. Comte did not believe – as Durkheim subsequently argued – that the spontaneous development of industrial society would lead to social solidarity through the social division of labour. Comte was convinced that the 'conformity of interests' (Early Essays, p. 234) could only be brought about by the restraint of a moral doctrine, just as Malthus had argued that it was essential if the inexorable increase of population was to be curbed. Similarly, Comte did

not believe that universal, peaceful economic and political co-operation could be achieved without the intervention of government guided by the spiritual power. In his fully worked out *Système de politique positive* (1851–4), Comte did not hesitate to proclaim that sociology as such was not sufficient; what was required was 'sociocracy' or 'sociolatry'! (vol. I, p. 403).

Though Comte retained his basic methodological and ideological convictions of the 1820s to the end of his life, what J. S. Mill called 'Comte's frenzy for regulation' and systematization (Mill, p. 196, cf. p. 141) assumed extravagant proportions in later years. In trying to understand how his propensity to mathematical megalomania developed into dogmatic, pseudo-scientific number mysticism, some responsibility must be attributed to the 'mental hygiene' Comte adopted at the age of 40. In 1838, the year which also marked the birth of the term 'sociology', Comte deliberately decided that he would stop reading new books, confining himself to writing and the reading of a few favourite poets; so confident was he that he knew all that was worth knowing that 'input' could now be sacrificed to 'output'. He therefore lost touch with common sense along with the corrective of what others thought, deciding that a hundred selected volumes would constitute the complete positivist library, the remainder being destroyed as superfluous (Mill, pp. 128–30, 179–81). He ended up in his *System of Positive Politics* and *Appeal to the Conservatives* (1855) in an outright advocacy of a conservative-capitalist dictatorship, with the proletariat having the pill of their subordination sweetened by public provision of guaranteed education and work for all, together with an assured minimum of social security. There was to be a twenty-one-year temporary dictatorship by three proletarians before temporal power was handed over to a triumvirate of three leading bankers, the High Priest of Humanity representing the countervailing spiritual power. This select group of self-recruiting and self-perpetuating oligarchs would be public functionaries acting in the general interest as they alone were able to conceive it.

Though the full implications of Comte's political system put to flight some of his greatest early admirers in Britain and France, the influence of his ideas has been enduring in a number of directions. His impact upon the philosophy of history and more especially sociology, notably through Durkheim and Lévy-Bruhl, has not been confined to France, nor has the attempt to develop a secular, scientistic morality to replace Christianity. However, whereas secularism commended Comte to the non-socialist left, his authoritarianism commended him to the non-Christian right, notably ' Charles MAURRAS. Positivism has also had a powerful impact on twentieth-century social science: through behaviouralism it virtually dominated American political science in the mid-twentieth century and to some extent still does (see POLITICAL THEORY AND POLITICAL SCIENCE). As 'the theorist of industrial society' (Aron, p. 77), his technocratic conception of politics has also had an enduring if more diffuse and unacknowledged influence, in association with the belief that democracy would lead to the dominance of ignorance and incompetence (see INDUSTRIAL SOCIETY). The engineers, applying scientific knowledge to industrial problems, were destined to combine the requisite spiritual and temporal capacities in harnessing the mass of the people in a peaceful, productive partnership. In his own homeland Comte's beloved École Polytechnique has to some extent lived up to his aspirations by providing an important component of the elitist interlocking directorate that runs French society. In 1977 a former *polytechnicien*, Giscard d'Estaing, while president of the French Republic, significantly created an Institut Auguste Comte in the buildings formerly occupied by the École Polytechnique which had moved to more spacious quarters. It was to provide a finishing school for technocrats – nearly half of them *polytechniciens* – but this venture did not survive d'Estaing's loss of the 1981 presidential election. So, despite Comte's fulminations against it, that much despised democratic device – election by universal suffrage – at least temporarily inhibited the symbolic consecration of scientistic managerialism as the handmaiden of political and economic power. However, the underlying tendency towards technocratic managerialism, detected by Comte, continues to make itself felt with almost deterministic force in most advanced industrial societies. JESH

Reading

†Aron, R.: *Main Currents in Sociological Thought*. Harmondsworth: Penguin, 1968.

†Charlton, D.G.: *Positivist Thought in France during the Second Empire*. Oxford: Clarendon Press, 1959.

Comte, A.: The Early Essays. In *The Crisis of Industrial Civilization*, ed. R. Fletcher. London: Heinemann, 1974.

——: *Cours de philosophie positive*, 6 vols. Paris, 1830–42; *The Positive Philosophy of Auguste Comte*, trans. and condensed H. Martineau. 2 vols. London: Chapman, 1853.

——: *Système de politique positive*. 4 vols. Paris: Mathias, 1851–4.

Gouhier, H.: *La Vie d'Auguste Comte*. Paris: Vrin, 1st edn 1931; 2nd edn 1965.

——: *La Jeunesse d'Auguste Comte et la formation du positivisme*. 3 vols. Paris: Vrin, 1933–41.

Hayek, F. von: *The Counter-Revolution of Science: Studies in the Abuse of Reason*. Glencoe, Ill.: Free Press of Glencoe, 1952.

Lévy-Bruhl, L.: *The Philosophy of Auguste Comte*. London: Sonnenschein, 1903.

†Mill, J.S.: *Auguste Comte and Positivism*. London: Trübner, 1865.

Popper, K.R.: *The Poverty of Historicism*. London: Routledge & Kegan Paul, 1957.

Voegelin, E.: *From Enlightenment to Revolution*. Durham, NC: Duke University Press, 1975.

conciliarism The representative assembly of the church, or council, acquired prominence in late medieval political theory and practice, largely because of the development of communal ideas by ecclesiastics who sought a solution to the Great Schism in the fourteenth- and fifteenth-century church. Conciliarism came to prominence at the church councils of Constance (1414–18) and Basle (1431–49) in which a theory of constitutional holism was proposed whereby the council was taken to be a visible manifestation of the invisible church's essence. The church as a whole is superior to any of its hierarchically arranged parts and the council, therefore, is superior in jurisdiction to the pope. Organically the whole council meeting together and voting by majority performs acts that no single member can perform.

Conciliarism was already legally developed by canon lawyers from the twelfth century onwards, but the most radical development of these ideas can be found in the writings of MARSILIUS OF PADUA, Henry Langenstein, Heimerich van de Velde, Conrad of Gelnhausen, Pierre d'Ailly, Jean Gerson, Juan de Segovia, Dietrich of Niem, Francesco Zabarella, Nicholas of Cusa and Niccolo de'Tudeschi, and others.

Conciliar theory, based as it was on earlier CANON LAW, also sustained important theological elements, owing to a renewed study of Scripture in place of civil jurisprudence. Conciliarism also owes much to contemporary secular corporative institutions such as guild constitutions. The themes of organic community and communal decision making were central to the ecclesiological attempt to reform a church in which three popes with differing national support contended for power. Originally deriving from the practice of the early church where synods made decisions in the areas of doctrine and discipline, conciliarism was eclipsed during the high Middle Ages by a doctrine of papal supremacy (see MEDIEVAL POLITICAL THOUGHT). Canonists, however, expounded on the correct relationship between head and members in lesser ecclesiastical corporations whereby 'authority in a corporation was not concentrated in the head alone but diffused among the various members'. With the increase in the number of late-medieval guild-governed towns, the foundation of many new universities, and a multiplication of religious associations for the laity and the clergy, conciliarism and communalism were living traditions which appealed to the organizational instincts of Europeans, and not least to political publicists. The conciliar period was fatal to any surviving claims of the papacy to oversee the norms or direct the policies of European states, because the fifteenth-century councils were, in effect, assemblies of secular as well as ecclesiastical leaders to reform the church.

Conciliarists anticipated many later theories of CONSTITUTIONALISM, REPRESENTATION and CONSENT, and the legacy of the fifteenth-century councils has been regarded as one of the major transitions from medieval to modern constitutionalism. But conciliarists themselves were largely interested in the theological deposit of faith and in ecclesiological reform. As a large-scale reform movement, conciliarism ended with Basle and its failure, defeated by concordats between popes and monarchs. Its failure led directly to the Protestant Reformation (see REFORMATION POLITICAL THOUGHT).

Vatican II (1962–5) is seen to have adopted some of the fifteenth-century conciliarist practices; Hans Küng is the most conciliarist of contemporary Catholic theologians. JC

Reading

Baker, D. ed.: *Councils and Assemblies*; vol. VII of *Studies in Church History*. Cambridge: Cambridge University Press, 1971.

Black, A.: *Monarchy and Community: Political Ideas in the Later Conciliar Controversy, 1430–1450*. Cambridge: Cambridge University Press, 1970.

†———: *Council and Commune: the Conciliar Movement and the Council of Basle*. London: Burns & Oates, 1979.

Coleman, J.: Transfert de théorie et des modèles d'organisation entre état et église: the influence of secular governmental structures on the theory and practice of conciliarism at Basle. *Église et État dans la genèse de l'état moderne*. Paris: CNRS, 1986.

Congar, Y. and Dupont, J.: *L'écclésiologie du haut moyen-âge*. Paris, 1968.

Figgis, J.N.: *Studies in Political Thought from Gerson to Grotius, 1414–1625*. Cambridge: Cambridge University Press, 1916.

Küng, H.: *Structures of the Church*. London: Burns & Oates, 1965.

Morrall, J.: *Gerson and the Great Schism*. Manchester: Manchester University Press, 1960.

Stieber, J.W.: *Pope Eugenius IV, the Council of Basel and the Secular and Ecclesiastical Authorities in the Empire: the Conflict over Supreme Authority and Power in the Church*. Leiden: Brill, 1978.

†Tierney, B.: *Foundations of the Conciliar Theory: the Contribution of the Medieval Canonists from Gratian to the Great Schism*. Cambridge: Cambridge University Press, 1955.

Condorcet, Marie-Jean, Marquis de (1743–1794) French philosopher. Condorcet was the youngest of the leading philosophers of the FRENCH ENLIGHTENMENT and the only one who lived to witness and participate in the French Revolution. He first made his name as a mathematician and, despite his noble rank, did not deign to climb to the top of the cultural institutions of the *ancien régime*. When TURGOT became Minister of Finance to Louis XVI, Condorcet, still only 30, was appointed governor of the Mint, and at that time he shared the former's belief that the path of reform in France lay in strengthening the powers of the king and subduing the legislative courts (*parlements*) and other traditional interests.

As the events of the Revolution unfolded, Condorcet changed from a royalist to a republican. He claimed that he was not inconsistent in doing so. For Condorcet had always believed in what he called the 'sovereignty of reason'. This notion he took care to distinguish from ROUSSEAU's theory of the supremacy of the 'general will', calling instead for the rule of the 'public reason'. In the context of the *ancien régime*, reason demanded a systematic and unified government which the monarch alone could provide. The monarch's title to rule was that he was the true representative of the nation as a whole (whereas the *parlements* were not).

After 1789 Louis XVI could no longer, in Condorcet's view, be seen as such a representative and new institutions were needed to articulate the public reason. Condorcet rejected democracy, since the generality of men were unenlightened, but he proposed to give the majority the right to choose, from among the educated elite, deputies to legislate on their behalf. He proceeded to devise some extremely elaborate techniques for elections to provisional and national assemblies to ensure that those assemblies were correctly representative of the 'public mind'. Condorcet's assemblies were, however, somewhat peculiar. Being eager to preserve reason from being obscured by passion and opinion, he recommended that the assemblies did not actually meet, but conducted their business by correspondence. In a word, politics was to be eliminated to make way for 'science'.

Condorcet wrote at length to defend his view that government could be as scientific as physics. In neither discipline, he argued, could there be certainty; both rested on probabilities. To make the calculation of probabilities in political science, experts would be needed. Condorcet envisaged the emergence of a bureaucrat class, dedicated to the 'public reason', and having as its task the formulation of rational solutions to such national problems as defence, sanitation, taxation, education, and general welfare, for he had an almost twentieth-century conception of the extent of the business of the state.

Condorcet secured election to more than one of the Revolutionary assemblies, and actually joined the Jacobin club in 1791; and although he did not vote (as an opponent of capital punishment) for the execution of the king, he did vote for the introduction of a republic. Yet his arguments for the sovereignty of reason were regarded by the champions of popular government as an endeavour to hand over power to a 'philosophical priesthood'. The constitution which he devised to realize his objectives found favour with the Girondins, but alienated his former friends among the Jacobins, and in 1793 Condorcet had to go into hiding.

While thus sheltering from the Terror, he wrote one of the most optimistic accounts of human history ever conceived – his *Sketch for an Historical Picture of the Progress of the Human Mind* (1795). In it he reaffirmed his belief that science not only could save mankind, but was going to do so. Condorcet was caught by 'patriots' when he emerged from hiding, and he died (perhaps by his own hand) in custody, at the age of fifty.   MC

Reading
†Baker, K.M.: *Condorcet*. London: University of Chicago Press, 1975.

Condorcet, M.-J.: *Sketch of an Historical Picture of the Progress of the Human Mind*, trans. J. Barraclough. London: Weidenfeld & Nicholson, 1955.

†Schapiro, J.S.: *Condorcet and the Rise of Liberalism*. New York: Octagon, 1934.

conscientious objection   The refusal to undertake compulsory military service, usually but not invariably on religious grounds. It may involve breaking the law (where no right of conscientious refusal is recognized), and has therefore been regarded as a form of CIVIL DISOBEDIENCE; but the assimilation is questionable, for the primary purpose of conscientious objection is normally to exempt the objector himself from military service rather than to arouse general opposition to the war in question. See PACIFISM.   DLM

consent   The notion of consent is used in political theory in at least three different ways:

(1) In the theory of POLITICAL OBLIGATION, by

those thinkers who want to provide an understanding of the duties that citizens owe to the state in terms of consent.

(2) In democratic theory, by those who hold that the distinction between democratic and non-democratic governments is that in the former the political elite rule by consent of the governed.

(3) In the appraisal of relationships among citizens within a political community, most notably sexual and economic relationships, where it may be important to define the criteria of consent.

In all these cases the emphasis placed upon consent has the same moral basis. To require that political arrangements and social relationships involve consent is to preserve the autonomy and self-direction of persons. Persons are not to be politically or morally committed to arrangements that they have not willed.

Given its widespread importance in political theory, it is useful to have a clear understanding of what the idea of consent involves. By defining the term clearly we can more readily identify an act of consent when it occurs and judge more reliably when someone has consented and what this involves. The trend in modern discussions is to analyse consent as a particular speech-act: that is, as a communication by a speaker intended to achieve a particular effect on those receiving the communication. The speech-act it most closely resembles is promising. When we promise, we communicate to another person that we will do something. When we consent, we indicate to others that it is all right by us if they do something, and we will not interfere with what they do. For example, if I consent to my neighbour holding a noisy all-night party next door, I am leading my neighbour to believe that I will not call out the police at two o'clock in the morning.

As with promising, the act of consent is assumed to involve a transfer of rights and obligations, and there are two ways in which this transfer has been viewed. According to the first interpretation, the giving of consent is simply a procedure by which we authorize someone to do or refrain from doing something. On this account consent is a specific type of performance which by its defining rule or conventions involves one person in transferring a right to another. This can be called the *normative* analysis of consent. On the alternative interpretation, consent involves no more than the communication of an intention to the effect that those with whom we are communicating can rely on our not interfering with their proposed course of action. Any moral claims which arise depend upon invoking further principles to the effect that we ought not to disappoint the reliance that others have been led to place in us. This can be called the *naturalistic* analysis of consent. Both interpretations can be supported by argument. For example, the normative analysis seems better able to account for the fact that the primary purpose of consent is to permit others to do something, not to induce in them the reliance that we will not interfere with what they do. On the other hand the naturalistic interpretation seems better able to explain how someone occupying a role within an organization could in fact have consented to something taking place, even though they were not empowered to give their consent. Someone may communicate an intention not to give their consent. Someone may communicate an intention not to interfere to another without the communication carrying any implication that the speaker is authorized to consent.

Under both the above interpretations the actual giving of consent in express form is required for there to be any moral consequences. However, as many writers point out, there are few occasions in the modern polity when citizens are even asked for their consent. So appeal is then made to the idea of tacit consent. This idea is best understood as the communication of a disposition not to interfere either by means of a failure to act or raise an objection, or by means of an act which has the foreseen, if unintended, consequence of inducing in others a reliance on one's not interfering. In this sense, voting in a free and fair election is sometimes taken to signal tacit consent to the result. A seemingly related idea is hypothetical consent, which involves a judgment about the sort of political arrangements to which people would consent if they were rational. However, this detaches the notion of consent too far from its grounding in the ideal of autonomy, and is best thought of as a judgment about the justice or fairness of social and political relationships.

APW

Reading

O'Neill, O.: Between consenting adults. *Philosophy and Public Affairs* 14 (1985) 252–77.

Pateman, C.: Women and consent. *Political Theory* 8 (1980) 149–68.

†Pitkin, H.: Obligation and consent. In *Philosophy, Politics and Society*, 4th ser., ed. P. Laslett, W.G. Runciman and Q. Skinner. Oxford: Blackwell, 1972.

Plamenatz, J.: *Consent, Freedom and Political Obligation*. London: Oxford University Press, 1968.

Simmons, A.J.: Tacit consent and political obligations. *Philosophy and Public Affairs* 5 (1976) 274–91.

†Weale, A.: Consent. *Political Studies* 26 (1978) 65–77.

conservatism By its critics, conservatism is frequently dismissed as a more or less obscurantist attempt by the 'haves' to defend their entrenched position of privilege against the 'have-nots'. Still worse, it is sometimes felt to be tainted by a vague connection with extremist movements like Nazism and the National Front. In what follows, by contrast, it will be argued that conservatism is a philosophy of human existence which not only deserves serious consideration but also is diametrically opposed to extremist movements of the kind just mentioned. The essence of this philosophy is the conviction that the human condition is characterized by tensions which can be mitigated, but never wholly eliminated, by political action.

The significance of the idea of ineliminable tension in the conservative philsophy of existence is most readily apparent when it is contrasted with the opposed radical doctrine, according to which the primary causes of evil and suffering are not rooted in the very nature of human existence, but originate in the structure of society. It is therefore at least possible to think of liberating men by eliminating these causes altogether, through a root-and-branch change in the appropriate part of the social order. In the modern world, the best example of such radicalism is MARXISM, according to which all the principal sources of human unhappiness can be removed by the revolutionary overthrow of capitalism. For conservatism, by contrast, evil and suffering are inseparable from existence, and wisdom therefore lies not in massive utopian schemes for abolishing them, but in modest proposals for containing and minimizing their impact. By their very nature, then, these tensions restrict politics to being a limited activity.

If the general vision of existence as a condition of ineliminable tension is now combined with the conception of politics as a limited activity, then conservatism may be defined as the art of political compromise, balance and moderation, in the interest of maintaining a limited style of politics.

It was the achievement of Edmund BURKE, the father of modern conservatism, to recognize immediately that the pursuit of liberty by revolutionary methods would not extend and perfect limited politics, as the French revolutionary democrats hoped, but would, on the contrary, destroy the conditions necessary for its maintenance. The first and most vital of these conditions is the RULE OF LAW; the second is an independent judiciary; the third is a system of representative government; the fourth is the institution of private property; and the fifth is a foreign policy designed to preserve political independence by maintaining a balance of power which, for conservatives, is the only stable and realistic principle by which to establish international peace.

It is in this form – that is, as the defence of limited politics – that conservatism is most persuasive. It may be objected, however, that limited politics is also the concern of the liberal tradition, and that it is therefore difficult to distinguish clearly between conservatism as defined here and LIBERALISM. The answer is that, whilst both liberalism and conservatism share common ground in Lockeian liberal principles, as transmitted by the Whig reform tradition to which Burke himself subscribed, conservatism nevertheless defends those principles in a wholly different way, and with major qualifications. As Burke made clear, conservatism rejects, for example, the abstract concepts of the individual, of the rights of man, and of a SOCIAL CONTRACT associated with Whiggism. Conservatism also rejects the UTILITARIANISM and belief in PROGRESS which subsequently characterized the reformulation of liberal principles during the nineteenth century.

From the vantage point afforded by the ideal of limited politics, it is now possible to proceed a step further and distinguish three different traditions within conservative thought. Although none of the three is the exclusive property of a particular nation, there is nonetheless a pronounced difference of emphasis in the degree of attention which each has received in French, German, and British conservative thought respectively. The difference between the three traditions can most easily be brought out by considering the standpoint from which each has sought to theorize the idea of tension.

The oldest standpoint is theological, and takes the form of Christian pessimism about human nature expressed in the myth of the Fall and original sin. Harnessed to the defence of the monarchy and the church, this pessimism has played a central part in French conservative thought, where it provided the basis of the reactionary tradition established in the nineteenth century by Joseph de MAISTRE, and best represented in the twentieth century (in a revised, secular form), by Charles MAURRAS and the Action Française. Although Christianity has also played an important part in the thought of men like Burke, what characterizes reactionary philosophy is a quest for a conservative utopia, usually located somewhere in the pre-revolutionary world, from which all the principal tensions of existence have been removed. In consequence, the reactionary begins by professing his commitment to the ideal of limited politics, but his futile quest for utopia inevitably ends by destroying it, because limited politics gives unrestricted play to the very tensions he dreads.

In German conservative thought, by contrast, theological interpretation of the human condition has characteristically been replaced by a secular philosophy of history which identifies the organic state as the perfect vehicle for human emancipation. The organic ideal, however, has tended to undermine rather than reinforce limited politics because freedom, in the German tradition, has been closely associated with a form of nationalist doctrine which subordinates everything to the requirements of cultural unity, or (in the case of Nazism) to racial purity (see NATIONALISM).

In Britain, finally, the distinctive feature of conservative thought has been a sceptical and flexible mood reflected, above all, in the ideal of a mixed constitution. Since the second world war, however, concern for this ideal has increasingly been all but eclipsed by an acrimonious debate within conservative ranks between defenders of the interventionist 'middle way', on the one hand, and defenders of an unregulated capitalist order, on the other. Before considering this contemporary development in more detail, however, it is necessary to locate modern conservatism at large in a broader perspective, by considering the principal task with which our age has presented it. This is the critique of the revolutionary style of politics inaugurated by the French Revolution. The nature of the critique can best be brought out by considering in turn the four characteristics of revolutionary politics which conservative thinkers have regarded as most disastrous.

The first of these is a quasi-religious fanaticism which converts politics from a limited activity, devoted to the piecemeal reconciliation of conflicts of interest and passion, into an all-embracing ideological crusade against evil. Such fanaticism follows almost inevitably from the belief, first enunciated in its modern form by ROUSSEAU, that man is naturally good and is corrupted only by bad social and political institutions. It has become only too familiar in the ideological conflicts of our century.

The second characteristic of revolutionary politics is rationalism, by which is meant the belief that satisfactory human institutions can only be created and legitimated by human reason. On this view, all existing institutions are rejected in principle, not because they have been found unsatisfactory by those who live under them, but because they are arbitrarily identified by the rationalist reformer as the irrational products of custom and tradition. In their place the rationalist seeks to put new institutions, chosen because they are believed to correspond to the requirements of wholly abstract ideals such as the rights of man, the greatest happiness of the greatest number, social justice, or the Great Society, to name only a few. From Edmund Burke to Michael OAKESHOTT, conservative thinkers have insisted that this politics of principle is not the key to human emancipation, but is merely a formula for dogmatism and inflexibility. They have argued, too, that reason cannot in fact perform the task of creating blueprints for achieving utopia, since it can offer no more than distillations (or 'abridgements' as Oakeshott calls them) of existing political traditions. More generally, they have maintained that the contempt for custom and tradition inherent in ideological politics undermines the voluntary social ties which they provide, with the result that the only means left of holding society together is coercion. It is therefore no accident, on this view, that every revolution since 1789 has ended in despotism.

The third characteristic is an unbounded optimism about the power of human will to shape and mould human destiny in any form which man desires. This optimism received its most spectacular and terrible expression in the fascist ideal of permanent revolution, according to which the meaning of life for a nation consists of constantly redefining its identity, and establishing its right to continued historical existence, by unquestioning obedience to a leader who will guide it to victory through the endless wars upon which it must embark, in order to prove itself (see FASCISM). This cult of will, and the political extremism that goes with it, is entirely alien to conservatism, which stresses the limitations imposed upon the will by the inescapable tensions of existence, not a futile titanism aimed at destroying them.

Finally, conservatives have criticized the naive faith, central to the new style, in popular sovereignty as the key to both municipal and international harmony. According to the doctrine of popular sovereignty, democracy automatically ensures both good government and world peace because it means self-government, and self-governing peoples (it is assumed) can surely have no interest in governing themselves badly, or in attacking each other. Against this view, conservatives have warned that democracy cannot be automatically identified with liberty and good government but, through the plebiscite, may easily be used to legitimate dictatorship.

From 1789 until 1945 it was this new revolutionary style of politics, surfacing again dramatically in 1848 and 1917, for example, and in the rise of fascism during the inter-war years, which haunted the conservative mind. During this intervening century and a half, various responses may be discerned. At one extreme, conservative thinkers might simply despair, abandon the ideal of limited politics, and resort to a cult of leadership pure and simple. Such was the theme, for example of Thomas CARLYLE and, at a later stage, of Oswald SPENGLER in Germany. Throughout the inter-war era, works like T. S. Eliot's *The Wasteland* (1922) and, in Spain, Ortega y Gasset's *The Revolt of the Masses* (1929) echoed the mood of conservative despair. Such responses to the modern world, however, served only to condemn conservatism to a sour-tempered impotence. At the other extreme, conservative thinkers like Lord Hugh Cecil seemed willing to place an almost limitless trust in the natural conservatism of the masses (*Conservatism*, 1912). In between these two opposed responses lay many possible permutations; in practice the most influential has been a long series of more or less ambitious compromise solutions, beginning with Disraeli's 'one nation' ideal and culminating in the post-1945 'middle way' ideology, originally advocated by Harold Macmillan in 1938, in a book with that title.

During the three decades following the second world war, the middle way ideal made substantial progress, partly because conservatives succumbed to the temptation of meeting the new socialist challenge, which had replaced the old liberal one, by stealing the enemy's clothes; partly because the controls introduced under the war economy seemed to have provided a practical demonstration of the ability of government planning to end the unemployment of the 1930s; and partly because the universal adoption of the welfare state committed every government to 'fine-tuning' of consumer demand, in order to maintain full employment. The result was a drift towards collectivism which, by the mid-1970s, had become so powerful that it seemed to many to have left conservatism without any coherent identity. It is against this background that the contemporary 'liberal-conservative' (or 'neo-conservative') reaction to middle way collectivism, which in varying degrees has marked European and American politics during the past decade, must be interpreted.

The liberal-conservative reaction was provoked by an acute awareness of five major limitations inherent in the middle way ideal. In the first place, middle way defenders had naively assumed that economic growth would automatically ensure an increase in general social well-being. The idea that affluence might instead create new problems of its own was never considered. In the United States in particular, this has been a central theme of neo-conservative critics of the Great Society, such as Daniel Bell, Patrick Moynihan, and Irving Kristol, who claimed that governments are now called upon to perform the impossible in matters of economic growth and employment, and are therefore inevitably judged by unrealistic criteria, with the result that the modern democratic state is condemned to increasing instability.

The second line of attack was upon the uncritical faith placed by proponents of the middle way in planning as the sovereign remedy for all human miseries. In *The Road to Serfdom*, a work which has steadily gained in influence since it first appeared in 1944, F. A. HAYEK claimed that planning sets a free society upon a path which inevitably leads directly to totalitarian rule. In particular, Hayek rejects out of hand the idea that the middle way represents a stable half-way house in which one can have the best of all worlds, by combining the benefits of planning with the advantages of liberty.

According to a third line of attack, the post-war government commitment to maintaining high levels of employment and economic growth was directly responsible for the rising level of inflation which began to emerge in the Western democracies during the 1970s. The solution proposed by leading liberal-conservative economists like Hayek and Milton Friedman was to deprive governments of all control over the money supply. Just how this is to be done, however, is a problem which has still not been solved, but has thus far produced only bizarre proposals like Hayek's demand for removal of the state monopoly of the issues of legal currency. More plausibly, another liberal-conservative thinker, W. Röpke, has stressed (*A*

Humane Economy, 1958) that the real cause of inflation is not the money supply at all, but the preference of democratic governments for 'soft' over 'hard' finance – that is, for borrowing in order to fulfil extravagant promises to the electorate rather than balancing the budget with all the constraints that entails. Inflation thus becomes a moral and political phenomenon, rather than a merely economic one, and the search for a cure, ironically, would seem to point liberal-conservatives in an authoritarian direction, since it is the democratic system itself which is called into question, once inflation is no longer regarded as a technical economic matter.

A fourth major criticism echoes TOCQUEVILLE's prophecy that modern democracy would end in a novel form of tutelary despotism, brought into existence not by government oppression but, on the contrary, by an excess of good intentions which leads governments to regulate the lives of their (supposedly) incompetent subjects to such an extent that nothing remains 'but to spare them all the care of thinking and all the trouble of living' (*Democracy in America*, pt 2, bk 4, ch. 6). It is precisely this unhealthy form of paternalism, liberal-conservatives maintain, which has been encouraged by the conversion of an older, restricted ideal of welfare (for instance that of Beveridge, based upon the twin concepts of social insurance and special need) into a comprehensive, cradle-to-grave version of the servile state.

Finally, an important critique of the middle way has stressed the incompatibility of the managerial politics which it entails with the survival of the mixed constitution itself. The executive, Lord Hailsham warned in his 1976 Dimbleby Lecture, now claims to be the only truly representative part of the constitution, and is growing so rapidly at the expense of the other parts that parliamentary government is being converted into a system of elective dictatorship. In a complacent editorial, *The Times* replied (on 15 October 1976) that Hailsham had ignored the growth of a new system of extra-constitutional checks and balances (such as political parties and pressure groups) which ensure that big government does not mean strong government. What *The Times* failed to see was that the new balance of power has no necessary tendency to promote the rule of law, or indeed any other requirement of constitutional government.

Liberal-conservatism clearly offers some salutary warnings, but it can scarcely be said to provide an adequate expression of conservative thought. Its central proposition is that liberty is indivisible, by which is meant that civil and political liberty can exist only within a capitalist economic órder; but at least three major difficulties emerge as soon as this position is examined.

In the first place, by identifying conservatism with the defence of capitalism, liberal-conservatism risks confusing the case for limited politics with the promotion of materialistic and consumer values that may well be incompatible with the moral, social, and political values which conservatism seeks to defend. Secondly, even on its own chosen terrain – the defence of free-market mechanisms – liberal-conservative economic theory is open to the charge of dogmatism. Finally, perhaps the most compelling criticism of liberal-conservatism is not that it is wrong, but that it is irrelevant. It is irrelevant because it flies in the face of the general trend of advanced western societies towards a 'post-industrial' social order within which capitalist attitudes and values have largely disappeared, with the result that there is no significant section of the population which desires a return to free-market conditions.

The future of conservatism looks bleak. On the one hand, it may well win votes by pandering to the collectivist ethos which Tocqueville so accurately foresaw, but in that case the nature of its identity will remain obscure. On the other hand, it may choose to defend the ideal of limited politics with which it has traditionally been associated. In that case, however, conservatives may find it very difficult to stay in office, since none of the institutions associated with limited politics – the rule of law, parliamentary accountability, and an independent judiciary, for example – has any obvious relevance for an age mainly concerned with the politics of prosperity.   NO'S

Reading

Burke, E.: *An Appeal from the New to the Old Whigs* (1791). New York: Bobbs-Merrill, 1962.

†Cecil, H.: *Conservatism*. London: Thornton Butterworth, 1912.

Hayek, F.A.: *The Road to Serfdom*. London: Routledge, 1944.

Kedourie, E.: *The Crossman Confessions and other essays*. London: Mansell, 1984.

Macmillan, H.: *The Middle Way*. London: Macmillan, 1938.

Oakeshott, M.: *Rationalism in Politics*. London: Methuen, 1962.

O'Sullivan, N.: *Conservatism*. London: Dent, 1976.

†Quinton, A.: *The Politics of Imperfection*. London: Faber & Faber, 1978.

Röpke, W.: *A Humane Economy*. Chicago: Regnery, 1971.

Santayana, G.: *Dominations and Powers*. London: Constable, 1951.

†Scruton, R.: *The Meaning of Conservatism*. London: Macmillan, 1980.

Shklar, J.: *After Utopia*. Princeton, NJ: Princeton University Press, 1969; London: 1970.

Smith, P. ed.: *Lord Salisbury on Politics*. Cambridge: Cambridge University Press, 1971.

Tocqueville, A. de: *Democracy in America*, ed. J.P. Mayer and M. Lerner. London: Fontana, 1968.

Constant de Rebeque, Henri Benjamin

(1767–1830) Swiss-born French liberal. Constant's Swiss Protestant origins were to play an important part in his life and thought, although he spent most of his life outside Switzerland. His father, a professional soldier, commanded a Dutch regiment. The precocious young Constant was educated first by tutors in Brussels, then at the University of Erlangen and, finally, at Edinburgh, where he came into contact with the social theory of the SCOTTISH ENLIGHTENMENT. Returning to the Continent, Constant fell under the sway of an older woman, Madame de Charrière, and the romantic pattern of his life was set. Older women, with whom he could share his passion for ideas, dominated that life. A marriage of convenience in 1789 (and another much later) scarcely interrupted the pattern. Constant's sympathy for the French Revolution brought a brief career as Chamberlain to the Duke of Brunswick to an end in 1794. Shortly afterwards he met Madame de Staël, who became the greatest influence on his life and thought for nearly two decades. Constant joined her liberal circle in Paris, and in 1796 published his first political essays, defending the Directory against 'reactionary' movements. In 1799 he was appointed to the new Tribunate, but his liberal opinions and relations with Madame de Staël soon made him *persona non grata* with Bonaparte. In 1803 Constant followed Madame de Staël into exile, and spent long periods at her château of Coppet near Geneva. Constant also visited Germany, where he came into contact with German romantic philosophy and religious thought (see ROMANTICISM).

The years of the Empire were Constant's most creative period, though he published little at the time. He began to compose major works on both politics and the 'religious sentiment'. Only the impending collapse of Napoleon's Empire led him to publish in 1813 his *De l'esprit de conquête et de l'usurpation dans leurs rapports avec la civilisation européenne* ... , a work in which he identified Napoleon's expansionist instincts as deeply contrary to the increasingly peaceful and commercial character of European society. The model of social and economic change implied by Constant's argument is redolent of the Scottish Enlightenment, though Constant does not employ it systematically. Returning to Paris, Constant rapidly became a leading liberal spokesman under the constitutional monarchy established by Louis XVIII's *Charte*. After Napoleon's return from Elba, however, Constant allowed himself to be persuaded (not least by a new Egeria, Madame de Recamier) of Napoleon's 'liberal intentions' and drafted a Constitutional Charter for the restored Empire. After Waterloo he fled to England where he published a novel, *Adolphe*, which was a masterpiece of introspection. Returning to Paris, Constant resumed his career as a publicist, defending liberty of the press with particular zeal and skill. He became a deputy in 1819, in time to witness and combat the ultra-royalist reaction after the assassination of the heir to the throne in 1820. Later in the 1820s his declining health together with a mounting fever for gambling reduced his political effectiveness. In the Chamber he never acquired the influence of Royer-Collard or De Serre, for he lacked the ability to improvise. He was known more for his incisive journalism. Constant died soon after the July Revolution, which he had welcomed and helped to sanction.

Like Madame de Staël's, Constant's social and political thought can be seen as a sustained commentary on the writings of ROUSSEAU. Rousseau's Genevan origins and conception of the just or GENERAL WILL, as well as the use made of his ideas by revolutionary figures such as Robespierre, meant that he could not be ignored, after 1795, by liberal Protestants who wrestled seriously with the question of why the Revolution had degenerated into the Reign of Terror. Did the conception of civic virtue incorporated into the notion of the General Will really capture the nature of modern Christian aspirations? Had Rousseau's admiration for the ancient *polis* and his defence of political participation in *Du contrat social* led him astray? It was by addressing such questions that Madame de Staël and Benjamin Constant began to move beyond the frontiers of eighteenth-century proto-liberal thought (see LIBERALISM). That movement involved criticizing Rousseau's concept of liberty on conceptual grounds and exploring the ways in which modern society differed from ancient society.

It was in this way that Constant came to draw his famous distinction between ancient and modern liberty. Observing that the ancients had understood liberty entirely in terms of CITIZENSHIP – that is, the right to take part in the assembly which debated and made public decisions – Constant pointed out that such a right did not guarantee any of the individual or private rights (against others) which modern Europeans associate first and foremost with the idea of liberty. For the ancient Greeks, the life of the citizen was the only life worth living, not least because it was the life of a privileged or aristocratic class in a slave-holding society. In modern Europe, on the other hand, equality before the law and the freedom it provides for individuals to define and pursue their own interests have created a radically different social and moral context. In place of the solidarity of a war-like governing caste, individual independence and freedom from harassment have become the uppermost social values. The peaceful, economic orientation of modern society means that 'public welfare' involves protecting private interests rather than sacrificing them to a reified, over-simple notion of public duty. Indeed, when transferred into the context of a modern nation-state, such a notion of civic duty becomes positively dangerous – for it tends to throw power into the hands of an oligarchy which conceals its power behind appeals to the General Will.

Thus Constant defends the modern 'discovery' of REPRESENTATION against Rousseau's use of the ancient *polis* to discredit it. Compared to the purely formal guarantee of individual liberty (by way of a principle of reciprocity) which Rousseau had introduced into his concept of the General Will, Constant argues that the representative system is the surest means of safeguarding individual independence. On the whole, Constant's anxiety to protect individual independence led him to underplay if not ignore the moralizing potential of political participation which Rousseau had emphasized – though when Constant revised some of his argument in 1819 during the struggle of Restoration liberals against the ultra-royalists he laid greater emphasis on the role of participation. But on the question of whether that participation was justified chiefly as a means to protecting civil liberty, or as something valuable in itself, his arguments remain ambiguous.

Constant's contrast between ancient and modern liberty – adumbrated in several writings, but given its final form in an 1819 lecture – has tended to receive attention at the expense of his other political writings. Yet, in fact, his *Principes de politique* (1815) offers subtle and original observations over a far wider range of questions. In particular, Constant helped to initiate the critique of the concept of SOVEREIGNTY, which younger French liberals such as Guizot and TOCQUEVILLE were to pursue and refine. Their new concern with the distribution of power within a nation-state helped to distinguish early nineteenth-century French liberalism from the eighteenth-century Enlightenment. Equally, Constant's interest in what he called the 'religious sentiment' separates him from the earlier *philosophes*. In his *De la religion* (1830), Constant sought to save the inwardness of religious feeling both from its exploitation by a religious priesthood *and* from the 'superficial' doctrine of self-interest – fighting on two fronts, against both eighteenth-century materialism and the clerical fanaticism of the ultra-royalists under the Restoration.

True to his Protestant origins, he sought to reconcile liberal principles and genuine religious feeling, thereby defending liberalism against the charge of being anti-religious.   LAS

Reading
Berlin, I.: Two concepts of liberty. In *Four Essays on Liberty*. Oxford: Oxford University Press, 1969.
Constant, B.: *Oeuvres*. Paris: Pléïade, 1964.
Holmes, S.: *Benjamin Constant and the Making of Modern Liberalism*. New Haven, Conn.: Yale University Press, 1984.
Siedentop, L.A.: Two liberal traditions. In *The Idea of Freedom* ed. A.J. Ryan. Oxford: Oxford University Press, 1979.

constitutionalism   Like the RULE OF LAW, for which it is arguably a synonym, constitutionalism can be used in at least two senses, one relatively formal and another more substantive. One sense reflects the definition of a constitution, as offered for example by Sir Kenneth Wheare in *Modern Constitutions*: 'the rules which establish and regulate or govern the government'. In Britain, he noted, this simply meant the collection of legal and non-legal rules that constitute the system of government. In almost every other country, however, the term relates to a selection of purely legal rules collected in one or a few closely related documents. In this sense constitutionalism would be simply the practice of establishing constitutions whatever their content might be.

Nevertheless, some writers – and probably over time a consensus of usage – have treated constitutionalism as the practice of establishing and working political systems of a particular kind that embody provisions reflecting the philosophy of limited government. Such systems have usually contained codes or charters of political or economic rights and liberties, together with other structural features designed to protect the rights of individuals against the state.   GM

Reading
†McIlwain, C.H.: *Constitutionalism and the Changing World*. Cambridge: Cambridge University Press, 1939.
†———: *Constitutionalism Ancient and Modern*. New York: Cornell University Press, 1940.
Morris-Jones, W.H.: On constitutionalism. *American Political Science Review* 59 (1965) 439–40.

Sartori, G.: Constitutionalism: a preliminary discussion. *American Political Science Review* 56 (1962) 853–64.

Wheare, K.: *Modern Constitutions*. New York and Toronto: Oxford University Press, 1966.

†Wormuth, F.D.: *The Origins of Modern Constitutionalism*. New York: Harper, 1949.

contradiction See DIALECTIC.

corporatism Long associated with the fascist regimes of the inter-war period, the concept of corporatism has been rehabilitated within political theory in the last ten years, and is now widely applied in studies of organized interests in democratic as well as authoritarian settings. It has made a significant contribution to the analysis of interest groups according to the extent to which they have become incorporated into the processes of public policy-making, reinterpreting the distinction between the public and private spheres characteristic of liberal theory.

The earlier meaning had a strong affinity with Catholic social doctrine and was closely bound to organic theories of society. Corporatism presupposed a classless social structure divided into various corporations according to the function each performed in the social division of labour. Organizations were created and licensed by the state to represent the interests of each category, but at the same time exercised close social control over the population. No society was ever wholly organized on corporatist principles, but the design for the Italian system under Mussolini came closest to this ideal.

The most widespread modern usage of the term focuses on the role of interest organizations which occupy an intermediary position between the state and civil society. Following Schmitter, most writers emphasize the differences between corporatism and PLURALISM. Whereas in a pluralist system a large number of voluntary interest associations compete with each other for members, resources and access to government in order to influence the direction of public policy, in a corporatist system there is a limited number of non-competitive organizations with compulsory or semi-compulsory membership. These organizations have a privileged status with respect to government in that they co-determine public policy and are responsible for its implementation by disciplining their members to accept bargained agreements.

Three key features of corporatism distinguish it from pluralistic processes of interest group politics. The first is the monopoly role played by corporatist bodies; the second is the fusion of the representative role with that of implementation; and the third is the presence of the state both in licensing monopoly representation and in co-determining policy. Whereas in pluralist theory interests are seen as existing before organization and political mobilization, in corporatist theory the state is identified as a crucial agent in shaping interests and affecting the outcome of group processes (see Cawson).

In contrast to liberal theory, which draws a sharp distinction between the public and the private and interprets society as an aggregation of individuals, corporatist theory focuses on organizations and social groups, and highlights the extent to which formally private bodies perform public tasks. The organizations which constitute a corporatist system are drawn from those which take their identity from the function which they perform in the social division of labour. A mutually interdependent relationship between the state and certain organizations develops to the extent that the latter can mobilize and deliver their constituent membership in exchange for favourable public policy decisions.

The difference between advanced capitalist societies where corporatism develops incrementally as a consequence of the growing monopoly power of interest organizations, and those where a corporatist design is imposed by the state, is captured in the distinction between societal (or liberal) corporatism and state corporatism (see Schmitter). Societal corporatism has become most strongly institutionalized in countries such as Austria or Sweden where a powerful labour movement has become a 'social partner' with the peak employers' association and the state in negotiating economic and social policies. State corporatism tends to be associated with peripheral or dependent capitalist regimes, such as those in Latin America (see Malloy).

Modern usage suggests the following as a concise definition of the concept:

Corporatism is a specific socio-political process in which a limited number of monopolistic organizations representing functional interests engage in bargaining with state agencies over public policy outputs. In exchange for favourable policies, the leaders of the interest organizations agree to undertake the implementation of policy through delivering the co-operation of their members.

There remains however some disagreement concerning what should be the focus of corporatist theory. The major approaches to corporatism can be summarized as follows:

(1) Corporatism is a novel system of political economy, different from capitalism and socialism, which consists of state direction of predominantly privately-owned industry according to the ideological principles of unity, order, nationalism and success (see Winkler).
(2) Corporatism is a form of state which develops alongside parliamentarism within capitalist society. Parliamentarism is based on a territorial-individual mode of representation, whereas corporatism fuses functional representation with an interventionist state (see Jessop).
(3) Corporatism is not a complete political system nor form of state, but is a form of interest intermediation different from pluralism in which a limited number of hierarchically ordered monopolistic organizations represent their members' interests in negotiation with the state and implement public policy (see Schmitter).

Where corporatism has become strongly entrenched at the macro-level, economic and social policies have been determined on the basis of tripartite negotiation. It has been argued that the ability of some countries to withstand economic recession without resorting to deflation and the creation of unemployment can be explained by the extent to which corporatism facilitates bargaining between capital and labour over the distribution of the social product (see Goldthorpe). In such cases corporatist processes involve class collaboration, and for this reason many Marxist critics (e.g. Panitch) have argued that corporatism can be understood as a strategy which is adopted by capitalist states in order to maintain the subordination of the working class.

A good deal of the literature has concentrated on the comparative analysis of nation-states, and several attempts have been made to rank countries according to the extent to which they conform to an ideal type of corporatism. Most authors seem to agree that the country which scores most highly is Austria, that the United States is the least corporatist country, and that in Britain corporatism has been relatively weak. Some attempts (discussed in Cawson) have been made to measure corporatism and correlate its incidence with other features of national political systems. The results are suggestive rather than conclusive, but there are indications that corporatism is linked to toleration of high levels of taxation and public spending. Other studies have suggested that the more 'governable' countries are the strongly corporatist ones, which also tend to have lower levels of unemployment.

The interest organizations that are most likely to achieve monopoly status and enter into a corporatist exchange with state agencies are those which represent producer rather than consumer interests, and that command resources of information or compliance necessary for the implementation of state policies. Empirical studies suggest that employers' and trade associations, trade unions and professional bodies are the most common interlocutors. The form that corporatism takes is bargaining, with a high degree of delegation of public authority to nominally private bodies. As a policy mode corporatism may be contrasted with legal-bureaucratic and market forms of regulation which involve a markedly different form of relationship between the state and interest organizations.

Corporatism can also be identified at an intermediate level, in the relationship between state agencies and organizations which have achieved monopoly representation of a particular sectoral interest. Even in countries such as the United States or Canada, which are weakly corporatist using national-level indicators, strongly entrenched forms of corporatist intermediation can be found in particular policy areas such as agriculture.

Corporatist theory has mounted a strong

challenge to pluralism as a model of interest group politics, but as empirical evidence feeds into successive refinements of the theory, it is becoming clear that corporatism and pluralism should not be seen as exclusive alternatives, but as end points on a continuum according to the extent to which monopolistic and interdependent relationships between interest organizations and the state have become established (see Cawson). AC

Reading

†Berger, S. ed.: *Organizing Interests in Western Europe: Pluralism, Corporatism and the Transformation of Politics*. Cambridge and New York: Cambridge University Press, 1981.

†Cawson, A.: *Corporatism and Political Theory*. Oxford: Blackwell, 1986.

Goldthorpe, J. ed.: *Order and Conflict in Contemporary Capitalism: Studies in the Political Economy of Western European Nations*. Oxford and New York: Oxford University Press, 1984.

Jessop, B.: Corporatism, parliamentarism and social democracy. In Schmitter and Lehmbruch eds.

†Lehmbruch, G. and Schmitter, P.C. eds: *Patterns of Corporatist Policy-Making*. Beverly Hills and London: Sage, 1982.

Linz, J.J.: Totalitarian and authoritarian regimes. In *Handbook of Political Theory*, vol. 3: *Macropolitical Theory*, ed. F.I. Greenstein and N.W. Polsby. Reading: Addison-Wesley, 1975.

Malloy, J. ed.: *Authoritarianism and Corporatism in Latin America*. Pittsburgh: Pittsburgh University Press, 1977.

Panitch, L.: The development of corporatism in liberal democracies. *Comparative Political Studies* 10 (1977) 61–90.

†Schmitter, P.C.: Still the century of corporatism? *Review of Politics* 36 (1974) 85–131.

——— and Lehmbruch, G. eds: *Trends toward Corporatist Intermediation*. Beverly Hills and London: Sage, 1979.

Winkler, J.T.: Corporatism. *European Journal of Sociology* 17 (1976) 100–36.

critical theory A body of neo-Marxist social theory originating in the Frankfurt Institute for Social Research (hence the later term 'Frankfurt School'). The Institute was founded in 1923 as a centre for interdisciplinary Marxist research and began to take on a distinctive character after Max Horkheimer (1895–1973) became director in 1930. Horkheimer and Theodor Adorno (1903–69)

formed the nucleus of the Institute, but many of the leading figures of German intellectual life were associated with it at one time or another. Probably the best known are the literary theorist Walter Benjamin, the philosopher Herbert MARCUSE and the psychologist Erich Fromm; others include Otto Kirchheimer and Franz Neumann (politics and law), Friedrich Pollock, Henryk Grossman and Arkady Gurland (political economy), Leo Löwenthal (literature) and Bruno Bettelheim, Nathan Ackerman and Marie Jahoda (psychology).

The Institute was forced to leave Frankfurt in 1933, settling in the USA in 1935. In 1950 it was re-established in Frankfurt, under the direction of Horkheimer and Adorno, with Marcuse and others remaining in the USA. It was the centre of a distinctive conception of society and culture, represented to a greater or lesser degree in the work of individual members and associates.

Critical theory may first be viewed as part of a more general trend in western MARXISM, dating from around 1930, towards a closer relationship with non-Marxist thought, a growing preoccupation with cultural and ideological issues at the expense of political economy, and a scholarly rather than a proletarian audience (see Anderson). In addition, critical theory must be seen in terms of the intellectual situation of western European Marxists, confronted in the 1930s by the unholy trio of liberal capitalism, Stalinism and FASCISM. The writers connected with the Institute were not content, like more orthodox Marxists, to analyse fascism as simply a mutant form of monopoly capitalism, nor, like the post-war theorists of TOTALITARIANISM, to equate Stalinism with fascism and to contrast both with an idealized image of liberal democracy. They were struck by the similarities in terms of organization, technology, culture and personality structure in all these forms of society, and hence gave these phenomena a more prominent place in their analyses than had the majority of Marxist writers.

Critical theory was understood from the outset as a totalizing theory which viewed society from the standpoint of the need to change it. The theory was to be reflexive about its own status and that of its interpretive categories: 'the critical acceptance of the categories which rule social life contains simultaneously their condemnation' (Horkheimer, *Critical Theory*, p. 208). Fascism, for example, could not really be understood in the categories of western liberalism, since this was the ideology of a social order which had produced fascism. 'He who does not wish to speak of capitalism should also be silent about fascism' (Horkheimer, cited in Jay, *The Dialectical Imagination*, p. 156). Critical theory was also hostile to traditional disciplinary boundaries: the early *Studien über Autorität und Familie* (1936) contained lengthy discussions of social and political thought as well as sociopsychological material, and *The Authoritarian Personality* (1950) was intended to be understood in terms of the more socio-cultural analysis of *Dialectic of Enlightenment* (1947), where anti-semitism is seen in the context of the rational domination inaugurated by the Enlightenment. Fascism 'seeks to make the rebellion of suppressed nature against domination directly useful to domination' (Horkheimer and Adorno, p. 185).

The concepts of domination and AUTHORITY pervade the Institute's work. Domination, although exemplified above all in fascism, was also the central principle of liberal societies, and possibly more important than the categories of Marxian political economy. As Adorno put it in a late article, 'Behind the reduction of men to agents and bearers of exchange value lies the domination of men over men'. Marcuse's concept of surplus-repression, developed in his critique of FREUD's *Civilization and its Discontents* (1930), is defined as 'the restrictions necessitated by social domination', over and above those which, as Freud had argued, were necessary for *any* ordered society and which Marcuse calls the 'rational exercise of authority' (*Eros and Civilization*, 1955, p. 45).

This distinction is crucial to the critical theorists' account of the relation between reason and domination. They criticized existing social arrangements in the name of reason and of a more rational alternative society, with the conviction that 'social freedom is inseparable from enlightened thought' (Horkheimer and Adorno, p. xiii). At the same time, however, they increasingly saw instrumental or technological rationality as the basis of the 'comfortable,

smooth, reasonable, democratic unfreedom [which] prevails in advanced industrial civilization' (Marcuse, *One-Dimensional Man* 1964, p. 19). And though Marcuse's critique drew heavily on his American experience, it applied increasingly, he thought, to state socialist societies: 'it is not the West but the East which, in the name of socialism, has developed modern occidental rationality in its extreme form' (p. 201).

Marcuse's critique of industrial society in *Eros and Civilization* and *One-Dimensional Man*, and some of his later writings, was prefigured in a more speculative form in Horkheimer and Adorno's *Dialectic of Enlightenment*. Here the domination of nature by means of reason leads inevitably to the domination of man. In the lapidary formula on p. 6, 'enlightenment is totalitarian'.

Dialectic of Enlightenment also contains a critique of mass culture, or as Horkheimer and Adorno preferred to call it, the 'culture industry'; they saw this as a homogeneous system of entertainment, devoid of the critical potential which high culture had once possessed and serving only to stabilize a system of domination. Here again one sees the emphasis on the interplay between politics, sociology and psychology: 'the might of industrial society is lodged in men's minds' (p. 127). Cultural theory is perhaps the area for which these writers will mostly be remembered; Adorno in particular produced a substantial body of work on aesthetic questions, especially on music. In philosophy, their contribution was mainly confined to expositions and critiques: Horkheimer's work on philosophies of history, Adorno's critiques of Husserl and Heidegger, and Marcuse's book on Hegel, *Reason and Revolution* (1941). But Adorno's major work, *Negative Dialectics* (1966), will surely remain one of the classic texts of twentieth-century philosophy.

Once the Institute was re-established in Frankfurt, the 'Frankfurt School', as it then came to be known, had a powerful influence in an otherwise rather conservative West Germany. The major intellectual event was the School's attack, in the fifties and early sixties, on POSITIVISM and empiricism in the social sciences, the *Positivismusstreit*; the main political event was of course the challenge of the student movement and the extra-parliamentary opposition, with which the Frankfurt School had an uneasy and ultimately hostile relationship. After the death of Adorno in 1969, critical theory developed in a more diffuse form, in the work of Jürgen HABERMAS, Karl-Otto Apel, Claus Offe, Alfred Schmidt, Albrecht Wellmer, and others.

Critical theory, then, aimed to transcend conventional distinctions between sociology and philosophy, psychology, and political thought. In particular, these writers attacked the whole idea of a distinction between normative political theory and empirical political science. In this respect at least they stand squarely within the Marxian conception which links social science to social criticism. At the same time, however, more orthodox Marxists see the critical theorists' abandonment of the concept of proletarian revolution and their 'eclectic' borrowing from non-Marxist sources as excluding them from the Marxist tradition. But this Marxist orthodoxy, like the positivist orthodoxy which insists on the separation of facts and values, has now been largely transcended in western social and political thought. In this respect, whether or not it survives as a distinct intellectual movement, critical theory has provided an important inspiration for more recent thinkers, even if they would not identify themselves with it.

Although, as noted above, the critical theorists rejected the distinction between normative and empirical theory, it may be used in an informal way to classify their contributions to modern political thought. In terms of political philosophy, they identify themselves with the ideals of classical liberal and democratic theory, while at the same time extending the Marxist critique of liberal democracy. Their claim is, in essence, that liberalism cannot sustain its ideals insofar as it remains tied to capitalism and hence to the instrumentally rational domination and oppression of wage labour. This comes out clearly in Marcuse's essay on 'The struggle against liberalism in the totalitarian conception of the state' (1934). In a generalized and more radical form it is also the guiding theme of Horkheimer and Adorno's *Dialectic of Enlightenment*. Habermas took up the same

theme in his early book, still not available in English, *Strukturwandel der Offentlichkeit* (Structural Change in the Public Sphere) (1962). He argued here that the liberal concept of public opinion, for all its limitations in terms of class (and, one could add, gender), had a critical purchase on state policy which is lacking in the modern world, where public opinion has become a mere quantity to be manipulated by politicians and the market research and advertising agencies which they employ.

Thus a classical conception of DEMOCRACY as the sphere of rational and open consensus formation and decision making combines with a factual critique of scientist positivism and technocratic politics. This theme is most fully developed by Habermas, but it is already present in the earlier critical theorists' analyses of fascism, Stalinism and monopoly capitalism, and, in more philosophical terms, in Horkheimer's discussions of bourgeois philosophy of history (1930) and in Marcuse's Hegelian/Marxist critique of positivism in *Reason and Revolution*. The 'Frankfurt' conception of politics has affinities with that of Hannah ARENDT but it is grounded in the broader and more sustained critique of advanced industrial society which has been perhaps the dominant counter-cultural movement of the post-war West. And where this counter-culture also stressed the themes of personal politics, sexual liberation and the critique of authoritarian family and educational structures, it was in large part following a direction mapped out in the Institute's early studies of 'Authority and the Family' (1936). These changes contributed in turn to the growth of feminist movements on a mass scale. And within the academy, the emergent sub-field of political psychology, where it escapes the bounds of scientist empiricism, has drawn on *The Authoritarian Personality* and on the work of Erich Fromm – in particular, *The Fear of Freedom* (1942).

The failure of the counter-culture of the 1960s to develop lasting political structures on a large-scale basis is also prefigured, in a sense, in the critical theorists' remoteness from 'practical' politics. (The very term 'practical' would attract their suspicion, insofar as it implied an accommodation to existing institutional structures.) This hostility to conventional or machine politics can be seen in the extra-parliamentary opposition in West Germany and elsewhere, and in the student movement(s), and more recently in the tensions within the West German 'Green' parties and among radical activists in social democratic parties such as the British Labour Party.

In all these ways, critical theory has had an important formative effect on the modern political consciousness. That such an uncom-promisingly severe intellectual style was able to attract such a widespread following in the sixties and seventies can only be explained by its having struck an important chord in western political awareness. Marx wrote that 'as philo-sophy finds its *material* weapon in the proleta-riat, so the proletariat finds its *intellectual* weapon in philosophy'. Critical theory never expected to find its material weapon in the proletariat. It sought a more diffuse basis of support and, perhaps to its surprise, found it in the political 'fragments' of the modern alterna-tive movements or counter-culture, whose intellectual weapons, whether or not they realized it, were often made in 'Frankfurt'. WO

Reading

Adorno, T.W.: Society. *Salmagundi* (1969–70) 10–11.

————: *The Authoritarian Personality*. New York: Harper, 1950.

————: *Negative Dialectics*. New York: Seabury, 1973.

————: *The Positivist Dispute in German Sociology*. London: Heinemann, 1976.

Anderson, P.: *Considerations on Western Marxism*. London: New Left, 1976.

†Bottomore, T.B.: *The Frankfurt School*. London: Horwood, 1984.

Habermas, J.: *Strukturwandel der Offentlichkeit*. Neuweid and Berlin: Luchterhand, 1962.

————: *Theorie des kommunikativen Handelns*. 2 vols. Frankfurt: Suhrkamp, 1981; *The Theory of Communi-cative Action*, vol. I, trans. T. McCarthy. London: Heinemann, 1984.

†Held, D.: *Introduction to Critical Theory*. London: Hutchinson, 1980.

Horkheimer, M.: Traditional and critical theory (1927). In *Critical Theory*. New York: Herder & Herder, 1972.

———— and Adorno, T.: *Dialectic of Enlightenment*. New York: Herder & Herder 1972; London: Allen Lane, 1973.

Institut für Sozialforschung: *Studien über Autorität und Familie*. Paris: F. Alcan, 1936.

Jay, M.: *The Dialectical Imagination*. Boston: Little, Brown; London: Heinemann, 1973.

————: *Permanent Exiles. Essays on the Intellectual Migration from Germany to America*. New York: Columbia University Press, 1986.

Marcuse, H.: *Reason and Revolution*, 2nd edn. London: Routledge & Kegan Paul, 1955.

————: *Eros and Civilization*. Boston: Beacon, 1966.

————: *One-Dimensional Man*. London: Routledge & Kegan Paul; Boston: Beacon, 1968.

Croce, Benedetto (1866–1952) Italian idealist philosopher and historian. Croce was born in Pescasseroli in the Abruzzi. His first writings were historical and antiquarian but the Marxist, Antonio LABRIOLA, awakened his interest in philosophy, leading him to write his essays on *Historical Materialism and the Econo-mics of Karl Marx* (1900). Although he is usually regarded as an Hegelian, the neo-Kantians, notably Herbart and Windelband, and the literary critic Francesco de Sanctis inspired Croce's 'realist idealism' and famous critique *What is Living and What is Dead in the Philosophy of Hegel* (1906). His main contri-bution was to the philosophy of aesthetics and history. His *Aesthetic* (1902) and journal *La Critica* (1903–44) had a profound impact on Italian culture. His collaborator, Giovanni Gentile, led him to adopt the doctrine of 'absolute historicism'. A thesis central to all his works published after 1909, it was developed in the three remaining volumes of his *Philoso-phy of Spirit*, the *Logic* (2nd edn 1909), the *Philosophy of the Practical* (1909) and the *Theory and History of Historiography* (1915), and his study of *The Philosophy of Giambattista Vico* (1911). In 1910 Croce became a senator and from 1920–1 he was minister of education under Giolitti. He opposed FASCISM and draf-ted the 'Protest against the "Manifesto of Fascist Intellectuals"' (1925) in opposition to Gentile. He turned his historicism into a 'religion of liberty', writing a number of historical works, notably a *History of Italy 1871–1915* (1927) and a *History of Europe in the Nineteenth Century* (1932), to illustrate his 'ethico-political' interpretation of human civilization, best expressed in *History as the Story of Liberty* (1938). After the war he was briefly a minister in 1944 and president of the ill-fated Liberal Party.

Croce's *Philosophy of Spirit* was intended as a secular religion capable of encompassing all aspects of human life. Spirit's activity is either theoretical or practical, the first subdivided into intuition and thought and the second into economic and moral willing. These subdivisions are so related that the second and fourth involve the first and third respectively but not vice versa. These four 'distinct moments' of Spirit's activity correspond to the 'pure concepts' of the Beautiful, the True, the Useful and the Good. Since these concepts are 'pure' they lack any determinate content beyond that which is supplied by Spirit's dialectical development through human activity in history. The Beautiful derives from the creation of works of art, the Useful from political and economic acts, and each provides in turn the material for our conceptions of the True and the Good. Croce was opposed to any 'transcendent' notion of an 'objective' standard of beauty, truth, etc., beyond those provided *post facto* by a cultural tradition of past acts. He identified philosophy with history, conceived as a progressive process in which previous systems of philosophy are incorporated within and transcended by present systems, a point he sought to illustrate with the histories of aesthetics, logic, ethics and historiography which accompanied the four volumes of his own system. All thought is 'historical judgment' and all history 'contemporary history' because the past is 'lived' and reworked in Spirit's, and hence humanity's, present experience.

Although Croce's philosophy is held together by an implied *telos* within history, he believed it was impossible to pronounce upon it. This had two divergent practical consequences: firstly, a subjectivism which endows all our acts and thoughts in the present with equal force; or secondly, resignation to the 'station and duties' which Spirit has accorded to us; a dilemma summed up in the Hegelian aphorism, 'What is real is rational, what is rational is real,' which was the keystone of Croce's historicism. Whereas Gentile's 'actualism' was to develop the first, Croce increasingly insisted on the moderate conservatism of the second, expressing it in semi-theological terms as a faith in the mysterious workings of Providence. However, twenty years of fascist rule produced a gradual revision of his ideas and in his last *Studies on Hegel* (1952) he had returned to the neo-Kantian position of his youth and maintained that a duality between the real and the rational, the *Sein* and the *Sollen*, was necessary for conscientious action in the present. He had a great influence on Italian contemporaries, notably GRAMSCI, but Vossler and COLLINGWOOD were his only important followers abroad. (See also HEGEL, HISTORICISM, IDEALISM.) RPB

Reading

Bellamy, R.P.: Liberalism and historicism: Benedetto Croce and the political role of idealism in Italy *c*.1880–1950. In *The Promise of History*, ed. A. Moulakis. Berlin and New York: Walter de Gruyter, 1985.

†———: Croce. In *Modern Social Theory: ideology and politics from Pareto to the present*. Cambridge: Polity, 1986.

Borsari, S.: *L'Opera di Benedetto Croce*. Naples: Istituto Italiano per gli Studi Storici, 1964.

Collingwood, R.G.: Croce's philosophy of history. *Hibbert Journal* 19 (1921) 263–78.

Croce, B.: *Opere*. 67 vols. Bari: Laterza, 1965.

———: *Filosofia – Poesia – Storia*. Milan and Naples: Ricciardi, 1951; *Philosophy, Poetry, History*, trans. C. Sprigge. Oxford: Oxford University Press, 1966.

———: *Autobiography* (1915), trans. R.G. Collingwood. Oxford: Oxford University Press, 1927.

Gramsci, A.: *Il materialismo storico e la filosofia di Benedetto Croce*. Turin: Einaudi, 1949.

†Hughes, H.S.: *Consciousness and Society: the Reorientation of European Social Thought, 1890–1930*, pp. 82–90 and 200–29. Brighton, Sussex: Harvester, 1979.

Jacobitti, E.E.: *Revolutionary Humanism and Historicism in Modern Italy*. New Haven, Conn. and London: Yale University Press, 1981.

Sasso, G.: *Benedetto Croce: la ricerca della dialettica*. Naples: Morano, 1975.

Crosland, Charles Anthony Raven (1918–1977) British socialist. The leading postwar revisionist theorist in British SOCIALISM, Crosland was a Labour MP from 1950 to 1955 and from 1959 to 1977, and a senior minister in the Labour governments of 1964–70 and 1974–77. He was the author of *Britain's Economic Problem* (1953), *The Future of Socialism* (1956), *The Conservative Enemy* (1961) and *Socialism Now*

(1974). His reputation as a political theorist rests upon *The Future of Socialism*.

Crosland set out to be, in his own words, the second Edward BERNSTEIN whose *Evolutionary Socialism* (1898) had rejected Marxist theories of capitalist collapse and the inevitability of socialism (see MARXISM). Like Bernstein, he rejected the Marxian analysis of capitalism and defined socialism in terms of values and principles to be achieved by democratic political action (see also SOCIAL DEMOCRACY).

Crosland claimed that by the mid-1950s capitalism had been so fundamentally transformed that it was no longer capitalism as Marx had understood it. This transformation, itself partly the result of democratic pressures, had come about by various means: the growth of trade unions had altered the balance of power in industrial bargaining; ownership was now less important than management; decision-making in industry was now in the hands of professional managers who did not necessarily share the values of traditional capitalists; a comprehensive welfare state had been developed in Britain; there was full employment; primary poverty had been eradicated; major industries had been taken into public control; governments had a range of techniques to manage the economy to keep employment high, inflation low and growth continuous. The combination of these factors had fundamentally altered capitalism and the power relations within it, Crosland maintained. Classical Marxism could not be a sure guide in such a changed world and the future of socialism had to be rethought.

Crosland defined socialism in terms of ideals and principles which were concerned with EQUALITY. The primary goal of socialism was the development of greater social equality, which would go far beyond the equality of opportunity favoured by liberals and conservatives, because it would be concerned not just with open recruitment to elite positions, but with a more egalitarian distribution of rewards, status and privileges, and the breakdown of existing class stratification. He argued the case for greater equality on four grounds:

(1) economic efficiency – under the existing reward structure high status and rewards were not clearly linked to economic function;

(2) a commitment to a more communitarian society – existing inequalities created resentment, which in turn had an effect upon economic progress;

(3) the injustice of rewarding talents and abilities for which an individual had only limited responsibility – these being to a large extent governed by nature and nurture;

(4) an appeal to a rather ill-defined notion of social justice which in *Socialism Now* is linked to RAWLS's *A Theory of Justice*.

Given such a definition of socialism, the means of achieving this egalitarian outcome had to be thought out in empirical rather than dogmatic terms. Traditionally, the British Labour Party was committed to wholesale nationalization under Clause IV of its constitution. Crosland, however, saw public ownership as no more than a means to achieving greater equality and a means which, given the changes in capitalism noted earlier, was growing less and less relevant. While there might be a need to use state action in the tax field to redistribute wealth directly, Crosland took the view that there were two other key means to the achievement of equality. The first was the development of comprehensive education, which would lead to a greater intermingling of classes and avoid the development of elite leadership of the type he thought both grammar and public schools fostered. The second was economic growth, that would yield a fiscal dividend which when used on social expenditure would radically improve the relative position of the worst-off while allowing the better-off to maintain their absolute standard of living. This was important in securing the allegiance of the better-off to a more egalitarian society. Quite where the push for equality would stop, Crosland refused to say. He was a strong pluralist – politically, economically and culturally – but he thought that greater equality could be achieved without threatening the values of a morally pluralist society.   RP

Reading

Crosland, C.A.R.: *Britain's Economic Problem*. London: Cape, 1953.
†———: *The Future of Socialism*. London: Cape, 1956.
———: *The Conservative Enemy*. London: Cape, 1962.

———: *Socialism Now, and other essays*. London: Cape, 1974.

Crosland, S.: *Tony Crosland*. London: Cape, 1982.

†Lipsey, D. and Leonard, D.: *The Socialist Agenda: Crosland's Legacy*. London: Cape, 1981.

D

Dante Alighieri (1265–1321) Italian poet. For Dante, the role of the poet included the moralist, the philosopher and, in his *Divine Comedy*, the prophet. Convinced by his brief but traumatic political career in his native Florence that the society which it represented required fundamental moral reform Dante, in the last twenty years of his life, gradually arrived at a vision of an ideal society where individuals would be free to follow the path of virtue leading to ultimate salvation, and it is in this essentially religious context that his political thought must be seen.

Dante's Florence was the wealthiest and most self-confident, but also the most turbulent, of the self-governing Italian cities. It acknowledged a nominal allegiance to the Holy Roman Emperor, but in practice took advantage of the ineffectuality of imperial authority in Italy to expand at the expense of its Tuscan neighbours, while keeping at arm's length the power which had sought to supplant the empire in Italy, the papacy. In November 1301 the governing party, to which Dante belonged, was overthrown in a coup with the connivance of Pope Boniface VIII, who hoped thereby to increase his influence over the city's affairs. Dante, who was in Rome on an embassy to Boniface at the time, was among those condemned in their absence by the new government, and so never returned to the city. This experience left him profoundly disillusioned both with Florence and with its economic and social values, and with a politically aggressive papacy; the conviction that both must be made to accept constraints on their political power underlies all his subsequent thought.

The works of the early years of his exile show Dante exploring the implications of this conviction, as it develops into the comprehensive vision of social and moral order of the *Divine Comedy*. These shorter poems and unfinished prose treatises reveal a marked preference for lay as against clerical institutions, and more sympathy than would have been normal in Guelph Florence for the last Hohenstaufen claimants to the imperial title. What is missing until the last book of the *Convivio* (*c.*1307) is that sense of the sacred destiny of Rome as the capital of the universal empire, which is evidently derived from Dante's re-reading of Virgil's *Aeneid*, and which is proclaimed as an article of faith throughout his mature works.

The *Divine Comedy* (begun about 1304) reflects the widening scope of Dante's political concerns. In the *Inferno*, Florence and its problems dominate the picture: a community where family and civic loyalties conflict, whose prevailing philosophy is materialism and whose prosperity rests on the socially sterile activity of usury, is shown as fundamentally unstable and corrupt. At the same time, the church is incapable of exercising its proper spiritual function because of the worldliness of its leaders; and the DONATION OF CONSTANTINE, whereby the first Christian emperor supposedly bestowed his temporal power in the West on the papacy, is seen as a fateful mistake which marked the beginning of the church's decline from its primitive faith. In the *Purgatorio* Dante turns to the larger political order which allows such developments to take place. There should ideally be two powers or 'suns' which should guide man's spiritual and temporal aspirations; but 'one has extinguished the other' (*Purg.* xvi, 106 ff), the church having trespassed on the competence of the empire, while the nominal emperors (the Habsburgs, since 1272) are too preoccupied with consolidating their power in Germany to challenge the papal usurpations in Italy. Finally, the *Paradiso* reflects the rise and fall of Dante's hopes with the career of Henry of Luxemburg, elected emperor as Henry VII in 1308, who briefly seemed to give substance to Dante's dream of an emperor claiming his crown and asserting his authority in Italy. But Guelph resistance led by Florence and King Robert of Naples revealed Henry's vulnerability, and he died, still leading the remnant of his army, in 1313. The turning-point in his fortunes was the withdrawal of support by the French pope, Clement V, under pressure from Philip IV of France. Dante's scorn for what he considered this act of treachery, and for the obduracy of the Florentines, is violently expressed in the *Paradiso*, and almost the last political reference in the poem (*Par.* xxx, 133 ff.) promises a throne in heaven for Henry and a place in hell for Clement.

The ideas underlying the political judgments of the *Comedy* are expounded in the prose treatise *De monarchia*, whose three books argue three uncompromising theses: that only a universal monarch can administer justice impartially between lesser powers; that special signs of divine favour have marked out the Roman Empire as the institution destined to exercise such a role; and that the emperor's authority is derived directly from God, not, as the church had long claimed and as Boniface vigorously reasserted, mediated through and hence subject to that of the church. CHURCH AND STATE were separate and autonomous; though in a much discussed conclusion, Dante argues that the emperor nonetheless owed to the pope 'that reverence which an eldest son should show to his father' (*Mon.* III, xv), since the spiritual realm was ultimately superior to the temporal.

The *Monarchia* makes no explicit reference to Henry VII, and so probably predates at least the *Paradiso*. Indeed, Henry's failure, and Clement's failure to support him in his prosecution of Robert of Naples for *lèse-majesté*, finally showed the untenability of Dante's notion of a universal monarch. In another respect too, the treatise stops short of Dante's definitive synthesis of his religious and political convictions in the *Comedy*: namely – and paradoxically – in that very insistence on the autonomy of the secular state, with its implied separation of the realms of nature and grace, which readers have always found its most strikingly modern feature.   MD

Reading

Dante Alighieri: *The Divine Comedy*, bilingual edn, ed. C.S. Singleton. 6 vols. Princeton, NJ: Princeton University Press; London: Routledge & Kegan Paul, 1971–5.

———: *Convivio*, Italian text ed. M. Simonelli. Bologna: Pàtron, 1966; English trans. C.J. Ryan. Saratoga, Calif.: Anma Libri, forthcoming.

———: *De monarchia*, Latin text with Italian trans., ed. B. Nardi. In *Opere minori*, vol. 2. Milan and Naples: Ricciardi, 1979 [with full commentary and bibliography]; English trans.: *Monarchy, and Three Political Letters*, ed D. Nicholl and C. Hardie. London: Weidenfeld & Nicholson, 1954.

†D'Entrèves, A.P.: *Dante as a Political Thinker*. Oxford: Clarendon Press, 1952.

†Holmes, G.: *Dante*. Oxford: Oxford University Press, 1980.

decretalists The name given to medieval commentators on the law of decretals, these being replies by the pope to questions of church law. The decretals were collected in a number of works, of which the most important are the *Decretum Gratiani* and the Decretals of Gregory IX. See CANON LAW, MEDIEVAL POLITICAL THOUGHT.

democracy An ancient political term meaning government by the people – in classical Athens where the word originated, rule by the *demos*. In current usage, it can refer to popular government or popular sovereignty, to representative government as well as direct participatory government, and even (not quite correctly) to republican or constitutional government, that is to say, government by law.

In earlier times, it was part of the standard classification of regime forms that distinguished rule by one (monarchy), several (aristocracy), and the many (democracy). It was sometimes identified as a conventional form and sometimes as a corrupt form of popular rule in the six-cell classification that included tyranny as the corrupt form of monarchy, oligarchy as the corrupt form of aristocracy, and ochlocracy as the corrupt form of government by the people.

Pure democracy was held in suspicion both by aristocratic philosophers such as SOCRATES and by proponents of mixed government such as ARISTOTLE, and was frequently contrasted with the so-called compound regimes (mixing monarchical, aristocratic and democratic elements) that typified classical Greece and republican Rome. Because 'the many' encompassed of necessity the poor and unpropertied, democracy was often associated not merely with the rule of the people but with the rule of the rabble, the hoi polloi, the mob. PLATO associated it with the subordination of reason to passion and compared it unflatteringly with his ideal of philosophical rule in his *Republic*; Aristotle, cautioning against the unsettling effect of regimes that polarized rich and poor, identified it with immoderation, regarding it (along with oligarchy) as a source of political instability and imprudence in his *Politics*.

Indeed, the model of government that emerged from the ancient world in the writings of Plato, Aristotle, Polybius, Cicero, and Augustine was one rooted in the ideal of a mixed constitution in which rulers were subordinated to virtue or to the law or, indeed, to one another, through a system of mutual checks; this ideal placed the rule of virtue and law above the rule of men. Monarchs guided by self-restraint and ruled by the law might be virtuous; aristocratic or democratic assemblies unhinged from moderation and reason might prove corrupt. Thus, in the modern political tradition that emerged during the Renaissance, philosophers such as MACHIAVELLI in his *Discourses* and MONTESQUIEU in his *Spirit of the Laws* took democracy to be a pure form of government that could be safely incorporated into statecraft only as one component of a mixed republican constitution. Even ROUSSEAU, the greatest early modern theorist of democracy, differentiated between a democratic sovereign (responsible for the enactment of basic law) and a democratic government (responsible for the quotidian execution of statutory law); the former he endorsed, the latter he deemed impossible – a form of government more suited to angels than to men.

In its early modern incarnation as SOCIAL CONTRACT theory, the democratic ideal offered a challenge to traditional dictatorship and the divine right of kings. The issue was the origin of political legitimacy under conditions where the state was increasingly understood as an artificial and mechanistic creation of man rather than an organic and historical body-politic. By arguing that the ultimate source of all governmental authority lay in individuals possessed of both natural liberty and natural rights, social contract theory established the foundations for later democratic government, and delegitimized once and for all the idea of kingly rule as a natural and incontestable prerogative of either divinity or heredity.

In its more recent incarnation, since the eighteenth century, democracy became a dominant standard by which regimes were judged rather than merely one among a number of regime forms. During this period, democratic theory and practice focused on the extension of the franchise, understanding universal suffrage to be a condition of that natural equality of all human beings that was bequeathed by the social contract tradition. Popular sovereignty, as the consequence of civil association by contract, had not guaranteed popular elections; nor had the theoretical equality of all citizens before the law guaranteed either membership in the citizen group (for the non-propertied in eighteenth-century England, for Indians and blacks in early America, and for women everywhere) or participation by those who were citizens in elections or office-holding.

With the winning of universal suffrage in the West at the beginning of the present century, democratic theory and practice turned to issues of democratic nation-building. The nationhood issue was raised by the aspiration to independence of the countries of the formerly colonized world. The assertion of national independence was reformulated in democratic terms by identifying democracy with the right to collective self-determination rather than with the actuality of self-government. Consequently, even where their newly formed internal governments were other than democratic, nations liberated from their

115

former colonial masters often declared themselves democracies or people's republics.

At the same time, the debate over democracy shifted from political questions to socioeconomic issues of production, distribution, property-holding, and class. The relationship between formal and legal equality and political democracy on the one hand, and systems of economic production and distribution on the other, have since that time come to dominate scholarly discussion as well as ideological politics. The 'people's democracies' of the second and third worlds assert their democratic legitimacy in the language of economics, pointing to their putatively egalitarian modes of ownership of capital, production and distribution, their guarantees of employment, and their devotion to public planning, while they neglect or even denigrate the role of multi-party electoral systems, political and legal rights, and parliamentary politics. The older democracies of the West, relying on traditional political and legal language, emphasize electoral and civic rights and the formal liberty and equality of the political system; if they associate democracy with economics it is only inasmuch as they hope to identify the freedom of the private market with the freedom of a democratic political regime, in the manner of Milton Friedman or Friedrich HAYEK.

This brief history indicates how controversial the idea of democracy has been from its earliest origins in classical Athens down to its most recent manifestation in East-West and North-South ideological politics. Indeed, even by the measure of a western political vocabulary that has been deeply contested, democracy has been marked by unprecedented ambivalence and dissent, arousing the fiercest philosophical and ideological debates. The issues that have emerged from these debates remain crucial to the politics and philosophy of modern democracy.

Among these basic issues are the following:

(1) *Who rules?* as a function of competing theories of human nature, and of citizenship;
(2) *Within what limits and scope?* as an aspect of the problem of limited and unlimited ('totalitarian') government and the proper extent of democratic rule;

(3) *In the name of which ends?* as an expression of the conflict between the individual and the community, or more generically between liberty (individual rights) and equality (social justice);
(4) *By direct or indirect means?* that is to say, by direct popular rule or through representative institutions? and with what impact on theories of 'elite-mass' relations?
(5) *Under which conditions and constraints?* as an encapsulation of the problem of the socioeconomic and cultural prerequisites of democracy; including (but not limited to) the class structure of society.

These questions need to be considered one at a time.

In answering the fundamental query as to who ought to govern in a just polity, theorists have long noticed the link between contradictory attitudes towards democracy and competing understandings of HUMAN NATURE. Democrats believe people possess the capacity for or can be educated to the arts of self-government; their critics believe people to be too base or too foolish to rule wisely. They must thus be subjected either to superior elements (aristocracy) or to abstract principle – reason, justice, law, or right, for example. Even thinkers such as J. S. MILL and John DEWEY accepted that democracy requires the subordination of the passionate element to the rational within individual citizens (which is the aim of civic education). In this way democrats seek to distinguish the rule of self-governing citizens from the rule of the masses (see CITIZENSHIP). In the words of JEFFERSON's memorable response to the political sceptics: 'If we think [the people] not enlightened enough to exercise their control with a wholesome discretion, the remedy is not to take it from them, but to inform their discretion.'

Current critics of democracy have been less concerned with civic competence than with the infernal logic of public choice, which raises serious problems for popular government. These include uncertainty about the nature of popular consent (does it entail a plurality? a majority? unanimity?), the difficulty of measuring intensity of feeling in egalitarian (one person one vote) electoral systems, and the paradoxes associated with attempting to rank preferences that cannot be hierarchically ordered by the logic of transitivity. The consequences of such problems are of crucial practical importance. Popular rule usually means the rule of a simple majority, but, as Rousseau noted, the interest of the majority may constitute the interest of a large faction rather than the interest of the whole. There may even be a disjunction between the interest of the whole, what Rousseau calls the will of all, and the GENERAL WILL or the public good. In modern terms, aggregating private interests may not produce a public interest (see INTERESTS). On the other hand, many post-war social scientists have accepted David Truman's contention that the idea of a public good is itself a myth, particularly in a representative democracy, where group politics creates a pluralist, polyarchal society (see PLURALISM).

Democracy can ordain the government of the active and interested (as Hannah ARENDT has suggested) or the government of everyone affected by government – the incompetent and apathetic no less than the educated and civic-minded. It can attempt to take into account the intensity of preferences through institutions that multiply the political effect of passionate convictions and heartfelt interests (primary elections, for example) or it can resist intensity altogether (requiring an absolute majority of the entire voting public, for example). The issue of transitivity in ranking preferences has been elevated through the work of Kenneth Arrow, Mancur Olson and other formal theorists into a critical dilemma of modern democracy (see POLITICAL THEORY).

These kinds of difficulties have suggested to theorists of rationality a certain internal incoherence in democracy. Others point out that such problems reveal weaknesses in formal rational choice paradigms and do not necessarily describe the politics of working citizen communities. At stake is the nature of RATIONALITY itself as it is defined from the perspective of competing theories of human nature. Both sides of the argument, however, assume the intimate link between democracy and theories of human nature, human reason, and human interests and motives.

The second major question that occupies democrats arises out of and reflects on the problem of who rules: namely, the question of the proper scope of democratic government. Because they understand government as an instrument of a competent citizenry for the achievement of public goods, proponents of democracy are prepared to extend the compass of government to a domain bounded only by the needs of the populace and the public good those needs disclose. Critics of democracy turn their inherent distrust of popular government into an argument for powerful constitutional limits on its scope. By limiting government's compass, an extended private sphere is preserved in which, they assert, liberty, property and conscience can be maintained. This critique of democracy associates a public domain of excessive scope with TOTALITARIANISM – the eradication of all boundaries between government and society.

These problems are related to the confrontation of liberals and democrats over the ends of democratic government, the third question arising out of the modern examination of democracy. For constitutional liberals who are democrats only to the extent of acknowledging the origin of government in popular consent, sovereignty can have as its end only the interests of the private individuals who constitute it. Behind this contractarian viewpoint lurks the distinction between government as a tool of liberty and property – of the rights of individuals – and government as a tool of equality and social justice, of a community that defines its members even as it is defined by them. The democratic paradox has been that government as the tool of individuals who are constituted in a community has appeared as the enemy of the rights of individuals. Both John Stuart Mill and Alexis de TOCQUEVILLE warned against the tyranny of an unbridled majority, a caveat that has haunted the fears of liberal critics of unlimited democracy from Ortega y Gasset to Karl Popper and Isaiah Berlin. 'Totalitarian democracy' has seemed to some of these critics to approach the oxymoronic.

This liberal fear of majoritarian tyranny has foundations in the palpable dangers of mass politics; nevertheless, democrats have responded that an educated and competent citizenry permitted to govern with due deliberation can insulate itself from such perils. 'Strong democracy' (see Barber) rooted in vigorous citizen participation can be distinguished from 'unitary' or totalistic democracy where the state is endowed with an abstract face defined by features such as race, blood, party, nation (*Volk*), or other such collectivist ideals.

Indeed the distinction between direct communitarian forms of rule and representative rule is the fourth area of concern in the examination of modern democracy. In its earlier historical manifestation, democracy was generally understood as a form of communal self-government that engaged the citizen body in direct legislation, popular assemblies, election by lottery, citizen-soldier military service, and other civic offices. The scale and complexity of modern society offer major obstacles to this classic form of participatory democracy. The invention of representative institutions can be viewed largely as a response to its apparent incompatibility with mass society (see REPRESENTATION). In America, the new constitution was organized around the prudent 'filter' of such devices as the Presidential electoral college, a Senate representing states rather than citizens, and an indirectly appointed Federal Court system. In Europe, too, representation brought in its train parliamentary styles of government, multi-party political systems and passive, privatized electorates. It rescued democracy from the scale of mass society, but it exacted a price.

An awareness that the device of representation interposes between the exercise of power and those to whom power is putatively accountable a widening gap that ultimately undermines democracy even in its weaker form underlay nineteenth-century theories of ELITISM. PARETO, MOSCA and MICHELS argued that democracy was often only a camouflage for the oligarchic tendencies of power, and that representation guaranteed little more than a circulation of ruling elites. Following in this tradition, Joseph SCHUMPETER defined democratic rule as a competition of elites through elections for the right to govern. In response Peter Bachrach and others have advanced the so-called 'neo-elitist' critique of democracy – a friendly 'progressive' critique worried about how easily money, property and power can manipulate representative institutions to the benefit of elites. Some of these same concerns

have sparked renewed interest in participation and community, initially from nostalgic admirers of the Greek *polis* such as Hannah Arendt, but also from students of Rousseau and Mill (Carole Pateman), the New England Town (Jane Mansbridge), communities of rational discourse (Jürgen Habermas), and civic participation and the new technologies that can facilitate citizen empowerment (Benjamin Barber). The contest between advocates of representative and participatory democracy raises questions for the survival of democratic institutions that are of grave importance; that the contest has been rejoined is a sign of the vigour of current democratic theory.

The final question that issues from the examination of democracy is also one of the most ancient. Students of government from Aristotle onwards have attempted to specify the conditions under which democracy is most successfully nurtured. Rousseau contended that it depended on special conditions, including a small state where citizens met face to face, great simplicity of manners, equality in rank and fortune, and an austerity of life and mores – conditions unlikely to be found in any but a handful of small-scale societies, such as the town republics and pastoral communes that graced the simpler world of ancient Greece or early modern Europe. In the presence of such conditions, democracy would seem almost inevitable; in their absence, no institutions, no contract, no constitution would be likely to preserve them. By these standards, modern mass society would appear to be a particularly inhospitable climate for democracy.

Recent social science has continued to explore the conditions that facilitate the growth of democracy. Gabriel Almond and Sidney Verba tried to extrapolate from the concrete historical experience of five democracies a set of indicators more favourable to its modern survival than Rousseau's stringent conditions. Seymour Martin Lipset offered a portrait of political man which aspired to capture something of the democratic personality – a mirror image of Theodor Adorno's authoritarian personality. This literature, classical and modern, yields a picture of democracy as an outgrowth of conditions of consensus, tolerance, a relatively peaceful, evolutionary history, and relative independence (if not autarky) that gives institutions and constitutions a secondary role in its emergence.

Perhaps most crucial among these conditions has been the socio-economic environment. Both classical economists and later Marxists perceived an intimate connection between patterns of class domination and patterns of government, between modes of production and distribution and modes of rulership. At the centre of the controversy were the relations between capitalism, socialism and democracy. Liberal democrats from Locke to Friedrich Hayek and Milton Friedman have focused on the role of liberty and free choice in democracy, and so have made capitalism's free market contractual relations both the model for and the necessary prerequisite of democratic political life. Egalitarian democrats from Rousseau to C. B. Macpherson have focused on the role of equality and social justice in democracy, and so have looked favourably upon public ownership and common goods as foundations for the political and legal equality on which democracy rests.

If this brief survey of the history and practice of democracy proves anything at all, it is that the democratic ideal remains one of the most cherished and at the same moment most contested of political ideals. Though it has failed as a practice to solve decisively the issues of social conflict and political justice to which it has been addressed, it continues as an aspiration to excite the hopes of humankind. For it remains, in Abraham Lincoln's phrase, a 'last best hope' for enlarging the sphere of common power in which human goods are achieved without diminishing the sphere of individual liberty in which human dignity is preserved.

BRB

Reading
Almond, G. and Verba, S.: *The Civic Culture*. Boston: Little, Brown, 1965.
Arendt, H.: *The Human Condition*. Chicago: University of Chicago Press, 1958.
Arrow, K.: *Social Choice and Individual Values*. New York: Wiley, 1951.
Bachrach, P.: *The Theory of Democratic Elitism*. Boston: Little, Brown, 1967.
†Barber, B.: *Strong Democracy*. Berkeley and Los Angeles: University of California Press, 1984.
†Dahl, R.: *Preface to Democratic Theory*. Chicago: University of Chicago Press, 1956.
Dewey, J.: *The Public and its Problems*. New York: Holt, 1927.
Habermas, J.: *The Theory of Communicative Action*. 2 vols. Boston: Beacon, 1984 and 1986.
Lipset, S.M.: *Political Man*. New York: Doubleday, 1960.
†Lively, J.: *Democracy*. Oxford: Blackwell, 1975.
†Macpherson, C.B.: *Democratic Theory*. Oxford: Clarendon Press, 1973.
†Pateman, C.: *Participation and Democratic Theory*. Cambridge: Cambridge University Press, 1970.
Schumpeter, J.: *Capitalism, Socialism and Democracy*, 5th edn. London: Allen & Unwin, 1976.

democratic centralism A doctrine developed originally by LENIN which subsequently passed into the canon of SOVIET COMMUNISM, democratic centralism combined two theses. First, the membership of each body in the political hierarchy (whether of party or state) was to be selected by the vote of the body below. Second, although free discussion on policy matters was to be encouraged at the stage of inception, once a decision had been reached by the highest body it was to be imposed rigidly at all lower levels in the hierarchy. Democratic centralism was thus hostile to any idea of political PLURALISM.   DLM

despotism Since the end of the eighteenth century the term despotism has been conflated with tyranny in western languages. As terms for governments with unlimited power, they have been joined or supplanted by ABSOLUTISM, dictatorship (in the modern, Bonapartist sense), and TOTALITARIANISM. But for two millennia despotism and tyranny were the distinctive regime types designating the total political domination of subjects by a single person. Today, both terms have been reduced to vague synonyms connoting arbitrary and coercive rule incompatible with political liberty, constitutional government, and the RULE OF LAW.

To retrieve the meanings once carried by despotism, its history must be studied in terms of its four most important phases:

(1) in classical Greek theory as summarized by ARISTOTLE;
(2) in early modern political thought of the sixteenth and seventeenth centuries, particularly that of BODIN, GROTIUS, PUFENDORF, HOBBES, and LOCKE;

(3) in the second half of the eighteenth century, when because of MONTESQUIEU's prestige despotism often replaced tyranny as the regime type designating vitiated or evil monarchies;

(4) in the nineteenth and twentieth centuries, when theorists such as de TOCQUEVILLE, J. S. MILL, HEGEL, MARX, and Wittfogel found new uses for despotism in their respective frameworks.

Throughout its history, despotism has with few exceptions carried pejorative associations derived from the Eurocentric perspective of its users. The one ostensible exception, the 'enlightened despotism' of certain eighteenth-century rulers, turns out to have been invented by nineteenth-century German historians in search of a respectable genealogy for Prussian monarchy.

(1) As a political concept, despotism first appeared during the wars of the fifth century BC between the Hellenes and the Persian Achaemenid Empire. It was ARISTOTLE who developed the concept most fully and contrasted it to tyranny. These were the two forms of rule that treated subjects as slaves. Despotism, or barbaric monarchy, was characteristic of Asian barbarians who, because they were slaves by nature, submitted willingly to an absolute ruler who alone was free. Such Asian empires were described as extensive and long-lived. Stable because resting upon tacit consent, they were governed by law and followed hereditary principles of succession. Aristotle's concept derived from three polar oppositions: between Hellenes and barbarians; freemen masters and natural slaves; Europeans and Asians. His most significant conclusion was that because of their superiority in mind and spirit Hellenes were meant to govern barbarians. Thus despotism became the first concept used by Europeans in an adversary anthropology that grouped together all Asian governments under the same pejorative category. This derived much of its force from the meanings of *despotēs*: (a) the head of a household; (b) a master of slaves; (c) a barbarian king ruling his subjects like slaves. Despotism was normal for Asians; tyranny was pathological for Greeks.

Tyranny both resembled and differed from despotism. Aristotle tended to restrict the use of tyranny to the usurpation of power in a *polis* by an individual using deception or force. This was characteristically done through employing a mercenary bodyguard of aliens. Traditionally, tyrants were said to rule exclusively in their own interest, to indulge their appetites, to disregard custom and law, and to base their power upon compulsion. Aristotle thought tyrannies were inherently unstable, because of the hatred inspired by coercive rule over resentful former citizens accustomed to ruling themselves.

The concept of tyranny was far more important than that of despotism in western political thought from the Roman period until the eighteenth century. It generated theories of justified resistance and even tyrannicide. Throughout the Middle Ages tyranny remained the most widely used term for the evil or usurped rule of a single person. But as the result of translations from Aristotle, the concept of despotism did not disappear entirely.

(2) By the sixteenth century conditions both within Europe and outside led to shifts in the meaning and prominence of despotism as a political concept. The assumption of European superiority found new applications, sometimes combined with belief in the civilizing mission of Christianity. Aristotelianism, revived once again, was applied by Sepúlveda to the debate among the Spanish conquerors about the justice of enslaving Indians. European travellers often carried with them Aristotle's classifications and invidious polarities on their voyages of exploration. Sovereignty, slavery and colonial conquest were justified by theories of despotism adapted in various forms by Bodin, Grotius, Pufendorf, Hobbes, and Locke. Bodin first incorporated into political theory new uses of despotism by using ROMAN LAW arguments justifying slavery, conquest, and seizure of property as a matter of right by victors in a JUST WAR. Grotius and Pufendorf certified as legitimate enslavement consented to by either a servile or a conquered people. Hobbes defined despotical dominion as power acquired by the consent of the conquered; this was an alternative to commonwealth by acquisition. Conquerors providing peace and union ought to be obeyed. Locke distinguished political from despotical power, defined by him as that of a

lord over such as are stripped of all rights because they have forfeited them in unjust war. Finally, civic humanists such as Algernon Sidney followed MACHIAVELLI in asserting that European republics produced better soldiers with greater *virtú* than did the governments of Asia and Africa. Once again, it seemed that free states could and should rule those lesser peoples unaccustomed to liberty.

(3) In the seventeenth and eighteenth centuries French aristocratic and Huguenot critics of Louis XIV first took the momentous step of applying the concept of despotism to a European state. This did not involve forgoing its former usage as a pejorative category for all near-, middle-, and far-eastern governments. Rather the new strategy entailed condemning domestic policies as identical with practices long attributed to oriental despotism. Montesquieu's *Lettres persanes* (1722) epitomized this mode of tacit attack upon the absolutism, centralization, bureaucracy, and religious persecution of Louis XIV. Thus 'despotism', now conceived as the importation of Asian government alien to ancient French constitutional tradition, became a potent weapon of the opposition groups led by Fénélon, Saint-Simon, and Boulainvillier. After the revocation of the Edict of Nantes, Huguenots also turned to the concept of despotism, as in *Les Soupirs de la France esclave*.

The salience of despotism as a regime type in the second half of the eighteenth century was largely due to Montesquieu's innovation. In his *De l'esprit des lois* (1748), he made despotism into one of the three basic types of government, and relegated 'tyranny' to a lesser place, related only to republics, aristocratic and democratic, Montesquieu's second type. At the centre of Montesquieu's analysis was his own stipulated definition of monarchy: constitutional, sharing power with intermediate groups, and based on the separation of powers. Despotism, defined as the alternative type of regime headed by a single person, became the other part of a binary opposition.

Montesquieu defined despotism, like the other two types, in terms of its nature (or structure) and its principle (or operative passion). The structure of a despotism consists of the despot, ruling through his viziers or ministers, who exercises virtually complete power over subjects, equal in that they and all property belong to the despot. As for the principle of despotism, it requires that all subjects must be so obsessed by fear that they obey completely and passively. Montesquieu concluded that despotism was a system natural to the Orient, but foreign and dangerous to European monarchy – that just and free order most appropriate to modern commercial states. Unlike early modern theorists of despotism, Montesquieu called into question all justifications of slavery, conquest, and colonial domination by Europeans.

Once the concept of despotism had been applied to European regimes by Montesquieu, it menaced the legitimacy of all absolute monarchies and those that aspired to become such. Montesquieu's enormous prestige thus placed the concept of despotism at the centre of political theory in the second half of the eighteenth century. Almost everyone writing about politics felt compelled to attack or defend Montesquieu's typology and the evidence he presented for his conclusions about the despotism of Asian governments. At issue was the case for applying the concept of despotism to European absolute monarchies. Their defenders could argue, as did VOLTAIRE, that Montesquieu had distorted evidence, and even worse, constructed a regime type of which there were no examples in Asia or elsewhere. In fact, many features of Asian government – as, for example, the Chinese Empire – were worth imitating. But the concept of despotism, applied both in the reformist sense Montesquieu advocated, and in revolutionary senses he would have repudiated, enjoyed great popularity both before and during the French Revolution.

(4) As politics and society were reconstructed between 1789 and 1815, some theorists such as CONSTANT began to feel that both despotism and tyranny were outmoded regime types applicable only to the *ancien régime*. Tocqueville followed Constant in considering these classifications as 'old words' inapplicable to the new egalitarian society he called democratic. Yet in diagnosing the dangers to liberty posed

by democracy, Tocqueville referred to 'democratic' and 'legislative despotism', as well as the 'tyranny of the majority'.

Both Hegel and Marx found uses for the concept of oriental despotism, as a common term for societies that otherwise diverged in their civilizations and experiences. For both, despotism retained its negative connotations, to which they added the notion of stagnation, as opposed to progressive development. Hegel described the movement of history as travelling from East to West. Despotism was the first stage of history; its final goal was monarchy in Europe, most exactly in Prussia. The unchanging East knows that only one is free, the despot; the progressive West knows that all are free. Thus oriental civilization has remained at the first world-historical phase. Marx also treated oriental societies as identical and unchanging. This he attributed to their shared mode of production and consequent political organization. In the first human mode of production, the 'Asian', Marx asserted, there was no private property in land. Rather a despotic centralized state power executed indispensable public works such as irrigation. Asiatic society was based on self-sufficient villages, which preserved the unchanging nature of the mode of production. The Orient could be brought into the progressive conflicts of the world capitalist economy only by European colonial expansion. 'England has to fulfil a double mission in India: one destructive, the other regenerating – the annihilation of old Asiatic society, and the laying of the material foundation of Western society in Asia' (Avineri, pp. 132–3). Using another political economy and concept of liberty, British utilitarians such as James and J. S. Mill shared many of the assumptions made by Hegel and Marx.

In the twentieth century, Karl Wittfogel has constructed a renovated theory of oriental despotism and applied it to the Soviet Union. Two aspects of his work have aroused interest: first, the attempt to establish a distinctive non-western system of despotic power, documented by extensive research and based upon a general theory much altered from its Marxist beginnings. Second, Wittfogel has interpreted 'communist totalitarianism as a total managerial, and much more despotic variant' of oriental despotism.

Another recent application of the concept of despotism comes in Kolakowski's *Main Currents of Marxism*, when he treats the origins of 'despotic forms of socialism'. He concludes that if there is a technique for establishing social unity, 'then despotism is a natural solution of the problem inasmuch as it is the only known technique for the purpose' (Kolakowski, vol. I, pp. 419–20). Here there is no reference to the eastern origins of despotism. But much recent discussion has been devoted to pejorative images of the Orient long associated with the concept of despotism. Intense controversy has centred around 'Orientalism' as treated by Edward Said, a presentation focused on the nineteenth and twentieth centuries, but curiously unhistorical in its neglect of the history and functions of despotism as regime type and political concept.   MR

Reading

Anderson, P.: *Lineages of the Absolute State*. London: New Left, 1974.

Aristotle: *The Politics*, ed. E. Barker. Oxford: Clarendon Press, 1946.

Avineri, S.: *Karl Marx on Colonialism and Modernization*. New York: Anchor, 1969.

Hay, D.: *Europe*. Edinburgh: Edinburgh University Press, 1968.

†Koebner, R.: Despot and despotism. *Journal of the Warburg and Courtauld Institutes* 14 (1951) 275–302.

Kolakowski, L.: *Main Currents of Marxism*. 3 vols. Oxford: Clarendon Press, 1978.

Marshall, P.J. and Williams, G.: *The Great Map of Mankind*. London: Dent, 1982.

†Richter, M.: Despotism. In *Dictionary of the History of Ideas*, ed. P.P. Wiener, vol. II. New York: Scribners, 1973.

———: *The Political Theory of Montesquieu*. Cambridge: Cambridge University Press, 1977.

Wittfogel, K.: *Oriental Despotism*. New Haven, Conn.: Yale University Press, 1957.

Dewey, John (1859–1952) American philosopher and educator. A reformer, critic and educator, Dewey was, above all, the most important American philosopher of his day. Born in Vermont, he graduated from that state's university and, after a short period as a public school teacher, went to the Johns Hopkins University to study philosophy. At Hopkins, Dewey undertook an intensive reading of

HEGEL and although, like Marx, he felt that Hegel too little valued the world of action and practice, he attributed to Hegel's account of the unified nature of human culture much of his own subsequent and lifelong opposition to the separation of theory from practice or knowing from doing. Earning his doctor's degree, Dewey went to the University of Michigan, next moving to the University of Chicago when it opened in 1893. During his time at Chicago, he founded the University Elementary School, more generally known as the Laboratory or Dewey School. In 1905 he joined Columbia University in New York City and remained a member of its faculty until his retirement in 1929.

Continuing to publish widely in philosophy and on public affairs, active in encouraging a third-party movement during the 1930s, and the most respected critic of the New Deal, Dewey earned a reputation as 'the guide, the mentor, and the conscience of the American people' (Commager, p. 100). This broader public reputation was largely due to the ease with which Dewey combined, in a manner more typical of philosophy in the nineteenth than in the twentieth century, the philosopher's passion for a comprehensive, because unified, account of human experience and the reformer's delight in solving the more particular problems of men. Insisting that these were complementary activities, Dewey's writings vary from formal works on logic, ethics, and aesthetics, complemented by numerous books on education and politics, to frequent columns for such journals as *The New Republic*.

Esteemed along with Charles Peirce and William James as the founder of pragmatism, Dewey is most responsible for the wider reputation that pragmatism enjoys as a philosophy for everyday experience. Denying that philosophy had any special claim to a knowledge that transcends the ordinary world of practical activity, Dewey sought to establish new and vital links between the two worlds of ideas and experience. Instrumentalism, his version of pragmatism, argues that theories and concepts are mainly tools for guiding action, that rationality is fundamentally a process of trial-and-error activity, and that the spread of this more experimental and practical intelligence is the key to resolving social conflicts. This same confidence in experimentalism also made him a naturalist in ethics. Moral choices, he argued, are no different from other practical judgments about how best to cope with some problematic experience so as to transform or reconstruct the experience in a more satisfactory direction.

Critical to Dewey's pragmatism is this sense of people trying to make their way in the world. Pragmatism is practical but not in the crude sense of celebrating whatever is useful. Rather, it is about the differences that intelligent action or enlightened practice make for a life of choice and freedom. Dewey's enemies were outmoded habits, oppressive routines, fixed ideas, rigid disciplines: all of which cramp experience and empty it of the creativity and satisfaction that enrich life. Typical of Dewey's faith in a life of creative intelligence is his defence of knowing and moral judgment as a continuous process of self-correction through practical action.

No amount of pains taken in forming a purpose in a definite case is final; the consequences of its adoption must be carefully noted, and a purpose held only as a working hypothesis until results confirm its rightness. Mistakes . . . are lessons in wrong methods of using intelligence and instructions as to a better course in the future. They are indications of the need of revision, development, readjustment . . . The end is no longer a terminus or limit to be reached. It is the active process of transforming the existent situation. Not perfection as a final goal, but the ever-enduring process of perfecting, maturing, refining is the aim in living . . . Growth itself is the only moral 'end' (*Reconstruction in Philosophy*, p. 177).

This commitment to a conception of knowledge and ethics as arts of social engineering made Dewey an especially harsh critic of all previous philosophy. In *The Quest for Certainty* (1929) he attributed philosophy's remoteness from the 'problems of men' to its mistaken search for fixed truths. In contrast, Dewey championed a reconstruction of philosophy that treats ideas as a guide to action, and the consequences of the action undertaken as the final confirmation or test of the idea's meaning. This pragmatic insistence that consequences count in measuring the worth of an idea has often been criticized as excessively practical and even anti-intellectual. But in a larger sense, it was part of Dewey's effort to replace the notion of philosophy as the 'quest for certainty' with an image of philosophy as the articulation of an intelligent method for resolving social conflicts.

As an educator, Dewey carried forward his opposition to any separation of knowing and doing, reflection and problem-solving. He constantly opposed that 'spectator' theory of knowledge that condemned students to a passive role in the classroom. While often criticized for celebrating the student's interest at the expense of a more formal curriculum, Dewey never wavered from his belief that education, indeed all modes of experience, should equip the individual with those dispositions and that understanding necessary to overcome problems as they arise.

When writing about politics, Dewey warned Americans that many of their ideas about liberalism, individualism, and economic freedom had failed to keep up with current conditions. Sympathetic to socialism, relentlessly opposed to any form of bigotry, critical of what is now often termed democratic elitism, impatient with the New Deal's cautious approach to economic problems, Dewey celebrated a more expansive and demanding understanding of DEMOCRACY as a way of life. In *Freedom and Culture* (1939) and other political writings, he often compared the democratic public to a community of inquirers and the democratic method to scientific method. Both pragmatism and democracy were understood by this very practical philosopher as a way of life for the co-operative reconstruction of experience in the common interest. Often criticized for being more imaginative about method than about the ends of life, Dewey always insisted that there was no real difference between intelligent action and a life lived well.　　AJD

Reading

†Bernstein, R.J.: *Praxis and Action*. Philadelphia: University of Pennsylvania Press, 1971.

†Cahn, S.M. ed.: *New Studies in the Philosophy of John Dewey*. Hanover, NH: University Press of New England, 1977.

Commager, H.S.: *The American Mind: an Interpretation of American Thought and Character since the 1880s*. New Haven, Conn.: Yale University Press, 1950.

†Damico, A.J.: *Individuality and Community: the Social and Political Thought of John Dewey*. Gainesville, Fla.: University of Florida Press, 1978.

Dewey, J.: *Democracy and Education* (1916). New York: Free Press, Macmillan, 1966.

———: *Reconstruction in Philosophy*. Boston: Beacon, 1957.

———: *On Experience, Nature, and Freedom*, ed. R.J. Bernstein. Indianapolis: Bobbs-Merrill, 1960.

———: *The Quest for Certainty*. New York: Putnam, Capricorn, 1960.

———: *Freedom and Culture*. New York: Putnam, Capricorn, 1963.

dialectic Originally understood as a method of reasoning, complementary to formal logic. In the dialogues of SOCRATES, for instance, the method consists primarily in rebutting various theses by showing that they lead to logical contradictions, until finally only one alternative is left holding the field. As a political idea, dialectic is important mainly for its use by HEGEL and MARX.

Hegel's use of dialectic seeks to arrive at truth by starting with a relatively primitive concept and demonstrating that it implies its opposite. From the juxtaposition of two such contradictory ideas, a new and more adequate notion emerges. This process is repeated until a completely adequate concept is reached. Because of Hegel's IDEALISM, this structure of thought was also held to be the structure of reality itself. Thus history exhibited a dialectical pattern of development, and the state could be understood only as a highly complex institution formed from the synthesis of contradictory elements at a number of different levels of social life.

Marx claimed to have taken over and 'inverted' Hegel's dialectical method, but the sense in which he did so remains controversial. Like his mentor he detected a dialectical pattern in history, but whereas for Hegel the relationships of contradiction and synthesis held between concepts embodied in human practices, Marx found them in material reality (thus he identified 'contradictions' between the forces and relations of production at certain moments in history; see MARXISM). Marx also held that his method of analysis was dialectical, meaning among other things that the concepts employed had a fluidity that corresponded to the transient quality of the reality they sought to depict. But whereas the content of Hegel's thought is hard to detach from its dialectical manner of presentation, Marx's major theses survive such detachment with relative ease. It is questionable, therefore, whether his thinking was dialectical in any very profound sense.

DLM

Reading

Norman, R. and Sayers, S.: *Hegel, Marx and Dialectic.* Brighton, Sussex: Harvester, 1980.

dialectical materialism The philosophy of MARXISM, as developed by Marx's successors, especially in Germany and the Soviet Union. It embodies two central assumptions: first, the primacy of matter, all mental processes being seen as ultimately derivative from material processes; second, the dialectical character of all processes, whether natural or human, expressed in three laws: the transformation of quantity into quality, the unity of opposites, and the negation of the negation (see DIALECTIC).

Dialectical materialism implies that the same cognitive procedures should be used in the human as in the natural sciences, a thesis stemming from ENGELS's work on the dialectics of nature. Later Marxists, including LUKÁCS and members of the Frankfurt School (see CRITICAL THEORY), rejected this doctrine as a form of POSITIVISM, and argued that only interactions between human subjects and the material world displayed a dialectical character.

DLM

Reading

Jordan, Z.A.: *The Evolution of Dialectical Materialism.* London: Macmillan; New York: St Martin's, 1967.

Dicey, Albert Venn (1835–1922) British jurist. Dicey is best known for his classic treatise on constitutional law, *Introduction to the Study of the Law of the Constitution* (1885) and for his *Lectures on the Relation between Law and Public Opinion in England during the Nineteenth Century* (1905). He read classics as an undergraduate at Balliol College, Oxford, and after a fellowship at Trinity College and practice at the Bar he was elected in 1882 to the Vinerian Professorship of English Law. His first published work was a short study of the Privy Council, but he wrote

also on the conflict of laws and later in life published a number of works on Irish Home Rule (which he opposed). Amongst these were *England's Case against Home Rule* (1886) and *A Leap in the Dark* (1893). In 1920, shortly before his death, he published with R. S. Rait *Thoughts on the Union between England and Scotland.*

Dicey's professional career appears not to have given him any great satisfaction; he seems to have felt some frustration at his failure to realize ambitions for a career in politics or on the Bench. His reputation was, however, securely enough founded on his law teaching and on his two major works, which although much criticized over the years stand out as masterpieces of critical exposition.

The Law of the Constitution deals with what its author called the two or three guiding principles which pervade the modern constitution of England. These were the sovereignty of Parliament, the RULE OF LAW, and the co-existence of law with constitutional convention. Dicey edited himself eight editions of his text between 1885 and 1923 and they included, besides the main themes, many short discussions of other topics (for example the right of public meeting, freedom of discussion, ministerial responsibility, the referendum, martial law, and the civil duties of the army).

Criticism of Dicey in the twentieth century has centred on his so-called Whig views on governmental discretion and his alleged misunderstanding of the French administrative law system. After a long period of Conservative governmental discretion it may be, however, that Dicey's views on the rule of law will enjoy a popular revival.

Dicey's exposition of parliamentary sovereignty and the role of constitutional convention have met with less criticism, though there has been much discussion in recent times of the implications of his analysis in new situations which Dicey could not have foreseen (for example in Commonwealth constitutions). A particular point of controversy has concerned the question whether a sovereign legislature as described by Dicey in the United Kingdom is legally capable of protecting its own legislation from repeal by enacting a special manner and form for legislation of special importance.

Many who have found fault with Dicey's views have nonetheless had much to say in his favour. James Bryce said of him that he had the power of bringing out certain main points with perfect clearness and convincing force; and Harold Laski called him 'the most considerable figure in English jurisprudence since Maitland'.

GM

Reading

†Cosgrove, R.A.: *Albert Venn Dicey, Victorian Jurist.* Macmillan: London, 1981.

Dicey, A.V.: *Introduction to the Study of the Law of the Constitution*, 10th edn. London: Macmillan, 1959.

———: *Lectures on the Relation between Law and Public Opinion in England during the Nineteenth Century*, 2nd edn. London: Macmillan, 1914.

†Lawson, F.H.: Dicey revisited. *Political Studies* 7 (1959) 109–26 and 207–21.

Rait, R.S. ed.: *Memorials of A.V. Dicey*. London: Macmillan, 1925.

dictatorship of the proletariat A phrase used occasionally by MARX, and more frequently by LENIN, to refer to the period immediately following a proletarian revolution, during which the working class would use the power of the state to suppress the capitalist class and create a socialist economy. See MARXISM.

Diderot, Denis (1713–1784) French philosopher. Diderot wrote no systematic work of political theory, and the writings in which he deals with the problems of politics are often constructed in a dialogue form which makes it difficult to determine which of the opinions expounded are those of the author. However, with the aid of Diderot's published correspondence, and various works which have been identified as his only in recent years, it is possible to trace a certain evolution of his political thinking in the context of his experience and the events of his time.

As a young man, Diderot seems to have been the disciple of Francis BACON as much in his politics as in his philosophy. The *Encyclopédie* (1751–65), the major work of Diderot's career, was dedicated to the idea of salvation through science. The conquest of nature through planned and collective empirical research was a project designed to improve the life of man on earth, and a strong centralized government was called for to put the programme into action. 'Enlightened despotism' is the usual name for this policy, but it is not altogether an exact one, because Diderot, even more than VOLTAIRE, had a sincere belief in individual freedom, and did not think it need be lost under wise absolutist rule. But, undoubtedly, he at one period in his life joined Mercier de la Rivière in calling for an all-powerful regime of experts which would leave no room for politics.

Diderot's way of thinking was 'dialectical', in the sense that having once completed the exposition of an argument, he set about refuting it. Like Voltaire and most of the *Encyclopédistes* he dreamed of himself becoming a philosopher at the side of a mighty monarch, controlling the mind of a sovereign with the power to control a whole kingdom. But when Diderot was actually given the chance to enact such a role, he promptly refused it. Catherine the Great, having read his books, invited him to St Petersburg to advise her on reforms. He sent Mercier de la Rivière instead. Then, when she finally prevailed on him to go in person, Diderot did his utmost to persuade the Empress to divest herself of her absolute sovereignty, and share it with a parliament.

Faced with an 'enlightened despot' Diderot overthrew his old Baconian politics, and set forth in essays and memoranda designed for the eyes of the Empress Catherine arguments which echoed those of MONTESQUIEU. Liberty, that most precious of all values, he argued, depended on a balance of power; the monarch should keep in permanent existence a legislative body to prevent the executive from lapsing unchecked into despotism. Catherine smiled on Diderot, but rejected his advice. Paradoxically, Diderot also told her that her empire was so backward that philosophers could not be of any help to her; in Russia, modernization should come first, conversations with the philosophers afterwards.

Diderot returned to France with political views which were rather to the left of most of the *Encyclopédistes* (see FRENCH ENLIGHTENMENT). He had never shared Voltaire's devotion to the idea of a natural right to property. Diderot was a poor man, with an acute sympathy for the workers. He opposed the physiocratic policy of economic *laissez-faire* because the removal of controls on the grain trade made food more costly for the lower classes. He bitterly attacked the imperialist and colonial policies of the European governments, partly because he considered the culture of the 'noble savage' far superior to the Christian culture which the imperialists tried to propagate among them, and partly because he believed that Europeans were wrong to impose their alien rule or their alien presence on communities which had a right to their own independence. With arguments such as these, Diderot separated himself from the fashionable progressive opinion of the Enlightenment that the spread of the more advanced European civilization into backward parts of the world was a useful step towards the ultimate triumph of science. Diderot's thought was less typical of the eighteenth century than any other Enlightenment thinker's; his views on politics, as on other matters, were well ahead of his time.   MC

Reading

Diderot, D.: *Le neveu de Rameau* (1820); *Rameau's Nephew*, trans. L. Tancock. Harmondsworth: Penguin, 1966.

————: *Selected Writings*, ed. L.G. Crocker. New York: Macmillan; London: Collier-Macmillan, 1966.

†France, P.: *Diderot*. Oxford: Oxford University Press, 1983.

†Mason, J.H.: *The Irresistible Diderot*. London: Quartet, 1982.

†Strugnell, A.: *Diderot's Politics*. The Hague: Martinus Nijhoff, 1973.

Diggers See LEVELLERS.

direct action A form of civil disobedience in which participants attempt to achieve their goal directly – e.g. by physically obstructing the carrying out of an objectionable policy – rather than by political lobbying or symbolic protest. See CIVIL DISOBEDIENCE.

discrimination In its most general sense the perception of a difference, a differentiation, or different treatment. In this morally neutral sense discrimination in certain circumstances may be required by the Aristotelian principle of JUSTICE, which tells us to treat like cases alike and different cases differently. For example, a teacher who fails to discriminate between an excellent and a poor student may be unfair to both.

But according to the most common social use of the term, discrimination violates the first clause of Aristotle's rule by treating persons differently when there are no morally relevant differences between them. In this sense discrimination occurs when social benefits and burdens are awarded according to criteria that are irrelevant to any legitimate purposes. Often such criteria are more unfair in appealing to inborn traits, although this is not always so, since we speak also of discrimination against the poor. Nor is all differentiation according to inborn traits unfair: a father is expected to favour his own children, for example. But unfair discrimination is made more so when its victims cannot aim their efforts at achieving the social benefits being distributed.

Most discrimination has been directed at members of groups defined by race, sex, or national origin. Individuals are considered only as members of such groups, which are singled out systematically for inferior treatment and opportunities. Sometimes such characteristics are thought to be correlated with others relevant to the benefits in question; but always these assumptions are false or irrelevant to individual cases. Discrimination of this sort forms an invidious pattern in education, housing, career opportunities, etc. It may be overt and legally sanctioned or more subtle and merely *de facto*, as when school districts are based on segregated geographical boundaries or when tests irrelevant to the performance of a job disproportionately eliminate black or female applicants.

Multiple wrongs are involved in such practices. First, the criteria applied in awarding benefits and burdens may serve no legitimate purpose and may be unrelated to the utility of assigning jobs according to qualifications. Second, as mentioned, race and sex are biologically determined and are therefore beyond the control of the individual. But these are not the only or even the main wrongs: criteria that do relate to probable performance on the job may be discriminatory if that performance is likely to be negatively affected by the prejudices of clients or customers. Similarly, discriminatory legislation may be irrational in being antithetical to the legislative aims in question; but it may be morally worse when the aim is to discriminate. The most serious wrong is that members of certain groups are assigned inferior status in society generally, that they are denied full moral status as persons with all the rights of other persons. Discriminatory attitudes are often deeply entrenched and manifested in interconnected ways so as to create fixed strata in society, which would be wrong no matter how individuals were assigned to the lower classes (see Wasserstrom).

Proposed remedies for discrimination have included programmes of preferential treatment or reverse discrimination for members of groups previously victimized. Reverse discrimination (also known as positive discrimination) utilizes criteria equally unrelated to performance in order to reverse prior patterns of discrimination. It may be directed at all members of groups such as blacks or women, or only at individual victims of previous discrimination. Its purported justification may appeal to utility or social harmony, to the creation of more equal opportunities, or to compensation for past wrongs.

If the justification is utilitarian, then backlash from resentment of the policy creates uncertainties. The policy may, for example, produce more disharmony than harmony. If the aim is compensatory, then it must be determined to whom compensation is owed and whether those owed will be repaid proportionately to their past injuries. It is not initially clear whether compensation is owed only to direct victims of overt discrimination, or to all those who have suffered indirectly (for instance from lack of motivation), or to some yet broader group. If the goal is equal opportunity, then proponents must determine when opportunities are relevantly equal, what is necessary for achieving such equality, and how rights to equal opportunity are to be balanced against others with which they may clash, for example the rights of those presently most qualified for the positions in question. It is usually assumed that equal opportunity entails awarding positions to those most qualified to perform in them. This assumption ignores the demand for equal opportunity to acquire qualifications. It may be that creation of more equal opportunities of the latter sort requires overriding the normal criterion for awarding positions in the short run (see EQUALITY).

In the United States some programmes aiming to correct past patterns of discrimination go under the name of Affirmative Action. Some of these have been ordered by courts after findings of discrimination; others have been instituted voluntarily; still others by executive order. Some involve preference or reverse discrimination; others do not, at least not overtly. Controversy centres on whether these programmes are preferential when they establish goals and timetables for inclusion of members of minority groups.   AHG

Reading

Babcock, B., Freedman, A., Norton, E. and Ross, S.: *Sex Discrimination and the Law: Causes and Remedies*. Boston: Little, Brown, 1975.

Baldwin, J.: *Notes of a Native Son*. Boston: Beacon, 1955.

Deckard, B.S.: *The Women's Movement*. New York: Harper & Row, 1979.

†Fullinwider, R.K.: *The Reverse Discrimination Controversy*. Totowa, NJ: Rowman & Littlefield, 1980.

†Goldman, A.H.: *Justice and Reverse Discrimination*. Princeton, NJ: Princeton University Press, 1979.

Millett, K.: *Sexual Politics*. Garden City, NY: Doubleday, 1970.

Wasserstrom, R.: *Philosophy and Social Issues: five studies* chs 1 and 2. Notre Dame, Ind.: University of Notre Dame Press.

Willhelm, S.M.: *Black in a White America*. Cambridge, Mass.: Schenkman, 1983.

Woodward, C.V.: *The Strange Career of Jim Crow*. New York: Oxford University Press, 1974.

divine right of kings   Divine right theories, which first appeared in the late sixteenth century, combined three essential theses: the authority of monarchs had been ordained by God for the benefit of mankind; their sovereignty was unlimited and indivisible (though they were morally bound to follow divine law); and all resistance to their commands was illegitimate. See ABSOLUTISM and PATRIARCHALISM.   DLM

Reading

Allen, J.W.: *A History of Political Thought in the*

Sixteenth Century, pt III, ch. 7. London: Methuen, 1960.

Donation of Constantine A late eighth-century forged document, probably of the Roman curia, meant to establish beyond doubt the legality of the pope's claim to central Italy and the western Roman provinces. It argued that Constantine, on his own conversion to Christianity in the early fourth century, had given the empire to the pope to govern, recognizing the spiritual overlordship of the church already implicit in his conversion. Constantine then removed himself to Byzantium (Constantinople). The story was based on an earlier legend telling how Pope Sylvester not only baptized Constantine but also miraculously cured him of leprosy, and in gratitude Constantine relinquished rule over Rome to the pope. Since the pope's city was the capital of the old Roman empire, whoever succeeded to its rule could claim the temporal, universal authority of the Caesars. By the fourteenth century this document would be recognized as the forgery it was and this was confirmed by Valla in the fifteenth century. (See MEDIEVAL POLITICAL THOUGHT.)   JC

Durkheim, Émile (1858–1917) French sociologist. A founding father of modern sociology, Durkheim taught first in Bordeaux, then in Paris, establishing sociology as an academic discipline. He founded a productive and wide-ranging sociological school, grouped around the *Année sociologique* (12 volumes, 1898–1912), and had a wide cultural and political influence in France, especially via primary school teachers who studied under him and his students and transmitted his ideas for generations. He wrote bold, original and pioneering works across a wide range that are still influential within sociology, social anthropology and elsewhere and that mark out a distinctive Durkheimian method and world view.

He saw sociology as offering extraordinary explanatory potential and as occupying the central position among the social sciences. Its object was a distinct reality, which was constraining and external to individuals but also (as he came increasingly to stress) internalized

within them. Its method was also distinct and set out in his *Rules of Sociological Method* (1895). There he developed the case for a social science that is absolutely objective, with its own specific reality and autonomous of non-scientific influences. Whether his sociological practice matched his account of it is another question.

To demonstrate sociology's possibilities, Durkheim sought to explore the limits of social determination. So in his classic study of *Suicide* (1897) he aimed to explain variations in the rate at which people commit this apparently most private and individual of acts in terms of social causes. In doing so, he offered a diagnosis of his own society that is reproduced and developed elsewhere in his work: there was, he argued, a breakdown in social integration and regulation, a condition of egoism and ANOMIE that led some to the extreme of suicide. This resulted from the rapidity of industrialization and from the corrosion of older normative frameworks, and had its impact in economic, industrial and domestic life. Durkheim saw it as 'abnormal', relative to the stage modern societies had reached and in relation to their 'conditions of existence' – that is, to the requirements of their harmonious functioning.

He spoke of those requirements as 'organic solidarity' – a notion elaborated in *The Division of Labour in Society* (1893, second edition 1902). Pre-modern societies (both tribal and traditional) were held together by 'mechanical solidarity', in which the principle of resemblance predominated, with segmental social structures, little interdependence, low population volume and density, repressive penal law and a highly developed and intense *conscience collective* that attached supreme value to society as a whole and its interests. By contrast, modern societies 'normally' cohered around the division of labour, with organized social structures, with fused markets and the growth of cities, involving interdependence, with high population volume and density, the prevalence of restitutive law, and an increasingly humane and secular belief-system, setting a high value on the individual and invoking equality of opportunity, the work ethic and social justice. He called this last the 'religion of individualism', seeing it as functional to the integration of modern societies, but capable of being threatened by atavistic social forces, as during the Dreyfus Affair (he was a strong Dreyfusard) and by the Germans in 1914 (he was a strong French patriot).

From this diagnosis, he drew various conclusions. Given their diversity and dynamism, a certain rate of suicide and crime was 'normal' in modern societies, even a 'factor in social health'. But he favoured the development of 'occupational groups' to provide a normative framework that could counteract the prevalent anomie – the 'malady of infinite aspiration'. He was a socialist in so far as he favoured the organization of economic life and a liberal in his advocacy of individualist values. The conservative thrust of his commitment to social integration and moral unity is evident, though some writers have overstated this. He was, however, quite averse to the politics of class conflict, seeing MARXISM as unscientific and revolutions as being as impossible as miracles. He saw socialism as a 'cry of pain' and the task of the sociologist, advising statesmen and public opinion at large, as offering a scientifically based remedy for the social illnesses inducing it.

More generally, his focus upon the conditions of social order and the integration of the individual within it meant that he always had a blindspot with regard to POWER – to all the asymmetrical relations of dependence, exploitation and domination, by which some harm the interests of others or gain at their expense. He tended to see the STATE as a communications system, an organ of conscious reflection upon society, not as a locus of power struggle or source of domination. Similarly, his theory of LAW was always about forms of normative regulation, never about contending social interests and their use of power.

These blindspots are serious but they are perhaps the obverse of, even the precondition for, the extraordinarily penetrating insights of Durkheim and his followers into one side of social life. This comes out most clearly in their work on primitive religion. Durkheim's own *Elementary Forms of the Religious Life* (1912) was his final exploration of the limits of social determination, this time upon the essentials of religious beliefs and practice. Examining the available literature on totemism and, in particular, the societies of Australian aborigines, he

advanced various bold hypotheses that he offered as having general explanatory implications for socially integrative belief systems centring upon sacred objects (which is how he saw religion). Not only did he seek to explain their beliefs and rituals by their social origins; he interpreted their 'real' meaning in social terms, seeing religion as reflecting society in all its aspects; and explored their functions for individuals' psychological integrity and social cohesion. He even went so far as to try to explain the fundamental categories of thought (time, space, causality, etc.) as stemming from early religion, and as social in origin. Despite its ethnographic weaknesses, and the flaws in its arguments, this book remains his masterpiece, compelling in its vision and theoretical ambition, and most clearly exemplifying the Durkheimian vision of the social world.   SL

Reading

Coser, L.A.: Durkheim. In *Masters of Sociological Thought*. New York: Harcourt Brace Jovanovich, 1971.

Durkheim, É: *The Division of Labour in Society* (1893), trans. W.D. Halls, intro. L. Coser. London: Macmillan, 1983.

———: *The Rules of Sociological Method* (1895) and *Selected Texts on Sociology and its Method*, ed. S. Lukes, trans. W.D. Halls. London: Macmillan, 1982.

———: *Suicide: a study in sociology* (1897), trans. J.A. Spaulding and G. Simpson. Glencoe, Ill.: Free Press of Glencoe, 1951.

———: *The Elementary Forms of the Religious Life* (1912), trans. J.W. Swain. London: Allen & Unwin; New York: Macmillan, 1915.

———: *Socialism and Saint-Simon* (1928), trans. C. Sattler, ed. A.W. Gouldner. Yellow Springs, Ohio: Antioch, 1958; London: Routledge & Kegan Paul, 1959.

———: *Professional Ethics and Civic Morals* (1950), trans. C. Brookfield. London: Routledge & Kegan Paul, 1957.

———: *Durkheim and the Law*, ed. S. Lukes and A. Scull. Oxford: Martin Robertson, 1983.

†Giddens, A.: Durkheim. In *Capitalism and Modern Social Theory*. Cambridge: Cambridge University Press, 1971.

†Lukes, S.: *Émile Durkheim: his Life and Work*. London: Allen Lane, 1973; Stanford, Calif.: Stanford University Press, 1983.

†Nisbet, R.A.: *The Sociology of Émile Durkheim*. New York: Oxford University Press, 1974.

Parsons, T.: Durkheim. In *The Structure of Social Action*. Glencoe, Ill.: Free Press of Glencoe, 1937.

E

ecclesiology The theory and practice of church government, developed by popes and medieval canon lawyers from the twelfth century onwards, which included the bases for and organization of papal and episcopal administration, with emphasis given to conciliar powers (see CONCILIARISM). At the heart of much ecclesiological doctrine lies the history of medieval representative institutions in general. (See MEDIEVAL POLITICAL THOUGHT.) JC

egalitarianism See EQUALITY.

elitism An approach to understanding politics and history which, in its strongest form, holds that societies are always dominated by a minority (the elite) which takes the major decisions within the society and which concentrates power in its own hands. By extension the term elitist is sometimes used pejoratively in political debates to describe policies which are alleged to promote the advantage of a minority and exclude the wider population. The term elite originally meant the 'elect' or the best. The term is still occasionally used in this sense in ordinary speech when policies are sometimes defended, particularly in education, as 'elitist', meaning that they are intended to produce the best or most able. In political thought elitism has a more technical reference to certain modes of explanation which derive from the work of the Italian sociologists MOSCA and PARETO.

These 'classical elitists' argued that the traditional classification of political systems into monarchies, aristocracies and democracies ignored the more important common feature that all were ruled by a minority, or elite. The elite gained its dominant position as a result of its possession of some resources or attributes which were valued in the particular society. This basis of the elite's domination was not necessarily economic, even though an elite might possibly use its domination to gain wealth and material advantage. In many societies authority was exercised by priests whose control of religious dogma and symbols granted them decisive power over the population. Alternatively, military officers might constitute the dominant group, governing the country either openly or covertly. In other systems the senior state officials might be the elite controlling political decisions. According to Pareto, the elite held power because it possessed appropriate psychological qualities, of cunning and deceit or of strength and decisiveness. In no case did the mass of the population exercise control, even in a democracy where the idea of the rule of the people was a myth concealing actual domination by an inner group of party leaders who manipulated the system of representation.

Most elitists argue that the elite maintains its domination by a combination of coercion and manipulation. The relatively compact size of the elite enables its members to act together in a conscious and cohesive manner. The elite's processes of communication are easier and its members can be rapidly mobilized to formulate a policy and take an initiative. The elite has the advantages of organization (particularly stressed by MICHELS). This is in sharp contrast to the 'mass' of the population who are typically regarded as atomized and incapable of rapid spontaneous action unless themselves led by an elite or 'counter-elite'. The elite normally uses

131

its position to perpetuate its domination. It controls entry into leading positions and may attempt to advantage its own family, relations or clients. Although an elite may use coercion to maintain itself, elitists often emphasize the role of IDEOLOGY in justifying the elite and perpetuating it. A successful ideology helps to unify the elite but, more importantly, it persuades the mass of the justice of the elite's rule by appealing to universal moral principles. Thus the doctrine of the DIVINE RIGHT OF KINGS provided a moral basis for the rule of kings and their courts.

Although elites wield an array of powers they are not always capable of maintaining their domination. For elitists history is the record of the displacement of elites. The fall of an elite is usually explained by some failure of political skill or political will. A common explanation is that an elite may have become excessively closed and have failed to open itself to new ideas and to assimilate new members. Elite values and priorities clash with those of the society at large, provoking the emergence of a counter-elite which is able to mobilize the mass to support the replacement of the established elite by a new ruling group, sometimes by violent means. By contrast a skilled elite will maintain its links with society and be prepared to absorb new interests, policies and personnel. Another account of 'elite circulation', as Pareto termed it, suggests that the elite may lack the qualities not only of flexibility but of sheer will – including the readiness to use brute force – needed to hold on to its position.

Elitist writers like Mosca, Pareto and Michels insisted that they were writing value-free social science and not making any prescriptions concerning elite rule. Their findings rested on the observation of a constant feature of human history. Nevertheless, certain political inferences could be drawn. In particular the socialist hope for an egalitarian society was misplaced if elite rule was an inevitable feature of human organization. Classical elitism was in large part a reply to MARXISM. While agreeing with Marx that past societies had been ruled by minorities, elitists argued first that such minorities were not necessarily owners of the means of production but might wield a variety of power resources, and second that any future society would also be subject to minority rule. The denial of this inevitable inegalitarianism showed socialism to be a pseudo-science concealing an ideological intention behind a facade of scientific terminology. Genuine democracy was also impossible in the face of elite rule – a view which led Pareto and especially Michels to sympathy with FASCISM.

Elitism and elitist political science have been challenged by Marxism and by PLURALISM. Marxists claim that elitists fail to explain the fundamental basis of elite domination (whether military, religious or political) in economic class relations. Pluralists argue that modern, developed and liberal societies are characterized by a multiplicity of interests, competing for power and influence. A small unified elite rarely achieves overall dominance. Instead, different and changing groups tend to influence different areas of decision-making. Pluralists often allege that the failure of elitists to appreciate the multiplicity of centres of decision making in liberal societies stems from an inadequate methodology for the study of POWER.

Many critics of pluralism have in turn argued that it gives a misleading picture of the working of liberal democracies (see DEMOCRACY). Accepting that a genuine competition for influence occurs between groups, they stress that these groups are themselves often controlled by leaders who are not always responsive to their members. The competition between groups must therefore be seen as competition between elites. Pluralist democracy has consequently been designated 'democratic elitism' and been interpreted as an elitist retreat from an earlier more participatory view of democracy. In democratic elitism the survival of democracy is often seen as depending more on the activity and commitment of the elites than on that of the relatively inactive citizenry. SCHUMPETER's Capitalism, Socialism and Democracy (1942) is often regarded as the major intellectual source of elitist theories of democracy.

Relatively few scholars now espouse the full classical elitist position although there has been a revival of a modified elitism, notably in the works of Field and Higley, and of Nordlinger. These writers argue that political science has over-emphasized the extent to which governmental decisions, even in liberal democracies, respond to social forces and has correspondingly neglected the degree to which the initiative for policy lies with elites relatively unconstrained by other groups or by the mass citizenry. Nevertheless, elitism has influenced contemporary political thought and political science in a number of ways. The study of politically influential elites has been incorporated into mainstream political science. These elites may include civil servants, trade unionists, businessmen, military officers or religious leaders. The elite approach focuses on the social and educational background of leaders, their recruitment to their positions and the persons who influence the recruitment (the 'selectorate'). It examines the beliefs of the elites and how far these beliefs affect policy. Where a multiplicity of sectional elites are identified in a society, elite analysis examines whether the elites are interconnected socially, economically, organizationally or ideologically to form a single cohesive elite, or whether they are disunified. Political systems may then be categorized according to the extent and nature of elite unity or disunity. Also central to elite analysis is the nature of the linkages between the elite and the non-elite or mass – the processes of communication upwards and downwards, the role of intermediary groups and relations between centre and periphery. The success or failure of linkage mechanisms is sometimes used to explain the patterns of elite replacement – by revolution, outside forces, colonial withdrawal or gradual change of personnel. Elite analysis is extensively undertaken in the study of communist systems, military governments and autocracies. Although the existence of a small and relatively autonomous group of decision makers is more widely accepted, elitism has been challenged by Marxists and pluralists.   GP

Reading

†Bachrach, P.: *The Theory of Democratic Elitism.* Boston and Toronto: Little, Brown, 1967.

†Bottomore, T.: *Elites and Society.* Harmondsworth: Penguin, 1966.

†Field, G.L. and Higley, J.: *Elitism.* London: Routledge & Kegan Paul, 1980.

Michels, R.: *Political Parties* (1911). Glencoe, Ill.: Free Press of Glencoe, 1958.

Mosca, G.: *The Ruling Class* (1896), trans. and ed. A. Livingston. New York: McGraw-Hill, 1939.

†Nordlinger, E.: *On the Autonomy of the Democratic State.* Cambridge, Mass.: Harvard University Press, 1981.

Pareto, V.: *The Mind and Society* (1916). New York: Harcourt Brace; London, Cape, 1935.

†Parry, G.: *Political Elites.* London: Allen & Unwin, 1969.

†Putnam, R.: *The Comparative Study of Political Elites.* Englewood Cliffs, NJ.: Prentice-Hall, 1976.

Schumpeter, J.: *Capitalism, Socialism and Democracy*, 5th edn. London: Allen & Unwin, 1976.

†Stanworth, P. and Giddens, A. ed.: *Elites and Power in British Society.* Cambridge: Cambridge University Press, 1974.

Engels, Friedrich (or **Frederick**) (1820–1895) German Marxist, who spent much of his life in England. Engels was born into a prosperous family of factory owners in the German Rhineland. At sixteen he left school for a career in the family firm, missing formal enrolment at university. The constitutional liberalism and rebellious literary nationalism of the 1830s appealed to him, despite his family's disapproval, and by the age of seventeen he was a published poet and at eighteen a social critic of some notoriety. In the 'Letters from Wuppertal' (1839) he attacked the mill-owners of his home community for hypocritically posing as good Christians while living on profits squeezed from workers. Their squalid housing, poor health and degrading poverty were vividly described. During the period 1839–42 Engels published nearly fifty short works, including accounts of the liberal-conservative debates in philosophy, politics and religion that were current in and around the university at Berlin, where he did his national service.

As a Berlin liberal Engels found little favour with the more radical Karl MARX whom he met in 1842 on his way to England, where the Engels family was in partnership with a firm of Manchester cotton-spinners. Whilst abroad Engels wrote on Chartist and socialist politics, investigated the condition of the working class in the home and workplace, began a history of

English industrialization and sent a critical review, 'Outlines of a Critique of Political Economy', to Marx for publication in Germany. Engels was then well received by Marx on his return in 1844, and the two agreed to collaborate on a political satire (*The Holy Family*, 1845). They travelled to England together that year and collaborated on a further political work (*The German Ideology*, posthumously published in 1932). By then a friendship was established that lasted until Marx's death in 1883 and continued, in a sense, when Engels became Marx's literary executor. Although Engels always presented himself as the junior partner in the relationship, it was his own works that were eventually to be taken as definitive of MARXISM.

Engels's masterpiece was *The Condition of the Working Class in England*, published in Germany in 1845, in which he combined an eye-witness account of industrial Manchester with material culled from the press. The work reflected his sympathy for the victims of industrialization, his democratic principles in politics and his communist view that collective control of the means of production must supersede the waste and disparity he associated with competitive production in capitalism. Engels drafted two documents for the League of Communists, which he and Marx joined in 1847, and *The Communist Manifesto*, predicting proletarian revolution, emerged under Marx's editorial direction in early 1848, just before the liberal revolutions which swept across Europe that year. Engels worked with Marx on a radical newspaper in Cologne and, like Marx, fled Germany for England when conservative regimes were re-established. In the early 1850s Engels wrote *The Peasant War in Germany*, an account of late medieval radicalism with an optimistic message for his recently defeated contemporaries, and *Revolution and Counter-Revolution in Germany* (for a time attributed to Marx), in which the recent upheaval was evaluated from the communist perspective.

Until 1869 Engels worked in Manchester, and at his retirement he was a partner in the family enterprise. During the decades of exile he supported the Marx family in London while Karl undertook the research for his magnum opus *Capital*, the first instalment of which was published as *A Contribution to the Critique of Political Economy* in 1859. Engels reviewed that work anonymously, at Marx's behest, and in a two-part article he established in outline the intellectual framework he used during the rest of his life. In his review Engels quoted the 'guiding thread' passage from the preface to Marx's little book and identified it as a 'materialist conception of history'. To explain how this materialist conception could be demonstrated with respect to historical examples, Engels employed three distinctions that reappear in his later, more influential works: Hegelian logic (divested of idealism) as opposed to a 'metaphysics' of 'fixed categories'; 'Marx's dialectic' as opposed to Hegel's; and the historical as opposed to the logical within Marx's method. Engels argued that in history 'action' originates from 'direct material impulses' which he then associated with both matter-in-motion and human economic activities in a way that was never satisfactorily spelled out.

Engels's single most influential work was *Anti-Dühring*, published under his own name in 1878 in Germany and originally entitled *Herr Eugen Dühring's Revolution in Science*. Dühring had propounded a socialist system which Marx's sympathizers in the German Socialist Party took to be a threat to their influence and authority. Engels was prodded to rebut the interloper, with Marx's blessing on the political character of the enterprise and a useful donation of background material for the economic sections. Engels opposed Dühring's views with a scientific socialism derived from 'dialectics' and encompassing two 'great discoveries' allegedly made by Marx: 'the materialist conception of history' and 'the revelation of the secret of capitalistic production through surplus value'.

Engels's DIALECTICS was a method purportedly derived from Hegelian logic which worked by deploying three universal laws of nature, history and thought. These were the interpenetration or unity of opposites or antitheses, the transformation of quality into quantity and vice versa, and the negation of the negation. Engels claimed that his laws were an exact representation of all processes within the universe, including its evolution, the development of mankind, logic and the human thought process. He presupposed motion and change, development and contradiction in all these phenomena and argued that our concepts must reflect this and cannot be 'fixed' in character. Further along in *Anti-Dühring* he considered political economy and socialism, presenting a compendium of Marx's views as correct. Extracts from Engels's book were published in French in 1880, and translated into German in 1883 and English in 1892 under the title *Socialism: Utopian and Scientific*, winning thousands of adherents to Marxism. After Marx's death Engels published further prefaces to *Anti-Dühring* and *Socialism: Utopian and Scientific*, advertising them as 'a more or less connected exposition of the dialectical method and of the communist world outlook fought for by Marx and myself', a claim not made in Marx's lifetime.

Engels applied this materialist method to anthropology in *The Origin of the Family, Private Property and the State* (1884). In that work he also incorporated an element of Darwinian natural selection as he understood it, claiming that it was compatible with and successfully subsumed under his historical materialism. He also argued that the position of women in society had deteriorated with the break-up of communistic households and the subsequent introduction of private property, modern monogamy and the patriarchal family. In *Ludwig Feuerbach and the End of Classical German Philosophy* (1888) he elaborated on the antecedents of his dialectics in Hegelian philosophy and positive science and developed its supposed implications for our own understanding of logic, epistemology and the history of society. Engels's account of the way that dialectics is confirmed by science, and in turn provides the ultimate criterion for scientific method, was contained in the posthumously published *Dialectics of Nature* (1927).

During his lifetime Engels's formulations of the materialist conception of history attracted considerable criticism, and in one of his attempts to explicate the doctrine he declared that 'the *ultimately* determining element in history is the production and reproduction of real life . . . [though] the various elements of the superstructure – . . . political, juristic, philosophical theories, religious views and their

further development into systems of dogmas – also exercise their influence' (Marx and Engels, vol. 2, p. 488). Engels's interactionism weakens his historical materialism, perhaps to the point of banality.

Engels was also editor of volumes II and III of Marx's *Capital*, and author, after Marx's death, of more than twenty prefaces and introductions to re-published versions of his works. He was Marx's lifelong correspondent, his eulogist and in a small way his first biographer, the first to present some of his early manuscript works to the public, and the author of canons of interpretation for Marx's life and works that are still commonly applied. Engels coined the phrases 'materialist interpretation of history', 'historical materialism' and 'false consciousness', the last in conjunction with his attempts to define the concept of IDEOLOGY. Engels's writings also form the basis for the 'DIALECTICAL MATERIALISM' currently accepted in Soviet philosophy and science. While Engels himself was in no doubt that his own views were accurate reflections of Marx's, or strictly justified expansions or modifications, critics have pointed to discrepancies between the works of Marx and of Engels. Those commentators who accept Engels's own version of the partnership are under increasing pressure to argue the case.   TC

Reading
Carver, T.: *Engels*. Oxford: Oxford University Press, 1981.

†———: *Marx and Engels: the Intellectual Relationship*. Brighton, Sussex: Wheatsheaf, 1983; Bloomington, Ind.: Indiana University Press, 1983.

Engels, F.: *The Condition of the Working Class in England*, trans. and ed. W.O. Henderson and W.H. Chaloner. Oxford: Blackwell, 1971.

†Henderson, W.O.: *The Life of Friedrich Engels*. 2 vols. London: Cass, 1976.

Lichtheim, G.: *Marxism: an Historical and Critical Study*. London: Routledge & Kegan Paul, 1964.

McLellan, D.: *Engels*. Glasgow: Fontana, 1977.

Marcus, S.: *Engels, Manchester and the Working Class*. New York: Random House, 1974.

Marx, K. and Engels, F.: *Selected Works*. 2 vols. Moscow: Foreign Language Publishing House, 1962.

Enlightenment, the A movement of intellectual change that penetrated every European country (and America) during the eighteenth century. It aimed essentially to emancipate human reason from the thraldom of prejudice and superstition (and especially from established religion), and to apply it to the cause of social and political reform. All Enlightened thinkers shared a belief in PROGRESS, but otherwise their political views diverged considerably: at one extreme stood advocates of enlightened despotism, at the other stood opponents of government such as GODWIN, who held that emancipated reason would have no need of political authority. For the major national schools of Enlightenment thought, see FRENCH ENLIGHTENMENT and SCOTTISH ENLIGHTENMENT. Representative figures from elsewhere include BECCARIA, BENTHAM, FRANKLIN, KANT, and PAINE.   DLM

Reading
Hampson, N.: *The Enlightenment*. Harmondsworth: Penguin, 1968.

equality Two uses of the concept of equality typically enter into political thought. The first is foundational: that of describing people as equal beings. The second is distributional: that of justifying a more equal distribution of economic goods, social opportunities, and/or political powers among people. Egalitarian theories generally invoke the foundational sense of equality to support more distributive equality.

Foundational equality
The claim that 'all men are created equal' seems to state a fact about the human condition. But to what fact does this claim refer? Surely not to equality in any measurable sense, such as equal height or weight. Nor to equality in a socially more significant and less measurable sense such as equal physical, mental, or moral capacity. People are not, as far as we can tell, equal in any of these respects. A more plausible, but some argue empty, claim is that all men are equal by virtue of being human beings, rather than plants or lower-order animals. The claim is not empty, however, if it implies that these ways in which human beings resemble each other are relevant to politics. The claim of natural rights theorists that people are endowed with the capacity to understand their rights and obligations establishes a presumption against

paternalistic government. The utilitarian claim that all human beings share a similar capacity for experiencing pleasures and pains lends support to the rule that everybody is to count as one, nobody for more than one. The Kantian claim that people share a dignity by virtue of being moral agents, capable of using their reason to formulate and follow moral laws, grounds the maxim that people should be treated as ends in themselves and never as means only.

Critics of equality point to the problem of not being able to derive the *value* that all people *should* be treated equally from the *fact* that all people *are* equal. But foundational claims of human equality are not factual in any straightforward sense. To say that people are equal – by virtue of their rationality, passions, or dignity – already entails an evaluation that a shared human characteristic is politically more significant than other apparent differences. 'Because men are men,' R. H. TAWNEY argued, 'social institutions . . . should be planned, as far as possible, to emphasize and strengthen, not the . . . differences which divide, but the common humanity which unites, them' (*Equality*, p. 49). Equality claims such as Tawney's are better viewed as judgments than as empirical facts about the human condition. If equality claims are already partly normative, then egalitarians can avoid the 'is-ought' problem. But they cannot avoid choosing and defending a theoretical framework within which foundational equality claims take on political significance. Several of the more historically and philosophically influential frameworks are described briefly below.

Relevant reasons
Justice, ARISTOTLE argued, is a form of equality: 'persons who are equal should have assigned to them equal things . . . But equals and unequals in what? (*Politics*, 1282b). Aristotle distinguished relevant from irrelevant reasons for distributions by determining the human virtue that merits a particular good. Talented flautists, not well-born or beautiful people, deserve flutes. Contemporary egalitarians extend the logic of relevant reasons beyond the realm of merit to that of need. Bernard Williams argues that 'the proper

ground of distribution of medical care is ill health'; for equally sick people to receive unequal medical treatment 'is an irrational state of affairs' (p. 128). But distributing health care according to merit rather than need would be neither irrational nor unjust in PLATO's *Republic*. Medical care, Plato suggested, might be justly denied a sick carpenter if it would not enable him to continue serving his social function (406c-7a). The logic of relevant reasons supports more or less egalitarian distributions depending on our foundational assumptions concerning human equality. (See also JUSTICE.)

Equality of opportunity

Equality of opportunity finds its first rigorous theoretical defence in Plato's *Republic*, whose educational system is designed to give equally talented and virtuous children an equal chance to achieve unequal social positions. Equal opportunity is often identified as an inegalitarian ideal because it affects *who* gets scarce social goods rather than *how equally or unequally* those goods are distributed. But if many of the observable inequalities among people are produced by nurture rather than by nature, then the ideal of equality of opportunity has radically egalitarian implications for social distributions. If talent and effort are considered an alterable part of children's environment rather than part of their identities, then equality of opportunity implies radical equalization of results, with limits set only by our practical knowledge of genetic engineering.

Liberal equality

Taken to its logical extreme, equality of opportunity undermines human freedom by preventing people from freely using their environmentally conditioned resources, talents, and virtues to achieve unequal results. A more liberal conception of equality leaves people free to pursue their own purposes, even if pursuit of those purposes conflicts with radical equalization of opportunity. Liberal equality, simply stated, is the state of affairs in which people are equally free to pursue their chosen life plans.

Philosophers commonly identified as liberal disagree over what constitutes equal FREEDOM. Libertarians identify equal freedom with the near absolute right to own property and to make contracts, regardless of the distribution of resources that results from such a right (see LIBERTARIANISM). For Robert Nozick, the condition of equal freedom does not entail, indeed it is likely in practice to preclude, distributing medical care or income according to need, merit, effort, or any other 'patterned' principle. Welfare-state liberals build upon Anatole France's criticism of the 'majestic equality of the law which forbids rich and poor alike to steal bread and to sleep under bridges'. The end of social justice, according to John RAWLS, is to maximize the *worth* of freedom to the least advantaged member of society, if necessary by redistributing income and wealth from rich and property-owning to poor and propertyless citizens.

Democratic equality

Democratic critics of the welfare state focus on another dimension of equality: the opportunity of citizens to participate in governing their society as political equals. ROUSSEAU, the classic exponent of democratic equality, was concerned with redistributing economic resources largely as a means of redistributing political power among citizens, by eliminating representative government and making society sufficiently small that citizens could care as much about their fellow citizens as about their own families. His contemporary disciples resign themselves to the fact that modern societies cannot be as small as Rousseau's Geneva. But some still argue for radical decentralization of political institutions as a means of providing all citizens with opportunities to participate directly in governing their society. Other defenders of democratic equality accept representative government but look for institutional means of making public officials more responsive to more of their constituents. Critics note that democratic equality may conflict with liberal equality: democratic majorities may decide to deprive minorities of their fair share of property or welfare. Democrats reply that a centralized state, however egalitarian in its distribution of economic goods and services, deprives most citizens of the goods of political participation and community. (See also DEMOCRACY.)

Socialist equality

Socialist equality extends the democratic critique of the welfare state from the political to the economic realm: just as a few public officials should not have the power to decide the political fate of all citizens, so a few property-owners should not have the power to decide the economic fate of all workers. 'What touches all should be decided by all' is a simple positive expression of socialist equality. But like most conceptions of equality, the socialist ideal is most often expressed negatively, as a critique of existing inequalities. Private ownership of industry violates socialist equality in so far as it permits a few people to exercise a great deal of control over many other people's lives. The socialist critique of capitalism builds upon the Marxian conception of man as a species being, who finds self-fulfilment in creative, socially valuable labour. Proponents of socialist equality criticize capitalism for creating inequalities not only in the distribution of wealth, but also in the satisfaction of human creativity. Industrial democracy is defended as a means of more equally distributing power over productive labour. Critics of socialist equality often point to the problem of bureaucracy, which perpetuates alienating labour in publicly as well as privately owned industries. Democratic socialists respond by combining the ideal of democratic equality with that of socialist equality, arguing for decentralization of economic along with political power.

Gender equality

Political philosophers have often applied foundational and distributional equality claims to only the male half of the human species. Although LOCKE argued that all 'mankind' are 'equal and independent', he assumed only men were parties to the social contract. Rousseau, like Aristotle, assumed that women were by nature unequipped for democratic citizenship. Plato and John Stuart MILL are two important exceptions. Plato introduces the idea of gender equality, suggesting that men and women are equally endowed with the virtues necessary for ruling. The price of gender equality, as of equal opportunity, in Plato's philosophy is the abolition of the family. Gender equality, in Mill's theory, is compatible with the freedom to form families. Mill argues that even if women play a greater role in child-rearing, they should be treated as the political, economic, and social equals to men. Some contemporary feminist theorists question whether gender equality in public life is compatible with gender inequality within the family. Others extend the logic of Mill's liberal argument: even if the priority of individual liberty prevents the state from mandating an equal division of labour within the family, the state is responsible for ensuring that women are treated as equals within all public realms, including the economy. (See also FEMINISM.)

Racial equality

Demands for racial equality, as for gender equality, often can be subsumed under a more general egalitarian framework. The American Civil Rights Movement, for example, pointed out the hypocrisy of professing belief in human equality and denying blacks the right to vote or to use the same public accommodations as whites. Most egalitarian frameworks speak clearly against such discrimination. But the more recent demand – for discrimination *favouring* blacks – raises a distinctive theoretical issue for egalitarian justice. 'Preferential treatment' or 'reverse discrimination' is sometimes defended on the basis of a principle of proportional representation of groups: income, power, and prestige should be distributed among distinct groups within a society in proportion to their size. Critics point out that proportional representation of groups often conflicts with treating individuals within those groups as equals. But reverse discrimination is also defended on individualistic grounds, as a means of compensating individual members of a disadvantaged group for having suffered from past discriminations. (See also DISCRIMINATION.)

For and against equality

Criticisms of equality as a distributional ideal tend to fall into three categories of claims: first, that the ideal is empty or redundant; second, that the ideal conflicts with other, more valuable ideals; and third, that the different ideals of equality are mutually incompatible. A critic of equality elaborates the first criticism as follows:

'To say that all men, because they are men, are equally men . . . is to import a spurious note of egalitarianism into a perfectly sound and serious argument. We may call it, if we like, the argument from Equality of Respect, but in this phrase, it is the word "Respect" . . . which is doing the logical work, while the word "Equality" adds nothing to the argument and is altogether otiose' (Lucas, p. 141). An egalitarian replies that the principle of equal respect is neither empty nor otiose: 'For it would be perfectly possible to consider the interests of everyone affected by a decision without giving them *equal* consideration. Elitist moralities . . . would allow that ordinary men have interests deserving some consideration, [but] the interests of the super-man, super-class, or super-race would always be preferred' (Benn, p. 158).

The second criticism focuses on the fact that a price must generally be paid for achieving greater equality. The price of a more equal distribution of income may be lower incentives and less efficiency in production. The price of more equality of opportunity may be less autonomy for the family and a more competitive, less communitarian society. When equality conflicts with other social values, hard moral choices must be made, which 'is an uncomfortable situation, but the discomfort is just that of genuine political thought. It is no greater with equality than it is with liberty, or any other noble and substantial political ideal' (Williams, p. 137). A similar analysis applies to the third criticism, that equality is not one but many, mutually incompatible ideals. Equality of opportunity, taken to its logical extreme, undermines liberal equality. Egalitarians may either sacrifice one ideal of equality for the sake of realizing the other, or defend the partial realization of each. Most contemporary egalitarians defend the latter alternative, often by invoking the foundational ideal of equal respect for persons as a reason for not sacrificing any intuitively appealing ideal of equality totally to any other.　　　　AGu

Reading
Aristotle: *The Politics*, trans. E. Barker. Oxford: Clarendon Press, 1946.

Bedau, H.A. ed.: *Justice and Equality*. Englewood Cliffs, NJ: Prentice-Hall, 1971.

Bell, D.: On meritocracy and equality. *Public Interest* 29 (1972) 29–68.

Benn, S.I.: Egalitarianism and the equal consideration of interests. In Bedau.

Berlin, I.: Equality. *Proceedings of the Aristotelian Society* 56 (1955–6) 301–26.

Cohen, M., Nagel, T. and Scanlon, T. eds: *Equality and Preferential Treatment*. Princeton, NJ: Princeton University Press, 1977.

Gutmann, A.: *Liberal Equality*. New York and Cambridge: Cambridge University Press, 1980.

Lucas, J.R.: Against equality. In Bedau.

Lukes, S.: Socialism and equality. In *The Socialist Idea*, ed. L. Kolakowski and S. Hampshire. London: Weidenfeld & Nicolson; New York: Basic Books, 1974.

Mill, J.S.: *The Subjection of Women* (1869). In *The Collected Works of John Stuart Mill*, ed. J.M. Robson, vol. XXI. Toronto: University of Toronto Press, 1984.

Pennock, J.R. and Chapman, J.W. eds: *Nomos IX: Equality*. New York: Atherton, 1967.

Plato: *The Republic*, trans. A. Bloom. New York and London: Basic, 1968.

Rae, D.: *Equalities*. Cambridge, Mass.: Harvard University Press, 1981.

Tawney, R.H.: *Equality*, 4th edn. London: Allen & Unwin, 1952.

Walzer, M.: *Spheres of Justice*. New York: Basic Books, 1983.

Williams, B.A.O.: The idea of equality. In Bedau.

Eurocommunism A portmanteau word used to describe the evolutionary process in modern communist parties operating in open democratic systems, typically in Western Europe. It gave rise to a considerable volume of analysis in the late 1970s, the result of which has been that it is an imprecise if not actually useless term of definition but that it covers a phenomenon of continuing importance. 'Reform communism' has too many Eastern European connotations to serve instead. If Eurocommunism had any founding manifesto, it was the declaration signed in Madrid in March 1977 by the leaders of the French, Italian and Spanish Communist parties; but each subsequently went its own way, and by the 1980s the phenomenon could be seen politically to be less immediately important, but on the other hand to be more broadly based and historically rooted than the somewhat fortuitous origins of the term suggested.

Eurocommunism may be dated variously, in the Italian party from Palmiro Togliatti's speculations about polycentrism in the late 1950s, from the French party's misgivings about the Soviet Union's action in Czechoslovakia in 1968 and during the 1974 Portuguese revolution, from the Spanish party's divisions in the mid-1960s and its emergence from clandestinity after Franco's death. Its characteristics – a divergence from Moscow, particularly over matters of foreign policy such as the Prague Spring, the invasion of Afghanistan, and Solidarity's suppression, accompanied by a measure of ideological heterodoxy, and internal party reform – can be traced in all Western European and Mediterranean parties. In Britain, Spain, Australia, Finland, Iceland and Greece these developments have either split the party or accentuated existing divisions. Only in Portugal and Cyprus have they been contained without serious depletion of membership and electoral support.

There is no standard text setting out the principles of Eurocommunism, apart from Santiago Carrillo's brief exposition of 1976. Eurocommunism is concerned with reform, not reformism; it centres on the proposition that, because under monopoly capitalism power is now concentrated in the hands of the very few, modern western states ought no longer to be seen in Leninist terms. It is assumed that these states are in crisis and that not only the working class but bourgeois and professional groups and even forces of law and order will have a common interest in reform.

Alliances in which communist parties will play a leading part, but not as sole representatives of the working class, will work democratically and non-violently, according to GRAMSCI's prescription of a war of position. A long transition is envisaged, rather than a revolution; democracy will be widened without need of a dictatorship of the proletariat. Such alliances will capture power piecemeal from a fragmented ruling class.

Although the communist party remains a vanguard, it will share power with social democrats and others at least during the transition. Internally, Eurocommunism implies greater participation for party members, and less application of democratic centralism.

Beyond national frontiers, combined action by parties of the left will create a Europe-wide momentum for disarmament, freer space between the super-powers, and closer links with the Third World. Eurocommunism also leads to a new sort of international communist movement, characterized by autonomy and mutual respect, and no longer dominated by the Soviet Union.

Historically, Eurocommunism involved the search for national ways to socialism which became necessary once communist parties made their transition from cold war isolation to working within existing political systems. Sectarianism did not disappear, however, nor did large sections of their memberships cease to defend the Soviet model as their primary guide to action; the reformers tended to lead from above, and acquired majority support only slowly in the early 1970s. In some parties, such as the Italian and Spanish, vigorous debates occurred about their own and Soviet history; in the French and Portuguese this tendency had much less effect, although at one point the former abandoned the theory of 'dictatorship of the proletariat'. Broadly speaking, each one set its theoretical analysis of the international communist movement within its practical party-to-party relationships with Moscow, Peking and other centres such as Belgrade and Hanoi. Occasionally critical language slipped into denunciation: Carrillo was perhaps the most outspoken, but Soviet spokesmen responded with equal vigour, and often encouraged orthodox minorities to resist what they called reformism.

In domestic politics, communist parties increasingly identified themselves with the governing process, having become contenders for parliamentary power through electoral competition. This involved them in acting as surrogates for government, and in seeking alliances or common platforms with socialist parties, from whom, however, they took pains to distinguish themselves. In France, after much tortuous negotiation, a rupture occurred over the terms of the Common Programme which may have lost the Union of the Left the 1978 election. When President Mitterand appointed his government in 1981, only four posts went to communists, who later withdrew as a protest against austerity. Two years' experience of association with the governing majority of Christian Democrats after 1977 finally forced the Italian party into opposition, where it hovers uneasily between seeking a bridge with the socialists and criticizing their policies – a dilemma similar to that of the Portuguese party.

The term Eurocommunism signifies a historical, continuing process, widely variable in its intensity, which is still germinating in European communist parties outside the Soviet sphere. It is likely to lead either to their virtual disappearance as small sectarian groups or to their regeneration as major contenders for political power.   KM

Reading

Boggs, C. and Plotke, D.: *The Politics of Eurocommunism*. London: Macmillan, 1980.

Carrillo, S.: *Eurocommunism and the State*, trans. N. Green and A.M. Elliott. London: Lawrence & Wishart, 1977.

Childs, D.H. ed.: *The Changing Face of Western Communism*. London: Croom Helm, 1980.

Machin, H. ed.: *National Communism in Western Europe*. London and New York: Methuen, 1983.

Middlemas, K.: *Power and the Party: Changing Faces of Communism since 1968*. London: Deutsch, 1980.

Tökes, R. ed.: *Eurocommunism and Détente*. Oxford: Martin Robertson, 1979.

Urban, G. ed.: *Eurocommunism: its Roots and Future in Italy and Elsewhere*. London: Temple Smith, 1978.

existentialism   Although existentialism has historical roots going back to the Greeks, it has only been fully articulated as a philosophy since the Enlightenment. The complete philosophy depended upon the conjunction of an ethical attitude with a particular method.

The ethical attitude was first seen in the work of Søren Kierkegaard (1813–55). This Danish philosopher, partly in reaction to HEGEL, firmly rejected universal and objective laws, whether of science or morality, on the grounds that they prevented the individual recognizing a much deeper reality, that of his subjective feelings. Refusal to pay attention to one's feelings was dubbed 'absentmindedness' by Kierkegaard, and he provided striking treatises on fear, guilt and anxiety to explain why and how this can happen. Kierkegaard encouraged the development of individual subjectivity, caring much

more for the manner in which people believe than in what they believe. He famously regarded Christian belief as depending upon a 'leap of faith' rather than upon rational demonstration or formal proof. Friedrich NIETZSCHE (1844–1900) was even more radical in his rejection of supposedly universal rules of whatever sort. To him such viewpoints could be reduced to claims for power on the part of those who propagated them. Nietzsche in consequence recommended a revaluation of all philosophies and his picture of the individual, bereft of certainty and forced to think through everything anew, has great and genuine pathos. He could not endorse any form of Christianity, which he regarded as a slave morality, but leaned instead towards a type of Darwinian naturalism. His own positive philosophy was, however, never fully worked out.

The existentialist stance in ethics thus has its roots in earlier philosophy. The methodology provided by phenomenology, most clearly articulated by Edmund Husserl (1859–1938), is in contrast altogether new. The importance of the method is that it validates the subjectivist ethic. One's feelings may become a full philosophy. The method seeks to 'bracket' received understanding so that a picture of the world may be built up on the basis of human perception. Such a view is fairly generally held in philosophy, and it is important to draw finer distinctions. There is no Cartesian belief that the purest and firmest ideas are those of mathematics, nor is there any Humean view of the individual as the passive receptor of sense experience. The individual is portrayed as an intentional agent coming into contact with the world on the basis of his life project. Reality is the 'life world' (*Lebenswelt*), and there is no clear attempt to go beyond this.

The great existentialists were Martin HEIDEGGER (1889–1976) and Jean-Paul SARTRE (1905–80), and on the basis of their respective key works *Being and Time* (1927) and *Being and Nothingness* (1943) it is possible to summarize the main tenets of existentialism. Existence is formless and without essence, and the individual discovers himself in the midst of a chaos of contingencies. There are no objective moral rules to guide the individual, nor is there some pre-existent human nature which gives life direction. Philosophy's task in this situation is to address the way in which the world feels to us. The greatest depths to existentialist thought are contained in analyses of dread, the sense of nothingness, fear of others and awareness of death. Perhaps the central paradox of existentialism is that it feels able to move beyond this rather gloomy view of the human condition towards more positive injunctions. These depend upon the individual being always free, able and obliged to make choices, and thereby to become something other than what he has so far been. At this point, moral injunctions differ considerably. Heidegger offers a more passive view whereby acceptance of human finitude will allow for acquiescence in one's life within the world. In contrast, Sartre came increasingly to advocate an activist political commitment.

The relationship of existentialism to politics is complex. At first glance, the search for an authentic moral life would seem to place existentialism on the left politically, supporting human freedom and liberation. There are many existentialist views which accord with this, and Sartre once proclaimed that existentialism must be a humanism. But the matter is more complex. Existentialists have occasionally been attracted towards men of action and will on the grounds that they do try to act authentically. Thus an ethics of commitment does not automatically encourage rationality, let alone the politics of the left. More seriously, there is no guarantee either that existentialism will ally itself with democratic politics. If most people lead inauthentic lives and fail to face up to the human condition, is it not appropriate that the great man, who has faced and survived loneliness, dread and anxiety, should be given his due and be served as a charismatic leader? It has been claimed that the general climate reflected in and reinforced by existentialism had some connection with the rise of Nazism. Certainly Heidegger was briefly and infamously involved with the Nazis; although he distanced himself from them later he did not thereafter abandon the search for a moralized politics. Such politics were memorably criticized by Gunter Grass in *Dog Years* (1963) as being, despite their self-advertisement, empty and metaphysical. The German existentialists' politics owed most to a general cultural reverence for Greek political life which has led, all too easily, to a blanket distrust of modern technology. French existentialism, in contrast, stands rather clearly aligned with the left because of the predominant place of MARXISM within French intellectual life. MERLEAU-PONTY and Sartre pondered deeply about the relationship between a supremely individualistic ethic and the collectivist spirit of Marxism, and the latter's *The Critique of Dialectical Reason* (1960) stands as the great monument to reconciliation. The attempt to marry the two approaches failed, but the political theories produced in consequence were of great interest. The *Critique* saw the emergence again of strikingly authoritarian politics designed to solve 'the problem of being', i.e. man's cowardly attempt to run away from responsibility for freedom. It is impossible not to think of ROUSSEAU's phrase about being 'forced to be free' in connection with such political theories.

Existentialism's greatest achievement has been to describe the pain endemic to the human condition. Here we must hesitate a little. Such evidence as we have suggests that most people in industrial society in normal circumstances do not feel themselves to be facing quite the amount of dread and anguish so marvellously portrayed in the great literary works that came from existentialism. Most humans find a great deal of meaning in their lives, and do not habitually feel that they are living in a void. Perhaps existentialism tells us more about the alienation of intellectuals in modern circumstances than it does about normal people. This point is reinforced by remembering that this philosophy had its great moments of popularity after defeat in war, i.e. at times when feelings of despair *were* quite generalized.

Existentialism has two great philosophical weaknesses. First, its philosophy of consciousness is facile and meretricious. The argument offered is simply that we are free because we feel free. Personally I do not feel *that* free, and there is everything to be said for attempts to explain human behaviour, as Noam Chomsky has argued, in ways that go behind the back of human consciousness. The second point is closely related. Existentialism has never concerned itself with modern science, except perhaps to dismiss its importance. This will not do. Science has transformed modern politics by providing affluence but, as Max WEBER insisted, there has been a human cost to this. The scientific outlook tends to destroy received opinions and practices. We can no longer trust our *Lebenswelt*, and there is the chance now that our own actions may become scientifically explicable.   JAH

Reading

Heidegger, M.: *Being and Time*, trans. J. Macquarrie and E. Robinson. Evanston, Ill.: Harper; London: SCM Press, 1962.

Sartre, J.-P.: *Being and Nothingness*, trans. H.E. Barnes. London: Methuen, 1953.

————: *Critique de la raison dialectique*, vol. 1. *Théorie des ensembles pratiques*. Paris; Gallimard, 1960. Trans. as *Critique of Dialectical Reason: Theory of Practical Ensembles*. London: New Left; Highlands, NJ: Humanities Press, 1976.

Spiegelberg, H.: *The Phenomenological Movement*. The Hague: Mouton, 1965.

†Warnock, M.: *Existentialism*. Oxford: Oxford University Press, 1970.

exploitation The idea of exploitation may be used either in a neutral sense ('exploiting the mineral resources of the North Sea') or in a critical one ('exploiting the black population of South Africa'). In political thought its use is nearly always critical: to exploit someone is to take unfair advantage of them. The concept is particularly associated with the work of Marx, although it can be employed by non-Marxists for non-Marxian purposes. A 'theory of exploitation' at its widest is an account of how a person or group exploits another person or group by obtaining from them goods or services to which the exploiter has no proper claim. Thus, on almost any account of justice, slaves are exploited, because the fruits of their labour are seized by their masters with no proper return made to the slaves. However, within most political theories exploitation neither needs nor receives any explicit treatment, because anything said about it follows very straightforwardly from the conception of JUSTICE implicit or explicit in those theories. Thus Tom PAINE treated the *ancien régime* as an exploitative regime because he held that the property rights of the landed aristocracy rested on brute force

backed up by superstition, and that those who monopolized landed property exploited those who worked on it by taking from them everything they could get out of them.

MARX's theory of exploitation is interesting because its author claimed to have no concern for justice, and because it is an integral part of his theory of profit under capitalism. The theory of exploitation is, so to speak, the other face of the theory of surplus value. Marx, as others had done before him, thought that within the LABOUR THEORY OF VALUE there was a problem about the capitalist's profits. Under perfect competition, the capitalist bought all his inputs at their full value; he could sell them for no more than their full value; it was therefore a mystery how putting the inputs together could increase the value of what was put together. What alchemy accounted for profit? It was no use saying that the capitalist's combinatory efforts were the source of value, for that turned the capitalist into another wage earner which he manifestly was not, since the size of his profits depended on the amount of capital he employed, not on the effort he devoted to his business. Answers such as J. S. Mill's, that profit was reward to the capitalist for his 'abstinence' – what later became the 'waiting' theory of interest and profit – were dismissed as beneath contempt. It was quite clear that capitalists did not abstain from anything, and if 'capital' meant capital equipment and the like, it was clear that it did not offer the alternative of consumption or investment in any case.

Marx concluded that his predecessors had not seen that what the capitalist bought from the worker was not *labour* but *labour power*, the ability to work for the period of the contract. That was bought and sold at its full value, namely the subsistence wage – which represented the amount of labour needed to produce a worker ready to work. What the capitalist got, however, was the actual work of the worker, and thus he got the value which that actual labour added. Profit was the difference between what it took to produce the worker and what the worker's efforts added. The extent to which workers were exploited was a matter of the proportion between the extra or 'surplus' value and the value of labour power.

Much ink has been spilled on the question of

Marx's view of the injustice of exploitation. It seems clear that Marx was eager to argue that the contrast between the 'forced labour' of the serf or slave and the labour done by the 'free labourer' under capitalism – on which the defenders of capitalism insisted – was, at a deeper level of analysis, an illusion. Just as the feudal landlord exploited his serfs by obtaining unpaid labour from them, so the capitalist exploited his workers in the same way. Whether this was unjust in Marx's eyes it is harder to say. He insisted that the capitalist had 'full right' to the labour power he purchased; he also denounced as utopians all those socialists who complained of the injustice of capitalism. He frequently said that no age could adopt a standard of justice higher than its production relations allowed. Nonetheless, it is hard to see why Marx should have insisted that the worker was engaged in forced labour whose fruits were stolen from him unless he wished to object to its injustice. The explanation of the difficulty, perhaps, is that Marx visualized communism as a society beyond rights and justice, and feared to encourage those who, as he thought, aimed at the chimera of a just capitalist society.   AR

Reading

†Elster, J.: *Making Sense of Marx*, ch. 4. Cambridge: Cambridge University Press, 1985.

†Lukes, S.: *Marxism and Morality*. Oxford: Clarendon Press, 1985.

Marx, K.: *Capital*. Moscow: Foreign Languages Publishing House, 1957–9.

†———: *Critique of the Gotha Programme* (1875). In *Marx and Engels: Selected Works*. London: Lawrence & Wishart, 1968.

Roemer, J.: Property relations vs. surplus value in Marxian exploitation. *Philosophy and Public Affairs* 11 (1982) 281–313.

Steiner, H.: A liberal theory of exploitation. *Ethics* 94 (1984) 225–41.

F

Fabianism The term is used to refer both to a general position within SOCIALISM and to the views of a specific group of late Victorian and early twentieth-century British socialists. The two uses are related.

As a general term Fabianism describes a style of socialism expressing the essential arguments of the historical Fabian Socialists. Its principal features are:

(1) an emphasis on meritocracy and the responsibility of trained experts in the management of public affairs;

(2) a distrust of radical or confrontational tactics and a confidence that planned and deliberate reform, carried out as a result of the triumph of reason and the presentation of evidence, can slowly but inevitably create a socialist society;

(3) a belief in reason as a possible and desirable motivating feature of government and politics;

(4) the pursuit of efficiency in public affairs, justified by empirically demonstrable criteria;

(5) commitment to a form of democracy in which individuals participate in their various roles as citizens, workers, etc., contributing by their efforts to the common good from which they benefit; and a corresponding disinclination to support the advocacy of forms of direct popular power.

In this last, broad sense a whole series of socialist thinkers and politicians from Hugh Dalton to Anthony CROSLAND have been deemed to be 'Fabian'.

As an historically specific term, Fabianism describes the views of the leading members of the Fabian Society from the society's formation in 1884 until the late 1930s. Although the word 'Fabian' was used to describe the views of the group as a whole, the Society had a heterogeneous membership which included the sometime secularist and theosophist Annie Besant, the future governor of Jamaica Sydney Olivier, and the political scientist Graham Wallas. What gave the Fabians unity was the presence of a large number of ambitious professional and intellectual men and women whose own skills and aspirations complemented the meritocratic ambitions of the Society itself. The principal exponents of Fabian views typified this characteristic of the membership. Beatrice Webb was an upper-middle-class social investigator, her husband Sidney Webb a civil servant turned politician and social scientist, and George Bernard Shaw a novelist, playwright and journalist. The most maverick member of the Society, H. G. Wells, was perhaps the most ambitious of all, both on his own behalf and on behalf of the meritocracy which on occasion he elevated to a caste of samurai or ironsides. The variety of opinions held by members went far beyond anything that could be presented as a single, distinctive position. There were differences even among the principal Fabians, between the Webbs' admiration for administration and participation, Shaw's belief in leadership (a view which, he said with characteristic modesty, he shared with LENIN and other natural Tories), and Wells's depiction of a dedicated oligarchic caste. Nonetheless, certain broad views can be said to characterize the classic Fabianism of the Webbs and Shaw.

By socialism the Fabians understood the

collective organization of society for the general good by the state, nationally and locally. The extension of the state's regulatory, administrative and provisory functions became the mark of the growth of socialism out of liberalism and capitalism.

The Fabian Society took its name from the Roman general who defeated Hannibal by waiting until the moment was right, wearing down his opponent and then striking hard. It was not an accurate description of the tactics of the Fabian socialists, however, or even of their own account of these. Their characteristic method and expectation were summed up in the phrase 'the inevitability of gradualness'. Critics of Fabianism have picked up the second part of the phrase, but for the Fabians the first part was equally important. Hard work, persuasion, and research would slowly but inevitably move society in a socialist direction. This work required generals just as the defeat of Hannibal had done, and Fabian socialism always placed high expectations on the contribution of trained experts and administrators. In the ideal Fabian state trained intelligence would play a central part, and its recognition and use would be one of the features that would mark off socialism from capitalism. Far from the hierarchies of capitalism being replaced by equality of power, it would be refined by a system of democratically accountable elites staffed by the most capable – whereas capitalism's elites had been staffed only by the most fortunate. There was often a high moral tone here, in praise of the ascetic dedication of the professional, and dismissively patronizing the 'average sensual man'. The high responsibility given to trained intelligence in national politics was exported in Fabianism to become an advocacy of the right and duty of the advanced industrial nations of Western Europe to administer the less developed parts of the world and raise them to the socialist heights which were to be attained at home.

The Fabians presented their argument as the natural extension of liberalism, continuing the development of democracy from the political into the social sphere, and their proposals were summed up in the term SOCIAL DEMOCRACY.

The Fabians were democrats in that they wanted an extension of the suffrage and expected that this would lead to the election of socialists. But they had a low opinion of the average elector, and were felt by many of their own female supporters to be insufficiently enthusiastic about the political emancipation of women. Moreover they saw democracy as the exercise of the political function of the people as a whole, in their collective role as consumers, and they were opposed to what they considered to be the sectional and potentially selfish self-government of groups organized on the basis of production in various forms of workers' control.

Though the Fabians disagreed with MARX's economics, their own theory of rent – derived from Ricardo – served a similar purpose to the LABOUR THEORY OF VALUE. It distinguished between the actual and the ideal distribution of rewards in the form of 'rent' to the various factors of production such as 'ability', 'labour' and 'capital'. The Fabian theory, however, had the distinction of attributing one part of rent to society as a whole and therefore to the state as society's representative for the purpose of either distribution or application to common purposes.   RB

Reading

Crossman, R.H.S. ed.: *New Fabian Essays*. London: Turnstile, 1952.

Durbin, E.: *New Jerusalems*. London: Routledge & Kegan Paul, 1985.

McBriar, A.M.: *Fabian Socialism and English Politics 1884–1914*. Cambridge: Cambridge University Press, 1966.

†MacKenzie, N. and MacKenzie, J.: *The First Fabians*. London: Weidenfeld & Nicolson, 1977.

Pimlott, B. ed.: *Fabian Essays in Socialist Thought*. London: Heinemann, 1984.

Pugh, P.: *Educate, Agitate, Organize: a Hundred Years of Fabian Socialism*. London: Methuen, 1984.

Shaw, G.B. ed.: *Fabian Essays* (1889). London: Allen & Unwin, 1962.

Webb, S. and Webb, B.: *A Constitution for the Socialist Commonwealth of Great Britain*. London: the authors, 1920.

————: *Industrial Democracy*. 2 vols. London: Longmans, Green, 1897.

Wolfe, W.: *From Radicalism to Socialism: Men and Ideas in the Formation of Fabian Socialist Doctrines, 1881–1889*. London: Yale University Press, 1975.

false consciousness A term used primarily

by Marxists to convey the idea that IDEOLOGY embodies a systematically distorted view of the world. It presupposes a distinction between the appearance of things and their underlying reality, and characterizes thought which takes appearances at face value and constructs specious theories on this basis.   DLM

Fanon, Frantz (1925–1961) Psychiatrist, political militant, and revolutionary. Born in Martinique, Fanon became Algerian by virtue of his participation in the Algerian liberation struggle (1954–62) but his powerful and passionate indictment of exploitation and oppression was not limited to Algerian experience. His language was universal. His vision transcended the world of North Africa and Africa to include all people struggling to free themselves of internal and foreign oppression. He emerged as one of the most articulate and eloquent theoreticians of twentieth-century liberation movements.

In 1947 Fanon left Martinique for France in order to study medicine and psychiatry. For the next five years he was involved in the literary, philosophical, and political movements that marked post-war France. The turning point came in 1953 when Fanon accepted appointment to the psychiatric hospital in Blida-Joinville, Algeria. Continuing his practice as psychotherapist, Fanon became an active supporter and militant in the FLN, the Algerian Liberation Front. In 1957, having resigned his position in Blida and been forced to move as a result of colonial government action, Fanon transferred to Tunisia where he joined the political/military cadre of the FLN and became one of the editors of *El Moudjahid* and *Résistance algérienne*, press organs of the FLN and ALN (Army of National Liberation). In time he was assigned to the Ministry of Information of the provisional government, established in 1958. Until his death of leukaemia in Washington, DC, in 1961, Fanon remained an indefatigable militant for the Algerian cause.

In addition to his important contribution to the Algerian revolutionary press, four major works, a collection of articles dealing with psychiatric theory and practice, and a number of unpublished essays and plays constitute Fanon's written legacy. In these diverse texts Fanon relentlessly exposed the psychological, social, and political dimensions of oppression and dependence. In *Peau noire, masques blancs* (1952), *L'An V de la révolution algérienne* (1959), *Les Damnés de la terre* (1961), and *Pour la révolution africaine* (1964), Fanon demonstrated the intimate relationship of language, personality, sexual relations, and political experience to social context. Though he focused on racism in his early works, the later writings extended his analyses to the colonial situation. Algeria and Africa provided the models of colonialism and resistance on the one hand, and the pitfalls of post-colonial statehood on the other.

Les Damnés de la terre was Fanon's most powerful and controversial work. In this masterful synthesis he developed interpretations of the Manichaean character of colonial society, the organization of revolutionary action, the personal and political roots of violence, and the critique of bureaucratized parties and compromised national bourgeoisies of post-colonial states. Fanon argued that the lumpenproletariat represented a revolutionary potential that had been overlooked by radical parties; and these he further criticized for their detachment from the rural peasant masses, whose importance in the Algerian experience he greatly emphasized. A partisan of decentralized politics, Fanon advocated the democratization and secularization of political parties and institutions, and the socialization of the post-independence economies of Third World states, drawing examples from Algeria and Africa.

Acclaimed for his prophetic power and passionate intellect, Fanon has generated considerable controversy among students of revolution, as well as of the Algerian state and society. None contest his singular ability or his commitment to the liberation of the 'wretched of the earth'.   ILG

Reading
†Caute, D.: *Fanon*. London: Collins; Fontana, 1970.
Fanon, F.: *Peau noire, masques blancs*. Paris: Éditions du Seuil, 1952.
———: *L'An V de la révolution algérienne*. Paris: François Maspero, 1959.
———: *Les Damnés de la terre*. Paris: François Maspero, 1961.
———: *Pour la révolution africaine*. Paris: François Maspero, 1964.

Geismar, P.: *Fanon.* New York: Dial, 1971.

†Gendzier, I.L.: *Frantz Fanon: a Critical Study*; 2nd edn. New York: Grove, 1985.

†Hansen, E.: *Frantz Fanon: Social and Political Thought.* Columbus, Ohio: Ohio State University Press, 1977.

Lucas, P.: *Sociologie de Frantz Fanon.* Algiers: Société Nationale d'Édition et de Diffusion, 1971.

†Perinbam, M.: *Holy Violence: the Revolutionary Thought of Frantz Fanon.* Washington, DC: Three Continents, 1982.

Zahar, R.: *Kolonialismus und Entfremdung.* Frankfurt am Main: Europäische Verlagsanstalt, 1969.

fascism Of all the major ideologies of the twentieth century, fascism was the only one to come into being together with the century itself. It was a synthesis of organic NATIONALISM and anti-Marxist SOCIALISM, a revolutionary movement based on a rejection of liberalism, democracy and Marxism. In its essential character, fascist ideology was a rejection of materialism – liberalism, democracy and Marxism being regarded simply as different aspects of the same materialist evil. It was this revolt against materialism which, from the beginning of the century, allowed a convergence of anti-liberal and anti-bourgeois nationalism and a variety of socialism which, while rejecting Marxism, remained revolutionary. This form of socialism was also, by definition, anti-liberal and anti-bourgeois, and its opposition to historical materialism made it the natural ally of radical nationalism. The fascist synthesis symbolized the rejection of a political culture inherited from the eighteenth century and the French Revolution, and it aimed at laying the foundations of a new civilization. Only a new communal and anti-individualistic civilization was deemed capable of assuring the permanence of a human collectivity in which all strata and all classes of society would be perfectly integrated, and the natural framework for such a harmonious, organic collectivity was held to be the nation – a nation enjoying a moral unity which liberalism and Marxism, both agents of warfare and disunity, could never provide.

An organic, tribal, exclusive nationalism based on biological determinism was a translation into political terms of the intellectual revolution of the turn of the century. With BARRÈS, MAURRAS and Corradini (who created the idea of the 'proletarian nation'), nationalism became a coherent political theory. It converged quite naturally with the second element in the fascist equation: the revision of Marxism undertaken at the beginning of the century by Georges SOREL and the theoreticians of Italian revolutionary SYNDICALISM. If one fails to take into account this initially socialistic revolt against materialism, fascist ideology can hardly be understood. Intellectually, it was greatly influenced by SOCIAL DARWINISM, by the anti-Cartesian and anti-Kantian philosophy of Bergson and NIETZSCHE, by the psychology of Le Bon and the sociology of PARETO. Its immediate context was the enormous changes which were taking place in the capitalist economy, in bourgeois society and in the life of the working class – changes which ran quite contrary to Marxist expectations.

Sorel replaced the rationalistic, Hegelian foundations of Marxism with anti-materialist, voluntarist, vitalist elements. This form of socialism was a philosophy of action based on intuition, and the cult of energy and *élan*, activism and heroism. To activate the masses, thought Sorel, one did not require reasoning but myths, systems of images which strike the imagination. When it became obvious that the myth of the general strike and proletarian violence was ineffective because the proletariat was incapable of fulfilling its role as a revolutionary factor, the Sorelians had no option but to abandon Marxism and to replace the proletariat with the great rising force: the nation as a whole. One arrived in this way at a socialism for all, embodying a new idea of revolution – a national, moral and psychological revolution, the only kind of revolution which does not bear the characteristics of class struggle. This was the real contribution of Sorel and the revolutionary syndicalists and non-conformists of France and Italy to Fascism.

Among these were the theoreticians of revolutionary syndicalism such as Arturo Labriola, Robert MICHELS, Sergio Panunzio and Paolo Orano, and their fellow-traveller Benito Mussolini. The connection between Mussolini and the revolutionary syndicalists was already very strong in 1902 and, throughout the period prior to the first world war, Mussolini's development took place under their shadow. In 1914, Mussolini and the revolutionary syndicalists together with Corradini's nationalists constituted the spearhead of the interventionist movement: the synthesis of a radical nationalism and a new type of socialism thus became a political reality. During the war, revolutionary syndicalism turned into national syndicalism and then into fascism.

In the sphere of political theory, this synthesis was already clearly expressed around the years 1910–12 in such publications as *Les Cahiers du Cercle Proudhon* in France, and above all *La Lupa* in Italy. The nationalists and revolutionary syndicalists wished to replace the mercantile civilization of their day with a civilization of monks and warriors, a warlike, virile and heroic civilization in which a sense of sacrifice would replace bourgeois hedonism and egoism. This new world would be created by an elite conscious of its duties which alone would be capable of leading the masses, who in turn were only a herd, to battle.

These constitutive elements of the fascist ideology, elaborated previous to August 1914, reappeared in an almost identical form in the 1920s and 1930s both in Italy and elsewhere: among the French fascists who had come from the right such as Georges Valois, Robert Brasillach and Pierre Drieu La Rochelle, and former French socialists and communists such as Marcel Deat or Jacques Doriot. Other examples were Jose Antonio Primo de Rivera in Spain, Léon Degrelle in Belgium and Corneliu Zelia Codreanu in Rumania.

From this perspective, it is clear that fascism was a pan-European phenomenon, and it existed on three levels – as an ideology, as a political movement, and as a form of government. From the point of view of the history of ideas, the first world war was not the watershed it appears to have been in so many other areas. Fascism did not belong only to the inter-war era but to that whole period of history which began with the modernization of the European continent at the end of the nineteenth century. The intellectual revolution of the turn of the century, the entry of the masses into politics, produced fascism as a system of thought, as a sensibility, as an attitude to the essential problems of civilization. The first

world war and the economic crisis of the 1930s produced the sociological and psychological conditions necessary to the construction of the fascist movement, but they did not produce fascist ideology.

The war did, however, contribute to the final crystallization of fascist ideology, not only because it provided a proof of the capacity of nationalism to mobilize the masses, but because it displayed the tremendous power of the modern state. It revealed quite new possibilities of economic planning, and of mobilizing the national economy as well as private property in the service of the state. The state was regarded as the expression of national unity and its might depended on the spiritual unanimity of the masses, but at the same time the state was the guardian of this unity which it fostered with every means possible. The war revealed how great the capacity of the individual for sacrifice could be, how superficial was the idea of internationalism, and how easily all strata of society could be mobilized in the service of the state. It demonstrated the importance of unity of command, of authority, of leadership, of moral mobilization, of the education of the masses, and of propaganda as an instrument of power. Above all, it had shown how easily democratic liberties can be suspended and a quasi-dictatorship gain acceptance.

The fascists felt that in many respects the war had proved the validity of the ideas expressed by Sorel, Michels, Pareto and Le Bon, namely, that the masses need a myth, they only want to obey, and democracy is merely a smokescreen. The first world war, the first total war in history, was a laboratory in which the ideas they put forward throughout the first decade of the century proved themselves in practice. Thus the fascism of the 1930s, as found in the writings of Gentile and Mussolini, Jose Antonio and Oswald Mosley, Léon Degrelle and Drieu La Rochelle, was made up both of the theoretical contribution of the pre-war nationalists and syndicalists, and of the experience of the war.

Basic to the political philosophy of fascism was a conception of the individual as a social animal. For Gentile the human individual is not an atom; in every respect man is a political animal. In so far as man is outside the organization of society with its system of reciprocal rules and obligations, he has no significant freedom. Ultimately, for Gentile and Mussolini, man has existence only in so far as he is sustained and determined by the community.

Fascist thought did not stop there, however, but went on to develop a conception of liberty that in Mussolini's terminology was 'the liberty of the state and of the individual within the state'. This is the reason why, according to Alfredo Rocco, Mussolini's minister of justice, individual rights were only recognized in so far as they were implied in the rights of the state. It was by way of such arguments that fascism arrived at the concepts of the new man and the new society so admirably characterized by the French fascist Marcel Deat: 'the total man in the total society, with no clashes, no prostration, no anarchy'. Fascism was a vision of a coherent and reunited people, and it was for this reason that it placed such emphasis on march-pasts, parades and uniforms, on a whole communal liturgy where deliberation and discussion were supplanted by songs and torches, by the cult of physical strength, violence and brutality. This unity found its most perfect expression in the quasi-sacred figure of the leader. The cult of a leader who embodied the spirit, will, and virtues of the people, and who was identified with the nation, was the keystone of the fascist liturgy. Gentile was quite correct when he defined fascism as a revolt against POSITIVISM.

Preserving the integrity of the nation and solving the social question means destroying the dictatorship of money. Wild capitalism must be replaced by the classic tools of national solidarity: a controlled economy and corporate organization topped by a strong state, a decision-making apparatus that represents the victory of politics over economics. The fascist state, creator of all political and social life and of all spiritual values, would of course be the undisputed master of the economy and of social relations.

The reform of the relations of power was the cornerstone of the fascist revolution. The most striking aspect of that moral and political revolution was TOTALITARIANISM. 'Ours will be a totalitarian state in the service of the fatherland's integrity,' said José Antonio. Innumerable passages in an identical vein are to be found throughout fascist literature. Totalitarianism is the very essence of fascism, and fascism is without question the purest example of a totalitarian ideology. Setting out as it did to create a new civilization, a new type of human being and a totally new way of life, fascism could not conceive of any sphere of human activity remaining immune from intervention by the state. 'We are, in other words, a state which controls all forces acting in nature. We control political forces, we control moral forces, we control economic forces . . . ,' Mussolini wrote, and, 'everything in the state, nothing against the state, nothing outside the state' (p. 40). For Mussolini and Gentile the fascist state is a conscious entity and has a will of its own – for this reason, it can be described as 'ethical'. Not only does the existence of the state imply the subordination of the individual's rights, but the state asserts the right to be 'a state which necessarily transforms the people even in their physical aspects' (p. 39). Outside the state, 'no human or spiritual values can exist, much less have value'; 'no individuals or groups (political parties, cultural associations, economic unions, social classes) outside the state' (p. 11).

The concrete consequences of such a conception of political power and the physical and moral repression it would engender are not hard to imagine. Here we see how communist and fascist totalitarianisms differ: whereas the Stalinist dictatorship could never be described as an application of the Marxist theory of the state, fascist terror was doctrine put into practice in the most methodical way. Fascism constitutes one of the best examples of the unity of thought and action.   ZS

Reading
Gentile, G.: The philosophic basis of fascism. In *Readings on Fascism and National Socialism*. Denver, Col.: Swallow, n.d.

Gregor, A.J.: *Young Mussolini and the Intellectual Origins of Fascism*. Berkeley and Los Angeles: University of California Press, 1979.

Hamilton, A.: *The Appeal of Fascism: a study of intellectuals and fascism 1919–1945*. New York: Macmillan, 1971.

†Laqueur, W. ed.: *Fascism: a Readers' Guide; analyses, interpretations, bibliography*. Harmondsworth: Penguin, 1979.

Lyttelton, A. ed.: *Italian Fascisms from Pareto to Gentile*. London: Cape, 1973.

Mosse, G.L.: *Masses and Man*. New York: Howard Fertig, 1980.

Mussolini, B.: *Fascism: Doctrine and Institutions*. New York: Howard Fertig, 1968.

†Nolte, E.: *Three Faces of Fascism: Action française, Italian Fascism, National Socialism*. New York: New American Library, 1969.

†Payne, S.G.: *Fascism: Comparison and Definition*. Madison: University of Wisconsin Press, 1980.

Primo de Rivera, J.A.: *Selected Writings*, ed. and intro. H. Thomas. London: Cape, 1972.

Rocco, A.: *La dottrina politica del fascismo*. Rome: Aurora, 1925.

Sternhell, Z.: *Neither Right nor Left: Fascist Ideology in France*. Berkeley and Los Angeles: University of California Press, 1986.

Turner, H.A. Jr ed.: *Reappraisals of Fascism*. New York: New Viewpoints, 1975.

Weber, E.: *Varieties of Fascism*. New York: Van Nostrand, 1966.

federalism A constitutional system of government is federal if law-making powers are divided between a central legislative body and legislatures in the states or territorial units making up the federation. Citizens are thus subject for different purposes to two different bodies of law, and normally in each unit of the federation there are also executive and judicial bodies corresponding to those at the federal level. The allocation of powers derives from the constitution and cannot be unilaterally changed by either set of legislators. It thus differs from unitary systems of government in which a measure of independent legislative power is devolved or delegated from the central legislature to local legislative bodies. The United States, Australia, Canada, West Germany, and India are federal states. In all of them the division of legislative authority is protected and policed by a power in the courts to declare invalid legislation that infringes the limits laid down in the constitution. In practice the degree of independence enjoyed by the units in a federal system depends in large measure upon political and economic factors as well as on the legal allocation of powers. GM

Reading
Birch, A.H.: Approaches to the study of federalism. *Political Studies* 14 (1966) 15–33.

Hogg, P.W.: *Constitutional Law of Canada*, 2nd edn, ch. 5. Toronto: Carswell, 1985.

Livingston, W.S.: *Federalism and Constitutional Change*. Oxford: Clarendon Press, 1956.

†Sawer, K.: *Modern Federalism*. London: Watts, 1969.

Vile, M.J.C.: Federalism in the United States, Canada and Australia. In *Royal Commission on the Constitution*, I, Cmnd 5460, Research Paper 2. London: HMSO, 1973.

†Wheare, K.: *Federal Government*, 4th edn. London, New York, Toronto: Oxford University Press, 1963.

Federalist Papers A series of eighty-five articles by Alexander HAMILTON (who wrote fifty-one of them), James MADISON (twenty-four), and John Jay (five). The papers were first published (under the pseudonym Publius) to support the campaign for ratification of the United States Constitution in 1787–8. They are generally acknowledged as the classic interpretation and defence of the basic principles and institutions of the American political system: self-government, REPUBLICANISM, REPRESENTATION, FEDERALISM, SEPARATION OF POWERS, and bicameralism. JZ

feminism A generic term for a complex phenomenon, feminism is defined in part by contests generated over its meaning. Understood broadly, it is a concern with the social role of women in relation to men in societies past and present, animated by a conviction that women suffer and have suffered injustices because of their sex. The political language and aims of modern feminism emerge from the French Revolution and the ENLIGHTENMENT. Associated historically with oppositional forces combating orthodoxy and autocracy, feminism defined itself as a struggle for recognition of the rights of women, for equality between the sexes, and for redefinitions of womanhood. Drawing upon liberal and rationalist as well as utopian and romantic ideas in Western Europe and America, feminism resists easy definition.

Although controversies about women's social role erupted explicitly during the Enlightenment, there are antecedents. Medieval and Renaissance writers took up the theme of women's social identity and defended expansion of female political power and influence, for example, Christine de Pisan's *Book of the City of*

Ladies (1405). Modern feminism, however, is more often traced to the publication of Mary WOLLSTONECRAFT's *Vindication of the Rights of Woman* (1792). Wollstonecraft adumbrated what were to become inescapable feminist preoccupations including, but not limited to, the defence of political and natural rights. She challenged received notions of the distinctive virtues of the two sexes; argued for a transformed education for male and female; attacked martial images of citizenship; and celebrated an androgynous notion of the rational self.

Reason became a weapon for women's emancipation, deployed against the exclusive identification of women with nature and with their sexual function and capacity. Faith in reason was then coupled with a strong belief in progress. These convictions, refined in and through an already deeply rooted tradition of liberal contractarianism and commitment to formal legalistic equality, are most manifest in John Stuart MILL's classic nineteenth-century tract, *The Subjection of Women* (1869). Counterposing 'Reason' and 'Instinct', Mill looks forward to a society based on rational principles. Reason, he contends, requires nullifying differences of treatment based on considerations of sex, among other 'accidents of birth'. Granting women equality of citizenship and civil liberty in the public realm will help to bring about a deeper transformation in the social relations of the sexes.

Liberalism has been attractive to feminist thinkers. The language of rights is a potent weapon against traditional obligations, particularly those of family duty or any social status declared 'natural' on the basis of ascriptive characteristics. To be 'free' and 'equal' to men became a central aim of feminist reform. The political strategy that follows from this dominant feminism is one of inclusion: women, as well as men, are rational beings. It follows that women as well as men are bearers of inalienable rights. It follows further that *qua* woman, there is no valid ground for discrimination against women. Leading proponents of women's suffrage in Britain and the United States undermined arguments which justified formal legalistic inequality on the basis of sex differences. Such feminists claimed that denying a group of persons basic rights on the grounds of some presumed difference could not be justified unless it could be shown that the difference was relevant to the distinction being made. Whatever differences might exist between the sexes, none, on this view, justified legal inequality and denial of the rights and privileges of citizenship (see EQUALITY).

Few early feminists pushed liberal universalism to its most radical conclusion by arguing that there were *no* justifiable bases for exclusion of adult human beings from legal equality and citizenship. Proponents of women's suffrage were also heirs to a tradition that stressed the need for social order and shared values, emphasized civic education, and pressed the importance of having a propertied stake in society. Demands for the inclusion of women did not often extend therefore to *all* women. Some women, and men, would be excluded by criteria of literacy, property-ownership, disability or, in the United States, race.

At times, feminist discourse turned liberal egalitarianism on its head by arguing *for* women's civic equality on grounds that served historically to guarantee women's exclusion from politics. One finds the case for greater female political participation argued in terms of women's moral supremacy or characteristic forms of virtue. These appeals, strategic though they may have been, were never *merely* strategic. They spoke to and from women's social location as mothers, using motherhood as a claim to citizenship and public identity. At various times, radical, liberal, democratic and socialist feminists have paid homage to women as exemplars of particular forms of social virtue.

From the vantage point of rights-based feminism, the emphasis on civic republican motherhood was a trap. But the discourse that evoked images of maternal virtue was one feminist response to a complex, rapidly changing political culture. That political culture, in the western democracies, was committed to liberalism but included as well civic republican themes of social solidarity and national identity. Women made their case within a male-dominated political order from *their* own sphere, a world of female-structured sensibility and imperatives that signified doubly their exclusion from political life and their cultural strength and importance. Less able than men to embrace an identity as a wholly autonomous social atom, often rejecting explicitly the individualist ideal, many feminists endorsed expanded familial values, stripped of patriarchal privilege, as the basis for a new communalism and social solidarity.

Feminists also turned variously to SOCIALISM, in its utopian and 'scientific' aspects, and to ROMANTICISM. Finding in notions of class oppression an analogue to women's social position *vis-à-vis* men, socialist feminists promoted notions of sex-class struggle and revolt. Feminists indebted to romanticism embraced a robust notion of a passionate, feeling self breaking the encrustations of social custom. Pressing a notion that women suffered as much from *repression*, or internalized notions of their own incapacities, as from *oppression*, or systematically imposed rules and customs that guaranteed sex inequality, feminist romantics stressed women's 'especial genius' (in the words of the American, Margaret Fuller), and hoped to see a social transformation that would free women's 'difference' and allow it to flourish.

The diverse history of feminisms in the plural forms the basis for current feminist discourse and debate. Varieties of liberal, socialist, Marxist and utopian feminism abound, including some indebted to psychoanalysis. Feminists debate equality understood in formal legalistic terms, or as equality of opportunity, or as equality of respect and treatment. Sexuality and sexual identity have become highly charged arenas of political redefinition. A minority of radical feminists urge women to separate entirely from male-dominated society while others see in this injunction a prescription for disaster. There are feminists who embrace a strong notion of women's difference and others who minimize distinctions between the sexes. Thus feminism remains an essentially contested concept.   JBE

Reading

Beauvoir, S. de: *The Second Sex*, trans. and ed. H.M. Parshley. London: Cape, 1953; New York: Bantam, 1968.

†Elshtain, J.B.: *Public Man, Private Woman: Women in Social and Political Thought*. Princeton, NJ: Princeton University Press, 1981.

Friedan, B.: *The Feminine Mystique*. New York: Norton, 1963.

Fuller, M.: *The Writings of Margaret Fuller*, ed. Mason Wade. New York: Viking, 1941.

Leach, W.: *True Love and Perfect Union: the Feminist Reform of Sex and Society*. New York: Basic, 1980.

Mill, J.S.: *The Subjection of Women* (1869). In *The Collected Works of John Stuart Mill*, ed. J.M. Robson, vol. XXI. Toronto: University of Toronto Press, 1984.

†Mitchell, J.: *Woman's Estate*. New York: Vintage, 1973.

†Richards, J.R.: *The Sceptical Feminist: a Philosophical Inquiry*. London: Routledge & Kegan Paul, 1980.

Taylor, B.G.: *Eve and the New Jerusalem*. New York: Pantheon, 1983.

Wollstonecraft, M.: *A Vindication of the Rights of Woman*, ed. I. Kramnick. Harmondsworth: Penguin, 1982.

Ferguson, Adam (1723–1816) Scottish philosopher and social theorist. His *Essay on the History of Civil Society* (1767) traced the evolution of the human mind from barbarism to civilization. See SCOTTISH ENLIGHTENMENT.

feudalism Feudal political arrangements relied on a mutual bonding of a military knight and his vassal knights who, in return for military services, received land which they eventually dominated in local and autonomous ways, demanding of their vassals in turn various dues in kind and service. Feudalism embodies a notion of obligation and loyalty that is strictly personal and hierarchical, in which legal equality is non-existent, and where honourable mutual ties are all. Serfs and villeins are virtually chattels rather than governed subjects. Feudalism is usually seen as a development after Charlemagne's short-lived empire, when Europe was subjected to the savage attacks of Vikings and Magyars from beyond its borders. All the tasks normally considered the responsibility of public authority embodied in central government were assumed by local lords who regarded such functions as private and profitable rights attached to their lands. Ecclesiastical lands and offices also fell under the control of feudal lords, seen as protectors. (See MEDIEVAL POLITICAL THOUGHT.)   JC

Reading

Bloch, M.: *Feudal Society*. 2 vols, trans. L.A. Manyon. London: Routledge & Kegan Paul, 1962.

Boutruche, R.: *Seigneurie et féodalité*. 2 vols. Paris: Aubier, 1970.

Strayer, J.R.: *Feudalism*. Princeton, NJ: Van Nostrand, 1965.

Feuerbach, Ludwig (1804–1872) German philosopher and theologian. A radical critic of HEGEL, Feuerbach's *The Essence of Christianity* (1841) portrayed religion as an expression of human alienation. See YOUNG HEGELIANS.

Fichte, Johann Gottlieb (1762–1814) German idealist philosopher; the father of modern philosophies of the will and preconscious drives. Born in Rammenau, Oberlausitz, Fichte was perhaps the first major German thinker of plebeian origins. After a long and painful struggle to establish himself, he held professorships at Jena, Berlin, and Erlangen, and became the first elected rector of Berlin University. His life was marked by abrupt breaks and changes, due not least to his eruptive temperament. Influenced at an early stage by the writings of Lessing, Rousseau, and especially Spinoza, whose determinism oppressed him deeply, his discovery of KANT came as a saving revelation.

'My system is the first system of liberty,' he wrote of his *Grundlage der gesamten Wissenschaftslehre* (Foundation of the Entire Science of Knowledge) (1794), a kind of ethical epistemology which went through some ten successive versions. He saw it as achieving in the realm of the spirit what the French Revolution had wrought in political life. Abolishing Kant's things-in-themselves, Fichte derived reality solely from the activity of the self-positing absolute ego (see IDEALISM). For him, the primal datum of the universe is ceaseless goal-creating, goal-pursuing activity: men's projects create the world, not the world their projects. Nature is so much mind-projected raw material to be subdued to human ends. The tendency of such thinking is to dissolve time-honoured distinctions between theory and practice, fact and value, finding and making. This was revolutionary indeed.

Fichte's political thought evolved in response to the imperatives of his system and the vicissitudes of the German peoples during the Napoleonic period. His early writings in defence of the French Revolution, *Die Zurückforderung der Denkfreiheit von den Fürsten Europas*

(Demand for Return of Free Thought from Europe's Princes) (1793) and *Beiträge* (Contributions) (1793), excoriate oppression and paternalism, and preach an extreme, almost anarchist individualism in the framework of a minimal contractual state. 'No man can be bound other than by himself.'

Legal and moral constraints loom larger in the *Grundlage des Naturrechts* (Treatise on Natural Law) (1796) and the *Sittenlehre* (Ethics) (1798): the state must now actively promote the welfare of its citizens, and freedom becomes the right (and duty) to develop one's 'higher', rational self.

With *Der Geschlossene Handelsstaat* (The Closed Commercial State) (1800) and *Die Grundzüge des Gegenwärtigen Zeitalters* (Characteristics of the Present Age) (1806), state power is further enlarged and its ends become identical with human life itself. Autarchy, rigidly centralized control of trade, tightly concerted collective action, turn society into an army on the march.

Manifesting wounded German pride at defeat by Napoleon, Fichte's *Reden an die Deutsche Nation* (Addresses to the German Nation) (1807/8) contain the classic exposition of the doctrine of modern NATIONALISM. The German nation, defined above all by language and an 'organic' collective character, will summon its untried spiritual forces and assume a civilizing mission. By education and indoctrination the German will be brought to see that his nation is 'his own extended self', in which he realizes his 'higher' freedom, and for which he must be permanently prepared to immolate his mere empirical self.

Fichte's later *Machiavelli* (1807) and *Politische Fragmente aus den Jahren 1807 und 1813* expound the doctrines of Pan-Germanism, naked *Realpolitik*, and the individual's forcible submission to the higher insight of the leader. In relations between states 'there is neither law nor right, but only the right of the stronger'; a nation has a natural propensity 'to incorporate in itself the entire human race'; and in order to be welded into an effective nation the Germans need a coercive national pedagogue, a *Zwingherr zur Deutschheit*. 'Compulsion is itself a form of education,' the *Zwingherr* says; 'you will later understand the reasons for what I am doing now.' Democratic numbers and common sense melt before him. 'No one has rights against Reason.' And he who possesses 'the highest understanding has the right to compel everyone to follow his insight'.

Fichte stood in the gateway to the future. With varying degrees of justification he has been described as an idealist, a liberal, an anarchist, and a modern Machiavelli; a Christian, a pantheist, an atheist; an anti-Semite, a nationalist, a chauvinist, a prophet of the politics of the masses, and a precursor of National Socialism; the first exponent of the doctrine of the inspired leader as an artist in human material; the philosopher of romanticism and the progenitor of depth psychology; a socialist, a communist, and a thinker with a secure place in the Marxist-Leninist pantheon; a nihilist, and a major forebear of existentialism, voluntarism, and philosophical pragmatism; an aggressive imperialist and a peace-loving cosmopolitan. He speaks with many voices, and his dark works bore the seeds of much that was fully developed only later in the nineteenth and twentieth centuries. The ideas he originated are still potent forces in our world.   RNH

Reading

†Aris, R.: *History of Political Thought in Germany from 1789 to 1815*. London: Allen & Unwin, 1936.

Fichte, J.G.: *Addresses to the German Nation*, trans. R.F. Jones and G.H. Turnbull. Chicago and London: Open Court, 1922.

————: *The Science of Knowledge*, trans. P. Heath and J. Lachs, New York: Appleton-Century-Crofts, 1970.

†Kelly, G.A.: *Idealism, Politics and History*, Cambridge: Cambridge University Press, 1969.

Léon, X.: *Fichte et son temps*. 3 vols. Paris A. Colin, 1922–27.

Reiss, H.S. ed.: *The Political Thought of the German Romantics 1793–1815*, Oxford: Blackwell, 1955.

Filmer, Sir Robert (1588–1653) English political theorist and controversialist. A defender of divine right absolutism and critic of 'populist' and social contract theories, Filmer is associated with 'patriarchal' political theory and is remembered principally as the author of *Patriarcha* (posthumously published in 1680),

whom LOCKE attacked in the *Two Treatises*. The eldest of eighteen children, he matriculated at (but did not graduate from) Trinity College, Cambridge, in 1604 and was called to the Bar in 1613. Filmer was knighted by James I in 1618/19; he inherited in 1629 the family home at East Sutton Park (near Maidstone), Kent, where he lived for the rest of his life. His wife, Ann, whom he married in 1610, was the daughter and co-heiress of the late Martin Heton, Bishop of Ely. Throughout his life, Filmer moved in circles that included high churchmen, antiquarians, and literary figures.

Though the last published, *Patriarcha* was the first written of Sir Robert's numerous political works, all but one other of which were anonymously published during his lifetime. These included a legal-historical defence of the superiority of the monarchy to parliament, criticisms of ARISTOTLE and some of the most important political writers of his day (including Hobbes, Milton, Grotius, Philip Hunton, and Henry Parker), a limited defence of obedience to the Cromwellian government, and a set of extracts from BODIN designed to prove that political power had always been absolute. All these writings were based upon the arguments of and in some cases derived from the text of the *Patriarcha* manuscript. The rest of Filmer's published works consists of discussion of witchcraft, a defence of the growing practice of lending money for interest, and *A Discourse concerning Power and Common Right* (published anonymously in 1680; previously attributed to Sir John Monson).

A mixture of biblical history, social structural inferences from the nature of household governance, reasoned arguments and assertions, and interpretations of English constitutional practice, Filmer's theories ultimately rested upon a Bodinian conception of SOVEREIGNTY. All authority, he insisted, was absolute and indivisible, owed its existence and nature to God, had its origin in the divine establishment of 'patriarchal' power in Adam, was passed on through the heirs to this original grant, and would still exist intact were those heirs known (see PATRIARCHALISM). Filmer's argument presumed the identity of patriarchal and political power rather than a metaphorical or analogical use of fatherhood. After the division of the world among the sons of Noah, the subsequent establishment of separate nations at the Tower of Babel, and the eventual loss of the identities of the true heirs to these titles, all power – including that of successful usurpers – remained patriarchal in nature. This was continually reconfirmed by the biblical history of the Hebrews, by the secular practices and philosophies of ancient Greece and Rome, and by the political history of England.

Kingship and fatherhood, Sir Robert insisted, had always been absolute, and the possessor of authority was answerable only to God. Rejecting or merely questioning the sovereign was to deny God's commands. Presenting one of the rare instances of a genuine doctrine of 'non-resistance' in modern political thought, Filmer held that rulers were entitled to the active obedience of their subjects even if their commands were contrary to God's law. It followed that there was no such thing as 'tyranny' and that any discomfort that was experienced at the hands of one's ruler had been decreed by God, who used human ministry to establish his mysterious order.

Filmer's theories were an important instance of the preoccupation of seventeenth-century political thinkers with origins: it was assumed that if the beginnings of political power (or specific institutions) could once be determined, their natures and functions would become clear. On these grounds Filmer criticized SOCIAL CONTRACT doctrines, replacing the state of nature with the natural power of fathers. Theorists of popular sovereignty as diverse as SUAREZ, GROTIUS, MILTON and HOBBES all made the mistaken and blasphemous presumption that people enjoyed a 'natural liberty' and that, collectively, they had once been sufficiently free to have voluntarily established political authority.

That was simply not true, Filmer countered, because people had always been born into families and were the natural and legitimate subjects of their fathers. Besides, only a contract that had been unanimously accepted would have been legitimate; any form of majoritarian agreement would have resulted in an unwarrantable denial of the liberty of the dissenters, and unanimous consent was impossible to obtain. Moreover, appeals to an 'original contract' ultimately denied their own principles and confirmed Filmer's patriarchalism by allowing the acts of one generation, the original contractors, to limit the freedom of the next, their heirs. Private possession of land was particularly troublesome for state of nature theorists, who, according to Filmer, allowed a human institution, ownership, to override what had been established by God, shared entitlement.

Claims of natural and original liberty and the rights of personal estate, of course, were generally used to justify limits on political authority. (Hobbes is a notable exception here, and in his criticism of Hobbes, Filmer pointed to this as an important contradiction.) Sir Robert contended that any attempt to define or impose restraints on political power would lead to a limited or mixed monarchy, which divided sovereignty and therefore violated the basic structural principle of governance, denied the possibility of authority, and resulted in an anarchic and unworkable government. The only conceivable alternative was the absolute, monarchical, patriarchal authority of Adam; the weakest links in that argument were the doctrines of prescriptive legitimation and usurpation.

It was of no moment, Filmer wrote, how people came to power, whether by succession, election, donation, or conquest; and it was equally irrelevant whether the form by which that power was exercised was monarchic, aristocratic, or democratic. All that mattered was that the content and nature of the authority were patriarchal and divinely ordained. On this ground, he was able to deal with the conflict that confronted royalists during the Interregnum and to defend obedience to Cromwell while remaining loyal to the exiled Charles Stuart. The cost, however, as his later critics were quick to observe, was the coherence of his doctrines, which came, in the end, to a theory of divine right prescription and to which the patriarchal power of Adam and the rest was irrelevant.

Filmer's political works were republished in 1679 and 1680 – when *Patriarcha* was first issued – as royalist contributions to the Exclusion Controversy. Their importance was immediately recognized, and they were singled out for attack by John Locke, Algernon Sidney, and others. The main lines of the criticisms consisted of a separation of political from patriarchal (or familial) authority – which was an important, early statement of the 'state/society distinction' – a reassertion on this firmer basis of the state of nature and consent theories of the origins of governance, and a shift from a static and strictly genetic view of history and manner of argument to a more dynamic and rationalistic conception of politics. In these respects, it was the need to frame answers to Filmer that set the stage for the articulation of a recognizably 'modern' mode of political discourse.   GJS

Reading
Daly, J.: *Sir Robert Filmer and English Political Thought*. Toronto: University of Toronto Press, 1979.

†Filmer, R.: *Patriarcha and other political works*, ed. and intro. P. Laslett. Oxford: Blackwell, 1949.

Greenleaf, W.H.: Filmer's patriarchal history. *The Historical Journal* 9 (1966) 151–71.

Hinton, R.W.K.: Husbands, fathers, conquerors. *Political Studies* 15 (1967) 291–300 and 16 (1968) 55–67.

Laslett, P: Sir Robert Filmer: the man versus the Whig myth. *William and Mary Quarterly* 3rd ser., 5 (1948) 523–46.

Locke, J.: *Two Treatises of Government* (1689), ed. and intro. P. Laslett. New York: Mentor, 1965; Cambridge: Cambridge University Press, 1970.

†Schochet, G.J.: *Patriarchalism in Political Thought*. Oxford: Blackwell, 1975.

———: Sir Robert Filmer: some new bibliographic discoveries. *The Library* 5th ser., 26 (1971) 135–60.

Sidney, A.: *Discourses concerning Government* (1698; written c.1682), ed. J. Robertson. London, 1772.

Sommerville, J.P.: From Suarez to Filmer: a reappraisal. *The Historical Journal* 25 (1982) 525–40.

Fortescue, Sir John (c.1385/95–c.1476)
Admitted to Lincoln's Inn before 1420, Fortescue became Lord Chief Justice of the King's Bench in 1442. He adhered firmly to the house of Lancaster until its final defeat in 1471, and spent much of the 1460s (when his most important works were written) in exile. After submitting to Edward IV he played no further part in public life.

All Fortescue's writings stemmed from the English political conflict through which he lived, but his importance in the history of political thought derives from the general ideas and categories he uses to expound his partisan case. Alike in *De natura legis nature* (1461–3), *De laudibus legum Anglie* (1471), and *The Governance of England* (1471), the foundations of his argument are laid in the Thomist/Aristotelian natural-law tradition. It is from the law of nature that human society derives; and its good order and welfare depend on government – specifically, on monarchical government. The lordship or dominion (*dominium*) exercised by rulers is thus itself in accordance with 'natural equity'. Fortescue, significantly, is not much concerned with the question of tyranny: he is very much concerned to differentiate one form of *dominium* from another. His primary distinction is between 'royal' or 'regal' lordship (*dominium regale*) and 'politic' or (in later terminology) 'constitutional' lordship (*dominium politicum*). The difference lies in the source of law in each of the two systems. Under *dominium regale* that source is the will of the ruler; under *dominium politicum* laws are made by 'the citizens' (*cives*).

Of these two basic forms, 'royal lordship', embodying in some sense the 'absolute' authority of the ruler, was for Fortescue exemplified in the French realm of his own day. *Dominium politicum*, on the other hand, was mainly important to him not in itself, but as an essential element in a third form – the *dominium politicum et regale* which, he believed, was found in the English monarchy. Here the effective and indispensable authority of an hereditary ruler is combined with the essential participation, through their representatives in Parliament, of the king's subjects (for *cives* are now *subditi*). Laws cannot be made nor taxes be levied without the full and active consent of both elements; and Fortescue carefully points the contrast with the French *dominium regale*, very much to the advantage of the English system. All this is related, further, to a complex account of the origins of human society in general as well as to an 'historical' version of the origins of specific political societies; and there are problematic affinities with earlier theological concepts of *dominium*.   JHB

Reading
†Chrimes, S.B. ed.: *Sir John Fortescue: De laudibus*

legum Anglie. Cambridge: Cambridge University Press, 1942; repr. 1949.

†———: *English Constitutional Ideas in the Fifteenth Century.* Cambridge: Cambridge University Press, 1936.

Ferguson, A.B.: *The Articulate Citizen and the English Renaissance.* esp. pp. 111–29. Durham, NC: Duke University Press, 1965.

Fortescue, Sir John: *The Works of Sir John Fortescue,* ed. Thomas Fortescue. 2 vols. London, 1869.

Gilbert, F.: Sir John Fortescue's 'dominium regale et politicum'. *Medievalia et Humanistica* 2 (1944) 88–97.

Plummer, C. ed.: *The Governance of England.* Oxford: Clarendon Press, 1885; repr. 1926.

Foucault, Michel (1926–1984) French philosopher, historian of ideas, and post-structuralist. Foucault was educated at the École Normale Supérieure, gaining a *licence* in philosophy in 1948, one in psychology in 1950 and a *diplôme* in psycho-pathology in 1952. He taught at a number of universities in France and abroad before being awarded a chair at the prestigious Collège de France in 1970. When he died he was widely regarded as one of the most eminent and original philosophers of post-war France.

Foucault started his career as a psychologist working with the mentally ill, and began to look critically at the way in which the concepts of sanity and madness, reason and unreason had emerged to define a category of mental illness. His work in this area culminated in his *Folie et déraison: histoire de la folie à l'âge classique* (Madness and Civilization) (1961). His interest in the origins of the concepts and practices of the human sciences also resulted in studies of the origins of clinical medicine and modern conceptions of the pathological (*Naissance de la clinique,* 1963), and of the emergence of the modern social sciences (*Les Mots et les choses* (The Order of Things), 1966). In 1969 he attempted a philosophical review of his methodological practice and procedures in *L'Archéologie du savoir.* The result was a highly complex analysis of what Foucault refers to as 'discourses' – that is, collections of statements, practices, classificatory schemas, and objects of analysis which, although seemingly disparate and contradictory, share a set of discursive rules which govern their functioning.

In these early works, Foucault related the knowledge and practices of the human and social sciences to seismic intellectual changes in the late eighteenth century – changes which could not be explained in terms of developments or advances in knowledge but which had to be seen as changes from one way of ordering and appropriating the field of human behaviour to another. Analogies are often drawn between Foucault's work and that of Thomas Kuhn, and these are not inappropriate, except that where Kuhn talks of paradigms Foucault talks of discourses and epistemes, and while Kuhn concentrates on the mature sciences, such as physics, Foucault deals specifically with those 'sciences' which claim knowledge of human nature and the human condition – particularly medicine, psychology, psychiatry, sociology, and social administration. Moreover, unlike Kuhn, who is more equivocal on this point, Foucault is unrelenting in his insistence on the arbitrary nature of discursive changes. Against those who see the history of civilization as a perpetual story of progress governed by humanity's increasing rationality and its increasing ability to understand human functioning, Foucault emphasizes the discontinuity, rupture, and contingency in our understanding of ourselves. The change from one constellation of discourses (the episteme) to another, and the reshuffling of configurations of statements, practices, and judgments which this involves, cannot be described as a self-justifying and self-explanatory form of rational progress, nor can it be reductively explained by references to determining material conditions (as in MARXISM). For Foucault, the arbitrary, the contingent, and the non-rational play a crucial and determining role in the history of ideas.

In 1970, in his inaugural lecture to the Collège de France, 'Orders of discourse' (see Sheridan, pp. 120–31), he first introduced the concept of POWER into his work. His next major work, *Surveiller et punir* (1975), was an analysis of the origins of the modern prison and its associated disciplinary practices which fully integrated his new concern with power and its relation to the truths of the human sciences, and which saw the prison as a field of practice in which the human sciences and their techniques of normalization could develop, before extending their surveillance to the rest of society.

Whereas Foucault's previous analyses of discourses often seem highly abstract studies of ideas, the concept of power allowed him to place much more emphasis on the social and material conditions in which these ideas developed and which they also transformed. For Foucault, power is an integral component in the production of truth – truth and power function interdependently: 'Truth is a thing of the world: it is produced only by virtue of multiple forms of constraint. And it induces the regular effects of power. Each society has its regime of truth, its "general politics" of truth: that is, the types of discourse which it accepts and makes function as true . . . ' (*Power/Knowledge*, p. 131).

The human sciences and their practices have increasingly come to monitor, discipline, and 'treat' the deviant elements in the social body. The ENLIGHTENMENT left a legacy of sciences and associated practices whose rules and norms provide criteria of normal functioning – whether in physical or mental health, or in social behaviour and personal and sexual conduct. Foucault's purpose is to show that these standards are as rooted in the irrational, the contingent, and the iniquitous as those which they have replaced. In his work on the prison, in his first volume of his *Histoire de la sexualité* (1976), and in a host of other minor essays (*Power/Knowledge*, 1980), Foucault offers a broad-ranging analysis of the way in which the modern individual or subject is produced. The human sciences have determined the very categories within which we conceptualize our own subjectivity and our implicit criteria for normality and pathology. In doing so they have created the disciplined subjects of the modern state and, by implication, the state itself. The modern state governs less through the use of force than through its use of the knowledge and practices of the human sciences to construct its subjects' subjectivity – through a 'micro-physics' of power.

In the month before his death, the second and third volumes of Foucault's *Histoire de la sexualité* were published and a fourth was said to be nearly ready to go to press. Foucault continued his attempt to locate the origins of modern conceptions of subjectivity and moral agency through the study of sexual ethics.

However, his analysis substantially revised his earlier work in two significant respects: he placed much less emphasis on the operation of power, and he now located the development of the subject of sexual ethics, not in the rationalism of the seventeenth and eighteenth centuries, but in the birth of western reason in the philosophizing of the Greeks. In both classical and Christian thought – albeit in different ways – sex, selfhood, and moral agency became intimately related. The two new volumes offer an account of the successive transformations of sexuality and its subjects to show that our current obsession with sex, far from being a sign of our liberation, indicates our lack of any non-coercive conception of how we should live.

Despite the frequent changes in Foucault's position, two themes can be recognized throughout his work. Foucault's analyses are 'genealogical' in character – the revealing of the irrational and iniquitous beneath the apparently rational – and as such they are profoundly influenced by NIETZSCHE; they are directed against the 'truths' and 'knowledge' of the modern world, and they aim to unmask operations of power in the practices which these truths legitimate so as to enable those who suffer from them to resist. They aim to show us that we have made ourselves perverted, mad, sick, and delinquent by subjecting ourselves to knowledge and practices which seek out the perversions, madness, sickness, and delinquencies of others. Behind this genealogical project lies a fundamental belief that there is no constant human subject in history, no valid philosophical anthropology, no 'true' human condition or nature: 'Nothing in man – not even his body – is sufficiently stable to serve as the basis for self-recognition or for understanding other men' (*Language, Counter-Memory, Practice*, p. 153). There is, then, no meaning or order to history; nor can there be any escape from the functioning of power and contingency. Struggle is always necessary to avoid domination, yet it cannot guarantee liberation since power is an inherent feature of social relations – we cannot act without affecting the conditions under which others act. It does not, however, follow that power will always take the particular form it has assumed in its alliance with the human sciences.

The commonest criticism levelled at Foucault arises from this denial of liberation and his apparent relativism. It looks as though Foucault can offer us no reason to prefer another state of affairs to the one we now live in. However, these criticisms partly miss the point: Foucault's purpose is to create uncertainties and doubts, to get us to re-think the categories and practices within which we live – that is, to free us, to at least some extent, by making us aware of what we have lost in becoming what we are; and thereby to loosen the grip which the human sciences currently exercise over the self-understanding of the subjects of the modern state.   MP

Reading

Foucault, M.: *Folie et déraison: Histoire de la folie à l'âge classique*. Paris: Plon, 1961; trans. R. Howard as *Madness and Civilization*; abridged edn, New York: Pantheon, 1965.

––––––: *The Birth of the Clinic: An Archeology of Medical Perception*, trans. A. Sheridan. London: Tavistock; New York: Pantheon, 1973.

––––––: *The Order of Things: An Archeology of the Human Sciences*, trans. A. Sheridan. London: Tavistock; New York: Pantheon, 1970.

––––––: *The Archaeology of Knowledge*, trans. A. Sheridan. London: Tavistock; New York: Pantheon, 1972.

––––––: *Discipline and Punish*, trans. A. Sheridan. London: Allen Lane; New York: Pantheon, 1977.

––––––: *History of Sexuality*, vol. I: *An Introduction*, trans. R. Hurley. London: Allen Lane, 1979. Vol. II: *L'usage des plaisirs* and III: *Le souci de soi*. Paris: Gallimard, 1984.

––––––: *Language, Counter-Memory, Practice*, ed. D.F. Bouchard. Ithaca, NY: Cornell University Press; Oxford: Blackwell, 1977.

––––––: *Power/Knowledge*, ed. C. Gordon. Brighton, Sussex: Harvester; New York: Pantheon, 1980.

†Sheridan, A.: *Michel Foucault: the Will to Truth*. London: Tavistock, 1980.

Fourier, Charles (1772–1837) French utopian socialist. Born in Besançon, Fourier was a small-time commercial traveller and lived mainly in Paris. During the French Revolution he observed and deplored the commercial machinations of merchants, hoarding or destroying grain at will; he also lost his patrimony. Otherwise, he led an uneventful, solitary life. Fourier was an autodidact, and rarely referred to other thinkers, although Enlightenment ideas of PROGRESS influenced his historical schema. His prolific works all reiterate the same basic ideas; their fullest statement appears in *Théorie de l'unité universelle* (1822).

Fourier's utopianism began with his analysis of 'the 144 evils of civilized society', which included commerce, deception and cuckoldry. He had a complex historical taxonomy, based on numerology, which showed Civilization (the society of his time) to be an inferior social form, barely removed from barbarism. Harmonism, the highest social form, would be followed by decline and the human historical cycle would take some 80,000 years.

Human beings, Fourier said, are endowed with twelve basic 'passions', which require satisfaction: the passions of the five senses; the passions of friendship, love, familism, and ambition; the 'cabalistic' passion for intrigue; the 'butterfly' passion for variety; and the 'composite' passion for combining physical and mental pleasures. In ideal circumstances, the thirteenth passion, for Harmony, unifies the others. Each individual's temperament is determined by a different combination of ruling passions, but in Civilization the passions are thwarted or perverted by bad institutions such as marriage and commerce and bring only misery to the self and to others.

Fourier's utopian community, the 'phalanstery', was a form of social organization in which everyone's passions would be fully developed and satisfied. The phalanstery, consisting of 1,610 people, each of a different temperament, was based on the principle of *attractive labour*. Everyone worked at what pleased him or her most: the rose-lover cultivated roses, while children, who delighted in playing with dirt, acted as dustmen. People worked in groups called *series*: they did twelve different jobs each day, to satisfy the butterfly passion, and also had nine meals! Because all social activity and work was based on natural attraction and inclination, no formal political organization was necessary: society operated spontaneously. Rewards were allocated in proportion to contribution, talent and investment, but the distinction between rich and poor ceased to matter, because everyone lived communally. Children were also raised communally, by those with a passion for child-rearing. In a parallel utopia, *The New Amorous World* (unpublished until 1967), Fourier described the sexual organization of the phalanstery, based on passionate attraction, free love and multiple relationships. Social cohesion would be strong because people would form attachments to their co-workers in different series and to a variety of sexual partners. Fourier envisaged a world-wide federation of independent phalansteries, and roving 'armies' of cobblers, pastry-cooks, lovers, etc., who would visit the communities to engage in competitions and festivals.

Fourier waited daily in a restaurant for a rich patron to implement his ideas. He found no takers, but he inspired many disciples. There were experiments on Fourier's lines in Rumania and the Swiss Jura, and more recently in California. Although branded by MARX and ENGELS as a 'utopian socialist' with no adequate historical or class analysis, Fourier was praised by Engels for his 'dialectical analysis' of social problems. The surrealist Breton's *Ode to Fourier* praised his psychological insight. Fourier's ideas were also acclaimed by many French students during the unrest of 1968, because he advocated spontaneity and personal development. The combination of social philosophy with psychological insight, and the emphasis on personal happiness, makes Fourier's theory permanently interesting, despite its many idiosyncrasies. (See also UTOPIANISM.)　　　BG

Reading

Fourier, C.: *Oeuvres complètes*, ed. D. Oleskiewicz. 12 vols. Paris: Anthropos, 1965–8.

†———: *The Utopian Vision of Charles Fourier*, ed. J. Beecher and R. Bienvenu. London: Cape, 1972.

†Goodwin, B.: *Social Science and Utopia*. Brighton, Sussex: Harvester, 1978.

Riasanovsky, N.V.: *The Teaching of Charles Fourier*. Berkeley: University of California Press, 1969.

Taylor, K.: *The Political Ideas of the Utopian Socialists*. London: Cass, 1982.

Frankfurt School   See CRITICAL THEORY.

Franklin, Benjamin (1706–1790) American statesman, diplomat, scientist, and essayist. Franklin, regarded as a founding father, was a member of the continental congress and a delegate to the constitutional convention. Before the Revolution, he served as a deputy postmaster-general, Pennsylvania assemblyman, and colonial diplomatic agent in England. During the war, he represented America in France. Earlier Franklin achieved considerable fame for his scientific experiments, particularly on electricity, and his invention of useful gadgets. His fortune came from printing and publishing, and he was editor of the *Pennsylvania Gazette* newspaper. He wrote numerous editorials, essays and pamphlets on politics, economics, science, morality and self-improvement. Under the pseudonym Richard Saunders, he produced for over twenty years *Poor Richard's Almanack* which contained information on science and technology, and numerous moral aphorisms associated with but not coined by Franklin. In his widely read *Autobiography* (1788–9), Franklin presents his life in terms of intellectual, social and moral development.

Franklin's multifarious ideas and recommendations achieve some unity as a broad political theory when considered in terms of the social evolution and PROGRESS which he constantly supported. Franklin rejected formal Christian dogma but saw order in the universe. Through reason and experience, man learned about nature, society and himself and should apply this knowledge to better his condition. For this improvement to occur, there must exist freedom of religion, speech and the press, and economic opportunity which is best created by territorial expansion and free trade. Implicit in these notions is Franklin's view that men are equal. He criticized the wealthy and the British aristocracy for their intellectual and political pretensions. He preferred the common sense and practical knowledge which he made available to all men through his publications. To encourage the productivity and social harmony necessary to achieve a higher standard of living, Franklin urged men to cultivate thirteen virtues – temperance, silence, order, resolution, frugality, industry, sincerity, justice, moderation, cleanliness, tranquillity, chastity, and humility.

Government could facilitate progress if it were unified, capable of purposeful planning and action, and mindful of man's liberty.

Franklin argued against proprietary government, taxation without representation, and slavery. After the Revolution, he supported universal male suffrage and a unicameral national legislature. Besides defending the interests of the common man, Franklin based his politics on practical considerations. Suffrage encouraged patriotism and obedience; unicameralism thwarted the rich and provided for united, efficient government. Such government should stimulate economic growth by land acquisition, trade and education in the useful arts, and by building bridges, roads and canals.

Prior to the Revolution, Franklin believed that progress could be achieved under a benign monarch. This view, along with his continual fear of factions and mobs, suggests some scepticism about democratic politics. His call for benevolent government projects, such as hospitals, was tempered by his criticism of social welfare programmes which might breed laziness. A more appropriate path to progress, he thought, was through the inspiration and guidance provided by his teachings, virtues and aphorisms. Franklin has consequently been criticized at times for reducing human progress to material well-being, moral and social philosophy to business ethics, and the justification of democratic government to political pragmatism.   DPR

Reading

†Becker, C.: *Benjamin Franklin: a Biographical Sketch*. Ithaca, NY: Cornell University Press, 1946.

†Conner, P.: *Poor Richard's Politics: Benjamin Franklin and the New American Order*. New York: Oxford University Press, 1965.

Franklin, B.: *The Autobiography of Benjamin Franklin*, ed. L.W. Labaree *et al*. New Haven, Conn.: Yale University Press, 1964.

———: *The Complete Poor Richard's Almanacks published by Benjamin Franklin*, ed. W.J. Bell. Barre, Mass.: Imprint Society, 1970.

———: *The Papers of Benjamin Franklin*, ed. L.W. Labaree *et al*. 23 vols. New Haven, Conn.: Yale University Press, 1959– .

†Stourzh, G.: *Benjamin Franklin and American Foreign Policy*. Chicago: University of Chicago Press, 1954.

†Van Doren, C.: *Benjamin Franklin*. New York: Viking, 1938.

fraternity   As a political idea, fraternity implies relationships between citizens or within a specific group which, like the ideal relation between siblings, are characterized by feelings of affection and commonality and by dedication to shared or similar goals.

Fraternity, like politics, is neither automatic nor free from conflict. The relation between brothers involves great rivalry as well as great affection. Fraternity requires that fratricidal impulses be subordinated and ruled by shared values and positive affects (Genesis 4:7; 33:1–11; 50:19–20). An element of volition is crucial in fraternity. Fraternal rituals, ancient and modern, assume that while the potential for fraternity may originate in accidents of birth and rearing, the actuality depends on willed or chosen commitments.

In this respect, fraternity is similar to friendship. Both fraternity and friendship, moreover, unite persons in the same role (as opposed to bonds like that between parent and child). To that extent fraternity, like friendship, implies equality. Yet unlike friendship, fraternity derives from and implies a common relationship to authority. Fraternal relationships, in fact, may be more likely among subjects in a hierarchical society than among citizens in a strictly egalitarian regime.

Ancient political theory regarded fraternity as a relationship between specific persons, involving intense affections and feelings of obligation. In this view, fraternity is a relatively exclusive bond, in practice if not by nature. Just as blood-brotherhood belongs in tribes and families, the *polis* is the natural home of political fraternity. Moreover, *adelphia* (brotherhood) nourishes *philia* (friendship): the higher forms of fraternity, like the theoretical city of philosophy, rest on habits of affiliation developed in less voluntary and less inclusive associations (Aristotle, *Politics*, 1262b8–25; 1263a41–1263b7).

While Christian teaching differed by proclaiming that all human beings are brothers by nature (Galatians 3:28), this spiritual and theoretical truth applied in practice only to reborn persons for whom 'Christ is all and in all' (Colossians 3:11). In classical Christian doctrine, most human beings, blinded by sin, are unable to recognize the fatherhood of God and unable to feel their fraternity with all humanity.

In the temporal world, even Christian fraternity, though informed by its vision of human kinship, will be relatively exclusive, with special affections and duties: 'Honour all men. Love the brotherhood' (I Peter 2:17).

Theorists of the ENLIGHTENMENT, by contrast, often aspired to realize the ideal of universal fraternity. In their doctrine, human beings have a 'fraternal instinct' or a drive toward 'species being' which is impeded by the barriers of nature and custom. Achieving human brotherhood requires, first, overcoming nature, principally through the advance of natural science, and, second, breaking the psychological hold of hierarchy and parochial loyalty by exposing the bonds which tie human beings to authority and to particular persons as only so many human contrivances. Fraternity is thus reduced to a sort of after-effect, neglected in favour of liberty and equality, the means which, it is thought, will make universal fraternity possible.

Earlier, more rationalistic theorists conceded that any cosmopolitan fraternity would rest on diffuse sentiments, like Hutcheson's 'universal calm benevolence', probably weaker than the affections uniting family, tribe and nation. Later, more romantic thinkers sometimes denied this limitation, as Emerson did in prophesying that eventually 'all men will be lovers'. In both cases, devotion to the brotherhood of man has been associated with suspicion and hostility toward the less inclusive forms of fraternity.

Modern political thought and practice are unfriendly to fraternity between specific persons. Modern political thinking generally presumes that, in public life, everyone is included who is not specifically excluded. In fraternal relationships, everyone is excluded who is not included. Modern regimes encourage a way of life which is mobile, specialized and extensive. Fraternity is fostered by stable and intense relationships which nurture similarity in character and fate. Modern political thought, recognizing the antipathy between fraternity and modern politics, unwisely has been inclined to slight or deny the human need for the support of brothers. (See also COMMUNITY.) WCMcW

Reading
Aristotle, *The Politics*, ed. E. Barker. Oxford: Claren

don Press, 1946.

Freud, S.: *Totem and Taboo*. In *The Complete Psychological Works of Sigmund Freud*, trans. and ed. J. Strachey, vol. XIII, pp. ix-161. London: Hogarth, 1971.

Hutter, H.: *Politics as Friendship*. Waterloo, Ont.: Wilfrid Laurier University Press, 1978.

†Ignatieff, M.: *The Needs of Strangers*. New York: Viking, 1985.

†McWilliams, W.C.: *The Idea of Fraternity in America*. Berkeley and Los Angeles: University of California Press, 1973.

Nelson, B.: *The Idea of Usury: from Tribal Brotherhood to Universal Otherhood*. Princeton, NJ: Princeton University Press, 1949.

Simmel, G.: *The Sociology of Georg Simmel*, trans. and ed. K. Wolff, pp. 307–76. Glencoe, Ill.: Free Press of Glencoe, 1950.

Stephen, J.F.: *Liberty, Equality, Fraternity*. London and New York: Holt & Williams, 1875.

freedom 'Liberty, what crimes have been committed in thy name!' said Madame Roland at the height of the French Revolutionary Terror. Madame Roland's view of the dangers of the pursuit of liberty is widely shared; but no analysis of its nature or of its value commands anything like universal assent. It is sometimes suggested that freedom resists analysis, because it is – like justice or democracy – an 'essentially contested concept': no one can deny that freedom is a good, but an endless and inconclusive conceptual battle takes place between those who try to persuade us to adopt their preferred account of its nature.

This is, however, exaggerated, for many writers have thought that while it was clear enough what freedom was, what mankind needs is order, leadership and enlightenment rather than freedom. This view received its first 'philosophical' defence in PLATO's *Republic*; for Plato, political freedom was the goal of democracies, and amounted to a more or less complete absence of control over the activities of individuals or the people as a whole. It led to the rule of demagogues, who swiftly set themselves up as tyrants exercising absolute and arbitrary power over their subjects. Plato's status as the fountain-head of western philosophy is confirmed by the way he combined this hostility to political liberty with a defence of the view that only virtuous action is fully voluntary – an argument which has proved perennially attractive to theorists of inner, or moral, freedom.

HOBBES did not share Plato's belief in rule by 'philosopher-kings', but agreed that what men needed was order, and that to achieve it they must renounce the useless liberty of the state of nature. This liberty to do anything whatever, even to injure or kill one another if it seemed necessary, must be useless because each person's exercise of his liberty is at odds with everyone else's. Hobbes's views have become the commonplace of subsequent conservative thinking about the state. They received an exaggerated expression in de MAISTRE's attack on the French *philosophes* who had let slip a tiger when seeking freedom for the ordinary man; and after de Maistre a philosophy of order and of discipline is the stock-in-trade of the European right's unappeased hostility to the French Revolution. To Rousseau's cry 'Man is born free and is everywhere in chains,' this sceptical conservatism has always replied, 'No, he is born in submission and will be mad and dangerous if he is liberated from his obedience to constituted authority.'

It does not follow that for such writers freedom is of no value. Hobbes was at pains to distinguish two views about freedom. One was the (mistaken) classical view that freedom was a matter of political self-government, and that only a popular republic could be free. This was MACHIAVELLI's view, and sometimes MILTON's. Hobbes insisted that once government was instituted freedom was a matter of 'the silence of the laws' and consisted in 'immunity to the service of the commonwealth'. Whether the form of government was monarchical, aristocratic or democratic was neither here nor there; the more we are left alone, the freer we are. This partly anticipated CONSTANT's distinction between 'the liberty of the ancients' and 'the liberty of the moderns'. Hobbes's 'non-interference' account of freedom is certainly an account of modern liberty; but where Constant agreed that self-government was a form of liberty, though one unsuited to the modern world, Hobbes denied that it was a form of liberty at all.

Hobbes's view of freedom, which identifies it with non-obstruction, is frequently described as 'negative' liberty, in contrast to theories which identify freedom with some form of positive self-government or self-mastery. The *locus classicus* of this distinction is Berlin's 'Two Concepts of Liberty' of 1957. While the 'negative' theory of liberty is simply described – my freedom is a matter of the range of things I may do without being stopped or punished by others – an equally simple account of positive liberty – I am free when I am my own master – hides underlying complexities only momentarily.

This is revealed by three well-known positive theories. The Stoic theory of freedom claimed that the slave could be as free as the emperor on his throne. This was obviously paradoxical, since the legal position of a slave was the paradigm of unfreedom, and the slave had a master in the most straightforward sense. The stoic riposte was that no matter what the master demanded of the slave, it was always up to the slave whether to comply or not. The choice was always his, even if it was only the choice between compliance and being beaten to death. The doctrine of *apatheia* – the idea that we should cultivate the ability to feel nothing – fits into this theory, less by trying to make the slave content with his powerlessness than by reminding us that if we fear nothing we are immune to threats and intimidation, cannot be coerced, and need never co-operate unless we so choose.

The Stoic theory flouts common sense: to have a choice only between humiliating obedience and a painful death is hardly to be 'free'. Yet this is all the choice the slave has; to insist that, even so, it is he who decides whether he obeys or not misses the point that what is open to him to choose from has been so narrowed that it is a denial of 'freedom'.

A second positive doctrine dates back to Plato, and was later espoused by KANT, and by many subsequent idealists. On this view, we act voluntarily only when we act rightly. All men aim to do good, and when they do not, it is the result of error or being swayed by passion; therefore no action other than a virtuous one is fully voluntary. In Plato, this argument rests on a teleological view of the cosmos, which implies that each of us has a proper goal or end which we would pursue if we were wholly rational and understood the universe adequately; in Kant, it rests on a view of what a wholly consistent moral will would inspire us to do. It also suggests that we are free only when our 'noumenal' selves are in control of our 'phenomenal' selves.

The view that freedom consists in the mastery of the higher element over the lower goes back to Plato at least, and finds echoes in St Paul, St Augustine, and other Christian writers. Its critics claim that it is an illiberal and dangerous view of freedom, because it allows those who claim to be more enlightened than we to dominate us in the name of our higher selves. This may feel like slavery to us, but 'really' it is freedom. It must be said that Kant at least was an impeccable liberal. He distinguished very precisely between this 'internal' freedom, which was a matter for each individual to achieve for himself or herself, and political freedom, which was a matter of limiting the law to the hindering of hindrances. Plato, by contrast, had no compunction about allowing the law to dictate the individual's moral convictions: 'freedom' – even in this strained sense – was not at stake, because he never thought that unforced virtue is the only virtue which matters.

The third, related, view is ROUSSEAU's identification of freedom with obedience to laws we prescribe to ourselves, and this in turn with obedience to the GENERAL WILL. Rousseau held that the basis of political life was a social contract which amounted to a unanimous agreement to obey *law* as opposed to individual inclination. Law is valid when it aims at the general interest; each of us is free only when we obey law. If we set out to break the laws we have helped to make, we shall be forced into obedience by the executive power of the state and in the process we shall be 'forced to be free'. It is this suggestion which alarms critics of positive theories of liberty. But Rousseau does not explain what he means, and it is possible that he chose only a misleading way of saying that we could not expect to be free – that is, free from the arbitrary interference of other men – unless we all obey the law.

The dangers of Rousseau's passion for 'ancient' liberty were seen very clearly by several post-revolutionary writers. Constant's discussion of the contrast between the liberty of the ancients and the liberty of the moderns explicitly contrasted the conditions of the Greek democratic city-states and nineteenth-century France, and pointed out that freedom for the Greek citizen rested on slavery on the one hand and the demands of more or less constant warfare on the other. TOCQUEVILLE and J. S. MILL were less explicit about the contrast between ancient and modern conditions, but both were at pains to defend liberty against an excess of democracy. The notion that individuals were entitled to a private sphere in which they might act and think as they pleased was the more important in an age of omnipotent public opinion. Though both were very attracted to the Greek ideal of the engaged citizen, both were more anxious to defend negative liberty against the despotism of opinion and the tyranny of the majority.

Recent writers have largely subscribed to some version of the modern or 'negative' account of freedom. Most of them have emphasized the distinction between freedom on the one hand and the value of our freedom on the other. To the old question whether an impoverished and propertyless labourer in a capitalist society can be free, the answer cannot be a simple yes or no – rather that the worker is not compelled by law or brute force either to work or not to work, but that this freedom is of little value, seeing that he has to work or starve. So John RAWLS, in arguing that one element in justice is the principle that everyone should enjoy the widest liberty consistent with a like liberty for all, moves on to interpreting this as the principle that we should maximize equal liberty on the basis of that liberty being of a fair value for everyone. This, in effect, implies that we should do what we can to ensure that even the least favoured can do enough with the freedom they have to make that freedom worth having.

This view, implying something like the welfare state's concern to secure equal opportunity, is repudiated by the fiercer libertarians on the one side and the fiercest critics of capitalism on the other. The purest libertarians identify freedom with the protection of all people and their property from violations of their natural rights (see LIBERTARIANISM). Wage labourers are free if they sell their labour in exchange for the capitalist's money, unfree if they are made to work for an employer they have not chosen from among the ranks of those willing to choose them. The limits of legitimate liberty are set by our natural rights, and they are best understood in a proprietary sense. That is, the right to freedom is one facet of the fact that I am my own person, and not the slave or partial slave of anyone else. By contrast, one strand of Marxist thought has held that under capitalism we are all the slaves of capital; thinking in proprietary terms betrays this fact (see MARXISM). Workers collectively are forced to labour – or starve – and the owners of capital are forced to compete and innovate – or lose their wealth. The unfreedoms of everyday life are in the end to be explained by the greater unfreedom of a society tyrannized over by its own institutions. Such claims can hardly be spelled out briefly, let alone be analysed. It is, however, worth observing that they cannot be criticized on purely conceptual grounds, that is, by insisting that what Marx calls freedom – that is, a society's rational control of its own productive activities – is not freedom.

The most general moral to be learned from the conceptual analysis of freedom is that because freedom literally 'means' little more than 'not obstructed, controlled or mastered', theories of freedom have invariably been accounts of the obstacles, forces or persons which most importantly master us. This is true even of existentialist accounts of the human condition (see EXISTENTIALISM). The existentialist association of freedom with a terrible anxiety, and the implication that freedom is something of a curse, is an account of the absence of the forces or persons which might have controlled us and spared us the anxiety of making decisions but, alarmingly, do not. To criticize such theories requires much more than a conceptual analysis of freedom; they must be taken seriously as psychological, social and political theories and criticized as such. AR

Reading

†Berlin, I.: Two Concepts of Liberty. In *Four Essays on Liberty*. Oxford: Oxford University Press, 1969.

Constant, B.: *Essai sur la liberté des anciens comparée à celle des modernes*. In *Oeuvres*. Paris: Pléiade, 1964.

†Gray, J. and Pelczynski, Z. eds: *Conceptions of Liberty in Political Philosophy*. London: Athlone, 1984.

Hobbes, T.: *Leviathan*, ed. C.B. Macpherson. Harmondsworth: Penguin, 1968.

Machiavelli, N.: *The Discourses*, ed. B. Crick. Harmondsworth: Penguin, 1950.

Marcus Aurelius: *Meditations*, trans. A.S.L. Farquharson. Oxford: Clarendon Press, 1944.

†Mill, J.S.: *On Liberty*. In *The Collected Works of John Stuart Mill*, vol. XVIII. Toronto: University of Toronto Press, 1977.

Plato: *The Republic*, trans. P. Shorey. London: Heinemann, 1956.

Rawls, J.: *A Theory of Justice*. Cambridge, Mass.: Harvard University Press, 1971; Oxford: Oxford University Press 1972.

Ryan, A. ed.: *The Idea of Freedom*. Oxford: Oxford University Press, 1979.

French Enlightenment A period in history which follows the end of absolutism, with the death of Louis XIV in 1715, and precedes the French Revolution of 1789, which it is often said to have provoked. The French Enlightenment was a time of ideological ferment and excitement, in which *les philosophes* captured the awed attention of almost all sections of society. It produced no great original thinkers like Descartes, Spinoza, Hobbes or Locke, but was rather the second stage of the Age of Reason, when intellectuals with remarkable literary gifts used the methods of seventeenth-century rationalism as instruments against traditional ideas about religion, society and culture, and adapted the innovations of seventeenth-century empiricism to develop popular theories based on an appeal to 'science'.

The *philosophes* were more divided in their opinions than is commonly supposed, but they all shared a conception of philosophy as action-oriented activity, and while some were Deists, some atheists, some lax Catholics, some sceptical Protestants, all were anti-clerical, united in their hostility to 'superstition', to the irrational and intolerant policies of the church, and to the cruelty of the secular authorities who tried to secure conformity by force. They were all humanitarians, committed to reform.

The political theorists of the French Enlightenment may be divided into three main competing schools: the royalists led by VOLTAIRE, the parliamentarians led by MONTESQUIEU, and the republicans led by ROUSSEAU. Both the parliamentary and the royalist schools were inspired by English philosophy, and both regarded the English system of government as a 'mirror of liberty'. They looked, however, to different English philosophers, and they understood English government in different ways. Montesquieu and his followers drew their inspiration from LOCKE, and what they admired in England was the constitution established by the Revolutionary settlement of 1689. Voltaire and his friends looked rather to Francis BACON, and what they admired in England was less its method of parliamentary government than its system of civil freedom and religious toleration. Montesquieu proposed to adapt to the situation of France Whiggish policies for sharing sovereignty between the executive, legislative and judicial authorities. Voltaire aspired to realize in France the Baconian dream of the sovereignty of reason, assured by the progress of science and technology, the centralization of government and the elimination of superstition.

Up to a point, the disagreement between Montesquieu and Voltaire reflected in eighteenth-century thought earlier, and deep-rooted, political antagonisms. Montesquieu, an hereditary nobleman and one-time president of a provincial legislative court or *parlement*, could be seen as an ideologue of his class, his theory a restatement in modern terms of the old *thèse nobiliaire*, according to which the ancient constitution of France established the king as nothing other than the first peer of the realm, subject to the law as defined by the noble magistrates of the *parlements* and the commands of God as expounded by the church. Voltaire could equally be thought to be restating the old *thèse royale*, according to which the king was the author of the law, and as the representative of every single one of his subjects stood above all the other estates and institutions of the realm in order to rule for the good of his kingdom as a whole.

And yet while the ideological content of Montesquieu's and Voltaire's theories to this extent continued two seventeenth-century *thèses*, both philosophers developed arguments in support of their ideas which were new in themselves, and were called forth by a new situation. The seventeenth century had witnessed the continuous expansion in France of royal absolutism at the expense of the nobility

and all other intermediate estates, so that the champions of the *thèse nobiliaire* could only appeal to fading memories and a dying tradition. An event in the early eighteenth century gave the *noblesse de robe* a totally new lease of life: the Duc d'Orléans as regent found it necessary to convoke the *parlements* to invalidate the will of Louis XIV which would rob him of the powers he sought. Thus unexpectedly re-animated, the parliamentary estate struggled throughout the decades that followed for more and more power. In Montesquieu it produced a theorist of genius to justify such claims.

Part of the novelty of Montesquieu is that he did not argue legalistically. His approach foreshadowed what was later to be known as 'political sociology'. He looked for general laws of social organization which would enable one to ascertain what constitutional forms and political institutions would best suit a given society, and which arrangements would produce predictable effects. On the basis of these investigations, Montesquieu concluded that freedom could be most effectively preserved in a state where no organ of government could monopolize power and so become despotic. Hence his formulae for divided sovereignty, for CHECKS AND BALANCES and the SEPARATION OF POWERS. The relevance of these conclusions to the situation of France was obvious.

The royalism of Voltaire and his friends was presented in no less modern terms. Voltaire, self-consciously and proudly bourgeois, did not dissimulate his personal antagonism towards aristocrats of all orders, and especially the *noblesse de robe*, which used its powers in the *parlements* to burn books and torture heretics; but as a 'scientific' thinker giving the lead to the contributors to the 'scientific' volumes of the *Encyclopédie*, his emphasis was placed on the rational case for ABSOLUTISM. Bacon, invoked by both DIDEROT and d'ALEMBERT, the editors of the *Encyclopédie*, as the prophet of their enterprise, had provided them with a double message: first the inauguration of scientific programmes for the improvement of men's life on earth and then the introduction of a centralized government to put those programmes into effect, a government such that only a powerful monarch unencumbered by churchmen, lawcourts and parliaments could be expected to provide. As a rule, the Enlightenment stood for reason; and while other, more 'old-fashioned' champions of absolutism appealed to tradition, the *Encyclopédistes* were eager to put reason on the side of the monarch's claim to a monopoly of power.

'Enlightened despotism' is an unfair name for what Voltaire, Diderot, d'Alembert and their collaborators had in mind when they called for enlightened absolutism; for they combined with their adherence to the Baconian political design a liberal or Lockeian belief in the natural rights of the individual to life, liberty and property. Montesquieu wrote for the *Encyclopédie*, and he was acknowledged by the younger *philosophes* as Voltaire's equal as a patriarchal theorist of the Enlightenment, but in the 1750s, when the first volumes of the *Encyclopédie* were published, few of its contributors had any sympathy for the claims of the parliamentary estate which Montesquieu represented. When Louis XV banished the Paris *parlement* in 1753 to make way for a royal court, the *Encyclopédistes* made no protest. They were more concerned just then to reform the Paris theatre and French music, a revolution in taste being seen as a step towards a revolution in thought.

It was at about this time that there emerged the third main strand in Enlightenment political thought, a *thèse républicaine*, so to speak, as an alternative to the modernized forms of both the *thèse royale* and the *thèse nobiliaire*. Its most important exponent, Rousseau, was then an intimate friend of Diderot and an active contributor to the pages of the *Encyclopédie*. His REPUBLICANISM was as rationalistic in its formulation as was the parliamentarianism of Montesquieu and the royalism of the *Voltairiens*. To a certain extent, moreover, it had been anticipated in the early writings of Montesquieu himself.

In *Les Lettres persanes* of 1721 Montesquieu had betrayed certain yearnings for republican government, and he undoubtedly did regard it as the highest ideal until the opportunity of witnessing republican government in action in Venice and Holland disillusioned him, and the happy surprise of finding liberty thriving under a constitutional monarchy in England changed his outlook. Montesquieu's vision of republican

virtue had been derived from reading about the republics of antiquity; it did not stand the test of experience, on which, as a scientifically minded man, he knew he must rely.

Rousseau, on the other hand, drew his republican inspiration from the modern world, from the city-state of Geneva where he had been born and bred. Until he was well over forty, Rousseau did not look below the surface of the liberal Genevan constitution to discern the ruthless domination of an hereditary patriciate. His model republic was Geneva as Calvin had designed it in the sixteenth century, not as it had become in the eighteenth, but Rousseau elaborated that model with such eloquence that a republican state became a living and potent ideal in the eighteenth-century imagination.

The success of Rousseau's presentation of his *thèse républicaine* was perhaps due in part to the fact that he did not simply rely on Geneva as his model, or introduce any elements of Protestant religion. He modified the Genevan model with features derived from Sparta and Rome, and with the ethics of civic humanism. He could thus appeal to readers who had received a classical education. It was one of the ironies of eighteenth-century France that the Catholic church, which the Bourbon Kings had gone to such lengths to protect, did not teach its pupils to venerate monarchy, but rather, in developing their study of antiquity, prompted them to admire the achievements of the Greek *polis* and the Roman republic. Rousseau's ideas took root in soil which the church had helped to prepare.

Montesquieu's Whiggish theory, temporarily out of fashion when he died in 1755, re-emerged a few years later, when the king's ministers at Versailles took more drastic action against the *parlements*. The *Encyclopédistes* then split into somewhat bitterly opposing camps; some, such as HOLBACH and Diderot, adopted Montesquieu's arguments for divided sovereignty as the only defence against despotism; while others, led by Voltaire, urged the king to resist the claims of the reactionary *parlements* and clergy and exercise his authority alone.

The success of the American Revolution in the 1770s prompted a new excitement around the idea of republican government. CONDOR-

CET, the youngest of the great *Encyclopédistes*, corresponded with several American intellectuals, developing ideas about the kind of constitution a republic the size of the United States could best adopt. Republican government need no longer be exclusively associated in the European mind with the Greek city-states or the cantons of the Swiss confederation. Rousseau's claim that only a small state could be genuinely republican was being refuted by events. Republicanism could, after what had happened in America, be contemplated as an option for France.

The French monarchy, having spent vast sums to help the Americans rebel against the king of England to punish the British for seizing Canada, soon found it had unleashed arguments which could call into question its own title to rule; and certain theorists who did not go the length of proposing republican government in France, challenged the king's right to enact the role of emperor abroad.

The French Enlightenment exalted the 'noble savage'; Rousseau was not the first nor the only *philosophe* to suggest that the half-naked inhabitants of the North American forests or the South Pacific islands were equally intelligent and indeed morally superior to the sophisticated denizens of European cities. The explorer Bougainville had suggested it – and dozens of fashionable writers besides Rousseau asserted it; Diderot and Raynal went even further and demanded that the European rulers should leave the 'noble savages' in undisturbed possession of their homelands; neither to invade them like the Spanish nor corrupt them like the Dutch, by introducing trade and settlements.

Other voices in the Enlightenment adhered to the strict Baconian ideology of progress. The spread of commerce, of industry and modern medicine into the continents beyond Europe was welcomed and encouraged as part of the conquest of nature, the triumph of science over ignorance. In place of missionaries carrying bibles, such *philosophes* envisaged technologists carrying the benefits of European civilization to savages whose very nobility would preserve them from the evils of European corruption.

Faith in the innocence of the exotic savage did not go together with any confidence in the simple people of the lower classes at home. Rousseau and Voltaire extolled the democratic elements in the Geneva constitution, but that was only because a system of universal public instruction had made the working class of Geneva an educated class. As a general rule, Rousseau favoured popular participation in legislation, but not in government; and Voltaire did not wish even universal education, let alone democracy, to be extended to France. If there was an exponent of democracy among the *Encyclopédistes* it was Condorcet, but even he proposed to limit the people's role in politics to voting for representatives, who in turn would ensure that the making of laws and policies was confined to persons of superior intellect. The expert was an ever-present figure in Enlightenment political thought, a simplified version of PLATO's philosopher-magistrate; and in Condorcet's writings the conception of democracy is fused with the idea of a cultured and public-spirited civil service running the state for the common good, an ideal which, if TOCQUEVILLE's analysis of the *ancien régime* is correct, was not far removed from the self-image of the bourgeois bureaucracy which served the Bourbon kings.

Voltaire in his celebrated novel *Candide* mocked optimism, but the Enlightenment itself was an age of optimism; although the Lisbon earthquake of 1755 shattered belief in a benevolent Deity, nothing seemed able to modify the *Encyclopédistes'* faith in progress. Even HELVÉTIUS, who conceived of man as a sort of machine built to a standard pattern, looked forward to continued improvement; and Condorcet himself, awaiting arrest by agents of the Terror in 1793, proclaimed the inevitable approach of human perfection.

Yet none of the *philosophes* offered much in the way of rational grounds for their optimism. Predictions of improvement in the future might be expected to find among empiricists a basis in evidence of improvements in the past. But much of the literature of the Enlightenment depicts the past history of man as a history of decay. Rousseau declared that man was naturally good, only to add that man's long experience since he had left the state of nature was one of increasing corruption. Condorcet said the human race was moving stage by stage

169

upwards towards perfection, yet he depicted the achievements of classical antiquity being succeeded by a thousand years of darkness and retrogression.

At odds with one another in their theories of politics, the *philosophes* were no less divided in their views on economics. Again, they often looked to English theorists for their inspiration, but some followed the mercantilist teaching of Locke, others the doctrine of free trade. François Quesnay, founder of the physiocratic school, was the most important of the latter (see MERCANTILISM and PHYSIOCRACY). He argued that each man was motivated by self-interest, but the natural law of harmony enabled unfettered private activity to generate the public good. Paradoxically, most of the physiocrats favoured at the same time the Voltairian policy of enlightened absolutism; they wanted *laissez-faire* in economics, but *dirigisme* in politics, if only as a means of abolishing traditional entrenched restraints on commerce. The failure in practice of the free trade policies adopted by the government of Louis XV in the 1760s to serve the interest of anyone except rapacious dealers prompted several philosophers of the Enlightenment – notably Galieni, Diderot and Holbach – to argue for state control of the economy; while others – Turgot, Morellet and Mercier de la Rivière – restated the physiocratic case for economic freedom.

Luxury was a subject much discussed in the course of this debate, and once more the *philosophes* disagreed among themselves. The champions of luxury argued that it was a motor of industrial progress, increasing both consumption and the quality of goods produced. The opponents held that it diverted industry from the production of things needed by everyone to the production of useless objects for the amusement of the favoured few. Some tried to separate their economic theory from considerations of morality, others to reconcile them. Greed, avarice, envy were even welcomed on the grounds that they stimulated the economy by spurring men to action. Voltaire's mistress, Madame du Châtelet, who translated MANDEVILLE into French, and even Voltaire himself in *La Défense du mondain*, eagerly took up the idea that private vices could generate public benefits.

Rousseau was the most eloquent of those who attacked luxury, but he was by no means alone. Diderot added a certain bitterness to his moral indignation at the rich being encouraged in their self-indulgence while the poor were left to starve. Even Holbach, who lived in luxury, denounced the doctrine of luxury. Some critics carried the attack to the point of challenging private property itself; one was the Abbé Mably, in a critique of the physiocrats published in 1768, *Doutes proposés aux philosophes économistes*; another was the author of the *Code de la nature*, commonly ascribed, on slender evidence, to the Abbé Morelly. These books were of small importance in the context of the Enlightenment, but they were later recognized as forerunners of the distinctively nineteenth-century theory of socialism (see COMMUNISM).

One tendency conspicuously absent from the political theory of the French Enlightenment is conservatism. One might have expected, as Holbach feared, that scepticism in the fields of religion and philosophy would lead to scepticism in matters of political and social reform and so encourage a conservative outlook. But there was in fact no systematic conservative thought in the French Enlightenment like that of David HUME in the Scottish Enlightenment or that of Alexander HAMILTON in the American Enlightenment. This is an indication of the universality of discontent in France. Hume and Hamilton were, after all, post-revolutionary theorists – Hume in the situation established in the British Isles by the settlement of 1689 and Hamilton in that established in America by the War of Independence; both could be conservatives because both had something – namely liberty – to conserve. The theorists of the French Enlightenment had no such motive; if they differed among themselves in their understanding of liberty, they agreed in thinking that liberty was something they did not yet have.   MC

Reading

†Brumfitt, J.H.: *The Enlightenment*. London: Macmillan, 1972.

Cassirer, E.: *The Philosophy of the Enlightenment*. Princeton, NJ: Princeton University Press, 1951.

†Cranston, M.: *Philosophers and Pamphleteers*. Oxford: Oxford University Press, 1986.

Darnton, R.: *The Literary Underground of the Old*

Regime. Cambridge, Mass.: Harvard University Press, 1982.

Frankel, C.: *The Faith of Reason*. New York: King's Crown Press, 1948.

Gay, P.: *The Party of Humanity*. London: Weidenfeld & Nicolson, 1964.

———: *The Enlightenment: an Interpretation*, 2 vols. London: Wildwood House, 1969.

†Hampson, N.: *The Enlightenment*. Harmondsworth: Penguin, 1968.

Havens, G.R.: *The Age of Ideas*. New York: Henry Holt, 1986.

†Hazard, P.: *European Thought in the Eighteenth Century*. London: Hollis & Carter, 1954.

Wade, I.O.: *The Intellectual Origins of the French Enlightenment*. Princeton, NJ: Princeton University Press, 1971.

Freud, Sigmund (1856–1939) Austrian psychoanalyst and social philosopher. Freud was born on 6 May 1856, in Freiburg, Moravia, in what is now Czechoslovakia. In 1859 the family moved to Leipzig, and then a year later to Vienna, which was Freud's home until 1938 – the time of the Nazi Anschluss. He spent his last year in London, where he died of long-standing cancer on 23 September 1939. Freud took medical training, practised neurology, and worked on hypnosis, especially with Breuer, in the 1890s. He was the founding father of the psychoanalytic movement; he had many disciples but dissident schools also emerged, e.g. those of Adler and Jung.

In his later years especially, Freud applied psychoanalysis to broader social problems. His social and political theory is expressed above all in *Civilization and its Discontents* (1930), *The Future of an Illusion* (1927), and his essays on war (1915 and 1932). The common descriptions of Freud's world-view – cold, unyielding, tenacious, stubborn, a Jewish vision – suggest, correctly, that it is harsh, uncompromising and pessimistic. He was determined to face the world directly, offering no salvation, no consolations, no prophecy. He was not an advocate of radical social change; nor was he – except tangentially – a critic of capitalism.

Freud aimed at the scientific understanding of mental phenomena through discovery of their causes and regular confirmation of the meaningful arrangements thereby established. He developed a structural account of the mind, according to which there are three psychical realms, regions or provinces. The basic drives are associated with the id, which is the oldest, darkest and least accessible of these psychical provinces. It is wholly unconscious, irrational and amoral, 'a cauldron full of seething excitations'. These predominantly sexual drives – of which genital sexuality is the highest but certainly not the exclusive form – demand immediate gratification and ignore the dictates of reality. The simple and dominating impulse is towards the satisfaction of the innate needs or drives of the organism.

The id cannot simply be left to follow its volatile and potentially destructive course. Hence there emerges from it an intermediary between it and the external world, with the task of finding out the circumstances in which id intentions can be realized. This region of mind, known as the ego, emerges out of the id during childhood, as a realistic response to external demands and conditions: it learns to adapt. It is predominantly but not completely conscious, and is therefore not equivalent to consciousness. Its function is that of self-preservation, and it is therefore dominated by the reality principle (as opposed to the pleasure principle).

The third constituent of mind is the super-ego, which is the home of repression, conscience and guilt. It is 'the vehicle of tradition' and the centre of prohibitions, taboos and censorship. It may be opposed to the ego, and readily goes beyond the needs of survival. But the superego, primarily through the guilt which it inculcates, is a primary instrument of civilization, transforming the child into 'a moral and social being', and gradually dispensing with external measures of coercion.

Freud's psychological model expresses, in dynamic and complex form, the common notion of a conflict between reason and passion. His account of the instincts altered, as he recognized non-erotic aggressivity and destructiveness, and he ultimately reduced the instincts on theoretical grounds to the erotic and the aggressive or destructive, presenting the evolution of civilization as an everlasting struggle between Eros and Death, Love and Hate, the instinct of life and the instinct of death. Even though he claimed that these instincts hardly ever operated in isolation, his grand theory is presented, commonly and correctly, as mythical.

Freud presented several speculative anthropologies portraying the acceptance of civilization as a kind of social contract, a rational exchange. 'Civilized man has exchanged a portion of his possibilities of happiness for a portion of security.' However, what particular individuals gain and lose differs. The redistribution of psychic energy demanded by civilization occurs mainly amongst men, who are compelled 'to carry out instinctual sublimations of which women are little capable'. Hence women, standing for the interests of family and of sexual life, easily become enemies of civilization. This picture, along with such particular theories as that of penis envy, helps explain the strong feminist opposition to Freud.

People bear the mutilation of their erotic lives in various ways. But central to the process of civilization as a whole is the strengthening of the sense of guilt, necessary to progress but costly to happiness. Civilization thus grows upon a basis of anxiety, of repressions, of sublimations and reaction-formations, 'by means of which a child with a quite other innate endowment grows into what we call a normal man, the bearer and in part the victim of the civilization that has been so painfully acquired'. Civilization also offers some outlets for inhibited aggressive drives, e.g. the punishment of criminals which allows vicarious satisfaction, and warfare.

Freud's interpretation of the masses as lazy, unintelligent, unruly, disinclined to instinctual renunciation, and in need of authority encouraged a vision of an upper stratum of 'men with independent minds', men who had 'subordinated their instinctual life to the dictatorship of reason'. He hoped, though fitfully, that they might act as educators and guides to lesser mortals.

The steady invasion of social life by reason has not destroyed the old Adam of aggressiveness, however. Socialists and communists – parodied in Freud's account as believing that 'man is wholly good and is well-disposed to his neighbour, but the institution of private property has corrupted his nature' – are dismissed for their idealism about human nature. Private property was not, for Freud, the source, but a result, of human aggressiveness which would, in the absence of private property, express itself in other forms, e.g. sexual competition. Aggression, 'this indestructible feature of human nature', will persist. Communism challenged basic human drives and was therefore bound to fail.

Freud has been criticized on many grounds. His clinical interpretations have been challenged, often because the relevant behaviour can be explained by (real) external events rather than by postulated internal events. Many other and broader factors than innate aggressive drives, themselves questionable, are causes of war. Existing resources – larger than Freud imagined – may make fuller instinctual satisfaction possible, and basic drives may be directed towards forms of gratification which minimize their destructive impact.

Nonetheless, Freud's larger speculations, resting on his earlier conclusions about the human psyche, remain challenging.   GCD

Reading

Freud, S.: *Civilization and its Discontents*, trans. J. Rivière. London: Hogarth, 1930.

——: *The Future of an Illusion*, trans. W.D. Robson-Scott. London: Hogarth, 1962.

——: *Two Short Accounts of Psychoanalysis*. Harmondsworth: Penguin, 1963.

Fromm, E.: *The Crisis of Psychoanalysis*. London: Cape, 1970; Harmondsworth: Penguin, 1978.

Marcuse, H.: *Eros and Civilization: a Philosophical Inquiry into Freud*. Boston: Beacon, 1955; London: Routledge & Kegan Paul, 1966.

†Roazen, P.: *Freud: Political and Social Thought*. New York: Vintage, 1968.

G

Gaius (active AD 130–80) Roman jurist. His *Institutes* anticipated those of JUSTINIAN. See ROMAN LAW.

Gandhi, Mohandas Karamchand (1869–1948) Great Indian leader, and a stimulating thinker. Gandhi was trained as a lawyer in England, and after an indifferent legal practice in India he left for South Africa. During his stay there of over two decades, he conducted many campaigns against racial discrimination and developed his well-known method of *satyagraha* or non-violent resistance. After his return to India in 1915 he became the unchallenged leader of the Indian nationalist movement. He evolved a new language of political discourse, an apparently archaic but historically evocative set of symbols, and a simple and austere life as a way of identifying himself with his poorest countrymen, and mobilized them under the leadership of the radically transformed Congress Party. He launched the Non-cooperation Movement in 1920, the Civil Disobedience Movement in 1930 and the Quit India Movement in 1942. He was largely responsible for India's independence in 1947. His moment of triumph was also his moment of failure, for independence was marked by widespread Hindu-Muslim riots, the ferocity of which shattered him and sapped his will to live. Although frail and broken, he trekked his way to distant trouble-spots and single-handedly restored peace and good will. When a fanatic Hindu assassinated him, Albert Einstein thought that future generations would 'scarce believe that such a one as this ever in flesh and blood walked upon this earth'.

Gandhi's moral and political thought is based on a relatively simply metaphysic. For him the universe is regulated by a Supreme Intelligence or principle which he preferred to call *satya* (Truth) and, as a concession to convention, God. It is embodied in all living beings, above all men, in the form of self-conscious soul or spirit. The spirit constitutes man's essence. Being merely a material construct, the body is ultimately unreal and has no moral claims. All wants and desires beyond the biological minimum are forms of sensual indulgence and spiritually degrading. For Gandhi contemporary western civilization is centred around the body, as is evident in its multiplication of wants, lack of self-restraint and the decline of moral and spiritual depth, and is unlikely to last long.

Gandhi argues that since all men partake in divine essence they are 'ultimately one'. They are not merely equal, but 'identical'. As such, love is the only proper form of relation between them; it is 'the law of our being', of 'our species'. Love implies care and concern for others and total dedication to the cause of 'wiping every tear from every eye'. Negatively it implies *ahimsa* or non-violence. Gandhi's entire social and political thought is an attempt to work out the implications of the principle of love in all areas of life.

For Gandhi the state 'represents violence in a concentrated form'. It speaks in the language of compulsion and uniformity, saps its subjects' spirit of initiative and self-help, and 'unmans' them. Since men are not yet morally developed and capable of acting in a socially responsible manner, the state is necessary. However, if it is not to hinder their growth, it ought to be so organized that its activities employ coercion as little as possible and that as large an area of human life as possible is left to voluntary efforts.

As Gandhi imagines it, a truly non-violent state is composed of small self-governing and relatively self-sufficient village communities relying largely on moral and social pressure. They elect district representatives, who in turn elect provincial and national representatives. The police in a non-violent state are basically social workers enjoying the confidence and support of the local community and relying on moral suasion and public opinion to enforce the law. Crime is treated as a disease, requiring not punishment but understanding and help. Decisions are taken by majority. However, the majority rule 'savours of violence' and is subject to two basic constraints. First, when a minority feels very strongly about an issue the majority must not override it. Second, since man is a moral being he must not be required to do things contrary to his conscience. Every citizen therefore retains the right to engage in CIVIL DISOBEDIENCE against policies he sincerely considers to be morally outrageous. For Gandhi, it is 'a birthright that cannot be surrendered without losing self-respect'.

A non-violent state is committed to *sarvodaya*, the growth or uplift of all human beings. As such, 'vested interests' have no place in it. Private property denies the 'identity' or 'oneness' of all men, and is immoral. It also leads to such evils as exploitation, sensual indulgence, and a contempt for one's fellow men. In Gandhi's view it is a 'sin against humanity' to possess superfluous resources when others cannot even meet their basic needs. Since the institution of private property already exists and men are attached to it, he suggests that the rich should take only what they need and hold the rest in trust for the community. Increasingly he came to appreciate that the idea of trusteeship was too important to be left to the good will of the rich, and assigned a considerable economic role to the state without evidently realizing that he was thereby contradicting his minimalist view of it. He advocated heavy taxes, limitations on the right of inheritance, state ownership of land and heavy industries, and even nationalization without compensation.

Gandhi's contribution to the creation of modern India was immense. Among other things he reformed Hinduism, undermined Untouchability, sensitized Indians to questions of social justice, set an example of amazing courage and fearlessness, and gave Indians a strong sense of cultural pride and their nationalism a rare breadth and depth. At the wider level, Gandhi's contributions consisted in his critique of VIOLENCE, his vision of a non-violent society and a novel method of political action. As for his limitations, he failed to appreciate the importance of industrial civilization, assimilated intergroup relations and conflicts to the interpersonal, and introduced an unacceptable degree of subjectivism into political life. Further, he blurred the dividing line between personal and political morality and encouraged the view that political life was basically an arena for working out personal moral and existential problems.   BCP

Reading
†Bondurant, J.V.: *Conquest of Violence: the Gandhian Philosophy of Conflict.* Berkeley: University of California Press, 1965.
Dhawan, G.: *The Political Philosophy of Mahatma Gandhi.* Ahmedabad: Navajivan, 1962.
Gandhi, M.K.: *The Collected Works of Mahatma Gandhi.* Ahmedabad: Navajivan, 1958.
———: *Hind Swaraj or Home Rule.* Ahmedabad: Navajivan, 1938.
———: *Non-violent Resistance* (1951). New York: Schocken, 1961.
†Iyer, R.N.: *The Moral and Political Thought of Mahatma Gandhi.* New York: Oxford University Press, 1973.

general will A phrase always (correctly) associated with Jean-Jacques ROUSSEAU, who gave the notion of *volonté générale* a central place in his political and moral philosophy. Rousseau himself insists that 'the general will is always right', that it is 'the will that one has as a citizen' – when one thinks of the common good and not of one's own particular will (*volonté particulière*) as a private person. Even virtue, he says, is nothing but a conforming of one's personal *volonté particulière* to the public *volonté générale* – a conforming which 'leads us out of ourselves', out of egoism and self-love, and toward 'the public happiness'. At roughly the same time as

Rousseau, DIDEROT used the notions of *volonté générale* and *particulière* in his *Encyclopédie* article, 'Droit naturel' (1755), saying that it is 'to the general will that the individual man must address himself in order to know how far he must be a man, a citizen, a subject, a father, a child'; and that *volonté générale*, which 'never errs', is 'the tie of all societies'.

These associations notwithstanding, the idea of *volonté générale* was well established in the seventeenth century, though primarily as a theological rather than as a political idea. It referred to the kind of will that God supposedly exercised in deciding who would be granted grace sufficient for salvation and who would be consigned to hell. The question at issue was: if God wills that all men be saved – as St Paul asserts in a letter to Timothy – does he have a general will that produces universal salvation? And if he does not, why does he will particularly that some men not be saved? Finally, would it be *right* to save some but not all? The first work of consequence to treat these questions through an appeal to 'general will' was apparently Antoine Arnauld's *Première apologie pour M. Jansénius* (1644), though Arnauld argued, following Augustine's *De corruptione et gratia*, that God's original general will to save all men before the Fall turned into a postlapsarian particular will to save only the elect through pity. That is also roughly PASCAL's view in the magnificent *Écrits sur la grâce* (1656–8); but Pascal's main achievement was to convert *volonté générale* from a purely theological concept into a social and political one by claiming that men, and not just God, should 'incline' toward what is general, that *particularisme* is the source of all evils, above all self-love. In the 1680s Malebranche both revived and transformed the language of general and particular will, saying that it is because God's operation is general and simple (through uniform laws) that he cannot particularly save each and every man.

That Rousseau was familiar with all of this is clear from remarks in the *Confessions* (1765–70) and from the theological exchange of letters between St Preux and Julie de Wolmar in book six of *La nouvelle Héloïse* (1761). Did he, then, use the notions of *volonté générale* and *volonté particulière* simply out of historical piety? By no means. Judith Shklar has argued that the notion of general will 'conveys everything he most wanted to say', that it is 'a transposition of the most essential individual moral faculty [volition] to the realm of public experience' (1975, p. 184). Rousseau's reasons for using *volonté générale* were essentially philosophical – however ready-made for his purposes the old theological notion may have been. After all, the component words of *volonté générale* – 'will' and 'generality' – represent two of the main strands in Rousseau's thought. 'Generality' stands for the rule of law, for civic education which draws us out of ourselves and toward the general (or common) good, and for the non-particularist citizen-virtues of Sparta and republican Rome; and the notion of 'will' stands for his conviction that 'civil association is the most voluntary act in the world'.

But it could still be asked: how can one reconcile Rousseau's insistence on an all-shaping, 'generalizing' educative authority with his equal insistence on choice and personal autonomy? Precisely *through* his theory of education, which is the heart of his entire philosophy. At the end of civic time, when men have been 'denatured' and transformed into citizens, they will *finally* have civic knowledge and a 'general will' – just as adults finally have the moral knowledge and the independence that they (necessarily) lacked as children. 'There is with nations, as with men, a time of youth, or, if you prefer, of maturity, for which we must wait before subjecting them to laws.' Autonomy arrives at the end of a process, and the general will is *at last* as 'enlightened' as it was always 'right'.

In the end the generality cherished by Pascal, Malebranche, Bayle, Diderot and Rousseau turns out to occupy a place midway between *particularity* and *universality*; and that *généralité* is something distinctively French. This becomes visible if one contrasts their thought with that of KANT, viewed as the perfect representative of German rationalistic universalism ('I am never to act otherwise than so that I would also will that my maxim should become a universal law . . . reason extorts from me immediate respect for such [universal] legislation'), and with that of William Blake, seen as a typical representative of English ethical 'empiricism':

175

He who would do good to another
must do it in Minute Particulars.
General Good is the plea
of the scoundrel, hypocrite and flatterer.

The discovery of an *ethos* that rises above 'minute particulars', that moves *toward* universality but has its reasons for not building *on* reason, and for drawing up short at a more modest 'generality': the advocacy of a kind of willing which is more than egoistic and self-loving and *particulière* but less than a Kantian, universal, 'higher' will – that is the distinctively French contribution to practical thought worked out by Rousseau, who socialized the 'general will' bequeathed to him by his greatest French predecessors.   PR

Reading

Bréhier, E.: Les lectures Malebranchistes de Jean-Jacques Rousseau. In *Études de philosophie modernes*. Paris: Presses Universitaires de France, 1965.

Postigliola, A.: De Malebranche à Rousseau: les apories de la volonté générale et la revanche du 'raisonneur violent'. In *Annales Jean-Jacques Rousseau* 39. Geneva: Julien, 1980.

†Riley, P.: *The General Will before Rousseau: the Transformation of the Divine into the Civic*. Princeton, NJ: Princeton University Press, 1986.

Shklar, J.N.: General will. In *Dictionary of the History of Ideas*. New York: Scribner, 1975.

———: *Men and Citizens*. Cambridge: Cambridge University Press, 1969.

Wokler, R.: The influence of Diderot on Rousseau. In *Studies on Voltaire and the Eighteenth Century*, vol. CXXXI. Oxford: Voltaire Foundation, 1975.

Gentile, Giovanni (1875–1944) Italian philosopher. In his early years an exponent of IDEALISM and a friend of CROCE, he later embraced FASCISM.

George, Henry (1839–1897) American economist, journalist and philosopher. Born into a pietistic family in prosperous Philadelphia, George received little formal education. In 1858 he made his way to California where he earned a meagre living as a journalist and editor for the next twenty years. In 1879 he completed his major work, *Progress and Poverty*; shortly afterwards he moved to New York City where he soon became embroiled in local politics. As the United Labour Party candidate, he registered an impressive electoral vote in the first of his two unsuccessful attempts to win the mayoralty. George spent the 1880s, his period of greatest fame, writing further books elaborating his 'single tax doctrine' and enjoying remarkable success as a public speaker on its behalf at large meetings in Britain, the United States and Australia. His last years were marked by political and intellectual controversies within the radical circles attracted to his ideas and by the relative neglect of academic economists.

George's doctrine is at once an ethical and an economic theory. It incorporates a Lockeian conception of natural rights which assigns exclusive unfettered ownership of labour's products to the owners of labour (see LOCKE) but subjects ownership of unproduced natural resources to some sort of egalitarian distributive constraint. Social injustice consists in the effects *both* of restrictions on the free disposal of labour and its products *and* of unencumbered private ownership of unproduced natural resources. The economic theory is an account of the manner in which such restrictions and ownership bring about those effects.

Working within the theoretical structure of CLASSICAL POLITICAL ECONOMY, George attempts to explain the apparent paradox of persisting poverty in the midst of growing productivity, of static wages in the face of increasing wealth. He deploys Ricardo's theory of rent to show that in an otherwise competitive economy all such increases ultimately accrue to landowners who, as owners of an indispensable production factor which is in fixed supply, enjoy a unique monopolistic bargaining position within any community. Increases in the rental and sale value of natural resources occur merely by virtue of technical progress and population growth, and the payments of this 'unearned increment' constitute deductions from the returns to labour and capital alike. Hence the true conflict of interests in capitalist society lies not between workers and capitalists but rather between both of these and landowners. Gross disparities in wealth distribution are largely attributable to this land monopoly, as well as to the monopolistic effects of other restrictions on competition.

George proposes the 'single tax' as a just and

efficient remedy for these social evils. Rather than institute each person's equal right to natural resources by nationalizing or constantly redistributing them, democratic governments should levy a 100% tax on the rental value of land. This measure would at once suffice as the source of a minimal state's revenue, discourage land speculation (seen as a primary cause of business cycles) and thereby introduce greater competition into the land market. The resultant distribution of wealth would be both less unequal and entirely congruent with what each person makes and saves.   HS

Reading

Andelson, R.V. ed.: *Critics of Henry George*. London: Associated University Presses, 1978.

†Barker, C.A.: *Henry George*. New York: Oxford University Press, 1955.

†Geiger, G.R.: *The Philosophy of Henry George*. New York: Macmillan, 1933.

George, H.: *Progress and Poverty*. London: William Reeves, 1884.

———: *Social Problems*. London: Henry George Foundation, 1931.

———: *A Perplexed Philosopher*. London: Henry George Foundation, 1937.

Gerson, Jean (1363–1429) French theologian. Chancellor of the University of Paris, and a leading figure in the conciliar movement. See CONCILIARISM.

Gierke, Otto von (1841–1921) German legal theorist. His account of voluntary associations has often been regarded as an early version of the pluralist theory of the state. See PLURALISM.

Gobineau, Joseph-Arthur (1816–1882) French diplomat and social theorist. His *Essay on the Inequality of Human Races* was a major influence on the development of RACISM.

Godwin, William (1756–1836) British political philosopher, novelist, and literary hack. The son of a poor Presbyterian minister, Godwin was educated by Dissenters and himself became a minister to a Presbyterian congregation in 1778. He showed little aptitude and diminishing faith. By 1783 he was living in London and earning a precarious living writing

rather undistinguished literary ephemera. During the 'Debate on the French Revolution' (see RADICALS, BRITISH) he persuaded his publisher to finance him while he produced a summary of developments in recent political philosophy. The result was Godwin's major work, *An Enquiry Concerning Political Justice*, published in 1793 and substantially revised for second and third editions in 1795 and 1797. In 1794 he further enhanced his reputation with the publication of his most successful novel, *Caleb Williams*. Godwin particularly influenced a younger generation of aspiring writers – most notably Wordsworth, COLERIDGE, Southey and Hazlitt, and later Shelley. In 1797 Godwin married Mary WOLLSTONECRAFT who died in childbirth some five months later (the child survived to become Mary Shelley, author of *Frankenstein*). Godwin's frank *Memoirs* of his consort, published in 1798, provoked licentious comment in the reactionary press and lost him much public support. He continued to write, producing essays, novels, biographies, some execrable plays, a number of children's books, and a few political pieces – most notably his *Reply to Parr* (1801), *On Population* (1820) (a reply to Malthus's attack on him in the *Essay on the Principle of Population*), and his last work, *Thoughts on Man* (1831). However, with the collapse of the radical literary culture of the 1790s, and with his name against him, much of his last thirty years was lived in debt and relative obscurity.

In *Political Justice*, Godwin rests his anarchist and utopian conclusions on a few simple axioms – namely, that sound reasoning and truth will always conquer error, that such reasoning and truth can be communicated, that truth is omnipotent, that the vices of man are the result of mistaken beliefs, and that man is, in consequence, a perfectible being. He begins from Thomas PAINE's position that society is always a blessing and government always an evil. Rather than being required to restrain the disruptive forces of human nature, government is itself responsible for these forces. Through their use of coercion, fraud, exploitation, and venality, governments corrupt their people, kindling in them conflicting and insatiable passions and setting each individual against his neighbour. To retain their power and authority, governments must keep their citizens ignorant. However, man being by nature rational and perfectible, society has gradually become more enlightened through the ages, and consequently some of the evils of government have been ameliorated. As our understanding of morals and politics improves and spreads through society we will no longer submit to arbitrary authority. The less we submit, the more our capacity for self-government develops and the more we come to act according to reason and justice. Government will find itself increasingly impotent; its sphere of influence will contract and it will finally disappear, leaving a natural society of men and women able to live their lives solely according to truth and justice through the exercise of their understanding and judgment and through the practice of full and free public debate and discussion. Because of reason's power to convince, because of the force with which truth strikes us, because errors are inevitably discomfiting for rational beings, and because we cannot willingly do wrong once we recognize that it is wrong, we will be able to live fully moral lives. Godwin is prepared to admit that there might need to be some form of representative assembly in the transition to this anarchic society, but he is reluctant to concede any arrangement or practice which interferes with the individual's right to act solely on the basis of the full and free exercise of his private judgment.

The first four books of *Political Justice* present Godwin's case for improvement and criticize other views of government and society. In these books Godwin argues that we ought always to act upon principles of justice and that these require that we do what in general produces the most benefit to mankind. The final four books go on to attack, in turn, established systems of government, attempts by government to interfere with political and religious opinion, systems of law and punishment, and forms of property. In his last book, 'On Property', Godwin argues that people's understanding will so improve that they will gain complete control over their physiological processes – they will be able to avoid both sleep (which arises from inattention), and the decline of their faculties. People will become immortal.

Modern commentators tend to dismiss God-win's utopian beliefs as fanciful, and they concentrate instead on his apparent UTILITAR-IANISM, arguing that this makes an important contribution to the history of political thought. However, although Godwin does believe that we ought to do that which produces the most happiness, he constrains the principle of utility by a more fundamental principle. This is most clearly seen in his account of PROPERTY. He argues that a distribution of property is just when it produces the greatest possible amount of happiness. He also claims that we have a right to the property which this optimal distribution would allot us. However, although he concedes that the present distribution is far from optimal, he nonetheless insists that we have stewardship rights over the property we presently hold. He moves away from utilitarianism by arguing that no one has a right to violate these stewardship rights – even if they do so to give people their rights under justice. Our right to judge how we should dispose of the property over which we have stewardship rights trumps our right to receive our share under a utility-maximizing distribution. Our right to judge is superior to our rights as derived from the principle of utility. Judgment is sacrosanct because it is only through the full and free exercise of private judgment that knowledge, truth, and understanding can make progress. We owe ourselves the development of truth because only thus do we perfect our natures by becoming more fully rational. In his commitment to this view Godwin betrays his continued debt to Rational Dissent, and to the view that in becoming more fully rational we are conforming our nature to the rational design of nature – or God's providence. We cannot detach Godwin's moral theory from his utopian beliefs – they are of a piece.　　　　MP

Reading

Clark, J.P.: *The Philosophical Anarchism of William Godwin*. Princeton, NJ: Princeton University Press, 1977.

Godwin, W.: *An Enquiry Concerning Political Justice*, ed. I. Kramnick. Harmondsworth: Penguin, 1976.

———: *Caleb Williams*, ed. D. McCracken. Oxford: Oxford University Press, 1977.

†Locke, D.: *A Fantasy of Reason: the Life and Thought of William Godwin*. London: Routledge & Kegan Paul, 1980.

†Marshall, P.: *William Godwin*. New Haven and London: Yale University Press, 1984.
†Philp, M.: *Godwin's 'Political Justice'*. London: Duckworth, 1986.

Goldman, Emma (1869–1940) Russian anarchist. Influential among American anarchists between 1890 and 1915, she introduced feminist ideas into anarchist thought. See ANARCHISM.

Gramsci, Antonio (1891–1937) Italian social theorist. Born in Sardinia, the son of a minor public official, Gramsci is generally regarded as one of the most distinguished Marxist thinkers since MARX. Because of his physical deformity (he was hunchbacked) and a family scandal (his father was imprisoned for corruption) Gramsci endured a miserable childhood, but misfortune encouraged his scholarly bent, and in 1911 he won a scholarship to the University of Turin, where he specialized in linguistics. In 1913 he joined the Italian Socialist Party (PSI) and soon wrote regularly for Party newspapers, including *Avanti*. Although a revolutionary, the young Gramsci displayed contempt for the 'scientific' determinism of the orthodox Marxists (see MARXISM). In contrast he much admired the romantic activism of SOREL and the neo-Hegelian 'spiritualism' of CROCE. Inspired by the Russian Revolution, a triumph of will-power over economic circumstances, Gramsci began to engage actively in political organization, becoming a prominent figure in the emergent factory council movement, whose theory was elaborated in *Ordine Nuovo*, a Party weekly, during the *biennio rosso* of 1919–20.

After the first world war Italy suffered from depleted agriculture, rampant inflation, and mass unemployment. Industrial unrest was rife, especially in northern Italy, but instead of promoting this revolutionary upsurge, both the PSI and the trade unions urged caution, much to Gramsci's dismay. He put this 'betrayal' down to the fact that the traditional working-class institutions owed their origins to the competitive capitalist system and were therefore inclined to obey the 'rules of the game', imposed by the proprietary classes. The PSI, for example, tended to become absorbed by parliamentary electioneering. The trade unions, for their part, expressed a view of labour as a commodity, to be bought and sold. Factory councils, on the other hand, could transcend the logic of capitalism since they embodied not the imperatives of bourgeois legality, but the everyday work experience of the proletariat. Council deliberations and activities would, Gramsci maintained, serve three purposes: they would raise the workers' consciousness, to develop solidarity as well as initiative; they would create a system of 'dual power' in the workplace, by restricting the decision-making capacity of the owners; and they would prefigure the future socialist state, in which the politico-administrative functions previously executed by bourgeois state organs would be assumed by the councils. The intention was not to *bypass* the PSI and the unions, but to demote them. The rapidly growing council structure would act as the 'prime mover' of the revolutionary process. Change would come 'from below'.

Gramsci did not succeed in resolving a central problem: how can spontaneity be reconciled with the discipline and co-ordination necessary for revolution? After some initial victories the council movement was defeated by the clever 'carrot-and-stick' policies of the top Italian industrialists, and, with FASCISM looming on the horizon, Gramsci effectively abandoned the *Ordine Nuovo* theory and accepted a more orthodox Leninist approach (see LENIN). In January 1921 he helped to found the Italian Communist Party, and became its general secretary (and a member of parliament) in 1924. Arrested two years later, he remained a prisoner of Mussolini's regime until his death, from natural causes, in 1937. While confined he produced his major theoretical achievement – a vast collection of notes and (mainly unfinished) essays, published posthumously as the *Prison Notebooks* (1929–35). Through this work, Gramsci earned a place alongside LUKÁCS as one of the great theoreticians of Hegelian Marxism, an interpretation of Marx's thought that lays emphasis on the reflective human subject.

The *Notebooks*, while focusing on politics and philosophy, range over a bewildering variety of subjects, among them sociolinguistics and literary criticism. Perhaps their most striking feature is their devastating attack on virtually every axiom of DIALECTICAL MATERIALISM. In Gramsci's opinion Marx did not want to substitute Matter for the Hegelian Idea but accorded priority to the productive organization of society – which of course incorporates conscious human action. *Contra* the orthodox Marxists Gramsci refused to view man as nothing more than a material object subject to the dialectical laws that govern the external world of nature. Elevation of the 'subjective factor' also led Gramsci to deny the standard Marxist belief that knowledge was merely the passive assimilation of a ready-made universe. Given the active, constitutive role of the cognizing mind it was erroneous, he maintained, to see Marxism as a scientific description of 'objective' reality', a reality independent of human purposes or interpretations. Marxism's validity, like that of any other doctrine, would be determined by 'practice', by the social functions it performs. But since 'truth' depends on the successful mediation (not reflection) of reality, theory must be constantly reconstituted to cope with historically modified living experience. Gramsci derided those who turned Marxism into a closed system, immune to empirical fact.

In consequence of his stress on 'man the creator', Gramsci resolutely opposed teleological and fatalistic conceptions of Marxism, which posited immutable laws underlying social evolution. More specifically, he rejected the notion that human liberation was an inevitable consequence of the internal dynamics of capitalism. He found such determinism not only false but a form of culpable self-deception, by means of which Marxists evaded their historical responsibilities. Economic determinism also impaired the Marxian explanation of why despite its contradictions capitalism persisted. By reducing thought to a 'reflex' of the productive process Marx's epigones underestimated the power of myths and ideas. The cohesion of modern bourgeois society stemmed, primarily, from the 'hegemony', i.e. the spiritual and cultural supremacy, of the ruling classes, who, through manipulation of 'civil society' (the mechanisms of socialization, such as the media, the churches, the trade unions), had managed to foist their own values

and beliefs on the rest of the populace. Here Gramsci departed fundamentally from the classical Marxian 'conflict' model of capitalist society, and this revision caused him to amend the Leninist strategy for revolution, then considered gospel. In backward countries, held together by a combination of apathy and coercion, a Bolshevik-style coup d'état was still appropriate; but in the advanced West, where the workers willingly consented to existing arrangements, revolution *presupposed* a transformation of mass consciousness, effected through a protracted 'battle of ideas', or 'war of position' (Gramsci liked military metaphors), within 'civil society'. As he scorned the idea that socialism would arise, inevitably, from the ashes of a doomed capitalism, he deemed the ideological struggle decisive, and pleaded with Marxists to end their obsession with economics and pay more attention to the realm of culture – to literature, moral and philosophical debate, etc.

Though Gramsci never advocated a 'parliamentary road' to socialism, proponents of EUROCOMMUNISM claim him, not without reason, as their spiritual ancestor. Certainly the *Notebooks* champion persuasion, consent, and doctrinal flexibility – essential elements of the Eurocommunist creed. It is, however, his discussion of social order under capitalism that is most interesting to political thinkers. While he wrongly ignores the *economic* reasons for working-class acceptance of capitalism, his theory of hegemony is a useful antidote to conventional Marxist assertions about pervasive class war.   JVF

Reading

Adamson, W.L.: *Hegemony and Revolution.* Berkeley and London: University of California Press, 1980.

†Femia, J.V.: *Gramsci's Political Thought.* Oxford: Clarendon Press, 1981.

Gramsci, A.: *Selections from the Prison Notebooks,* trans. Q. Hoare and G. Nowell Smith. London: Lawrence & Wishart; New York: International Publishers, 1971.

——: *Selections from Political Writings, 1910–1920,* trans. J. Mathews, ed. Q. Hoare. London: Lawrence & Wishart; New York: International Publishers, 1977.

Gratian (*c.*1100–*c.*1150) Italian canon lawyer.

Author of the *Decretum Gratiani*, an influential compilation of canon law texts. See CANON LAW.

Greek political thought This cannot be examined before the earliest Greek literature, the *Iliad* and *Odyssey*, and the poems of Hesiod, of the late eighth or early seventh century BC. Whatever political thinking there may have been in the preceding millennia is wholly lost, in the absence not only of belles-lettres but also of such epigraphical texts as the royal inscriptions and annals familiar in contemporary Egypt and the Middle Eastern kingdoms. It is impossible to exaggerate the difficulty of analysing the beginnings of Greek intellectual thought: source material before PLATO (writing in the first half of the fourth century BC) either is restricted to fragmentary or marginal texts embedded in historiography or poetry (especially fifth-century Athenian tragedy) where it is extremely elusive, as is clearly demonstrated by Aristophanes or by Thucydides' *History of the Peloponnesian War*; or it has disappeared, as in the case of the writings of Protagoras; or it is very late and falsely attributed to earlier times, as with the works of Pythagoreans under the Roman emperors.

Plato and ARISTOTLE in the next generation were the first systematic political theorists in the proper sense of the term, though immediately before them at least two men, the Sophist Protagoras and SOCRATES, had taken steps towards a science or philosophy of political behaviour, which became full-fledged with Plato. That Plato and Aristotle had only a fragmented tradition behind them is suggested by the way in which Plato changed his mind drastically on fundamental questions between the *Republic* of his 'middle period' and the later *Statesman* and *Laws*, and by Aristotle's failure to complete his *Politics* or even to convert it into a fully coherent work. After Aristotle the development came to an abrupt end. It appears that Greek political thought was coterminous with the small autonomous city-state, the *polis* (from which the words 'politics' and 'political' were derived): thinking about politics began with the emergent city-state and ended with its death. Thus Zeno, the founder of the Stoic philosophical school, who was born thirteen years before the death of Aristotle, also wrote a *Republic*, but, its title apart, it had nothing in common with Plato's book. What little is known of this 'republic' reveals that it had neither social nor economic nor political institutions, reflecting the way in which the Greeks after Alexander the Great turned their moral and political concerns away from the *polis* and politics to the inner psyche of the individual. The real world had become increasingly monarchical, and what passed for political writing was soon concentrated on superficial analysis of the 'good king', symbolized by the four orations entitled *On Kingship* of Dio Chrysostom (who died after AD 112).

It is hardly surprising that there was no interest in antiquity in Aristotle's *Politics*, with its basic premise [1253a2–3] that 'man is by nature a being designed to live in a *polis*'. Aristotle's *Nicomachean Ethics* had closed by looking ahead to the *Politics*. 'As then the question of legislation has been left uninvestigated by previous thinkers, it will perhaps be well if we consider it for ourselves, together with the whole question of the constitution of the state' [1181b12–14]. There follows in a few lines a rough table of contents of the *Politics* (except for Book 1), closing with the sentence, 'Let us then begin our discussion.' Whether Aristotle himself or a later ancient editor wrote this conclusion, the points it makes are first that the study of politics is a branch of ethics, and second that it can be examined only within the framework of the city-state. Hence the discussion of the good citizen becomes closely enmeshed with the account of the good man. The demise of the *polis* after Alexander inevitably entailed the end of both aspects of the fundamental premise. And the pivotal problem, the nature of JUSTICE, was replaced, in so far as one may speak of any replacement, by the qualitatively different question of the nature of the good ruler.

A major stimulus to the lively though unsystematic political discussion that began in the sixth century BC was the institutional variety that emerged among the numerous more-or-less independent city-states of the Greek world. Some idea of this variety may be deduced from the fact that Aristotle and his school produced 158 booklets, each called 'The Constitution of X', of which only the one on

Athens survives, thanks to its rediscovery in the late nineteenth century on an Egyptian papyrus first published in 1891. Presumably it is typical of all of them with its mixture of historical and contemporary descriptive data and, at some fifty pages, it was probably the longest.

Once politics became a subject of speculation and debate, this extraordinary variety invited comparative value-judgments. Which was better or best, and why? These questions were already being asked by poets such as Solon and Theognis in the first half of the sixth century BC and they were the subject of public discussion in Athenian tragedy in the next century. But the answers were brief, almost gnomic, as moralists asserted their conflicting views. In the exchange between King Theseus of Athens and a Theban herald the former declares: 'This city is ruled by no one man. The *demos* reigns, taking turns annually. They do not give supremacy to the rich; the poor man has an equal share in it.' 'That's mob rule,' replies the herald. 'The *demos* is not the right judge of arguments; then how can it give right guidance to the city?' (Euripides, *Suppliant Women*, lines 399–419). This is assertion and counter-assertion, argument without a rational progression. For the latter to emerge, a whole series of more systematic discussions was required, of the nature of truth and of justice, of the virtues and their limits, of human nature and the possibilities of changing or controlling it. In that context the famous dichotomy between nature (*physis*) and convention (*nomos*) became prominent in political analysis for several decades.

The men who initiated those first more systematic theoretical discussions of ethics and society in the second half of the fifth century BC were professional itinerant teachers known as Sophists. They were in no sense a school of thinkers; on the contrary, they often disagreed sharply among themselves, most obviously in their political allegiance. The illusion that they were in some ways a group with essential coherence is a tenacious but false image created by Plato and it has remained dominant to this day. It was Plato, too, who has made it virtually taboo to accept the contemporary view that counted Socrates among the Sophists, though, as Kerferd has phrased it, '*in function* he was

correctly so regarded' (p. 57). That Socrates took no pay from his pupils is essentially an irrelevance, though it is customarily adduced as central in distinguishing the activity of Socrates from that of the other Sophists. The place of neither in the history of political thought is influenced, let alone determined, by anything so marginal to their thinking about politics.

Much as the Sophists (and others) disagreed among themselves on matters as fundamental as the nature of justice or the relative superiority of democracy or oligarchy, there was more or less universal agreement on the inequality of men and almost as much unanimity, in consequence, on the necessity for social and political hierarchy in a well-functioning community. Not even the utopian thought of the classical Greek period was egalitarian. Nor, to move from Utopia to existing Greek society, was such a figure as the Sophist Protagoras of Abdera an egalitarian, though, as Kerferd has pointed out, he 'produced for the first time in history a theoretical basis for participatory democracy' (p. 144). Protagoras held that all men – or, more correctly, all free adult males – were endowed with the capacity to share in the process of political decision-making, but not in equal measure. Hence the need for educators, for Sophists like himself and, at least by implication, for a political leadership. There is reason to think that some such view was widely shared in democratic circles: that is the implication of the acceptance in practice of elite leadership, even in Athens. In the final century of Athenian democracy the paradoxical situation then arose in which democracy was virtually unchallenged as a working political institution at the same time that the small articulate intelligentsia were anti-democratic, while the spokesmen for democracy, such as Demosthenes, were content to repeat familiar slogans without any attempt to elaborate and deepen the Protagorean doctrine or any other.

It was also universally believed, by Plato and Aristotle along with nearly everyone else, that the essential condition for a true *polis*, and therefore for the good life, was 'rule by laws, not by men'. Of the frequent statements of that position it is enough to quote one, again from Euripides' *Suppliant Women* (lines 312–13): 'The power that keeps cities and men together is noble preservation of the laws.' To be sure, that kind of ideological slogan is easily shown to be incapable of withstanding rigorous analysis, but it was eminently practical. It meant in practice the stability of the city-state, its freedom from civil strife. Without fixed, publicly known laws that were regularly enforced as the basis of all social behaviour, stability could not have been achieved. The formulation and publication of the laws was the work, in the archaic period, of shadowy figures known by the Greek as lawgivers (*nomothetai*), often taking action in direct or indirect consequence of civil strife. Thereafter, rule by laws remained unchallenged in Greek history, by and large for practical rather than theoretical reasons, even when absolute monarchs became increasingly the norm.

This lack of theoretical justification or sanction for whatever law was held to rule is striking. Neither LEGITIMACY nor POLITICAL OBLIGATION was a serious concern among Greek writers on politics. Modern scholars have managed, after a desperate search, to produce a few examples among the Sophists of a rudimentary SOCIAL CONTRACT notion, and there is the extraordinary and unique passage in Plato's *Crito* in which Socrates insists on his moral obligation to accept the death penalty that had been imposed on him by an Athenian court. However, that all adds up to a negligible harvest when compared with the long line in modern political thought stretching back to William of Ockham and Jean Bodin. Rule by law, in short, was upheld because the alternative was chaos, not because the content of the law, whatever it was, could be justified on theoretical grounds.

Especially striking was the lack of religious sanction for the law. Justice came from Zeus, to be sure, and there were punishable offences of blasphemy and sacrilege, but both the content of the law and the procedure had become secularized by the early classical period. All ideas, all proposals, had to be defended, argued, supported or challenged by human reason. On that score, at any rate, Socrates, Plato and Aristotle were not rebels but representatives of a fundamental strain in Greek thought.   MIF

Reading

†Aalders, G.J.G.: *Political Thought in Hellenistic Times*. Amsterdam: Adolf Hakkert, 1975.

Aristotle: *The Nicomachean Ethics*, trans. H. Rackham. London: Heinemann, 1934.

†Barker, E.: *From Alexander to Constantine*. Oxford: Clarendon Press, 1966. [An anthology, with massive commentary on passages and documents, 338 BC to AD 337.]

Ehrenberg, V.: *The Greek State*, 2nd edn. London: Methuen, 1969.

Euripides: *The Suppliant Women*, trans. F. Jones. Chicago: University of Chicago Press, 1958.

Finley, M.I.: *Politics in the Ancient World*. Cambridge: Cambridge University Press, 1983.

————: *Democracy Ancient and Modern*, 2nd edn. London: Hogarth Press; New Brunswick: Rutgers University Press, 1985.

Guthrie, W.K.C.: *A History of Greek Philosophy*, vol. III, pt 1, *The Fifth-Century Enlightenment*. Cambridge: Cambridge University Press, 1981.

Kerferd, G.B.: *The Sophistic Movement*. Cambridge: Cambridge University Press, 1981.

Nippel, W.: *Mischverfassungstheorie und Verfassungs-realität in Antike und früher Neuzeit*, pt 1. Stuttgart: Klett-Cotta, 1980.

Raaflaub, K.: Zum Freiheitsbegriff der Griechen. In *Soziale Typenbegriffe im alten Griechenland*, vol. IV, ed. E. Weiskopf. Berlin: Akademie-Verlag, 1981.

Vlastos, G.: Isonomia politike (in English). In *Isonomia*, ed. J. Mau and E.G. Schmidt. Berlin: Akademie-Verlag, 1964.

†Winton, R.I. and Garnsey, P.: Political theory. In *The Legacy of Greece*, ed. M.I. Finley. Oxford: Clarendon Press, 1981.

Green, Thomas Hill (1836–1882)   British philosopher and social reformer. Green's major achievement was to transform LIBERALISM by recasting it in the terms of an idealism adapted to the political practices and religious crisis of his time. From about 1880 to 1920, his political philosophy did more to shape university teaching and public policy in Great Britain than did J. S. MILL's UTILITARIANISM. Green merits attention because he attacked the empiricism, utilitarianism, and *laissez-faire* doctrines that had been used by previous liberals. Green's version ought not to be written off as a transient phase of liberalism. As its most prominent British form for two generations, Green's school provides a set of instructive counter-examples to unhistorical generalizations about liberalism in general.

Green began with the assumption that liberals had to face up to a crisis at once philosophical and political. A philosophy was needed to deal rigorously with the problems left by what he perceived as the bankruptcy of earlier British empiricism and utilitarianism. No moral and political principles had won general acceptance; Green was particularly concerned by the absence of any alternative to the calculation of individual and national self-interest, as in the case of British support for the Confederacy in the American Civil War. General principles, philosophically adequate, were wanted, not only in international politics, but in domestic policy to support necessary expansions in suffrage, education, and social legislation.

In Green's view the empiricist tradition had failed to provide either an adequate theory of knowledge or a proper account of rational human conduct. Embracing philosophical IDEALISM, he held that nature and our consciousness of nature alike presuppose an eternal, self-differentiating, and self-identical subject, which both connects thoughts and provides their material. Equally the rational determinants of action are will and choice, rather than passive compliance with the suggestions of desire or passion. Such a view, he claimed, provides citizens not only with sound theories of knowledge and ethics, but also with a guide to their political ends. A set of principles are immanent in the moral, social, and political practices of a society. When the presuppositions of these practices are reconstituted, they provide principles which help citizens to define their goals and standards for common action. Once in possession of the proper ends of action, we have a guide to the principles we ought to apply in the present and future. Such a method considers persons, not abstractly in isolation from their actual membership of groups, but concretely in the full complexity of the social and political relationships in which they are necessarily enmeshed. Idealists, Green argued, can avoid the errors of an unmediated individualism, whether secular or religious.

At the centre of Green's thought, moral and political, is the doctrine that persons do not seek pleasure directly. Rather they seek to realize a conception of themselves. As self-conscious subjects, they have integrated into that conception an idea of the good which they share with other members of the associations to which they belong. It is because of such ideas that humans acknowledge the legitimacy of duties entailing the sacrifice of individual inclinations or interests. Such shared ideas of the good have 'been the parent of the institutions and usages, of the social judgements and aspirations through which human life has been so far bettered' (*Prolegomena to Ethics*, 1883, p. 206). Individuals accept duties thus prescribed because they can realize themselves only through being conscientious children or parents, citizens or public servants. Ideals must be recognized by the society of which they are members. All other ideals remain, in Hegelian language, 'abstract'. That this notion posed a threat to the liberty and conscience of individuals was conceded by Green. This is why he refused to grant that self-realization could occur anywhere else other than in individuals.

Which, then, is prior – the individual or the society? This question Green considered meaningless: 'Without society, no persons; this is as true as that without persons . . . there could be no such society as we know' (*Prolegomena*, p. 218). The basis of society is the recognition by its members of one another as all being ends in themselves. And the proper purpose of both ethics and politics, in Green's view, is to develop individuals with moral characters. This is the criterion by which the value of institutions and laws ought to be judged. Their value is to be determined by the extent to which they realize the capacities of will and reason by giving citizens scope for their exercise. If existing arrangements hinder the moral development of any class of citizens, the present order must be reformed to remove such impediments.

When Green turned from ethics to politics in his *Lectures on the Principles of Political Obligation* (1879–80), he continued to apply this same criterion: the worth of arrangements is to be measured by their effects upon the character of individuals. Applied to proposed legislation, this criterion creates a presumption against state action, but not an interdiction in all circumstances. Law can force men to perform certain actions. But such actions are external. No law can make its subjects moral, for morality depends upon a freely willed motive. Thus law should be used only to maintain the conditions necessary for individuals to exercise will and reason. Only those acts should be prohibited by law which are 'so necessary to the existence of a society in which the moral end stated can be realized that it is better for them to be done or omitted ... from fear or hope of legal consequences than not to be done at all' (*Works*, vol. II, p. 344). The fewer such laws, the better.

Yet Green's view of the proper scope and function of state legislation differed sharply from the pure negativism of Spencerian INDIVIDUALISM. Green's goal was to reconcile the claims of individuality with those of COMMUNITY, and to do so through a moral psychology of the self. Green bristled when confronted by older forms of liberalism based upon theories of natural rights brought into society by individuals. These theories, from LOCKE to SPENCER, derived, Green thought, from the unexamined assumptions that individuals have rights, but no obligations; that every exercise of state power is an illegitimate restraint upon this original, asocial freedom. Such theory 'affords a reason for resisting all positive reforms ... which involve an action of the state ... promoting conditions favourable to moral life' (*Works*, II, p. 345). Utilitarians held that men should obey the law because thereby more pleasure is attained, or pain avoided. But utilitarians had no way of using ethical terms such as 'ought' in either those instances where a moral obligation exists to resist the powers that be, or the more usual cases where actors ought to perform actions even though they produce unpleasant consequences for the agent.

This is not to say that Green broke entirely with earlier liberal positions. He would have preferred that voluntary organizations such as unions and co-operatives provide old age and unemployment insurance, as well as other services. If feasible, this would meet workers' needs without creating dependence upon the state. He believed that private property was an indispensable means for developing individual character; he denied that the capitalist economy was responsible for existing poverty and unemployment.

Yet it would be a mistake to disregard the deliberate rejection by Green of strict *laissez-faire* principles. He asserted positive, although limited, functions for the state. Certain situations require that the state free its citizens from hindrances or disabilities that keep them from realizing their moral selves. Which sorts of legislation did Green have in view? Public health and education were perhaps the most significant, although he was a committed advocate of restrictions on drinking. To the question of whether state action might not diminish the self-reliance of citizens, Green replied with characteristic pragmatism in his lecture 'Liberal Legislation and Freedom of Contract' (1880). No doubt it would be preferable to have a society where spontaneous action supplied necessary education and protected public health. But, he concluded, until these things are done by voluntary action, it is the business of the state to ensure that they are available to all equally. Without education, 'the individual in modern society is as effectually crippled as by the loss of a limb' (*Works*, III, pp. 373–4). Nor were freedom of contract, freedom to do what one wills with private property, absolute rights, good in themselves. Such freedoms were valuable, in Green's view, only as means to that end by which all rights are to be measured: 'freedom in the positive sense: the liberation of the powers of all men equally for contributions to a common good' (*Works*, III, p. 372).

Green's ambivalence towards state action accounts for the fact that after his death his students went on to embrace very different causes. But it was also a source of strength, inspiring two generations of liberals who might have been put off by a more specific programme. By his expanded and concerned liberalism, Green demonstrated how much more comprehensive liberalism could be than its critics today are prepared to admit. Whatever its philosophical standing, liberalism in its idealist form went beyond merely negative liberty and narrow individualism. Green's liberalism, without abandoning the concern for individual rights and liberties, sought to reconcile freedom with equality and community. Green stressed political participation as an obligation of citizenship; he insisted upon the overriding value of the common interest as essential both to the moral life of the individual and to the definition of the proper goals of a democratic state.   MR

Reading

Green, T.H.: *Prolegomena to Ethics*, ed. A.C. Bradley. Oxford: Clarendon Press, 1883.

──────: *The Works of Thomas Hill Green*, ed. R.L. Nettleship. 3 vols. London: Longmans, Green, 1885–8.

†Milne, A.J.M.: *The Social Philosophy of English Idealism*. London: Allen & Unwin, 1962.

Pucelle, J.: *La Nature et l'esprit dans la philosophie de T.H. Green*. Louvain: Éditions Nauwelaerts; Paris: Béatrice-Nauwelaerts, 1961–5.

†Richter, M.: *The Politics of Conscience: T.H. Green and his Age*. London and Cambridge, Mass.: Weidenfeld & Nicolson, 1964; repr. Lanham, Md: University Press of America, 1983.

Grotius, Hugo (1583–1645) Dutch jurist and philosopher. Hugo Grotius (the Latinized name of Huig De Groot) was born at Delft in the United Provinces on 10 April 1583 into a family of professional lawyers. He began his career as a humanist prodigy, writing extremely accomplished Latin verses from an early age and entering Leiden University at the age of eleven. He studied the arts course at Leiden, and then led the life of a typical humanist, editing classical texts, writing poetry and history, and acting as a diplomat and political adviser for the leading statesman of the United Provinces, Jan van Oldenbarnevelt. Oldenbarnevelt arranged for Grotius to enjoy a number of political offices, culminating in that of Pensionary or chief executive of the city of Rotterdam in 1612.

In 1619 his period as political adviser and politician came to a dramatic end. During the previous decade Grotius and Oldenbarnevelt had tried to prevent factional fighting within the United Provinces' church between Arminians and orthodox Calvinists, and they had done so principally by trying (against great opposition) to elevate the power of the state over that of the church. In 1619 Oldenbarnevelt decided that the only course left to him in order to prevent a complete social and political breakdown was to seize control of the army of the province of Holland from the *statholder* (the equivalent of a governor of an American state). His attempt failed, and both he and Grotius were tried for treason; Oldenbarnevelt was executed, and Grotius (who betrayed his master in the trial) was sentenced to life imprisonment. Two years later he escaped, and lived the rest of his life in exile, mainly in Paris. From 1634 he was employed by Queen Christina of Sweden as her ambassador in France, and while sailing from Sweden in 1645 he was caught in a shipwreck near Rostock, where he died on 28 August. His body was carried back in honour to Delft, where he had not been allowed to return during his lifetime.

Most of Grotius's major ideas were developed during his political activity before 1619, though they did not receive public expression in any substantial form until the famous *De iure belli ac pacis* which he published in 1625. In some unpublished essays dating from 1599 to 1610 and in his published *De antiquitate reipublicae batavicae* (1610) he argued strongly for the aristocratic and republican character of the Netherlands constitution, attacking (for example) the idea of a mixed constitution, and countering the idea that the Netherlands had ever been a limited monarchy even under the dukes of Burgundy or the kings of Spain. At the same time he urged the prosecution of the Dutch imperial mission, chronicling its development in his *Annales et historiae* (published posthumously in 1657). This theory of aristocratic, imperialist republicanism, which he and others in Oldenbarnevelt's circle developed, was the forerunner of similar theories in mid-seventeenth-century England and the United Provinces, and helped to underpin the growing empires of the English and Dutch. In 1605 Grotius composed a long, substantially unpublished work justifying the Dutch aggression against the Spaniards in the East Indies (a work which he entitled *De Indis*, but which has been known since 1864, when it was rediscovered, as *De iure praedae*; in 1609 one chapter was published as *Mare liberum*). In this manuscript, Grotius confronted the central problem of early seventeenth-century Europe – how to cope with radical moral conflict and its derivative, armed warfare (see JUST WAR and INTERNATIONAL LAW). He asserted (against contemporary sceptics such as MONTAIGNE) that there could be universal moral standards which might be used to adjudicate questions of international conflict, but (against contemporary Aristotelians) he also argued that this universal morality would have to depend ultimately on two principles. The first was that self-preservation must always be legitimate, and the second was that *wanton* injury of another (i.e. not for reasons for self-preservation) must always be illegitimate. Upon this foundation of self-preservation, rules for reconciling conflict (or advancing it) could be erected, and the existence of civil societies explained. The acquisition of PROPERTY, too, could be justified in these terms: a 'sort of property' would appear whenever people seized from an unowned natural world the necessities of life, and this would develop gradually through economic and technical change into a modern system of private property – though with the proviso that *in extremis* men must always be entitled to seize what they needed.

In *De iure belli ac pacis* he extended and systematized these ideas. He also put them in a fuller philosophical framework, claiming that these principles constituted the foundations of 'sociability' (i.e. no society could be envisaged which would deny them) and that they were therefore the basis of the 'laws of nature'. Given that they seemed to be *necessarily* functional to a social or moral life, they could be seen as obligating men independently of all other considerations, even (he asserted in a famous phrase) 'if we concede that there is no God'. He also systematized ideas about toleration he had developed during the religious conflict in the United Provinces, arguing that there could be no justification in enforcing *any* religious beliefs upon anyone, other than the minimal proposition that there is at least one God who cares for human welfare. This minimalist ethics and theology was compatible with a reluctance to condemn any arrangement freely arrived at by the parties, even voluntary slavery or a civil society's putting itself under an absolute ruler; though Grotius was always careful to stress that such arrangements were unlikely and not to be presumed without clear evidence.

Writers in the early ENLIGHTENMENT hailed Grotius as the founder of a modern moral science, and they focused on his new answer to moral relativism. Post-Kantian historians for the same reasons despised him as a 'sorry comforter' who could not have answered the new scepticism of Hume. We can now see that he was indeed in many ways the founder of the classical 'natural rights' theories of seventeenth- and eighteenth-century Europe, and he has not deserved the contempt into which his enterprise fell after KANT's criticism of it, nor his coralling in the enclosure of the history of international law.   RFT

Reading

Grotius, H.: *De iure praedae*, trans. G.L. Williams. Oxford: Clarendon Press, 1950.

———: *De iure belli ac pacis*, trans. F.W. Kelsey. Oxford: Clarendon Press, 1925.

Haggenmacher, P.: *Grotius et la doctrine de la guerre juste*. Paris: Presses Universitaires de France, 1983.

†Knight, W.S.M.: *The Life and Works of Hugo Grotius*. London: Sweet & Maxwell, 1931.

†Tuck, R.: *Natural Rights Theories*. Cambridge: Cambridge University Press, 1979.

———: Grotius, Carneades and Hobbes. *Grotiana* new ser. 4 (1983).

Guicciardini, Francesco (1483–1540) Italian historian and statesman. A critic of MACHIAVELLI, nonetheless sharing many of his ideas. See RENAISSANCE POLITICAL THOUGHT; REPUBLICANISM.

guild socialism A doctrine and a movement that arose in Britain during the first two decades of the twentieth century; its essence was a non-statist, self-governing socialism, rooted in the producer democracy of industrial 'guilds' formed out of the trade unions.

The medieval idiom reflects one of the doctrine's sources, a parentage first established by Arthur Penty ('that shabby stammering architect' in Margaret Cole's phrase) in *The Restoration of the Guild System* (1906). However, Penty's uncompromising medievalism was joined, and soon submerged, by other contemporary sources of anti-state sentiment, such as SYNDICALISM, PLURALISM and distributivism, and it was out of these diverse sources that the guild socialist position developed. Its early development occurred largely under the auspices of A. R. Orage; the first editorial of his journal *The New Age* in 1907 declared in general terms that 'socialism as a means to the intensification of man is even more necessary than socialism as a means to the abolition of economic poverty'.

A distinctive theory and programme had evolved by 1912, when a series of *New Age* articles written by S. G. Hobson (but unsigned) began to outline a scheme for a 'co-partnery' between the state and the trade unions, in which the unions became 'responsible bodies, approximating in spirit to the ancient gilds'. These articles, which attracted a good deal of interest among political intellectuals, were published in book form in 1914 as *National Guilds: an Inquiry into the Wage System and the Way Out*. It was the 'wage system' under capitalism that was identified as the cause of the worker's subordination and passivity, but it was to be replaced not by any of the available socialist alternatives to capitalism but by 'what we may call a system of National Guilds, under which the state enters into partnership with the organized craftspeople and manages the industry jointly with them' (Wright, p. 26). In 1915 the National Guilds League was formed to propagate the new doctrine, which was now summarized in manifesto form in what became known as the 'Storrington Document'.

If Penty, Orage and Hobson should be acknowledged as the immediate progenitors of guild socialism, it was the young Oxford academic, G. D. H. Cole (1889–1959), who equipped it with its distinctive political theory. In a prolific series of books, beginning with *The World of Labour* (1913) and culminating in *Guild Socialism Re-stated* (1920), Cole set out to establish the theoretical credentials of the guild position and to relate this to its practical programme.

In particular, this involved a revised theory of the STATE and of the nature of REPRESENTATION. Cole advanced a pluralist critique of theories of political monism and state sovereignty (most succinctly, in a paper on 'Conflicting Social Obligations' to the Aristotelian Society in 1915), in which the state was to be seen as 'only an association among others', as a geographical grouping for the performance of certain common purposes, while 'speciality of function' was the central principle of modern social life requiring a recognition of group autonomy alongside the need for a structure of associational co-ordination. No longer could there be any 'facile identification of the community and the state', although the aim was 'not to generalize the association, but to particularize the state'. Much of Cole's guild socialist system building was an attempt to give structural form to this general social theory. If it provided a theoretical basis for industrial self-government, it also involved the need to devise a structure that would reconcile producer and consumer interests, particular interests and a general community interest. Dissatisfied with his original nomination of the state as the representative of the consumer, Cole developed increasingly complex models of associational co-ordination (the final version of which appears in his *Guild Socialism Re-stated*).

Alongside the pluralist critique of the state, Cole offered a revised view of the nature of democratic representation. The democratic idea had been subverted by the false belief that one person could 'represent' another in a general sense, whereas genuine representation had to be 'specific and functional' not 'general and inclusive'. This required a system of co-ordinated functional representation throughout society. As Cole put it, the democratic principle applied 'not only or mainly to some special sphere of social action known as "politics", but to any and every form of social action' (Guild Socialism Re-stated, p. 12). If the guild socialists were primarily concerned with extending democracy to industry it was because they believed this was the key to a wider, 'social' democracy.

Indeed, guild socialism was essentially a theory of DEMOCRACY. Common to all the diverse strands of thought that contributed to its development was a belief in the need to find the basis for an active citizenship in a twentieth-century context. If this meant resisting the claim of capitalism to treat labour as a commodity, it also meant avoiding the centralist, bureaucratic tendencies of socialist collectivism. Widely influential for a time, after the early 1920s guild socialism receded from view and could be disregarded as a utopian diversion from the serious business of parliamentary or revolutionary socialism. A generation later Cole's *History of Socialist Thought* (1958) could still plausibly present guild socialism as 'the outstanding contribution to new non-Communist theories of socialism during and immediately after the first world war' (p. 25); while at the end of the twentieth century many of its concerns have again come to seem strikingly contemporary.

AWW

Reading

Cole, G.D.H.: Conflicting social obligations. *Proceedings of the Aristotelian Society* 15 (1915) 140–59.

———: *Self-government in Industry*. London: Bell, 1917.

———: *Guild Socialism Re-stated*. London: Leonard Parsons, 1920.

———: *Social Theory*. London: Methuen, 1920.

———: *A History of Socialist Thought*, vol. 4, pt 1. London: Macmillan, 1958.

Cole, M.: Guild socialism and the labour research department. In *Essays in Labour History 1886–1923*, ed. A. Briggs and J. Saville. London: Macmillan, 1971.

———: Guild socialism: the Storrington Document. In A. Briggs and J. Saville eds.

†Glass, S.T.: *The Responsible Society: the Ideas of the English Guild Socialist*. London: Longman, 1966.

Wright, A.W.: *G.D.H. Cole and Socialist Democracy*. Oxford: Clarendon Press, 1979.

H

Habermas, Jürgen (1929–) German philosopher and social scientist. Habermas is the most important contemporary thinker of the Frankfurt School of CRITICAL THEORY. Like other thinkers in that tradition he rejects the orthodox Marxian notion that the normative standpoint for a radical critique of capitalist society is the privileged role of the proletariat. Habermas's work as a whole can perhaps be best understood as a wide-ranging search for 'adequate normative foundations for a critical social theory'.

Habermas's efforts have focused on the concept of RATIONALITY and the problem of societal rationalization. He has criticized the reduction of the former to purely instrumental calculations and tried to construct a 'more comprehensive' account. The development of such an account is necessary for an adequate understanding and critique of the 'one-sided' process of societal rationalization which has characterized the development of capitalism. This notion of one-sidedness refers to an increasing tendency for a technical, instrumental orientation to social life to marginalize more reflective, normative and aesthetic, expressive orientations.

This dual focus on rationality and rationalization has meant that Habermas's work has continually engaged both abstract topics in epistemology and the philosophy of language, as well as more concrete questions in social theory such as legitimation problems in advanced capitalism and the importance of new social movements (e.g. women, radical ecologists, counter-cultural movements, gays).

In the course of his writings Habermas has shifted his strategy for treating rationality and rationalization. His first major book, *Knowledge and Human Interests* (1968), attempted an epistemological critique of the prevailing positivist model of knowledge (see POSITIVISM). Briefly, he argued that this model incorporated only one knowledge-constitutive interest of the human species: the technical interest in control. This model threatened to usurp the place of other, equally basic, models of knowledge which are grounded in two other knowledge-constitutive interests and which can help illuminate the problems of societal rationalization. Hermeneutic or interpretive knowledge answers to the practical interest in expanding communicative interaction, and critical, emancipatory knowledge (such as critical social theory) answers to the emancipatory interest in removing structures of domination.

By the mid-1970s Habermas was becoming increasingly dissatisfied with this framework linking knowledge and reason to universal, 'anthropologically deep-seated' interests. He shifted his focus away from epistemology to language. He decided that a proper understanding of rationality would emerge not from speculation about knowledge-constitutive interests, but from a theoretical reconstruction of the competence actors demonstrate in linguistic interaction. Whenever actors engage in 'communicative action', that is, orient themselves towards 'reaching an understanding', they mutually impute a certain accountability to one another in relation to the validity of the claims they raise in their speech acts. Habermas argues that there are three universal claims: truth, normative legitimacy, and sincerity. Each actor has an intuitive understanding of the differences between these claims as well as of how one goes about redeeming them. The most important of these claims for critical theory is normative LEGITIMACY. For Habermas, the legitimacy of any norm can, in principle, be assessed according to the argumentation rules of 'practical discourse'. Together these rules define an 'ideal speech situation' in which the only influence which is allowed to count is the 'force of better argument'. The formal rules of practical discourse are intended by Habermas to lay the basis for a minimal, 'communicative ethics'.

This attempt to derive a normative foundation from the 'universal validity basis of speech' has been subjected to criticism on the grounds that it manifests a variant of western ethnocentrism. Habermas has tried to accommodate this criticism by admitting that his analysis of 'communicative competence' is directly valid only for 'members of *modern* societies'. But this has meant that in order for him to continue to maintain a universalist position on practical reason, he has had to provide a sophisticated defence of 'modern structures of consciousness'. And that is exactly the direction his thought has taken in the 1980s, particularly in *The Theory of Communicative Action* (1981) and *Philosophical Discourse on Modernity* (1986).

Together these works defend the 'rational potential' of the differentiated structure of modern thought which allows learning to occur in 'cultural spheres' corresponding to the three validity claims: science and technology, modern law and post-conventional ethics, and modern art and art criticism. It is from the perspective of this three-fold potential for learning made available with 'cultural *modernity*' that Habermas now gains his critical perspective on *modernization* or societal rationalization, since this process has made a one-sided use of the three-fold potential.

On the level of social theory this perspective yields a thesis about the 'colonization of the lifeworld'. Functionalist rationalization of growing areas of social life, according to the imperatives of the economic and political-administrative systems, means that the opportunity for actors to use their critical, rational competence in organizing their own lives is increasingly being denied. This line of analysis exhibits some important changes in Habermas's thinking about advanced capitalist society. In *Legitimation Crisis*, written in the early 1970s, he speculated that capitalism was experiencing severe and possibly insoluble legitimation problems. But, at the same time, he was quite vague about which social classes or groups would press towards an emancipatory solution to these problems. In other words there was no social 'addressee' for his critical analysis.

In Habermas's recent work advanced capitalism is portrayed as rather more resilient and the colonization problem more threatening. Nevertheless he has become more specific about those who constitute, at least initially, the addressees of critical theory: new social movements. What links these groups is that they operate, to differing degrees, outside the normal give and take of political life. 'In short, the new conflicts are not sparked by *problems of distribution*, but concern the *grammar of forms of life*.' These political struggles cannot be adequately understood simply as attempts to control the state, but rather must be seen as protracted 'border conflicts' along those points in society where the rationalization process (now interpreted as lifeworld colonization) is being pushed forward by systemic imperatives.

SKW

Reading

Bernstein, R. ed.: *Habermas and Modernity*. Cambridge, Mass.: MIT Press; Cambridge: Polity, 1985.

Habermas, J.: *Knowledge and Human Interests*. Boston: Beacon, 1971.

————: *Theory and Practice*. Boston: Beacon, 1973.

————: *Legitimation Crisis*. Boston: Beacon, 1975.

————: *Communication and the Evolution of Society*. Boston: Beacon, 1979.

————: *The Theory of Communicative Action*. 2 vols. Boston: Beacon, 1984 and 1986.

————: *Philosophical Discourse on Modernity*. Cambridge, Mass.: MIT Press, 1986.

†Held, D. and Thompson, J. eds: *Habermas: Critical Debates*. Cambridge, Mass.: MIT Press, 1982.

†McCarthy, T.: *The Critical Theory of Jürgen Habermas*. Cambridge, Mass.: MIT Press, 1978; Cambridge: Polity, 1984.

†Outhwaite, W.: *Habermas*. Cambridge: Polity, 1986.

Hamilton, Alexander (1755–1804) American statesman, delegate to the Constitutional

Convention (1787) and secretary of the treasury (1789–95). Hamilton was the author, with James MADISON and John Jay, of *The Federalist* (1787–8), a series of newspaper articles supporting ratification of the federal Constitution, the most authoritative exposition of the thought of the Constitution's framers; he also wrote numerous policy papers, pamphlets, addresses and letters. Hamilton's advocacy of a strong central government and an economic policy favourable to industrialization, combined with his relative distrust of the people, made Hamilton the arch-antagonist of Thomas JEFFERSON in early American politics.

Hamilton believed in natural rights but, influenced by HUME and BLACKSTONE, emphasized the power necessary, in practice, to secure those rights. In Hamilton's view, the STATE OF NATURE is or becomes a state of war because it involves a private right to execute natural law. Civil society is defined by an agreement to establish a public executive power in which rulers pledge to uphold the rights of the ruled. 'Energy in the executive' is thus the heart of civil government. Moreover, the ways in which natural rights can best be secured vary with circumstances. Hence Hamilton's constitutional doctrine of 'implied powers': government must be permitted any means appropriate to its ends not specifically forbidden by law.

Human beings, Hamilton considered, are moved by self-love and self-interest. However, ambition and enlightenment may extend the sense of self and interest beyond the body and its subsistence. The love of wealth, for example, leads to a concern for one's property and an interest in civil order. The love of power, less tied to material well-being, inclines toward public life. The 'noblest minds', however, are ruled by the passion for fame, which allows the soul to be governed by higher principle. Those who love power pose the greatest danger to liberty, especially in popular governments where ordinary citizens – inexpert, parochial and short-sighted – are liable to be swayed by demagogy. Free government, Hamilton reasoned, needs those who love fame to check those who crave dominion.

For this reason, Hamilton admired the British constitution – 'the best in the world' –

with its aristocratic admixtures. In the United States, however, 'representative democracy' was the best practicable regime, and Americans in general, caught up in the pursuit of gain, seemed unsuited to civic virtue. In a commercial society, Hamilton argued, virtue is most likely as a 'graceful appendage of wealth', attracting those whose desire for riches has been somewhat sated. Through public life, Hamilton thought it possible to sharpen the taste for honour among the rich, but there was always a forlorn quality to his hope.

The 'science of politics' taught Hamilton, like Madison, that a large and diverse republic lessens the need for civic virtue by weakening individual 'factions' as parts of the whole. He rejected the ancient case for a small state on the further ground that political societies were naturally in conflict with one another. Since the commercial spirit is 'domineering' as well as enterprising, a commercial regime changes only the object of conflict, honour yielding to wealth. Consequently, Hamilton's *Report on Manufactures* urged that any nation should aim to possess 'the essentials of national supply', a goal which implies a large and diverse economy. Yet an acquisitive regime scorns 'unprofitable heroism' while its foreign policy requires a certain amount of military virtue. Once again, Hamilton concluded that liberal principles, in practice, must be balanced and edified by moral virtue and an element of honour.

Increasing democratization, exemplified by the election of Jefferson, led Hamilton toward political despair. In 1802, he referred to the Constitution as a 'frail and worthless fabric', though he proclaimed, and demonstrated, his willingness to defend it to the end.　　WCMcW

Reading

Hamilton, A., Madison, J. and Jay, J.: *The Federalist*, ed. M. Beloff. Oxford: Blackwell, new edn 1987.

†Kenyon, C.: Alexander Hamilton: Rousseau of the right. *Political Science Quarterly* 73 (1958) 161–78.

†Miller, J.C.: *Alexander Hamilton: Portrait in Paradox.* New York: Harper, 1959.

†Mitchell, B.: *Alexander Hamilton.* 2 vols. New York: Macmillan, 1962.

†Rossiter, C.: *Alexander Hamilton and the Constitution.* New York: Harcourt Brace & World, 1964.

†Stourzh, G.: *Alexander Hamilton and the Idea of*

Republican Government. Stanford, Calif.: Stanford University Press, 1970.

Harrington, James (1611–1677) English political theorist. A member of a long-established aristocratic family, Harrington studied at Trinity College, Oxford, and the Middle Temple, and then embarked on a prolonged and extensive continental tour, serving in an English regiment in the Low Countries and observing at first hand the functioning of the Venetian political system. After attaching himself to King Charles I between 1647 and 1649 he returned to a life of study (perhaps to seek an explanation for the King's martyrdom), publishing his *The Commonwealth of Oceana* in 1656. Between 1656 and 1660 he wrote a number of shorter political works which, in general, amplify and defend the ideas of *Oceana*. Arrested (on an unsubstantiated charge of conspiracy) in 1661, Harrington suffered a mental collapse while imprisoned, and though upon his release he resumed his life in Westminster he published nothing further.

So great was Harrington's admiration for 'ancient prudence' (as opposed to the political teaching of the moderns) that his works are sometimes overburdened with a heavy-handed classicism. But though he often employed classical republican arguments and categories he also regarded his theory as offering for the first time a rigorous treatment of issues not previously fully understood, namely the role of property and of military power in the state, and the connection between the two. For Harrington property is the foundation of all else, and it occurs in three distinct distributions, being possessed by one, few, or many. Although governments 'against the balance' (tyranny, oligarchy, anarchy) were possible they could not long exist, and thus there were only three stable forms of government. 'Absolute monarchy' is a system in which property is monopolized by the monarch, and where rule is maintained by a mercenary army. 'Mixed monarchy' is characterized by landownership by great magnates, and where this aristocracy and their retainers are the bearers of arms. A 'commonwealth' comes into being where landownership is sufficiently dispersed amongst those who can 'live of themselves' that no aristocracy can be formed, and thus the armed forces are a citizen militia.

Much of Harrington's *Oceana*, however, is given over to a detailed sketch of a baroque constitutional order to be brought into being by Olphaus Megaletor (a lightly fictionalized Cromwell). Harrington's theory is not entirely historical since it is his belief that an appropriately engineered constitution, which ensures that the dictates of reason and the impulses of interest coincide, may achieve immortality by preventing the development of oligarchy and controlling the ownership of property in such a way that it is always dispersed. Once again Harrington considers his achievement to have been the rigorous presentation of problems not previously comprehended. Here he records his indebtedness to the example of the physician William Harvey, and considers his 'political anatomy' of past constitutions to have exposed their mainsprings as surely as Harvey had described the circulation of the blood.

The constitutional model expounded in *Oceana* shows a clear indebtedness to ARISTOTLE's conception of the polity, and to other theorists of the mixed or balanced constitution. It incorporates two legislative chambers indirectly elected by all property holders, a senate of wealthier landholders possessed of sole powers to frame legislation, and an assembly of smaller freeholders with sole power to accept or reject legislation thus proposed. An executive magistracy is also to be established, and from the parish upwards civil, military, and religious hierarchies are largely identified. Regular rotation of office-holding checks any tendency to oligarchy, and a limitation on the size of landed estates in the form of an 'Agrarian Law' prevents any retrogression to feudal aristocracy.

It was Harrington's intention to show his fellow countrymen that 'the dissolution of this government caused the [civil] war, not the war the dissolution of this government'. The property and with it the military basis upon which monarchical power was founded had, in the Tudor period, suffered a series of fatal erosions: this basis having disappeared, the governmental 'superstructures' could not long exist. In these circumstances the ancient constitution was but a relic and could never undergo restoration; constitution-making was therefore a legitimate necessity. And if this fundamental alteration in forms of government was a secular process involving 'the people' as a whole, then any demand for the rule of the 'Saints' was defused, and the exclusive claims for dominion by the party of the Good Old Cause (or the Rump oligarchs) were diluted, if not submerged, in the more embracing character of Harrington's populism. To cap the theory, not only could Harrington claim that the commonwealth which issued from these proceedings was the best form of government, embodying as it did the common interest of all the citizens, he could also point the way, by his reading of history, to a stable, if not immortal, polity.

Early interpretations of Harrington linked his historical analysis to the debate concerning the rise (or decline) of the gentry. More recently, scholars (notably John Pocock) have emphasized his original fusion of the civic humanist and classical republican belief (particularly as expounded by MACHIAVELLI) that the bearing of arms is the foundation of citizenship, with the insight that such arms-bearing rests in turn upon the possession of land sufficient for the citizenry to live independently rather than be beholden to superiors (see REPUBLICANISM). And Harrington has been shown to be the originator of the arguments against ABSOLUT-ISM which began to be propounded around the time of his death. Pocock has termed this school of thought 'neo-Harringtonian', its position being that in the later Stuart era the constitution was in danger of being undermined by an executive in command of a public exchequer sufficiently large to corrupt parliament with placemen and overawe the country with a standing army. There is some irony in Harrington's theory being associated with this school since, although common to both is the belief that the popular bearing of arms is a check on absolutism, the neo-Harringtonians offer a fundamentally revised view of the past. For Harrington a mixed monarchy is to some extent a disorderly system where no power is strong enough to check the others; for the neo-Harringtonians it is a balanced order in which, though there is a dependency upon the great magnates by the lesser orders, some degree of liberty is preserved because power is not held in a single hand but is dispersed. JSC

Reading
Cotton, J.: James Harrington as Aristotelian. *Political Theory* 7 (1979) 371–89.
†Greenleaf, W.H.: *Order, Empiricism and Politics.* Oxford: Oxford University Press, 1964.
Macpherson, C.B.: *The Political Theory of Possessive Individualism.* Oxford: Oxford University Press, 1962.
Pocock, J.G.A.: *The Machiavellian Moment.* Princeton, NJ: Princeton University Press, 1975.
†———: *The Political Works of James Harrington.* Cambridge: Cambridge University Press, 1977.
Raab, F.: *The English Face of Machiavelli.* London: Routledge & Kegan Paul, 1964.
Russell Smith, H.F.: *Harrington and His Oceana.* Cambridge: Cambridge University Press, 1914.
†Tawney, R.H.: *Harrington's Interpretation of His Age.* Oxford: Oxford University Press, 1942.

Hayek, Friedrich August von (1899–) Austrian economist and political philosopher. Hayek was born in Vienna into an academic family. In his youth, he was attracted to socialism. He studied economics under Wieser, and also law, at the University of Vienna. He also had interests in philosophy and theoretical psychology.

After the first world war he worked with Ludwig von Mises, first in official service, and then in an Institute for Trade Cycle Research. Hayek applied the capital theory of the Austrian School of economics to problems of trade cycles. Although he did not fully agree with Mises on economics or politics, he was profoundly influenced by Mises's critical work, *Socialism.* He was appointed to a chair at the London School of Economics in 1931.

Hayek continued his technical work in economics into the 1940s. Thereafter, he wrote largely on political philosophy and the methodology of social science. He was a professor at the University of Chicago from 1950 to 1962, and subsequently held positions in Freiburg and Salzburg. In 1974 he was awarded a Nobel Prize for his work in economics.

In a series of papers (collected in his *Individualism and Economic Order*, 1948), Hayek extended Mises's work on economic calculation under socialism. He argued that a centrally directed economy could not utilize the tacit knowledge of individuals, as could a market economy. Thereafter, Hayek's work emphasizes the importance of dispersed and tacit knowledge, and markets as institutions that help us to utilize this knowledge, and also to cope with ignorance and learn through trial and error.

Hayek's ideas on economic calculation underpin his *Road to Serfdom* (1944). This presents TOTALITARIANISM as an unintended consequence of the attempt to pursue economic planning. It also contains a powerful restatement of classical LIBERALISM. Hayek allows for a fair degree of governmental activity. But this is limited to forms compatible with his (*Rechts-staat*) conception of the RULE OF LAW.

Hayek's liberalism includes an appreciation of many useful social institutions as the products of human action but not of human design. This theme, developed with emphasis on Hume and the Scottish Historical School as his precursors, comes gradually to prominence in Hayek's work. The good society rests not simply on the pursuit of self-interest within a legal framework provided by government but, rather, on a complex framework of law, moral tradition and rules of behaviour, the character of which is – and can be – known only tacitly to the bulk of its members.

All this gives Hayek's work a Burkean edge. It has led him into issues of social evolution and group selection – and into some difficult problems. The relation between his account of the characteristics of selective mechanisms and his liberalism is not always clear. And the non-rationalistic character of these themes contrasts with his highly rationalistic and almost utopian schemes for a new liberal constitution. But these schemes, in their turn, draw inspiration from Hayek's ideas about the character of the 'spontaneous orders' of the market place and other undesigned institutions.

Hayek is not a rights theorist in the sense of, say, Nozick (see LIBERTARIANISM). His liberalism is founded, ultimately, on his belief that a social order of a classical liberal character best enables the individual citizen to satisfy his preferences and to avoid coercion by others. His argument is consequentialist, and broadly utilitarian in character. But all this is qualified by the almost Kantian requirement that laws should treat every citizen equally. Hayek's emphasis on the ignorance of individuals, and on their general inability to judge what the

long-term consequences of particular actions will be, leads him far away from the more usual forms of UTILITARIANISM.

Hayek has also written on the methodology of the social sciences. He here defends methodological INDIVIDUALISM. The phenomena of the social world should, for Hayek, be understood as the products, intended and unintended, of meaningful human action. Hayek also argues that human action is orientated towards objects as classified by 'subjective' human criteria, rather than by the 'objective' properties they might be described as possessing by the natural scientist. When dealing with complex phenomena in both the natural and the social sciences, our knowledge is limited to an 'explanation of the principle' upon which they function, and to making 'pattern predictions', as contrasted with the detailed predictions possible in some areas of natural science.

This work was in part a reaction to the physicalism of members of the Vienna Circle (Neurath, Carnap) and to 'scientism' in the social sciences. It is also related to Hayek's work on the cognitive psychology of perception – and to his political thought. For in Hayek's view, these mistaken methodological ideas blind people to the merits of the market and of 'evolved' social orders, and to the *kind* of knowledge we can have of such institutions.

In 1960, Hayek published a major work, *The Constitution of Liberty*. This gave an account of a classical liberal social order as one which minimizes coercion and brings material benefits to its citizens. He also discusses practical problems of public policy, and explicitly allows that the government should provide a welfare safety net, outside the market. This was followed by a trilogy, *Law, Legislation and Liberty* (1973–9), which combines classical liberalism with 'evolutionary' themes – and attacks legal positivism. Hayek criticizes the ideal of social JUSTICE as unrealizable in a market economy, and its pursuit as mischievous in its consequences, and he criticizes the pluralist politics of interest groups. He also discusses the problem of the stability of a market order, and offers radical proposals for a new liberal constitution, involving a new division of powers. This, he suggests, if citizens imposed it upon themselves, might stop them from taking measures that would ultimately prove destructive of both liberty and human well-being.

Hayek has recently returned to economic and policy-related themes. He has proposed the 'denationalization of money', and has offered criticisms of Keynesian economic policies which draw on his own early economic writings. He is currently at work on a further trilogy on liberalism and the market order.

Hayek's writings are complex, and cover a vast range of topics, historical and theoretical, through which run certain common themes. They should be appreciated as exercises in political economy, which focus upon individual freedom and the market order and their functional prerequisites – and *not* perhaps as the analytic philosophy to which Hayek occasionally lays claim. Although Hayek's work raises many problems of consistency and interpretation, it has greatly influenced some younger scholars, and has been a major influence on the revival of interest in classical liberalism in British political thought.   JS

Reading

†Barry, N.P.: *Hayek's Social and Economic Philosophy*. London: Macmillan, 1979.

Bosanquet, N.: *After the New Right*. London: Heinemann, 1983.

Cunningham, R.L. ed.: *Liberty and the Rule of Law*. College Station: Texas A & M University Press, 1979.

†Gray, J.: *Hayek on Liberty*. Oxford and New York: Blackwell, 1984. [Contains full bibliography.]

Hayek, F.A. von: *The Road to Serfdom*. Chicago: University of Chicago Press; London: Routledge & Kegan Paul, 1976.

———: *Individualism and Economic Order*. Chicago: University of Chicago Press; London: Routledge & Kegan Paul, 1976.

———: *The Constitution of Liberty*. Chicago: University of Chicago Press; London: Routledge & Kegan Paul, 1960.

———: *Studies in Philosophy, Politics and Economics*. Chicago: University of Chicago Press; London: Routledge & Kegan Paul, 1969.

———: *New Studies in Philosophy, Politics, Economics and the History of Ideas*. Chicago: University of Chicago Press; London: Routledge & Kegan Paul, 1978.

———: *Law, Legislation and Liberty*. Chicago: University of Chicago Press; London: Routledge & Kegan Paul, 1982.

Hegel, Georg Wilhelm Friedrich (1770– 1831) German philosopher. Born in Stuttgart, Hegel studied at Tübingen, then worked as a private tutor in Berne and Frankfurt; he was a university lecturer (*Privatdozent*) at Jena (1801–7), editor of a pro-French newspaper in Bamberg (1807–8), and headmaster of a *Gymnasium* in Nuremberg (1808–16). In 1816 he was appointed professor of philosophy at Heidelberg, and in 1818 professor of philosophy at Berlin University to succeed Fichte. While at Jena he founded, together with Schelling, the *Kritische Jahrbücher der Philosophie*. His major works are *Phenomenology of Spirit* (1807), *The Science of Logic* (1812), *Encyclopaedia of Philosophical Sciences* (1817; twice revised), and *Philosophy of Right* (1821). Among the posthumously published lectures are those on *Philosophy of History*, *History of Philosophy*, and *Philosophy of Religion*.

The core of Hegel's political thought is to be found in his *Philosophy of Right*. His earlier writings show him groping for an overall theory capable of relating both the classical philosophical tradition and the heritage of KANT and FICHTE to the changing political realities inaugurated by the French Revolution and its aftermath. His unpublished essay of *c.*1801, *The German Constitution*, is his first attempt to reach a viable definition of the state which could confront the radical impact of the French revolutionary wars on the traditional political system in Germany. And in the *Phenomenology of Spirit*, written in the immediate shadow of the Napoleonic victories, he tries to evoke the historical achievement of the Greek *polis* as the epitome of political cohesion and integration, while showing at the same time why the modern world, based as it is on the principle of subjectivity, cannot realize the pristine immediate identity of the self with the polity, which had been the cornerstone of the classical commonwealth. In his *Science of Logic* and in his *Encyclopaedia* he systematically set out his dialectical method, within which he placed his political philosophy as expounded in his *Philosophy of Right*. (See DIALECTIC.)

To Hegel, the STATE – the political community – is not a mere instrumental entity concocted by human practical reason for the furtherance of individually-oriented goals. While incorporating the elements of 'subjective freedom' (which he sees as the main achievement of modern society), he regards the state as an ethical entity, whose aims are anchored in a web of interpersonal relationships transcending the wishes of any given single individual.

This ethical nature (*Sittlichkeit*) of social existence has, according to Hegel, three 'moments', whose totality encompasses the multi-faceted nature of human life. They are the family, civil society, and the state. Each of these is a network of human relationship organized according to a different principle, and it is the dialectical relationship among the three which gives full meaning to the richness of human life. A person lacking any of these three relationships is deeply impaired in his quality as a human being.

The family is the kind of human relationships based on *particularistic altruism*: the willingness to act not in one's own interest but for the good of the other members of the family – parent, spouse, offspring, etc. In caring for the nourishment and education of one's children, or the welfare of one's ageing parents, action is determined not by self-interest but by willingness – sanctified in the social mores as a duty – to benefit another person. It is, on the other hand, a relationship limited to a particular set of people, and thus its altruism is severely circumscribed.

The second moment of interpersonal relationships is called by Hegel 'civil society' (*bürgerliche Gesellschaft*) and this is the sphere of *universal egoism*: a person relates to all other human beings (except, of course, members of his own family) on the basis of his own interests; he tries to maximize these interests, and views the interests of all other human beings as mere means to this end. The sphere of civil society is therefore the specific arena of economic activity, since a person who engages in commerce, for example, is not working in order to ensure the livelihood of others, but is using the felt needs of others as the means through which he may satisfy his own needs. Private property is the external mark of a person's standing in society – property is the objectification of a person's existence for others; Hegel's political philosophy therefore entails wide distribution of private property, and he recognizes that the emergence of widespread poverty in modern

society may undermine the efficacy of the structure he proposes.

To guarantee the well-regulated working of the market, a set of rules and universal principles is needed (e.g. agreed weights and measures), leading to the development of laws and courts capable of enforcing these rules. This mechanism of civil society Hegel calls 'the external state' (*Philosophy of Right*, §184); he is well aware that modern political thought, from HOBBES and LOCKE onwards, has identified this 'external state' with the state proper, and has thus anchored political obligation in rational self-interest.

Yet the third moment, the state proper, cannot according to Hegel be based on perceptions of mere individual self-interest: how is it possible, on the basis of self-interest, to legitimize the call to arms which may put a citizen's life in jeopardy? (Hegel is aware that this is a weak point in Hobbes's attempt to base political obligation on self-interest.) Hence Hegel posits the state as founded on *universal altruism*. Within the dialectical structure of Hegel's thought this also means that the state is a synthesis of the constitutive elements of the family and civil society. On the one hand, the state is analogous to the family in that the citizen is expected to act not in his own interest but in ways that promote the welfare of others: paying taxes, serving in the army, etc. These acts can only be justified and legitimized in terms of solidarity with other members of what thus becomes the body politic. On the other hand, the state integrates into its structure the universal element of civil society, and this synthesis gives rise to a consciousness of citizenship based on universal criteria: 'It is part of education, of thinking as the consciousness of the single in the form of universality, that the self comes to be apprehended as a universal person in which all are identical. A man counts as a man in virtue of his humanity alone, not because he is a Jew, Catholic, Protestant, German, Italian, etc.' (*Philosophy of Right*, §209).

Hegel affirms the public nature of the state, yet the private and the public spheres are not altogether severed from each other as they are in ARISTOTLE's distinction between the *oikos* and the *polis*: in modern society man has to contend both with his private relationships and with the public sphere, being at the same time both *bourgeois* and *citoyen*. Political freedom is the delicate balance emerging from these contradictory yet ultimately integrated orientations. This integration is possible, according to Hegel, only in the modern state, which legitimizes a sphere of subjectivity: civil society is the sphere of the autonomy of the subjective will. The classical *polis*, on the other hand, with its unmediated politicization of private matters (including religion), did not possess such an autonomous sphere. Modern political philosophy, from Hobbes onwards, tried by contrast to analyse the public realm in terms of individual self-interest, and thus did not, according to Hegel, progress beyond 'civil society'. The height and ultimate self-destruction of this reign of unbridled egoistic individualism Hegel saw in the Reign of Terror of the French Revolution (*Philosophy of Right*, §258).

The interplay of these forces Hegel then formally institutionalizes in the political constitution of the modern state as envisaged in the *Philosophy of Right*. The various interests of civil society find their expression in the corporations and the Assembly of Estates which represent the aggregate interests of the various elements of civil society. Yet Hegel opposes any republican idea of parliamentary sovereignty, which he fears could become a tyranny of special interests. The power of the Assembly of Estates is circumscribed by the power of a career civil service ('the universal class' in Hegel's parlance). This class, like PLATO's Guardians, has the interests of the common weal as its end: it should be open to all citizens on the basis of ability and education, and fixed salaries should inoculate its members against the temptations of civil society – an innovative proposal in the early 1820s.

But while the Platonic Guardians wield absolute power over a society otherwise lacking a political structure, Hegel's 'universal class' operates within a system where special interests have their legitimate expression in autonomous corporations and the Assembly of Estates. Moreover, this whole political structure is headed by a hereditary monarch, who symbolizes the idea that the state is based on subjective will, as it is the monarch's assent to the laws which gives them formal validity. But the monarch's powers are extremely limited and he is a mere symbol of the unity of the body politic in a single formal will, whose function is to rubberstamp the decisions of the Assembly and the public servants (*Philosophy of Right*, addition to §280).

The historical impact of Hegel's political philosophy has been greatly enhanced by the fact that his theory of the modern state was embedded within an overall philosophical system which saw historical development as part of the objectification in the temporal and spatial world of what Hegel called 'Spirit'. Hegel's view of the rationality of the world and its perceptibility by human reason follows Aristotle and is, within the tradition of German IDEALISM, a radical critique of KANT. But in contrast to Aristotle, Hegel maintains that the rationality of the world is not an *a priori* given, but evolves over time together with the concrete human consciousness which recognizes it as such. Philosophy is thus the ever-unfolding vehicle of human reason's comprehension of the world, and hence the stages of the development of philosophy evolve *pari passu* with the stages of historical development itself. Philosophy is 'the thought of the world, appearing only when actuality is already there cut and dried after its process of formation has been completed' (*Philosophy of Right*, Preface, pp. 12–13). History, and the political realm as its most visible aspect, is by itself of philosophical significance. In this context Hegel used the phrase 'what is rational is actual, and what is actual is rational' (Preface, p. 10). Though some critics interpret this as a complete vindication of existing reality, Hegel himself explicitly took this statement to mean that what is rational has the potential of actualizing itself, and hence historical development, far from being an undifferentiated aggregate of incomprehensible accidents and human foibles, has a rational structure. This structure may not always be perceptible at the time that any given event occurs, but philosophy has the key to decipher the hieroglyph of reason as embedded in history.

It was this insistence on reason's power to actualize itself in history that became the cornerstone for the critical work of the YOUNG HEGELIANS, who measured all existing institutions by the standards of Hegelian political philosophy – and found them wanting. Ultimately, this use of philosophy as a vehicle of social criticism became the philosophical underpinning of MARXISM.

Hegel maintained that the march of reason in history was a complex dialectical process, in which individuals (and nations) were mere tools, mostly unaware of the import and significance of their own deeds. Changes were often introduced by 'world-historical individuals' like Alexander, Caesar and Napoleon; but Hegel was explicit that their role derives not from their conscious intentions or political platforms, for they were motivated, like all other human beings, by base desires such as ambition, greed, and the quest for glory. It was the objective consequences of their deeds, and not their subjective intentions, that made them historically significant.

By thus downgrading the 'great men of history' from the idealized role allotted to them by the romantic tradition, Hegel turned them into unconscious tools in the hand of the 'cunning of reason' (*List der Vernunft*), an idea which implies that reason may have to use irrational means to guarantee its realization. It is the role of the philosopher to go beyond external appearances and discover the rational kernel hidden even within apparently irrational phenomena. The acknowledgement of this tension between subjective intention and objective consequences also distinguishes the philosopher from the pedantic moralist.

History to Hegel is, then, development towards the consciousness of freedom as expressed in the political, cultural, and religious institutions of a community. The sum total of these characteristics Hegel calls – following both MONTESQUIEU and HERDER – 'the spirit of the nation' (*Volksgeist*). It is expressed externally in the formation of objective institutions – i.e. in the emergence of a state. Hegel discerns three basic stages of historical development, each representing a further evolution of the consciousness of freedom:

(1) the *Oriental World*, in which *one* person was free, while all others were unfree; hence oriental despotism was its political structure;

(2) the *Classical World*, in which *some* people were free; hence the *polis*, whose franchise might be wider or narrower but was not universal, was its historical expression;

(3) the *Germanic World*, where on the basis of the universal nature of the Christian gospel *all* people were considered capable of freedom. In this world, comprising all of Western Europe where people of Germanic origin settled on the ruins of the Roman Empire, the potential of freedom for all underlay the evolution of political institutions. This is the world of modern England, France, Germany and Italy; the Reformation and the French Revolution were, according to this scheme, crucial milestones on the road to the full consciousness of freedom. Hegel thus secularized and politicized the meaning of the universality of Christian salvation, yet his thought remained anchored in Protestantism and he therefore shied away from the nationalist ROMANTICISM of his age.

While no concrete historical state ever served Hegel as a model for the full realization of freedom, the modern constitutional monarchy as it evolved out of the French Revolution and the Restoration seemed to him to move clearly in that direction. His essays on political conditions in Germany and England plainly suggest this.

While Hegel has been criticized for the conservative bent of his political philosophy, it is essentially a refinement of ENLIGHTENMENT thought as filtered through both German Idealism and the harrowing experience of the French Revolution. History is indeed progress, but, as the French Revolution suggests, it moves in violent spirals. The modern state is based on subjective freedom, but to prevent it from degenerating into an unbridled war of all against all, mediation through rational institutions is required, as the only guarantee against arbitrariness and the threat of tyranny posed by absolute monarchy and absolute majoritarianism.

It is ironic that while Hegel's basic philosophical premises led to the development of the revolutionary social critique culminating in Marxism, the need for mediating institutions ultimately became – though not necessarily through the influence of Hegel himself – the cornerstone of the modern Western state as we know it. Despite obvious differences, the role of political parties and other aggregating institutions makes the modern democratic state much more similar to the Hegelian state than to the undifferentiated and unmediated democracy of ROUSSEAU, with its inherent totalitarian proclivities.   SA

Reading

†Avineri, S.: *Hegel's Theory of the Modern State.* Cambridge: Cambridge University Press, 1972.

†Harris, H.S.: *Hegel's Development.* Oxford: Oxford University Press, 1972.

Hegel, G.W.F.: *Early Theological Writings*, ed. R. Kroner, trans. T.M. Knox. Chicago: Chicago University Press, 1948.

———: *Lectures on the Philosophy of World History*, trans. H.B. Nisbet. Cambridge: Cambridge University Press, 1975.

———: *Political Writings*, ed. Z. Pelczynski, trans. T.M. Knox. Oxford: Oxford University Press, 1964.

———: *Phenomenology of Spirit*, trans. A.V. Miller. Oxford: Clarendon Press, 1977.

———: *Philosophy of Right*, trans. T.M. Knox. Oxford: Oxford University Press, 1942.

Kaufmann, W. ed.: *Hegel's Political Philosophy.* New York: Atherton, 1970.

Pelczynski, Z.A. ed.: *State and Civil Society: Studies in Hegel's Political Philosophy.* Cambridge: Cambridge University Press, 1984.

†Plant, R.: *Hegel*, 2nd edn. Oxford: Blackwell, 1983.

Rosenzweig, F.: *Hegel und der Staat.* Munich and Berlin: Oldenbourg, 1920.

Shklar, J.N.: *Freedom and Independence: a Study of the Political Ideas of Hegel's 'Phenomenology of Mind'.* Cambridge: Cambridge University Press, 1976.

†Taylor, C.: *Hegel.* Cambridge: Cambridge University Press, 1975.

hegemony A term used principally by GRAMSCI and his followers to refer to the non-coercive aspects of class rule, i.e. to the ability of a dominant class to use agencies of socialization to foist its own values and beliefs on to the remainder of the population.   DLM

Heidegger, Martin (1889–1976) German philosopher. After early studies in theology, logic, mathematics, and natural science, Heidegger turned his attention to philosophical studies, and became assistant to Edmund Husserl, founder of the school of phenomenology. The work for which Heidegger is most famous is *Being and Time* (1927). For many, the legacy of Heidegger has been seriously clouded by his infamous involvement with the Nazis during his brief tenure as rector of the University of Freiburg in 1933, but the actual significance of this episode has been hotly contested.

Heidegger's contribution to twentieth-century philosophy has been a comprehensive re-examination of the basic ontological assumptions of western thought, and a radical probing of the metaphysical tradition as a whole. Like NIETZSCHE, he sees western thought from Plato onwards as a gradual but inexorable development in the direction of contemporary nihilism, culminating in the rampant subjectivism of modern man's relationship to Being. In particular, Heidegger tries to offer a root-and-branch critique of the subject-object dichotomy as it has been unfolded in the tradition of western metaphysics, as well as to spell out the far-reaching implications that this idea has had for our civilization as a whole. (See also EXISTENTIALISM.)

Heidegger's project, then, is to scrutinize the deficiencies of traditional ontology (the study of Being in general); this necessarily has implications for our evaluation of the history of political thought. Heidegger's metaphysics commit him to rejecting three major traditions of political thought, each of which offers a different account of man and of man's place in Being. One account, the classical, portrays man as a being within nature, but a being who can also ascend to a rational apprehension of nature; the political order is a microcosm of the natural order. Another account, the contractarian, sees man ranged against an alien nature; men must band together in order to resist collectively the pressure of natural necessity. A third account, the Hegelian-Marxist, tries to reconcile freedom and nature by depicting the re-establishment of unity between man and nature as the definitive accomplishment of human freedom. For Heidegger, however, the differences between these accounts are less important than what is common to them, namely, a set of metaphysical assumptions about man as a being of a certain kind, related in a specific way to the rest of Being. To expose and challenge these metaphysical assumptions is to subvert the whole tradition of political philosophy as such.

For instance, how can one base one's understanding of politics on a conception of HUMAN NATURE and of man's place in nature when one is no longer certain whether nature is an object-domain waiting passively to be contemplated, or whether it is – to use Heidegger's language – an historically revealed 'realm of disclosure'? Again, how can one base a theory of sovereignty on a notion of man as a being who freely enters into contracts if one is no longer clear about the status of the human subject (namely, whether the subject can be said to have transparent access to its own subjectivity)? And finally, how can one claim to reconcile freedom and nature when fundamental metaphysical assumptions concerning both subject and object have been thrown into radical question? We find ourselves forced to reconsider the roots of our tradition of thought about man and politics.

Political philosophies typically take their point of departure from philosophical anthropology, that is, some conception of human nature. Heidegger, however, contends that the prevailing philosophical anthropologies have failed to secure themselves at the ontological level and are, unknowingly, ontologically biased. In the 'Letter on humanism' (*Basic Writings*, pp. 193–242), he argues that the traditional understanding of the man as *animal rationale* is fatally contaminated by metaphysics in that it tries to specify the generic property that defines a particular class of beings – animals with 'something extra' added, namely soul or reason (hence man conceived as a 'synthesis' of *animal* and *ratio*). According to Heidegger, man does not have a nature in the sense in which objects in the natural world might be said to have a nature; therefore all those political philosophies that are grounded upon a definition of human nature are compelled to address Heidegger's charge that metaphysical determinations of human nature necessarily fall short of an authentic grasp of the 'human essence' – which for Heidegger is constituted not as an object-domain (specifying properties of objects) but as a 'realm of disclosure' (a particular way of being open to Being).

Heidegger believes that the destiny of our civilization has been irrevocably shaped by the traditional philosophic understanding of man and being, both classical and modern. For instance, he argues that the contemporary aspiration to 'planetary domination' of the earth and technological mastery of nature is the outcome of an understanding of man as a 'subject' ranged against a passive and submissive object-world. This dichotomous understanding of Being was, Heidegger claims, first introduced in PLATO's allegory of the cave in the *Republic*, and became enshrined in western metaphysics through the subject-predicate logic of ARISTOTLE. It culminates in rationalism and empiricism on the one hand (both of which share a notion of self-transparent subjectivity) and German IDEALISM on the other hand. For idealism, the object is actually constituted by the activity of the subject: thus the world is the product of human will, and nature waits passively to be shaped by human creativity. Heidegger therefore combines a critical analysis of the most basic presuppositions of ancient and modern thought with an historical account of how these assumptions have shaped everyday experience in the modern world.

Although many students of Heidegger have seen important implications in his thought for their own reflections on social and political life, its full relevance has yet to be explored. Aside from its far-reaching implications for the reinterpretation of the history of western philosophy as a whole, the most direct bearing that Heidegger's work has upon political theory arises from the critical interrogation, contained in his later writings, of what Heidegger calls 'the essence of technology', namely that dispensation of Being that brings forth all beings as objects at the unlimited disposal of the human subject. Heidegger's crowning thought seems to be that philosophy as a tradition fails to possess the resources necessary to contend with this ultimate dispensation, and that therefore we must have recourse to a new kind of meditative thinking (closer to the poetic than to the conceptual) that will foster a more receptive relationship to Being.   RSB

Reading

†Gillespie, M.A.: *Hegel, Heidegger, and the Ground of*

History, ch. 5. Chicago and London: University of Chicago Press, 1984.

Heidegger, M.: *An Introduction to Metaphysics* (1953), trans. R. Manheim. New Haven and London: Yale University Press, 1959.

————: *Being and Time*, trans. J. Macquarrie and E. Robinson. New York and Evanston: Harper & Row, 1962.

————: *What is Called Thinking?* (1954), trans. F.D. Wieck and J.G. Gray. New York: Harper & Row, 1968.

———— *Basic Writings*, ed. D.F. Krell. New York: Harper & Row, 1977.

†Murray, M. ed.: *Heidegger and Modern Philosophy*. New Haven, Conn.: Yale University Press, 1978.

Helvétius, Claude-Adrien (1715–1771) French philosopher of German origin. Helvétius turned to philosophy after he had made his fortune as a tax farmer. Only marginally less rich than Holbach he was considerably more to the left, the most egalitarian and democratic of the theorists of the FRENCH ENLIGHTENMENT. As an exponent of UTILITARIANISM, Helvétius was the acknowledged master of Jeremy BENTHAM and the English school of philosophic radicals; he was a personal friend of Jefferson and Franklin, but he stood somewhat apart from the French *Encyclopédistes* who often regarded him as a wealthy amateur, lacking intellectual finesse.

His egalitarianism was based on his belief – considered absurdly extravagant by such contemporaries as DIDEROT and HOLBACH – that all men are uniform or fundamentally alike. The differences between one man and another, he claimed, were entirely due to differences in upbringing and environment. 'The existing inequality of minds is the effect of a known cause, and that cause is inequality of education' (*A Treatise on Man* I, p. 94). Existing differences of education explained why some men were more virtuous or more accomplished than others. Helvétius denied that there were any innate qualities, or indeed any innate talents or aptitudes. Education could be used to train anyone to do anything that anyone else could do. All skills were acquired; none was the gift of nature.

Helvétius criticized Rousseau's view that men had ceased to be equal when they left the state of nature to enter society; he maintained that men were still naturally as equal as they had always been. To demonstrate that equality, it required only a system which would provide each person with the education needed to bring him up to standard.

Helvétius's democratic politics derived from his utilitarian ethics. Having defined good actions as those which promote the greatest happiness of the greatest number, Helvétius went on to suggest that good legislation was that which enlarged the pleasure of the majority of the community as distinct from the pleasure of privileged minorities. While he located the pleasure of all men in the enjoyment of life, liberty and property, he acknowledged no natural right to such things in individual persons which could be given priority over the happiness of all. As to what policies would contribute most to the greatest happiness of the greatest number, Helvétius argued that only the greatest number – the majority – could tell; hence the case for democracy.

However, Helvétius's plea for democracy was modified by another plea – more characteristic of Enlightenment thinking – for wise legislation. The majority might recognize what gave it pleasure and what gave it pain, but it did not have the foresight to see by what means it could maximize pleasure in future. Hence, Helvétius did not propose the immediate introduction of democracy, but called for a legislator to set down a new constitution. He suggested that such a legislator, like the founder of a religious order, would have to ignore all existing prejudices, and be guided by the light of philosophy.

While he seemed to have a enlightened monarch in mind to enact the role of legislator, Helvétius looked forward to a further arrangement whereby the state would take the form of a federation of small quasi-autonomous provinces, virtually republics. He went even further to suggest the subdivision of the land into as many parcels as there were families. He did not advocate common ownership or socialism, but rather the introduction of a system of property-owning democracy. Since it was part of his theory of human motivation that each person was directed by nature to seek his own advantage, Helvétius argued that the only way to make everyone work for the common good was to bring about a fusion of the private and the public interest. This could be accomplished, he believed, only if every family had a share in the national wealth.   MC

Reading
†Cumming, I.: *Helvétius*. London: Routledge & Kegan Paul, 1955.
Helvétius, C.A.: *Essays on the Mind*. London, 1759.
——: *A Treatise on Man*, trans. W. Hooper. London, 1777.
†Smith, D.W.: *Helvétius*. Oxford: Clarendon Press, 1965.

Herder, Johann Gottfried (1744–1803) German philosopher and founding father of cultural history. Herder was the son of a pietist schoolmaster at Mohrungen in the backward province of East Prussia. As a student at the University of Königsberg he came under the influence of KANT, who introduced him to the writings of ROUSSEAU, HUME, and MONTESQUIEU. Here he also formed a lifelong friendship with the irrationalist thinker, J. G. Hamann. In 1764 he took a teaching post at Riga, and was ordained as a Lutheran clergyman the following year. In 1769 Herder embarked on a period of travel which took him to many places including Nantes, Paris, and Strasbourg, where he made a lasting impression on the young Goethe. In 1776 he went to Weimar to become clerical head of the Grand Duchy, a post he held to the end of his life.

Though Herder began as a disciple of the FRENCH ENLIGHTENMENT and its German followers, retaining some of its attitudes to the end of his life, his most original and influential works mark a fundamental break with it. Among his most original works are *Abhandlung über den Ursprung der Sprache* (Treatise on the Origin of Language) (1772) which contains some of his earliest Counter-Enlightenment views on mind and language and won a prize offered by the Berlin Academy; *Auch eine Philosophie der Geschichte* (Yet Another Philosophy of History) (1774) which marked a further step in his break with the Enlightenment; and his massive *Ideen zur Philosophie der Geschichte der Menschheit* (Ideas for the Philosophy of the History of Mankind) (1784–91).

Against the Enlightenment ideal of timeless, universal, rational standards in knowledge, action, and aesthetics, Herder advocated the claims of the unique and particular in a specific time and place. Every authentic activity, outlook, culture, must be understood from within in terms of its own peculiar purposes and goals. Herder thus rejected the Enlightenment ideal of a unified science of all reality, and was one of the first (after VICO) to draw a sharp distinction between the methods required for the study of physical nature and those demanded for understanding the self-developing spirit of man.

Herder's stress on the central formative role of language and poetry in the collective life of men – 'language expresses the collective experience of the group', 'a poet is a creator of a people', and 'we live in a world we ourselves create'; his belief that nations are natural units and that a man is defined by belonging to a specific group, culture, nation, within which alone he can flourish; his conviction that all the works of man are above all acts of self-expression which embody a total vision of life; his connected conception of a culture as a unique self-developing totality, each strand of which is indelibly marked by the style of the whole; his passionate assertion that there is no 'superior' people – no *Favoritvolk* – with a historic right to impose its ways on 'inferior' peoples; his claim that no culture is a mere stepping-stone to its successors, since each is incommensurable and exists in its own right; his passionate advocacy of variety for its own sake; and his resolute battle against the faculty psychology of thinkers such as Descartes and Kant who dissect the total personality into the dead segments of will, reason, understanding, etc.; all these ideas contributed to a revolutionary shift in European awareness.

Herder was above all the intellectual father of the doctrine of nationalism which first took root in Germany, spread to the Slav world, and is widespread today in Africa and Asia (see NATIONALISM). Though bitterly opposed to the state which 'robs us of ourselves', rejecting all his life all forms of coercion, Herder's doctrines flowed into the thought of later nationalists like FICHTE, Arndt, Görres, Jahn, and Treitschke, all of whom distorted his ideas, and through them into the insane excesses of NATIONAL SOCIALISM. And though he did not himself conceive of cultures as superindividual entities to which real individuals might be sacrificed, his notion of the *Volksseele* (the collective soul of the people) was developed in that direction by Fichte, HEGEL, and their followers. Again, Herder's conception of the undivided creative personality, whose works express his own authentic experience and that of his group, inspired both the ideal of artistic commitment among radical writers in nineteenth-century Russia, and also the vision of *der ganze Mensch*, the whole man, with its corollary of alienated human nature, as developed by the YOUNG HEGELIANS and by Marx in his youthful, humanist phase. Herder's impact on Jakob Grimm, the Schlegels, and the growth of folk studies and comparative philology, on Savigny and the Historical School of law, as well as on ROMANTICISM and its later intellectual offshoots, was incalculably great.

Whatever sinister forms they may have taken at the hands of later irrationalist thinkers, Herder's own doctrines were (and are) powerfully liberating. He was the first great champion of the right of all men, whether as individuals or groups, to pursue their own natural bent, free of oppression by centralized authority, alien forms of life, narrow, dogmatic, and distorting views of what men are and should be, and artificial shackles of all kinds.   RNH

Reading
†Berlin, I.: *Vico and Herder*. London: Hogarth Press, 1976.
Herder, J.G.: *Herder on Social and Political Culture*, a selection of texts, ed. and trans. F.M. Barnard. London: Cambridge University Press, 1969.
†Nisbet, H.B.: *Herder and the Philosophy and History of Science*. Cambridge: Modern Humanities Research Association, 1970.
Wells, G.A.: *Herder and After*. The Hague: Mouton, 1959.

Herzen, Alexander Ivanovich (1812–1870) Russian philosopher and publicist. Herzen was the illegitimate but pampered son of a Russian aristocrat and a German mother. A pivotal figure in nineteenth-century Russian thought, he stands midway between Westerners and Slavophiles and between liberalism and socialism. Before 1847 he was a leading Westerner; afterwards he wrote his major works as an emigré in Western Europe, responding to the failure of the 1848 revolutions and to his own personal tragedy – the infidelity and, in 1852, the death of his wife. He founded the Free Russian Press and his publications, especially *The Bell* and *The Polar Star*, influenced Russian opinion in the years before the reforms of Alexander II. He is regarded as the founder of Russian POPULISM and his memoirs, *My Past and Thoughts* (1861–7), are a major contribution to Russian literature.

Greatly influenced by HEGEL, Herzen accepted the dialectic as an explanation of historical progress, but rejected historical inevitability or any rational force in history. His early philosophical works divided history into three periods: of natural immediacy, of thought, and – the current stage – of action. He firmly believed in man's capacity to shape his own destiny. His socialism, derived from PROUDHON and FEUERBACH, always remained anarchist, utopian, and anti-Marxist in inspiration, and uneasily co-existed with his overriding concern with the development of the individual personality.

In the name of individualism he opposed the Slavophile emphasis on orthodoxy and conciliarism, exemplified in the peasant commune and pre-Petrine Russian government. Although defending Peter I's westernization policies he also broke with the Russian liberals, who saw in Europe a political model for Russian development. Herzen rejected parliamentary democracy, seeing it as a contract between masters and slaves. He was never a constitutional democrat and his experience in 1848 merely completed his disillusionment with bourgeois, capitalist society. His moralistic rejection of bourgeois mediocrity and vulgarity reflected his aristocratic upbringing.

From the Other Shore, written after the failure of the French revolution in 1848, is a passionate defence of individual freedom against ideologies that demand present sacrifices for future utopias. Yet, despite this rejection of all myths, he was soon to rediscover one of his own. Losing faith in a socialist revolution in Europe, he came to identify the Russian peasant commune as an embryonic socialist organization which might enable a young and vigorous Russia to pass directly from feudalism to socialism, overtaking a decadent capitalist

West. But for all his involvement with nineteenth-century European progressivism, Herzen was never tempted to see an inevitable pattern in history, nor to idealize the Russian peasant. His ultimate ideal lay in a fusion between intellectual individualism and peasant collectivism; but in his more realistic moods he was aware of the chasm between the intelligentsia and the masses, and feared the destruction of European civilization by a violent (if, for him, justified) communist revolution.

Never an economic thinker, his vision of socialism remained rural and co-operative. His calls for Russia's elite to go to the people, to learn as well as to teach, inspired the central strand of Russian populism and he bequeathed to that movement its anarchist and idealistic character.   BW

Reading

Acton, E.: *Alexander Herzen and the Role of the Intellectual Revolutionary*. Cambridge: Cambridge University Press, 1979.

†Berlin, I.: *Russian Thinkers*. London: Hogarth Press, 1978.

Herzen, A.: *From the Other Shore* and *The Russian People and Socialism*, trans. M. Budberg, intro. I. Berlin. Oxford: Oxford University Press, 1979.

————: *My Past and Thoughts: the Memoirs of Alexander Herzen*, trans. C. Garnett, rev. H. Higgens, intro. I. Berlin. 4 vols. London: Chatto & Windus, 1968.

†Malia, M.: *Alexander Herzen and the Birth of Russian Socialism 1812–55*. Oxford: Oxford University Press, 1961.

Walicki, A.: *A History of Russian Thought*, chs 7 and 10. Oxford: Clarendon Press, 1980.

Hindu political thought Unlike the Hindu philosophical tradition which is subtle, rich and complex, the Hindu tradition of political thought, spanning the centuries between the Vedic period around the second millennium before Christ and the consolidation of Muslim rule in the fourteenth century AD, is relatively simple, homogeneous and lacking in diversity. It did, of course, undergo changes in response to the theoretical and practical problems posed by such events as the rise of new religious and philosophical movements, new castes, guilds and corporations, and waves of foreign invasions. Amidst all these changes, however, its basic categories of thought, questions and

manner of answering them remained substantially the same.

For the Hindu political thinkers the universe is characterized by *Rta*, an inviolable cosmic order brought about by the operation of laws representing divine intelligence. The laws are not imposed or created by God, rather they are God. They are thus not merely natural but also rational and moral in nature. Order in the universe is maintained by each entity keeping to its ordained place and obeying the relevant laws. Human society is an integral part of the universe. It reproduces the order and 'truth' of the universe when all men keep to their proper place and discharge their relevant *dharma*. *Dharma* means what is right or, broadly, duties. Unlike natural objects, human beings have a capacity to think and will. They can fall victim to illusions and temptations, and deviate from *dharma*. *Danda*, meaning force and punishment, therefore becomes necessary to keep them to the path of rectitude.

Dharma and *danda* are the master concepts of Hindu political thought. Governing a territorially organized community ultimately consists in using *danda* to maintain *dharma*. It thus raises related but distinct questions about, first, the nature, basis, sources and content of *dharma* and second, the nature, basis and organization of *danda*. While the earlier Hindu writers discussed both, they later began to concentrate on one or other set of questions. Some wrote *dharmasastras* or treatises on *dharma* whereas others wrote *dandaniti* or *arthasastras*. The term *artha* means, among other things, territory and prosperity, and *arthasastra* refers to the study of the ways of acquiring and maintaining territory and promoting its prosperity. This is how it is defined by Kautilya, the greatest Hindu political thinker. Strictly speaking the two groups of writers are complementary, and this was fully appreciated by them. The two together constitute the Hindu tradition of political thought. Over time, however, the complementarity was lost sight of, and the term political thinker came to be confined to the authors of *arthasastras*.

Although the Hindu political writers acknowledged that some duties pertained to men *qua* men, they thought that the bulk of them were contextual. Some devolved on men as members of specific social groups (*varnadharma*) and others as occupying specific stages in life (*ashramadharma*). For the Hindu writers a society is not a collection of individuals but a community of communities. It is articulated into specific castes, each with its appropriate economic functions and place in the social hierarchy. An individual's *dharma* is derived from the caste of his birth. His birth into a particular caste is not an accident but a result of his actions or *karma* in previous life. *Karma* means both action and fate. For the Hindus every action both reflects and shapes the agent's character and is an interplay of human freedom and fate. In addition to the caste, an individual also occupies other social positions such as a father or a son, a husband or a wife, a brother, a neighbour and so on, and there are specific duties pertaining to each of them.

When each individual does his *dharma* there is no disorder in society, and obviously no need for *danda* or government. For most Hindu thinkers men were once in such a state. Thanks to the decline of moral sense, or the emergence of greed, or the appearance of *ahamkar*, a pregnant Sanskrit term meaning at once a sense of individuality, self-love and pride, men became corrupt, and began to ignore their *dharma*. This led to *varnasankara* or confusion of castes, *arajakata* or lawlessness, and *matsyanyaya* or the law of the sea according to which the big fish devour the small. Government became necessary to put an end to all this.

Although nearly all Hindu political thinkers concentrated on the monarchical form of government, India knew many other forms as well, including oligarchies and republics. Republics thrived in many parts of India. They had popular assemblies and councils of leading citizens, elaborate rules of public discussion, elections and strong corporate identities. A beautiful verse in the *Rigveda* captures the kind of sentiment that characterized the popular assembly; 'Common be your intentions, common be your hearts, common be your thoughts, so that there may be a thorough union among you.' Rather strangely the republics did not throw up a systematic body of political thought, let alone a thinker of the stature of Kautilya, the greatest theorist of the Mauryan empire. Much of what they seem to have

produced is either lost, or survives in fragmentary discussions in the epics, the Puranas and literary plays.

For the Hindu political thinkers the king's main function was *loksangraha*, the co-ordination and preservation of people as constituted into a specific community. It involved not just maintaining internal order and the territorial integrity of the community, but also promoting the reign of *dharma*, the spirit of righteousness, trade, commerce, prosperity, the arts, and so on. In these and other ways the king was to create an environment in which his subjects could attain the four main goals of human life, namely *dharma*, wealth, satisfaction of desires, and liberation from the cycle of births and deaths. Since he made a vital contribution to their moral growth, he was described as *acharpreraka* (the inspirer of moral conduct) and *kalasya karanam* (the primary determinant of the ethos and moral climate of his community). The behaviour of his subjects was thus a result not only of their own efforts but also of his. Hence he shared part of the responsibility for their conduct, and acquired a portion of their moral and religious merit or demerit as the case might be.

The king's duty to enforce *dharma* raises the question about the sources of *dharma*. Most Hindu political writers regarded the Vedas, the Smritis and *Vyavahara* (custom) as its three major sources. The Vedas enunciated abstract moral principles and contained little concrete discussion of duties. The Smritis were mainly digests of the prevailing practice. For all theoretical and practical purposes custom, defined as 'what is in vogue and is of long standing', was therefore the dominant source of *dharma*.

Although the Hindus recognized the universality of some moral principles, they insisted that the operative morality of a social group was profoundly shaped by time and space. Every social group inhabits a specific geographical environment, represents a particular stage of moral and cultural development, its members have a specific 'temperament' and disposition, and so on, and it develops its own distinctive way of life to which they are deeply attached and which must be respected. Over the centuries the social structure of India underwent important changes, and many new castes, foreign settlements, guilds, corporations, religious organizations and groups of heretics and atheists came into existence. The Hindu writers extended the traditional theory of *dharma* to them and recognized their right to regulate their affairs according to their own customs and usages, the king having a right to intervene only when these were ambiguous or harmful to public interest. The king thus ruled over a highly differentiated and uncentralized social order, and his power and authority were rigidly circumscribed by the relatively inviolable autonomy of the various fairly powerful corporate entities. The concept of 'oriental despotism' does not apply to ancient India.

As for the structure and mode of operation of government, the Hindu writers displayed little divergence of views. For all of them the polity was composed of seven 'organs' or elements, namely the king, ministers, a territorially settled community, fortification, the treasury, the army and the allies, the organization of each of which they described in considerable detail. For all of them there were four ways of maintaining oneself in power, namely persuasion, bribery, intrigue and force. Nearly all of them insisted on the importance of an efficient and professional civil service and an extensive network of spies. All Hindu writers freely acknowledged that the king was fully justified in resorting to violence, cruelty and deception, if necessary for the preservation of the community, his highest *dharma*. In *Mahabharata* even Krishna, the Lord Himself, resorts to lies and deceptions on a few occasions, thereby demonstrating that even God cannot cope with the imperatives of political life without occasional recourse to otherwise immoral deeds.

The Hindu political writers also took substantially similar views on such questions as political obedience, punishment and taxation. The king was to be obeyed because he upheld and sustained the social order and enabled his subjects to live disciplined and moral lives. Many Hindu writers acknowledged that a king lacked legitimacy unless duly crowned, but argued that even a usurper acquired authority and deserved obedience if he properly discharged his royal duties. They were divided about what to do when a king turned tyrannical. Some

advocated continued obedience, some urged that his subjects should desert his kingdom, whereas others advocated his removal and even his assassination.

Most Hindu writers advanced a functional theory of taxation. Taxes were the 'price of protection' which people paid in order to ensure the security of their person and property. Some pressed the argument to its logical conclusion and contended that the ruler must reimburse his subjects for theft and forfeit his right to the taxes for a systematic failure to protect them.

For the Hindu writers punishment was designed to achieve five objectives: it restrained the individual concerned; deterred others; preserved the social order; signified society's collective determination not to tolerate evil; and purified the criminal by making him suffer the consequences of his deed, thereby wiping out its effects on his soul. They insisted that the kind and degree of punishment should vary with the social status of the individual concerned. The higher castes were to receive lighter punishment and were exempted from corporal punishment.

Buddhism represented an important stage in the development of Hindu political thought. It was atheistic, rejected the caste system, founded monasteries, gave India the first experience of an organized but non-theological religion, admitted women, and enjoyed the support of such neglected and socially inferior classes as traders, artisans, merchants and foreign settlers. It accepted the Hindu view that the king's basic duty was to maintain *dhamma* (the Buddhist word for *dharma*), but rejected its caste-based definition and content. This meant that the king now had to determine the content of *dhamma*. For the first time in the history of Indian thought, Buddhism introduced the idea of legislation, a view that laws can be made, are acts of will and derive their authority from secular sources. It also advanced a quasi-contractualist theory of the origin of government and argued that political authority was derived from the people.

The impact of Buddhism on Hindu political thought was limited. While its philosophy was revolutionary, its political theory was not. It accepted such basic Hindu beliefs as that life is full of sorrow, desires are bad, a man's *karma* in his previous life determines his character in this one and the ruler's supreme duty is to maintain *dharma*. It did not extend social and political equality to the poor and the *Sudras*, and confined political power to the higher castes. While it challenged the power and authority of the Brahmans, it upheld that of the Ksatriyas, and only replaced the Ksatriya-Brahman alliance with that of the Ksatriyas and Vaisyas. It thus amounted to a reconstitution rather than a rejection of the traditional form of political domination.

Before concluding this brief summary of the Hindu tradition of political thought, it would be useful to highlight some of its central features. First, the Hindu tradition was basically descriptive and didactic and lacked analytical, theoretical and speculative interests. As a result it did not generate works in political philosophy comparable to its brilliant texts in logic, epistemology, moral philosophy and metaphysics. Second, it was essentially conservative and apologetic and lacked a critical thrust. With the exception of the Buddhists, no Hindu political thinker challenged the caste-based social order. Third, it saw man primarily as a member of different social groups, as a player of roles, and therefore emphasized duties rather than rights. Fourth, thanks to its epistemology, it saw truth as inherently plural. While this allowed it not only to tolerate but also respect and welcome diversity of beliefs and practices, it also prevented it from developing general principles with which to evaluate and criticize them. Finally, since custom played a powerful role in Indian life, the Hindu writers did not find it necessary to develop the idea of legislation and generally regarded political authority as judicial rather than legislative in nature. As a result they did not formulate such ideas as sovereignty, will, political rationality, a single legal system for the country and the government as an agent of social change, all of which have played such a vital role in the development of the modern European state.   BCP

Reading

†Ghoshal, U.N.: *A History of Hindu Political Theories*. Calcutta: Oxford University Press, 1966.

Jayaswal, K.P.: *Hindu Polity*. Calcutta: Butterworth, 1924.

Jolly, J. and Schmidt, R. ed.: *Arthasastra of Kautilya*. Lahore: Motilal Banarasidas, 1923.

Kane, P.V.: *History of Dharmasastra*. Poona: Bhandarkar Oriental Research Institute, 1930.

Sinha, H.N.: *The Development of Indian Polity*. Bombay: Asia Publishing House, 1963.

†Spellman, J.: *The Political Theory of Ancient India*. Oxford: Clarendon Press, 1964.

Varma, V.P.: *Studies in Hindu Political Thought and its Metaphysical Foundations*. Delhi: Motilal Banarasidas, 1974.

historical materialism   The view, espoused chiefly by MARX and his followers, that the course of human history, especially political change and the growth of ideas, is determined ultimately by the way in which people produce their means of subsistence and organize their economic relations. See MARXISM.

historicism   The belief that philosophical explication of historical knowledge provides the basis and rationale for all valid knowledge about human activities and achievements. It envisages a comprehensive reconstruction of the social and cultural sciences, in so far as they have been founded upon assumptions and methods alien to such a principle.

Because there is fundamental disagreement about the philosophical explication of historical knowledge, and because rhetorical and analytical renderings of concepts cannot be neatly distinguished in social and political theory, it is necessary to consider two largely incompatible uses of the term; the second of these uses 'historicism' as a polemical label for a variety of positions seen as mutually inconsistent by their proponents. In the first sense historicism refers to a philosophical doctrine deriving from the epistemological presuppositions of critical historiography; in the second, it refers to theories centered upon substantive philosophies of history of the sort which critical historiography rose up to challenge. The first kind of historicism, moreover, mostly concerns itself with the limits of scientific knowledge and its unsuitability as a means for controlling future events, while the second kind is linked to ambitions for subjecting all human happenings to rational control. Yet the dual usage does have a certain justification: both views reject an approach to the presuppositions and structure of knowledge grounded upon a universal theory of human nature, in favour of an approach grounded upon historically-localized knowledge of a historically-changing world (see Cumming, Strauss).

The original German term, *Historismus*, was coined at the end of the nineteenth century to embrace numerous challenges to the prevailing ideal of science (derived from the then current philosophy of the physical sciences) within such disciplines as economics, law, aesthetics, and political studies, as well as within various branches of philosophy. Inspired by the mid-century counter-attack on positivism and its application to historiography itself, culminating in the work of Wilhelm Dilthey (see Makkreel, 1975), the common theme was the need to build knowledge in the human sciences upon the distinctive qualities of the subject matter thought to be revealed by the study of human history. Originally the debate concerned methodological issues, posed in conjunction with actual detailed studies, as was the case with the foremost members of the 'historical school' in economics or law, but subsequent reflections upon those debates and studies sought to work out a common philosophical doctrine and cultural programme of 'historicism'.

Despite important differences, the various attempts at such a doctrine share three common elements: an emphasis on qualitative variation among particular occurrences (uniqueness), a conception of the cumulative and irreversible, but not predetermined, development of larger contexts as a source for these qualitative variations (development), and an insistence on the irrationally founded subjective designs of historically particularized human actors as the principal plane upon which variation and development take place (subjectivism). Knowledge of such a reality must be largely concrete, descriptive and hermeneutic in character, rather than abstract, explanatory and universal. It will above all eschew the search for universal natural laws, and it will recognize itself as an historically concrete occurrence rather than as a manifestation of timeless reason. Finally, social and cultural sciences drawn to this design will accept a purely contemplative role, abandoning the Baconian yearning for knowledge as a

source of power (see Collingwood, Croce, Mannheim (*Conservatism*), Meinecke and Ortega y Gasset; see also entries on COLLINGWOOD, CROCE and MANNHEIM).

The polemical sense of historicism originated in England during the second world war, in arguments against certain popular political conceptions, especially concerning the need for public planning and coordinated control, which were commonly justified by reference to Marxist or similar diagnoses of the new objective requirements of a new historical age (see Hayek; also entry on HAYEK). In a series of influential publications during the period of greatest disillusionment with and political mobilization against Soviet Marxism, authors such as POPPER, Aron and ARENDT maintained that any argument postulating an explicable logic and sequence in historical development, taken as a whole, and claiming to derive from it projections of future developments and directions for present conduct, is devoid of philosophical merit and must be grasped as a power-seeking ideology rather than as genuine social theory. Historicism in this sense then came to be a central feature in the structural analysis of IDEOLOGY, where that concept was taken in its negative sense, as a mode of thinking antithetical to rational thought. Whatever their plausibility as a response to a certain class of vulgar political argument, these denunciations of historicism do not have much critical purchase on contemporary non-official offshoots of Marxism, which have moved far from the stereotyped scientistic account attacked as 'historicist' by the critics. The continued use of the concept is itself to be understood as a merely rhetorical or ideological manoeuvre.

Where historicism in its original sense approaches Marxism or similar theoretical interpretations of the historical process, it is in an attempt to overcome the potentially self-undermining relativism and total passivity which its philosophical conclusions seem to imply. But, as Troeltsch and Mannheim ('Historicism') indicate, that marks a return to the problems which generated Hegel's conception of dialectics and similar theoretical strategies and can no longer be profitably comprehended as integral to historicism. A more promising strategy for broadening the reach of the concept without ideological stereotyping builds on the general contrast between structures of knowledge grounded on universal theories of human nature and those grounded on concrete historical experience, as a way of analysing important phases in intellectual history and formulating pivotal philosophical problems (see Cumming). DK

Reading

Arendt, H.: *The Origins of Totalitarianism*, 2nd enlarged edn. New York: Harcourt Brace, 1957.

Aron, R.: *The Opium of the Intellectuals*. New York: Doubleday, 1957.

Collingwood, R.G.: *The Idea of History*. Oxford: Clarendon Press, 1946.

Croce, B.: *History as the Story of Liberty*. New York: Norton, 1941.

Cumming, R.D.: *Human Nature and History*. Chicago: University of Chicago Press, 1969.

Hayek, F.A.: *The Counter-Revolution of Science*. Glencoe, Ill.: Free Press of Glencoe, 1952.

Makkreel, R.A.: *Dilthey: Philosopher of the Human Studies*. Princeton, NJ: Princeton University Press, 1975.

†Mannheim, K.: Historicism. In *Essays on the Sociology of Knowledge*. London: Routledge & Kegan Paul, 1952.

————: *Conservatism*. London: Routledge & Kegan Paul, 1986.

Meinecke, F.: *Die Entstehung des Historismus*. Munich: Leibniz, 1946.

Ortega y Gasset, J.: *History as a System*. New York: Norton, 1961.

Popper, K.: *The Open Society and its Enemies*. London: Routledge, 1945; Princeton, NJ: Princeton University Press, 1950.

†————: *The Poverty of Historicism*. Boston: Beacon, 1957.

Strauss, L.: *Natural Right and History*. Chicago: University of Chicago Press, 1953.

Troeltsch, E.: *Der Historismus und seine Probleme*, vol. III of *Gesammelte Schriften*. Tübingen: J.C.B. Mohr (Paul Siebeck), 1922.

Hobbes, Thomas (1588–1679) English philosopher. Hobbes's birth at Malmesbury, Wiltshire, on 5 April 1588, was supposedly precipitated by his mother's hearing about the Spanish Armada. His family were of the 'middling sort', his mother a farmer's daughter and his father a minor clergyman who abandoned the family; Hobbes was brought up by his uncle. Displaying an early aptitude for classical languages, he went up to Oxford and was then recommended to the Earl of Devonshire as a tutor to his son; he stayed in the household of the Cavendishes for the rest of his long life. Between 1610 and 1615 he accompanied his pupil William Cavendish on a European tour of which the most important part was a visit to the republic of Venice where they learned about the struggle the intellectual leaders of Venice were having to preserve its temporal supremacy over ecclesiastical matters – a theme which was to preoccupy Hobbes. On his return he acted (at the request of one of these Venetians) as an amanuensis to Francis Bacon, and, probably also at the Venetians' suggestion, translated Thucydides. Cavendish, Hobbes's patron and pupil until his death in 1629, fostered Venetian, anti-Spanish interest in England and was frequently in opposition to the king (and sometimes even accused of sympathy with republicanism). His son, also educated by Hobbes, was much more royalist, and during the 1630s Hobbes too seems to have become clearly committed to upholding the crown's authority against its critics.

During travels on the Continent in the 1630s, Hobbes became a member of the group of philosophers centred around Marin Mersenne in Paris. The common aim of these philosophers (who included Descartes and Gassendi) was to go beyond the kind of scepticism which, for example, the Venetians such as Paolo Sarpi had endorsed, and provide a new kind of post-sceptical physical and moral science. Although Hobbes consistently alleged that his own philosophical discoveries predated those of Descartes, there is no good evidence that this is so; there is some probability that it was reading the *Discourse on Method* that led Hobbes into a new kind of philosophy. In 1640 he produced the *Elements of Law*, his first substantial essay on the theme. This circulated only in manuscript; it contains the essentials of all his later political thought. Having tried (and failed) to be elected to Parliament, Hobbes left for Paris again, and there published in an extremely limited edition the Latin *De cive* (1642), intended to be the last part of a three-part compendium of his philosophy. It was reprinted in a much larger edition in 1647, and was closely studied, particularly on the Continent (where it remained the best known political work by Hobbes for many generations).

The political theory outlined in *De cive* was not very different from that in the *Elements* or the later *Leviathan*; but it did contain a defence of the Church of England's peculiar status vis-à-vis the monarch. The sovereign, Hobbes wrote, is *obliged* to make ecclesiastical regulations on the basis of consultation with an episcopate. During his exile in the 1640s, Hobbes became disenchanted with the Church of England, and excited by the prospect that all ecclesiastical power would be broken in his native land. The result was *Leviathan*, written extremely quickly during 1649–50 and published by April 1651. The bulk of the work (the last two parts) was a systematic exposition of the secular ruler's independent authority over all religious matters, including the ascertaining of doctrine. Hobbes returned to England in 1651, and lived contentedly in the new order until the Restoration.

After 1660 Hobbes was in some danger from the restored Church of England, but he managed to survive. He wrote a number of pieces attacking the church, the common lawyers and the scientists of the new Royal Society – all, in his eyes, gangs of professionals seeking autonomous power over other citizens which the sovereign should not allow. His last contribution to political literature seems to have been a paper advising the future Duke of Devonshire on the legitimacy of Parliament's attempt to exclude the heir to the throne from the succession (1679); Hobbes died in December of that year. In addition to his political writings, and a succession of works on literary matters, he also wrote a number of highly important works of general philosophy; the most striking are perhaps the *Critique of Thomas White* (written in 1643, but not discovered and published until the 1950s), *De corpore* (published in 1655) and *De homine* (published in 1658), the latter two completing the scheme he had in view with *De cive*.

His political thought rested on an acceptance of the radical attack launched by late sixteenth-century writers, for example MONTAIGNE, on orthodox theories such as Aristotelianism or Ciceronian humanism, but he sought to transcend their sceptical relativism. In all three of his major political works he argued that there could be no *real* moral properties, any more than there were any *real* phenomenal properties of a physical object. 'Every man . . . calleth that which pleaseth, and is delightful to himself, GOOD; and that EVIL which displeaseth him: insomuch that while every man differeth from each other in constitution, they differ also one from another concerning the common distinction of good and evil. Nor is there any such thing as . . . [the] simply good' (*Elements* 1.7.3.). But this ethical disagreement could be overcome, for all men would acknowledge that each of them was justified in defending himself, and would also recognize that there could be no general agreement *beyond* this – there could be no agreement (for example) that a man was justified in harming other people for reasons *other* than self-defence.

The possibility of this general acknowledgement enabled Hobbes to claim that there was one fundamental right of nature, and one equally fundamental law: the right was 'the Liberty each man hath, to use his own power, as he will himselfe, for the preservation of his own Nature', while the law was 'every man, ought to endeavour Peace, as farre as he has hope of obtaining it; and when he cannot obtain it . . . he may seek, and use, all helps, and advantages of Warre' (*Leviathan*, ch. 14). The 'right' represented what all men would think was justified; the 'law' represented their recognition that *wanton* injury could not be similarly justified. Upon this foundation (prompted in some respects by the work of Hugo GROTIUS and John SELDEN), Hobbes hoped to erect a structure which would command general assent.

He postulated that there is a deep uncertainty about the circumstances under which we are actually in danger and should use our right of self-defence, and that because of this uncertainty, in the absence of a civil power we would play safe and indulge (for example) in pre-emptive strikes. This would give rise to a STATE OF NATURE in which (in the famous phrase from *Leviathan*) man's life would be 'solitary, poore, nasty, brutish, and short'. But certainty could be created artificially, if men agreed not to exercise their right except in cases where it was uncontentiously obvious that they were already under attack, and to hand over the power of defending themselves to an agent, a sovereign, who would make the appropriate judgments about difficult cases. This sovereign was 'Leviathan', but his power was ambiguous: he possessed it only in so far as he protected the individuals whose agent he was, and if he failed the state of nature was resumed. Moreover, like any man or group of men, he possessed only the right to preserve himself or (in his unique case) other people: he did not possess the right to do anything which he knew was not conducive to this single end. As to whether a monarchical or republican form of government was to be preferred, Hobbes provided some rather low-level arguments in favour of monarchy, but intended his theory to apply to any form of government.

This argument succeeded in disconcerting almost all contemporary readers. Hobbes removed from the men opposed to royal policies in the 1630s and early 1640s their central justification, that they had as much right as the king to determine (for example) whether or not England was threatened and therefore whether a ship money tax should be levied. But he also argued that a condemned criminal had a right to resist the sovereign, for his life was *clearly* and *unarguably* at risk from the sovereign's actions. Hobbes thus completely overturned the political assumptions of the parliamentary leadership, while not giving what they expected to the advocates of divine right monarchy. It is true that particularly in the *Elements* and *De cive* he was much more sympathetic to the king's supporters than to his opponents, but the other major aspect of his thought totally alienated them after the appearance of *Leviathan*, for in that work he could see no place in his system for any independent Anglican authority. Indeed, one of his former friends, the Anglican theologian Henry Hammond, described *Leviathan* as 'a farrago of Christian atheism'. This referred to the fact that Hobbes's political theory was accompanied by a materialist metaphysics, though it is a matter of some debate as to how far it was *entailed* by it. Hobbes argued that the only form a scientific explanation could take was a hypothesis about the interaction of moving material objects, and he claimed that he could

provide such an explanation of the universality of the human urge to defend oneself. He did so using the idea that 'vital spirits' circulate in the body to keep it alive, and that these spirits give rise to all emotions, being in turn affected by perceptions. It was this aspect of his philosophy that seemed 'atheistical', for he allowed no ontological space for immaterial beings or a disembodied mind. His main intention in putting it forward seems to have been to correct Descartes's answer to the sceptic, with its reliance ultimately on a proof of God's existence: Hobbes claimed that while we cannot say of any particular scientific theory that it is necessarily true, we can say that its form is that of any true theory, and that scientific debate must be conducted in materialist terms.

This materialism still allowed some room in his theory for religion. It was, he argued, possible for people to have genuine religious beliefs which did not *conflict* with his own civil and natural philosophy, though the beliefs would not derive from it. For a Christian, 'all that is NECESSARY *to Salvation*, is contained in two Vertues, *Faith in Christ*, and *Obedience to Laws*' (*Leviathan*, ch. 43). Christians believed in the history of man's fall and redemption contained in the Scriptures, and therefore in the special role played in that history by Christ; but (according to Hobbes) they need believe nothing else which could not be derived by natural reason from his own principles, for what God required of us was simply obedience to the laws of nature. Moreover the reward of eternal life in heaven, and the punishment of a second death in hell, could both be interpreted in materialist terms. Hobbes's remarks about God have led a number of scholars in this century (notably the major British student of Hobbes, the late Professor Warrender) to conjecture that he intended theistical beliefs of some kind to play a much larger part in his theory than contemporaries such as Hammond would have believed; but in view of Hobbes's refusal to answer his many critics in such a way, this conjecture remains rather implausible.

Hobbes was arguably one of the two greatest British philosophers (the other being HUME, who resembled him in many ways). His work in both politics and metaphysics has always seemed to be in some sense peculiarly representative of modern thought as a whole. As long as the post-Renaissance European state survives, his will be one of the key accounts of it.   RFT

Reading

Brown, K.C., ed.: *Hobbes Studies*. Oxford: Blackwell, 1965.

†Goldsmith, M.M.: *Hobbes's Science of Politics*. New York: Columbia University Press, 1966.

Hobbes, T.: *Elements of Law*, ed. F. Tönnies, rev. M.M. Goldsmith. London: Cass, 1969.

——: *De cive*, ed. H. Warrender. Oxford: Clarendon Press, 1983.

——: *Leviathan*, ed. C.B. Macpherson. Harmondsworth: Penguin, 1968.

Nagel, T.: Hobbes's concept of obligation. *Philosophical Review* 68 (1959) 68–83.

†Raphael, D.: *Hobbes*. London: Allen & Unwin, 1977.

Skinner, Q.R.D.: The ideological context of Hobbes's political thought. *Historical Journal* 9 (1966) 286–317.

†Warrender, H.: *The Political Philosophy of Hobbes*. Oxford: Clarendon Press, 1957.

†Watkins, J.W.N.: *Hobbes's System of Ideas*. London: Hutchinson, 1973.

Hobhouse, Leonard Trelawny (1864–1929) British social and political philosopher. Hobhouse's career combined academic and journalistic activities and reflected the synthetic approach of his work. Oxford educated, he was a philosophy tutor in the 1890s; during this time he wrote *The Theory of Knowledge* (1896). From 1897 he began a long and fruitful association with the *Manchester Guardian* and its editor, C. P. Scott, and in 1906–7 served as the political editor of the short-lived *Tribune*. His journalism brought him into close contact with the new liberals, and he became a leading exponent of their ideas, opposing the Boer War, attacking imperialism (*Democracy and Reaction*, 1904), and supporting the emerging social-reformist policy of the Liberal Party. In 1907 he became the first holder of the Martin White chair of sociology at the University of London, while maintaining his output for the *Manchester Guardian* and playing an active role in developing Trade Boards.

Evolutionism and IDEALISM were the two main intellectual influences on Hobhouse's thought, though in his systematizing efforts he employed the teachings of the two schools selectively. He regarded evolution as a framework setting out the purposive development of mind towards a harmonious rationalism that could be empirically demonstrated. To that end he utilized physiological studies of animal life as well as psychological theories that dwelt on the connection between instincts, drives, and rational-gregarious human behaviour. His purposive-developmental perspective drew him towards sociological, anthropological and comparative-historical studies, as in his trilogy *Mind in Evolution* (1901), *Morals in Evolution* (1906), and *Development and Purpose* (1913). Hobhouse viewed human progress as a process in which mind was, in contradistinction to some versions of SOCIAL DARWINISM, a major factor in evolution. The orthogenic development of mind led to a growth in mutual sympathy and harmony and to a conscious awareness of its power to direct human affairs. This rational self-direction, with its ability to control the external and internal conditions of life, was the teleological unfolding of the highest human ethics. In political terms it endorsed the movement of modern societies towards a greater degree of collectivism, embodying a large measure of co-operation and mutual responsibility.

Hobhouse's attitude to idealism was complex. Although a product of Oxford idealism, he reacted strongly both against its apparently non-empirical base and against the conservative political vehicles to which British idealism was frequently harnessed. He especially took exception to German Hegelianism, both for its remoteness from processes of induction and deduction and for its illiberal impact on British political thinking. On the other hand he was close to T. H. GREEN's variant of idealism inasmuch as it postulated a common good arrived at by freely co-operating rational individuals, rather than reflecting the separately identifiable will of a social entity. To that extent Hobhouse rejected a supraindividual organicism. Nevertheless the implicit organicism of idealism fuelled his holism and his predilection for general systems. Hobhouse also adopted the idealist rational bias, its concern with harmonizing the private and the public spheres, and its purposive approach to social development. His political conclusions, however, transcended the idealism of his times and derived their force from a concatenation of arguments typical of turn-of-the-century new liberal thought (see LIBERALISM).

As a liberal theorist Hobhouse continued the break with nineteenth-century liberalism that has been accredited to Green, and helped significantly to adapt liberal tenets to emerging social theories and political pressures alike. In *Liberalism* (1911) and other writings, he firmly embedded individual liberty in a social setting, emphasizing both that human personality consisted of strongly socially-oriented characteristics and that its development had to be abetted by communal assistance. The harmonious balance of individual and social ends within each person led to a theory of rights in which, although rights were seen as essential to self-development, they were granted by society. It also led to a view of property that attempted to distinguish the social from the individual factors in wealth, arguing that if private property was necessary to the fulfilment of individual personality, common property was valuable for the expression of social life. At the same time Hobhouse asserted that wealth could only be acquired by social service.

Central to the new liberalism which Hobhouse espoused was an insistence on the paramount role of the state in promoting both the individual and the social good. The state became the repository and guardian of the moral and spiritual interests of its members. As an ethical and responsible institution, it was entitled to use compulsion if individuals were unable to do justice to the social conscience, though never at the expense of individual development. The state was cast in the role of intelligent regulator of human behaviour and socio-economic forces, while concurrently representing a common good that could rise above sectional interests. Hence also Hobhouse's ambivalence towards organizations such as trade unions which on the one hand protected the rights and needs of the less privileged members of society and appealed to the egalitarian element in his liberalism, yet on the other hand pursued particularist gains without adopting a broader social purview. This reflected Hobhouse's typical liberal underplaying of problems of power and class.

In his later years, after the first world war, Hobhouse's political thinking underwent remarkable changes. His growing pessimism concerning human nature and the possibilities of progress was deepened by the restrictions on civil liberties imposed on the British public. He now feared that an omnipotent state would strike at the moral autonomy of the individual, and he demanded a reinstatement of economic and political liberty within the liberal tradition, even lauding his ideological opponent, Herbert SPENCER. Yet Hobhouse still held, though more cautiously, that the state could be the trustee of the final good of society, so long as it respected individual liberty. This notion of liberty combined choice and the absence of constraint with the harmonious working out of an individual's potential, linked to prevalent 'hormic' psychological theories.

Hobhouse's reputation as a major exponent of twentieth-century social-liberalism is well deserved. His influence has been diffuse rather than dramatic, but his ideas have contributed to the left-liberal tradition both in Britain and on the Continent.   MSF

Reading

†Clarke, P.: *Liberals and Social Democrats*. Cambridge: Cambridge University Press, 1978.

†Collini, S.: *Liberalism and Sociology: L.T. Hobhouse and Political Argument in England 1880–1914*. Cambridge: Cambridge University Press, 1979.

†Freeden, M.: *The New Liberalism: an Ideology of Social Reform*. Oxford: Oxford University Press, 1978.

†———: *Liberalism Divided: a Study in British Political Thought 1914–1939*. Oxford: Oxford University Press, 1986.

†Hobhouse, L.T.: *Liberalism*. New York: Oxford University Press, 1964.

———: *Development and Purpose*. London: Macmillan, rev. edn, 1927.

———: *The Metaphysical Theory of the State* (1918). London: Allen & Unwin, 1960.

———: *The Elements of Social Justice* (1922). London: Allen & Unwin, 1965.

Hobson, J.A. and Ginsberg, M.: *L.T. Hobhouse: His Life and Work*. London: Allen & Unwin, 1931.

Holbach, Paul Henri Thiry, Baron d' (1723–1789) French philosopher. Born in

Germany and educated at Leyden in Holland, Holbach made a notable contribution to the thought of the FRENCH ENLIGHTENMENT as the exponent of an uncompromising form of POSITIVISM and behaviourism. He had an unusually thorough knowledge of the sciences, yet in his writings on political and moral theory, he was at once the most utopian and the most puritanical of the *Encyclopédistes*. He argued for what he called *Éthocratie*, or the rule of morality, consciously devised as an alternative to the more worldly political ideas of MONTESQUIEU and VOLTAIRE.

Rejecting Montesquieu's suggestion that virtue could be the animating principle only of a republic, Holbach envisaged a kingdom where virtue would be found in monarch and subjects alike. He outlined the institutional arrangements which might make this possible. Education was the first method. The state should remove royal princes from their family and train them from birth to be philosopher-kings. The character of the subjects should be moulded by a system of compulsory moral instruction for all children. Holbach's second method was censorship. A tribunal of morals would watch over and correct the behaviour of adults. Sumptuary laws would curb the luxurious living of the rich. Gambling, prostitution, theatres, balls and other such amusements would be forbidden. Holbach's programme for reform had striking affinities with those of Savonarola and CALVIN, despite the fact that Holbach himself, an immensely rich man, lived and entertained lavishly.

He preached austerity. Far from sharing the liberal hedonism of Voltaire, Holbach drew a sharp distinction between happiness and pleasure. Nature had so devised the universe, he argued, that the man who sought immediate gratification was punished and the man who pursued high ends was rewarded. Holbach could not accept DIDEROT's claim that the South Sea Islanders, who had no sexual taboos, were happy; for Holbach it was a law of nature that unrestrained indulgence brought misery. Hence, all the laws he proposed for the purpose of imposing austerity were seen by him as instruments for the enlargement of true felicity.

He did not believe in equality, and went out of his way to attack the egalitarian ideas of his friend HELVÉTIUS; but he held that labour was the only basis for a right to property, and he proposed that owners of large estates should be made to earn their entitlement by working as managers of their farms and improvers of the land. The idleness of the existing aristocracy was one of the reasons for the prevalence of vice.

When Louix XVI came to the throne in 1774 Holbach invited him to use his absolute sovereignty to enforce the rule of virtue. Paradoxically, a year or two later, Holbach demanded the restitution of the powers of the *noblesse de robe* in the legislative courts or *parlements*, which meant that the king would no longer have 'absolute sovereignty' to enforce any kind of rule. It seems that Holbach had come to believe that the *parlements* were the only institutions in France which could serve as a barrier against despotism. Despite his absolutism, and his pleas for the enforcement of virtue, Holbach did *not* approve of despotism, which by definition meant the annihilation of liberty. He believed that his particular form of absolutism was compatible with freedom, with true freedom, that is with freedom understood as doing what you ought to do rather than doing what you want to do.

Not unnaturally, when Holbach rallied to the defence of the *noblesse de robe* against the king, he was charged by his critics of putting, as a member of the ennobled bourgeoisie, the interests of his class before the principles of his philosophy; but at least Holbach could never be accused, as were Montesquieu, Voltaire and Rousseau in their different ways, of formulating an ideology for the class to which he belonged.

MC

Reading

d'Holbach, P.: *Le Christianisme dévoilé*; trans. as *Christianity Unveiled*. London, 1767.

———: *Système de la nature*; trans. as *The System of Nature*. London, 1770.

———: *Le bon-sens*; trans. as *Common Sense*. London, 1772.

†Topazio, V.W.: *D'Holbach's Moral Philosophy*. Geneva: Institut et Musée Voltaire, 1956.

†Wickwar, W.H.: *Baron d'Holbach*. London: Allen & Unwin, 1935.

holism A doctrine, contrary to INDIVIDUALISM, that gives privileged status to social wholes, which may be seen as organic unities, cultural wholes, functioning systems or determining structures. Methodologically, it proposes that social factors alone are explanatory. Ontologically, it excludes reduction to the individual level. As a moral and political doctrine, it subordinates the individual to the collective good. None of these positions entails the others; nor are holism and individualism the only possible alternatives.   SL

Hooker, Richard (1554?–1600) English political philosopher and theologian. Educated at the Latin School in Exeter and at Corpus Christi College, Oxford, which in 1577 elected him to a fellowship, Hooker was Master of the Temple Church in London (where he clashed with Walter Travers, a leading Presbyterian) from 1585 to 1591, and rector of Bishopsbourne, Kent, from 1595 until his death. Although he wrote various sermons and tracts, he is remembered for a single work: *Of the Laws of Ecclesiastical Polity*, a magisterial treatise in eight books. The first five were printed between 1593 and 1597, the sixth and eighth in 1648, and the seventh in 1662. Restoration royalists – who objected to Hooker's suggestion that the authority of monarchs and bishops derived from the consent of the community rather than from divine right – fostered a myth that Puritans had tampered with the posthumous books prior to publication, but it is now accepted that the entire work is authentic. Hooker defended the constitution and practices of the Church of England against the Puritan charge that they were unscriptural and therefore morally untenable. In providing theoretical foundations for the Elizabethan church, he reflected also upon such issues as the nature of law, the relationship between CHURCH AND STATE, and the origins of government. The *Ecclesiastical Polity*, in consequence, is the most systematic political treatise written in English during the sixteenth century, as well as a classic statement of the Anglican Church's claim to walk a middle way between Rome and Calvin's Geneva.

Hooker took his philosophical bearings from the medieval natural-law tradition, in which reason was considered to complement faith. According to Puritans, reason was so impaired by sin that the Bible offered the only reliable guide to human conduct. Hooker retorted that rigid scripturalism was an essentially subversive doctrine which sanctioned the unbridled exercise of private judgment in public affairs, because anyone who disapproved of the civil and ecclesiastical establishment could imagine themselves inspired by revelation. His refutation of scripturalism hinged upon a distinction between central issues of faith and matters 'indifferent' to salvation, such as particular ceremonies and forms of ecclesiastical administration found to be expedient but not prescribed by scripture. Following Thomas AQUINAS and other scholastic writers, Hooker argued that laws controlling 'things indifferent' were morally sound in so far as they had been shaped by reason from the principles of natural law to suit the needs of time and place. Such matters were properly determined by corporate authority rather than by individual conscience, for whereas private judgment was fallible, the accumulated experience of society served as a principal channel through which divine wisdom flowed into the arrangements of church and state. Opponents of the ecclesiastical establishment were probably misled by their own dogmatism, 'for in all right and equitie that which the church hath received and held so long for good, that which publique approbation hath ratified, must cary the benefite of presumption with it to be accompted meete and convenient' (vol. I, p. 286).

The Church of England, then, was both a fellowship of believers who with Christians everywhere sought to observe scriptural injunctions, and also an organization competent to frame regulations and patterns of worship according to its particular traditions. In the latter aspect it resembled any civil association. This conception of the church as a political – as well as spiritual – society enabled Hooker to discredit the tendency of Puritans to challenge the royal supremacy in religious affairs. Church and state were not separate communities, because they shared an identical membership – the church, in fact, was society organized for the practice of Christianity. Logically, therefore, supreme authority over both should reside in a single person. On practical grounds, also, the monarch should be head of the church, given that divided authority was likely to provoke political conflict.

Church and state were coextensive, too, in so far as they shared the same legislative procedures: 'the *Parlament* of *England* together with the *Convocation* annexed thereunto' (vol. III, p. 401). Here Hooker blended a theory about the origins of government with the assumptions of English common law. He rejected Aristotle's proposition that the superiority of certain individuals endowed them with a natural right to rule. Legitimate government emerged instead from an agreement, tacit or formal, between people who through reason grasped the advantages of living in political society. The English, according to Hooker, had long ago consented to the creation of a system of government which constitutional theorists judged to be excellent: a limited monarchy in which arbitrary power was precluded by the rule of law, and both civil and ecclesiastical statutes were enacted or amended by a parliament representing the whole society. The founding fathers of the nation had thereby bequeathed constitutional mechanisms for enabling the affairs of church and state to be determined by the evolving corporate wisdom of the community. Given that communal consensus was a sign of the influence of divine reason in public life, there could be no grounds for dissent from the practices of the Anglican Church.

It was once fashionable to describe Hooker as a forerunner of seventeenth-century SOCIAL CONTRACT theory. John LOCKE, indeed, quoted extensively from the *Ecclesiastical Polity* in his *Two Treatises of Government* (1689), which used a contractual account of political society to refute the absolutism of Restoration royalists. Yet the theories of Hooker and Locke were designed to serve different ideological purposes. Locke made the exercise of political authority conditional upon the terms of an original contract, as a means of demonstrating that the community might depose a tyrant who infringed the natural rights of his subjects. Hooker, by contrast, neither approved of popular resistance to arbitrary power nor acknowledged the existence of individual natural rights. And whereas Hooker's concern was to preserve religious uniformity, Locke argued that the sovereignty of private judgment in matters of belief sanctioned a policy of

toleration towards individuals who dissented from the Church of England. Hooker emphasized the consensual foundations of government to illustrate the excellence of English polity, thereby reminding his audience of their duty to uphold the Tudor church and state. Rather than anticipating the liberal assumptions of writers such as Locke, he was in essence a conservative thinker.   RRE

Reading
†Cargill Thompson, W.D.J.: The philosopher of the 'politic society'. In *Studies in Richard Hooker: essays preliminary to an edition of his works*, ed. W. Speed Hill. Cleveland and London: Case Western Reserve University Press, 1972.
Eccleshall, R.: Richard Hooker and the peculiarities of the English: the reception of the 'Ecclesiastical Polity' in the seventeenth and eighteenth centuries. *History of Political Thought* 2 (1981) 63–117.
Faulkner, R.K.: *Richard Hooker and the Politics of a Christian England*. Berkeley and Los Angeles: University of California Press, 1981.
Hooker, R.: *The Folger Library Edition of the Works*, ed. W. Speed Hill. 4 vols to date. Cambridge, Mass.: Harvard University Press, 1977– .
McGrade, A.S.: The coherence of Hooker's Polity: the books on power. *Journal of the History of Ideas* 24 (1963) 163–82.
Wolin, S.S.: Richard Hooker and English conservatism. *Western Political Quarterly* 6 (1953) 28–47.

Horkheimer, Max (1895–1973) German philosopher. Horkheimer was director of the Institute of Social Research in Frankfurt, and was chiefly responsible for establishing the philosophical foundations of CRITICAL THEORY.

human nature It might be thought that a theory of human nature is an indispensable part of any political theory. A political theory is *inter alia* a theory of the ways in which social and political organization contribute to the well-being of the members of a society: how can we know what constitutes the well-being of the members of a society, or what institutions they are capable of sustaining, unless we know their 'nature'? Nobody can build a bridge without knowing the qualities of the materials; how can anyone lay down principles for social and political organization without a thorough knowledge of the human materials from which it is to be constructed?

This argument has seemed compelling to innumerable writers from Greek antiquity onwards. But the analogy with engineers and their needs has often been resisted on the strength of an argument almost as simple and almost as ancient. The nature of wood, stone and metal is invariant: iron has the same properties in Athens as in Persia, and had the same properties in antiquity as it has today. People, however, are profoundly affected by their surroundings. This, too, was a Greek discovery. Herodotus told how King Darius had asked Greeks and Indians about their burial practices; it appeared that the Greeks burned their dead and the Indians ate theirs, and found each other's customs absolutely appalling. The moral was obvious; if men differed so much in what they valued so deeply, the behaviour of humanity at any particular time and place was not a conclusive guide to what constituted human nature. Men might want what was to others 'unnatural'; even more alarmingly, it might be that they had no fixed nature at all, only local desires and beliefs.

In the reaction of PLATO and ARISTOTLE to this kind of relativism, two issues are entangled. The first is whether nature is to be understood normatively, whether the natural order is a guide to conduct. Plato is, notoriously, ambivalent on this: the world of appearance is delusive, only in the world perceived by reason is order apparent. Accordingly, we can find only limited help in deciding 'how to live' from an empirical investigation of the world about us. Nevertheless, such order as the empirical world contains is the gift of the underlying, mathematically intelligible world; its order and organization does provide norms for us. Aristotle is disinclined to draw such a sharp distinction between the world of appearance and the rational cosmos. Unlike Plato, he sees the world as a biologist might, and tries to discover the various goods that suit different kinds of beings. Empirical investigation is relevant to finding out what the good life is, and how politics can help us attain it. But both Plato and Aristotle subscribe to a teleological understanding of the universe; were we to understand the world thoroughly, we should also know what constituted the goodness of everything in it.

The second issue, which is not entirely settled by a decision on the first, is whether this means that the good is invariant. Aristotle asks the question, 'Is there one justice, as fire burns here and in Persia?' and decides that the answer is that there is one justice. Nonetheless, Aristotle's conception of the good is not monistic as Plato's is. Aristotle sees that what is good for different people may differ according to what kind of people they are; moreover, there may be no single scale of values along which different people can be ranked, so there is no question of their different goods being – as they must be for Plato – better or worse as they participate more or less fully in The Good. There is, of course, no doubt in Aristotle's mind that men are superior to women, free men to slaves and Greeks to barbarians; nonetheless, there is a good life for a woman which does not consist in being a pale imitation of a good man. And even if there is one justice, it allows for local variations in its application. Aristotle approaches human nature more as a biologist than as a mathematician, willing to recognize a variety of goods and ills and a variety of ways of life which promote the first and ward off the second.

The difficulty of deciding how large a part a theory of human nature plays in a particular political theory is evident in Plato's work. The *Republic*'s assumption that men are born to be carpenters, soldiers or rulers is on the face of it an assumption about human nature; Plato's assumption, shared with most Greek thinkers, that virtue and happiness coincide with the fulfilment of our nature again assimilates human flourishing to the flourishing of any other natural creature, such as a plant or an animal. But Book X of the *Republic* defends the claim that the practice of virtue is good for us by an appeal to the immortality of the soul and its welfare in an indefinite series of lives. This is not in any straightforward sense a 'naturalistic' approach to 'human nature'.

It is, however, the bond that unites Plato's moral and political philosophy with that of AUGUSTINE and of Christian Europe generally. The Christian conception of the politics of this world, as we have it in Augustine's *City of God*, is not at ease with Aristotle's view that nature designed man to live in the *polis*; it is at ease only with the thought that our true home is elsewhere, and that our earthly allegiances are at best temporary shelters from the evils of our fallen condition. Plato's suggestion that philosophers will never be kings and must concentrate on surviving the storm finds an echo in Augustine's ambivalence about the values of earthly politics. The heavenly city has no politics; neither the theory nor the practice of elections, committees, government by the rule of law and the rest can make any sense. Nevertheless, too detached a view of the things of this world brings its own dangers also. We are not to be antinomian and strive for individual salvation in an anti-social fashion. We need the shelter of earthly justice and we have a duty to act as citizens of the earthly city as well as the heavenly city.

Even if it is true that nothing that happens in earthly politics is of any importance compared with our standing with God, it is not true that earthly politics is of no importance. Man, having fallen, cannot act well without restraint. Law is necessary to keep us in the path of goodness. Salvation is a divine gift and not to be attained by good works; nonetheless, we must act justly in the things of this world, and law is the indispensable tool to achieve this. Similarly, although there is no ultimate authority but that of God, it is ordained by God that there should be subordinate and earthly forms of authority; these must practise justice if they are to have any claim on our consciences – for if justice is absent, a state is nothing but a troop of bandits writ large. It is thus true that Christianity – at least as understood by Augustine – has a conception of human nature though, importantly, it is neither a naturalistic nor a political one.

The issue of how rich a conception of human nature a political theory must have is raised quite strikingly in MACHIAVELLI's work. For Machiavelli belongs to a school of thought which may not exactly reject the engineering analogy with which we began, but which certainly treats the political manipulation of whatever characteristics we 'naturally' have as the central issue. Machiavelli's famous realism involves an acceptance of the limits of human nature, but it does not imply that the politician's task is to rule in accordance with nature, let alone that there are natural rulers and natural subjects. As much as any Christian thinker,

Machiavelli takes the fallen condition of mankind for granted; or, to be more precise, he takes it for granted that 'men are naturally evil' and will do whatever seems good to them without reference to justice, equity or virtue, so long as they are not held in check. Political management consists in the creation of institutions which hold men's evil impulses in check and which, indeed, trade on those impulses to bring about the security of the state and enable it to pursue survival at least and glory at best.

Is this a theory of human nature at all? It is quite unlike those of both Plato and Aristotle; they rely heavily on the thought that nature has created us with specific capacities and specific goals which we ought to fulfil and which we shall find happiness in fulfilling. Machiavelli accepts nothing of the sort. If anything explains the goals people pursue it is the social conditioning they receive; aristocrats are proud and seek power, the ordinary man is timid and seeks security, but there is no suggestion that the social structure of ancient Rome or sixteenth-century Florence reflects 'nature'. On the other hand, Machiavelli's method is strikingly naturalistic. If a theory of human nature plays little part, the nature of things plays a large part in his politics. A ruler who acquires power from humble origins must expect jealousy and resentment from the upper classes; no elaborate theory of human nature supports this claim, only the observation that this is how it almost always turns out, and that it is in the nature of politics that it will always be so. The assumption he shares with the Christian moralists – that men will do the evil that lies in them unless prevented – does not play the same role in his work that it might play in other writers. It is, so to speak, only a constraint on the pagan politics of self-aggrandisement and the search for glory, not a fundamental premise of his political theory.

If we compare Machiavelli with HOBBES, the case is strengthened. Hobbes's account of human nature is, of course, not only unclassical, but anti-classical; it is, in crucial ways, unChristian, too, even if Hobbes himself had many ways of defusing the accusation of 'atheism' which his contemporaries so often hurled at him. Hobbes insists that in order to understand the nature of sovereignty, authority, law and therefore what we nowadays would call the state, we must start from human nature. Indeed, we must start from the barest account of human nature we can give, considering men as if they were new sprung out of the ground like mushrooms, unsocialized, and uneducated by social and political intercourse with one another. In so saying Hobbes was contradicting Aristotle. This was less a matter of disbelieving what Aristotle said about *human* nature than of rejecting the fundamental assumptions which Aristotle made about all of nature. Hobbes repudiated Aristotle's teleology; explanation by ends or final causes was no explanation at all. To give an account of anything we had to give an account of its construction and its motive power. Mechanisms replaced entelechies.

Thus for Hobbes there was nothing natural about the state; in the 'state of nature' men lived without law, without authority, and without any means of curbing one another's aggression. Considered scientifically, each man is a self-maintaining mechanism which will do anything rather than submit to extinction. Between his earlier and his later writings Hobbes modified his account of the selfishness of mankind: in *De cive* he seems to think that men are narrowly self-interested; in *Leviathan* he suggests only that all their goals have *some* reference to themselves; but everywhere he insists that it is irrational of anyone to lay down the means of his own preservation unless he can be sure others will do so too. Unlike Aristotle who, as it were, sees us drawn into political society by our shared desire for the good life, Hobbes sees us naturally impelled into the war of all against all. Each will be an enemy to all the rest, not because we are 'sinful' by nature – Hobbes insists that we are not – but because we are both timid and competitive. Fear impels us to strike down our competitors before they can strike us down; competition excites in us the desire to do better than everyone else which in turn gives rise to fear. The creation of a government armed with absolute power is the only solution to this situation.

After Hobbes, a good deal of political theory revolved around contested views of 'natural man'. ROUSSEAU insisted that the competitive and fearful man of Hobbes's pages was not natural man, but man in modern society; the 'war of all against all' was not a natural condition but a social condition. Natural man, untouched by society, must be like the orang-utan or the 'missing link' of the travellers' tales – speechless, solitary, devoid of any notion of time and devoid of self-consciousness. Both anxiety and aggression would be foreign to him. This was widely understood at the time as an attack on the idea of original sin, though Rousseau took care to say that his account of natural man was purely hypothetical and was not in competition with the Book of Genesis. If Rousseau's vision of human nature was a vision of innocence, some of his contemporaries went further in asserting the natural goodness of mankind. DIDEROT's *Supplément aux voyages de Bougainville* is in part a high-spirited joke at the expense of the Catholic Church. All the same, the thought that the Polynesians were happy, sexually liberated, and unbothered by religious controversy, was a familiar item in the argument that civilized man had become removed fron nature and was unhappy in consequence.

But what Rousseau also put into circulation was the thought that human nature was strikingly different from anything else in nature – so different that it might well be a mistake to talk about human nature at all. Alone among all creatures human beings have a history; apes are mature at a few months, and an ape in 500 BC has the same character as an ape in AD 1800, but the human infant changes greatly until it is twenty-odd and may change a good deal thereafter, while the human race is altogether different in 500 BC and AD 1800. Perhaps human beings are made so malleable by circumstances that we cannot usefully talk about human nature at all. The engineering analogy we began with would break down entirely if it were true that societies themselves created what their inhabitants took to be 'human nature'. Rousseau did not go so far. DURKHEIM, deliberately basing himself on the insights of Rousseau, did.

Rousseau took seriously the changes wrought by history on our nature. HEGEL followed him in this, while repudiating much else in his work. But Hegel also argued that the historical process was one of self-education, not the education of any one individual, but that of the whole human species. In this he followed

KANT's *Proposal for a Cosmopolitan History*. But where Kant had said that it was only an 'idea of reason' that history possessed the ulterior purpose of bringing human capacities to their fullest development, Hegel held that philosophy demonstrated this. The philosophy of history is a philosophy of freedom; the human essence is freedom, and history finally reveals this, and at the same time brings it about that we live in a social and political setting which allows our freedom its full expression. Hegel would have been reluctant to call this a theory of human nature, since he wished to distinguish eighteenth-century fantasies about natural man from his own rigidly philosophical approach; but it is hard to deny that his political and historical theory imply a (historicized) account of human nature.

It is a moot point how far MARX and MARXISM generally dispensed with an idea of human nature. It is often and rightly remarked that Marx has a vision of human emancipation which makes sense only if there is something in human beings which cries out for fulfilment in creative work under conditions of self-government; it is equally often pointed out that Marx condemned appeals to 'nature' as generally reactionary – they assimilated how things were organized at some particular place and time to the timeless dictates of nature – and that he was deeply hostile to the way CLASSICAL POLITICAL ECONOMY explained the existence of market economies in terms of a natural disposition to truck and barter. Adam SMITH's 'simple system of natural liberty' was, he thought, neither simple, nor natural, nor libertarian. Moreover, Marx's sociological 'holism' explains the beliefs and attitudes of the members of a society in terms of the society's pressures upon them rather than in terms of human nature. No wonder that some energetic defenders of Marx have claimed that what is distinctive in his work is its 'structuralist' and 'anti-humanist' elements. This is going too far. Marx may well have believed that human nature explains little compared with the dictates of the social, economic and political systems, but he could hardly have been the critic of exploitation, overwork and sheer misery that he was if he had no conception of what it is in human nature that these outraged. It is, moreover, the inadequacy

of his opponents' view of human nature that he savages – memorably denouncing Bentham as a 'leathern-tongued apostle of the bourgeoisie', for instance – not their having a view of human nature at all.

Similarly, Durkheim's claim that the social sciences cannot be truly *social* if they appeal to human nature in explanation of social behaviour does not go to the length of denying that there is such a thing as human nature, nor does it go to the length of suggesting that happiness and unhappiness owe nothing to that nature. Durkheim held that human nature and sociability are not at odds with each other. It is part of human nature, not an adventitious piece of socialization, that we want to live in a society where our own deeply felt sense of justice is also expressed in institutions. Mere nature supplies the raw material of human existence; it is society which makes it the expression of human nature.

As in so much else, we live still in the shadow of the nineteenth-century social theorists. One important attempt to extend their work has been the research programme of 'sociobiology', an attempt to extend the insights of evolutionary biology to human behaviour. So far, most of such work has progressed no further than the early followers of Darwin such as Leslie Stephen; that is, what we have seen so far is little more than conjectural accounts of how familiar moral attitudes and familiar features of political organization *might have* arisen as solutions to problems of survival. The critics of sociobiology have attacked it as crudely deterministic and reductionist; and they have denounced the comfort it gives to conservatism just as Marx denounced classical economics. Those who are not *parti pris* agree that at some point in the development of the social sciences a link will surely be forged between them and the biological sciences; and when that happens the scientific study of human nature will be properly under way. But it is hard to believe that that day has already dawned. Until it has done so, readers will turn to Aristotle, Hobbes, Rousseau and Marx out of more than merely antiquarian interest.   AR

Reading

†Aristotle: *The Nicomachean Ethics*, trans. H. Rackham. London: Heinemann, 1934.

Augustine, St: *The City of God*, ed. D. Knowles, trans. H. Bettenson. Harmondsworth: Penguin, 1972.

†Benthall, J. ed.: *Human Nature*. London: Allen Lane, 1974.

Durkheim, E.: *The Rules of Sociological Method* (1895), ed. S. Lukes, trans. W.D. Halls. London: Macmillan, 1982.

†Hobbes, T.: *Leviathan* (1651), ed. C.B. Macpherson. Harmondsworth: Penguin, 1968.

Machiavelli, N.: *Discourses on the First Decade of Titus Livius*, trans. L.J. Walker, ed. B. Crick. Harmondsworth: Penguin, 1970.

Plato: *The Republic*, trans. A. Bloom. New York and London: Basic, 1968.

Rosenberg, A.: *Sociobiology and the Preemption of Social Science*. Oxford: Blackwell, 1981.

Rousseau, J.-J.: *The First and Second Discourses together with the Replies to Critics*, and *Essay on the Origin of Languages*, ed. and trans. V. Gourevitch. London: Harper & Row, 1986.

Wilson, E.D.: *Sociobiology: the New Synthesis*. Cambridge, Mass.: Belknap, 1975.

human rights Rights possessed by human beings simply as human beings. The term 'human rights' has only come to the fore in this century; in earlier centuries these rights were more commonly spoken of as 'natural rights' or the 'rights of man'.

Not every age or civilization has possessed the concept of a human right nor, indeed, the concept of a right of any kind. There is controversy, for example, over whether the concept of a right figured in ancient Greek and Roman systems of law. In a recent study, Tuck has argued that the concept of a right did not appear in Europe until the twelfth century, but that a fully-fledged theory of natural rights had already emerged by the end of the fourteenth century, to be found in the writings of Gerson and those associated with him. The theory was developed virtually afresh at the beginning of the seventeenth century, particularly in the work of Hugo GROTIUS. Subsequently there emerged two different schools of thought about natural rights. The more conservative of these, exemplified by SELDEN and HOBBES, attributed a virtually unlimited right to freedom to men in their 'natural' (i.e. pre-political) condition, but held that that right was surrendered more or less completely when men entered civil society. On this view, therefore, acceptance of a theory of natural rights was quite compatible with advocacy of absolute governmental authority. By contrast, more radical theorists held that, while some natural rights were surrendered to governments for the sake of social peace, others were not and could be appealed to by a people against an oppressive government. Thus natural rights were asserted in defence of both the English Revolution of the 1640s and the English Rebellion of 1688. It was this more radical theory that became the dominant theory of natural rights. It received its most influential expression at the end of the seventeenth century in the writings of John LOCKE.

According to Locke, God's natural law provided that 'no one ought to harm another in his life, health, liberty or possessions'. That law could therefore be said to give each a natural right to his life, liberty and property, though it also imposed upon each a natural duty to respect the lives, liberties and properties of others. In their natural condition men would also possess the right to do what was necessary to protect the natural rights of themselves and others. It was this 'executive right of nature' which would be a source of conflict in a state of nature and men would seek peace by handing it over to a common authority, so establishing a political community. Very importantly for Locke, men had not given up their natural rights to life, liberty and property. On the contrary, the whole point of their establishing a political community was the better to protect those rights. Those rights were inalienable – no man was morally empowered to place his life or liberty entirely at the disposal of another (although he might 'forfeit' his natural rights if he infringed the rights of others).

Natural rights yielded three main political consequences in Locke's theory. First, since men enjoyed equal rights under the law of nature, no one could come under the political authority of another except by his own consent. Second, the maintenance and protection of natural rights constituted the primary function of government. Third, natural rights set limits to the authority of governments so that a government which violated the rights of its citizens lost its claim to obedience and could be legitimately overthrown.

In subsequent centuries, these three political implications remained closely associated with assertions of natural rights. The American Declaration of Independence (1776), for example, enunciated as self-evident truths that 'all men are created equal, that they are endowed by their Creator with certain unalienable rights, that among these are Life, Liberty and the pursuit of Happiness.' It then went on to assert that governments were instituted to secure these rights, that they derived their just power from the consent of the governed, and that a government which sought to destroy these rights could be abolished by the people. The French Declaration of the Rights of Man and of Citizens (1789) made similar claims in relation to the 'natural, imprescriptible and inalienable' rights that it enumerated.

Twentieth-century doctrines of human rights are direct descendants of the liberal theory of natural rights. Indeed many would use the terms 'natural right' and 'human right' interchangeably. The idea of a human right remains that of a right which is 'natural' in that it is conceived as a moral entitlement which human beings possess in their natural capacity as humans, and not in virtue of any special arrangement into which they have entered or any particular system of law under whose jurisdiction they fall. Human rights can be, and are, asserted against private individuals and against private associations such as firms and trade unions. But their principal context remains political; they describe the minimum entitlements that governments must protect and secure and that governments must themselves respect.

Eighteenth- and nineteenth-century declarations of natural rights have been matched by twentieth-century declarations of human rights – most notably the United Nations Declaration of Human Rights of 1948 and the various UN Covenants and Conventions that have followed it, and the European Convention on Human Rights. Statements of rights have also become common ingredients of the constitutions of particular states and, in so far as these are conceived as acknowledging rather than creating the rights that they announce, they belong to the same tradition.

Which rights have been most commonly claimed as human rights? Judging by formal declarations, these fall roughly into six categories. First, and often foremost, is the right to life. This may be understood variously as the right not to be murdered or physically assaulted, or the right to be protected from murder and assault, or the right to receive the material essentials of life and a minimum of health care (see below). Second, FREEDOM has always figured prominently in declarations of rights. Sometimes it appears as a right to freedom in some generalized sense; sometimes as rights to particular freedoms of which freedom of thought, expression, religion, association and movement are the most favoured. Third, the right to PROPERTY, which figured importantly in early statements of rights, has remained in many twentieth-century statements, although it is now often conceived as a more limited right – particularly in the extent to which it can restrain public policy. Fourth, there are rights concerning the individual's status as citizen such as the right to nationality and democratic rights. Fifth are rights concerning the conduct of government, in particular rights concerning the RULE OF LAW and the administration of justice such as the right not to be subjected to arbitrary arrest and the right to a fair trial. These last two categories of right would not have been intelligible in terms of the original conception of natural rights as those rights enjoyed by men in their 'natural condition' which was, by definition, a condition without government. However, they are intelligible as natural or human rights, for the moral status attributed to persons may well have implications for how they are entitled to be treated in and by political institutions and private associations.

Finally, human rights are claimed to certain social, economic and cultural goods. The UN Declaration, for example, asserts, *inter alia*, human rights to education, work, social security, rest and leisure, and a standard of living adequate for one's health and well-being. While claims to these sorts of rights are not completely unprecedented, they have only become prominent within the human rights tradition in this century. Their status as human rights has also proved controversial. In part this is because they raise disputed questions about social JUSTICE, but it is also because of doubts about their intelligibility as human rights. Many Third World countries do not currently have the resources to provide the goods concerned. Is it not absurd to tell people they have rights to goods which cannot possibly be provided? And would it not be equally absurd to attribute different *human* rights to people in different parts of the world or living at different times? The other questionable feature of socio-economic 'human' rights is that for any specific person the corresponding obligation to provide the good falls upon a particular government: a right to that good would therefore seem to be held as citizen of a particular society rather than as member of the human race. Yet although drafters of declarations may not have been fully sensitive to the distinction between human rights and desirable social goals, the case against socio-economic rights is not unanswerable. A right can be fully intelligible as a right even though its possession is conditional upon circumstances. It can also be universally held, even though for any particular holder the corresponding duty falls upon a particular body such as a government. Finally, whatever the intentions of those who have drafted declarations of rights, it is not *logically* nonsensical to hold that human beings have a responsibility on a world scale for one another's economic well-being.

How are human rights to be justified? Declarations of rights have sometimes been presented as statements of self-evident truths which therefore require only to be announced. This approach is, at best, implausible and invites the opponent of human rights to dismiss them as no more than a set of prejudices. In the past natural rights have commonly been regarded as the offspring of natural law, so that they form part of a general theory of natural law and stand or fall with it (see LAW). While this remains an important approach, the concept of human rights has been increasingly detached from traditional natural law thinking. Contemporary moral and political philosophers are more likely to found a case for human rights upon a commitment to fundamental values such as freedom, autonomy and equality together with other considerations relating to the essentials of human well-being (see RIGHTS). What form might such an argument take?

Human beings are complex; so too are the circumstances of their lives. There is no reason, therefore, to suppose that a theory justifying human rights need be or can be a simple matter. Nor is there reason to suppose that only one set of moral principles or one form of moral argument will yield an idea of human rights. Nor, again, is there reason to suppose that different justifications will yield lists of human rights with the same contents. Theories of human rights are, therefore, capable of greater diversity and can be more sophisticated than critics of the notion have typically allowed. But these points also indicate that there is no reason to suppose, *a priori*, that proponents of human rights need be agreed upon the ground nor, therefore, upon the content of human rights, so that their shared aim of producing a single, universally accepted, statement of human rights may not be easily achieved.

Despite the widespread popularity achieved by the idea of human rights, it is far from universally accepted. In some cases rejection is a corollary of a general critique of the rights approach to morality and politics. Other criticisms are directed specifically at human rights. One of the most persistent concerns their epistemological status. Followers of BENTHAM have complained that natural or human rights are asserted as though their existence were as much a matter of fact as the existence of legal rights. An orthodox natural law theorist might well reply that God's natural law and the rights it confers are as much facts about the world as are the legal rights created by human enactment. However, most contemporary exponents of human rights would accept that there is a difference between the empirical claim '*A* has a legal right to *x*' and the moral claim '*A* has a human right to *x*'. Provided that that distinction is recognized, the claim that humans have rights as humans is no more illicit than any other moral claim.

The need to take account of the details and complexities of social life has also been turned against the doctrine of human rights. BURKE, for example, complained that the rights asserted by the French Revolutionaries were 'all extremes', whereas, in reality, government was about securing balances and compromises between competing goods and competing evils.

Certainly the more one conceives political decisions as calling for the balancing of complex and conflicting considerations, the less sympathetic one is likely to be towards theories which demand the honouring of a list of more or less inviolable rights.

Finally, the universalist character of human rights thinking has led some to express fears of cultural imperialism. If individuals the world over must be accorded their 'human rights', that may seem to grant a licence to enthusiasts for this peculiar outgrowth of European culture to ride roughshod over other cultures which do not share its conception of the good life and the just society.   PJ

Reading

Brownlie, I. ed.: *Basic Documents on Human Rights*, 2nd edn. Oxford: Clarendon Press, 1981.

Cranston, M.: *What are Human Rights?* London: Bodley Head, 1973.

†Donnelly, J.: *The Concept of Human Rights*. London: Croom Helm, 1985.

Finnis, J.: *Natural Law and Natural Rights*. Oxford: Clarendon Press, 1980.

Gewirth, A.: *Human Rights: Essays on Justification and Applications*. Chicago and London: University of Chicago Press, 1982.

Locke, J.: *Two Treatises of Government* (1689), ed. P. Laslett. New York: Mentor, 1965.

†Melden, A.I. ed.: *Human Rights*. Belmont, Calif.: Wadsworth, 1970.

————: *Rights and Persons*. Oxford: Blackwell, 1977.

Paine, T.: *Rights of Man* (1791/2), ed. H. Collins. Harmondsworth: Penguin, 1969.

†Raphael, D.D. ed.: *Political Theory and the Rights of Man*. London: Macmillan, 1967.

Tuck, R.: *Natural Rights Theories*. Cambridge: Cambridge University Press, 1979.

Waldron, J.J. ed.: *Theories of Rights*. Oxford: Oxford University Press, 1984.

Humboldt, Wilhelm von (1767–1835) German thinker, educational reformer and founder of the University of Berlin (1809). Humboldt came from a Prussian aristocratic family (his younger brother, Alexander, was the famous scientist and explorer of South America). As a student of Heyne at Göttingen (1788–9), where he already exhibited a dazzling linguistic versatility and philological competence, he laid the foundations for a life-long study of classical antiquity (and for the pioneering work in the philosophy of language that occupied the last phase of his life). Influenced by Winckelmann's vision of ancient Greece and by his friendship with SCHILLER and Goethe, the young Humboldt developed the ideal of *Bildung* – of the original, many-faceted and harmonious personality – that became the major inspiration of his philosophical and aesthetic theories as well as of his practical reform programmes.

His most important work as a political thinker – and the one best known to English-speaking readers through J. S. MILL's *On Liberty* – was written in 1792: *Ideen zu einem Versuch die Grenzen der Wirksamkeit des Staats zu bestimmen* (Some Ideas Concerning the Attempt to Define the Limits of State Action). In it Humboldt claimed that the commonly accepted duty of governments to promote the welfare of their subjects entailed the most objectionable despotism. For no matter how enlightened its purpose, state intervention always removed the conditions and incentives for *self*-development.

Individuality of character – conceived in analogy with the work of creative genius – and the greatest possible diversity of human pursuits and life-styles were the twin pillars of Humboldt's aesthetic liberalism. It denied not only the legitimacy of legal constraints upon individual behaviour (with only minimal concessions to the security functions of the state) but was equally wary of the threat to freedom posed by the collective identities of social rank, religion and race (Humboldt's unequivocal support for the emancipation of the Jews, for example, flowed from the premises of this radical individualism). Unlike Mill he did not link individual self-development to the exercise of political freedom. Active CITIZENSHIP, i.e. the direction of individual energies towards common goals, would, he feared, submerge individuality in uniformity and one-sidedness.

This ideal of *Bildung* was put into practice – ironically by means of state action – when Humboldt became involved in the liberal reform movement of the Stein-Hardenberg era (1809). He built the reorganization of Prussia's educational system upon the strict separation between general human education (*allgemeine Menschenbildung*) divorced from any utilitarian concern, and the instruction in particular skills required by occupations and social roles later in life (the latter having no place in the school). The corner-stone in this edifice was the humanistic *Gymnasium* (grammar school). Based on the teaching of classical, especially Greek, languages and literatures, it remained the dominant educational institution in Germany until the second half of the twentieth century. Humboldt conceived the university as a domain of pure research, equally free from state regulation and from the demands of social relevance.

Through the imprint which they left on a key sector of social life, Humboldt's ideas have had an enduring influence on German intellectual and political development. The apolitical notion of freedom, confined to a sphere of private fulfilment, has often been held responsible for Germany's failure to adapt to the complex realities of modern industrial society and to the demands of democratic citizenship. Yet Humboldt's liberal principles have also been invoked – after 1918 and, again, after 1945 – as a potent defence against the encroachment of an authoritarian and totalitarian state. With regard to more recent debates on the conceptual foundations of modern LIBERALISM, the association of FREEDOM and self-development offers an interesting argument for the inseparability of the negative and positive meanings of liberty. Moreover, with their emphasis (often ignored by critics) on voluntary association and spontaneous individual co-operation as the corollary and practical consequence of individual freedom, Humboldt's arguments challenge the widespread belief that the individualistic premises of liberal thinking necessarily exclude the conditions of sociability and community.   UV

Reading

†Humboldt, W. von.: *The Limits of State Action*, ed. J.W. Burrow. Cambridge: Cambridge University Press, 1969.

Krieger, L.: *The German Idea of Freedom*. Chicago: Chicago University Press, 1957.

Sweet, P.R.: *Wilhelm von Humboldt: a biography*. 2 vols. Columbus: Ohio State University Press, 1978–80.

†Vogel, U.: Liberty is beautiful: von Humboldt's gift to liberalism. *History of Political Thought* 3 (1982) 77–101.

Hume, David (1711–1776) Scottish philosopher and historian. Hume was the second son of a family of small Scottish landowners, and was educated at the University of Edinburgh. After attempting to train as a lawyer he became interested in philosophy, and composed his first and most important philosophical work, *A Treatise of Human Nature* (1739–40), while living in France. To his great disappointment the book was neither a financial nor a critical success. He turned his hand instead to miscellaneous essays – some philosophical, some literary, some political – written in a lighter and more popular style. These appeared as *Essays Moral and Political* (1742) and *Political Discourses* (1752). Meanwhile he attempted to cast the academic philosophy of the *Treatise* in a more accessible form, the outcome being *An Enquiry Concerning Human Understanding* (published, under a different title, in 1748) and *An Enquiry Concerning the Principles of Morals* (1751).

Hume was prevented by clerical opposition from obtaining a regular academic post, but in 1751 he was appointed Keeper of the Advocates' Library at Edinburgh, which enabled him to work on his magisterial *History of England*, published in eight volumes between 1754 and 1761. In later life he held public offices in Paris and London, before returning to Edinburgh to spend his last years in the company of friends such as Adam SMITH and John Home. His *Dialogues Concerning Natural Religion*, written many years earlier but suppressed, was published posthumously in 1779.

Hume's philosophy began from the empiricist assumption that all substantive knowledge must ultimately be derived from sense experience. But whereas his predecessors and heirs in that tradition sought to provide a rational warrant for most of our ordinary beliefs (e.g. beliefs about material objects), Hume's sceptical conclusion was that many beliefs – including, most notoriously, beliefs about causation – had no such warrant. Instead they were to be explained in psychological terms, as the results of mental processes of a non-rational (though practically irresistible) kind. In particular he drew attention to the role played by the imagination, guided by customary associations of ideas, in generating belief.

In ethics, likewise, Hume sought to discredit the prevailing view that moral judgments could be given a rational basis. Moral belief depended on our experiencing feelings of a special type when contemplating other people and their activities, feelings generated by sympathy with the affected parties.

The upshot of Hume's philosophical enquiries was a mitigated form of scepticism. Human reason was powerless to establish types of belief that were vital to everyday life. Yet there were natural processes at work – imaginative and sensitive processes – which made it impossible to suspend belief, except momentarily. Moreover, uniformities in the human mind meant that on both empirical and moral questions people's beliefs tended to converge, creating at least the appearance of objectivity. Philosophers might still discriminate between more and less adequate beliefs, without being able to show that any belief was rational in the strong sense.

The implication of this doctrine for political thought was that ideas with rationalist underpinnings – such as the traditional conception of natural law, or the SOCIAL CONTRACT – had to be discarded. Instead social and political institutions should be understood as devices developed in response to the exigencies of the human condition. According to Hume, men were creatures of limited benevolence placed in an environment in which goods were scarce relative to their desires. Although naturally sociable, they tended to think first of themselves, their families and their friends, and so found themselves in conflict with strangers over resources. To secure social peace, conventional rules concerning the stability of possessions and the keeping of contracts had emerged more or less spontaneously. Hume called these 'rules of justice'. It was in everyone's interest to have them, though agreement in detail depended on the common properties of the imagination, which made connections between (for instance) people and particular material goods. Thus justice and property were artificial devices, because dependent on convention, but at the same time rooted in human nature.

Government was necessary because people were often too short-sighted to realize that their interests were best served by adhering to the rules of justice. It arose less by deliberate decision than through people coming to see that it was to their advantage to support any authority that enforced the rules effectively – a military chieftain, say (thus the social contract depicted by HOBBES, LOCKE and others was both historically improbable and philosophically unnecessary to explain allegiance). As to who should be granted authority in an established government, Hume once again relied on the imagination as a source of conventional rules.

Hume's theory of government was primarily a theory about the function of government; he was less interested in who was morally entitled to rule than in who was likely to rule well and command the allegiance of the people. As he once wrote (*New Letters*, p. 81), 'I look upon all kinds of subdivision of power, from the monarchy of France to the freest democracy of some Swiss cantons, to be equally legal, if established by custom and authority.' This did not mean that he had no preferences about forms of government; rather, no form could be defended from abstract principle alone, but only by taking local circumstances into account.

His preferences emerge most clearly in the *History of England*, where he depicts the gradual emergence of 'regular' government – government conducted according to general and uniform laws – from the 'barbarism' of Anglo-Saxon and Norman times. Such government was his strongest desideratum. On the question whether monarchy on the French model or a 'free' (i.e. mixed) constitution on the British model was preferable, he was very cautious. In his essays he explored the consequences of the two systems: free governments encouraged commerce, but were liable to contract a runaway public debt; free governments encouraged the sciences, monarchies the arts; free governments gave their subjects more liberty, but were in greater danger of sacrificing their authority; and so forth. Hume's general message was that, where regular government of any form existed, the choice between regimes was finely balanced enough to make support for the existing regime the prudent policy.

Hume has sometimes been labelled a Tory, but the only grounds for such an attribution are that he criticized Whig dogmas such as the

Original Contract, and that he painted a relatively sympathetic portrait of the early Stuarts in his *History*. In fact he consciously stood aloof from party conflict, urging moderation on all sides, and trying to persuade both Whig and Tory to abandon historical dogmas that had little relevance to the political establishment of the time; in particular he wished to cure his fellow Scots of their residual Jacobite leanings. As we have seen, his political attitudes were broadly conservative, but it was a conservatism born of scepticism rather than of abstract principle. He defended the oligarchical regime established in Britain because it governed effectively, because it commanded popular allegiance, and because rationalist arguments for change could be exploded philosophically; not, however, because it fulfilled divine purpose or was sanctioned by an historic contract.

Hume wrote a number of essays on economic subjects, some of them foreshadowing themes developed more fully by Adam SMITH and the classical economists. He favoured the growth of commerce and defended policies such as free trade and the abolition of monopolies which encouraged it. He should not, however, be regarded as an advocate of unbridled capitalism, for he lived in a society in which the landed interest was still predominant, socially and politically, and he accepted this state of affairs with equanimity. His vision was of a society in which land and trade blended harmoniously, commercial activity providing dynamism and economic growth, land providing social stability and moderation in government. The virtues he admired were not the 'Protestant' virtues – work, abstinence, self-discipline and the like – but rather characteristics such as good manners, constancy in

friendship, dignity, wit and eloquence, qualities that would endear a man to the mobile but still predominantly aristocratic society of Hume's day.

Hume's legacy to later political thought was a theory constructed on a wholly secular basis in which social and political institutions were to be judged by their consequences and by their correspondence to 'natural' human attitudes and sensibilities. BENTHAM said that, on reading the *Treatise*, 'I felt as if scales had fallen from my eyes', but Hume's true heirs were less the rationalistic utilitarians than students of human nature and the historical development of society such as Adam Smith and his fellow participants in the SCOTTISH ENLIGHTEN-MENT.   DLM

Reading

†Forbes, D.: *Hume's Philosophical Politics*. Cambridge: Cambridge University Press, 1975.

Hume, D.: *A Treatise of Human Nature*, ed. L.A. Selby Bigge. Oxford: Clarendon Press, 1978.

———: *Essays Moral, Political, and Literary*, ed. E. Miller. Indianapolis: Liberty Classics, 1985.

———: *Enquiries Concerning Human Understanding and Concerning the Principles of Morals*, ed. L.A. Selby Bigge. Oxford: Clarendon Press, 1975.

———: *The History of England from the Invasion of Julius Caesar to the Revolution in 1688*, ed. W.B. Todd. Indianapolis: Liberty Classics, 1983–5.

———: *New Letters of David Hume*, ed. R. Klibansky and E.C. Mossner. Oxford: Clarendon Press, 1954.

†Mackie, J.L.: *Hume's Moral Theory*. London: Routledge & Kegan Paul, 1980.

†Miller, D.: *Philosophy and Ideology in Hume's Political Thought*. Oxford: Clarendon Press, 1981.

Mossner, E.C.: *The Life of David Hume*. Oxford: Clarendon Press, 1980.

Whelan, F.G.: *Order and Artifice in Hume's Political Philosophy*. Princeton, NJ: Princeton University Press, 1985.

I

Ibn Khaldūn, Abū Zayd ʿAbd al-Rahmān Ibn Muhammad (1332–1406) Arab courtier, condottiere, judge, historian, and polymath. Born in Tunis, Ibn Khaldūn spent more than half his stormy career pursuing elusive ambitions at the courts of Fez, Granada, Tlemcen, and Bougie. In the more stable conditions of Cairo, where he settled in 1378, he pursued a successful and controversial career as judge and professor; in 1401 he had a colourful encounter with Tamerlane outside the walls of Damascus. Ibn Khaldūn is best known for his *Muqaddima* (1377), the prolegomenon to his *Universal History* (1377–82); he is also the author of a treatise on mysticism, a juvenile theological commentary, and of other juvenilia no longer extant.

Ibn Khaldūn's was an historical enterprise. He set out to compose his *Universal History* of truthful and connected narratives, and in this spirit he wrote the *Muqaddima*. In it he discussed the emergence of human collectivities (*ʿumrān*) as a result of propitious ecological and climatic factors which made possible the continuity and the preservation of organized habitation; this in itself had come into being after men, naturally fractious and predatory but unable to survive singly, had together contracted to live in society. In order for society to cohere, it places over and above itself a coercive authority, much as a living organism is held together by the dominance of a particular temper. This coercive authority starts under tribal conditions as chieftaincy, and chieftaincy, animated by the animal faculty of the psyche, yearns for greater glory, and when successful becomes kingship with the establishment of a state, *daula*. As coercive authority, political leadership wields together a community as a cohesive political unit, *ʿasabiyya*. But with the foundation of the state this unity, based on real or fictitious bonds of kinship, ultimately breaks down as the sovereign dissociates himself in practice from his original constituency and embarks upon an absolutist course. This brings in its wake great wealth and prosperity, but eventually develops into a tyranny which has a deleterious effect on the welfare of the subjects, with the increasing use of monopolies and extortionate taxation, with the fragmentation of the state at its extremities, and with a high incidence of pestilential and other calamities. Thus within the space of three generations the state runs through five phases which brings about its senescence with effeminacy and tyranny; the life-span of the state is thus, under optimal circumstances, 120 years, the length of the Grand Lunar Year of the astrologers. Finally, the *Muqaddima* provides a unique sketch of social, cultural, scientific, and economic conditions that prevail under the aegis of a prosperous state before it atrophies and is taken over by new claimants for another dynastic round.

Ibn Khaldūn's discussion is learned, and informed by a robust realism derived from political activity and historical knowledge. His observations have often been construed as a basis for ascribing to him sociological and other modern theories of the state. The state in the *Muqaddima*, however, is cast in a mould derived directly from Arabic historical writing, and the paradigm Ibn Khaldūn developed was meant to serve as a gauge for differentiating true from false historical narratives, *ʿUmrān* and *ʿasabiyya* are unthinkable without the context of the state construed as an abstract agency of power, bereft of a body politic; in other words, the state is conceived as a succession of dynasts connected by nothing but temporality. Ibn Khaldūn's discussions of *badāwa* (rude rural life) and *hadāra* (urbanism, civilization) are geared towards the conceptual requirements of the state as constituted by historical writing, and the 'sociological' substance they contain is the result of a vernacular retrospective realism. For the rest, the transition of the power group from the wild to the city and the acquisition of kingship is interpreted in terms of an Aristotelian teleological metaphysics, where statehood consummates chieftaincy and the *'asabiyya* which surrounds and sustains it, and where *badāwa* and *hadāra* relate as matter and form.   AA

Reading

Al-Azmeh, A.: *Ibn Khaldūn in Modern Scholarship*. London: Third World Centre for Research and Publishing, 1981.

†———: *Ibn Khaldūn: an Essay in Reinterpretation*. London: Cass, 1982.

Ibn Khaldūn: *Les prolégomènes d'Ibn Khaldoun*, trans. W.M. de Slane. 3 vols. Paris, 1863–8; reissued Paris: Geuthner, 1934–8.

———: *Ibn Khaldūn's Muqaddimah*, trans. F. Rosenthal. 3 vols. New York: Pantheon, 1958.

———: *at-Ta'rif bi-Ibn Khaldūn* [autobiography], trans. A. Cheddadi as *Le voyage d'occident et d'orient*. Paris: Sindbad, 1980.

†Nassar, N.: *La pensée réaliste d'Ibn Khaldoun*. Paris: Presses Universitaires de France, 1967.

†Schmidt, N.: *Ibn Khaldūn: Historian, Sociologist and Philosopher*. New York: Columbia University Press, 1930; repr. 1967.

idealism Although the work of many philosophers can be described as idealist, in the context of political theory the most important features of idealist thought were developed by KANT, FICHTE and HEGEL and subsequently by British Idealists such as T. H. GREEN, W. Wallace, E. Caird, H. Jones and B. BOSANQUET. The most important of these thinkers are dealt with as individuals, so the aim here is to describe the general character of Idealist thought in Germany at the end of the eighteenth century and its subsequent influence in Britain, particularly in Oxford and Glasgow in the nineteenth century. All Idealist philosophers saw a very close link between their idealism and their political philosophy.

One of the major themes running through Idealist thought is the relationship between Subject and Object, or how the knowing mind relates to the world it claims to know and within which the human agent acts, whether this world is to be understood as the natural physical world or as the world of political and social institutions. It is in trying to develop an adequate understanding of this relationship that the distinctiveness of Idealism lies. Hegel held that it is the sense of the divorce between Subject and Object that is the source of the need for philosophy, and that it was Kant above all who began to develop an adequate account of the Subject-Object relationship – a theory which, in Hegel's view, was to receive its final and coherent form in his own philosophical work.

Kant had argued, against Hume in particular, that the human mind is not some kind of passive organ which receives impressions from the external world, with conceptions of objects being formed by a mechanism of association. On the contrary, in Kant's view the objects which we experience are structured by the human mind. The mind itself transforms and transposes the chaotic manifold of sense impression into an objective and intelligible world by means of the understanding, deploying a fundamental categorical structure such as causality, substance, reciprocity, quantity, etc., and by the faculty of intuition in the forms of space and time. The experienced world in this sense is a human creation, the product of the activity of the mind. The experienced world could be seen as embodying the creative activity of the Ego, although as the presupposition and not the object of experience, this Ego is transcendental – that is to say it could not be described in empirical terms, because its activity is itself the basic condition of empirical description and experience. This meant that for Kant the human Ego *qua* deployer of categories was not to be understood as part of the empirical or phenomenal world bounded as that is by causality. The Kantian self is noumenal, rational and autonomous, acting in such a way as to produce the ordered world of our experience. These transcendental features of the self were, in addition, for Kant necessary for us to make sense of the possibility of human morality and the possibility of acting on principle – a sphere of our experience which presupposes human rational agency and autonomy. If human nature was wholly constrained by causal necessity, then the possibility of morality would be incomprehensible. These same aspects of human nature are also important for Kant's ideas about human dignity and worth, and the kind of respect which human beings deserve. His ideas about the kingdom of ends, and what respect for persons means in terms of mutual duties and obligations, likewise depend upon this account of the self.

However, it was precisely the transcendental nature both of the self and of things in themselves in the external world as they are unexperienced by us which in Hegel's view posed the major problem with Kant's theory. Elements within it, crucial both to Kant's metaphysics and epistemology and to his moral and political philosophy, were placed beyond investigation as transcendental objects – necessary presuppositions of, but beyond the reach of, empirical inquiry. Hegel therefore regarded the work of Fichte as a major improvement on Kant, because Fichte made it the explicit aim of his philosophy to eliminate transcendental objects, but from within a Kantian perspective. Fichte argued that the experienced world, as the world we know, is the only world, it is not an indirect representation of things in themselves, and as such is wholly dependent upon the Ego. The task of philosophy is to explain in detail for both the natural and the social world how the activity of the Ego can be understood as positing this world, and thus to demonstrate the Ego-dependence of the external world. For obvious reasons this theory became known as Subjective Idealism. For Fichte, however, the reconciliation of Subject and Object, by showing the complete dependence of the Object upon the Subject, would never be finally achieved – the struggle to show the Ego-dependence of the natural and social worlds has to be done in detail and without residue, but this process, while the historical process is going on, has no terminating point. Because of this, Hegel finally rejected Fichte. He had not in the end produced a coherent

theory of the relationship between Subject and Object, it was a *Sollen*, a mere 'ought to be', not a completed theory. In addition, Hegel took the view that Fichte's means of overcoming the residue of things in themselves or transcendental objects in Kant's theory was a sham because, in a sense, Fichte had denied the ultimate externality of the world and had left the nature of the Ego on which it depends opaque.

The Objective Idealism of Schelling was almost the reverse of Fichte's view. He argued that both Ego and Nature had to be taken as real, neither having a privileged position in the scheme of explanation. Both Ego and Nature are aspects of the same basic substance or Absolute, or what Schelling called 'the point of indifference' in which Nature and Ego are not differentiated. Nature and Ego do not exist in opposition or in one-sided dependence: rather the Ego makes explicit in science and philosophy the quasi-spiritual forces at work in nature. However, in Schelling's view the position which would ground the ultimate identity of Nature and Ego is known only through intuition. It cannot be argued for, it can only be understood in its results. Hegel rejected this view, arguing that the relationship between Subject and Object has to be capable of rational demonstration, not based upon some private intuitive experience.

Hegel's own form of idealism, usually known as Absolute Idealism, has to be seen against this background. He takes from Kant the need for an adequate account of the relationship between Subject and Object (construing Object to include social and political forms, as well as natural phenomena). He accepts from Fichte the argument in favour of exorcizing transcendental objects from idealism; he takes from Schelling the idea that the objectivity of the world has to be taken seriously, while wishing to avoid Schelling's intuitionism. Hegel's idealism is therefore an attempt to produce an account of the nature of the human subject in relation to the world and to make this relationship wholly transparent and rational. This project has a number of key features.

First of all, philosophy must be systematic, it must cover the whole range of human thought and action, otherwise there would be areas left out of the reconciliation of Subject and Object.

Philosophy must be historical in the sense that we cannot, as Kant thought, explain the relationship between the knowing subject and the world which it knows in a timeless way, according to a set of universal categories. The concepts which human beings bring to the understanding of their world change and develop through time, becoming more and more adequate to the encapsulation of the objective world in thought through a process of dialectical contradiction and subsequent development. So, as Hegel argues in the *Philosophy of Right* (1821), 'the shapes which the concept assumes in the course of its actualization are indispensable for the knowledge of the concept itself' (§1): that is to say, an analysis of the concepts and categories in terms of which the mind seeks to comprehend the world cannot be detached from the historical understanding of the ways of life in which these concepts were articulated. Philosophy also has a practical aspect in Hegel's Idealism, in that he believed that the attempts at reconciliation between Subject and Object made by Kant and Fichte were too intellectualist, based clearly in Kant's view on the operation of the Ego as a transcendental object, whereas in Hegel's view the relationship between Subject and Object involves embodied human activity in such things as labour, political action and artistic endeavour. We cannot understand the relationship between mind and the world in a vacuum: our concepts arise in relation to human activity, in the attempts through labour, science and art of all sorts to mould the world to human projects and purposes. So philosophy has to be based on a knowledge of the practical ways in which human beings attempt to shape the world through their major life activities. In addition, this account of the relationship between Subject and Object has to be exoteric and open to rational appraisal by all who will take on the 'labour of the concept', as Hegel puts it. This means that the philosophical explanation of particular forms of social life and their attendant concepts has to be in terms of general concepts and categories which can be made transparent and the *grounds* for the employment of such concepts made evident, in contrast to the intuitive approach of Schelling. Hence, the purpose of Hegel's two major works on logic is

to try to elaborate the general categorical framework in terms of which the dialectical evolution of a particular conceptual framework is rationally compelling, because it can be shown to emerge as a matter of necessity from the most basic assumption which any categorical framework must make – namely the acknowledgement of *Being* (that is to say that there *is* something or other).

Hegel's Idealism is referred to as 'Absolute' for a cluster of reasons. It is absolute in the sense that Hegel claims to provide us with the set of categories in terms of which all of human experience, in the past and the present, can be understood and set in a developmental pattern to which there is no alternative. It is also absolute in the sense that the absence of any alternative interpretative framework is given some kind of metaphysical guarantee by Hegel. The rationality of the world and the development of human history and institutions is not a Kantian regulative idea, one which we must presuppose in our approach to the world, both material and human; it is rather, in Hegel's view, capable of being given a metaphysical justification and this in two parallel ways: by being shown, as has already been noted, to emerge by necessity out of the basic assumptions of *any* categorical framework (the argument in *The Science of Logic*) and by being shown to emerge by necessity out of the most basic and inescapable forms of consciousness (the argument of the *Phenomenology of Spirit*).

The view of the world and history which philosophy gives us is, in Hegel's view, implicit in a more or less developed way in non-philosophical forms of human activity and most particularly in art and religion. The link between philosophy and religion is important for Hegel's Idealism and vital for understanding most subsequent forms of British Idealism. This point is borne out by considering the argument hitherto in the light of T. H. Green's position developed in the *Prolegomena to Ethics* (1883). The central issue of philosophy, as Green poses it, is whether the objective world as revealed to us in science and common sense presupposes a principle or set of principles which is not itself part of this world of facts. Green's answer to this question is an interesting combination of Kant and Hegel and he clearly relates his answer to religious and theological conceptions. Like Kant, Green argues that our experience is not of a chaotic manifold but rather an awareness by an enduring subject of a unified world of objects. He differs from Kant, however, in arguing that the 'objectivity' of objects has to be considered in terms of the necessary *relations* in which objects stand to one another. This enables Green to say that the manifold of experience cannot be provided independently of the mind, because only minds or consciousness can make relationships, and this is just what objectivity *means*. The self is indispensable to the world which it knows and thus the objectivity of the world cannot be explained naturalistically. This view of the nature of the world as a set of relationships requires an order of relationships which is a presupposition of all intersubjective enquiry and activity, and this in turn requires the operation of a spiritual principle: 'an eternal intelligence realized in the related facts of the world, or as a system of related facts rendered possible by such an intelligence' (§36).

Kant had seen the unifying and categorizing power of the Ego as a transcendental presupposition of all our experience but he did not think it was possible to ground this in anything other than the fact that it is a necessary precondition of experience, whereas Green, following Hegel, argues that this intersubjective power of the Ego reveals and reproduces in its own operations in each individual the unifying power of the spiritual principle, or the eternal intelligence which Green identified with God. In this sense, therefore, philosophy puts into a rational form what is put in a symbolic and religious way in the Christian religion. However, unlike Hegel, he argues that the eternal intelligence does not reproduce itself fully in any human consciousness and so our knowledge of relationships and objectivity is always piecemeal and never finally completed; whereas Hegel had argued that his philosophy reproduced in a final way the working of such an eternal principle, what he called the Absolute Idea, which, when fully articulated and developed in detail for all the forms of experience with which philosophy deals, leads the human mind which comprehends this to *Geist* or Spirit.

In Green's view and in Hegel's the role of the Idea, or the eternal intelligence which transcends but is revealed in the operation of the individual mind, is central to escaping the potential solipsism of Kant and Fichte. If the objectivity of experience is a product of mind, then there can only be a sense of intersubjective reality in so far as the operations of individual minds reproduce the operations of a mind or idea in which we all share. So we are all part of the Divine Life which reproduces itself in us – finally for Hegel, progressively but never finally for Green – and this is necessary to explain the intersubjective nature of experience. Indeed, when the objectivity of experience is based upon the operation of the Subject rather than in the nature of the Object, as it is for all Idealists, it is difficult not to raise the question of what secures the agreement or objectivity in the way that Hegel and Green pose it for us. Most of the British Idealists follow Green and Hegel here, the major disputes being about the nature of the Absolute – for example whether it is really another term for God and, if so, whether it has personal characteristics, and how such a view of the Absolute and its role can be made compatible with the freedom and individuality of human agents.

What, then, is characteristic of the Idealist approach to politics and political philosophy? The most obvious general point is that an account of political life has to be situated in a structure of philosophical explanation of wide generality, in which, as a distinctive form of human association and activity, politics has to be seen in relation to human life and experience in the round, that is in relation not just to things such as economics but also to morality, history, art and religion. Second, political life has to be understood in terms of history, but a history which has a progressive rationality to it. Human beings are seen as forming political relationships which reflect both the needs of human nature as this develops in history and their patterns of behaviour in other areas of life. So, at least for Hegel, the modern state meets the needs for human nature as it has come to be modified by profound cultural changes in art, literature, religion, philosophy and economic activity. It follows from this that political life has to be understood teleologically rather than naturalistically or in terms of causal laws.

Political institutions have to be explained in terms of the progressive needs and sense of self of a developing human subjectivity, a point which Hegel makes generally in the *Philosophy of Mind* when he says: 'The ego is by itself only a formal identity. . . . Consciousness . . . appears differently modified according to the difference of the given object and the gradual specification of consciousness appears as a variation in the characteristics of its objects' (§415). As the human mind cannot be a subject for scientific causality, so political activity as the product of mind cannot be exhaustively explained in terms of causal laws.

The particular problem in the modern world for the reconciliation between the human subject and objective institutions is the reconciliation between the growing sense of personal freedom, independence and dignity which has been a marked feature of western culture since the time of Socrates, and a world of institutions within which that sense of individual worth can both be recognized and made compatible with a similar recognition of the worth of others. In Hegel's view this sense of individualism has been enhanced by the whole history of the West: by the figure of Socrates questioning the moral conventions of his society, by Roman law, by Protestant Christianity with its idea of a personal relationship to God, by the growth of subjectivism in moral thought and practice, by the experience of the French Revolution, by the development of the modern economy, and the idea of control over the external world which comes from science. All of these factors have radically changed our sense of self, and this poses the problem of finding objective institutions that are potentially compatible with a subject with this type of self-understanding. However, Hegel and most of the British Idealists rejected a Rousseauian solution to this problem, involving a radical change in the nature of society and the structures of politics. They took the view that the institutions of the modern state, as these were developing in the advanced societies in the West, did have the potential for accommodating a range of spheres of life such as private morality and economic activity within which individualism could flourish, but which at the same time were held within a set of political institutions capable of securing social unity and stability. For Hegel, Caird, Bosanquet, Wallace and to a lesser extent Green, the political reconciliation between Subject and Object was not a *Sollen* to be projected into a different type of political arrangement (whether of a utopian Rousseauian sort or a regulative Kantian 'kingdom of ends') but was intimated in the institutions of the modern world. As Hegel writes in the *Philosophy of Right*: 'The principle of the modern state has prodigious strength and depth because it allows the principle of subjectivity to progress to its culmination in the extreme of self-subsistent personal particularity and yet at the same time brings it back to the substantive unity and so maintains this unity in the principle of subjectivity itself' (§260). Correctly understood, therefore, the institutions of the modern state provide the basis for a reconciliation between an historically developed sense of self, marked by individualism, and the world of institutions. However, such a reconciliation is a philosophical task, because this potential is obscured in everyday experience and its misconceptions. It is precisely this point which MARX criticizes, for example in the *Theses on Feuerbach*. In his view the reconciliation between Subject and Object is not a matter of understanding or interpretation of what is, but has rather to be achieved by a struggle to change the world to meet the real needs of human nature.   RP

Reading

Fichte, J.G.: *The Science of Knowledge*, trans. P. Heath and J. Lachs. New York: Appleton-Century-Crofts, 1970.

Green, T.H.: *Prolegomena to Ethics*. Oxford: Clarendon Press, 1883.

Hegel, G.W.F.: *Philosophy of Right*, trans. T. M. Knox. Oxford: Clarendon Press, 1952.

———: *Philosophy of Mind*, trans. W. Wallace and A.V. Miller. Oxford: Oxford University Press, 1971.

Milne, A.J.M.: *The Social Philosophy of English Idealism*. London: Allen & Unwin, 1962.

†Plant, R.: *Hegel*, 2nd edn. Oxford: Blackwell, 1983.

Richter, M.: *The Politics of Conscience: T.H. Green and His Age*. London: Weidenfeld & Nicolson, 1964.

†Taylor, C.: *Hegel*. Cambridge: Cambridge University Press, 1975.

†Vincent, A. and Plant, R.: *Philosophy, Politics and Citizenship: the Life and Thought of the British Idealists*. Oxford: Blackwell, 1984.

Wood, E.M.: *Mind and Politics*. Los Angeles: University of California Press, 1972.

ideology Ideologies are patterns of symbolically-charged beliefs and expressions that present, interpret and evaluate the world in a way designed to shape, mobilize, direct, organize and justify certain modes or courses of action and to anathematize others.

The term was coined by Destutt de Tracy in 1796 to designate a systematic critical and therapeutic study of the sensationalist grounds of ideas (see Cox; Lichtheim). But modern uses of the neologism in social and political theory derive rather from a mocking metonymic use of the term to stand for all systems of ideas which exaggerate their importance in the constitution and transformation of reality. It carries a strong implication that this lack of realism has its source in the self-infatuation or self-interest of the ideologist, viewed as representative of some partisan social type or collectivity, and that it performs merely propagandistic functions, even when this is not deliberately intended by those who promulgate the ideas. This rhetorical twist forms the starting point for the Marxist development of the concept as an instrument for discrediting the beliefs, theories and practices of opponents (see MARX; MARXISM). The alternative line of development, less judgmental in its applications, also begins with the semiological shift from theory of ideas to type of ideas.

Where non-Marxist commentators have retained the twofold pejorative connotation associated with the original metaphorical use of the term, they have generalized it; and they have offered a variety of additional explanations for the systematic distortion of knowledge and exploitative manipulation of belief which they mean to indicate when they designate certain politically-oriented symbolic systems as ideologies (see Bell; Shils).

The original polemical uses of the term ridiculed the political pretensions of speculative doctrines remote from reality, and ideology, in all its interpretations, is still understood in terms of its practical bearing upon a domain characterized by the play of power and resistances, not always political in an obvious sense. The most common models for ideologies, in non-Marxist uses of the term, are nevertheless the more or less systematized political doctrines expressly professed by the major organized partisan tendencies which emerged during the nineteenth and early twentieth centuries, and the most common classification schemes for ideologies build upon this historical material (see Mannheim), frequently also incorporating the conventional ranging of the tendencies across a spectrum from left to right. Accordingly, 'ideology' usually presupposes the continued political significance of integrated patterns of thought whose outlines follow the historical doctrines of liberal, conservative or socialist parties, although this assumption itself has increasingly appeared problematical to some recent investigators, such as Converse, Marcuse, and Habermas.

Among those non-Marxist writers for whom the term carries a strong pejorative sense, however, only the more manifest, elaborate, self-contained and monopolistic of these partisan doctrines are selected as paradigmatically ideological. In a paradoxical (and frequently polemical) reversal, accordingly, Marxism has often been taken, since the second world war, as the prime example of an ideology in this sense, although this critical conception of ideology was largely built up through the analysis of fascist movements and regimes. From this point of view ideologies are contrasted with value systems, outlooks and creeds (see Shils), and other types of interpretive frames of reference said to lack the exclusiveness and the domineering character of ideologies. The special feature of ideology, according to both Marxist and non-Marxist proponents of the concept in its developed negative sense, is that it is not only a 'prescriptive doctrine that is not supported by rational argument' (Raphael, p. 17) but also a prescriptive scheme which operates so as to destroy the possibility of rational argument.

A different line of development, suggested by MANNHEIM's sociology of knowledge and subsequently taken up in certain anthropological writings, attempts to neutralize the concept of ideology by functionally differentiating it from systems of scientific knowledge, practical deliberation or moral argument. Ideologies are then said to be symbolic systems which cannot be faulted for lacking the qualities of scientific theories, pragmatic strategies or reasoned moral philosophies. They represent a distinct type of cultural formation, providing expressively formulated, value-laden and directive interpretations of the world, when traditional guidelines cease to perform this practical function. As such, they cannot but be partisan and designing (see Geertz; Seliger). But they are functionally indispensable in all non-traditional societies.

Other investigators arrive at a similarly neutralized concept by different routes, as in the case when ideologies are defined operationally, as clusters of co-variant opinions (or attitudes) about major political questions, including questions about the subjective assessment of political experiences, major contested policy preferences, and the desired organization, scope and purposes of government. More sophisticated versions of these approaches make room for differences in types of political reasoning as well, rather than limiting themselves to the classification of responses to opinion surveys. This whole literature, then, links up with the study of attitude and opinion formation and systematization, as practised by contemporary academic psychology. Except where this empirical work concerns itself with patterns in non-western societies, it does not address the question considered by anthropological approaches, whether ideology is simply any kind of symbolic pattern which may serve to provide people with a political identity and direct their political attitudes, or whether it has special distinguishing features. Where the issue is addressed, the concept is confined to organizationally-grounded belief systems in modernized (or modernizing) societies with an autonomous political domain.

In the literature of the sociology of knowledge, the two ways of developing the concept are commonly distinguished as evaluative and non-evaluative (see Mannheim); but in fact both are evaluative, at least in the sense that neither recognizes the validity of the ideas which it considers to be ideological. An exception to this is a theoretically unreflective use of the term current among English academic writers on political subjects, who simply consider ideologies as popularized, informal and incompletely argued social or political philosophies, to be philosophically tidied up, and debated. But this conception is as indifferent to the actual rhetorical-cognitive structures of the patterns of thinking or discourse to which it refers as it is to their provenance, actuality or functions. Accordingly, it fails to encounter the materials and problems at issue in the contest about the concept. The contest is between critical and empirical senses of the term. This distinction serves to indicate that the proponents of the empirical version do not expressly address questions about the epistemological or ethical implications of ideologies, having stipulated that such issues are not germane to the study of ideologies, while those such as Mannheim and Habermas who deploy the critical concept expressly attend to the relationship between knowledge and political or social action.

The persistence of the original pejorative connotation in ordinary language is such, however, that discussions operating with the empirical concept rarely escape contamination by inadequately considered critical judgments on the ideologies they are treating. Political analysis, moreover, is constantly forced back to questions about the rationality of the structures and processes it considers (or to assume unargued answers to such questions); and the disinterested study of ideologies, in the context of such analyses, can in consequence hardly avoid critical questions about their relationships to rational patterns of political judgment (see Connolly).

Marxist social theory has produced the richest theoretical elaborations of the critical sense of the concept, especially as writers in this tradition have sought to account for the failure of the working class to develop the revolutionary consciousness which Marx had projected as antithesis to the dominant ideologies he undertook to unmask (see ALTHUSSER, CRITICAL THEORY, GRAMSCI, LENIN and LUKÁCS). In the definitive form of their doctrine, Marx and Engels had interpreted ideology in terms of a conceptual distinction between a 'base' constituted by the dynamic processes of production and a 'superstructure' corresponding to the development of the base, and made up of ideas and institutions reflecting the unequal class structure and embodying 'false consciousness'. The revolution against the order thus constituted would be generated by the cumulative dynamism of production, but it would appear in the form of class struggle within the superstructural domain, pitting the increasingly self-assertive and self-conscious political activities of the structurally subordinated productive class ('class-consciousness') against the ideologically encoded structure of domination. This abstract but elegant theoretical formulation became less empirically plausible towards the end of the nineteenth century. Where Marx had envisaged a polarized confrontation between regimes uncompromisingly and visibly subservient to the requirements of capitalist property, and a growing labour movement apparently inclining towards ever more political and sweeping demands for social transformation, there emerged instead complex patterns of accommodation in some places and radically changed terms of conflict in others.

The sharp differences among theorists commonly claiming to derive inspiration from Marx's conception and analysis of ideology arise from this challenge to their shared theoretical and political heritage. Official Marxism has simplified the concept so as to equate ideology with any explication of the interests imputed to a social actor deemed to possess specifiable interests (usually economic) for purposes of a given political analysis. This makes no consistent distinction between cases where the presumed explication is rhetorically deployed by the actor in question as a doctrinal weapon to further his interests, and those where the explication purports to lay out the hidden unified rationale underlying practices which may be mediated by different sorts of symbolic schemes. Since the term may be used, at least in the former of these emphases, to refer to the doctrinal weapons of Marxist regimes or movements themselves, a qualifying adjective ('bourgeois', 'proletarian', etc.) is commonly added to indicate whose ideology is intended. This means that the negative evaluation and theory of distortion almost always implied in the concept in Marx's own formulations is largely muted or only opportunistically revived.

In contrast, most other Marxist-inspired currents build upon this critical aspect. They are marked and differentiated by substantial modifications of the original distinction between base and superstructure, as well as by attempts to incorporate novel theories of rhetoric and meaning, which undermine the notion of ideas as expressions of actors' intentions and as the material of practical deliberation. Accordingly, for example, some thinkers include the technological organization of material production among the ideological, superstructural elements in society and expand the concept of the base to comprehend the work of the artist as producer. Similarly, conceptions of directional verbal and non-verbal semiotic structures, discourses, languages, and implicit symbolic logics (see HABERMAS and FOUCAULT) increasingly displace the notion of ideologies as systems of ideas which are either openly expressed as such or can be extracted fairly readily from the frames of reference actually used in communication.

At some point in this theoretical development, with its distinctions between types of cultural formations which the older critical conceptions of ideology had attempted to unmask as ultimately integrated by a common ideological rationale, the question arises whether it is still useful to construe this complex critical theory as a critique of ideology. Does such an inclusive concept distract from the need to work out in detail the various ways in which symbolic domains may be constituted? The distinction between the material forces shaping human experience and the inverted images of this reality captured in ideas, upon which Marx built his concept, appears to have been abandoned by those who continue his radical critique of modern civilization. There is much to be said, accordingly, for restricting the concept of ideology more narrowly to the sorts of political phenomena which the empirical line of enquiry has distinguished. The explanation of such phenomena may still be couched in terms of the critical theories which have their historical origins, at least in important measure, in attempts to explore and deepen the understanding of ideology in its widest sense.

DK

Reading
Bell, D.: *The End of Ideology*. New York: Free Press, 1960.
Connolly, W.E.: *The Terms of Political Discourse,*

expanded edn. Princeton, NJ: Princeton University Press, 1983.

Converse, P.E.: The nature of belief systems in mass publics. In *Ideology and Discontent*, ed. D. Apter. New York: Free Press, 1964.

†Cox, R.H.: *Ideology, Politics, and Political Theory*. Belmont, Calif.: Wadsworth, 1969.

Geertz, C.: Ideology as a cultural system (1964). In *The Interpretation of Cultures*. New York: Basic, 1973.

Habermas, J.: *Knowledge and Human Interests*. Boston: Beacon, 1971.

†Lichtheim, G.: *The Concept of Ideology, and other essays*. New York: Random House, 1967.

Mannheim, K.: *Ideology and Utopia*. New York: Harcourt, Brace, 1936.

Marx, K. and Engels, F.: *The German Ideology* (1846). London: Lawrence & Wishart, 1967.

Raphael, D.D.: *Problems of Political Philosophy*. London: Macmillan, 1976.

†Seliger, M.: *Ideology and Politics*. London: Allen & Unwin, 1976.

Shils, E.: Ideology: the concept and function of ideology. In *International Encyclopedia of the Social Sciences*, vol. VII. New York: Macmillan and Free Press, 1968.

imperialism The word 'imperialism' is used in many senses. It may refer to a world system of political domination or economic exploitation, to a policy of defending or expanding an empire, to an ideology which supports imperial ambitions (the original sense of the word), or even to individual acts of aggression. All of these different usages refer to different aspects of a complex historical process, culminating early this century, in which a few countries came to dominate most of the world, either by direct conquest or by less formal military and economic pressures. (Pre-capitalist empires are clearly a different phenomenon, and will not be discussed here.)

The study of imperialism has mainly been the province of Marxists (see MARXISM) who have presented a variety of theories. All agree that capitalism is the root cause of imperialism, though they agree on little else. They generally explain imperialism in terms of the economic interests of private capital, but they often fail to explain exactly how private interests succeeded in enlisting state support. Some non-Marxists argue for non-economic explanations, some argue that no generalization is possible. Whether a single theory can cover the whole history of modern imperialism is certainly debatable.

The 'classical Marxist' theorists of imperialism, writing in the early years of this century, wanted to explain the emergence of intense inter-imperialist rivalry and bellicose nationalism in Europe in their own time. They therefore had little to say about earlier periods or about the impact of empire on those who were conquered. The main line of argument, following Hilferding and Bukharin, made inter-imperialist rivalry the result of the rise of monopoly. Emerging nationally-based monopolies, linked to banks, sought protection from foreign rivals behind tariff walls, and then sponsored a policy of conquest to expand their protected markets. LENIN, the most quoted if not the most original member of this school, dated the start of the 'imperialist stage' of capitalism at 1900. He blended the Hilferding/Bukharin argument with that of Hobson (a non-Marxist economist), who had argued that surplus capital had to be invested in colonies because home markets were limited by mass poverty.

These theories explain at best only one episode in the history of imperialism. It is hard to see how they could account for the subsequent collapse of formal empire and the effective cessation of inter-imperialist rivalry (unless the USSR is counted as imperialist). Their factual basis is doubtful, anyway, since monopoly was less widespread in the period around 1900 than Marxists claimed, and colonies accounted for only a small fraction of exports and of investment.

Many modern writers, by contrast, focus on the historical roots of the technical and economic backwardness of the Third World. 'Dependency' theorists argue that capitalism is, and has been since the fifteenth century, a world system, in which the 'centre' exploits the 'periphery'. The centre develops, but the periphery suffers the 'development of underdevelopment'. Frank, for example, treats formal imperial rule as almost irrelevant; the centre can always find collaborators to rule on its behalf. The problem with dependency theory, however, is that it cannot explain why some peripheral areas have developed rapidly while others have not.

A third stream of Marxist writing descends from MARX's articles on India (1853). Marx argued that the immediate effects of British rule in the sub-continent had been disastrous, but that the end result would be to start a process of capitalist development. Warren revived this theme; he argued that imperialism ('the pioneer of capitalism') laid the basis for general post-independence development. Again, his theory can be criticized for not explaining the very different fates of different areas.

Marxist writings on 'modes of production' (which are surveyed by Foster-Carter) aim to explain the variations in the impact of imperialism around the globe in terms of the different socio-economic systems encountered by capitalism as it expanded. Non-Marxist historians, notably Robinson and Gallagher, have also stressed conditions in the periphery, arguing that imperial powers preferred to exercise informal control, but were sucked into local conflicts and ended up imposing direct imperial rule for want of a workable alternative. These theories perhaps represent the best way forward for the study of imperialism, but they lack an account of the forces which impelled central states to involve themselves in the affairs of the periphery in the first place. This missing link is provided by an analysis of the economics of capitalism on the lines of Marx (and SCHUMPETER): capitalism fosters continuous economic and technical advance; it was first established in Europe, so Europe gained a decisive lead. At the same time the search for new markets, for exotic products, and for cheap materials drove traders, backed by their home governments, out into the less developed world. The pattern of imperialist penetration depended on the opportunities and costs of the available strategies in each case.

The fall of (formal) empire remains to be explained. After 1945 direct imperial rule became prohibitively costly because of popular resistance, and also unnecessary once capitalism was well established. Trade and investment could proceed without direct political control. Decolonization was accelerated by the weakness of European colonial powers. The USA emerged as the dominant power, and pursued a policy of (relatively) free trade and informal control, subsidizing friendly governments and harassing unfriendly ones. Whether this is 'imperialism' is a debatable matter. As in earlier periods, the future of the periphery will depend mainly on developments in the periphery itself. Some countries are developing rapidly, and will achieve real political independence, while others seem likely to remain weak and dependent, at least for the foreseeable future.   AAB

Reading
†Brewer, A.: *Marxist Theories of Imperialism: a Critical Survey*. London: Routledge & Kegan Paul, 1980.

Bukharin, N.: *Imperialism and World Economy* (1915). London: Merlin, 1972.

Foster-Carter, A.: The modes of production controversy. *New Left Review* 107 (1978) 47–77.

Frank, A.G.: *Capitalism and Underdevelopment in Latin America*. New York: Modern Reader Paperbacks, 1969.

Lenin, V.I.: Imperialism: the highest stage of capitalism (1916). In *Selected Works*, vol. I. Moscow: Foreign Languages Publishing House, 1950.

Marx, K.: *On Colonialism and Modernization*, ed. S. Avineri. New York: Doubleday Anchor, 1969.

Robinson, R.E. and Gallagher, J.E. with Denny, A.: *Africa and the Victorians*. London: Macmillan, 1961.

Warren, B.: *Imperialism, Pioneer of Capitalism*. London: New Left, 1980.

Indian political thought   See HINDU POLITICAL THOUGHT.

individualism   The concept covers a wide variety of ideas, attitudes and doctrines, whose common factor is the systematic according of centrality to the 'individual'. But the 'individual' can be conceived of in many ways, as can the antithesis between 'individual' and 'collective'. Many forms of individualism rely on that antithesis, some on denying it.

The term's history is of interest. Nineteenth-century in origin, it exhibited different meanings in different countries, though by now these have merged. Originating in France in reaction to the Enlightenment and the French Revolution, its French meaning has always tended to be pejorative, signifying the sources of anarchy and social disorder. This was so whether the idea was used by reactionaries, nationalists, socialists or liberals, and despite wide differences about the causes of social dissolution and the nature of a feasible and desirable social order. Its German usage has tended to stress the Romantic idea of individuality, the notion of individual uniqueness, originality and self-realization, applied initially to the cult of individual genius, notably the artist, and developing into an organic theory of community, notably the nation or the state (see ROMANTICISM). In England, the term tended to be used as an epithet for non-conformity in religion, for the sterling qualities of self-reliant Englishmen, especially the middle classes, and for features common to the various strands of English LIBERALISM. In this sense it came to signify the minimum of state intervention, as opposed to socialism or collectivism. In the United States, it early became a catchword for free enterprise, limited government and personal freedom, and the attitudes, forms of behaviour and aspirations held to sustain these. One influential version of this usage was Herbert Hoover's campaign speech celebrating 'rugged individualism'.

Various notable syntheses of these usages can be found. Jacob Burckhardt, fusing the French and German senses, saw in the Renaissance the growth of individualism – with the growth of self-assertion, the cult of privacy and an 'impulse to the highest individual development'. John Stuart MILL brought a German-influenced conception of individuality to his classic statement of liberalism in his essay *On Liberty* (1859). And Alexis de TOCQUEVILLE, observing the individualism of democratic America, was acutely conscious of its threat to public life, through the weakening of social bonds.

Tocqueville's usage is perhaps the most influential among contemporary writers. 'Individualism' was, he argued, of democratic origin and threatened to develop as equality grew: it was 'a new expression to which a new idea has given birth . . . a deliberate and peaceful sentiment which disposes each citizen to isolate himself from his fellows and to draw apart with his family and friends', abandoning 'the wider society to itself', first sapping 'the virtues of public life', then attacking and destroying all others, eventually being 'absorbed into pure egoism' (*Democracy in America*, Book 2, pt 2, ch.

2). He was torn between his admiration for this trait of the American character and his anxieties about its consequences, not least the danger of a pervasive social conformism. This analysis, and its attendant paradoxes, have reappeared many times, not least in American social and cultural criticism.

Another influential contemporary usage of the term is to denote what has also been called 'atomism' in social and political theory – a view of society as constituted by individuals for the fulfilment of ends that are primarily individual, which gives priority to the individual and his rights, seen as existing antecedently to any particular form of social life. The view is typically seen as stemming from the seventeenth century and as exemplified in the SOCIAL CONTRACT theories of Hobbes and Locke and later in the utilitarian tradition (see UTILITARIANISM). Thus Charles Taylor sees atomism as rooted in 'those philosophical traditions . . . which started with the postulation of an extensionless subject, epistemologically a *tabula rasa* and politically a presuppositionless bearer of rights' ('Atomism', p. 210). And C. B. Macpherson writes of 'possessive individualism', also rooted in the seventeenth century, as based on 'a conception of the individual as essentially the proprietor of his own person or capacities, owing nothing to society for them' (*The Political Theory of Possessive Individualism*, p. 3).

A third, commonly understood sense is 'methodological individualism' – a doctrine about explanation, which asserts that no explanation in social science or history can be fundamental or 'rock-bottom' unless couched wholly in terms of facts about or features of individuals: their properties, goals, beliefs and actions. Social wholes or aggregate patterns of behaviour must always be explained, or ultimately explained, in terms of individuals. This doctrine can take various forms, and it continues to be controversial. Some, such as POPPER, see its defence as crucial to liberal politics. Others, from DURKHEIM onwards, have seen its rejection as the first step in sociological understanding. Still others see the debate as fruitless, trading upon different ways of conceiving the individual. The less abstract (and more social) such conceptions, the less contentious methodological individualism becomes, or should become.

A further way in which individualism may be defended, increasingly prevalent in contemporary analytical political philosophy, is to argue for basic HUMAN RIGHTS, protecting the fundamental liberties and interests of individuals, whether on grounds of respecting the separateness of persons, or of according them equality of concern and respect. On both grounds, utilitarianism is now seen as anti-individualistic, summing all individuals' desires into a single system of desire. Whether individualism, thus conceived, requires self-ownership or methodological individualism is in dispute, as is the question whether taking it seriously yields libertarian, liberal or socialist conclusions.   SL

Reading

Arieli, Y.: *Individualism and Nationalism in American Ideology*. Cambridge, Mass.: Harvard University Press, 1964.

Bellah, R.N., Madison, R., Sullivan, W.M., Swidler, A. and Tipton, S.: *Habits of the Heart: Individualism and Commitment in American Life*. Berkeley and Los Angeles: University of California Press, 1985.

Burckhardt, J.: *The Civilization of the Renaissance in Italy*, trans. S.G.C. Middlemore. London: Phaidon, 1955.

Hayek, F.A. von: *Individualism and Economic Order* (1948). Chicago: University of Chicago Press; London: Routledge & Kegan Paul, 1976.

†Lukes, S.: *Individualism*. Oxford: Blackwell, 1973.

Macpherson, C.B.: *The Political Theory of Possessive Individualism: Hobbes to Locke*. Oxford: Clarendon Press, 1962.

†O'Neill, J. ed.: *Modes of Individualism and Collectivism*. London: Heinemann, 1973.

Popper, K.R.: *The Poverty of Historicism*. London: Routledge & Kegan Paul, 1955; Boston: Beacon, 1957.

Taylor, C.: Atomism. In *Philosophical Papers*, vol. 2. Cambridge: Cambridge University Press, 1985.

Tocqueville, A. de: *Democracy in America*, trans. G. Lawrence, ed. J.P. Mayer and M. Lerner. New York: Harper, 1966; London: Fontana, 1968.

industrial society A major concern of nineteenth-century social thinking was to identify the nature of industrialization and to trace its social and political effects. The concept of industrial society was central for some social theorists, pre-eminently SAINT-SIMON and Herbert SPENCER, but the term had a general usage and this common understanding was shaped by other thinkers employing a different terminology to identify modernity – Adam SMITH and commercial society, COMTE and positivist society, MARX and capitalist society.

The main feature of industrial society was taken to be its dedication to material production. From the SCOTTISH ENLIGHTENMENT there emerged the theory that societies were to be distinguished by their characteristic modes of production and economic life. However, what was thought to distinguish the new industrial society was not solely a new mode of production, but a new social imperative – the raising of material production; and when contrasts were sought with past societies, they were found in terms of alternative social objectives – the protection of political hierarchies and the achievement of military dominance. Both this new social imperative and the expectation of its being satisfied were seen as the product of industrialization, and this process was analysed by means of discussion of the division of labour, the market, rationality, and mechanization.

Adam Smith brought the idea of the division of labour into the centre of social debate. For Smith, the division of labour, in the sense of a division of productive effort between town and country and between artisanal skills, was characteristic of all advanced economies. However, a special form of the division of labour had brought about the rapid expansion of production in his own day: the breakdown of the production of artefacts into detailed mechanical tasks which could then be allocated to different workers. The attribution of economic growth to this form of the division of labour became the common coin of socio-economic thinking, and most notably was accepted by Marx.

The development of the concept of the market and the analysis of market operations was the main objective and achievement of CLASSICAL POLITICAL ECONOMY. The expansion of the market came to be seen as one central characteristic of industrialization. Indeed, it seemed an inevitable consequence of increasing division of labour; for Smith, the natural propensity to truck and barter was the basis of an exchange economy, and the greater the specialization of production the more extensive and complex would be market operations. This, it was generally assumed, would be socially beneficial, for the market was the context within which the actions of the self-interested were co-ordinated for mutual benefit.

The third general characteristic attributed to industrialization was a rational and scientific tendency. Faith in science as an engine of social PROGRESS, inherited from the Enlightenment, was based on a number of expectations. Scientific progress would bring technological progress; it would encourage the growth of a moral consensus which would either reinforce or replace crumbling Christian certainties; it would aid the rational organization of production.

Increasingly, it was the first of these, technological improvement, which was seen as the major contribution of science, and the mechanization of production, more especially through the utilization of new power resources, came to be identified as another general feature of industrialization. In this context, the function of capital as a factor of production came to be considered more as the provision of plant and machinery and less as a wage-fund.

What would be the general social consequences of such industrialization? Broadly, there were two different responses to this question. One, which dominated socialist thinking, was that it was not the industrial character of the society that would be ultimately determinant, but the prevailing pattern of property relations. Given the irreconcilable conflict of interests between capital and labour, the outstanding feature of capitalist society would be class conflict. Nevertheless, even Marx could see an opposite tendency within industrialism; one of the sharpest contradictions of capitalism was precisely that between the social character of production and the individualist basis of ownership. It was this tendency that was stressed in the alternative response, which saw the new society as shaped primarily by its industrial character and identified that character as essentially co-operative and consensual. Theorists of industrial society did foresee social conflict as a feature of the transition between older and newer social orders. Ricardian economics indeed explicitly marked out the battle lines between land on the one side and capital and labour on the other. However, it also stressed the identity of interests between capital and labour. Other aspects of industrialization encouraged co-operative and social harmony. Industrial division of labour intensified the economic interdependency of individuals, classes and enterprises, and this in turn would nurture the spirit of co-operation. A market economy depended on competition, but economic competition, in contrast to political rivalry, was essentially pacific and non-violent. What was emphasized was the market as a system of free exchanges rather than as an arena of competition; the persistent association of free trade and the pacification of international relations relied on this emphasis.

The pacific nature of the new order was pointed up in the contrast made by both Saint-Simon and Spencer between military and industrial societies. The weakening of the martial spirit with the advance of civilization had been a common theme of eighteenth-century thought, but those who took up the theme – like Rousseau, Ferguson and Smith – mostly regretted this as a decline. Theorists of industrial society welcomed it as progress. Past military societies had been idle and decadent; the emergent society would foster the higher virtues of industry, foresight and productivity. Above all, past societies had posed political and military domination as the founts of honour. The emergence of alternative values of production would have profound effects upon the state. The role of the state in a society devoted to co-operative production would be minimal. The task of co-ordination of productive activity was managerial and would not require the state, at least in the sense of an apparatus of coercion.

With heightening class conflict and a growing tendency to look to state intervention as a remedy for social and economic dislocation, this vision of industrial society had lost much of its intellectual appeal by the beginning of the twentieth century. The concept had a new lease of life in the 1950s and 1960s as part of the convergence thesis, that western and eastern systems would grow more alike largely under the pressures of a common industrial organization. In part, convergence would come about through the increasing complicity of the state in economic activities in the West; but mainly, it was argued, a more technically skilled and educated workforce, growing affluence and increasing pluralism within the economic sphere would produce a gradual liberalization and democratization in Soviet systems.　　JL

Reading

†Aron, R.: *Eighteen Lectures on Industrial Society*. London: Weidenfeld & Nicolson, 1967.

Brzezinski, Z. and Huntingdon, S.P.: *Political Power: USA/USSR*. New York: Viking, 1965.

†Manuel, F.E.: *The New World of Henri Saint-Simon*. Bloomington, Ind.: Notre Dame University Press, 1963.

Peel, J.D.Y.: *Herbert Spencer: the Evolution of a Sociologist*. London: Heinemann, 1971.

Saint-Simon, H.: *Selected Writings*, trans. and ed. F.M.H. Markham. Oxford: Blackwell, 1952.

Spencer, H.: *The Principles of Sociology*, ed. S. Andreski. London: Macmillan, 1969.

interests　　The idea of interest, as when an individual or group is said to 'have an interest' in a policy or programme, assumes special prominence in a modern society where individuation is highly developed and the role of tradition is attenuated. In such a society the concept of interests is joined to conceptions of RIGHTS, obligations, responsibility, and rationality, and this cluster functions together to define the modern self as an agent and a citizen. Individuals and citizens are the paradigmatic bearers of interests, and to say that an individual has an interest is to provide a presumptive reason for fulfilling it, since one of the ways to show respect for persons is to take their interests seriously, to treat their interests as worthy of support because they (agents or subjects) are the sort of beings whose welfare is intrinsically important. Of course other relevant considerations might override this presumption, in particular the claim that 'special interests' threaten the public interest or the common good or that they are unjust. Each of these reasons for overriding interests refers back to other ways of respecting persons that sometimes come into conflict with supporting their interests.

There are two initial points to note about the vocabulary of interests, then. First, talk about interests in politics is normatively loaded, and this normative investment explains why academic contests over the criteria to govern the ascription of interests are so intense and protracted. Second, the role of interests in political discourse depends upon its established relation to the idea of the self as a person or subject. If this more basic idea were altered in any fundamental way the role and meaning of interests would be disturbed as well.

The most common definition of an interest is probably that of a policy or programme which is preferred by the party involved over other stated alternatives. This definition has the advantage of apparent simplicity and it also appears to respect the choices and judgments of the parties involved over the judgment of the observer (or investigator or activist or official) who takes it upon himself to decide not merely what will be done to the party but what is in the party's interest. But the simplicity and moral superiority of this definition dissolves upon inspection. First, party X may prefer one policy to another, not because it is in X's interest, but because it is just or supportive of the common good even though it goes against X's interests. To reduce all preferences to interests is to place all claims on the same moral plane before appraisal has proceeded very far. Second, X may, through misinformation or, in a more complicated way, through a failure to understand the longer term implications of the policy, prefer a policy which is not in X's best interests. Third, the range of alternatives publicly debated may foreclose consideration of possible options which, had they been on the agenda, would have received the reflective endorsement of the parties involved. Such exclusions might be relatively simple, as when people are able to choose between two types of health insurance but, because of the power of the medical establishment, are not presented with the option of prepaid health care. The issues may be considerably more complex and difficult to appraise, as when it is claimed that the interests of the working class are fostered more fully in a competitive market system than in a system of state ownership of the means of production, or when it is claimed that the

243

interests of future generations require a complete restructuring of the styles of consumption governing modern life.

For all these reasons the simple conception of interests must be abandoned, but it is hard to ascertain what conception to endorse instead. The concept of interests is supposed to guide appraisals of what is best for the self (or, better, it functions in conjunction with a family of such terms to guide those appraisals), but each conception advanced seems to presuppose its own answer. Further, the common intuition that 'interest' is a crucial term of appraisal in politics appears to presuppose that the welfare of the individual should be given primacy in political life.

So debates about the definition of interests soon become invested in larger debates over the appropriate conception of self and the role of the common good in politics. It is indeed the desire to avoid these larger and more theoretical debates which probably explains the persistence with which many social scientists cling to the simple conception of interests despite its defects. To glimpse some of the complexity in the latter debates consider one possible definition of interests designed to avoid problems in the simple conception: 'Policy y is in the best interests of party X if, when enacted, it supports the needs of X over other articulated and possible alternatives.' This definition corrects some of the defects in the simple one. It makes it possible for a policy preference to be at odds with a policy interest. It can be clarified so as to distinguish between moral support for a policy and support because the policy is in one's interests. But the definition shifts the difficult issues from one place to another. It now becomes necessary to determine what human needs are, how they are to be identified, what hierarchy can be established among them, and how competing interpretations of need are to be adjudicated. Is a need a felt disposition or the choice an agent would make upon reflection? If the latter, what establishes one as an 'agent' capable of making rational choices, and what distinguishes an agent from a disturbed or irrational or immature or unreflective human? HOBBES, ROUSSEAU, MILL, HEGEL, and HABERMAS would answer each of these questions somewhat differently. When we start

tracing these connections it soon becomes clear that it is impossible to define 'interests' with sufficient specificity outside the frame of a larger theory and that the appraisal of alternative conceptions of interest eventually becomes bound up in the appraisal of alternative political theories. Those who attempt to bypass this larger process end up presupposing the answers they are trying to establish.

It is understandable, then, that recent literature has shifted away from the attempt to provide an abstract answer to the question of interests towards the question: what is the relation between the interests of an individual and the good of the community? This takes us back to the questions which govern the classic tradition of political theory. Some theorists, led perhaps by John RAWLS, Robert Nozick, and Ronald Dworkin, give priority to the individual in the appraisal of interests, while others, led perhaps by Charles Taylor, Michael Sandel, and Alasdair MacIntyre, give priority to the common good in identifying and appraising the interests of individuals. The latter claim can be stated briefly in this way: the very commitment to the priority of the individual is the endorsement of one contestable conception of the common good over other possible conceptions, and this is so because every specific conception of interests must move within a larger frame which gives it its specificity. To be an individual with specific ideas, standards, interests, and principles one must first be a member of a particular society. Participating within that way of life provides the individual with a settled set of criteria (pre-understandings) within which to make judgments about his or her interests. The common good, in short, has priority over the interests of the individual.

Now the point of making this claim is to pave the way for saying that the conception of the common good which has governed modern, individualist, capitalist, liberal societies has given too much priority to the inclinations of individuals over the claims of the community, the present over the future, and the hopes of the future over understandings inscribed in traditions received from the past (though certainly each theorist will emphasize some of these points over others). Societies that give primacy to individual interests, it is claimed, undermine their own preconditions of existence over the long term. The conception of the common good within which their readings of individual interests are housed contains a self-defeating dialectic.

According to this critique we need to give greater attention to a conception of the common good that emphasizes what we share in common, our obligations to the future, and the relation between the identity of the self and the way of life with which the self identifies. When this is done we become more alert to how common understandings of the good we share sets the frame within which particular interests are defined and evaluated. In an individualist society where economic growth is a precondition of the good life and itself part of the good life, it is in one's interest to improve one's income level, even though there may be overriding considerations which limit the ways or extent to which this may be done. In a communal society where the cultivation of virtue is central to the good shared in common, the single-minded pursuit of wealth is not even conceptualized as an interest to be restricted; it is defined as vice or avarice or as a perversity in need of correction. Similarly, the single-minded pursuit of civic virtue in an individualist society is not conceived as an interest; it is so far outside the institutionalized frame of possible attainments that its pursuit becomes a piece of foolishness or a fantasy or utopian. It certainly becomes too unrealistic to fit within the hard-headed idea of protecting one's own interests. In these · ways the established understanding of the common good licenses a set of pursuits as interests (which may or may not then be accepted as legitimate) and shuffles other pursuits outside this frame. Thus to criticize the common good implicitly or explicitly governing a way of life is also to criticize the range of interests it enables and disables.

Debates over interests can assume many appearances. They can focus on whether rights should have priority over interests, whether real interests should have priority over perceived interests, whether one conception of the common good provides a superior frame to others in defining and appraising interests. They can also centre on the conception of self most appropriate to the characterization of interests. The communalist and the individualist diverge in their conception of self and this difference infiltrates into their respective conceptions of interests. But the importance of the conception of self might best be brought out by seeing how a genealogist in the tradition of FOUCAULT would challenge both the above conceptions of self and interest. Any particular formation of self and the common good, says the Foucaultian, is a social artefact imposed upon material which is, at least in some respects, resistant to the formation. For the self to be formed as an interest-bearing subject (or person or agent) it must be organized in a particular way. There is thus a politics by which the self becomes an agent of self-interest as well as one by which its interests are fulfilled and contained. An examination of the politics of modern individualization and collectivization should concentrate on the disciplines which constitute the self as a bearer of rights, interests, and virtues, and the losses which accompany these achievements.

The Foucaultian account is of course highly contestable, but the terrain he has charted in one particular way is itself ripe for exploration. Debates concerning the primacy of rights over interests, or the individual over the community, are now infiltrated by considerations which reveal what these opponents have in common and what political issues have been obscured by the predominance of these debates. This is all to the good, since the established debates have become rather sterile.   WEC

Reading

Barry, B.: The public interest. *Proceedings of the Aristotelian Society* supp. vol. 38 (1964) 1–18.

†Benn, S.I.: Interests in politics. *Proceedings of the Aristotelian Society* 60 (1959–60) 123–40.

†Connolly, W.E.: The public interest and the common good. In *Appearance and Reality in Politics*. Cambridge: Cambridge University Press, 1981.

†Flathman, R.: *The Public Interest*. New York: Wiley, 1966.

Foucault, M.: *Discipline and Punish* (1975), trans. A. Sheridan. London: Allen Lane; New York: Pantheon, 1977.

MacIntyre, A.: *After Virtue*. Notre Dame, Ill.: University of Notre Dame Press, 1981.

Sandel, M.: *Liberalism and the Limits of Justice*. Cambridge: Cambridge University Press, 1982.

Schultze, C.: *The Public Use of Private Interest.* Washington DC: Brookings Institute, 1977.

international law That body of rules and usages which collectively govern the relations between and among states. Depending on context, 'international law' can refer to any of four somewhat different things, singly or in combination.

(1) *Positive international law* is the corpus of specific agreements (treaties, conventions, declarations, protocols) that states have made between or among themselves and by which they have formally consented to be bound.

(2) *Customary international law* is the unwritten body of customary behaviour known by historical record and followed by informal consensus.

(3) The *principles of international law* are those ideal principles, such as that of 'humanity' in the law of war, that are held to underlie both customary and positive international law.

(4) Finally, the *theory of international law* is the province of the class of writers, collectively called publicists, analogous to 'jurisprudence' in domestic law.

Properly understood these four categories are not independent types of international law but various aspects of the same reality or, as in Article 38 of the Statute of the International Court of Justice, four definitive sources for the determination of law in the adjudication of particular cases. The four are not, in any case, formally equal: the principles of international law underlie both positive and customary international law, while the writings of the publicists provide systematic theoretical commentary on the other three, their inter-relations, and how to apply them concretely in specific kinds of cases.

In its narrowest sense, as positive law, the sanctions of international law and the agents of sanction are those explicitly stated in the agreements themselves; further, the interpretation of the meaning of these agreements lies with the states party to them – except when the parties to a dispute consent to be bound by some third party, as in cases submitted to the International Court of Justice and cases of arbitration where some other state or group of states besides the disputants are given the right

to settle the conflict in question. This is not positive law in the sense Georg Schwarzenberger has called the 'law of power', by which a superior authority legislates for those it governs and possesses the force to impose obedience to the rules of behaviour it lays down. In international law there exists no such single superior authority, and the ability to use force to impose a desired pattern of international behaviour always depends on the agreement of the states actually possessing that force to employ it in the service of such ends.

Still, even domestic law meets the tests implied by the 'law of power' ideal only in the case of totalitarian or authoritarian societies where the ruling individual or party is unambiguously in control. In societies where the law is based, like international law, on the principle of consent of the governed, there are also elements of what Schwarzenberger has called the 'law of coordination' and the 'law of reciprocity', and in fact international law almost entirely reduces to these two types.

'Coordination' refers here to the orchestration of efforts by the whole body of individual states so as to promote and serve their collective good; such functioning can be seen clearly in such instruments as the General Agreement on Tariffs and Trade (GATT), rules relating to international use of certain constricted waterways, and efforts to control environmental pollution across international boundaries. Apart from anything that may be explicitly stated in particular agreements, the sanctions implicit in such law of coordination are precisely the undesirable results that could be expected should the effort at coordination break down. These are none the less real for not being imposed by some higher authority.

Reciprocity in international law is most often present in the negative cautionary principle that states ought to avoid taking actions detrimental to other states, with the latter having the right to retaliate for such actions. Whereas the principle of coordination has to do with matters in which all parties benefit from orchestrating their efforts communally and unilateral action produces results disadvantageous to the actor, the principle of reciprocity has to do with matters in which unilateral action may produce benefits to the actor. In such cases the fear of reciprocal reaction serves to inhibit self-seeking. Much international law, particularly the law of war, depends on the deterrent force of such fear. Thus, for example, the Charter of the United Nations (in Articles 2 and 51) explicitly preserves the right of national or regional self-defence because without it some states might be encouraged to become predators. Except for the case of gratuitous harm, which it is in no nation's interest to sanction, the protection given in the Geneva Convention rests on the principle of reciprocity. The killing of prisoners of war, for example, might at times be militarily advantageous were it not for the threat of having one's enemy do the same to one's own captured combatants. Examples of the incorporation of the principle of reciprocity in international law outside the law of war include the conventions protecting ambassadors and the mutual recognition of national boundaries and territorial limits at sea.

While today it enjoys a general consensus of nations all around the globe, international law is fundamentally a product of western cultural experience and reflection upon that experience. Its deepest roots reach back into the classical era, and specifically to conceptions of law and the inter-relations among peoples framed in the late Roman empire (see ROMAN LAW). In the Middle Ages civil and canon lawyers alike reflected on the ideas of natural law (*jus naturale*) and law of nations (*jus gentium*) inherited from Roman civilization. The nascent JUST WAR tradition, the direct progenitor of the modern law of war, incorporated many of the benefits of such reflection. The ideas of *jus gentium* and *jus naturale* remained strong in the modern period, and early naturalistic publicists such as VITORIA, SUAREZ, and GROTIUS recast the medieval inheritance so as to define the conceptual basis on which modern international law is founded. Medieval canon lawyers and theologians had held that it was possible to know natural law through such sources as Hebraic and Roman law, but also through revelation, since revealed law encompassed the law of nature. Later theorists rejected the latter claim; for Grotius, Roman law and practice, together with what he knew about more primitive peoples, provided the best window on natural law. For him it set down only minimal standards of conduct. Beginning with Vattel the law of nature assumes the more lofty character of general principles from which particular positive laws may be derived. When a modern writer such as Myres McDougal employs the term 'the principle of humanity' he is invoking a natural-law concept like that found in Vattel, but very different from that present earlier in Grotius.

The idea of *jus gentium* has undergone a similar transformation. For the Romans it meant the specific laws of the various tribal groups or settled peoples with whom the Romans were in contact. Within the empire the various *jure gentii* were to be tolerated so long as they did not conflict with Roman law or custom. In the Middle Ages, though, and more explicitly in Grotius, *jus gentium* or 'law of nations' comes to denote the customary 'laws' according to which European states behaved. More restrictive than *jus naturale*, this concept of customary right and justice was broader than the corpus of specific agreements among sovereigns or states that existed at any one time. This latter sense of the term has come down into contemporary usage: when a contemporary international lawyer speaks of *jus gentium*, he is referring to customary international law.

The term 'international law' was first used by BENTHAM, but the idea behind it, that of a settled body of rules by which sovereign entities could conduct their mutual relations, is much older. Perhaps the oldest single element in international law is the idea that ambassadors should be protected while on a mission; yet the oldest major portion of modern international law is the law of war, which derives directly from earlier just war tradition. Antecedents for contemporary ideas of international organization may be pushed back through medieval Christendom to the *pax Romana*; yet a more plausible (and more recent) source of this part of international law is the various schemes of 'perpetual peace' that were produced during the Enlightenment era. Probably the earliest systematic precedent for a set of mutual agreements among sovereign entities regulating their inter-relationships were those among the Italian city-states in the late medieval–early modern period.

The immediate antecedents of contemporary international law belong chiefly to the nineteenth century. The law of maritime war and the rights and duties of neutrals began to be developed in the Napoleonic period. The basic principles on which maritime international law has been built were first stated in the Declaration of Paris (1856), and codification of the law of war began with the United States army's *General Orders No. 100* (1863) and the first Geneva Convention (1864). All these aspects of international law have become greatly more specific since their initial statements. In particular the law of war (or, as it is now generally termed, the 'law of armed conflicts') has moved markedly from the realms of custom and morality to that of positive international agreements on specific issues in the conduct of hostilities.

Besides the types of subject matter mentioned above, which have been perennial elements in international law, an important development in twentieth-century international law has been towards the definition of HUMAN RIGHTS (as distinct from the rights of persons implicit in their citizenship in one or another state) and the effort to extend protection to individuals in the name of such rights.

Structurally, two major and somewhat conflicting lines of development may be noted in contemporary international law. One is the effort to identify and incorporate into codified positive agreements elements of customary international law and the principles of international law. In short, this is an effort to make positive law out of *jus naturale* and *jus gentium*. The developments within the law of war and, recently, the law of the sea best illustrate this trend. In general, this line of development assumes the continuation of the present system of state sovereignty and remains within that system. By contrast, the second broad theme is that of efforts to enhance international order (or 'world order') at the expense of national sovereignty. These two approaches to the development of international law are not entirely contradictory; yet they clearly represent two diverse conceptions of what is possible in relations among nations and in the legal regulation of such relations. JTJ

Reading

De Visscher, C.: *Theory and Reality in Public International Law*. Princeton, NJ: Princeton University Press, 1967.

†Falk, R.A.: *The Status of Law in International Society*. Princeton, NJ: Princeton University Press, 1970.

Hyde, C.C.: *International Law*, 2nd edn. Boston: Little, Brown, 1945.

Kelsen, H.: *Principles of International Law*, 2nd edn. New York: Holt, Rinehart & Winston, 1966.

Lauterpacht, H.: *The Function of Law in the International Community*. Hamden, Conn.: Archon, 1966.

——: *International Law and Human Rights*. New York: Garland, 1973.

McDougal, M.S. and Feliciano, F.P.: *Law and Minimum World Public Order*. New Haven and London: Yale University Press, 1961.

Oppenheim, L.: *International Law*, 8th edn. London and New York: Longmans, Green, 1955.

Schwarzenberger, G.: *A Manual of International Law*, 5th edn. London: Stevens, 1967.

Stone, J.: *The Province and Function of Law*. Cambridge, Mass.: Harvard University Press, 1950.

investiture controversy Sparked off by a reforming papacy under Gregory VII (Hildebrand) (1073–85), this was a three-sided battle between secularized bishops with vast temporal wealth and power at their disposal, an imperial power that sought to become more than a pliant head of a hierarchy of feudal vassals of near-equal power, and a morally reforming papacy. The papacy was concerned to remove the investiture of spiritual authority from the hands of laymen, leaving royalty with the power to invest only with temporalities. Gregory also appears to have argued for the papal use of deposition of a temporal monarch – 'that the Pope may absolve subjects of unjust men from their fealty' (*Dictatus Papae*). The conflict came to a head in 1077 when the German emperor Henry IV was made to do penance for his 'misdeeds' in the snows of Canossa. (See MEDIEVAL POLITICAL THOUGHT.)

JC

Reading

Fliche, A.: La réforme grégorienne et la reconquête chrétienne (1057–1123). In *Histoire de l'Église*, vol. VIII, ed. A. Fliche and V. Martin. Paris: Bloud & Gay, 1950.

Tierney, B.: *The Crisis of Church and State*. Englewood Cliffs, NJ: Prentice-Hall, 1964.

Islamic political thought The Koran does not contain a theory of politics. Like other scriptures, it is a text for all occasions, to be referred to, deferred to, and quoted, all in a ceaseless interpretative enterprise. What the Koran does contain are general maxims and injunctions to which specific meaning has been imputed by generations of Muslim authors. The three broad genres of political theorizing in Islam – the religious and juristic, the philosophical, and that expressed in Mirrors-for-Princes – have all drawn on the Koran in support of the severe hierarchical (though not inclement) authoritarianism which they share.

Religious and juristic thought
The religious and juristic genre is available in two versions, corresponding to the major denominational division of Islam into Sunnite and Shiite; Sunnites hold that political and religious authority should be vested in the person of an imām-caliph belonging to the tribe of Quraish, to which Muhammad belonged, while Shiites limit legitimacy to the line of Muhammad's cousin Ali with differences regarding the narrower definition of the incumbent. And while the Shiites hold that their position is justified by the specific designation by Muhammad of Ali as his successor, and consequently regard the imamate in the line of Ali as an article of dogma, Sunnites have generally based their position on traditional consensus – consensus being a major source for legislation. Scholars of both denominations have occasionally employed another argument for the necessity of having an imām, that political authority in general is rendered necessary by the innate inadequacy of individual men, who therefore convene to appoint an authority capable of imposing order and justice on the community thus formed.

As Sunnism was the party of order and government, it relegated the issue of the perfect caliphate to the realm of utopia; only the first four caliphs, the last of whom was Ali (d. 661), conformed to the ideal in varying degrees. True caliphate had become sullied with kingship (*mulk*), but the eschatological corollaries of this implicit assumption, which provided much sustenance to the Shiites, were subdued and removed from the political to the devotional

sphere of life. The early history and prehistory of Sunnism, and of the theory of the caliphate, still awaits detailed research, but from the days of the great traditionalist and unambiguous Sunni, Ahmad Ibn Hanbal (d. 851), the Sunni conception of the caliphate became concrete legislation rather than speculative theory. Ibn Hanbal himself conceded that the caliphal office need not necessarily be held by 'the most excellent' (*al-afdal*), but could legitimately be discharged by 'the less excellent' (*al-mafdūl*).

The most systematic exposition of the Sunni theory of the caliphate is that of Māwardī (d. 1058). The caliphate, according to the tradition he represented and formalized as statutes of public law, is incumbent upon the community and falls under *mu'āmalāt*. Islamic law divides rights into those of God (*ibādāt*, devotions), and those of man (private and public law, *mu'āmalāt*). The caliphate is instituted as a vice-regency of the Prophet Muhammad, and its incumbent is the guardian of religion as well as pastor of worldly affairs. A caliph is either designated by the community represented by an elite (*ahl al-hall wal-'aqd*), or named by a ruling caliph. In a later development, Ghazālī (d. 1111) introduced the idea that a caliph might legitimately be designated by an overpowering temporal, usually military, authority, whereby caliphal and sultanic authorities may co-operate in the maintenance of order and the upholding of Islamic law. This same idea of a temporal-spiritual co-operation implying the stripping of the caliphate of its political and military functions had been foreshadowed by Māwardī, who decreed admissible the usurpation by a powerful martial authority of the political prerogatives of the caliphate, provided the sultan protected the caliphate, applied Islamic law, and extracted canonical taxes.

In this context of reduced temporal competence, the caliphal incumbent had to conform to a number of conditions, including moral probity as required by legal witnesses, Quraishite descent, and learning as required by a judgeship. Though Ghazālī relaxed some of these requirements, and though some jurists admitted the legitimacy of the coexistence of more than one caliph, the canonical theory was never shelved, but kept in abeyance. The essential conception of state institutions such as the Vizirate, the Mint, military command, and the legal and devotional hierarchies as extensions of the caliphal office was never revised.

There were, however, alternative theories arising from the temporal powerlessness of the caliphs. Ibn Jamā'a (d. 1333) regarded any authority as legitimate and transferred to sultanic authority the provisions of constitutional theories worked out in the Sunni legal tradition. His more radical contemporary Ibn Taimiyya (d. 1328) characteristically confronted mundane imperfection in a direct manner, and denied the mandatory character of the caliphate outright. The presence of a caliph is not, as in classical theory, an obligation incumbent upon the community of Muslims. The heirs of the Prophet are the class of 'ulamā, religious and legal scholars, he maintained, in line with many members of this learned class. State and religion are indissolubly linked, for without the state religious authority and duties cannot be properly maintained, and without religion the state will become sheer tyranny. Ibn Taimiyya then put forward legal statues for the proper order of life in accordance with the sharā'a, Islamic law, which the sovereign was to enforce and guard.

The question of order lies at the root of all these theories and variations on theories. The good order of the world requires absolutist authority, and obedience is owed to the caliph as it is owed to the sovereign. Insurrection against a ruler, no matter how tyrannical or impious he might be, was ruled out in the mainstream of Sunni theory. The caliphate cannot be impeached, though it might be forfeited by insanity or captivity; the institution of a new caliphal order is meant to accomplish the same providential purpose of keeping the good order of the world, assuring the exercise of religion, and thus preparing for the good order of the world to come.

The Shiites provided the most consistent theories of the public order most conducive to the fulfilment of divine purpose. In an imperfect world not complicated by political involvement such as that incumbent upon Sunni legists, the Shiite conception of the imamate assured the maintenance of absolute religious purpose as well as of order by the community in this world. With the caliphate definitively usurped and transformed into mulk in 680 with the death in the battlefield of Husain, the son of Ali and the third imam, divine purpose is assured in the world by obedience to the impeccable imams in the charismatic line. The Sunnite conception of traditional legitimacy embodied in consensus is rejected in favour of the belief in the divine designation of legitimate authority. The imām is not only impeccable, but infallible by virtue of an esoteric omniscience transmitted from imām to imām and originally conveyed to the world by God; the difference between an imām and a prophet is that the former does not transmit to the world a divine scripture, as Muhammad did the Koran.

To this impeccable authoritarianism is wedded the belief that the good order of the world could not be maintained if in any age an imām were absent. When the twelfth imām disappeared in a cave in 873, it was held that his absence had inaugurated the Occultation, and that he would return as the Mahdī (Messiah) to fill the iniquitous world with justice and rectitude, and to inaugurate a period which prepares for the apocalypse. Thus the coming of the Mahdī closes the cycle of history and returns things to the original Adamic order.

Rather more elaborate is the cyclical theory of the Ismailis, so-called because they vested the legitimate imāmate in Muhammad, the second son of Ismā'īl Ibn Ja'far and the seventh in the line of Ali by their reckoning. Like the Twelvers (so called because of their belief in the return of the twelfth descendant of Ali), the Ismailis too believed in the return of their own Mahdī, albeit within a more elaborate conception of history as consisting of seven great cycles of prophecy and iniquity, the penultimate having been inaugurated by the Prophet Muhammad and the last to be signalled by the return of Muhammad Ibn Ismā'īl. This doctrine was subjected to a variety of adjustments necessitated by the worldly complications connected with the foundation and prosperity of the Ismailis' own mighty state, the Fatimid caliphate (909–1171). Among other things, the Druze faith arose from the belief that the Fatimid caliph al-Hākim, who disappeared in 1021, was God incarnate. It is doubtless proto-Ismaili undercurrents which led to the rise of many a messianic Sunnite political movement, especially in North Africa and Spain, based on belief in the semi-divine character of mystical thaumaturgues and wonder-workers and in the cyclical conception of history involving the transformation of caliphate into kingship. One such movement led to the short-lived state in the Algarve under the mystical saint Ibn Qasī (d. 1151).

Philosophy

Allied to both the mystical and the Ismaili conceptions of the imamate was a very elaborate cosmology and cosmogony, in which analogies and correspondences were established between cosmic and mundane principles. Less literal analogies between the cosmic and political orders were drawn by the philosopher Fārābī (d. 950). In line with the neo-Platonic Aristotelianism prevalent in Islamic philosophy, Fārābī saw creation as a process of emanation along a descending hierarchy. In the same way, the good order of the world depends on placing everything in its proper station. Only thus will the mundane microcosm correspond to the heavenly macrocosm. The world contains a variety of imperfect cities described as oligarchies and other systems. The 'virtuous city' (*al-madīna al-fādila*) is one in which good order is kept by a sovereign in full possession of ethical, rational, and practical virtues. On to this Platonic conception Fārābī attempted to graft Islamic conceptions of prophethood and the imamate. He sometimes called his philosopher-king 'imām', and attributed to him some of the qualifications normally attaching to the caliph. Fārābī accepts the requirement of Islam that the prophet be a lawgiver, but philosophizes this by assuming the soul of the prophet to be united with the Active Intellect. But there is no true attempt at synthesizing Islamic dogma and metaphysics in the work of Fārābī.

In contrast to this bookish utopia, the great neo-Platonic Aristotelian Ibn Sīnā (Avicenna – d. 1037) deduced the necessity of human association along the familiar conventional lines, and then unambiguously affirmed the centrality of *sharī'a* for the good order of the world. He made no attempt to equate the philosopher with the prophet, but elevated the latter to cosmic rungs higher than the former. The prophet, according to Ibn Sīnā, has an intuitive and immediate perception of intelligibles, much like that obtaining in mystical gnosis. It is the prophet, not the philosopher, who is the lawgiver, and authority in this world belongs to an *imām* defined in terms not dissimilar to those already encountered in the classical theory of the caliphate. Philosophy therefore has no immediate bearing upon the world, but seems to be a form of participation in the world of intelligibles, intellectual and gnostic, which is the preserve of the few.

The most pronounced development of this conception came with Ibn Rushd (Averroes – d. 1198). For him, philosophy is a mode of apprehending this world and the heavenly world of which few persons are capable. Dialectical and sophistical modes of apprehension are fitting for the mass of humanity. The letter of dogma, suitable for the mass, is not in itself false, but has an additional, parallel sense to which philosophy provides access. But philosophy does not abrogate dogma, for 'truth does not contradict truth'. Philosophy therefore has no direct bearing on public law; the caliphal order guaranteeing the rule of *sharī'a* is the best form of government. And in this connection Ibn Rushd actively worked on the refinement of *sharī'a* in the context of the theory of *maqāsid al-sharī'a*, of legal 'purpose', a conception akin to that of natural law.

Mirrors-for-Princes

The same practical purpose is clearly behind the Mirrors-for-Princes. Such books are conceived as instruments of rule, from the work of the state secretary Ibn al-Muqaffa' (d. 759), through that attributed to the theologian and littérateur Jāhiz (d. 868), on to the book by the celebrated Vizier Nizām al-Mulk (d. 1092), a treatise by the jurist Turtūshī (d. 1126), the book by Abū Hammū (d. 1386), king of Tlemcen, and many others. Kingship is usually seen as falling into three categories: that based on religion, clearly the best and the most conducive to salvation, that based on reason and assuring the good order of the world, and that of passion and caprice, the sure road to perdition in this world and the next. As instruments of rule, Mirrors-for-Princes contain ethical and practical maxims, sentences, and a wealth of historical examples of rule, good and bad, which are meant to warn and serve as models. They contain no explicit theory of politics except in so far as they affirm the primacy of the sovereign, almost his transcendence, in relation to his subjects, who are a formless mass rather than a body politic, and whose cohesion is assured only by hierarchy. The sovereign is the shadow of God on earth, and relates to his subjects as God relates to His creation, much as in Fārābī's city.

Mirrors-for-Princes thus consist of collections of topics germane to the maintenance of a hierarchical order in which religion is protected by the state and acts, for some, as the foundation of its ethos. The ethical idea that is perhaps most privileged is justice. Justice is the maintenance of things in their proper stations and the regulation of practical life in accordance with the requirements of stability. Abū Hammū expressed this well in his statement that there can be 'no power without an army, no army without money, no money without taxation, no taxation without prosperity, no prosperity without justice'. Justice thus assures the maintenance of both religious and rational government. Caprice fosters injustice.

The same historical presentation and analogical use of example was elevated by IBN KHALDŪN to the status of a systematic science. Ibn Khaldūn was heir to all three Islamic traditions, which are fused in his work, but he had few followers, and he was understood by posterity as a particularly acute contributor to the tradition of Mirrors-for-Princes. Ottoman 'Khaldunism' was of this variety.

Modern Islam
Modern Islamic political thought is differently cast from the tendencies described above, although the juristic and eschatological currents are still present. Perhaps the first significant modern Islamic reformer was Muhammad Ibn Abd al-Wahhāb (d. 1792), whose doctrine is official dogma in Saudi Arabia. He sought to revivify the political and social doctrines of Ibn Taimiyya, and combined with the head of the House of Saud to set up a regime sustained by the *sharī'a* and legitimized by it. But sovereignty (*hākimiyya*) is the preserve of God.

Wahhabism, though attractive to some, had little relevance to more complex societies.

Islamic political thought in the nineteenth century is associated with the names of Jamāl al-Dīn Asadābādī (alias Afghānī – d. 1897) and his pupil Muhammad Abdu (d. 1905). The efforts of the former were concentrated on an attempt to unify all Muslim powers in order to counter colonial encroachment, while Abdu agitated along with him and finally settled in the position of Grand Mufti of Egypt where he worked on reforming the *sharī'a*. Both believed that the Muslims were weak because they had abandoned authentic Islam and allowed non-Islamic superstitions and thoughts to corrupt it. The answer to this situation was a return to fundamentals (Asadābādī was a keen admirer of Luther); like all fundamentalism, this one sought to obliterate what was generally accepted as Islam in order to introduce modernist ideas which could be sustained by reference to canonical texts. Ideas of constitutionalism and positivist motifs are apparent in this reformist effort, especially with Abdu.

Muhammad Rashid Rida (d. 1935) constitutes the culmination of Islamic modernism. A number of fundamental ideas were elaborately formulated during the course of his political, legal, and literary career, which started under Abdu. The caliphate in its classical mould is not possible in the present age, and the next best thing is a caliphal office of an apostolic and supervisory nature. The reform of *sharī'a* along modernist lines and the introduction of extra-*sharī'a* legislation is necessary; such matters are anyway well catered for in terms of the auxiliary, non-canonical provisions and legal methods known to classical Islamic jurisprudence. Of particular importance is Rida's conception of popular sovereignty, which is clothed in the Islamic conception of *shūra* (consultation). Equally modernist are certain strands in Arab nationalist polities, and certain modern Islamic activists such as Mustafa Sibā'ī (d. 1956) have formulated socialist principles of economic and social organization in Islamic language.

More prominent today than accomplished Islamic modernism is radical Islamism that refuses to countenance any compromise with the corrupt present. Hence the generic appellation *salafiyya*, the emulation of pious predecessors at the head of whom is Muhammad. Salafi theory is mainly the work of

Abul-A'lā Mawdūdī (d. 1979) and has had dramatic adepts in radical Egyptian Islamic groups, who are also under the influence of Sayyid Qutb (d. 1965). The main features of this line of thought are emphasis on the concept of *hākimiyya* (already encountered in Ibn Abd al-Wahhāb), and the equally Wahhabi-inspired notion of *hijra*. This last term, used to designate the flight of Muhammad from Mecca to Medina in 622, indicates for its modern adepts the necessity of stepping apart from corrupt society in order to form a *salafi* alternative which adheres to all examples set by pious predecessors. Outside the *hijra*, society is not only corrupt, but impious, and the sole manner of dealing with it is by direct political and military action which seeks to bring about the foundation of a political system conforming to pious paradigms in every sense.

The idea of *hākimiyya* as pertaining to God only has been used by Shiite political theory as well. Unlike Shiite constitutionalism and modernist trends, the theory identified with Ruhollah Khomeini (1902–) grounds in the exclusive sovereignty of God the corollary, unorthodox among Shiites though not without important precedent, that viceregency on earth resides in Shiite ecclesiastics (*velayat-e faqih*). This can be represented by one person – Khomeini himself at the time of writing – or a council of such ecclesiastics. The function of this office is to oversee the establishment of an order according to what one might term a Shiite *salafiyya*. Radical modern Shiite thought which has been influenced by modernist trends, such as that of Abol-Hasan Bani Sadr (b. 1933), sought to grapple with the despotic consequences of this notion, and developed a theory of generalized imamate, whereby every individual is so formed by the Islamic state that he will be able to exercise the judgment and behaviour one expects from a pious ecclesiastic. As in the case of Sunnism, primitivist utopia in Shiite fundamentalism is liable to interpretations both modernist and traditionalist.

AA

Reading

Bosworth, E. *et al.* eds: *Encyclopedia of Islam*. Leiden: Brill, 1960.

†Enayat, H.: *Modern Islamic Political Thought*. London: Macmillan, 1982.

Fārābī: *Idées des habitants de la cité vertueuse*, trans. P. Jaussen. Beirut: UNESCO, 1960.

——: *Al-Fārābī on the Perfect State*, trans. R. Walzer, ed. G. Endress. Oxford: Oxford University Press, 1985.

†Gardet, L.: *La cité musulmane: vie sociale et politique*. Paris: Vrin, 1969.

Ibn Taimiyya: *On Public and Private Law in Islam*, trans. O. Farrukh. Beirut: Khayat's, 1966.

Kerr, M.: *Islamic Reform: the Legal and Political Theories of Muhammad Abduh and Rashid Rida*. Berkeley and Los Angeles: University of California Press, 1966.

Laoust, H.: *Essai sur les doctrines sociales et politiques d'Ibn Taymiyya*. Cairo: Institut Français d'Archéologie Orientale, 1939.

Māwardī: *Les status gouvernementaux*, trans. E. Fagnan. Algiers, 1915; repr. Paris: Sycomore, 1982.

Nizam al-Mulk: *The Book of Government or Rules for Kings*, trans. H. Darke. London: Routledge & Kegan Paul, 1960.

†Rosenthal, E.: *Political Thought in Medieval Islam*. Cambridge: Cambridge University Press, 1958.

Turtushi: *Lámpara de los príncipes*, trans. M. Alarcón. 2 vols. Madrid: Instituto de Valencia de Don Juan, 1930–1.

J

Jacobinism The term derives from the Jacobins, the revolutionary group which, under Robespierre's leadership, imposed the Reign of Terror on France during 1793–4. Used more widely, it is the belief that the will of the people can be represented by a small elite group who act in their name but are not formally accountable. In this sense it has been applied, usually in a critical spirit, to the theory and practice of later groups and individuals, including BLANQUI and LENIN.   DLM

Jefferson, Thomas (1743–1826) American statesman and political philosopher. Jefferson served as governor of Virginia, delegate to the Continental Congress, and third president of the United States, 1801–9. He wrote the Declaration of Independence, the Virginia Statute for Religious Freedom, *Notes on the State of Virginia*, and numerous addresses and letters. Near the end of his life, Jefferson founded the University of Virginia.

Jefferson's early political writings centred around the revolutionary cause of the North American colonies seeking independence from the British Empire. Drawing on the English theory of liberties derived from an ANCIENT CONSTITUTION, and upon John LOCKE's political theory, Jefferson developed a federated theory of the British Empire. In this federated view, all legislative bodies within the Empire (e.g. the British Parliament and the Virginia House of Burgesses) were 'free, equal and independent', and the Crown served merely as an impartial arbiter among these separate legislatures, preserving the rights of each. Given this view, the British Parliament's regulation of the American colonies in the 1760s and 1770s was regarded as a usurpation of the colonial legislatures' prerogatives, and the Crown's support of Parliament was considered tyrannical. Jefferson's views during this period are most succinctly expressed in *A Summary View of the Rights of British America* and the Declaration of Independence.

After the American War of Independence, Jefferson's political writings focused on the formation of a new republic in America. Following ARISTOTLE, Jefferson considered man naturally social, but requiring participation in small democratic communities to cultivate his social and political faculties. Jefferson encouraged the division of Virginia into 'Wards' of 5–6 square miles and 100 citizens to replicate the classical Greek *polis*. He also believed that through participatory DEMOCRACY citizens would recognize the best among them, those of 'wisdom and virtue', whom Jefferson called the Natural Aristocracy. This Natural Aristocracy would then be elected to prominent positions of political leadership and would serve as representatives to the increasingly centralized governments (county, state and national) of the large American republic. In support of this ideal of local direct democracy, Jefferson advocated universal public education and rough economic equality. Advancement in the educational system was to be according to merit, and the state was to grant 50 acres of land to every citizen not holding such. Jefferson opposed the institution of slavery, but advocated a gradual emancipation of black slaves and their resettlement in Africa. He was opposed to women participating in politics.

Jefferson's religious beliefs corresponded to his political theory. A conservative Unitarian, he considered Christian ethics essential to man's virtue as a social being, and to the just, harmonious state. In response to the Established Anglican Church in Virginia, he advocated 'freedom of religion', which he understood as the full expression of all religious beliefs (and non-beliefs), and he hoped that through exposure to such diversity the citizenry would distil the basic ethical teachings of Jesus. (See also CHURCH AND STATE.)

Thomas Jefferson is considered an idealist who lived to see most of his ideals frustrated. The trend in American politics towards centralized national power and an industrial, capitalist ethic led Jefferson to champion the causes of states' rights and agrarian virtue. As such, his late political writings bear a striking resemblance to his early Revolutionary writings: just as he attacked the British Parliament and Crown for usurping the legislative power of the colonial governments, he attacked the national Congress and courts for usurping the power of the state governments.

Because of the depth and variety of his political ideas, Jefferson continues to be cited by a wide range of political movements, including Third World revolutionaries, conservative democrats and radical socialists.   GS

Reading
Becker, C.: *The Declaration of Independence: a Study in the History of Political Ideas*. New York: Vintage, 1958.
Jefferson, T.: *The Writings of Thomas Jefferson*, ed A.A. Lipscomb and A.E. Bergh. 20 vols. Washington, DC: memorial edn, 1903.
————: *The Papers of Thomas Jefferson*, ed. J. Boyd and C.T. Cullen. 22 vols to date. Princeton, NJ: Princeton University Press, 1950–82.
Koch, A.: *The Philosophy of Thomas Jefferson*. New York: Columbia University Press, 1957.
Malone, D.: *Jefferson and His Time*, vols I–VII. Boston, Mass.: Little, Brown, 1948–83.

John of Paris (*c.*1250/4–1304) Dominican publicist. John wrote his *De potestate regia et papali* at the turn of the fourteenth century as a contribution to the debate between France's king Philippe the Fair and the pope Boniface VIII. Here he argued for a separation of politics from theology by insisting that civil authority was autonomous and sovereign in the realm of temporal property, free of ecclesiastical coercion. He took the origins of the state to be natural and the origins of property to be prior to the state. The community has the ultimate sanction of authority. He sketched a middle road which separated ecclesiastical and secular realms of jurisdiction regarding the different, respective internal structures of CHURCH AND STATE, the differing relationship of each to property, and the separate moral influence of each. Unlike MARSILIUS OF PADUA he did not represent the church as an organ of an omnipotent state. John allows the church, corporately, to possess *dominium* (lordship, property ownership) with the pope as dispensator or steward of this collectively owned property. The *dominium* of the corporate church or of individual priests over temporal things does not come to them because they are vicars of Christ and successors of the apostles but by virtue of the concession and permission granted them by pious rulers or from donations of pious laymen.

John's whole argument concerning church and state jurisdiction depends on his narrow understanding of *dominium in rebus* (PROPERTY rights). He established that the traditional *de facto* independence of the monarch and the independence of property-holding individuals could be vindicated *de jure*, because all men have inalienable property rights chronologically prior to secular and spiritual institutions. They acquire rights in things by means of their own labour and industry. Neither prince nor pope has *dominium* or stewardship in the lay world. Indeed, governments are set up to arbitrate in private property disputes. Although God gave men the earth in common, men thereafter came to differentiate private property through labour, and rulers were established to prevent the discomforts of not having an impartial arbiter when property was usurped by those without just title to *dominium*. The prince has the power of jurisdiction over his subjects' property, without subjects alienating their private property rights to him. Rulers are therefore elected by popular consent. Deposition is not only possible but obligatory when the relation of trust between subjects and their rulers is destroyed by the ruler not representing the common welfare but his own. John also discussed the circumstances under which a pope may be deposed, and argued the case for the will of the council as sovereign where the council is made up of members of the whole church.

This radical tract which not only limits papal power in the temporal sphere but also circumscribes monarchs was cited throughout the following centuries, and it has been argued that LOCKE was familiar with its contents.   JC

Reading

†Coleman, J.: Medieval discussion of property: *ratio* and *dominium* according to John of Paris and Marsilius of Padua. *History of Political Thought* 4 (1983) 209–28.

†——: *Dominium* in thirteenth and fourteenth-century political thought and its seventeenth-century heirs: John of Paris and Locke. *Political Studies* 33 (1985) 73–100.

John of Paris: *On Royal and Papal Power*, trans. J.A. Watt. Toronto: Pontifical Institute of Mediaeval Studies, 1971.

John of Salisbury (*c.*1115/20–80) Medieval political theorist influenced by Ciceronian republicanism. John of Salisbury's varied, cosmopolitan interests, scholastic, ecclesiastical and political, brought him into contact with most areas of twelfth-century public life. He is usually recognized as one of those twelfth-century humanists with a taste for ancient authorities and high Latin rhetoric. He was a mirror of his age. Born in Old Sarum, a student in the French schools *c.*1130–40, he studied under the great luminaries of the age including Abelard, William of Conches and Thierry of Chartres. As an ecclesiastical administrator for Archbishop Theobald of Canterbury and an advocate in church courts, he came to work under Archbishop Thomas Becket, playing a role in the latter's tragic life. At the end of his life he was the Bishop of Chartres.

His political theory is expressed in his *magnum opus*, the *Policraticus*, as well as in his *Historia Pontificalis*, his philosophical *Metalogicon*, and in his letters. He travelled widely in France and Italy and is a primary, often unique, source for the period, witnessing the transformation of papal monarchy through the increasing use of appeals to the curia. His knowledge of ROMAN LAW and CANON LAW was extensive, although he does not appear to have been formally trained.

The *Policraticus* (1156–9) is a many-faceted work of political theory. It is a manual of government, a mirror for princes, a moralist's criticism of courtly life, a didactic philosophical treatise, and an encyclopedia of letters and learning. It is perhaps best known for its treatise on tyranny and its examples of evil tyrants who, through God's working, come to bad ends. John is often said to be the first medieval defender of a theory of tyrannicide, but his real position appears to be that tyrants are dealt with by God. His advice therefore is not to take things into one's own hands, since violent resistance, revolution, civil war in state and church have terrible consequences; it is better to suffer, tolerate, and pray, for in the end the tyrant has no safety and no peace. John wrote to warn tyrants, not to advise murderers; rather than defending tyrannicide, his is a theory of tyrants as an extreme opposed to good princes.

According to John, law is a gift from God and is taught to secular rulers by priests. But there is also a natural knowledge of moral law which each man reads in himself through his use of reason. His understanding of this natural law is similar to Cicero's. He calls it *aequitas*, the application by man of his own capacity for reason and right; thus man can answer moral questions where divine law appears to be silent. A true society is both a natural entity and a spiritual body, a mean where men are both animals and saints, and this he says was known in the classical world as a *polis* or a *respublica*. Human society is both a confederation of men and a congregation of Christians, where the natural and divine work together. Thus the decree of the prince must conform to canon law. The good ruler must be a man of the state, a physical expression of the body of right as both a vicar of God and an image of natural equity. John compares the republic to a living organism composed of head and members, the ruler forming the head. His task is to bring subjects' actions into line with divine *aequitas* so that secular law (*lex*) is the form in which *aequitas* is mediated on earth. Because the ruler maintains justice as a servant of divine equity, a free choice in conscience, he is free of outside legal obligation. As God's representative the ruler is the public person and any resistance to governmental power is rebellion against God. The ruler is raised above the terrestrial sphere but he is not autonomous because he is obliged, in conscience, to maintain *aequitas*. The *policraticus*, as an ideal political being, must blend the animal and divine nature of the *polis* he governs. John believed that Henry II had acted like a wild animal in attacking clerical immunities, disrupting the balance of kingly rule by nature and spirit. The clergy and the populace must unite to restore the balance, removing the tyrant who rules only by animal domination and not by *aequitas*.

The *Policraticus* greatly influenced fourteenth-century Italian jurists and French humanists. John's works were also prized as collections of ancient stories, serving as a gateway to antiquity.   JC

Reading
†John of Salisbury: *Policraticus*, bks 4–6 and parts of 7–8, trans. J. Dickinson. New York: Alfred A. Knopf, 1927; bks 1–3 and parts of 7–8, trans. J.B. Pike. Minneapolis: Pol. sci. classics ser., 1938.
†———: John of Salisbury's Memoirs of the Papal Court (*Historia Pontificalis*), ed. and trans. M. Chibnall. London: Nelson, 1956.
Wilks, M. ed.: *The World of John of Salisbury*. Studies in Church History, subsidia 3. Oxford: Blackwell, 1984.

just war In its broadest sense, the term refers to the entire tradition of thought and practice in western culture aimed at determining when the use of force for political purposes is justified, and at setting limits upon even such a justified use. Understood in this way, its component sources and its expressions include religious and philosophical moral thought, legal theory, domestic and international customary and positive law, and military theory and practice. In many contexts, however, the term is used in more restricted ways. One common specialized use attaches only to the classic form of just war theory achieved in the Middle Ages, with different terminology for other stages in the development of the broader tradition. In this light international lawyers such as J. B. Scott regard just war theory (medieval) and international law (modern) as two phases of development of the same continuous body of thought (see also INTERNATIONAL LAW); similarly, W. V. O'Brien speaks of 'just war–limited war tradition', arguing that the idea of limited war is the

contemporary expression of the just war idea. Theological ethicists such as Paul Ramsey employ the term to refer mainly to that component of the broader tradition derived from Christian theological sources, and Roman Catholic authors typically narrow the meaning still more when they speak of the 'just war doctrine' of Catholic moral theology. The breadth and continuity of the overall tradition may be recognized even when the meaning of the term 'just war' is restricted in such ways as these or others. (See further Johnson, *Ideology, Reason, and the Limitation of War* and *Just War Tradition*.)

Content of just war tradition
The just war tradition has displayed noticeable diversity in adapting to the particular needs of time and place and the changing character of war. It is not a single theory or doctrine, but is best conceived as a framework of thought containing many theories and doctrines, whose continuing relevance is the result of constant debate over the precise meaning or content of the various just war criteria. J. F. Childress refers to these criteria as statements of 'prima facie duties' regarding the morality of the use of force; this emphasizes their character as a framework of thought typical of western moral reflection on war.

In its classic form as achieved by the close of the Middle Ages the just war tradition has two main divisions, usually designated by the Latin terms *jus ad bellum* and *jus in bello*, having to do respectively with the question of whether force is justified in a given instance and with the restraints that ought to be imposed on justified uses of force. Each of these divisions is further specified by various criteria.

The *jus ad bellum* of just war tradition includes the requirements that there be a *just cause*, a *right authority* for initiating the use of force, a *right intention* on the part of the party/parties employing such force, that the resort to force be *proportional* (not doing more harm than good), that it be a *last resort*, that it be undertaken with *the end of peace* as its goal, and that there be a *reasonable hope of success*. In the Middle Ages three types of 'just cause' were recognized: to retake something wrongfully taken, to punish evil, and to defend against an attack either planned or in progress. All three ideas can also be found in Roman thought and practice of war in the late classical era. In twentieth-century international law self-defence against an armed attack in progress is the major justification admitted for resort to force; stress on arbitration for the settlement of disputes before the 'last resort' tends to undercut the other classic justifications for use of force. 'Right authority' for the Romans meant the highest civil authority; in the late Middle Ages it referred to nobles with no feudal superior; in the modern period it is associated with the *compétence de guerre* that attaches to a state and, implicitly, to the sovereign (person or parliamentary body) that rules that state; finally, recent international law has drifted towards allowing some measure of 'right authority' to revolutionary insurgent groups. 'Right intention' is a specifically moral concept; in the words of its originator, St AUGUSTINE, it rules out 'the desire for harming, the cruelty of avenging, an unruly and implacable animosity, the rage of rebellion, the lust of domination and the like'.

These are the major concepts within the *jus ad bellum* of just war tradition; the others are essentially prudential concerns that remain in much the same form throughout history. Two exceptions to this general observation may be noted: one is that, as mentioned above, international law has strengthened the criterion of 'last resort' by stressing arbitration as the morally preferred way of settling international disputes; the other is that for many persons the destructive potential of nuclear weapons implies that in any nuclear war the criterion of proportionality would necessarily be violated. This last is the position variously known as 'nuclear pacifism', 'modern-war pacifism', or 'just-war pacifism'. Rather than a genuine instance of PACIFISM, it is a particular judgment about the morality of this kind of modern war from the perspective of just war tradition.

The *jus in bello* is defined by two main ideas, the principle of *proportionality of means*, requiring that means of force be avoided that cause gratuitous or otherwise unnecessary destruction, and the principle of *discrimination* or *noncombatant immunity*, requiring that noncombatants should be protected so far as possible from the ravages of war and, in any case, should enjoy protection from direct and intentional harm. The classical period did very little about *in bello* restraints on war; as GROTIUS remarks, the main *in bello* restraint observed in classical antiquity was that instead of killing conquered peoples (combatants and noncombatants alike) the victor might enslave them. Proportionality of means was, in any case, always imposed until the industrial age by the scarcity of resources available for military purposes. In the modern period the term 'economy of force' renders the main idea of the principle of 'proportionality of means'. Yet for a while in the Middle Ages, and at various times since, efforts have been made to outlaw certain types of weapons as necessarily disproportionate. Such efforts are an important feature of twentieth-century international law and moral reflection about restraint in war.

As for the principle of 'noncombatant immunity', medieval efforts defined noncombatancy in terms of two criteria: social function and ability to bear arms. Ecclesiastics, pilgrims, townspeople, and peasants on the land were noncombatants for the first reason; women, children, the aged, and the infirm were noncombatants for the second. Persons of either sort could forfeit their protected status by bearing arms. Much of modern international law, especially the various Geneva Conventions, has to do with designating noncombatants and specifying their rights; yet in the twentieth century noncombatants have by no means been spared the effects of war. Indeed, one element in strategic nuclear deterrence is the threat to noncombatant populations posed by the weapons in question, even though they may be nominally targeted on legitimate military objectives.

Historical development of just war tradition
The deepest roots of just war tradition are to be found in classical Hebraic, Greek, and Roman practices and reflection on the experience of war. By the end of the classical era Roman law and practice had developed notions of just cause, of the authority necessary to make war, and of the necessity of calculating the evil likely to be done against the good to be achieved by resort to arms (proportionality). Christian theorists such as St Ambrose of Milan and St

Augustine simply took these ideas into their own thought on war, adding the Hebraic idea of war commanded by God (holy war) and introducing mitigations implied by Christian *caritas* (love). Both Ambrose and Augustine argued that the innocent should be defended in war, but neither they, nor Roman law in their time, developed a coherent notion of noncombatant immunity.

All these restraints on the use of military force were generally ignored in the West from the time of Augustine (fifth century AD) to the era of the Peace of God and the Truce of God (tenth and eleventh centuries). Like the earlier developments from the classical era, these early medieval efforts to restrain war in themselves formed no systematic body of thought on right usage in war. Development towards coherence began with Gratian's *Decretum* (*c.*1148), a magisterial compilation of CANON LAW that knitted together various fragments from Christian tradition under topical headings. On the subject of war two successive generations of canonists (the Decretists and the Decretalists) and theologians such as Peter of Paris and Thomas AQUINAS built further on the base laid down by Gratian. At about the same time secular theorists were rehabilitating elements from Roman law, and within the knightly class the code of chivalry was coalescing, contributing its own restraints on the use of armed force. By the time of the Hundred Years War these various lines of development had converged into a broad cultural consensus on the justification and limitation of war in which all the major structural elements of just war theory as identified above were in place.

In the sixteenth and seventeenth centuries a succession of theorists including VITORIA, SUAREZ, Gentili and GROTIUS brought about a transformation in the received just war tradition and out of it defined the theoretical basis of modern international law. At the same time the chivalric code was transformed into a body of externally imposed rules of military discipline. In the eighteenth century this discipline combined with strategic concerns to produce the classic era of limited warfare. Vattel's work on international law in this century reflects both the thought of previous theoretical writers such as Grotius and the contemporaneous practice of limited warfare. In the nineteenth and twentieth centuries positive international law both clarified the inherited tradition and, as seen above, somewhat modified it.

The twentieth century also brought a recovery of just war tradition by moralists. Historical work (see Scott; Vanderpol) began during the first world war. Following the second world war the nuclear age spurred normative debate over morality and the use of force: theologians such as John Courtney Murray and Paul Ramsey and philosophers such as Elizabeth Anscombe began explicitly to employ just war criteria as tools of moral analysis. Michael Walzer and William V. O'Brien are notable examples of political scientists who have done the same. Historical work continued (see Johnson, *Ideology, Reason, and the Limitation of War* and *Just War Tradition*; Russell) alongside more focused applications of just war reasoning to contemporary issues (see Childress; Johnson, *Can Modern War Be Just?*). Other contemporary lines of development of the broad just war tradition include the continuing expansion of the international law of war and refinement of military manuals on the law of war. JTJ

Reading

(See also under GROTIUS, INTERNATIONAL LAW, SUAREZ and VITORIA.)

Childress, J.F.: *Moral Responsibility in Conflicts*. Baton Rouge and London: Louisiana State University Press, 1982.

Gentili, A.: *De jure belli libri tres*, trans. J.C. Rolfe. Oxford: Clarendon Press; London: Humphrey Milford, 1933.

†Johnson, J.T.: *Ideology, Reason, and the Limitation of War*. Princeton, NJ and London: Princeton University Press, 1975.

†———: *Just War Tradition and the Restraint of War*. Princeton, NJ and London: Princeton University Press, 1981.

†———: *Can Modern War Be Just?* New Haven, Conn. and London: Yale University Press, 1984.

Murray, J.C.: *Morality and Modern War*. New York: Council on Religion and International Affairs, 1959.

O'Brien, W.V.: *The Conduct of Just and Limited War*. New York: Praeger, 1981.

Ramsey, P.: *The Just War*. New York: Scribner, 1968.

———: *War and the Christian Conscience*. Durham, NC: Duke University Press, 1961.

†Russell, F.H.: *The Just War in the Middle Ages*. Cambridge: Cambridge University Press, 1975.

Scott, J.B.: *The Spanish Origin of International Law*. Oxford: Clarendon Press; London: Humphrey Milford, 1934.

Vanderpol, A.: *La Doctrine scholastique du droit de guerre*. Paris: A. Pedone, 1919.

Vattel, E. de: *The Law of Nations; or Principles of the Law of Nature*, trans. C.G. Fenwick. Washington: Carnegie Institution, 1916.

†Walzer, M.: *Just and Unjust Wars*. New York: Basic, 1977.

justice At least since the time of Plato, justice has been regarded by political thinkers of all persuasions as one of the primary qualities of a good political order. Indeed there has been a temptation to regard justice as the all-encompassing political virtue, so that the good society and the just society are one and the same. Strong though this temptation is, it should be resisted. The idea of justice draws our attention to a particular feature: namely that people, as separate individuals, receive the treatment that is proper or fitting for them. This marks it off from other desirable qualities, especially from those attaching to the overall character of a society: a country can be economically prosperous, successful at war, or artistically fertile without necessarily being just. The best general definition is still Justinian's: justice is the constant and perpetual will to render to everyone his due.

The first distinction that needs to be drawn in amplifying this definition is between what is due to a person by way of benefit and what is due by way of PUNISHMENT. Justice in punishment requires that three conditions be met:

(1) that punishment should only be inflicted on those found guilty of wrongdoing, using proper procedures;
(2) that punishments be uniformly imposed, i.e. that differences in penalty should always correspond to differences in wrongdoing;
(3) that the scale of penalties should be proportionate to the various misdemeanours being punished – neither too severe nor too lax.

The interpretation of the third condition depends on how punishment in general is viewed – e.g. whether as a means of deterrence or as retribution – and it is therefore more contestable than the first two.

Punishments that exceed the three conditions are unjust; but it is less clear what view we should take if the conditions are fulfilled and yet the offender is let off part or all of his punishment. This has traditionally been seen as an exercise of clemency or mercy, but there is dispute as to whether it is proper to set justice aside in this way. Some philosophers have held that justice sets upper limits to punishment, but does not stand in the way of mercy, which is the quality that perfects it, an idea famously expressed by Shakespeare: 'And earthly power doth then show likest God's/When mercy seasons justice.' Others have echoed KANT's view that the demands of justice must be carried out regardless of circumstances: 'Even if civil society were to dissolve itself ... the last murderer remaining in prison must first be executed, so that everyone will duly receive what his actions are worth ... ' (*Metaphysical Elements of Justice*, p. 102).

When we turn to the broader question of what justice requires in areas where no wrongdoing is involved, we find an enormous diversity of view. Historically there has been a strong tendency to see close connections between justice and LAW; to be just, whether for a person or for a public authority, is to be law-abiding. The law embodies general rules specifying how people are to behave towards one another, and in particular cases determines what each is entitled to by way of property, services and so forth. Justice means respecting those conventions and entitlements. For most thinkers in this tradition, however, the law itself had to meet certain moral requirements if it was to be regarded as just. This was often expressed in the terminology of natural law: behind the positive law there stood a moral law, discoverable by reason, and in cases of conflict it was the latter that defined justice. Yet although this doctrine approached human law critically, it was usually interpreted so as to have broadly conservative implications. The assumption was that, in most cases, existing laws simply filled out natural law more explicitly. Justice, therefore, also had a conservative character. It was the virtue that protected a social order in which each person had a legally defined place.

Yet even in pre-modern times, this dominant understanding co-existed with other ideas that to some extent prefigured the modern notion of social justice. The exchange of goods and services in the market could not be entirely regulated by law and yet it seemed to raise questions of justice between the contracting parties. ARISTOTLE, in a famous discussion, gave a separate treatment of commercial justice. For exchanges to be fair, he argued, there had to be a common standard of value by which the products of the two parties could be measured. A somewhat similar idea lay behind the medieval notion of the just price. It was not sufficient for justice that an exchange was voluntary and within the bounds of law. The parties to it were obliged to sell their commodities at a just price – though as to how the latter was to be established, whether by tradition or by observing current prices in the market, the medieval commentators were less clear.

A second idea, again to be found in Aristotle, was that goods ought in certain circumstances to be distributed on the basis of merit. Aristotle had mainly in mind distribution of public funds, though he may also have been thinking of the division of benefits within private clubs and partnerships. As a principle regulating public distribution, this was clearly more at home in a republic such as Athens, where all citizens were nominally equal, than in later feudal societies, where hierarchy and tradition were the main determinants of distribution.

In contrast, the idea of need had a firmer place in medieval thinking about justice. Although the general duty to relieve the needy was usually regarded as a duty of charity, it was often said that people with superfluous goods – goods over and above those required to maintain them in their station – had an obligation of justice to help those in need. AQUINAS went further still when he argued that a man in extreme need was entitled to take another man's property to sustain himself.

We see here how beliefs about justice have reflected prevalent social relationships, which they have at the same time helped to constitute. As we move forward into the modern period, the major change is the emergence of the idea of social justice.

Social justice and its critics

To speak of 'social justice' implies that it is realistic to attempt to bring the overall pattern of distribution in a society into line with principles of justice. The term first appeared in political debate in the early nineteenth century (it was employed by, among others, John Stuart MILL) and its use has since become widespread. It rests on two assumptions: first, that social processes are governed, at least in broad outline, by discoverable laws, so that it makes sense to try to reshape society deliberately; second, that it is possible to find a source of power – usually in government – sufficient to carry out the reshaping. There have been two major conceptions of social justice, one embodying the notions of merit and desert, the other those of need and equality.

The first conception entails that each person's social position and material rewards should as far as possible correspond to their place on a scale of merit, an idea also expressed in demands for 'careers open to talents' and 'equality of opportunity'. It implies the ending of hereditary privilege and an open society in which people have the chance to display their desert. So much is common ground; but there are differences of view about what 'desert' means and how it can best be assessed in practice. For some, desert is a matter of contribution: what talents someone has, and how effectively they employ them. Others would argue that talent as such has nothing to do with desert: people deserve reward only for the effort they expend, and perhaps for choosing to expend it in a more or less useful direction. On the issue of assessment, liberal thinkers have often seen the free market as the best mechanism for rewarding desert in practice, arguing that the price someone can command for his products or services is a reasonable indicator of their value to others. Socialist critics of this view have pointed out that market receipts are often affected by factors such as luck and social background which have nothing to do with merit; some have proposed instead that desert should be measured directly, for instance by a public body responsible for fixing salaries in a planned economy.

The second conception entails that goods

should be allocated according to each person's various needs. It is closely allied to an idea of EQUALITY, since a programme which success-fully satisfies needs makes people materially equal in one important respect. The idea of need is, however, notoriously difficult to define precisely (see also INTERESTS). It has to be distinguished from desire or preference, since these notions may encompass quite frivolous items; on the other hand, the needs that someone has must clearly vary according to their basic purposes in life. Although there is a biological core to the concept of need, as manifested in needs for food, clothing and shelter, there is also a large periphery in which needs depend on culturally specific lifestyles. In the face of this variability, need-based concep-tions of social justice have followed one of two broad patterns. The more radical, found in COMMUNISM, allows each person to define his or her needs, and assumes that sufficient resources can be created to meet all needs so defined. The more cautious, found in SOCIAL DEMOCRACY, assumes that a public authority must define needs according to the standards prevailing at a particular time and place. The latter view may allow for a compromise between the claims of need and those of desert – some social resources being allocated on the basis of need through the welfare state, others being allocated according to desert through an econo-mic market or through bureaucratic processes. This is the most popular interpretation of social justice in the West today.

Some theories of social justice avoid giving fundamental place to either desert or need. According to UTILITARIANISM, all questions of distribution are to be resolved by reference to overall consequences; a socially just allocation is ultimately an allocation that produces the greatest sum of happiness. John Stuart Mill's *Utilitarianism* (1861) contains perhaps the most persuasive presentation of this position. RAWLS has developed an alternative theory, the most distinctive element of which is the principle that inequalities in the allocation of goods are permissible if and only if they work to the benefit of the least well-off members of society. This gives the notion of justice an egalitarian flavour, but allows for departures from equality when these serve (for example) as incentives,

creating a greater stock of goods for redistri-bution to the worse off.

A more far-reaching challenge has been posed by critics such as HAYEK and Nozick (see LIBERTARIANISM) who reject the notion of social justice altogether, and argue instead for a return to the traditional understanding of justice as respect for law and established rights. Their arguments begin from different philosophical starting-points, but contain three central claims. First, the notion of social justice assumes that there is some agency responsible for the distribution of benefits in society, whereas in fact this distribution arises through the uncoordinated activity of many agents, none aiming at the overall result. Second, the quest for social justice involves replacing the market economy with a stultifying bureaucracy which tries (albeit unsuccessfully) to exercise complete control over the flow of resources to individuals. Third, this quest also involves fundamental interference with personal FREE-DOM, in so far as people must be prevented from doing as they please with the resources they are allocated if the preferred distributive pattern is to be maintained. Justice, these neo-liberals argue, is a property of processes rather than of outcomes. If the correct procedures for acquir-ing and transferring benefits have been followed, it makes no sense to describe the resulting distribution of resources as either just or unjust.

These arguments, although forceful, are not decisive. The notion of social justice does not presuppose a single distributor of resources, but only that the pattern of distribution depends on major social institutions which may them-selves be altered politically. For instance the relative incomes of employers and employees in a market economy will depend partly on the way in which the law defines the contractual rights of either party, a matter for political decision. This observation also helps to counter the second and third objections. If conceptions of social justice are intended to shape institutions, the idea need not imply that all resources are to be allocated by a central bureaucracy. It might, for example, be preferable to allow many benefits to be distributed spontaneously through a market, while at the same time regulating the background institutions, such as tax and property systems, so that the general shape of the distribution conformed to substantive principles of desert or need. This would also permit each person a considerable, albeit not unlimited, degree of freedom in the use of resources, without sacrificing the justice of the overall distribution.

The debate about social justice illustrates a tension in our thinking about justice in general. On the one hand, justice has to do with rules and procedures: treating people justly means applying the relevant rules to them in a fair way. On the other hand, it has also to do with outcomes: people should end up with whatever it is they deserve or need. A dilemma arises when procedures that appear generally just lead to particular outcomes that are not. Here we are torn between the justice of consistent rule-application and the justice that demands that rules should be abandoned or revised if their results are unacceptable. A satisfactory theory of justice needs to straddle both horns of this dilemma. DLM

Reading

Aquinas, T.: *Selected Political Writings*, ed. A. P. d'Entrèves. Oxford: Blackwell, 1959.

Aristotle: *The Nicomachean Ethics*, ed. W.D. Ross, ch. 5. Oxford: Clarendon Press, 1925.

Hayek, F.A. von: *Law, Legislation and Liberty*, vol. II: *The Mirage of Social Justice*. London: Routledge & Kegan Paul, 1976.

Kant, I.: *The Metaphysical Elements of Justice* (1797), trans. J. Ladd. Indianapolis: Bobbs-Merrill, 1965.

Mill, J.S.: *Utilitarianism* (1861). In *The Collected Works of J. S. Mill*, vol. X. Toronto: University of Toronto Press, 1969.

†Miller, D.: *Social Justice*. Oxford: Clarendon Press, 1976.

Nozick, R.: *Anarchy, State and Utopia*. New York: Basic; Oxford: Blackwell, 1974.

†Pettit, P.: *Judging Justice*. London: Routledge & Kegan Paul, 1980.

†Raphael, D.D.: *Justice and Liberty*. London: Athlone, 1980.

Rawls, J.: *A Theory of Justice*. Cambridge, Mass.: Harvard University Press, 1971; Oxford: Oxford University Press, 1972.

Walzer, M.: *Spheres of Justice*. New York: Basic; Oxford: Martin Robertson, 1983.

Justinian I (482–565) Byzantine emperor. Born in the village of Tauresium near Nis in modern Yugoslavia, and a native Latin-speaker, Justinian was brought to Constantinople as a boy by his uncle, a soldier, who adopted him and had him educated there. The uncle became the Emperor Justin I and Justinian succeeded him as emperor in 527. He immediately initiated a comprehensive programme to restore the greatness of Rome in all its aspects. Like Napoleon, he slept little and had great nervous energy and command of detail. He was much influenced by his wife, Theodora, a former actress, and after her death in 548, he was less active as a ruler.

Territorially, Justinian was able to maintain the eastern frontier with Persia and through the efforts of his generals, Belisarius and Narses, he recovered North Africa from the Vandals and re-established imperial authority over the Ostrogothic kingdom in Italy. At the same time he strengthened the administration of the empire and improved the collection of taxes. These reforms were so unpopular that they resulted in the Nike riots of 532 which nearly cost him his throne.

Exploiting the talents of his brilliant minister Tribonian, Justinian in 528 ordered a complete re-statement of Roman law, with the aim of restoring it to its technical peak of three centuries earlier. Its three main parts, the Digest, Code and Institutes, were completed in 534 (see ROMAN LAW). Justinian regarded the well-being of the state as linked with that of the church and regarded himself as holding supreme religious as well as supreme temporal power. His policy is sometimes called 'caesaropapism' (the subjection of church to state), but in his own view there was no distinction between CHURCH AND STATE. He legislated to enforce ecclesiastical discipline and orthodox doctrine, particularly the view of the Council of Chalcedon that the human and divine natures co-existed in Christ, against the Monophysites who held that Christ was essentially divine and the Nestorians who held that the incarnate Christ had two distinct persons, human and divine. In his great church of Hagia Sophia in Constantinople, consecrated in 537, Justinian claimed to have surpassed Solomon.

In the pragmatic sanction of 554, Justinian ordered the application of his laws to Italy and it was probably then that copies of his codification came there. Although they had no immediate influence, at least one Digest manuscript, later discovered at Pisa and subsequently held in Florence, survived to form the basis for the revival of Roman law studies at Bologna in the late eleventh century.

Justinian's likeness is familiar from the mosaic in the church of San Vitale at Ravenna.

PGS

Reading

Browning, R.: *Justinian and Theodora*. London: Weidenfeld & Nicholson, 1971.

Jones, A.H.M.: *The Later Roman Empire, 284–602: a social, economic and administrative survey*. 3 vols. Oxford: Blackwell, 1964.

K

Kant, Immanuel (1724–1804) German philosopher. Kant was born and died at Königsberg, East Prussia. His philosophical reputation rests on the three *Critiques – Pure Reason* (1781), *Practical Reason* (1788) and *Judgment* (1790). In 1785 he published the *Groundwork of the Metaphysic of Morals*, which first set forth the celebrated categorical imperative always to have a 'good will', to treat persons as ends in themselves, never merely as means to arbitrary ends. Kant's political thought was developed after the French Revolution in *Toward Eternal Peace* (1795), the *Metaphysical Elements of Justice* (1797), and *The Conflict of the Faculties* (1798); its central idea is that politics must 'bend the knee' to morality.

It is plainly Kant's *central* political conviction that morality and politics must be related, since 'true politics cannot take a single step without first paying homage to morals'. At the same time, however, Kant drew a very strict distinction between moral motives (acting from good will or respect for the moral law) and legal motives, and insisted that moral and legal incentives must never be collapsed into each other; this is why he argued (in *The Conflict of the Faculties*) that even with growing 'enlightenment' and 'republicanism' there still will not be a greater quantity of moral actions in the world, but only a large number of legal ones which roughly correspond to what pure morality would achieve if it could. (At the end of time, a purely moral 'kingdom of ends' will predictably not be realized on earth – though it ought to be – but one can reasonably hope for a better legal order which is closer to morality than are present arrangements.) Morality and public legal justice must be related in such a way that morality *shapes* politics – by forbidding war, by insisting on 'eternal peace' and the 'rights of man' – without becoming the *motive* of politics (since politics cannot hope for 'good will').

Given this tension between a morality and a public legal justice which must be related but which equally must remain distinct, it may be that the notion of 'ends' can help to serve as a bridge: for public law certainly upholds some moral ends (e.g. no murder), even though that law must content itself with a legal motive.

Using teleology as a bridge connecting the moral to the political-legal realm is not a very radical innovation, since Kant himself used 'ends' in the *Critique of Judgment* to unite his whole philosophy. He did this by arguing that nature can be estimated (though never known) through purposes and functions which mechanical causality fails to explain, that persons as free agents both have purposes which they strive to realize and view themselves as the final end of creation, and that art exhibits a 'purposiveness without purpose' which makes it (not directly moral but) the symbol of morality. Surely, then, if ends can link – or be thought of as linking – nature, human freedom and art, they can link (much more modestly) two sides of human freedom: namely the moral and the legal realms.

Now if 'good will', in the moral realm, could mean never universalizing a maxim of action which would fail to respect persons as ends in themselves, then morality and politics-law could be connected through Kantian teleology. If all persons had a good will, then they would respect all others as ends – indeed as members of a 'kingdom of ends'; but, although it ought to, this does not actually happen, thanks to the pathological fact that man is radically evil. If, in sum, good will means respect for persons as ends in themselves, and if public legal justice sees to it that some moral ends (such as non-murder) get *observed*, if not respected, then public legal justice in Kant might be viewed as the partial realization of what would happen if all wills were good. In addition Kant frequently suggests that law creates a kind of environment for good will, by bracketing out occasions of political sin (such as fear of others' domination) which might tempt (though never determine) people to act wrongly.

Perhaps Kant's whole position on politics as the legal realization of moral ends is best summed up in two passages, the first from his *Metaphysical Principles of Virtue* (1797), pp. 96–7.

Man in the system of nature . . . is of little significance and, along with the other animals, considered as products of the earth, has an ordinary value . . . But man as a person, i.e. as the subject of a morally practical reason, is exalted above all price. For as such a one (*homo noumenon*) he is not to be valued merely as a means to the ends of other people, or even to his own ends, but is to be prized as an end in himself.

In *The Conflict of the Faculties* Kant translated this very passage – or so it almost seems – into the language of politics:

In the face of omnipotence of nature, or rather its supreme first cause which is inaccessible to us, the human being is, in his turn, but a trifle. But for the sovereigns of his own species also to consider and treat him as such, whether by burdening him as an animal, regarding him as a mere tool of their designs, or exposing him in their conflicts with one another in order to have him massacred – this is no trifle, but a subversion of the ultimate purpose of creation itself. (See *Political Writings*, p. 185.)

On this teleological view, sovereigns deny the rights of man (or perhaps more properly the rights of persons) by treating men as mere means to a relative purpose (e.g. territorial aggrandizement); in Kant's view war, which necessarily treats men as mere means to an immoral purpose, causes the state to attack and subvert morality, when in fact the state and the legal order ought (as qualified goods) to provide a stable context of peace and security within which men can safely exercise the sole unqualified good, a 'good will'. So the notion that

persons are ends who ought never to be used merely as means to arbitrary purposes provides 'good will' with an objective end which is the source of the categorical imperative, and it sets a limiting condition to what politics can legitimately do. Despite what HEGEL says, then, Kantianism is not merely a formal doctrine in which (to quote Hegel's language) 'chill duty is the final undigested lump left within the stomach'.

Kant is clear, moreover, that *citizens* (not mere subjects) in a republic would dissent from war, out of the legal motive of self-love. Therefore republicanism (internally) and eternal peace (externally) are interlocked, absolutely inseparable. This is why Kant says that in 'a constitution where the subject is not a citizen, and which is therefore not republican, it is the simplest thing in the world to go to war' – despite the fact that 'reason as the highest legislative moral power, absolutely condemns war as a test of rights'. Therefore republican citizenship is instrumental to an essential moral end that good will alone may never realize, thanks to human pathology. For Kant, the outside is shaped by the inside; it is that which leads him to say that the first definitive article of eternal peace is that 'the civil constitution of every state shall be republican'.

All of this is brought out by Kant himself in the splendid last pages of the *Metaphysical Elements of Justice*:

Moral-practical reason within us pronounces the following irresistible veto: There shall be no war, either between individual human beings in the state of nature, or between separate states, which, although internally law-governed, still live in a lawless condition in their external relationships with one another. For war is not the way in which anyone should pursue his rights . . . It can indeed be said that this task of establishing a universal and lasting peace is not just a part of the theory of right within the limits of pure reason, but its entire ultimate purpose (*Endzweck*). (See *Political Writings*, p. 174.)

This simply confirms, and ties together, what has been said above: that it is morality itself that vetoes war (doubtless because war treats ends as mere means, persons as mere things); that peace as a moral end can be legally approached by establishing that constitution (namely 'republicanism in all states, individually and collectively') that brings self-loving rational citizens to veto war; that to think that the moral law that forbids war might be misleading is to renounce reason and to fall back on the 'mechanism of nature'; that right, which legally realizes some moral ends (even without good will), has universal and lasting peace as its 'entire ultimate purpose' (*Endzweck*). It is doubtful whether there is any other passage, anywhere in Kant, that so vividly and movingly fills out his notion of a politics that pays homage to the ends of morals. It is a passage whose visionary but sane breadth redeems the drier parts of the *Metaphysical Elements of Justice*. And it confirms what should never have been doubted: that Kant is a political philosopher of the very first rank whose evolutionary political goals would, if actually realized, constitute a valuable revolution in history.   PR

Reading

Cassirer, E.: *Kant's Life and Thought*, trans. J. Haden. New Haven, Conn.: Yale University Press, 1982.

†Kant, I.: *Political Writings*, ed. H. Reiss, trans. H.B. Nisbet. Cambridge: Cambridge University Press, 1970.

————: *Metaphysical Principles of Virture*, trans. J.W. Ellington. Indianapolis: Bobbs-Merrill, 1964.

Kelly, G.A.: *Idealism, Politics and History*. Cambridge: Cambridge University Press, 1969.

Nell, O.: *Acting on Principle*. New York and London: Columbia University Press, 1975.

Paton, H.J.: *The Moral Law*. London: Hutchinson, 1948.

Rawls, J.: *A Theory of Justice*. Cambridge, Mass.: Harvard University Press, 1971; Oxford: Oxford University Press, 1972.

†Riley, P.: *Kant's Political Philosophy*. Totowa, NJ: Rowman & Littlefield, 1983.

Shklar, J.: *Ordinary Vices*. Cambridge, Mass.: Harvard University Press, 1984.

Yovel, Y.: *Kant and the Philosophy of History*. Princeton, NJ: Princeton University Press, 1980.

Kautsky, Karl (1854–1938)   German socialist theoretician. As editor of *Die Neue Zeit*, the German Social Democratic Party's principal theoretical journal, Kautsky played a major role both in German Social Democracy and in the Second International. His influence as a leading exponent of MARXISM was much diminished during the last two decades of his life.

Kautsky's Marxism was evolutionary and determinist. He was a Darwinian before he was a Marxist and, to some extent, remained a Darwinian all his life, his conception of social evolution being always tied to that of natural evolution, hence his excessive emphasis on productive forces and objective necessity. Much of Kautsky's time was spent defending what he considered to be traditional Marxist orthodoxy. He insisted that the appearance of monopolies and cartels was evidence of the final involution of capitalism: the ever more serious crises brought about by underconsumption were proletarianizing even the growing middle class and would shortly cause the whole system to collapse. In two areas, however, Kautsky's thought was distinctly innovative. First, in his book *Die Agrarfrage* (1899) he attempted to show in detail that the interests of the German peasantry – in particular in protective tariffs and private ownership of land – were directly opposed to those of the proletariat; on the other hand the peasants were also becoming proletarianized through their increasing dependence on capitalist investment. Second, Kautsky developed a notion of 'ultra-imperialism'. In his earlier writings and in keeping with his underconsumptionist views, he had held that the export of capital was an effort to limit productivity and stabilize the system. Later Kautsky pointed to the possibility of capitalism's achieving this, at least for a time, by organizing international cartels which would prevent both the arms race and war.

Kautsky was always insistent on the reality of class conflict and the impossibility of class compromise. But his generally determinist attitude led him into a certain political passivity. He anticipated something of LENIN's doctrine of socialist consciousness originating outside the working class, for he considered that scientific socialism was a theory derived from observation and then applied by skilled scholars in a kind of social technology. He held to the idea of the radical transformation of the state under a dictatorship of the proletariat. By this he meant that the task of the forthcoming proletarian revolution was to make Germany fully democratic. This merely involved the majority rule of the proletariat under fully democratic – and parliamentary – institutions.

But this side of Kautsky's thought was never very well developed as he was always more at home in the sociological and historical areas of Marxism. DTMcL

Reading
Kautsky, K: *Die Agrarfrage*. Stuttgart: Dietz, 1899.
———: *The Road to Power*, trans. A.M. Simmons. Chicago: Bloch, 1909.
———: *The Dictatorship of the Proletariat* (1919), trans. H.J. Stenning. Ann Arbor: University of Michigan Press, 1964.
†Kolakowski, L.: *Main Currents of Marxism*, vol. II, ch. 2. Oxford: Oxford University Press, 1978.
McLellan, D.: *Marxism after Marx*, ch. 2. London: Macmillan, 1980.
Salvadori, M.: *Kautsky and the Socialist Revolution*. London: New Left, 1979.

Kelsen, Hans (1881–1973) Austrian legal theorist and constitutional draftsman and author of the 'pure' theory of LAW. Of a Jewish family from Galicia, Kelsen studied law in Vienna and was professor of law both there (1911–30) and in Cologne (1930–3). On Hitler's rise to power he moved to Prague (1933–8) and then to Geneva; eventually he went to the USA, finally settling in Berkeley for the last three decades of a prodigiously long life dedicated unremittingly to juristic labours. These labours produced the most brilliant and rigorously elaborated doctrine of legal positivism yet stated.

The most fundamental problem in Kelsen's thought is one of epistemology: how can there be a scientific (*wissenschaftlich*) and objective cognition of normative law? In the neo-Kantian spirit of turn-of-the-century Vienna this translates easily into a quest for the transcendental presuppositions which make possible such objective cognition. Just as a presupposed principle of causality grounds the particular types of linking of events (causal links) whose cognition and elucidation is the task of natural science in the realm of the 'is', so must there be some presupposed principle ordering our cognition of the specifically normative link ('if A is, then B ought to be') the cognition and elucidation or rational reconstruction of which is the defining task of normative science, studying the realm of the 'ought'. For Kelsen this governing principle is that of 'imputation' or 'attribution' (*Zurechnung*).

In the cognition of any actual legal order, the required presupposition is one taking the 'historically first' act of constitution-making as valid: it regulates how force *ought* to be used in the community constituted by the given constitutional order, with the subordinate legal norms validly created in the exercise of constitutional powers. This presupposed – but not posited – norm, or *Grundnorm* ('basic norm'), is what transforms our appreciation of human acts as having actual or possible causal influence on others into an appreciation of them as setting binding standards of conduct for other persons who in turn can be aware of these as such. The *Grundnorm* is Kelsen's most celebrated and widely known if not widely understood intellectual artefact.

This suggests a dynamic view of legal order, and such is Kelsen's view. Seen diachronically, a legal order of positive law is an order which regulates its own creation. A constitution as established by human acts or customs validates acts of superior legislation as and when these are performed by qualified legislators; primary legislation may likewise validate secondary legislation; all forms of general legislation authorize the invocation of judicial sanctions and so validate imposition of sanctions in cases of proven breaches of law; and judicial orders for sanctions authorize sanctioning acts by officials and citizens. The legal system is a process whereby norms are made more concrete, issuing finally in individualized directives to individuals. Concretization is also disambiguation; general norms always leave discretions and leeways of choice in interpretation. The general norm as a schema for evaluation of actions (as 'lawful' or 'unlawful', etc.) never exhaustively covers particular cases – only individualized norms do that. Hence, at all levels in the dynamic hierarchy, acts of discretionary will are called for to fill in the gaps and to narrow the range of indeterminacy – but only individualized norms are ever wholly determinate. The process is not deductive; specific norms cannot be deduced from general ones, they can only be *made* by persons whom general norms authorize to do so.

Such acts of norm-creation enable us to understand the meaning of 'oughts' and hence the category of the normative. Every act of will addressed at another's behaviour has the subjectively intended meaning that the other should do something. But this 'subjective meaning', this subjective 'should' or 'ought', is not necessarily an objective or even an intersubjective meaning. Kelsen's thesis is that only in the case of a validly authorized act of will do subjective and objective meanings converge. Only given a rationally grounded presupposition of a *Grundnorm* is objective (intersubjective) normative judgment possible. And the conditions for rational presupposition of a *Grundnorm* are that the constitutional order whose validity is in issue be a by-and-large efficacious one.

As law viewed diachronically must be conceived as a dynamic order, regulating its own creation, so can it at any one moment in time be viewed synchronically and thus in a static aspect. This perspective on legal order reveals its other salient characteristic, viz. as a *coercive* order. For in a static representation of law every legal element – not excluding *Grundnorm* and constitution – becomes a condition upon the authorization of some sanction; given the validity of the constitution, given the validity of legislation on contracts, given valid execution of some contract, given breach by one party and a validly made claim by another, given proof of breach and damage, then a court ought to order an award of damages against the party in breach – and so on. Conversely, every act of coercion by one human against another is, from a legal point of view, either a delict or a sanction. In thus envisaging the universal regulation of coercion, law can be perceived as an order of peace; and so Kelsen represents it.

The state is brilliantly explained by Kelsen in the light of all this as a personification of the unity of the legal order. Given an efficacious and relatively centralized legal order covering a definite territory, we impute the acts of organs of the legal order when acting in their official capacities to a single personified entity – 'the state'. Talk of the state is talk about law in another aspect, and vice versa; no dualism of law and state is thinkable, and so theories which regard law as being created by the state are empty.

States and state legal orders are themselves subjects of INTERNATIONAL LAW, whose princi-

ple of efficacity guarantees the validity of the acts of all lawfully authorized state-officials. In this light, Kelsen advances the highly controversial (and probably erroneous) theory of the unity of international and municipal law. All municipal legal systems become, in this view, essentially sub-systems of the international legal order. Normative monism prevails.

The same monistic view leads Kelsen to the thesis that a conflict of valid norms is inconceivable. If legal and moral norms were to clash, one or other must be wholly invalid. Being himself a subjectivist in meta-ethics, Kelsen therefore concludes that the only prospect for an objective and interpersonally effective normative order is that of the law, with all such faults as it may have. But the idea that legal validity could be conditional upon objective moral value is, to him, absurd.

The inevitable indeterminacy of general legal norms does, however, entail that the implementation of legal norms or application of law to individual cases must always involve an ideological element. Ideology is inevitable in legal activity, but it is not the same as, and should not be confused with, either legal science or the pure theory of law. On these points Kelsen maintained a long-standing quarrel with Marxist jurists; for Kelsen's side of this see *The Communist Theory of Law* (1955).   NMacC

Reading

Harris, J.W.: *Law and Legal Science*. Oxford: Oxford University Press, 1979.

Kelsen, H.: *General Theory of Law and State*, trans. A. Wedberg. Cambridge, Mass.: Harvard University Press, 1945.

———: *The Pure Theory of Law*, trans. M. Knight. Berkeley: University of California Press, 1967.

———: *The Communist Theory of Law*. London: Stevens, 1955.

———: *What is Justice?* Berkeley: University of California Press, 1957.

———: *Law and Peace in International Relations*. Cambridge, Mass.: Harvard University Press, 1942.

———: *Essays in Legal and Moral Philosophy*, intro. O. Weinberger, trans. P. Heath. Dordrecht: D. Reidel, 1973.

†Moore, R.: *Legal Norms and Legal Science: a Critical Study of Kelsen's 'Pure Theory of Law'*. Honolulu: University of Hawaii Press, 1978.

Keynes, John Maynard (1883–1946) British

economist. Raised in the Cambridge of Sidg-wick, Marshall and G. E. Moore, Keynes revolutionized economics with his *General Theory of Employment, Interest and Money* (1936), which was taken to justify deficit spending to stimulate employment. In 1919 he urged a magnanimous peace with Germany. He co-founded the International Monetary Fund (1944).

Keynes believed that poverty and 'the economic struggle between classes and nations' (which could produce war) could be overcome by social reorganization. Rejecting 'state socialism', he held that capitalism safeguarded personal liberty and promoted efficiency, through decentralizing decisions and appealing to self-interest. But the 'economic anarchy' of *laissez-faire* capitalism did not ensure full employment or sufficient equality of income and wealth. This required collective action. An enlargement of the functions of government (especially through semi-autonomous agencies) and greater governmental control over savings and investment (through low interests rates and public works programmes) were the techniques of promoting 'social justice and social stability'. This would preserve a modified capitalism, in which Keynes hoped 'money-motives' would diminish in importance.

While economists debate the meaning of Keynes's writings, 'Keynesian' economic policies are now widely criticized as promoting inflation and the growth of government. They are seen by others, however, as significantly responsible for post-war economic growth and high employment (at least until the 1970s).

DJM

Reading

Harrod, R.F.: *The Life of John Maynard Keynes.* London: Macmillan, 1951.
Keynes, J.M.: *The Collected Writings of John Maynard Keynes*, esp. vols II, VII and IX. London: Macmillan; Cambridge: Cambridge University Press, for the Royal Economic Society, 1971–.
†Robinson, E.A.G.: John Maynard Keynes. *Economic Journal* 57 (1947) 1–68.

Kollontai, Alexandra (1872–1952) Russian socialist and feminist. She attempted to incorporate a feminist critique of the family and 'bourgeois' sexual mores into MARXISM. See FEMINISM.

Kropotkin, Peter (1842–1921) Russian anarchist. Kropotkin was born into a noble family and at an early age entered the service of Tsar Alexander II. His liberal views, and above all his scientific interest in geography, however, led him away from the Russian court to Siberia, where he began to observe peasant agriculture at close quarters and to reflect on the inadequacies of centralized government. In 1872 he made his first trip to Western Europe, where in the villages of the Jura he encountered anarchist theories at first hand. After his return to Russia his association with a radical group, the Chaikovsky circle, led to his imprisonment in 1874. Two years later he escaped in dramatic circumstances and fled to Western Europe, where he quickly became prominent in the anarchist movement. He founded *Le Révolté* and contributed a number of articles setting out the basic principles of anarcho-communism (some collected later in *The Conquest of Bread*, 1906). In 1883 he was caught in a round-up of anarchists in Lyons and once again imprisoned. On release he emigrated to England where he lived for over thirty years, composing a number of theoretical works in support of anarchism, of which the best known is *Mutual Aid* (1897). He returned to Russia shortly before the October Revolution, and lived long enough to record his disillusionment with the Bolshevik regime. His funeral was the last occasion on which libertarian opponents of the regime were allowed to demonstrate in public.

Kropotkin accepted the general principles of ANARCHISM. His special contribution was to set out the case for anarcho-communism, and to ground it in a putatively scientific theory of social evolution. He envisaged a society made up of largely self-sufficient communes in which freely associated producers would provide goods to meet all essential needs. He tried to show (especially in *Fields, Factories and Workshops*, 1901) that industry could be effectively decentralized, while on the other hand improved methods of agriculture would allow even large cities to grow their food nearby. He denied that it was either possible or desirable to reward people for their individual contributions at work. The means of production were properly regarded as the collective product of the human race; where labour was divided it was arbitrary to single out people for special reward; and attempting to do so would create social divisions. Natural human solidarity meant that people would willingly work for the common good once property distinctions were abolished.

To achieve such a society, Kropotkin advocated revolutionary change; but in comparison to BAKUNIN, for instance, he said very little about the form of organization that revolutionaries should adopt. He saw the role of anarchist intellectuals as one of broadcasting subversive ideas, which would one day coalesce with the revolutionary instincts of the masses and destroy capitalism and the state together. He was adamant that the task of social reconstruction needed no central political body. Not only would such a body create a new ruling class, but it would hinder the work of rebuilding, which required the local knowledge of ordinary people.

As a scientist, Kropotkin was always interested in the Darwinian theory of evolution, and in *Mutual Aid* he tried to show that Darwinian ideas, properly understood, could be invoked in aid of libertarian communism (thereby rebutting the normal implications of SOCIAL DARWINISM). Beginning with animals and moving on to human societies, he argued that those groups which had proved most successful in evolutionary terms had done so by developing practices of mutual aid – practices whereby each member came to the help of others in need. He traced the course of human development through the clan, the village community and the medieval city, the last representing for Kropotkin the most advanced form of human solidarity yet achieved. However, the demise of the medieval city at the hands of the centralized state signified the triumph of the contrary impulse – the instinct of self-assertion and

domination. Mutual aid practices still survived, but only in the interstices of modern society – in the trade unions, and above all in voluntary associations such as the Red Cross and the Lifeboat Association.

Kropotkin's account does not really amount to a theory of *evolution*. For although it successfully sets forth a large number of examples, both animal and human, that refute the view that life is a continual struggle for survival between members of the same species, it nowhere shows that the extent of mutual aid increases as we move up the evolutionary scale. Indeed, by admitting the existence of self-assertive instincts alongside solidaristic instincts in man, Kropotkin is left with no reason to predict the eventual triumph of the latter except pious hope.

Kropotkin's achievement, nonetheless, was to give anarchism an empirical basis of sorts. Even if the coming of anarcho-communism was not inevitable, Kropotkin could point to examples suggesting that a decentralized society without a formal apparatus of coercion was not just a pipe-dream. Although some of his fellow anarchists attacked him in later years for withdrawing from active politics and immersing himself in scholarly research, he did more than anyone to present anarchism to the thinking public as a doctrine to be taken seriously.   DLM

Reading

Baldwin, R.N. ed.: *Kropotkin's Revolutionary Pamphlets*. New York: Dover, 1970.

Kropotkin, P.: *The Conquest of Bread*. New York: Vanguard, 1926.

———: *Fields, Factories and Workshops*. London: Nelson, 1912.

———: *Mutual Aid*. London: Heinemann, 1902.

†Miller, D.: Kropotkin. In *Rediscoveries*, ed. J. Hall. Oxford: Clarendon Press, 1986.

†Miller, M.A.: *Kropotkin*. Chicago: University of Chicago Press, 1976.

Woodcock, G. and Avakumović, I.: *The Anarchist Prince: a biographical study of Peter Kropotkin*. New York: Schocken, 1971.

L

labour theory of value This theory maintains that every commodity – every good produced by human labour and capable of being exchanged for other goods – has a value that is determined by the total quantity of labour needed for its production; this includes both the labour expended directly on making it and the labour required to produce the raw materials and implements used in the process of production.

This thesis has played an influential role in social and political theory, but the use made of it has varied a great deal. In some hands it has been used to defend private PROPERTY: LOCKE, for example, claimed that nine-tenths or even ninety-nine hundredths of the value of anything depended on the labour employed in making it, and used this to support his argument that the person who labours on something becomes its legitimate owner. In CLASSICAL POLITICAL ECONOMY, the labour theory of value was used primarily as an explanatory tool, the claim here being that the ratios in which all commodities would tend to exchange were governed largely by their labour-determined values. MARX made an additional and more critical claim. He argued that labour, as a commodity like any other, would normally exchange for the equivalent of its own cost of production – the minimum subsistence required to maintain and reproduce the labourer. The labour power sold would, however, be used by the capitalist to create surplus value, hence the working class was the victim of EXPLOITATION.

The labour theory of value has been attacked on a number of grounds: it overlooks the fact that capital accumulation requires deferred consumption, and capital therefore unavoidably commands a premium over and above the labour it embodies; it mistakenly assumes that the labour used in production is homogenous; and it neglects the influence of demand on the relative prices of commodities. As a result it has now been abandoned outside Marxist circles, and even within them it remains a matter of controversy how essential the labour theory is to the Marxist critique of capitalism.

DLM

Reading
Meek, R.L.: *Studies in the Labour Theory of Value*, 2nd edn. London: Lawrence & Wishart, 1973.

Labriola, Antonio (1843–1904) Italian Marxist philosopher. Labriola was born in southern Italy and studied under the Hegelian Bertrando Spaventa at Naples University. He is principally known as the first Hegelian Marxist, although VICO, SPINOZA and the psychology of Herbart were equally important to his intellectual development. He was the first to stress, some thirty years before the publication of MARX's *Early Writings*, the role of consciousness and of *praxis* in MARXISM, and criticized the evolutionary materialism of his fellow Italian Marxist, Achille Loria. Labriola's principle writings are *In Memory of the Communist Manifesto* (1895), *On Historical Materialism* (1896) and *Talking about Socialism and Philosophy* (letters to Sorel, 1897). None of these works is a systematic treatise; rather they are 'preliminary clarifications' of the materialist conception of history. The first two pieces, published in French by SOREL and in Italian by CROCE, became minor classics of Marxist literature, winning the praise of

ENGELS, Plekhanov and LENIN (which casts doubt on how well they understood Labriola's work).

Labriola's chief contribution was to attack all crude determinist readings of Marx. He was particularly critical of the Darwinian-inspired view, favoured by Loria and Enrico Ferri, which identified the progressive development of the means of production with the dynamics of natural evolution. In Vichian manner he distinguished the study of the natural world from that of the human world, since the latter is the product of the conscious shaping of the former by human labour in order to produce an artificial environment. Similarly he rejected the vulgar Marxist thesis that the economic base determines institutions and consciousness. He frequently quoted Engels's caveat that the economy is the determining factor only 'in the last analysis', but his critique went further to question the base–superstructure model altogether. He argued that Marxism is essentially a practical philosophy. *Praxis* means man's conscious reshaping of nature and the creation of history via intellectual and manual labour. Revolution is not simply a consequence of a progressive change in the economic base, but only occurs when and if the proletariat have consciously created the necessary material conditions and so organized themselves that the transition to a new socialized mode of production can proceed.

Although a gradualist, Labriola attacked both the reformism of Turati and Jaurès and Bernsteinian REVISIONISM, which he believed wanted only to ameliorate bourgeois capitalism rather than foster a proletarian consciousness of the future. He was equally opposed to the voluntarism of Sorel and Croce, whom he regarded as separating the political ideals of socialism from the materialist conception of history, and his last writings were bitter polemics against them. His work was a major influence on GRAMSCI.   RPB

Reading
†Bellamy, R.P.: Labriola. In *Modern Italian Social Theory: ideology and politics from Pareto to the present.* Cambridge: Polity, 1986.
Dal Pane, L.: *Antonio Labriola nella politica e nella cultura Italiana*, 2nd edn. Turin: Einaudi, 1975.
†Kolakowski, L.: Antonio Labriola: an attempt at an

open orthodoxy. In *Main Currents of Marxism*, vol. II, trans. P.S. Falla. Oxford: Oxford University Press, 1968.
Labriola, A.: *Opere*. 3 vols. Milan: Feltrinellia, 1959.
————: *La concezione materialistica della storia*, ed. E. Garin. Bari: Laterza, 1965; trans. C.H. Kerr as *Essays on the Materialist Conception of History*. Chicago: C.H. Kerr, 1903.
————: *Socialism and Philosophy*, trans. E. Untermann. Chicago: C.H. Kerr, 1934.

laissez-faire   The doctrine that the state should intervene as little as possible in economic affairs, restricting its role to the protection of persons and property, national defence, and the provision of a small number of public goods such as roads and harbours. This doctrine, which is usually premised on the assumption that economic activities will naturally harmonize to everyone's benefit if left alone, was first espoused by the French physiocrats (see PHYSIOCRACY). It was endorsed in the major works of CLASSICAL POLITICAL ECONOMY, though usually with qualifications: J. S. MILL's remark, '*Laissez-faire*, in short, should be the general practice: every departure from it, unless required by some great good, is a certain evil', sums this up. Recent defenders of the doctrine are to be found in the camp of LIBERTARIANISM.

DLM

Reading
Robbins, L.C.: *The Theory of Economic Policy in English Classical Political Economy*. London: Macmillan, 1952.
Viner, J.: The intellectual history of *laissez-faire*. *Journal of Law and Economics* 3 (1960) 49–69.

Lassalle, Ferdinand (1825–1864)   German socialist leader. The son of a prosperous Jewish businessman, Lassalle studied Hegelian philosophy in Berlin and took an active part in the 1848 revolution. After a decade during which he devoted himself to writing weighty books on philosophy and law, he re-entered active politics and, during the last two years of his flamboyant and tempestuous life, was responsible for founding the General Union of German Workers – Germany's first socialist party. He met his death in a love duel.

Lassalle's main contributions to socialist thought lay in his economic analysis and the political conclusions he drew therefrom. In the economic field his aim was to give a socialist turn to Ricardian principles. He produced an incisive account of how most state revenue derived from indirect taxation which was paid disproportionately by the poor whereas political power was based on direct taxation of property which actually contributed very little. Lassalle stressed the exploitative nature of production relationships and coined the phrase 'iron law of wages' whereby the average wages of labour remained at the level necessary for the subsistence of the worker and his or her family. Under contemporary capitalism, production was divorced from ownership and anarchy reigned in the field of distribution. To remedy these evils, Lassalle proposed, in a manner reminiscent of Louis Blanc, the establishment of producers' co-operatives in which ownership and control would be vested in the workers who would then retain the full value of their labour. Politically Lassalle advocated, first, the introduction of universal, equal and direct suffrage to make the state reflective of the workers' interests; and second, that the state viewed, at least potentially, as the organized working class should provide the necessary capital for funding the producers' co-operatives. Lassalle thus rejected the concept of the state as (in his phrase) 'a nightwatchman': he perceived the political weakness of the German bourgeoisie and was prepared to negotiate directly with Bismarck in order to implement his proposals. This tendency to make the implementation of SOCIALISM dependent on the intervention of an active and benign state provoked much criticism from the Marxists (see MARXISM). Although lacking both coherence and common sense, Lassalle had enormous energy and his enthusiastic amalgam of Ricardo and Hegel continued to have a powerful influence on German socialism until almost the end of the century.   DTMcL

Reading

Footman, D.: *The Primrose Path: a Life of Ferdinand Lassalle*. London: Cresset, 1946.

Lassalle, F.: *Ausgewählte Texte*, ed. T. Ramm. Stuttgart: Koehler, 1962.

———: *Eine Auswahl für unsere Zeit*, ed. H. Hirsch. Bremen: Schünemann, 1963.

†Morgan, R.: *The German Social Democrats and the First International 1864–1872*, chs 1–3. Cambridge: Cambridge University Press, 1965.

Na'aman, S.: *Lassalle*. Hanover: Verlag für Literatur und Zeitgeschehen, 1970.

law   The term has two quite distinct applications, the first to denote whatever establishes some normative order in the affairs of rational beings (consider: the law of the land, the laws of God, moral law, or the laws of golf), the second to denote statements of supposedly universal regularities or necessities in natural or social processes (compare: the laws of motion, the laws of thermodynamics, the law of supply and demand, or the law of diminishing returns). Law in the former sense we may call 'normative law'; in the latter sense, 'descriptive law' or 'scientific law'. Whether what is involved here is a pure pun on the word 'law', or is genuinely a pair of senses of a single idea, is itself a contested question in jurisprudence, legal philosophy and the philosophy of science. Questions of the existence and the knowability of 'laws' of either kind have been strongly contested over a long period of intellectual history.

One prominent approach to the understanding of law insists upon the firmest possible differentiation of normative and descriptive law, and of this approach the strongest case is known as 'legal positivism'. According to legal positivists, the existence of normative laws is always dependent upon the will or the conscious practice of some rational agent or, more probably, some group or community of rational agents. Laws in the relevant sense are norms or rules or standards of some sort determining how people ought to conduct themselves in community. They are exhibited in practices of human beings or communities, and depend on human wills to sustain them and even to give them being. Only so long as the relevant will or practice is sustained does the law exist and govern conduct; any putative law not so sustained is indeed only a putative law. On such a view there is a clear-cut distinction between normative laws and scientific laws, the latter being universal statements of regularities in nature or in social affairs, testable by reference to empirical evidence.

Scientific laws are sometimes called 'laws of

nature'; yet 'law of nature' or 'natural law' has another sense also. This other sense of the term refers to a law which is normative as well as natural, that is, to some principle or principles of objectively right conduct, the rightness of which is immanent in human nature or the nature of things. If such objective and immanent principles hold good, then any humanly established norms will depend for whatever obligatory quality they have on their derivability from, or at any rate compatibility with, the presupposed fundamental principles. A natural law theory is one which conceives human law as being in some sense subordinated to or grounded in natural law.

At least some natural law theories diminish the difference between normative and descriptive laws, for they are committed to the view that fundamental principles of right are basic discoverable truths about human existence, just a 'laws of nature' in the other sense are fundamental truths discoverable in respect of processes in the world of nature. Of course, proponents of natural law theories in the normative sense do not (except in a few cases) suppose that there is any relationship of mutual entailment between descriptive and normative laws of nature. Positivists have sometimes accused natural law theorists of making this mistake, and no doubt some natural law theorists have made it, but it is not a feature of natural law theory as such.

Most prominent in the discussion between positivism and natural law is debate about the relationships of the legal and the moral. The positivists hold that the existence and legal validity of norms is one thing, their moral merit or demerit quite another. The decision whether to obey or not is a moral question, but the decision whether a law is valid or not is a technical question dependent upon legal criteria and upon the derivability of a legal proposition from one of a fixed range of legal sources. The natural law thesis is, as already mentioned, some variant upon the theme that law in its very essence must be some kind of derivative from, or determination of, basic principles of right. Where there is direct conflict between enacted norms and the moral order, such enactments lack what is definitive of legality in its central or focal meaning.

Such discussion may in turn be reconsidered as debating the nature of the 'normativity' of normative law. There is a minimalist view about normativity which would say simply that whatever can be conceived as a standard for the judgment of conduct and the guidance of conduct, however hypothetically, is properly understood as a norm. Hence any order of positive law in the human community can provide such a set of standards, perhaps hypothetically; that is, one can say what the legal judgment of a certain course of behaviour would be, and thus one can say what in a given case ought to be done according to law, but one does not thereby answer whether one ought, all things considered, to accept that judgment or to do that act. A naturalist view would go farther and say that this concept of hypothetical normativity is merely derivative from a more fundamental notion of that which is categorically binding upon or obligatory for human beings. So law is 'normative' only in so far as it is or aspires to be a genuine and morally binding order of right conduct among human beings.

Normativity either in the conception here ascribed to positivism or in that here ascribed to natural law is a much disputed concept. Various approaches to legal thought which have been given the label 'realist' assert that normativity in either of these senses is illusory. For realism ascribes reality only to physical entities and their states, which does not embrace norms as envisaged either by positivists or by natural lawyers. Admittedly, there are psychologically investigable experiences of 'feeling bound' or of 'ought-ness'. These feelings, moreover, may be causes of or motives to action. Supposedly 'normative' laws have real existence only insofar as they actually do affect behaviour. Thus, from a realist point of view, statements of law have validity as scientific statements only if interpreted as some kind of prediction about human behaviour. As predictions they are, of course, testable. Thus realism leads to an assimilation of descriptive and normative law somewhat different from that considered above in connection with certain forms of natural law theory.

This reduction of normative legal statements to hypothetical predictions, if sound, would certainly diminish the supposed gap between normative and scientific law. This, however, is a ground for one of the gravest objections to a so-called realist approach. While from a certain sort of detached social-scientific point of view it may be satisfactory enough to think of legal rules as being essentially qualified predictions, this can hardly be true from the point of view of legal agents themselves. Knowing a certain rule of law may enable us to predict what a judge will do if a certain sort of case is brought before him or her; but this is so only if the judge considers the rule of law normatively, not as a mere prediction of his or her own future action. To take this point is to see that law may be considered, and for some purposes has to be considered, from what is sometimes called the 'internal point of view'. And if, as many think, such a viewpoint is essential to an understanding of normative law, it follows that some sort of hermeneutic explanation of law is essential to an adequate understanding of it for what it is. It is a disputed question whether such an explanation necessarily leads to our thinking of law in moral terms, or leaves open the possibility of legal normativity being distinct from moral normativity.

Another aspect of this last-mentioned debate concerns the relationship between obligatoriness and coerciveness. The normativity of law is commonly viewed as having at least something to do with the idea that conformity to law is not optional but obligatory. This obligatory quality may be seen as closely tied to the use of coercion in human communities. To be obliged to do something is to have no choice about doing it. The simplest way of having no choice about doing something is being forced to do it or not do it. It is certainly the case that systems of positive law within modern states, and indeed within feudal monarchies, rely heavily upon the use of coercive sanctions to back up legal requirements or imperatives. Such a coercive quality may be less noticeable in other legal orders such as public INTERNATIONAL LAW, or the customary law of primitive societies or, for example, CANON LAW. Those, however, who regard coerciveness as of the essence of the obligatory quality of law are apt to treat these other instances as at best subsidiary or substandard instances of law.

Against the view that the obligatoriness of law depends upon the coercive imposition of sanctions can be ranged two rival ideas. The first of these points out that *legal* sanctions are such only when imposed by those having a duty or obligation to do so. Hence not all legal obligations can owe their status as such to the attachment of some sanction. Furthermore, it is obvious that by no means all rules of law are themselves obligation-imposing. Many laws may confer or regulate the exercise of power or the enjoyment of rights. Such laws may be perfectly genuinely instances of legal norms without being themselves supported by or directly related to any sort of coercion. This point is not necessarily conclusive, since most of those who uphold it do also believe that valid exercises of legal powers or of legal rights necessarily result in changes in the legal state of affairs such as may be upheld by recourse to coercive measures in the last resort. Even so, it remains the case that legal obligations at the highest level are not coercively sanctioned, and hence obligatoriness must be given some alternative account in terms of the seriousness or importance or peremptoriness of laws as reasons for conduct. The idea of peremptory reasons for conduct can be developed in positivistic terms as one involving no necessary moral content.

The rival view to this accepts that obligatoriness is explicable only in terms of practical reason; but it goes further and, asserting the practical primacy of the moral, argues that the obligatory quality of law, and the existence of obligations under law, must depend on law's being morally obligatory. Only if and insofar as law has a morally peremptory quality can it be truly (as distinct from purportedly) obligatory. In such a natural law view, legal obligation becomes a special and derivative case of political obligation, and questions of the nature of law require answers to the problem of the legitimacy of authority in human communities. It is not the coerciveness of legal enforcement that explains obligation; rather, it is the obligatoriness of law that justifies coercion.

As to the upholding of legal measures by coercive powers, it is commonly taken to be a further especial characteristic of normative law, at least of the normative law of the modern state, that it is in several senses institutionalized. Above all else, the making of, the adjudication about, and the enforcement or administration of, law requires the establishment of and recourse to organized social institutions such as legislatures, judiciaries and executive branches of government. Furthermore, the whole structure of legal administration to which this gives rise, can be seen as a species of so-called 'institutional' facts. So in an important way legal systems are institutional systems. Thus, from the standpoint of political science, legal systems constitute many of the institutions which it is most important for political scientists and political theorists to analyse, interpret and otherwise study.

Some would object that an excessive concentration upon the institutional character of law in the above senses overrides a necessary and proper attention to one of the fundamental characteristics of legal orders. That is, it might be thought to obscure the way in which legal orders especially and uniquely exist to uphold the RIGHTS of human beings. The rights of human beings for this purpose can be envisaged either as principally individual rights or as principally the rights of collectives of human beings, or some mixture of rights of both sorts. But in any case, it can be contended that rights are of the very essence of law. Moreover, it is argued by some that the sense in which laws uphold rights is not exhausted by any of the senses in which laws are obligatory. The rights of human beings are to be seen as grounds for the imposition of legal obligations, not merely results of that imposition.

It is not difficult to correlate such views with the natural law positions mentioned above. If it can be held that human beings have certain fundamental rights which they would enjoy even in a STATE OF NATURE (see HUMAN RIGHTS), then it is easy to proceed by argument to the thesis that the essential function of law is the upholding of such rights. Where we envisage a strictly 'state-of-nature' theory about rights, we necessarily envisage rights as obtaining between human beings regardless of the existence of any form of state institutions. Law as the upholder of rights is then logically prior to law as institutionalized.

Theories of rights and of law as the upholder of rights do not necessarily require commitment to state-of-nature theorizing. Law may be seen as an institutionalized technique for protecting the fundamental claims of individuals against utilitarian policies aiming at the greatest happiness of the greatest number (see UTILITARIANISM). An argument in favour of such a view, as advanced most notably by Ronald Dworkin, is revealed by scrutiny of practical reason in the legal process. Characteristic of legal reasoning and argumentation is appeal to arguments of principle as contradistinguished from arguments of policy. This contrast of principle and policy is taken to be identical with that between rights and utility. Rights are individuated goods secured to persons as a matter of principle and of justice, policies the collective goals of a community as a whole. Fully to identify the rights guaranteed by a legal system, one must construct the most plausible system of political morality which fits the rules and institutions of the system. Such a body of institutional morality is then identified with the true body of the law. This view, if sound, is said to subvert the possibility of positivism and its doctrine of the sources of positive law in human wills and human practices.

Whether it actually does so may be doubted. That law is a practical concept necessarily illuminated by the place it takes in practical reasoning is a point of capital importance. It is far from the truth, however, that this is incompatible with a positivistic view of the sources of law. Indeed, the very point of an institutional morality of law is that it is a moral theory designed to fit rules which are derivable from those sources and ultimately identifiable in terms of what H. L. A. Hart calls a 'rule of recognition'. Moreover, while it is certainly the case that arguments of principle figure prominently in legal reasoning, and can for some purposes be contrasted with arguments of policy, no non-stipulative ground has yet been advanced for the supposition that legal principles always and only declare rights as distinct from, for example, liberties, powers or duties. The focus of contemporary debate having shifted to disputations about practical reason, it is by no means clear that positivists cannot give reasonable accounts of practical reason in the law. Rights theories, whether in institutional or in state-of-nature form, do not hold uncontested sway in contemporary legal thought.

Rights as envisaged in terms of state-of-nature theories (even if only hypothetical states of nature be envisaged) furnish the basic idea behind one of the most famous internal distinctions in the idea of law. It is by no means uncommon, especially in civilian legal systems, to differentiate sharply between private law and public law. Private law consists essentially of those rights which can be envisaged as obtaining among human beings regardless of the existence of a state. Thus it is concerned with rights of personal security against other persons' violence, with rights to fidelity in interpersonal dealings, with familial relations and with rights of and over property. Where there is a state, its function in relation to private law is to uphold relevant rights. Private law is the sphere of 'CIVIL SOCIETY', and this the state guarantees without necessarily being required to constitute it.

Public law, on the other hand, defines and constitutes the existence of the state and the rights (if any) which citizens may vindicate against the state or the state against the citizen. Thus public law includes constitutional law, administrative law, the law of taxation and of social welfare and – on many views – the criminal law. This makes it clear how much the internal divisions of legal material into the branches such as torts, contract or property law on the one hand, or revenue law, administrative law or criminal law on the other (which are standard divisions for purposes of legal practice and – even more – academic legal studies) owe to a historically influential, but no longer widely held, theory of law and society. The subdivisions remain intelligible even if their original intellectual foundations are rejected. Such a rejection necessarily follows if one accepts a positivist theory of the nature of law. For on such a theory, there can be no radical differentiation as between different forms of human legal regulation according to their subject matter or according to the private or official character of persons as regulated by different rules.

Nevertheless if one contemplates the division between private and public law as real or as really held for true by humans as social agents, it can be contended that this simply exhibits the alienated character of those human beings who have recourse to law. Human beings freed from the ALIENATION implicit in class societies would neither need to relate to each other in terms of rights nor need to establish public institutions to enforce rights, and thus also to exploit those least advantaged by the system. To pose this issue is to raise one of the most fundamental questions about law. The question is none other than whether law is an ineluctable feature of human society or merely, in its normative forms, a feature of some sorts of human society. One could not pretend to certainty in either direction unless one believed that human societies were subject to law in some other, perhaps descriptive, sense. It does, however, seem more certain that there are normative laws than that there are natural ones, at least in the descriptive sense. On the other hand, reflections such as those advanced by critical jurists in the Marxist mode, or indeed other insights from different sociological or anthropological viewpoints, remind us of the danger of mistaking features special to particular societies for general or even universal elements in human experience.

Even if it were true that in some conditions of humanity, law and state might wither away as coercive institutions, it appears that there are elements in contemporary western legal order which would always be of value to human beings. Human arrangements do require a stable institutional framework and mutual expectations of the firmest sort facilitate co-ordination and communication between people. The commonly praised ideal of the RULE OF LAW with its stress upon the certainty and foreknown quality of legal rules, their generality and lack of arbitrariness, their relative constancy in time and freedom from internal contradiction, and above all the congruence of official and individual conduct with rules, is surely an ideal of real value in contemporary societies, whether or not definitive of law as L. L. Fuller has claimed. That which it secures in human life seems of real value in any imaginable human circumstances. But this does not imply (nor is it true) that all uses of law are of positive human value, or that the goods it secures always outweigh the mischiefs it can procure. NMacC

Reading

Collins, H.: *Marxism and Law*. Oxford: Oxford University Press, 1982. [On critical theory]

†Cotterell, R.: *The Sociology of Law: an introduction*. London: Butterworth, 1984.

Dworkin, R.: *Taking Rights Seriously*. London: Duckworth, 1978.

Finnis, J.M.: *Natural Law and Natural Rights*. Oxford: Oxford University Press, 1980.

Fuller, L.L.: *The Morality of Law*, rev. edn. New Haven, Conn.: Yale University Press, 1969. [On natural law]

†Harris, J.W.: *Legal Philosophies*. London: Butterworth, 1980.

Hart, H.L.A.: *The Concept of Law*. Oxford: Oxford University Press, 1961. [On positivism]

Kelsen, H.: *The Pure Theory of Law*, trans. M. Knight. Berkeley: University of California Press, 1967. [On positivism]

MacCormick, N.: *Legal Reasoning and Legal Theory*. Oxford: Oxford University Press, 1978.

Olivecrona, K.: *Law as Fact*, 2nd edn. London: Stevens, 1971. [On realism]

Raz, J.: *Practical Reason and Norms*. London: Hutchinson, 1975. [On normativity]

Twining, W.: *Karl Llewellyn and the Realist Movement*. London: Weidenfeld & Nicolson, 1973.

legitimacy Every complex form of human society somehow confronts the issue of legitimacy, the question of whether and why the order deserves the allegiance of its members. But the issue is both more salient and more pervasive in modern societies. Perhaps ROUSSEAU's formulation of the issue in the early modern period can help us to see how this is the case.

Man is born free, and everywhere he is in chains. How did this change occur? I do not know. What can make it legitimate? I believe I can answer this question. But the social order is a sacred right that serves as the basis for all others. However, this right does not come from nature; it is therefore based on convention. The problem is to know what these conventions are (*Social Contract*, pp. 46–7).

This manifesto, radical enough in its own day, could not have been enunciated a few centuries earlier. For the world was experienced then as a cosmic order in which human beings were situated, provided with a station and a purpose. In such a world custom is touched by divine purpose and political authority is anchored in the larger cosmic order.

The interlocking concepts of freedom, legitimacy, will, consent, agency and convention governing Rousseau's statement were not yet in place. His declaration of independence from the old world of signs and meanings is joined to an intensified experience of 'unfreedom' in society. The kernel of modern experiences of ALIENATION, ANOMIE, and legitimacy crisis is contained in this formulation. For if the established order does not reflect a cosmic order then any of its prohibitions, demands or rules that go against the will constitute infringements of freedom – infringements of my freedom and our freedom. Unwilled limits become chains; limits can now only attain legitimacy if they are validated by human will.

No one today can accept Rousseau's own solution to the problem of legitimacy – the theory of the GENERAL WILL – but we all define the issue of legitimacy within the broad frame of conceptions deployed by him. This leads to the suspicion that the failure of his particular answer may not be merely the failure of a particular theory of legitimacy but indicative of more pervasive difficulties lodged in the frame itself.

Contemporary theories of legitimacy can be divided into three types. There are those that try to restore aspects of the world we have lost, interpreting the customs and norms of the order as traditions touched by divinity or reflective of a purpose immanent in nature; they attempt, in the words of Hannah ARENDT, to restore a doctrine of 'legitimacy [that] derives from something outside the range of human deeds' (p. 82). Other theories acknowledge the conventional character of modern life but then try to limit the question of legitimacy to those conventions that govern the relation of the citizen to the state, and to secure that legitimacy through the rational consent of citizens. And there are theories that insist that conventionalization of norms and standards has penetrated into all areas of life and then attempt to apply a criterion of discursive consent to an entire way of living.

George Kateb presents a recent example of the second theory. Modernity represents the desacralization of nature, the conventionalization of life, the crystallization of the state, and the primacy of the consenting agent in bestowing legitimacy, but the question of legitimacy is to be restricted to the consent of the citizen to the basic constitutional principles governing the state. Criticizing theories of actual or immanent legitimacy crisis within democratic-capitalist states, Kateb finds no 'deep and widespread feelings and opinions marked by disaffection from . . . constitutional representative democracy' (p. 180). There may be estrangement and alienation in many sectors of life, but this condition is itself part of the modern idea of freedom and conventionality; it is neither a sign of the illegitimacy of the state nor is it removable without returning to a mystified condition in which nature or God provide external standards of legitimacy.

Another tradition, led by Jurgen HABERMAS, insists that in contemporary societies the field in which the question of legitimacy arises must be broadened. For, in those societies, practices, norms and standards previously thought to be governed by tradition or the impersonal market are increasingly and correctly experienced as conventions shaped by power and politics. To the extent that these conventions are at odds with the reflective will of those implicated in them they will either mystify (and thus contribute to unfreedom) or be experienced as hateful constraints rather than media of freedom. And the state's legitimacy – though not necessarily its operative ability to maintain order – will turn on its ability to adjust these conventions to the reflective will of its citizens formed discursively through open, democratic processes. Issues of income distribution, the structure of work life, the social composition of consumption, the character of the natural environment, the sexual division of labour, the relations between parents and children, the treatment of old people – issues previously seen as located outside the field of will, convention, politics, and legitimacy – now become drawn into this field; and it is difficult to see how an order functioning within the assumptions of modernity can resist this development without doing so in authoritarian (illegitimate) ways.

We can now understand the concerns governing the most typical responses to the contemporary problem of legitimacy: conservatives and neo-conservatives try to find ways to de-conventionalize areas of life by restoring the sense of naturalness or necessity to those limits essential to capitalist-constitutional democracies; liberals try to limit the question of political legitimacy to constitutional principles governing the state by maintaining lines of separation between the state and the economy, and by adopting different standards of legitimacy for each sphere; and radicals try to visualize an enlarged set of conventions that might receive and deserve the reflective allegiance of an entire populace. Each of these responses runs into grave difficulties: the conservative restoration must be experienced as an attempt to mystify conventions in the contemporary era; the liberal division between the economic and the political increasingly appears artificial in a setting where power and politics have penetrated deeply into economic life (and vice versa) and the radical vision of an entire order of conventions receiving the reflective allegiance of a whole populace must appear to be a utopian dream. Creative thinking about legitimacy requires a deepening of thought about the epistemic circumstances within which the modern problem of legitimacy is located.   WEC

Reading

Arendt, H.: What was authority? In *Nomos I: Authority*, ed. C. Friedrich. Cambridge, Mass.: Harvard University Press, 1958.

†Connolly, W.E. ed.: *Legitimacy and the State*. Oxford: Blackwell; New York: SUNY Press, 1984.

Habermas, J.: *Legitimation Crisis*, trans. T. McCarthy. Boston: Beacon, 1973.

Hirschman, A.O.: *The Passions and the Interests*. Princeton: Princeton University Press, 1977.

Kateb, G.: On the legitimation crisis. In W.E. Connolly ed.

Lowi, T.: *The End of Liberalism*. New York: Norton, 1979.

Rousseau, J-J.: *On the Social Contract*, ed. R. Masters and trans. J. Masters. New York: St Martin's, 1978.

Sandel, M. ed.: *Liberalism and its Critics*. Oxford: Blackwell; New York: SUNY Press, 1984.

Taylor, C.: *Philosophical Papers*, vol. II, ch. 10. Cambridge: Cambridge University Press, 1985.

Lenin, Vladimir Ilich (pseudonym of V. I. Ulynanov) (1870–1924) Theorist of MARXISM, party organizer, and first leader of the Soviet state. Lenin is the principal figure in the development of Marxism in the twentieth century. He contributed to it a distinctive revolutionary politics that is of continuing importance. He is celebrated in particular for his account of the proper organization of a revolutionary party, its relationship to the class system and its role in political mobilization, and for his characterization of a new and final epoch of capitalist development that had created all the sufficient conditions for global socialist transformation. Immediately before the Bolshevik revolution of October 1917, which he largely inspired, he developed MARX's teaching on the state, integrating Marx's enthusiasm for the Paris Commune with his conception of the potential of the soviets. Experience of power in dealing with the succession of crises faced by the new regime led him to alter fundamentally this initial conception and to amplify a theory of the dictatorship of the proletariat that was to have a lasting impact on the Soviet state. As leader of the Communist International he was instrumental in enforcing acceptance of Bolshevik organizational precepts and the Russian revolutionary progression upon member parties, precipitating a breach with gradualist and constitutional SOCIAL DEMOC-RACY. During his lifetime he engaged in and provoked an almost constant stream of polemic and disputation, and almost every aspect of his thought and activity continues to be the subject of scholarly controversy. Detailed dispassionate academic study of his texts in their contexts remains however in its infancy.

Lenin's early work, culminating in his major study *The Development of Capitalism in Russia* (1899), may, in some regards, be accounted his most original contribution to Marxist theory. Utilizing contemporary Russian data he traced the phases of the evolution of capitalism from natural economy and situated differing bran-ches of industry and social strata within this complex progression. His conclusion was that wage labour (and therefore capitalist exploitation) permeated all levels of Russian society, but only the industrial proletariat could adequately articulate its grievances. He went on to argue that the consciousness, articulation and organization of classes also traversed distinct phases of development. Only in so far as the proletariat transcended the localized and particular nature of economic grievances, and

emerged with a national political organization capable of articulating the interests of all Russia's wage workers, could it claim to exist as a CLASS properly so called. To achieve this in conditions of illegality it would need a particular organizational structure in which a pre-eminent role would be played by cadres – or professional revolutionaries under the disciplined control of a party centre. The object of the vanguard party was to lead the advanced workers and, after them, the mass of the exploited into political activity that would expose the irreconcilability of class divisions within society and thereby accelerate the growth of adequate conscious-ness. These ideas were set out in Lenin's *What Is To Be Done?* (1902). Class war, in its most literal sense, expressed for Lenin the essence of Marxism, and the party was to be its organizer. Politics, as the organization and articulation of the generalized interests of economic group-ings, was but a phase in this war and would close with its termination. Politics could not resolve the problems of a class-divided society and was to be replaced by national non-coercive administration under COMMUNISM.

Up to 1914, however, Lenin was insistent that, given the level of capitalist development in Russia, the party's objective was to act as the vanguard of the democratic revolution against landlordism and autocracy. Success in this struggle was possible only if the proletarian party won the support of the wage-earning peasantry. They, and not the radical bourgeoi-sie, were the natural allies of the proletariat. This strategy informed Lenin's tactics in the revolution of 1905 and crystallized the dif-ferences between Bolsheviks and Mensheviks at that time.

With the outbreak of the Great War Lenin began to formulate a new theory of contempo-rary capitalism which he completed in *Imperia-lism, the Highest Stage of Capitalism* (1916) (see IMPERIALISM). In it he contended that the innovative and progressive role of capitalism in refining the productive forces was a product of its competitive market structure, and conse-quently ceased when capitalism became monopolistic at around the turn of the century. It then became retrogressive and parasitic upon colonial exploitation, thereby universalizing its own contradictions and preparing the ground for the fusion of the European socialist revolution with the colonial struggle for national liberation. The uneven development of capitalism made wars for the division and redivision of the economic territory of the world inevitable. Competition between enterprises in the home market was replaced by the global confrontation of militarist state capitalist trusts whose state structures became increasingly swollen and oppressive. Capitalism, Lenin concluded, had outlived its historical mission. Simultaneously, however, monopoly capitalism had, by concentrating capital in the hands of the banks and by rationalizing the processes of production and distribution in the trusts and cartels, itself created the mechanisms through which a rational allocation of scarce resources and equitable distribution of the product could be achieved under popular control. Capitalism, in its imperialist stage, had created the objective conditions for international socialist transformation.

In 1916 and 1917 Lenin rescued from the oblivion into which it had fallen Marx's account of the commune as the administrative structure proper to socialism. The soviets, based on immediate democracy with delegates subject to recall, combined the legislative, executive, judicial and policing powers hitherto balanced against one another in institutions unresponsive to the popular will. The soviets realized the ideal of popular self-administration, and the simplified structures inherited from finance capitalism, especially the big banks, at last made national administration of the economy under popular control a feasible proposition. The emphasis throughout was on dismantling the old structures of domination and subordination and restoring to the agencies of popular administration the powers arrogated to the centralized state.

These optimistic projections did not long survive the series of crises the regime had to face in its early years. Centralized, military and administrative methods of dealing with them dramatized the disparity between theory and practice. Lenin, along with Bukharin and TROTSKY, began to elaborate a revised theorization of the state that was essentially completed by 1920 (see SOVIET COMMUNISM). Faced with external isolation and the dramatic decline in the social base of the regime, the dictatorship of the proletariat emphasized policy content more than popular forms of administration and accountability; transformation of property relations more than elimination of patterns of domination and subordination in productive process and public life. Lenin now acknowledged that the diminishing stock of socialist virtues resided predominantly within the party, that therefore it would have to assume control of government and oblige all its agencies to dress by its norms of democratic centralism: that is the disciplined accountability of lower bodies to higher ones in the new hierarchy of power. In his last writings of 1922 and 1923, disturbed by evidence of the high-handedness and incompetence of the swollen state and party apparatuses, Lenin proposed a radical reorganization of the party and the state, but by that time he was largely incapacitated by illness, had himself earlier disposed of those who might now have been his allies, and was outmanoeuvred by colleagues who feared the implications of his proposals.

NH

Reading
Carr, E.H.: *The Bolshevik Revolution*. 3 vols. Harmondsworth: Penguin, 1966.

†Harding, N.: *Lenin's Political Thought*. 2 vols. London: Macmillan, 1977, 1981.

Lenin, V.I.: *Collected Works*. 45 vols. Moscow: Foreign Languages Publishing House, 1960–3; Progress Publishers, 1964–70.

Lewin, M.: *Lenin's Last Struggle*. London: Pluto, 1975.

Lieberman, M.: *Leninism under Lenin*. London: Cape, 1975.

Polan, A.J.: *Lenin and the End of Politics*. London: Methuen, 1984.

†Ulam, A.B.: *Lenin and the Bolsheviks*. London: Secker & Warburg, 1966.

Leninism The interpretation of MARXISM offered by LENIN, stressing in particular the vanguard role of the party in creating a revolutionary working class. Often used loosely in socialist debate to connote elitism in political practice (cf. JACOBINISM).   DLM

Levellers The term 'leveller' was originally an abusive name given to reformers whose proposals were thought to entail an unacceptable degree of equality, especially of property. It was current from the seventeenth to the nineteenth century. More particularly it refers to a loosely cohesive movement of radicals active during the English Civil War. Most prominent between 1646 and 1649 they re-emerged briefly, if weakly, at the end of the Protectorate before apparently disintegrating.

The principal demands of the Civil War Levellers were for a guaranteed fundamental law, reform of the franchise, religious tolerance, and redress of a wide range of social and economic grievances. However, their pro-gramme varied as they sought alliances in the shifting pattern of Civil War politics. Their support came mostly from London and the soldiers of the New Model Army, but there is evidence of provincial sympathizers too. While the leaders were men of some limited education and property, the rank and file were drawn from the smaller traders, artisans, and apprentices, well outside the political classes of the day. The Levellers represent the first substantial emergence in Britain of 'the people' as a secular political force, and for this reason the movement has been the focus of much atten-tion; their pamphlet literature is the first considerable body of radical secular political theory, made possible by the breakdown of censorship in the Civil War, and unmatched by anything until at least the 1790s. The shorthand record of their debates with the officers at the Army Council meetings at Putney and else-where provides a dramatic and unique insight into political argument of the day and has been the subject of several dramatizations.

The principal Leveller spokesmen were John Lilburne (*c*.1614–57), William Walwyn (1600–?), John Wildman (*c*.1621–93), and Richard Overton (*fl*. 1646). Lilburne was born of minor Durham gentry and apprenticed to a cloth merchant in London. Whipped and pilloried for publishing unlicensed books critical of the Church of England in the late 1630s, Lilburne led a turbulent career of often individual opposition to whatever he saw as tyranny. Walwyn was from Worcestershire, a grandson of a bishop of Hereford. He was apprenticed as a silk mercer, and became a silk merchant on his own account; he too attained notoriety as an advocate of freedom of con-

science before the emergence of the Leveller movement. Wildman, later Sir John Wildman, was educated at Cambridge, and continued his political career long after the movement col-lapsed, being associated with the republican Algernon Sidney, the Rye House Plot of 1683, and the Duke of Monmouth. After the Revo-lution of 1688 he sat for Wootton Bassett in the Convention Parliament and was briefly Postmaster-General. Little is known of Overton, but he seems to have spent time in Holland, was a known anticlerical, and published a famous mortalist pamphlet, *Man's Mortalitie*, in 1643. To these should perhaps be added the name of Colonel Thomas Rains-borough, a career soldier and the Leveller spokesman at Putney.

It is difficult to speak of a coherent Leveller political theory, since there is some dispute about even the degree of organizational unity they managed to achieve. Moreover their policies underwent continual modification and compromise. To achieve their effects with a politically unsophisticated audience they were apt to use a wide range of arguments many of which were dramaturgic rather than theoretical. These derived from Christianity and the classics, common and natural law, and English history as well as personal experiences; scholars have assigned different degrees of priority to these sources in understanding their thought. Two arguments, however, have rightly claimed much attention. The first is the Levellers' striking appeal to radical and libertarian natural rights, particularly in the case of Overton, foreshadowing a line of thought later adopted by John LOCKE in his much more moderate defence of resistance. The second is their radical view of English history, a version of the 'ANCIENT CONSTITUTION' argument used by parliamentarians and later by Whigs. For the Levellers, English liberties had been suppressed by the Normans and were difficult to discern in the subsequent legal record. The constitution since the Conquest they regarded as burdened by the 'Norman yoke'. Radicals used this argument as late as the 1890s.

The Levellers' central demand was for the abolition of arbitrary power, whether located in the king, Lords, or later, as they claimed, in the House of Commons itself. Despite their belief in the 'Norman yoke' such demands were often justified by appeals to common or constitutional law, but a psychologically deeper argument seems to have been the radical Protestant idea that the individual had a duty (to God) and therefore a natural right to retain responsibility for himself (not usually herself) and that it was not merely imprudent, but wicked, to give up political control over one's leaders, and thereby resign one's fate to them. From this basic position a number of other Leveller demands followed.

Political authority, they thought, could derive only from the people. But unlike parliamentarians such as Parker the Levellers showed an embarrassingly persistent interest in the precise mechanism of that derivation. The most famous consequences of this were their *Agreements of the People*, a series of attempts to draft a basic constitution and to promulgate it through subscription in a literal implementation of the SOCIAL CONTRACT. They argued that the arbitrary rule of the traditionally constituted powers had rendered all political power in England morally bankrupt, and that legitimate authority could only be reconstituted on the basis of the voluntary consent of prospective citizens through taking *The Agreement*. Prohibited from subscribing were supporters of the king and others who had shown themselves morally delinquent through their acceptance of arbitrary power. On a number of occasions the Levellers considered the exclusion from voting rights in the new polity of a variety of other groups such as almstakers, apprentices, and house-servants on the grounds that they lacked moral independence. Nevertheless, even on the most narrow interpretation their franchise would have doubled the number of voters, and their wider versions would have increased it over five times. It was these franchise demands which gave them their 'levelling' reputation, for as Ireton, the officers' spokesman at Putney argued, if the poor can outvote the rich, 'why may not those men vote against all property?'

Interest in the problem of interpreting the Levellers' basic position on the franchise has to some degree distorted appreciation of their wider social and religious aims. They showed a typically populist concern with limiting the scope and power of learned professions such as the law. Trading monopolies granted by royal charter or patent, and surviving 'base tenures' (property rights encumbered by service or held insecurely) were to be abolished; and rudimentary social services ensured for all. They also sought safeguards against arbitrary power through the establishment of fundamental constitutional law (see CONSTITUTIONALISM); and in religion, compulsory maintenance of the state church through tithes was to be abolished and a relatively wide degree of toleration allowed.

A more radical group of agrarian communards, the 'True Levellers' or Diggers led by William Everard and Gerrard Winstanley, did indeed preach a kind of COMMUNISM from their commune on St George's Hill in Surrey in 1649. Drawing inspiration from the radical strains in the Christian tradition, their pamphleteer Winstanley equated private property with original sin and saw the gradual spread of his agrarian communism heralding a kind of egalitarian millennium.

Recognition of the importance of the Levellers as pioneer radicals and proto-democrats has fuelled fierce debate about their true status and significance. The terms of this debate have depended too much on scholars' own judgments about the characteristics of modern society that the Levellers are supposed to have anticipated. Early socialists tended to read into them the first strivings of a working-class movement. Conversely the Marxist political theorist C. B. Macpherson has argued that their thought is essentially petit-bourgeois because it is based on the assumption that only property-holders (albeit minor ones) could have political rights. Liberal historians in the Whig tradition have tended to see them as trailblazing constitutional democrats, even as the first extra-parliamentary party organization. Despite their extensive pamphlet literature it has not proved easy to fit Levellers into modern categories. IWH-M

Reading

†Aylmer, G.E.: *The Levellers in the English Revolution*. Ithaca, NY: Cornell University Press, 1975.

Brailsford, H.N.: *The Levellers and the English Revolution*. London: Cresset, 1976.

†Frank, J.: *The Levellers*. New York: Russell & Russell, 1969.

Haller, W. and Davies, G.: *Leveller Tracts 1647–53*. New York: Columbia University Press, 1944.

†Hampsher-Monk, I.W.: The political theory of the Levellers. *Political Studies* 24 (1976) 397–422.

Hill, C.: *The World Turned Upside Down*. London: Temple Smith, 1972; Harmondsworth: Penguin, 1976.

——— ed.: *Winstanley: The Law of Freedom, and other writings*. Cambridge: Cambridge University Press, 1983.

Kishlansky, M.A.: The Army and the Levellers: the roads to Putney. *Historical Journal* 22 (1979) 795–824.

Macpherson, C.B.: *The Political Theory of Possessive Individualism*, pt 1. Oxford: Oxford University Press, 1962.

Schenk, W.: *The Concern for Social Justice in the Puritan Revolution*. London: Longman, 1948.

Wolfe, D.M.: *Leveller Manifestoes of the Puritan Revolution*. London: Cass, 1967.

Woodhouse, A.S.P.: *Puritanism and Liberty*. London: Dent, 1938.

liberalism A way of thinking about humanity and politics which has inspired several political movements in Europe and in countries influenced by European culture during the last four centuries. Because of the lengthy prominence of liberalism in western politics it has sometimes seemed impossible to define it without identifying it with western civilization in its entirety, back as far as the pre-Socratic philosophers. This problem of definition is exacerbated by the fact that the most powerful radical and conservative rivals of liberalism have often reached their non-liberal positions from liberal premises; conservatives conserve liberalism, and radicals° radicalize it. This blurs distinctions, and makes it difficult to decide whether or not certain political thinkers were liberals (for example, Thomas HOBBES, Immanuel KANT, G. W. F. HEGEL, Edmund BURKE). Furthermore, liberalism itself has appeared in various shapes in different times and places, depending on the circumstances or the enemies it has confronted. For example, liberalism in secular periods differs from liberalism in religious times; liberals in Catholic countries differ from those in Protestant ones. Finally, like other schools of thought, liberalism has been internally divided, and therefore resistant to tight definition.

Helpful distinctions can nevertheless be made. In the first place there are clear differences between the liberalisms of the classical and modern West. The 'liberalism' of philosophers such as Democritus and Lucretius is not liberal in the modern sense of the word. Such classical 'liberals' disagreed with the Socratic philosophers, by denying that political life is a natural and worthy activity, and in this way they seem to anticipate the modern liberal elevation of private life over and against the claims of the community or the state. However, these classical 'liberals' differ from most of their modern counterparts and agreed with Socratic philosophy by maintaining that human reason can discern a naturally best way of life. The moral latitudinarianism of modern liberalism is not characteristic of classical philosophy, which considers only the best individuals, not all individuals as such, to have claims against political authority. Moreover, classical 'liberals' differ from modern ones by maintaining that political action is unnatural and inadvisable. For the most part, modern liberalism has been politically active, although a more retiring mood has occasionally descended upon it. Modern liberalism questions political authority, but typically seeks to reform it rather than merely to evade it.

This political questioning of politics is at the heart of modern liberalism. (The self-contradiction inherent in this posture helps to explain some of the characteristic intricacies and problems of liberalism.) The basic principle of modern liberalism is the view that politics is artificial. Government is necessary, but it is not natural. Liberty is the natural human condition. Political authority is conventional. Reason can guide politics, but nature furnishes reason no positive goals for political conventions, only negative ones, chiefly the avoidance of death, disease, and poverty. There are no ways of life and therefore no classes of human beings that can claim to rule by natural or supernatural right. The legitimate ends of government are limited to securing the conditions of all ways of life, and therefore consist largely of the secular goals of peace and prosperity.

The first and formative battle of modern liberalism was its fight against the distortion of politics by other-worldly religions. Some political thinkers and actors had advanced a policy of one country, one religion, in order to reduce conflicts among competing claims to rule for the sake of saving souls; the liberal strategy went beyond this policy, to redefine and to narrow the scope of politics, so that one country, many religions would no longer be a recipe for civil war. Alongside this policy of religious toleration, liberals looked favourably on commerce as an area in which the energies of citizens could be more profitably employed. These are the foundations of liberal thinking, on which its later varieties as well as conservative and radical departures from it have been built: the absence of positive moral guidance in nature, the priority of liberty over authority, the secularization of politics, and the promotion of constitutions of government and principles of law that establish the limits of government and the rights of citizens against government.

Liberal thinking has been associated with numerous practical political parties. Although the label 'liberal' was first applied to a political party in Spain in 1810, that party's programme consciously imitated English constitutionalism. The origins of modern liberalism, in spite of continental anticipations in the tolerant and commercial regimes of the Venetian and Dutch republics, can be seen most clearly in the thinking and policies linked to the English Revolution of 1688. The constitutionalism, religious toleration, and commercial activity promoted by this 'Glorious Revolution' became a standard for European and American liberals in the eighteenth century. The French philosopher MONTESQUIEU's somewhat idealized portrait of England was his model of the kind of regime that was worthiest of imitation by modern men. The successful American revolutionaries of the last quarter of the eighteenth century were attracted to republican sentiments, and were of course fighting against Britain, but the republic that they constructed owed much to John LOCKE's political philosophy, which was seen as the classic justification for the Revolution of 1688. The motives and results of the French Revolution of 1789 were more mixed, and less clearly liberal; in this more turbulent revolution, democracy, nationalism, and socialism became rivals to liberalism. Nevertheless, during the century before the first world war liberal revolutions and reforms occurred throughout the European continent, although often in alliance with nationalist and democratic movements. Liberal thinkers such as Alexis de TOCQUEVILLE, J. S. MILL, and Lord ACTON began to consider how to reconcile democracy with liberty, and particular national (ethnic) loyalties with universal human rights.

It is often noticed that the preoccupation of many continental liberals with national unification – particularly in Germany, Italy, and Central Europe – made them less opposed to the unifying and centralizing power of the state than many of their British and American liberal contemporaries, who in the nineteenth century were more attracted to anti-statist, *laissez-faire* doctrines and policies. However, it should also be noticed that British and American liberalism was not originally so anti-statist; for example, Locke and James MADISON favoured government that was reduced in its scope (ends) but not in its powers (means). Although the fact that state action is called 'intervention' even by liberals who favour it betrays a belief that the state is not natural and requires justification; the arguments against the use of the economic and social powers of the state that were made by liberals such as Herbert SPENCER and William Graham Sumner were distinctly one-sided versions of liberalism.

This is shown by the correction (some would say over-correction) of these arguments by twentieth-century liberals. In the late nineteenth and early twentieth centuries the liberal justification for state intervention was redeployed, in Britain by the new social liberalism spoken for by T. H. GREEN and L. T. HOBHOUSE and the new political economics of J. M. KEYNES, and in the United States by the 'progressive' reformers, whose thinking was expressed by such writers as Herbert Croly and John DEWEY. These writers disowned the extreme INDIVIDUALISM of certain nineteenth-century liberals, and tried to reconcile individual liberty with recognition of the extent to which societies and states rather than individuals are responsible for human welfare, in particular for the material and educational conditions of the poor. Parallel developments of liberal thinking occurred in continental Europe, where social liberals could trace their origins back to Rhenish industrialists such as Friedrich Harkort in the 1840s.

These liberal redeployments and revisions seemed like alien departures to many at the time, and have done ever since; many liberals have refused to go along with them, distrusting the state-directed economic strategies and the new welfare goals of social liberalism, which have seemed more akin to SOCIALISM than to liberalism. However, social liberalism has become well established. Even many conservative liberals have accepted the desirability of the welfare state, although they have worried about the temptation of total reliance on the state. In Britain as on the Continent, the new liberalism was not (at least at first) wholeheartedly accepted by the official liberal parties, but social democratic parties have harboured it; in the United States, the political acceptance of the new methods and goals is symbolized by the fact that since the Great Depression of the 1930s, the progressives have captured the 'liberal' label, and the older liberals are now called 'conservatives' (see SOCIAL DEMOCRACY and CONSERVATISM).

The new liberalism was in part a response to the rise of socialist parties, and the question arose whether the division between old and new liberals was really between true and false liberals. Conservatives alleged that the new liberals had conceded too much to socialism. New liberals complained that conservatives were clinging to outdated liberal policies that no longer served the ends of liberalism. This dialogue has been one of the major debates animating western politics in the twentieth century. During and after the second world war, conservative liberalism recovered some of its popularity, especially when tyranny of the left rather than of the right came to be seen as the more durable threat to liberal regimes. For a brief period in the 1950s, some liberal intellectuals even entertained the idea that ideas no longer mattered: that liberalism was superior to its totalitarian rivals because it was not ideological, and that healthy, liberal politics consisted merely in the conflict of interest groups, not in ideological disputes (see IDEOLOGY). This idea did not not survive the return of ideological polarization in the 1960s and 1970s. The failure of liberal economic management to extend the post-war economic boom into the last quarter of the twentieth century has helped to revitalize conservative liberalism, and to put social liberalism on the defensive. However, the dialogue continues.

Do the division and diffusion of liberalism into social democracy and modern conservatism amount to a triumph or a decline of liberalism? Perhaps they show that liberalism is alive and well in practice but is in trouble theoretically. These theoretical troubles have practical consequences. Both conservatives and social democrats tend to adopt a dogmatic approach towards the question of state intervention, in contrast to older liberals such as Montesquieu who encouraged a more prudential approach. From this point of view the debate between old and new liberalism seems stifling rather than animating. Furthermore, liberal thinking has become altogether less confident, at times retreating from the battles of the political arena to the relatively serene privacy of the arts, in particular to the modern liberal novel, in which only personal relationships, not political ones, reveal the possibilities of liberal humanism.

The central difficulty for liberal thinking in the twentieth century does not stem from the challenge of socialism. Liberals old and new have a good stock of reliable responses to socialism: that it takes material wealth for granted, failing to see that economic freedom and the prospect of unequal rewards are its prerequisites; that it reduces politics to economics, thereby exacerbating instead of limiting class selfishness and conflict; that it makes society everything and the individual nothing, thereby encouraging individual irresponsibility; and that liberal labour organizations and liberal parties can overcome the exploitative economic practices that have 'permitted unscrupulous employers to conceal a policy of slavery beneath a cloak of Liberalism' (Ruggiero, p. 394). Liberals must concede that their refusal to consider dispensing with the family and its private property makes their commitment to equal economic opportunity less than absolute, but they argue that their acceptance of less than perfect justice is more conducive to human happiness than is any utopian attempt to abolish these elements of privacy, and that much can and has been done to improve equality of opportunity without going as far as socialists demand.

The greater challenge to the confidence of liberal thinking has come from those of its critics who have gone beyond allegations about liberalism's economic shortcomings to question its moral basis and outlook. Critics on both right and left have protested against the tendency of liberalism towards either moral indifference – morality being seen as a strictly private matter, not politically relevant – or moral philistinism, promoting narrow, selfish, middle-class virtues to the exclusion of nobler and more public-spirited virtues. They argue that this moral aimlessness and narrowness have made political community less viable, by destroying old economic and social ties and failing to replace them with anything beyond a destructive, isolating, atomistic individualism. The experience of the interwar Weimar Republic in Germany is often cited to demonstrate the fragility of liberal politics in the absence of restraints provided by the Protestant or other older moralities that have been necessary to prop up liberal regimes.

In response to this criticism, liberals have been able to point out that none of the best liberal thinkers has overlooked the need for social virtues in liberal regimes. This is especially clear in French liberal writers such as Tocqueville and François Guizot, who emphasized the political importance of morals, manners (*moeurs*) and associations. But it is also evident in such classical English liberals as John Locke, who understood and justified certain moral virtues and social institutions as products of individualism rightly (that is, non-atomistically) understood. Liberals characteristically distrust the mixture of governmental power with the educational power of social institutions, but their relegation of sociality and morality to non-governmental spheres is not tantamount to social atomism and moral indifference. Understanding individual human beings rather than families or other groups as the units of political society is not to claim that politics can dispense with such groups. Nor does the absence of a naturally highest good for human beings necessarily mean that all ways of life are equally eligible.

This response meets many but not all of the charges against liberalism. There remains the accusation that liberalism, while perhaps not morally indifferent, is nevertheless morally unambitious; that liberal virtues such as self-denial, industry, honesty, civility, and liberality, even if not destructively individualistic, do fail to bring out the best in human nature. The safe, productive, and blandly sociable sides of humanity are cultivated, but the more aspiring and imaginative faculties are neglected.

Many liberals (intellectuals more than economists or businessmen) have responded to this indictment by emphasizing a more ambitious side of liberalism. In fact, there has been an ambiguity in the thrust of liberal thought from its earliest days. The tough-minded liberalism of Hobbes, Locke, Adam SMITH and their successors has been content to help reason serve natural human passions more reliably, by replacing institutions and conventions that hinder the pursuit of peace and prosperity with those that assist it. The more ambitious strand of liberalism has aspired to use reason to construct a realm of freedom that escapes natural constraints much more completely. For this liberalism, human freedom means freedom for the active development of the personality, rather than merely freedom from material insecurity and poverty. It pursues Benedict SPINOZA's insight that human life consists not in enduring (however comfortably) the natural passions, but in free, rational activity. The opposition between humanity and nature, observable in the tougher but less ambitious liberalism's denial that nature provides positive goals for humans, is greatly intensified in this softer but more ambitious liberalism, which suspects that the natural limits of human projects and conventions can be largely if not completely left behind. By emphasizing the intersubjectivity of the mind or spirit that enables humans to escape nature, it is also better placed to explain and support human sociality.

However, this intensified detachment from nature, that enables liberals to avoid pedestrian morality and corrosive individualism, may at the same time lead towards moral nihilism. The less ambitious liberalism of Hobbes and Locke – in spite of the theoretical doubts about the intelligibility of nature raised by their own epistemologies – proposed natural goals at least in the negative sense; the more ambitious liberalism, abandoning these, had to rely (as seen in the philosophies of Kant and Hegel) on the rational realization of freedom in the progress of human history to provide and to secure moral and political goals. When (in the late nineteenth and early twentieth centuries) the rationality and progress of history became less credible, the quest for authentic, truly free selves tended to withdraw from politics to poetry, to the novel, and to the psychiatric couch. Lockeian liberalism, by restricting such ambitious quests to non-political spheres from the outset, tries to allow them to flourish without distorting politics by making it too aspiring, and without causing political disillusionment should they falter.

The revival of liberal political theory among English-speaking academic circles in the 1970s and 1980s has not addressed this radical challenge to liberalism. It has been preoccupied instead with the question as to whether utilitarian or rights-based arguments provide the better justification for the kinds of political institutions and policies that find favour in these circles (see UTILITARIANISM and RIGHTS). This division between utilitarians and deontologists makes contemporary liberal theory less able to rise to the radical challenge than was the older, Lockeian liberalism, which at least provided a united front by combining utilitarian and rights-based arguments. Current critics of the deontological alternative to utilitarianism accurately note that this alternative embodies a Kantian notion of the human self, but what they dislike is not its high contrast between the human and the natural (which they accept), but its universalism. The critics argue that what is needed is more appreciation of the moral depth given to human selves by their being parts of a particular community, rather than unencumbered, Kantian selves (see Sandel, pp. 125–63). English-speaking liberal theorists thus seem to be repeating – somewhat belatedly and much more drily – the continental movement away from utilitarianism through Kantian deontology to Hegelian historicism. Neither the deontologists nor their critics want to shoulder the burden of maintaining that human rights are

natural, 'that rights have some special metaphysical character' (Dworkin, p. xi). It seems doubtful that liberalism can relieve itself of that burden without either collapsing into a Burkeian conservatism that relies on history to maintain liberal traditions without the benefit of a liberal creed of universal rights, or progressing into a radical rejection of liberalism as a once useful but now exhausted way of thinking.

JZ

Reading
†Arblaster, A.: *The Rise and Decline of Western Liberalism*. Oxford: Blackwell, 1984.
†Bramsted, E.K. and Melhuish, K.J. eds: *Western Liberalism: a History in Documents from Locke to Croce*. London and New York: Longman, 1978.
Dworkin, R.: *Taking Rights Seriously*. London: Duckworth, 1977.
MacLean, D. and Mills, C. eds: *Liberalism Reconsidered*. Totowa, NJ: Rowman & Allanheld, 1983.
Manning, D.J.: *Liberalism*. London: Dent, 1976.
†Mansfield, H.C. Jr: *The Spirit of Liberalism*. Cambridge, Mass. and London: Harvard University Press, 1978.
Minogue, K.R.: *The Liberal Mind*. London: Methuen, 1963.
Orwin, C. and Pangle, T.: The philosophical foundations of human rights. In *Human Rights in Our Time*, ed. M.F. Plattner. Boulder, Colo.: Westview, 1984.
Ruggiero, G. de: *The History of European Liberalism* (1925). Boston: Beacon, 1959.
Ryan, A. ed.: *The Idea of Freedom*. Oxford and New York: Oxford University Press, 1979.
Sandel, M.J. ed.: *Liberalism and its Critics*. Oxford: Blackwell, 1984.
Strauss, L.: *Liberalism Ancient and Modern*. New York: Basic, 1968.

libertarianism   What are the legitimate functions of government? Libertarianism, a twentieth-century political movement with adherents principally, though not entirely, in the United States and Britain, answers this fundamental question of political theory in a radical way. More accurately, there are two main branches of libertarianism and each has a radical answer to the query. One group, the anarchists (see ANARCHISM), holds that all government is illegitimate. The other group, generally called 'minarchists', maintains that government may appropriately engage in police protection, enforcement of contracts, and national defence, but that is all. Included under the first two of these legitimate functions of government is a system of civil and criminal courts. Definitely not included, according to most minarchists, is the power to tax, even to secure money for the functions just mentioned. The anarchists think that this 'nightwatchman state' is too extensive; they believe that the government activities accepted by minarchists should be performed by private protection agencies. Few libertarian anarchists, however, take the further step of rejecting altogether the use of force, even in self-defence.

The question at once arises: why do libertarians endorse these views, so sharply at variance with most political theory? There are two principal reasons. First, libertarians hold an extremely strong doctrine of individual RIGHTS, particularly the right of individuals to acquire and hold PROPERTY. Their conception of property rights and freedom of contract excludes welfare rights, since claims to these rights require, in the libertarian view, compulsory labour of some on behalf of others. Second, libertarians believe that the operation of an unrestricted system of *laissez-faire* capitalism is the most desirable social system. People unfettered by state compulsion would be likely to establish this sort of economic system, and it is all for the best that they do so.

This view of economics has been urged in a large number of books and articles by the movement's most active intellectual advocate since the second world war, the American economist Murray N. Rothbard. A student and disciple of the Austrian economist Ludwig von Mises, Rothbard combined the *laissez-faire* economics of his teacher with the absolutist views of human rights and rejection of the state he had absorbed from studying the individualist American anarchists of the nineteenth century such as Lysander Spooner and Benjamin Tucker. (Rothbard himself is on the anarchist wing of the movement.) Both by his writings and by personal influence, Rothbard is the principal founder of modern libertarianism.

The movement received large-scale academic attention with the appearance in 1974 of *Anarchy, State, and Utopia* by the Harvard philosopher Robert Nozick. The work achieved great acclaim for its brilliance of argument and was frequently bracketed with RAWLS's *A Theory of Justice* (1971) as having revived normative political philosophy in the scholarly world. Nozick devotes the first part of his book to showing that individuals in a state of nature (a Lockeian rather than a Hobbesian one) would find it in their interest to allow a 'dominant protective agency' to emerge which would have a *de facto* monopoly of force in a given territory and hence would constitute a 'state-like entity'. The formation of such an entity, if done in the appropriate way, need violate no one's rights. The dominant agency, however, has no power of taxation. In part II of his book Nozick argues that the state has no legitimate powers beyond the functions of protection, justice, and defence that he has set forward in part I. Against what he calls a 'patterned theory' of justice, i.e. one that advocates that property or income be distributed in a certain way based on people's characteristics, he deploys his famous 'Wilt Chamberlain' example. He shows by this example that patterns can be easily upset by seemingly minute actions. Suppose, he says, that everyone in an egalitarian society offers to give Wilt Chamberlain (a well-known American athlete) a quarter of a dollar to induce him to play basketball. As a result Chamberlain will have a very large income. Thus to preserve a pattern would require constant interferences with individual liberty.

Nozick avoids the problems of a patterned theory of justice by substituting a historical theory. In this account, which borrows from the theory of LOCKE, individuals need not morally deserve their property. Instead, they need only be entitled to it. An individual can be entitled to property either by initially justly acquiring unowned property or by receiving property from someone who has just initial title to it. The details of the system are best left to the book itself, which also includes a penetrating criticism of Rawls's very different system. Part III of the book attempts to demonstrate that a libertarian society fulfils the most plausible definition of a utopian social order, since in it persons or groups can establish forms of life as they wish.

Nozick's arguments for libertarianism rely at crucial points on moral intuitions. One group of libertarians opposes this approach, attempting instead to derive libertarian conclusions from an Aristotelian philosophical framework. Those in this group have been heavily influenced by the American novelist Ayn Rand, for whom the basis of ethics is rational egoism: each individual's highest goal is to promote his or her own flourishing as a rational human being. From this foundation, members of this school attempt to derive a system of libertarian rights. Among the most prominent supporters of this approach are the American philosophers John Hospers, Eric Mack, and Tibor Machan.

Although most libertarians base their views upon a belief in individual rights, not all do so. Some, such as David Friedman, stress arguments from economics and the theory of public choice to support the unhampered market economy. In so doing they become hard to distinguish from classical liberals and supporters of capitalism not usually considered part of the libertarian movement in the strict sense, such as Milton Friedman and Friedrich von HAYEK. The latter's distinctive approach to the rule of law, in particular, has been widely influential among libertarians.   DG

Reading

†Friedman, D.: *The Machinery of Freedom*. New York: Harper & Row, 1973.

Hayek, F. von: *The Constitution of Liberty*. London: Routledge & Kegan Paul, 1960.

Machan, T.: *Human Rights and Human Liberties*. Chicago: Nelson-Hall, 1975.

†Nozick, R. *Anarchy, State, and Utopia*. New York: Basic; Oxford: Blackwell, 1974.

Rand, A.: *The Fountainhead*. New York: Bobbs-Merrill, 1943.

————: *Atlas Shrugged*. New York: Random House, 1957.

†Rothbard, M.: *Ethics of Liberty*. Atlantic Highlands, NJ: Humanities Press, 1982.

————: *Man, Economy, and State*. Menlo Park, Calif.: Institute for Humane Studies, 1970.

————: *Power and Market*. Menlo Park, Calif.: Institute for Humane Studies, 1970.

liberty See FREEDOM.

Lilburne, John (*c.* 1614–1657) British radical pamphleteer. He was active during the English Civil War as a champion of religious freedom and constitutional reform, and a leader of the LEVELLERS.

Lincoln, Abraham (1809–1865) American statesman and political philosopher; president of the United States, 1861–65. Lincoln eloquently and effectively reasserted natural right philosophy at a time when powerful intellectual and political forces were assembling against it. John Caldwell CALHOUN's pro-slavery theory rejecting the doctrine of natural human freedom and equality was complemented by Stephen Douglas's policy (adopted by the United States Congress in 1854) of 'popular sovereignty'. This policy required official indifference to the extension of slavery into territories then being organized into new states, by leaving it to the people of each territory to decide for themselves whether to permit or to forbid slavery.

Lincoln failed to unseat Douglas from the United States Senate in the electoral campaign of 1858 (during which many of the famous debates between Lincoln and Douglas occurred). But he did succeed in spoiling Douglas's chances of becoming president, and helped elevate himself to that office by insistently raising the slavery issue that Douglas sought to bury. Lincoln charged that official indifference to slavery encouraged a change in American public opinion that gravely endangered the prospects for self-government everywhere. The declared indifference to the extension of slavery not only 'deprives our republican example of its just influence in the world – enables the enemies of free institutions, with plausibility, to taunt us as hypocrites', it also 'forces so many good men amongst ourselves into an open war with the very fundamental principles of civil liberty – criticizing the Declaration of Independence, and insisting that there is no right principle of action but self-interest'. The conviction of 'the great mass of mankind' that slavery is 'a great moral wrong' tolerable only as a necessary and temporary evil 'lies at the very foundation of their sense of justice . . . ' (*Collected Works*, II, pp. 255, 281–2). To undermine that conviction is to undermine justice in regimes that depend on public opinion. Lincoln argued that there are limits to the allowable diversity of public opinion in popular governments, under which it would be disastrous to adopt Douglas's 'policy of "don't care" on a question about which all true men do care ... ' (*Collected Works*, III, p. 550).

Lincoln thought that some popular prejudices denying some of the implications of human equality would always persist, and he himself did not challenge many of the racial prejudices associated with American slavery. However, he argued that to allow public opinion to deny the truth of natural human equality was to give up the possibility of moving public opinion towards less prejudice and more justice. It was also to deprive public opinion of the only ground justifying its power. The same natural equality that requires and justifies government by consent (and thus justifies the power of public opinion) also requires government that secures equal natural rights. The drift of intellectual and popular opinion in the nineteenth century away from the recognition of the natural right basis of LAW towards legal positivism and reliance on the inevitability of historical progress absolutized the first requirement and neglected the second.

Like other liberals in the nineteenth century, Lincoln moved beyond the STATE OF NATURE theories that had been erected against tyrannical governments by liberals in the seventeenth and eighteenth centuries and recognized that, popular government having become well established, the danger of tyranny now came not (as in the earlier centuries) from ignorance and neglect of the people's rights against government, but from the denial of HUMAN RIGHTS by governments responding to popular pressure (see LIBERALISM). However, unlike many liberals in the nineteenth and twentieth centuries, Lincoln did not abandon nature as a political standard. He transformed natural equality from an attribute of a pre-political state of nature in a doctrine about what political society should not be, into a goal describing what political society should be. He set up the equal natural rights of the Declaration of Independence as 'a standard maxim for free society, which should be familiar to all, and revered by all; constantly looked to, constantly labored for, and even though never perfectly attained, constantly approximated, and thereby constantly spreading and deepening its influence and augmenting the happiness and value of life to all people of all colors everywhere' (*Collected Works*, II, p. 406).   JZ

Reading

†Jaffa, H.V.: Abraham Lincoln. In *American Political Thought: the philosophical dimension of American statesmanship*, ed. M.J. Frisch and R.G. Stevens. Itasca, Tex.: Peacock, 1983.

———: *Crisis of the House Divided: an interpretation of the issues in the Lincoln-Douglas debates*. Chicago: University of Chicago Press, 1982.

Lincoln, A.: *The Collected Works of Abraham Lincoln*, ed. R.P. Basler. 9 vols. New Brunswick, NJ: Rutgers University Press, 1953.

Thurow, G.E.: *Abraham Lincoln and American Political Religion*. Albany, NY: SUNY Press, 1976.

Locke, John (1632–1704) English philosopher and politician. Locke's most important works, *A Letter Concerning Toleration* (1689), *Two Treatises of Government* (1689), *An Essay Concerning Human Understanding* (1690), *Thoughts on Education* (1693), and *On the Reasonableness of Christianity* (1695), were published in the decade following the 'Glorious Revolution' of 1688. Before that, Locke's career had taken him from a well-born country family in Somerset, to a studentship in medicine at Christ Church, Oxford, to the household of the Whig politician and Exclusionist agitator, Anthony Ashley Cooper, first earl of Shaftesbury, and eventually into subversive intrigue and hasty exile in Holland during the reign of James II. Though a couple of early works are known from his Oxford days – *Essays on the Law of Nature* (1660) and *An Essay on Toleration* (1667) – Locke's mature political theory was developed during his time with Shaftesbury. Historical research has indicated that his most influential work, the *Two Treatises*, may have been written as early as ten years before Locke deemed it safe to publish it and that therefore the position he adopts in this work is not, as it appears to be, an apology for a revolution that has succeeded, but a call for a revolution to take place – a call that might easily have cost its author his life had it been published in the 1680s. The year 1688 was a turning point for Locke: though some of his works were published anonymously, they soon acquired for him a very considerable reputation, and he enjoyed both political influence and high political office in the last fifteen years of his life. The success of recent historical work by Peter Laslett and others, investigating the circumstances of the composition and publication of Locke's writings, his acquaintance with other works in the area, and the political context in which he was writing, has greatly bolstered the case of those scholars who insist that the study of political thought should not be left to philosophers who are ignorant of its historical context.

Of Locke's *Two Treatises of Government*, the second has been the more important and influential. The *First Treatise* (which exists in an incomplete form) attempts a detailed refutation of the particular version of the divine right of kings theory associated with the patriarchalist thinker, Robert FILMER. Much of this work is concerned to show that Old Testament texts do not establish a case for regarding Adam and his heirs as the God-given rulers of the whole world; as such it is of limited interest to anyone who does not share Locke's conviction that biblical revelation can pre-empt argument in this respect. But the thrust of Locke's case in this treatise is that nobody has been singled out by God with any mark of natural authority over others.

This view forms the background to the argument of the *Second Treatise*. The starting-point of Locke's political philosophy is that by nature human beings are equal and therefore nothing can put anyone under the authority of anybody else except his own consent. Locke is at pains to distinguish political authority from a number of other relations of dominance: master and servant, man and wife, parent and child, just conqueror and vanquished aggressor, and in his later work on toleration, priest and flock. Locke insists that each of these relationships is confined to a particular function or to particular circumstances, and that nothing but confusion and oppression is caused by using them (in the way, for example, that PATRIARCHALISM does) as analogies for the political.

These premises place Locke firmly in the natural law tradition of early liberal political thought. He makes use of the idea of a STATE OF NATURE – that is, the idea of men living together,

without a common superior on earth, subject only to the dictates of natural law, until such time as they move voluntarily into political society. Natural law, according to Locke, constitutes and protects RIGHTS of life, liberty and property; it requires men to keep their promises and to do what they can to secure the well-being of others; and it empowers them to punish transgressions. Like other theorists in this tradition, Locke identified natural law with the law of God on the one hand, and the dictates of reason on the other. He failed, however, in the endeavour which in many ways dominated his life's work, to demonstrate the rational foundations of this law. In the *Essay*, he eschews the benefit of any appeal to innate moral knowledge and his empiricism threatens to undercut the possibility of the ethical rationalism he hoped for; if the epistemology of the *Essay* was intended by its author to culminate in a vindication of ethical knowledge, then it must have been a disappointment. Certainly Locke's political theory treats the law of nature as something whose detailed elaboration can be undertaken elsewhere.

The only aspect of natural law expounded in any detail is the theory of PROPERTY. Though Locke shared the view of his predecessors, GROTIUS and PUFENDORF, that the earth and its fruits were given by God to men in common, he rejected their claim that the distribution of this common heritage to individuals must have been a matter of convention (see Tully). Instead he argues that appropriation of natural resources by labour and cultivation is sufficient to generate exclusive individual rights which are not dependent on other people's consent to be so excluded. The argument has a number of strands. Sometimes Locke argues that only a system of property rights based on labour is capable of fulfilling God's intention that human need should not be left unsatisfied. (But in the *First Treatise* he suggests that need may create rights directly even to property presently owned by others.) Sometimes, he uses a version of the labour theory of value to show that the labour which generates entitlements creates almost all the value which property has. And sometimes he uses a straightforward historical entitlement argument, maintaining that an object which has been worked on has been literally *mixed* with labour that belonged to the person who worked on it, and is accordingly marked out as his own. In any case, the acquisition of property is limited by Locke's insistence that an owner must not let resources spoil uselessly in his possession. This would be sufficient to generate a rough equality of possessions, were it not for the fact that the invention of money, a conventionally-sanctioned durable means of exchange, made it possible for men to own and get the benefit of much more land than they themselves could use the produce of. This legitimation of inequality, and the emphasis on private acquisition and enclosure in Locke's theory, have led many to see him as an ideologist of early modern capitalism (see Macpherson).

The move from the state of nature to political society is seen as a response to problems of covetousness, conflict, and ethical uncertainty caused by the development of money and the growth of inequality. Though Locke presents a gradualist account of the actual development of political institutions, the process is described abstractly in terms of the SOCIAL CONTRACT. Contract and consent have three stages in Locke's description: first, men must agree unanimously to come together as a community and pool their natural powers so that they can act together to uphold one another's rights; second, the members of this community must agree by a majority vote to set up legislative and other institutions; third, the owners of property in a society must agree, either personally or through their representatives, to whatever taxes are imposed on the people. On this basis, Locke develops his normative theory of politics. ABSOLUTISM of the kind Thomas HOBBES envisaged is ruled out on the grounds that people hold their natural rights to life and liberty as a sort of trust from God and therefore cannot transfer them to the arbitrary power of another. Since government is set up to protect property and other rights, and not to undermine them, the government may not take or redistribute property without consent. The task of human legislation is not to replace natural law and natural rights but to give it the precision, the clarity, and the impartial enforceability that were lacking in the state of nature. Natural rights remain in place and constrain all men, 'legislators as well as others'.

Locke is sometimes regarded as an early theorist of DEMOCRACY, the SEPARATION OF POWERS, and the RULE OF LAW, but neither of the first two themes is developed at any length in his political writings. The desirability of balancing the power of government by placing the various parts of it in different hands is mentioned but not discussed; elsewhere Locke is at pains to stress that the legislature must be in a position to dominate the other branches of government. The responsibility of the executive to summon regular parliaments is discussed at greater length, but only as an application, in the contemporary English context, of the principle that the executive magistrates must not undermine the legislative institutions set up in the second stage of the social contract. There is nothing in Locke's theory to warrant any particular theory of the franchise: taxpayers, of course, must be represented, but it is only a contingent matter that in England the taxpayers' representatives are also members of the legislature. The emphasis on the rule of law is much stronger and more sustained. Unless magistrates are subject to law, Locke argues, men remain in a state of nature with their rulers; absolute monarchy, he says, is a form of war, not of government. It may be necessary occasionally for officials to exercise prerogative power, but only for the public good and in cases where the law is silent. Locke rejects utterly the view that prerogative should be regarded as a distinct source of authority or as an area on which legislation should not be allowed to encroach.

What about the duties of the citizen? Few of us have the opportunity to participate in the contractual formation of a political society, but Locke considers that our POLITICAL OBLIGATION is nevertheless still based on our CONSENT. All are born free; none is naturally subject to any government. Our obligation to obey the laws of the land where we live arises either from an explicit pledge of allegiance or from what Locke calls 'tacit consent'. The latter is deemed to be given to a society when a person enjoys or makes use of any property under the jurisdiction and protection of its laws, whether this involves enjoying the ownership of land or, as Locke puts it, 'barely travelling freely on the

Highway'. This doctrine has been subject to a lot of criticism. It should be emphasized, however, that the obligation is a qualified one, and does not preclude the possibility of justified disobedience, resistance or revolt when natural rights are violated or when government or legislature exceeds the limits of its authority.

Above all, Locke's is a theory of resistance. It treats magistrates who exceed their power and legislators who violate natural rights as no more than thieves or robbers; they have put themselves into a state of war with those who are nominally subject to them and may be resisted, with violence if necessary. To the objection that this will lead to anarchy and chaos, Locke makes two replies: first, that as a matter of fact, tyrants will not be resisted unless their abuses have affected a large number of people; and second, that if resistance is occasioned, the blame for the ensuing chaos lies with the tyrant who occasioned it, not with the subject who acts to protect his life and liberties. Though the test of justified resistance is not the subject's belief but the objective fact that his rights have been violated, there can be no authority on earth to determine this matter. Those who resist tyranny must appeal to heaven for their justification, and they are responsible to God for the legitimacy of their decision. Locke argues that resistance becomes REVOLUTION if either the legislature betrays its trust by seeking to destroy or overturn the property of the people, or if the magistrates prevent the legislature from assembling or attempt to transfer the legislative power to other hands. In these cases, political authority shifts away from institutions and officials altogether and reverts back to the community constituted in the first stage of the social contract; thus the people recover their original freedom to set up new political institutions as they see fit.

Locke's views on TOLERATION are based, first, on his own Christian beliefs and, second, on his conception of the proper functions of government. The first argument views persecution and intolerance as contrary to the spirit of the gospel. The second argues that magistrates have no business making laws on matters of religion. Religious practice is a personal matter: each individual is responsible only to God in this, and the heresy of one man is no prejudice to the salvation of any other. Since magistrates have no special competence in religious affairs, no one can afford the gamble with his salvation that obedience to their dictates in the face of his own conscience would require. Finally, since the essence of true religion is sincere belief, and since belief is not subject to the will, it follows that it is irrational to attempt to compel religious faith with the means available to the magistrate.

The influence of Locke's political theory has been enormous. His writings are a watershed in the theory of natural rights, CONSTITUTIONALISM, and toleration. Their impact can be discerned in the American Constitution, in the manifestos of the French Revolution, and in the subsequent development of modern LIBERALISM. His theory of property remains the natural starting-point for all modern discussions of the subject, and its emphasis on labour as a source of value and entitlement sets the scene for the later economics of Adam SMITH and Karl MARX.   JJW

Reading

†Coleman, J.: *John Locke's Moral Philosophy*. Edinburgh: Edinburgh University Press, 1983.

†Cox, R.H.: *Locke on War and Peace*. Oxford: Clarendon Press, 1960.

†Cranston, M.: *John Locke: a Biography*. London: Longman, 1957.

†Dunn, J.: *The Political Thought of John Locke*. Cambridge: Cambridge University Press, 1969.

†Gough, J.W.: *John Locke's Political Philosophy*. Oxford: Clarendon Press, 1973.

Locke, J.: *A Letter Concerning Toleration*, ed. A. Montuori. The Hague: Martinus Nijhoff, 1963.

———: *Two Treatises of Government*, ed. P. Laslett. New York: Mentor, 1965; Cambridge: Cambridge University Press, 1970.

———: *An Essay Concerning Human Understanding*, ed. P. Nidditch. Oxford: Clarendon Press, 1975.

———: *The Educational Writings*, ed. J. Axtell. Cambridge: Cambridge University Press, 1968.

Macpherson, C.B.: *The Political Theory of Possessive Individualism*. Oxford: Oxford University Press, 1962.

†Parry, G.: *John Locke*. London: Allen & Unwin, 1978.

Ryan, A.: *Property and Political Theory*. Oxford: Blackwell, 1984.

Tully, J.: *A Discourse on Property: John Locke and his Adversaries*. Cambridge: Cambridge University Press, 1982.

LUKÁCS, GEORG

†Yolton, J.W.: *John Locke: Problems and Perspectives*. Cambridge: Cambridge University Press, 1969.

Lukács, Georg (1885–1971) Hungarian philosopher and literary critic. The son of a wealthy banker, Lukács was born in Budapest. He graduated from Budapest University in 1906, then studied with Georg Simmel at the University of Berlin (1909–10) and with Max WEBER at Heidelberg (1913–14). From his youth he was attracted by the neo-romantic, anti-positivist outlook that prevailed at the turn of the century. Despite his contempt for bourgeois culture, he recoiled from the 'vulgar' materialism of orthodox MARXISM; but, following the Russian Revolution, he unexpectedly joined the Communist Party of Hungary, and became Commissar of Education during the ill-fated Hungarian Soviet Republic of 1919. Following its collapse, Lukács emigrated to Vienna, where he composed a number of theoretical essays, published in book form in 1923 as *Geschichte und Klassenbewusstsein* (*History and Class Consciousness*).

This work, considered Lukác's magnum opus, laid the foundation for the renaissance of Marxist philosophy that has occurred in recent years. Reflecting Lukács's earlier ethical idealism, *History and Class Consciousness* endeavoured to 're-Hegelianize' Marxist thought, to rediscover the power of the subjective agent, and to attack those who, allying Marxism to physical science, turned the doctrine into a form of evolutionary POSITIVISM. Small wonder that the book incurred the wrath of the Bolsheviks, who officially condemned it at the Fifth Comintern Congress in 1924. This repudiation did not shake Lukács's Communist allegiance; as an exile in Stalin's Russia in 1933 he retracted some of his main positions, an exercise in self-criticism that was repeated on several other occasions. In the post-Stalin era, Lukács periodically withdrew or modified these recantations, causing some confusion as regards his true beliefs. In any case, *History and Class Consciousness* remains his most profound and influential philosophical work, expressing a core of ideas now recognized as 'the essential Lukács'.

Lukács's criticisms of orthodox Marxism stemmed from his Hegelian stress on the creative role of human consciousness (see HEGEL). He was scornful of naturalistic materialism as well as the 'copy' theory of knowledge, according to which thought 'mirrors' a ready-made empirical reality, divorced from mental activity. Nor could he endorse ENGELS's proclamation that human behaviour is subject to timeless dialectical laws, similar to those of nature. Indeed, Lukács ridiculed the very idea of a 'dialectic of nature', for the crucial determinant of dialectics – the interaction of subject and object – is absent from the world of nature, whose operations exclude human thought.

If human action is *free* (not necessitated by external stimuli) then, *pace* the 'vulgar Marxists' (p. 68), socialist revolution could not be viewed as the automatic consequence of the ever-worsening contradictions of capitalism. While Lukács accepted that these contradictions would eventuate in 'the downfall of capitalism' (p. 196), he insisted that no objective economic process could, *in itself*, transform mass consciousness: this required vigorous ideological struggle. Still, he did not see the future as open-ended. For he followed Hegel in arguing that history manifests an 'inner logic' (p. 15), which propels mankind towards its 'essential', predetermined goals. But Hegel had found the demiurge of history in the domain of 'Absolute Mind', whereas Lukács dismissed this as mythical nonsense and replaced it by a concrete historical force – the proletariat, the representative of mankind's highest aspirations. As he maintains, 'ultimately – the proletariat will be victorious' and build communism (p. 43). The 'realm of freedom' is not, however, something that we foresee on the basis of an analysis of unbreakable economic laws; rather, it is the meaning of history, immanent in man's nature, and it arrives through self-conscious human (proletarian) activity.

The workers, according to Lukács, come to know the world only in the act of reshaping it. Contrary to the scientific dogma of the orthodox Marxists, knowledge and action, theory and practice, coincide. By claiming that there are objective historical processes, immune to human control, and that we merely observe or 'contemplate' these, after the fashion of a scientist gathering data, these Marxists had, in

Lukács's opinion, succumbed to the most debilitating feature of bourgeois thought – 'reification'. Deriving from MARX's discussion of 'commodity fetishism', reification refers to the process whereby the products of human labour become autonomous 'things', 'given' phenomena, ruling men through apparently inexorable laws. Both subjectively and objectively, men become passive spectators instead of active subjects: they surrender their essential human creativity to alien, impersonal forces. This dehumanization is especially evident in the capitalist system of production, where human labour power is turned into a marketable commodity, and confined to narrow, repetitive, mindless tasks. But eventually the internal organization of the factory becomes the microcosm of the entire structure of capitalist society, as rationalization and specialization penetrate every sphere of life. The result is a fragmented world of stunted human beings, for whom the unity of society and history becomes unintelligible.

This brings us to the notion of 'totality'. On Lukács's interpretation the Marxist method of analysis regards the social/historical universe as a single, dynamic whole, or 'totality', which determines and gives meaning to all its constituent parts. Alas, Lukács fails to explain how we come to understand the nature of the 'totality'. Global comprehension cannot be achieved by factual analysis, since the meaning of isolated facts is only revealed in relation to the (logically prior) 'Whole'. He simply rests content in the assumption that the proletariat, by virtue of its social situation, enjoys privileged insight. Possession of total truth requires adoption of the proletarian class standpoint. There seems to be a paradox in Lukács's theory: the proletariat is spiritually crippled by capitalist reification, yet only the proletarian perspective can (and does) apprehend history in its totality. The apparent paradox is resolved when we look more closely at his conception of working-class consciousness. This consciousness is 'neither the sum nor the average of what is thought or felt by the single individuals who make up the class'; it is, on the contrary, an 'ideal-type', the rational expression of their 'true' interests, as defined by the Communist Party (p. 51).

Lukács's *political* orthodoxy is also reflected in his literary criticism, which offers a sophisticated defence of 'socialist realism'. For him, this did not involve a flat, photographic reproduction of everyday socialist life. The progressive artist must *transform* the individual experience of his characters into images of universal validity. Lukács also praises the so-called 'bourgeois' or 'critical realists' (e.g. Balzac, Scott) who evoke – without fully grasping – the structural conflicts of their time, through the medium of individual destinies. Contrasted with realism is the whole of modernist and *avant-garde* literature – naturalism, expressionism, surrealism, etc. What unites these 'decadent' art forms is a fatal 'subjectivism', which never attempts to link personal experience to an objective representation of the world.

Critics note that Lukács's aesthetic judgments provided a respectable rationalization for Stalinist cultural despotism, and that his notion of party infallibility amounted to a justification for the extinction of dissent. Certainly his unwavering commitment to an oppressive political system is hard to reconcile with his humanistic insistence on 'man as the measure of all things' (p. 190).   JVF

Reading

†Kolakowski, L.: *Main Currents of Marxism*, vol. III, ch. 7. Oxford: Clarendon Press, 1978.

Lukács, G.: *History and Class Consciousness*, trans. A. Livingstone. London: Merlin, 1971.

———: *The Historical Novel* (1937), trans. H. and S. Mitchell. London: Merlin, 1962.

———: *Lenin* (1924), trans. N. Jacobs. London: New Left, 1970.

†Parkinson, G.H.R.: *Georg Lukács*. London: Routledge & Kegan Paul, 1977.

Luther, Martin (1482–1546) German theologian, reformer and translator of the Bible. As theology professor at Wittenberg in Saxony from 1512, Luther articulated a theology of justification, utilizing primarily St Paul and St AUGUSTINE (he was himself an Augustinian monk). Its practical implications embroiled him with the papacy and its German supporters. As a churchman and polemicist he addressed himself to the practical difficulties and needs of 'evangelical', 'Lutheran' or

'Protestant' congregations. His theologically derived reflections about the polity do not always square with those which are pastorally oriented.

In its most abstract formulation (see especially *On Secular Authority*, 1523), Luther's view of the polity depends on his conception of God's government of the world. As a consequence of original sin, mankind becomes incapable of even understanding God's will, let alone following it, and instead idolizes its own will and reason: this is the *Reich* (kingdom, empire) of the World or Satan. God has instituted two 'governments' (*Regimente, Obrigkeiten*), the spiritual and the temporal, which together make up His *Reich*, in order to combat and finally to vanquish the *Reich* of Satan at the end of the world, which Luther thought close at hand.

The spiritual government is exercised only over the true Christians, a community (*Gemeinde*) whose only head is Christ. This is a community of love and mutual service; it entirely excludes coercion, and the only 'authority' exercised by Christians over Christians is the authority of the Word and persuasion. In a polemical contrast to the 'tyrannical' distinction between clerical and lay 'estates' (statuses) of unequal spiritual dignity in the Romanists' church, Luther asserted the equal 'priesthood of all believers'. He also described Christians as enjoying 'Christian liberty' in that no earthly person, office or law, whether civil or ecclesiastical, has any authority over the consciences of true Christians. Even God's law is not, for true Christians, an external imposition but rather becomes their own will, and is followed freely. Like St Augustine's 'city of God', this 'true Church' is not identical with any 'external' church in the world, especially not the 'Romanist tyranny'.

Temporal, worldly or secular government (*weltliches Regiment, weltliche Obrigkeit*) stands in complete contrast to the freedom and equality of God's spiritual government over the church. It is instituted by God to prevent the complete dominance of Satan, to keep men from 'tearing each other apart', and therefore cannot and must not govern in the same way as the church. Luther symbolizes it by 'the Sword'. Its task is the coercive enforcement of an 'outward justice', a conformity of conduct to laws and commands which have the safety of persons, reputation and property as their aim. The intentions prompting such outward justice are not the ruler's concern; he cannot induce true or inner righteousness, since that is a free gift of God to true Christians alone. True Christians do not need (though they benefit from) secular government and may not use it for their personal benefit. However, out of love for their neighbour, they freely support this divine institution, accepting public office, and doing more than civil law requires. (Luther here made the conventional assumption that positive laws merely declare and enforce moral norms.) The outward conduct of Christians is therefore indistinguishable from that of (merely 'outwardly') good citizens. If the laws and commands of rulers violate God's law – the acid test is Scripture – Christians must of course refuse compliance. But the spiritual status of Christian conveys no right to use violence against anyone, least of all against the occupants of the divinely ordained office of governor. The Sword is reserved to rulers, and violent resistance of 'inferiors' to 'superiors' is therefore ruled out. Theological considerations aside, events confirmed Luther's rooted conviction about the futility as well as the hideous consequences of political insubordination.

This theological account of the two *Reiche* and the two 'governments' leaves ambiguous the relationship between their worldly embodiments. Against the Romanists Luther insisted that 'external' or 'bodily' churches must mirror the true, invisible church in eschewing coercion (even in self-defence or for the repression of heresy), as well as any claim to temporal superiority or immunity (cf. REFORMATION POLITICAL THOUGHT). Their only right is to preach, administer the sacraments, admonish, and ultimately to excommunicate. In his writings of the early 1520s Luther left judgment of doctrine, ecclesiastical organization and choice of personnel to the congregations, as 'Christian liberty' and 'the priesthood of all believers' seemed to require. This communal tendency was quashed by wars, disorders and sectarianism, all of them blamed on the Reformation, and by the vulnerability of evangelicals to 'Romanist' authorities. The support and protection of well-disposed secular rulers was indispensable. Luther's theology had assigned no specifically ecclesiastical function to them. However, even in his *Appeal to the German Nobility* (1520) he had already urged Christians in positions of authority to use that authority to punish the wicked (namely the Romanists), to protect the good (namely the partisans of reformation) and to remedy abuses in the church, which *any* Christian may do, provided it be done peaceably. In the later 1520s and 1530s, Luther expanded this more favourable view of secular authority to include the right of secular rulers to repress heresy and blasphemy and to support the ministers of the gospel, especially in consideration of the needs of 'weaker brethren'. When confronted by hostile rulers (as he had been when he wrote *On Secular Authority*), he reverted to the narrower definition of the rulers' office, excluding them from competence in 'spiritual' matters altogether (see also CHURCH AND STATE).

Furthermore, his argument against political resistance had not allowed for disputes between 'superiors' themselves, Luther having always assumed that all members of commonwealths are either subjects or 'superiors' (*Herren, Oberen*), themselves hierarchically subordinated to one supreme overlord; in the Holy Roman Empire, the emperor. When Protestant rulers went to war not only against their Catholic equals (which was unproblematic for Luther) but also against the emperor, Luther acquiesced in the opinion of Protestant lawyers that the laws and customs of the Holy Roman Empire permitted 'lesser magistrates' (rulers below the rank of emperor) to resist a tyrannous emperor, treating this as a legal question in which theology was (for once) incompetent. In this way he saved his primary doctrine that violent resistance is always impermissible for *private* persons, but without explaining why merely human laws of the land had such authority with Christians. Nor did he ever resolve the question of the legitimacy of the 'Christian commonwealth', whose rulers *de facto* controlled the doctrine and worship of their subjects and appointed and salaried the clergy, the price Lutherans paid for protection.   HMH

Reading

Atkinson, J.: *Martin Luther and the Birth of Protestantism*, rev. edn. London: Marshall, Morgan & Scott, 1982.

Cargill Thompson, W.D.J.: *The Political Thought of Martin Luther*. Brighton, Sussex: Harvester, 1984.

†Heckel, J.: *Lex Charitatis*, rev. edn. Cologne: Boehlau, 1973.

Luther, M.: *Luther's Works*, ed. H.T. Lehman *et al.*, vols. 44–47. Philadelphia: Fortress, 1966–71.

———: *Martin Luther: selections from his writings*, ed. J. Dillenberger. Garden City, NJ: Doubleday, 1961.

†Skinner, Q.: *The Foundations of Modern Political Thought*, vol. II: *The Age of Reformation*. Cambridge: Cambridge University Press, 1978.

†Wolin, S.S.: *Politics and Vision*, ch. 5. Boston: Little, Brown, 1960.

Luxemburg, Rosa (1871–1919) Polish Marxist and revolutionary. A prominent figure in three socialist movements, the German, the Polish, and the Russian, Rosa Luxemburg wrote on most of the important theoretical and tactical issues that occupied European socialism before the first world war. From a middle-class Jewish family, she was obliged because of her youthful political activities to flee Poland in 1889, studied political economy in Zurich, where she wrote a doctoral thesis on Poland's industrial development, then moved in 1898 to Germany and remained there until her death. She was, from 1894, one of the principal founders and leaders, and the main theoretician, of the Social Democracy of the Kingdom of Poland, opposing the principle of Polish independence and national self-determination in favour of a unified working-class movement of the whole Russian empire. In Germany she became identified as the foremost representative of the left within the German Social-Democratic Party (SPD). She produced a vigorous riposte to Edward BERNSTEIN's revisionist arguments; then from 1905 began to sponsor, against the SPD's 'good old' parliamentary tactic, the more radical alternative of the mass strike; opposed and denounced the party's support for the German war effort from 1914 to 1918. A friend and a critic – a friendly critic – of LENIN and the Bolsheviks, in 1905 and again in 1917 she was in broad agreement with the strategic perspectives of Bolshevism concerning the Russian revolution, though she had earlier taken issue with Lenin's views on party organization and would express serious reservations too about some of the Bolsheviks' policies in the months after they came to power. Luxemburg spent most of the first world war in prison for her antiwar activities. Released late in 1918 during the German revolution, she was brutally murdered by counter-revolutionary officers.

Luxemburg's first important work, the anti-revisionist *Social Reform or Revolution* (1899), challenged the claim that socialism could be created gradually, from within capitalism, by a long, cumulative series of social reforms. Necessary and desirable as these were, a revolutionary conquest of political power by the proletariat would, she insisted, be indispensable. The contradictions and crises of the capitalist economy could never be smoothed away by reform, and economic breakdown of the system was ultimately inevitable. These ideas were developed further in subsequent works. Her major treatise, *The Accumulation of Capital* (1913), sought to give theoretical foundation to the economic breakdown argument. The capitalist market, she argued, was unable to absorb all the surplus-value generated in the sphere of production, and IMPERIALISM offered only a temporary – and increasingly violent, militaristic – solution to this problem: securing access to a non-capitalist environment and new markets, it simultaneously eroded that environment to the point where capitalism must eventually prevail universally and, without further possibility of such relief, collapse.

In her *Mass Strike, Party and Trade Unions* (1906), the most interesting and original of her political writings, Luxemburg also elaborated her view of proletarian revolution. A vast wave of strikes and demonstrations, meetings and marches; giving free play to the spontaneous initiatives of the working-class masses, their own efforts and experience, their trial and error; to be influenced and guided but never cramped or dominated by a revolutionary socialist party; fusing economic and political struggles, the workers' everyday concerns with far-reaching revolutionary demands – it was the school and the substance of socialist democracy itself. It was owing to the commitment reflected in this conception that she had criticized Lenin, in

Organizational Questions of Russian Social Democracy (1904), for wanting a too narrow, rigidly centralized vanguard party; and that she would criticize him again, in *The Russian Revolution* (1918), for the inroads being made upon Soviet democracy, albeit, she acknowledged, in a situation for the Bolsheviks of the gravest pressure and difficulty.

Rosa Luxemburg's was a very civilized voice in the cause of international socialism. Clear, forceful, and forthright without ever being ugly or abusive, combining courage and combativity with a deep and transparently genuine humanity, engaged – thought and feeling – on the side of the exploited everywhere, it conveyed above all a potent sense that the socialist revolution – whatever else it may be – is, has to be, a process of education, an *enlightenment* of the masses of the working class. Her writings are alive with and inspired by this as those of no other Marxist to quite the same degree. It is reflected in two classical Marxian themes she was fond of invoking: that the emancipation of the working class must be won by the working class itself; and that the proletarian revolution is, as Marx described it in *The Eighteenth Brumaire of Louis Bonaparte*, self-critical in its very nature – tortuous, drawn out, fraught with difficulty. Around these classical references, Luxemburg developed some characteristic themes and emphases of her own. Socialism could not be simply decreed, legislated into existence by government. It must be made out of the many-faceted, million-headed efforts and activities of the proletarian masses. And their struggle for and conquest of power would always be, was inherently, premature, since there could be no school of socialism outside this struggle and the experience it vouchsafed. The political experience of the working class, that was the key, and through experience, its organization, strength, and knowledge. Successes, triumphs, victories, would make up one part of this. But equally failures, mistakes, and defeats would make up another. As she herself put it in the very last article she wrote, 'Revolution is the sole form of "war" . . . in which the final victory can be prepared only by a series of "defeats"!'

Luxemburg's work has often been misconstrued as putting unlimited faith in mass spontaneity and as a form of fatalism. Neither criticism withstands close scrutiny. For her there was nothing automatic about socialism. Capitalist collapse threatened humanity with the alternative of barbarism, and effective socialist leadership must play its part in averting that threat.   NG

Reading
†Geras, N.: *The Legacy of Rosa Luxemburg*. London: New Left/Verso, 1976.

Luxemburg, R.: *The Accumulation of Capital*. London: Routledge & Kegan Paul, 1963.

†Nettl, J.P.: *Rosa Luxemburg*. Oxford: Oxford University Press, 1966.

Waters, M.A.: *Rosa Luxemburg Speaks*. New York: Pathfinder, 1970.

M

Macaulay, Thomas Babington (1800–1859) British historian, politician and essayist. Macaulay was the son of a leader of the movement against the slave trade, and was brought up among Evangelicals. He attended Trinity College, Cambridge, and later became a barrister. His brilliant essays on literary, historical and political topics in the *Edinburgh Review* made him its leading contributor and led to his election to the House of Commons as a Whig (1830–4, 1839–47, 1852–6); his speeches made him a leading figure, especially during the Reform Bill debates (1831–2). He was Law member of the Governor-General's Council in India (1834–8), and produced the Penal Code for India. His lasting fame rests on his *History of England* (1848–61).

In speeches and writing Macaulay discussed authors and problems that are within the province of political philosophy. His essay on MACHIAVELLI addressed issues of political morality. His speech on the civil disabilities of the Jews used arguments that had a close affinity with LOCKE's *Letter Concerning Toleration*. His articles on the utilitarian theory of government defended BENTHAM's contributions to law reform but criticized James MILL's method of deductive reasoning, and here he used arguments that can be traced back to BURKE. His essay on MILTON allowed him to present a rationale for liberty of expression. In speeches in support of parliamentary reform he analysed the causes of revolution and defended gradual and conciliatory constitutional change as a way of avoiding it.

Macaulay's position on these issues lend support to the conventional view in which he is labelled a liberal Whig and moderate liberal (see LIBERALISM). This view, however, fails to recognize that both in his political career and in his writing he put forward the politics of trimming. As a distinguishable and principled theory of politics trimming is associated with George Savile, Marquess of Halifax, author of *The Character of a Trimmer* (1688). In this theory, for Macaulay as for Halifax, regimes were threatened by centrifugal forces that drove those representing diverse opinions to extremes – some, who were excessively critical of the regime, threatening anarchy, others, zealous to defend established ways with repression, threatening despotism. The task of the politician was to avoid such extremes, to combine liberty that stops short of anarchy with order that stops short of despotism. This goal would be achieved by frustrating the fanatics, zealots and irreconcilables that represented extremist sects and factions, and by promoting gradual change, reconciliation, stability and centrist politics. Those who shared this understanding were given heroic status, most notably William III and Halifax, and, to a certain extent, Burke; those whose extremism made them obstacles to trimming were villains, e.g. James II, Titus Oates, Paine, Ultra-Tories, philosophic radicals, doctrinaires. As a politician Macaulay was sensitive to discontents that could lead to revolution and that could provoke demands for repression. He sought a middle course between the extremes of radicalism and Ultra-Toryism, and he sympathized with flexible Tories, especially Canning, and became spokesman for the conciliatory Whigs (see PHILOSOPHIC RADICALISM).

Macaulay's trimming was especially evident in the *History of England* which contained the political lesson that inherent risks of extremism leading to anarchy, despotism and perhaps civil war required politicians to recognize the wisdom of trimming as a way of maintaining consent for a constitutional regime which combined liberty and order. By incorporating this teaching into his account of the past, Macaulay claimed, the historian influenced politics in the future and became a 'philosophical' historian.   JH

Reading

†Clive, J.: *Macaulay: the Shaping of the Historian.* New York: Knopf, 1973.

†Hamburger, J.: *Macaulay and the Whig Tradition.* Chicago and London: University of Chicago Press, 1976.

Lively, J. and Rees, J. eds: *Utilitarian Logic and Politics: James Mill's Essay on Government, Macaulay's Critique and the Ensuing Debate.* Oxford: Clarendon Press, 1978.

Macaulay, T.B.: *History of England,* ed. H.R. Trevor-Roper. New York: Washington Square, 1968.

———: *Speeches,* ed. G.M. Young. London: Oxford University Press, 1952.

†Millgate, J.: *Macaulay.* London and Boston, Mass.: Routledge & Kegan Paul, 1973.

Machiavelli, Niccolò (1469–1527) Florentine secretary and political writer. Born in Florence, the son of a civil lawyer, Machiavelli was ineligible for political office in the post-1494 republican regime and was thus dependent on paid employment in the chancery for the experience on which he based his acclaimed new political method. His life falls into three main periods:

(1) 1469–1498: the early years in Florence during Lorenzo de' Medici's ascendancy and, after his son Piero de' Medici's expulsion in 1494, the four turbulent years of republican government dominated by the Dominican friar Girolamo Savonarola;

(2) 1498–1512: active involvement in politics as head of the second chancery and trusted confidant of the new permanent head of state after 1502, Piero Soderini; during this period Machiavelli was also secretary of the war magistracy of Ten, secretary of the new Nine of Militia which he was largely responsible for creating in 1506, and government envoy on some thirty-five missions, including four to

France (1500–11) and Siena (1501–10), two to Cesare Borgia (1502) and to the Papal Court (1503 and 1506), and one to the emperor in Germany (1507–8);

(3) 1512–1527: loss of office and brief imprisonment on the restoration of the Medici, and the beginning of his literary career, 'because Fortune has decided that, being unable to discuss either the silk or wool businesses, profits or losses, I must talk about politics (*lo stato*)'. Attempts to gain the favour of the Medici through *The Prince* resulted in 1520 in a commission from Cardinal Giulio de' Medici to write a history of Florence, as well as a blueprint for the government of Florence on the death of Lorenzo Duke of Urbino, the *Discursus*. After a series of minor missions outside Florence, he was appointed chancellor of the Supervisors of the Walls in May 1526, a year before the Sack of Rome and fall of the Medici regime in Florence. Machiavelli died on 21 June 1527, eleven days after failing to recover his former position in the chancery on the re-establishment of republican government.

Machiavelli is principally known for his two writings, *The Prince* (henceforward *Pr.*), composed in 1513 and dedicated to Lorenzo de' Medici in 1515–16, printed in 1531, and *The Discourses on the First Ten Books of Titus Livy* (henceforward *Disc.*), *c.*1513–17, dedicated to two republicans, Zanobi Buondelmonti and Cosimo Rucellai in 1519, printed in 1531. Also relevant to his political thinking are the *Arte della guerra*, composed *c.*1520, printed in 1521, and various political writings, including the *Discursus* (1520), Legations, Letters, the *Istorie Fiorentine*, and various theatrical writings. All Machiavelli's writings were on the Papal Index from 1557 until 1850.

Machiavelli's reputation as a political theorist is due, first, to his new 'scientific method' producing maxims such as that described by David HUME in his essay 'That politics may be reduced to a science' as 'one of those eternal political truths which no time nor accident can vary'; second, to the doctrine of moral expediency and deviousness which led to the verbs 'to Machevallize' or 'Machiavellianize' being coined to mean 'to practise Machiavellianism or cunning subtil policy'; third, to the theory of political REPUBLICANISM, which according to

J. G. A. Pocock exercised an important influence on English and American political thought in the seventeenth and eighteenth centuries. None of these interpretations has gone unchallenged. In the mid-twentieth century, there were more than twenty leading theories about Machiavelli's political writings, with a bibliography of over three thousand items.

New political method

Machiavelli claimed novelty for his method, which he defined as drawing maxims or rules for successful political behaviour from history and experience, in order to write something 'useful to the enquirer' (*Pr.* ch. 15, *Disc.* I, preface; cf. the preface to the Giuntine edition of the *Discourses* (1543), where it is claimed that Machiavelli was 'the first to reduce public and civil actions to rules, drawn from the most useful field of history'). The method is illustrated in *Pr.* ch. 3, where 'the general rule' (*regola generale*) that 'he who enables someone to become powerful ruins himself' is drawn from Machiavelli's practical experience of Louis XII's campaign in Italy that made Popes Alexander VI and Julius II strong at his own expense; and *Disc.* III, 43, where ancient Roman and contemporary Florentine experience of French avarice and treachery provides the maxim 'don't trust the French', since the affairs of the world 'are conducted by men who have and always have had the same passions, which of necessity produces the same result' (cf. *Disc.* I, 39). Machiavelli's method has been called inductive or scientific in drawing conclusions from practical or historical experience of human nature that is unchanging in political regimes experiencing a natural cycle of growth and decay. Although the method as Machiavelli applies it contains fallacies (discussed by Anglo, ch. 9, and Hulliung, ch. 5), his originality lies in his use of the growing Renaissance emphasis on man's behavioural patterns instead of Christian moral precepts as a basis for politics (see RENAISSANCE POLITICAL THOUGHT).

His method is based on a pragmatic and utilitarian approach to politics, trying to be useful (*utile*) by getting at the real truth of the matter (*verità effettuale*) instead of dealing merely with imaginary situations. This involves a realistic assessment of politics in terms of power and control ('in all republics the number of citizens who reach positions of command is never more than forty or fifty; they can be kept quiet with honours or by being done away with; the rest only want security', *Disc.* I, 16; 'government consists in nothing else but in so controlling subjects that they will not be able to nor have cause to do you harm') and of human nature in terms of its passions and animality, to control which he must be like a centaur, half man and half beast, combine the cunning of a fox with the strength of a lion, cruel or parsimonious as 'necessity' demands (*Pr.* ch. 18). Machiavelli is original in *Disc.* I, 4–6, in accepting conflict as a positive force in politics, provided it is institutionalized as it was in Rome, and in rejecting consensus or 'the middle way'. Although limited by his humanist belief in cyclical history, he develops a more sophisticated economic and social analysis of the problem of conflict in his late *Istorie Fiorentine*.

Closely related to Machiavelli's realism and natural determinism is his view of the STATE as an organic structure governed by its own laws of development and enjoying its own justification in terms of its success. This encouraged Meinecke in 1924 to call him 'the first person to discover the real nature of *raison d'état*'. As Gaines Post has subsequently argued, the concepts of public necessity and *ratio publicae utilitatis* were entirely familiar in the later Middle Ages; nor does Machiavelli, unlike his contemporary Guicciardini (1483–1540), use the words *ragione di stato* (reason of state) or argue that the end justifies the means: rather, he claims that a ruler's success will be judged by popular verdict, and the means he uses will be *excused* if they are successful, for in politics, 'where there is no court of appeal, one judges by the result' (*Pr.* ch. 18, *Disc.* I, 9). Nevertheless, if not as original as Meinecke claimed, Machiavelli's frequent use of the word *stato* and his emphasis on the dichotomy between successful politics and traditional morality reveal him to be precociously aware of the problems posed by the growing powers of the secular state.

Morality and religion

As suggested above, Machiavelli did not

subordinate moral standards to political ones, recognizing 'how praiseworthy it is for a prince to keep his word and to live by integrity and not deceit' and that 'it is wrong not only according to Christian standards but by any human standards' to treat people as inhumanely as Philip of Macedon did in moving them from province to province (*Pr.* ch. 18, *Disc.* I, 26). Nor does he deny the important role of religion in the state in making citizens good and obedient (*Disc.* I, 11–12). Nevertheless, in confronting the politician with a choice between public success and private goodness, Machiavelli threatens traditional morality. For although honesty is praiseworthy, men's nature is such that 'a wise ruler . . . cannot and should not keep his word when it would be to his disadvantage' (*Pr.* ch. 18). He is consistently critical of Christianity for teaching the wrong virtues for a strong and successful state and for setting a bad moral example itself (*Disc.* I, 12; II, 2); his deterministic view of men who 'never do good unless driven by necessity' and 'proceed as the force of nature compels them' (*Disc.* I, 3; III, 9) also limits the role of Christian free will and encourages moral flexibility and relativism. In Reformation Europe *The Prince* was condemned as a book 'written by the hand of Satan (*c.*1539), 'the *Koran* of the French Courtiers and the Breviary of the French politicians' (1576). Although Berlin argues that there is no conflict for Machiavelli between the two systems of values he espouses, Christian and pagan, the question how far political success excuses immoral behaviour remains as controversial as in Machiavelli's own day.

Machiavelli's belief that fortune controls half our lives (*Pr.* ch. 25) also has important moral and political implications. It is the ruler's need to be 'ready to turn where the winds of Fortune and the changeability of affairs require him' that obliges him 'often to act against his promise, against charity, against humanity and against religion' (*Pr.* ch. 18). It also raises the question of political virtue and who should rule. Not only do men find it difficult to change their behavioural patterns in order to adapt to fortune but it is uncertain what behaviour results in success, the cruel Hannibal and the pious Scipio being equally successful by different means (*Pr.* ch. 17, *Disc.* III, 21). So for

Machiavelli political *virtù* has nothing to do with moral virtue or traditional prudential behaviour but consists in boldness, courage and flexibility. Since these qualities are rarely found in one person, Machiavelli concludes that republics are preferable to principates because they offer a wider range of characters to adapt to changing circumstances (*Disc.* II, 2).

Republicanism

The need for flexibility prevents Machiavelli from offering a definitive solution to the problem of government. Single rulers are necessary to found and reform states, republican governments are better at sustaining them once established (*Disc.* I, 58). Nevertheless, despite the difficulty, which has monopolized so much attention, of reconciling the republican *Discourses* with *The Prince*, Machiavelli's thought is consistently republican both on a practical and on an ideological level, as Pocock and Skinner demonstrate. Not only can republics adapt better to changing circumstances due to their mixed citizenry, but the opportunity they offer of political and military participation provides greater fulfilment for human beings (*Disc.* II, 2; on citizen militias, an important theme in Machiavelli's political theory, see *Pr.* ch. 12, *Disc.* I, 4, and *Arte della guerra*). Machiavelli shows an early awareness of the power of the people or masses (*moltitudine*), not least because they are the final judges of all political action: 'in the world there are only the common people' (*Pr.* ch. 18, cf. chs 9 and 19). Machiavelli's model was the Roman republic and, although accused of lack of realism in admiring Rome so uncritically both at the time and later, the citizen militia he established in 1506 and his blueprint for the government of Florence in 1520 shows its practical importance. In the hands of Machiavelli and his contemporaries, classical republicanism also served to justify the growing power of the state, for, as Machiavelli wrote in the 1520 *Discursus*, 'I believe the greatest good that can be done and the most pleasing to God is that which is done to one's country.' Recently Hulliung has argued that Machiavelli's republicanism offers a tough theory of power politics that is perfectly consistent with the political argument of *The Prince*.

Conceptual analysis plays an important part in current studies, Skinner recently helping to defuse the problem of Machiavelli's republicanism by treating *The Prince* and *The Discourses* as part of different literary traditions with different intentions. Analysis of Machiavelli's use of the concepts of *gloria, virtù, fortuna*, etc., help to clarify his political language, while social and 'gender' approaches now attempt to interpret his political thought in a wider context. ABr

Reading

†Anglo, S.: *Machiavelli: a Dissection*. London: Gollancz, 1969.

†Berlin, I.: The originality of Machiavelli. In *Against the Current: Essays in the History of Ideas*. London: Hogarth Press, 1980.

Geerken, J.: Machiavelli studies since 1969. *Journal of the History of Ideas* 37 (1976) 351–68.

†Hulliung, M.: *Citizen Machiavelli*. Princeton, NJ: Princeton University Press, 1983.

Machiavelli, N.: *The Chief Works, and others*, trans. A. Gilbert. Durham, NC: Duke University Press, 1965.

———: *The Portable Machiavelli*, selected writings trans. P. Bondanella and M. Musa. Harmondsworth: Penguin, 1979.

———: *The Prince*, trans. G. Bau. Harmondsworth: Penguin, 1961.

———: *The Discourses*, trans L.J. Walker, ed. B. Crick. Harmondsworth: Penguin, 1970.

———: *The History of Florence, and other selections*, trans. J. Rawson. New York: Washington Square, 1970.

Meinecke, F.: *Machiavellianism: the Doctrine of Raison d'État and its Place in History*, trans. D. Scott. London: Routledge & Kegan Paul, 1957.

Pitkin, H.: *Fortune is a Woman: Gender and Politics in the Thought of Niccolò Machiavelli*. Berkeley, Los Angeles and London: University of California Press, 1984.

Pocock, J.G.A.: *The Machiavellian Moment*. Princeton, NJ: Princeton University Press, 1975.

Post, G.: Ratio publicae utilitatis, ratio status and 'reason of state', 1100–1300. In *Studies in Medieval Legal Thought*. Princeton, NJ: Princeton University Press, 1964.

Skinner, Q.: *The Foundations of Modern Political Thought*, vol. I: *The Renaissance*. Cambridge: Cambridge University Press, 1978.

†———: *Machiavelli*. Oxford: Oxford University Press, 1981.

Mackintosh, James (1765–1832) British liberal politician and philosopher. His *Vindiciae Gallicae* (1791) contained a philosophically sophisticated defence of the principles of the French Revolution. See RADICALS, BRITISH.

Madison, James (1751–1836) American statesman and political philosopher. James Madison grew up in Virginia in the years leading up to the American Revolution (1776–83). In 1780 he became one of Virginia's delegates to the Continental Congress where he was a leading advocate of American nationalism, respected for his quiet, penetrating arguments. From 1784 to 1786 he was a member of the Virginia legislature where he led a successful resistance to the conservatives who were trying to reverse the liberal religious policies of the state. Madison was one of the most important figures in the United States Constitutional Convention of 1787 and in the ratification contest that followed. He was elected to the new United States House of Representatives from 1788 to 1797. Here he surprised many observers by becoming the leader of an opposition to the centralizing and industrializing policies of Alexander HAMILTON in spite of the fact that he had hitherto co-operated with Hamilton, both by advocating similar policies in the early 1780s, and by supporting the nationalist side in the ratification contest. In his opposition to Hamilton and other Federalists he helped to form the Republican Party – the first modern political party – which secured the election of Thomas JEFFERSON to the presidency in 1800. Madison served as secretary of state from 1801 to 1809, when he succeeded Jefferson as president. During his sixteen years in executive office Madison again seemed to reverse his position, moving away from his hostility to initiatives by the national government. He stopped opposing the national government's protection of manufactures and the establishment of a national bank, and he was compelled to substitute war (against Britain, 1812–15) for the more passive and pacific original Republican policy of economic coercion. After his retirement from the presidency in 1817 he held no public office (apart from a brief appearance as a member of the Virginia Constitutional Convention in 1829), but he continued to make known his political opinions.

As in the case of many other American political thinkers (and some European ones, such as Edmund BURKE) Madison's political thought is expressed not in systematic treatises but in polemical pamphlets, essays, state papers, speeches, and letters. Some of these are deeply theoretical, and Madison was no stranger to the classics of western political thought, especially those in the liberal and republican traditions. However, it is characteristic of Madison that he did not restrict himself to political theory, but made himself a master of the history of ancient and modern confederacies when he was preparing for his part in the reform of the American confederation in 1787. His political thought is distinguished by its unswerving but well-reasoned loyalty to liberal REPUBLICANISM, coupled with a healthy appreciation of the imperfections of all practical arrangements and the shortcomings of all theories.

This sceptical attitude did not lead Madison to abandon political theory, although he did reject such theories as socialism and utilitarianism because of their impracticability. The principles of Madison's politics were the theoretical tenets of Lockeian natural rights adjusted to the republican world of the Anglo-American colonies, which was more rigorously opposed than Lockeian liberalism to government containing non-elective offices. Madison reaffirmed LOCKE's argument that religious freedom is a fundamental natural right because the human mind by its nature cannot be coerced into conviction, and that legitimate government is instituted by a compact not for heavenly salvation but for earthly utility. This compact must be understood as a unanimous agreement, and at least the implied assent of individuals coming of age under an established government is necessary to maintain the legitimacy of its constitution. The least imperfect constitution is republican in form, establishing majority rule through a scheme of representation. In one of his most telling interventions into political controversy during his retirement, Madison objected to John Caldwell CALHOUN's doctrine supporting nullification of acts of the United States government by individual states, on the ground that this doctrine, by trying to convert the natural right of resistance to tyrannical government into an ordinary constitutional device, would in fact result in minority rule.

Madison's best-known writings are his con-

tributions to *The Federalist*, a collection of essays first published in 1787–8. *The Federalist* (to which Hamilton and John Jay also contributed) remains the classic interpretation and defence of the American Constitution. Madison's first and most brilliant essay in this series (no. 10) makes clear the reasons why he supported majority rule only as the least imperfect system of government, and specifies the main advantages of the American republic over previous popular governments. The characteristic defects of popular government, in which majorities ultimately prevail, are majority folly (short-sightedness and instability) and majority tyranny (injustice to minorities). Madison argues that the cure for these defects is not (as traditional republican thinking held) to keep republican societies small and simple (so that the public good is easier to see and insular minorities are less likely to exist), but to enlarge and to diversify them. A system of representation can address the problem of folly if able representatives are elected, and in the larger electoral districts of a large republic, the number of worthy candidates in each district will be greater, and, because electoral corruption is more difficult when more interests and voters are involved, such candidates will have greater chance of success. The problem of majority tyranny also becomes easier to solve: 'the greater variety of parties and interests' in the large republic makes it 'less probable that a majority . . . will have a common motive to invade the rights of other citizens; or if such a common motive exists, it will be more difficult for all who feel it to discover their own strength and to act in unison with each other' (*The Federalist*, no. 10, p. 83).

Madison completes his argument by adding that the separation of the government into three branches and the division of the legislative branch into two houses form a necessary 'auxiliary precaution' against the defects of republicanism. Each division of government can prevent the others from ruling unjustly; moreover, the more permanent branches (the executive and the judiciary) and the upper legislative house can add an element of steadiness and useful delay, so that 'the cool and deliberate sense of the community' can prevail over any 'temporary errors and delusions' that infect the public mind (*The Federalist*, no. 63, p. 384).

This Madisonian system of a pluralist society and a divided government has drawn fire from twentieth-century critics who see it as too negative. Madison's elaborate precautions against unwise and unjust government seem to make any government very difficult. Defenders of Madison's thinking (and of the American political system, which incorporates this thinking) reply that Madison neither desired nor expected the delays of the legislative process to amount to immobility; after all, Madison was one of the leading promoters of the strengthening of government, and his arguments were intended not to neutralize this strengthening but to assure doubters that it would be safe.

As an opponent of Hamilton, Madison became one of his own best critics. Many of the essays that he published in the 1790s contradict the arguments of his Federalist period, by their greater confidence in the competence of majorities and by their encouragement of social solidarity rather than diversity. The party system of Madison the Republican provides a way of overcoming some of the divisions and delays in the constitutional system of Madison the Federalist. Some of those who have noticed this second Madisonian system have charged that Madison was a less able thinker and statesman than the more consistent Hamilton or Jefferson. A defence of Madison against this charge could suggest that Madison's superiority lay precisely in his sceptical attitude to both of the theoretical systems that he espoused.   JZ

Reading

Brant, I.: *James Madison*. 6 vols. Indianapolis: Bobbs-Merrill, 1941–61.

†Epstein, D.F.: *The Political Theory of 'The Federalist'*. Chicago: University of Chicago Press, 1984.

†Hamilton, A., Jay, J., and Madison, J.: *The Federalist Papers*, ed. C. Rossiter. New York: New American Library, 1961.

†Madison, J.: *The Mind of the Founder*, ed. and intro. M Meyers. Hanover, NH and London: University Press of New England, 1981.

———: *The Papers of James Madison*, ed. T. Hutchinson, W.M.E. Rachal, R.A. Rutland *et al.* 15 vols to date. Chicago: University of Chicago Press; Charlottesville: University Press of Virginia, 1962–84.

———: *The Writings of James Madison*, ed. G. Hunt. 9 vols. New York: Putnam, 1900–10.

†Zvesper, J.: The Madisonian systems. *Western Political Quarterly* 37 (1984) 236–56.

Maine, Henry Sumner (1822–1888) British jurist, legal historian and political thinker. Born the son of a medical practitioner, in Kelso, Scotland, Maine was educated at Christ's Hospital and Pembroke College, Cambridge. He became Regius Professor of Civil Law at Cambridge in 1847, and then Reader in Roman Law and Jurisprudence at the Inns of Court in 1852. He established himself in London literary life, writing numerous unsigned articles for the *Saturday Review*. His first book, *Ancient Law: its Connection with the Early History of Society and its Relation to Modern Ideas* (1861), by which he is still chiefly remembered, at once established his reputation as a scholar, and led to his appointment in 1862 as Legal Member of the Council of India. On returning to England he became Corpus Professor of Jurisprudence at Oxford (1869) and, subsequently, Master of Trinity Hall, Cambridge (1877).

Maine's chief scholarly achievement was to introduce in Britain the methods and ideas of the German school of historical jurisprudence developed by Savigny and Jhering. He was also an original social theorist, and exercised a substantial influence in a variety of fields other than jurisprudence, notably in historiography, political science and what was to be called anthropology. In *Ancient Law* Maine used the development of Roman jurisprudence as a basis from which to try to reconstruct the early history of European concepts of law and justice. In subsequent works, *Village Communities in East and West* (1871), *The Early History of Institutions* (1875), *The Effects of Observation of India on Modern European Thought* (1875), and *Early Law and Custom* (1883), he advocated and employed his characteristic comparative approach to questions of legal and social history. Doing this, he used analogies from modern India, in particular, to eke out and interpret the available evidence of early European tribal custom, especially in relation to property. The validity of this method was guaranteed for Maine by the notion, derived largely it seems from the philologist F. Max

Müller, of an original stock of 'Aryan' institutions possessed by the ancestors of all the peoples speaking the languages of the Indo-European group. In this way, though he sometimes disclaimed pretensions to speak of the early history of mankind generally, Maine became one of the chief authorities for the later nineteenth-century concept of 'social evolution'. He was particularly identified with the theory of a primitive, patriarchal social organization, which was challenged by J. F. McLennan and F. Bachofen who stressed the prevalence of matrilineal descent in primitive societies.

Essentially, Maine saw human society as developing from a corporate form of social existence in which all relations were determined by status in the kin-group, to the modern individualism grounded in the free individual ownership of property; the movement of the progressive societies, as he put it in a famous formula, had been 'from status to contract'. A good deal of Maine's writing was by implication and intention polemical, though only in *Popular Government* (1885) did he deal directly with modern political questions. He passed, later in life, for a 'conservative', though in fact he was a *laissez-faire* liberal like his colleague Alfred DICEY, deploring what he regarded as 'socialistic' tendencies as a reversal of progress. His polemics had two chief targets. He was a respectful critic of the theories of BENTHAM and John AUSTIN, which he thought oversimplified law and social behaviour by failing to consider them historically. His other target was Rousseauist ideas of the original natural rights of man; these he associated with the demands for universal suffrage which he deplored. He always saw theories of natural rights as resting on (false) factual claims about an original state of individualism and equality, and saw it as his task to refute these by historical evidence.   JWB

Reading

†Burrow, J.W.: *Evolution and Society*, ch. 5. Cambridge: Cambridge University Press, 1966.

†Collini, S., Winch, D. and Burrow, J.: *That Noble Science of Politics*, ch. 7. Cambridge: Cambridge University Press, 1983.

Grant Duff, M.E.: *Sir Henry Maine: a Brief Memoir of his Life*. London: Murray, 1892.

Feaver, G.A.: *From Status to Contract: a Biography of Sir Henry Maine, 1822–1888*. London: Longman, 1969.

Maine, H.S.: *Ancient Law: its Connection with the Early History of Society and its Relation to Modern Ideas*. London: Murray, 1861.

———: *Popular Government*. London: Murray, 1885.

Stein, P.: *Legal Evolution*. Cambridge: Cambridge University Press, 1980.

Maistre, Joseph de (1753–1821) Savoyard political theorist. Born in Savoy, Maistre was the son of a recently ennobled public legal official. He was brought up in a deeply pious family and remained a committed Catholic, although in early adult life he was attracted to mystical freemasonry. Following his father as a public lawyer, his life until the French Revolution was one of provincial placidity. An initial enthusiastic response to the Revolution soon waned and by the time the new French Republic invaded Savoy in 1792 he had taken up a firm counter-revolutionary stance. Fleeing from Savoy he moved to Lausanne where he represented the Sardinian crown and began his career as a political commentator. Much that he wrote there was not to be published for nearly a century, but his *Considérations sur la France* appeared in 1796 and was influential in shaping the counter-revolutionary credo. After a brief return to Italy he was sent, again representing the Sardinian crown, to St Petersburg where he remained until his return home in 1817. During these years in Russia he produced the works which were to establish his European reputation, particularly *Soirées de Saint-Pétersbourg*, *Du pape*, *Essai sur les principes générateur des constitutions politiques* and *Examen de la philosophie de Bacon*.

In these bitter, mordant and polemic writings Maistre expressed all the hatred of the *emigrés* for the authors of their sufferings. In his assault on revolutionary attitudes and the ENLIGHTENMENT thought that he believed had given rise to them, he did however achieve a coherent statement of reactionary beliefs, reactionary in that protest against the revolutionary present was their constant stimulus and also in that the alternative presented was an idealized and perhaps distorted vision of the past.

There can be no mistaking the moral revulsion Maistre felt towards the Enlightenment. He attacked individual thinkers more for their moral than their intellectual inadequacies and it was pride, the deadliest of sins, which he saw as the central characteristic of Enlightenment philosophy. It had been in rebellion against all authority. Its rejection of traditional political leadership went naturally with its rejection of Christianity. Indeed he claimed the Enlightenment was 'an insurrection against God'. In parallel, the French Revolution was strictly satanic, finding a precedent only in the biblical revolt against heaven.

The rebellious pride of the revolutionaries and their intellectual precursors was manifested most clearly in their faith in perfectibility, their belief that through political action and social reconstruction a moral Nirvana could be reached. Against these to him vain and impious hopes, he posed man's dualistic nature and original sin. Man was made in the image of God, yet had fallen from grace; he had the god-like attribute of free will, yet was inclined towards evil choice; he was capable of the social virtues, yet was infected with a lust for power. This human nature was not the subject of political choice but the very condition of human existence, and the revolutionary aspiration to reform it was itself evidence of man's propensity to sin.

Although Maistre, like BURKE, saw the Revolution as 'a fond election of evil', he nevertheless believed in a constant Providential ordering of human history. Corrupt human will could affect the course of things, but ultimately God's purposes would prevail in humanly unintended and unforeseeable ways. The Revolution itself demonstrated this, since this instance of man's wickedness was also an instrument of God's justice. Like Enlightenment thinkers, Maistre returned obsessively to the theodicy problem, why evil should exist in a God-ordained world, and more particularly to the question, peculiarly poignant to the *emigrés*, why the innocent should suffer while the guilty prospered. His answer was bleak; moral and physical evils are the instruments of God's just wrath, but that wrath is directed against a sinful nature in which all men share. In consequence, it fell and must fall on saints and sinners as indiscriminately as bullets on a battlefield.

Men could revolt against the ordained order, but their revolt must be both vain and punished. Nevertheless, God had given some indications of divine purposes. Curiously, Maistre seldom mentioned biblical revelation or even, outside his work *Du pape*, the guidance of the church and the pope. Generally, he emphasized rather national traditions, the inner sentiments of the heart and the work of men of genius as God's way of revealing his will. Traditional beliefs were the vestiges in the collective mind of the original primitive intuitive knowledge of ultimate causes enjoyed by men before the Fall. This primitive knowledge was also retained in the inner sentiments of the righteous, uncorrupted, unsophisticated heart. Against these traditions and sentiments given by God, reason and scientific empirical investigation were as nothing. In pressing these convictions, Maistre laid the way for anti-rationalist, populist NATIONALISM. But, like other nationalists, he associated POPULISM with an admiration for the 'hero in history'. Great men of thought, art and action were also voices of God. 'Genius is a grace', and stems from divine inspiration.

Following tradition and prejudice, listening to inner conscience and attentive to men of genius, the people could both discern and enforce God's will. Yet neither social unity nor political authority rested or could rest on popular consent. Maistre attacked the ideas of SOCIAL CONTRACT and popular sovereignty. Society was not an artefact and 'the people' became a people not by self-ordination but by God working through historical circumstance. Equally, the people could not be the source of a sovereign whose purpose was to force them into social discipline and on whom there could therefore be no theoretical limitations. At the same time he could defend those representative institutions rooted in national histories and not constructed by 'artificial' written constitutions or purporting to represent a popular will which could find true expression only in general traditions of thought and habits of behaviour.

Reacting against the ideas of the Revolution, Maistre nonetheless moved towards some of those ideas, at least in his populism and nationalism.   JL

Reading

Bayle, F.: *Les idées politiques de Joseph de Maistre*. Paris: Domat Montchrestien, 1945.

Laski, H.J.: *Studies in the Problems of Sovereignty*, ch. 5. London: Allen & Unwin, 1968.

Lebrun, R.A.: *Throne and Altar: the Political and Religious Thought of Joseph de Maistre*. Ottawa: Ottowa University Press, 1965.

†Maistre, J. de.: *The Works of Joseph de Maistre*, selected, trans. and intro. J. Lively. London: Allen & Unwin, 1965; New York: Schocken, 1971.

Morley, J.: *Biographical Studies*, ch. 3. London: Macmillan, 1923.

Triomphe, R.: *Joseph de Maistre*. Geneva: Droz, 1968.

Malthus, Thomas (1766–1834) British economist. In *An Essay on the Principles of Population* (1798) he argued that population growth would always tend to reduce living standards to subsistence level, a view that he modified in his later writings. See CLASSICAL POLITICAL ECONOMY.

Mandeville, Bernard (1670–1733) British satirist and social theorist. Born in Rotterdam, Mandeville studied philosophy and medicine at the University of Leyden where in 1691 he received the degree of doctor of medicine. He moved to England in the mid-1690s, married, and lived in London as a prosperous physician until his death.

Mandeville's most famous work was *The Fable of the Bees: or Private Vices, Public Benefits* (1714). *The Fable* was based on a satirical poem, 'The Grumbling Hive: or Knaves Turn'd Honest' (1705), but only became infamous with the 1723 edition which included 'An Essay on Charity and Charity-Schools'. Among Mandeville's other important works are *Aesop Dress'd* (1704); *The Virgin Unmask'd* (1709); *The Fable of the Bees Part II* (1729); *Free Thoughts on Religion, the Church, and National Happiness* (1720); and *An Enquiry into the Origin of Honour, and the Usefulness of Christianity in War* (1732).

In 'The Grumbling Hive' Mandeville wrote of a hive of bees who found their prayers answered that all vice be abolished. But instead of a better society the bees experienced disaster, for much of their prosperity was based on their vices – 'luxury employ'd a million of the Poor, and odious Pride a Million More' (vol. I, p. 25).

Mandeville concluded that the bees should 'leave Complaints' and enjoy the real pleasures of private life. The obvious political implications of this poem are that people should be accepted as they are and large-scale reform avoided. These sentiments were behind his Whig political allegiance, that is, his defence of William III in 1703 and later of the House of Hanover.

Like the French moralists of the late seventeenth century he so admired, Mandeville saw human nature as passionate and egoistic rather than rational or public-spirited. But instead of simply chiding his readers to moderate their passions, he tried to understand how the passions, especially pride, envy, and avarice, were responsible for the development and operation of society. The famous subtitle of 'private vices, public benefits' captures this intent. The outrage that ultimately greeted *The Fable* was based on the belief that Mandeville was justifying immoral activity; and in a sense this belief was correct, for in criticizing Christian self-denial, aristocratic honour, and civic devotion to the common good, his work was undermining the dominant moral ideals of his society. Moreover he not only criticized these ideals, but also specifically legitimated a life dedicated to profit-seeking.

Mandeville's defence of self-interest, luxury, fewer restrictions on international trade, and the advantages of the division of labour are noteworthy contributions to the history of economic thought. But his constant reminders that self-interested people need restrictions, 'The dextrous management of a skillful Politician,' should temper any attempt to see him as an early exponent of the *laissez-faire* philosophy. In moral philosophy he is often credited with playing an important role in the development of UTILITARIANISM, while in social theory his emphasis on the long and gradual development of human faculties and institutions, and his analysis of socialization and unintended consequences, are significant.   TAH

Reading

†Goldsmith, M.M.: *Private Vices, Public Benefits*. Cambridge: Cambridge University Press, 1985.

†Horne, T.A.: *The Social Thought of Bernard Mandeville*. New York: Columbia University Press, 1978.

Mandeville, B.: *The Fable of the Bees*, ed. F.B. Kaye. London: Oxford University Press, 1924.

Mannheim, Karl (1893–1947) Hungarian-born sociologist, classical innovator in the sociology of knowledge, active in Germany until 1933 and then in England. Mannheim was twice displaced, first in 1919 by counter-revolution in his native Budapest, and then again in 1933 by National Socialist measures against 'alien' professors. He spent ten years as private scholar and *Privatdozent*, or unestablished university lecturer, in Heidelberg, until he was appointed professor of sociology in Frankfurt in 1930 on the strength of his eagerly discussed publications on the political element in knowledge and its social foundations. After his forced emigration in 1933, he was lecturer in sociology at the London School of Economics, and became a professor in the Institute of Education at the University of London in the year before his death. During his stay in England he was noted for his advocacy of comprehensive planning and social education, as responses to the general crisis of which he thought German events were symptomatic (see *Man and Society*).

After early studies in the philosophy and sociology of culture influenced by Georg Simmel, Georg LUKÁCS and Alfred Weber (see *Structures of Thinking*), Mannheim turned more specifically to the social dimensions of thinking. He agreed with the Marxist contention that all varieties of modern thought have a formative principle which is volitional and political, and that they can best be interpreted by being related to the collective social actors to which they can variously be imputed. But he maintained that a refinement and generalization of this Marxist insight into the 'ideological' character of thought would yield a politically neutral 'sociology of knowledge', the practice of which might lay the foundation for a 'science of politics' (see Kettler *et al.*). Groups in conflict could be brought to acknowledge the partiality of their perspectives and the complementary partialities in those of their opponents, opening the way to a 'synthetic' common knowledge of the prevailing historical situation and a realistic assessment of actual possibilities (see *Ideology and Utopia*).

Apart from such broad theses, Mannheim treats numerous issues in the sociological interpretation of intellectual production, including the social formulation and functions of conservative thinking (*Conservatism*) and economic ambition (*Essays*), as well as the importance of utopian strivings (*Ideology and Utopia*), generational differences and intellectual competition (*Essays*) in the constitution of thought. Especially controversial were his attempts to characterize the functions and missions of intellectuals and to distinguish between ideological and utopian thinking (see *Ideology and Utopia*; Meja and Stehr).

Mannheim wrote only essays and deliberately experimented with mutually inconsistent theoretical attempts upon his most basic themes, pending a never-achieved systematic integration of his thinking. This has somewhat perplexed and divided his many commentators: professional sociologists have drawn on his innovations in the sociological analysis of belief systems but discounted his speculations about philosophical problems in the relationship between knowledge and socially grounded politics, whereas social theorists have been challenged by his ideas about the activist and historical character of knowledge in society. Some among the former have criticized Mannheim's way of specifying the objects for sociological interpretation, as well as conceptual and methodological imprecisions in the interpretive work itself (see Merton). Among the latter, a recurrent objection relates to Mannheim's historicist strategy for grounding his claims about the cognitive status of ideologies or 'synthesis' (see HISTORICISM). He is often charged with falling into a special form of a relativistic vicious circle ('Mannheim's paradox') (see Meja and Stehr). When Mannheim's work is viewed in the context of contemporary hermeneutic method (see Simonds) and in relation to recent explorations in 'functionalist' theories of truth (see Ludz), his 'experimentalism' proves to be more fruitful than the positions upon which the most prominent criticisms are founded.   DK

Reading
†Kettler, D., Meja, V. and Stehr, N.: *Karl Mannheim*. Chichester, Sussex: Ellis Horwood, 1984.
†Loader, C.: *The Intellectual Development of Karl*

Mannheim. Cambridge: Cambridge University Press, 1985.

Ludz, P.C.: *Ideologiebegriff und marxistische Theorie*. Opladen: Westdeutscher, 1976.

Mannheim, K: *Ideology and Utopia*. London: Routledge; New York: Harcourt Brace, 1936.

——: *Man and Society in an Age of Reconstruction*. London: Routledge, 1940.

——: *Essays on the Sociology of Knowledge*, ed. P. Kecskemeti. London: Routledge; New York: Oxford University Press, 1952.

——: *Structures of Thinking*. London: Routledge & Kegan Paul, 1982.

——: *Conservatism*. London: Routledge & Kegan Paul, 1986.

Meja, V. and Stehr, N.: *The Sociology of Knowledge Dispute*. London: Routledge & Kegan Paul, 1987.

Merton, R.K.: *The Sociology of Science*. Chicago: University of Chicago Press, 1972.

†Simonds, A.P.: *Karl Mannheim's Sociology of Knowledge*. Oxford: Clarendon Press, 1978. [Includes a bibliography.]

Mao Zedong (Mao Tse-Tung) (1893–1976) Chinese political leader and Marxist theorist. Born into an upwardly mobile peasant family in Shaoshan, Hunan province, Mao received a desultory education, part classical, part modern. He served as a soldier in the provincial army during the 1911 revolution, and after further education in the provincial capital, Changsha (where he was much influenced by his teacher, the Kantian Yang Changji), he moved to Beijing where Li Dazhao (a leading intellectual radical and an early proponent of Marxism) arranged for his employment at the university library. Returning to Changsha Mao engaged in political activity while employed as a teacher; at this stage his writings reveal the influence of MARX as well as of the Russian anarchists. One of the twelve original members of the Chinese Communist Party, Mao then engaged in the organizing of mine workers in Anyuan. Between 1921 and 1925 he travelled widely, working for the Communist Party in Shanghai, Guangzhou, and his native province. During the period of Communist–Guomindang (Nationalist Party) co-operation Mao began to develop an interest in the peasant question. After the Guomindang purge of the Communists (1927) Mao was entrusted with the task of organizing a peasant rebellion in Hunan and Jiangxi. In his writings of this time he identifies the class struggle of the peasantry with that of the proletariat and states that the revolutionary potential of China's peasantry is greater than that of any other class.

After the failure of the Autumn Harvest peasant uprising Mao retired in 1928 with the remnants of his peasant levies to Jingangshan. Thus began the guerrilla peasant phase of the Chinese Communist Party, the CCP setting up a series of Soviet areas in south-east China. Until 1934 the CCP was dominated by Russian-trained cadres who endeavoured to follow or interpret the Comintern revolutionary line of the time, which sought to employ Communist peasant guerrillas in attempts to capture urban areas. With the failure of this strategy, and the successful encirclement of the Soviet areas by Guomindang armies, the CCP was forced to engage in the 'Long March' to the north-west. In January 1935 at a meeting in Zunyi Mao was promoted to undisputed leadership over the CCP, a position he occupied until his death.

The years in Yanan in the north-west after 1937 were formative for Mao and the CCP. Mao began a serious study of Marxist philosophy and published writings on this topic. He ensured that his own thought and role became indispensable to the organization through the 'rectification campaign' of 1942–3 in which all possible leadership rivals were induced to engage in self-criticism of past conduct, and all party members were required to study his works. He also organized the people of the Soviet area by way of the 'mass line' for a protracted nationalist struggle against the Japanese, writing a number of theoretical works on guerrilla warfare.

Hopes of continuing the wartime Guomindang-Communist co-operation soon foundered, and Mao became head of state of the new People's Republic in 1949 (a post he held until 1958). After a period during which Soviet precedents were followed, Mao led experiments in social and economic organization which departed fundamentally from previous Marxist models. The commune movement (1958) and the Great Leap Forward (1958–9) sought to mobilize by way of moral incentives and mass enthusiasm the one resource China had in abundance – labour – for a quick forced march to communism. Neither was a success, the latter ending in near catastrophe with industry disrupted and large-scale food shortages, and as a result Mao was forced to relinquish some of his powers of management of the economic and political systems. Mao's response, after an initial period of quiescence, was to fight back on the ideological front. As his increasingly strident and critical remarks did not generate wide enthusiasm among the leadership of the CCP he resolved to sweep them aside, launching the Cultural Revolution in 1966. Successful in his first aims, Mao was then forced to turn to the army to restore order as the nation descended into chaos and bloodletting. From that time until his death an uneasy coalition of Cultural Revolution radicals, army members, and reha-bilitated state and CCP leaders dominated Chinese politics. Since 1976, though Mao has continued to be revered as the founder of the regime, his successors have become increas-ingly critical of his later role, now holding the view that the Cultural Revolution was a totally negative episode, and that the radical policies of 1958–9 incorporated serious errors.

Mao's MARXISM is a curious blend of Stalinist orthodoxy and innovation. His political writings of the 1940s conform to the Comintern interpretation of national revolution in the neo-colonial world, and his first excursions in philosophy follow closely their Soviet dialectical materialist originals. He was one of the first Marxists to give serious attention to military questions, and his view of guerrilla warfare was seminal for later practitioners of this art. And at the heart of the practice of the CCP after 1928 was the successful organization of the peas-antry. Thus, though Mao was careful (after his initial enthusiastic pronouncements) to declare that the proletariat (via their Party) should have hegemony over the overall struggle, he is in essence a theorist of peasant revolution. The protracted nature of the CCP struggle, and in particular the experience during the Yanan period, account for many of the idiosyncrasies of Mao's theory. To harness the support of a peasant population in what was principally a national rather than a social struggle, the CCP evolved the 'mass line', echoes of which can be seen in Mao's later orchestration of mass

struggles to transform the economy and rectify the political system. And the practice of 'rectification' in the campaign of 1942–3 was undoubtedly an influence on Mao's later view of the correct way to deal with those who commit errors: 'cure the sickness to save the patient' by way of exhaustive self-criticism.

After 1958, and particularly after 1962, Mao's Marxism took on a new aspect. He became more and more critical of the means by which the transition to socialism was organized (bureaucratic direction, reward according to 'bourgeois right' or labour), coming round to the view that China had taken the same wrong turn as the Soviet Union. In works widely disseminated during the Cultural Revolution but still not officially published in China, he rejected the formula put forward by Stalin in 1936 that classes (apart from remnants of the old order) could not exist or be generated under socialism. This he founded on a new inter-pretation of the universal and unceasing nature of the Marxist dialectic which thus understood would engender struggle and contradiction, even during the socialist phase. Mao warned of the possibility that a new bourgeoisie or privileged class could emerge from those who were the principal beneficiaries of the transition period, ultimately locating the headquarters of this new class in the CCP itself. While this was a convenient justification for purging the CCP of most of its senior cadres, Mao drew back when confronted (in the form of the 'Shanghai Commune' organized in 1967) with the anar-chist implications of his new theory, the period from 1969 seeing a gradual reconstruction of the communist system on more conventional lines.

It is significant that Mao was almost alone among his peers in having no experience of study abroad or knowledge of foreign lan-guages. For these reasons Chinese influences predominate in his works, some interpreters finding in them similarities to neo-Confucianism in his emphasis on the role of correct consciousness and the will in making revolution, others pointing to continuities after 1949 with the absolutist practice of the legalist-inspired first emperor of China, Qin Shihuang (see Ch'in, CHINESE POLITICAL THOUGHT). But there can be no doubt that orthodox Marxism-Leninism had a great impact on his thinking, particularly during the Yanan period when he was able to study for the first time by way of translations a considerable sample of the Marxist and Soviet canon.   JSC

Reading

Ch'en, J. ed.: *Mao Papers: Anthology and Bibliography*. London: Oxford University Press, 1970.

Leys, S.: *The Chairman's New Clothes: Mao and the Cultural Revolution*. London: Allison & Busby, 1977.

Mao Zedong: *Selected Works*, I-V. Peking: Foreign Languages Press, 1965–77.

———: *Miscellany of Mao Tse-tung Thought (1949–68)*, pts 1–2. Springfield, Va: National Technical Information Service, 1974.

†Schram, S.: *Mao Tse-tung*. Harmondsworth: Penguin, 1966.

———: *The Political Thought of Mao Tse-tung*, rev. edn. Harmondsworth: Penguin, 1969.

†——— ed.: *Mao Tse-tung Unrehearsed: Talks and Letters: 1956–71*. Harmondsworth: Penguin, 1974.

———: *Mao Zedong: a Preliminary Assessment*. Hong Kong: Chinese University Press, 1983.

Snow, E.: *Red Star over China*. London: Gollancz, 1937.

†Starr, J.B.: *Continuing the Revolution: the Political Thought of Mao*. Princeton, NJ: Princeton University Press, 1979.

Wakeman, F.: *History and Will: Philosophical Perspectives of Mao Tse-tung's Thought*. Berkeley: University of California Press, 1973.

Marcuse, Herbert (1898–1979)   German neo-Marxist social theorist and founding member, with Max Horkheimer and Theodor W. Adorno, of the so-called Frankfurt School of CRITICAL THEORY. In 1922 Marcuse received his doctorate from the University of Freiburg for a dissertation on *The German Artist Novel* which explored the relationship between art and society. Highly integrated societies, Marcuse argued, produce art that conforms to unified systems of belief. Fractured societies give birth to artistic works that do not reflect the dominant ideology but oppose it. Art flourishes on the basis of such conflict. Through new art forms the artist depicts a vision of a rational society able to develop its conflicts creatively towards an ideal of human freedom.

Marcuse's interest in art was deeply political as well as theoretical. It was his view that the struggle of the bourgeois artist, notably Thomas Mann, to create an aesthetic representation of a rational society was symbolic of the real historical struggle in Germany for a socialist community. But with the waning of socialist politics in Western Europe during the 1920s Marcuse began to entertain the possibility that MARX's theory of historical materialism provided an inadequate account of the conditions precipitating the emergence of class consciousness. His doubts about MARXISM surfaced clearly in 'On the Problem of the Dialectic' (1930). Marcuse maintained that the concept of 'correct class consciousness', particularly as it appeared in Georg LUKÁCS's *History and Class Consciousness*, was too abstract to grasp the individual's complex social existence and the tendencies to action imbedded in it. The abstractness of the concept of historical (class) agency blinded Marxism to the individual's potential for radical politics and to the question of how that potential might be developed. Consequently, Marxist theory was responsible for the apparently unbridgeable chasm between theory and practice, between the theoretical expectations for historical change and the practical possibilities for realizing those expectations.

Marcuse's argument was part of a project to ground the Marxist theory of historical change in the everyday practical activity of the individual rather than in the abstract historical activity of a class agent. This project unfolded between 1928 and 1932, a period Marcuse spent studying with the philosopher Martin HEIDEGGER at the University of Freiburg, following the publication of Heidegger's *Being and Time* in 1927. As Marcuse understood it, the fundamental ontology described in *Being and Time* could reorient Marxism towards forms of action that constitute every individual's existence and which cannot be suppressed totally by capitalism. The Heideggerian foundation for Marxism could serve as the new starting point for radical social action at a time when class struggle was subdued.

Integrating Marx and Heidegger did not end the predicament created by historical materialism. In his first major published work, *Hegel's Ontology and the Foundations of a Theory of Historicity* (1932), Marcuse offers an interpretation of HEGEL's *Logic* and *Phenomenology of*

Spirit that roots Heidegger's ontology in Hegel's dialectic. By this means Marcuse could see the individual as author of the determinants of his or her social existence and as becoming theoretically self-conscious about the structure of his or her existence and his or her part in shaping that structure. The individual is no longer, as with Heidegger, the unreflective product of pre-given ontological determinants. However, although Hegel's individual was reflexively self-creative, the Hegelian foundation for theory and practice (praxis) still relied upon pre-given ontological determinants of individual thought and action and was not entirely suitable groundwork to release historical materialism from its abstract leanings.

The problem was finally solved to Marcuse's satisfaction as a consequence of the discovery and publication in 1932 of Karl Marx's *Economic and Philosophical Manuscripts*. These uncompleted essays of the young Marx provided Marcuse with the philosophical arguments to complete his revision of historical materialism and to free the concept of praxis from an ontology that predetermined the structure and ends of human activity. The influence of the early Marx on Marcuse's project crystallized in 'The Foundation of Historical Materialism' (1932) and 'The Concept of Labor' (1933). The significance of the *Manuscripts* for Marcuse cannot be overestimated. The solution to the problematic in Marxist theory that Marcuse had framed imperfectly through the philosophies of Heidegger and Hegel was ironically provided by Marx himself.

At the collapse of the Weimar Republic and the Nazi assumption of power in 1933, Marcuse initially fled with other German Jews to Geneva and then left Switzerland to seek refuge in America. He abandoned his project to place historical materialism on a foundation that incorporated a theoretical recognition of the practical significance of the individual. The project no longer appeared viable in light of the virtual absence of any opposition to fascist totalitarianism. All individuals and classes appeared to be swept up into the torrent of mass politics. Marcuse now became associated with the so-called Frankfurt School and spent the next three decades accounting for the failure of historical materialism and reconstructing the theoretical foundations of Marxism in the wake of this failure.

The first major work in this period of Marcuse's theoretical development was *Reason and Revolution* (1941). Here Marcuse returns to Hegel, though to a much different Hegel from that encountered earlier in *Hegel's Ontology*. He now assigns Hegel's concept of reason the task of articulating the standards against which all societies must be assessed. Theory, Marcuse insists, is necessarily thrown back to such a high level of abstraction in historical settings where there is no historical agency opposing domination. And where there is no political movement critical of a repressive regime, there only can be a critical theory.

Along with the other members of the Frankfurt School Marcuse pursued an explanation for the evolution of FASCISM from capitalism. He focused on the role of technology in securing fascist repression, and with the assistance of Max WEBER's work developed a general theory of technological domination. According to Marcuse, because of their commitment to scientific and technical progress all advanced industrial societies, regardless of differences in political institutions and beliefs, increasingly conform to the rationality of technological production. Technological rationality organizes all cultural, political, social, and economic sectors of society to follow the central ideological principle of material productivity. Social relations are shaped into a totally administered, completely integrated, perfectly uniform and comfortable existence to which there is no challenge and from which there is no escape. Marcuse's theory of technological domination forms the basic argument of *Soviet Marxism* (1958) and his most famous work, *One-Dimensional Man* (1964).

Although the domination of technological reason reduced all of human experience to a single, uniform dimension, Marcuse argued also that the rational reorganization of technology could render obsolete many forms of labour and by so doing create the preconditions for new modes of human freedom and development. He turned to the metapsychology of Sigmund FREUD to derive these radically different types of human expression. His vision of a non-repressive society is set forth in *Eros and Civilization* (1955) and *An Essay on Liberation* (1969).

With the NEW LEFT and the student movement gaining political prominence through their opposition to the Vietnam war, from 1968 to 1974 Marcuse looked to these groups as potential agents of resistance to advanced industrial society and of social change. During this period he appeared to depart from his earlier argument that technological reason destroyed all political bases for criticism of the established society. His hope that these new political forces would serve as the vanguard of sweeping historical transformation was expressed in *An Essay on Liberation* and in *Counterrevolution and Revolt* (1972). Once the New Left and the student movement faded at the close of the Vietnam era, however, Marcuse returned to the pessimism of *One-Dimensional Man*.

During the final years of his life Marcuse devoted increasing attention to the role of art in the modern world. He embraced more strongly than ever his long-held view: in a one-dimensional society only the most abstract forms of expression could offer a vision of a way of life that could rationally exploit the progress of a technological reason that had come to enslave us. In his last work, *The Aesthetic Dimension* (1977), Marcuse came full circle to the arguments of his doctoral dissertation, and he completed his life's work on the note where it had begun more than half a century earlier. MS

Reading
†Geoghegan, V.: *Reason and Eros: the Social Theory of Herbert Marcuse*. London: Pluto, 1981.
†Jay, M.: *The Dialectical Imagination: a History of the Frankfurt School and the Institute of Social Research, 1923–1950*. Boston: Little, Brown; London: Heinemann, 1973.
Kateb, G.: The political thought of Herbert Marcuse. *Commentary*, 49.1 (1970) 48–63.
Katz, B.: *Herbert Marcuse and the Art of Liberation*. London: Verso/New Left, 1982.
Marcuse, H.: *Hegels Ontologie und die Grundlegung einer Theorie der Geschichtlichkeit* (*Hegel's Ontology and the Foundations of a Theory of Historicity*). Frankfurt: Klosterman, 1932.
———: *Reason and Revolution: Hegel and the Rise of Social Theory*. New York: Oxford University Press, 1941; 2nd edn, London: Routledge & Kegan Paul, 1955.

———: *Eros and Civilization: a Philosophical Inquiry into Freud*. London: Routledge & Kegan Paul, 1966.
———: *Soviet Marxism: a Critical Analysis*. New York: Columbia University Press, 1958.
———: *One-Dimensional Man: Studies in the Ideology of Advanced Industrial Society*. Boston: Beacon; London: Routledge & Kegan Paul, 1968.
———: *An Essay on Liberation*. Boston: Beacon; London: Allen Lane, 1969.
———: *Counterrevolution and Revolt*. Boston: Beacon; London: Allen Lane, 1972.
———: *The Aesthetic Dimension: Toward a Critique of Marxist Aesthetics*. Boston: Beacon, 1978.
†Schoolman, M.: *The Imaginary Witness: the Critical Theory of Herbert Marcuse*. New York: Free Press, 1980.

Maritain, Jacques (1882–1973) French philosopher. A leading exponent in the twentieth century of the theory of natural law, developed along Thomist lines. See THOMIST POLITICAL THOUGHT.

market socialism A form of SOCIALISM which advocates combining social ownership of the means of production with extensive use of market mechanisms in the economy – for instance by basing production in autonomous and competing workers' co-operatives. In this way, it is hoped, the distributive and democratic aims of socialism can be married to the efficiency-inducing properties of market competition. DLM

Reading
Nove, A.: *The Economics of Feasible Socialism*. London: Allen & Unwin, 1983.

Marsilius of Padua (Marsilio dei Mainardini) (1275/80–1342) Italian political theorist. Marsilius probably studied medicine at the University of Padua. In 1313 he was rector of the University of Paris, where he met such leading Averroists as Peter of Abano and John of Jandun. He is chiefly famous for his antipapalist treatise *Defensor pacis* (Defender of Peace) (1324), a landmark in the history of political philosophy. When his authorship of this work became known in 1326 he was forced to flee to the court of Louis of Bavaria in Nuremburg; Pope John XXII thereupon branded him a heretic. Marsilius subsequently assisted Louis in various imperial ventures in Italy. He was also the author of some minor political works. There is a disputed attribution to him of some commentaries on Aristotle.

The primary purpose of the *Defensor pacis* was to refute the papalist claims to 'plenitude of power' as these claims had been advanced by Pope Innocent IV, Egidius of Rome, and others in the thirteenth and fourteenth centuries (see MEDIEVAL POLITICAL THOUGHT). So crushing was the refutation produced by Marsilius that it completely reversed the papalist position. This held that secular rulers must be subject to the papacy even in 'temporal' affairs, so that they must be established, judged, and, if necessary, deposed by the pope. Marsilius, in contrast, undertook to demonstrate that the papacy and the priesthood in general must be subject not only in temporal, but even in 'spiritual', affairs to the whole people and to the secular ruler acting by the people's authority. The powers of the priesthood were to be reduced to the administration of the sacraments and the teaching of divine law, but even in these functions priests were to be regulated and controlled by the people and its elected government. The upshot of Marsilius's doctrine was that the attempt to base human society on religious values under priestly control was decisively overthrown; instead, the way was opened for a purely secular society under the control of a popularly elected government. Hence, it is understandable that Marsilius has been hailed as a prophet of the modern world. His treatise exerted a marked influence on the Conciliar movement (see CONCILIARISM) and during the period of the Reformation.

Equally as important as these revolutionary conclusions are the premises from which Marsilius derived them. These premises are found in his general theory of the state, which is noteworthy for its fusing of three distinct themes. The first is ARISTOTLE's teleological view of the state as subserving the good life. The various parts of the state, including government, are defined by the contribution they make to the rational 'fulfilment' of man's natural desire for a 'sufficient life'. The first theme, then, stresses an affirmative and maximal utilitarianism – what is required for the attainment of the highest ends of the 'sufficient life', the common benefit, and justice.

The second theme of Marsilius's political theory, in contrast, is a negative and minimal utilitarianism. It emphasizes the inevitability of conflicts among men and the consequent need for the formal instrumentalities of coercive law and government in order to regulate these conflicts. Without such regulation, Marsilius repeatedly insists, human society itself must be destroyed. In developing this theme, Marsilius presents a positivistic concept of LAW, which stands in contrast with his nonpositivistic conception of justice (a distinction often overlooked in discussions of his ideas). Unlike most medieval political philosophers Marsilius holds that justice is not a necessary condition of law. What is necessary is that the legal rules have coercive force, such that with regard to their observance 'there is given a command coercive through punishment or reward to be distributed in the present world'. These rules and the government which enforces them must be unitary in the sense that, if a society is to survive, it cannot have two or more rival coercive bodies of law and government.

The third theme of Marsilius's political theory is that the only legitimate source of all political authority is the people. It is the people, the whole body of citizens or its 'weightier part', which must make the laws either by itself or through elected representatives, and it is also the people which must elect, 'correct', and, if necessary, depose the government. Marsilius presents many arguments for this republican position.

Although all three themes of Marsilius's general political theory were found in earlier medieval political philosophers, no other philosopher had given the second and third themes as central a position as did Marsilius. The full consequence of these emphases emerges in the applications he makes of his general political theory to the problems of ecclesiastical politics.

In keeping with his first theme, Marsilius views the Christian priesthood as one of the parts of the state dedicated to achieving the 'sufficient life' for all believers. Unlike the other parts of the state, however, the priesthood subserves the 'sufficient life' to be attained primarily 'in the future world' rather than the present one. Like the other Averroists, Marsilius manifests scepticism about the rational demonstrability of such a future life; nevertheless, he officially accepts the Christian doctrine that the future life is superior to the present life. He also holds, however, that secular and religious values are in basic opposition; here he seems to be applying in the realm of the practical the Averroist doctrine of the contrariety of reason and faith in theoretic philosophy.

At this point, however, Marsilius's second and third themes have their effect. Since the essence of political authority is the coerciveness required for the minimal end of preserving society, it follows that the higher end subserved by the priesthood does not entitle it to superior political authority. What determines the order of political authority is not the greater excellence of one end over another but, rather, the specifically political need for unified coercive authority in order to prevent unresolved conflicts from destroying society. Hence, the secular government, as bearer of this coercive authority, must be politically superior to the priesthood.

In addition to this political argument against diverse centres of coercive power in any society, Marsilius also stresses, from within the religious tradition itself, that in order to be meritorious religious belief must be purely voluntary. Hence, in order to fulfil its mission, divine law and the priesthood which teaches and administers it cannot be coercive in this world.

Marsilius's third theme, REPUBLICANISM, also plays an important role in the political subordination of the priesthood and papacy. The only rules and persons that are entitled to the status of being coercive laws and government officials are those ultimately chosen by the people; hence, there can be no crediting the claims of divine law and the priesthood to a separate derivation of coercive political authority from God. This republicanism operates not only in the relation of the priesthood to the secular state but also in its relation to religious affairs. Because the whole people is superior in virtue to any of its parts and because freedom requires popular consent or election, the priesthood itself must be elected by the people of each community rather than being appointed by an oligarchically chosen pope, and the pope himself must be elected by the whole of Christendom. Similarly, the whole people must elect general councils to provide authoritative interpretations of the meaning of divine law. In these ways Marsilius's general political theory leads to a republican structure for the church as against its traditional monarchic structure.   AG

Reading

†Gewirth, A.: *Marsilius of Padua and Medieval Political Philosophy*. New York: Columbia University Press, 1951.

Lagarde, G. de: *La Naissance de l'esprit laïque au déclin du moyen âge*, vol. III: *Le Defensor pacis*. Paris: Béatrice-Nauwelaerts, 1970.

Marsilius of Padua: *Defensor pacis*, trans. A. Gewirth as *Marsilius of Padua, the Defender of Peace*. New York: Columbia University Press, 1956.

Quillet, J.: *La philosophie politique de Marsile de Padoue*. Paris: Vrin, 1970.

Martov, Yulii Osipovich (1873–1923) Russian Marxist. The leading theorist of MENSHEVISM and an opponent of LENIN. See SOVIET COMMUNISM.

Marx, Karl (1818–1883) German social scientist, historian, and revolutionary, whose critical analysis of capitalist society laid the theoretical foundations for the political movement bearing his name. Marx's main contribution to social and political theory lay in his materialist conception of history which emphasized the importance of the economic sphere – the conditions under which men and women produced and reproduced their means of subsistence – in shaping the other areas of social activity. Politics in the narrow sense was, therefore, an activity unintelligible without reference to the larger study of history and economics on which its forms were dependent; and Marx's theories of the state, revolution, etc., have to be understood in the context of this general outlook which has had considerable influence on the whole of the social sciences over the last century.

During the early period of his life, Marx progressed from the idealist Hegelianism of his student days to the humanist communism that characterized his stay in Paris in 1844. Born into a professional middle-class home, Marx early assimilated both the rational Enlightenment views of his father, a respected Trier lawyer, and the enthusiasm for romanticism and utopian socialism of Baron von Westphalen (whose daughter Jenny he later married). As a student at the University of Berlin, however, Marx embraced the dominant philosophy of Hegelianism. The increasingly reactionary politics of the Prussian government meant that Marx's chosen career of university teaching was closed to him and he took up journalism instead, becoming the editor of the leading Rheinish newspaper. This journalistic experience brought Marx into contact with contemporary debates on law and economics and led him to re-evaluate HEGEL's political philosophy from a more materialist viewpoint, a process for which the closure of his newspaper gave him unexpected leisure. Convinced that socialism of some sort would shortly be on the agenda for Germany (and elsewhere), Marx moved in late 1843 to Paris, the home of socialist theory. Here he rapidly became an ardent communist and, in the *Economic and Philosophical Manuscripts* (1844), set out the first systematic version of his ideas. Influenced by the philosophy of Ludwig Feuerbach (see YOUNG HEGELIANS), he based his conception of COMMUNISM on a contrast between the ALIENATION of labour under capitalism and a communist society in which human beings could freely develop their nature in co-operative production. In the society described by the classical political economists, workers were alienated in that they forfeited the products of a labour which was imposed on them and thus were separated both from their fellow human beings and from the natural world. All these alienations would be overcome in communism, which would involve a reunification of human beings with the products of their labour, with their work process, with each other, and with the natural world.

A historical and material basis for these somewhat utopian views was provided by Marx two years later in *The German Ideology* (1846), of which the basic thesis was that 'the nature of individuals depends on the material conditions determining their production' (*Selected Writings*, p. 161). In this materialist conception of history, the sum total of the relations of production – the way human beings organized their social production as well as the instruments they used – constituted the real basis of society, on which there arose a legal and political superstructure and to which corresponded definite forms of social consciousness. Thus the way in which people produced their means of subsistence – and particularly the classes yielded by the different relationships of social groups to the means of production – conditioned the whole of intellectual, political and social life.

Marx's only substantial engagement in practical politics was during the revolutionary years of 1848–9 when he combined with great difficulty the radicalness demanded of him as leader of the German emigré workers' organization known as the Communist League with the more muted tone appropriate to his editorship of the left-liberal *Neue Rheinische Zeitung*. Marx's more reflective views on politics, following his move to London in 1849, are to be understood in the context of his materialist conception of history. Thus Marx saw the STATE, for example, as an instrument of class domination within the framework of the rise and fall of successive and progressive modes of production. In his earlier writings Marx had seen the proclaimed liberty and equality of the liberal state as compensation for the defects of economic life under capitalism, as alienated social power; later he concentrated more on an analysis of the function of the state in society. In his most simplistic formulation, 'the executive of the modern state is but a committee for managing the common affairs of the whole bourgeoisie' (*Selected Writings*, p 223). A more subtle analysis of the relative independence of state power is to be found in Marx's writings on contemporary French (and British) politics, particularly in *The Eighteenth Brumaire of Louis Bonaparte* (1852) where he discusses the role of different class fractions in establishing Bonaparte's power. Elsewhere, Marx allowed that the state might not represent the whole of a class but only a section of that class (for example, the financiers under Louis-Philippe); or that one class could control the state for the benefit of another class (for example, the Whigs on behalf of the middle class in England). In relatively backward countries, where classes were not fully developed, Marx thought that the state could play an independent role; also in the European absolutist monarchies in the transition between feudal and bourgeois rule.

The materialist conception of history also involved the view that at a certain stage in their evolution the forces of production would develop beyond the relations of production, which would then act as a fetter, so inaugurating a period of social revolution. Marx describes revolution as 'the driving force of history' and all his studies in other fields were devoted to uncovering the springs of that driving force. In particular, his voluminous *Capital* (1867–), the main product of his lengthy exile in London, was designed to uncover the origin and destiny of capitalist EXPLOITATION. Marx's analysis of the nature of surplus value under capitalism, the increasing severity of crises, and the tendency of the rate of profit to fall, convinced him that capitalism could not long survive. The proletarian revolution which would mark its demise would generally be violent (though Marx conceived of the possibility of a peaceful transition to socialism in certain countries), would be centred on the most industrially advanced countries (though he foresaw the possibility of its originating in Russia) and would rapidly become international.

On the subject of post-revolutionary politics, Marx's views are necessarily sketchy. The experience of the Paris Commune showed Marx the possibility of closing the gap between the state and civil society that had been opened up by liberal democracy. As an instance of the abolition of the division of labour in politics, Marx welcomed the Commune's proposal to have all officials, including judges, elected by universal suffrage and revocable at any time; to pay officials the same wages as manual labourers; to replace the standing army by the armed people; and to divest the police and clergy of their political influence. Marx also considered that the initiative of the Commune could have yielded a decentralized, federal political structure and an economy based on co-operatives united by a common plan – in contrast to the more centralized and authoritarian suggestions in the *Communist Manifesto* (1848). In his *Critique of the Gotha Programme* (1875), Marx talked of a revolutionary dicta-

torship of the proletariat which would convert the state 'from an organ superior to society to one completely subordinate to it'. Most of what little Marx says of communist society indicates that it will have dispensed with the need for politics.

Unlike most earlier theorists of politics, Marx did not produce a systematic treatment of the subject. There are several reasons for this. Given the structure of his theory, politics was derivative of economics. It was the latter that claimed most of his attention, and his project of a major work tracing political to economic forms remained incomplete, with the result that any picture of Marx's views has to be reconstructed largely from *ad hoc* comments on contemporary politics. Such a reconstruction has been hampered in the past by the fact that the elevation of Marx's ideas into the official doctrine of the movement bearing his name has made them the subject of acute political controversy, not to say distortion. In addition, the fact that Marx's thought obviously developed considerably throughout his life led to arguments as to whether there was a continuity in his thought or whether there were not two radically different Marxes – the young humanist philosopher of the early 1840s and the later, more rigorous and apparently determinist, social and economic theorist. Given, also, the conceptual fluidity and open-endedness that Marx acquired from his Hegelian origins it is no wonder that the meaning and import of the Marxian dialectic has given rise to the most diverse interpretations.

The strength of Marx's account of present and past politics is the way in which he anchors it firmly in the social and economic world and, through the doctrine of IDEOLOGY, traces the self-description of political actors back to the conflict between social groups over the production and distribution of scarce resources. Within this framework, Marx's analysis is most impressive when it is least reductionist – as in his account of the rise to power of Louis Bonaparte. The predictive and prescriptive side of Marx's ideas is less satisfactory. His own theory precluded him from offering what he called 'recipes for the cookshops of the future', but his clear expectation of proletarian revolution in the West has, to date, been frustrated and his picture of future communist society has been thought by many to rest on a naive and one-sided conception of human nature. Nevertheless, over the whole range of the social sciences, Marx has proved probably the most influential figure of the twentieth century.

DTMcL

Reading

†Avineri, S.: *The Social and Political Thought of Karl Marx*. Cambridge: Cambridge University Press, 1968.

Cohen, G.: *Karl Marx's Theory of History: a Defence*. Oxford: Clarendon Press, 1978.

Elster, J.: *Making Sense of Marx*. Cambridge: Cambridge University Press, 1985.

Hunt, R.: *Marxism and Totalitarian Democracy*. 2 vols. London: Macmillan, 1974 and 1985.

†McLellan, D.: *The Thought of Karl Marx*, 2nd edn. London: Macmillan, 1981.

Marx, K.: *Selected Writings*, ed. D. McLellan. Oxford: Oxford University Press, 1977.

Plamenatz, J.: *Karl Marx's Philosophy of Man*. Oxford: Clarendon Press, 1975.

Wood, A.: *Karl Marx*. London: Routledge & Kegan Paul, 1981.

Marxism The economic, social and political theory and practice originating in the works of Karl MARX and Friedrich ENGELS and subsequently elaborated by their various followers. What Marxism is and what it is not is a matter of considerable dispute, partly because of the very wide variety of theories so described and partly because of the use of the term as one of political approval or disapproval.

Nevertheless there is general agreement that most varieties of Marxism typically contain three main strands. First, and most important, there is an explanation and critique of present and past societies. The explanation consists in according some privilege to the economic factor over other factors in accounting for social change and development. More specifically, prime importance is given to the forces of production (the tools and instruments that are at the disposal of human beings at any given time) and the relations of production (the way in which human beings organize themselves in order to use the same forces of production) as shaping the political and cultural arrangements in any given society. This view, known as 'historical materialism', is often jejunely formulated in the proposition that the economic base determines the political and ideological superstructure. Although it is granted that the political and ideological elements can influence the economic structure, it is the development of the latter which produces social change. At a certain state of their evolution the forces of production develop as far as they can under the existing economic and political organization of society, which then becomes a barrier to their further development, ushering in a period of social revolution in which new economic and political relationships, corresponding to the expanded forces of production, are established. In accordance with this pattern it is possible to pick out the asiatic, ancient, feudal and modern bourgeois modes of production as progressive epochs in the economic formation of society.

The critical component in this first strand consists in the view that in these successive modes of production the crucial elements in society – the forces of production – have been controlled by a minority who have used their economic power in order to exploit the mass of the population by appropriating the economic surplus for their own benefit. This inherently conflictual situation gives rise to a CLASS struggle which centres around the ownership and control of the means of production. All political institutions and cultural beliefs are shaped by the prevailing economic arrangements and the holders of economic power – the ruling class – so as effectively to bolster the unequal distribution of resources. This yields the Marxist concept of IDEOLOGY as a set of beliefs and practices which serve to maintain an asymmetrical allocation of economic and political power.

The second strand of Marxist thought is the notion of an alternative to a society based on exploitation and divided along class lines. This can only consist in a society based on the common ownership of the means of production in which the human potential, stunted by the division of labour characteristic of class societies, will be enabled freely to develop its manifold facets. Such a society will obviously have no classes and therefore no need for a state apparatus defined as an instrument of class domination. In an initial stage, generally known as socialism, distribution of goods will be made in the first instance according to the contribution of each individual; later it will be possible to move to a communist organization of society which will embody the famous principle of 'from each according to their ability and to each according to their needs'. Any detailed description of such a society is bound, on Marxist assumptions, to be highly speculative.

The third strand is some account of how to move from the first to the second. Clearly the materialist conception of history outlined in the first strand implies that the capitalist mode of production is as transitory as all previous ones. Marxists have disagreed over the exact mechanism – whether, for example, it is the tendency of the rate of profit to fall or the growth of underconsumption – but there is general agreement that the capitalist system is inherently unstable, crisis-ridden and will inevitably collapse. However, the advent of socialism will also require the revolutionary activity of those whom capitalist society is producing as its own gravediggers – the working class, whose growing numbers and relative impoverishment will lead to revolt. Following on a revolutionary upheaval, there will have to be a transitional period, referred to as the dictatorship of the proletariat, before a fully communist society can be inaugurated. The relationship of any Marxist-inspired party to the class it represents is subject to more varying accounts than any other aspect of Marxism. Since the era of the mass party only arrived after Marx's death, he himself did not have to cope with this problem and anyone – from a Leninist proposing a highly centralized 'vanguard' party to lead workers (who would otherwise have the most inadequate views about politics) to a libertarian socialist who believes that political power should be vested directly in workers' assemblies – can claim, without fear of refutation, to stand in the true Marxist tradition.

Of these three strands, the second – the delineation of a viable alternative socialist society – is not much further advanced than when Marx himself wrote. The third – how to get from capitalism to socialism – has proved increasingly problematic and controversial, at least in the West. The result is that most of the efforts of Marxist theorists have gone into elaborating variations on the first theme – the critical analysis of past and present societies.

Nevertheless during the 'Golden Age' of Marxism, from the death of Marx in 1883 to the outbreak of the first world war, Marxism did present a fairly coherent appearance. This coherence was largely due to the power and prestige of the German Social Democratic Party whose Erfurt Programme of 1891 reiterated what had become the traditional doctrines of the drive to monopoly within capitalism, the decline of the middle class, the impoverishment of the proletariat and the inevitability of the socialization of the means of production in a classless society, while at the same time containing such immediate demands as universal suffrage, freedom of expression, free schooling and a progressive income tax.

Around the turn of the century two new elements came to the fore. A comprehensive account of the nature of the universe was provided by the metaphysics that came to be known as DIALECTICAL MATERIALISM. Originating with Engels and taken up by Soviet orthodoxy, dialectical materialism finds a dialectic in nature as well as in history and declares matter to move according to various laws such as the transformation of quantity into quality and the negation of the negation. More interestingly, the scramble for colonies at the end of the nineteenth century had led Marxists to produce theories of IMPERIALISM of which the most impressive was that of Hilferding who pointed to the growing control of credit institutions over industry and to the rise of corporate ownership. The power of national cartels led to heightened international tension through growing competition to monopolize markets and sources of raw materials. There was also an increase in the practice of dumping abroad goods unsaleable at home at monopolistic high prices and a tendency to export capital by founding businesses abroad. This led to economic warfare between nations and armed expansion into underdeveloped regions to enlarge potential markets, in a process where freedom, democracy and equality were the first casualties.

This Second International Marxism – as it came to be called – whose most prominent representative was Karl KAUTSKY, emphasized the determinist aspects of Marx's materialist conception of history and owed more to Darwin than to Hegel. The belief in the inevitability of the decline of capitalism and the growth of socialist forces produced an underlying political passivity in that it always made sense to wait for the preconditions for revolution to ripen still further rather than risk all in premature revolutionary activity. The Kautskyan orthodoxy was attacked from the right by Edward BERNSTEIN who advocated the revision of many of Marx's doctrines which had in his view been rendered obsolete by economic developments in the industrial societies; and from the left by Rosa LUXEMBURG who detected a dangerous enthusiasm for electoral politics and a concomitant coolness towards such genuinely revolutionary concepts as that of the general strike. Nevertheless the impressive organization and electoral success of the German Social Democrats gave their fragile combination of revolutionary doctrine and passive political practice a leading role in the Marxist movement as a whole until the outbreak of the first world war.

The fate of German Social Democracy during and immediately after the war had the most decisive influence on the evolution of Marxist doctrine. Marxists had hitherto paid little attention to the phenomenon of NATIONALISM (the working class had no fatherland) and thus were ill-equipped to deal with its violent expression in world war. The splintering of the German party over the question of support for the war and the crushing of its left wing in the abortive rising of 1918–19 deprived them of their hegemonic role, which passed to LENIN and the successful Bolsheviks. Although Lenin's ideas on imperialism, culled mainly from Hilferding and Bukharin, have undoubtedly proved very influential, his main contribution to Marxist doctrine was his theory of the vanguard party. The innovation here was not so much the idea that a party was needed to instil socialist consciousness into the workers (Kautsky would have agreed with that) as that the party organization should be composed exclusively of revolutionaries who were professional in the double sense that they would devote themselves full time to party work and that they would be fully trained. Lenin's prognosis of a bourgeois revolution in Russia carried out under proletarian leadership and his description of a libertarian socialist society in *The State*

and Revolution (1917) were both overtaken by the circumstances of the 1917 revolutions and the ensuing civil war, where TROTSKY's more hard-headed theory of permanent revolution was found more suitable. Left alone on the world stage by the failure of the German revolution, the Russian Marxists were confronted with a set of problems concerning the organization and development of a socialist economy which the Marxist tradition had simply not equipped them to answer. The questions were the subject of lively debate during the early and mid-1920s, until the triumph of Stalin's version of 'socialism in one country' imposed a sterile orthodoxy from which the Soviet Union has yet to emerge (see SOVIET COMMUNISM).

The success of Russian Marxism in 1917 provoked a split in the Marxist movement outside Russia between, on the one hand, those in the newly formed national Communist parties who accepted both the Bolshevik method of internal party organization and the predominance of Soviet views on world politics in the context of the Third International and, on the other hand, those who strove to maintain a non-Soviet form of Marxist theory and practice despite its evidently gloomy prospects. The efforts of the latter have been dogged by two related problems. The first was the legacy of Stalinism. Not only did the Bolshevization of most of Western European Marxism mean that the practical, if not intellectual, energies of many Marxists became subordinate to the dictates of Moscow; in addition, those who refused such obedience had to come to terms with the awkward fact that in the one country where Marxism had apparently triumphed a sort of bureaucratic collectivism had emerged to which they – and still less their fellow-citizens – were little inclined. The second problem confronting Marxists in the West was the evidently non-revolutionary nature of the central agency of revolution in the Marxist tradition – the working class.

One response to these difficulties has been that of the small Trotskyist parties who have combined a continued confidence in the revolutionary potential of the working class with a virulent criticism of the Soviet Union. More significant, though, has been the inevitable divorce of most Marxist theory from active politics (GRAMSCI being the last Marxist theoretician of note to combine these roles) and the consequent twin tendencies to give more emphasis to intellectual and cultural questions than had previously been the case and to explore what could usefully be borrowed from other philosophies. Since most leading Marxist theoreticians in Western Europe and the United States over the last half-century have been academics rather than activists and have been writing in a period of decline of working-class activity, philosophy, epistemology, methodology, even aesthetics bulk larger in their work than do politics or economics and their outlook is more resignedly pessimistic than that of the previous generation.

The two decades after 1917 nevertheless yielded important writers in LUKÁCS and Gramsci, both of whom were, at times, political activists, and whose influence continues to be felt today. In the work of the early Lukács the strong emphasis on consciousness can be seen as a theoretical reflection of the Bolshevik revolution. Lukács's criticism of the bourgeois world-view as reified – that is, unacceptably static, fragmented and objective – and his confidence in the heightening capacity of proletarian consciousness – ascribed rather than actual, and embodied in an elite of revolutionary intellectuals – marks the high point of Marxist optimism in the West. But Lukács's picture remained at some distance from reality as the revolutionary movements in Germany, Austria and his native Hungary proved a failure and he found himself theorizing in a socio-political vacuum.

Gramsci is perhaps the central figure in the whole of the western Marxist tradition. He is the most original Marxist thinker of the last fifty years: his contribution spanned the entire spectrum of Marxist politics in the decade following the October Revolution. His general aim was to re-evaluate the place of the superstructure in the Marxist account of historical change. He achieved this first by stressing the role of intellectuals in politics and pointing to the problem now facing the working class of producing its own organic intellectuals; second, by underlining the importance of establishing hegemony, the process by which the proletariat gained leadership over all the forces opposed to capitalism and welded them into a new political bloc capable of resisting and eventually overthrowing the hegemony of the bourgeoisie. His analysis of this process led Gramsci to pose the question of the relationship of civil society to the state, and to contrast here Russia, where state power had been vulnerable to frontal attack, with the West, where the weakening of bourgeois ideological and institutional hegemony would be a precondition for any successful revolution.

Marxism as it emerged from the second world war has been characterized by two opposite tendencies, both of which sought rejuvenation through the aid of some more recent philosophy. The first, largely embodied in the Frankfurt School and the later SARTRE, stressed the subjective side of Marxism. Whereas Sartre attempted to combine a form of Marxism with his own version of EXISTENTIALISM, the Frankfurt School was most influenced by psycho-analysis, and its members' work tended to move from the traditional Marxist version of politics and economics into a more general critique of bourgeois culture (see CRITICAL THEORY). The second trend was influenced by structuralist ideas and conceived of Marxism as a science. The work of the most prominent of these Marxists, Louis ALTHUSSER, in particular his concept of the problematic and his insistence on the relative autonomy of the sciences, was a good antidote both to all types of reductionism and to extreme forms of Hegelian Marxism. Nevertheless neo-structuralist Marxism, too, was cut off from the influence of the conditions of social production and ultimately appeared as the preserve of an intellectual elite disconnected from the revolutionary activity of the working class. As the influence of structuralism declined there have been recently, and particularly in the Anglo-Saxon world, some interesting attempts to re-examine Marxist concepts with the aid of linguistic analysis and game theory.

It is evident from the above account that Marxism has become extremely diffuse as the twentieth century has progressed. At the present time, four very different kinds of Marxism can be discerned. First, there is the rigidly orthodox Marxism of such established socialist societies as the Soviet Union and China where it serves as an ideological framework within which to conduct social and political discussion; second, there is the more pragmatic Marxism of Western European Communist parties, where a much simplified version of Gramsci's ideas is often used to justify compromises with the prevailing parliamentary ethos (see EUROCOMMUNISM); third, in much of Africa, Central and Latin America and South-East Asia, Marxism is used as a vehicle for protest against economic exploitation and, often in combination with nationalism, functions as an ideology for mass participation in the modernization process. Finally, in the West, many Marxists have turned their attention to philosophy almost as an end in itself and to subjects – such as literary criticism – far removed from politics.

As a political doctrine, Marxism has encountered severe difficulties: the continuing resilience of capitalism in the West and the disappointing results of existing socialist societies in the East have frustrated most Marxist expectations. As a social and political theory, the same broad difficulties confront Marxism as confront any other general theory: its precise statements are liable to refutation and a more defensive formulation tends to be so vague as to be almost vacuous. In the case of Marxism, again as with other such theories, argument has centred largely on how to dissect the social whole in the first place and how to describe the relationship of the elements thus picked out. Although the crude metaphor, derived from heavy engineering, of base and superstructure has long been abandoned by most Marxists, it is essential to a Marxist perspective to be able to distinguish in one way or another the economic from the political and ideological – a task which has turned out to be increasingly difficult. A convincing description of the relationship of the economic to the political and the ideological has proved even more elusive. Whereas most early Marxists talked of the one causally determining the other, it has latterly become more usual to talk in terms of correspondence, or even to analyse the relationship in an explicitly functionalist manner.

Given that Marxism has come to borrow so much from other social theories, it is perhaps misguided to look too hard for the specificity of Marxism. It is much more as a general approach, a perspective, a broad conceptual framework that it continues to exercise its influence. As such, it is clear that much excellent contemporary work on subjects such as the nature and function of the capitalist state, the economics and politics of underdevelopment, or contemporary theories of aesthetics and ideology owe much to Marxism. In its analysis of persisting economic inequality both inside nation-states and between them, and of the concomitant systems of power and domination, together with a critique of such arrangements, Marxism can claim to be the most influential paradigm of our age.   DTMcL

Reading
Anderson, P.: *Considerations on Western Marxism.* London: New Left, 1976.

Boggs, C. and Plotke, D. *The Politics of Eurocommunism.* London: Macmillan, 1980.

Carr, E.H.: *A History of Soviet Russia.* London: Macmillan, 1950– .

Diggens, J.: *The American Left in the Twentieth Century.* New York: Harcourt, Brace, Jovanovich, 1973.

Gay, P.: *The Dilemma of Democratic Socialism: Edward Bernstein's Challenge to Marx.* New York: Schocken, 1962.

Howard, D. and Klare, K. eds: *The Unknown Dimension: Post-Leninist Marxism.* New York: Basic, 1972.

Jay, M.: *Marxism and Totality.* Berkeley: University of California Press, 1984.

†Kolakowski, L.: *Main Currents of Marxism.* 3 vols. Oxford: Oxford University Press, 1978.

Lenin, V.I.: *The State and Revolution.* In *Collected Works*, vol. 25. Moscow: Progress Publishers, 1969.

Lichtheim, G.: *Marxism.* London: Routledge & Kegan Paul; New York: Praeger, 1961.

†McLellan, D.: *Marxism after Marx.* London: Macmillan, 1980.

Salvadori, M.: *Kautsky and the Socialist Revolution.* London: New Left, 1979.

Schorske, C.: *German Social Democracy, 1905–1917.* Cambridge, Mass.: Harvard University Press, 1955.

Marxism-Leninism   The official ideology of the Soviet Union, and of countries in Eastern Europe within the Soviet sphere of influence. See SOVIET COMMUNISM.

mass society   The term is largely used at the

present time to denote a kind of society that is at once large in population and rather loose and amorphous in its social structure, polity, and economy. In the ideal-type of mass society individualism is rampant in morals, hedonism permeates consumer behaviour, and a generalized laxness pervades family, neighbourhood, church, and school. Moreover, in the stereotypes of mass society which are associated with the names of SPENGLER, Hannah ARENDT, and many others of the last half-century, the masses are perceived as the breeding ground of despotism. By its very looseness, its atomized rather than organic nature, mass society is held to be not only conducive to the rise of centralized power – in part because of an endemic search for political community – but an ideal kind of society for the aims and desires of totalitarian leaders, who therefore encourage its growth. In all, mass society is perceived as a highly probable consequence of industrialism and democracy.

The idea of mass society first arose as a capsule for disturbed reactions to the French Revolution and also the industrial revolution. For such minds as BURKE, BONALD, HEGEL, COLERIDGE, and TOCQUEVILLE, both revolutions brought the erosion and destruction of the ancient bonds of kinship, caste, church, guild, and village or town. Burke wrote his influential *Reflections on the Revolution in France* essentially around this theme of disintegration of the traditional under the impact of a new, revolutionary, popular power and of the consequent formation of the mass, that is, 'an unsocial, uncivil, unconnected chaos of elementary principles' (p. 195). Conservative, and some liberal, thought in Europe closely followed Burke's image of the masses and the kind of power that creates them.

The industrial revolution as the focus of traditionalist fears for social order is particularly vivid in the writings of the French and German conservatives, but we should not overlook such English moulders of thought as Coleridge, Southey, and Matthew Arnold, all of whom thought the 'commercialism', the 'mechanism', and the 'philistinism' of the economic revolution highly destructive of the disciplines and the bonds of a genuine culture. Tocqueville thought that the onset of manufacturing industry promoted class warfare as well as the dissolution of old communities.

Throughout the nineteenth century we find striking expressions of fear or apprehension with respect to a coming 'age of the masses'. Tocqueville, Kierkegaard, Burckhardt, and NIETZSCHE are among those who gave specific statement to this apprehension. They saw such an age as the almost direct outcome of democracy and its elevation of majorities, of secularism and its erosion of sacred, unifying beliefs, of individualism and its fragmentation of community, and of the spread everywhere of what Tönnies called *Gesellschaft* and Max Weber 'rationalization'. The ultimate and overriding result, almost all philosophers of mass society were agreed, would be the appearance of a new, unprecedented form of absolute power: power at once the result of mass society and the sole means of its governance.

The idea of mass society has spread widely in the twentieth century. Spengler, writing before the first world war, saw the masses and Caesarism as the future of western society. The Spanish philosopher Ortega y Gasset published *The Revolt of the Masses* in 1929, in which he described not only mass society but 'mass man', the human creature spawned by cultural disintegration and social atomism and rendered the natural prey of totalitarian despots. Peter Drucker, Herman Rauschning, and Emil Lederer were among the earliest to see mass society as the cocoon of totalitarianism, a position Hannah Arendt made notable after the second world war in her monumental study of Russian and German TOTALITARIANISM.

Although 'mass society' is a widely used concept in modern writing, it has had its critics – for instance, Edward Shils, Joyce Cary, and Daniel Bell. They are antagonistic not to the idea itself so much as to its over-application to contemporary democratic and industrial populations. They charge that the organic structure of the past, pre-mass society is exaggerated, and it is misguided to give the negative labels 'mass society', 'mass culture', and 'the age of the masses' to the greater freedom, mobility, and openness of the modern democratic-industrial age. Although there is justification for these criticisms, the term 'mass society' is unlikely to lose its unfavourable connotations.   RN

Reading

Arendt, H.: *The Origins of Totalitarianism*. New York: Harcourt Brace, 1951.

Burke, E.: *Reflections on the Revolution in France*, ed. C.C. O'Brien. Harmondsworth: Penguin, 1968.

†Nisbet, R.: *The Quest for Community*. New York: Oxford University Press, 1953.

Ortega y Gasset, J.: *The Revolt of the Masses*. New York: Norton; London: Allen & Unwin, 1932.

Tocqueville, A. de: *Democracy in America*, trans. G. Lawrence, ed. J.P. Mayer and M. Lerner. New York: Harper, 1966; London: Fontana, 1968.

Maurras, Charles (1868–1952) French writer, journalist and politician. Maurras was a theoretician of integral nationalism and the leader of the nationalist movement Action Française founded in 1899.

The Action Française movement was always small in numbers, but nevertheless had an enormous political and literary influence, both in France and in Italy, Spain, Belgium and Eastern Europe. This influence was due first and foremost to Maurras's writings and to his journal *L'Action Française* which became a daily newspaper in 1908. *L'Enquête sur la monarchie*, published in 1900, was Maurras's most famous work. Among his many subsequent works, the most significant for a definition of Maurrassian thought are *Athinea* (1901), *La Politique religieuse* (1912), *Romantisme et révolution* (1922), *Mes Idées politiques* (1937) and *La Seule France* (1941). Elected to the Académie Française in 1939, Maurras attempted to play the role of the theoretician of the Vichy regime. From 1940 to 1944 he fostered a violent anti-semitic campaign and praised the Vichy racial laws, very close to Nazi legislation; he fought the Resistance, Gaullism and the Allied war effort as a whole. At the Liberation, he was given a life sentence for collaboration with the enemy.

The starting-point of Maurrassian thought is an affirmation of the overriding importance of the nation as such. Maurras came to the conclusion that in order to arrest the decadence of the nation and to assure the perpetuity of that harmonious and unique entity, the 'goddess France', it was necessary to repudiate all the philosophical foundations that underlay the Republic and the French Revolution, including the theory of natural rights, and to replace them by the monarchical principle. This solution, he believed, was the necessary conclusion of all nationalist thinking and represented 'integral nationalism'.

NATIONALISM, for Maurras, was first of all an aesthetic conception: he believed that France was a marvel unequalled in the entire world. But he also maintained that nationalism possessed a metaphysical essence, and the nation could be regarded as an end-in-itself, in an absolute sense. France is endowed with a body, a soul, and natural beauties. But a goddess can perish: she demands homage at every instant. This absolute nationalism requires the elimination of everything that weakens the national organism, and first of all democracy. An acceptance of democracy, he thought, can only mean the destruction of the country, and for that reason patriotism requires a strong, stable, permanent regime, one that is not the expression of the caprice of changing majorities or special interests: in other words, a monarchical regime. The king, the servant of the nation, represents its unity, its sovereignty, its perpetuity.

In order to ensure the survival of the nation, he held that it had to be defended not only against foreign invaders, but also against the enemy within. The Republic, he taught, had abandoned the national, Catholic heritage to the 'Four confederated Estates' – the Jews, the foreigners, the Freemasons and the Protestants. Only a hereditary monarchy could liberate the nation from this appropriation, just as it was the only form of government which could resolve the social question by reintegrating the proletariat into the national community. In the name of this reconciliation of the proletariat with the nation, Maurras and his followers opposed capitalism and liberalism and advocated a form of CORPORATISM and an alliance with revolutionary SYNDICALISM.   ZS

Reading

Capitan, P.C.: *Charles Maurras et l'idéologie d'Action Française*. Paris: Éditions du Seuil, 1972.

†Curtis, M.: *Three Against the Third Republic: Barrès, Maurras, Sorel*. Princeton, NJ: Princeton University Press, 1959.

Maurras, C.: *Oeuvres capitales*, 4 vols. Paris: Flammarion, 1954.

Nolte, E.: *Three Faces of Fascism: Action Française, Italian Fascism, National Socialism*. New York: Holt, Reinhart & Winston, 1966.

†Sutton, M.: *Nationalism, Positivism and Catholicism: the Politics of Charles Maurras and French Catholics 1890–1914*. Cambridge: Cambridge University Press, 1982.

Weber, E.: *Action Française*. Stanford, Calif.: Stanford University Press, 1962.

medieval political thought A major aspect of the intellectual history of the Catholic West that deals specifically with man and his social organization from the collapse and fall of the Roman Empire to the Reformation of the sixteenth century. It is the story of the attempts made by a society, fragmented after Rome's dissolution and experiencing economic, social and structural decline, to come to terms with the attitudes to man of ancient pagan philosophy in the light of competing and often conflicting Christian doctrine. No understanding of the political texts of this extended period, many of which are historical or theological in genre, can be achieved without some knowledge of the economic and material conditions alongside the contemporary beliefs and traditions of ideas that served as components of daily life from the fifth to the sixteenth century in Western Europe.

The early middle ages

The political thinking of the period *c.*500–1000 was primarily concerned with preserving philosophical and institutional aspects of pre-Christian antiquity, especially universal ROMAN LAW, combining these with the philosophical and theological writings of the church Fathers such as AUGUSTINE and Jerome, and then squaring this tradition with particularist and local, usually oral, customary practices of various barbarian peoples. The barbarian tribes, which settled in the West alongside the Roman population, often found imperial law, designed for the government of an empire of diverse peoples, irrelevant to the needs of an agrarian society whose major concern was survival. The regulation of land possession and the respective rights of jurisdiction and administration, once the preserve of the Roman centralized system, became in an agricultural economy the domain of decentralized loci of power, dominated by military kings who waged war to protect their kin. The politics of illiteracy

and custom and the non-universality of the folk law degraded but did not completely destroy Roman law. Byzantium in the East maintained the tradition and practices of the old empire, making the emperor the head of the church (Caesaropapism); however, in the politically fragmented West, the only near-universal organization was the church which, in effect, ruled the city of Rome and held the whole of Europe together by its parochial organization based on the Roman diocese, and by its appeal to a single spiritual fellowship rather than to a single political obligation.

The political thought of the early Middle Ages focuses on three active influences on the shape of society and its ideals: the institutional, hierarchical church and its head, the bishop of Rome, the pope; the waning influence of imperial Rome and her institutions and law; and the Germanic barbarians with their separate development of a royal divinity and their understanding of military and personal leadership, and loyalty to that person rather than to office. Rome represented loyalty and obligation to an idea; barbarian Europe represented loyalty and obligation to kin and personal kingship. The papacy, bolstered by the arguments of theologians such as Augustine, represented loyalty and obligation ultimately to God, and not to men or to earthly institutions.

Augustine, writing when the Roman state had just become officially Christian, argued against the traditional pagan notion of a Ciceronian republic, and substituted the idea of a true and just commonwealth being one that gave due reverence to God. Early on this became despiritualized and misinterpreted as a blueprint for sharing out jurisdictions and *dominium* (lordship) between two functioning institutions, CHURCH AND STATE, uniting Christendom according to supposedly harmonizing spheres of influence over spiritual and temporal aspects of Christians' lives. In the fifth century, Pope Gelasius wrote to the Byzantine emperor that there were two powers by which the world was ruled – the sacred authority of the priesthood and the royal power. The responsibility of priests was the weightier, for they answered for kings of men at the Last Judgment. Gelasius asserted that the imperial office itself was conferred by divine dispensation and that priests obey imperial laws regarding public order but the emperor obeys priests who have been charged with the administration of the sacred mysteries. This much-discussed Gelasian theory of, in effect, two swords to govern the world, with the spiritual ultimately of higher authority than the temporal, was to be the beginning of a long tradition of conflict between church and state, *sacerdotium* and *regnum*, that is, between spheres of authority in one society.

Competing with this view was the Germanic idea of divine kingship which became, by the seventh and eighth centuries, controlled by the church through coronation ceremonies carried out by the clergy. Royal authority was Christianized, and the Germanic kings were viewed in Old Testament terms. In the year 800 Charlemagne, the most powerful of western rulers and king of the Franks, was crowned by the Pope in Rome and this revived the western idea of the Roman Empire, Charlemagne being viewed as western emperor as well as Frankish king. It was to be argued by the church that the creation of an emperor was in its gift.

Apart from Augustine's writings and ecclesiastical pronouncements of church councils supplemented by theological and institutional statements of the church Fathers, the early Middle Ages had little intellectual tradition of its own; indeed one might argue that practice gave rise to justificatory polemic, drawing on imperial and theological language during the Carolingian period. Charlemagne's court at Aachen, serving as a centre of administration and of European (largely Irish and English) intellectual endeavour, helped to create the reality of a Christian empire with a single legal and educational system and liturgical uniformity. It was, however, shortlived. With the division of Charlemagne's empire among his sons, the later ninth century and the tenth became the true 'Dark Ages' as Magyars and Vikings invaded, totally disrupting whatever tenuous civilized structure of society had been created by church and Germanic kingdom. It was during and after this period of disruption that the tradition of imperial supremacy over clerical and lay aspects of society was revived (under Otto III, at the end of the tenth century) and the counterattack by the church was mounted, through forgeries of documents including the notorious DONATION OF CONSTANTINE.

During the tenth and eleventh centuries royal power across Europe decomposed into FEUDALISM; vassal dukes and counts were the small local units of government and safety, and society was overarched by the theory of the Donation, a theory of a church-ruled Christian commonwealth. Kings saw themselves as the suzerain heads of pyramids of personal loyalties. Local lords assumed rights over the persons and property of their followers, to judge, punish, levy taxes, and receive rents and services. Such petty lords viewed the local churches and monasteries in their area as part of their own domains, and they put in their own men as bishops and abbots, men who often cared little for their spiritual duties and offices. Indeed, kings throughout Europe chose bishops, enriched them with lands (fiefs), and invested them with the symbols of their spiritual office – the ring and staff. The feudal degradation of centralized political and administrative rule and of the spiritual role of the church was challenged by a monastic movement of reform, first of the spiritual monastic life and then of the relationship between monasteries and local feudal lords. Cluny in Burgundy drew up its charter in the year 910 making certain that the monks themselves would elect their own abbot and that they were subject to no external authority other than the papacy – an island of autonomy in feudal society. This was followed by a revival of the papacy itself through an internal reform movement that sought to purify its own institutions and rid the papacy of imperial and feudal interference.

The eleventh and twelfth centuries

Medieval political thought and practice from the eleventh century onwards owed much to the successive waves of purifying reforming movements in the church itself which attempted to realize the *ideals* of church and state. The INVESTITURE CONTROVERSY stimulated an unprecedented outburst of political pamphleteering, which was a new departure in the medieval tradition of political thought. The continuing belief in the supernatural authority of kings was sufficiently widespread to help in the ultimate defeat of extreme political papal claims. The issue at stake was whether there was a clearly defined division of authority between spiritual and temporal rulers. The eleventh-century Gregorian reform provided the impetus for what would eventually be Gratian's systematic collection of CANON LAW, culled from centuries of church councils and the theology of the church Fathers along with the decrees of popes, all in an effort by the papacy to gain centralized control of the administrative machinery of the church. At the same time, German emperors, especially Frederick I (Barbarossa), encouraged a massive revival of Roman imperial law: an elaboration through glosses and commentaries on Justinian's Code (see ROMAN LAW) which was the means by which (along with the thirteenth-century rediscovery of ARISTOTLE's ethical and political writings) major theoretical revisions and novelties, in harmony with economic changes in society, would help to transform medieval political thought and practice. Thus from the eleventh century, Roman and canon laws served as the theoretical foundations on which political theories of various persuasions, concerning the nature of government and of man governed, were to be built. Augustine's model of sinful, dependent, irrational man was replaced by a more rational and natural man whose reason was not impaired by the Fall.

By the late eleventh century the chief agent in the disruption of feudalism was the re-establishment of towns and attendant international commerce and trade. Simultaneous with the attempts to codify and standardize customary feudal practices throughout whole territories was the emergence of a corporate view of society based in practice on the development of guilds of craftsmen, and in theory on Roman law justifications for self-authenticating autonomous groupings of men. Cathedral schools gave way to nascent universities to train not only ecclesiastics but administrators in secular government and the professions. At universities – which were, like Paris and Oxford, corporations of teaching masters, each member receiving a licence from the church to teach – a secular clergy developed with a monopoly of literacy and systematic learning. They were joined by members of the mendicant orders such as the Franciscans and Dominicans. As students in minor orders when at university, many of these clerks moved into the emergent bureaucracies of royal government. Like JOHN OF SALISBURY they wrote 'mirrors for princes' in order to educate monarchs in the learned, 'schools' view of political society as an organism dependent on a re-reading of Cicero and Roman law. It is from this legal tradition, Roman and canon, that the emergence of concepts like natural law, right reason, the *lex regia* and equity, and discussions of the role of the king in relation to the law of the land, developed in the twelfth century.

We begin to see fully-fledged arguments that the power of a monarch or emperor is conferred by the people. Does this popular sovereignty, however, entail an eventual and complete alienation of the people's power to the monarch? (See JOHN OF SALISBURY and Henry de BRACTON.) A compromise was struck between feudal law and Roman theory. Likewise the development of canon law was dependent on the terminology of civil law, presupposing, as did Roman law, the equality of all men. Certain institutions, such as slavery and property, were seen as the results of the Fall. Sovereign authority that was delegated or alienated to a ruler was seen as coercive in both church and state, necessary as a result of sinful man. This would change to the notion of law serving to make habitual what was already naturally virtuous in man. Those who commented on the canon law (DECRETALISTS) saw the pope as the holder of the powers of binding and loosing of men, powers that were initially committed by Christ to the church in the person of St Peter. Discussion as to the meaning of 'the church' – was it pope and bishops, or the whole body of honest and faithful people? – pointed out the stark contrast between an earlier feudal hierarchical understanding of order and the most recent revival of Roman corporation theory applied to the corpus of the church as a mystical entity. Just as the twelfth-century writers expounded on the issue of the limits to temporal authority and the nature of tyrants (is the king beneath or above the law of the land?), so too the question was asked in canonist circles whether the pope was circumscribed by Scripture, by general church councils, by the sayings of the church Fathers; and could an heretical pope be removed? Most decretalists argued that the council was superior to the pope in defining articles of faith, for the corporate council embodied universal consent, with its decisions ratified only with the corporation's head, the pope, present.

Likewise, in monarchies of increasing administrative and bureaucratic centralization (such as that of Henry II in England), and especially as the requirements of defence policies made it impossible for the king to manage without additional taxation of his subjects, incipient representative institutions emerged. These parliaments initially comprised the king and his counsellors, and then powerful and wealthy representatives of various localities in attendance on the king; their duties were to go back home and inform local communities of decisions of the king in council. Gradually, by the end of the thirteenth century and more definitely during the fourteenth century, the king was not only seen as preserving the customs of the realm where he acted as the court of last resort in a national and uniform system of justice; he was also seen as ruling more or less in concert with his wealthier noble and non-noble subjects whose discussions of and agreement to royal policy were vital since it was they who, for the most part, footed the bills via taxation. In fourteenth-century England, this is evident in the increasing importance of the Commons in Parliament. The medieval theory and practice of representation and corporation has led historians to consider how far we can speak of the origins of modern, European democracy in the Middle Ages.

The thirteenth century
During the thirteenth century strong kings who sought to centralize jurisdiction and administration in geographically-unified and prosperous regions confronted a series of strong and juridically-minded popes, such as Innocent III, Gregory IX and Innocent IV. Innocent III argued in his decretal *Per venerabilem* (1202) that the papacy had the right to confirm elections to the imperial office on the ground that the papacy had transferred the empire from the Byzantine Greeks to the Germans in the days of Charlemagne; although this was not quite a claim to direct papal supremacy over secular authority, the decretal *Novit* further asserted the power of the papacy to arbitrate between warring kings because of the church's authority over cases where sins were committed, *pro ratione peccati*. This could lead to an unlimited capacity for papal intervention in secular affairs. Some pro-papal theorists argued that the papacy's power was *de iure* while the secular powers had a *de facto* sword to do the coercive work in human society, in effect on the church's command. Heresy was therefore determined by the church but punished by temporal rulers as a civil crime. The 'two keys' of the church were interpreted to mean that the pope ultimately could be called upon to provide justice since the emperor or monarch had no secular superior. Only in relatively strong monarchies such as Capetian France and Angevin England were monarchs able to use indigenous bodies of customary law, and expand royal jurisdiction in uniform ways so that, by what some have called a 'juristic accident', feudal vassals were replaced by the king's centralized courts; these monarchies alone were capable of challenging the papacy's dominance. Germany and Italy were less successful. It is the progress of political thought towards a theory of the autonomous and secular early modern state that is visible in France and England in the writings of the monarchies' respective publicists.

During the thirteenth century two conflicting theories of the origin of the state and sovereignty were expounded: one that strengthened the autonomous monarchy as representing God's will for human society, the king standing in for God's power; the other, a civilian emphasis on popular sovereignty seen in terms of communal, guild or urban self-rule or transference of a collectivity's original powers to a proctor who represents the majority decision of the corporation. The latter theory is thought to have issued from earlier Germanic custom which asserted the right of resistance of individuals in groups to royal misrule and which merged with Roman law principles. It also developed from practice in those urban areas where a merchant and craft bourgeoisie formed, originally to protect a trade but expanding to self-government and eventually to collective government of the commune, as in France and northern Italy. At the same time abbeys, cathedral chapters of canons, and mendicant orders further developed the practice of electing abbots, bishops, or representatives of their respective communities; indeed it was argued that the very ownership of church property was collective, with a bishop or even the pope merely acting as steward of property given to communities, the pope ruling over such material interests for the good of the community. The notion of the common good received its final theoretical justification in matters spiritual and temporal with the rediscovery of Aristotle's works on politics and ethics.

All these developments helped to promote the Roman principle of public law with the king as a public persona ruling for the welfare of the community. The argument was advanced that the public authority in the person of the king had the right to demand contributions to the common welfare in emergency or for defence of the realm – in effect, for the general utility of the realm. Only in the thirteenth century does the word status, something near the early modern notion of the state, emerge to mean the welfare of the general fabric of the community expressed in its uniform laws and customs, geographically bound by a sphere of legal jurisdiction to which all members of the society of whatever degree may appeal. Sovereign monarchs come to be seen and to see themselves as the supreme legislative authority in the community, some arguing that the king's will is law but that he is bound in conscience rather than by law to observe the community's welfare and to make new laws with the advice of his council, others arguing that law is made by the community which the king enforces in the community's name. Personal royalty and allegiance to it receded in favour of the notion of monarch as an office with duties. Indeed Bracton argued that the king cannot alienate the judicial and administrative functions of the crown. The appeal, especially concerning the increasing financial needs of the crown to carry out its duties, was to the non-noble, non-feudal subjects of the realm who by the end of the thirteenth century were seen as arriving in parliament with the *plena potestas* (fullness of power) of their respective communities.

The papacy also used this notion of proctorial representatives in the ecclesiastical corporations within the hierarchy. But despite this growth in representative government in church and state, pope and monarch still had the last word most of the time. Each moved decisively away from feudalism towards notions of sovereignty, *dominium*, legitimacy, obligation, that were justified by Aristotle's theory that man was by nature political, living naturally in a community that was more than the survival unit of family and village; man lived in a natural polity whose characteristics were rational. Thomas AQUINAS provided perhaps the best theoretical account of contemporary ideals of kingship and good governance for his generation and beyond. But what is perhaps most revealing is that political theory in its most systematic form was written by theologians who sought during this high point of scholasticism to provide a summa in which a single work would bring together the sum total of human knowledge and divine truth, not only about politics but also about man's otherworldly aim, salvation. Out of this theological tradition, for the first time, we have a treatment of the political realm with recognizable aspects of the modern secular state. The *regnum* has a right of existence; it is a God-sanctioned natural phenomenon, necessary to the well-being of individuals, and in existence for the good of the whole. Loyalty is defined by its object: the common good, which is different in kind from the sum of individual goods. From the thirteenth century onwards the trend was towards the transformation of the *regnum*, previously seen as a functioning branch of a unified Christian commonwealth, to an autonomous, self-sufficient, self-authenticating corporate body.

The fourteenth century onwards

This rational, secular argument aroused the strongest opposition from the papacy's yet further enhanced claims to *plena potestas* in matters spiritual and temporal. The pope was now explicitly called the vicar of Christ on earth and Christ's royalty was emphasized. The most comprehensive statement of this papal hierocratic theory of government was expressed in the publicist writings of the Augustinian canon Giles of Rome (*De ecclesiastica potestate*) (1301) and in Pope Boniface VIII's *Unam sanctam* (1302). An attempt to revive Augustine's understanding of legitimate government, where the church sanctioned property and secular rule, was countered by the equally radical writings of JOHN OF PARIS where emphasis was on the notion of the individual's rights to private property prior to the setting up of governments or any ecclesiastical organization. This was taken to final extremes by MARSILIUS OF PADUA who defined the state's purpose as the securing of peace and the materially sufficient life for subjects. The rule of law made by the sovereign people is superior to the rule of one man so that collective wisdom and experience of the people retain sovereignty. The prince is merely the executive enacting the people's will, a will that, when legally formulated, has the sole coercive force in society. The transference of authority from the people to the prince is not irrevocable. Furthermore, politics is an autonomous realm separate from religious, non-coercive instruction. The priesthood is subsumed into the *regnum*, the church being made up of the whole body of the faithful in congregation, with secular control of clerical appointments and even excommunication.

This transformation of the *regnum* into an autonomous state was brought about not only by the influence of Aristotle and Roman law's corporation theory, but by the increasing political involvement across Europe of a literate, wealthy, administratively competent lay bourgeoisie. The clerical monopoly over education and therefore administration was on the wane from the fourteenth century onwards. The collective whole, the state, was seen as having rights of survival of its own, the sovereign prince already being able to take extraordinary measures for the common good long before MACHIAVELLI made the doctrine of *raison d'état* a central tenet of his 'new politics' in the sixteenth century. The state as an abstraction above the members who govern and above the governed, with an end superior to that of any individuals within its territories, emerged at this time, especially in the writings of Italian jurists such as Bartolus. But it is not yet clear that such an abstract whole exists

without the physical presence of representatives of the corporation meeting together.

The idea of a public law, superior to private law, rights and interests, was gradually emerging through the decline of localism and the rise of a centralized, reliable public authority, the safety of which 'knew no law', the king acting as the state's agent. In effect, late medieval cities in Italy were their own princes. Corporation theory along with the secularization of society (which does not imply that men were no longer pious), the separation of ethics from politics, along with the parallel growth of constitutional thought in ecclesiology *and* secular political theory, were taken further during the attempted conciliarist solutions to the Great Schism in the church at the end of the fourteenth century (see CONCILIARISM). The central tension between simultaneous affirmations of the overriding right of a sovereign to rule and the overriding claim of a community to defend itself against abuses of power was central to the development of church *and* state constitutional theory into the seventeenth century. Medieval theorists established the foundations of later consent theory; by the fourteenth century the major outlines of a theory that the community has a right to constitute government independent of church sanctions (see WILLIAM OF OCKHAM), and to change the form of such government without dissolving the community itself (see JOHN OF PARIS) were present. The competing doctrine of hierarchy being ordained from above also persisted into the seventeenth century. The major debates over the sources of legitimacy and sovereignty, the nature of obligation, the right of resistance, and the spheres of authority found in theological, ecclesiastical and civilian texts from the twelfth century onwards were not unfamiliar to Reformation thinkers (see REFORMATION POLITICAL THOUGHT) or to seventeenth-century theorists of the early modern state. JC

Reading

Black, A.: *Guilds and Civil Society in European Political Thought from the Twelfth Century to the Present*. London: Methuen, 1984.

Coleman, J.: Property and poverty. In *The Cambridge History of Medieval Political Thought*, ed. J.H. Burns. Cambridge: Cambridge University Press, 1987.

Gierke, O.: *Das deutsche Genossenschaftsrecht*. 4 vols. Berlin: Weidmannsche Buchhandlung, 1868–1914.

Michaud-Quantin, P.: *Universitas: Expressions du mouvement communautaire dans le moyen-âge latin*. Paris: Vrin, 1970.

Milsom, S.F.C.: *The Legal Framework of English Feudalism* (the Maitland lectures, 1972). Cambridge: Cambridge University Press, 1976.

Sayles, G.O.: *The King's Parliament of England*. London: Arnold, 1975.

Skinner, Q.: *The Foundations of Modern Political Thought*. 2 vols. Cambridge: Cambridge University Press, 1978.

†Strayer, J.R.: *On the Medieval Origins of the Modern State*. Princeton, NJ: Princeton University Press, 1970.

Tierney, B.: *Foundations of the Conciliar Theory: the contribution of the medieval Canonists from Gratian to the Great Schism*. Cambridge: Cambridge University Press, 1955.

†————: *Religion, Law and the Growth of Constitutional Thought, 1150–1650*. Cambridge: Cambridge University Press, 1982.

Ullmann, W.: *Principles of Government and Politics in the Middle Ages*. London: Methuen, 1961.

Wilks, M.: *The Problem of Sovereignty in the Later Middle Ages*. Cambridge: Cambridge University Press, 1963.

menshevism The ideas of the Mensheviks, a faction of the Russian Social Democratic Labour Party formed in 1903 after the split with the Bolsheviks (see BOLSHEVISM). The Mensheviks wanted a more open party, and arguably remained closer than their opponents to classical MARXISM in believing that a socialist revolution must await the further industrialization of Russia. See SOVIET COMMUNISM.

mercantilism The ideas and policies that surrounded the doctrine of the balance of trade in European economic thinking of the seventeenth century and most of the eighteenth. Thomas Mun (1571–1641) expressed this doctrine in *England's Treasure by Foreign Trade* (1664): 'The ordinary means to increase our wealth and treasure is by foreign trade, wherein we must ever observe this rule: to sell more to strangers yearly than we consume of theirs in value.' Since bullion or treasure are limited in the world, economic activity necessarily involved conflict as one country's gain required another's loss. Just as national interests were believed to conflict, mercantilist writers saw potential disharmony between national interest and private interest within states. An open acceptance of profit-seeking by nations and individuals and the need for regulations to order economic life were common assumptions of mercantilist thought. The inseparable goals of mercantilism – national power and plenty – are best understood against the background of intense international rivalry that characterized the seventeenth century.

To create a favourable balance of trade mercantilists relied upon government bounties and duties to encourage exports and discourage imports. Limiting imports to cheap raw materials and emphasizing the export of finished products seemed to guarantee a trade surplus. Associated with this policy was the need for colonies, the protection of domestic industry, the granting of monopoly privileges to trading companies, and the control of shipping (e.g. England's Navigation Acts). To keep the price of goods competitive in the world market, low wages were often recommended. High population growth was also defended in mercantilist thought. Along with Thomas Mun, important figures in this tradition were Sir William Petty (1623–87), Josiah Child (1630–99) and Jean-Baptiste Colbert (1619–83), who was minister of finance under Louis XIV.

'Mercantilism' or 'the mercantile system' were terms first used by the French physiocrat Mirabeau in 1763 and later popularized by Adam SMITH in *The Wealth of Nations* (1776). Both disparaged the protectionism they found in the economic writers of the preceding century in order to defend free trade. Smith argued that mercantilists confused wealth with money or bullion and that this error was used by merchants and manufacturers to obtain government regulations that unfairly protected them from competition. Smith's attack on mercantilism led to its disfavour throughout most of the nineteenth century.

Mercantilism received its first defence from German historians, most notably Gustav Schmoller in 1884, who were sympathetic to its obvious nationalism. According to Schmoller, mercantilism was above all a system of state building, in which governments worked to tear down internal barriers to trade and better the nation's position in the world economy. Mercantilism was also defended by J. M. KEYNES in *The General Theory* (1936). His recommendations for government action led him to view favourably the mercantilist use of state regulation to maintain the domestic stock of money and to keep interest rates low. Contemporary scholarship is interested less in dismissing mercantilism than in understanding the forms it took in different countries and the circumstances of the seventeenth century that brought it forth.   TAH

Reading

†Coleman, D.C. ed.: *Revisions in Mercantilism*. London: Methuen, 1969.

Heckscher, E.: *Mercantilism*. London: Allen & Unwin, 1935.

Keynes, J.M.: *The General Theory of Employment, Interest and Money*. London: Macmillan, 1936.

Merleau-Ponty, Maurice (1908–1961) French philosopher. Merleau-Ponty made a major contribution to political thought in his attempt to reconcile MARXISM with phenomenology. He joined the Resistance during the second world war and it was here that he befriended a number of radical intellectuals, among them Jean-Paul SARTRE with whom he founded *Les Temps Modernes* in 1945. Until 1950 he was the journal's political editor, contributing to an existentialist analysis of world events. He was sympathetic to the Communist Party, though antipathy towards Stalinism kept him from membership. In 1952 he resigned from the journal because of what he saw as the Soviet Union's imperialist role in Korea. He quarrelled with Sartre, then moving closer to the Communists, and by 1955 he declared that he was disillusioned with Marxism itself. He subsequently wrote little about politics, although he did support the shortlived socialist government of Mendès-France. In any case, Merleau-Ponty's life was one of a writer and academic rather than a political activist. In 1952 he had been appointed to the prestigious chair of philosophy at the Collège de France. At his death, he was engaged in a reappraisal of the philosophical foundations of politics, although his interests were now more focused on language and aesthetics.

Merleau-Ponty's major political works are *Humanism and Terror* (1947) and *Adventures of the Dialectic* (1955). The former offers a defence of revolutionary violence while the latter more cautiously examines the fate of dialectic in those post-Marxian philosophies advocating such acts. Additional essays on political themes appeared in *The Primacy of Perception* (1947), *Sense and Non-Sense* (1948), and *Signs* (1960). However the key to Merleau-Ponty's political writings lies in his underlying philosophy. This is adumbrated in *Phenomenology of Perception* (1945), the preface to which offers the clearest account of his existential phenomenology. The posthumously published extracts of the unfinished *The Visible and the Invisible* (1964) suggest a profound rethinking of this position.

Merleau-Ponty's political philosophy combines three major approaches: phenomenology, EXISTENTIALISM and Marxism. Phenomenology entailed descriptions of how meaning makes its appearance in the world and involved a systematic interrogation of all those meanings we daily take for granted. Merleau-Ponty claims that we first structure our environment through acts of perception involving a complex interplay between our bodies and the world. These yield us shifting and equivocal, but nevertheless significant, forms. We do not rely on consciousness to constitute a coherent world out of chaos, since we are incarnate minds caught in meaningful situations before any reflection. He argues that the theories and articulations we subsequently impose on this 'lifeworld' can only be provisional and second-order accounts of the fuller and more vibrant experience that they can never exhaust. They retain the partial and perspectival nature, as well as the openness and ambiguity, of original sense perception. These studies thus reach a profoundly anti-Cartesian conclusion, facilitating rejection of subject-object dualism in both its idealist and its empiricist form.

This leads to Merleau-Ponty's existentialism, with its claim that existence always precedes essence: we can never step outside our situation to sum it up, nor aspire to absolute knowledge; rather, it is through action that we bring meaning into the world. If we discern meaning in history, it is by experiencing the logic of events from our perspective as engaged actors. And if we offer accounts of such meanings, we are obliged to acknowledge that their nature is provisional and not exclusive of additional interpretations.

It is this existential phenomenology that underlies Merleau-Ponty's Marxism and indeed his entire politics. It implies a sustained attack on all doctrines and movements which purport to offer complete understanding or require the imposition of final historical solutions. He equates such beliefs with a rationalism which thinks the world can be fully known and thereby controlled. This chimera is shared by LIBERALISM when it believes in the capacity of well-meaning individuals to attain rational decisions, and by orthodox Marxism when it claims to comprehend history's laws. When Marxism discerns a single development within history and equates the proletariat with its truth, it becomes a rationalist rather than a dialectical philosophy. Regimes predicated on this approach inevitably become inertial, closed, violent, for they cannot adapt themselves to the struggles and exigencies all provisional solutions must engender.

What Merleau-Ponty calls for instead is a style of politics recognizing that history is contingent and that political activity is a risky and violent affair. He originally refers to such an approach as Phenomenological Marxism but later calls it a New Liberalism. Such a politics attempts to impose no preconceived solution on events. It recognizes that we cannot control history because its institutions arise in an 'interworld' where individual acts converge in a result for which none bears responsibility. Yet since history is a consequence of intersubjective acts it is redolent of human purposes. Like perceptual forms, its sense is open though not arbitrary; it offers various possibilities and thus a limited freedom to push events in a progressive direction if we elicit options and galvanize support behind one of them.

A phenomenological Marxism thus recognizes that reason enters the world only as a concrete and ongoing project. It must be painfully forged by an integrating of perspectives, achieved through struggle and communication. It has no guarantees; it is no pre-existing idea that an elite might impose on our behalf. Accordingly this is a politics that interprets

events as they unfold. It attempts to inform and expand mass consciousness, recognizing that it is on the level of mass actions that meanings are etched into history. It is a politics without illusions. It remains revolutionary because it has no final goals, although it is committed to the humanist value of enriching and expanding opportunities for co-existence. It sees that freedom lies in our capacity continually to transcend the given, thereby opening up new possibilities while accumulating traditional truths. It must therefore challenge reified structures that inhibit our capacity for creative response and exchange. Rationalism is especially dangerous here, as it claims definitive solutions without any alternative.

Merleau-Ponty ultimately found Marxism's commitment to the proletariat as sole historical agent inimical to so dialectical and open-ended an undertaking. He switched allegiance to the non-communist left, while registering general pessimism about the aimlessness of the politics of the 1950s. His critics accused him of lacking any real analysis of power and of succumbing to the very idealism he attacked. Yet Merleau-Ponty never claimed to offer an exhaustive account of his times, nor any programme to rectify its problems. Instead he invited us to engage in a permanent questioning of the meanings we encounter daily and offered us philosophical and political reasons for continuing this task.   DHC

Reading

†Kruks, S.: *The Political Philosophy of Merleau-Ponty.* Brighton, Sussex: Harvester, 1981.

Merleau-Ponty, M.: *Phenomenology of Perception,* trans. C. Smith. London: Routledge & Kegan Paul, 1962.

———: *Humanism and Terror,* trans. J. O'Neill. Boston: Beacon, 1969.

———: *Adventures of the Dialectic,* trans. J. Bien. London: Heinemann, 1974.

†O'Neill, J.: *Perception, Expression and History: the Social Phenomenology of Maurice Merleau-Ponty.* Evanston, Ill.: Northwestern University Press, 1970.

†Schmidt, J.: *Maurice Merleau-Ponty: between Phenomenology and Structuralism.* London: Macmillan, 1985.

Michels, Robert (1876–1936)   German sociologist. Michels taught at the universities of

Turin, Basle and Perugia. Under the influence of MOSCA, PARETO and WEBER he became an exponent of ELITISM, and made a major contribution to the sociology of political parties. He is celebrated as the inventor of the 'iron law of oligarchy'.

Michels began his intellectual life as a Marxist. From the outset he was critical of those socialist parliamentary parties which permitted bourgeois constitutionalist considerations to undermine belief in revolutionary direct action, and which allowed a concern for the preservation of party organization to prevail over socialist principle. In his most famous book, *Political Parties* (1911), he developed the thesis that society in general and all organizations were subject to oligarchical domination: 'Who says organization, says oligarchy' – the 'iron law of oligarchy'. Michels applied this general theory to socialist parties to demonstrate that the law would apply even in the most unfavourable test case of a party committed to the principle of internal democracy.

Constitutionally, leaders of socialist party organizations are elected by the mass of the members, are accountable to them, and are expected to carry out the policies of the party. Michels argued that the leadership escapes from these constraints and acts autonomously. Two main reasons are given. First, organizations of any size and complexity require specialization of function and expertise. It becomes impossible for the ordinary membership to supervise the specialists who take decisions for the party on their own initiative. The habit of leadership helps confirm its position. The leaders accumulate influence over the organization, including elections to executive positions. The external need for leadership stability in party competition in parliament and in general elections also reinforces the internal position of the leaders and involves the leadership in compromises on matters of socialist principle. Second, Michels held that the mass of people have a psychological need to be led. Again following elitist theory, he saw the masses as atomized, disorganized and incapable of collective action unless led by the activist minority. They are not merely apathetic but inclined to venerate the strong leader.

The oligarchy becomes almost invulnerable. Changes in leadership occur less through elite displacement than through a process of absorption of new members into the existing oligarchy. Democracy in any strict sense is impossible. At best it consists of competition between oligarchical organizations.

In his later writings, Michels pursued his ideas of the superiority of the elite and of the psychological deference of the mass further in an anti-democratic direction and became an open supporter of FASCISM.

Despite its forceful presentation, the Michelsian analysis of party oligarchy is not always clear. Michels does not always distinguish technical expertise from political leadership. Pressures internal and external to the party are sometimes confused. He fails to recognize the extent to which complex organizations generate a plurality of competing leadership groups. Nevertheless the 'iron law of oligarchy' has had a major impact on studies of parties, unions, pressure groups and other major organizations.   GP

Reading
Beetham, D.: From socialism to fascism: the relation between theory and practice in the work of Robert Michels. *Political Studies* 25 (1977) 3–24, 161–81.

Hands, G.: Roberto Michels and the study of political parties. *British Journal of Political Science* 1 (1971) 149–72.

McKenzie, R.T.: *British Political Parties*, 2nd rev. edn. London: Heinemann, 1964.

Michels, R.: *Political Parties*. Glencoe, Ill.: Free Press of Glencoe, 1949.

†Parry, G.: *Political Elites*. London: Allen & Unwin, 1969.

Putnam, R.: *The Comparative Study of Political Elites*. Englewood Cliffs, NJ: Prentice-Hall, 1976.

Mill, James (1773–1836) British philosopher, economist and radical pamphleteer. Mill was trained at Edinburgh to be a Presbyterian clergyman, but his agnosticism led him to give up this profession. He became a freelance writer in London and lived impecuniously until the publication of his *History of British India* (1817) led to his appointment with the East India Company. He was closely associated with BENTHAM and actively propagated Bentham's ideas about the principle of utility, law, government, education, and psychology. He was more a popularizer than an original thinker, yet he played an important role by mediating between those with theoretical views, such as Bentham and the political economists, and those whose political activities were give direction by his interpretations of political and economic theory. He was a catalyst to the intellectual development and political activities of Ricardo, Grote, Parkes, many of the philosophic radicals (see PHILOSOPHIC RADICALISM), and above all his son, John Stuart MILL.

Mill was a spokesman for Bentham's UTILITARIANISM, Hobbesian individualism and associationism in psychology, Malthusianism, and the principles of CLASSICAL POLITICAL ECONOMY as developed by Adam SMITH. As a utilitarian, Mill claimed to be seeking the 'greatest happiness of the greatest number', and like Bentham he analysed established institutions, especially aristocratic government, the legal system as celebrated by Blackstone, schools, the church, and the mercantilist economy, to show that they were obstacles to the greatest happinesss; and he proposed new institutional arrangements designed to promote the greatest happiness. The most notable of these concerned politics, and appeared in his influential *Essay on Government*. He prescribed democratic institutions as a way of achieving good government, that is, government in the interest of the governed. Defects, especially corruption, originated in the free play of sinister interests, which were the separate interests specific to each individual. The main beneficiary of sinister interests was the aristocracy, for in the absence of obstacles to its sinister interests it exploited the mass of the people. The remedy was representative government, including a greatly extended, close to universal suffrage, frequent elections, and secret ballot. Until these democratic checks were adopted, politics was a struggle between Aristocracy and People; once adopted, there would be an identity of interest between government and community.

Mill's extravagant praise of the middle rank has led some scholars to adopt the incorrect view that he wished to limit the suffrage to the middle class. His praise of the middle rank however was coupled with the forecast that the people beneath them would be guided by the middle rank's advice and example, so this was not a qualification to his advocacy of a democratic suffrage.

Mill's political thought was severely criticized by MACAULAY, who rejected his argument for 'pure democracy' and ridiculed his use of deductive reasoning in political argument. John Stuart Mill, influenced by Macaulay's critique, questioned his father's use of a scientific format for what in fact was a political pamphlet, and criticized him for neglecting to provide for enlightened leadership in his proposed democracy.   JH

Reading

Bain, A.: *James Mill: a Biography* (1882). New York: Augustus Kelley, 1967.

†Hamburger, J.: *Intellectuals in Politics: John Stuart Mill and the Philosophic Radicals*. New Haven and London: Yale University Press, 1965.

†Lively, J. and Rees, J. eds: *Utilitarian Logic and Politics: James Mill's Essay on Government, Macaulay's 'Critique' and the Ensuing Debate*. Oxford: Clarendon Press, 1978.

Mill, J.S.: (1873) *Autobiography*. In *The Collected Works of John Stuart Mill*, vol. I, ed. J. Robson. Toronto: University of Toronto Press, 1981.

†Thomas, W.: *The Philosophic Radicals*. Oxford: Clarendon Press, 1979.

Mill, John Stuart (1806–1873) British philosopher, economist and statesman. Mill was the first of the six children of James MILL and Harriet Burrows. He was educated by his father, with some assistance from Francis Place and Jeremy BENTHAM, to be the intellectual leader of the philosophic radicals (see PHILOSOPHIC RADICALISM). Although he did not wholly fulfil their hopes, having become disillusioned with the radicalism of his father and Bentham in the 1820s and 1830s, he did gain an extraordinary intellectual ascendancy over his contemporaries. By the time he was fifty, his *System of Logic* (1843) and his *Principles of Political Economy* (1848) were the established textbooks of the ancient universities; *On Liberty* (1859) alarmed as many readers as it inspired, but was almost universally recognized as a masterpiece, and *Considerations on Representative Government* (1861) set the tone of discussions of the prospects and perils of democracy for another twenty years. The little essay on

Utilitarianism (1861) made less stir in its own time, though it has made up for it by being incessantly controverted and reinterpreted ever since.

This is not to say that Mill was an uncontroversial figure: he was by no means 'sound' on most subjects – at the age of sixteen he was jailed overnight for disseminating birth-control literature in a working-class district in London, and his essay on *The Subjection of Women* (1869) alarmed many of its readers; he was ready to see an independent Ireland, and ready to solve the problem of Irish agriculture by compulsory purchase of the lands of absentee landlords; he was an unrepentant defender of the French revolution of 1848; and it was generally known that he was at best an agnostic. But he was acknowledged to be the intellectual superior of almost anyone in public life.

Mill's *Autobiography* (1873) gives a persuasive picture of his career and opinions. It is a readable work, but a deceptive one; its internal chronology is sometimes incoherent, it is very selective, and it is primarily a work of propaganda. Mill describes it as an account of his education, which does indeed bulk large; but it is much more than that. What he has to say about the deficiencies of the education which led him into a nervous collapse at the age of twenty, and his account of his long friendship with and eventual marriage to Harriet Taylor, reflect his views on nineteenth-century politics more accurately than they reflect the facts of his career. His education was – he said – excessively analytical: it cultivated his intellect but not his emotions; it gave him an abstract concern for human well-being, but no passion for it. In this, it reflected the shortcomings of the radicalism of his father and of Bentham; they were men of the eighteenth century, analysing the defects of the old order, but incapable of suffusing their picture of a better world with the emotional warmth and the richness of texture it required. Harriet Taylor seemed to Mill to embody the poetic sensibility and quickness of imagination he was seeking; his relationship with her therefore symbolized the union of heart and head, emotion and intellect which radicalism required. She was certainly passionately hostile to what she thought of as the dead weight of Victorian respectability, and the tone of Mill's essay *On Liberty* owes a good deal to her. Considered more narrowly, it is less clear that she had much influence on the argument.

Mill, in fact, learned most of the lessons he was eager to pass on not from her but from a miscellany of other sources. As a coming man, he was pursued by Saint-Simonian 'missionaries' in the late 1820s, and later by Auguste COMTE; in revolt against Bentham he was mistaken for a disciple by CARLYLE. So he became convinced that a theory of government required a theory of history and a philosophy of progress to support it; he thought it futile to discuss institutional issues except against the background of a wider social culture; and he began to speculate about the possibilities of socialism. At the same time, he had to earn his living in the East India Company, where practicality was the test of policy.

So we find Mill steering his course between his original teachers and their critics. The *System of Logic* is an uncompromising defence of 'the inductive school' in science and social science; its intention is to defend two claims, the first that social science is possible, and that politics, economics and sociology are capable of scientific study, the other that no science discovers necessary truths about the world, that all science can ever discover is how things are, not how they must be. The ulterior target of this second claim is ethical 'intuitionism', the doctrine that moral truths are a branch of necessary truth, and are shown to be true by the revelations of intuition. *Utilitarianism* was conceived by Mill as an attack on intuitionism as well as a defence of UTILITARIANISM. All his life he thought conservative politics was propped up by people mistaking their own prejudices for ultimate truths about the world; the *System of Logic* and *Utilitarianism* assault that bad habit at one level, while *On Liberty* and *The Subjection of Women* attack the practical consequences of an inability to believe that what is obvious to us may nevertheless be false.

But if conservatism was one enemy, the simplicities of 'philosophic radicalism' were an equally tempting target. Towards the end of his life, Bentham had relied on universal suffrage and majority rule as almost infallible devices for securing good government. Mill became more and more sceptical of their efficacy. There was no reason to suppose that a simple majority of the population would be more often right than wrong: the bulk of the middle class was simply dull and obsessed with making money; the working class was ignorant, ill informed, and through no fault of its own generally dishonest. This was not an argument against democratic reform, since an unchecked governing class would infallibly behave selfishly and corruptly; but it was an argument against the old simplicities.

Under the influence of TOCQUEVILLE, Mill came to think that preserving 'the antagonism of opinions' was one crucial need; another was ensuring that wherever expertise was applicable it would be applied. So in his *Considerations on Representative Government*, Mill offers some complicated solutions to complicated problems. To prevent the majority swamping the minority, he offers a system of proportional representation, and to prevent the ignorant swamping the informed, he offers a system of plural voting which entitles the educated to additional votes. All but the illiterate, the criminal and those who cannot support themselves must have at least one vote – Mill does not *argue* for the inclusion of women in the electorate, other than to observe in passing that their exclusion is as irrational as the exclusion of red-haired men. All must have a vote, since all must be encouraged to participate and must have a voice; it does not follow that all must have an equal voice. To ensure that even this adjusted electoral system yields sensible results, he advocates a parliament which does not draft or amend legislation but instructs legislative commissions to prepare what is needed; and he advocates a degree of independent influence for civil servants.

In essence, he balances the two things he is anxious to achieve – widespread participation and progressive government on the one hand, and the influence of an intellectual and moral elite on the other. The mixture is unstable, and was in any case overtaken by the rise of party organization in the last quarter of the nineteenth century – Mill was in principle hostile to political parties, though in practice he was a good party MP for the three years he was in parliament himself (1865–8).

Mill's doubts about pure majority rule led him in a somewhat conservative direction. His enthusiasm for SOCIALISM led him in a more radical direction. He was sceptical of the ambitions of both the Saint-Simonians and the Owenites when he encountered them in the 1820s, but he reacted to the defeat of the French revolution of 1848 and to the promptings of Harriet Taylor with a qualified defence of socialism. He looked to the future to see a society of producer co-operatives, securing the good of private property without its evils. Capitalism he rejected, because workers were not self-governing and the division between owners and employees was no foundation for political democracy. Centralized communism was intolerable, but a competitive economy featuring worker-owned enterprise was greatly to be desired. In the same spirit, Mill proposed that until the advent of socialism, much could be done to make private property more legitimate – by introducing inheritance taxes, for instance, and by preventing landlords from taking the benefit of their tenants' efforts.

As this suggests, Mill was obsessed with the defence of FREEDOM in a democratic society. One element of his defence of freedom was his reinterpretation of the demands of utilitarianism; where his predecessors had given freedom a large but not a central place in utility, Mill argued that the main contribution to happiness was a developed character, and the main need of such a character was freedom: freedom was part of happiness, and indispensable to the search for new forms of happiness. Later writers have been preoccupied by such things as Mill's 'proof' of the Principle of Utility; this ignores the fact that the proof mattered little to Mill, while the attempt to reconcile the demands of individual liberty with the demands of the general welfare mattered a great deal.

It is in *On Liberty* and *The Subjection of Women* that Mill's most eloquent defence of freedom is found. In *On Liberty* he defends 'one very simple principle' – that society may not coerce unwilling individuals except in self-defence. PATERNALISM is absolutely illicit; 'moral' legislation is absolutely illicit – though Mill would not have expressed himself in such terms. Whether it is possible to defend such an absolute position on utilitarian grounds is much debated; what is clear is that Mill himself rejected any attempt to defend it on the grounds of a 'natural right to liberty'. In essence, the negative argument was that a proper understanding of morality and social life would show that prohibition could only be justified as a defensive measure, and the positive argument that all the great goods of life demanded 'experiments in living' and individual liberty. *The Subjection of Women* is avowedly devoted to condemning the legal inferiority of women in Victorian England, but it ends with an argument from the absolute value of liberty: no country would surrender its independence for any amount of prosperity, and no human being who has tasted freedom would give it up at any price. What further proof could there be of the supreme value of liberty, for women as well as for men?   AR

Reading

†Berger, F.R.: *Happiness, Justice and Freedom.* Berkeley: University of California Press, 1984.

Gray, J.A.: *Mill on Liberty: a Defence.* London: Routledge & Kegan Paul, 1983.

†Mill, J.S.: *The Collected Works of John Stuart Mill*, ed. F.E.L. Priestley. Toronto: University of Toronto Press, 1963–84.

†Packe, M. St J.: *The Life of John Stuart Mill.* London: Secker & Warburg, 1954.

†Robson, J.M.: *The Improvement of Mankind.* London: Routledge & Kegan Paul, 1968.

†Ryan, A.: *J.S. Mill.* London and Boston: Routledge & Kegan Paul, 1974.

Schwartz, P.: *The New Political Economy of J.S. Mill.* London: Weidenfeld & Nicolson, 1972.

Ten, C.L.: *Mill on Liberty.* Oxford: Clarendon Press, 1980.

Milton, John (1608–1674) English poet and controversialist. Milton, a Londoner, set out to be a poet but was drawn into political and religious polemics in 1641. The disputes in which he engaged were partly generated by his domestic concerns – a bad marriage elicited from him four pamphlets justifying divorce on grounds of incompatibility of mind and temperament (1643–5). But it was the great public issues of religion and politics heralding and accompanying the English civil wars and interregnum which drew him into public life in

1641 and kept him there until 1660. He wrote five undistinguished pamphlets against prelacy in 1641–2 and his famous – and, as to its content, overrated – *Areopagitica*, defending freedom of the press, in 1644.

In 1649 Milton began to publish more directly on what nowadays would be thought of as more obviously 'political' matters, though it must not be forgotten that his tracts against prelacy had large political implications. In *The Tenure of Kings and Magistrates* he justified the trial, execution and deposition of Charles I. In the same year he also published *Eikonoklastes* which poured scorn and derision on the famous *Eikon basilike*, a book which was often wrongly attributed at the time to Charles himself and which, if his authorship were accepted, contained the maudlin, religiose and authoritarian reflections of the martyr-king.

By March Milton had been appointed Secretary of Foreign Tongues to the Council of State set up under the revolutionary Rump Parliament. This amounted to a commission to justify the English revolution to continental Europeans, and he was indeed his country's principal defender in that arena. He wrote one Latin defence of the revolution and the 'commonwealth' of the Rump – *Pro populo anglicano defensio* – in 1651, and in 1654 he produced a second Latin work, *Defensio secunda*, which justified the first Protectorate under Oliver Cromwell. His final political polemic during this period, *The Readie and Easie Way to Establish a Free Commonwealth* (1660), was written in the shadow of inevitable restoration.

Though Milton was famous abroad as a polemicist he was justly ignored in England. His tracts on divorce caused some stir, but otherwise his contemporaries judged him to be a figure of only peripheral interest. It was not until his fame as a poet was established that he was elevated to the Whig and libertarian canon. His prose works, it must be said today, remain too occasional, too unoriginal, too little informed by a feel for the detail and structure of social and political reality, and too lacking in passion for consistency or depth of analysis to have occasioned much general interest. Nevertheless, he produced some powerful expressions of his beliefs; historians of political and religious ideas and of the practice of rhetoric have found much of interest in his mannered prose and in his poems. Evidence of the correspondence of his interests with those of his time is to be found in the fact that the Yale edition of his prose works provides the best chronologically presented introduction to the polemics of his age available.

Milton's guiding passion was for the Christian liberty of virtuous men guided only by reason and by scriptural knowledge. Nothing must stand in the way of it. It was for that reason that he opposed episcopacy, and then presbytery, and finally any form of church government at all. And it was as much for Charles's encroachment on Christian liberty as for his denial of legal rights that Milton, a monarchist in the early forties, became a republican by 1649. 'To live safe and free, without suffering violence and wrong, to this end it was that men first entered into a polity; to live piously and religiously, into a church,' he said in 1651. But both organizations must conform with the law of nature and God, and his prescriptions as to the forms of both varied with his perceptions of how that vaguely stated ideal might be achieved. As he moved towards an antinomian individualism in religion, so his politics, by 1660, issued in the prescription for the rule of a godly oligarchy, free from the control of a licentious and corrupt people. Despite his history of opposition to the Stuart church and state for nearly twenty years, he escaped persecution at the restoration of the Stuart monarchy in 1660, and retired again from public life to ensure his lasting fame with the publication first of *Paradise Lost* in 1667 and then in 1671 of *Paradise Regained* and *Samson Agonistes*. Christopher Hill and others have recently suggested that it would be wrong to see these works as other than his continuing reflections on the defeat of the libertarian religious revolution he had looked to. But it may be said that he died as quietly in 1674 as he had seemed to live since the restoration.   RAS

Reading

Davies, S.: *Images of Kingship in 'Paradise Lost': Milton's Politics and Christian Liberty*. Columbia: University of Missouri Press, 1983.

†Hill, C.: *Milton and the English Revolution*. London: Faber & Faber, 1977.

Milton, J.: *Complete Prose Works of John Milton*, ed. D.M. Wolfe. 7 vols. New Haven, Conn.: Yale University Press, 1980.

†Wolfe, D.M.: *Milton in the Puritan Revolution*. London: Nelson, 1941.

Zagorin, P.: *A History of Political Thought in the English Revolution*, 2nd edn. London: Routledge & Kegan Paul, 1965.

Montaigne, Michel de (1533–1592) French philosopher and essayist. Montaigne is best known as one of the most important figures in his country's literary history, particularly for his invention of the genre of the 'essay'. Ultimately however his greatest historical significance may lie in his role as one of the earliest philosophic architects of, and propagandists for, modern liberal doctrine and regime (see LIBERALISM).

Born into a prosperous merchant family, Montaigne spent most of his life in the Bordeaux area. He retired from the local magistracy in 1571 to begin writing the only book he ever wrote for publication, the *Essays*. Yet he continued to maintain an active, mostly informal, political role, negotiating among the leaders of the opposing parties in the religious wars, and advising the future Henry IV, who finally brought those wars to an end. Montaigne served as mayor of Bordeaux from 1581 to 1585.

Outwardly rambling and disorganized, the *Essays* were first published in two books in 1580; Book III appeared in the fifth edition (1588), and Montaigne made many subsequent revisions and additions to the text. The two most obvious unifying themes of the book are the author's purported self-revelation and his 'scepticism'. The work loosely follows an 'evolutionary' pattern, moving from the 'Stoical' and impersonal tone of many of the earlier chapters – which often consist largely of a string of quotations from classical authors – through the systematic 'sceptical' critique of religion and philosophy in the 'Apology for Raymond Sebond' (by far the longest chapter), and culminating in the more 'personal' or conversational chapters of Book III, in which the author professes an 'Epicurean' attitude of hedonism and tolerance. While some scholars have interpreted this evolution as reflecting a change of thought and mood undergone by the author as he wrote, the text is far from fully consistent with this interpretation. In view of

Montaigne's avowals of his consistency, his apparent evolution may be better understood as an instrument of his rhetoric, by which he seeks to effect a transformation in his readers.

Beginning with a conventional appeal to the wisdom of the ancients, Montaigne gradually reveals the limitations of that wisdom – particularly its incapacity to alleviate the bodily miseries of human existence. The real object of Montaigne's 'sceptical' attack, however, is Christianity, which rests on an unwarranted 'presumption' about man's status in the universe and his capacity to decipher its meaning, and is the cause of tyranny, persecution, and needless suffering. As an alternative to both classical and Christian teachings, Montaigne tempts the reader with the attractiveness of the way of life he professes to pursue – an 'unambitious' but harmless and infinitely tolerant pursuit of pleasure. Despite outwardly professing opposition to all political changes, Montaigne demonstrates the irrationality of the existing political order, and aims to replace it by a form of government whose goal would be limited to protecting men's freedom to live as they please. He also aspires to transform philosophy into a science of 'medicine', broadly understood, dedicated to conquering nature so as to make life more comfortable. Human contentment requires the moderation of man's vain spiritual demands, but the concomitant enlargement of the sphere of earthly enjoyments.   DLS

Reading

Armaingaud, A.: Étude sur Michel de Montaigne. In *Oeuvres complètes de Michel de Montaigne*, vol I. Paris: Louis Conard, 1924–41.

†Frame, D.M.: *Montaigne: a Biography*. New York: Harcourt, Brace & World, 1965.

†Keohane, N.O.: Montaigne's individualism. *Political Theory* 5 (1977) 363–90.

Montaigne, M. de.: *Essays*. In *The Complete Works of Montaigne*, trans. D.M. Frame. Stanford, Calif.: Stanford University Press, 1957.

†Sayce, R.: *The Essays of Montaigne: a Critical Exploration*. London: Weidenfeld & Nicolson, 1972.

†Schaefer, D.L.: Montaigne's intention and his rhetoric. *Interpretation: a Journal of Political Philosophy* 5 (1975) 57–90.

†———: Montaigne's political reformation. *Journal of Politics* 42 (1980) 766–91.

Villey, P.: *Les Sources et l'évolution des Essais de Montaigne*. 2 vols. Paris: Hachette, 1908; repr. New York: Burt Franklin, 1968.

Montesquieu, Charles-Louis de Secondat (1689–1755) French political philosopher. Montesquieu is the author of three works of premier importance. The first, published when he was thirty-two, is his epistolary novel, *Les Lettres persian*. Scandalously sensual and yet gracefully humane, a penetrating *jeu d'esprit* and a profound allegory of love, morals, politics, and religion, the book soon made famous its initially unknown author. No adequate interpretation of this enchantingly mysterious creation has yet appeared. The work may be tentatively characterized as presenting the negative or ground-clearing portion of Montesquieu's philosophy: his critique, in a spirit informed by BAYLE, LOCKE, and SPINOZA, of the reigning traditions of Judaeo-Christian religion and Aristotelian natural right.

Having been introduced to the court under the patronage of the exiled Duke of Berwick, and elected to the French Academy in 1728 (after considerable opposition), Montesquieu spent the following four years as an attentive traveller on the Continent and in England. Returning to France, he spent two years of solitude in his provincial château and then published *Considerations on the Causes of the Greatness of the Romans and Their Decline* (1734).

This work seems best understood as an attempt to come to terms with MACHIAVELLI, whose 'new path, never before followed by anyone' (*Discourses*, bk. 1, Intro.) led to a new and dramatically lowered conception of virtue or excellence, opposed not only to Christian charity but also to ARISTOTLE's 'moral' as well as to his 'contemplative' virtue. The true 'virtue' that is in accord with man's selfish nature and enables that nature to fulfil its genuine needs is exemplified in the history of the wolfish Roman republic, where citizens honed their emotions and intellects in a severe competition for security, dominion, and – rarest but most gratifying – lasting glory.

Montesquieu does not defend either the biblical or the classical tradition against Machiavelli's attack. He limits himself to drawing into question Machiavelli's specific characterization of humanity's largely selfish passions. The history of Rome, Montesquieu in effect argues, is too much the product of distorting accidents to be the revealing expression of that towards which human nature tends when it is liberated or allowed to express itself in a shrewdly self-conscious way. What Rome manifests is a fascinating perversion of human nature – a pathology to which republics are, indeed, all too prone. Montesquieu thus sets the stage for his new, post-Machiavellian political theory.

Before attempting to sketch that theory as presented in his masterpiece, *De l'esprit des lois* (1748), we must first confront the difficulty posed by Montesquieu's manner of writing. Since the time of Voltaire's review of the work, most readers and commentators have been unable to find in it order, plan, or coherence. Montesquieu himself insisted, in the preface and the body of the work as well as in private replies written to critics, that his book had a precise if hidden plan and that his teaching could only be understood by those who deciphered the plan. D'ALEMBERT, after long study of *De l'esprit des lois*, strongly concurred. Montesquieu furthermore claimed that his covert manner of presentation was not untypical of the previous tradition of political philosophy; in various of his published and unpublished reflections on writing and writers he mentioned in particular Plato, the leading Stoics, Descartes, and Spinoza as examples of philosophers who wrote in such a way as to hide their key teachings. One obvious – but, it turns out, secondary – reason for such a mode of communication is the threat of censorship and persecution (Montesquieu felt that all three of his major works had to be published anonymously and in foreign lands). More important, in Montesquieu's eyes, is the danger unmuted philosophy poses to the foundations of many decent societies; for it must inevitably raise and pursue subversive or disturbing questions. But Montesquieu makes it clear that the weightiest reason for indirect communication is educative. Philosophic education is best served not by a teacher's delivering a message, but by his trying to stimulate the best of his students to rethink the problematic path of questioning and puzzlement that he himself has travelled.

De l'esprit des lois opens with a compressed discussion of 'laws in general', or 'the necessary relationships that derive from the nature of things'. We are assured, on the theological authority of Plutarch, that even God the creator must follow 'rules as invariable as the fatality taught by atheists'. The 'natural laws' of human behaviour define or arise directly from the most powerful and least resistible human needs (secure survival and procreation); as such, they describe the fundamental limits, goals, and hence norms of our existence. The human species differs from both the merely animal and the divine because its existence is left mainly to the guidance not of instinct, but of a very fallible 'intelligence', whose power of reasoning remains undeveloped unless wrenched into motion by accident or external pressure. Human beings by nature frequently cannot discern the best ways, or even very adequate ways, to satisfy the dictates of their natural laws. In particular, the natural laws are prior to, and distinguished from, 'the relationships of equity anterior to positive law': for equity, or justice, presupposes society and 'intelligence', and humanity by nature lacks both. At the core of our natural constitution is a radically disconnected, subrational individuality, filled with anxiety and longing desperately for peace and security. Foreshadowing ROUSSEAU, Montesquieu rejects the Hobbesian state of nature, with its warlike desires for honour and dominion, as still too sociable. But against Rousseau, and in more basic agreement with HOBBES, Montesquieu teaches that the state of nature is a state of terror and misery.

Partly as a consequence, the state of nature is not a static condition. Mankind soon becomes aware of the pleasures and advantages that accrue from sociability. Unfortunately, the primary outcome of this natural desire for society is destructive: taking humanity out of the state of nature, it plunges our species immediately into 'the state of war'. Once we lose our overwhelming fear of other men, our selfish needs for security and material welfare tend to predominate, leading us to try to exploit our fellows or to protect ourselves, by anticipation, from their exploitation.

Responding to the horrors of the state of war, reason discovers certain more or less universally valid rules of reciprocity which, if enforced in positive law, will maintain peace, security, and a substantial degree of fairness within each civil society in all but extreme circumstances. The essence of legitimate political law appears then to be the rule or rules of reason devised with a view to security, the overwhelming imperative of the natural law. Yet the few quasi-universal laws which reason can discover provide only very minimal standards. They show us that DESPOTISM, or government based on terror, is against nature; but they do not show us which, if any, non-despotic (or 'moderate') form of government is best by nature in all times and places. The laws of reason do not even provide us with a universally applicable principle of legitimacy like the Social Compact or the Consent of the Governed. This is because humanity as we know it in society is in fact the product not merely of nature, but of vastly differing historical and natural environments. The 'general spirit' of each nation gives its people a second, quasi-natural stratum of needs, or a unique way of expressing the needs they share with all men. The adaptation and modification of reason's goals and precepts in the light of the 'general spirit of each nation' is what Montesquieu means by, and intends to teach as, the science of 'the spirit of the laws'.

Because Montesquieu lays such unprecedented emphasis on the sub-political influences, like climate, that shape society, he has frequently been honoured as the father or the chief precursor of sociology and social history. This would seem to be an exaggeration. Montesquieu continues to conceive of politics, law, and legislation – above all the fundamental laws constituting the 'form of government' – as the chief determinants of any society.

In classifying each form of government, Montesquieu speaks first of its 'nature' (the institutional distribution of 'sovereign power') and then of its 'principle' (the specific passions, the 'modification of the soul' required in the inhabitants as the 'spring' which makes each institutional mechanism work). Non-despotic forms of government, based on a principle other than fear, have flourished only in Western Europe, and there in two very different varieties. The first is the civic republic typified by the ancient *polis*, and a few modern republics like

Venice; the second is feudal monarchy, with its tense and shifting balance between king, nobility, and clergy. The principle of monarchy is honour, or a proud and prickly sense of rank and place. The principle of republics is 'virtue', by which Montesquieu means (he stresses) neither moral nor religious virtue but instead a passionate, unreflective patriotism which can for a time induce citizens to subordinate or redirect their selfish energies for the sake of an austere and egalitarian spirit of fraternity. Montesquieu bows to the apparent grandeur of this 'virtue', and the freedom, security, and equality it produces – especially in contrast to the decadent or somewhat slavish and almost bizarrely contrived form of honour he sees around him in eighteenth-century France. Yet as his analysis proceeds the inhumanity and irrationality of 'virtue' is quietly but steadily pressed upon our attention. Virtue requires a conformism, enforced by a strict and censorious watchfulness, that represses some of humanity's strongest natural impulses: in a vivid passage (bk V, ch. 2), Montesquieu likens the virtuous republican city at its best to a monastery.

As the reader's disenchantment with virtue grows, he starts to appreciate Montesquieu's occasional and seemingly paradoxical praise for the commercial spirit that infects some republics. That spirit saps – but, by the same token, mitigates – the rigour of virtue (compare III, 3 with V, 6). At the same time, monarchic honour or vanity, which may heighten but surely does not stifle individuality, begins to appear in a more favourable light. Our sensibilities are thus gradually prepared for Montesquieu's famous celebration of the English constitution and commercial way of life. England, at least in its aspiration or in a somewhat idealized portrait, represents the first and thus far the only nation in history dedicated to liberty, properly understood not so much as political participation or power but rather as the security of each individual's life, family, and peaceful or non-exploitative pursuit of property. In England the old monarchic government rooted in honour has been integrated into a broader and more effective system of checks and balances (culminating in the famous SEPARATION OF POWERS), a system that liberates and efficiently mobilizes each individual's natural anxiety and peaceful acquisitiveness so as to produce ever greater prosperity for all.

The English nation as painted by Montesquieu sets the rational standard which should guide reform in every nation. Some of its institutional features (for example, the independent judiciary) may, with circumspection, be transplanted. But any application of the English standard requires painstaking familiarity with the history of the nation to be affected: it is to the sort of history required, in the case of his own nation, that Montesquieu devotes the last part of his great work – partly as an act of patriotic public spirit, partly as a model to other philosophic and statesmanlike 'legislators'.

What *can* be promulgated and spread universally with great likelihood of success, what can be counted on to transform human existence in the direction of the equal protection of all human beings, is the 'spirit of commerce', guided by the new science of finance or economics. The books devoted to commerce, its past history and world-historical future implications, reveal the truly revolutionary thrust of Montesquieu's philosophic 'legislation'. For in them it is argued that commercialism tends to cure human beings of the prejudices that veil their true needs. In recognizing the common neediness that constitutes its nature, mankind discovers a sense of 'humanity' that replaces previous religious, ethnic, and national sectarianisms. Once captivated by the allure of peaceful trade, men look with increasing disgust at military exploits and the risks of war. They learn to appreciate the charms of national diversity and individual singularity; if commerce threatens to vulgarize or trivialize the arts, it also tends to release the arts, along with everything else, from parochialism and the restraints of moral censorship. Besides, commerce brings virtues of its own: 'frugality, economy, moderation, work, prudence, tranquillity, order, and rule' (V, 6); more precisely, the spirit of commerce 'produces in men a certain spirit of exact justice, opposed on the one hand to brigandage, but opposed on the other hand to those moral virtues which restrain one from always pressing one's interests with rigidity, and allow one to neglect one's interests for the sake of the interests of others' (XX, 2). Montesquieu sums up his view of *the* great choice as follows: 'The Greek political thinkers knew of no other power that could sustain popular government except that of virtue; today we hear only of manufactures, commerce, finance, riches, and even luxury' (III, 3). With the fullest awareness of what was at issue, Montesquieu took his stand with the moderns and against the Greeks. (See also FRENCH ENLIGHTENMENT.)   TLP

Reading

Althusser, L.: *Politics and History*, trans. B. Brewster. London: New Left, 1972.

†Aron, R.: Montesquieu. In *Main Currents in Sociological Thought*, vol. I. Garden City, NJ: Doubleday Anchor; Harmondsworth: Penguin, 1968.

Carcassonne, E.: *Montesquieu et le problème de la constitution française au XVIIIᵉ siècle*. Paris: Presses Universitaires de France, 1926.

Durkheim, E.: *Montesquieu and Rousseau: Forerunners of Sociology*, trans. R. Manheim. Ann Arbor: University of Michigan Press, 1960.

Lowenthal, D.: The design of Montesquieu's 'Considerations'. *Interpretation: a Journal of Political Philosophy* 2 (1970) 144–68.

Montesquieu, C.-L.: *Oeuvres complètes*, ed. R. Caillois. Paris: Gallimard, 1949–51.

———: *Considerations on the Causes of the Greatness of the Romans and Their Decline*, trans. D. Lowenthal. Ithaca, NY: Cornell University Press, 1968.

———: *The Spirit of the Laws* , ed. F. Neumann, trans. T. Nugent. New York: Hafner, 1949. [A sometimes misleading translation but the only one in English; must be used with caution.]

†———: *The Political Theory of Montesquieu*, ed. M. Richter. Cambridge: Cambridge University Press, 1977. [A reasonably accurate translation of excerpts from all of Montesquieu's major works.]

†Pangle, T.L.: *Montesquieu's Philosophy of Liberalism: a Commentary on 'The Spirit of the Laws'*. Chicago: University of Chicago Press, 1973.

Shackleton, R.: *Montesquieu: a Critical Biography*. London: Oxford University Press, 1961.

More, Thomas (1478–1535) English statesman and author, saint of the Roman Catholic Church. More is today best known as the author of *Utopia* (1516) and for his execution by Henry VIII. In his day he was a lawyer, politician and diplomat, and was known as one of the leading members of the Renaissance of northern Europe and, later, as a defender of the faith.

Born the son of John More, a barrister of Lincoln's Inn, Thomas More was a page for John Morton, Archbishop of Canterbury. He was educated in the City of London and at Oxford before entering one of the Inns of Chancery in 1496 and being called to the bar in 1502. His career was to culminate in his appointment as Chancellor. With the rise of Protestantism he devoted much of his energy to rooting out heresy within the church. He was unable to reconcile this role as defender of the faith with support for the Act of Supremacy which made Henry the head of the church in England, and he was executed for treason. He was beatified in 1886 and canonized in 1935.

In the history of political thought More is remembered solely as the author of *Utopia*, a little book that gave rise to a genre of literature and a name for a mode of theorizing (see UTOPIANISM). *Utopia* has bedevilled critics for over four hundred years; there is still basic disagreement over its meaning. Scholars agree that *Utopia* presents a non-existent society located in space and time and that there are substantial satiric elements in the book, but there is no agreement on the meaning and importance of the satire.

The satire is most obvious in the play on words. Utopia means 'no place' but is a play on the word *eutopia*, meaning 'good place'. In the same way, Hythlodaeus (the surname of the main character) means speaker of nonsense but Raphael (his first name) means healer from god. This play on words tells us nothing about More's intentions.

More addresses a number of issues in *Utopia*. The society (each family and the country as a whole) he presents is authoritarian, patriarchal and hierarchical in a setting of complete economic equality (the inhabitants even exchange homes on a regular basis). Age is honoured and given authority, as are husbands and fathers. Property is held in common; there is no competition; and everyone works under direction for the common good (see COMMUNISM).

The direction is provided by political and religious hierarchies who administer a law code, established by the founder of the country, which provides detailed regulations for all aspects of life. The main purpose of the administrators is to ensure that no one is idle. They move people about the country as need arises (even from family to family or into and out of colonies). But the economic equality ensures that no one has to work too hard, everyone has enough to eat, and everyone is housed and clothed simply but adequately.

Reason is one of the guides for the inhabitants of Utopia, although they conclude that revelation may provide a higher standard. Their rational religion provides the major problem for contemporary commentators. Some way must be found, scholars argue, to reconcile More's devout Catholicism with the Utopian institutions of religious toleration and voluntary euthanasia. (The institution of common property was also once a difficulty but is nowadays rarely thought to pose a problem.) Elaborate analyses have been developed to show that More did not support these institutions, but none of these analyses has been wholly satisfactory. In making *Utopia* a complex puzzle, they take away any good reason for reading the book.

We simply do not know what More intended, but it is reasonable to conclude that *Utopia* was, among other things, a thought experiment in which More attempted to see where the dictates of reason might lead. In later life More rejected *Utopia*, refusing to allow it to be translated into English from the original Latin because it might infect the uneducated. To More, the defender of a beleaguered faith, his youthful *jeu d'esprit* was of little interest.

More's *Utopia* was a product of the Renaissance and Age of Discovery during which many people in Western Europe were rethinking their relationships with the church, the state, and each other (see RENAISSANCE POLITICAL THOUGHT). In *Utopia* More posed fundamental questions about all those relationships. He asked his contemporaries whether poverty and human degradation were really necessary. By presenting a society of economic equals cooperating for the common good, he suggested that the answer could be negative. By portraying that society as authoritarian, hierarchical and patriarchal, he suggested that human beings must be controlled; reason was not enough to provide order in society. Reason must be embodied in a set of detailed rules and regulations, and the people must be both encouraged and forced to obey.

Undoubtedly, More's model was the monastery. The whole system is a monastery writ large; even such minor points as common meals accompanied by edifying readings show this influence. More drew heavily on this medieval institution, but he added the insights of the Renaissance and the Age of Discovery together with his extensive reading of the classics to produce something new and different.   LTS

Reading

Fox, A.: *Thomas More: History and Providence*. Oxford: Blackwell, 1982.

Guy, A.: *The Public Career of Sir Thomas More*. New Haven, Conn.: Yale University Press, 1980.

†Hexter, J.H.: *More's Utopia: the Biography of an Idea*. New York: Harper & Row, 1952.

†Logan, G.M.: *The Meaning of More's 'Utopia'*. Princeton, NJ: Princeton University Press, 1983.

†Marius, R.: *Thomas More: a Biography*. New York: Knopf, 1984.

†More, T.: *Utopia*, trans. P. Turner. Harmondsworth: Penguin, 1965.

Surtz, E.L., SJ: *The Praise of Pleasure: Philosophy, Education and Communism in More's 'Utopia'*. Cambridge, Mass.: Harvard University Press, 1957.

————: *The Praise of Wisdom: a Commentary on the Religious and Moral Problems and Backgrounds of St Thomas More's 'Utopia'*. Chicago, Ill.: Loyola University Press, 1957.

Morris, William (1834–1896) British writer, artist, socialist, and communist. Morris began his short and energetic public life as a painter, poet, and designer. His concern for the quality of work led him in the 1880s into politics. He was briefly associated with H. M. Hyndman's Social Democratic Federation, before leaving to form, with Eleanor Marx and E. Belfort Bax, the Socialist League. His principal political writings were a series of essays on the actual and possible nature of work, and two socialist utopias, *A Dream of John Ball* (1888) and *News from Nowhere* (1891).

Morris's main contribution to socialism was his account of work. He saw work as the characteristically human occupation and its 'useless' and 'toilsome' character as the chief blemish, together with the absence of FRATERNITY, of contemporary industrial society. Work could, he believed, be a pleasurable and creative

activity, in which the workers could express and fulfil themselves. He thus approached from the point of view of the working artist the matter which Marx had dealt with from a different perspective in his account of ALIENATION. Morris's politics were to this extent a tactic for achieving his moral and aesthetic aspirations, and the best of his political writing occurs in works which are not in their immediate appearance political.

Morris saw little point in conventionally political tactics, believing rather that persuasion and propaganda would prepare the way for an eventual transformation. He envisaged that the existing order, which he stigmatized as 'commercial slavery' and 'patriarchy', would be overthrown by popular uprising, and that the ensuing communist society would conduct its communal business through *ad hoc* local assemblies. It would lack any of the central coercive functions of the modern state, an institution which he considered an instrument for 'the protection of the rich from the poor, the strong from the weak'.

Morris was for many years effectively dismissed as a romantic eccentric, but was 'rediscovered' in the second half of the twentieth century, partly in the movement of ideas and politics gathered under the umbrella title NEW LEFT. He is now regarded as a figure of major importance, and is consequently the subject of some dispute as to whether he is best described as 'socialist', 'anarchist', or 'communist' in outlook.   RB

Reading

Morris, W.: *News from Nowhere*. London: Routledge & Kegan Paul, 1970.

————: *Political Writings*, ed. A.L. Morton. London: Lawrence & Wishart, 1979.

†Thompson, E.P.: *William Morris: Romantic to Revolutionary*. London: Merlin, 1977.

Mosca, Gaetano (1858–1941) Italian political sociologist. Mosca was professor of constitutional law at Turin from 1895 to 1923, then professor of public law at Rome until 1933. He was also involved in politics, a member of the Chamber of Deputies from 1908 to 1918, and subsequently a senator. Alongside PARETO, he is regarded as the founder of ELITISM.

Mosca provided the most concise exposition of elitism in his book *The Ruling Class* (1896): 'In all societies . . . two classes of people appear – a class that rules and a class that is ruled.' The ruling class monopolizes power and enjoys the advantages of power. It uses both legal and arbitrary methods to sustain its domination. Mosca believed that political science could discover laws based on the study of history, which displays certain constant tendencies. He rejected the general explanations offered by Marxists, evolutionary theorists and racialists.

The domination of a ruling or political class (or 'elite' as this minority was to be termed in political science) was a law supported by evidence from all periods of history and from all parts of the world. Each ruling group possesses some resource or attribute which is esteemed or influential in the particular society and which it exploits in order to advance its own power and advantage. This might be, as MARX held, the ownership of the means of production but Mosca rejected any such unidimensional explanation of social and political power. Military force, priestly status or administrative expertise were equally plausible bases of political domination. In every case the elite tries to convert itself into a form of hereditary rule by using its power to perpetuate its control. As a minority it can act in a conscious, cohesive manner. Even liberal democracies are subject to manipulation in that free elections are controlled by party elites and open examinations to official positions routinely favour the established ruling class. The ruling class rules not only by violence and manipulation but through ideology or 'the political formula' which convinces the general population of the moral legitimacy of the elite's domination. Universal 'illusions', including religious or nationalist sentiments, hold societies together. The will of the majority was the prevailing democratic formula which Mosca sought to expose as fraud.

Political and social change occurs as a result of conflict between ruling classes seeking to hold on to power and new forces, also led by minorities, striving to displace them. Elites often lose power because they fail to assimilate new social forces by opening ranks to new personnel or by adapting their policies and ideas. An elite which is excessively introverted and immobile gradually loses its political and ideological hold on society and may itself be overthrown. Mosca classified forms of elite rule according to the kinds of legitimating ideology and the processes by which elites are recruited and replaced. Societies will always be elite-dominated. Mosca predicted, in particular, that communist states would be managed by the officials controlling both political and economic life. Change never results in political equality.

GP

Reading

Albertoni, E.: *Mosca*. Oxford: Blackwell, 1987.

†Bobbio, N.: *On Mosca and Pareto*. Geneva: Droz, 1972.

Bottomore, T.: *Elites and Society*. Harmondsworth: Penguin, 1966.

†Meisel, J.H.: *The Myth of the Ruling Class: Gaetano Mosca and the Elite*. Ann Arbor: University of Michigan Press, 1962.

Mosca, G.: *The Ruling Class*, trans. and ed. A. Livingston. New York: McGraw-Hill, 1939.

†Parry, G.: *Political Elites*. London: Allen & Unwin, 1969.

Mussolini, Benito (1883–1945) Italian dictator. See FASCISM.

mutualism A social theory expounded by PROUDHON and a number of his French disciples that sought to find a middle way between the principles of private PROPERTY and COMMUNISM by means of workers' associations and mutual credit. The mutualists were broadly anarchist in outlook, but advocated gradual rather than revolutionary change. See ANARCHISM.

N

national socialism   The ideology of the National Socialist German Workers Party (NSDAP), better known as the Nazi party, which was formed in 1919 and under Hitler ruled Germany between 1933 and 1945. National socialism essentially combined two doctrines: the fascist belief that national unity could best be secured by an all-encompassing state directed by a party with one supreme leader embodying the national will, and the racist belief in the superiority of the Aryan peoples, implying that other races might justifiably be subjugated or eliminated entirely. Although national socialism was the most spectacular, and in some respects the most successful, of all forms of fascism, it was intellectually less sophisticated and less interesting than French or Italian fascism.

Its political success lay in its ability to synthesize often contradictory elements into a doctrine with universal appeal – 'socialism' for the working class, anti-bolshevism for the employers, nationalism for traditional conservatives, and anti-semitism for all who looked for a scapegoat on whom to pin the blame for the loss of world war one and the economic disasters of the 1920s. Domestically, this recipe was a great success; internationally, it weakened the so-called Axis, or wartime alliance between Italy, Germany and Japan. Italy had every reason to fear German nationalism, which could only revive separatist aspirations in the former South Tyrol and boded ill for Italian ambitions in Africa; Japan could hardly be unaware that Hitler's ambitions for the Aryan race left little room for its own, and that the 'Yellow Peril' had frequently featured in the rhetoric of his pre-war speeches.

Nazism had intellectual pretentions, but they came a poor second to an enthusiasm for brute force and the cult of the leader. Liberals have often accused Hegel of laying the foundations of Nazism (see Popper, vol. II); the Nazis themselves frequently claimed an intellectual kinship with Nietzsche. In fact, Hegel's conservative liberalism was at worst intermittently authoritarian, and his insistence on the rule of law and constitutional safeguards for private rights was utterly uncongenial to Nazism, while Nietzsche's contempt for the pretensions of the German Empire is an indication of how removed his ideals were from anything in national socialism. Where Italian fascism could boast of Gentile, and French fascism of BARRÈS and MAURRAS, Nazism was intellectually barren. Alfred Rosenberg (born 1893, hanged as a war criminal October 1946) was its only 'philosopher', and his best-known work, *The Myth of the Twentieth Century* (1930) is a discordant jumble of racist and *volkisch* ideas loosely attached to a history of European culture which bizarrely attempts to prove that everything worth having in European history is of Nordic origin.

National socialism is of sociological rather than intellectual interest. It has been handled best by writers who have understood it as an intellectual pathology, whether that has been interpreted as an episode in the history of mass society (see Arendt) or as a response to the desire for the transcendental (see Nolte). Its 'socialism' meant little more than that the state's rights transcended those of private owners; its appeal to the *Volk* was hardly more than an excuse to destroy the secondary organizations of liberal society, trade unions in particular, and to arouse the population for war. The most interesting feature of Nazi ideology was its ambivalence about revolution; although Barrès and Maurras were articulate enemies of the French Revolution and subsequent liberalism, Mussolini was always as much attracted by Marxism as repelled by it. Nazism was the apotheosis of this ambivalence, simultaneously presenting itself as counter-revolutionary and yet revolutionary. Its psychological appeal was evidently very similar to the appeal of revolutionary utopianism of all kinds (cf. Cohn) and while lip-service was paid to the static ideal of the corporate state, the more characteristic aspect of national socialism, rhetorically and in practice, was something akin to permanent revolution. All institutions were valuable only in so far as they expressed the spirit of the *Volk* and advanced the triumph of the Aryan race, and all might therefore be swept away at any moment if necessary. This is but one of many ways in which national socialism defies assimilation to previous forms of conservatism or authoritarianism, and in which the Nazi version of fascism is much more than an assemblage of responses to the problems of economic dislocation which affected almost all countries in the inter-war years.

Its embodiment in the febrile genius of Hitler is, in this sense, more than an accident. For it was his political opportunism and his galvanizing energy which allowed the Nazis to gain support by promising both nationalization and the protection of private ownership, by stressing both industrial might and the unique virtues of the peasant, and by emphasizing the necessity of both radical and conservative measures. The only constant was an emphasis on national expansion, racial purity and the 'leadership principle'. War was the inevitable outcome of combining these aspirations with the explicit claim that in international politics might is right; total defeat in 1945 was a verdict with which no national socialist could quarrel. See FASCISM, NATIONALISM, RACISM.

AR

Reading
Arendt, H.: *The Origins of Totalitarianism*. New York: Harcourt Brace, 1951.
Bullock, A.: *Hitler: A Study in Tyranny*. Harmondsworth: Penguin, 1962.
Cohn, N.: *The Pursuit of the Millennium*. London: Paladin, 1970.
Mosse, G.L.: *The Crisis of German Ideology*. Weidenfeld & Nicolson, 1966.
Neumann, F.: *Behemoth*. New York, 1966.
Nolte, E.: *Three Faces of Fascism*. New York: Holt, Rinehart & Winston, 1965.
Popper, K.R.: *The Open Society and its Enemies*. London: Routledge, 1945; Princeton, NJ: Princeton University Press, 1950.
Rosenberg, A.: *Race and Race History*, ed. R. Pois. London: Weidenfeld & Nicolson, 1970. [Includes excerpts from *The Myth of the Twentieth Century*.]
Stern, F.: *The Politics of Cultural Despair*. Berkeley: University of California Press, 1974.

nationalism If an IDEOLOGY is a general way of thinking about the world that has prescriptive implications for politics, then nationalism is an ideology – and by far the most potent ideology in the world. As a way of thinking about the world it emphasizes the importance of nations in explaining historical developments and analysing contemporary politics, and also typically claims that 'national character' is a pervasive factor in differentiating human beings. Prescriptively, nationalism carries the implication that all human beings should have one and only one nationality, which should be their primary focus of identity and loyalty. This means that people should see themselves as members of a nationality before they are members of any narrower, more inclusive, or cross-cutting grouping; and that they should be prepared to make any sacrifices required to defend and advance the interests of the nation, whatever the expense may be to other interests.

Nationalism characteristically issues in the demand for each nationality to be organized in a sovereign state. Most scholars have indeed equated it with this demand. Gellner writes: 'Nationalism is primarily a political principle, which holds that the political unit and the national unit should be congruent. . . . Nationalist *sentiment* is the feeling of anger aroused by the violation of the principle, or the feeling of satisfaction aroused by its fulfilment. A nationalist *movement* is one actuated by a sentiment of this kind' (p. 1). This entails (as Gellner recognizes) that every nationalist movement must be a separatist movement if its nationality is wholly contained within the boundaries of some larger existing state, and must be committed to some more complex redrawing of state boundaries if members of the same nationality occupy a contiguous area of more than one state.

In spite of the weight of scholarly authority to the contrary, the position to be taken here is that making the demand for independent statehood the defining characteristic of a nationalist movement is to mistake the effect for the cause. What is central to a nationalist movement is that it claims to represent members of the nationality in virtue of the material and cultural interests that they share. It calls on its supporters to subordinate the common interests (based on class, religion, or party, for example) that they share with their fellow citizens to those that they share with other members of the national group. Hence, we find in the nineteenth century Irish Nationalists standing outside the division between Liberals and Conservatives in the rest of the United Kingdom the better to pursue distinctively Irish interests in land reform, the recision of penal legislation, and Home Rule for Ireland. In the period since 1945 nationalist parties in Quebec, Flanders, Scotland and Wales have similarly called upon the members of the national group to desert parties with a country-wide basis and join with their fellow nationals in seeking to advance the interests that they share in respect of common nationality.

Most, though not all, nationalist movements of this kind have a demand for independent statehood in their programme, but it would be highly artificial to deny the bona fides of nationalist movements that do not. Moreover, it is no easy matter to determine the extent to which a demand for independent statehood is seen by the leaders of a nationalist movement as a bargaining lever with which to secure other concessions, including increased political autonomy falling short of statehood. Conversely, a nationalist movement's official demands may not include statehood because its leaders calculate that the best way towards that ultimate goal is to aim in the medium term for increased political autonomy. Thus, while the Irish Nationalists were officially in favour of Home Rule, leader Charles Stewart Parnell said in a speech in 1885, 'No man has a right to fix the boundary of the march of a nation; no man has the right to say to his country – thus far shalt thou go and no further.' There may indeed be

no fact of the matter to discover: even a nationalist leader who wanted to tell the truth might be unable to say which is goal and which is strategic move.

By putting at the centre of our analysis of nationalism the claim of the overriding importance of nationality, we can keep demands for political autonomy or independence in perspective as means to the pursuit of the nationalist end of advancing the collective cultural and material interests of those united by common nationality. An independent state is naturally conceived of as a means because this maximizes the power of representatives of the nationality, but independence may have counterbalancing economic costs. A nationalist movement that settles for a high degree of political autonomy (including control of the educational system and the cultural apparatus), combined with economic concessions from the rest of the country to its region, is not the less a nationalist movement for that.

The insistence that a nationalist movement *must* seek independent statehood is derived from an assumption imposed on reality by the scholar who takes it as axiomatic that: 'the only insurance of political survival under modern conditions is protection from interference by hostile outsiders in a separate political organization, or State' (Smith, p. 217). This assumption rests on too limited an appreciation of the capacity of states to adapt their forms so as to accommodate nationalist aspirations. The most dramatic illustration of this is the transformation of Belgium in the past quarter century from a centralized state on the French model to something more like a configuration of two national sub-states. The deflation of separatist sentiment in Quebec during the same period is only less remarkable because Canada started as a federal state.

Nationalism as a doctrine of universal applicability claims that all people should give their highest loyalty to their own nation. Membership of a nation is thus seen as an essential good for every human being. Nationalism can also take a particularistic form. Nationalist sentiment here means an emphasis in politics on the pursuit of the national interest at the expense of the interests of other countries and without regard to other values such as the avoidance of bloodshed, respect for international law, or the maintenance of international co-operation through bilateral or multilateral treaties. This particularistic nationalism bears the same relation to universal nationalism as selfishness does to individualism, selfishness being the pursuit of one's own interests without regard to the interests of others, and individualism being the doctrine that it is legitimate to pursue one's own interests on the same terms as those on which others are free to pursue theirs. When elaborated as an ideology it is IMPERIALISM, and is taken to legitimate a country's seizure of territory not occupied by its own nationals, either with the object of settling it with nationals or extracting some advantage (typically military or economic) from its possession.

As an ideology, nationalism gives one particular answer to the question of the proper basis of human association. It is therefore inherently in conflict with any ideology that gives a different answer. An obvious example is classical MARXISM, with its slogan that 'the workers have no country'. (MARX's theory of history may, indeed, owe an intellectual debt to nationalism, in that it takes the idea of collective actors as progressive forces in history from HEGEL but changes the identity of the collectivity from nations to classes.) Nationalism also conflicts with what we might call 'personalism', the position epitomized in E. M. Forster's assertion that if he had to choose between betraying his country and betraying his friends he hoped he would have the courage to betray his country. This position – the moral primacy of personal relations – has recently been advanced by a number of American feminist writers (see, for example, Noddings). At the opposite pole from personalism, with its emphasis on the supreme importance of personal relations and rejection of all general obligations, is 'cosmopolitanism'. According to this, the interests of all human beings have in principle an equal claim on all of us (see, for example, Beitz). It is obvious that cosmopolitanism is just as much a denial of nationalism as is personalism.

At the same time, nationalism can in practice combine with the ideologies of LIBERALISM, SOCIALISM and COMMUNISM in spite of their cosmopolitan implications when abstractly stated. Everywhere in the world nationalism comes first and the other ideology occupies a subordinate position, partially defining the content of the national ideal. Stalin's slogan 'Socialism [i.e. communism] in one country' applies to all other ideologies prescribing forms of social organization, which are simply fitted into the nationalist matrix. Little intellectual discomfort is apparently felt at this subversion – even by the great majority of intellectuals.

Most of the literature on nationalism consists of attempts to categorize the bases on which nationality or nationhood has been attributed to various groups in history. The main division is between 'objective' ideas of nationality according to which nationality is a natural fact about people, constituted by mother tongue, ethnic descent, etc. (see Ergang), and the 'subjective' view, according to which nationality is a psychological phenomenon (see Mill, ch. 16). On this view, 'a "nationality" . . . represents a common feeling and an organized claim rather than distinct attributes which can be comprised in a strict definition' (*Encyclopaedia Britannica*).

The various versions of the first conception are compounded of historical myth and pseudobiology (see also RACISM). The second conception is better able to accommodate the actual negotiability and mutability of national identity. (It has been said with some truth, for example, that a language is a dialect with an army and a navy.) The protean nature of nationality doubtless contributes greatly to its popularity as an ideology. At the same time it renders dubious the value of any attempt to offer a single explanation of that popularity.

BMB

Reading

Barry, B.: Self-government revisited. In *The Nature of Political Theory*, ed. D. Miller and L. Siedentop. Oxford: Clarendon Press, 1983.

Beitz, C.: *Political Theory and International Relations*. Princeton, NJ: Princeton University Press, 1979.

Encyclopaedia Britannica, 11th edn. *sub.* 'Nationalism', vol. XIX. Cambridge: Cambridge University Press, 1911.

Ergang, R.R.: *Herder and German Nationalism*. New York: Columbia University Press, 1931.

†Gellner, E.: *Nations and Nationalism*. Oxford: Blackwell; Ithaca, NY: Cornell University Press, 1983.

†Kohn, H.: *The Idea of Nationalism*. New York: Macmillan, 1946.

Mill, J.S.: *Considerations on Representative Government*. In *Essays on Politics and Society*, ed. J.M. Robson. Toronto: University of Toronto Press, 1977.

Noddings, N.: *Caring: a Feminine Approach to Ethics and Moral Education*. Berkeley and Los Angeles: University of California Press, 1984.

†Smith, A.D.: *Theories of Nationalism*. London: Duckworth, 1971.

†Snyder, L. ed: *The Dynamics of Nationalism*. New York: Van Nostrand, 1964. [Contains selections from earlier writers on nationalism.[sr

natural law See LAW.

natural rights See HUMAN RIGHTS.

needs See INTERESTS and JUSTICE.

New Left An umbrella term for a group of radical thinkers who, between the late 1950s and the early 1970s, sought to revitalize socialist thought. The New Left were critical of 'existing socialism' in Eastern Europe, and distanced themselves from communist parties in the West. They also questioned the orthodox Marxist belief in the impending economic collapse of capitalism, focusing instead on ideological and cultural factors which prevented the victims of capitalism from becoming aware of their authentic needs. The New Left had little by way of a concrete political programme: the anarchist strain in their thought showed up in their distrust of conventional party politics, and they are best regarded as social critics. Nonetheless they succeeded in reshaping the socialist agenda, placing on it questions about personal (especially sexual) relationships, cultural change, and the value of material progress. (See SOCIALISM.)   DLM

Reading
Long, P.: *The New Left*. Boston, Mass.: Porter Sargeant, 1969.

New Right A term used somewhat vaguely to describe a group of thinkers who, in the 1970s and 1980s, attacked the ideas and practices of SOCIAL DEMOCRACY as embodied in existing western states, as well as the form of SOCIALISM established in Eastern Europe. Their ideological affiliations ranged widely between LIBERTARIANISM and CONSERVATISM, but they shared a commitment to 'rolling back the state', in some areas if not in all. Their novelty consisted less in the content of their ideas (which owed much to nineteenth-century liberalism) than in the political context in which these were deployed.

DLM

Reading

Levitas, R. ed: *The Ideology of the New Right*. Cambridge: Polity, 1986.

Niebuhr, Reinhold (1892–1971) American theologian, social critic and political thinker. Born in Missouri, USA, Niebuhr attended Elmhurst College, and Eden and Yale Divinity schools. He was admitted to the Evangelical Synod of North America in 1915, and was pastor in a working-class Detroit church until 1928 when he joined the faculty of Union Theological Seminary in New York, where he held the chair in Christian ethics until his retirement in 1960. Niebuhr was the author of many books and articles and the recipient of several honorary degrees; in 1939 he was invited by the University of Edinburgh to give the Gifford Lectures, from which resulted his magnum opus *Human Nature and Destiny* (1942). But the central themes of his lifelong interest in politics had already been set forth in his first book, *Moral Man and Immoral Society* (1932).

These concerns focused on the operations of the forces of sin and grace in secular society and politics. Though for Niebuhr human consciousness is graced by awareness of and yearning for the transcendental, human institutions – including even language – are prevented by the power of sin from framing ultimate meaning in secular life. His social criticism was accordingly aimed at what he considered the falsity of all secular claims to universal justice. For this reason Niebuhr was considered, and considered himself, an Augustinian (see AUGUSTINE). Highly self-critical – self-criticism being his method – he consistently adhered to a realism according to which secular authorities undermine themselves by their claims to self-righteousness, even when those claims grow, as they characteristically do in contemporary times, under the guise of scepticism.

Niebuhr's particular defence of democracy, as opposed to all authoritarianism, rested on the argument that only democratic practices encourage the puncturing of illusions; from this view stemmed his famous definition of democratic politics as 'the proximate solution of insoluble problems' and his best-known prayer:

God, give us grace to accept with serenity the things that cannot be changed, courage to change the things that should be changed, and the wisdom to distinguish the one from the other.

Niebuhr's theological mentor was Jonathan Edwards; his political hero was Abraham LINCOLN. As the former asked infinite respect for the mysteries of the world, including those of cruelty and suffering, so the latter advanced the necessary political stance – a 'combination of moral resoluteness about the immediate issues with a religious awareness of another dimension of meaning and judgment' and an 'awareness of a contradiction between divine and human purposes, even on the highest level of human aspirations' (*The Irony of American History*, p. 72). Only this awareness, Niebuhr argued, could ground human charity, proceeding, as it must, from a 'broken spirit and contrite heart'. Even as politics must be understood as a matter of conflicting interests expressed through force, and even as every community, especially the nation, defends its own interests by force, the final judgment on the use of force can never be merely pragmatic.

Niebuhr therefore emphasized the dependence of political resoluteness on biblical injunction and prophecy. His guiding principle, he wrote in *Man's Nature and His Communities*, was to relate religious responsibility to politics in such a way that 'a realistic conception of human nature should be made the servant of an ethic of progressive justice . . . and not a bastion of . . . a conservatism which defends unjust privileges.'   JBK

Reading

†Davis, H.R. and Good, R.C. eds: *Reinhold Niebuhr on Politics*. New York: Scribner, 1960.

Niebuhr, R.: *Moral Man and Immoral Society*. New York: Scribner, 1932.

————: *Beyond Tragedy*. New York: Scribner, 1937.

————: *Human Nature and Destiny*. New York: Scribner, 1942.

————: *The Children of Light and the Children of Darkness*. New York: Scribner, 1944.

————: *The Irony of American History*. New York: Scribner, 1952.

————: *Man's Nature and His Communities*. New York: Scribner, 1965. [The introduction describes the evolution of his thought as Niebuhr himself understood it.]

Nietzsche, Friedrich Wilhelm (1844–1900) German philosopher. Nietzsche first came to the public eye when he was awarded the chair of classical philology at the University of Basle in 1869. For most of the academic profession, this early promise was not fulfilled when, three years later at the age of twenty-seven, he published his first major work, *The Birth of Tragedy from the Spirit of Music* (1872). This book, dedicated to the then highly controversial composer Richard Wagner, called into question most of the nineteenth-century received wisdom about ancient Greece and the origins and purposes of tragedy. It was subject to a withering critique by Nietzsche's philological rivals. Increasingly in ill health, Nietzsche abandoned the hope he had had for spurring the revival of culture by means of educational institutions and Wagner's music-drama, broke with Wagner and, in 1879, resigned from the university. He spent the next ten years of his life in southern Switzerland and northern Italy. The writings of this period, especially *Thus Spoke Zarathustra* (1883–4), *Beyond Good and Evil* (1886), *On the Genealogy of Morals* (1887), *The Twilight of the Idols* (1889), *The Antichrist* (1895), as well as his autobiography and posthumously published last work, *Ecce Homo* (1908), remain the core of his work. There is in addition a work published from a compilation of Nietzsche's notebooks by his executors and entitled by them *The Will to Power* (1901); this work has recently been shown to be composed mainly of material that Nietzsche discarded and must be treated with caution.

In 1889 Nietzsche became insane; he spent the last eleven years of his life in the care of his mother and sister. A few years before this his work had started to attract the attention of important intellectual figures in Europe; by the time of his death he was recognized as one of the most important of European thinkers. Since then his reputation has fallen and risen, in part because of the (fallacious) use the Nazis made of his work; it is fair to say that he has been a seminal thinker for the twentieth century.

It is apparent from the shape of Nietzsche's writings that his intellectual intentions far transcend academic philosophy. Instead of soberly persuasive essays we find poetry, invective, riddles, aphorisms, confession, all interwoven with passages that appear to be conventional arguments. The intention behind this apparently dismaying mixture of genres rests with Nietzsche's conviction that his teaching must penetrate the listener at a level so much deeper than that of assessment that it changes the nature of assessment itself. Instead of merely interpreting the world, Nietzsche sets out to change it. Ultimately, therefore, he cannot persuade us in terms that reflect only the sources and structure of the world as we now encounter it. Rather he tries to make his work strike us in such a way that our mode of being-in-the-world is transformed. It is only a slight exaggeration to say that all who read Nietzsche find themselves reflected in some fashion in Nietzsche's text.

The difficulties and dangers of such an approach are with Nietzsche from his earliest work. In *The Birth of Tragedy* he focused on the role of tragedy in creating and maintaining the culture of the *polis*. He is interested not only in the individual but also in the collectivity – or, more accurately, in the structure that makes possible the special culture of a particular collectivity. For Nietzsche the Greeks had solved what we would call the problem of AUTHORITY. They had found a way of determining what it meant to be Greek that did not rest on anything other than their own actions. Nietzsche argued that tragedy had played a central role in the maintenance and productive renewal of this self-certainty. When he turned his attention to the modern world he found the same problem. On what can a culture rest without authority?

For Nietzsche the modern world faces a crisis. It has been brewing for a long time, having its origins ultimately in Socratic aporia and Christianity. The most immediate manifestation of this crisis is what he calls 'the death of God', the general phenomenon he calls 'nihilism'. By these terms he means the state in which humans continue to look for a principle

of authority, while making it and its coming to consciousness impossible to attain. This state of affairs will dominate, he thought, the next two hundred years.

Part of Nietzsche's enterprise is addressed to those unexamined self-protective presuppositions that humans employ to keep themselves from confronting the reality of their condition. In this aspect of his work Nietzsche continues the critique of ideology that has its origins in KANT and had begun to preoccupy social science in the nineteenth century. The 'idols' of whom Nietzsche predicted the 'twilight' are close cousins to the 'fetishes' that MARX saw lurking under the appearance of commodities and to the 'totems' by which FREUD thought humans protected themselves against direct confrontation with the bases of civilization.

Nietzsche, however, is more relentless in his critique than are Kant, Marx, or Freud. He argues in *On the Genealogy of Morals* that both the practices and the understandings of the world are to be understood 'genealogically', as a common family that has its origin in specific acts that reflect relations of power and selfhood. Here his argument is a conscious parody and critique of HEGEL. Hegel had, famously, given the names of 'lord' and 'bondsman' to the poles of the relationship in which the oppressed discover in the conditions of their oppression the very source of their own liberation. Nietzsche, likewise, designates as 'master' and 'slave' moralities the two broadest forms that morality has assumed and argues, like Hegel, that it is in the logic of slave morality to undermine the epistemological foundations of master morality. The triumph of slave morality is for Nietzsche not a step towards new and higher forms of consciousness. It is rather the progressive domination by a form of selfhood that requires the existence of oppression to maintain a sense of self. Oppression does not lead, as it had with Hegel, to liberation, but merely to more and more sophisticated and internalized forms of self-oppression. Nietzsche traces these through the last two books of the *Genealogy*. To the degree then that slave morality has completely triumphed as a way of being-in-the-world – and Nietzsche thinks its sway great and increasing – human life becomes one-dimensional, an empty repetition of the same. If everything is shaped by slave morality, then all that human beings do will repeat back to themselves the conditions of their own imprisonment. Nietzsche does not think, as did Marx and the liberals, that our present condition contains the conditions of its own self-transcendence.

Nietzsche calls 'will-to-power' the inevitable characteristic of all actions to reproduce the presuppositions and conditions that make them possible. 'Will to power' is thus characteristic of all actions, including the most 'slavely moral'. Contrary to many commentators, Nietzsche does not think of the will to power as a positive value, but rather as the core of any human action. (The German for power is *Macht*, which derives from *machen*, to make; the English fails to catch this resonance.)

There are many scattered comments about politics throughout Nietzsche's work. In relation to modern times they are almost all negative; most commentators, however, fail to notice that they are negative about *modern* politics. The 'time comes', he writes in a note of 1886, 'when one will have to transform one's views on politics.' Nietzsche is particularly distressed by the development of the modern state and European nationalism, 'this perpetuation of European political particularism, of small politics [that has] deprived Europe of its meaning, of its reasons, . . . [and] has driven it into a dead-end street' (*Ecce Homo*, 'The Case of Wagner', §2). He is opposed to nationalism because he sees it as a rear-guard resistance to the disintegration of the modern state. He anticipates 'war such as no one has ever seen'. These wars, for 'mastery of the earth', will be characteristic of the coming century. Nietzsche's point is that in the twentieth century wars will be fought not for gain as measured in terms of the categories that people already have, but rather in order to define what counts as having something. In the coming century, he writes, 'the concept of politics will have been entirely merged with a war of and for minds' (*Ecce Homo*, 'Why I am a destiny', §1). In Nietzsche's understanding, politics and epistemology have merged in the twentieth century: politics is no longer a question of who gets what, where and when,

but of the terms in which the world is to be understood.

At the end of his life, in *Ecce Homo*, Nietzsche criticizes his early work for being unpolitical. Standing on the brink of insanity, he has no time and perhaps no means to develop a substantive political theory. He has argued that modern conditions are breaking down the old orders of rank and privilege that have kept Europe decadent; yet he knows that at the same time the present power structures continue to maintain the old orders. It is in desperation and mania, then, that he announces in several very late letters that he is having all the representatives of the older orders shot. He is going to make it possible for there to be once again those who have 'the right to command'. Nietzsche did not describe the substance of this new principle of authority. It is revealing of the politics that he predicted for the twentieth century that his most explicit practical political pronouncements and his madness came at the same time.

TBS

Reading
†Allison, D. ed.: *The New Nietzsche: Contemporary Styles of Interpretation*. New York: Dell, 1977.

Heidegger, M.: *Nietzsche*, trans. and ed. D.F. Krell. San Francisco: Harper & Row, 1979.

Nehamas, A.: *Nietzsche: Life as Literature*. Cambridge, Mass.: Harvard University Press, 1985.

Nietzsche, F.W.: *Nietzsche Werke: Kritische Gesamtausgabe*, ed. G. Colli and M. Montinari. Berlin and New York: de Gruyter, 1967–. (English edn in preparation.)

——: *Basic Writings of Nietzsche*, trans. and ed. W. Kaufmann. New York: Random House, 1968. [Includes *The Birth of Tragedy from the Spirit of Music*; *Beyond Good and Evil*; *On the Genealogy of Morals*; and *Ecce Homo*; also available in separate edns.]

——: *The Portable Nietzsche*, selected, trans. and ed. W. Kaufmann. New York: Viking, 1954. [Includes *Thus Spoke Zarathustra*; *Twilight of the Idols*; and *The Antichrist*.]

——: *On the Advantage and Disadvantages of History for Life*, trans. and intro. P. Preuss. Indianapolis: Hackett, 1980.

†Strong, T.B.: *Friedrich Nietzsche and the Politics of Transfiguration*. Berkeley and Los Angeles: University of California Press, 1975.

Williams, W.D.: *Nietzsche and the French: a study of the influence of Nietzsche's French reading on his thought and writing*. Oxford: Blackwell, 1952.

O

Oakeshott, Michael Joseph (1901–) British political philosopher. Oakeshott graduated from Cambridge University in 1923, and two years later became a fellow of Gonville and Caius College. In 1951 he was appointed to the university chair of political science at the London School of Economics, from which he retired in 1968.

In his first major philosophical work, *Experience and its Modes* (1933), Oakeshott set out to elucidate the constitutive characteristics of different forms of understanding human experience. For him experience is a single whole of which the mind and the external world, the subject and the object, are one-sided abstractions. All attempts to understand it fall into one of two categories. They understand it either from specific standpoints, or 'as a whole' and 'for its own sake'.

By its very nature every standpoint is based on certain assumptions or presuppositions, which it does not and cannot question. It abstracts relevant aspects of the totality of experience and offers a homogeneous, sovereign and self-contained account of them. Oakeshott distinguishes three such standpoints or 'modes', namely practice, science and history, to which he later added poetry. The practical mode views experience *sub specie voluntatis* (under the aspect of will). It presupposes separate, unique and self-contained individuals wanting to satisfy their diverse desires, and understands the totality of experience in terms of such concepts as the self, the other, change, desire, good, bad, ought, pleasure and pain. History views the totality of experience *sub specie praeteritorum* (under the aspect of the past) and science *sub specie*

quantitatis (under the aspect of quantity).

Unlike the modes, philosophy is concerned to offer unconditional and unabstracted experience. As such it avoids all partial standpoints and assumptions. For Oakeshott philosophy is unique among all intellectual inquiries in being radical, self-conscious and rigorously self-critical. A constant and relentless critique of assumptions, its own and those of the modes, is its most distinctive characteristic.

In *Experience and its Modes* Oakeshott said little about the nature of politics and political philosophy. He began to write about these a few years later, for example, in his Introduction to Hobbes's *Leviathan* (1946), several essays in *Politica* and the *Cambridge Journal*, and his Inaugural Lecture (1951). Some of these essays were later collected in his *Rationalism in Politics and other essays* (1962). During this period Oakeshott advanced several different views on the nature and task of political philosophy, such as the exploration of 'the nature and earthly destiny of man', a critical examination of contemporary civilization, and conceptual analysis. As for POLITICS, he saw it as the activity of attending to the periodically highlighted incoherences in the 'at once coherent and incoherent' pattern of arrangements obtaining in every community. It does not and cannot consist in deciding each day what to do and how as the empiricists maintain, nor in implementing some abstract principles, ideas or doctrines as the rationalists maintain, but in pursuing the intimations of the existing traditions of behaviour. For Oakeshott the empiricists and rationalists wholly misunderstand the nature of time and knowledge, the two central dimensions of political life. For one, time is a series of disjointed moments and for the other it is unreal; for one, knowledge is a bundle of information and for the other it is a body of timeless general truths. Neither appreciates the vital importance of TRADITION in ordering a community's perception of time or historical continuity and providing the practical or concrete knowledge required for conducting its affairs.

Oakeshott's *On Human Conduct* (1975) provides his most systematic statement of political philosophy. His latest book *On History and other essays* (1983) contains only one theoretical essay on politics and does not signify a new departure. *On Human Conduct* is a complex book written in different modes and idioms and using old Latin terms to express modern ideas. Oakeshott argues that political, or what he now prefers to call civil, philosophy is concerned to analyse the ideal character and postulates of human conduct in general and civil association in particular. For him every human association is structured in terms of practices. Practices are either prudential or moral. Prudential practices serve a common substantive purpose or purposes, whereas moral practices are non-instrumental in nature. There are thus two 'categorially distinct modes' of constituting human associations. Prudential or 'enterprise' association is united in terms of a common purpose, and moral association in terms of the acknowledgement of the authority of common practices.

For Oakeshott civil association is not enterprise but moral association constituted in terms of practices consisting entirely of different types of interdependent rules, which he calls *respublica*. As he puts it, 'what relates *cives* to one another and constitutes civil association is the acknowledgement of the authority of *respublica* and the recognition of subscription to its conditions as an obligation' (p. 149). Of all the rules constituting *respublica*, *lex* is unique to civil association and lays down the norms of conduct to which *cives* are required to subscribe. *Lex* is morally binding because it is made by authorized men according to established procedures. In order to ensure that it is adequately subscribed to, civil association requires ruling, consisting of adjudication and administration, and an 'apparatus of rule'.

Although the rules constituting the *respublica* are obligatory because of their authoritative nature they may be examined in terms of their desirability, an activity which Oakeshott calls politics. Politics involves accepting the authority of *respublica* and criticizing its specific rules. Political deliberation is guided by considerations of *bonum civile*, of what is civilly just or desirable and to which all *cives* can be required to subscribe under threat of civil penalty. It rules out such objectives as the pursuit of a perfect society or bettering the lot of mankind, because civil association is not enterprise association, and distributive justice, because civil rulers own nothing and have 'nothing to distribute'. Evidently Oakeshott does not think that an apparently formal distribution of rights and obligations may in fact involve a substantive distribution of powers, opportunities and property.

Although civil association can be only moral and not enterprise association, Oakeshott contends that almost from its very beginning every modern European state has harboured tendencies in both directions. In different states or in different historical epochs one of them gained ascendancy although the other was not wholly absent. In his view the conflict between the two offers a better key to the understanding of the modern state than such conventional ideological labels as right and left or free enterprise and collectivism. He does not adequately explain how such radically contradictory tendencies arose, are able to co-exist and even reach a working compromise.   BCP

Reading

†Greenleaf, W.H.: *Oakeshott's Philosophical Politics*. London: Longman, 1965.

Oakeshott, M.: *Experience and its Modes*. Cambridge: Cambridge University Press, 1933.

———: *Rationalism in Politics and other essays*. London: Methuen, 1962.

———: *On Human Conduct*. Oxford: Clarendon Press, 1975.

†Parekh, B.: *Contemporary Political Thinkers*. Oxford: Martin Robertson, 1982.

Political Theory 4 (1976): a symposium on Oakeshott.

Ockham, William of   See WILLIAM OF OCKHAM.

Ortega y Gasset, José (1883–1955) Spanish philosopher. Best known as a social thinker, especially for his critical account of MASS SOCIETY in *The Revolt of the Masses* (1929).

Owen, Robert (1771–1858) British socialist. Owen did not see himself as a great intellectual figure. He was largely self-educated, and often boasted with pride that he did not read scholarly books. Yet through his early practical experience in managing cotton mills, especially those at New Lanark which he took over in 1800, he became passionately interested in social questions. Convinced that the character of men was shaped by the environment in which they lived and worked, he devoted himself to the promulgation of this theory and to practical experiments designed to reveal the validity of his ideas as a basis for schemes for social improvement. This mission took him from his model village in New Lanark to a communitarian project in America (at New Harmony, Indiana, from 1824 to 1829) and back to England where, in the 1830s, he became involved with the emergent co-operative and trade union movements. From the mid-1830s onwards Owen committed himself to a strong ethical sectarianism, rooted in millennarian expectations of the coming of a 'New Moral World', and the cause of 'SOCIALISM' (a new term at this time) was espoused.

Owen's best known work is *A New View of Society* (1812–13). Although far from being an expression of his socialism, it contains the initial statement of his theory that character is formed by environment. This appeared to be a strikingly novel idea because it questioned the prevailing orthodoxy: that idleness, ignorance, crime, poverty, and other social evils were unavoidable manifestations of the inferior way of life led by the lower orders in society. Owen insisted that these evils were the result of ameliorable social conditions and he attempted to demonstrate this in a series of environmental, industrial, and educational reforms at New Lanark. The consequences of these reforms were presented by Owen as evidence enough of the possibility of changing the character of an entire community by intelligent reorganization.

This materialistic approach was defended by Owen as a 'rational system of society', and one of his chief preoccupations, throughout his life, was to wage war on what he regarded as the major source of irrationality in society: religion. Religion was one of three great barriers to progress; the others were marriage and private property. To be more precise, it was the particular forms that religion and marriage assumed in nineteenth-century society, rooted in unenlightened supernatural belief and outmoded moral values, that Owen rejected. His objection to private property, as the effective basis of inequality and poverty, was absolute.

Despite his unremitting attack on the church and the priesthood Owen always saw religious life as a natural and indispensable expression of man's innermost aspirations and sentiments. In the first issue of *The New Moral World* (November 1834) he described the new society of the future, the alternative to the individualistic order, as 'the Second Coming of Christ', and he confidently announced the beginning of the millennium. Socialism was presented as a comprehensive world-view to be disseminated in the manner of an inspirational gospel. Not surprisingly, the Owenite movement which now arose exerted an appeal of a thoroughly sectarian kind. This was a far cry from the *New View of Society* and the early communitarian experiments, although Owen always insisted that he foresaw a socialist transformation based on small-scale units of mutual co-operation in which principles of democratic self-government operated. The limit he placed on the size of such units in his *Report to the County of Lanark* (1820) was between 300 and 2000 persons, ideally in the range 800–1200, which would require a land area of some 600–1800 acres. In later works the upper limit was increased to a population of 3000 with the ideal size being about 2000. There has been much discussion of whether such small units, which would inevitably be primarily agricultural, could possibly be regarded as a suitable framework for economic development in a country such as Britain, especially as Owen himself seemed to welcome mechanization as an instrument of progress and wealth-creation.

Owen wrote a great deal about the importance of work as an essentially creative human function, and he alerted his contemporaries to the danger that machinery would enslave men rather than liberate them for a fulfilling life. He believed that small-scale co-operation, such as he recommended, would prevent the domination of men by machinery, since it would be based on communal ownership and control of the major means of production, and on the elimination of money as a medium of exchange, to be replaced by free distribution of essentials according to need and the trading of surpluses on the basis of new 'labour notes' (paper currency in units of labour time related to actual work done).

It can be seen that Owen's proposals amounted to a form of COMMUNISM, although in using this term care should be taken to distinguish between Owen and other contemporary thinkers such as Blanqui, Cabet, Weitling and, of course, MARX and ENGELS: thinkers whose communism was revolutionary and directed, ultimately, at seizure of the central state. Owen's small-scale communitarian proposals were much closer to those of FOURIER, although Fourier always reserved a role for private property.

Owen's strategy for bringing about the necessary social change remained gradualistic and pacific – one reason why, in company with Saint-Simon and Fourier, he was attacked by Marx and Engels for being a 'utopian' dreamer. Yet Owen left a legacy of great *practical* importance. His communitarian ventures were alternative societies in miniature and, on a broader canvas, he contributed much to the development of co-operation and trade unionism. (See also UTOPIANISM.)   KT

Reading

†Butt, J. ed.: *Robert Owen – Prince of Cotton Spinners*. Newton Abbot, Devon: David & Charles, 1971.

Owen, R.: *A New View of Society, and other writings*, ed. G.D.H. Cole. London: Dent, 1927.

———: *The Book of the 'New Moral World'* (1836–44). New York: Kelley, 1970.

———: *The Revolution in the Mind and Practice of the Human Race* (1849). New York: Kelley, 1973.

†Pollard, S. and Salt, J. eds: *Robert Owen – Prophet of the Poor*. London: Macmillan, 1971.

†Taylor, K.: *The Political Ideas of the Utopian Socialists*. London: Cass, 1982.

P

pacifism The belief that all wars are wrong, however good the cause that is being fought for or whatever the threat to one's own country. This belief has often been based on religious conviction but it also has humanist and political roots. Pacifism is closely linked to resistance to war, but not identical with it, since some movements have opposed wars for non-pacifist reasons and by non-pacifist means.

Pacifism in the West springs from early Christianity, which interpreted literally the New Testament teaching to 'resist not evil' and to turn the other cheek. Christians refused to serve in the imperial Roman armies. Gradually the Christian church evolved a theory of JUST WAR, which tried to limit warfare by specifying just causes and just methods of war, but enabled Christians to fight when their governments required them to do so. Nevertheless a utopian strain within the Christian faith has kept reappearing and reasserting a pure pacifism. Sects which uphold a pacifist witness include the Quakers, the Mennonites, the Dukhobors and Jehovah's Witnesses. Some Christians have therefore viewed pacifism as primarily a religious rather than a political commitment, although the Quakers have always been active in politics as well.

By the Renaissance, political writers were putting forward secular arguments against war. Erasmus, the Dutch philosopher of the sixteenth century, attacked the cult of chivalry and the glorification of war to expose the barbarity of warfare. Over the next two centuries a number of political theorists concerned themselves with the problem of how to secure international peace, and after the end of the Napoleonic wars in 1814 popular peace movements grew up in Europe and the United States. These movements drew primarily on a liberal belief that economic progress and cooperation and the spread of reason through education should make the brutality and destructiveness of war obsolete.

The majority of pacifists have been liberal democrats, and pacifism is usually dismissed by Marxists as 'bourgeois'. But the socialist international congresses at the beginning of this century advocated working-class resistance to capitalist and imperialist wars, and a minority of socialists were also pacifists who opposed all wars. Resistance to war, including strikes, desertion and mutiny, is part of the anarchist tradition, and linked to anarchist opposition to the state (see ANARCHISM). Most anarchists have accepted the need for violent methods of political resistance against the state, but some anarchists have also been pure pacifists. The best known example is Leo TOLSTOY, whose writings influenced GANDHI's experiments in non-violent resistance.

During the first world war the introduction of conscription in Britain and the United States led to widespread conscientious objection by individuals who refused to fight. Since then pacifism has been defined more strictly to mean a personal commitment never to serve in the armed forces. In this sense it has been most common in countries with a Protestant and a liberal tradition, which encourages individuals to take a conscientious stand and also tends to make governments more tolerant of religious conscientious objection to war.

Many pacifists have become increasingly committed to the use of non-cooperation or non-violent resistance to oppose racialism or other forms of injustice, and to oppose wars and war preparations. Gandhi's methods of non-violent struggle against the British in India influenced contemporary pacifist thought. Pacifists looking for an alternative to war have also elaborated possibilities of organized non-violent resistance as the basis of a defence policy. Interest in these ideas has greatly increased since the development of nuclear weapons.

There are differences of emphasis within pacifism, for example between those who stress the need for international negotiations and conciliation between nations and those who stress popular non-violent resistance to militarism. A distinction is also sometimes made between pure pacifists, committed to personal refusal to take part in war and opposed to all uses of armed force, and pacificists, who support political measures to prevent war, but who may also support the use of force by international bodies such as the League of Nations or the United Nations. Many members of peace movements have been pacificists and not pure pacifists.

Pacifism has still wider connotations. Many pacifists refuse to use any violence at a personal level, either as a form of punishment or in self-defence. Some also try to extend the principle of non-violence to the organization of society, arguing that this entails the end of all forms of coercion or exploitation. Pacifism usually includes the belief that the ends are determined by the means, so violent means always have violent consequences. AFC

Reading

Bondurant, J.: *Conquest of Violence: the Gandhian Philosophy of Conflict.* Princeton, NJ: Princeton University Press, 1958.

†Brock, P.: *Twentieth Century Pacifism.* New York: Van Nostrand Reinold, 1970.

Howard, M.: *War and the Liberal Conscience.* London: Temple Smith, 1978.

Huxley, A.: *Ends and Means: an Enquiry into the Nature of Ideals and into the Methods Employed for their Realization.* London: Chatto & Windus, 1937.

†Mayer, P. ed.: *The Pacifist Conscience.* Harmondsworth: Penguin, 1966.

Sharp, G.: *The Politics of Nonviolent Action.* Boston: Porter Sargent, 1973.

Tolstoy, L.: *Letter to a Hindu* (1908). In Mayer ed.

Paine, Thomas (1737–1809) British-born radical pamphleteer and international revolutionary. Born into a Norfolk Quaker family, Paine, was, in his own words, given 'an exceedingly good moral education, and a tolerable stock of learning'. He worked in a number of trades – sailor, staymaker, exciseman and shopkeeper – and developed a number of skills as a lay preacher and debater. His first pamphlet, written at the age of thirty-five, presented the case for an increase in wages for the excisemen. The several months he spent petitioning on their behalf in London cost him his marriage, his job and his shop. He emigrated to America in 1775, found employment on a Pennsylvania journal, and in 1776 published *Common Sense.* The pamphlet pleaded the case for American independence at a time when few Americans were prepared openly to adopt this policy. It was extremely successful, going through twenty-five editions in its year of publication alone. Paine was subsequently involved in drawing up a liberal state constitution for Pennsylvania (which incorporated universal suffrage, annual elections, democratic representation, a unicameral legislature, and full religious freedom) and in working for Washington's Revolutionary Army.

In 1787 Paine visited Europe and was quickly caught up in political activity in both France and England. He sprang to his radical friends' defence in 1791 when they were attacked in BURKE's *Reflections on the Revolution in France* (see RADICALS, BRITISH). Paine's *Rights of Man* (1791 and 1792) attacked hereditary and monarchical systems, insisted on popular sovereignty and individual rights, and delivered a withering critique of Burke's arguments. Unsurprisingly, the British government prosecuted and outlawed Paine for seditious libel, while the French elected him to the National Assembly. Despite his fervent republicanism, Paine spoke out against the Jacobins' demands for the king's execution and was later imprisoned and narrowly escaped execution under the Terror. During his stay in France he published his deist treatise, *The Age of Reason* (1794) (which, by attacking established religion, ensured him public notoriety and condemnation until well into the present century), and his most radical political pamphlet, *Agrarian*

Justice (1796). Paine finally returned to America in 1802, only to be vilified by the Federalist press. He died, a rather neglected and isolated figure, in 1809.

Paine was not an especially profound or original political thinker, and he interpreted the work of those he claimed as influences rather liberally. From LOCKE he drew material to support his defence of natural rights and his belief that men join society to secure their rights, not to give them up. Thus government can have no right to violate our natural rights; its sole duty is to ensure that we are fully able to preserve our life, liberty, and possessions. People contract with each other to form society, and they entrust government with certain powers in order to preserve social order; but the people must always retain sovereignty – they can withdraw their trust and set up another system of government whenever they collectively decide to do so. Paine also believed that he was faithful to Adam SMITH when he argued that people's wants, rather than producing conflicts of interests, naturally bring them into society and make them dependent on each other. Commerce, and the 'hidden hand' which serves to reconcile interests, bear witness to the fact that society is natural to man. This is also confirmed by the social affections which nature has implanted in man to ensure that he can only find his happiness in society. Indeed, Paine argues, so natural is society to mankind, that government is hardly necessary at all.

Starting from these assumptions Paine produced a series of savage attacks on the monarchical and aristocratic systems of eighteenth-century Europe. Hereditary government is government by fraud – it relies on people's ignorance and on superstition: 'the idea of hereditary legislators . . . is as absurd as an hereditary mathematician, or an hereditary wise man; and as absurd as an hereditary poet laureate' (*Rights of Man*, p. 105). The principle is irrational and the practice of such governments is riddled with war, corruption, and expense. The only system of government free from such abuses is a representative democracy founded on a constitution which has been drawn up by a convention of the whole people and approved by them. Paine's model of government was rooted in his American

experience, and his later writings are essentially appeals to the people of France and England to abolish their corrupt hereditary systems and replace them with republican government of the American form, which will secure their rights and produce cheap, responsible, and peaceable government. Such a government, because it must explain its actions to its people, will tend to see the best and wisest men elected to it.

Paine's most original writing is to be found in the second part of the *Rights of Man* and in *Agrarian Justice*. In both he advances beyond the libertarian idea of a minimal state and offers a justification and a blueprint for a welfare state. In the former he offers Britain a national system of poor relief, state finance for education for the poor, old age pensions, death and maternity grants, and sheltered workshops for the indigent, all to be financed from the savings in expense arising from replacing monarchical government by a republican constitution. He also argues for the replacement of taxes on consumption by a progressive tax on property. This would remove burdens from the poor that condemn them to hardship, and it would also encourage the rich to spread their wealth more equally among their children, thereby ending the unnatural system of primogeniture.

In *Agrarian Justice* Paine provides a more principled defence of redistributive taxation and a welfare state. He argues that each person is born with a natural right to use the earth and its produce, and that while people have a right to the value they create through their efforts, this does not extend to the land they work on which remains common property. Furthermore, most personal property is acquired through society rather than through labour with our hands. We thus owe both a form of ground-rent, and a part of our accumulation, to society 'from whence the whole came'. Paine proposes a property tax, to be levied in the form of death duties, which can be used to pay a lump sum to every person at the age of twenty-one, and an annual payment to all those over fifty years old and to those who are blind or lame. By this method, no individual would be denied the start in life, or the comfort in distress, which he is owed by right of nature.

Paine's claim on posterity lies less in his originality or depth as a political philosopher than in his great abilities as a communicator of political ideas. He spoke to the common man, and to men of commerce, who sought to improve their situation through their own labour and talents, and who resented the rule of hereditary wealth and power. His democratic principles, and his assertion that each individual has the right to judge how best to secure his natural rights, communicated themselves to his audiences with great effect. This does not mean that Paine necessarily convinced his audience of the virtues of the republican system, but he did convince many who had previously played little part in politics that they had the right to discuss political principles and agitate for political reforms. MP

Reading

†Fennessy, R.R.: *Burke, Paine and the Rights of Man.* The Hague: Martinus Nijhoff, 1963.

Foner, E.: *Tom Paine and Revolutionary America.* New York: Oxford University Press, 1976.

Paine, T.: *The Life and Major Writings of Thomas Paine,* ed. P.S. Foner. 2 vols. Secaucus, NJ: Citadel, 1948.

———: *Rights of Man,* ed. H. Collins. Harmondsworth: Penguin, 1969.

———: *Common Sense,* ed. I. Kramnick. Harmondsworth: Penguin, 1976.

†Williamson, A.: *Thomas Paine: His Life, Work and Time.* London: Allen & Unwin, 1973.

Pareto, Vilfredo (1848–1923) Italian economist and political sociologist. Pareto was originally trained as an engineer, but worked in business from 1870. In 1889 he began writing on economics, and held a professorship in this subject at Lausanne from 1893 to 1907. His major contributions were to equilibrium theory and the theory of social choice. His chief sociological work is *Trattato di Sociologica generale* (1916), translated as *The Mind and Society.* Pareto was a critic of democracy and socialism, and with MOSCA the originator of ELITISM.

Pareto's theory of elites is his chief contribution to political science but it forms part of a wider treatise on society. He divided human activity into logical conduct, in which means and ends are objectively related, and non-logical conduct, where they do not correspond. Logical conduct guides science, including economics. Most social actions are, however, non-logical, prompted by a non-rational state of mind. Psychological forces are therefore the bases of human conduct but Pareto does not study psychology directly. Though sentiments and impulses are the real sources of action, human beings tend to believe that action results from rational deliberation based on theory which is, however, mere rationalization. Theory consists of two elements. One varies over time and place, is made up of justifications and explanations and is termed a 'derivation'. It is 'derived' from the constant element in theory which corresponds to deep-rooted psychological drives and is termed a 'residue'. Human conduct is therefore to be explained by the underlying residues and not by the overt derivations, such as political philosophies, metaphysics or theology.

Pareto identified two main classes of residue. Class I is the 'instinct of combinations', an inventive, imaginative capacity. Class II is the 'persistence of aggregates', a stolid, conservative tendency. Each class corresponds to a broad set of attitudes and behaviour on the part of all social actors, including elites.

Pareto held that all societies are divided into leaders (the elite) and the led. The elite comprises a governing and a non-governing element. The governing elite maintains its power through a combination of coercion and (manipulated) consent. Government requires contrasting qualities. It needs flexibility, cunning and the powers of persuasion. It also requires readiness to use violence to suppress opposition. These qualities correspond to the two opposed psychological types – Class I or 'foxes' and Class II or 'lions' – and are rarely combined in any elite. Political change occurs through the displacement of one elite by another ('circulation of elites'). This results from the psychological unfitness of the elite to deal with events. The 'foxes', excellent at generating consent through political manoeuvres, are incapable of wielding violence when needed. They will be overthrown by a counter-elite with Class II attributes who are ready to act decisively. The 'lions' typically employ coercion in organized fashion but tend to become excessively conservative, stultified and remote from the population and to require the assistance from those with Class I attributes who gradually infiltrate and transform the elite. History shows a constant pattern of circulation between these two types of elite.   GP

Reading

†Bobbio, N.: *On Mosca and Pareto*. Geneva: Droz, 1972.

†Parry, G.: *Political Elites*. London: Allen & Unwin, 1969.

†Parsons, T.: *The Structure of Social Action*. Glencoe, Ill.: Free Press of Glencoe, 1949.

Pareto, V.: *The Mind and Society*, trans. A. Livingston and A. Bongioro. 4 vols. New York: Harcourt Brace, 1935.

———: *Sociological Writings*, ed. S.E. Finer. Oxford: Blackwell, 1976.

Pascal, Blaise (1623–1662) French mathematician, physicist and religious philosopher. Pascal achieved eminence for his scientific and mathematical work before abandoning such pursuits to enter the Jansenist monastery of Port-Royal at the age of thirty-one. Among his various writings, his most significant work for philosophy and political theory is his post-humously published *Pensées* (Thoughts) (1670), an uncompleted but rhetorically powerful series of aphoristic reflections on the theme of 'the evidences of religion'.

Pascal endeavoured to defend the Christian faith at a time when it was under attack as a consequence of the revival of philosophic atheism and of the popularization of modern science, which seemed to reveal an infinite, godless universe governed by purely mechanical causation. His mode of defence was to take seriously this picture of the universe, and to demonstrate the consequent meaninglessness of man's life if he is bereft of faith. Pascal rejects teleological proofs of the existence of God, just as he uses the conception of an infinite universe to undermine the philosophers' hopes of discovering the meaning of existence, or the sovereign human good, through reason. Instead, it is God's very absence from the visible universe that compels man, terrorized by the meaninglessness of his existence, to seek Him.

Pascal follows MONTAIGNE in disparaging human justice, which is founded merely on custom or prejudice. Governments and laws should be obeyed not because they are just, but only because they are necessary to prevent the ultimate earthly evil of civil war. Governments are incapable of engendering human virtue or excellence; they exist merely to mediate the conflict among men, who naturally hate their fellows. Our radical separateness as individuals, constituted most manifestly by the fact of our mortality, prevents there being a true community among men.

Like Montaigne, Pascal mocks the seriousness with which men pursue such goals as glory, knowledge and power; such pursuits are merely attempts to 'divert' ourselves from the transitory and meaningless character of our existence. But unlike Montaigne, he denies that man can rest content with a comical view of life, which sees no ultimately higher purpose in it than diversion or pleasure. Being aware of the meaninglessness of mere earthly life compels men to 'wager' that God exists, despite the impossibility of proving that belief, and therefore to live as Christians, in the hope of achieving salvation.

Pascal was perhaps the first thinker fully to confront the problematic consequences of the modern scientific world-view for the meaning of human life. His sense of the absurd disproportion between the infinite demands that man's soul makes on the universe, and the incapacity of the infinite and purposeless universe discovered by reason to satisfy those demands, recurs in the nihilist and existentialist movements of the nineteenth and twentieth centuries – this time without Pascal's hope that that disproportion could be overcome through faith (see EXISTENTIALISM).   DLS

Reading

†Löwith, K.: Man between infinities. In *Nature, History, and Existentialism*. Evanston, Ill.: Northwestern University Press, 1966.

†Mesnard, J.: *Pascal: His Life and Works*. New York: Philosophical Library, 1952.

Pascal, B.: *Pensées*, ed. L. Brunschvicg, trans. W.F. Trotter. In *Pensées/Provincial Letters*. New York: Modern Library, 1941.

———: Pascal's conversation with Monsieur de Saci on Epictetus and Montaigne. In *Great Shorter Works of Pascal*, trans. E. Cailliet and J.C. Blankenagel. Westport, Conn.: Greenwood, 1974.

paternalism In modern use the term usually refers to those laws and public policies which restrict the freedom of persons in order that their interests may be better served. Examples of paternalism in this sense would include consumer safety laws to prevent persons buying cheap, but unsafe, products, or prohibitionist policies to limit the consumption of harmful substances such as addictive drugs, alcohol, and tobacco. There are two main questions which arise in the theoretical discussion of paternalism: first, how do we identify laws and policies that are genuinely paternalist? and second, what might be the justification of paternalism in the modern state?

The problem of identification arises because it may be difficult to determine whether a policy or piece of legislation is predominantly or only incidentally paternalist. For example, compulsory pensions provision may involve making people save more than they otherwise would, and in that sense might be regarded as paternalist; but also it may involve a redistribution of income from rich to poor, and in that sense may be regarded as egalitarian. To this definition of paternalism should be added the condition that the law or policy must be intended to benefit the interests solely of those whose freedom it restricts. This definition raises its own problems, since there are well-known difficulties associated with the notion of legislative intent. But it seems preferable to face those difficulties, rather than risk extending the scope of paternalism to cover all those laws and policies which might have the unintended, and even unforeseen, effect of promoting people's interest against their own choices.

The justification of paternalism seems particularly difficult in the modern liberal democratic state. Paternalism runs against the main currents of liberal thinking, for typically liberals insist that each person is the best judge of his or her own welfare. (Note, incidentally, that the principle stipulates the best, not perfect, judge.) This principle was upheld by J. S. MILL, in *On Liberty* (1859), with his declaration that the sole aim of legislation and state coercion should be to prevent harm to others; and modern welfare economics, which continues the traditions of classical LIBERALISM, usually identifies a person's welfare with his or her expressed preferences. Nonetheless, despite these strong currents of thought, many writers of a liberal persuasion, for example H. L. A. Hart (1963), have felt bound to admit that paternalism may well be justified for certain purposes and on certain occasions. Their argument is simply that it is a gratuitous assumption to assert that persons are always the best judges of their own welfare, and that there might well be opportunities for promoting someone's long-term welfare by restricting freedom now.

Because the appeal to paternalism is controversial, liberal writers who accept the necessity for some paternalism have sought to devise criteria to justify its use which do not rely upon strong statements of value or the notion that there is one ideal of life that individuals ought to follow. The most popular criterion in this respect requires that the person whose freedom is restricted comes to see and accept the validity of the restrictions. However, the trouble with this criterion is that it makes justifiable paternalism difficult to distinguish from successful brain-washing. Hence there seems no alternative, if one is a liberal and also convinced of the necessity of paternalism, but to fall back on a value pluralism which accepts that there are two distinct values, choice and interests, and that these values may conflict with one another under the law and as a result of public policies. In these circumstances, the best that the liberal can hope for is that the acceptance of paternalism is surrounded by institutional safeguards to prevent personal freedom being restricted too greatly.   APW

Reading

Ackerman, B.: *Social Justice in the Liberal State*. New Haven, Conn. and London: Yale University Press, 1980.

Gert, B. and Culver, C.M.: Paternalistic behaviour. *Philosophy and Public Affairs* 6 (1976) 45–57.

Hart, H.L.A.: *Law, Liberty and Morality*. London: Oxford University Press, 1963.

Mill, J.S.: *On Liberty*. In *Essays on Politics and Society, Collected Works*, vol. XVIII, ed. J.M. Robson. Toronto: University of Toronto Press, 1977.

†Sartorius, R. ed.: *Paternalism*. Minneapolis: University of Minnesota Press, 1983.

†Weale, A.: Paternalism and social policy. *Journal of Social Policy* 7 (1978) 157–72.

patriarchalism   Historically, the theory or

doctrine that political authority is a consequence or derivative of (or is discernible in terms of) the governance of the household. Centring upon the powers and entitlements of the father/husband, which were taken to be strong, and emphasizing the 'natural' existence of authority, patriarchalism has traditionally been absolutist. It is associated primarily with the English royalist of the mid-seventeenth century, Sir Robert FILMER, and his book, *Patriarcha* (not published until 1680 and attacked by LOCKE in the *Two Treatises*).

Aspects of patriarchal doctrines can be found throughout the history of western political thought, especially in the form of quasi-anthropological accounts of the development of political organization from the primary and natural association of the family. From the Reformation, Protestants used the Decalogue injunction to 'Honour thy father and thy mother' (Exod. 20:12) to explicate and defend the duties to obey all superiors, including masters, teachers, ministers, and magistrates. That doctrine was regularly incorporated into catechistical instruction, and helped to convey an image of the world in which household, economy, and polity were all in harmony. The widespread use of the familial or patriarchal conception of the origins of civil society to counter STATE OF NATURE and SOCIAL CONTRACT theories and to defend divine right ABSOLUTISM in Stuart England marks the emergence of patriarchalism as a comprehensive theory of political obligation; it was that theory that was finally undone by the attacks of Locke and others, although the anthropological doctrine and the traditional structure of the household were immune to those criticisms.

'Patriarchalism' is used by contemporary social critics to refer to the male-dominated household and to the unjust and repressive practices and institutions in the society at large that spring from it. It is argued that these practices cannot be eliminated until the household itself is altered.   GJS

Reading

Filmer, R.: *Patriarcha and other political works*, ed. and intro. P. Laslett. Oxford: Blackwell, 1949.

Schochet, G.J.: *Patriarchalism in Political Thought*. Oxford: Blackwell, 1975.

————: Patriarchalism, politics, and mass attitudes in Stuart England. *Historical Journal* 13 (1969) 413–41.

patriotism A love of one's homeland, implying a readiness to act in its defence and to favour it in other dealings. It is often confused with NATIONALISM, but is a far older idea, and carries with it less theoretical baggage. Nationalism presupposes that nations exist as real and distinct entities; patriotism, on the other hand, may simply involve attachment to a physical locality or a way of life, and need not involve any abstract idea of 'country'.

Patriotism is really a sentiment rather than a political idea, but one that can be pressed into service by creeds of many different sorts, most notably in time of war. It might be thought to affiliate most naturally with CONSERVATISM, but it is noticeable in this century that socialist regimes have made extensive appeals to patriotic loyalties, for instance in the course of the Soviet Union's so-called Great Patriotic War (the second world war). In particular contexts, patriotism may serve as a party label, as happened in eighteenth-century England where 'patriot' came to refer to a Country ideologue, but such associations are never more than short-lived.   DLM

philosophic radicalism A doctrine of British origin, associated with the disciples of Jeremy BENTHAM and James MILL, most notably John Stuart MILL. It combined Bentham's UTILITARIANISM; CLASSICAL POLITICAL ECONOMY as developed by Adam Smith, Malthus and Ricardo; a jurisprudence, propounded by Bentham and John AUSTIN, that tried to rationalize the law; and a rationale for DEMOCRACY that was formulated by Bentham and James Mill. Although the doctrine originated in philosophical and economic theories, philosophic radicalism was concerned with practice; it provided a justification for radical changes in the established regime that had survived into the early nineteenth century and was associated with reform movements that were opposed to the landed aristocracy, economic monopolies, and the established church. Its main thrust was to accelerate the movement to transform the traditional aristocratic regime into a modern, secular, democratic, market, liberal society.

Utilitarianism was the most important component of philosophic radicalism, for it was the philosophic foundation for all the rest. It was axiomatic for utilitarians that all individuals sought to maximize their own happiness and that the purpose of government was to promote the greatest happiness of the greatest number. Utilitarianism relied on an individualism and premises about psychology that can be traced back to HOBBES; it was opposed to tradition and to theories of natural law, and in addition it was implicitly critical of religion. Utilitarianism in its practical consequences served to undermine the legitimacy of the established regime, but it also provided the basic principles with which alternatives were designed and justified.

Philosophic radicalism also included Bentham's jurisprudence, which was severely critical of common law for being traditional, self-contradictory, arbitrary, and difficult to understand (see LAW). BLACKSTONE, in particular, was attacked as the most prominent defender of common law and the legal profession on which the public was dependent for access to the law and the courts. Bentham's utilitarian jurisprudence included opposition to all use of the language of nature, including natural law and natural rights, for being intolerably ambiguous and for providing an unwarranted justification for arbitrary decisions. As an alternative Bentham created a jurisprudence which boasted of rationality and clarity, qualities which were to be achieved through codification.

The third major component of philosophic radicalism was political economy which, with its individualism and its emphasis on maximizing satisfactions, had affinities with utilitarianism. The principles of political economy were incompatible with monopoly and protectionism and were implicitly critical of the economic foundations of aristocratic power; this gave it affinities with other parts of philosophic radicalism. The philosophic radicals consistently supported agitation against protectionist corn laws.

The fourth and perhaps most visible component of philosophic radicalism was its rationale for democracy, which can be found in Bentham's *Plan of Parliamentary Reform* (1817) and James Mill's *Essay on Government* (1820), which was said by his son to have been a textbook for the philosophic radicals. The goal of politics was to establish an identity of interests between rulers and ruled. The obstacle to this was the existence of sinister interests, that is, interests separate from those of all other persons or the community. It became necessary to prevent those with sinister interests from using positions of power to gain benefits by corrupt means. An aristocratic regime provided the best example of predatory rulers using the powers of government to gain sinecures and places in the state bureaucracy, church, and army – clearly interests not shared with the remainder of the populace. The remedy was to frustrate those with sinister interests by establishing a representative system based on the universal or general interest of the entire people. This was to be achieved by placing democratic checks on rulers and allowing the universal interest of the entire populace to prevail. To achieve this, organic reform, i.e. fundamental constitutional change, was necessary and such reform was to include a greatly extended, preferably universal, suffrage, frequent elections, and secret ballot – in short, democracy.

Belief in only some of these doctrines did not make a philosophic radical. There were many who supported one or some of these constituent parts of philosophic radicalism while rejecting others, and they cannot be regarded as belonging to the movement. Most political economists, for example McCulloch and Nassau Senior, were neither utilitarians nor radical democrats and so they were not philosophic radicals. There were utilitarians who rejected democracy, and therefore placed themselves outside the boundaries of philosophic radicalism, for example William Paley, and John Austin at the time he wrote *The Province of Jurisprudence Determined* (1832). There were law reformers, including critics of common law, who were neither democrats nor utilitarians and therefore not philosophic radicals, for example Mackintosh and Brougham. There were also radical democrats who rejected utilitarianism and the teachings of political economy and were anything but philosophic radicals, for example Hetherington and the Chartists. Among notable intellectual figures

Bentham, James Mill, and John Stuart Mill were unusual for their commitment to all the constituent parts of philosophic radical doctrine.

Although Bentham and James Mill were the intellectual architects of philosophic radicalism it should be noted that they did not use the term itself, which was an invention of historians eager to attribute to a particular group of intellectual figures the ideas that fostered the growth of liberalism in politics and economic policy (see below). The term philosophic radicals, however, was the label adopted by John Stuart Mill and his like-minded associates for whom it had a specific meaning which did not encompass the several doctrines later attributed to philosophic radicalism. It referred to a small group of radical journalists and politicians who, while they accepted utilitarianism, Benthamite jurisprudence, the principles of political economy, Malthusianism, and the rationale for democracy, were distinguished by their commitment to the belief that a parliamentary party ought to be and could be formed with the primary goal of seeking constitutional reform along democratic lines. (In addition to John Stuart Mill, the most prominent persons in this enterprise were: George Grote, banker, MP, and later famous for his *History of Greece*; Harriet Grote, who conducted the philosophic radical salon; Sir William Molesworth, MP, financial supporter and contributor to philosophic radical journals, and later the organizer and editor of *The Works of Thomas Hobbes*; Francis Place, organizer and pamphleteer; and John Roebuck, MP, colonial reformer, and later prominent critic of Crimean policy.)

As philosophic radicals Mill and his associates developed a rationale and a strategy for a parliamentary party committed to democracy in opposition to an aristocratic party. Democracy versus aristocracy was the fundamental issue; all other issues were thought to be either derivative or comparatively insignificant. This issue was fundamental because it reflected the underlying social reality that consisted of conflict between aristocracy and people. Therefore realignment of parties was proposed and expected. It would require a combination of the two established parties, since they were both dominated by aristocrats and promoted aristocratic interests. This realignment would allow for the emergence of a radical democratic party representing the people in opposition to a single aristocratic party. Party conflict would ensue between those who defended aristocratic principles, termed philosophic Tories, and those who had a principled defence of democracy, namely the philosophic radicals. This realignment would also allow parties to reflect both underlying reality and pure principles. In this view doctrinal parties representing extreme positions had the greatest claim to legitimacy and it is not surprising that philosophic radicals were called ultras and doctrinaires. During this time (1824–40), John Stuart Mill was hostile to centre parties and criticized compromisers and trimmers as unprincipled.

This understanding distinguished philosophic radicals from other types of radicals – from those, such as Thomas PAINE and his followers, whose radicalism rested on a belief in natural rights; from those devoted to particular issues for whom democratization was only a means to their particular end; and from those such as Cartwright or Cobbett, who justified their belief in constitutional change by the argument that it would be a restoration of popular institutions as they existed in the ancient past (see RADICALS, BRITISH).

The philosophic radicals formed a small faction in the House of Commons and mounted a vigorous campaign in the public journals during the 1830s; because of the balance of parties in the Commons they were able to entertain hopes for success. These hopes collapsed, however, when the rise of Chartism, the Anti-Corn Law agitation and other political circumstances led to their disillusionment and the break-up of their tiny faction.

The name survived the demise of the small self-styled philosophic radical party. The term philosophic radicalism was adopted by much later historians, notably Elie Halévy, whose *Formation du radicalisme philosophique* was published in 1904 and translated into English in 1928. By calling attention to his early political activities in his *Autobiography* (1873), Mill probably contributed to this development. In contrast to Mill's fairly precise definition, Halévy's loose usage, which included Benthamism, utilitarianism, liberalism, *laissez-faire* doctrine and a generalized radicalism, became conventional.

The most notable criticism of philosophic radicals was directed at their doctrinairism by centrists affiliated with the Whig party. Francis Jeffrey thought they encouraged civil conflict and made reconciliation of classes and parties difficult to achieve. MACAULAY had many complaints: they used deductive reasoning which was inappropriate in politics; they resembled seventeenth-century Puritans and Jacobins; their support lent ridicule to good causes; they were arrogant and intolerant; and they made the reform movement too revolutionary. In a less sophisticated formulation Stephen repeated some of these criticisms in his *English Utilitarians* (1900). From a different point of view CARLYLE directed his ire at philosophic radicalism for its individualism, its insensitivity to spiritual needs, and its support for a market economy. MARX regarded philosophic radicalism as bourgeois ideology.   JH

Reading

Halévy, E.: *The Growth of Philosophic Radicalism*, trans. M. Morris. London: Faber & Gwyer, 1928.

†Hamburger, J.: *Intellectuals in Politics: John Stuart Mill and the Philosophic Radicals*. New Haven and London: Yale University Press, 1965.

Mill, J.: *An Essay on Government*. New York: Liberal Arts Press, 1955.

Mill, J.S.: *Autobiography*. In *Collected Works*, vol. I, ed. J.M. Robson. Toronto: University of Toronto Press, 1981.

————: *Essays on England, Ireland, and the Empire*. In *Collected Works*, vol. VI, ed. J.M. Robson. Toronto: University of Toronto Press, 1982.

†Robson, J.M.: *The Improvement of Mankind: the Social and Political Thought of John Stuart Mill*. Toronto: University of Toronto Press, 1968.

Stephen, L.: *The English Utilitarians*. London: London School of Economics and Political Science, 1950.

†Thomas, W.: *The Philosophic Radicals: Nine Studies in Theory and Practice, 1817–1841*. Oxford: Clarendon Press, 1979.

physiocracy Meaning 'rule of nature', this was the first theory of political economy to account for the complete economic cycle and view the economy as a continuous, interdependent flow. Physiocracy resulted from the interaction of the pathbreaking economic analysis of François Quesnay (1694–1774) with the social theory of Victor de Riqueti, Marquis de Mirabeau (1715–89). It has been interpreted as foreshadowing CLASSICAL POLITICAL ECONOMY and even MARXISM in its analysis of capitalist production and reproduction, including surplus value. But the physiocrats insisted that land constituted the only source of wealth. Although they clearly analysed capitalist production in agriculture, they denied that manufacture or trade produced new values. Manufacture, or industry, and trade only elaborated the values produced by the agricultural sector. Labour alone could produce no value; even agricultural labour produced value only because of the land it worked.

Except for its insistence on the unique productivity of agriculture, physiocracy strongly resembled the political economies that would succeed it by emphasizing absolute private property, economic individualism and the market as the cornerstones of economic life. The physiocrats were the first theorists to identify economic growth as an organic process that did not require beggaring others. They even denied potential conflict between economic sectors. A high price for grain would benefit consumers as well as producers since prosperous agricultural producers would provide a strong market for the goods and services of non-agricultural producers, thus permitting the latter to pay more for grain while feeling the pinch of its price less.

For the physiocrats, a healthy economy required that land be held in absolute property, unencumbered by any dues or services; that labour be similarly unfettered; and that landlords command the resources to develop agricultural production. They further assumed that actual farming would be supervised by 'farmers' – agricultural entrepreneurs – who rented the land on long leases from the landlords. Agricultural production must begin with adequate investment not merely in seed, but in livestock (or labour and fertilizer) and in improved fields and agricultural buildings. If they enjoyed completely free markets, such agricultural enterprises would necessarily produce a profit – a net product, or surplus value – above and beyond the costs of production, including the remuneration of the farmer. That net product provided the only legitimate fund for taxation and all taxes must be taken from it.

Any attempt to tax agricultural wealth, other than the net product, would result in the depredation of the entire economy. To tax funds needed for advances would reduce the advances and thus reduce the succeeding crop. Similarly, any barrier to the absolutely free circulation of agricultural products would have the same effect. To lower prices artificially for the benefit of urban workers would rob the farmers and decrease the capacity for reinvestment. The urban classes' short-term gain would result in their long-term loss. The physiocrats presented these prescriptions as absolute and inviolable laws of nature. Quesnay designed a diagram, his celebrated *Tableau économique* (1758–9), to demonstrate with mathematical rigour the inexorability of his findings.

For Quesnay, Mirabeau, and the other original physiocrats including Baudeau, Le Mercier de la Rivière, Le Trosne, Roubaud, and Du Pont de Nemours, physiocratic political economy carried a heavy political component. Quesnay insisted that government must be simultaneously non-interventionist and absolute. He coined the term 'legal despotism' for his ideal and proposed China as the best existing model. These political views sharply distinguished the physiocrats from British political economists who assumed that free economic development and secure private property required a representative political system that would mirror and promote the freedom of the market.

As a political economy, physiocracy remained closely tied to that pre-revolutionary French society in which it originated. During the 1760s, the physiocrats lobbied vigorously for the freedom of the grain trade and the abolition of any restraints on the market. During the 1770s and 1780s, the doctrine gradually moved away from the doctrinal rigidity of Quesnay's formulations and merged into more general liberal programmes for absolute property, economic individualism and political reform. Few of the purported adherents of physiocracy in the United States and elsewhere actually deserved the label. From the original doctrine, they took little except the reverence for agriculture as a privileged form of economic activity.   EF-G

Reading
Du Pont de Nemours, P.S.: *Autobiography*, ed. and trans. E. Fox-Genovese. Wilmington, Del.: Scholarly Resources, 1986.

†Fox-Genovese, E.: *The Origins of Physiocracy: Economic Revolution and Social Order in Eighteenth-Century France*. Ithaca, NY and London: Cornell University Press, 1976.

Institut National d'Études Démographiques: *François Quesnay et la physiocratie*. 2 vols. Paris, 1958.

†Meek, R.L.: *The Economics of Physiocracy: essays and translations*. London: Allen & Unwin, 1962.

—— and Kuczynski, M. eds.: *Quesnay's Tableau Économique*. London and New York: Macmillan, 1972.

Quesnay, F.: *Oekonomische Schriften*, ed. M. Kuczynski. 2 vols. Berlin: Akademie-verlag, 1972, 1976.

——: *Oeuvres économiques et philosophiques de F. Quesnay, fondateur du système physiocratique*, ed. A. Onken. Frankfurt and Paris, 1888.

Weulersse, G.: *Le mouvement physiocratique en France de 1756 à 1770*, ed. F. Alcan. 2 vols. Paris: Libraires Félix Alcan et Guillaumin Réunies, 1910.

Plato (427–347 BC)   Greek philosopher. The political philosophy of Plato of Athens as opposed to that of SOCRATES of the early Platonic dialogues begins with the *Republic*. We know nothing of Plato's own attitudes to contemporary politics; he came from an aristocratic family and was related to some of the aristocrats who overthrew the Athenian democracy, but he took no part in their regime, nor in that of the restored democracy. Several pupils from his school, the Academy, took part in anti-democratic coups in various cities, but we do not know Plato's attitude to these. The so-called 'Seventh Letter' ascribed to Plato presents him as disillusioned by Athenian politics, and as intervening in an idealistic but disastrous way in the politics of Syracuse. But we have no reason to think any of the 'Letters' genuine, still less to use them to interpret the political theory of the dialogues.

The *Republic* begins as Plato's attempt to answer the question, why should I, an individual agent, be just? Plato's answer is that, ultimately, being just is in my interests; but this cannot be convincingly shown until we start to spell out the nature of JUSTICE in the 'larger letters' of the state. That is, we can see the just agent properly only in the ideal conditions of the just state. So it does not matter if the ideal state is unrealizable in practice; even if it is only a 'pattern laid up in heaven' it serves as an ideal for the would-be just agent. The just society must be compatible with human nature; Plato is uncompromisingly uninterested in its empirical practicability. We should remember, however, that he is not sketching a complete Utopia, but reforming a Greek city-state so as to make it just. He assumes the continuation of unideal features like inter-city warfare, and he takes over unchanged the basis of economic life, including slavery.

States, Plato argues, are based on our lack of self-sufficiency. Division of labour accords with natural distribution of talents and also enables us to rise above primitive conditions and develop a richer life. Plato finds uncontroversial, and does not bother to defend, two assumptions which liberals find uncomfortable. He sees humans as essentially social, finding their natural fulfilment in political association. It does not occur to him that there is any problem in justifying POLITICAL OBLIGATION, or that individuals might have rights which they lose or modify in political association. Further, he sees the state not as external machinery for regulating conflict, but as a natural context in which citizens can develop both private and public virtues.

Justice in the state casts light on justice in the agent in a very specific way; state and individual have analogous parts and are just in analogous ways. Plato develops from the original division of labour the thought that each should do only what he or she is best fitted to do. Since he thinks that only a few have the right combination of theoretical and directive intelligence fitting them to rule, this leads to a drastic relocating of power. While all the money stays in the hands of the producing classes, the city's political life is run entirely by a class of 'Guardians' (with the aid of a third, military class, the 'Auxiliaries', whose status is a little unclear but whose way of life is like that of the Guardians). The Guardians live a totally communal life, with no private property, no privacy or family life and no personal ambitions. Plato's claim that this is required for a city to be just rests on the claim that only the Guardians have the capacity to reason impartially for the good of the whole city, while ordinary people cannot rise above their personal goals; only in a city ruled by those who care only for the common good will conflict be abolished, unity achieved and the just state attained where each 'does what is his own', i.e. fills the role for which he (or she, for Plato remarkably includes women Guardians) is naturally fitted.

The just state is paralleled by a picture of the just individual. A person is just when particular desires are ruled and reformed by impartial reason, which works out the good of the whole, with the aid of the semi-rational 'spirited' or emotional part. The result is a kind of inner harmony in which all the parts do what is appropriate for them, enjoy their own highest pleasures and produce a stable and happy life. In both state and person the impersonal nature of reason is taken to extremes; the reason ruling the just person turns out to require years of philosophical training and depends on what this ultimately achieves: insight into the goodness of the universe.

The state/individual parallel leads Plato to a problem which he does not solve. In the individual, the particular desires are educated and retrained by reason so that they produce no felt opposition to what is best for the whole person. In the state, what is the condition of the individuals of the producing class, who must subordinate their individual projects to the Guardians' direction for the common good? Sometimes Plato suggests that they will be happy with their subordination, producing a happy and united state where all in their appropriate ways feel and think alike. But sometimes he suggests a darker picture: the producing class, precisely because they cannot rise to an appreciation of the common good, must be ruled by force and rhetorical persuasion. If so, in the just state not all will be fully just. Plato ignores the problems latent in divorcing power from money and its use, and in giving power only to those with expert knowledge; his interest is with the fully just, the Guardians, and revealingly he drifts into talking as though they formed the whole city.

In the *Republic* Plato is confident that people can attain the rational insight which entitles its possessor to rule those who lack it, and that the only way to achieve political justice is to give absolutely wise and just people absolute power: philosophers must become kings. Institutional changes are despised as ineffective, and in the ideally just state there are no independent checks on the Guardians. Plato has enough faith in human nature to think that such a system could work; he sees only personal and private ambitions, not political power itself, as corrupting forces.

Plato's later political theory is just as ideal, as opposed to practically applicable, but displays two drastic shifts. One is a loss of the confidence that individuals could become completely just and so be entrusted with absolute power. In the *Statesman* he argues that while an expert like a doctor may overrule his own prescriptions, in the doctor's absence one should stick to his rules; until the appearance of the philosopher-king, who can rule without laws because of his knowledge, we are better off with laws.

This signals a major concession. The attractive side of the idea that ruling is an expertise grounded in knowledge is the idea that the expert can deal with each situation as it arises, in an authoritative but personal and flexible way. Laws are by contrast necessarily general and apply mechanically to unlike cases. Even in the *Statesman* Plato ridicules the idea of bureaucratic insistence that doctoring and other skills be done by the rule-book. Yet Plato now takes this 'second-best' very seriously. The doctor's prescription is not adaptable to changing need, as the doctor is, but in a world without the doctor it is the nearest we will get to his knowledge, and preferable to nothing, or guesswork. Once he has come to this conclusion, Plato's interest in the ideal philosopher-ruler wanes; his major concern shifts to the question of whether states are or are not law-abiding. If a state abides by its laws, monarchy is the best form of government; next best is minority rule, and majority rule is worst. However, if a state is not law-abiding, majority rule is best, because least open to abuse of power; next comes minority rule, and monarchy is worst. Plato's considered view of the merits of different forms of government is thus sensible and pragmatic.

Laws, then, are clumsy because of their generality, but they are at least the product of rational thought, and obeying them is the nearest we get to running the state in a rational and stable way. Indeed, in his later works Plato comes to be somewhat obsessed with the stability and authority that laws can provide. His last work, the *Laws*, sketches an ideal state in which every detail of life is organized by laws (the Greek word, *nomoi*, covers many kinds of regulations as well as formal laws). The laws are ultimately shaped and maintained by the wise, who now form the Nocturnal Council (which among other things 're-educates' or liquidates atheists). But the council represents only a remnant of the Guardians' function in the state. There is less scope for rule by expertise in a state where every aspect of life from ante-natal exercises to funerals is firmly regulated. The result is oppressive and authoritarian, yet more egalitarian than the *Republic*; individuals do have, in the many laws, safeguards against the activity of their rulers. Further, Plato has so far overcome his distaste for bureaucracy as a clog on expertise that he follows the practice of democratic Athens in having enormous numbers of officials checking up constantly on other officials.

So Plato comes to reverse his emphasis: our best rational insight must still take second place to the collective wisdom expressed in laws, and work indirectly through them; and the defining virtue of a good citizen comes to be the self-control needed to obey them in every detail of life. This is a retreat from his earlier optimism about the possibilities for human nature; and many of the *Laws*' provisions are notoriously harsh and betray a pessimism about humans. Yet its *approach* is more moderate, and everywhere introduces compromise and recognition of the diversity of our needs. Plato here for the first time faces rather than denies the complexity of political problems.

The second major shift in Plato's thought is a new interest in the political relevance of history. Instead of *a priori* accounts of ideal political organization, Plato looks to the past. The *Statesman* uses a version of the Golden Age myth to help define statecraft. (Admittedly it is an extremely bizarre version of the idea that life was perfect in the past; the Golden Age is an exact reversal of ours, to the extent that people live their lives backwards, from the grave to the cradle.) The fascinating and unfinished *Critias* turns the very different myth of Atlantis into a kind of historical fiction about Atlantis and ancient Athens, with moral implications. These projections of the ideal state into the past are fanciful, complex and often hard to interpret. More straightforwardly, Book III of the *Laws* sketches prehistory and history from the Flood to the present day to bring out desirable or successful features of states which the ideal state is to embody. Plato's history is unreliable, selective and biased toward his theory; but it marks a decisive break with the approach of the *Republic*. Now the politician must learn from the past political successes and failures that history shows us; and the main lessons that we find are that cities suffer collapse of morale if they abandon their original laws, and that a 'mixed' form of government produces stability, while extremes of repression or licence lead to instability. Both the method and the realistic conclusions point forwards to ARISTOTLE, who stresses the importance of securing good institutions and bases his political theory on detailed examination of how states have developed in the past. The main difference is that Plato is not as concerned as Aristotle to collect many facts, and to get them right, before theorizing. JEA

Reading

†Annas, J.: *An Introduction to Plato's Republic*. Oxford: Clarendon Press, 1981.

Gill, C.J.: Plato and politics: the *Critias* and the *Politicus* [*Statesman*]. *Phronesis* 24 (1979) 148–67.

Plato: *Critias, Republic, Timaeus*. All in Loeb Classical Library; London: Heinemann.

————: *Laws*, trans. and annotated T.J. Saunders. Harmondsworth: Penguin, 1970.

————: *Statesman*, trans. and intro. J. Skemp. London: Routledge & Kegan Paul, 1952.

†Stalley, R.: *An Introduction to Plato's Laws*. Oxford: Blackwell; Indianapolis: Hackett, 1983.

Weil, R.: *L'archéologie de Platon*. Paris: Klincsieck, 1959.

†White, N.: *A Companion to Plato's Republic*. Oxford: Blackwell; Indianapolis: Hackett, 1979.

†Woozley, A.: *An Introduction to Plato's Republic*. London: Macmillan, 1964.

Plekhanov, Georgii Valentinovich (1856–1918) Russian Marxist. At first a supporter of POPULISM, Plekhanov was chiefly responsible for introducing MARXISM into the revolutionary movement in Russia. See SOVIET COMMUNISM.

pluralism An ideology which does not accept any single account as the ideal but which itself functions in a plurality of ways. It provides an alternative to the competing ideologies of communalism and individualism, both defective in their purest form, as recipes for the good life. Communalism is defective because the measures implemented to unify a people will be interpreted by many as coercive impositions which undermine their individual rights, ignore their interests and contravene their sense of justice. Individualism is defective because, though presenting itself as worthy of universal acceptance by giving primacy to the rights, interests and dignity of the individual, it falls prey to the criticism that the institutional arrangements needed to sustain it require a background of common understandings and commitments which compromise the individual as the source and end of the good life.

Pluralism is variously defined as an ideal of the good life; as a characterization of politics in western, capitalist democracies; as a theory of ethics relevant to the politics of liberal societies; and as a doctrine of cultural diversity that endorses neither a relativist nor a monist assessment of alternative cultures.

It is possible to endorse any one of these views without endorsing all the others, but most 'pluralists' will endorse several of them. The closest relation, perhaps, is that established between the theory of ethics and the ideal of the good life endorsed. A pluralist in ethics holds that though deontological variants of individualism are insufficient to generate an ethical theory, there is no single purpose or good that deserves the highest support of all rational people. Instead there is a plurality of goods, each capable of rational support and all appropriately included as options for individual choice (free choice itself being one). A pluralist society promotes a plurality of goods modestly, each being confined only by the degree necessary to make space for the others. Pluralist politics (it is said) combines features from the individualism of LOCKE, the participatory ethic of DEWEY and the concern with the virtues of continuity and stability of BURKE.

Active involvement in a variety of partial associations helps to develop the reflective and ethical powers of a person; it provides a variety of agencies to appeal to in protecting one's interests and rights. This diversity of associations funnels a diverse set of concerns, values and interests to the state for deliberation and resolution. Society as a whole also benefits from pluralism. The many intermediary institutions with which individuals are associated inhibit unreason in more than one way: if most individuals are implicated in more than one association, the individual self becomes an arena within which debates between groups are internalized; and if each association must appeal to others to obtain enough power to advance its most militant claims, it will often find it necessary to forgo its lesser demands and initial priorities out of deference to the highest priorities of its potential allies. Pluralism fosters stability without depending too heavily on direct state coercion or communal unity.

Nevertheless the theory asserts that innovation and change are also possible in pluralist politics. New groupings, formed perhaps by changes in economic position or in generational experience, can enter into politics and shift the balance of power in the give and take of pluralism. Pluralism slows the pace of change so that the older generation will not become too alienated from the younger; yet it maintains the pace sufficiently for the younger generation to be able to establish a stake in the future.

It would be difficult to oppose such an ideal, especially once the pure forms of individualism and communalism have been discounted. Debates over pluralism, therefore, have focused on the question of the degree to which the ideal is actually approximated in western, capitalist democracies. But competing interpretations of pluralism have been applied to those debates. Critics who claim that capitalist democracies do not measure up to the ideal can be grouped into several types. There are those who claim that the rise of the welfare state and the related bureaucratization of public life have given too much weight to the incentive-coercive power of the state, upsetting the balance between the plural associations and the state

apparatus in favour of the state. There are those who claim that the progressive oligopolization of capital has given it both too much independent power and too much power over the state apparatus. There are those who claim that the dual relation between the state and the economy and the state and the electorate spawns a series of contradictions which reduce the ability of the state to respond to the plurality of claims made upon it and force it to give priority to one subset of demands over others. There are those who claim that the background consensus a pluralist polity needs to thrive has been eroded, resulting in the formation of single issue constituencies who in aggregate render the order ungovernable through traditional pluralist channels. There are those who claim that institutions cannot achieve their intended aims; that this impasse, while not embodied in the official political dialogue, inspires a variety of expressions of disaffection from the order (such as the underground economy, high divorce rates, high rates of crime), and that changes in the ends governing the political economy are essential to the restoration of pluralist politics.

Testimony to the power of the pluralist ideal resides in the fact that most critics of pluralism – right, left and centre – applaud it as an ideal. The critics disagree amongst themselves, though, about the relative weight to be given to the various elements in the pluralist ideal. Some would give special emphasis to the pluralist appreciation of diversity; others to its modes of stabilization; others to its protection of rights; others to the openness and creativity of its politics; others to its commitment to reduce inequality sufficiently to enable all adult residents to participate as citizens; others to its quest for consensus on common aims.

There is a further consideration which, if endorsed, adds still more complexity to this already complex doctrine. In response to the debate between those who support a doctrine of cultural relativism and those who endorse a conception of one good life superior to all others, a theory of cultural pluralism might be defended. According to this view, there are a few social forms that can foster some of the values and standards worthy of human admiration while subordinating others. The character of the human condition, including the requirement that any way of life must establish limits in some areas to enable it to flourish in others, leads to this result.

Such a doctrine, plausibly named cultural pluralism, acknowledges that the good life endorsed by any particular pluralist society will sacrifice some recognizable virtues that other ways of life would allow. This understanding brings the pluralist up against the limits to diversity entailed by any particular manifestation of pluralism in one country, supports the case for rethinking the ways in which 'otherness' is defined and treated within pluralist societies, opens the door to reflection about the human costs and benefits of subordinating plurality in the self, and advances the case for extending the ideal of pluralism to relations between societies as well as to relations within them. Once its complexity has been appreciated pluralism can be seen to be more than the two-dimensional doctrine endorsed by, say, James MADISON. It not only aims to constrain factions in the interest of political stability and the protection of a small set of individual rights, but it moves at a number of levels all pertinent to the quality of political and ethical life.   WEC

Reading

†Bachrach, P.: *The Theory of Democratic Elitism: a Critique*. Boston: Little, Brown, 1967.

Berlin, I.: *Against the Current*. Harmondsworth: Penguin, 1982.

Connolly, W.E.: *Appearance and Reality in Politics*. Cambridge: Cambridge University Press, 1981.

†Dahl, R.: *A Preface to Democratic Theory*. Chicago: University of Chicago Press, 1956.

Hirschman, A.O.: *The Passions and the Interests*. Princeton, NJ: Princeton University Press, 1977.

Huntington, S.: *The Promise of Disharmony*. Cambridge, Mass.: Harvard University Press, 1981.

†Lindblom, C.: *Politics and Markets*. New York: Basic, 1977.

Tocqueville, Alexis de: *Democracy in America*, trans. G. Lawrence, ed. J.P. Mayer and M. Lerner. New York: Harper, 1966; London: Fontana, 1968.

Walzer, M.: *Spheres of Justice*. New York: Basic; Oxford: Martin Robertson, 1983.

political obligation Much of the history of modern (post-sixteenth-century) political philosophy revolves around the problem of political obligation. The problem has three main aspects: (1) To whom, or to what, do I owe my political obligations? – the *identification* of political authority; (2) Precisely how far, or in what respects, am I obligated to those in political authority? – the *extent* of political obligations; and (3) How is it that I come to have political obligations, or even, do I have any at all? – the *origins* of political authority.

Political obligation is correlative with political AUTHORITY. Thus, if I have an *obligation* to do or to refrain from doing some action x, there must be someone else (or some body) who has the *right* to require me to do or not to do x and consequently possesses *authority* over me in respect of x. Typically, the political authority is taken to be the state, or the government, or its representatives. However, *my* political obligations are not owed to any or to all states, only to the state of which I am a member (though I may have legal obligations as an alien in another state). The fact that my political obligations are 'particularized' in this way has been thought to pose difficulties for any attempt to derive political obligations from higher general moral principles, such as general utility or justice. For it is far from obvious that either must invariably best be served by adherence to the commands of one's own state. Hence the attractiveness, despite other disadvantages, of 'contract' theories of political obligation which argue that it is precisely because I promised or consented to obey the commands of my state that I am obligated to it rather than to any other.

In so far as the state is thought to enjoy political authority over its members, this is usually taken to imply that it possesses the sole right to pass laws and to monopolize the use of coercion in enforcing them. Hence the minimum content of my political obligation is not simply to obey *this* or *that* law as I happen to choose but to obey *the* law. In addition to obligations of obedience it is often held that we have obligations of civility – to support and sustain the main political institutions of the state by participation therein, e.g. voting, jury service, military duty. However, philosophers in the liberal tradition typically argue that one's political obligations are significantly limited in a number of ways. In the first place, they are merely one kind of moral obligation among others – along with, for example, familial, professional and religious obligations.

Moreover, moral obligations in general must be distinguished from moral duty, that is to say from what, all things considered, one ought to do. So, if I ought to do x, then x is my morally required action. But if x is an obligation upon me then it may be overridden, either by more exigent obligations, or by other higher moral considerations (see CIVIL DISOBEDIENCE). Consequently, liberal theories of political obligation are usually not offered as final answers concerning our moral duties in regard to the state. On the other hand, some critics of liberalism argue that conformity to one's political obligations constitutes one's highest moral duty (see below, pp. 381–2).

Until roughly the beginning of the sixteenth century the answer given to the question, How do we come by our political obligations? was either that we simply inherit them, as a given fact of nature like our parents and parental obligations, or that we must simply accept them as God's will. Modern political philosophy may be distinguished by its rejection of the older idea of the inevitableness of political authority and by adherence to the principle that all valid obligations must be voluntarily incurred or self-assumed – a view which immediately raises the question of justification: Why should we incur such obligations at all? Answers to this central question fall into two main kinds: either it is because of self-interest – the state is a necessary means to things we want (physical safety, or security of property) and if we will the end we must will the means; or it is because we have certain basic moral duties (such as maximizing human happiness or securing justice) and these cannot be discharged except through the mechanisms of political authority. In the liberal tradition the view that our political obligations must be self-assumed is marked by a strong, though by no means entirely unambiguous or even consistent, tendency towards 'radical voluntarism' – the idea that if authority is to be legitimate it must not simply be *accepted* but must be *created* by an act of will. The difficulties associated with giving a plausible or coherent expression to this idea by way of the notion of a SOCIAL CONTRACT, and the alternatives proposed to it, utilitarian, idealist, democratic and anarchist, largely constitute the modern history of the philosophical treatment of the concept of political obligation.

Unconditional obligation: As long as it is generally believed that political authority is an immutable fact, natural or divine, the question of whether we really have political obligations or not cannot even be raised. Reflective defences of unconditional obligation appear only when circumstances begin to change and the source of the state's claims to authority come to be questioned. Thus, in the political turmoil accompanying the religious Reformation in the sixteenth century, LUTHER responded to those who claimed the right of individuals to follow their conscience in all things, including their political duties, simply by reiterating St Paul's severe injunction passively to obey the powers-that-be. A century later FILMER presented kingly power as a kind of paternal authority, thus invoking the traditional reverence for the 'natural' hierarchy of the family in support of the absolutist pretensions of the Stuart monarchy. Neither form of argument is of course likely to impress those who lack a predisposition to piety; consequently more modern advocates of unconditional obedience have tended to follow HUME in defending submission to the state on the grounds that the advantages of a reliable system of political authority of virtually any kind must almost invariably outweigh the disadvantages of disturbing it.

Conditional obligation: Utilitarians with a less jaundiced view than Hume's of the likely consequences of political innovation usually advocate some form of conditional political authority. Historically, however, absolutist claims of the kind advanced by Luther and Filmer were opposed largely by thinkers in the contractarian tradition, a style of political thinking first hinted at by PLATO in the *Crito*, systematically developed from the sixteenth century by thinkers such as Buchanan, HOOKER, ALTHUSIUS, GROTIUS and MILTON, and crowned in the seventeenth century by the masterpieces of HOBBES and LOCKE.

The essence of the classical contractarian position is that political authority is legitimate only in so far as it is conditional upon the wills or the consent of those subject to it, and only as long as it is restricted in scope. These two distinct conditions are brought together by way of the idea of a social contract. As men cannot live, or at least live well, without the necessary amenities of civil order, the state must be regarded as being designed to serve a specific purpose (avoidance of the dangers and difficulties of the STATE OF NATURE), and political authority seen as being restricted to what is necessary to achieve this end. As men all must wish to live, or to live well, this necessary authority must be regarded as arising from their common agreement to alienate or transfer their natural rights to a political sovereign. Leaving aside the details and difficulties involved in the notional transition from the state of nature to civil society, it is sufficient for our purposes to note that in the process the individual is thought to retain and to carry into civil society at least some of the rights he enjoyed in the state of nature. The crucial effect is to set limits to the obligations of the subject or citizen to the state by erecting a sharp conceptual barrier between the sphere of political authority and the sphere of individual rights.

The point at which the line is drawn between these two spheres differs of course according to the particular view taken of HUMAN NATURE, of the deficiencies of the state of nature, and hence of the account given of the terms of the contract. For Hobbes people are by nature distrustful and insecure, and the state of nature is a 'war of all against all' which can be avoided only by a mutual alienation of all our natural rights, with the sole exception of our right to defend ourselves when immediately attacked. The third-party beneficiary of this profound renunciation of freedom then becomes sovereign and assumes virtually absolute authority to act in whatever way is thought necessary for the security of his or her subjects, even as far as having unqualified rights over their property and consciences. Locke, having a less desperate view of the natural state than Hobbes, is able to preserve a much wider sphere of individual liberty. According to Lockeian theory, political authority arises in two stages: first a unanimous contract of society, in which men form themselves into a political society by renouncing their natural right to execute the laws of justice, and then a majority decision of those so incorporated as to the particular form of government to which to entrust powers of legal execution. By

merely entrusting their natural rights to the state, rights which include the right to property as well as to life, they also reserve the right to resume their executive powers if the state fails to discharge its trust, either through incompetence or tyranny; although Locke is unclear about how such dereliction is to be identified, and whether it is the individual who has the right to withdraw recognition, or the majority of political society.

This lack of clarity is significant. For although contractarians insist that political obligation must be conditional upon the state's fulfilling its restricted purposes and going no further, the circumstances under which the individual might properly consider himself to have been released from his obligations are usually specified either so stringently (as with Hobbes) or so ambiguously (as with Locke) that the effect is often to attenuate or even to nullify the element of individual consent. In addition, CONSENT itself is usually characterized so broadly or vaguely that it becomes difficult to envisage conditions under which it may be said that it has been withdrawn. Indeed, it has been argued that the contract idiom adopted by writers such as Hobbes and Locke is potentially misleading, in that what really legitimizes political obligation for them is not consent at all but rather the nature of the state itself – its being just, for example, and hence the kind of state to which people ought to consent, or to which they would consent if they were rational or moral.

Difficulties of this kind with classical contractarian theory have led in two directions: via ROUSSEAU to contemporary attempts to give the act of consent more reality by attaching it to specifically democratic processes, and via Hume to utilitarian theories of obligation. Each of these, however, is not without its difficulties. Democratic theories of consent face the problem of the obligations of dissenting minorities or of disaffected individuals; and utilitarian theories, which ground both the practice of promising and the practice of political allegiance upon general utility, stumble both over the aforementioned 'particularity' problem and over the fact that the distinctive element in political authority is that the state lays claims upon its citizens to obey the law not because it maximizes utility, but simply because it is the law (see DEMOCRACY and UTILITARIANISM).

Unconditional freedom: The radical notion that the individual is free from any obligation to the state has historically taken two main forms – anarchism and revolutionary socialism. Of the latter by far the most influential view has been that of the Marxists (see MARXISM). Marxists offer two distinct arguments against political authority, although they are rarely distinguished. The first is that the vast majority of people have no political obligations because the state is merely the instrument of a particular economic minority (landlords, capitalists) for the exploitation of workers – a position which leaves open the possibility that workers may have obligations of a political kind to others of their class to change the form of the state, and would have political obligations in a just state. The second is more radical: moral principles, including principles of political obligation, have no independent and objective force. They are merely ideological expressions of economic class interests, and shift as the balance of economic and political power changes. It is not clear what the implications of this reductionist argument might be for obedience in a post-revolutionary workers' state, or for the classless communist society.

Political ANARCHISM is exemplified in the writings of such nineteenth-century anarchists as PROUDHON and KROPOTKIN. For them, all governmental authority is invalid because the state is of its essence a coercive institution and coercion occurs only in corrupt or unjust societies. As the individual has a moral obligation to act justly, his primary moral duty must be to oppose the state in every way he can and to strive for a society in which all members co-operate voluntarily according to principles of justice. Political anarchism by no means entails the rejection of all forms of authority, only of those involving the claim to a right to coercion. But, although it involves no obvious logical absurdity, political anarchists have found difficulty in giving a convincing account of a non-political form of social authority.

Philosophical anarchism is, however, much more radical in that it involves the rejection of the very idea of legitimate authority, political or otherwise. The basis of this doctrine is to be found in the writings of GODWIN and it has been developed in recent years by R. P. Wolff. The nub of this position is that the individual's primary moral duty is always to maintain his moral autonomy, that is to say, never to subordinate his own judgment to that of another, and as the essence of political authority is that the state's imperative 'Do x!' is itself a moral reason for doing x, moral autonomy and political obligation are necessarily incompatible. Perhaps the main difficulty with philosophical anarchism lies in the uncertainty of its practical political implications. For, even if we are prepared to accept the claim that the state's commanding something can never be a moral reason for doing that thing, it may still be the case (and surely very often is) that what the state demands is morally required of us anyway as being right or just. The major significance of the doctrine may be in reminding us of the profound moral dangers of automatic and unreflecting conformity to political authority.

Political obedience as self-determination: Rousseau's position in the development of the idea of political obligation is a complex and ambiguous one, for although he argues in the same contractual idiom as Hobbes and Locke, he develops a line of thought which, in the hands of the Idealist philosophers of the nineteenth and early twentieth century such as HEGEL, GREEN and BOSANQUET, culminates in the most rigorous critique of the liberal individualist tradition of conditional obligation. The crucial point, perhaps, at which Rousseau differs from classical contract theorists is in arguing that, in order to create a legitimate political sovereign, men in a state of nature must alienate *all* their natural rights. In one sense, then, Rousseau is a proponent of unconditional authority. His originality, however, lies in his view that this radical act of alienation of rights not only creates political authority, but also recreates the parties to the contract in that, in becoming morally incorporated into the sovereign, their individual wills are modified or merged into the GENERAL WILL. The implications are immense. For, in the light of such a moral transformation of personality, the oppositions which characterize liberal political theory and which create the classical 'problem' of political obligation are fundamentally redefined. Certainly, it can still be said that the individual has obligations to the state, and indeed that these represent his primary duties. But, in so far as he is rational, his individual will is identical with the general will and so his obligations are, in a sense, really to himself. From this perspective the central problem of political philosophy ceases to be that of identifying the proper line to be drawn between individual rights and political authority and becomes one of specifying the conditions under which the individual may achieve true self-determination and freedom by merging his own will with the general will.

What is in Rousseau an essentially ethical ideal of moral self-determination becomes in Hegel and later Idealists a systematic philosophical critique of the metaphysical basis of liberal political thought, especially of its individualism and empiricism (see IDEALISM). The result is the dissolution of the problem of political obligation as it is understood in the liberal tradition, although it is peculiarly vulnerable precisely because of its dependence upon difficult, and in the opinion of many thinkers, entirely insubstantial philosophical premises. It must, however, also be remarked that in recent years there has been an attempt by philosophically sophisticated Marxists to reformulate the purported insights of this line of approach in the language of historical materialism.

Writing on the topic of political obligation in the 1960s, one eminent Oxford political philosopher confessed the need to apologize for even considering a subject that was 'old-fashioned, even in Oxford'. The reason for the undoubted decline in philosophical interest in the topic in the decades following the first world war is complicated, but it must at least in part be attributed to developments in logic and epistemology, for both of the main contenders in the field – contract theory and political idealism – suffered severely at the hands of positivistically inclined philosophers (see POSITIVISM). Political idealism fell before the logical atomism of Moore and RUSSELL – for, if wholes are necessarily reducible to their constituent parts, as they argued, then general wills must be analysed into individual wills and hence the

obligations of the latter cannot without circularity be accounted for by appeal to the former. In the 1940s and 1950s the debunking style of ordinary language philosophy was destructive not only of the ambitious metaphysical edifices of idealism but equally of contract theory. Practical problems of political obligation, it was maintained, are always specific – Why should I obey *this* law, or *this* government *now?* – and are susceptible of fairly straightforward (if sometimes factually complicated and morally difficult) answers, usually in terms of the likely consequences of alternative decisions. The so-called problem of political obligation arises, it was argued, because philosophers pose the question too generally – Why should I obey *any* law, or *any* state? For, once raised, the general question catches the philosopher in a mystifying logic which ends in a high-sounding but essentially spurious appeals to such fictions as natural rights, states of nature and social contracts. Since the mid-1960s, however, positivism in its various forms has been on a steady retreat and theory has regained respectability in most areas of philosophy; and with it serious consideration of the question of political obligation. Perhaps the best evidence for this is to be found in RAWLS's ambitious and immensely influential theory of justice, which incorporates as an essential element within it a subtle and sophisticated account of the scope and limits of our political obligations.   GWS

Reading

Bosanquet, B.: *The Philosophical Theory of the State*, 4th edn. London: Macmillan, 1923.

†Flathman, R.: *Political Obligation*. New York: Atheneum, 1972.

Green, T.H.; *Lectures on the Principles of Political Obligation* (1882). London: Longman, 1966.

Hobbes, T.: *Leviathan* (1651), ed. C.B. Macpherson. Harmondsworth: Penguin, 1968.

Hume, D.: Of the original contract. In *Essays Moral, Political and Literary*, ed. E. Miller. Indianapolis: Liberty Classics, 1985.

Locke, J.: *Two Treatises of Government* (1689), ed. P. Laslett. New York: Mentor, 1965; Cambridge: Cambridge University Press, 1970.

†Pateman, C.: *The Problem of Political Obligation*. New York: Wiley, 1979.

†Pitkin, H.: Obligation and consent. In *Philosophy, Politics and Society*, 4th ser., ed. P. Laslett, W.G. Runciman and Q. Skinner. Oxford: Blackwell, 1972.

†Plamenatz, J.: *Consent, Freedom and Political Obligation*, 2nd edn. Oxford: Oxford University Press, 1968.

Plato: *The Last Days of Socrates*, trans. G.H.P.P. Tredennick. Harmondsworth: Penguin, 1954.

Rawls, J.: *A Theory of Justice*. Cambridge, Mass.: Harvard University Press, 1971; Oxford: Oxford University Press, 1972.

†Simmons, A.J.: *Moral Principles and Political Obligations*. Princeton, NJ: Princeton University Press, 1979.

Wolff, R.P.: *In Defense of Anarchism*. New York: Harper & Row, 1970.

political science See POLITICAL THEORY AND POLITICAL SCIENCE.

political theory Systematic reflection on the nature and purposes of government, characteristically involving both an understanding of existing political institutions and a view about how (if at all) they ought to be changed. It is an intellectual activity that has gone on since people first saw the form of their government, and their social institutions, not as dictated in all aspects by immutable tradition, but as open to modification. It is only recently, however, that this critical enterprise has been labelled 'political theory' and turned into an academic discipline. Previously those engaged in it would have regarded themselves as philosophers or scientists; now political theory is often marked off from political philosophy on the one hand, and from political science on the other (see POLITICAL THEORY AND POLITICAL SCIENCE).

This demarcation originates in a general shift of intellectual outlook that has accompanied the rise of modern science. Under the influence especially of POSITIVISM, it has become common to distinguish between, first, empirical statements, true or false by virtue of what observation shows to be the case; second, formal statements, such as the propositions of mathematics, true or false by virtue of the meanings of their constituent terms alone; and third, evaluative statements, such as moral imperatives, which are often said not to be true or false in any sense at all, but in any case are not entailed by either empirical or formal statements. If these distinctions are accepted, then science will be seen as a discipline that deals entirely in empirical statements, and philosophy as one that deals entirely in formal statements. Since political theory deals in evaluations – recommendations about what ought to be done, politically – it appears to follow at once that it cannot be assimilated either to science or to philosophy.

By the same token, however, it becomes hard to see how political theory can claim to be a discipline at all, as opposed to the mere airing of subjective preferences; and this has led a number of critics to present obituaries for the whole enterprise. An alternative response has been to cast the subject in a new role, different from that assumed by the classic political thinkers from Plato to Marx. A number of such interpretations have been proposed, each with some merit, but none ultimately satisfactory.

Political theory as the history of political thought: Political theory is seen here as the activity of scrutinizing the works of the classical writers themselves, with the aim of establishing the authentic meaning of the texts, and thereby recapturing the vision of politics which each contains. This programme is sometimes underpinned, as in the case of Leo Strauss, by the conviction that modern political thought – and especially modern political science – represents a falling away from the level of political insight achieved by these pre-modern philosophers.

Most political theorists do, in fact, spend part of their time reflecting on the achievements of their predecessors, and there seem to be at least two good reasons for this. Such reflection reveals the range of contrasting interpretations of politics that are possible, and dispels any illusion that the study of politics is a cumulative science, in which each theory merely improves upon its forerunner. Moreover the classic texts enjoy that status precisely because of the power of the analyses they contain, and these often turn out to be fruitful starting-points for thinking about contemporary politics. Yet as a wholesale programme for political theory, the historical approach is inadequate.

To begin with, if there really is a logical error involved in moving from empirical or formal statements to evaluative statements, this error cannot be avoided by pointing out that it has frequently been committed in the past. The challenge posed by the advent of modern science has to be met head on. Furthermore, there is an implicit tension between treating the history of political thought as *history* and as *political theory*. An historical approach which seeks to establish the texts' authentic meaning must increasingly pay attention to the precise intellectual context in which they were composed: the audience to which they were addressed, the author's aims in addressing that audience, the language available to him in making his approach, and so forth (see Skinner). As this contextual meaning is established, it becomes steadily more difficult to use the classic works to illuminate contemporary issues posed in a radically different context. Thus a gulf appears (reflected in the academic discipline) between those whose main concern is accurate historical interpretation, and those who wish to appropriate the classics for their own purposes with little regard to context.

Political theory as conceptual clarification: An alternative view sees political theory as a process of clarifying the meaning of the terms in which political argument is conducted, terms such as democracy, freedom and justice. It is clear that there is ample scope for such clarification, since these terms are frequently employed in ways that disguise the structure of the argument being advanced; as, for example, when a shift of meaning allows a protagonist to conceal a logical gap in a chain of reasoning. In particular, some political theorists, under the influence of linguistic philosophy, have seen their task as one of close examination of the use of political concepts in ordinary, pre-theoretical, language (see Weldon).

The difficulty with this view is that the ambiguities and inconsistencies displayed by the concepts used in political argument are reflected in ordinary language itself. Moreover it turns out that these variations are not random, but correspond broadly to the political outlook of the speaker in question. Thus a liberal and a socialist will characteristically use the notion of freedom in different ways, the socialist seeing impediments to personal freedom where the liberal sees only natural incapacities of various sorts. This is not to say that conceptual clarification is impossible, but it cannot be carried out in a wholly neutral manner;

defending one interpretation of a political concept usually means defending the general ideological stance with which that interpretation is linked. This means in turn that those who engage in conceptual clarification are actually engaged, overtly or covertly, in precisely the more substantive form of political theory that the classical authors undertook.

Political theory as formal model-building: A third view, mainly popular in the US, sees political theory as a matter of constructing formal models of political processes, in a manner inspired by theoretical economics. In broad outline, such models begin by postulating a group of rational actors, each with his or her own goals whose achievement he or she aims to maximize, but constrained by a set of procedural rules. The model then deduces how the actors will behave, and what the final outcome of their actions will be.

Such models have two possible purposes. They may aim primarily to be explanatory: that is, they may seek to present, schematically, the mechanisms that underlie political processes in the real world. On the other hand, their intentions may be primarily normative, in the sense that they may be seeking to show what consequences will follow from the adoption of particular rules for, say, reaching collective decisions. A well-known example of an explanatory model is Antony Downs's theory of electoral competition, in which voters are presented as trying to gain maximum utility from the outcome of elections, and parties as teams attempting to maximize their chances of winning. Downs then shows how parties will develop political ideologies to win support and how, on certain assumptions, the ideologies of all parties will converge to the centre of the political spectrum. This pioneering work has been considerably refined by later theorists. An equally famous example of a model with normative intentions, albeit of a somewhat negative kind, is Kenneth Arrow's impossibility theorem. Arrow postulates a population of voters having to choose between a range of policies, each voter being able to rank these policies in a particular order of preference. How should these preferences be combined to select one policy as the collective preference? Arrow demonstrates that there is no method of doing so which simultaneously meets a number of reasonable-sounding conditions (such as that if each person prefers x to y, y should not be chosen collectively in preference to x). This theorem implies, among other things, that where a democratic choice has to be made between more than two alternatives, the outcome is likely to be arbitrarily affected by the procedure used to make the choice; a result of concern to democratic theory generally.

Although it has established some significant results, the formal modelling approach suffers from at least one grave weakness. It depends on postulating actors as rational goal-maximizers, a postulate that seems far more questionable in politics than it does in economics. For political actors typically have principles and commitments that constrain their pursuit of goals; and moreover these goals themselves are liable to be modified by political persuasion. Many political phenomena – for example the rise of charismatic leaders – appear quite impervious to formal analysis of this type.

Political theory as theoretical political science: The rise of political science in the twentieth century has led some practitioners to regard political theory as simply the more theoretical aspect of that discipline (see POLITICAL THEORY AND POLITICAL SCIENCE for a fuller discussion). It synthesizes particular observations and low-level empirical generalizations into a general explanatory framework, rather as theoretical physics provides a systematic explanation of our everyday experience of the physical world. According to this view, the normative element in traditional political theory – the recommendations it contained for political change or conservation – was merely a dispensable addition to an essentially scientific enterprise.

Although several general frameworks for the explanation of political phenomena have been developed, it is noticeable that none has established itself on empirical grounds alone as the most adequate. It is also noticeable that each framework carries with it a practical stance of a rather general kind towards political life. This is especially clear in the case of MARXISM, where an explanation of politics in capitalist societies as the expression of class conflict is linked to a practical stance of opposition to capitalism.

Thus the attempt to construct a political theory free of normative elements seems doomed to fail. The reason, it appears, is that any explanation of political events involves an interpretation of the actions and intentions of the participants; and such an interpretation will draw on an disputable general view of human needs and motives that in turn carries normative implications with it (see Taylor).

None of the recent attempts to redraw the syllabus for political theory is therefore convincing. On the one hand, the need for political theory in the traditional sense – for a more reflective understanding of political phenomena than is provided by IDEOLOGY – is clear enough. On the other hand the credentials of the undertaking have been put in question by the positivist separation of empirical, formal, and evaluative statements. A defence of political theory must begin by rebutting this positivist view. It must show how explanation in the human sciences combines empirical and normative elements, and how the formal analysis of political concepts draws upon such explanations. The weakening hold of positivism on the social sciences has made such a defence easier.

The greatest practical difficulty that now faces political theory is simply the immense body of empirical material that modern political science has collected. Whereas the classical political theorists were unavoidably amateur political scientists – gathering information by casual observation and hearsay in a fairly haphazard way – their would-be successors are liable to be overwhelmed by systematically gathered data. Although there have been some important contributions to political theory in the last two decades – for instance the work of OAKESHOTT, RAWLS, Nozick, and Dworkin – it is noticeable that none of these combines the philosophical analysis of political principles with an empirical understanding of political processes in a wholly successful way. Their work is philosophically sophisticated but poorly-grounded empirically, and highly vulnerable to criticism by social scientists. Further progress in the field must involve rectifying this imbalance, a task that is, however, easier to set than to achieve. DLM

Reading

Arrow, K.: *Social Choice and Individual Values*. New Haven, Conn.: Yale University Press, 1963.

†Berlin, I.: Does political theory still exist? In *Philosophy, Politics and Society*, 2nd ser., ed. P. Laslett and W.G. Runciman. Oxford: Blackwell, 1964.

Connolly, W.E.: *The Terms of Political Discourse*. Lexington, Mass.: Heath, 1974.

Downs, A.: *An Economic Theory of Democracy*. New York: Harper & Row, 1957.

†Miller, D. and Siedentop, L. eds: *The Nature of Political Theory*. Oxford: Clarendon Press, 1983.

†Runciman, W.G.: *Social Science and Political Theory*. Cambridge: Cambridge University Press, 1969.

Skinner, Q.: Meaning and understanding in the history of ideas. *History and Theory* 8 (1969) 3–53.

Strauss, L.: *Natural Right and History*. Chicago: University of Chicago Press, 1953.

Taylor, C.: Neutrality in political science. In *Philosophy, Politics and Society*, 3rd ser., ed. P. Laslett and W.G. Runciman. Oxford: Blackwell, 1967.

Weldon, T.D.: *The Vocabulary of Politics*. Harmondsworth: Penguin, 1953.

political theory and political science Before the 1970s, 'political theory', outside American political science, was principally a categorical term referring to the canon of classic texts from Plato to Marx and to a loosely related body of contemporary literature in fields such as philosophy, political science, and history. In the United States political theory was principally a subfield of political science, and to the extent that any wider nascent interdisciplinary field of political theory existed, it tended to reflect issues that were generated within political science. The situation changed dramatically during the 1970s as the more general field of political theory began to take institutional form.

Although many of the current images of political theory and many of the issues that now define the literature originated in American political science, the subfield of political theory in political science is today largely, and increasingly, a microcosm of the wider field of political theory. Even though there are elements of political theory that distinctly reflect the research programme of contemporary political science, and notwithstanding 'remnants' of issues that are basically indigenous to that field, the subfield tends to exist somewhat anomalously within the parent discipline. There are also strong separatist forces both in political theory and mainstream American political science. To speak about political theory in political science as something distinct from political theory more generally conceived is necessarily to speak somewhat historically and parochially.

Although it is important to look carefully at the current conceptions, or dearth of conceptions, of political theory within orthodox political science, it is equally important to stress what is peculiar to the discipline and not simply reiterate those aspects of political theory that reflect the more general field. But one of the most striking features of political science today is its denial of the centrality of theory to the discipline and its tolerance of pluralism within the subfield of political theory. The explanation for what might be called the devolution and dispersion of political theory in political science is complex, but two principal and complementary developments must be emphasized. The first is the attenuation, by the early 1970s, of the conflict between what had characteristically been referred to as 'traditional' and 'scientific' political theory. The second is the growing differentiation, autonomy, and institutionalization of the interdisciplinary field of political theory. To understand these developments requires some general sense of the context and background of political theory in political science.

When political science, as a distinct professional discipline, was (in 1903) created with political theory itself as one of six subfields, there was little notion of political theory as a particular kind of activity. 'Political theory' referred principally to a subject matter that had traditionally been part of the field of political science during the second half of the nineteenth century and to the study of that subject matter. Political scientists had largely taken the state as their object of inquiry and, in Hegelian fashion, divided their concerns between the theory and practice, or between the subjective or ideational as opposed to the institutional and objective dimensions of the state. Political theory was also the repository of that part of the traditional university curriculum devoted to the study of the classics, of moral philosophy and ethics which were concerned with politics and government. As a concept, political theory was generic or categorical and designated certain types of claims and kinds of literature as well as ideas in and about politics.

In American political science of the late nineteenth and early twentieth centuries, the 'scientific' study of politics was basically historical, evolutionary, and comparative – following the perspectives of Hegel, Comte, and Spencer. Political theory became, in the work of individuals such as William Dunning, beginning around the turn of the century, the study of the history of political thought, from the Greeks to the present. The emphasis was on the evolutionary progress of democratic ideas and the scientific understanding of politics. The study of political theory was also assumed to yield a stock of analytical concepts for scientific political inquiry which was essentially understood as an applied science of political and governmental reform, social control, and citizen education. By the early 1920s the emphasis had shifted to the creation of a more analytical, descriptive, and explanatory (but, in this era of 'progressive' ideology, ultimately practical) science; yet political theory was primarily studied and taught as the history of political ideas and their relationship to political institutions in various social and historical contexts.

During the 1920s Charles Merriam, who in many ways must be regarded as the founder of modern political science, emerged as an influential spokesman for the development of a theory of politics that would form the core of an objective and methodologically sophisticated mode of social scientific inquiry. He placed considerable emphasis on the application of concepts and methods from other fields such as psychology and sociology and on the development of quantitative techniques to deal with the growing body of facts that the discipline was accumulating. Merriam argued that political science had progressed from an *a priori* deductive approach, which had characterized the first half of the nineteenth century, through a historical/comparative phase in the second half. Although in the early years of the twentieth century progress had been made in the development of inductive science concerned with observation and measurement, the future demanded a more theoretical and psychologically grounded treatment of politics and political behaviour if the scientific promise of the field was to be realized and its practical democratic goals achieved.

There are two characteristics of this period that deserve emphasis. First, despite the growing commitment to scientism in the work of individuals such as Merriam, there was little or no tension between their notions of empirical scientific theory and the study of the history of political thought. These were seen as complementary endeavours, the one devoted to the contemporary analysis of political processes, the other to their development over time. Second, the idea of science remained practical. The purpose was to further political reform and contribute to rational public policy.

The domestic and international problems of the 1930s diverted concern away from metatheoretical questions about the science of politics. Political theory, as exemplified in the work of individuals such as George Sabine, remained principally the study of the history of political theory, with considerable attention devoted to articulating liberal democratic ideas, their historical development, their contrast with the totalitarian aberrations of Nazism, fascism, and communism, and their identity with scientific principles. Merriam's claims, however, were not forgotten and were further developed by Harold Lasswell in this period, but, in practice, political theory was understood primarily as the history of political ideas.

Although the behavioural 'revolution', and the 'movement' that by the mid-1960s came to constitute mainstream political science, did not take shape until the 1950s, the sentiments that it represented had already been expressed in the 1940s. These sentiments were in many respects those of Merriam and Lasswell, and part of the problem was the sense that little progress had been made toward realizing the scientific ideal that political scientists had, at least in principle, increasingly come to embrace. The central tenet of behaviouralism, as articulated by individuals such as David Easton, was the development of a science of politics modelled after the methodology of the natural sciences. This goal was in itself hardly novel, but the behavioural persuasion had some special features.

First, for several reasons (including the delicate context created by the Cold War

387

ideology, the growing domestic post-war complacency, and funding that benefited basic research), behaviouralism depreciated the idea of political science as serving practical reform and citizen education and gave priority to the idea of pure science. Second, it succeeded in fundamentally changing the research programmes of political science – particularly through the introduction of systematic and quantitative methods of analysis. Third, it was in many respects a *theoretical* revolution. Its leaders were largely individuals who had been originally trained as historical and normative political theorists; it saw the development of empirical theory as the key to scientific advancement and focused much of its efforts on creating such theory; it introduced an unprecedented metatheoretical self-consciousness about scientific theory and explanations; most notably, it pointedly rejected the history of political theory as the basic meaning of theory in political science (this represents another important characteristic of the behavioural movement).

Why, after years of co-existence, did the historical and scientific approaches to political theory come into conflict? Ostensibly, it was because behaviouralists understood the study of the history of political theory as representing an unscientific humanistic/antiquarian approach that stood in the way of scientific development, and as occupying the ground that should have been the province of theory as the core of empirical inquiry into political behaviour and political processes. But although the history of political theory may have become an object of attack in part simply because the revolution needed something to revolt against, there was a deeper but seldom articulated issue. Beginning in the late 1930s, emigré scholars from Germany such as Leo Strauss, Eric Voegelin, Hannah ARENDT, Theodor ADORNO, and Herbert MARCUSE had begun to make a significant impact on the subfield of political theory. Their ideas, whether ideologically to the right or the left, were fundamentally antithetical to the basic values that had traditionally informed American political science including its faith in science, its commitment to liberal democracy, and its belief in historical progress. Thus the behavioural revolution, despite the

transformations it effected in the research programmes of the discipline, was in many respects a conservative revolution which reasserted those basic values of the field.

The behavioural critique of what it took to be the 'decline' of political theory, mounted by individuals such as Easton, was, during the 1950s and the 1960s, countered by historians of political theory who, like Strauss, claimed that the new science of politics was the real symptom of decline and that it both reflected and abetted a general political crisis of the West through its positivist tendencies and its failure to come to grips with normative issues. Throughout the 1950s, the controversy over behaviouralism was to a large extent most clearly manifest in the debate over political theory. Those committed to evaluative and prescriptive analysis and to the study of the 'great tradition' and the classic canon saw the scientism of behaviouralism as a threat to the very existence of political theory, while behaviouralists argued that such traditional political theory represented the dead hand of the past and constituted a barrier to progress in genuine scientific inquiry. It was from these debates that many of the subsequent images of political theory – whether as a world-historical activity concerned with criticism and restructuring of political life or as a mode of cognitive science – would emerge.

By the mid-1960s, behaviouralism had gained a position of dominance in the discipline of political science. Although scientific and traditional political theory maintained their antagonistic postures during this decade, they increasingly tended to go their separate ways. Critics of behaviouralism such as Sheldon Wolin charged that the preoccupation of political science with method represented an abdication of the true 'vocation' of political theory. Many such as Wolin held out little hope for political theory in political science, and mainstream political scientists were, in the wake of their professional success, largely disengaging from the critique of political theory and pursuing their scientific goals. By the late 1960s, the profession had officially divided political theory into three parts: historical, normative, and empirical. For most political scientists during this period, the attempt to realize the behavioural vision of scientific theory took the form of either the development of abstract 'conceptual frameworks' such as those represented in the 'systems' analysis of individuals such as Easton and Karl Deutsch or, as in the case of Heinz Eulau and Robert Dahl, the attempt to build theory inductively from empirical propositions of increasing generality. The enthusiasm for science and the concern with developing such 'strategies of inquiry' continued into the next decade, but certain developments began to change the image and practice of theory in the discipline.

Toward the end of the 1960s, behaviouralism began to attract criticism from several quarters for its 'pure science' stance and its failure to study, and speak to, the pressing social and political issues of the period. In 1969, Easton announced a 'new revolution' in political science, a 'post-behavioural revolution', that represented, at least initially, less emphasis on scientific method and technique and a greater concern with the public responsibilities of the discipline and with political problems. This reconstituted public policy image of the discipline developed consistently through the 1970s and, by the 1980s, represented the basic identity of the field. The shift also meant that less emphasis was placed on developing general empirical theory. The various subfields of political science continued to be occupied with their regional or particular theoretical concerns, but there was a progressive retreat from issues at the theoretical core of the discipline.

This retreat was complemented, and hastened, by a new critique of the behavioural image of scientific theory and explanation. This image had been informed and justified by logical positivist arguments in the philosophy of science (see POSITIVISM) which, by the late 1960s, had begun to come under attack from individuals such as Thomas Kuhn. This work, along with new challenges in the philosophy of social science (such as those advanced by Peter Winch and Alfred Schutz) to the idea of positivistic social science, began to spill over into political theory. Much of the discussion in the 1970s was devoted to metatheoretical debates about the nature of social scientific theory and explanation. While the earlier critique of behaviouralism had raised questions about the value of science as such and had

largely accepted the same positivist conception of science as behaviouralism, the new critique questioned not only the idea of the methodological unity of science but the adequacy of the prevailing conception of natural science.

These debates had the effect of weakening the hold of positivist assumptions in the field, but political scientists were in general now more concerned with policy relevance than with scientific identity. At the same time, political theorists were beginning to disengage from issues in political science and to direct their attention inward toward methodological and substantive issues connected with their own particular endeavours. By the end of the 1970s, political theory, or at least those aspects not directly tied to mainstream political science, had come to constitute a differentiated but tolerated enclave within the discipline of political science, and became absorbed in the diverse range of issues that defined the wider interdisciplinary field of political theory which had developed during the decade. These issues were generated by the work of individuals such as Jürgen HABERMAS, John RAWLS, Robert Nozick, and various other developments in a growing literature that many believed signalled a revival of political theory in the post-positivist age.

Quite diverse assessments can be made of the present condition of political theory and its prospects for the future. Many welcome the pluralism and vitality, which has characterized political theory in general in the post-positivist years, as well as the disengagement from issues in mainstream political science. Others believe that there is little sense of intellectual identity in the field and that although the debate between scientific and traditional political theory may have been properly interred, the issues have been more retired than resolved, and political theory has relinquished an important task by withdrawing from a critical appraisal of political science. Some hold out hope for a reunification both of the various branches of political theory and of political theory and political science, and believe that there are signs of such accommodation in, for example, the convergence of concerns between public policy analysis in political science and normative political theory. At least a few are somewhat pessimistic about such trends and believe that the apparent pluralism and growth in political theory in fact signify alienation and overproduction; and that, despite a new sense of practical relevance, little progress has been made in sorting out the persistent issues regarding the relationship between political theory and politics.

Political science, and political theory as a subfield of the discipline, have primarily been American inventions and, from the beginning, the issues that have emerged within and between these fields have revolved around the question of the relationship between public and academic discourse. Even when the general discipline of political science, during the behavioural era, withdrew from the traditional idea of political science as primarily a practical science, this notion was sustained within political theory. Yet, despite the appearance of several images of political theory as addressing relevant social problems, as in the case of CRITICAL THEORY and the Frankfurt School or the attention of normative and analytical theorists to a wide variety of social issues, the question of the relationship between political theory and politics remains unsolved. Some of these same problems are inherent in the idea of political science as a policy science, and it may be that this range of issues will ultimately serve to foster a re-engagement of political theory and political science.   JGG

Reading
†Crick, B.: *The American Science of Politics*. Berkeley: University of California Press, 1959.
†Finifter, A. ed.: *Political Science: the State of the Discipline*. Washington, DC: American Political Science Association, 1983.
Gunnell, J.G.: Political theory: the evolution of a subfield. In Finifter ed.
———: *Between Philosophy and Politics: the Alienation of Political Theory*. Amherst, Mass.: University of Massachusetts Press, 1986.
Nelson, J.S. ed.: *What Should Political Theory Be Now?* Albany, NY: SUNY Press, 1983.
Ricci, D.: *The Tragedy of Political Science*. New Haven, Conn.: Yale University Press, 1984.
†Seidelman, R.: *Disenchanted Realists: American Political Science 1884–1984*. Albany, NY: SUNY Press, 1985.
†Somit, A. and Tanenhaus, J.: *The Development of American Political Science*. New York: Irvington, 1982.
Waldo, D.: Political science: tradition, discipline, profession, science, enterprise. In *The Handbook of Political Science*, vol. 1, ed. F. Greenstein and N. Polby. Reading, Mass.: Addison-Wesley, 1975.

politics Politics may be defined briefly as a process whereby a group of people, whose opinions or interests are initially divergent, reach collective decisions which are generally regarded as binding on the group, and enforced as common policy. This definition includes several elements which need to be examined separately if the complexity of the idea of politics is to be understood.

(1) Politics presupposes diversity of views, if not about ultimate aims, at least about the best means of achieving them. Where people agree spontaneously on a course of action, or more importantly where they are able to reach unanimity simply through unconstrained discussion, they have no need to engage in politics. Groups of friends or communities of scientists may approach this ideal of apolitical consensus; so, in fiction, did the perfectly rational Houyhnhnms of Swift's *Gulliver's Travels*. Politics occurs when no such consensus is forthcoming, but when the group in question needs to act collectively.

(2) Politics implies something about the way in which collective decisions are reached. It typically involves three elements: persuasion, bargaining and a mechanism for reaching a final decision. Persuasion is a matter of trying to convince your opponents of the merits of your case, by good arguments or bad; it embraces that most characteristic of political events, the rhetorical speech. Bargaining involves agreeing to meet your opponents' demands in one respect in order to win a concession from them in another. After persuasion and bargaining, in varying proportions, have occurred, a decision is made. This may at one extreme involve a formal mechanism – say democratic voting; at the other extreme, the decision may emerge quite informally – for instance as the will of an autocratic monarch after lobbying by his courtiers. What politics excludes, however, is the resolution of disagreements by simple *force*. A man who obliges his companions to do as he wishes by pointing a gun at their heads is not engaged in a political relationship with them.

Persuasion and bargaining are frequently

unedifying activities, typically involving deception of opponents and sacrifice of principle for political advantage. This largely accounts for the negative connotations that the word 'politics' holds, a view immortalized in the second verse of the British National Anthem:

Confound their politics,
Frustrate their knavish tricks . . .

(3) Politics implies, though, that the decision reached, in however underhand a way, is regarded as authoritative by the group in question. It becomes *policy* – a separate term in the English language, but not clearly differentiated from *politics* in others, including French and German. This aspect casts politics in a more favourable light, for it suggests a settled endeavour to achieve results that are beneficial to the group. It draws attention to ends that can only be realized by agreed-upon collective action.

(4) Although politics is unthinkable without AUTHORITY, it is in practice inseparable from POWER, the imposition of decisions on recalcitrant members. It is this face of politics that is distasteful to libertarians; and the ideologies which look forward to the eventual disappearance of politics, ANARCHISM and MARXISM, have this coercive aspect chiefly in mind.

Given these four characteristics, it is no surprise that the chief arena of politics, in the modern world, should be the STATE. For the state is the most comprehensive authority that we encounter, and therefore the institution which it is most worthwhile to try to influence by persuasion and bargaining. This has led some analysts to tie 'politics' definitionally to the state, and of course in common parlance a politician is someone engaged either in directing the state or in trying to displace the current directors; and 'political' may mean 'having to do with affairs of state'. Yet there is an equally well-established practice of referring to politics within corporations, trade unions, universities and other such sub-state institutions. Since in all these cases we find the four elements referred to – a diversity of views, a procedure for reaching decisions, acceptance and enforcement of the decision reached as common policy – the description seems proper and illuminating.

On the other hand, over-extension of the term 'politics' is to be avoided. Recent feminist literature has employed the catchphrase 'the personal is the political'. The meaning of this slogan is unclear. If it means that personal matters – the rights of men and women in their relationships with one another – should become an object of political (i.e. state) concern and action, then it may well be valid, but only in the sense in which any issue – protection of rare breeds of animals, or the construction of a tunnel under the English Channel – may properly become political. If it means that personal relationships *are* political relationships, then it may be drawing attention, in a misleading way, to the power exercised (typically) by men over women. But although all political relationships involve the exercise of power, the converse does not hold: the relationship between a master and his slave is not political, nor that between officer and private. 'The personal is the political' probably means, in practice, something like: personal relationships, styles of life, etc., are matters of the greatest importance, not to be given second place to conventional politics. This may or may not be true, but the point can and should be made without widening the idea of politics to the point of vacuity.   DLM

Reading
†Crick, B.: *In Defence of Politics*. Harmondsworth: Penguin, 1964.
Dahl, R.: *Modern Political Analysis*. Englewood Cliffs, NJ: Prentice-Hall, 1963.
Lasswell, H.: *Politics: Who Gets What, When, How*. New York: McGraw-Hill, 1936.
†Laver, M.: *Invitation to Politics*. Oxford: Martin Robertson, 1985.
†Leftwich, A. ed.: *What is Politics?* Oxford: Blackwell, 1984.
†Miller, J.D.B.: *The Nature of Politics*. Harmondsworth: Penguin, 1962.

Polybius (before 200–after 118 BC)   A Graeco-Roman historian. Polybius began his career with the junior military and political offices of the Greek community of which he was a member, the Achaean League. This had been formed in the third century BC and covered most of southern Greece. When the Romans first intervened militarily on a significant scale in the Greek world, against the kingdom of Macedon in 200 BC, the Achaean League after some hesitation threw in its lot with them. Just thirty years later, when Macedon made its last attempt to assert its independence from Rome, the Achaean League tried to distance itself very slightly from Roman policy. The result was that, after the defeat of Macedon, Polybius and many others were taken to Italy and interned. There he fared substantially better than his companions and was accepted as a friend by members of the Roman elite. This was no doubt the result of his intellectual capacities, in a Rome already hungry for Greek culture.

Polybius rapidly formed the idea of writing an account of how the Romans had conquered the known world; he initially intended to cover the period from the Roman crossing to Sicily in 264 to the final defeat of Macedon in 167, but soon decided to extend his treatment to the destruction of Carthage in 146, in order to provide material whereby the quality of Roman rule might be judged (see ROMAN POLITICAL THOUGHT).

A central part of the *Histories* of Polybius is formed by Book Six, where he describes the Roman political system at its acme. It is important to his conception of Rome that he provided an account both of her more strictly political aspects and of her military system. But Polybius, writing for Greeks among others, also attempted to locate Rome in the general context of Greek writing about constitutions and to analyse Rome in terms of Greek theoretical arguments about the development of states.

Probably influenced by his Roman friends, Polybius argued that the Roman political system was the result of collective effort by the community as a whole over a long period of time. So far, so good. But he also wished to relate the history of the Roman political system to two theoretical approaches of Greek origin. One held that states underwent a cyclical process, monarchy degenerating into tyranny, to be replaced by aristocracy; this in turn degenerated into oligarchy, to be replaced by democracy; after this had degenerated into ochlocracy, the rule of the mob, a period of anarchy was followed by the emergence again of primitive monarchy. But Polybius also operated within a framework dominated by a model

drawn from the human or animal world, of birth, growth, acme, decline and end. Finally, he also wished to hold that the Roman state had somehow succeeded in breaking out of the necessity to obey any kind of cyclical law or that imposed by a biological model. Rome, in fact, was a perfect blend – Polybius nowhere succeeds in explaining exactly how this was achieved – of monarchy, aristocracy and democracy.

This notion of the mixed constitution has had a long history in later political thought and it is important to observe that Polybius did not propound a system of CHECKS AND BALANCES between executive, judiciary and legislature, but a system where each of his elements had its own sphere of action. This sphere of action was circumscribed by the spheres of action of the other two elements in the state; and it was also the case that in some contexts the co-operation of one or more of the other elements was necessary for any action to take place at all.

MHC

Reading
Ferrary, J.-L.: Ciceron entre Polybe et Platon. *Journal of Roman Studies* 74 (1984) 87–98.

Musti, D.: Polibio. In *Storia delle idee politiche, economiche e sociale*, ed. L. Firpo. Turin: UTET, 1983.

Nippel, W.: Mischverfassungstheorie und Verfassungsrealität. In *Antike und früher Neuzeit*. Stuttgart, 1980.

Polybius: *The Histories*, trans. W.R. Paton. 6 vols. London: Heinemann, 1922–7.

†Walbank, F.W.: *Polybius*. Berkeley, Los Angeles and London: University of California Press, 1972.

Popper, Karl Raimund (1902–) Philosopher. Born in Vienna, Popper left Austria shortly before the Anschluss; he taught philosophy in New Zealand from 1937 to 1945, and from 1946 until his retirement was professor of logic and scientific method at the London School of Economics. Best known as a philosopher of science – for example, see *Logik der Forschuung* (1934), translated as *The Logic of Scientific Discovery* (1959) – Popper is a passionate defender of liberal values, which he sees embodied in the best scientific work.

As a young man, Popper was influenced by Marxism and by psychoanalysis, both of which he came to dismiss as pseudo-sciences. The need to explain their shortcomings was one stimulus of his work in the philosophy of science. But Popper's most direct contributions to political theory are *The Open Society and Its Enemies* (1945) and *The Poverty of Historicism* (1957). The former is a two-volume work, the first volume an attack on Plato, the second an attack on Hegel and Marx. *The Poverty of Historicism* criticizes the idea that there are 'historical laws' which it is the business of social science to discover – and which should dictate our politics. The book is dedicated to the countless victims of the fascist and communist belief in historical destiny.

The Open Society and Its Enemies lives up to its title by arguing that science and freedom flourish together in a society which is open in the sense of being willing to accept new ideas. The philosophy of PLATO is authoritarian and totalitarian; the rule of the Guardians is propped up by myths, not by intellectual competence. Plato is a theorist of the closed society, a reactionary who tries to prevent social change by giving absolute power to the philosophical elite. But Popper's most devastating objection is that in politics as in science it is a great error to ask 'How can we be certain?' and 'How can we secure perfect rulers?' The proper question is, 'How can we detect and remedy our mistakes as quickly as possible?' and 'How can we minimize the damage that bad rulers may do?'

It is in this light that HEGEL and MARX are condemned in *The Open Society and Its Enemies*: Hegel is beneath contempt, a mere windbag pretending to Absolute Knowledge. Marx, however, was a serious social theorist. Popper praises him for the way he distinguishes between 'human nature' – about which we know almost nothing, and which does not explain how people behave in the situations in which they find themselves – and the motivation of actors in a given social situation. But Marx was a 'holist' and a determinist, and he subordinated explanation to prophecy – to announcing the 'inevitable' downfall of capitalism and, inconsistently, calling on his followers to bring about the inevitable by rising in revolt.

The explanation of the errors committed by Marx (and many others) comes in *The Poverty of Historicism*, where Popper elaborates the distinction between genuine laws and historical trends. There can be no law of 'the historical process' as a whole, since it is a unique occurrence and not an open-ended class; so-called 'laws', such as the 'law of the increasing concentration of capital' are not laws, but at most statements of a trend. Notoriously, extrapolating from a trend is the weakest form of prediction. The self-confidence of historicists is thus at odds with the feebleness of their results (see also HISTORICISM).

Popper's positive allegiances are somewhat obscure. He avows a general commitment to the sanctity of the individual and to equality before the law, and he advocates that governments should concentrate on reducing misery rather than on trying to do the most good possible. This goes beyond the LIBERALISM that confines the state to the repression of force and fraud, but it stops short of suggesting that governments ought to engage in elaborate and far-reaching economic planning for the purpose. His emphasis on the unpredictability of human affairs would, in any case, suggest scepticism about the possibility of successful planning. In many ways his liberalism is like that of KANT, with its emphasis on the RULE OF LAW and individual security, and the positive good that governments can do limited to the 'hindering of hindrances to the good life'.   AR

Reading

Currie, G. and Musgrave, A. eds: *Popper and the Human Sciences*. The Hague: Nijhoff, 1985.

†Magee, B.: *Popper*. London: Fontana, 1973.

†Popper, K.R.: *The Open Society and Its Enemies*. London: Routledge & Kegan Paul, 1945.

†———: *The Poverty of Historicism*. London: Routledge & Kegan Paul, 1957.

populism A term with a wide variety of meanings which can be grouped into two broad categories: 'agrarian populism', a set of radical movements and socio-economic doctrines concerned with the interests of peasants and small farmers, and 'political populism', a number of attitudes, activities and techniques based on an appeal to 'the people'. Each of these categories includes a range of different phenomena.

Agrarian populism

The two paradigm cases here, American and Russian populism, are very different from one another. The USA's People's Party of the 1890s, whose supporters coined the term populist, was a grass-roots movement growing out of the economic grievances of farmers in the western and southern states. Declaring their aim 'to restore the government of the Republic to the hands of "the plain people"', the populists denounced financiers and demanded government action to help small producers, notably free coinage of silver to combat deflation. The movement collapsed after the defeat in the 1896 presidential election of W. J. Bryan, a Democrat who campaigned on a largely populist platform.

Narodnichestvo (populism), by contrast, was a phase of the nineteenth-century Russian revolutionary movement during which radical intellectuals idealized the peasantry and hoped to build a new socialist society upon the traditions of communal cultivation which survived in the Russian village. At the height of the movement, in 1874, young intellectuals went 'to the people', flocking to the countryside to preach the gospel of agrarian socialism. When the peasantry proved unresponsive, some of the *Narodniki* took to terrorism and succeeded in assassinating the Tsar.

The term populism is also applied to a wide range of movements and theories concerned with the problems of small-scale rural producers faced with modernization. Movements of this kind often idealize the communal traditions of rural life and aim to find a humane middle way between large-scale capitalism on the one hand and bureaucratic socialism on the other. Whether looking towards widely-distributed private property or towards decentralized versions of socialism, such populists oppose hierarchical organization and aim at local co-operation between equals. By these criteria, the following may be categorized as populist: PROUDHON; GANDHI; Nyerere; Distributism; much Roman Catholic social thought; the 'Green' movements of Eastern Europe after the first world war. Populism of this kind has generated a good deal of economic thought, much of it directed towards the problems of the Third World (see e.g.

Schumacher). Kitching provides a critique of such theory.

Political populism

As a political stance, populism means above all an appeal to 'the people', usually against the elite, often also against outsiders and foreigners. This can take a number of different forms. Trust in the people can result most directly in populist DEMOCRACY, which is hostile to representation and seeks to keep as much power as possible in the hands of the ordinary citizen. Its characteristic institutional devices are the referendum on legislation passed by the representative assembly; the popular initiative, whereby voters can bypass their representatives and initiate legislation to be voted on in a referendum; and the recall, whereby representatives can be forced to undergo an early election if their constituents are dissatisfied. As a result of populist pressure in the early twentieth century many USA states have constitutional provisions of this kind. Populism in this sense may be seen as an extreme form of democracy.

Direct appeals to the people can be ambiguous in their effects, however, and the term populist is also applied to charismatic dictators who gain power by appealing past conventional politics and bribing the masses with bread and circuses. Peron's rise to power in Argentina is often regarded as a classic case, while both Hitler and de Gaulle have been called populist. Within parliamentary systems, politicians may be accused of populism if they break the liberal elite consensus by playing to popular prejudice against foreigners, deviants or ethnic minorities. Populism in this sense has derogatory overtones, suggesting reactionary views, intolerance of diversity and hostility to individualism, intellect and culture.

Another way of appealing to 'the people' is to concentrate on the sense of that ambiguous expression in which it refers to the nation as a whole, emphasizing its integrative connotations. Politicians may be called populist if they avoid ideological commitments and claim to speak for the whole people rather than any faction or class, or if they belong to 'catch-all people's parties' that are short on principles and eclectic in their policies. Populist rhetoric is often used in such circumstances to evade issues, although it can also provide a language in which to articulate views and grievances not catered for within established political conventions. The content of populist politics can therefore vary widely from one political system to another, sometimes including the themes of agrarian populism, sometimes having little connection with them.

Although it is possible to identify proto-populists in pre-modern times, populism is essentially a modern phenomenon, generated in its agrarian forms by economic modernization and in its political forms by the political mobilization of the masses. Within the last half century the status of populist ideas and attitudes in academic circles has altered sharply. In the mid-twentieth century, agrarian populism was dismissed by liberal and Marxist economists, while political populism was associated with Nazism and McCarthyism and feared by intellectuals. Since the 1960s, however, interest in the Third World has given a new topicality to agrarian populism, while the simultaneous attack on 'democratic elitism' brought populist devices such as referenda back into fashion. One result has been a more sympathetic rewriting of the history of populist movements, notably American populism (see e.g. Goodwyn).

MEC

Reading

†Canovan, M.: *Populism*. London: Junction, 1981.

Goodwyn, L.: *Democratic Promise: the Populist Moment in America*. New York: Oxford University Press, 1976.

†Ionescu, G. and Gellner, E.: *Populism: Its Meanings and National Characteristics*. London: Weidenfeld & Nicolson, 1969.

Kitching, G.: *Development and Underdevelopment in Historical Perspective: Populism, Nationalism and Industrialization*. London: Methuen, 1982.

Schumacher, E.: *Small is Beautiful*. London: Blond & Briggs, 1973.

Venturi, F.: *The Roots of Revolution*. London: Weidenfeld & Nicolson, 1960.

positivism Many different proposals as to what positivism is have found favour with different individuals and groups at different times. This makes it particularly difficult to decide which thinkers should properly be regarded as positivists. A number who call themselves anti-positivists because they disagree with one or other thesis usually associated with positivism, are still regarded as positivists by their critics (see Stockman). In its most general current sense, to be positivist means no more than to be self-consciously scientific. But without further specification, this general characterization does not differentiate positivism from other positions that also claim to be scientific, such as realism within the philosophy of the social sciences and MARXISM within political thought. The different positivist theses are mainly (but not all) different specifications of what it is to be scientific.

'Positivism' is a contraction of 'positive philosophy', the name coined by COMTE to describe his vast systematic reconstruction of the history of scientific knowledge. But Comte was not the first to espouse the ideas that have since been identified with positivism. The themes he brought together to organize his historical conspectus derived from the FRENCH ENLIGHTENMENT and earlier. It is arguable, on the basis of his consistent empiricism, that HUME was the first thoroughgoing positivist (see Kolakowski), for empiricism is central to most conceptions of positivism, including Comte's, even though the precise form of empiricism incorporated into positivism has varied. Empiricism, in general, maintains that the only way to ensure that knowledge of matters of fact is sound or scientific is to base it on observation or, more generally, experience. In Comte's positivism, this thesis was combined with two others. First, he undertook his review of the development of the sciences in order to support the unity of science thesis, according to which all scientific disciplines, natural and social, can be (and ultimately will be) integrated into a single system of knowledge; for there are no essential differences between them, only differences in the degree to which they have progressed to the positive ideal of discovering the invariable natural laws to which all phenomena are subject. Second, Comte's efforts to complete the unified system of observational sciences by founding social physics or sociology – the positive science of society – was motivated by a practical thesis:

scientific knowledge provides the necessary basis for control over both nature and society.

Under the influence of these three theses – empiricism, unity of science, and control – positivist political thought in the nineteenth century did not address the state or other specifically political institutions, but concerned itself with society in general, with advancing and applying the positive science of society to overcome the present social malaise and promote a better future. Within this general approach, political programmes as different as those of SAINT-SIMON, Comte and SPENCER were devised. What united them was their common desire to put political choices on a sound scientific basis.

By the early twentieth century, interest in social and political cosmologies was waning, and those that remained were based on alternatives to positivist ideas, especially Marxism. But meanwhile another positivist thesis, another suggestion as to what it is to be scientific, gained strength. This had its roots in the political arithmetic of the seventeenth century and was nurtured by the social surveys of nineteenth-century philanthropists, administrators, and reformers. It claimed that being scientific involved collecting and manipulating quantitative data, and it was accompanied by rapid developments in all branches of statistics. Political thought under the influence of this positivist thesis saw itself as the natural scientific study of political actions and institutions through the collection and statistical analysis of quantified political facts. (See POLITICAL THEORY AND POLITICAL SCIENCE.)

A revitalized form of positivism appeared in the 1920s and 1930s in the works of a group of philosophers, mathematicians and scientists known as the Vienna Circle. The Circle's philosophical programme, given the name logical positivism, centred on phenomenalism (a radical form of empiricism that limits the basis of science to experiences of sensations alone) and logical analysis, and the aim was to unify science (see Neurath *et al.*). Immediate experience provided the content of all science, and logic the formal language through which to connect descriptions of experiences and so construct laws and theories. This combination of empiricism and logical analysis is captured by the principle of verifiability. This is a rule for demarcating science, in which all propositions must be analysable into basic statements verifiable by experience, from metaphysics, which, lacking direct empirical reference, is without meaning. Early logical positivism was also reductionist, in that the basic statements describing immediate experience were to be expressed in the same observational vocabulary, initially that of physics.

Logical positivism had two different effects on political thought (see POLITICAL THEORY). One stemmed from the support given by the principle of verifiability to the view that politics is metaphysical, beyond science, a matter of essentially arbitrary choices and non-rational commitments, for science tells us only what will happen, under certain conditions, not what should happen. This was in marked contrast to the nineteenth-century positivist view that politics could itself become scientific. The second and contrary effect of logical positivism stemmed from its dominance as a philosophy of science and the consequent widespread acceptance that to be scientific meant to adopt those aspects of science that logical positivism identified as essential. These included the view that physics is the paradigm of a unified science, and that science proceeds inductively from observations to laws. Hempel was influential, through his formalization of the logic of explanation in his deductive-nomological schema, in promoting the view that explanation and prediction are formally symmetrical, both involving the subsumption of particular occurrences under general laws. These various ideas lent general support to statistical positivism, where there have been considerable technical advances in operationalization, measurement, and data analysis undertaken by statisticians seeking to make social surveys the analogue of controlled experiments for the discovery and verification of social and political laws. These ideas, together with reductionism, also lent weight to behaviourism, to a concentration on the observable aspects of individuals and institutions as opposed to intangibles, especially the social meanings considered central by those opponents of positivism who draw a radical distinction between the hermeneutic human sciences and the natural sciences.

Early logical positivist philosophy of science has undergone many modifications as attempts have been made to solve or circumvent internal problems. Social scientists have mostly ignored these refinements, except the contribution of POPPER, a self-avowed anti-positivist but a positivist to his critics. He has been particularly successful in promoting, as an alternative to verifying laws through induction, his hypothetico-deductive method of first conjecturing laws and then trying to refute them by empirical test. This method is followed by empirical political analysts when they subject hypotheses to significance tests.

Positivism is now unfashionable, having come under attack from (a) realism, which rejects empiricism and for explanations looks to the working of real mechanisms beyond experience that are causally responsible for what we observe; (b) hermeneutics, which rejects the unity of science thesis and accords primary attention within the human sciences to the meaningfulness that pervades the social world; and (c) CRITICAL THEORY, which rejects the control thesis in favour of human emancipation through interpretive analysis of society.   PH

Reading

†Ayer, A.J. ed.: *Logical Positivism*. London: Allen & Unwin, 1959.

Comte, A.: *Cours de philosophie positive* (1830–42); *The Positive Philosophy of Auguste Comte*, trans. and condensed H. Martineau. London: Chapman, 1853.

Fay, B.: *Social Theory and Political Practice*. London: Allen & Unwin, 1975.

†Halfpenny, P.: *Positivism and Sociology: Explaining Social Life*. London: Allen & Unwin, 1982.

Hempel, C.G. ed.: *Aspects of Scientific Explanation*. New York: Free Press, 1965.

Kolakowski, L.: *Positivist Philosophy: from Hume to the Vienna Circle*. Harmondsworth: Penguin, 1972.

Neurath, O., Hahn, H. and Carnap, R.: The scientific conception of the world: the Vienna Circle. In O. Neurath, *Empiricism and Sociology*, ed. M. Neurath and R.S. Cohen. Dordrecht: Reidel, 1973.

Stockman, N.: *Antipositivist Theories of the Sciences: Critical Rationalism, Critical Theory and Scientific Realism*. Dordrecht: Reidel, 1983.

positivism, legal See LAW.

power The concept of power is ubiquitous in political discourse and in political analysis. Yet, like many of the concepts constitutive of political discourse, 'power' is defined and used in different ways by different analysts. Some contemporary commentators have, indeed, suggested that power is an 'essentially contested concept' whose meaning and criteria of application are forever in dispute (see Lukes, *Power: a Radical View*; Connolly). Yet, despite their disagreements as to how the concept should be defined, most analysts are agreed that 'power' refers, at a minimum, to one agent or agency affecting the attitudes and/or actions of another.

The English word 'power' comes by way of the French *pouvoir* which in turn derives from the Latin *potestas* or *potentia*, meaning 'ability' (both from the verb *potere*, to be able). For the Romans, *potentia* referred to the capacity or ability of one person or thing to affect another. *Potestas*, having a more narrowly political sense, referred to the peculiar abilities possessed by people communicating and acting in concert; we capture something of that concept today when we say that there is strength in numbers. CICERO drew the distinction, *Potestas in populo, auctoritas in senatu* ('power in the people, authority in the senate'); and it is important to note that power was carefully distinguished from other concepts such as AUTHORITY, coercion, force, and VIOLENCE.

Since the seventeenth century, however, these older distinctions and discriminations have been eroded or obliterated. The revolution in the natural sciences brought in its wake an attempt to make the study of politics similarly scientific and rigorous. One of the first philosophers to extend the idiom of the new science to the study of politics – and to 'power' in particular – was Thomas HOBBES. True to the mechanistic imagery of the new science, Hobbes redefines power as a relation between cause and effect, between an active pushing 'agent' and a passive 'patient':

Power and Cause are the same thing. Correspondent to cause and effect, are power and act; nay, those and these are the same things . . . For whensoever any agent has all those accidents [i.e. combined features] which are necessarily requisite for the production of some effect in the patient, then we say that the agent has the *power* to produce that effect, if it be applied to a patient. . . . Wherefore the *power of the agent* and the *efficient cause* are the same thing (*De corpore*, ch. 10).

Although this mechanistic-causal picture of the power relation had all the advantages of simplicity, it was not without its difficulties. For example, despite Hobbes's hope of reducing human action to mechanistic pushes and pulls, he could not get away from the older Aristotelian view that all things aim at some end and that human action necessarily involves some view of the good. This is especially evident in the exercise of power. So far as human beings are concerned the acquisition and exercise of power is inevitably connected with an agent's having some view of the good and an intention to bring it about. (There is, needless to say, no counterpart to this in the natural sciences.) For Hobbesian egoists living in a world of scarcity, all agents will attempt to bring about their own good, which each equates with the satisfaction of his desires. Hobbes therefore 'put[s] for a generall inclination of all mankind, a perpetuall and restlesse desire of Power after power, that ceaseth onely in Death' (*Leviathan*, vol. I, ch. 11). This desire can only be kept under control by the supreme power of the sovereign.

Variations on these Hobbesian themes are to be found in the writings of twentieth-century social scientists and social philosophers. Max WEBER, for example, defined power as 'the probability that one actor in a social relationship will . . . carry out his own will' against the resistance of others (*Economy and Society*, vol. I, p. 53). Nor has Hobbes's mechanistic, push-pull picture entirely lost its lustre. Robert Dahl suggests that 'our ideas about underlying measures of [power or] influence rest on intuitive notions very similar to those on which the idea of force rests in mechanics'. The 'underlying idea in both cases' is essentially the same (*Modern Political Analysis*, p. 41). Similarly, A. S. McFarland maintains that: 'The idea of force essentially refers to a cause that *pushes*; definitions of power based on force differentials refer to what happens when a first causal agent pushes one way (force) and a second causal agent pushes another way (resistance). The stronger push or stronger force is the "stronger" cause, i.e. the more powerful agent' (*Power and Leadership*, p. 11).

For 'behavioural' political scientists – particularly those of the 'pluralist' persuasion – an exercise of power is a relation in which one actor C makes an observable attempt to cause another actor R to do what C intends but that R would not otherwise do. If C's 'power attempt' succeeds, then C is said to have power over R with respect to the particular 'issue area' over which they openly disagreed (see the essays by Simon, Dahl, Polsby, and Riker in Bell *et al.*) Until quite recently this understanding of 'power' was predominant in political science, particularly in the United States.

Over the last two decades, however, the behavioural-pluralist conception of power has come under increasingly heavy attack, less because it is mistaken than because it is partial and one-sided or 'one-dimensional' (see Lukes, *Power: a Radical View*). According to the 'two-dimensional' account advanced by Peter Bachrach and Morton Baratz (in Bell *et al.*), political power is Janus-faced. They readily concede that the pluralists are right about one aspect or 'face' of power, namely power that is exercised in an overt and observable way. But power has another, hidden face. Power may in some instances be exercised covertly and in ways that are not directly observable. For instance, C might exercise power by controlling the agenda, thereby limiting discussion, debate, and decision-making to 'safe' issues which do not threaten C's interests. Or C might be able to take advantage of biases built into the political system that tend to favour C's interests over R's. Or again R, anticipating defeat and/or reprisal, might be unwilling to challenge C on a particular issue. The fact that there are no observable challenges or overt power attempts does not necessarily mean that no power is being exercised. On the contrary, it may well mean that power is being exercised even more effectively.

The one- and two-dimensional views of power have in their turn been challenged by an alternative, 'three-dimensional' view. According to Steven Lukes (*Power: a Radical View*), the two-dimensional critique of the pluralist account does not go far enough. For although all three views agree in assuming that C has power over R when C affects R 'in a manner contrary to R's interests', the first two

make the further and more problematic assumption that would-be challengers do in fact know what their real INTERESTS are. This, Lukes objects, is a large and often unwarranted assumption. For *R* may have mistaken beliefs about *R*'s interests. Indeed, the most effective way in which *C* can exercise power over *R* is to shape *R*'s very beliefs about what is and is not in *R*'s interest. To the degree that *C* can instil and take advantage of *R*'s false or mistaken interpretation of *R*'s interests, *C*'s power is well-nigh complete, and all the greater for its being virtually invisible to those over whom it is exercised.

With its emphasis upon 'objective' interests, the three-dimensional view of power has affinities with the Marxian notion of 'false consciousness'. Someone suffering from false consciousness labours under the illusion that his 'subjective' or perceived interests – those instilled by, and benefiting, a ruling class, caste, or group – are his real or 'objective' interests. These may be individual, group, or class interests. But there are also, Lukes insists – in a way that owes more to KANT than to Marx – interests that we have simply by virtue of being human. Whether they are aware of it or not, human beings have an objective (or, in Kantian terms, a transcendental) interest in autonomy. Hence slaves who see their lot as normal and natural, or wage-labourers who are utterly uncritical of the capitalist system, or Indian 'untouchables' who accept the Hindu caste system, are arguably unaware of their objective interests.

Not surprisingly, much of the criticism of the three-dimensional view of power has centred upon its quasi-Kantian, neo-Marxian conception of objective interests, along with the claim that 'power' is an 'essentially contestable' concept. Lukes's critics contend that he cannot coherently claim that power is essentially contestable *and* that his three-dimensional view is analytically superior to alternative conceptualizations (see Oppenheim; Gray). Other critics claim that the three-dimensional view cannot be empirically applied and tested, while defenders (most notably, Gaventa) argue that it can. This controversy continues.

Another current controversy concerns the apparent incompatibility of 'intentionalist' and 'structuralist' understandings of power. According to the former, every exercise of power necessarily involves the intentions of an identifiable agent. According to the latter, however, intentions are analytically irrelevant, because power is a property of impersonal social 'structures', not of individual agents and their aims or aspirations. Socio-economic systems are self-maintaining structures in which individuals figure only as interchangeable and readily replaceable 'role-bearers'. This structuralist perspective on power is not tied to any particular political or ideological perspective; indeed it is, in different versions, common to conservative sociologists (e.g. Talcott Parsons) and to some neo-Marxists alike (e.g. Louis ALTHUSSER and Nicos Poulantzas). Some social theorists suggest that the two perspectives are compatible after all, since each stands in a 'dialectical' relation to the other (see Lukes, *Essays*). More recently, Michel FOUCAULT has proposed a radical reconceptualization of 'power'. Attempting to move beyond Hobbes's and Weber's negative or conflictual characterization, Foucault emphasizes the positive 'empowering' possibilities of power relations.

The continuing controversy over 'power' is not traceable to any lack of ingenuity on the part of proponents of different views. On the contrary, it may be because 'power' is such a central concept in political discourse that its meaning is so often and so heatedly contested. Simply to stipulate a definition will surely not suffice, since that is not to avoid conceptual controversy but to participate in it.   TB

Reading

Ball, T.: Models of power: past and present. *Journal of the History of the Behavioral Sciences* 11 (1975) 211–22.

†Bell, R., Edwards, D.V. and Wagner, R.H. eds: *Political Power: a Reader in Theory and Research.* London: Collier-Macmillan, 1969.

†Connolly, W.E.: *The Terms of Political Discourse*, 2nd edn, chs 1–3. Princeton, NJ: Princeton University Press, 1983.

Dahl, R.A.: *Modern Political Analysis.* Englewood Cliffs, NJ: Prentice-Hall, 1963.

Foucault, M.: *Power/Knowledge*, ed. C. Gordon. New York: Pantheon; Brighton: Harvester, 1980.

†Gaventa, J.: *Power and Powerlessness: Quiescence and Rebellion in an Appalachian Valley.* Urbana, Ill.: University of Illinois Press, 1980.

Gray, J.: Political power, social theory, and essential contestability. In *The Nature of Political Theory*, ed. D. Miller and L. Siedentop. Oxford: Clarendon Press, 1983.

Hobbes, T.: *Leviathan* (1651), ed. C.B. Macpherson. Harmondsworth: Penguin, 1968.

†Lukes, S.: *Power: a Radical View*. London: Macmillan, 1974.

———: Power and structure. In *Essays in Social Theory*. London: Macmillan, 1977.

McFarland, A.S.: *Power and Leadership in Pluralist Systems*. Stanford, Calif.: Stanford University Press, 1969.

Oppenheim, F.: *Political Concepts: a Reconstruction*, chs 2 and 3. Chicago: University of Chicago Press, 1981.

Weber, M.: *Economy and Society*, vol. I, ed. G. Roth and C. Wittich. New York: Bedminster, 1968.

†Wrong, D.: *Power: its Forms, Bases, and Uses*. Oxford: Blackwell, 1979.

Price, Richard (1723–1791) British moralist. Price was an ethical rationalist whose sermon in defence of the French Revolution, *Discourse on the Love of Our Country* (1789), provoked BURKE's celebrated attack. See RADICALS, BRITISH.

Priestley, Joseph (1733–1804) British chemist, theologian and philosopher. His *Essay on the First Principles of Government* (1768) helped to inspire BENTHAM's utilitarianism. Later he enraged public opinion through his attack on BURKE. See RADICALS, BRITISH.

privacy Concern with privacy is as old as life in society; however, discussions of the concept and calls for its protection are of relatively recent origin. It is by now generally admitted that privacy is an important element in human relationships, and it has been accorded protection in a number of international documents enumerating universally recognized human rights.

The scope of the concept itself is rather controversial, but all agree that it is related to issues of information, seclusion, and attention. Some add to the list concerns with liberty of action in 'private' affairs, presentation to others in a false light, use of one's name or identifying features (such as voice or picture) for another's purposes, mainly in commercial contexts, and freedom from unwanted exposure to noise, smell, or sight. Determination of exact conceptual boundaries are thus necessarily to some extent a matter of stipulation.

The core of the concept of privacy includes issues related to the acquisition, maintenance, and dissemination of information about a person; to the extent the person can control access of others to him; and to the power of the individual to maintain anonymity. All these are related, but they form distinct parts of the concept of privacy. This core concept distinguishes privacy from secrecy, and connects the former to *persons* only; the secrecy of commercial organizations or of government are not seen as raising issues of privacy.

There is a pervasive descriptive-normative ambiguity in uses of 'privacy' and 'private', which must be attended to if we want to avoid confusion. Thus 'private' may at times mean 'that which is in fact unknown (inaccessible)', and at times it means 'that which should be unknown' either according to existing norms, or according to norms which the speaker wishes to advocate. In many arguments about the desirable extent of protection, unjustified moves are made from the descriptive to the normative. In other cases, arguments are circular because they switch without warning from an appeal to existing norms to an appeal to ideal norms (for example, in the statement that there is no justified claim of privacy concerning events occurring in public places).

The modern intensification of concern with privacy as related to information stems from a combination of new and greater threats to privacy on the one hand, and a strengthened awareness of the relationship of privacy to important ideals of the person and society on the other. The greater threats are related in part to technological developments. There is now a variety of sophisticated devices for acquisition of information (such as electronic following and eavesdropping, and long-range photography). Computers provide almost unlimited capacities for retention, accumulation, processing, merging, and retrieval of information. In addition, dissemination of information and attracting attention may be instant and worldwide. In some other respects our societies are more private than those our ancestors lived in: most of us have more anonymity than they could have hoped (or maybe wished) for. Nonetheless, the nature of the new technological threats does mean that the precautions we usually take to protect our privacy from others would not be adequate against a determined attempt to invade our privacy. Some regulation may therefore be necessary.

It is not universally agreed that privacy, in the sense of some areas in which the individual can control information, access, and attention, is indeed an ideal: some say that the modern preoccupation with privacy is just another indication of a dangerous individualism which is an aspect of ALIENATION. Others claim that the main function of privacy is to facilitate deceit: people do not need privacy if they have nothing to conceal. Most scholars agree, however, that some balance of privacy is essential both to individual ideals such as autonomy, mental health, creativity, growth, learning, and the capacity to form human relationships; and to the social ideals of an open, free, and democratic society. The new intensity of the concern with privacy is based on the awareness that only by cherishing it can we develop the kind of persons and institutions we deem desirable.

Claims of privacy become an issue whenever there is a conflict of wishes or interests regarding the quantity and quality of information about an individual others should have. Typical conflicts concern areas where people claim to need the information as the basis of some decision that they are required or permitted to make, or in satisfaction of their 'right to know', whereas the individual involved either denies the need or argues that his or her own interest in privacy is overriding. In general, such conflicts cannot be decided merely on a want-satisfaction level. Resolution of the conflicts must go beyond the wishes to the interests and values which their satisfaction may promote.

By now most legal systems have accepted that privacy is a proper subject for *legal* protection, thus settling a long-term controversy between scholars on this question. Legal protection involves both a resolution of the moral conflict and a decision that the law is the proper way of protecting this solution. Some legal systems

protect privacy as such, others protect areas of privacy under other labels. The regulation of computerized data-banks seeks to limit indiscriminate dissemination of information, and to put limits on acquisition, access and retention. In addition to privacy, this regulation seeks to promote accuracy, updatedness, and completeness of data. The law is also concerned with modes of acquisition of information both by law enforcement officials and by private individuals. The right not to incriminate oneself is partly justified in terms of the wish to protect privacy and the values supported by it. Wiretapping, searches and seizures, mandatory medical examinations are all seen to raise issues of privacy. In some contexts the law imposes duties of confidentiality and privileges in order to guarantee privacy. The most controversial question is that of regulating dissemination of true information about individuals, conflicting with freedom of expression, which is designed to promote some of the ideals deemed to be connected to privacy as well, notably democracy. RG

Reading

Benn, S.I. and Gaus, G.F. eds: *Public and Private in Social Life.* London: Croom Helm, 1983.

Parent, W.A.: Recent work on the concept of privacy. *American Philosophical Quarterly* 20 (1983) 341–55.

†Pennock, J.R. and Chapman, J.W. eds: *Nomos XIII: Privacy.* New York: Atherton, 1971.

†Schoeman, F. ed.: *Philosophical Dimensions of Privacy.* Cambridge: Cambridge University Press, 1984.

†Westin, A.: *Privacy and Freedom.* New York: Atheneum, 1967.

progress The idea of progress is one of the master-ideas of western civilization, reaching back to ancient Greece and Rome. Other civilizations have known ideas of perfectibility and of achievement of virtue, wisdom, and happiness, but these concepts have been directed to individuals alone, not to all humanity or whole peoples. The western idea of progress is distinctive because it centres exactly upon all humanity; mankind is envisaged as having begun its history in ignorance, squalor and fear, and thereafter having risen slowly and continuously to ever-higher levels in the arts and sciences, in its command of environment, and in knowledge generally. The idea of progress is more than a eudemonic idea: it is, as J. B. Bury termed it, 'a synthesis of the past and prophecy of the future'; it is a framework of perception and thought.

Although we tend to think of it as exclusively modern, the idea of progress is clearly present in ancient Greek and Roman, and also early Christian, thought. Protagoras, PLATO, Zeno, Lucretius, and SENECA all wrote of the ascent of humanity from primitivism to ever-greater knowledge in the arts and sciences. Moreover this advance was firmly held to extend to the future, occupying 'thousands of centuries' in Seneca's rendering. While classical thought also contains ideas of cyclical recurrence and of fall or decline from an original golden age, the Greek and Romans were well acquainted with the idea of linear progress.

So were the Christian fathers in their work of constructing what we know as the Christian epic. St AUGUSTINE, in *The City of God*, made the 'education of the human race' fundamental; moreover, as we see in Book 22 of that work, his envisagement of this education through time could be quite as secular in substance as that of any Greek or later westerner. St Augustine's greatest contribution to the perspective of progress was the idea of necessity, of inevitability. Not only, he tells us, has man's knowledge, sacred and profane, advanced through distinct stages, but such advance has been *necessary*; necessary because God in his very creation endowed humanity with the appropriate capacity. The remarkable Joachim de Fiore in the twelfth century depicted Augustinian faith in divine progress as a three-stage process, an image that would remain evocative for the next six centuries in western thought.

A great deal of the philosophy of progress of the eighteenth and nineteenth century is simply a secularization of Augustine's Christian epic. Such influential minds as Leibnitz, KANT, CONDORCET, HEGEL, COMTE, and MARX carry forward into modernity the Augustinian vision of a unitary and progressive human race, of a single time-frame for all humanity, one into which the histories of all known peoples can be fitted in ascending order, of conflict as the motor of human progress, and, finally, of the causal necessity of the entire panorama of development. What we see in the modern period pre-eminently is the translation of divine necessity into a claimed natural or purely human necessity. For Marx, struggle between classes occupied the same causal role in human history as the struggle between the Two Cities had in Augustine.

In many ways the greatest use of the idea of progress in the modern West has been as a kind of taxonomy for the world's peoples. From the sixteenth century, the question was asked: how do we account for, give order to, the vast diversity of peoples and their cultures which missionaries and explorers revealed to westerners in their reports? There were several possible answers of course, but one of them, destined to be the most popular, was furnished by the idea of progress. Geo-cultural differences could be seen simply as differences in stages of development. Thus TURGOT, Comte, Marx, Tylor, and many other students of social evolution, past and present, have chosen to explain all major social and cultural differences among the world's peoples as differences in degree of progress in a single time-frame, and one, of course, in which Western Europe is deemed the most developed, the most progressive.

In the eighteenth and nineteenth centuries little if any differentiation of meaning existed between 'progress', 'evolution', and 'development'. This was as true in the study of biology as of the social sciences. The social evolutionary schemes of Condorcet, Comte, Hegel, Marx, and J. S. MILL all had their origins in pre-Darwinian channels of thought, though in the latter part of the nineteenth century there arose theories of human progress based upon mechanisms of struggle and conflict which were labelled SOCIAL DARWINISM. Darwin himself had full confidence in the progressive course of biological evolution that he set forth in his *Origin of Species* in 1859. When Marx read this work, he was initially impressed by the parallels between Darwin's thesis and his own (though his later verdict was more guarded). It was Herbert SPENCER, though, at once biological and sociological evolutionist, and prophet of progress in every sphere, who appeared in the later nineteenth century as probably the foremost herald of progress. He said that progress, by virtue of its inextricable root in purely natural, human processes, 'is not an accident but a necessity'.

The picture is certainly different in the twentieth century. There are probably more visions of disaster, of decadence, and decline, than there have been since the ancient world. Even so, as in that classical civilization, the twentieth-century mind continues to have room for the idea of progress. It remains the official vision of all Marxist countries, it has been sanctified by the Roman Catholic Teilhard de Chardin, at once archaeologist and prophet, and all recent studies of 'Small Town', 'Middle Town', and 'Metropolis' show that with varying degrees of fervour, faith in the progress of humanity persists. Equally telling, perhaps, is the increasing, and largely unquestioned, adoption of the philosophy of progress as national and international policy – the last seen most vividly in the continued division of the world's peoples into the 'undeveloped' and the 'developed' and in the unapologetic parading of the West's own peculiar pattern of development as a universal norm.   RN

Reading

†Bury, J.B.: *The History of the Idea of Progress*. London: Macmillan, 1920.

Cochrane, C.N.: *Christianity and Classical Culture*. New York: Oxford University Press, 1957.

Edelstein, L.: *The Idea of Progress in Classical Antiquity*. Baltimore: The Johns Hopkins University Press, 1942.

Lovejoy, A.O.: *The Great Chain of Being*. Cambridge, Mass.: Harvard University Press, 1942.

Nisbet, R.: *Social Change and History*. New York: Oxford University Press, 1969.

†——: *History of the Idea of Progress*. New York: Basic, 1980.

Teggart, F.J.: *Theory of History*. New Haven, Conn.: Yale University Press, 1925.

—— ed.: *The Idea of Progress: a collection of readings*. Berkeley: University of California Press, 1929.

Tuveson, E.L.: *Millennium and Utopia: a study in the background of the idea of progress*. New York: Harper Torchbooks, 1964.

proletariat   A value-laden term for the poorest class in society, implying that its members lead a hand-to-mouth existence and are excluded from the full benefits of citizenship. In Marxist usage, the proletariat are identified with the urban working class in contrast to peasants, etc., but other thinkers use the term synoptically to cover all the 'dispossessed'. See CLASS, MARXISM.   DLM

property   The rights and duties associated with property distribute between individuals and collectivities a variety of powers and liabilities to determine what shall happen to 'things' which are property. These things may be more or less material or abstract: a house is a physical object, but a copyright is not. The indeterminacy of the 'things' which may be property is compounded by a dual meaning of property. In many contexts the term refers to the thing, the house or copyright. But it is also used to refer to the legal relation which exists between a person and the thing, which is of course always an abstraction. The difference may be brought out by considering the example of lost property offices. These take care of things which have been misplaced, either by the owner or by someone who had the use and possession of them. Whilst the 'thing' may be misplaced, like the briefcase left behind inadvertently at the end of a railway journey, the property considered as a legal relation does not come to an end and is not extinguished unless the person to whom the property belongs fails to claim it within a set period.

As a social institution, property has exhibited great variety both in the sorts of things it has encompassed and in the ways in which the relation between a person and the object of property has been conceived. A full description of the legal arrangements governing property in any particular society would necessarily be complicated by these facts. As a contributor to a nineteenth-century encyclopaedia observed:

A complete view of property, as recognized by any given system of law, would embrace the following heads, which it would be necessary to exhaust, in order that the view should be complete. It would embrace an enumeration of all the kinds and classes of things which are objects of property: the exposition of the greatest amount of power over things which a man can legally exercise; and, connected with this, the different interests which persons may have in a thing which is an object of property; the modes in which property is legally transferred from one person to another, or acquired or lost; the capacity of particular classes of person to acquire and transfer property as above understood, or, to take the other view of this division, an enumeration of persons who labour under legal incapacities as to the acquisition and loss of property. (*National Cyclopaedia of Useful Knowledge*, vol IX, p. 871.)

We might conclude that such an account of a legal property system would exhaust the researcher as well as the headings listed by this encyclopaedist. Two further points arise. First, property is subject to social convention and the operation of public opinion as well as to law. For example, many Christian writers have felt that the possession or ownership of private property carries with it a duty of charity, a willingness to relieve the need of others. This duty, however, need not be imposed by legal provision. For this reason, even the complete exposition of a legal system of property would not reveal all that we might want to know about its social implications. Second, property is obviously related to ownership; the greatest amount of power over things which a man can legally exercise is usually in the hands of the person treated as owner. Providing an account of 'liberal ownership', A. M. Honoré lists a number of rights and liabilities (which he calls collectively 'incidents') which, taken together, make up this 'greatest' power. Ownership thus conceived may be split or divided, since the incidents in question may be attached to a number of different persons each of whom has some property interest, making it difficult to identify any one owner. Nor can we say with confidence which of the rights is most important, since this will depend on the purpose of our inquiry. Honoré draws attention to the rights to possess, to use, to manage, and to an income, to the capital and to security. Similarly, although 'public ownership' is usually intended to denote the antithesis of private ownership, it is used vaguely to cover a range of property arrangements, including nationalization and municipal ownership. Both private and public ownership are compatible with a dispersal of property interests, and the practical consequences may be very similar.

The distinction between the description of the legal system, and argument surrounding the moral status of property, draws attention to the fact that property is an institution which needs justification. We saw earlier that a description of property would attend to the mechanisms by which title to objects of property could be transferred. But knowledge of these mechanisms does nothing to explain the origins of property titles. An inquiry into the origins of property titles could, of course, be an historical investigation into the way in which property has developed or how in fact the present distribution of property has come about. For example, part of MARX's analysis of capitalism was an historical inquiry into the division which had emerged between those who owned capital and those who sold their labour-power. An inquiry into the origins of property could also, however, be concerned with the conditions under which a particular property system would be legitimate.

Legitimacy here could be tested by a range of considerations, such as harmony with God's purpose, compatibility with natural rights, or ability to realize a great range of values such as justice or liberty. Lawrence C. Becker has classified a range of such arguments for private property, and examined their coherence, in *Property Rights – Philosophic Foundations*. Of course, whatever system of property any particular person might favour (whether it be private property, common ownership, state property), some argument must be produced to explain why this is to be valued. Because productive activity has such a central role in society, property in productive resources is subjected to special scrutiny in assessments of the relationship between property and values such as liberty and justice. In addition, particular writers' conceptions of the nature of labour and of work (often, of course, derived from some particular conception of human nature) inform their theories about property. Alan Ryan has suggested that a useful distinction may be drawn between theorists who take an 'instrumental' view of property, and those who take a 'self-developmental' view. The instrumental view 'regards work or labour as a cost incurred by men who want to consume the goods thus made available to them' (p. 7). The self-developmental view is that work 'is, or can be, and certainly should be, intrinsically satisfying' and 'that the relationship between a man and what he *owns* is intrinsically significant; there is a substantial bond between a man and his property, a bond which repays philosophical analysis' (p. 11). But Ryan also brings out clearly that the holding of one or other of these views does not closely determine a writer's practical stance in property questions. A similar point may be made about commitment to values like liberty and justice: shared starting points do not always lead to shared conclusions about the legitimacy of property systems. This may be because of differences in the interpretation of those values. More frequently it occurs because of different analyses of the operation of economic systems.

Another aspect of the distinction between the description of legal practice, and the justification of property systems, is the issue of whether property is a legal institution which can exist only in the presence of political power, or whether it might be pre-political. Although utilitarians such as BENTHAM argued that property is a creature of law, impossible without a coercive apparatus to enforce sanctions, other writers have held that property could be pre-legal or non-political. They thought that convention or the law of nature would regulate property; or (and, sometimes, in addition) that individuals have rights which may be conceived as property rights (for example, over their bodies or their labour) which exist independently of legal recognition (see HUMAN RIGHTS). Such rights could therefore be the basis for an assessment of the legitimacy of a socially enforced property system. There are two problems with this approach. The first is concerned with the status of universal, non-legal or natural rights which are dismissed by some writers as without foundation. The second is connected to a broader issue, namely which of our rights should we think of as property rights?

There are two popular ways of answering this question in private property systems. The first draws on a distinction between property and contract as explanations for the origins of a person's rights. It is argued that a property interest may be asserted against anybody, whereas a contractual right may be asserted only against the other contractor. In the one case the property title grounds the claim, in the other the content of an agreement. The

distinction is not, however, very sharp. HOBBES, for example, thought that 'conjugal affection' was part of a man's property (p. 383). Furthermore, any general and non-consensual right might be treated as a property right, and was so treated by writers such as LOCKE. The second answer emphasizes another characteristic of property rights – their transferability. This view is favoured by some economists, who stress that the structure of property rights may be adjusted to make individuals, as far as possible, bear the costs and reap the benefits of their own activities, thus increasing efficiency. Property rights are thus treated as those which are transferable in a market.

Although neither answer is entirely satisfactory, each draws upon a central feature of private property, namely the power of exclusion which usually accompanies it. A person who owns private property is able to exclude others from using it or benefiting from it, even if the owner is subject to regulation of the uses to which the property may be put, and even if this exclusion is not complete. According to C. B. Macpherson, who has provided an interpretation of modern liberal theory, drawing attention to its 'possessive individualist' assumptions, the crux of the distinction between private property and common property is that the former should be conceived as a right to exclude others (from the use of the property) and the latter should be conceived as a right not to be excluded (p. 124). Of course, those with common property rights might be able to exclude non-commoners. Similarly, the use of public property is available to anybody who qualifies as a member of the relevant public.

Although private property is associated with rights to exclude, so that the right of use, for example, has to be granted by the owner, either freely or for value received in the market, common property may also require rationing procedures, even thought they are not necessarily ones provided by the market. A right not to be excluded does not guarantee access, any more than a right to exclude necessarily denies it. Everyone may have a right to sit on a seat in a public park, but not everyone can exercise the right at the same time. For this reason, those who argue that private property is undesirable have to specify alternative methods of allocating access to things, especially productive resources, and to show that the features of market-orientated private property to which they object will not be reproduced by those methods. Much of the controversy about property arises from rival claims about the market and alternative methods of allocation.   AWR

Reading

Anon.: Property. In *National Cyclopaedia of Useful Knowledge*. London: C. Knight, 1850.

†Becker, Lawrence C.: *Property Rights – Philosophic Foundations*. London: Routledge & Kegan Paul, 1977.

†Chapman, J. and Pennock, R. eds: *Nomos XXII: Property*. Chicago: Aldine Atherton, 1980.

Hobbes, T.: *Leviathan* (1651), ed. C.B. Macpherson. Harmondsworth: Penguin, 1968.

Honoré, A.M.: Ownership. In *Oxford Essays in Jurisprudence*, ed. A.G. Guest. Oxford: Oxford University Press, 1961.

Locke, J.: *Two Treatises of Government* (1689), ed. P. Laslett. New York: Mentor, 1965; Cambridge: Cambridge University Press, 1970.

Macpherson, C.B.: *Democratic Theory*. Oxford: Clarendon Press, 1973.

Marx, K.: *Capital*, vol. I, pt 8. Moscow: Foreign Languages Publishing House, 1957–9.

Reeve, A.: *Property*. London: Macmillan, 1986.

†Ryan, A.: *The Political Theory of Property*. Oxford: Blackwell, 1984.

†Snare, F.: The concept of property. *American Philosophical Quarterly* 9 (1972) 200–6.

Protagoras (*c.*490–*c.*415 BC) Greek philosopher. A leading Sophist, famous for his scepticism about claims to absolute knowledge, and one of the first political philosophers. See GREEK POLITICAL THOUGHT.

Proudhon,   Pierre-Joseph   (1809–1865) French anarchist. Proudhon grew up in Besançon, the son of a failed and litigous cooper. After being forced by his family's destitution to give up his scholarship at the local high school, he became a printer and continued his education by reading proofs, including one of a work by Fourier. In 1839, with a fellowship from the Besançon academy, he spent a year in Paris. After a time as managing clerk of a barge company in Lyons, where he associated with that city's radical textile workers, he returned to Paris, and remained there, except for his exile during the Second Empire, until the end of his life.

Proudhon first attracted wide attention during his period as an activist in the revolution of 1848 by winning a seat in the Constituent Assembly and, from his post as editor of a successful newspaper, by deftly criticizing all the revolutionary leaders. Perhaps his most famous act as a representative was to vote against the constitution which the assembly enacted, 'just because it was a constitution'. Before 1848 Proudhon had published several obscure books, one of which, *What is Property?* (1840–1), contains his famous dictum, 'Property is theft.' But it was in the decade of the 1850s that, disillusioned with politics by the failure of the revolution, he achieved most as a theorist in two works, *General Idea of the Revolution in the Nineteenth Century* (1851) and *On Justice in the Revolution and the Church* (1858), which, taken together, advance the first systematic argument for ANARCHISM. Proudhon died in 1865, just as he was softening his anarchism by seeking an alliance with the labour movement and admitting the need for a minimal state.

The chief contributions of Proudhon to political theory are his case against legal government and his model of a good 'mutualist' society in which social co-operation is secured without coercion by the state. Both his criticism and his proposal express his deep commitment to communal individuality, the goal he shares with other anarchists, who all seek to merge the greatest communal unity with the fullest self-development.

His argument against legal government proceeds by identifying characteristics which all legal governments possess and showing why these characteristics stunt individuals and break communal ties. Legal government is characterized by its location of authority in public officials who control behaviour with fixed, general rules, enforced by threats of physical punishment. Proudhon focuses on the concentrated authority and the coerciveness of this arrangement, but not the generality of its rules, as what make it inadmissible. By concentrating authority – the right to command – in a small number of officials who ensure obedience with physical force, legal government prevents ordinary people from acting on the basis of their independent judgments. Since the basis of self-development and communal solidarity lies, for Proudhon, in mental independence, he must forthrightly reject legal government.

Proudhon nonetheless recognizes the utility of legal government for maintaining social order. His scheme for the mutualist society which is to replace government therefore includes arrangements designed not only to encourage communal individuality but also to ensure peace. Rejecting the market for being exploitative and coercive, but above all for presupposing legal government, Proudhon looks instead to the bargaining process as the organizing mechanism in his good society. Under mutualism, individuals and groups negotiate directly with one another for whatever they want, until they reach acceptable terms of agreement. Since people who bargain freely exercise and follow their independent judgments, mutualist society seems to be a place where communal individuality will flourish.

Yet Proudhon recognizes the numerous deficiencies in the bargaining process which prevent it from serving as the sole organizing mechanism for a society that is either free or safe. His theory of mutualism is most penetrating where it specifies how bargaining must be regulated to secure its promised but elusive benefits. Insecurity is the most obvious danger in a society organized by means of bargaining. For such a society offers no protection to parties who are poor in negotiable assets from being crushed by their rivals. To give security to all the parties in a mutualist society, Proudhon insists that they have roughly equal power and that they be numerous, diverse, and self-sufficient enough to be reciprocally but not essentially dependent on one another. In a society with this kind of structure parties have an incentive to negotiate rather than fight for the things they seek, because they need but cannot dominate their rivals. Yet Proudhon, rather than counting on the structure of incentives to make mutualist society secure, relies also on moral principle by requiring a commitment from all parties to commutative justice, which imposes on each bargainer the duty of equivalent exchange. The members of a mutualist society are thus constrained by duty as well as interest to act safely as they exercise their independent judgment.

Faced with the practical problem of how to achieve mutualism in a hostile world, Proudhon vacillated between ineffective strategies in tune with his objective and more promising strategies which his objective rules out. At first he relied solely on reasoned argument. He then turned successively to a scheme for free credit, to collaboration with Louis-Napoleon Bonaparte, and, after 1863, to withdrawal by the partisans of mutualism into their own exemplary institutions. During the period 1855–63 he scarcely concerned himself with strategy, being content to await the revolution while composing theoretically-oriented books.

Proudhon has always been a controversial figure among interpreters. His first reputation was that of a revolutionary leveller. MARX derided him as an apologist for *petit bourgeois* private property. Sections of the Catholic Right, following Charles MAURRAS, have revered him for his defence of traditional values. A case has even been made for calling him a fascist. Part of the reason why Proudhon has been so variously interpreted is that he thought aloud in print, writing polemically and discursively on a vast range of topics from stock market speculation to religion and art. But when attention is focused on his political writings, unity and coherence are evident. His description and defence of a society where persons who exercise independent judgment achieve self-expression and social unity establish Proudhon as one of anarchism's most persuasive exponents.   AIR

Reading
Haubtmann, P.: *La philosophie sociale de Pierre-Joseph Proudhon*. Grenoble: Presse Universitaire de Grenoble, 1980.

Hoffman, R.: *Revolutionary Justice: the Social and Political Thought of P.-J. Proudhon*. Champaign-Urbana, Ill.: University of Illinois Press, 1972.

Proudhon, P.-J.: *What is Property?*, trans. B.R. Tucker. London: William Reeves, n.d.

———: *General Idea of the Revolution in the Nineteenth Century*, trans. J. Robinson. New York: Haskell House, 1969.

———: *De la Justice dans la révolution et dans l'église*. Paris: Marcel Rivière, 1930–5 .

———: *The Principle of Federation* (1863), trans. R. Vernon. Toronto: University of Toronto Press, 1979.

†Ritter, A.: *The Political Thought of Pierre-Joseph*

Proudhon. Princeton, NJ: Princeton University Press, 1969.

Watkins, F.: Proudhon and the theory of modern liberalism. *Canadian Journal of Economics and Political Science* 13 (1947) 429–35.

†Woodcock, G.: *Pierre-Joseph Proudhon: a Biography*. New York: Macmillan, 1956.

public interest See INTERESTS.

Pufendorf, Samuel (1632–1694) German natural law philosopher. Born in Lutheran Saxony, Pufendorf was educated at Leipzig and Jena, taught at Heidelberg (1660–7) and Lund (1667–86), and from then until his death was historian to the Brandenburg court under the patronage of the Great Elector, Frederick William of Prussia. His major works on natural law are *Elements of Universal Jurisprudence* (1660), an attempt to apply geometrical reasoning to political and moral philosophy, and his two most famous works: the monumental *On the Law of Nature and Nations* (1672), which served as an essential textbook for European law and philosophy students for over a hundred years, and its epitome, *On the Duty of Man and Citizen according to Natural Law* (1673). He replied to the widespread Aristotelian and Scholastic criticism of his natural law theory in a series of articles, published as *Scandinavian Polemics* (1686). In addition, he wrote a contentious analysis of disunited Germany, *On the Constitution of the German Empire* (1667) and defended it in *Select Scholarly Essays* (1675). His later career was dominated by historical and religious writing: the lectures, *Introduction to the History of the Great Empires and States of Contemporary Europe* (1682–5), a history of contemporary Swedish affairs, a Protestant consideration of religious policy in response to the revocation of the Edict of Nantes, *On the Relation of the Christian Life to Civil Life* (1686), and a posthumously published history of Frederick III containing a defence of the Glorious Revolution of 1688–9 in England.

Like most seventeenth-century political thought Pufendorf's theory is a response both on the practical side to the horrors of the Thirty Years War and to the consolidation of sovereign, mercantile states, and on the intellectual side to the complementary destruction of traditional Aristotelian, Scholastic and Humanist moral and political certainties by the sceptical crisis, initiated by MONTAIGNE and Pierre Charron. Pufendorf followed GROTIUS in reconstructing political theory on the basis of a minimum natural law of self-preservation. From this base natural duties and rights of self-defence and protection of property could be deduced with certainty, and these in turn could be used as moral standards to determine the rightness, wrongness or indifference of any action or social relation. This minimum notion of preservation was thought to be immune to attacks by moral sceptics, acceptable to all the warring Christian factions in Europe, and free of the higher moral claims of the old theories which, Pufendorf argued, led to the wars of religion. The duty of preservation provided a basis for a modern theory of INTERNATIONAL LAW. It also furnished absolute monarchs with a non-sectarian justification for internal and external defence and for the new mercantile policies of preserving the strength and power of the population.

In response to Grotius's rationalist conclusion that natural law would exist even if God did not, Pufendorf re-introduced the view that sanctions are an essential feature of law and so natural law is binding in virtue of the threat of divine punishment and the hope of divine reward. The fear of God is thus an essential feature of any moral-political order. Furthermore, the reduction of natural law to rights and duties of self-preservation undercut any justification of distributive justice, as HOBBES had shown in *De cive*. Pufendorf therefore introduced the idea that, in certain situations, 'imperfect' rights (moral claims on others to basic needs) could become legal claims, thus opening the door to a larger role for the preservationist state.

Pufendorf also responded to Hobbes's disturbing argument that the natural condition of man was one of rights without duties, by advancing his immensely influential thesis that all rights necessarily correlate with duties. Man's duties are underwritten by a natural motive of sociability, and this Stoic device counter-balances the Epicurean motive of self-interest that Hobbes had correctly discerned.

Finally, Pufendorf provided a more logically and historically complex account of the transition from the state of nature to the formation of the state, which produced a more sophisticated defence of the view that the absolute monarchies of Europe were formed by the people individually *alienating* (not delegating) their rights of preservation to the monarch. Even writers such as LOCKE and ROUSSEAU, who sought to transform this tradition, turned to Pufendorf for their general framework.

Pufendorf's influence in the eighteenth century was enormous. He was particularly well served by Jean Barbeyrac, who republished his major works in Latin and French with copious notes and commentary. Through these texts Pufendorf's detailed application of the natural law tradition was transmitted to the thinkers of the ENLIGHTENMENT.   JT

Reading

†Kreiger, L.: *The Politics of Discretion: Pufendorf and the Acceptance of Natural Law*. Chicago: University of Chicago Press, 1965.

Pufendorf, S.: *Elementorum jurisprudentiae universalis, libri duo* (*Elements of Universal Jurisprudence*), Latin-English edn, trans. C.H. and W.A. Oldfather. In *The Classics of International Law*, ed. J.B. Scott. Oxford: Clarendon Press, 1931.

†————: *De jure naturae et gentium* (*On the Law of Nature and Nations*), Latin-English edn, trans. C.H. and W.A. Oldfather. In *The Classics of International Law*, 1934.

————: *De officio hominis et civis juxta legem naturalem* (*On the Duty of Man and Citizen according to Natural Law*), Latin-English edn, trans. F.G. Moore. In *The Classics of International Law*, 1927.

Welzel, H.: *Die naturrechtslehre Samuel Pufendorfs*. Berlin: de Gruyter, 1958.

punishment Within political society punishment is generally defined as the infliction by a state authority of some measure which is generally regarded as unpleasant upon an individual or, more rarely, a group, as a response to the commission by that individual or group of an offence against the criminal law of the state. The basic elements of this definition are relatively uncontroversial, the main debate focusing on the nature of the justification for the practice of state punishment.

Two main theories of punishment have been advanced in the history of political thought; one is retributivist, the other utilitarian. The retributivist or just deserts theory, defended in its strongest form by KANT, argues that the voluntary commission of an offence constitutes both a necessary and a sufficient condition for justified punishment, by reason of the moral desert of the offender. Desert is defined in terms of the culpability of the offender, culpability being a function of the state of mind with which the offence was committed (such as intention, recklessness, or, more controversially, negligence) combined with the gravity of the harm which the offence has caused. For the retributivist, the offender's desert indicates not only who may be punished and for what reason, but also what measure of punishment is justified; that which is proportionate to the offender's culpability. The primitive law of the talion, 'an eye for an eye and a tooth for a tooth', has been displaced by a more subtle approach to the explication both of the desert principle and of the relationship of equivalence or proportionality between offence and punishment. This approach, perhaps best understood in the context of a SOCIAL CONTRACT view of political society, argues that when an offender voluntarily breaks the criminal law, he or she takes an unfair advantage as compared with his or her law-abiding fellow citizens. This creates a moral disequilibrium which must be redressed by punishment, the severity of which is dictated by the need to remove the unfair advantage, however great or small it may be.

By contrast, the utilitarian or consequentialist position, well illustrated by the writings of BENTHAM, seeks to justify punishment not on the basis that it is a fair response to past voluntary action but on the basis that it is effective to increase the balance of pleasure over pain in society, typically by deterring future offences by both the offender and other members of society (see UTILITARIANISM). Many different types of beneficial consequences have been claimed by utilitarian writers to justify state punishment. Apart from individual and general deterrence secured by the unpleasantness of the experience of punishment and by the threat of its infliction, writers have argued that it should be used to reform or rehabilitate the offender, to educate and maintain moral standards in society, to denounce crime, to satisfy the grievance-desires of victims, and to uphold respect for the legal system. Given this variety, it would be a mistake automatically to classify all utilitarian theories in one category, for the various aims disclose very different conceptions of the role of the state in maintaining and enforcing the criminal law. However, all utilitarian theories do share the feature, in sharp distinction to retributivism, that they are in principle susceptible of empirical validation. Thus the twentieth century has witnessed a growth of interest among sociologists who are engaged not only in theorizing about the place of punishment in society but also in attempting to test the efficacy of punitive programmes designed to reform, deter, or educate actual or potential offenders.

Clearly, each of these main traditions captures an important feature of our settled intuitions about the proper basis of punishment. Yet there is little consensus among philosophers and political theorists, except perhaps as to the view that there must exist some justification for a practice so widely felt to constitute a fundamental cornerstone of a well-ordered society. Utilitarians argue that the retributivist theory is fraught with mystery and confusion, and that when its metaphorical language is cleared away, what we are left with is a mere axiom that past culpable acts generate a reason for present punitive action on the basis of desert; a proposition which is uncomfortably close to the assertion that two wrongs make a right. The opponents of retributivism argue that a theory which would dictate punishment even where it could achieve no benefits in either social or individual terms purports to justify what is pointless and indeed unjust. Furthermore, doubts have been raised about the adequacy of retributive theory when tested against criminal justice systems approximately like our own: does all offending really involve moral culpability? How can retributivism explain the fact that we believe that not all actions which are morally culpable should be proscribed and punished by the criminal law? These arguments point not so much to the incoherence of the desert principle as to its need for supplementation by arguments about the nature of the obligation to obey the law and the proper limits of the criminal law; but they nevertheless add to the impression that retributivism alone cannot capture all that is important about the practice of punishment.

The utilitarian is equally vulnerable to the retributivist's counter-arguments. These aver that the utilitarian treats the subject of punishment merely as a means to a social end, and not as an end in itself, which offends against the fundamental principle of respect for persons as moral agents. Moreover, in the pursuit of certain utilitarian aims, it is not clear that the punishment needs to be inflicted at all, or, if it must be imposed, it may not matter whether it is inflicted upon the offender or upon a scapegoat. For a generally deterrent effect to be secured, all that is strictly necessary is that citizens should believe in the threat of punishment; if a pretence could be maintained, it might never be necessary or even justified to punish anyone. Furthermore, if social anxiety about a particular offence was very great, and the offender could not be traced, would not the apparently correct conviction of an innocent person have great beneficial potential, overriding the misery of the innocent scapegoat and his or her family? This argument against utilitarian theories of punishment is similar to the fundamental objection to utilitarianism as a general moral principle: it fails to incorporate an adequate distributive principle and thus does not take the separateness of individuals seriously, since it focuses only on the maximization of happiness aggregated over the whole citizenry, however distributed. Thus whilst utilitarian theories seem to accommodate our views about why it is that a state needs to punish offenders, they fail to accommodate equally strong intuitions about whom it is right to punish. There are also doubts about whether a utilitarian theory can generate an adequate principle limiting the amount of punishment, given the gains to be made in deterrent terms by occasional especially severe sentences when a particular form of offending has become prevalent.

Not surprisingly, therefore, a third category of theories of punishment has emerged in the second half of this century. These may be called the mixed theories, for they aim to incorporate the insights of both their retributivist and utilitarian predecessors. Their development was precipitated by an important article by

H. L. A. Hart, 'Prolegomenon to the principles of punishment' (1959), in which he argued that the way forward in theorizing about punishment lay in distinguishing three separate questions. The first was that of the definition of punishment; second there was the question of the general justifying aim of punishment – why a society has an institution of punishment at all; and third the question of liability to punishment. This last question had two aspects: that of distribution, or who may be punished, and that of amount, or how much they may be punished. Once these questions have been distinguished, Hart argued, it becomes clear that it is possible to give a retributive answer to one and a utilitarian answer to another. Thus his own position, employing a standard definition, is that the general justifying aim of punishment is utilitarian, whereas the question of distribution should be answered in retributive terms: only an offender may be punished, and only for an offence voluntarily committed. The question of amount is answered partly by reference to a retributive principle of proportionality, and partly by utilitarian considerations. We thus have a theory with a strong utilitarian component, but in which the pursuit of utility is limited by an independent principle based on the value of fairness, which cannot simply be absorbed into a utilitarian calculation. The lead given by Hart has been followed by many others, some of whom answer the question about the general justifying aim in retributive terms but subject this to a limiting utilitarian distributive principle. Thus desert is argued to be a necessary but not a sufficient condition for punishment: it would only be just to punish a deserving offender if there were also compensating social benefits to be gained by doing so.

The attractions of such mixed theories of punishment are obvious, but their development has not led to any greater consensus about the justification of punishment. Apart from substantive disagreements about whether the general justifying aim should be utilitarian or retributive, certain doubts remain about the hybrid approach to principles of punishment. Taking Hart's theory as our example, the difficulty lies in the fact that most people are not in fact willing to contemplate the principle

of retribution in distribution as an *absolute* constraint on the pursuit of social goals. This is well reflected in the widespread existence of no-fault criminal liability, typically in areas where the penalties are not heavy and where the advantages of strict liability in terms of preventing socially harmful behaviour are expected to be substantial. This suggests that even in relatively normal cases we are in fact willing to balance the values of fairness and utility in just the way which Hart rules out. Thus the further question arises of how this balancing is to be accomplished, given that the two values are incommensurable: how shall we give fairness the special weight which our intuitions seem to dictate, without extensively curtailing our pursuit of the great benefits which we may reasonably expect a criminal justice system to have in terms of preventing the misery and other costs associated with crime?

It is clear, however, that only a pluralistic theory will turn out to be adequate to accommodate our ideas of what is right and proper in the area of punishment. The difficulty is to reconcile the consequentialist and retributive principles at a deeper level than has so far been accomplished. This would probably be by way of a greater effort to reflect about punishment in the context of all the other features which we take to make up a just society. What sort of obligation do individuals have to obey the laws of their state? What constitutes a just law? How far is the state justified in intervening in individual lives by means of criminal controls? Not until thinking about punishment is undertaken in this natural theoretical context will progress be made towards the development of a theory which is both coherent and pluralistic.   NML

Reading
Beccaria, C.: *On Crimes and Punishments* (1764), trans. H. Paolucci. Indianapolis: Bobbs-Merrill, 1963.
Benn, S.I. and Peters, R.S.: *Social Principles and the Democratic State*. London: Allen & Unwin, 1959.
Bentham, J.: *An Introduction to the Principles of Morals and Legislation* (1789), ed. J. Burns and H.L.A. Hart, chs 1–5, 13–15. London: Methuen, 1982.
Durkheim, E.: *The Division of Labour in Society* (1893), ch. 2. Glencoe, Ill.: Free Press of Glencoe, 1960 .

Feinberg, J.: *Doing and Deserving*. Princeton, NJ: Princeton University Press, 1974.

†Hart, H.L.A.: *Punishment and Responsibility*. Oxford: Clarendon Press, 1968. [Includes 'Prolegomenon to the principles of punishment'.]

†Honderich, T.: *Punishment: the Supposed Justifications*. Harmondsworth: Penguin, 1984.

Kant, I.: *The Metaphysical Elements of Justice* (1797), trans. J. Cadd. Indianapolis: Bobbs-Merrill, 1965.

Von Hirsch, A.: *Doing Justice*. New York: Hill & Wang, 1976.

Wootton, B.: *Social Science and Social Pathology*. London: Allen & Unwin, 1967.

Q

Quesnay, François (1694–1774)   French economist. Intellectual leader of the physiocrats, and an early exponent of the doctrine of LAISSEZ-FAIRE. See PHYSIOCRACY.

R

racism   As a political theory and as the basis for a theory of history, racism became a factor in European history in the second half of the nineteenth century. As a political force, it came to the fore in the anti-semitism of the turn of the century and it constituted the intellectual foundation of Nazism.

The intellectual origins of racial explanations of the human world go back to the eighteenth century. It was at that time that anthropology came into being, a new scientific discipline which attempted to determine, by the use of empirical methods, the place of man in nature. Men were observed, evaluated, compared. At the same time, a search for unity and harmony in human affairs gave rise to a belief in the unity of the flesh and the spirit. This unity, it was believed, could also be observed and evaluated.

Although the great naturalists and anthropologists of the eighteenth century – such as Lamarck (1744–1829), the author of *Philosophie zoologique* (1809), whose studies on the mutation of species heralded those of Darwin, or Buffon (1707–88), the author of the celebrated *Histoire naturelle de l'homme* (1778) – offered a materialist and environmentalist explanation of racial differences, their criteria of classification were already of a highly subjective character. The use of stereotypes became very common, and variations in physical characteristics were held to indicate the existence of mental, psychological and cultural differences. From the beginning of the nineteenth century many scientific texts, such as works of natural history or anthropology, were already openly racist. The new sciences of humanity, modelling themselves as far as possible on the highly respected physical sciences, tended, at that period, to attribute to mental or moral characteristics the same hereditary immutability as was attached to physical characteristics. Since black people were black by heredity, they must also, therefore, be hereditarily 'idle and negligent'.

Throughout the nineteenth century, we find this attempt to approach the soul via the body constituting the outstanding characteristic of racism. In Europe at this time, two ideas gained wide acceptance: first, the notion that there are intrinsic psychological differences between the various races, and second, that only people of one 'blood' can share the same cultural and intellectual heritage. The rise of NATIONALISM, which involved a search for objective criteria for the definition of national collectivities, and attributed importance to national histories and languages, as well as the long struggle in Europe against the French Revolution and the rationalist heritage of the age of Enlightenment, helped to create the conditions in which racism could develop until it became both the basis of a theory of history and a political force.

In this connection, one should draw attention to the work of HERDER. In many respects he was a rationalist and a humanist who rejected the principle of racial classification, but he nevertheless exerted a decisive influence on European nationalism and indirectly on racialist thinking by introducing the subjective idea of the *Volksgeist*. For Herder the nature of a people was expressed in its unchanging spirit refined through history. What gives unity to the life and culture of a people, he surmised, is the persistence of the original juices which are its basic strength. The *Volksgeist* revealed itself to Herder through mythologies, songs and sagas. These go back to the origins of a people and, if conserved, will rejuvenate their spirit. This organic concept of the nation had an enormous influence on the growth of European particularisms and provided fuel for tribal nationalism, the nationalism of the earth and the dead – the nationalism of 'blood and soil' (*Blut und Boden*).

The systematization of racist thought in the nineteenth century was the achievement of Arthur de Gobineau who wrote *Essai sur l'inégalité des races humaines* (1853–55), a synthetic, interdisciplinary work based on history, anthropology and linguistics. Gobineau claimed that the principle of race elucidated the past, the present and the future; it determined

the fate of civilizations. When a civilization became decadent, this was due to the mixture of races. No race could preserve its purity indefinitely, and the more mixed it became, the more it became degenerate.

Gobineau said there were three principal races: the yellow, the black and the white. The yellow race was materialistic and lacking in imagination, and its language incapable of expressing metaphysical thought. The black race lacked intelligence. Among the whites, the Aryan race, which first formed the elite of India and then created the Teutonic heritage, possessed the virtues of a nobility: a love of freedom and honour and a cult of spirituality. Gobineau was not anti-semitic and he condemned slavery, but in explaining universal history by a racial theory and in affirming the superiority of the Aryan element, he lent himself to adoption by the pan-Germanic movement which used his theory to provide a conceptual framework for its nationalism and anti-semitism.

England too had its Gobineau, in the person of Robert Knox (1798–1862), whose *Races of Men* (1850) asserted the superiority of two Aryan races, the Saxons and the Slavs (in this he was unique) and the inferiority of the Jews. James Hunt (1833–69), an admirer of Knox and the founder and president of the London Anthropological Society, contributed to the spread of racism by seeking to rid science of unfortunate prejudices such as the theory of the rights of man and a belief in the equality of mankind. They both believed that racial qualities are innate and unchangeable, embracing the moral and intellectual as well as the physical aspects of a person.

An explanation of history which laid stress on ethnic factors in the development of civilizations greatly influenced some of the outstanding figures of the intellectual establishment of the second half of the nineteenth century. Hippolyte Taine (1828–93) undoubtedly dominated French intellectual life at this time. In his monumental *Histoire de la littérature anglaise* (1863), he claimed that a civilization is always the product of three main elements: the race, the milieu and the moment. He thought that men were bound together primarily by a 'community of blood and spirit'. Taine is usually regarded as a positivist and a liberal, and this is also the case with that other giant of the French intellectual life of the period, Ernest Renan, who was strongly influenced by Gobineau.

However, it was only when racial thought adopted SOCIAL DARWINISM that racism gave rise to a coherent political theory. The ideas of 'natural selection', of the struggle for existence and of the 'survival of the fittest' were immediately seized upon by the theoreticians of racism; biological determinism, applied to the human sciences, became for them a norm, justifying existing inequalities or those which had to be introduced in order to re-establish a natural order destroyed by liberalism, democracy, the French Revolution or Marxism.

By the end of the nineteenth century, this synthesis of social Darwinism and racism was already very common in Europe. It was expressed most characteristically in the work of the 'anthropo-sociologists' Georges Vacher de Lapouge in France and Otto Ammon in Germany. They not only asserted the absolute physical, moral and social superiority of the Aryan (which they based on measurements of the skull as well as on other social, anthropological and economic criteria), but also put forward a new concept of human nature and a new idea of the relationships between men. Ammon and Vacher de Lapouge believed that the distribution of men in society is subject to a strict determinism and nothing can eliminate the predestination of the race. It is the Aryan element which always bears the weight of history, founding civilization and creating the arts and sciences, discovering new countries and everywhere generating economic activity. For the representatives of this school there is an absolute correlation, not only between the organism and spiritual activity, but even between people's measurements and degree of spiritual adventurousness, or between the dimensions of the skull and their chances of rising in the social scale.

Social Darwinism allied to racism had the immediate effect of desacralizing the human being and assimilating social with physical existence. For such racists, society was an organism regulated by the same laws as living organisms, the human species was subject to the same laws as the other animal species, and human life was nothing but an incessant struggle for existence. The world, they believed, belonged to the strongest who was accordingly the best, and there came into being a new morality (which Vacher de Lapouge called 'selectionist') to replace the traditional Christian morality.

The idea of the ethnic inequality of the different peoples had become prevalent by the turn of the century. Works of a racist and very often anti-semitic character expressing a synthesis of racism and social Darwinism were legion. Some of them became best-sellers: *Die Welträtsel* (1899) by Ernst Haeckel, the father of Darwinian 'monism', *Rembrandt als Erzieher* (1890) by Julius Langbehn in Germany, and Drumont's *La France juive* (1886) in France. Gustave Le Bon's works of social psychology, which gave a place of particular importance to the racial factor, were translated into sixteen languages. For Drumont as for Lagarde, the author of *Deutsche Schriften* (1876), or for Wagner who wrote *Judentum in der Musik* (1850), the Jew is the eternal enemy who wages an all-out war against the Aryan.

This idea was central to the thought of one of the most famous theoreticians of racism, the Germanized Englishman Houston Stewart Chamberlain, author of *Die Grundlagen des XIX Jahrhunderts* (1899) who, together with the Austrian Otto Weininger who wrote *Geschlecht und Charakter* (1903), directly influenced Hitler. Chamberlain believed that the Jews represented absolute evil, while the Germans were the chosen people. The fate of civilization depended on the struggle between Aryan and Semite. The victory of the Jew meant its destruction, whereas that of the Aryan was the starting-point of a spiritual revolution, the end of the present degeneration and the birth of a new era.

The spread of racist ideas of an allegedly scientific character, including the idea that the Jews were a branch of humanity which could be demonstrated to be inferior, played a major part in the long process of undermining an entire political culture based on rationalism, individualism and the rights of man. These ideas were victorious not only in Germany but also in other countries, such as Italy where racist legislation was adopted in 1938, or France where in 1940, after the Vichy regime had been established, racist legislation very similar to the Nuremberg Laws was promulgated.   ZS

Reading

Ammon, O.: *Die Gesellschaffisordnung und ihre natür-lichen Grundlagen.* Jena: Fisher, 1895.

Barzun, J.: *Race: a Study in Superstition.* New York: Harper & Row, 1965.

†Biddiss, M.D.: *Father of Racist Ideology: the Social and Political Thought of Count Gobineau.* New York: Weybright & Talley, 1970.

Guiral, P. and Temime, E. eds: *L'Idée de race dans la pensée politique française contemporaine.* Paris: Éditions du CNRS, 1977.

Gobineau, J.A. de: *Selected Political Writings,* ed. M.D. Biddiss. London: Cape, 1970.

Le Bon, G.: *The Crowd: a study of the popular mind.* New York: Viking, 1972.

Mosse, G.L.: *The Crisis of German Ideology: intellectual origins of the Third Reich.* New York: Grosset & Dunlop, 1964.

†————: Toward the final solution. In *A History of European Racism.* New York: Howard Fertig, 1978.

Sternhell, Z.: Anthropologie et politique: les avatars du darwinisme social au tournant du siècle. In *L'Allemagne nazie et le génocide juif.* Paris: Gallimard – Le Seuil, 1985.

Vacher de Lapouge, G.: *Les Sélections sociales.* Paris: Fontemoing, 1899.

radicalism The term may be defined as a disposition to subject existing arrangements to critical questioning, and to advocate the reform or abolition of those which cannot be given a principled justification. It is therefore a stance rather than a fully-fledged political creed; its practical content will vary according to the political circumstances in which radicals find themselves. Most radicals have been liberals or socialists, but it is possible to envisage a critical opposition to institutions that are already liberal or socialist in character, and thus creeds such as fascism may be described as ideologies of the radical right. The true contrary of radicalism is CONSERVATISM, understood as the view that political action can improve the human condition only in very minor respects. For major schools of political radicals, see LEVELLERS; PHILOSOPHIC RADICALISM; RADICALS, BRITISH; RICARDIAN SOCIALISTS.   DLM

radicals, British (1789–1815) In Britain in the last decade of the eighteenth century the principles of politics were subjected to wide-spread popular debate in a stream of pamphlet literature demanding various forms of political reform. The debate was furthered through the meetings of a number of radical political associations which sprang up to organize the distribution of this literature and to campaign for parliamentary and electoral reform. The movement drew on a number of strands of radical thinking which had developed in the previous decades. The American Revolution had prompted a good deal of criticism of the administration, particularly from the Whig opposition, from Dissenters who sympathized with their fellow Puritans, and from those whose commercial and business interests were affected. Many also saw the revolution as heralding a new era by successfully abandoning the monarchical system in favour of a republican and democratic order. The revolution and the earlier Wilkes controversy, in which the rights of the citizen against the power of parliament and the crown were successfully contested, also revived the older 'real Whig', 'Eighteenth Century Commonwealthman', and 'Country Party' traditions of political thought. These looked back to the writings of HARRINGTON, LOCKE, MILTON and Sidney, and argued that civil liberty required both a strong body of landed gentry who could remained independent from the patronage of the king, and a mixed constitution which would maintain a delicate balance of monarchical, aristocratic and democratic elements (see Robbins). These controversies stimulated the formation of metropolitan and provincial political associations which petitioned for parliamentary reform and arranged for the printing and circulation of their traditions' canonical texts. Although these associations foundered in the early 1780s, they provided a valuable model for their successors in the next decade. They also attracted considerable support from Dissenters who increasingly came to see the cause of religious toleration as dependent upon political reform (see Lincoln; Goodwin).

However, it was events in France in 1789 which revived these earlier traditions and provoked extensive controversy in both parliamentary and extra-parliamentary circles in

Britain over the nature of the revolution (was it merely a French version of 1688?), its legitimacy (by what right had the Estates acted?), and its lessons for Britain (should France be a lesson to Britain's ruling class, or an example to its people?). The 'Debate on France' was opened, unwittingly, by Dr Richard Price, an Arian Dissenting Minister, statistician, and moral and political philosopher. In his sermon at the annual service organized by the London Revolution Society to commemorate the Glorious Revolution of 1688, Price welcomed events in France and restated the principles of 1688, which he took to be: the right to liberty of conscience; the right to resist power when abused; and the right to choose our own governors, cashier them for misconduct, and to frame a government for ourselves. Price's account of 1688 and his enthusiastic welcome for the revolution provided the initial focus for Edmund BURKE's attack on the 'French experiment' and its British sympathizers in his *Reflections on the Revolution in France* (1790). The *Reflections* provoked more than a hundred further pamphlets on 'French principles' in the following two years in what has been described as 'perhaps the last real discussion of the fundamentals of politics in our country' (Cobban, p. 31). The debate deserves this description both because of the quality of many of the contributions, and because it extended to such a wide extra-parliamentary audience. At times it became a struggle for the allegiance of those who were denied representation and had hitherto stood outside the orbit of political debate and organization.

The debate ranged over three main areas: writers disputed over Price's and Burke's competing interpretations of the events and principles of 1688; they argued over Burke's account of events in France in the summer of 1789; and they contested the principles on which their political system should be based. The most important single contribution was Thomas PAINE's *Rights of Man* (1791 and 1792), which espoused a radical republican ideology based on the American experience and which achieved sales in excess of 150,000 copies in the two years following its publication (Thompson, p. 117). However, for all Paine's popularity, especially amongst the radical associations

which circulated his works, his political principles were not characteristic of the pamphlet debate. Radical contributions only rarely followed Paine's advocacy of natural rights, popular sovereignty, and universal suffrage; most invoked older traditions. Many contributors demanded the restoration of Britain's ANCIENT CONSTITUTION; see in particular Major John Cartwright's much reprinted *Give us our Rights* (1782) and David Williams's *Letters to a Young Prince from an Old Statesman* (1792). Others, including Price, simply referred back to Whig and Country Party traditions of the mixed constitution, claiming that reform was necessary to strengthen the democratic element against the overweening ambition and power of the crown. However, the debate was not restricted to such concerns. Joseph Priestley, the theologian, chemist and philosopher, in his *Letters to the Right Hon. Edmund Burke* (1791), attacked Burke's discussion of the proper relations between church and state, restated the case for complete religious toleration, and looked forward to a time when government would conduct itself solely according to the public good, leaving all men the enjoyment of as many of their natural rights as possible. Once such true principles of government had been established, he prophesied the 'extinction of all *national prejudice* and enmity, and the establishment of *universal peace* and good will among all nations' (quoted in Butler, p. 88).

The hope for improvement also found expression in James Mackintosh's *Vindiciae Gallicae* (1791), a philosophically sophisticated defence of 1688 and 1789 which provided a clearly argued rule-utilitarian justification for rights, thereby combining Mackintosh's inheritance from the SCOTTISH ENLIGHTENMENT with the newer 'French principles'. For Mackintosh 'all rights, civil or natural, arise from expediency. But the moment the moral edifice is reared, its basis is hidden from the eye for ever. . . . It then becomes the perfection of virtue to consider not whether an act is useful, but whether it is right' (pp. 216–17).

However, whereas Paine and Mackintosh, to some extent Priestley, and many others, relied on appeals to the rights and interests of individuals, an alternative current ran through the debate stressing disinterested benevolence and man's rational duties. Mary WOLLSTONE-CRAFT in her *Vindication of the Rights of Man* (1790), William GODWIN in his *Political Justice* (1793), Thomas Holcroft in his political novel *Anna St Ives*, Price in his *Discourse on the Love of our Country* (1789), and others (e.g. George Rous, Thomas Christie, John Adams, and Catherine Macauley) all stressed the duties of the individual to moral and political truth (a duty derived for many writers from our duties to God). They argued that the vision of a community of egoistic individuals pursuing their interests within a system of rules which allows each the maximum freedom (the view canvassed by Paine and Mackintosh) was too narrow. Catherine Macauley expressed her hope 'that we shall not be so much *blinded* with the splendour of dazzling images, as to confound those *narrow affections* which bind small bodies together by the ties of interest, to that *liberal benevolence*, which, disdaining the consideration of every selfish good, cheerfully sacrifices a *personal interest* to the welfare of the community' (pp. 38–9).

This division might also be seen as reflecting the distinction between the Scottish and French heritages, which stressed the role of the passions and interests (HUME and SMITH; HOLBACH, HELVÉTIUS and ROUSSEAU), and the more rationalist tradition of English Dissent which found its classic expositions in Price's *Review of the Principal Questions of Morals* (1756, enlarged edition 1787) and in the first edition of Godwin's *Political Justice*. However, these two very different traditions were frequently merged (if not altogether coherently) in the writings of liberally-minded humanitarians from the middle ranks of society who were persuaded by the American and French revolutions, by the developing prosperity of Georgian England, and by their own success and social advancement, that they were witnessing the dawn of a new era. These multiple influences show through in the later editions of Godwin's *Political Justice* (1795, 1797), in the novels of Godwin, Holcroft, Robert Bage, Wollstonecraft, and others, and in the brief flirtation with radicalism in the poetry of William Wordsworth and Samuel Taylor COLERIDGE. (More millennial influences are evident in the work of William Blake.) Just as the underlying political

ideologies of writers differed, so too did their objectives. These ranged from expectations of a utopian future peopled by fully rational men and women, through demands for a people's convention to draw up a new constitution, and assertions of the people's right to universal suffrage and annual parliaments, to more modest proposals for an extension of the franchise to a wider class of property owners.

After 1792 the debate increasingly became a more direct struggle to capture the allegiance of metropolitan and provincial artisans. This campaign was at first directed by the Society for Constitutional Information (SCI) but was taken over by the London Corresponding Society (LCS) – a society composed of 'a class of Men who deserve better treatment than they generally meet with from those who are fed and cloathed, and inriched by thier labour, industry or ingenuity' (quoted in Thale, p. 8). While these societies contained many moderates, their rhetoric was dominated by the language of natural rights and popular sovereignty. In 1794 their zeal for reform led them to plan a convention with elected delegates from throughout Britain to draw up proposals for the reform of Parliament and to act as a mouthpiece for the people's demands. Such a convention tacitly threatened parliamentary claims to sovereignty – or so the government claimed as it arrested and tried the leaders of the societies for high treason. They were eventually acquitted in December 1794, but their long imprisonment and the defection of their secretary broke the SCI, and the LCS only recovered slowly. The LCS did have a resurgence of support in 1795 as public unrest grew over the war with France, rising food prices, and the predation of the recruitment officers, but under the leadership of John Thelwall, as under his predecessor Thomas Hardy, it never moved beyond a demand for political rights and an end of the war with France. Thelwall argued: 'Remember, I do not mean equality of property. This is totally impossible in the present state of human intellect and industry. . . . The equality I mean, is the equality of rights' (p. 14). Only outside the society, in the writings of Thomas Spence and William Godwin, and in Paine's rather belated *Agrarian Justice* (1796), did the radicals move on to countenance an alternative theory of property to the traditional Lockeian view. Spence in particular, an isolated and largely neglected figure in the 1790s, advanced a doctrine of rights to equal property to be managed collectively by the community which influenced nineteenth-century radicals. For Spence, a right in land was an essential prerequisite for meaningful political rights and proper representation – a view which linked the republican tradition of the early part of the eighteenth century to the socialist traditions of the nineteenth.

The radical societies were increasingly harassed by government spies, propaganda, prosecutions, and arrests (facilitated by the repeated suspension of *habeas corpus* throughout the decade). The more respectable elements of the LCS – such as Thelwall and Francis Place – retired from it and it became increasingly dominated by men with more insurrectionary ambitions but little political ideology. In 1799 the LCS was finally outlawed.

Although popular radicalism and reforming activity revived in the early years of the nineteenth century under Sir Francis Burdett, Henry Hunt, and William Cobbett (the last two sharing some of Paine's ability to communicate and arouse the working man), little of the activity was as vital, as threatening, or as innovative as it had been in the last decade of the eighteenth century. Although Paine's works were still circulated, and Spence continued to turn out demands for common ownership, political debate was dominated by writers from the 1780s rather than the 1790s, and was consequently more moderate in its demands and expectations.

How far the radicals of the 1790s and their principles posed a threat to the prevailing aristocratic order of Georgian Britain remains much debated. The order certainly reacted as if the threat was serious, and in doing so it doubtless provoked some radicals to consider more violent methods of reform, but the movement is probably more significant for having developed a political theory of natural rights and popular sovereignty which underlay the democratic and socialist demands of the nineteenth-century labour movement in Britain. It is also important because it brought the tradition of radical political inquiry to a new audience which had previously remained firmly outside the arena of political activity. In these ways the British radicals came to play a major part in the theory and practice of parliamentary democracy in Britain.   MP

Reading
Burke, E.: *Reflections on the Revolution in France*, ed. C.C. O'Brien. Harmondsworth: Penguin, 1968.

†Butler, M.: *Burke, Paine, Godwin, and the Revolution Controversy*. Cambridge: Cambridge University Press, 1984.

†Cobban, A.: *The Debate on the French Revolution*. London: Black, 1950.

†Goodwin, A.: *The Friends of Liberty*. London: Hutchinson, 1979.

Knox, T.R.: Thomas Spence: the trumpet of liberty. *Past and Present* 76 (1977) 75–98.

Lincoln, A.H.: *Some Political and Social Ideas of English Dissent*. Cambridge: Cambridge University Press, 1938.

Macauley, C.: *Observations on the Reflections of the Rt. Hon. Edmund Burke . . . .* London, 1790.

Mackintosh, J.: *Vindiciae Gallicae*. London, 1791.

Paine, T.: *Rights of Man*, ed. H. Collins. Harmondsworth: Penguin, 1969.

Robbins, C.: *The Eighteenth Century Commonwealthman*. Cambridge, Mass.: Harvard University Press, 1959.

Thale, M. ed.: *Selections from the Papers of the London Corresponding Society*. Cambridge: Cambridge University Press, 1983.

Thelwall, J.: *Peaceful Discussion and not Tumultory Violence the means of Redressing National Grievances*. London, 1795.

†Thompson, E.P.: *The Making of the English Working Class*. Harmondsworth: Penguin, 1968.

rationality   Rationality and irrationality are predicated in the first instance of human beings and of human beliefs and actions. Talk about the rationality or irrationality of historical processes, institutions, methods of collective decision-making, and so on, requires interpretation on a case-by-case basis and must always be regarded as problematic, at best.

Rationality is attributed to *homo sapiens* in virtue of the ability to reason and act upon the results of deliberation. To say that an individual person possesses rationality is to say that that person measures up to the minimum standard that establishes a presumption of competence. Absence of rationality is taken to warrant a diminution of legal rights and commonly some kind of supervision or even constraint. Rationality is here a threshold concept. It may also be used as a scalar concept. In this sense, people who pass the first test can have greater or smaller degrees of rationality ascribed to them. Thus someone who always engages in elaborate calculations before acting may be said to be excessively rational. Rationality harnessed to the pursuit of self-interest is prudence, which is similarly a virtue that it is possible to have too much of. 'For . . . that man, which looks too far before him, in the care of future time, hath his heart all the day long, gnawed on by fear of death, poverty, or other calamity; and has no repose, nor pause of his anxiety, but in sleep' (*Leviathan*, p. 169).

The concept of rationality requires for its elucidation reference to the concept of a reason, and the words reason and rational ultimately derive from the same Latin root *ratio*. In the past, rational and reasonable could be used interchangeably: HOBBES said that 'children . . . are called Reasonable Creatures, for the possibility apparent of having the use of Reason in time to come' (p. 116). But the two words have become specialized, so that reasonableness is now seen as a more social virtue than rationality. The *Oxford English Dictionary* gives under 'reasonable' for modern usage: 'Having sound judgement; sensible, sane', in which it is noted to be equivalent to a sense of 'rational', and also 'not asking for too much'. The connection between reasonableness in this second sense and rationality in general is, it may be suggested, that in conflicts about the terms of social co-operation, willingness to listen to the reasons offered by others amounts to an openness to their perspectives and interests. 'Not asking too much' may be seen as a sign of (if not a criterion for) the existence of this openness. The contrast with 'rationality' is further increased by the tendency in contemporary usage for rationality to be equated with prudence rather than with the disposition to act on reasons of all kinds.

Rationality in belief and action is the successful exercise on a particular occasion of the rational faculty. A belief is held rationally if the person holding it can give reasons in its favour and is prepared to reassess it in the light of arguments against it. Rationality in belief is related to truth in the same way as a fair trial is to a correct verdict. A fair trial is more likely to lead to a correct verdict than a procedurally defective trial, but a fair trial may sometimes issue in an incorrect verdict, while a correct verdict may on occasion emerge from a procedurally defective trial. Rationality refers to the manner in which beliefs are held; it can be attributed to beliefs themselves only elliptically. No belief (i.e. possible content of an assertion) is rational or irrational in itself. What we can say is that, given a person's other beliefs, the prevailing canons of evidence, and so on, it is rational or irrational for someone to believe a certain thing. Thus, 'what entitles us to call the belief in witchcraft [in sixteenth- and seventeenth-century Europe] irrational is not its falsity, but the fact of its incoherence with other beliefs and criteria possessed by those who held it' (MacIntyre, p. 248).

Rationality in action is the exercise of the capacity to formulate and to act on reasons for acting. Since the formulation of reasons for acting requires the deployment of beliefs about the situation in which one finds oneself and the consequences to be expected from alternative courses of action, it follows that rational action is parasitic upon rational belief. No action can be more rational than the beliefs upon which it is based. One who believes himself to be made of glass does well, given his belief, to avoid sharp contact with hard surfaces. But his following this precept with care scarcely makes his actions rational *tout court*. Rationality neither guarantees nor is guaranteed by success. Just as a rational belief may be false, a rational act may turn out badly; and just as an irrational belief may be true, so an irrational act may turn out well.

The most straightfoward and uncontroversial reason for acting is to secure something that one wants. According to this notion, a rational action is one that is rationally adapted to the pursuit of some end of the actor. This entails that the actor has rational beliefs (in the elliptical sense defined above) about the situation and the nature of the available alternatives, that the actor chooses the option that offers the best prospect of achieving the desired end, and actually performs the action recommended by this process of deliberation and not some other that is inconsistent with it. The paradigm of what is usually called means–end rationality requires elaboration in order to accommodate two phenomena: the existence of multiple ends and of rational uncertainty about the connection between acts and outcomes. Easy extensions are possible for easy cases. For example, other things being equal, where one alternative would achieve an end while another would achieve that plus another end, the second alternative should be preferred; and if one alternative is more likely to achieve an end than another then the first alternative should be preferred. (These are RAWLS's second and third 'principles of rational choice', pp. 412–13; the first is the principle already put forward for a single end, to choose the most efficient means, pp. 411–12.) More difficult cases give rise to unresolved (perhaps unresolvable) controversies.

Both Rawls and Brandt, for example, have proposed that the principle for establishing ends rationally is that one should create a harmonious system of ends such that one is maximally satisfied by it. But this is easier said than done, as critics have pointed out (see Copp and Zimmerman). A less demanding and more obviously plausible demand is that desires should be consistent. A good pragmatic reason for this is that if someone prefers a to b, b to c, and c to a, he is liable to find himself on a treadmill, expending time and money to get back to his starting point (see Epilogue in Barry and Hardin).

The problem of decision-making under uncertainty has attracted much attention from philosophers and decision theorists in the past thirty years, but disagreements remain at the most basic level about the criteria for a rational choice. Allan Gibbard has proposed cutting the Gordian knot by saying that to call something rational is to commend it as 'making sense'. On this view, when Bayesians and non-Bayesians, say, have conflicting views about what it makes sense to do in the face of uncertainty, the concept of rationality is itself part of the dispute. Although we can say if we like that rational action is whatever action will do best for us, each decision-rule is itself a conception of what doing best consists of. There is no independent criterion of rationality to act as a benchmark.

Gibbard professes to believe that arguments about rational action continue to be important, yet it is hard to see what, on his view, the arguments are supposed to be *about* – except what to do! But the promise of rationality was that it would tell us what to do, not that we should decide what to do first and then award our choice the accolade of rationality. Even so, most everyday uses of the concept of rationality will still stand because they rest on uncontroversial criteria. All that will have to go is the hope that resort to the concept of rationality will help us to solve normative problems that we have notoriously failed to solve by direct argument.

Other disputes are: how irrational people actually are, and what the implications of human deficiencies in data processing are for public policy (see Slovik *et al*.); how far rationality has to be assumed in interpreting any culture (see Hollis and Lukes); whether the assumption that actors are rational seekers of their own interest provides the best research programme in the social sciences (see Popkin); how far the concept of rationality can usefully be extended from individual human beings to societies, so as to apply, for example, to the prospect of mutual frustration in prisoner's dilemma situations or to the possibility of an intransitive social preference ordering arising from the aggregation of individual transitive preferences (see Barry and Hardin).   BMB

Reading

†Barry, B. and Hardin, R. eds: *Rational Man and Irrational Society? an introduction and sourcebook*. Beverly Hills, Calif.: Sage, 1982.

Brandt, R.: *A Theory of the Good and the Right*. Oxford: Clarendon Press, 1979.

†Copp, D. and Zimmerman, D. eds: *Morality, Reason and Truth: New Essays on the Foundations of Ethics*. Totowa, NJ: Rowman & Allanheld, 1984.

Gibbard, A.: Moral judgements and the acceptance of norms. *Ethics* 96 (1985) 5–21; Reply to Sturgeon, pp. 34–41.

Hobbes, T.: *Leviathan* (1651), ed. C.B. Macpherson. Harmondsworth: Penguin, 1968.

†Hollis, M. and Lukes, S. eds: *Rationality and Relativism*. Oxford: Blackwell; Cambridge, Mass.: MIT Press, 1979.

MacIntyre, A.C.: Rationality and the explanation of action. In *Against the Self-Images of the Age*. London: Duckworth, 1971; Notre Dame, Ind.: University of Notre Dame Press, 1978.

†Popkin, S.L.: *The Rational Peasant: the Political Economy of Rural Society in Vietnam*. Berkeley and Los Angeles: University of California Press, 1979.

Rawls, J.: *A Theory of Justice*. Cambridge, Mass.: Harvard University Press, 1971; Oxford: Oxford University Press, 1972.

Slovik, P., Fischhoff, B. and Lichtenstein, S.: Regulations of risk: a psychological perspective. In *Regulatory Policy in the Social Sciences*, ed. R.G. Noll. Berkeley and Los Angeles: University of California Press, 1985.

Rawls, John (1921–) American philosopher. In 1971 Rawls published his book *A Theory of Justice*, which has since emerged as the greatest single influence on Anglo-American political philosophy over the last fifteen years. Earlier papers in learned journals had foreshadowed the major themes of that book, and later articles and lectures have incorporated a number of theoretical revisions. Philosophically, Rawls's main contribution has been to present an alternative ethical theory to UTILITARIANISM. Politically, his account of justice has been regarded as a defence of LIBERALISM in the American sense, or SOCIAL DEMOCRACY in the European sense.

Rawls's books has sometimes been interpreted as a revival of the SOCIAL CONTRACT tradition in political thought; but in fact his interests and method of proceeding are very different from the mainstream of that tradition. He is not directly concerned with justifying political authority, but with establishing principles of social JUSTICE. In order to do so, he imagines people placed in what he calls 'the original position'. This is a purely hypothetical situation in which people are deprived of knowledge about their talents and abilities and about the place they occupy in society. They are then asked to formulate principles of distribution by which they will be governed when they return to normal society. They do not know what their particular purposes in life are; but they do know that it will be useful to have various 'primary goods', which Rawls lists as rights and liberties, opportunities and powers, income and wealth, and the bases of self-respect. Everyone is assumed to want as many of these goods as possible, but because of the ignorance imposed in the original position, they are constrained to put forward distributive principles that are quite general in form.

Rawls claims that this construction avoids the major weakness of utilitarianism, namely that the interests of particular individuals may be sacrificed to the aggregate welfare of the whole, while at the same time yielding principles of justice that reflect the beliefs we already hold most deeply. Neither claim is uncontentious. Some critics have argued that the upshot of the original position would actually be a form of utilitarianism; others that the principles Rawls claims to derive from it conflict with at least some deeply-held beliefs. The principles themselves are as follows:

(1) Each person is to have an equal right to the most extensive liberty compatible with a similar liberty for others.

(2) Social and economic inequalities are to be arranged so that they are both: (a) to the greatest benefit of the least advantaged; and (b) attached to positions and offices open to all under conditions of fair equality of opportunity.

The first principle embodies a familiar liberal idea, but Rawls's use of it has three noteworthy features. First, he interprets 'liberty' in a fairly narrow way, to refer to such legally-defined freedoms of movement, speech and political participation (see also FREEDOM). Second, recognizing that the value of such liberty to each person must depend on the material resources they possess, he nevertheless requires only that liberty itself, not its value, should be equally distributed. Third, he gives the principle of liberty strict priority over the second principle, at least in economically developed societies. Freedom may never be sacrificed for an increase in material well-being.

If the first principle reveals Rawls's commitment to liberalism, the second, and especially part (a) – the so-called 'difference principle' – appears to give the theory a more egalitarian flavour. The difference principle requires us to regulate social inequalities in such a way that those with the least material goods (income, wealth and the bases of self-respect) will nonetheless be given as large a share as possible. Rawls assumes a market economy in which material inequalities serve as incentives, increasing the overall stock of goods available for distribution. In practical terms his principle implies that the tax system should be used progressively to redistribute goods to the worst off, until a point is reached at which the disincentive effects of further taxation would lower the total yield.

How egalitarian Rawls's principles would be in their effects depends on empirical facts about human psychology. His critics on the left see this as a weakness, arguing that the need for incentives is not a brute fact, but at least in part a product of prevailing economic institutions. Conversely, his critics on the right argue that those who succeed in a competitive market deserve to keep their rewards, even if it would be economically feasible to tax them away.

Rawls's theory has also been challenged at a more fundamental level. Some have seen his notion of primary goods as embodying an unwarranted individualism: it appears to overlook the value most of us attach to collective aspects of social life (such as living in a harmonious society). Others have argued that the theory is indefensibly ahistorical in attempting to derive principles of justice entirely from general assumptions about human purposes. Rawls has responded to these challenges in his more recent work, especially his Tanner and Dewey lectures. In particular he now regards his theory of justice not as an eternal verity but as reflecting the 'traditions of a modern democratic state'. Primary goods are to be understood in terms of a 'Kantian' conception of persons as moral agents, capable of following public principles of justice and at the same time devising and pursuing their own ideals of the good life.

Although Rawls's theory of justice has won few complete adherents, it has stimulated an impressive critical literature in political philosophy; and politicians of a liberal or social-democratic persuasion have been drawn to it as an appropriate philosophical basis for the policies they favour.   DLM

Reading

†Barry, B.: *The Liberal Theory of Justice*. Oxford: Clarendon Press, 1973.

†Daniels, N. ed.: *Reading Rawls*. Oxford: Blackwell, 1975.

Rawls, J.: *A Theory of Justice*. Cambridge, Mass.: Harvard University Press, 1971; Oxford: Oxford University Press, 1972.

————: Kantian constructivism in moral theory. *Journal of Philosophy* 77 (1980) 515–72 (The Dewey Lectures).

————: The basic liberties and their priority. In *The Tanner Lectures on Human Values*, vol. III, ed. S.M. McMurrin. Salt Lake City: University of Utah Press, 1982.

Sandel, M.: *Liberalism and the Limits of Justice*. Cambridge: Cambridge University Press, 1982.

†Wolff, R.P.: *Understanding Rawls*. Princeton, NJ: Princeton University Press, 1977.

Reformation political thought The Reformation is a periodization retrospectively applied to those movements for religious reform which began about 1520 and rapidly hardened into separate churches. They saw themselves as furthering the 'cause of the Gospel', a 'restoration', 'renovation', 'reformation', or 'restitution' of true religion, a return *ad fontes*, to the unsullied well-springs of scriptural Christianity, without accretions and corruptions.

The principal aim of the reformers of the 1520s (among whom Luther, Melanchthon, Zwingli, Oecolampadius, Bucer and Farel stand out) was to bring about an 'inner' conversion of individuals from 'false' to 'true' religion. In their view, what currently passed for religion was a compound of Aristoteleian (and therefore pagan) notions of virtue and self-serving fabrications of the papacy. On the reformers' interpretation, which perhaps had some justification as an account of popular teaching and belief but was a parody of scholastic theology, what the faithful were being taught by the Roman church was that they must attempt to 'merit' salvation by 'good works', especially by practices and rituals so designated. According to the reformers, this imposed an impossible task because truly good works presuppose a good will, which fallen human nature cannot attain. The true, scriptural doctrine, as they interpreted it, is that human nature is totally incapable of *deserving* salvation as a 'reward' for just conduct; on the contrary God 'accounts' sinners just *despite* their wickedness, because of His mercy through the redeeming work of Christ. A conversion from false to true religion is effected by the power of the Gospel, which those whom God has chosen receive in faith, that is, in confidence and trust (*fides*) in the saving mercy of God. Hence the watchwords of the Reformation: salvation 'by faith alone', and 'Christian liberty' (the title of one of Luther's most famous pamphlets, 1520): the Christian is freed, liberated from bondage to impossible duties, false teachers and illegitimate 'authorities'. The only indispensable 'outward' prerequisite of true religion is the preaching of the Word of God, which all must judge for themselves. Other 'external' agencies, arrangements and matters are of importance only in so far as they impede or promote the Word.

Although the early reformers invariably sought to enlist rulers in the service of reformation, they did not regard it as their task to articulate a theory of the polity. According to the commonplace distinction they employed in this context, their concerns were with 'spiritual' not 'temporal' (or 'secular') matters, although on their own showing any matter whatever may be regarded under either aspect. This spiritual/temporal distinction was later superseded by the equally porous distinction between 'religion' and 'politics' (see MEDIEVAL POLITICAL THOUGHT and CHURCH AND STATE).

Polity and religion were, however, inextricably connected in the ordinary arrangements and assumptions of the time. No clear distinction was usually made between crime and sin; thus, for example, adultery and heresy were crimes punishable by civil law. Likewise, the civil duties of subjects included religious duties, and conversely the orthodoxy, piety and morals of subjects were regarded as a proper concern of secular rulers. Furthermore, the church was part of the public order of all Christian commonwealths, having its own personnel, courts, laws and punishments, to which all Christians were subject, and enjoying various privileges and immunities. Any religious reformation was therefore bound to impinge on the public order of Christian commonwealths.

This was immediately apparent in the confrontation between 'true religion' and the papacy and its supporters. Both the spiritual and temporal authority of the papacy were gravely compromised by memories of the Great Schism and the Conciliar movement, by the real or presumed failings of learning, morality and pastoral zeal of the personnel of the papal church from top to bottom, and by the time-honoured intervention of secular rulers in ecclesiastical affairs (see MEDIEVAL POLITICAL THOUGHT). Nevertheless, the papacy remained everywhere the visible symbol of the universal, supra-territorial character of the church. However, it was plainly the mainstay of false religion and the prime obstacle to reformation, and the reformers came rapidly to deny its claims to spiritual as well as temporal authority. Their interpretation of the 'church' was that in the true, scriptural sense it was the 'congregation', 'community' or 'assembly' (in German *Gemeinde*) of all the Elect (see MEDIEVAL POLITICAL THOUGHT), united under the headship of Christ alone by their common faith. This definition preserves the universality of Christ's church (a scriptural postulate), while denying that the papal hierarchy is a necessary precondition of that universality. The Reformers also rejected the 'Romanist' distinction of two classes of Christians, a governing (clerical) and a subject (lay) 'estate', and the supporting doctrine that the so-called 'religious' (that is, clerical) life is a more meritorious 'good work' than any other lawful Christian vocation: all Christians are equal in spiritual dignity. This was polemically formulated by LUTHER as 'the priesthood of all believers'. An educated, preaching clergy is indispensable, but its principal task is to teach, and there was consequently no justification for most of the existing large population of clerics, or for their wealth, temporal authority, or juridical exemptions. The anticlericalism of the reformers had great popular appeal.

The church in this sense is by definition 'invisible', transcending the boundaries of any organized collectivity in the world. But this says nothing about the order of any 'visible church' as an organized, earthly collectivity, composed of true and nominal Christians alike (see AUGUSTINE). It merely implies that such a 'church' will be identified as a 'congregation' or 'community', not as a hierarchy. The Anabaptists (the 'Radical Reformation') construed this to mean that a true church must be a voluntary association composed only of those who had experienced conversion, with adult baptism – or as opponents said, 're-baptism', hence 'Anabaptists' – as the outward badge of membership. Such 'gathered churches' of the Elect were complete and self-sufficient communities, separating themselves totally not only from the established church, but from the civil commonwealth and civil subjection as well. Anabaptists generally acknowledged secular government as a providence of God, but only for the unrighteous, and they denied its authority over their congregations; some Anabaptists indeed claimed that the Sword (symbolizing authority) had now passed to the Elect. The church as a voluntary association was an idea utterly at variance with established order and belief; nonetheless its proximity to the liberating, egalitarian and conversionist tendencies in the beliefs of the orthodox early reformers (see LUTHER) allowed their opponents to blame them for Anabaptist insurrections, peasant wars and political insubordination generally. The reformers responded by re-emphasizing their original doctrine that secular government is a divine ordinance, that political obedience to the powers established is a Christian duty, and that passive non-compliance with the laws and commands of ungodly rulers is the most that is permitted (see AUGUSTINE); the bed-rock evangelical doctrine of *Christian liberty*, so far from diminishing the authority of secular rulers, actually increases it by reducing clerics to the political subjection proper to all Christians. Romans 13 and 1 Peter 2 were the Reformation's favourite political proof-texts.

For orthodox reformers, then, secular authority was the defining and constitutive characteristic of the polity. In any case European vernaculars (in the use of which reformers, notably Luther and Calvin, excelled) habitually identified political collectivities by their overlords or form of government (empire, kingdom, electorate, principality, dukedom, and so on). More abstract concepts like 'commonwealth' or 'polity' were of course available; the term 'state', however, was generally unknown in northern Europe as a designation for the political collectivity until the 1560s, in Germany later still. In short, the authority of secular governors over the commonwealth did not admit of any doubt amongst evangelicals.

By contrast, Reformation theologians had identified 'churches' only as 'congregations' or, in their typically polemical, 'abuse-removing' idiom, as being *not* the Romanist establishment. This left opaque which agency was now competent to reform churches, or to act representatively on their behalf. There were three possible candidates: private individuals, the clergy, or rulers. Reformations by private persons persistently resulted in civil disturbances and sects. The pre-eminence of clerics within the church was explicitly repudiated by Reformation theology. And the nascent evangelical churches depended on rulers for protection against papists without and Anabaptists within; in any case, false religion was entrenched in laws and arrangements which only secular authority could change in an orderly fashion. It was therefore a foregone conclusion that it would be rulers who would supervise the reforming work. The reformers from the beginning encouraged them to do so, on the basis of more or less *ad hoc* legitimating interpretations of rulers as 'emergency bishops', as 'representatives' of Christian congregations, or as Christians who happened to be in a position to use secular power for spiritual purposes. They also argued that ecclesiastical order and organization are *adiaphora*, that is, matters on which Scripture is silent (except in demanding decency and good order) and which fall within the secular rulers' function of maintaining 'outward' peace and order.

The upshot of government-fostered, endorsed or protected reformations was polities recognizing no superior spiritual authority except Scripture, and compulsory evangelical church-membership for the subjects of 'evangelical' princes or magistrates. There was no reason in early Reformation theology why 'churches' should be co-extensive with polities. The ambition of the early reformers had been to reform the whole of Christendom: they had not anticipated 'reformed' commonwealths confronting 'papist' ones and refused to recognize the permanency or even legitimacy of the denominational divisions amongst themselves. The first step in the legitimation of this state of affairs was the introduction (perhaps by Melanchthon) of the idea of a 'Christian commonwealth'.

425

Again, evangelical secular authorities now appointed the personnel of 'their' churches, and decreed which doctrines and practices were in accordance with Scripture. The reformers had never intended to authorize political control of doctrine or worship: they were confident in the self-interpreting and unequivocal character of Scripture as the unique 'rule of faith'. They belatedly recognized their churches' need for a degree of political independence, and therefore for independent agents (a reformed clergy) to act on their behalf. But rulers were by then entirely unwilling to surrender the ecclesiastical power they had acquired, and congregations, attracted by Reformation anti-clericalism, were reluctant to submit again to clerical rule, however 'evangelical'. By 1531, Zwingli and Oecolampadius were both dead; Luther lived in expectation of the last days and despaired of more than a holding operation; his attitude to the ecclesiastical power of 'evangelical' princes and magistrates was always permissive. The most (and even then only partially) successful attempt to re-establish a measure of ecclesiastical independence was that of CALVIN and his followers, especially in Geneva, France, the Netherlands and Scotland. What was aimed at here was co-operation, on relatively equal terms, of 'godly ministers' and 'godly magistrates'. No orthodox reformer ever contemplated the idea of the church as intrinsically a private association.

Originally, conversion from false to true religion had been conceived as God acting on the soul of individuals through the preached Word, without any suggestion that coercion might be employed. Indeed Luther – in, for example, *On Secular Authority* (1523) – insisted that faith cannot be coerced and that persecution is counter-productive. This might have made for religious toleration. Nonetheless, the orthodox reformers reluctantly endorsed compulsion in religion, in part because they could always regard coercion as being directed not at false belief itself but at its deleterious consequences for public order.

Since Catholic princes claimed an equal authority over their subjects to proscribe *reformed* doctrine, worship and literature, and to extirpate 'heresy' inside and even outside their jurisdictions, the stage was set for a prolonged period of confessional belligerence and religious persecution. In the Holy Roman Empire this was terminated by the Peace of Augsburg of 1555; the principle that a subject's religion should be that of his ruler (*cuius regio eius religio*) was not formulated until the end of the century, but was implicit in the Pacification, which was however denounced by the Catholic Counter-Reformation as *politique*, that is, as subordinating religion to merely temporal convenience. France alternated between persecution, toleration, and (from 1560) civil war until the 1590s.

The reformers' insistence on the duty of private Christians to obey secular authorities was principled, but not always expedient or even capable of being followed. Given the indeterminate and overlapping jurisdictions of European polities, it often happened that the Reformation enjoyed support amongst some of the rulers of a polity while being opposed by others. In such cases there were strong reasons, both of self-preservation and of religious conviction, to seek to justify political (that is, organized and often armed) resistance, and both Luther's and Calvin's followers did so, with equivocal support from their respective spiritual mentors. This involved raising questions long familiar to political theory but initially ignored by the reformers. For example, granted that all legitimate authority comes ultimately from God, does it redound to persons or to offices, and mediately or directly? And what is the scope of the authority of kings or emperors over 'lesser magistrates', individually or collectively, or over 'the people' as a whole? Answering such questions meant recourse to the works of scholastic theologians and lawyers whom the reformers had derided in favour of Scripture as the ultimate authority in all, even political, questions.

Evangelical arguments for resistance seem to follow a broadly similar pattern. The question of resistance was always first formulated as a legal-historical question about who had legal authority to command whom. It was assumed without discussion that the positive (in this case customary) law of, say, the Holy Roman Empire or France was binding on evangelicals. Thus François Hotman, who published shortly after the St Bartholomew's

Day Massacre, devoted the largest part of his *Francogallia* (1573) to a demonstration that in the past supreme authority over the 'kingdom' (the term was alas unavoidable) of France had lain with the Estates General, who had formerly even elected the kings. The implicit assumption here is that 'ancient law' is more authoritative than anything more recent. A very similar argument had been used by Lutherans from *c.*1530 about the relative authority of the Holy Roman Emperor and the laws, 'lesser magistrates' and institutions of the Empire. Calvin too, in a single line of his *Institution*, had allowed 'popular magistrates' to resist tyrants, guardedly citing Estates General as examples. The French Huguenots in the 1560s sheltered their political and military activities under this exception to 'passive obedience', with Calvin's reluctant approval while he lived, interpreting the Estates General and the Princes of the Blood as 'lesser magistrates' authorized by the ancient laws of France. However, even Hotman had not contented himself with merely historical argumentation, interpreting the ancient arrangements of France as an indigenous version of that 'mixed government' favoured by the best philosophers of antiquity. Other theorists of resistance, notably Théodore de Bèze (Calvin's successor at Geneva), George Buchanan and Philippe du Plessis-Mornay, argued that kingship, like other forms of magistracy, originates in an unequal contract, by which 'the people' agree to obey a ruler, on condition that he governs them in accordance with divine and human laws; the term 'fundamental laws' was invented in this context (perhaps by de Bèze) to distinguish those laws which specified the conditions of the ruler's authority. If the king breaks his contract, 'the people', or rather their representative 'lesser magistrates', may revoke the authority they entrusted to him. Whether monarchy was a desirable form of government at all was an open question.

What were taken to be the chaotic implications of this doctrine of 'resistance to tyranny' were met, both in and out of reformed circles, by the doctrines of SOVEREIGNTY and of divine hereditary right monarchy (see DIVINE RIGHT OF KINGS). HMH

Reading

(See also under CALVIN and LUTHER.)

Allen, J.W.: *A History of Political Thought in the Sixteenth Century*. London: Methuen, 1967.

Davies, R.E.: *The Problem of Authority in the Continental Reformers*. London: Epworth, 1946.

Elton, G.R.: *Reformation Europe 1517–1559*. London: Collins, 1963.

†Franklin, J.H.: *Constitutionalism and Resistance in the Sixteenth Century*. New York: Pegasus, 1969.

Grimm, H.J.: *The Reformation Era, 1500–1650*, 2nd edn. New York: Macmillan, 1973.

Lecler, J.: *Toleration and the Reformation*, vol. I, trans. T.L. Westow. New York: Association Press; London: Longmans, 1960.

Leonard, E.G.: *A History of Protestantism*, vol. I. London: Nelson, 1965.

†Skinner, Q.: *The Foundations of Modern Political Thought*, vol. II: *The Age of Reformation*. Cambridge: Cambridge University Press, 1978.

Stayer, J.M.: *Anabaptists and the Sword*. Lawrence, Kan.: Coronado, 1972.

Tonkin, J.: *The Church and the Secular Order in Reformation Thought*. New York: Columbia University Press, 1971.

Walton, R.C.: *Zwingli's Theocracy*. Toronto: University of Toronto Press, 1967.

Williams, G.H.: *The Radical Reformation*. Philadelphia: Westminster, 1962.

Reich, Wilhelm (1897–1957) Austrian/American psychoanalyst and critic of civilization. Reich was born on 24 March 1897, in an outlying part of the Austro-Hungarian Empire. He was of Jewish origin though his upbringing was not Jewish. His mother committed suicide in 1911 and his father died three years later. He joined the Austrian army in 1916, then studied psychoanalysis in Vienna, though unqualified medically. He sought to combine psychoanalysis and communism, and was expelled from the professional associations of both. He lived in America from 1939 until his death in prison, from a heart attack, in 1957. His life was tormented and miserable, some of his claims were unusual and highly speculative, and he is often dismissed as a crack-pot, particularly because of his later work.

Reich's central claim was that civilization was threatened by a permeative repression of sexuality, the loss of what should be free, spontaneous and joyful. The healthy person, or 'genital character', experiences genuine orgasm, i.e. instinctual freedom. Such persons do not immediately gratify every instinctual drive, but are capable of self-regulation, without any externally enforced 'compulsive morality'. Genital characters, whom Reich thought to be found most commonly amongst industrial workers, were equipped with 'natural sexuality', which made monogamy unlikely, though it did imply that each of the successive close relationships which were likely to occur would be truthful.

This instinctual basis for an optimistic development of FREUD's ideas underlay Reich's far-reaching critique of modern civilization. Most civilized people suffered from 'character neurosis', and were capable at best of fake orgasm (or joy), but not of the 'ultimate vegetatively involuntary surrender' of the genital character. They develop 'character armour', which may solidify into 'muscular armour', against threatening, spontaneous impulses. Muscle relaxation may lead to emotional liberation and gives an important role to the analyst.

These obsessional defences often have disastrous consequences, as undischarged sexual energy takes the noxious form of anxiety, sadism and aggression. The damming-up of biological energy leads to all kinds of emotional behaviour, including violent mass phenomena such as FASCISM. Life-negating ideologies dominate an inert and submissive population.

The process through which most people lose themselves, by dissipating their 'primordial cosmic energy', is presented as social and economic rather than biological in origin. Society in its various aspects produces a particular kind of character-structure, the primary source being the authoritarian family, led by the dominant, repressive father. The process begins in childhood with rigid house-training and the outlawing of masturbation. 'From infancy people are trained to be falsely modest, self-effacing and mechanically obedient, trained to suppress their natural instinctual energies' (*Character and Society*). The crippling of the young has a purpose – 'the older generation's fear of youth's sexuality and fighting spirit' (*The Function of the Orgasm*,

1927). The process is completed in inevitably miserable bourgeois marriage, characterized by conflict between naturally polygamous sexuality and economic needs. A revolt of the young, demanding sexual freedom, was one of Reich's paths to liberation.

Reich's grand theories of a universal struggle between constructive and destructive forces, possibly reconciled in a oneness of self and nature, and his powerful indictment of western civilization, are more poetic and prophetic than scientific. Rycroft (p. 89) discovers in his work 'a nature poet struggling to escape'. There are sharp observations on the costs of civilization, and some constructive suggestions for reducing them, e.g. confronting character armour or the resistance of patients, rather than chasing the elusive unconscious. But Reich's grandiosity and pretension, some absurd proposals such as the 'orgone box' for capturing cosmic energy, and his difficult personality, have led to his ideas being dismissed indiscriminately.   GCD

Reading
Reich, W.: *Listen, Little Man!* trans. R. Mannheim. New York: Octagon, 1971.
——: *The Function of the Orgasm*, trans. V.R. Cartagno. New York: Simon & Schuster, 1973.
——: *The Mass Psychology of Fascism* (1933), trans. V.R. Cartagno. Harmondsworth: Penguin, 1975.
†Rycroft, C.: *Reich*. London: Fontana, 1979.

reification A process of thought whereby human relationships are falsely regarded as relationships between things, and thereby endowed with a spurious objectivity and immutability. According to Marxists, and especially LUKÁCS (who popularized the term), reification is a crucial attribute of bourgeois IDEOLOGY.
      DLM

Renaissance political thought The growth of Renaissance political thought from the mid-thirteenth century to the sixteenth was closely related to the growth of independent city-states in Italy. From as early as the twelfth century Italy was distinctive in being divided into cities governed by annually elected consuls drawn from the 'plebs' as well as the military class; already, this type of government was described as republican. Though these cities were still subject to the overlordship of the emperor, their long battle with the Hohenstaufen and the effective independence they won on Frederick II's death in 1250, when many established 'popular' governments, gave them a *de facto* SOVEREIGNTY not enjoyed elsewhere. This created problems for these new regimes at a time when prevailing political thought favoured monarchical rule within a Christian framework (see MEDIEVAL POLITICAL THOUGHT). On the one hand it encouraged a revived interest in classical REPUBLICANISM with its preference for 'political' or mixed government, its humanist ethics and its cyclical theory of history; on the other, the need to justify their *de facto* sovereignty encouraged the development of new ideas about 'absolute power', 'sovereignty' and 'the state' that can be regarded as the most original contribution to this period. For this reason Renaissance political thought cannot be described simply in terms of the classical revival, important though this was, but rather as a new blend of concepts that stemmed from both the medieval and the classical traditions.

The development of 'Italian republican ideology' after the translation of ARISTOTLE's *Politics* around 1260 has been analysed by C. T. Davis and N. Rubinstein, who show how the priorities of medieval political thought were reversed by writers such as Brunetto Latini (d. 1294), Ptolemy of Lucca (d. 1327) and Remigio de' Girolami (d. 1319). Although the first book of the *De regimine principum* of Thomas AQUINAS (*c.*1265) shows the influence of Aristotle in recognizing three types of government, Aquinas still preferred the government of one to that of many, despite admiring some advantages of the latter. Brunetto Latini, however, already preferred communal government to monarchy as 'by far the best' in his *Trésor*, written in exile in Paris in the 1260s, after his time in office as chancellor of Florence's first popular government. His republicanism was reinforced by Ptolemy of Lucca's continuation of the *De regimine principum* (*c.*1302–5), which not only states a preference for republican government but draws a close analogy between the Greek *polis* 'which is a plurality or city' and 'the political rule' of Italian cities (see Rubinstein, p. 158).

The Dominican reader in Florence, Fra Remigio de' Girolami, drew out the implications of republicanism in his two treatises *On the Common Good* (1302) and *On the Good of Peace* (1304). Quoting Aristotle, he writes 'he who is not a citizen is not a man for "man is by nature a civic animal"' and illustrates this in the striking image of a citizen whose city is destroyed remaining 'a painted image or a form of stone, because he will lack the virtue and activity of former times'; as a result, quoting again from Aristotle's *Politics*, 'the city is prior to the home and the individual, for the whole is necessarily prior to the parts', and, now quoting Plato from Cicero's *De officiis*, 'for the utility and benefit of the whole body of citizens' men must forget their own interests, for 'we are not born for ourselves alone but for our country and our friends as well' (see Matteis, pp. 5–8, 18, 61, 62). Remigio's sense of the priority of state interest led to the concept of reason of state and the patriotism enunciated so clearly by MACHIAVELLI and his followers in the sixteenth century.

In contrast to this 'organic' corporatism, the guilds in Florence were at the same time developing a different and more egalitarian concept. Following the Roman law principle 'quod tangit omnes', they argued that all the guilds should contribute an equal voice in the government of the whole. Although not destined to survive the wool carders' revolt of 1378, guild republicanism offered a contrasting vision of corporate politics that served to stimulate political debate in the fourteenth century (see Canning; Najemy).

The inherent problem that Remigio raises, that of the individual and the state, emerges even more clearly in the *Defensor pacis* (1324) of MARSILIUS OF PADUA. Believing like Aristotle in man's political nature, Marsilius argues that laws should be made by 'all the people or its weightier part' through its will expressed in the general assembly, and that this assembly should also possess coercive authority over the church. This theory of popular sovereignty seems to anticipate majoritarian theories and, according to Skinner, 'was destined to play a major role in shaping the most radical version of early modern constitutionalism' (p. 65).

All these writers lived in France as well as Italy and were influenced by thinking in the University of Paris, yet it was their experience of communal life and factionalism in Italy that makes their work distinctive. With the collapse of most communes into lordships or 'despotisms', freedom and equality became increasingly important themes of republican theory. Although 'liberty' in the fourteenth century usually meant freedom from external over-lordship, in the writings of the humanist chancellors of Florence, Coluccio Salutati (d. 1406) and Leonardo Bruni (d. 1444), it also came to mean constitutional freedom to live under laws passed 'by the action of the whole citizen body', as Bruni wrote in 1402 in his *Panegyric to the City of Florence*; equality meant the special protection afforded by the state to the poor by laws against the rich and powerful. By 1439, however, in his treatise *On the Constitution of the Florentines*, Bruni had modified his earlier description of Florence's popular constitution by defining it instead as Aristotle's middle or mixed state, in which popular features such as short-term offices drawn by lot were modified by oligarchic control of legislation and the army.

Republican theory in Florence was further modified in the second half of the fifteenth century under Medicean control. Bruni's defence of republican liberty as the rule of law was reversed by a later chancellor of Florence, Bartolomeo Scala (d. 1497), who argued in his 1483 dialogue *On Laws and Judgments* that the flexible rule of one good and wise man is preferable to the rule of unchanging laws and (elsewhere) that specialization is preferable to pluralism and interchange of function in government. This new republicanism was influenced by PLATO, the translation and printing of whose writings between 1463 and 1484 encouraged the widespread diffusion of Platonic ideas. But although Florentines such as Machiavelli, Francesco Guicciardini (d. 1540) and Francesco Vettori (d. 1539) rejected Platonic idealism after the fall of the Medici in favour of the new realism, their writings nevertheless reflect his continuing influence on elitist political thought in the early modern period.

The fifteenth century was the period of so-called 'civic humanism' when ideas about man's essential political nature, drawn from the republican tradition described above and from the *ars dictaminis* tradition, were widely diffused. According to this view, 'man is the measure of all things' and he expresses himself through language and history. Political debates show how by the 1420s civic humanism had become an integral part of Florentine political experience, providing not only rhetorical techniques by which the ruling elite 'persuaded', 'exhorted' and 'argued' their policies before fellow-citizens, but also a new attitude to history as a practical guide to formulating these policies.

This new attitude to history had important implications for political thought. Influenced by Arabic astrology as well as by classical history, Renaissance writers believed that 'the world is conditioned in such a way that everything that exists at present has existed under different names in different times and different places in the past' – provided one is sharp enough to spot the similarities, as Guicciardini put it (*Dialogo del reggimento*, p. 17). According to this cyclical view, history not only describes man and the world he lives in but it can suggest what is going to happen in the future, hence its value to the political theorist. For although man is limited by behavioural patterns imposed by the stars at his birth, as well as by 'the times that run' and the arbitrary play of fortune, he can learn from history the importance of flexibility and readiness to act when times are favourable (see MACHIAVELLI). The determinism and the relativism implied by this outlook contrasted with the Christian view of history as an account of redemption by God's grace and it contributed to the revolution in political values at the end of the Renaissance period.

This revolution was encouraged by political events, in particular by the rise of lords, or 'despots' as the church as well as rival communes liked to call them. Yet these new rulers often fulfilled a vital function in ending factionalism, and new arguments were needed to justify their *de facto* authority. This situation encouraged the development of a princely literature eulogizing the merits of peace and security brought about by single rulers.

Petrarch (d. 1374), despite his avowed republicanism, preferred the tyranny of one man to popular tyranny and wrote a eulogistic letter to Francesco Carrara, Lord of Padua, on 'How a ruler ought to govern his city'. The princely literature that developed in the courts of *condottieri* rulers such as the Visconti and Sforza in Milan, the Gonzaga in Mantua and the Montefeltro in Urbino was the counterpart to republican eulogies of cities, Bartolomeo Platina's *On the Prince*, written for the Gonzaga, paralleling his *On the Best Citizen* for the Medici in Florence. At the same time, however, histories of rulers such as Simonetta's *Commentaries* on the life of Francesco Sforza display a new realism that anticipates Machiavelli's overturning of the princely model in *The Prince*.

Parallel with this development of courtly literature was the recognition by lawyers and political writers of the *de facto* authority of these new rulers. An important step was taken by the lawyer Bartolus of Sassoferrato (d. 1357) when he argued that the cities of Italy 'and especially those of Tuscany where no superior is recognized' are in fact free, 'and hence possess *merum imperium* in themselves.' According to Bartolus's distinction between tyrants *ex defectu tituli* (lacking a legal title) and those *ex parte exercitii* (behaving tyrannically), Obizzo d'Este, appointed 'permanent lord' of Ferrara in 1264 by common consent, would have been recognized as legitimate, whereas Lorenzo de' Medici (d. 1492) was condemned by opponents as a tyrant on both counts. The contrast between Lorenzo's obvious power in Florence and his lack of constitutional status acted as a stimulus to new political thought that came to maturity in the years of crisis following his death and the French invasions of Italy.

By 1530 it was agreed by Machiavelli, Guicciardini and Vettori that there was little distinction between republics and tyrannies, nor could it be argued that someone lacking a legitimate title was a tyrant. By the late 1520s Francesco Vettori had condemned all government as tyrannical, French and Venetian as well as Florentine, and Guicciardini agreed: 'all political power is rooted in violence, there is no legitimate power' (*Maxims*, p. 119), and in 1536 it was he who justified Duke Alessandro de' Medici's absolutism on the grounds that, once

established, a state has unlimited power. In his 1520 *Discursus* Machiavelli also agreed, by giving full sovereign powers to the Medici in Florence for their lifetimes. Thus in their writings the old distinction between good and bad government was eradicated.

Emerging from this new view of politics are new concepts. The concept of 'absolute power' that WILLIAM OF OCKHAM was using in the fourteenth century to describe God's omnipotence was applied in the fifteenth to political power. Related to this is the concept of sovereignty, which as Jean BODIN rightly said was not new but was the equivalent of 'the political constitution' in the Greek *polis*, *signoria* in Italian communes, and *summum imperium* in ancient Rome, the total powers that Machiavelli and Guicciardini now accepted as an essential attribute of effective government (*Methodus*, p. 175). This in turn is closely related to the idea of the state, a word that was transformed in the fifteenth and sixteenth centuries from 'estate' or condition to mean 'respublica', a public entity with full sovereignty, 'reason of state' in Guicciardini's usage being the public interest that should override Christian morality: 'When I said one should murder and imprison all the Pisans, I perhaps spoke not as a Christian but according to the reason and practice of states' (*Dialogo del reggimento*, p. 163). Although Machiavelli does not use the term, he too contrasts the political interest of the state with private morality. The word became familiar after Giovanni Botero's *Ragione di stato* was published in 1589, meaning the maxims of political prudence that create a healthy state, but as we have seen it was already a concept familiar to Italian writers.

Italy provided the right conditions for traditional constraints on government to be weakened during the Renaissance period, thanks to its new rulers and their critical attitude to the church. A Florentine merchant's maxim at the beginning of the fifteenth century, that it is impossible to control governments and states according to Christian precepts if you want to hold them as they are held today, was echoed by Machiavelli and Guicciardini a century later, encouraging greater separation of politics and religion. Towards the end of the sixteenth century, as Venice became involved in conflict with the papacy, Fra Paolo Sarpi agreed with Guicciardini that, provided justice was administered impartially, no one cares about the nature of the state, and in France and later in England Bodin and HOBBES agreed.   ABr

Reading

Bartolus: *De tyrannia*, chs 8, 9; trans. E. Emerton, *Humanism and Tyranny*. Cambridge, Mass.: Harvard University Press, 1925, repr. 1964.

Bodin, J.: *Method for the Easy Comprehension of History* (1566), trans. B. Reynolds. New York: Columbia University Press, 1945.

Brown, A.: Platonism in fifteenth-century Florence. *Journal of Modern History* 58 (1986).

Canning, J.P.: The Corporation in the political thought of the Italian jurists of the thirteenth and fourteenth centuries. *History of Political Thought* I (1980) 9–32.

Cochrane, E. and Kirschner, J. eds: *The Renaissance*. Chicago: University of Chicago Press, 1986. [Includes translated excerpts of Bartolus, above; Bruni, *On the Constitution of the Florentines*; and B. Scala, *Dialogue on Laws and Judgments*.]

Davis, C.T.: An early Florentine political theorist: Fra Remigio de Girolami. *Proceedings of the American Philosophical Society* 104 (1960) 662–76.

Guicciardini, F.: *Dialogo e Discorso del Reggimento di Firenze*, ed. R. Palmarocchi. Bari: Laterza, 1932.

———: *Ricordi*; trans. M. Domandi, *Maxims and Reflections of a Renaissance Statesman*. New York: Evanston and London: Harper & Row, 1965.

Kohl, B.G. and Witt, R.G. eds: *The Earthly Republic*. Manchester: Manchester University Press, 1978. [Includes F. Petrarch, *How a Ruler ought to Govern his State*; and L. Bruni, *Panegyric to the City of Florence*.]

Matteis, M.C. de: *La Theologia politica e comunale de Remigio de' Girolami*. Bologna: Patron, 1977.

Najemy, J.: Guild republicanism in Trecento Florence. *American Historical Review* 84 (1979) 53–71.

†Rubinstein, N.: Political theories in the Renaissance. In *The Renaissance: Essays in Interpretation*. London and New York: Methuen, 1982.

†Skinner, Q.: *The Foundations of Modern Political Thought*, vol. I.: *The Renaissance*. Cambridge: Cambridge University Press, 1979.

Vettori, F.: *Scritti storici e politici*, ed. E. Niccolini. Bari: Laterza, 1972. [Includes 'Sacco di Roma' and 'Sommario della Istoria d'Italia'.]

representation Making present through an intermediary persons, groups, or abstractions not actually present. In politics representation means the arrangements by which some persons stand or act for others. A monarch, a diplomat, even a flag may represent, but modern representative government is characterized particularly by an elected legislature. Modern representation is usually based on numbers or territorial groupings of population. Electoral districts may correspond to political subdivisions or be conventionally drawn; each may choose one representative (single-member district system) or several; where several are chosen or no districts set up, representatives may be apportioned among political parties in proportion to the number of votes each received (proportional representation); or representation may be based on work-groups or other functional groups (functional representation) or weighted in favour of certain such groups (hereditary aristocracies, the educated, etc.).

Historically, the idea of representation is associated with persistent theoretical controversies and incompatible definitions. Some theorists distinguish representative government from other forms; others argue that every government represents; still others, that representation is impossible.

Thomas HOBBES defined representation as acting in the name of another who has authorized the action, so that the representative's act is ascribed to and binds the represented. Although Hobbes thought that representation can be limited in time or scope, when people authorize a sovereign in the SOCIAL CONTRACT, they make him their unlimited representative. Whatever the sovereign does is authorized and binds them; consequently every effective government represents. Other theorists stress the diametrically opposite view: that, above all, a representative is someone ultimately held to account by the represented. Not initial authorization but final accountability defines representation; the representative has special obligations, the represented special rights and powers.

Both these views are formal, focusing on how the representative relationship begins or ends. Other theorists look to the substance of what goes on during representation, i.e. how one represents. Of these, some conceive representation as a 'standing for' something or someone absent, either by resemblance or by symbolization. A representative legislature may be regarded as a replica, mirror, map, or sample of the nation; an individual representative as epitomizing his constituency. Here representation is representativeness. Or the representative may be regarded as an artist or stage-actor, presenting, depicting, or making allegations about the represented. He makes rather than is the representation. In symbolic representation, no resemblance or depiction is required; the representative symbolizes either by convention, or because his qualities have psychological impact on the represented or on his audience.

Finally, representation may be seen as 'acting for' others in a substantive sense that goes beyond formal authorization or accountability to a kind of activity. Many expressions have been invoked to characterize this activity, i.e. the representative's role: he or she acts on behalf of the represented, in their place, stead, or name, as they would have acted, as they should have acted if rational, for their sake, in accord with their wishes, desires, or opinions, or in pursuit of their welfare, needs, or interest.

Each definition has some foundation in our ordinary use of the term 'represent', yet each is partial, ignoring other aspects of its meaning. Besides the difficulties of definition, persistent fundamental questions plague representation theory. One is the 'mandate-independence controversy', usually formulated as a dichotomous choice: should a representative do what his constituents want or what he thinks best? Mandate theorists stress the representative's obligation to his or her constituents, arguing that they are not really represented if the representative's actions are unrelated to their needs and wishes. Independence theorists stress the representative's role in a national legislature and obligation to the public good; they say that the representative is not really representing if he or she merely acts as a mechanical transmitter of decisions others have made. This view was eloquently argued by Edmund BURKE.

A second issue concerns the value and the very possibility of genuine representation. Jean-Jacques ROUSSEAU argued that so-called representative institutions only substitute the will of a few people for that of the whole community, with no guarantee or even likelihood that these would coincide. He concluded that voters are free only at the moment of elections; as soon as they are represented they are once more subject to an alien will. Since the seventeenth century, representation has been seen as a substitute for direct DEMOCRACY where a people is too numerous to govern itself directly. But this view has been subject to recurrent democratic challenges along Rousseauian lines: that participation in self-government is intrinsically, not just instrumentally, valuable, that only a politically involved and active people is free, and that representative institutions have come to discourage active citizenship.

Political representation thus remains beset by many theoretical and practical issues: to whom or what are representatives obligated – their supporters, their entire district, their party, the public interest? Should representation be based on traditional subdivisions, parties, functional groupings, or numbers ('one man, one vote')? If districts are conventionally drawn, what constitutes a fair apportionment? Which matters most in political representation: representativeness (likeness of legislature to nation, proportional presence of minorities), symbolic expressiveness (capacity to make people feel included and cared for), agency (representatives instructed and supervised by constituents), judgment (deliberation and independent decisions by unbound representatives), or loyalty to leader, policy, or political party?   HFP

Reading

†Birch, A.H.: *Representation*. London: Pall Mall, 1972.

Burke, E.: *Burke's Politics*, ed. R.J.S. Hoffman and P. Levack. New York: Knopf, 1949.

Hobbes, T.: *Leviathan* (1651), ed. C.B. Macpherson. Harmondsworth: Penguin, 1968.

Mill, J.S.: *Considerations on Representative Government* (1861). In *Collected Works*, ed. J.M. Robson, vol. XIX. Toronto: University of Toronto Press, 1977.

†Pennock, J.R. and Chapman, J.W. eds: *Nomos X: Representation*. New York: Atherton, 1968.

†Pitkin, H.F.: *The Concept of Representation*. Berkeley, Los Angeles and London: University of California Press, 1967.

Rousseau, J.-J.: *The Social Contract* (1762), ed. R.D. Masters. New York: St Martin's, 1978.

republicanism   The term is defined by contrast with monarchy. Whereas a traditional king enjoys personal authority over his subjects and rules his realm as his personal possession, government in a republic is in principle the common business (*res publica*) of the citizens, conducted by them for the common good.

Although monarchy has been the norm for most of history, republican ideas have been prominent in European political thought ever since its origins in the city-states of Greece. It was in Rome, however, that the republic came to form the centre of an ideology. Contrasted with the personal rule of the kings and, later, the emperors, the Roman Republic was turned by orators, satirists and historians into a myth combining military glory with liberty and virtue. 'Liberty' in this connection meant freedom from the arbitrary power of tyrants, together with the right of the citizens to run their common affairs by participating in government (see CITIZENSHIP). 'Virtue' meant patriotism and public spirit, a heroic willingness to set the common good above one's own or one's family's interests, typified by the acts of the heroes chronicled by Livy and Plutarch.

Many republicans, such as Sallust, attributed Rome's freedom to the virtue of her citizens, and the loss of that freedom to corruption caused by luxurious living. Others offered more institutional explanations for republican success, pointing to the complexity of Rome's political system. The ideal of the mixed constitution, which had first appeared in PLATO's *Laws* and been developed further by ARISTOTLE, was given its most influential form by POLYBIUS, who claimed that forms of government change into one another in an endless cycle of instability unless their movement is halted by a balance of the different elements within them. Rome owed its greatness, therefore, to the balance between monarchical, aristocratic and democratic elements: a belief which became an essential part of classical republicanism.

After being overshadowed for many centuries by Christian monarchism, republicanism revived in the later Middle Ages in the city-states of northern Italy. Its supporters drew upon several different theoretical resources: MARSILIUS OF PADUA used Aristotelian concepts to construct a radical argument for popular sovereignty, while the lawyers Bartolus and Baldus showed that the monarchical structure of ROMAN LAW could be turned to

republican purposes if the city were regarded as *sibi princeps*, legal sovereign in its own territory. Above all, Florentine humanists applied the myth of the Roman Republic to their own circumstances, once again proclaiming that the highest political ideal was the civic freedom of a self-governing republic (see RENAISSANCE POLITICAL THOUGHT).

Renaissance republicanism was, however, a creed developed in increasingly dark times, as the Italian cities succumbed one after another to princely rule. By the early sixteenth century it seemed clear that republican liberty was a rare and fragile artefact, easily destroyed by the turn of fortune's wheel. Faced with the problem of how civic freedom could be secured, Florentine writers stressed two complementary prescriptions, one moralistic, the other institutional. In the first place, as MACHIAVELLI and Guicciardini agreed, a stable republic was impossible without patriotic virtue. Citizens must set the public good above their private interests, especially the pursuit of wealth; they must refrain from factional squabbles; they must be prepared to fight in person for their *patria*, not leaving its defence to hired mercenaries. Patriotism, kept alive by continual participation in civic affairs, must in effect be their religion, in preference to Christianity.

Alongside the stress on civic virtue went an equal concern for wise constitutional contrivance. Many republicans, notably Giannotti, attributed the continuing success and stability of Venice to her constitution, in which the combination of Doge, Senate and Council could be readily interpreted as a classical mixture of monarchical, aristocratic and democratic elements. Machiavelli, his eyes on turbulent Rome rather than static Venice, suggested that in a dynamic system, powerful tensions between patricians and people could actually contribute to the greatness of the whole.

For two centuries after the demise of the Florentine Republic in 1530 republican ideas shrank to an underground current in European political thought, subordinate to the main preoccupation with relations between kings and subjects. During the English Civil War, HARRINGTON produced a republican utopia, *Oceana* (1656), which showed great faith in the power of institutional arrangements to secure liberty, and adapted the classical mixed constitution to contemporary conditions. Harrington's influence was partly responsible for the curious semi-republicanism of much eighteenth-century English political thought. 'Country' publicists saw contemporary politics in classical terms, with the crown-in-parliament standing for the mixed constitution, the freeholders of the shires for Roman citizens, and the court and national debt for the luxury and corruption that proverbially destroyed all free states. In face of the traditional assumption that republican government was suitable only for small states, the presence of this vocabulary made it easier for the American revolutionaries to see a republic as the solution to their problems.

This change of scale is one of the ways in which republican ideology altered in the course of the American and French revolutions. As republicans ceased to think in terms of city-states and aspired to self-government for nations, the principle of direct political participation by citizens rotating in office was replaced by REPRESENTATION of the people's will (though, paradoxically, the people thus represented were credited with the unlimited sovereignty that had formerly been claimed only by kings). In another significant change, classical pessimism was replaced by modern optimism. Republics had hitherto been thought of as rare exceptions to the ordinary run of monarchical governments, possible only in privileged circumstances and likely to be short-lived. Success in America meant, however, that republics were now seen as a universal challenge to kings. And whereas classical republicans had thought of history in cyclic terms, their successors were buoyed up by a confident belief in the progress of enlightenment, which was (as Tom PAINE, for example, believed) simultaneously undermining both churches and kings. So strong was this belief that even the failure of the French Revolution could not destroy it. It is ironical that the pessimistic ROUSSEAU, in some ways the last truly classical republican, became the prophet of a new secular faith promising the future to the GENERAL WILL of the sovereign people.

Like their classical predecessors, republicans of the revolutionary era differed in the relative emphasis placed on 'virtue' or on institutional arrangements in preserving liberty. French republicanism, following Rousseau, was moralistic in tone. To Robespierre and Saint-Just, who saw themselves in Roman terms and talked a great deal about virtue and devotion to the *patrie*, freedom was positive, geared to the common life rather than to individualism. Even TOCQUEVILLE, coolly confronting classical ideals with American realities half a century later, still saw absorption in private life as a danger to republican liberty, and the public spirit induced by citizen participation as its cure.

Republicanism in the late eighteenth century could, however, also take more bourgeois and instrumental forms, playing down the need for heroic patriotism and building on the old tradition of institutional CHECKS AND BALANCES. Defending the new United States Constitution, which owed much to the republican theory of mixed government, MADISON argued that even to aim at unity among the citizens was utopian. The way to avoid the factional strife that had so often destroyed republics was to contrive the institutions so that rival interests would check one another. Arguing along similar lines, and with even less respect for the tradition of civic virtue, BENTHAM and his followers conceived of a republic simply as a businesslike answer to the problems of government. Taking for granted the self-interest of political man, they argued that any kind of irresponsible authority is dangerous, but that good government can be secured by making power-holders elective and subject to continual oversight by those they represent.

During the nineteenth century, republicanism remained an ideal to be fought for against traditional monarchies. In the twentieth century it has virtually disappeared from the political agenda, partly because there are now no old-style kings to fight, but also because the ancient conception of a free republic, in which participation in public affairs takes precedence over the citizens' private life, does not appeal to liberals holding more negative and individualistic conceptions of liberty. In recent years, however, classical republican ideals, and particularly this understanding of FREEDOM as a matter of public rather than private activity, have been revived by Hannah ARENDT. More generally, a new pessimism among students of politics and a renewed emphasis upon the importance of political culture in sustaining a free public life perhaps recall the classical republican themes of the fragility of republics, and the need for virtue to overcome fortune.

MEC

Reading

Arendt, H.: *On Revolution*. New York: Viking; London: Faber, 1963; Harmondsworth: Penguin, 1973.

Guicciardini, F.: *Selected Writings*, ed. and trans. C. Grayson. London: Oxford University Press, 1965.

Hamilton, A., Madison, J. and Jay, J.: *The Federalist*, ed. B.F. Wright. Cambridge, Mass.: Harvard University Press, 1961; ed. M. Beloff. Oxford: Blackwell, new edn 1987.

Machiavelli, N.: *The Discourses*, ed. and intro. B. Crick. Harmondsworth: Penguin, 1970.

Pocock, J.G.A.: *The Machiavellian Moment: Florentine Political Thought and the Atlantic Republican Tradition*. Princeton, NJ: Princeton University Press, 1975.

†Skinner, Q.: *The Foundations of Modern Political Thought*, vol. 1: *The Renaissance*. Cambridge: Cambridge University Press, 1978.

Tocqueville, A. de: *Democracy in America*, trans. G. Lawrence, ed. J.P. Mayer and M. Lerner. New York: Harper, 1966; London: Fontana, 1968.

revisionism A term used primarily within the socialist tradition to describe the views of those who seek to revise the prevailing orthodoxy, usually in a more moderate direction. The term was originally coined by the German opponents of BERNSTEIN, the latter having abandoned a number of Marx's theses concerning the development of capitalism, and drawn from this reformist conclusions. LENIN and his successors (see SOVIET COMMUNISM) applied the label less discriminately to individuals and parties who departed from the political analysis favoured by the Bolsheviks, and later by the Soviet regime. In the socialist parties of the West, the term has been used specifically to designate those who deny the necessity of taking the means of production into public ownership.   DLM

Reading

Labedz, L. ed.: *Revisionism*. London: Allen & Unwin, 1962.

revolution, theories of Revolutions are dramatic episodes of political change. A revolution is not a single event, but a complex process. In a revolution the central government of a society loses the ability to enforce its laws over a significant part of its territory or population. Varied groups, including the former government, struggle to establish themselves as the central authority; this power struggle may take the form of extensive civil war, quick coups d'état, or long-drawn-out guerrilla warfare. The competitors attempt to build new political (and often economic) institutions to replace the old.

These three aspects of revolution – state breakdown, competition among claimants for central authority, and building new institutions – do not occur in clearly separated stages or in a consistent order. Each aspect influences the others. State breakdown due to bankruptcy or military collapse may lead to struggles for power among competing claimants to authority; this pattern occurred in the English, French, and Russian revolutions. On the other hand, competition for power and building alternative institutions may lead to state breakdown. Competitors for central authority may begin by organizing their followers and building new institutions on a small scale as a basis for challenging and eventually overthrowing the central government; the Chinese and Nicaraguan revolutions followed this pattern. State breakdown, competition for central authority, and building new institutions thus constitute a revolution like threads in a tapestry, or like atoms in a molecule: it is the interdependent combination of the parts that makes the whole.

These aspects can also occur separately or in partial combinations: state breakdown without competition for central authority occurs in secession movements, peasant uprisings, and urban riots; state breakdown and competition without attempts at building new institutions occur in dynastic civil wars (for example, the Wars of the Roses); competition and institution-building occur without state breakdown in coups and elite reform movements. What distinguishes revolution from other forms of political violence is precisely the interwoven combination of all three aspects.

Theories of revolution attempt to explain why revolutions have occurred in specific times and places, and to account for the various forms of struggle and different outcomes that have ensued. The complexity of revolution makes explanation difficult. In examining historical revolutions, theorists have often differed on the starting and ending dates for revolution, and even over which historical events qualify as 'true' revolutions. Theorists also dispute which aspects are most crucial, and thus argue over what is the primary thing to be explained. As a result, most 'theories of revolution' have in fact been partial theories, addressed mainly to explaining state breakdown, or to explaining why new institutions emerge, or to clarifying some characteristics of competing groups in the struggles for power.

PLATO wrote that all governments inevitably go through the same sequence of changes, with aristocracy eventually giving way to democracy, and then to tyranny. ARISTOTLE countered with evidence to show that the causes of changes in government were numerous and highly varied. The truth about revolutions lies somewhere in between – the causes of revolutions are numerous, and no two revolutions are exactly alike; yet certain patterns of events and causal relationships do consistently recur.

After Aristotle, however, the debate on the causes of revolutions lapsed for two thousand years. From the time of Rome through the eighteenth century the theory of revolutions was preoccupied not with why revolutions occurred but with when, or if, they were justified. Livy's history of Rome, which treated the founding of the Roman republic as a morality play in which virtuous Romans triumphed over the tyranny of Tarquin kings, set the tone for discussions of revolution for a millennium. POLYBIUS adopted the notion of 'revolution' as a resetting of things in their proper order – thus tyranny was an aberration to be corrected by a revolution to restore a just and properly ordered society. In the Middle Ages political theorists such as Nicholas of Cusa considered whether, given that kings were trustees of God to watch over society, the people were ever justified in revolting against their king, and concluded that revolt was justified only when monarchs violated their trust. In the seventeenth century

LOCKE argued that kings had responsibilities to their subjects, not merely to God; revolt was justified when kings failed to protect the rights of their subjects. When the English labelled their deposition of James II in 1688 the Glorious Revolution, or when in the following century the colonists in North America declared their war of independence the American Revolution, both were still using the word in the sense of Polybius, as the restoration of proper political order which a tyrant had violated. BURKE argued that the French were not justified in their revolution, for their monarch had not been a tyrant and only tyranny could justify the overthrow of authority.

Some political theorists thought that revolution was never justified: HOBBES argued that the chaos and bloodshed of revolution were far worse than the most severe tyranny. BODIN and FILMER maintained that the authority of a king over his subjects came from God, like a father's authority over his children, and thus was absolute and irrevocable. MACHIAVELLI, in pragmatic fashion, saw revolution as a risk that rulers justifiably incurred if they were both weak and tyrannical; he counselled that monarchs could preserve their power if they avoided this fatal combination of flaws.

In the French Revolution a new sense of 'revolution' emerged. Instead of presenting themselves as removing a temporary aberration and restoring a traditional order, the leaders of the French Revolution sought to discredit the entire *ancien régime* and to erect political and social institutions that would begin a new age. Thus ever since 1789 the idea of 'revolution' has come to stand not merely for opposition to tyranny, but for establishing an entirely new organization of society.

The problem of the decay and replacement of older forms of social organization dominated the thought of the two most influential writers on revolution in the nineteenth century – MARX and TOCQUEVILLE. Marx (together with his collaborator ENGELS) viewed European development since the Middle Ages as a progression through various modes of production: feudal, capitalist and, in the future, socialist. They postulated that the transition between these modes had not been – and would not be – peaceful, since in feudalism and capitalism a particular class dominated others. This dominant class would have to be dislodged by a revolution in order for the transition to the next mode of production to take place. The French Revolution of 1789 was an example of a revolution waged to dislodge the privileged feudal aristocracy and clear the way for capitalism. However, Marx and Engels argued that conflict would appear again, for the new political freedoms and economic benefits following the overthrow of the aristocracy went only to the class of professionals and businessmen – the bourgeoisie – who dominated the new capitalist society: the French Revolution was essentially a bourgeois revolution. The revolution of the working class was necessary to extend the benefits of modern industrial technology to all. This socialist revolution by workers would occur when capitalism had fully developed, and capitalists' domination of workers become so oppressive that there was no alternative but revolt. Once the workers themselves had taken control of production, work would be organized on a communal, egalitarian basis, and the state, whose main purpose under capitalism was to preserve the interests of the bourgeoisie, would 'wither away'. The major tenets of this view – that revolution is a necessary agent of change, and that such change leads to greater freedom – have embodied the idea that revolutions are progressive and beneficial.

Whereas Marx was trained as a philosopher, Tocqueville was a civil servant. He too saw a historical trend toward equality as inevitable, yet with very different consequences. He agreed that the French Revolution destroyed the power of the old aristocracy and those laws and practices associated with feudal society. But where Marx and Engels saw the defeat of feudalism as a triumph for a new class – the bourgeoisie – that a later socialist revolution would in turn dislodge, Tocqueville saw the triumph of the centralized state. To Tocqueville, when the French Revolution destroyed class privileges and set all men equal before the law it also removed all the obstacles to the authority of the state. Before the Revolution, privileged and powerful groups had existed alongside the state; after the Revolution the state stood alone, gathering all power to itself. If

Marx has inspired a tradition that sees revolution as progressive and beneficial, Tocqueville inspires caution, noting that revolution often strengthens the power of the state rather than weakening it.

In the late nineteenth and early twentieth centuries attention shifted from institutional change *per se* to the psychological trends that underlay violence and political change. DURKHEIM argued that as modern society became more complex, individuals became more isolated; bereft of traditional guideposts, they were more prone to erratic and violent behaviour. Le Bon dealt specifically with the violence of revolutionary crowds, and attributed revolutionary violence to mass disorientation and irrationality. FREUD also argued that revolutionary crowds acted irrationally, seeking release from deep feelings of powerlessness and dissatisfaction by attaching themselves to a leader and following wherever he might lead. WEBER saw political history as a process of oscillation between the tendency of states to become more rationally organized and more bureaucratic, and the periodic rise of charismatic leaders who presented new visions of society, attracted followers, and sought to build new institutions. Throughout most of history, kings and emperors had often faltered in war or when confronted by economic change, and were liable to be overthrown by charismatic leaders promising to establish a new order. However, Weber noted that modern authorities combined more thoroughgoing bureaucratization with a rapidly improving scientific technology of communication and production. Echoing Tocqueville's pessimism, Weber feared that history was leading to the rise of an indispensable and unassailable bureaucratic state that would place individuals in an 'iron cage' of bureaucratic rule.

In 1917, events once again changed the context of debate, as Russia fell to a socialist revolution. The fact that Russia – a relatively backward nation in which capitalism had made little progress – underwent a socialist revolution fundamentally challenged Marx's view of history. Scholars thus began to re-examine the great revolutions, the English, American, French, and now Russian, to seek new patterns. Brinton, Edwards, and Pettee developed a 'natural history' of revolutions that sought recurrent sequences of events, with some success. They discovered that old regime ministers were generally not blindly stubborn conservatives, but instead vigorous reformers who recognized their difficulties and sought to amend their ways. Unfortunately, their reforms more often than not prompted demands for still greater change and loosened the grip of the central authority. In addition, it was found that the major changes in a revolution did not occur when the old regime fell. Instead of Marx's new 'class' that sought to institute reforms, the opposition to the old regime was divided into 'moderates' and 'radicals'. It was only when moderates, unable to resolve the problems they inherited from the old regime, fell to the radicals that the violent restructuring of society occurred.

The 'natural history' theories of revolution were useful in elucidating the complex processes of state breakdown, competition for power, and institution-building. However, they had little to say about why revolutions occurred. The widespread outbreak of revolutions following the second world war prompted scholars to search for the causes of revolutions.

The answer was found, echoing Durkheim, in variations on the theme of how modernization bred widespread disorientation and discontent. Davies, Gurr, and the Feierabends argued that modernization, by rapidly spreading education and communication, raised expectations faster than material progress, thus creating frustration and aggression. Smelser and Johnson argued that not merely individual expectations, but the co-ordination of social institutions – political, economic, educational, cultural – was thrown into disarray by the tendency of certain sectors to modernize more rapidly than others. Huntington suggested that education and cultural change raised people's desires for political participation, and that revolutions occurred when the masses, lacking any legitimate means of political expression such as voting, violently expressed their desire to be heard.

Such theories were quite influential, but several correctives soon appeared. Tilly noted that individuals who are unorganized and powerless, no matter how discontented, were unlikely to revolt. Emphasizing the competition for power that marks revolution, Tilly argued that revolution was only likely when alternative claimants to power appeared with the resources to press their claim effectively. Modernization might spur revolution, but by redistributing resources and giving rise to new groups pressing claims to power, not by creating diffuse individual discontent. Moore recast the issue entirely through a comparative study of modernization that demonstrated that modernization was not a single uniform process; instead different nations modernized along entirely different routes. Modern states included democracies, fascist dictatorships, and communist societies; each type traced its own path of modernization, and its own type of revolutionary experience, according to differences in its pre-modern class structure and political organization. Skocpol noted that revolutions often did not arise from revolutionary movements planned by discontented groups, but began unexpectedly when states collapsed in the face of military pressures or financial crises. Modernization theorists had said little about the problems that governments faced in international conflicts, or about how states with different forms of government and different levels of economic development responded to such conflicts. Yet these are clearly important issues.

Skocpol's work has been amongst the most influential of recent theories of revolution. Her 'social-structural' theory focuses on how different political and social institutions affect states' ability to cope with international conflicts. Comparing the French, Russian, and Chinese revolutions, she noted that each revolution occurred when the state faced pressures from wars with more advanced capitalist states. Skocpol also observed that in each of these countries there was some combination of structural weaknesses that limited the ability of the state to respond to international pressures, and thus created the potential for revolutionary crises: underdeveloped agriculture that could not support a competitive military (Russia); autonomous elites who could block attempts to raise taxes or raise the efficiency of state administration (France and China); or autonomous peasant villages which could readily organize for attacks on landlords in the event of the weakening of the central government (France and Russia). The conjunction of military pressure from economically more advanced states, structural constraints on state actions, and peasant autonomy that abetted effective rural uprisings, produced revolutions.

Further contributions to theories of revolution have been diverse: the most important recent work is discussed briefly below (see Goldstone and Gurr for extensive bibliographies).

Skocpol's theory has been subject to some criticism. Gugler, Bonnell, and Dix have suggested that Skocpol understates the role of urban workers in bringing about revolutions. Eisenstadt, Arjomand, and Sewell have maintained that cultural factors, which Skocpol neglects, played a large role in shaping revolutionary possibilities. Goldstone has argued that Skocpol's theory should be combined with attention to long-term economic and population dynamics. He has observed that while international military pressures were a nearly constant aspect of European politics from 1500 to 1850, revolutions in this period occurred in two major clusters, from 1550 to 1650 and from 1750 to 1850. Noting that both these periods were times of rapid population growth, Goldstone has pointed out that in densely populated pre-industrial states rapid population growth can adversely affect price stability, government finances, elite recruitment, and popular living standards. This conjunction of effects could create strains on state administrations and intensify conflicts among groups competing for power and status, increasing the risk that routine wars or domestic conflicts would lead to revolutionary crises.

Recent work on the theory of revolutions has also examined particular problems through more tightly focused historical and comparative studies. Goldfrank has used Skocpol's structural model to explain the origins of the Mexican Revolution; Abrahamian has used a similar model to analyse the revolution in Iran. Trimberger has extended the structural theory of revolutions to cover cases of 'revolution from above': she noted that Japan in 1868 and Turkey in 1921 experienced state breakdown and new institution-building, but that state breakdown and the conflict for power were relatively brief and confined largely to elites. She maintained that this kind of elite revolution was due to states coming under pressures from more advanced states abroad, but where instead of the structural weaknesses cited by Skocpol there existed a highly professional bureaucratic elite, devoted to government service rather than ownership of land, which had the flexibility to reshape institutions to meet external pressures. Wolf, Paige, Migdal, Scott, and Popkin have waged a debate over the factors that govern peasant participation in revolutions, with Scott stressing the role of shared peasant culture, Paige stressing the economic relations of cultivators to landlords, Migdal and Wolf stressing the penetration of villages by capitalist enterprise and population growth, and Popkin emphasizing peasants' efforts to gain advantages at the expense of their fellow villagers. All of these factors no doubt play a role in peasants' behaviour, but their relative importance in specific situations has not been resolved. One thing does seem clear however: the appeal of communist movements to peasants does not lie in the intrinsic appeal of communist ideology; rather it is that communist parties have been more responsive to peasant ideals, and more flexible and persistent in organizing peasants, than the pre-communist government authorities. Rudé has studied police records of revolutionary crowds and argued that they were not the irrational mobs of Le Bon but were made up chiefly of established workers and artisans clearly seeking to defend their economic interests. Further studies of workers' movements by Traugott, Calhoun, and Aminzade have demonstrated the manner in which revolutionary movements drew power from the workers' defence of traditional rights. Rejai and Phillips have examined revolutionary leaders, and argue that those leaders in fact were generally not charismatic, and did not create revolutions; instead revolutionary situations – state breakdown and conflicts over state authority – gave scope for individuals who otherwise would probably have followed traditional professions to emerge in revolutionary roles.

Theorists of revolution have also devoted increasing attention to the long-term outcomes of revolutions. Where ARENDT once argued that only those events that established liberal democracies were 'true' revolutions, current consensus is that revolutions have a wide variety of possible outcomes. Skocpol, Eckstein, Walton, and Tardanico have identified a series of factors that affect outcomes. They suggest that socialist governments are most likely to emerge when economic resources are concentrated in a few capital-intensive centres, when mass mobilization is extensive, and when external pressures from capitalist countries are modest; capitalist governments are more likely when the reverse is true. However, as Kelley and Klein have argued, neither socialist nor capitalist revolutions have been able greatly to reduce inequalities of income or opportunity, except for very brief periods. Tendencies for stratification evidently run strong in all human societies, even those that have experienced revolutions.

Current theories of revolution thus stress variety. Ranging over a large number of cases and problems, they use multi-causal, conjunctural explanations. They trace variation in revolutionary conflicts and outcomes to differences in military pressures, differences in the autonomy of elites and of peasants, variations in the resources of states, long-term economic and demographic shifts, and differences in economic development among states competing in the international economy.   JAG

Reading

Brinton, C.: *The Anatomy of Revolution*. New York: Vintage, rev. and expanded edn, 1965.

Eisenstadt, S.N.: *Revolutions and the Transformation of Societies*. New York: Free Press, 1978.

†Goldstone, J.A. ed.: *Revolutions: Theoretical, Comparative, and Historical Studies*. New York: Harcourt Brace Jovanovich, 1986.

Gurr, T.R. ed.: *Handbook of Political Conflict*. New York: Free Press, 1980.

Huntington, S.P.: *Political Order in Changing Societies*. New Haven, Conn.: Yale University Press, 1971.

Moore, B. Jr: *Social Origins of Dictatorship and Democracy*. Boston: Beacon, 1966.

†Skocpol, T.: *States and Social Revolutions*. Cambridge: Cambridge University Press, 1979.

Tilly, C.: *From Mobilization to Revolution*. Reading, Mass.: Addison-Wesley, 1978.

Wolf, E.R.: *Peasant Wars of the Twentieth Century*. New York: Harper & Row, 1969.

Ricardian socialists A group of radicals writing in the 1820s and 1830s, who tried to show that workers in a capitalist system were unjustly deprived of (part of) what was due to them. Since the name was not used as a form of self-identification by the writers usually held to answer to the description 'Ricardian socialist', a number of doubts may be raised about the adequacy of the term. Three related problems have been discussed. First, who should be included in the group? Second, in what sense were they Ricardians? Third, were any or all of them socialists, and if so on what understanding of SOCIALISM?

The term itself was used as the title of a book written by E. Lowenthal in 1911. The immediate source for Lowenthal was the Introduction, written by H. S. Foxwell in 1899, to Anton Menger's study of *The Right to the Whole Produce of Labour*. It is largely from these two sources that the term has passed into use, but Noel Thompson has identified an earlier application of it in a book about Malthus written in 1895. Early uses of the term were informed by the perception that some writers had apparently employed propositions associated with Ricardo's political economy (see CLASSICAL POLITICAL ECONOMY), particularly those relating to the determination of value, to criticize capitalism and to defend the interests of the labouring classes. It was this anti-capitalism which appeared to warrant the name of socialists, and this provenance of the ideas which appeared to warrant the adjective 'Ricardian'.

More recent studies, however, have raised the doubts mentioned above. First, the membership of the group cannot be determined by their self-identification, since the term was used not by them but by subsequent historians. There were a good many writers willing to criticize contemporary economic arrangements, particularly their consequences for the labouring classes, or the poor, in the early nineteenth century. As MARX noted in *The Poverty of Philosophy* (1847), a long list would result from the application of this test. One further filtering device, employed by Thompson, is to examine the degree of sophistication in the analyses offered. On this basis, Thompson argues for the inclusion of four writers: John Bray, John Gray, William Thompson and Thomas Hodgskin. These four are indeed conventionally regarded as the core of the group. Burkitt's account of radical political economy, however, includes Piercy Ravenstone among the most prominent Ricardian socialists, while ENGELS, referring back to *The Poverty of Philosophy*, mentioned:

an entire literature which in the twenties turned the Ricardian theory of value and surplus value against capitalist production in the interest of the proletariat [and] fought the bourgeoisie with its own weapons. The entire communism of Owen, so far as it engages in polemics on economic questions, is based on Ricardo. Apart from him, there are still numerous other writers, some of whom Marx quoted as early as 1847 against Proudhon, such as Edmonds, Thompson, Hodgskin etc. etc. (Preface to *Capital*, vol. II, p. 13).

Although Burkitt points out that if the criterion of inclusion is to have been influenced by Ricardo, then Marx himself must be included, Thompson argues that the *only* Ricardian socialist is Marx. This is because he, unlike the others named, employed Ricardo's analysis of value, rather than Adam SMITH's, as a point of departure. This leads us to the second problem, as to which of these writers adopted or adapted Ricardo's doctrines. If we concentrate on the theories of EXPLOITATION they put forward (even if they did not use that term) the weight of evidence favours Douglas's and Thompson's conclusion that it would be more appropriate to think of them as Smithian socialists. They insisted that the model of early society developed by Adam Smith, in which goods exchanged in proportion to the quantity of labour they embodied, should be made applicable to modern society – even if they were not entirely clear about how this was to be achieved. Some specifically criticized views which they attributed to Ricardo. While nineteenth-century historians may have associated these writers with Ricardo because he was a prominent exponent of a LABOUR THEORY OF VALUE, they themselves referred to Smith.

Even when we have identified the most important members of the group, whether by prominence or sophistication of analysis, their Ricardianism is still in doubt. But so, too, is the extent of their socialism. W. Stark contrasted the egalitarian liberalism of Thomas Hodgskin with the libertarian communism of William Thompson. Although both were critical of the economic system they observed, Hodgskin emphasized the need to remove defects in the market and in property rights: he did not want to abolish property in the means of production, except when it was capital owned by those who neither made nor used it. Thompson, by contrast, hoped for the creation of communities in which exchange would be abolished. It may well be that concentration on what these writers have in common, a natural consequence of their having been identified as a group, has led to insufficient attention being given to the differences between them.

It has been suggested that the influence of these writers on popular thought did not last beyond the mid-1830s. But they remain of considerable interest to historians of political economy, and to political theorists, because of their attempt to locate the causes of the labourers' ills primarily in the economic system (although Hodgskin ultimately blamed a defective political system for guaranteeing property rights which violated natural rights of property). Even if they did not articulate, individually or collectively, a coherent theory of exploitation, the difficulties they faced and the approach they adopted are illuminating. In some ways, the present-day theory of MARKET SOCIALISM attempts to repair their omissions.   AWR

Reading
†Burkitt, B.: *Radical Political Economy*. Brighton, Sussex: Wheatsheaf, 1984.
Douglas, P.H.: Smith's theory of value. In *The Development of Economic Thought*, ed. H.W. Spiegel. New York: Wiley, 1961.
Engels, F.: Preface to *Capital*, vol. II. Moscow: Foreign Languages Publishing House, 1957.
Foxwell, H.S.: Introduction to Anton Menger, *The Right to the Whole Produce of Labour*. London: Macmillan, 1899.
†Lowenthal, E.: *The Ricardian Socialists*. New York: Longmans Green, 1911.
Marx, K.: *The Poverty of Philosophy*. In *Collected Works of Marx and Engels*, vol. VI. London: Lawrence & Wishart, 1975–.
Stark, W.: *The Ideal Foundations of Economic Thought*. London: Kegan Paul, Tench, Trubner, 1943.

†Thompson, N.: *The People's Science: the popular political economy of exploitation and crisis 1816–34.* Cambridge: Cambridge University Press, 1984.

Ricardo, David (1772–1823) British economist. Ricardo provided a systematic exposition of the principles of CLASSICAL POLITICAL ECONOMY in his *Principles of Political Economy and Taxation* (1817), a work that was drawn upon both by defenders of capitalism and by its critics, including MARX and the so-called RICARDIAN SOCIALISTS.

rights The term is used in three main ways in political philosophy:

(1) to describe a type of institutional arrangement in which interests are guaranteed legal protection, choices are guaranteed legal effect, or goods and opportunities are provided to individuals on a guaranteed basis.

(2) to express the justified demand that such institutional arrangements should be set up, maintained and respected.

(3) to characterize a particular sort of justification for this demand, viz. a fundamental moral principle that accords importance to certain basic individual values such as equality, autonomy, or moral agency.

The term 'legal right' is used for the first sense and the term 'moral right' (and in older uses 'natural right') for the other two. The term 'human right' may be used in any of these three senses. A number of authors – notably Jeremy BENTHAM – have suggested that the term 'right' should be confined to the first sense on the grounds both that the demand for a right is no more itself a right than a hungry man's plea is bread, and that the substance of rights, taken as moral considerations, can be expressed more clearly in terms of duties and utility. On the whole, these strictures have not been followed, and there has been a considerable proliferation of political theories of rights and 'right-based' political theories in recent years.

Even if we confine ourselves to the first sense we find that the term 'right' is ambiguous. Jurists have followed W. N. Hohfeld in distinguishing four types of legal relation that may be described as 'rights':

(a) *privileges* or *liberties*, where a person is described as owing no duty (to a particular person or to people in general) not to do a certain thing – for example a person who is attacked has the right to defend himself;

(b) *claim-rights*, where a person is described as having a duty owed to him (by some other person or by people generally) – for example a person has a right not to be attacked;

(c) *powers*, where there is something a person can do to alter the legal relations between him and other people – for example a proprietor has a right to leave his property to anyone he chooses in his will;

(d) *immunities*, where a person's legal position is not susceptible to being changed by the exercise of another's power – for example a proprietor has a right not to be expropriated by the state. What we think of as legal rights or human rights may be analysed as complex clusters of any or all of these elementary legal relations. In political theory, however, most attention is concentrated on (b), claim-rights, and on the relation between rights of an individual and the duties they impose on other people, and particularly on governments.

The simplest account of the relation between rights and duties is expressed in the idea of *correlativity*: X's right to some good is just another way of talking about Y's duty to provide that good for X. On this view, sometimes known as the 'Benefit Theory', to have a right is to be the intended beneficiary of someone else's duty.

Some philosophers reject this view in favour of the 'Choice Theory' of rights: X may be said to have a right only if Y's duty is owed *to him* in the sense that he has the power to waive it if he pleases. Thus the recipient of a promise has a right not merely because the promisor has a duty to carry out his undertaking but because the recipient is in a position to release him from that duty. On this account, rights are necessarily waivable; no rights are inalienable in the sense that they cannot be set aside by the say-so of the person who holds them.

The controversy over the alienability of rights has dominated the history of the concept since its introduction into early modern political thought. If rights are alienable, tyranny and slavery may be defended on a conventionalist basis; but if rights are inalienable, as they were in the political theory of John LOCKE, they cannot be thought of as having been renounced at the time of the SOCIAL CONTRACT. In modern discussions, this issue is important for the way we think about the rights of children, paternalistic legislation, and freedom of contract.

A somewhat different alternative to the strict correlativity view of rights and duties is the 'Interest Theory' of rights: an individual is said to have a right whenever an interest of his is regarded as sufficiently important in itself to justify holding others to be under a duty to promote that interest in some way. On this account, rights and duties are not simply correlative; rather the former are thought of as *generating* the latter. Those who take this view do not say that *every* interest is the subject of a right. So far the view is a purely formal one and needs to be married to a substantive theory indicating which interests are sufficiently important to be regarded as a basis for generating duties and which are not. The function of a theory of rights is to pick out certain crucial individual interests and give them priority over interests generally in political justification (see Dworkin).

The dispute between the 'Benefit', the 'Choice' and the 'Interest' theories concerns the *form* of the language of rights. More substantial issues concern the justification of rights, the possibility of a right-based theory of politics, and the relationship between rights and other moral considerations.

Issues of justification arise in the first instance because legal rights are *costly* to governments and others whose decisions they constrain. These costs arise not merely because rights get in the way of political power and personal ambition, but also because they require legislators to offer stable guarantees to individuals in circumstances where the benefits to society of doing so may vary considerably from day to day. On the one hand, rights dictate an inflexible mode of administration which cannot be adapted quickly to changing circumstances: for example, measures such as internment without trial or trial without jury in the unusual circumstances of Northern Ireland would be unthinkable in America where suspects have guaranteed rights to certain forensic procedures. On the other hand, where

rights protect choices, they create uncertainty and unpredictability for the administrator: parents' rights to choose schools for their children make it difficult for education authorities to plan efficient use of buildings and teaching resources. Even among rights-theorists, few believe that rights should be the sole determinant of policy decisions. Rights should be confined to those special areas of life where it is important for people to enjoy stable guarantees even in the face of social costs and constantly changing economic and political conditions.

For these reasons, it is commonly thought that theories of UTILITARIANISM are incapable of justifying individual rights. The pursuit of general utility in the changing circumstances of a complex society seems to require, on the one hand, the pragmatic flexibility and, on the other hand, the capacity to plan ahead of individual choices which as we have seen rights tend to frustrate. It is easy to think of cases in which more preferences would be satisfied or greater happiness promoted by simply interning suspected terrorists than by putting them on trial, by the central planning of housing, employment and education than by allowing people choices in these matters, or by neglecting poverty and deprivation for the time being than by guaranteeing everyone a minimum income. Some utilitarians are happy with this position: like Bentham, they deny flatly that men have any moral right to legal guarantees that cannot be supported by specific utilitarian calculations. 'Intuitions' to the contrary are dismissed as the psychological flotsam and jetsam of discredited moral theories. Others take a softer line, arguing that even if act-utilitarian calculations cannot generate the guarantees that rights require, nevertheless one or other of the modern forms of 'indirect' utilitarianism might. (See UTILITARIANISM for further discussion.)

Similar points can also be made about the relation between rights and DEMOCRACY. If political decisions are taken on the basis of majority-rule, there is no guarantee that the majority will not impose unacceptable burdens or sacrifices on a minority of fellow citizens. In some countries (the United States, for example) Bills of Rights impose constraints on the decisions that may be taken by the people or their representatives. From the point of view of the majority, these constraints are anti-democratic because they frustrate the satisfaction of the political preferences of most of the members of the society concerned. Some theorists have insisted that they are compatible with a more sophisticated understanding of democracy. Rights protect democracy itself against the threat of being abolished by democratic decision-making; and rights do not so much impede majority-rule as constrain political majorities to consider soberly the effect of their decisions on *all* the members of their society. But this seems true of only some of the rights that are constitutionally protected in this way.

If neither utilitarianism nor the theory of democracy is capable of supporting individual rights, what can be adduced in their favour? Historically, appeal was often made to natural law or the laws of God: John Locke, for example, maintained that since we are all God's creatures, we are subject to certain constraints in the way that we treat one another and these constraints are the basis of our inalienable rights. But the modern age is sceptical of revelation as a basis for political morality, and the idea of 'natural' rights suffers from doubts about the concept of HUMAN NATURE, and also from the general disrepute associated with naturalistic arguments in meta-ethics.

Recent theories have tried instead to identify the deep moral values and principles that underlie the idea of rights, rather than to establish natural foundations for them. The most interesting theories have based moral rights on considerations of freedom, autonomy and equality.

According to H. L. A. Hart and others, rights are distinguished from other moral considerations by the fact that they protect and promote the specifically human interest in FREEDOM. Rights alone among moral considerations carry with them the idea that their *enforcement* is morally appropriate; and if freedom is to be overridden only for the sake of freedom, then the inherent enforceability of rights shows the importance of the freedom-related values they embody. Moreover, many of those who associate rights with freedom hold

some version of the 'Choice Theory' (discussed above): the right-bearer is presented in an active light, rather than as the mere beneficiary of another's duty. On this account, then, rights cannot be ascribed to animals or foetuses, since these are beings incapable of exercising the choice and the freedom which it is the function of rights to protect. Some of these theorists are also critical of the inclusion of so-called 'socio-economic' rights – such as the right to social security, to education, to a job (with paid holidays), and to minimum health care – in documents such as the Universal Declaration of Human Rights. Not only are these aspirations utopian so far as most countries are concerned, but they are insufficiently connected with the idea of freedom to be dignified with the label of 'rights' (see HUMAN RIGHTS).

In recent years, this freedom-based view has become increasingly unpopular. The 'Choice Theory' is no longer believed, even by its original proponents, to capture the logic of many characteristic rights-claims. And the idea that considerations of freedom alone have the urgency and force associated with the concept of rights is now no longer accepted. Many freedoms (such as the freedom to drive along a street that is to be turned into a pedestrian precinct) are not thought worthy of this protection, and those that are (such as religious and political freedom) must be distinguished from them in terms of values other than the notion of freedom itself.

Recently, some have sought to derive rights from the idea of respect for human agency or autonomy, an idea associated with the moral philosophy of KANT. The idea is that rights may be seen not as the main principles of our moral system, but as the necessary preconditions for moral thinking and moral agency. People find it difficult to exercise their responsibilities of deliberation, choice and moral action if, for example, their lives are threatened, their options are limited beyond a certain point, they are subject to overwhelming pain, or they are preoccupied with desperate needs. Though autonomy and respect for human agency are freedom-related values, they view moral freedom in a much more positive light, as something that must be nurtured and achieved, rather than taken for granted in human life.

445

These considerations have important affinities to the political tradition of LIBERALISM and the liberal view of justice: if the role of a theory of justice is to enable people to justify to one another the basic arrangements for the distribution of benefits and burdens in their society, then rights can be seen as the basic principles of respect for persons that the business of justification presupposes.

The third idea – that of equality – is connected with this. Liberals believe that governments must treat their citizens with equal concern and respect, whatever their particular talents or deserts, in justifying social and political arrangements. Perhaps moral rights can be derived from this basic obligation, for example, in the way RAWLS derives principles of liberty and social distribution from the egalitarian premises of his theory of justice. Ronald Dworkin has suggested that utilitarian calculations may perhaps embody the principle of equal concern, but only if they leave out of account what he calls 'external preferences', i.e. preferences that some people have about the treatment that *others* should receive. He argues that many rights can be seen as constraints on (or 'trumps over') utility in cases where it is difficult to avoid counting external preferences and where they are likely to be otherwise decisive. Controversy continues to surround this distinction, between 'external' and 'personal' preferences, and the theory of rights that Dworkin attempts to build on it.

Not everyone is convinced that the idea of rights has an important contribution to make to moral or political philosophy. Even among those who are, many would argue that rights do not exhaust morality. For one thing, rights seem to represent specifically individualist values. We talk of rights where it is thought to be important to secure some good to an individual or to individuals severally. In the case of goods of which the value cannot be accounted for in terms of value to individuals one by one – collective goods, for example, like FRATERNITY or COMMUNITY – the language of rights seems inappropriate. A number of socialist writers have gone further, arguing that rights represent the political morality of bourgeois egoism, and that a genuinely socialist morality would not need to find room for these strident individualist demands. But this is difficult to accept: though a morality composed of nothing but rights seems singularly unattractive, all but the most fanatically collectivist theories must accept that individuals have certain interests which it is not only morally permissible but morally imperative for them to protect.   JJW

Reading

†Bentham, J.: Anarchical fallacies. In *Human Rights*, ed. A. Melden. Belmont, Calif.: Wadsworth, 1970.

Campbell, T.: *The Left and Rights*. London: Routledge & Kegan Paul, 1983.

Dworkin, R.: *Taking Rights Seriously*, rev. edn. London: Duckworth, 1979.

Feinberg, J.: *Rights, Justice and the Bounds of Liberty: essays in social philosophy*. Princeton, NJ: Princeton University Press, 1980.

†Finnis, J.: *Natural Law and Natural Rights*. Oxford: Clarendon Press, 1980.

Fried, C.: *Right and Wrong*. Cambridge, Mass. and London: Harvard University Press, 1978.

Hart, H.L.A.: *Essays in Jurisprudence and Philosophy*. Oxford: Clarendon Press, 1983.

——: Are there any natural rights? In Waldron ed.

Hohfeld, W.N.: *Fundamental Legal Conceptions*. New Haven, Conn.: Yale University Press, 1923.

Lyons, D. ed.: *Rights*. Belmont, Calif.: Wadsworth, 1979.

†Raphael, D.D. ed.: *Political Theory and the Rights of Man*. London: Macmillan, 1967.

Rawls, J.: *A Theory of Justice*. Cambridge, Mass.: Harvard University Press, 1971; Oxford: Oxford University Press, 1972.

†Tuck, R.: *Natural Rights Theories: Their Origin and Development*. Cambridge: Cambridge University Press, 1979.

†Waldron, J. ed.: *Theories of Rights*. Oxford: Oxford University Press, 1984.

Roman law Transmitted to later ages mainly through the so-called *Corpus iuris* of the sixth-century Byzantine emperor, JUSTINIAN, Roman law was the product of a thousand years of continuous legal development, of which the peak was the 'classical period' in the first two centuries AD. It was concerned with private law, dealing with the relations between private individuals, rather than public law, governing the organs of the state, which was relatively undeveloped until the Byzantine period.

The law of the early Roman Republic in the fifth century BC was a set of unwritten customs, which were considered as part of the heritage of the Romans, and applicable only to Roman citizens (*ius civile*, civil law, law for *cives*, citizens). In cases where the custom was doubtful, the interpretation of the pontiffs, a body of patrician aristocrats, was decisive. According to tradition, the disadvantaged plebeians agitated for the customary law to be written down and doubtful points settled in a comprehensive series of written rules (or *leges*), known as the Twelve Tables, approved by the popular assembly in 451–450 BC.

For the rest of the Republic there was little legislation affecting private law, which was developed largely through the control of legal remedies. An action was divided into two stages. In the first, the parties appeared before an annually elected magistrate, the praetor, to settle in legal terms what was the issue between them; in the second, a private citizen chosen by the parties (the *iudex*, a kind of single juryman) heard the evidence and arguments and decided that issue. From the late Republic, the praetor set out the issue in a written formula which instructed the *iudex* to condemn the defendant if he found certain allegations proved, and otherwise to absolve him. This system allowed the praetor to grant new formulae, and so create new causes of action when he thought fit. They were set out in the edict published by each praetor on taking up office.

The formulary system is thought to have been introduced originally for cases involving non-citizens, *peregrines*, to whom the *ius civile* did not apply. Such cases were governed by the *ius gentium*, the law of nations, rules considered to be part of the laws of all civilized people (the sense of 'law governing the relations between states' did not exist in antiquity). These rules were applicable to citizens and peregrines alike. They were explained as being dictated by the common sense or natural reason shared by all men, so that *ius gentium* was often identified with natural law.

Surprisingly, in view of the technical character of the formulary system, neither the praetor nor the *iudex* nor the advocates who represented the parties before them (the last-named being trained in the art of rhetoric) were lawyers. Yet from the middle of the Republic there was a class of legal experts, jurists, who had no formal role to play in the administration of justice but who took over from the pontiffs the function of expounding the law to those who sought their advice. Their concern with problems put to them by praetors, *iudices* and parties encouraged them to adapt the law on a case by case basis to the new conditions created by Rome's territorial expansion over the whole of the Mediterranean littoral. Thus Roman law, like the English common law, was elaborated through discussion of cases by legal experts, who then collected and published their opinions. Their authority depended on the reputation of the author.

When the Empire replaced the Republic, *leges* in the sense of statutes passed by the popular assemblies soon ceased. The praetorian edict was codified by the jurist Julian on the orders of the Emperor Hadrian (AD 117–138), and its text became the object of commentaries by the jurists. The emperor himself assumed legislative powers, and 'imperial constitutions' were recognized as a source of law. Though the emperor occasionally legislated directly by edict, his constitutions were more frequently rescripts, or answers, drafted by jurists in the imperial chancery, to questions of law either from litigants or from officials. Normally such rescripts clarified the existing law and did not introduce substantial changes.

The main agency of legal development in the classical period was the writings of the jurists, whether in the imperial service or not, in commentaries on the edict or on the traditional law and in collections of opinions on actual or hypothetical cases. The classical jurists gave Roman law great technical sophistication but also made it very complex, and the mid-second-century jurist Gaius, an obscure law teacher, introduced the 'institutional' system for the benefit of students.

Gaius's system divided all the law into three parts, concerned respectively with persons, things and actions. The category of persons was concerned with the rules governing different kinds of status, considered from three angles: liberty (freemen and slaves), citizenship (citizens and peregrines) and position in the family (those who were independent and those subject to the power of another). The category of things bore the main brunt of the classification. It included anything that was quantifiable in money terms. Gaius recognized both corporeal and incorporeal things. Under the latter head he included, first, obligations, considered as assets in the hands of the creditor, which arise either from contracts or from delicts (civil wrongs), and second, collectivities of things, which pass *en bloc* from one person to another, such as the inheritance of a deceased person, which passes as a whole to his heirs. The third category included procedure and classified different kinds of action. Although this scheme had little immediate influence, it was increasingly adopted as a structure for the private law system as a whole, and its influence can be seen in modern codes of civil law.

The classical period of Roman law ended in the third century, with the great synthesizing commentaries of Paul and Ulpian, who successively held the highest imperial office of praetorian prefect. Thereafter the breakdown of stable government meant that legal development became impossible. The next three centuries, the so-called post-classical period, were marked by a sharp decline in the level of legal science and the growth of so-called 'vulgar law', i.e., Roman law modified to fit the special conditions of the provinces. The empire was divided for administrative purposes into two parts, one governed from Rome and the other from Constantinople, and bureaucracy increased. The formulary procedure was replaced by the *cognitio* procedure, in which the lay element was abandoned and a state-appointed judge heard the whole case, deciding questions both of law and of fact. This procedure was adopted by the courts of the church and formed the basis of the medieval Romano-canonical procedure, characterized by professional judges, elaborate written pleadings and the putting of all evidence into writing (see CANON LAW).

In the fifth century the Roman Empire in the West crumbled before the incursions of Germanic tribes who set up their successor states. They followed the personal principle in law, which the Romans themselves had followed a thousand years before, and made no attempt to apply their Germanic tribal law to their Romanized subjects. For the latter they provided collections of Roman law, based on simplified post-classical editions of classical juristic writings and extracts from collections of imperial constitutions, mainly the Theodosian Code of AD 438. The most important of these barbarian collections was the *Lex Romana Visigothorum*, published by Alaric II, king of the Visigoths, in AD 506. This collection of Gallic vulgar law remained the main source of knowledge of Roman law in the West until the eleventh century.

The Roman empire in the East, now largely Greek-speaking, continued until 1453. In 527 Justinian was able to take advantage of a revival of legal science in law schools at Constantinople and Beirut to commission his minister, Tribonian, to restate the law in permanent form. The most important part of his codification is the Digest, or Pandects, an anthology of extracts from classical jurists, but with over one third from Ulpian and one sixth from Paul. They are collected into titles, each title being devoted to a particular topic, and the titles arranged in fifty books. The whole is about one and a half times the size of the Bible, but represents only about a twentieth of the material extracted. The order of the titles is that of the edict but the fragments do not appear in any obvious order. The compilers were instructed to attribute each fragment to its source but also to make whatever changes were necessary to eliminate out-of-date matter, contradictions and repetitions. The extent of these so-called interpolations, or *emblemata Triboniani*, has been a matter of debate since the sixteenth century. The Code is a collection of imperial constitutions based on the Theodosian Code, but with much recent legislation, especially by Justinian himself – some of his constitutions settling disputes that had remained unresolved since the classical period. The constitutions are arranged in chronological order in titles, and fill twelve books. These two main collections were supplemented by the Institutes, in four books, based on Gaius's manual. The whole work, which later came to be known as the *Corpus iuris civilis*, included also *novellae constitutiones* or *Novels*, legislation enacted by Justinian after the completion of the Code in 534.

By his codification Justinian turned the whole of the law into statutory form. As he put it, he made it entirely his own, and all parts (even the Institutes) were henceforth to have the same legal force. Reference to the earlier material was forbidden, as also were commentaries. In fact the great work, being mainly in Latin, made little impact on the Greek-speaking lawyers of the eastern empire (although a Greek version, the *Basilica*, was published in the ninth century). Copies were probably sent to Italy later in the century but, in view of their bulk and complexity, they were ignored until the revival of legal science in Bologna in the twelfth century.

The Bolognese doctors treated Justinian's texts with the same reverence as Holy Scripture and glossed the whole *Corpus iuris* with explanations and cross-references, which were synthesized in the Great Gloss of Accursius (*c*.1240). Since without the Gloss the original texts were barely comprehensible, it was treated as having as much authority as, and always copied with, the original. The Glossators fostered the view that somewhere in the *Corpus iuris* one could find the answer to any conceivable problem of law or government. What was important was the support of a text, but it could come from anywhere in the *Corpus iuris*.

Subsequent generations treated the *Corpus iuris* as a quarry from which arguments of various kinds could be extracted, often without regard to their original context. For example, the famous maxim *quod omnes tangit*, 'what touches all should be approved by all', comes from a constitution of Justinian dealing with the position of several guardians of the same ward, who must all agree to certain acts on behalf of their ward (Cod. 5.59.5.2).

The strength of the Digest and Code is in the closely reasoned discussion of cases. There are few texts which deal explicitly with the sources of law, and they hardly speak with one voice. One text (Dig. 1.3.32.1) justifies treating custom as law on the ground that, since statutes are binding because they are approved by formal vote of the people, what the people have approved by their conduct, without putting it into writing, should also be binding. Another text (Cod. 8.52.8), however, says that custom is only valid when it is not contrary to law or reason. Again, Cod. 1.14.4 states that the emperor should declare himself bound by the law, since his own authority depends on that of the laws. On the other hand, Dig. 1.3.31, which referred originally to the imperial practice of dispensing individuals from the operation of particular rules, describes the emperor as *legibus solutus*, 'released from the laws', and Dig. 1.4.1 pr. states that what pleases the emperor has the force of law.

The Commentators of the fourteenth and fifteenth centuries, led by Bartolus of Sassoferrato, identified principles which were alleged to be latent, although not expressly stated, in the texts. They created out of Roman law a learned 'common law' (*ius commune*) for contemporary Europe which, apart from the canon law, was the only law taught in universities (including Oxford and Cambridge) until the eighteenth century, and was drawn on whenever local customary law was deficient. The justification for such a 'reception' of Roman law was sometimes that it was the imperial law of the revived Holy Roman Empire, but more usually that its doctrines were more rational and sophisticated than any alternative – 'reason in writing'. Encouraged by the adoption of the Romano-canonical procedure on the continent, the process occurred at different periods and in different degrees in different countries – gradually and sporadically in France, but suddenly and almost totally in Germany (*c*.1500). England adopted some Roman categories through BRACTON's treatise in the thirteenth century and later the Chancellor drew on Roman doctrine in the development of equity, but the strength of the English common law prevented any general reception, such as was required in Scotland in the sixteenth and seventeenth centuries through the weakness of the local law.   PGS

Reading

Gilmore, M.P.: *Argument from Roman Law in Political Thought 1200–1600*. Cambridge, Mass.: Harvard University Press, 1941.

†Jolowicz, H.F. and Nicholas, B.: *Historical Introduction to the Study of Roman Law*, 3rd edn. Cambridge: Cambridge University Press, 1972.

†Nicholas, B.: *Introduction to Roman Law*. Oxford: Clarendon Press, 1962.

Stein, P.: *Legal Institutions: the Development of Dispute Settlement*. London: Butterworth, 1984.

Thomas, J.A.C.: *Textbook of Roman Law*. Amsterdam and New York: North Holland, 1976.

Roman political thought Already under the Monarchy and certainly from the foundation of the Republic at the end of the sixth century BC, the Romans were presumably capable of formulating arguments to recommend or justify action in terms of shared moral and political values. There survive from the third century BC several brief contemporary accounts of the careers of great men, which allow us a glimpse of these values. Similar values are presupposed in the works of the early Roman poets, both drama and epic.

What the Romans would have done if left to their own devices is unknowable. For in the third century members of the Roman aristocracy began to come into close contact with the Greek world, with its long-standing traditions of philosophical investigation. The early Roman poets, around 200 BC, already show traces of experiments with the deliberate creation of new abstract nouns in Latin.

From this point onwards, the principal interest of Roman political thought lies in the fact that its exponents were for the most part actively engaged in public life and made sustained attempts to relate what they knew of GREEK POLITICAL THOUGHT to their perceptions of the Roman political process.

The early stages of the story are obscure. POLYBIUS, a Greek active in the affairs of his community of origin, who was interned in Rome from 167 BC, has left us a clear account of the Roman political system. Unfortunately, there is no evidence that it was read by anyone until the first century BC. Nonetheless, it is possible to observe that Polybius held the same view of the development of the Roman political system as Cato the Censor (234–149 BC), a view which was also later adopted by CICERO: that the Roman political system as they knew it was the result of collective effort by the community as a whole over a long period. This view contrasts with the naive view widespread in the Greek cities that their constitutions were the work of single founder figures. It is likely that Polybius and Cato evolved their theories in the general context of discussions within the Roman elite about the changing nature of Roman society in the second century BC.

The principal contact made by Polybius in Rome was P. Scipio Aemilianus (*c.*185–129 BC), and Aemilianus also travelled in the company of the Greek Stoic philosopher Panaetius. His association with Aemilianus was emblematic of the future, for it was Stoic philosophy which eventually predominated at Rome, rather than any of the other three main schools of philosophy in the Greek world after Alexander: the followers of PLATO (the so-called Academy), those of ARISTOTLE (the Peripatetic school), and those of Epicurus (342/1–271/0 BC).

Again, little is known about the nature of the contacts between Panaetius and Aemilianus; but it is in the period immediately following these contacts that the first traces at Rome of theoretical argument about the nature and desirability of democracy, drawing on both Greek and Roman historical examples, can be detected. This period is that of the tribunates of Ti. Sempronius Gracchus and his younger brother C. Sempronius Gracchus (133 BC and 123–122 BC). They both attempted, in part successfully, to reform certain aspects of the Roman political system and met their deaths as a result. It is here that the beginning of the revolution which replaced the Republic by the Principate is conventionally placed. This revolution undoubtedly provoked reflection about the tensions between the freedom of action of individual office holders and the need for some form of collective control. The final stage of these reflections is shown to us in the works of Cicero.

On a broader front, the Romans needed to analyse and understand their possession of an empire, which by the end of the second century BC covered much of the Mediterranean world. Polybius had already taken it for granted that a ruling state should consider the welfare of its subjects, if only on prudential grounds, and also that the subjects of Rome were entitled to criticize her conduct.

The early first century BC saw a number of major uprisings against Roman rule and it is in this context that one can place the work of Posidonius (*c.*135–50 BC), another Stoic philosopher, a pupil of Panaetius and, like Panaetius before him, a close friend of members of the Roman elite. Most of Posidonius' works are lost, but it is clear from the fragments which survive that they covered almost the whole range of geography, ethnography, natural science and ethical philosophy, as well as including a history of the Roman world from the end of Polybius' *Histories* down to his own day. Posidonius was concerned in general terms with the nature of the relationship between ruler and ruled and with the obligations which existed on both sides; but he was also concerned in particular with the Roman empire and its subjects and with the position of the Roman ruling elite.

Posidonius was not unique. Just as in Greece works of history stood alongside works of philosophy in the history of political thought (the classic case being Thucydides), so in Rome the writing of history formed one approach to the problems of political analysis. This is particularly clear in the case of a younger contemporary of Posidonius and Cicero, the Roman historian Sallust (86–34 BC). He chose two episodes of recent history, the attempt by Catiline to seize power in 63 BC and the war against an African kinglet, Jugurtha, in the late second century BC, principally to analyse the conduct of the Roman elite at home and abroad, but also to allow him to reflect on the reasons for the gradual disappearance of the consensus which had earlier existed within the elite and within the population of Rome as a whole. His general explanation, expounded in the prefaces to the two works, in terms of a decline in political morality brought about by greed for the riches of the Mediterranean world, is argued with much vehemence, and little sophistication. On the other hand, the speeches attributed to Marius or Caesar, for instance, contain subtle analyses of the distribution of political power in the state and of the limits of tolerance.

In general the age of Cicero marks the Roman conquest of almost all forms of intellectual activity invented by the Greeks and the development of new forms on a substantial scale for the first time. Creative activity over the whole range lasted into the Principate of the first Emperor, Augustus, but hardly beyond.

What did occur in the Principate, however, was a revival of intellectual activity in the Greek world under Roman rule, on a vast scale, if not of great originality. Once again, the principal vehicle of analysis was works of history. For Greek historians, from Dionysius of Halicarnassus, Diodorus (both late first century BC) and Strabo (64/3–after AD 23) in the age of Augustus to Dio at the turn of the second and third centuries AD, the Roman Empire was above all a system which worked and worked well, requiring no further justification. This approach remained alien to Latin historians and was perhaps for all practical purposes unknown to them. On the whole, they used only the Greek material already available in the age of Cicero. Their concerns were very different.

The Principate, when there was an heir available, was from the outset a hereditary monarchy: in the words of Edward Gibbon, a despotism tempered by assassination. The convenient fiction was very early developed that the Roman people vested its supreme power in each successive emperor, which led to important developments in Roman views about the sources of law (see ROMAN LAW). The elite which had held power as a group under the Republic had undoubtedly lost it, despite the fact that the Principate could not of course dispense with their services. What is interesting is that new members of the Roman elite absorbed so rapidly the ideals of the traditional aristocracy. The early Principate saw continuing, if intermittent, opposition, not simply by those ambitious for supreme power, but above all to emperors regarded as enemies of freedom. Yet all depended on the personality and good will of the emperor. This fact underlay both the attempt of SENECA to develop a theoretical account of the proper conduct of a monarch and the harsher analysis by Tacitus of the tension between Principate and liberty.

Tacitus (*c.*55–early second century) composed his *Histories* (originally covering the period AD 69–96) and his *Annals* (covering the period from the death of the Emperor Augustus in AD 14 to 68) during the reign of the Emperor Trajan. The beginning of this reign witnessed the delivery of a *Panegyric* by Pliny the Younger (AD 61 or 62–early second century), in the course of which he claimed that Trajan had succeeded in reconciling Principate and liberty. Yet this reconciliation had no institutional basis, only a personal one. And the only conclusion to be drawn from the writings of Tacitus is that the two were essentially incompatible. One of his minor works, the *Agricola*, praises a man who was the loyal servant of a tyrannical emperor; the *Dialogue on Orators* concludes that the decline of oratory is the result of the end of the Republic. In his conclusion that a member of the Roman elite should serve even a bad master, Tacitus approaches the view of the Greek sources, though from a different direction, that the Roman Empire demanded acceptance because it was a system which worked and there was in any case no real alternative.

The most interesting document of the second century AD, however, is the so-called *Meditations* of the Emperor Marcus Aurelius, who ruled from 161 to 180. His early upbringing was the normal one of a member of the Roman elite; it was not until he was seventeen that he was adopted as heir by Antoninus Pius, who had no male child, and had himself been adopted by Hadrian as the latter's successor. In the course of his upbringing, Marcus did more than absorb the Stoic philosophy familiar in a diluted form to any educated Roman; he acquired a considerable knowledge of its principal doctrines. In a Stoic utopia, only the wise were to rule. The Roman Empire, however, was not a utopia and everyone had a general duty to perform the functions which were appropriate to his or her station in life. In the case of Marcus, these happened to be those of a Roman emperor. In general terms, the attraction of this aspect of Stoicism to members of the Roman elite is obvious. It was a world with strictly limited possibilities for change, and someone whose station in life was near the top of the pyramid of society was doubtless pleased to find that it was his duty to accept the position. Marcus, however, as we can see, agonized over his weakness and unworthiness. It is striking how extensively he uses military metaphors to describe his calling and duty. The language no doubt underlies the developments of the late Empire, where all forms of public service were described as *militia*.

Also of interest is Marcus's impatience with, and indeed contempt for, the men who formed his entourage. In the Greek world, there was a long tradition of blaming the misconduct of a ruler on the bad advice given by his courtiers, of saving the institution by attaching the blame for its malfunctioning elsewhere. But the Roman emperors seem to have accepted the absolute nature of their position and their responsibility. What there is little trace of, as long as the Roman emperors remained pagan, is any kind of theory of the divine right of kings.   MHC

Reading

†Beard, W.M. and Crawford, M.H.: *Rome in the Late Republic*. London: Duckworth, 1985.

Brunt, P.A.: Marcus Aurelius in his meditations. *Journal of Roman Studies* 64 (1974) 1–20.

Earl, D.C.: *The Political Thought of Sallust*. Cambridge: Cambridge University Press, 1961.

Firpo, L. ed.: *Storia delle idee politiche, economiche e sociali*. Turin: UTET, 1982. [Esp. essays by J.-L. Ferrary and S. Mazzarino.]

Gabba, E.: The historians and Augustus. In *Caesar Augustus: Seven Aspects*, ed. F.G.B. Millar and E. Segal. Oxford: Clarendon Press. 1984.

Nicolet, C. ed.: *Demokratia et aristokratia*. Paris: Sorbonne, 1983.

Nock, A.D.: Posidonius. *Journal of Roman Studies* 49 (1959) 1–15.

Syme, R.: *Tacitus*. Oxford: Clarendon Press, 1958.

———: *Sallust*. Berkeley: University of California Press, 1964.

Strasburger, H.: Posidonius on problems of the Roman Empire. *Journal of Roman Studies* 55 (1965) 40–53.

romanticism Taking a broad view of the conceptual structure of romantic thinking, and of its historical origins, one can identify 'romanticism' with a belief in the cardinal role of art in human life, and a claim to its paradigmatic function for the understanding of all cultural and social phenomena. These new conceptions of art and artistic creation arose initially from a revolt against a particular strand of eighteenth-century rationalism: neo-classicist aesthetics. The ground for the revolt was prepared by the cult of sensibility in the novels of ROUSSEAU and Richardson, by the violent anti-authoritarianism of the Storm and Stress movement and by the religious revival fostered in Methodism and Pietism.

The seminal ideas of this aesthetic critique received their first and most systematic expression in Germany in the last decade of the eighteenth century. In the early works of the brothers Friedrich Schlegel (1772–1823) and August Wilhelm Schlegel (1767–1845), and of their friends and literary collaborators Novalis (Friedrich von Hardenberg, 1772–1801), Friedrich Schleiermacher (1786–1834), and Ludwig Tieck (1773–1853), the term 'romantic' was self-consciously used to differentiate the characteristic attributes of 'modern' poetry from those supplied in the model of classical antiquity, and to formulate a programme for the future regeneration of art. Expanded into a comprehensive theory of modern civilization, this new conception of poetry subsequently influenced romantic thinkers in England, such as COLERIDGE (1772–1834) and CARLYLE (1795–1881) and, through Madame de Staël (1776–1817), imparted vital impulses to the evolution of romantic doctrines in France and Italy.

In rejecting the neo-classicist canon of rules and pure genres, the German romantics stressed originality, spontaneity and the power of the artist's imagination as the essential qualities of the creative process. Against an ahistorical aesthetics bound by uniformity of standard and the servile imitation of the ancients, they affirmed the equal, because incommensurable, value of all art forms in which the genius of nations and peoples had found expression. Individuality, diversity and organic unity were established as the normative categories that should guide the understanding of art and, beyond it, of life in all its manifestations.

In its rejection of the major postulates of ENLIGHTENMENT rationalism, romanticism could appear as a revolt against modernity as such. For the same reasons for which it opposed uniformity of standards in the evaluation of cultural phenomena, it turned against the methodological foundations of the Newtonian paradigm of scientific knowledge: romantic thinkers dismissed the achievements of modern physics and of associationist psychology because the search for general laws, premised upon the quantifiability and calculability of all subject matter, rendered only an impoverished, abstract notion of human persons and could give no account of the intimate and emotive quality of the relationships that bound them to

nature and to each other. A strongly pantheistic strain in Schelling (1775–1854), Schleiermacher, Wordsworth (1770–1850), Coleridge, and Shelley (1792–1822) portrayed man and nature as essentially adapted to each other – integral parts of a living universe which was accessible to human understanding through intuition and empathy.

Similar objections to the dissecting and fragmenting effects of modern analytical reasoning marked the romantic attitude in other fields of knowledge: against the universal tenets of the Enlightenment's natural religion and its explication in rational discourse, Schleiermacher and Chateaubriand (1768–1848) defended private feeling and spontaneous communication with the divine as the only authentic basis of religious faith. Adam Müller (1773–1825), Coleridge and Carlyle criticized the methods of CLASSICAL POLITICAL ECONOMY for reducing the human dimension of economic life to the barren schema of the cash nexus. All romantic thinkers found fault with the simple contractual model of political obligation dominant in liberal and democratic doctrines (see SOCIAL CONTRACT). The supreme value which they attached to individuality and diversity of national and local traditions, furthermore, explains why the romantics stood opposed to the major political changes of their time. They condemned the trend towards bureaucratic rationalization (manifest in the machine-like state of Frederick's Prussia), the attempt at legal unification (as, for example, Savigny's critique of the Code Napoléon), and, most emphatically, the revolutionary demand for equal political rights based upon a false uniformity of human nature.

However, as far as actual political commitments are concerned, romanticism cannot simply be equated with conservatism and reactionary nationalism. The predominance of aesthetic values in romantic thinking ensured a flexible – or, as has sometimes been argued, an essentially apolitical – disposition, which could align itself with any ideological stance between the poles of revolution and reaction. Thus in Germany, due mainly to the effective polemics of the Young Germans and the YOUNG HEGELIANS, romanticism became virtually synonymous with the reactionary policies of the

Metternich era. In France and Italy, on the other hand, romantic ideas harnessed to the cult of Napoleon and to revolutionary patriotism could form a natural alliance with liberal forces. Divisions of a similar magnitude can be said to separate the political convictions of the Lake poets from those held by Shelley, Keats (1795–1821) and Byron (1788–1824).

Despite the variety of political causes championed by individual romantic writers one can, nonetheless, speak of a distinct contribution of romanticism to modern political thinking. By joining the idea of the 'state' to that of the 'nation', romanticism extended the focus of political argument beyond the institutional framework of law and government and drew attention to the manifold non-rational and non-formal bonds of social cohesion given in common language, religion, folk art, customs, etc. Moreover, given its organicist assumptions, romanticism could not accept the separation of private and public spheres which is constitutive of liberal political theory. That is, it did not consider the state as an umpire or guarantor of individual rights nor as an instrumental device for the promotion of social happiness. Rather, the state embodied the highest human aspirations, the 'totality of human affairs' (Müller; in Reiss, p. 157). This transcendence of the conventional delineation of politics was already manifest in the romantic attitude towards the French Revolution. Enthusiasm for the events in France – initially hailed as the harbinger of an imminent total transformation of society – was soon followed by disillusionment when it became clear that the changes amounted to no more than a 'political' revolution, affecting merely the external and formal arrangements of social life.

A similar vacillation between utopian and reactionary elements can be discerned in the idea of COMMUNITY (*Gemeinschaft*) through which romantic thinking made perhaps its strongest impact upon later political doctrines. This postulated the total identification of the individual with the whole – without reference to constitutional guarantees of individual rights or to active participation in the institutions of the state. Instead, 'community' invoked feelings of loyalty, fellowship and belonging by welding together different types of social relationships:

the intimacy of friendship and love; the personal character of obligations characteristic of small groups (such as the manorial community of the Middle Ages); the emotive bonds of a common religious faith; and the strength of patriotic feelings.

In the early romantic projects of communal living ('Sympoetry' and 'Symphilosophy' in the language of Friedrich Schlegel and Novalis, 'Pantisocracy' in the schemes of the Cambridge circle around Coleridge and Southey), the 'congregation of artists', united by bonds of love and friendship, was to be the beginning of a new world. Liberated personal relationships – predicated upon the emancipation of women (and men) from traditional sexual stereotypes – were conceived as the inner cells from which true freedom would radiate outwards and permeate the whole of social life. Romantic medievalism – the rehabilitation of the 'Dark Ages' – is often taken to denote an escape into a haven of unquestioned beliefs and stable hierarchical forms of authority. Yet Novalis's famous essay *Die Christenheit oder Europa* (Christendom or Europe) (1799) called not for the return to a golden age in the past, but rather for the poetic anticipation of a future when Europe would once again be united by a common faith – analogous to, but not identical with, medieval Catholicism. Even where (as in the writings of Adam Müller, Coleridge, Southey and Carlyle) the romantic re-valuation of the Middle Ages became more closely associated with a politically motivated defence of 'feudal' institutions, it cannot be explained merely as a conservative reaction to revolution and democracy. It was also an effective vehicle of social criticism. In an idealized hierarchical order rooted in personal relations of service and protection, romantic writers found a vantage-point which allowed them to depict the destructive effects of modern commercialism and industrialism, and to expose new modes of exploitation and domination behind the façade of formally equal rights.

In considering the links between romanticism and NATIONALISM it should not be forgotten that the romantic idea of the nation, with its emphasis upon cultural rather than political factors, bore as yet little resemblance to the quest for power and self-aggrandizement prominent in later nationalist ideologies. The feeling for national peculiarities that the romantics had learnt from HERDER was not incompatible with a sympathetic understanding of traditions other than one's own. Indeed, one of the lasting achievements of romantic thinking lies in the inspiration which it gave to the comparative study of languages and cultures across a wide historical and geographical spectrum (including non-European civilizations). In the historical school of law and the historical school of economics this romantic influence generated new methods – opposed to classical economics and legal positivism – of apprehending the nature of economic and legal practices through their concrete historical development and their interdependence with all other institutions of society.

The wars against Napoleon gave rise to a more narrowly-bounded concern with nationality which centered upon political unity and military strength. But even here the legacy of Romanticism cannot be pressed into a simple formula. The ideas which inspired demands for national self-determination in Poland (Mickiewitz, 1798–1855) were mystical and Messianic (extolling the virtues of an uncorrupted peasantry); Mazzini's appeal to the Italian people to throw off the yoke of an alien power rested upon libertarian and egalitarian beliefs. The glorification of war as a catalyst of national awakening and the overt tones of anti-semitism (to be found in some romantic circles in Germany), on the other hand, contained the seeds of aggressive doctrines in which the idea of a nation's unique character and special mission could obliterate any universal norms of conduct.

Concentration upon the causes of twentieth-century FASCISM, RACISM and militarism has no doubt generated important insights into the processes through which the romantic critique of rationalism, the polemical opposition of *Gemeinschaft* and *Gesellschaft*, and organicist conceptions of state and nation as ends in themselves, could be adapted to serve the goals of anti-modernist and anti-liberal ideologies. However, by divorcing romantic political ideas from their broader aesthetic and philosophical foundations, this focus has obscured the extent to which romanticism revolutionized our understanding of history and culture, and thus the nature of politics.   UV

Reading

Abrams, M.H.: *Natural Supernaturalism: Tradition and Revolution in Romantic Literature*. New York: Norton, 1971.

Berlin, I.: The counter-enlightenment. In I. Berlin, *Against the Current: essays in the history of ideas*, ed. H. Hardy. London: Hogarth, 1979.

Halsted, J.B. ed.: *Romanticism*. London: Macmillan, 1969.

Lovejoy, A.: *Essays in the History of Ideas*. Baltimore and London: The John Hopkins University Press, 1948.

————: *The Great Chain of Being: a Study of the History of an Idea*, ch. 10. New York: Harper & Row, 1960.

Mannheim, K.: Conservative thought. In K. Mannheim, *Essays in Sociology and Social Psychology*, ed. P. Kecskemeti. London: Routledge & Kegan Paul, 1953.

Müller, A.: Elements of politics (1808–9). In Reiss ed.

Reiss, H. ed.: *The Political Thought of the German Romantics, 1793–1815*. Oxford: Blackwell, 1955.

Wellek, R.: *A History of Modern Criticism 1750–1950*, vol. II: *The Romantic Age*. Cambridge: Cambridge University Press, 1981.

Rousseau, Jean-Jacques   (1712–1778) French moral and political philosopher. The private life of Jean-Jacques Rousseau has been the focus of more public attention than that of almost any other serious philosopher. His mother died in childbirth, leaving Jean-Jacques to be reared first by his father, then by relatives. As a teenage apprentice, he ran away from his native Geneva in 1728 and set out to find his fortune on foot, with nothing but his shirt on his back. Self-educated, Rousseau became one of Europe's most extraordinary thinkers and writers: composer and music critic, novelist, botanist, and essayist as well as the author of serious works of political and moral philosophy.

Taken under the protection of Mme de Warens, a Catholic proselytizer who became his lover, he educated himself – particularly during a stay in her house outside Chambéry. After moving to Paris in 1742, Rousseau spent a short period as secretary to the French ambassador in Venice (1743–4); returning to the French capital, he became intimate with Diderot and the other leading intellectuals of the day.

In 1749, on the way to visit Diderot, who was imprisoned in Vincennes for his subversive writing, Rousseau read the announcement of an essay contest sponsored by the Academy of Dijon and, he claimed, had a sudden inspiration of a 'noble and sad system' explaining human evolution, misery, and injustice (the so-called 'Illumination of Vincennes'). The resulting *Discourse on the Sciences and Arts* (1750) not only won the prize in Dijon, but made him famous.

As a Genevan whose career was primarily established in France, Rousseau was socially a 'marginal' man. Endowed with an extraordinarily sensitive – some would say paranoid – personality, he made enemies among the leading figures of the FRENCH ENLIGHTENMENT (the group known as the *philosophes*); in part as a consequence of his *Discourse on the Sciences and Arts*, he moved from Paris to the countryside and ultimately broke with his friend Diderot. After *Émile* (1762) and *Du contrat social* (1762) were condemned in Paris and Geneva, he fled France and spent a number of years seeking a tranquil refuge in Swiss, Prussian, and English territory. Convinced of a plot to persecute him, Rousseau wrote, between 1764 and 1770, his autobiographical *Confessions*, an extraordinary work of self-relevation that was to be followed by two further autobiographical writings, the *Dialogues* (written 1772–6) and the *Rêveries d'un promeneur solitaire* (written 1776–8).

Although biographical details may explain the apparent contradictions of Rousseau's thought, they do not indicate either the breadth of his experience or the depth of his philosophical understanding. As the quintessential outsider, Jean-Jacques had an uncommonly deep awareness of both the isolation of the self and the sweetness of social harmony. To an unusual degree, his experience spanned different countries, different social classes, and different ways of life. Despite the fascinating personality and experiences that he reveals in his autobiographical writings, the major works that formed the basis of what he called his 'system' constitute a turning-point in the history of western political and social thought.

Rousseau's contribution to moral philosophy is principally based on the insights set forth in his two *Discourses*. In the first – the prize-winning *Discourse on the Sciences and Arts* –

Rousseau asserted that the spread of scientific and literary activity was morally corrupting for society at large. In the second – the *Discourse on the Origin of Inequality* (1755) – he explained the foundations of this critique of the Enlightenment, arguing that humans had evolved from an animal-like 'state of nature' in which isolated and stupid individuals lived peacefully. Originally, humans were naturally equal and free beings animated by the principles of self-preservation and pity; differences of status, wealth, and political power were thus produced by a historical transformation of the 'natural man' (who was 'good' without being either rational or virtuous) into a competitive and selfish 'social man' capable of intentionally harming others (see also HUMAN NATURE).

A century before Darwin, Rousseau thus elaborated an evolutionary foundation for political thought. He rejected both the traditional doctrine of 'natural sociability', derived from the ancients, and the modern or Hobbesian teaching according to which humans are naturally competitive and self-seeking. Perhaps even more important, in place of the general assumption that historical change constitutes progress and improvement, Rousseau took a profoundly pessimistic view of history. For him, primitive societies like those of the indigenous Americans and Africans were the 'best for man'; civilization, far from being a boon, is always accompanied by costs that are greater than the benefits.

These premises were consciously radical. They led Rousseau to challenge all existing political and social institutions on the grounds that they were inherently unnatural; to cite the famous words of the *Social Contract* (I, ii, p. 46): 'Man was [or is] born free, yet everywhere he is in chains.' But Rousseau combined these radical principles with praise of the 'virtue' of the pagan city-states of antiquity. Sparta and republican Rome became his models, because only in such small-scale communities could citizens be educated to prefer the good of the community to their private self-interests.

Rousseau's positive political teaching, summarized in *Émile* and set out in more detail in the *Social Contract*, thus seems to contradict the concept of human nature developed in the second *Discourse*. This contradiction is more apparent than real, however. At the beginning of history, humans were fundamentally equal, wandering in the forests as isolated and free individuals. Moral corruption and injustice arise from social inequality and the resulting dependence of one individual on another. To mitigate these evils, it is necessary to establish human laws that treat all individuals equally and that give each member of the community the guarantee of a free vote on all laws.

Rousseau's political principles are based on the oft-debated concept of the GENERAL WILL. In addition to each individual's self-interest (the private will), the citizen has a collective interest in the well-being of the community. Rousseau therefore traced the foundations of the law and political society itself to the 'general will' – i.e. the citizen body acting as a whole and freely adopting rules that will apply equally to each individual. The forerunner of the rational choice theory of 'collective goods' developed by twentieth-century economists, this concept of political right stresses the importance of freely chosen social obligations as the basis of civic virtue.

Rousseau thus presented a radically 'democratic' challenge to the political principles of the *ancien régime*. It follows from his principles that the citizen body is the only legitimate 'sovereign' of a political community. Hence, at a time when the term sovereign was typically reserved for the king of France and other hereditary rulers, Rousseau distinguished between the people as 'sovereign', and the 'government' as an agent of the popular will (and capable of being organized in various ways).

It also follows from Rousseau's principle of the general will that, for a society to be legitimate, political decisions must be in accord with laws that are not only enacted by the sovereign people, but binding on all citizens equally. For a citizen to submit to decisions in the name of the public interest without becoming dependent on others, legal rules must apply to all without exception. Only in this way, Rousseau claimed, could each individual freely vote for and obey the law as an expression of the common good without contradicting his own interest and needs.

Since all acts of the government should be subordinated to popularly enacted laws, and since all laws should apply to every citizen equally, Rousseau claimed that his 'principles of political right' could explain why a rational and self-interested individual would join with others in a political community. As a result, Rousseau felt he had resolved the dilemma of human selfishness and collective interest posed by HOBBES without denying – as Hobbes seemingly had done – the existence of a positive or active form of civic freedom based on self-sacrifice for a legitimate political community.

The resulting political philosophy strikes many readers as paradoxical. On the one hand Rousseau outlined the cardinal principles of modernity – freedom and equality – a generation before they were enshrined in the French Revolution; on the other, he criticized the characteristically modern concept of political and economic progress, choosing instead to propose the city-state of antiquity as the model of the virtuous political community. The paradox is not due, however, to contradictory or confused thought on Rousseau's part: quite the contrary, for he saw – as many of his critics did not – that what Europeans called historical progress was purchased at the cost of social inequality, violence, and the morally degrading domination of the indigenous peoples of Africa and the New World.

It would be unnecessarily narrow to focus on Rousseau's political thought without indicating his more general contributions to western culture. Works such as *Émile*, the *Confessions*, and the *Rêveries d'un promeneur solitaire* changed the way many people felt, just as Rousseau's political works contributed to a fundamental change in the way people thought. Jean-Jacques can be said to have rediscovered 'nature': his writings stressed the primacy of natural feelings and moral corruption due to social convention, rationality, and complex political life. His *Émile* contributed to radical educational reform by insisting that teaching conform to the developmental process, emphasizing 'lessons of things' and 'negative education' in place of rote learning and formalized curricula.

Rousseau's more autobiographical works – notably the *Confessions* and the *Rêveries* – had important literary consequences, celebrating the 'self' of the creative artist. He also wrote a best-selling novel, *Julie ou la Nouvelle Héloïse* (1761), which portrayed many of his principles in a romantic form that did much to legitimize sentiment as a counterweight to reason. Consistent with his philosophic criticism of civilization, language, and the Enlightenment in the name of 'nature', these works challenged rationalism in the name of feeling.

Given the range of his erudition, the depth of his reflection, and the variety of his interests, it is hardly surprising that Rousseau's influence has changed markedly over time. In the eighteenth century, he was the *enfant terrible* of the Enlightenment, denying the legitimacy of the status quo while challenging the concept of progress. In the nineteenth century, he was more often viewed either as the apostle of the French Revolution or as the founder of the romantic movement (see ROMANTICISM). For twentieth-century critics, he is often praised as a founder of the western democratic tradition or vilified as a forerunner of totalitarianism. This very range of interpretation suggests that his thought cannot be reduced to a single stereotype or category: Rousseau – like Plato, Hobbes, and Marx – deserves to be considered as one of the most profound and complex political thinkers in the history of the West.

RDM

Reading

Cranston, M.: *Jean-Jacques: the Early Life and Work of Jean-Jacques Rousseau, 1712–1754*. New York: Norton, 1982; London: Allen & Unwin, 1983.

Gilden, H.: *Rousseau's Social Contract: the Design of the Argument*. Chicago: University of Chicago Press, 1983.

Goldschmidt, V.: *Les principes du système de Rousseau*. Paris: Vrin, 1974.

Launay, M.: *Jean-Jacques Rousseau, écrivain politique*. Grenoble: ACER, 1971.

†Masters, R.D.: *The Political Philosophy of Rousseau*. Princeton, NJ: Princeton University Press, 1968.

†Miller, J.: *Rousseau: Dreamer of Democracy*. New Haven, Conn.: Yale University Press, 1984.

Rousseau, J.-J.: *Correspondence complète*, ed. R.A. Leigh. Geneva: Institut et Musée Voltaire, 1965– .

——: *Oeuvres complètes*. Éditions de la Pléiade. 4 vols to date. Paris: Gallimard, 1959–69.

——: *First and Second Discourses*, ed. R.D. Masters. New York: St Martin's, 1964.

——: *Politics and the Arts: Letter to M. d'Alembert on the Theatre*, ed. A. Bloom. Glencoe, Ill.: Free Press of Glencoe, 1960.

——: *The Social Contract, with Geneva Manuscript and Political Economy*, ed. R.D. Masters. New York: St Martin's, 1978.

——: *Émile*, ed. A. Bloom. New York: Basic, 1978.

Starobinski, J.: *J.-J. Rousseau: la transparence et l'obstacle*. Paris: Gallimard, 1971.

rule of law An expression associated in England with A. V. DICEY's classic description of the English constitution. Dicey himself related it to the old legal phraseology of the Year Books: 'La ley est le plus haute inhéritance que le roy ad; car par la ley, il même et toutes ses sujets sont rulés.'

In his *Introduction to the Study of the Law of the Constitution* (1885), Dicey assigned three particular meanings to the phrase. It stood first, he said, for the idea that LAW excluded the exercise of arbitrary power. Englishmen could be punished for breaches of law and for nothing else. Arbitrary punishments inflicted by prerogative power or by uncontrolled bureaucratic discretion were inconsistent with the rule of regular law.

Second, the rule of law stood for equality of all persons before the law and the equal subjection of both subjects and officials to the ordinary law administered by the ordinary law courts. It excluded special exemptions for governmental action or special tribunals for the consideration of cases involving state officials.

Third, the rule of law in England stood for the idea that the constitution was not the source of citizens' rights, but the result of the benefits and liberties conferred on individuals by the remedies provided by the ordinary law of the land.

Dicey's ideas have been subjected to much criticism. The proposition that Englishmen can only be punished (legally) for a breach of law sounds like a plain tautology. The subjection of both private citizens and government officials to a single set of courts is not, moreover, a guarantee of equal rights or liberties. The ordinary law itself may embody privileges for state officials or confer unequal benefits. Given a sovereign legislature of the English kind, it can be argued that Dicey's concept is formal and empty. Procedural regularity and a common set of courts is compatible with legal tyranny.

Dicey, it is true, argued somewhat implausibly that parliamentary sovereignty reinforced the rule of law, since it could only be exercised (by King, Lords and Commons) in a manner prescribed by law, and since Parliament itself had never exercised direct executive power. Neither argument seems of much account compared with the possibility that sovereignty, when exercised in the properly prescribed manner, has an unrestricted capacity for removing all the liberties of those who are subject to it.

Nevertheless the general view of Dicey's theory that has become popular amongst his twentieth-century critics is unfair, when the argument of *The Law of the Constitution* is more carefully considered. Dicey's definition is not, in fact, a purely formal or procedural one. The exclusion of broad or independent executive power is a substantive restriction imposed upon legislation. Moreover, it is worth noticing that Dicey's consideration of the 'Rule of Law' immediately precedes six chapters on aspects of civil liberty, and he concludes his discussion by saying that what the principle really means can only be understood by examining with care the manner in which the law of England deals with the right to personal freedom, freedom of discussion, public meeting, martial law, the rights and duties of the army, the collection and expenditure of the public revenue and the responsibility of ministers. Thus the rule of law embraces the idea that individual rights must receive legal protection. They are not legally guaranteed rights, given the unrestricted sovereignty of Parliament in England; but the sovereignty of Parliament is controlled by constitutional conventions designed to make those who wield it accountable to the political sovereign or electorate.

If we widen the perspective, we can see that the rule of law has often been a shorthand phrase for all the devices of limited government that are customarily promulgated under the head of constitutional protections for citizens' RIGHTS. Where, as is usual outside the United Kingdom, these are codified in constitutional instruments the term 'constitutional rights' or 'constitutionalism' seems to be more or less coterminous with the wide interpretation of Dicey's 'rule of law'. The provisions that figure in a typical catalogue of such constitutional rights can be easily listed. Most obviously they include protection for freedom of expression and movement, religious freedom, guarantees of equal protection, and anti-discrimination provisions. They include also procedural guarantees of due process of law, fair legal procedures, fair trials, natural justice, judicial independence and access to the courts for the enforcement of rights conferred by law. In this wide sense (which is not universally admitted – see Raz) the rule of law or constitutionalism may be taken to imply also a number of propositions about the character and form of law making – for example, that laws should be precisely drafted, not retrospective in operation (at least in criminal matters) and that they should not impose penalties on named individuals, cruel or unusual punishments, or delegate ill-defined or unduly broad discretionary powers.

In the international sphere, the phrase 'rule of law' has been commonplace as reflecting an aspiration to subject the behaviour of nation states to generally agreed rules applied by international courts or adjudicators whose decisions are generally accepted and obeyed by those subject to their jurisdiction (see INTERNATIONAL LAW).   GM

Reading
Dicey, A.V.: *Introduction to the Study of the Law of the Constitution*, 10th edn, ed. E.C.S. Wade, chs 4, 12 and 13. London: Macmillan, 1939.

Fuller, L.L.: *The Morality of Law*, ch. 19. New Haven, Conn. and London: Yale University Press, 1964.

Jennings, I.: *The Law and the Constitution*, 5th edn. London: University of London Press, 1959.

†Lyons, D.: *Ethics and the Rule of Law*. Cambridge: Cambridge University Press, 1984.

Marsh, N.S.: The rule of law as a supra-national concept. In *Oxford Essays in Jurisprudence*, ed. A.G. Guest. Oxford: Oxford University Press, 1961.

†Raz, J.: The Rule of Law. In *The Authority of Law*. Oxford: Clarendon Press, 1979.

The Rule of Law in a Free Society. Geneva: International Commission of Jurists, 1960.

Ruskin, John (1819–1900) British art critic and social philosopher. Ruskin secured his reputation as a critic and writer with three works on art and architecture: *Modern Painters* (1843–60), *The Seven Lamps of Architecture*

(1849) and *The Stones of Venice* (1851–3). In them he argued that the character of societies is revealed in their art and finds its clearest expression in their building. Architecture requires social organization and subordinate labour: it is built upon men's work. He concluded that corrupted society and inhuman work could produce no art and nothing else of any value. He therefore turned, at the age of forty, from the field in which he had established his authority to social criticism, convinced that civilization, art and society would be destroyed by Victorian capitalism's rejection of traditional values. This concern was to dominate him from 1859, when *The Two Paths* was published, until the end of his life. *Unto This Last*, his most influential social examination, was published in 1862. *Fors Clavigera* or *Letters to the Workmen and Labourers of Great Britain* (1871–84) was his last great work apart from his unfinished autobiography, *Praeterita* (1885–9).

In his social analysis of Victorian England he sustained a savage attack upon its values and the economists' 'damned lie' about the dominant importance of material reward, acquisition and selfish competition. His social criticism was connected to his earlier work on art and architecture, by the unity that he sought to establish between Christian teaching, morality, justice, truth, nature and social relationships. His violent attack upon capitalism emerged from his moral indignation at its distortion of the affection and responsibility that should underlie all sound social relationships. His criticism of economics set out to correct its misuse of the terms 'value' and 'wealth', arguing, in a manner that invites comparison with Marx, that use value was more significant than exchange value and that true wealth meant the accumulation of things that sustain life. Mechanization and the obsessive pursuit of efficiency had, he believed, dire consequences: it was not the work but the worker that was divided, most cruelly, by the separation between intelligence and labour.

He saw no hope in socialist egalitarianism because it would share and spread the contamination of capitalism's values. Short of revolutionary breakdown, the only solution lay in a change of values established by precept and education; without it, political action would be useless and democracy moribund. His moral paternalism demanded that leaders should exercise responsible care and accept more than their share of sacrifice rather than riches, which were always the product of other men's labour.

His influence was considerable, although it has since waned. It encompassed William MORRIS and GANDHI, continued and extended a radical tradition quite distinct from Marxism, and helped to form the idea of the welfare state.

PDA

Reading

Abse, J.: *John Ruskin, the Passionate Moralist*. London: Quartet, 1980.

†Anthony, P.D.: *John Ruskin's Labour*. Cambridge: Cambridge University Press, 1983.

Clark, K. ed.: *Ruskin Today*. Harmondsworth: Penguin, 1983.

Hilton, T.: *John Ruskin: the Early Years, 1819–59*. New Haven, Conn.: Yale University Press, 1985.

†Landow, G.: *Ruskin*. Oxford: Oxford University Press, 1985.

Ruskin, J.: *The Works of John Ruskin*, ed. E.T. Cook and A. Wedderburn. 39 vols. London: George Allen, 1903–12.

Sherburne, J.S.: *John Ruskin or the Ambiguities of Abundance*. Cambridge, Mass.: Harvard University Press, 1972.

Russell, Bertrand (1872–1970) British philosopher. Russell's godfather was John Stuart MILL and he spent most of his ninety-eight years in the defence of causes dear to his godfather's heart – the emancipation of women, the reform of education, the lessening of the power of the owners of property, and a great expansion of social freedom. The last decade and a half of his life was spent above all in combating the threat of nuclear warfare: his campaign against nuclear weapons and the superpower politics of mutual nuclear blackmail led him to an increasing impatience with conventional politics on the one hand and to the conviction that the United States was the chief danger to world peace on the other. Russell was therefore associated in his last years with the politics of non-violent CIVIL DISOBEDIENCE in Britain and with the world-wide hostility to the American presence in Vietnam. In the 1950s, he had hoped that calm persuasion would be effective in getting the superpowers to reject nuclear weapons and had been instrumental in setting up the Pugwash conference which created a permanent network for discussion and propaganda by concerned scientists.

Russell was born into the Liberal aristocracy: his grandfather was Lord John Russell, who had piloted the First Reform Bill through the Commons, and he himself was an 'advanced Liberal' from 1890 to 1914 – that is, he approved of the Asquith government's moves towards a welfare state, and went a little beyond the government in advocating votes for women and a swingeing tax on landed property. But he became an unyielding opponent of the first world war and, to a large extent, disillusioned with everyday politics. He declared himself a hesitant socialist – he thought GUILD SOCIALISM acceptable, but unlikely to gain converts – but became obsessed with the need to educate children out of the frame of mind in which war was thinkable. So his *Principles of Social Reconstruction* (1916) argued for the training of the 'creative impulse' which, he thought, led to a happy and open personality immune to the urge to fight. In the 1920s, he and his second wife, Dora, owned and ran a school at Beacon Hill to put into practice the ideas which he set out in *On Education* (1926) and *Education and the Social Order* (1932).

Russell was always hostile to MARXISM, although he had a considerable sensitivity to the attractions of Marx's own views. But from his first book, on *German Social Democracy* (1896), Russell argued that Marxism was more religion than science and that the cataclysmic overthrow of capitalism was a needlessly destructive route to socialism. This message was reinforced by the Russian Revolution of 1917, which he welcomed in so far as it took Russia out of the war, but attacked in *The Theory and Practice of Bolshevism* (1920) as a despotism much like the one it had replaced. Russell never retreated from this view, except perhaps in the last few years of his life when his hostility to American brutalities in Vietnam persuaded him that the Soviet Union was on the side of freedom after all.

From 1914 onwards, Russell's predominant preoccupation in politics was the need to avoid another world war; he abhorred warfare as an irrational outlet for pride, boredom and greed.

He looked to some form of world government to provide a framework within which reformed national governments would re-educate their citizens. In depressed moments, he envisaged the United States dominating the world by might and enforcing a version of the *pax Romana* – which would be a *pax Americana* for the benefit of American capitalism. In more optimistic moments, he looked forward to a development of the United Nations. He was always brutally realistic about the need for a world government to possess the means to make itself obeyed.

It was this realism which in 1945 and several times thereafter made him suggest that the United States should employ its then monopoly of nuclear weapons to force the Soviet Union to disarm. He admitted that it was likely that the Soviet Union would resist and that war would follow: this, however, seemed to him a lesser evil than the utter destruction which a nuclear war would cause. The same frame of mind had in 1936 made him advocate complete PACIFISM in the face of Hitler's Germany. Always the evil to avoid was the destruction of European civilization: in 1936 pacifism seemed the way (he changed his mind in 1941 when it became clear that Nazism was quite unlike anything he had imagined), while in 1945 and for a few years thereafter a policy of nuclear bullying seemed the way. The end never changed, though the means did. He was much criticized for these changes of mind, but was genuinely puzzled by the complaints: a sensible man changes his mind when circumstances alter.

Once both great powers possessed nuclear weapons, the case was again altered. Blackmail and pre-emptive strikes became impossible and the rational course of action was to find ways of lessening the risk of accidental war. As time passed, Russell became more convinced than ever that governments were hostile to peace, and largely run by the criminally insane: but his recipes for the prevention of war were generally commonsensical – he was one of those who demanded a ban on nuclear tests in the atmosphere, advocated a non-proliferation treaty, and held that if nuclear weapons could be confined to the superpowers and they could negotiate their numbers down, the peace might be kept. But this moderation in theory did not inhibit his denunciation of the political morality of the great powers: one of his more famous claims was that modern statesmen were more wicked than Hitler. His last years made KEYNES's summary of Russell's views more apt than ever. 'He thinks the world is terrible because everyone is mad: happily the remedy is simple, they must all behave better.'   AR

Reading

†Clark, R.: *The Life of Bertrand Russell*. London: Weidenfeld & Nicolson, 1975.

†Russell, B.: *The Principles of Social Reconstruction*. London: Allen & Unwin, 1916.

†———: *The Theory and Practice of Bolshevism*. London: Allen & Unwin, 1920.

†———: *Freedom and Organization*. London: Allen & Unwin, 1934.

———: *Authority and the Individual*. London: Allen & Unwin, 1949.

———: *Common Sense and Nuclear Warfare*. London: Allen & Unwin, 1959.

———: *War Crimes in Vietnam*. London: Allen & Unwin, 1967.

Vellacott, J.: *Bertrand Russell and the Pacifists in the First World War*. Brighton, Sussex: Harvester, 1980.

S

Saint-Simon, Claude-Henri de Rouvroy
(1760–1825) French socialist. An aristocrat by
birth, Saint-Simon absorbed from the
eighteenth-century ENLIGHTENMENT an interest in philosophy and the sciences, and the
application of knowledge to the solution of
social problems. Yet his own first pronouncements on these matters did not appear in print
until the first decade of the nineteenth century,
by which time his experience of violent
upheaval in the American and French revolutions had convinced him of the urgent need for
a programme of systematic social reorganization. He subsequently undertook pioneering
investigations concerned principally with the
establishment of a scientific study of man and
society – a 'social physiology'. As a social
reformer he put forward proposals which at first
could hardly be distinguished from liberal
doctrines, but he gradually moved away from
orthodox liberalism towards 'industrialism', a
theory which contained many socialistic
elements.

One of the most significant features of
Saint-Simon's 'social physiology' was its
underlying conception of history. Inspired by
the mechanical determinism of the Newtonian
world-view and the optimism of Enlightenment
philosophies of PROGRESS, Saint-Simon
attempted to reveal the inexorable pattern of
historical change, not only in the past and
present, but also through scientifically-based
anticipations of the future. This perspective led
him to stress the relationship between science
(theoretical knowledge) and industry (meaning,
at this time, all productive activity, not just
manufacturing) as the key agents at work in
shaping successive types of society in the course

of man's evolution from primitive to modern
times.

Saint-Simon was one of the first thinkers to
identify the main features of an emergent
INDUSTRIAL SOCIETY (or 'industrial system'),
and to try to show how such a society was likely
to develop out of the collapse of feudalism.
Central to this endeavour was the argument that
every type of society is built on the foundations
of a particular system of beliefs, and that once
these beliefs lose credibility, the social order
must itself disintegrate. Thus, for Saint-Simon,
it was ultimately the Enlightenment attack on
theology which precipitated the destruction of
the feudal system; and it followed that only a
new, alternative set of beliefs – modern
'positive' science – could furnish the basis for
the post-feudal, industrial order. This would
happen only when the old ruling classes of
landed nobility and clergy (the twin pillars of
feudalism) had been replaced by the new,
ascendant classes of scientists, engineers and
artists (in the intellectual sphere), and entrepreneurs, industrialists and producers (in the
more practical sphere of politics and
administration). Such an image of modern
society does perhaps suggest rule by technocrats, or it might be seen as another variation on
the theme of capitalistic utilitarianism. Both
these interpretations have some justification,
since Saint-Simon clearly hoped to elevate
professional experts of various kinds to positions of authority, experts whose main task
would be to promote human satisfactions within
an essentially capitalistic framework based on
the maintenance of private property rights. Yet
other more collectivistic tendencies in Saint-
Simon's thought must be taken into account,

tendencies which were given clearest expression in his writings of the period 1820–5: *Du système industriel, Catéchisme des industriels, Nouveau christianisme.*

These works criticize the individualistic morality of LIBERALISM, for its heavily legalistic and metaphysical approach to social questions. In Saint-Simon's view such an approach was unduly negative and insufficiently dynamic to furnish the basis for a new, progressive social order. Liberalism's most serious failure was its incapacity to deal with the condition of the vast majority of people in society – the working or 'industrious' classes – who suffered enormous hardship and deprivation, even though they were directly responsible for the creation of most of society's wealth. The church (especially the Catholic church) must also accept its share of responsibility for this situation, since the moral guidance it provided clearly did nothing to promote greater equality, even though the original teachings of Christ could reasonably be interpreted as a call to intervene in society on behalf of the poor and the oppressed.

The title of Saint-Simon's last work – *Nouveau christianisme* (1825) – conveys the force of his moral argument: that a new religion, Christian in spirit but led by the most knowledgeable thinkers in society (principally scientists and artists) rather than theologians, must be established in order to formulate and disseminate beliefs relevant to a modern society, a society capable of harnessing the forces of science and industry to create an earthly paradise in which all basic human needs would be fulfilled. Productivity must become the key social goal, and political power, exercised by skilled administrators, would be nothing more than the applied science of production.

Saint-Simon identified class conflict as a major factor in social development, but he did not believe that in modern times this must necessitate violent struggle. He did not foresee a future classless society, but assumed that all types of society must be divided into various functional ranks. Under industrialism, for example, the working classes would be in one sense subordinate to their 'natural' leaders, but at the same time their interests would be integrated harmoniously into an overall conception of the social good. Furthermore all workers, from labourers to entrepreneurs and managers, were seen to belong to a single class of producers sharing a common concern to eliminate, through peaceful reform, all non-productive groups from society. Once this was done the natural harmony of interests uniting all those engaged in productive occupations would lead to a new sense of social solidarity.

Together with FOURIER and OWEN, Saint-Simon has traditionally been regarded as one of the three great founding fathers of modern SOCIALISM. After Saint-Simon's death, a group of disciples founded a Saint-Simonian School which quickly transformed itself into a religious sect advocating complete collectivism. Another of Saint-Simon's followers, Auguste COMTE, went on to elaborate theories of positivist science and philosophy, including a conception of what he considered to be the new science of 'sociology'. (See POSITIVISM.)   KT

Reading
Ionescu, G. ed.: *The Political Thought of Saint-Simon.* London: Oxford University Press, 1976.

†Manuel, F.E.: *The New World of Henri Saint-Simon.* Cambridge, Mass.: Harvard University Press, 1956.

Saint-Simon, C.-H. de: *Oeuvres de Claude-Henri de Saint-Simon.* 6 vols. Paris: Éditions Anthropos, 1966.

———: *Selected Writings on Science, Industry and Social Organization*, ed. K. Taylor. London: Croom Helm, 1975.

†Taylor, K.: *The Political Ideas of the Utopian Socialists.* London: Cass, 1982.

Sartre, Jean-Paul (1905–1980) French philosopher, dramatist and novelist. Sartre was the most celebrated and perhaps the most influential intellectual of modern times. He graduated from the École Normale Supérieure in 1929, and taught in various *lycées* from 1931 to 1945, except for a short period in the armed forces and thereafter as a prisoner of war. Sartre's work combined literary and philosophical viewpoints. His earliest philosophical essays dealt with the emotions, the imagination and the nature of the self, and these issues are treated in his first novel, *La Nausée* (1938), a book which also makes explicit his visceral loathing of bourgeois society. According to Simone de Beauvoir and Raymond Aron, Sartre had no interest in politics before the war. His novel cycle *Les Chemins de la liberté* (1945–9) shows him moving towards a more activist stance as the result of the war and his participation in the Resistance. His major philosophical work *L'Être et le néant* (Being and Nothingness) was published in 1943. A companion volume on ethics was promised but never appeared, most immediately because Sartre's political commitment was becoming more pressing. Many ethical problems are dealt with, however, in the gripping plays he wrote at this period: *Huis clos* (1945), *Les Mains sales* (1948), and *Le Diable et le bon dieu* (1952). Sartre was for a long period a fellow-traveller who involved himself in various apologetic gymnastics, and he was close first to the French and then to the Italian Communist parties. His main theoretical work on politics, *Critique de la raison dialectique* (The Critique of Dialectical Reason) (1960), attempted to marry EXISTENTIALISM with MARXISM. The book was a huge, complex, and fascinating failure. Parisian intellectuals realized that Sartre was trapped in individualistic categories, and gave their allegiance to various structuralist thinkers who proclaimed the exact opposite – that subjectivity was an illusion, and a bourgeois one at that! In his last years Sartre continued to meditate upon the antinomy of situation and choice. *Les Mots* (1963) offers a brilliant and limpid account of his own early years, while *Flaubert* (1971–2) considers part of the French novelist's career at interminable length.

Being and Nothingness is Sartre's masterpiece. The influence of Husserl is seen in its being a phenomenology, and of HEIDEGGER in its concentration on 'being'; in other words, we are offered a description of how it feels to be alive. Life is associated with nothingness because our imagination always makes it possible for us to imagine that any situation might be different. We exist in a wholly contingent world, and must impose some pattern upon it; there are no pre-ordained essences, and we make of the world what we will. Sartre's vision is essentially pessimistic. His genius is best employed when describing the evasions and excuses most people find to avoid taking responsibility for their actions: 'bad faith' is the desire to shirk the burden of freedom. Such evasion is seen as peculiarly bourgeois, but Sartre argues that the

very presence of others is a constant reminder of our own limitations (as is made clear in his stunning pages on sadism and masochism). His description of personal relationships resembles that of Proust, but he has none of the humour of the great novelist. When he said 'hell is other people', he really meant hell. This pessimistic vision by far outweighs the moral uplift that comes towards the end, and which was to have been the centre of the volume on ethics. His argument is that the individual should take responsibility for his or her actions at all times and at all costs; one's life must become a project that can be questioned at any particular time. This position has often been criticized on the grounds that its instability would undermine the trust necessary to social life *per se*: I may love someone today, but just as authentically abandon them tomorrow. However, the greater criticism of Sartre's vision is that it lacks any conception of sociability. Freedom is always freedom from the interference of others, never the possibility of co-operating with them.

The Critique of Dialectical Reason operates at one level as a philosophy of history. A type of dialectical reason is suggested by means of which the project of every individual will somehow come to be seen as part of the totality of history. The brilliance of Sartre's account of individuals undermines this larger aim, the full justification of which was left to another volume (which, again, never appeared). But the second level of the treatise shows Sartre once again in his true colours as a moralist. A crucial contrast is drawn between human beings caught in 'series' and in a 'group-in-fusion'. By the former – illustrated, bizarrely, by people queuing for a bus – Sartre had in mind daily lives devoid of purpose and will, caught in bad faith, and related only by an accidental similarity of aim. Examples of the latter were revolutionary groups whose members achieved authentic moral FREEDOM through participating in a common project to change history. Interestingly, his political theory is centred much more on 'the problem of being' than on, for example, any actual measures for the poor and deprived. The argument contains a justification for VIOLENCE of a striking kind. As bad faith lurks so close to the surface of the individual, anyone who reneges on the 'group-in-fusion' loses his rights. The attempt to produce a collective vision can only be secured by violence because Sartre cannot escape his lack of any concept of sociability. His appreciation of the weakness of the autonomous individual reminds one of ROUSSEAU, but in Sartre there is no equivalent respect for law.

Sartre's political thought is exceptionally interesting. His was perhaps the greatest expression of an individualistic, puritanical viewpoint in France since Rousseau, and he allows us to see the limits of a politics which has no conception of sociability.   JAH

Reading

Aron, R.: *History and the Dialectic of Violence*, trans. B. Cooper. Oxford: Blackwell, 1975.

†Aronson, B.: *Jean-Paul Sartre: Philosophy in the World*. London: New Left, 1980.

Jameson, F.: *Sartre after Sartre*. New Haven, Conn.: Yale University Press, 1985.

†Manser, A.: *Sartre*. London: Athlone, 1966.

Sartre, J.-P.: *Being and Nothingness*, trans. H.E. Barnes. New York: Philosophical Library, 1956; London: Methuen, 1957.

———: *The Critique of Dialectical Reason*, trans. A. Sheridan-Smith. London: New Left; Highlands, NJ: Humanities, 1976.

Schiller, Friedrich von (1759–1805) German poet and dramatist. Schiller was born the second child of an army doctor in Marbach, in southern Germany. His unhappy years at the military academy in Stuttgart (1773–80) instilled in him the hatred of tyranny and the enthusiasm for freedom and republican virtue that were the hallmarks of his early plays – most notably *Die Räuber* (The Robbers) (1781). As powerful statements of the rebellious spirit of Storm and Stress ('Sturm und Drang') they excited and shocked theatre audiences everywhere in Germany (and earned Schiller, in 1792, the title of an honorary citizen of the French Republic). After a dramatic escape from his native Würtemberg he finally settled in Jena, in close proximity to Weimar which, as the residence of Goethe, Wieland and Herder, was then becoming the cultural centre of Germany.

Schiller's mature work was inspired by KANT's philosophy and, most decisively, by his friendship (from 1794) with Goethe. From their fruitful alliance dates an unprecedented flourishing of German literature known as Weimar Classicism. Schiller's particular contribution to this partnership – apart from masterpieces such as *Wallenstein* (1796–99), *Maria Stuart* (1800) and *Wilhelm Tell* (1804) – was the development of an aesthetic theory that attempted to place art in a systematic relationship with morality and politics.

In two seminal essays – *Über die ästhetische Erziehung des Menschen, in einer Reihe von Briefen* (On the Aesthetic Education of Man) (1795), and *Über naive und sentimentalische Dichtung* (On Naive and Sentimental Poetry) (1795–6) – Schiller discussed the conditions of FREEDOM in modern society. The failure of the French Revolution testified to a dilemma that he also discerned in Kant's dualistic account of moral agency: the discrepancy between men's aspiration towards freedom and their present incapacity, as sensuous beings, to act in accordance with the dictates of reason. 'It is only through Beauty that man makes his way to Freedom' (*Aesthetic Education*, p. 9): Schiller credited the aesthetic faculty activated in *Spieltrieb* with the power of closing this gap. Only if human beings attained wholeness of character (*Totalität des Charakters*) in the harmonious interplay of all their faculties – freed both from the one-sided domination of moral imperatives and from the tyranny of outward necessity – would they become capable of citizenship in the rational state.

Ferguson's account of the division of labour (see SCOTTISH ENLIGHTENMENT) and ROUSSEAU's paradox of civilization, moreover, provided Schiller with the means of linking individual experience to the dominant conflicts of contemporary social and political life. Although, like many German writers of his time, he derived the images of harmony and totality from an idealized vision of ancient Greece, he significantly restated the traditional contrast between classical and modern civilization. Instead of seeing in the latter symptoms only of degeneracy and irretrievable loss, he identified in the operation of the 'all-dividing intellect' itself a dynamic of historical progression that would allow mankind to restore unity on a new and higher level.

In thus casting modern experience – the

dichotomy of reason and feeling, the fragmentation of knowledge through specialization, the separation of the individual from the state – into a dialectic of ALIENATION and regeneration Schiller opened new avenues for philosophical and political argument, that can be traced in the evolution of German ROMANTICISM, in HEGEL's *Phenomenology*, and in the early writings of MARX. UV

Reading

Abrams, M.H.: *Natural Supernaturalism: Tradition and Revolution in Romantic Literature*, ch. 4. New York: Norton, 1971.
†Miller, R.D.: *Schiller and the Ideal of Freedom*. Oxford: Clarendon Press, 1970.
Schiller, F. von: *On the Aesthetic Education of Man* trans. and ed. E.M. Wilkinson and L.A. Willoughby. Oxford: Clarendon Press, 1967.

Schumpeter, Joseph Alois (1883–1950) Austrian economist and social scientist. As early as 1908 Schumpeter published an important book on the nature and content of economic theory (*Economic Doctrine and Method*) which established his fame as the ablest among the younger group of Austrian economists. His teachers had been Menger and Böhm-Bawerk. After being nominated at the University of Czernowitz, he became professor of economics at the University of Graz in 1911. His well-known *Theory of Economic Development* was published in 1912. Much of Schumpeter's later work on business cycles and the evolution of CAPITALISM into SOCIALISM represents an elaboration and improvement of the global ideas and analysis presented in this book. By the time of its publication it was already clear that Schumpeter could not be regarded narrowly as an economist. His thinking displays the broader concerns of the historian and social scientist.

In Schumpeter's interpretation of capitalism the entrepreneur, who applies new combinations of factors of production, plays a central role. He is the innovator and the agent of economic change and development. The rise and decay of capitalism also centre around the Schumpeterian entrepreneur. Innovations carried out by the gifted few, pioneering new technologies, new products and new markets, initiate the short and long new cycles in economic life, joined as they are after some time

by many imitators. Because of the competitive illusion, over-investment and over-expansion of credit take place.

Schumpeter became a permanent professor of economics at Harvard University in 1932. His impressive *Business Cycles* appeared in 1939, and in 1942 he published *Capitalism, Socialism and Democracy*, in which he predicted the gradual decay of capitalism. This prediction is based on the idea that it is not the economic failure but the economic success of capitalism that causes the march into socialism. Social rather than economic factors are, according to Schumpeter, responsible for the structural change in the organization of society.

At the heart of the capitalist economy, in Schumpeter's view, lies the process of creative destruction. It can be seen at work in the opening of new markets, new methods of production, new products and new types of organization that incessantly modify the economic structure from within. The competitive character of capitalism is determined more by creative destruction than by the textbook mode of competition, in which prices play such a dominant role.

Schumpeter had the highest possible opinion of the dynamic character and productive capability of capitalism. In counterposing the static optimal allocation of resources in the case of perfect competition to the dynamic efficiency of monopolistic structures (in particular with regard to innovative activities) he expressed an outspoken preference for monopoly and oligopoly and a disdain for free competition. He did not adhere to the theory that vanishing investment opportunities and a slowdown of technical change would lead to stagnation and in the end to a breakdown of capitalism. The present climate of economic revival, the application of new technology, and the introduction of new products (as well as the general air of optimism) suggest that Schumpeter was right in this respect.

Why does the success of capitalism bring about its decay? As Schumpeter puts it, capitalism undermines the social framework which protects it. This framework includes the remnants of the feudal system and the existence of many small businesses and farmers. Their disappearance weakens the political position of the bourgeoisie. The elimination of the socio-economic function of the entrepreneur further undermines the bourgeoisie, especially in large corporations where technical change is a matter of routine and management is bureaucratized, reinforced by the growing influence of the public sector. Above all capitalism produces an army of critical and frustrated intellectuals who by their negative attitude contribute to the decline of capitalism and help to establish an atmosphere in which private property and bourgeois values are daily subjected to attack by journalists and political opinion. Looking back to the general political atmosphere of the 1960s and 1970s one cannot deny the element of truth in Schumpeter's vision.

It seems, however, that on the basis of technical possibilities, there is much more room for Schumpeterian entrepreneurial activity, especially in smaller scale operations, than Schumpeter himself foresaw. Furthermore socialism looks increasingly less attractive as an alternative to capitalism.

One of Schumpeter's important innovations as a social thinker is his distinction between political and methodological INDIVIDUALISM. In particular, the concept of methodological individualism seems to be crucial for the analysis of social phenomena, outside the sphere of the market mechanism. As a method of analysis, methodological individualism prescribes starting from the individual in order to understand, for example, the working of the political process and the behaviour of groups. In this sense Schumpeter's social thinking is the opposite of MARX's thinking in terms of the class struggle. The modern theory of public choice, which has recourse to the maximization of individual welfare by politicians and bureaucrats in order to describe their social behaviour as part of the government, is a direct application of methodological individualism.

Strongly related to this development is the economic theory of DEMOCRACY of which Schumpeter is a forerunner. In his view the democratic method is that institutional arrangement for arriving at political decisions in which individuals acquire the power to decide by means of a competitive struggle for the people's vote. In other words Schumpeter introduces the idea that democracy is a type of

horizontal co-ordination in the public sector that can be compared to the role of the market mechanism in the private sector of the economy. The political process is regarded as a market process in which the voters are the demanders and the politicians and bureaucrats are the suppliers. This idea appears to be very fruitful both in theory and in practice, and contributes to Schumpeter's fame as a social and economic thinker of lasting significance.

AH

Reading

Frisch, H. ed.: *Schumpeterian Economics*. New York: Praeger, 1982.

†Harris, S.E. ed.: *Schumpeter, Social Scientist*. Cambridge, Mass.: Harvard University Press, 1951.

†Heertje, A. ed.: *Schumpeter's Vision*. New York: Praeger, 1981.

März, E.: *Joseph Alois Schumpeter*. Vienna: Verlag für Geschichte und Politik, 1983.

Schumpeter, J.: *Economic Doctrine and Method*. London: Allen & Unwin, 1954.

———: *The Theory of Economic Development*. New York: Oxford University Press, 1962.

———: *Ten Great Economists*. London: Allen & Unwin, 1962.

———: *Business Cycles*. New York: McGraw-Hill, 1939.

†———: *Capitalism, Socialism and Democracy*. London: Allen & Unwin, 1976.

Seidl, C. ed.: *Lectures on Schumpeterian Economics*. Berlin: Springer, 1984.

Scottish Enlightenment Between 1740 and 1790 Scotland was the setting for a concentrated burst of intellectual activity now known as the Scottish Enlightenment. David HUME and Adam SMITH were the pre-eminent figures; alongside them clustered a galaxy of thinkers, including Adam Ferguson, Francis Hutcheson, William Robertson, Lord Kames, Thomas Reid, Sir James Steuart and John Millar. Their interests ranged from metaphysics to the natural sciences; but the most notable and characteristic achievements of the Scottish Enlightenment as a whole lay in the fields of history, moral and political philosophy, and political economy – in the study of what was called 'the progress of society'.

In the context of the wider European ENLIGHTENMENT, Scotland's should be seen as characteristically 'provincial', comparable with the Enlightenment in the provinces of France, or in the provincial states of eighteenth-century Italy and Germany. The Scottish thinkers naturally cultivated connections with Paris, the metropolitan centre of the Enlightenment, but their concerns were perhaps closer to those of the philosopher-reformers of the Enlightenment in the distant kingdom of Naples. The priority attached to economic improvement, the urgent interest in its moral and political conditions and consequences were equally features of Scottish and Neapolitan thought, and reflected fundamental similarities of European provincial experience.

At the same time the experience of eighteenth-century Scotland differed from that of other provinces in important respects, which shaped Scottish thought. The achievement of slow but real economic growth in Scotland within the period of its Enlightenment gave Scottish thinkers an unusually direct acquaintance with development and its social consequences. The Union of 1707 with England, by which the Scots exchanged their independent parliament for the opportunity of free trade with England and its empire, was in no simple sense the cause of Scotland's economic growth or the inspiration of its Enlightenment. But it naturally called attention to the relation between institutions and economic development. Religious liberalization (the taming of the fierce covenanting presbyterianism of the seventeenth century by the 'Moderate' churchmen under William Robertson), university reform (making Edinburgh, Glasgow, Aberdeen and St Andrews into the leading universities of Protestant Europe), and the growth of voluntary societies and clubs such as the Select Society of Edinburgh – these certainly were preconditions of the Enlightenment. They also provided a setting in which Scottish thinkers learnt and asserted for themselves the importance of the moral and cultural framework of society, and its relation to material progress. None of these distinguishing aspects of Scotland's experience, moreover, encouraged its Enlightenment to be particularly radical. Though not complacent, and in different ways anxious to influence their country's development, the Scottish thinkers were sufficiently sanguine about the future to devote most of their energies to understanding, relatively few to reform. It was a rare opportunity, which the Scottish Enlightenment did not waste.

Scotland not only offered its thinkers the stimulus of its particular, unusually successful provincial experience. It was also intellectually cosmopolitan, having been since the late seventeenth century increasingly open to new developments in European thought. In Scotland as elsewhere nothing did more to enlarge intellectual horizons than the triumph of Newtonianism in the natural sciences. The impact of the Newtonian philosophy in Scotland (other than on Hume) has yet to be examined thoroughly: but it is clear that Hume was not alone in being inspired to attempt a comparable revolution in the science of man and society. For the content of such a science the Scots drew on all the main European traditions of moral and political thought. The natural jurisprudence of PUFENDORF and LOCKE and the moral philosophy of Shaftesbury had a particular impact in the universities. In the lectures of Hutcheson, professor of moral philosophy at Glasgow, these were combined to produce an academic discourse capable of exploring the full range of social phenomena. Further inspiration was provided by the institutional and moral concepts of classical or civic humanism. Here the seminal figure was Andrew Fletcher, whose eccentric, uncompromising pamphlets stimulated the development of a less formal style of political discourse. The academic and political discourses of eighteenth-century Scotland were not mutually exclusive; nor did they inhibit continued openness to European thought. The Neapolitan historian Giannone (but not Vico), the French *philosophes* MONTESQUIEU, VOLTAIRE, ROUSSEAU, Quesnay and Turgot were all quickly familiar to the Scots. But the development of specifically Scottish idioms of discourse was indicative of intellectual self-confidence, and enabled the Scottish thinkers to respond to the work of their European contemporaries with distinctive contributions of their own.

Setting aside the fields of metaphysics and natural sciences in order to concentrate on the enquiry into 'the progress of society', there were three areas in which the Scottish Enlightenment made a major contribution.

The first was in the analysis of the origins and development of society and government. Following Hume no Scottish thinker subscribed to the juristic notion that society and government had been founded on an original contract. For Hume and Smith an *a priori* theological assumption that Natural Law entailed a duty to keep contracts was inadmissible; and all the Scots agreed that the accounts of the contract given by earlier jurisprudential thinkers, Locke in particular, were historically inadequate. In the *Treatise of Human Nature* (1739–40) Hume conjectured that society developed from the family, and government from the need for defence and the security of property. Following his lead, the most substantial expositions of a new, properly historical approach came in Smith's Glasgow University *Lectures on Jurisprudence* (1762–3, 1766), Ferguson's *Essay on the History of Civil Society* (1767) and Millar's *Origin of the Distinction of Ranks* (1770). Smith provided the classic statement of the theory that society developed in four distinct stages, corresponding to the means of subsistence – the hunting, the pastoral, the agricultural and the commercial; at each stage the sophistication of government was related to the nature and scale of property-holding. Ferguson likewise underlined the historical role of property, but offered a different classification of social forms, and was particularly penetrating in his analysis of the martial culture of savage and barbarian societies. In addition Lord Kames in his *Historical Law Tracts* (1758) specifically related the development of law to the progress of society, while William Robertson made use of the new theories to order his historical narratives, notably the 'View of the Progress of Society in Europe' with which he introduced his *History of Charles V* (1769).

The Scots did not transform the old jurisprudential approach without some analytical loss. Locke's characteristic concern to establish a standard against which to assess the legitimacy of a society's arrangements for property and government was neglected. But the new historical perspective was successful in making it possible to view society as a system of interrelated parts, and thus offered the basis of a science of society.

The Scots' second major contribution lay in their analysis of morals and institutions in the final, commercial stage of social development. Here the terms of classical humanism were joined to those of natural jurisprudence; and greater divisions of opinion became manifest. Hume, responding to MANDEVILLE, took the offensive by deriding the classical shibboleth that luxury led to moral corruption. Luxury, he maintained in his *Essays*, was both economically and morally beneficial, fostering a more graduated hierarchy of ranks and the refinement of personal and public values. The classical ideal of virtue, on the other hand, was unnatural and dangerous. Smith followed Hume, arguing in the *Theory of Moral Sentiments* (1759) that propriety was the appropriate standard for a civilized society, and that the modern hierarchy of ranks, by raising expectations, served to improve the condition of all. Even so, Smith subsequently added the qualification that admiration for wealth and rank could have a corrupting effect on men's morals.

Much less confident of the moral consequences of commerce were Kames, Millar and Ferguson. In his *Essay* Ferguson argued that the specialization of professions had irredeemably debased the lower ranks of commercial society, and was threatening the upper ranks with imminent moral corruption. Anti-sceptical in his moral philosophy, Ferguson defiantly reasserted the classical idea of virtue, and urged the cause of a citizens' militia as the means to inculcate it.

Ferguson's concern over the moral condition of commercial society did not extend to its institutions. With most of the Scottish thinkers, he tended to believe that the institutions of government adapted naturally and more or less adequately to economic and social change, and he emphatically discounted the notion of a founding legislator. Such indifference towards institutions was not, however, shared by Hume and Smith. They believed that the advent of commercial society placed new demands on institutions, demands which required a constructive response. It was essential first of all to limit the burden of government, confining it to the minimum necessary provision of defence, justice and public works, and in the longer run it would also be necessary to extend the opportunities for political participation by citizens. Hume, who was doubtful of the stability of the British system of government, suggested a federal republic as a model for commercial society. Smith adopted the principles of parliamentary sovereignty and offered the – admittedly utopian – model of a British-American imperial union. Neither Hume nor Smith can be said to have constructed a theory of the modern state, a nineteenth-century achievement. But their analyses acknowledged that institutional questions must now be related to economic life, and offered a suggestive treatment of the implications for personal and political liberty.

The third and most important contribution of the Scottish Enlightenment was the virtual creation of political economy. As the Scots conceived it, political economy was embedded in the larger enquiry into the progress of society. It built upon the historical account of the emergence of a commercial stage of social development. It presupposed the moral analysis of luxury, and the recognition that men's expectations could no longer be considered primarily in relation to subsistence needs. Finally, it assumed an understanding of the institutional conditions of economic activity. But political economy was not simply the sum of these historical, moral and political analyses. The crucial insights on which the Scots founded political economy were that economic life was self-regulating, and that economic growth was a dynamic, self-sustaining process. Once again it was Hume who launched the discussion, in his provocative but fragmentary economic essays. Sir James Steuart sought both to answer Hume's arguments and to provide a comprehensive treatment of the subject in his *Principles of Political Oeconomy* (1767). Unfortunately for Steuart, his work was promptly and definitively eclipsed by the publication of Smith's *Wealth of Nations* in 1776. In this the natural, self-adjusting mechanism of the market was laid bare, and a systematic model of economic growth, explaining the respective contributions of the division of labour and capital, of agriculture and manufactures, was set forth. In Smith's mind political economy

might still be but 'a branch of the science of a statesman or legislator'; but the *Wealth of Nations* could be understood by itself. Better organized, more accessible, more convincing and simply more intelligent than Steuart's *Principles* – or the European alternatives, Quesnay's *Tableau économique* (1758–9) and Genovesi's *Lezioni di commercio* (1765) – it established the science of political economy in its own right.

Smith's death in 1790 provides a convenient terminal date for the Scottish Enlightenment. In Scotland as throughout Europe the French Revolution transformed the conditions and assumptions of intellectual life. Between 1790 and 1830 a new generation of Scottish thinkers set about adapting the inheritance of their Enlightenment to the challenge of political radicalism. Dugald Stewart, professor of moral philosophy at Edinburgh, strove to develop a synthesis of Thomas Reid's Common Sense moral philosophy and Smithian historical and economic theory. His pupils, the literary lions of the *Edinburgh Review*, tried to refurbish the political ideology of Whiggism. With more conservative inclinations, Sir Walter Scott combined the Scottish Enlightenment's historical perspective with the new German-inspired interest in national culture to write the Waverley Novels. But the most enduring legacy of the Scottish Enlightenment was CLASSICAL POLITICAL ECONOMY, which from 1800 was cultivated in England. The political economy of Malthus, Ricardo and their successors largely dispensed with the wider framework of historical, moral and political theory to which the Scots were committed: if it was related to any political theory it was to PHILOSOPHIC RADICALISM. Nevertheless, it was still recognizably the creation of Adam Smith and the Scottish Enlightenment. JCR

Reading

(See also HUME and SMITH.)

Bryson, G.: *Man and Society: the Scottish Enquiry of the Eighteenth Century.* Princeton, NJ: Princeton University Press, 1945.

Campbell, R.H. and Skinner, A.S. eds: *The Origins and Nature of the Scottish Enlightenment.* Edinburgh: John Donald, 1982.

Ferguson, A.: *Essay on the History of Civil Society*, ed. D. Forbes. Edinburgh: Edinburgh University Press, 1966.

†Hont, I. and Ignatieff, M. eds: *Wealth and Virtue: the Shaping of Political Economy in the Scottish Enlightenment*. Cambridge: Cambridge University Press, 1983.

†Phillipson, N.T.: The Scottish Enlightenment. In *The Enlightenment in National Context*, ed. R. Porter and M. Teich. Cambridge: Cambridge University Press, 1981.

Robertson, J.: *The Scottish Enlightenment and the Militia Issue*. Edinburgh: John Donald, 1985.

Selden, John (1585–1654) English jurist and philosopher. Selden was the son of a small farmer in Sussex. From his local grammar school he went to the University of Oxford, and became a professional lawyer and political adviser to a group of aristocratic families. With their support, in the 1620s and again in the 1640s he was a member of Parliament, taking a leading part in the opposition to Charles I and his ministers in the former decade, and being a prominent member of the moderate Parliamentarian group in the latter. His prestige with the Parliamentarians even after 1649 was so high that Cromwell is said to have considered asking him to write the constitution of the new republic. His friends ranged from Clarendon to HOBBES, with whom he had much in common and who was one of the last people to see him before he died.

Selden's principal contribution to the history of political thought rests on his speeches in Parliament, which were widely circulated, and two works of general political theory – *Mare clausum* (1635) (an answer to GROTIUS's *Mare liberum*) and *De iure naturali et gentium juxta disciplinam ebraeorum* (1640). In addition he published a large number of other works on English and classical history which usually had a political purpose (for example, the famous *History of Tythes* (1617), which was a major statement on an Erastian position on church government). Selden was a kind of English Grotius, critical of both traditional Aristotelianism and modern scepticism, hostile to any claims for ecclesiastical power, and insistent on the validity of any bargains made between men (even voluntary slavery). *Mare clausum* turned some of Grotius's arguments against him on the specific question of freedom of navigation, while *De iure naturali* offered a completely novel account of natural law.

Selden argued that men were in principle totally free of all moral restraints, unless they came to fear punishment by a superior (notably God) for a specifically promulgated set of actions. Natural reason could not provide men with the list of such actions; only an historical record of God's pronouncements to all mankind, or direct revelation, could do so. The record he found in the Talmudic description of God's dealings with men after the Flood, the only suitable universal promulgation (the Decalogue was merely for Jews). This eccentric view was nevertheless widely respected by writers of the late seventeenth and early eighteenth centuries for its freedom from the conventional idea that (for example) the Aristotelian virtues or the Decalogue could be seen as rationally founded in human nature, and Selden may have been one of the first writers to state clearly that man's essential condition was one of absolute moral freedom.   RFT

Reading

Christianson, P.: Young John Selden and the Ancient Constitution. *Proceedings of the American Philosophical Society* 128 (1984) 271–315.

Selden, J.: *Mare clausum* and *De iure naturali et gentium juxta disciplinam ebraeorum*. In *Opera Omnia*, ed. D. Wilkins. London, 1726. English edn of *Mare Clausum: Of the Dominion or Ownership of the Sea*, trans. M. Needham. London, 1652.

†Tuck, R.: *Natural Rights Theories*. Cambridge: Cambridge University Press, 1979.

———: The ancient law of freedom. In *Reactions to the English Civil War 1642–1649*, ed. J. Morrill. London: Macmillan, 1982.

Seneca, L. Annaeus (*c.*4 BC–65 AD) Roman philosopher and statesman. Born in Cordoba in Spain, the son of a local teacher, Seneca came early to Rome and embarked on a political career, a normal decision for a scion of the upper orders of one of the Romanized cities of the provinces. Nearly executed under Gaius and exiled under Claudius, he survived to become the teacher of Nero who eventually succeeded Claudius in AD 54. A principal adviser of Nero in the early years, Seneca progressively lost favour. In AD 65 he was believed to have been implicated in a conspiracy against Nero and felt compelled to commit suicide.

Seneca wrote two overtly political tracts, a satirical account of the deification of Claudius and a treatise on clemency, as well as numerous philosophical treatises and dramas in verse. In so far as the piece of satire contains a consistent political message, it is a criticism of the arbitrary exercise of power, but its name alone, the *Apocolocyntosis divi Claudi*, translatable as *The Pumpkinification of the Deified Claudius*, implies that we should not take it too seriously.

The theme of the exercise of power returns in the *De clementia*. This was dedicated to Nero and written while Seneca was still in favour. Its composition is certainly to be dated after Nero had murdered his step-brother, Britannicus. Our assessment of the work must start from the fact that clemency is the characteristic virtue of a monarch whose power is unlimited and who may exercise that power as he pleases. Seneca certainly wished to recommend clemency to Nero as a policy, but it is a policy for which in the last resort it is possible only to hope.

Elements of political analysis are detectable in the more general philosophical works of Seneca, although these are primarily devoted to moral instruction. He considers the problems of republican and imperial government, as well as slavery and the entire social order. But although he was certainly dealing with matters of major current concern, his analyses always return to the moral character of individual rulers on the one hand and the moral code of the individual politician on the other. There is no real attempt to relate the behaviour of an individual to the institutional framework. MHC

Reading

†Griffin, M.T.: *Seneca: a Philosopher in Politics*. Oxford: Clarendon Press, 1976.

Seneca: *Apocolocyntosis*, ed. P.T. Eden. Cambridge, New York, Melbourne: Cambridge University Press, 1984.

———: *De clementia*. In *Moral Essays*, vol. I, trans. J.W. Basore. London: Heinemann, 1928.

separation of powers The doctrine that the various functions of government should be separated was formulated in a fragmentary way by a number of writers including John LOCKE, but most notably by MONTESQUIEU, and in its modern form by the authors of the FEDERALIST

PAPERS, who embodied into it some elements of the English constitutional notion of CHECKS AND BALANCES. In its purest form, which it most nearly attains in the United States, the separation of powers doctrine implies that:

(1) Executive, legislative and judicial powers are conferred by the constitution on different persons and bodies.
(2) The branches of government are regarded as co-ordinate and autonomous, none of them being subordinate or accountable to any of the others. (For example, the legislature cannot remove the executive, nor can the executive dissolve the legislature.)
(3) No branch of government can in principle exercise the powers allocated by the constitution to the other branches. (For example, the legislature cannot delegate its powers entirely to the executive branch, or confer an undefined rule-making power, nor can judicial power be exercised otherwise than by the judicial branch of government.)
(4) The judicial branch acts independently of political influence and enjoys security of tenure. It may have the power to declare legislation constitutionally invalid (though outside the United States this power is not universally regarded as entailed by the separation doctrine).

Many constitutions contain some of the above elements without others. Even in the United States the powers of government are intermingled in a number of ways. The President, as executive, has a part in the legislative process. The Senate has a role in executive appointments and treaty-making. By way of the impeachment process both branches of the legislature can remove the President and the Judiciary from their offices. Moreover, many rule-making powers have been conferred on executive agencies.

In France the separation of the judicial and legislative powers is differently regarded as creating a prohibition on the judicial review or nullification of legislative action. In Australia the allocation of powers by the constitution to different branches of the Commonwealth government has significantly limited the capacity of the Commonwealth parliament to delegate powers and to create adjudicatory or arbitration bodies. GM

Reading

The *Federalist Papers*, nos 47 & 48. London: Everyman, 1948 (reissued 1986).

Finnis, J.M.: Separation of powers in the Australian Constitution. *Adelaide Law Review* 3 (1968) 154.

†Gwyn, W.B.: *The Meaning of the Separation of Powers.* New Orleans: Tulane University; The Hague: Nijhoff, 1965.

†Marshall, G.: *Constitutional Theory*, ch. 5. Oxford: Oxford University Press, 1971.

†Vile, M.J.C.: *Constitutionalism and the Separation of Powers*. Oxford: Oxford University Press, 1967.

Shaw, George Bernard (1856–1950) British playwright and pamphleteer. A leading member of the Fabian society, he edited *Fabian Essays in Socialism* (1889). See FABIANISM.

Sidgwick, Henry (1838–1900) British philosopher. The Knightbridge professor of moral philosophy at Cambridge, 1883–1900, Sidgwick is still regarded as a grey figure of late-Victorian irresolution, a reputation given him by the next Cambridge generation, who attempted to tackle as separate problems the issues he treated as parts of a comprehensive ethico-political system.

Sidgwick was the last reputable philosopher to attempt, like J. S. MILL, major works on ethics, economics and politics (*The Methods of Ethics*, 1874; *The Principles of Political Economy*, 1883; and *The Elements of Politics*, 1891), yet he still remains the confuser of Benthamite certainties, the pre-Marshallian economist, and a political scientist insulated from the impact of post-Marxian sociology.

Yet J. M. Keynes's famous dismissal: 'He never did anything but wonder whether Christianity was true and prove that it wasn't and hope that it was' (quoted in Skidelsky, p. 34), echoed by Skidelsky's image of Sidgwick 'moving effortlessly – if not painlessly – between the several worlds of Victorian *Angst*' (p. 34), is more than unfair about an active and fruitful career in which involvement in intellectual and political controversy led not – as has been usually the case in the twentieth century – into sociological generalization, but into a reconsideration of the premises of political thinking careful enough to have enduring value.

Sidgwick was the son of an Evangelical clergyman; he attended Rugby School with T. H. GREEN and was part of the energetic and productive generation that carried through the reform of Oxford and Cambridge in the 1860s and 1870s, attempting both to marry the universities to the needs of the new democracy and to devise some form of civic ethics which would replace the dwindling credibility of revealed religion.

The religious-political controversies of the 1860s underlie the argument of *The Methods of Ethics*, with its examination of the inadequacies of egoism as a basis of utilitarian ethics (see UTILITARIANISM). What, Sidgwick asked, happened when the greatest good could only be secured by personal self-sacrifice, a predicament he had experienced when he resigned his own fellowship in 1869. This book – and to a great extent all Sidgwick's subsequent economic and political philosophy – examines the relationships that *a priori* moral injunctions and political axioms bear to calculations of general utility and hence to the action of governments. His contemporaries, of whom James Bryce was typical, realized that the distinction of his contribution lay in his treatment of the customary terms of ethical and political reasoning: 'the student who had already some knowledge of the topic . . . gained immensely by having so many fallacies lurking in currently accepted notions detected, so many conditions indicated which might qualify the amplitude of a general proposition' (p. 333).

It was Sidgwick's careful analysis of concepts such as 'justice', 'authority', 'liberty of contract', that gave his economic and political studies their lasting value, often better conveyed in essays rather than in his formal works. Although he was the last reputable economist to dispense with mathematical techniques, Alfred Marshall praised his treatment of the functions of government in the economy as 'by far the best thing of the kind in any language', and his British Association address 'On the Economic Exceptions to Laissez-Faire' is a small classic. His *Principles of Political Economy* drew the wrath of the Manchester school for its argument that economic efficiency might on strictly utilitarian grounds require a considerable element of state intervention, but this apparent radicalism was qualified by an apprehensiveness about the competence of a democracy to undertake such economic management. *The Elements of Politics*, while following the schema of argument from principles to institutions, stressed the need for government by the well-qualified and disinterested but, unlike PARETO and MOSCA, without formulating any sociological theory to account for the hegemony of such elites. This paralleled what he referred to as the 'Liberal principles and Tory votes' of his later life, as a leading Liberal Unionist and brother-in-law of the future Conservative premier, Arthur Balfour. For all his reputation as a doubter, Sidgwick's energetic career as a university reformer, and the catholicity of his political critique, laid many of the foundations of consensus *étatisme* in the twentieth century.   CTH

Reading

Bryce, J.: *Studies in Contemporary Biography*. London: Macmillan, 1903.

†Harvie, C.T.: *The Lights of Liberalism: University Liberals and the Challenge of Democracy, 1860–86*. London: Allen Lane, 1976.

Havard, W.C.: *Henry Sidgwick and Later Utilitarian Political Philosophy*. Gainesville: University of Florida Press, 1959.

†Schneewind, J.B.: *Sidgwick's Ethics and Victorian Moral Philosophy*. Oxford: Clarendon Press, 1977.

Sidgwick, H.: *The Methods of Ethics*. London: Macmillan, 1874.

———: *The Principles of Political Economy*. London: Macmillan, 1883.

———: *The Elements of Politics*. London: Macmillan, 1891.

Skidelsky, R.: *John Maynard Keynes*, vol. I. London: Macmillan, 1983.

Sieyès, Emmanuel Joseph (1748–1836) French publicist and politician. Born into a prosperous bourgeois family, Sieyès was educated by Jesuits, became a priest, and held posts as an ecclesiastical official until the Revolution, despite a scepticism towards traditional theology and a taste for secular philosophy. In August 1788 the king announced a meeting of the Estates General the following May, and Sieyès wrote four pamphlets, appearing between November and February, that were intended to shape the agenda of the Third Estate: *Essay on Privileges, What is The Third Estate?, Views on Means of which the French People Dispose*, and *Plan of Deliberations*. These pamphlets, particularly the second, brought Sieyès into political prominence and ensured his election as a delegate for Paris to the Estates General. During June he played a major part in the merging of the three separate Estates into the National Assembly, and contributed much to the shaping of the 1791 Constitution. Thereafter, during the republican and Napoleonic periods, his political importance declined and his influence, though crucial at times, was spasmodic. His political life ended in 1816 when, after Napoleon's final fall, he fled into exile in Brussels.

Sieyès's combination of intelligence with intellectual arrogance and an acute sensitivity to criticism at least partly explain his limitations as a politician – and also perhaps his limitations as a political theorist. He was essentially a publicist who caught and articulated popular ideas and aspirations at a moment of political crisis, and thereby helped to shape the ideology and rhetoric of revolutionary politics.

The major themes in his pamphlets of 1788–9 were an attack upon legal privileges, a defence of popular sovereignty and representative government, and an assertion of NATIONALISM. Any truly social state must be based on legal equality and all legal privilege must be corrupting. It created vested class interests, subordinated government to the protection of those interests, promoted false pride and vanity, and undermined the recognition of the real merit of those who work. Far from a privileged order being or representing the nation, it lay outside it. The nation consisted in the Third Estate – all those who contribute to the social good – and it is the national will alone that should be represented. Society originated in the wish of individuals to act collectively and their consequent agreement to act through a common will. Population increase might require the construction of representative institutions, but the national will remained supreme, most particularly in that it could at any time determine changes in the political constitution. How far Sieyès's support for the idea of popular sovereignty committed him to full democracy is doubtful; certainly, even before the waning of his enthusiasm for popular elections in the late 1790s he backed constitutional devices, such as the distinction between active and passive citizenship, which suggested that the poor as well as the nobility lay outside the nation. Nevertheless, he did give a populist face to French nationalism. In basing nationhood upon neither culture, language nor tradition but upon the common contribution of citizens to the national will, Sieyès followed MONTESQUIEU and ROUSSEAU in associating patriotism with political participation.   JL

Reading

Sieyès, E.J.: *What is the Third Estate?*, trans. M. Blondel, ed. S.E. Finer. London: Pall Mall, 1963.

Van Deusen, G.G.: *Sieyès: His Life and His Nationalism*. New York: Columbia University Press, 1932; repr. AMS Press, 1968.

Smith, Adam (1723–1790)   British moral philosopher and political economist. Smith was born in Kirkcaldy, Scotland, the posthumous only child of a civil servant. He was educated at the local burgh school and later at Glasgow College (1737–40), where he was chiefly influenced by Francis Hutcheson. He spent the next six years at Balliol College, Oxford, before returning to Scotland, where the success of public lectures on rhetoric and *belles lettres* given in Edinburgh led to his appointment to the chair of logic at Glasgow in 1750. He transferred to the chair of moral philosophy two years later and held this position until his resignation in 1764. Smith's teaching on ethics, jurisprudence, and politics provided the framework for both of his main published works, the *Theory of Moral Sentiments* (1759) and *An Inquiry into the Nature and Causes of the Wealth of Nations* (1776), though for a fuller understanding of the ambitious system of knowledge which he passed on to his students it is now possible to supplement these by students' notes on his lectures on jurisprudence. Smith left Glasgow to act as tutor to the Duke of Buccleuch; this made it possible for him to visit France and Geneva, and to make the acquaintance of French economists and *philosophes*. It was also while on this tour that he began the work which emerged twelve years later at the *Wealth of Nations*. Largely as a result of the reception given to this work, Smith was appointed Commissioner of Customs in Edinburgh, a post which placed his expertise on economic subjects at the disposal of such statesmen as Pitt, North, and Shelburne.

Although later to be chiefly known as the founding father of a school of CLASSICAL POLITICAL ECONOMY that encompasses Malthus, Ricardo, J. S. MILL and MARX, Smith was primarily a moral philosopher whose views on ethics and jurisprudence are essential to an understanding of his politics and economics. The famous 'system of natural liberty and perfect justice' expounded in the *Wealth of Nations* serves simultaneously as an explanatory and normative model for the conduct of human affairs in economic matters. It seeks to show that the untrammelled pursuit of individual self-interest under competitive conditions can (ought to be allowed to) create a harmonious public order in which the benefits of economic growth and efficiency, chiefly in the form of rising wages and lower prices and profits, will be most widely diffused throughout society. The growth of opulence is treated as the unintended consequence of short-sighted behaviour largely directed towards meeting private needs and motivated by a persistent desire to improve both personal condition and social status. The economic mechanisms producing growth are the expansion of markets, the enhanced productivity resulting from the division of labour, and capital accumulation arising from private thrift under conditions ensuring political security. The *Wealth of Nations*, therefore, contains a detailed argument, conducted along national and cosmopolitan lines, for free trade and competitive markets; and it was buttressed by a 'very violent attack' on mercantile restrictions and monopoly privileges granted by the state (see MERCANTILISM).

In contradistinction to later, more extreme versions of *laissez-faire* individualism, however, Smith paid as much attention to the institutional preconditions required to produce a socially beneficial result as he did to the internal connections forged by economic activity itself. By contrast with modern economics, he did not employ rational economic man assumptions; and he was at least as concerned with the political and moral byproducts of economic activities in modern commercial societies as he was with material benefits for their own sake. Indeed, with regard to the latter his position must be regarded as distinctly sceptical and ascetic.

Smith's contributions to social and political thought are best understood as original variations on themes in Scottish moral philosophy first enunciated by Hutcheson, and as more systematic developments of various ideas on natural jurisprudence and politics that can be found in the writings of his close friend, David HUME (see also SCOTTISH ENLIGHTENMENT). In common with Hume, Smith adopted a Newtonian or naturalistic approach to morals and politics which entailed rejection of the SOCIAL CONTRACT as an account of the origins of government. In place of such rationalistic constructs, Smith treated POLITICAL OBLIGATION as an outcome of psychological dispositions at work in all societies, namely habitual deference to established authority and a sense of the public utility attached to regular forms of government. As a result, political obedience was linked with the sociological phenomenon known as the distinction of ranks and made subject to the prevailing climate of 'opinion', whether expressed in representative institutions or not.

In opposition to more individualistic accounts of society and government, Smith, in his *Theory of Moral Sentiments*, developed the concept of 'sympathy' as an explanation for our capacity to seek and achieve the approbation of our fellow human beings, and hence to form objective moral norms and rules of justice as internal and external guides to conduct. This emphasis on socially acquired habits exercised through customs and institutions which differed according to time and place was also expressed in Smith's pioneering treatment of law and government as historical phenomena which had emerged via a process that could be divided into a progressive sequence of four stages, each of which corresponded to a particular mode of subsistence: hunting, pastoral, agricultural, and commercial. The last of these stages, described interchangeably as commercial society or CIVIL SOCIETY, was the form that had emerged throughout modern Europe as a result of the silent revolution that had undermined feudal institutions. An account of this revolution is given in Book III of the *Wealth of Nations*, and the nature of

commercial society, together with its implications for liberty, gives unity to the whole work.

Again in common with Hume, Smith's conception of liberty was primarily juristic. It centred on security of personal and property rights under the rule of law, where JUSTICE was defined as abstention from injury to the rights of others. It involved precise negative rules of commutative justice rather than the positive, yet less easily codifiable and hence enforceable, moral codes underlying benevolence and distributive justice. No social existence was possible without some such negative rules, but the need became acute with the development of inequalities arising from property and the expansion in the number and complexity of potential injuries that could be inflicted. Personal liberty in the modern sense, therefore, was a product of the process of civilization itself, dependent on the capacity of strong centralized governments to administer law effectively and impartially.

Together with defence of the realm, justice was one of the main duties of the sovereign; and it is clear that Smith believed that legislative as well as judicial intervention was necessary to discharge this function properly. He frequently appealed to ideas of injustice and oppression, as well as economic inexpediency, when criticizing attempts by governments to regulate economic life, especially when this entailed granting special privileges to particular orders or groups within society. It was his opinion that the most common departures from principles of natural justice in modern states were attributable to pressures exerted on government by vested interests, particularly those associated with commerce and manufacturing. Indeed, Smith singled out such groups as being especially unfit to advise on legislative matters where notions of public good ought to prevail.

Smith also believed that government had significant duties to perform with respect to education and the provision of public works that could not be left to private initiative. Thus state-supported education was particularly important as an antidote to the effects of the division of labour in undermining the mental, moral, social, and political capacities of the populace at large. Smith expected, therefore, that the duties and even size of government would grow with opulence; but he was anxious to devise means by which essential functions could be supplied without undue burden in the form of taxes and the growth of 'unproductive' activities. Hence his interest in proposing extra-market institutions designed to achieve this result by methods that matched incentive to performance.

Smith's concern with institutional machinery that would curb harmful proclivities and harness energies to serve the public good was based on a hard-headed realism about human nature which emphasized man's vanity, self-interestedness, and propensity to dominate others when given the opportunity to do so. It lends to his politics a non-idealistic, or deeply anti-utopian cast which is best summarized in his criticisms in the *Theory of Moral Sentiments* of the 'man of system' who seeks to implement an ideal plan of government without regard to the motives and interests of those individuals and orders which comprise civil society and underpin its constitution. State and civil society are mutual spheres of interaction. A knowledge of the 'science of the legislator' was useful in animating public spirit and in encouraging the attitudes of the statesman as opposed to those of the mere politician; but legal and other machinery should be relied upon to control anti-social behaviour and ensure the coincidence of private and public interest.

Smith did not expect his system of natural liberty to be implemented as a whole, and he never laid claim to extensive foresight. Nevertheless, he has been criticized either as an apologist, or for his failure to appreciate many aspects of later, more industrial stages of capitalism, notably by underestimating the role played by technology and the growth of factory methods of production, with all their apparent consequences in terms of inequality and exploitation. With somewhat greater justification, he can be criticized for excessive faith in the self-regulating properties of competitive markets. It is also sometimes charged that Smith was responsible for deflecting political discourse towards economics and sociology, and hence away from the larger moral issues of classical political discourse. This charge can be linked with a more general attack on his non-idealistic, naturalistic stance. Smith's politics can also be criticized for relying too heavily

on 'opinion' and the persistence of deference within a society of ranks to ensure the stability and legitimacy of government. In other words, the durability of his political vision has been called into question by the very same forces of social fluidity which he believed were one of the welcome byproducts of economic progress; it has created situations in which political obedience and social hierarchy no longer seem to be mutually reinforcing.

The positive/normative distinction is not entirely appropriate as a means of understanding Smith's position because, like other writers in the natural law tradition, the fruitful ambiguities embedded in the term 'natural' allow Smith to move freely between what is normally the case under actual conditions, and what ought to be the case under ideal conditions. Thus Smith's ideals of liberty and justice, though real enough, were accompanied by a desire to establish explanations for how human affairs had actually come to be the way they were. The attempt to combine the approaches of social scientist and political moralist could in fact be Smith's main source of interest to later generations.   DNW

Reading

Campbell, T.D.: *Adam Smith's Science of Morals.* London: Allen & Unwin, 1971.

Forbes, D.: Sceptical Whiggism, commerce and liberty. In *Essays on Adam Smith*, ed. A. Skinner and T. Wilson. Oxford: Clarendon Press, 1976.

Haakonssen, K.: *The Science of a Legislator.* Cambridge: Cambridge University Press, 1981.

†Raphael, D.D.: *Adam Smith.* Oxford: Oxford University Press, 1985.

Rosenberg, N.: Some institutional aspects of the *Wealth of Nations. Journal of Political Economy* 68 (1960) 537–70.

†Skinner, A.: *A System of Social Science.* Oxford: Clarendon Press, 1979.

Smith, A.: *The Glasgow Edition of the Works and Correspondence of Adam Smith*, ed. R.H. Campbell and A.S. Skinner. Oxford: Clarendon Press, 1976–.

†Winch, D.: *Adam Smith's Politics.* Cambridge: Cambridge University Press, 1978.

social contract   At the heart of social contract theory is the idea that legitimate government is the artificial product of the voluntary agreement of free moral agents – that there is no such thing as 'natural' political authority. Thus Michael Oakeshott is right to call contractarianism a doctrine of 'will and artifice'; indeed one might epitomize the theory in LOCKE's assertion that 'voluntary agreement gives political power to governors'. While there are traces of contract theory in ancient and medieval thought, and while the doctrine has recently been revived by certain modern liberals, the golden age of social contract theory was the period 1650–1800, beginning with HOBBES's *Leviathan* and ending with KANT's *Metaphysical Elements of Justice*.

Why voluntarism came to hold such an important place in western thought is debatable. What is probable is that ancient theories of the good regime and the naturally social end of man gave way, under the influence of Christianity, to thinking about politics after the model of 'good acts': just as good acts required both knowledge of the good and the will to do the good, politics required moral assent, the implication of the individual in politics through his own volition. The freedom to conform voluntarily to absolute standards had always been important in Christian doctrine, and the Reformation doubtless strengthened the element of individual choice and responsibility in moral thinking, while subordinating the role of moral authority. It was natural enough that the 'Protestant' view of individual moral autonomy should spill over from theology and moral philosophy into politics, providing an intellectual basis for social contract theory. After the unfolding of the essential social ideas of the Reformation, the mere excellence of an institution would not, of itself, legitimize it; that required authorization by individual men understood as authors. However voluntarism and social contract theory arose, it is certain that ideas of the good state increasingly gave way to ideas of the legitimate state; and after the seventeenth century this legitimacy was often taken to rest on the notion of *willing*.

The decisive turn in the voluntarization of western social thought came with St AUGUSTINE, who appropriated the *bona voluntas* of CICERO and SENECA and deepened it into a central moral concept. Although not a voluntarist or contractarian in his explicitly political writings, Augustine forged in his moral theory the strong link between consent and will

without which social contract theory would be unthinkable. This voluntarism became less indirect, more explicitly political, in some of the Christian political philosophers who succeeded Aquinas – most notably WILLIAM OF OCKHAM and Nicholas Cusanus, both of whom argued that legitimate political authority depended on the free consent of subjects.

But the most advanced and subtle form of political voluntarism before the social contract school itself is contained in Francisco SUAREZ's magisterial *Tractatus de legibus ac Deo legislatore* (Treatise on the Laws and God the Lawgiver). For Suarez, free will and political consent are analogous or even parallel; will is the 'proximate cause' of the state. Suarez summarizes his doctrine with the observation that 'human will is necessary in order that men may unite in a single perfect community', and that 'by the nature of things, men as individuals possess to a partial extent (so to speak) the faculty for establishing, or creating, a perfect community'. Plainly for Suarez that faculty is will: men can be gathered together into one political body only by 'special volition, or common consent'; the people cannot manifest consent 'unless the acts are voluntary'.

The modern contractarian position involves just such an effort to view politics as legitimized through consent, so that obligation and authority are products of everyone's original freedom and responsibility, effects of everyone's will as a moral cause. It is perfectly possible, of course, to treat contractarianism in more modest terms: as an extension of certain medieval ideas about contracts between rulers and peoples, as conciliarism writ (very) large, or as a theory about the rational boundaries of government (see POLITICAL OBLIGATION). The disadvantage of more modest treatments, however, is that they take inadequate account of the revolution introduced into political and moral philosophy by Christian ideas and thereby underemphasize the ethical components of contractarianism, such as autonomy, responsibility, duty, authorization, and willing.

CONSENT, or agreement based on will, understood as a moral faculty, came to occupy a place in political philosophy in the seventeenth, eighteenth, and early nineteenth centuries that it had never occupied so completely before. HOBBES, for instance, urges in *Leviathan* (1651) that 'the right of all sovereigns is derived originally from consent of every one of those that are to be governed' (ch. 42), and he insists that human wills 'make the essence of all covenants' (ch. 40). In his earlier *De cive* (1642) he had even urged: 'I say that . . . a man is obliged by his contracts, that is, that he ought to perform for his promise sake; but that the law ties him being obliged, that is to say, it compels him to make good his promise, for fear of the punishment appointed by law' (ch. 14, §2 n.). Here Hobbes clearly states that obligations are derived from promises, from contracts of which will is the essence, and not from fear of punishment, which simply reinforces the intention that results from a promise. Passing over Locke, who nonetheless argues that 'voluntary agreement gives . . . political power to governors for the benefit of their subjects', and turning to ROUSSEAU, one finds an insistence that 'I owe nothing to those whom I have promised nothing . . . Civil association is the most voluntary act in the world; since every individual is born free and his own master, no one is able, on any pretext whatsoever, to subject him without his consent' (*Du contrat social*, bk 4, ch. 2). (This passage shows clearly how the ideas of consent, contract, and voluntary actions are tied together.) As for Kant, in the *Rechtslehre* (Metaphysical Elements of Justice) (1797) he urges that it is just for the nobility to be allowed to die out gradually, since the people could never have willed the establishment of a hereditary class that does not merit its rank, and that all legitimate laws must be such that rational men *could* consent to them. Even HEGEL explicitly argues that while 'in the states of antiquity the subjective end simply coincided with the state's will', in modern times 'we make claims for private judgment, private willing, and private conscience'. When a social decision is to be made, Hegel continues, 'an "I will" must be pronounced by man himself'.

His voluntarism notwithstanding, Hegel was an influential critic of the contractual theory of the state. For more than a century after his death in 1831, social contract theory was eclipsed by, on the one hand, UTILITARIANISM, and on the other by historical theories of the state stemming largely from Hegel himself and finding their most powerful expression in MARXISM. Only recently has it been given new life in the work of, especially, John RAWLS, who attempts to present his principles of justice as 'the principles that free and rational persons concerned to further their own interests would accept in an initial position of equality as defining the fundamental terms of their association' (p. 11). Rawls is not directly concerned with justifying political authority, and he makes little explicit use of the ideas of *will* and *consent*, yet his attempt to present the just society as a 'voluntary scheme of co-operation' links him to the contractarian tradition. A mode of political thought which has its roots in Augustine, and which dominated the Enlightenment, seems to have made a remarkable recovery.   PR

Reading
†Barker, E.: *The Social Contract*. London: Oxford University Press, 1946.

Hobbes, T.: *Leviathan*, ed. C.B. Macpherson. Harmondsworth: Penguin, 1968.

——: *De cive*, ed. S.P. Lamprecht. New York: Appleton-Century-Crofts, 1949.

Hume, D.: Of the original contract. In *Political Essays*, ed. C.W. Hendel. New York: Liberal Arts, 1953.

Kant, I.: *The Metaphysical Elements of Justice*, trans. J. Ladd. Indianapolis: Bobbs-Merrill, 1965.

Locke, J.: *Two Treatises of Government* (1689), ed. P. Laslett. New York: Mentor, 1965; Cambridge: Cambridge University Press, 1970.

Oakeshott, M.: Introduction to *Leviathan*. Oxford: Blackwell, 1946.

Plamenatz, J.: *Consent, Freedom and Political Obligation*. London: Oxford University Press, 1938.

Rawls, J.: *A Theory of Justice*. Cambridge, Mass.: Harvard University Press, 1971; Oxford: Oxford University Press, 1972.

†Riley, P.: *Will and Political Legitimacy*. Cambridge, Mass.: Harvard University Press, 1982.

Ritchie, D.: *Darwin and Hegel*. New York: Macmillan, 1893.

Rousseau, J.-J.: *The Social Contract* (1762), ed R.D. Masters. New York: St Martin's, 1978.

Suarez, F.: *A Treatise on the Laws and God the Lawgiver* (1612). 2 vols. Naples, 1872.

social Darwinism   Attempts by social and political thinkers to borrow the authority of Darwinian biology for their own theories are conveniently referred to as 'social Darwinism'; in this sense the heyday of social Darwinist theories was the last quarter of the nineteenth century. There are, however, several important qualifications which need to be made. Biological analogies for society, various forms of organicism, and the use of the word 'evolution' to refer to aspects of historical change, were widespread, but in many cases their connection with Darwinism proper was remote. Much of this theorizing, and the use of evolutionary language, was inspired by Herbert SPENCER, whose own evolutionist doctrines were derived chiefly from Lamarck. Sometimes, claims to present a view of 'social evolution' amounted to little more than a rechristening of nineteenth-century historicist ideas in a fashionable 'scientific' idiom.

The term 'social Darwinism' is most properly applied to attempts to find social analogies for the Darwinian law of natural selection (or, as it came to be called, 'the survival of the fittest') and to explain the course of human history in terms of its operation. Such theories were typically philosophies of history, often of a determinist kind, with conflict or competition as their 'law' or controlling agency. The earliest to appear after the *Origin of Species* was *Physics and Politics* (1869) by Walter BAGEHOT, and over the next three or four decades a great variety followed, ranging from extreme *laissez-faire*, individualist versions, in the Spencerian tradition, as in the work of the American sociologist William Graham Sumner (1840–1910), to the more collectivist interpretation of Benjamin Kidd (1858–1916) in England and the racial version of the Austrian Ludwig Gumplowicz (1838–1910). The Russian anarchist, Peter KROPOTKIN (1842–1921), offered in his *Mutual Aid* (1902) a version in which co-operation rather than competition was the key factor in social evolution, and the leading propagandist for Darwinian evolutionism in biology, T. H. Huxley, became an early and trenchant critic of social Darwinism in *Evolution and Ethics* (1893).

No theoretical consensus among social Darwinists approached that of Darwinians in biology. Social Darwinism was a vocabulary and a set of argumentative and explanatory tendencies in social theory rather than a coherent paradigm. Four sets of historical and intellectual conditions shaped the forms taken by social Darwinist arguments in the later

nineteenth century and help to explain their popularity:

(1) the emergence of sociology as a branch of learning and the need to give it a theoretical basis;
(2) the centrality, in political argument, of the debate between individualist and collectivist political theories (see INDIVIDUALISM);
(3) imperialism and the tendency fostered, if not created, by social Darwinism, to see global issues in quasi-biological terms, as conflict or competition between races (see RACISM);
(4) European international tension and the arms race, culminating in the outbreak of war in 1914.

Despite an inclination to speak deterministically about social change, and to claim the authority of 'science', social Darwinist arguments were rarely, if ever, put forward in a purely explanatory way. The almost unquestioned identification of social evolution with progress, and the use of the phrase 'survival of the fittest', provided a clothing for the diversity of political opinions, adaptable to all. Theoretical ambiguities, such as the units (individuals or collectivities) between which competition took place, were polemically exploited, and social Darwinism could be individualist, socialistic, racist or militarist. Essentially such arguments were about which forms of competition to legitimate and which to reject – an issue irrelevant to, and incomprehensible within, Darwinian biological theory.   JWB

Reading

†Banton, M. ed.: *Darwinism and the Study of Society*. London: Tavistock, 1961.

Bock, K.E.: Darwin and social theory. *Philosophy of Science* 22 (1955) 123–34.

Crook, D.P.: *Benjamin Kidd: Portrait of a Social Darwinist*. Cambridge: Cambridge University Press, 1984.

†Himmelfarb, G.: *Darwin and the Darwinian Revolution*. London: Chatto & Windus, 1959.

†Jones, G.: *Social Darwinism and English Thought*. Brighton, Sussex: Harvester, 1980.

social democracy The idea of social democracy is complex; originally a form of dogmatic MARXISM, it has come to have a very different meaning. In order to account for this change and subsequent complexity, reference must be made to the history and institutional development of social democracy and particularly its relationship to SOCIALISM and to New Liberalism.

The origins of social democracy in its modern sense may be traced back to divisions within the Social Democratic Party in Germany, formed in 1875 through an accommodation between the reformism of LASSALLE and orthodox Marxism. The Gotha Programme which defined the outlook of the new party was severely criticized by MARX in *The Critique of the Gotha Programme* (1875), and in this critique we can see the main outlines of what were to become major differences between Marxism and what became subsequently social democracy. The Programme embodied a number of errors in Marx's view but two stand out as being of major theoretical importance. One is the theory of the state presupposed by the Programme. It had advocated the development of a free state by means of universal suffrage, direct legislation, civil rights and a popular militia, and it assumed that these changes could be brought about by peaceful means. Marx, however, argued that this was to assume the Hegelian view that the state stood over and above the economic and social forces at work in society, a universal and neutral instrument which could be used, once political power was attained, to secure socialist advances. For Marx the state was an instrument of class domination, and socialism could only be achieved by revolutionary transformation.

The second important theme of the Programme which Marx rejected was the attempt to define socialism at least in part in terms of social justice or what the Programme calls 'a fair distribution of the proceeds of labour'. In Marx's view this was to strike at the heart of the coherence of historical materialism or 'scientific' socialism because it assumes that moral values like justice and fairness can operate independently of dominant class relations. Thus a democratic socialist government could, by political action, develop a fair and just distribution of the social product. For Marx, however, moral values are part of the ideological superstructure and cannot operate as

independent political motives for reform to the basic structure of society.

These issues, on the social democratic side of the argument, were clarified by BERNSTEIN, a leading member of the Social Democratic Party and Engels's literary executor. Bernstein set out to make a fundamental revision of the Marxian analysis of capitalism and its own assumptions about socialism, and it was this that led to the idea of 'revisionism'. He was impressed by the fact that most of Marx's predictions about the development of capitalism had simply not come true, and he argued that the failure of the predictive part of the theory indicated a weakness in the analysis on which the predictions were based. Since the foundation of the German Reich in 1870 a period of great prosperity had been experienced, a prosperity which, Bernstein argued, had benefited all classes, not just the capitalists and the leading members of the working class. Marxian theory could, of course, accommodate the view that at certain stages in its development capitalism could generate periods of relative prosperity, but such prosperity would always be restricted to the capitalists themselves, and perhaps to the elite of the proletariat whose revolutionary fervour was thus 'bought off'.

It was not only in its account of economic changes that Bernstein found Marxian theory lacking. He argued that it could take no account of correlative changes in social structure. Marx had contended that as capitalism developed a polarization of classes would take place, between the oppressed and exploited proletariat on the one hand, and the exploiters, the capitalists, on the other. Such class polarization had not occurred, Bernstein argued. Indeed, on the contrary, a greater differentiation in social structure had taken place in trade, industry and commerce, and in the bureaucracies middle-class occupations were therefore on the increase.

The prediction of the polarization of classes and the greater and greater impoverishment of the working class were widely taken to be the two cornerstones of Marx's theory of revolution. The development of these two factors would exacerbate the tensions in capitalism to such a degree that the system would eventually collapse. As these predictions were not, in

Bernstein's view, correct, the emphasis on revolution, he argued, could be dismissed. Furthermore the failure of the predictive part of the theory undermined the scientific pretensions of the analyses which underpinned it, and in his influential lecture *How is Scientific Socialism Possible?* (1901), Bernstein broke with *scientific* socialism which was considered to be the major hallmark of the Marxian system. He argued that socialism was not an inevitable outcome of the development of capitalism, but rather a moral ideal for which those committed to it must struggle.

Bernstein's critique very clearly had practical consequences. Revolution was not needed, since the twin bases upon which such a necessity had been predicated did not exist; rather the struggle for socialism had to be gradualist and reformist. Politically it would consist in the attempt to achieve full democracy; economically in the appropriation by the workers, through both political power and trade union pressure, of the means of production in society. The projected socialization of German economic power had in Bernstein's view been made easier by the development of cartels in the economy, rendering the ownership of economic power less diffuse. The task was therefore to struggle for particular socialist objectives, not to wait for socialism to emerge fully complete from the womb of history.

The emergence of social democracy in Britain was heavily influenced by the New Liberalism of theorists such as HOBHOUSE and Wallas. In *Fabian Essays* (1889) Wallas wrote of his political goal as a 'tentative and limited social democracy', and Hobhouse in *Social Evolution and Political Theory* (1911) linked liberalism and social democracy. Whereas old or classical liberalism had as its aim the removal of restraints and restrictions, particularly in the civil and trading spheres, 'New Liberalism' was concerned with the achievement of greater social justice and a fairer distribution of economic rewards in order to secure greater freedom, understood in a positive and not just a negative sense. The mechanism for this was to be state intervention in the economy. In this sense, therefore, there is some overlap between the revisionism of someone like Bernstein and New Liberalism in that both saw the state and

political reform as instruments which with the appropriate political will would be able to secure their social goals, and these goals were in their turn seen in moral terms. Initially some Fabians, particularly the Webbs, did not see the need for a socialist party – the need was to permeate the leadership of existing parties – in particular the progressive elements of the Liberal Party – so that socialism would be arrived at in a cumulative way, as the result of a long period of social reform (see FABIANISM). Thus socialism required no decisive break with capitalist society but would be, as Cole and Postgate argue, 'the logical consummation of a progressive policy of social reform' (p. 410). The simultaneous development of Fabianism and New Liberalism contributed to the formulation in Britain of a non-Marxist form of socialism, to the extent that some writers such as P. F. Clarke in *Liberals and Social Democrats in Historical Perspective* (1978) and Alan Warde in *Consensus and Beyond* (1982) have seen the social democratic tradition in Britain as being more closely bound up with these developments, rather than as an internal revision of Marxism. Socialism, in the social democratic understanding of it, was a combination of political democracy, a welfare state, educational opportunity and greater social justice, all to be developed in the context of a mixed economy. These themes were to become important in the subsequent development of social democracy in Britain.

During the late 1930s the social democratic position received a major theoretical boost with the publication of Keynes's *General Theory of Employment, Interest and Money* (1936). Although Keynes was himself a Liberal, his arguments were taken up by social democrats such as Durbin in *The Politics of Democratic Socialism* (1940) and Douglas Jay in *The Socialist Case* (1938) as fresh evidence for the falsity of Marx's analysis of capitalist society. Keynesian techniques looked as though they were able to resolve the contradictions of capitalism, if a government capable of implementing them were to be elected. So great was the force of the case developed by Jay, in particular, that it convinced the doyen of British Marxist theorists in the 1930s, John Strachey, to abandon Marxism for a more social democratic approach in his *Programme for Progress* (1940). Other factors too helped the growing ascendancy of the social democratic case over the Marxism of the mid-thirties by the end of the decade, particularly the thesis developed by James Burham in *The Managerial Revolution* (1941) which seemed to many to undermine part of Marx's analysis of capitalism by insisting upon the political importance of the growing divorce between ownership and control in capitalist enterprises.

In the post-war period, particularly in Britain and Germany, social democratic ideas gained the ascendancy on the left. In 1959 at its Bad Godesberg Conference the German SPD abandoned its residual Marxism and fully embraced social democratic principles, and in Britain the Labour Party under the leadership of Hugh Gaitskell turned more and more in practice, if not according to its constitution, to social democratic ideas, and particularly to ideas about equality and social justice. This process was helped considerably by the publication in 1956 of *The Future of Socialism* by C. A. R. CROSLAND and in 1962 of Douglas Jay's *Socialism and the New Society*. Writing in the spirit of Bernstein, Crosland argued that the Keynesian techniques of economic management adopted by the Labour governments of 1945–51 and by the subsequent Conservative administration had resolved many of the tensions in capitalism. Ownership of industry was now more widely spread and its control was in the hands of professional managers; trade unions had increased their power; the war years had shown to the whole country how state power could be used for the common good, given the political will; primary poverty had been reduced; key industries such as gas, electricity, railways and the mines had been nationalized, and a comprehensive welfare state had been established. In Crosland's view these responses had had such a far-reaching effect on the distribution of power in society and on the nature of the economy that Britain was no longer a capitalist society as that term was understood by Marx. The social democrat had to look for inspiration and guidance elsewhere, to values such as social justice, equality, and the diffusion of power. Of these Crosland put EQUALITY in the highest place on the agenda

(see CROSLAND for his interpretation of this idea).

Greater equality was to be achieved by two major means. The first and most general was economic growth. In Crosland's view, in a democratic society greater equality could be achieved with the least social tension by levelling up rather than down, and the fiscal dividends of growth would allow the better off to retain their absolute standard of living while improving the relative position of the worst-off members of society. The other major element in the pursuit of equality was to be comprehensive education, both to widen educational opportunity and to bring children of different social groups and ability into the same educational environment.

Despite Crosland's and Jay's efforts, a significant section of the Labour Party remained opposed to social democratic ideas. In the 1950s these disagreements were fought out between the Gaitskellite and the Bevanite factions in the party, and came to a head after the 1959 election defeat when, at the subsequent conference, Gaitskell attempted to change the party constitution so that under the terms of Clause IV it was no longer committed to wholesale nationalization. Although he was defeated on this issue, subsequent Labour governments acted more on social democratic principles than on those enshrined in its constitution. This divergence of view became very severe in the late 1970s, and in 1981 the Social Democratic Party was formed. Although there is no real equivalent to *The Future of Socialism* to define the new party's philosophy for the 1980s, a number of theoretical books have been written by social democrats, for example David Owen's *Face the Future* (1981) which combines traditional concerns with the mixed economy and redistribution of wealth for greater equality. However, there is now an emphasis not really present in the works of the 1950s and 1960s on the importance of political and industrial decentralization.

As the history of social democracy shows, political ideologies resist strict definition. To characterize the socialist left, we perhaps need a threefold distinction, between Marxism, democratic socialism, and social democracy. Marxism on this view involves accepting historical materialism and the limits on political change within capitalist society which this entails; democratic socialism shares the Marxist belief in the prime importance of bringing the means of production into social ownership but adds the view that this change can be secured by democratic means; social democracy shares the democratic socialist's commitment to democracy, but rejects the primacy of ownership which both the Marxist and the democratic socialist hold as central, and defines socialism largely in terms of redistribution and greater equality within the context of the mixed economy.   RP

Reading

Bernstein, E.: *Evolutionary Socialism* (1898). New York: Schocken, 1961.

†Clarke, P.F.: *Liberals and Social Democrats in Historical Perspective.* Cambridge: Cambridge University Press, 1978.

Cole, G.D.H. and Postgate, R.: *The Common People, 1746–1938.* London: Methuen, 1938.

†Crosland, C.A.R.: *The Future of Socialism.* London: Cape, 1980.

Durbin, E.: *The Politics of Democratic Socialism.* London: Routledge, 1940.

†Gay, P.: *The Dilemma of Democratic Socialism.* New York: Columbia University Press, 1952.

Jay, D.: *The Socialist Case.* London: Faber & Faber, 1938.

———: *Socialism and the New Society.* London: Longman, 1962.

Marx, K.: *The Critique of the Gotha Programme.* In *Selected Works.* London: Lawrence & Wishart, 1968.

Owen, D.: *Face the Future.* London: Cape, 1981.

Strachey, J.: *Programme for Progress.* London: Gollancz, 1940.

†Warde, A.: *Consensus and Beyond: the development of Labour Party strategy since the second world war.* Manchester: Manchester University Press, 1982.

socialism   As an identifiable body of argument, socialism developed in Europe from the end of the eighteenth century as a response to industrialization. Once its general character was established, attempts were made to discover intellectual precedents; by the twentieth century there was no part of the world in which elements of socialist argument had not been articulated. Nonetheless it remains in origin a European set of ideas, and specifically of ideas first expressed in France, Germany and the United Kingdom, the three principal original industrial nations.

Socialism is a range of related arguments rather than a single doctrine. There is disagreement amongst both academic commentators and political supporters and opponents over the identity or existence of 'essential' elements. There is disagreement too about the relative priority of the various arguments which contribute to socialism. All socialists would probably agree, nonetheless, in describing human activity in the first place in terms of social relationships rather than in terms of individual actions, though without denying significance to the latter. Such an understanding supports the belief that the credit for providing goods and services of all kinds cannot be claimed by any single individual, since production is the result of the labour of society as a whole. In so far as an attempt is made to allocate the rewards of production, they are therefore due to society as a whole, and to its members equally, rather than to particular individuals. The major themes in socialist thought, though they do not characterize all socialists, are as follows:

Property and labour: The control of goods and services, which are seen as social products, is central to socialism. Hence socialist arguments do not go very far before they address themselves to PROPERTY. Socialists have generally used the term property to refer to private property, and particularly private property in the means of production. In this sense of the word 'property', socialism is its antithesis, and is sometimes used to indicate a state of affairs where the means of production are commonly possessed, and hence where property in the familiar sense has disappeared. But there is great disagreement as to the most appropriate means of effecting common possession, whether it is the state, nationally or locally, or associations of producers, or collectives of producers and consumers organized around particular forms of production. A valuable distinction was made by the anarchist PROUDHON between proprietorship and possession. The first is an ultimate claim over some form of capital, the second is the effective right to its day-to-day use. Socialists have often found ways of stating and effecting claims to the former, but their proposals for the latter have been less prominent.

A further problem is that property is only one of the elements in production, the other being labour. The problem with property was that it was unjustly distributed; with labour, that it was inappropriately rewarded. Hence FOURIER and MARX attempted to link the rewards of production to the input of labour. This attempt draws on earlier liberal theories of labour, and has individualist as well as socialist implications, seeking as it does to identify individual claims to the result of production.

The attempt to reward society and the attempt to reward labour can lead in different directions. Nor is rewarding labour an easy matter. In a peasant society, or even in one of artisans and craftsmen, the entire production of any good can be viewed as encompassed by the labours of one person, and linking the fruits of production to the effort involved seems simple and direct. Industrial production and the division of labour destroys this simplicity, and creates a diffuse responsibility for production. There are three responses to this: to attempt nonetheless to attach rewards to effort through some form of workers' control; to remodel production so that the units *are* simple, direct, and self-contained, as was done by anarchists, and by socialists such as William MORRIS; or to give up the whole enterprise and return to rewarding society as a whole through some form of centralized socialism.

A further problem is that socialist conceptions of production have in general been limited to industrial production, and labour has been thought of as an activity undertaken for a wage. Socialist feminists have pointed out that a great part of the production of goods and services in any society is carried out within the household by women, who work without wages of any kind. The discussion of domestic labour and of the reproduction of the labour force has taken an increasingly large part in socialist argument over production in the second half of the twentieth century.

Equality and justice: The justification for socialist proposals is frequently found in a notion of equality, an idea which is expressed in various versions:

(1) that there are some intrinsic or super-historical rights of humanity – this argument begins with radical expression by Babeuf and Buonarotti of the revolutionary French assertion of equality;
(2) that all human beings share a common, super-historical human essence which gives purpose to life – this view is most clearly expressed in Marx's account of ALIENATION;
(3) that the political doctrine of equality implicit in the liberal view of democracy leads logically to the wider equality of socialism;
(4) that the social nature of life and production demands that rewards be allocated equally and in common rather than to separate individuals;
(5) that all people are equally children of God, an argument used by the English socialist R. H. TAWNEY.

The socialist belief in equality has been a moral rather than an empirical one – an assertion not that all people are the same but that their claims are equal. Thus Louis Blanc presented inequalities of capacity not as a justification for unequal rewards, but as the reason for unequal contributions – hence his much quoted, 'From each according to his ability, to each according to his needs.'

Co-operation and fraternity: Socialism seeks to replace capitalism and individualism with a form of production and distribution which is communal and co-operative. To that extent it expects to change not only the organization of society but the motivation of its members, to replace selfishness with altruism, and competition with co-operation. There have always been therefore those socialists who have expressed their arguments in moral, psychological, or even religious terms. When they have done so, they have often come close to the arguments of ANARCHISM. In the United Kingdom, Edward Carpenter advocated a social transformation based on the manner of life of communally living individuals, William Morris depicted a communistic society based on fellowship or fraternity and joy in creative work, and Oscar Wilde wrote of the 'soul of man' under socialism. Other British socialists spoke of their beliefs as a 'religion' and of being 'converted' to socialism, and Tawney drew on Protestant Christianity to condemn the 'acquisitiveness' of human nature under capitalism.

There have been conceptions of reformed human nature dependent upon reformed institutions. Robert OWEN rejected the idea of character as individually formed; his criticism of the consequences of industrial capitalism on character were complemented by proposals for a reformed and beneficent industrial system that would shape a similarly improved humanity.

The transformation of work: Charles FOURIER proposed making work pleasurable by a rotation of tasks within the day amongst members of the phalanx, the model balanced communities into which his ideal society was to be organized. This concern with the nature or quality of work as something experienced by the individual worker was to be a recurring, though subordinate, theme of socialism, expressed by Marx in his writings on alienation, by Morris, and by the various movements for workers' control of production, in particular the ideas expressed by Tawney and Cole as part of GUILD SOCIALISM.

Social democracy: Socialism has been presented both as the fulfilment of liberal democracy and as its antithesis. There is within socialism an emphasis both on the 'formal' freedoms of politics and on the 'real' freedoms of economic and social capacity. The first leads to an argument for democracy, the second either to its expansion into an argument for social democracy, or into a dismissal of democracy as merely 'bourgeois' freedom.

There is a distinction also between those socialists for whom the democratic state can be an instrument of what they wish to achieve, and those for whom it can be at most a transitional institution. For Marx the latter was the case, and hence a purely social democratic programme was inadequate both for this reason, and because for him – and more particularly for followers such as LENIN – the democratic method could not, anyway, lead to control by the working class of the state apparatus, since that apparatus, with the constitutional structure within which it operated, was a bespoke institution of capitalism. A different view, of socialism as a desirable condition in itself and one attainable by electoral and persuasive politics based on working-class power, was articulated by Ferdinand LASSALLE. Universal suffrage was to be a means of giving the workers power to use the state to promote producers' co-operatives in order to provide for the workers the full fruits of their labour. At the same time the state, in a view derived from HEGEL, was seen as the (potentially) highest expression of the communal welfare.

In the United Kingdom the clearest expression of social democracy was given by the Fabians (see FABIANISM), in Germany by Edward BERNSTEIN. Particularly as advocated by the Fabians, social democracy was not simply about the democratic control of the state, but also about the use of that control to extend popular power beyond the political institutions of society and into its social and economic ones.

Working-class power: CLASS occupies a central place in the analysis by socialists of capitalism. Capitalism is a society which forms itself into exploiting and exploited classes, and members of the working class are, in this view, both the particular victims of capitalism and the basis for opposition to it and for its final overthrow. There has been in socialism an assumption both that desired changes will come about as a result of the rise to power and influence of the working class, and that the empowering of the working class is itself a desirable component of socialism. The ambivalence between workers' power directly exercised, which could be seen as an expression of liberty, and power exercised through the state, which could threaten to be a form of paternalism, was evident in the proposals of the nineteenth-century French socialist Louis Blanc. He advocated replacement of individual capitalist production by social workshops, which the state would initially fund and administer, but which should develop into self-managing communal enterprises. In France also, Georges SOREL argued for workers' power through unions, a form of SYNDICALISM aiming at a general strike which would overthrow capitalism and inaugurate a workers' regime. In the United Kingdom a non-insurrectionary version of workers' power exercised from the point of production was elaborated in guild socialism, which sought to combine a rediscovered satisfaction in work with both decentralized producers' power and an overall co-ordinating and regulating task for a reconstituted state. Various forms of workers' control continued to attract socialists throughout the twentieth century, and some of them drew encouragement from what appeared to be the success of practical schemes for its implementation in Yugoslavia after the establishment of Tito's regime there.

There is also a problem in deciding who are the members of the working class, whether they consist solely of the industrial wage earners, or include the service sector. And even if the working class can be defined, there is a further divergence between the assumptions of those who base their arguments on the make-up of the working class as they suppose it actually to be under capitalism, and the expectations of those who look to a working class with a heightened political consciousness. A good deal of socialist energy in the second half of the twentieth century has gone into describing the qualities of existing or previous working-class culture. Socialists such as George Orwell, however, who have relied on a notion of existing working-class decencies for their depiction of possible socialist futures, have been criticized for blunting the radical and progressive edge of socialism, and giving it too much in common with conservatism. Those, on the other hand, who have relied on an account of the working class as it might be, have been open to the criticism of, for the moment therefore, relying not on the working class at all but on a political elite of different social origins.

Rationalization and efficiency: Capitalism and industrial production were for socialists both inefficient and harmful, and there were many proposals for reorganization that would be either more beneficial, more rational, or more 'efficient'. Owen, starting from this belief in the environmental determination of human character, argued that a system of production which was exploitative and individualistic should be replaced by a regulated and harmonious environment in which social virtues would be cultivated. SAINT-SIMON advocated the rational organization of industrial production under the direction of an elite of intellect and science. His argument, which implied recognition of the social nature of production, drew on a notion of 'brotherhood', and laid heavy emphasis on the contribution of manual workers, has been often taken to constitute one of the roots of modern socialism. It also expressed a frequent theme of later socialists: the greater efficiency which would result from the organization of society from above by a skilled and trained elite who would in some sense represent the interests of all. The presentation of socialism as the rational use of economic resources led, after Saint-Simon, to the technocratic elitism of Fabianism and, after the first world war, to the advocacy of planning, a method of achieving both economic efficiency and economic equality which drew much strength from the supposed successes of the Soviet Union.

Culture: The mid-twentieth century revisionist CROSLAND argued for the importance of culture in any conception of a socialist society – by which he meant not high culture, but the ordinary manner of life of the people. This concern was expressed with even greater force during the intellectual and political episode known as the New Left from the late 1950s till the early 1970s. Drawing on anarchism, on writers such as Morris, and on Marx's early writing on alienation, socialists in Western Europe and North America saw the aesthetic and sensual aspects of life and work as important matters for both socialist criticism and socialist recommendations. These recommendations were both for a life enhanced by new possibilities and experiences, and for one based on a recognition of the existing virtues of working-class culture. They were not always compatible, especially when the former was presented as progressive, libertarian, and experimental, and the latter as traditional, proletarian, and heroic.

Beyond the working class: The New Left had extended the critical and creative attention of socialism to all forms of human activity. The phrase 'the personal is the political' which was associated particularly with the women's movement meant not that private and personal relations were to be subsumed under the political struggle, but that all human activities had aspects which were both individual and collective, and hence both private and political. The 'private' and 'individual' decisions of men and women, whilst made by individuals, were no more independent of institutions such as capitalism and patriarchy than were the 'individual' decisions of workers to accept wages at a particular factory. Hence sexual relations and the relations of power and wealth within the household were all matters of political concern, and subject to change by political activity (see FEMINISM). In consequence socialism in the last quarter of the twentieth century has had to take account of the place of people who are defined by characteristics other than being a member of the waged manual working class, in particular gender and ethnicity.

Planning, liberty, and markets: That strand within socialism which is suspicious of the central national state has recently been strengthened by the attempt to articulate, or re-state, the place within socialism of property, markets, and individual liberty. For all its repudiation of individualism, socialism has within it a strong liberal inheritance. Alec Nove has argued that the kinds of popular and workers' power which socialism supports are best achieved in a balance between the state as the representative of all equally, and smaller associations which, whilst representing people collectively, do not represent them universally. This 'feasible socialism' draws together the concerns both of those who have wanted direct and therefore decentralized popular power in the workplace, and of those who have believed it possible to maximize choice and variety through the market. It also raises a matter which socialists have frequently found difficult, and generally avoided: the ownership and control of material resources expressed in the term property.

There are important disagreements, therefore, about the manner in which socialism will develop as a form of social organization. But what they indicate is not a failure to define or grasp socialism, but the many and contradictory elements and aspirations which constitute the socialist tradition.   RB

Reading

†Berki, R.N.: *Socialism*. London: Dent, 1975.

Cole, G.D.H.: *A History of Socialist Thought*. 7 vols. London: Macmillan, 1953–60.

Durkheim, E.: *Socialism and Saint-Simon* (1928), trans. C. Salter. Yellow Springs, Ohio: Antioch, 1958; London: Routledge & Kegan Paul, 1959.

†Fried, A. and Sanders, R. eds: *Socialist Thought: a Documentary History*. Edinburgh: Edinburgh University Press, 1964.

Laidler, H.W.: *History of Socialism*. London: Routledge & Kegan Paul, 1948.

Landauer, C.: *European Socialism: a History of Ideas and Movements*. Berkeley and Los Angeles: University of California Press, 1959.

Lichtheim, G.: *A Short History of Socialism*. London: Weidenfeld & Nicolson, 1970.

Nove, A.: *The Economics of Feasible Socialism*. London; Allen & Unwin, 1983.

Socrates (469–399 BC) Greek philosopher. 'This indictment and affidavit is sworn by Meletus son of Meletus of Pitthos against Socrates son of Sophroniscus from Alopece; Socrates does wrong in not recognizing the gods which the city recognizes, and in introducing other new divinities. He also does wrong in corrupting the young men. The penalty demanded is death' (Diogenes Laertius, *Lives of the Philosophers*, II, 40). Socrates of Athens was tried and condemned to death by a jury of his fellow-citizens in 399 BC. Then as now it was thought that the charge was extremely vague and the religious element in it disingenuous. Socrates was put to death because of his philosophical activity, which was not popular. To use his own metaphor, the Athenians swotted the gadfly which irritated them by questioning everything and demanding that people defend their beliefs (*Apology* 30d–31a). Yet Athens was a democracy priding itself on its tolerance; Socrates' fate as well as his ideas raises unresolved questions about the threat which intellectuals pose to a state, and it has led to the most diverse interpretations of his life and its significance. Standard views tend to be over-simple: Socrates has been seen both as an individualistic liberal (see Popper) and as an authoritarian reactionary (see Wood and Wood). The latter view relies on the undoubted fact that he influenced many of the aristocrats who had led a coup against the democracy. But we know little of his personal attitudes; even his social standing is unclear (his father was a stonemason, but there are indications that he may originally have been well off, though he ended his life poor). His personal life is unrecoverable through layers of later hagiography, and since he wrote nothing himself we inevitably have to reconstruct his ideas from

Xenophon and from PLATO's early dialogues. The former presents him as a conventional thinker; only Plato explains why he should be found intellectually challenging.

Socrates, in Plato's version, insists continually that wisdom in politics is a skill; like any other skill it presupposes some intellectual grasp of what you are doing, and an ability to teach it. He finds contemporary politics fundamentally faulty in two ways. First, important decisions are made by majority vote, though most people, he thinks, lack both the time and the temperament to become capable of any such intellectual grasp of the issues. Second, even political leaders depend on the majority for election or support; although the city demands proper intellectual qualifications from its doctors and architects, politicians' power rests not on knowledge but on mere popular appeal. Socrates is frequently pictured showing prominent public figures that their views lack any intellectual backing. He is also depicted as shocking Greek expectations by discouraging talented young men from entering politics. They will, he claims, merely harm themselves and others until they have searched themselves and by hard philosophical scrutiny of their political beliefs achieved at least as much as Socrates has: awareness of their own ignorance. Practical experience, muddling through with no consistent intellectual justification, positively unfits one to become a politician in what Socrates takes to be the true sense: a person with the knowledge necessary for competent handling of political matters. Hence the consciously outrageous claim (*Gorgias* 473c–474a, 521d) that Socrates, ignorant of the proper procedure when chairing a meeting, is the only real politician in Athens.

This stress on philosophically grounded knowledge undermines the claim of democracy to be either an efficient or a fair method of government; we can discern here the seeds of Plato's insistence that political power should belong to those with the appropriate knowledge. Socrates, however, is presented as aporetic as to whether and how such knowledge could be achieved. If knowledge matters so much, freedom of discussion and action will have no intrinsic value; Socrates has nothing but bitter criticism for the freedoms of Athens. In the *Menexenus* he satirizes their most famous ancient defence, Pericles' Funeral Speech in Thucydides; in the *Gorgias* he criticizes Athenian politicans for producing merely the 'trash' of external prosperity and show (517–19). He prefers the rigid oligarchies of Sparta and Crete, where moral education and discipline are thought more important.

Nonetheless, Socrates performed all his civic duties, including army service. And in the *Crito*, offered escape from execution, he imagines the laws of Athens demanding from him, and getting, submission to his sentence. This is not what we would expect. And there is a notorious further problem: how we are to reconcile the *Crito* with Socrates' insistence in the *Apology* (29c–d) that he would pursue his god-given duty to philosophize even if the court required him to stop. On this point scholars are deeply divided. But, whether consistent with the rest of Socrates' political philosophy or not, the *Crito* introduces several key characterizations of political obedience.

(1) The state is compared to a parent; citizens owe obedience to the state both because of benefits received and because of the natural unchosen fact of dependence.

(2) The state-citizen relation is as asymmetrical as that of parent-child or even master-slave; the latter may not return blow for blow, but must put up with unequal treatment.

(3) Living in a city which one may leave, but does not, is represented as a tacit agreement to obey its law.

(4) Disobedience to any given law is seen as arising from a spirit of disobedience to the entire system of law.

We can see why Socrates would think these claims justifiable in ideal conditions; why he thinks the laws of Athens entitled to make them remains a puzzle.   JEA

Reading

Allen, R.E.: *Socrates and Legal Obligation*. Minneapolis, Minn.: University of Minneapolis Press, 1980.

Kraut, R.: *Socrates and the State*. Princeton, NJ: Princeton University Press, 1984.

Plato: *Apology, Crito, Charmides, Laches, Protagoras, Menexenus, Gorgias, Alcibiades, Lovers*. All in Loeb Classical Library; London: Heinemann.

Popper, K.: *The Open Society and its Enemies*, vol. I. London: Routledge, 1945.

Sprague, R.K.: *Plato's Philosopher-King*. Columbia: University of South Carolina Press, 1976.

Wood, E.M. and Wood, N.: *Class Ideology and Ancient Political Theory*. Oxford: Blackwell, 1978.

Woozley, A.: *Law and Obedience*. London: Duckworth, 1979.

Xenophon: *Memorabilia* (with *Oeconomicus*). London: Heinemann, 1923.

solidarism A reformist doctrine which became virtually the official ideology of the French Third Republic during the two decades before the first world war. Opposed to *laissez-faire* liberalism, Marxist collectivism, Catholic corporativism and anarcho-syndicalism, it advocated state intervention, social legislation and voluntary associations. Opposed to class conflict and social reconstruction, it was friendly to SOCIALISM which it attempted to neutralize in practice.   SL

Sorel, Georges (1847–1922) French theorist of SYNDICALISM and author of *Réflexions sur la violence* and many other works on various topics. Born in Cherbourg, Sorel graduated from the École Polytechnique in 1867 and worked as a highway engineer, mostly in Perpignan, until early retirement in 1892. He then moved with his companion Marie-Euphasie David to Boulogne, outside Paris, where he lived until his death.

Sorel adhered to a variety of political persuasions, but he stated that the great concern of his life was the investigation of 'the historical genesis of morals'. In his 'early' writings (he published nothing before he was thirty-nine) he formulated what emerged as three historical principles on which a strong moral structure was supposedly based: a sturdy family structure; a 'warrior' mentality based on soldiers struggling against a respected foe or, analogously, on workers struggling against the malign forces of nature or against opposing classes; and an 'epic state of mind' rooted in a social poetry or 'myth' which sustains the warrior outlook, resists the lure of philosophic rationalism, and prevents a rustic community of warrior-craftsmen from degenerating into a decadent society of consumption and leisure ruled by a hierarchy of intellectuals. In *Le procès de Socrate* (1889) and *La ruine du monde antique*

(1894, 1901), Sorel argued that the decline of classical civilization came about as a result of the failure of these three standards.

After Sorel became a socialist in 1892 he elaborated, in various writings on natural science, on the theme of workers struggling against nature. He rejected the older rationalist view of a unified natural science which, when perfected, would allow for predictions in all branches of science, including social science, as precise as those in astronomy. Sorel argued instead that there were many sciences with varying degrees of precision. Inspired by VICO and MARX he asserted that the more precise sciences developed knowledge based on what men build and produce: in physics, practitioners build models for experiments which create an 'artificial nature' that is closed off from the rest of nature ('natural nature'). Such a foreclosure inevitably changes nature and leaves us with only a partial and segmented view of phenomena that makes an all-embracing science of nature or of society absurd.

The 'production' of physics models also means that there are fewer and fewer differences between the physics laboratory and the manufacturing workshop, or between scientists and workers. In both cases, according to Sorel, the amount of energy and vigilance that is expended to sustain the separation of 'artificial nature' from 'natural nature' is a rough index of the virtue of the practitioner. There is also a heroic dimension in the struggle of workers to overcome their own 'natural natures', that is, their inclination to relaxation and sloth, analogous to the law of entropy or energy loss in the second law of thermodynamics.

In his works on Marxism such as *Insegnamenti sociale della economica contemporanea* (Social Foundations of Contemporary Economics) (1906), Sorel praised some of Marx's writings but criticized others as being based on the old-fashioned, unitary view of knowledge that he had rejected. He dismissed Marx's theories of 'inevitable' class conflict and increasing misery; he especially scorned the transformation of these so-called laws into a totalistic utopianism that envisioned a final end to history. Such ideas would allow the proletariat to slide into quiescence and abandon the class struggle in the expectation that the 'progress of history' should automatically produce a revolution.

In *Les illusions du progrès* (1908) Sorel traced the development of the ideology of PROGRESS to the justification of ever-expanding state power in eighteenth-century France, a development that contributed to the decadence of the old regime. As early as 1902 Sorel had foreseen a similar development in socialism: the Marxian version of dialectical progress, if triumphant, would help sap the vitality of workers' organizations and replace them with an effete aristocracy of theoreticians and politicians governing through 'the magical power of the state'. Sorel therefore abandoned political socialism in favour of syndicalism, the view that socialism should be upheld by autonomous workers' organizations acting through strikes and direct action rather than through political activity. In his syndicalist works Sorel praised the writings of Marx that stressed the practical side of socialism. This 'other side' of Marxism is essentially a pragmatic doctrine of prudence based on the view that tasks are rooted in already-existing solutions; that socialism exists already in workers' organizations as well as in the hearts and moral energy of workers.

In *Réflexions sur la violence* (1908) Sorel discusses the 'social poetry' that sustains this moral energy: the 'myth of the general strike' links the workers' constant struggles against capitalists to the never-ending struggle against nature by transmuting labour and struggle into creative acts. Such myths are not passive or utopian descriptions of things but 'expressions of the will' or wish images of forthcoming epic battles that are bound to come. Myths are active, poetic replacements for the philosophic quietism of the idea of progress; they retain the sense of certainty necessary for action.

True to his pragmatic inclinations, Sorel cared less about the details of the myth or whether the material revolution will actually take place than whether the myth succeeds in making existing workers' organizations more militant. After 1908 and a series of setbacks for syndicalist organizations, Sorel became pessimistic about the future of the proletarian movement. He thought briefly that royalism was the only movement left in France that was capable of inspiring social and moral regeneration, but by 1914 he abandoned it as statist and reactionary. After the first world war he made a few statements that seemed sympathetic to Mussolini, but this sympathy was extremely circumscribed and he condemned the street terrorism of the fascists. In his last years, he supported the Russian Revolution on the (mistaken) grounds that it embodied a movement of independent, self-governing workers' councils.

JLS

Reading

Horowitz, I.L.: *Radicalism and the Revolt against Reason*. London: Routledge & Kegan Paul, 1961.

Humphrey, R.: *Georges Sorel: Prophet Without Honor*. Cambridge, Mass.: Harvard University Press, 1951.

†Jennings, J.: *Georges Sorel*. London: Macmillan, 1985.

Meisel, J.H.: *The Genesis of Georges Sorel*. Ann Arbor, Mich.: George Wahr, 1951.

Portis, L.: *Georges Sorel*. London: Pluto, 1980.

Roth, J.: *The Cult of Violence: Sorel and the Sorelians*. Berkeley: University of California Press, 1980.

Sorel, G.: *The Illusions of Progress*, ed. and trans. J. and C. Stanley. Berkeley: University of California Press, 1969.

———: *Reflections on Violence*, trans. T.E. Hulme and J. Roth. New York and London: Macmillan, 1950.

———: *Social Foundations of Contemporary Economics*, trans. J. Stanley. New Brunswick, NJ: Transaction, 1984.

———: *From Georges Sorel*, ed. J. Stanley. New York: Oxford University Press, 1976.

†Stanley, J.L.: *The Sociology of Virtue: the Political and Social Theories of Georges Sorel*. Berkeley: University of California Press, 1981.

Vernon, R.: *Commitment and Change: Georges Sorel and the Idea of Revolution*. Toronto: University of Toronto Press, 1978.

sovereignty The power or authority which comprises the attributes of an ultimate arbitral agent – whether a person or a body of persons – entitled to make decisions and settle disputes within a political hierarchy with some degree of finality. To be able to take such decisions implies independence from external powers and ultimate authority or dominance over internal groups. A sovereign is a person or group of persons (including a representative assembly) possessed of sovereignty.

The first attribute of sovereignty is location: it is the *highest* power in a politico-legal hierarchy. The second attribute is sequence: it is the *final* or ultimate power of decision within a politico-legal hierarchy. The third attribute of sovereignty is effect: it involves the notion of *generality*, meaning to influence the overall flow of action. The fourth attribute of sovereignty is autonomy: a sovereign must have *independence* in its relations with, cannot be subject to, other agents (internal or external, domestic or foreign).

The highest power: Sovereignty adverts to the topmost element of a hierarchy; it is not identical with the entire politico-legal system. Most decisions taken within a system – by the traffic policeman, by the local councillors, by the city mayor – do not directly emanate from the top, even if they have much the same effect as those that do. Decisions that emanate directly from the top of a hierarchy represent only a small proportion of all decisions taken within it. Sovereignty is the point one reaches, in moving from appeal to appeal, when no higher competence can be reached.

At the most elementary level this notion of a highest power takes the form of an individual ruler. Where any matter of import is to be settled, it is pushed up to some given individual who is presumed competent to attend to it. Modern government, and sovereignty in such government, has lost – if ever it had – this simplicity. Sovereignty as a legal notion has become both significantly circular and diffuse.

First, where we look for authority in a modern democratic state, we proceed from lower to higher competences. But when we reach these higher competences (such as the prime minister, president, chairman), we discover a still higher competence – namely the 'people', or '*le pays réel*', or simply the electorate, which somehow simultaneously constitutes the base of the political hierarchy. Hence circularity. Second, in proceeding from lower to higher, especially in federal states, we find no one person or body that is competent to decide all important matters arising – juries, administrative tribunals, legislative committees, ordinary courts, local (especially 'state') authorities, special investigators, private corporations, all enjoy various forms and degrees of autonomy and cannot all be overridden from any one centre. Hence diffuseness.

Under an eighteenth-century monarch such as Louis XIV, who could declare '*l'état, c'est moi*', the highest power/authority could perhaps credibly be accorded a single locus. In a complex federal democracy such as the United States the 'highest' power tends to reduce to a 'final' power: a decisional procedure may lead to distinct power centres.

The final power: Sovereignty involves the exercise of final control over a hierarchy. An absolute power (as of the Sun King) may well be final, but a final power need not be absolute. Given that a sovereign power, at a later date, may amend or even reverse a law decreed earlier, finality is not to be equated with irreversibility. A sovereign decision is final in the specific sense that no *inferior* (subordinate) agent within the hierarchy can (or is entitled to) reverse it. Where sovereignty is collective or 'popular', it is more difficult to be sure that any particular decision is final, any matter closed. But it is not the case that no decisions under collective sovereignty are final. Finality is often imposed by time: the decision to jail the accused, to build a dam, not to protect a rare species, to launch a war, may be final in the sense that once these decisions are taken, and despite the possibility of further debate and appeal, the accused may already have been jailed, the dam built, the rare species wiped out, the war (perhaps nuclear) engaged.

The finality of sovereignty, where held by an individual, differs from that held by a collectivity. The finality exercised by an individual can be absolute; that exercised by a collectivity cannot be. A collective (or 'popular') sovereign may draw the same conclusions and take the same decisions as an individual sovereign. But the procedural differences are such that the two cannot be equated. Procedurally, an individual sovereign is not required to consult others in order to issue a directive. A collectivity, by contrast, simply in order to know its own 'mind', has to accept the indispensability of some form of public discussion or debate (however irrational), and must therefore be bound by certain principles such as, perhaps, 'majority rule' or 'free and full debate'. It is a source of law, but cannot unqualifiedly set itself above the law.

Generality of effect: In the case of an individual sovereign, a distinction is made between person and office (e.g. king and crown), such that the individual sovereign makes many decisions which are not themselves 'sovereign' – perhaps to hunt, feast, sleep, etc. A similar distinction applies to collectivities; but here no *decisions* can be made which are not sovereign, i.e. 'public'. The individual sovereign, because individual, makes many particularized decisions which not only do not, but cannot, serve as guides to inferior levels. A collective sovereign, by contrast, is only sovereign when collective, i.e. when 'public', and thus can take few or no decisions without some general effect. Generality of effect may pertain to scope (as when fixing a procedure) or to accomplishment (as in pursuing a particular substantive goal of public importance).

Independence: No social or political entity is entirely or absolutely independent of every other. As individuals, we may be slaves to passion, to fashion, to ideologies, and more. Some nations may regularly imitate others, and in diverse ways betray reciprocal influences. Some, certainly, have far greater power than others, and over others. Autonomy in matters political does not indicate an absence of interaction. It signals, rather, a particular form of interaction – that obtaining between political entities, each of which has its own separate hierarchy – with its own apex, finality and generality of effect.

A distinction has been made (by Dicey) between legal and political sovereignty, but it is of little relevance here. For politics (e.g. electoral competition) designates those who make and manipulate laws. And laws (e.g. electoral rules, whether of proportional representation, 'first-past-the-post', etc.) provide an active and non-neutral framework within which politics unfolds. There will be powerful groups within any state seeking influence, preference or control. Many external groups (not least among these being other states) will betray the same purpose. The point is that for a sovereign (meaning independent) state to be subject to non-sovereign influences does not mean that, in this, it loses its sovereignty and independence, any more than it follows that an individual, persuaded in some matter or matters by another, becomes, by virtue of this, subject to that other. Nevertheless, it remains open as to how regularly one sovereign entity may sway another before it becomes inappropriate to speak of the latter as 'sovereign'.

There is a vast literature on the subject of sovereignty. At least three different questions are raised: first, what is the nature of political rule? second, who (in any system) does rule? and finally, who ought to rule? Perhaps the most important writers on the subject since the Renaissance have been Jean BODIN, Thomas HOBBES, Jean-Jacques ROUSSEAU and John AUSTIN. These writers (and many others) differ over the questions who does, and who ought to, rule. On the nature or attributes of sovereign rule, they are constant. This constant element may be referred to as the 'traditional doctrine' of sovereignty, one arguing for the concentration of power at a given centre, power which must be absolute, total, illimitable and indivisible.

Bodin assumed that any form of state organization other than the monarchical was seriously defective. The state, for him, achieved true stability or unity or peace through the sovereign, this agent being inadequate to the purpose if not a specific individual. Hobbes, unlike Bodin, at least allowed (explicitly) that a group, as well as an individual, might be sovereign. But the acknowledgement was only nominal. For Hobbes's argument implied that collective sovereigns, if sovereign, really only reduce to the will of some specific representative, and that democracies (in this reductionist sense) must prove as absolute as monarchies. The implication in Hobbes makes it plain that he, too, took monarchical government to be best – the only genuine guarantee of peace and unity. Austin was more alive to the viability of collective sovereigns. But, like Rousseau (who had provided the first serious argument for a democratic sovereign), he still contended that, to be sovereign, their power must be illimitable. Even very recent writers can be observed to subscribe, in however qualified a fashion, to the unlimited power of parliament. The survival of this view derives from the failure to take seriously the difference between individual and collective sovereignty, which encompasses the difference between monarchical and democratic sovereigns.

The 'classical' doctrine of sovereignty proved far too absolutist to account accurately for the order obtaining especially in democratic states. It viewed order as exclusively a relationship of command and obedience. It assumed finality of decision to be possible only in circumstances where some distinct agent commands the rest. This classical view made it difficult for a democratic state genuinely to qualify as 'sovereign', for we may take 'democracy' to encompass a sharing of power, a limiting of power and the rule of law. A sovereign democratic state (if it qualifies as such) is necessarily bound by some rules from which it cannot free itself.

Where we hold that the attributes of sovereignty consist in the highest, final and most general power/authority within an autonomous state, we exclude claims to total, illimitable, perpetual and indivisible power. The chief mark of sovereignty is not indivisibility (normally projected in the person of a monarch), but finality. Sovereignty can clearly be divided among a plurality of agents (whether legislators in a sovereign assembly voting upon a measure, or different branches of a government or states in a federation), without in any way detracting from finality of decision.   PK

Reading

Austin, J.: *The Province of Jurisprudence Determined.* London: Murray, 1832; ed. H.L.A. Hart. London: Weidenfeld & Nicolson, 1954.

Bodin, J.: *Six Books of a Commonweal* (1576). Cambridge, Mass.: Harvard University Press, 1962.

Dicey, A.V.: *Introduction to the Study of the Law of the Constitution*, 10th edn. London: Macmillan, 1959.

†Hinsley, F.H.: *Sovereignty*. London: Watts, 1966.

Hobbes, T.: *Leviathan* (1651), ed. C.B. Macpherson. Harmondsworth: Penguin, 1968.

†Jouvenel, B. de: *Sovereignty*. Cambridge: Cambridge University Press, 1957.

Kelsen, H.: *General Theory of Law and State.* Cambridge, Mass.: Harvard University Press, 1949.

†King, P.: *The Ideology of Order: a Comparative Analysis of Jean Bodin and Thomas Hobbes.* London: Allen & Unwin, 1974.

†———: *Federalism and Federation.* London: Croom Helm, 1982.

Merriam, C.E.: *History of the Theory of Sovereignty since Rousseau.* New York: Columbia University Press, 1900.

Rousseau, J.-J.: *The Social Contract* (1762), trans. M. Cranston. Harmondsworth: Penguin, 1968.

Stankiewicz, W.J.: *Aspects of Political Theory: Classical Concepts in an Age of Relativism*. London: Collier-Macmillan, 1976.

Soviet communism Now the official ideology of the Soviet Union, the roots of Soviet communism lie in the impact of MARXISM on Russian intellectuals in the late nineteenth century. The ramshackle and oppressive but economically dynamic Russian Empire provided fertile soil for revolutionary ideas. Industrial development was fostered by the tsarist state so that Russia could confront the major European powers on less unequal terms. It brought the growth of a bourgeoisie, a proletariat and a professional middle class. But the regime failed to accommodate the political aspirations of the new social classes, or to satisfy the economic grievances of the peasantry which still made up 80 per cent of the population. Revolution seemed to provide the only way forward, first to a minority within each class, and eventually to almost the entire nation.

Marx's ideas gained a foothold in radical circles in the aftermath of POPULISM, which had failed to win mass support. Plekhanov (1856–1918), a former populist, argued in 1883 that the industrial wage-earning working class (or proletariat) would become the main revolutionary force in Russia. The peasantry was no longer a single potentially revolutionary class, but was dividing into exploiting and exploited groups under the impact of capitalism. In the 1890s LENIN, whose populist brother was hanged in 1887 for attempting to assassinate the tsar, broadly endorsed the Plekhanov line.

At the turn of the century two trends within Marxism moved away from the viewpoint represented by Plekhanov and Lenin. The first group, including Struve, Tugan-Baranovskii and other 'revisionists', were dubbed 'legal Marxists' by their opponents because they confined themselves to writings which could be published legally in Russia. They argued that in Russian conditions capitalist development was progressive. In the remote future, after a long period of capitalist development, socialism would be introduced by evolution, not revolution. The second group, including Kuskova and her husband Prokopovich, were called 'Economists' by their opponents because they argued that in view of Russian backwardness workers must concentrate on the struggle for better economic conditions, leaving the political struggle against the autocracy to the middle class. This view was broadly shared by workers' groups in St Petersburg between 1897 and 1899.

These new trends collapsed as a result of the conversion of leading 'legal Marxists' and 'Economists' to constitutional liberalism, the growth of revolutionary political ideas among the workers, and Lenin's vigorous campaign against revisionism. By the time of the 1905 revolution two major revolutionary parties were contending for the support of workers and peasants: the Socialist-Revolutionary Party (SRs) and the Russian Social-Democratic Labour Party (RSDLP). The SRs, founded in 1901, continued the peasant-revolutionary and terrorist policies of their populist predecessors. The RSDLP, nominally founded at a congress of 1898, but fully formed at its second congress in 1903, followed the traditions of Plekhanov.

The 1903 congress of the RSDLP saw not only the defeat of revisionism but also the beginning of the division of the party into 'hards', headed by Lenin, and 'softs' headed by Martov (1873–1923) and Axelrod (1849/50–1928). The main dispute at the congress concerned the duties of a party member. Lenin insisted on 'personal participation in one of the party organizations', while Martov merely required from members 'regular personal assistance under the direction of one of the party's organizations'. Lenin's definition was defeated, but his group eventually secured a majority at the congress after the rejection of the Jewish Bund's demand for organizational autonomy led the Bund to withdraw from the congress. Henceforth 'hards' and 'softs' were known as 'Bolsheviks' and 'Mensheviks' from the Russian words for 'majority' and 'minority'. This dispute was symptomatic. In the conditions of tsarist oppression, the Bolsheviks advocated a centralized party, dominated by full-time revolutionaries and geared to clandestine activity. The Mensheviks favoured a more broadly based and loosely knit structure.

This disagreement about organization was soon associated with a more profound difference of political strategy which emerged between the two groups. Bolsheviks believed that the RSDLP should not co-operate with the liberal bourgeoisie in the struggle against the autocracy but should act entirely independently. In 1905, insisting that the Russian bourgeoisie was too weak and pusillanimous to overthrow the autocracy, they urged the working class, led by the RSDLP, to mount an armed insurrection which would establish a democratic republic. Lenin also argued (and here he parted company with Plekhanov) that the mass of the peasantry could be won over to revolutionary action under the leadership of the proletariat. Following a successful armed uprising the RSDLP, in alliance with the SRs, would establish a 'revolutionary democratic dictatorship of the proletariat and peasantry', which would force through democratic reforms. The Bolsheviks did not aim at a socialist as distinct from a 'bourgeois-democratic' revolution. They took for granted the classic doctrine that socialism could not be achieved in peasant Russia until it received the support of a successful proletarian revolution in a more advanced country.

Among the Mensheviks, there was no unanimity about strategy. But they tended to believe that the liberal bourgeoisie occupied a dominant position in the political struggle, and that the role of the RSDLP should be restricted to building up the political strength and understanding of the proletariat. The proletariat would move to the centre of the political stage only after a period of industrial development under a democratic government. During the 1905 revolution, the Mensheviks therefore maintained that 'social democracy should not aim to seize power or share it in a Provisional Government, but should remain a party of extreme revolutionary opposition'. (For Trotsky's advocacy of 'permanent revolution', see TROTSKY.)

With the outbreak of the first world war, what had seemed mere vexatious disputation on Lenin's part now acquired the quality of a profound ability to separate opportunists from true revolutionaries. The unity of the Bolsheviks in opposition to their own government and to the imperialist war distinguished them from most other European socialist groups. The Mensheviks were divided on their attitudes to the war. Martov denounced it but many Mensheviks, including Plekhanov (who went over to the Mensheviks after 1905), supported the patriotic Russian cause.

In 1917, following the overthrow of the autocracy in the February revolution, divisions again appeared among the Bolsheviks. The majority of the party supported Lenin's call for a further revolution of the proletariat and poorest peasantry, epitomized in the slogan of autumn 1917 'All power to the Soviets!' (the Soviets were the councils directly elected by the masses at their place of work). But before, during and after the Bolshevik revolution of October 1917, a shifting series of Bolshevik groups, which could perhaps be seen as an early 'Right Opposition', urged compromise and coalition with those Mensheviks and SRs who opposed the continuation of the war and supported further revolutionary change. This 'Right wing' included such notables as Zinoviev (1883–1936), Kamenev (1883–1936), Rykov (1881–1938) and Lunacharsky (1875–1933). The fundamental difference between them and Lenin was their belief that the weakness of the industrial working class in Russia meant that the Bolsheviks, drawing support primarily from the working class, could not survive in power alone. This position was, of course, shared by all the Mensheviks.

During the civil war and foreign intervention which in 1918–20 followed the October revolution, all Bolsheviks and many Mensheviks and SRs rallied to the Soviet cause. Within the Bolshevik party criticism of official policy came mainly from the Left. In the spring of 1918 the 'Left Communists' headed by Bukharin (1888–1938) called for a revolutionary war, against Lenin's insistence on signing a peace treaty with Germany. The Left Communists also objected to several major features of internal policy: the over-centralization of decisions, the employment of bourgeois specialists, and the introduction of one-man management in place of elected committees in industry. This line of criticism was continued by the 'Democratic Centralists' and the 'Workers' Opposition' in 1920–1. The successive oppositions regarded these policies as symptoms of the degeneration of the revolution under the influence of the overwhelming mass of the individual peasants. Lenin in turn diagnosed the unrealistic views of the 'Leftists' as typical petty-bourgeois vacillations. According to Lenin, Soviet military weakness made the Peace Treaty essential, the inexperience of the Russian working class meant that it must learn to run the economy from the capitalist trusts, and the strength of counter-revolution impelled tighter political control. The Bolsheviks had seized power knowing that the proletariat in Russia was weak and the economy backward; and Lenin now strove to adapt to these circumstances. But he certainly did not anticipate that the close control of political life from the centre and the appointment of administrators and managers from above would remain permanent features of the Soviet system.

After Bolshevik victory in the civil war, the party known since 1918 as the 'Communist Party (Bolsheviks)' retained and even strengthened its monopoly of power; and its internal discipline was tightened. These measures were held to be essential in view of the hostile capitalist encirclement and the continued overwhelming predominance in Soviet Russia of individual peasant family farms. But the New Economic Policy (NEP) launched in 1921 permitted peasants to trade freely on the market, and replaced arbitrary state requisitioning of their products by a tax. Lenin and his supporters held that the restoration of the alliance between worker and peasant would provide a basis for a gradual transition to socialism, while Russia awaited the economic support which the victory of socialism in a more advanced country would bring. In view of the desperate state of the economy at the beginning of 1921, and the widespread social unrest, the introduction of NEP met with little resistance within the party. But from the autumn of 1923 a 'Left Opposition' headed by Trotsky correctly diagnosed the rise of bureaucratism in the party but wrongly feared that this would make industrialization and social transformation impossible.

After Lenin's death in January 1924, Soviet political thought was increasingly dominated by Stalin (1879–1953), who presided over the triumphs of industrialization and the horrors of famine and purges in the 1930s, and was commander-in-chief during the bitter struggle against the Nazi invasion in 1941–5.

The pervasive ideology designed by Stalin was of major importance in consolidating the Soviet regime. As early as April 1924, in his lectures *The Foundations of Leninism*, he insisted that Leninism was not merely a version of Marxism applicable to a peasant country, but was 'Marxism of the era of imperialism and proletarian dictatorship', of world-wide validity. Lenin's democratic centralism (see LENIN) now acquired a new tone: for Stalin the party was not only the 'leading and organizing detachment of the working class', it was 'the embodiment of unity of will' and 'becomes strong by cleansing itself of opportunist elements'. The Leninist style of work combined 'Russian revolutionary sweep' with 'American efficiency'. A few months later Stalin announced, with the support of Bukharin and others, and against bitter opposition from TROTSKY, Zinoviev and Kamenev, that it was possible to complete the construction of socialism in the Soviet Union without a socialist revolution elsewhere.

Stalin's version of 'socialism in one country' soon divided the majority of the Politburo from Bukharin, Rykov and other members of the 'Right deviation'. Bukharin, who abandoned his earlier Leftism and enthusiastically supported NEP, believed that peaceful collaboration with the peasantry could gradually lead to socialism. But Stalin in 1928 argued that the class struggle would be intensified as the advance to socialism proceeded, and later also ruled that the proletarian state would not wither away during the transition to socialism, but must be strengthened owing to the capitalist encirclement.

This ideology, distinctive of Stalinism, underpinned the industrialization drive and the forcible collectivization of agriculture. In the early 1930s the Soviet definition of 'socialism' was substantially modified. All Marxists hitherto supposed that 'socialism', while retaining the 'bourgeois' principle of payment in accordance with work done, would involve the public ownership of all means of production, the abolition of trade and the introduction of some kind of moneyless economy. But from the

mid-1930s onwards Soviet Marxists held that the personal plot of the collective farmer, and the free market associated with it, were part of the socialist economy, and that a money economy would continue until the establishment of COMMUNISM. In June 1931 Stalin also attacked petty-bourgeois 'egalitarianism' as alien to socialism. The subsequent drive for greater inequality in the interests of efficiency was against the spirit if not the letter of the earlier understanding of 'socialism'.

On the basis of this changed definition Stalin was able to announce in December 1936 that socialism had been established 'in principle' in the USSR. Exploitation of class by class had been eliminated, and replaced by an alliance of two non-antagonistic classes – the workers in state-owned industry and the collective farmers. The December 1936 Constitution accordingly described the Soviet Union as 'a state of workers and peasants'. Stalin insisted, however, that the state management of society remained in the hands of the working class. The peasants thus continued to be a junior partner in the alliance.

At the time of the 1936–8 purges, Stalin also announced that the absence of antagonistic contradictions within socialist society meant that all hostile actions and beliefs came from outside that society. Shortly before his death he slightly modified this harsh doctrine, admitting the possibility that relations of production could lag behind forces of production (see MARXISM) within socialist society, and stressing the value of a 'clash of opinions' within Marxism. It can perhaps be plausibly argued that Stalin himself tentatively launched, if unsuccessfully, the de-Stalinization of Soviet ideology.

The far-reaching criticisms of Stalin and the 'cult of the individual' launched by Khrushchev in 1956 did not involve any substantial change in the Soviet definition of 'socialism', or in the notion that the political system must be managed by a single monolithic party. But Stalin's doctrine of 'the intensification of the class struggle' during the transition to socialism was sharply attacked. At the end of the 1950s, Khrushchev and his advisers turned from criticism of the past to positive prescriptions about the bright future. While the 1936 Constitution described the USSR as 'a state of workers and peasants', the party's long-term programme adopted in 1961 endorsed Khrushchev's doctrine that the dictatorship of the working class had given way to the 'state of the whole people'. According to Khrushchev, by 1961 socialism had triumphed '*fully* and *finally*' in the USSR, and the period of the 'construction of communism' had begun; the programme rashly asserted that communism would be constructed 'in principle' in the USSR by 1980. Other utopian features were associated with this remarkable foreshortening of goals. With Khrushchev, the 'state of the whole people' and the transition to communism implied a decline in coercive control from above, a great increase in popular participation in government, and a substantial and continuing transfer of educational and cultural functions from the state to voluntary or social (*obshchestvennye* – the word does not have an exact English equivalent) organizations. The withering away of the state, except for its purely external defensive functions, had again become a practical possibility.

Under Brezhnev (1906–82), who was party general secretary from 1964 until his death, the description of the Soviet state as 'a socialist state of the whole people' was retained, and was enshrined in the 1977 Constitution (the first since 1936). The importance of popular participation continued to be stressed in words, but it was Khrushchev's utopian hopes rather than the state which withered away. At the end of 1966, two years after the dismissal of Khrushchev, the claim that the USSR had entered the period of construction of communism was withdrawn, and a new stage of 'developed socialism' (*razvitoi sotsializm*) was interposed between the 'completion of the construction of socialism' and communism. In 1982, a few months before he briefly became Brezhnev's successor, Andropov (1914–84) declared in an important pronouncement that developed socialism would be a 'lengthy historical stage', which in its turn would have 'its own periods, its own stages of growth'. He admitted that possibility of 'the non-coincidence of the interests of various social groups', and, while declaring on familiar lines that this would 'not go as far as antagonism', he conceded that mechanisms should be established 'to record, compare and reconcile various interests'. All

this provided a certain framework for political analysis and reform. The self-analysis of Soviet communism has always suffered, however, from tunnel vision. It does not substantially account for two major features of Soviet socialism not anticipated by Marx or Lenin: the concentration of decision-making in a self-selecting Politburo, and the dominant position in Soviet politics and society of an elite commanding considerable social and economic privileges.

With these important limitations, political and economic reform is clearly on the Soviet agenda. Published discussions in recent years have turned on such major issues as the centralized power of the state, the role of the market, one-man management and the functions of the party. Much more remains unpublished. The rise of Solidarity in Poland in 1981 may indicate that hidden stresses also lurk beneath the relatively calm surface of Soviet political life. Even the Politburo itself acknowledges the paramount necessity of reform. 'We cannot delay, we cannot wait; there is no time left for hesitation, it has been used up in the past' (Gorbachev, June 1985).   RWD

Reading

†Carr, E.H.: *The Bolshevik Revolution, 1917–1923,* vol. I, chs 1–9. London: Macmillan, 1950.

Evans, A.B.: Developed socialism in soviet ideology. *Soviet Studies* 29 (1977) 409–28.

Harding, N. ed.: *Marxism in Russia: Key Documents, 1879–1906.* Cambridge: Cambridge University Press, 1983.

Kanet, R.: The rise and fall of the 'All-People's State'. *Soviet Studies* 20 (1968–9) 81–93.

†Lewin, M.: *Political Undercurrents in Soviet Economic Debates.* London: Pluto, 1975.

†Marcuse, H.: *Soviet Marxism: a Critical Analysis.* London: Routledge & Kegan Paul, 1958.

Stalin, J.V.: *Works*, vols I–XIII [covering 1901–34]. London: Lawrence & Wishart, 1952–5.

———: *The Essential Stalin: Major Theoretical Writings, 1905–52,* ed. B. Franklin. London: Croom Helm, 1972.

†Venturi, F.: *Roots of Revolution: a History of the Populist and Socialist Movements in Nineteenth-Century Russia.* London: Weidenfeld & Nicolson, 1960.

Spence, Thomas (1750–1814) British economic reformer and radical journalist. He was celebrated chiefly for his attacks on the private ownership of land. See RADICALS, BRITISH.

Spencer, Herbert (1820–1903) British philosopher and sociologist. An only child, Spencer was brought up in the austere non-conformism of newly industrializing Derby. His father's influence predisposed him towards self-reliant individualism, radical politics and an interest in natural science and technology. Upon completion of a largely technical education he embarked upon a career as a railway engineer and subsequently as a columnist for the *The Economist*. During this period Spencer involved himself in numerous radical causes, publishing articles on a variety of public issues and laying the foundations of the theoretical doctrines to which he devoted the rest of his working life. After 1853 he supported himself (with the assistance of several legacies) as an independent writer, contributing to various journals and elaborating his *Synthetic Philosophy*, published in multiple instalments from 1860 to 1896. Spencer reached the peak of his acclaim in the 1880s but in his declining years suffered increasingly from the onslaughts of illness and of intellectual controversies which tended to erode his reputation as a principled and consistent thinker.

The recriminatory exchanges which so embittered Spencer's later life reflect the fact, true of many political philosophers, that his mature views differ significantly from his earlier published ones. Whether these differences are ultimately only changes of focus and emphasis or represent a more fundamental theoretical divergence is a matter of considerable dispute. Doubtless, his negative or minimalist conception of the role of the state and his championship of *laissez-faire* are continuous themes from his earliest to his last political writings. Where change occurs, it is in the type of reason offered for that position and in the status of those reasons themselves. Spencer's political theorizing is unified by a rationalist quest for a scientific morality. Its duality is marked by a shift in the basic premises from which that morality is derived.

The early political theory is most systematically set out in the first edition of *Social Statics* (1850) where Spencer develops a natural rights doctrine from the 'law of equal freedom'. Acknowledging the inconclusiveness of his attempt to ground this basic principle of political morality in considerations of evolutionary adaptation, he does succeed in showing that it generates a set of individual rights which imply universal suffrage, children's rights, private property and *laissez-faire*, land nationalization and 'the right to ignore the state'. Even in this work there is some latent tension between an underdeveloped evolutionism and the predominantly prescriptive character of his individualism. But the presumed universality of adaptive capabilities allows Spencer to attribute most forms of social misery to inequitable restrictions on personal liberty and to the impact of private ownership of natural resources to which all persons are held to be equally entitled. For the early Spencer, natural rights set limits on the extent to which persons may exercise their capabilities at the expense of others.

The later Spencer's embrace of his characteristic SOCIAL DARWINISM was a process in which his sociological beliefs came gradually to eclipse his radical convictions. An important factor in this transition was the growing prominence assigned to natural selection as the mechanism of adaptive change. Social evolution, from militaristic barbarism to civilized industrialism, is fostered by increasing interpersonal differentiation of socio-economic functions. And it vitally depends upon the subordination of the interests of the less capable to those of their superiors. Activities mitigating the harsher effects of the natural tendency toward survival of the fittest succeed only in disrupting that benign historical progression by insulating idleness and incompetence from the consequences of their non-productivity, perpetuating them at the expense both of the industrious and of future generations.

In the light of this evolutionary perspective Spencer's mature political theory rescinds support for suffrage extension which is seen as likely to result in such 'over-legislation'. On more obscure grounds he also repudiates land nationalization. These recanted rights are said to be demands of 'absolute ethics' which, though ideally valid, must give way to the more pragmatic claims of 'relative ethics' until society has evolved to the point where recognition of these egalitarian entitlements would pose no danger to further social progress. In general differential political and legal rights conform to the requirements of human character development along the evolutionary lines indicated in the rest of Spencer's work. They are instruments for the eventual attainment of maximum human wellbeing rather than, as previously, symmetrical restrictions on the manner in which it may be attained. The mature theory thus represents a shift in the foundation of Spencer's antistatism, from considerations of justice to those of historically computed social utility. HS

Reading

History of Political Thought 3.3 (1982) [articles on Spencer by various authors].

†Peel, J.D.Y.: *Herbert Spencer*. London: Heinemann, 1971.

Spencer, H.: *Social Statics*. London: Chapman, 1850.

———: *The Man versus the State* (1884), ed. E. Mack, intro. A.J. Nock. Indianapolis: Liberty Classics, 1981.

———: *The Principles of Ethics* (1892–3), ed. T. Machan. Indianapolis: Liberty Classics, 1982.

†Wiltshire, D.: *The Social and Political Thought of Herbert Spencer*. Oxford: Oxford University Press, 1978.

Spengler, Oswald (1880–1936) German historian and philosopher. Spengler was educated at the universities of Munich, Berlin and Halle, and worked for a time as a schoolteacher before opting for a life of private scholarship. His fame rests entirely on his two-volume work, *Der Untergang des Abendlandes: Umrisse einer Morphologie der Weltgeschichte: I: Gestalt und Wirklichkeit* (1918); II: *Welthistorische Perspektiven* (1922) (translated as *The Decline of the West*), which made an immediate impact when published in Germany.

Spengler formulated a cyclical theory of historical change and a comparative approach to the study of the culture. He called his method 'morphological'. The conceptual framework of his work is provided by the application to history of the biologist's concept of living forms. According to him each culture is an organism which experiences its spring, summer, autumn and winter. For the traditional succession of ancient, medieval and modern periods, Spengler substituted Chinese, Ancient Semitic, Egyptian, Indian, 'Apollinian' (Greco-Roman), 'Magian' (Iranian, Hebrew and Arabian), Mexican and 'Faustian' (Western) – although in fact he gave a full account only of the Greco-Roman and Western cultures. It was his analysis of the West European culture that won him his popularity with the general public.

In terms of historical research, philosophy or social science, Spengler's work cannot stand serious scrutiny. As a work of literature, however, it is an extraordinary achievement, and in the atmosphere of defeat that prevailed in Germany after the first world war, his vision of the doom of western civilization, his pessimism, his determinism and his revolt against reason exercised an enormous influence.

In Spengler's view 'Faustian' culture was born in the tenth century. It manifests itself with the articulation of feudal society and the emergence of Romanesque architecture. After the triumphs of Gothic architecture and medieval scholasticism, 'Faustian' culture breaks down in internal contradictions. The Renaissance was a failure, the Reformation marked the urbanization of Europe and the end of its youth. In the new society of cities, 'Faustian' culture was to experience its summer; the eighteenth century was its autumn and with the nineteenth century began the winter of the West. It brought the victory of materialism and scepticism, of socialism, parliamentarism and money.

But in the twentieth century a new aspect of the 'Faustian' spirit reveals itself. Blood and instinct will regain their rights against the power of money and intellect. The era of individualism, liberalism and democracy, of humanitarianism and freedom, was reaching its end. The new era will be that of Caesarism and of great wars. The mass of mankind will accept with resignation the victory of the Caesars and will be willing to obey strong leaders. Life will descend to a level of general uniformity, of a new kind of primitivism.

A prophet of authoritarianism and a visionary of a German apocalypse, full of hatred for rationalism, Spengler played a major role in undermining the liberal and democratic ideas of the Weimar Republic. If he cannot be considered as one of the direct precursors of

Nazism, his importance in the creation of a moral climate in which the Nazi takeover became possible was even greater than that of the 'conservative revolutionaries' such as Arthur Moeller van den Bruck, author of *Das Dritte Reich* published in 1923, or of the prophet of German irrationalism, Julius Langbehn, author of *Rembrandt als Erzieher* (1890), who became immensely famous in the last years of the nineteenth century.   ZS

Reading

Bojeman, A.B.: Decline of the West? Spengler Reconsidered. *Virginia Quarterly Review* 59 (1983) 151–207.

†Hughes, H.S.: *Oswald Spengler: a Critical Estimate.* New York: Scribner, 1962.

Killmer, H.: Figures in the Rumpelkammer: Goethe, Faust, Spengler. *Journal of European Studies* 13 (1983) 142–67.

Sorokin, P.A.: *Social Philosophies of an Age of Crisis.* London: Black, 1952.

Spengler, O.: *The Decline of the West.* London: Allen & Unwin, 1932.

Stutz, E.: *Oswald Spengler als politischer Denker.* Berne: Francke, 1958.

Vogt, J.: *Wege zum historischen Universum: von Ranke bis Toynbee.* Stuttgart: Kohlalhammer, 1961.

Spinoza, Baruch or **Benedict** (1632–1677) Descended from Jewish refugees from Spain, Spinoza spent all of his short life in the Netherlands. He wrote on political, metaphysical and ethical theory, corresponded with leading European philosophers, and maintained himself modestly as a lens-grinder. His political writings seem, at first glance, a collage of religious, scientific and political concepts drawn from classical, medieval and modern literatures. He blends MACHIAVELLI with HOBBES, ARISTOTLE with Descartes, is a partisan in Dutch politics, an ENLIGHTENMENT precursor, even a 'bourgeois ideologist'. Yet we must include him among the pre-eminent political philosophers because he actually synthesized all these disparate themes, transcended the history of his ideas, and produced a lasting unified vision of the condition and potentialities of the political animal, man.

Spinoza is essentially a moral philosopher. He belongs, with Aristotle and HUME, to that nonreductionist, naturalistic, 'emotivist' school of value theorists which explains and justifies human values in terms of man's biological nature. Our species nature, crucially our species-specific pattern of feelings, determines, not our actions but what for us shall be, the better and the worse. He introduces this value theory with a metaphysics and completes it with a political theory.

Metaphysical reality is a unity which can, with equal validity, be understood as a conceptual or as a material system. Called 'Substance', 'God', or 'Nature', it is a brute fact which exists for no purpose beyond its own unconscious internal necessities. It is, roughly, the world of our contemporary sciences. The constituent partial elements of this total system have each their own agendas and each of them – hydrogen atoms, bacilli, foxes, man – has a nature which determines that it shall struggle to persist in its characteristic being, if necessary at the expense of all other natures. Spinoza continues this model of contained conflict, characteristic of most modern thought from Machiavelli through Adam SMITH to the present, into his account of the war of the passions within each individual man and among men in the political arena.

Our species is 'a part of Nature, not a kingdom within it'. Its essence, its nature, is its species-characteristic pattern of emotions. We realize our nature in the satisfaction of those emotions. Unfortunately – 'all good things are as difficult as they are rare' – we are not very good at this. First, all the other elements of Nature go their own way without concern for us. Men succumb to predatory species, to bacteria, to meteorological phenomena, to the indifferent environment. Scientific knowledge of the forces of Nature can help to prolong and improve our lives. Second, man faces the complexity of his own nature in himself and in other humans. Here again, ignorance entails defeat and misery while knowledge promises at least some success and happiness.

Minimally our happiness is found in the satisfaction of our major and enduring passions, but men are misled by ephemeral or minor passions and fail to see the consequences of their actions for their future feelings. Their mistaken or confused representations of reality result in that state of dissatisfaction or misery which we see as normal. Knowledge and self-control are our best tactics for happiness. Spinoza's general conclusions are not dissimilar to those reached by the tradition epitomized in SOCRATES, Epictetus and Hume.

Ethical philosophy is as perennial as the social alienation which provokes it. Political philosophy, by contrast, emerges only when, as in Spinoza's time, there is political hope. Although a few can always find some degree of personal salvation in any kind of society, such individual success is severely limited by the fact that we are intensely social creatures, social both by necessity and by natural feeling. Because the power and therefore happiness of individuals is multiplied in social groupings, we have an obligation to support the general welfare by support of social and political institutions.

Social and individual salvation are different. Communities may help or hinder their members in the acquisition of true philosophy, but cannot themselves acquire it. The great majority of men are so far below the level of understanding needed to make their communities rational and happy, the chance of the wise becoming statesmen is so remote, that no sudden or comprehensive improvement in politics is likely. The task of the ethical philosopher turned political thinker is to learn from historical experience how polities have succeeded or failed and to show what political institutions, under what circumstances, best meet the constraints and opportunities presented by human nature and the environment.

Spinoza found it particularly interesting that the non-philosophic majority interpret the world and act on the basis of poetic metaphors or myths such as that of religion. Myths make a society possible in the first instance and also constitute the greatest danger both to society itself and to philosophers. Religion, taken to include ideology and civic culture, has the vital function of promoting civic virtue and social solidarity; it fails in these functions when priests gain political influence and myths are taken literally.

Of the major political philosophers, Spinoza stands alone as the unequivocal advocate of democracy. He argues that it most completely concentrates the collected strengths of all citizens and so can most effectively forward their interests. But democratic institutions are an ideal, for they require a people disposed toward moderation, with a strong traditional civic culture and reasonable standards of education and living. Until these requirements are met, monarchy or aristocracy will have to do; either can be so constituted as to minimize its inherent evils and to prepare a people for democracy.

Duff concludes of Spinoza's political theory: 'From the premises of *The Prince* he reaches a conclusion analogous to that of the *Civitas Dei*; and on the basis of Hobbes's absolutism he builds a superstructure of popular liberties better secured than that of either Locke or Rousseau' (p. 11). Spinoza's political thought has not been as widely studied as has that of some other writers, but it may be that more of it survives to be useful to us today.   RJMcS

Reading
Duff, R.A.: *Spinoza's Political and Ethical Philosophy.* Glasgow: James Maclehose, 1903.
†McShea, R.J.: *The Political Philosophy of Spinoza.* New York: Columbia University Press, 1968.
Wernham, A.G.: *Benedict de Spinoza: The Political Works.* Oxford: Clarendon Press, 1958.

Stalin, Joseph Vissarionovich (pseudonym of J. V. Dzhugashvili) (1879–1953) Soviet political leader. Originally a disciple of LENIN, Stalin's main intellectual achievement was to devise a version of MARXISM that could underpin the Soviet regime of which he became undisputed leader.

The term Stalinism was applied by critics to the ideas and policies of Stalin and the Soviet regime that he led (see SOVIET COMMUNISM). It is often used more loosely to characterize the repressive features of other communist parties and regimes.   DLM

state The word 'state' can be used to mean a historical entity or a philosophical idea, a perennial form of human community or a specifically modern phenomenon. These different meanings are not necessarily contradictory, but need to be carefully distinguished.

Probably the most common use is to equate 'state' with the body politic or political community as such, something that has existed

503

throughout history in a wide variety of differing forms, and whose mutations provide traditionally the central subject matter for the science of history. Only the primitive nomadic form of political community is customarily excluded from the designation, the implication being that such communities lack the firmly defined order that seems inherent in the concept. A state requires a fixed relationship between a community and territory.

Used in this general way the term expresses the idea that the political community has certain universal characteristics that cut across time and space; that, for example, the Greek *polis*, the medieval *regnum*, and the modern republic share a certain quality. Can this quality be defined more closely? Clearly any definition that reduces the state to an eternal and immutable substance or thing, simultaneously reduces the process of change and development in history to an insubstantial shadow play. A valid definition must hence be couched in different terms, in terms of action. The state as a universal phenomenon is a kind of activity or undertaking, one that history shows to be imposed on man as a necessity. The recurrent features of this activity would appear to be the following. First, it forms or shapes a fixed relationship between human beings together with their possessions, or in other words it creates a unity or society, in the most basic sense of this term, between human beings. The end or achievement of the state is hence peculiarly fundamental. Second, it presupposes an ordering potency or a form of rule, or a relationship of command and obedience between human beings. The unity or society that the state achieves is hence coterminous though not necessarily identical with a hierarchy. Finally, the activity that makes and upholds the state is always exclusive and particularistic, asserting itself in contrast to that of others who are not part of the community in question.

This definition of the state, as an exclusive totality of rulers and ruled that founds an ordered relationship between men and things, is intended to convey solely the state's minimal characteristic as a species of human activity. It points to another characteristic which opens up a fresh dimension of the state. In so far as it is a kind of activity concerned with ends, it

necessarily raises the question of the rightness of the end it seeks and the means that it employs in a given instance. Is the right order of society being realized? Is the form of rule rightful? Are the external relations of the community being conducted in the right manner? Seen from this angle the state is not merely a necessity imposed on man, a form of activity that, come what may, he has to engage in, it is also a persistent problem, a problem of right. The state involves a struggle to establish not merely an order in place of anarchy, but an order that is true, authentic and just, as distinct from distorted, hollow and despotic.

The great classical works of political theory, whether they be those of Plato, Aristotle, Hobbes or Hegel, can be seen as so many definitions of the state as it ought to be, according to its own inherent logic. Much of their work was devoted to distinguishing the state from other types of human association with which, in empirical or historical reality, it has often been blended and overlaid. ARISTOTLE begins his famous work on *Politics* by distinguishing the form of rule typical of a political community from that of a household. In the seventeenth century LOCKE was equally concerned to make this distinction. A political community, he argued, was not an extended family and political rule was not paternal. The distinction between a political community and a religious or spiritual community came to be drawn sharply in the wake of the religious strife caused by the Reformation. HOBBES, for example, was at pains to demonstrate that ecclesiastical power in and for itself was not of a political nature; it was not a form of rule, command or coercion, but a form of teaching and persuasion. A clerical body could not claim power over a state. On the contrary, only through acts of state could religious doctrines acquire a political status. At the end of the eighteenth century and the beginning of the nineteenth, following the French and industrial revolutions, another distinction came into prominence, that between state and society. Society in this context meant not the fundamental union between human beings established by the state, but rather the network of interaction and exchange formed by individuals exercising the right to pursue the satisfaction of their particular needs in their own way. HEGEL was one of the first to articulate this distinction when he argued in the *Philosophy of Right* that the state proper should not be confused with 'CIVIL SOCIETY'.

The twentieth-century 'totalitarian' state can be seen as marking a movement to remove these historically developed distinctions. Society in the sense of an arena of spontaneous activity comes to be reabsorbed into the state, and the state itself is subordinated to a party which bears not a few of the characteristics of a religious movement, and often to a paternalistic leader (see TOTALITARIANISM).

There has also been a noticeable tendency in recent times to define the state in a much more restricted and instrumental fashion than in classical political theory. It has come to be seen by many as merely an apparatus of rule, an apparatus distinguished pre-eminently by the fact that it involves a monopoly of coercion or, as WEBER expresses it, 'a monopoly of the legitimate use of force'. The distinction between state and DESPOTISM becomes very thin indeed.

This tendency may be traced to a number of different sources. The rise to prominence of positivist methodology, with its insistence that a true science of society must eschew all value judgments and metaphysics, and devote itself to the ascertainment of facts and the deduction or construction of the laws they instantiate, is one such source (see POSITIVISM). Sociology in general, because of its links with positivism, and its tendency to see public institutions as the agencies of social classes, has undoubtedly been another. Oppenheimer's self-styled 'sociological' idea of the state is a good illustration. MARXISM, particularly in its Leninist form, has been an important factor. The state according to Marxist theory is a transitory phenomenon, an outcrop of class-divided society, which is destined to wither away when classes are abolished by communism. LENIN argued vehemently that the state was no more than an apparatus of force used by one class to oppress another, and his definition has played a crucial role in differentiating the political tactics of his own followers from those of social democrats within non-communist regimes. Finally radical LIBERALISM, of the kind that has achieved a certain popularity in the West in recent decades, tends to contrast the state as embodying coercion with society as embodying the free and spontaneous exchange of individuals, and to argue in consequence that the state's sphere of activity should be whittled down to an absolute minimum. HAYEK's ideas are a good example of the last tendency. There has always been an anti-state stream within liberalism.

It may be questioned whether any of these methodologies or doctrines are equipped to do justice to the state as the constant reproduction of human society, guided, strengthened and refined by ideas of its own right constitution. It is significant perhaps that Russian scholars, over the past few decades, have tried to progress beyond Lenin's reductionist theory of the state towards a more constructive analysis.

The state as a universal historical phenomenon, and the state as a philosophical concept, require to be supplemented by consideration of the state as a specifically modern phenomenon. There are a significant number of historians and political theorists who argue that the term 'state' should be used only to denote the kind of body politic that developed in Europe in the aftermath of the Renaissance and Reformation; that the theory of the state is the theory of this particular kind of body; and that to use the term in a blanket fashion for all kinds of body politic is to distort and confuse the process of historical development.

This usage has etymology on its side. The word state gradually evolved into a general term for the body politic between the fourteenth century and the end of the seventeenth century. According to Mager its main roots would appear to have been *status* used to denote the condition, power, office, income, or dignity of the prince (*status regalis*) and *status* meaning the form or constitution of the polity.

The contention that the state is properly a modern concept does not rest on etymology alone, however. It is founded principally on the idea that the state emerges at the same time as the concept of SOVEREIGNTY, and that a state which is not sovereign is not properly a state. In other words a state must be equipped – following the doctrine of sovereignty developed by BODIN and Hobbes in the sixteenth and seventeenth centuries – with a public office or person endowed with the incontestable right and power to decide upon the resolution of the extreme situation. It must be a self-determining body in this sense. It cannot be a loose conglomerate or composite structure held together by some tacit or open bargain between the parts, which is liable to fall apart *in extremis*. It cannot be subordinate to the decision of other bodies when crisis looms. Sovereignty means a much sharper drawing of the line between public and private within the body politic, and also a much sharper drawing of the boundary between one body politic and another. It means that law within the body politic becomes far more 'positive' or ruler-created than ever before.

Concomitantly with the idea of sovereignty – and partly in opposition to it – there grew up another idea that can be said to distinguish the state as a modern phenomenon, namely the idea that the form of rule within a body politic is rightfully decided and constituted by the people or nation as a single entity. This idea was carried further in the French and American revolutions, which established the representative character of public institutions and also developed the notion that one of the major ends of such institutions is to secure the rights of the individual citizens. The state as a modern phenomenon may thus be defined as the institutional representation of the people's will, enabling it to act effectively in both the normal and the extreme situation to secure the defence and welfare of the whole and the rights of the parts – together with this very activity itself.

The idea of the state as a specifically modern phenomenon does not necessarily contradict the two other notions of the state that were developed earlier. Those who use the word in the restricted sense of the 'modern body politic' must nevertheless use some general term to convey the earlier forms, and can scarcely deny that, however deep the change brought about by the doctrine of sovereignty, all continuity was not broken. The state as a universal phenomenon, the state as a modern phenomenon, and the state as a philosophic idea are complementary conceptualizations of a fundamental dimension of human existence.   MGF

Reading

Bosanquet, B.: *The Philosophical Theory of the State* (1899). London: Macmillan, 1958.

†Dyson, K.: *The State Tradition in Western Europe*. Oxford: Martin Robertson, 1980.

†D'Entrèves, A.P.: *The Notion of the State*. Oxford: Clarendon Press, 1967.

Hayek, F.A.: *Law, Legislation, and Liberty*. London: Routledge & Kegan Paul, 1982.

Lenin, V.I.: *The State and Revolution* (1917). Moscow: Foreign Languages Publishing House, 1951.

†MacIver, R.M.: *The Modern State*. Oxford: Clarendon Press, 1926.

Mager, W.: *Die Enstehung des modernen Staatsbegriffs*. Wiesbaden: Steiner, 1968.

Nozick, R.: *Anarchy, State, and Utopia*. New York: Basic; Oxford: Blackwell, 1984.

Oppenheimer, F.: *The State*. Montreal: Black Rose, 1975.

†Poggi, G.: *The Development of the Modern State*. London: Hutchinson, 1978.

Weber, M.: Politics as a vocation (1919). In *From Max Weber*, ed. H.H. Gerth and C. Wright Mills. London: Routledge & Kegan Paul, 1948.

state capitalism   In its classic sense this term meant a private capitalist economy under the control of the state; it was frequently used to refer to the controlled economies of the great powers during the first world war. Soviet Marxists now regularly use the term 'state monopoly capitalism' to refer to the most recent phase of capitalism, in which the state exercises its power on behalf of the monopolies against the small capitalists as well as the mass of the population. Extending the concept to Soviet Russia in the aftermath of the proletarian revolution, LENIN in April 1918 argued that 'state capitalism' could be under the control of either a bourgeois or a proletarian state; in Russia private capitalism, under the control of the proletarian state, constituted a transitional phase to the establishment of a fully socialist economy. In 1921, after the devastation of the civil war, Lenin called for 'state capitalism' in the form of concessions to foreign capitalists which would help to provide goods for the peasantry – but little came of this scheme.

In 1925, the Leningrad Opposition headed by Zinoviev and Kamenev endeavoured to revive Lenin's 1918 use of the term in relation to Soviet Russia, claiming that the Soviet economy was still 'state capitalism'. The party majority rejected this formula on the grounds that socialist ownership was already predominant in the USSR in the mid-1920s.

Since the late 1930s, one wing of the international Trotskyist movement has argued that the present-day Soviet system is 'state capitalism' (or 'bureaucratic state capitalism'). On this view, while the state owns the means of production, the 'bureaucracy' controls and uses the state to exploit the workers and accumulate capital; it thus performs the same functions as the individual owner in a capitalist economy. In one variant, the theory claims that the Soviet economy is driven to accumulate capital not by any internal mechanism but by international military competition.   RWD

Reading

Cliff, T.: *State Capitalism in Russia*. London: Pluto, 1974.

Jessop, B.: *The Capitalist State*. Oxford: Martin Robertson, 1982.

†Lane, D.: *Soviet Economy and Society*, ch. 3. Oxford: Blackwell, 1984.

state of nature A term of art employed by SOCIAL CONTRACT theorists to describe a state of affairs in which there is no settled political authority. Its role may be to justify the existence of the state, to deny its necessity, to contrast the happy state of civilized man with the miserable state of the savage, or to turn that comparison on its head. It is to be found in the writings of HOBBES, LOCKE, PUFENDORF, GROTIUS, ROUSSEAU, KANT and many other thinkers of the seventeenth and eighteenth centuries. Its role in their thought yields different accounts of the state of nature: is it a social but non-political condition, or a non-social condition? Is it peaceful or is it equivalent to the state of war? Is it a purely hypothetical condition or is it the actual condition of some of mankind now or in the past? Is it an essentially juridical concept or is it a factual one? To all these questions writers have given very different answers. All writers agree that people who owe allegiance to no settled political authority are in the – or at least 'a' – state of nature with respect to each other; most agree that this means that the rulers of sovereign states are in the state of nature with respect to one another.

The fierceness of HOBBES's insistence that the state of nature is the state of war is unmatched by any other writer; even GROTIUS,

who legitimates the domination of the weak by the strong, is more eager to insist that the state of nature is governed by the law of nature. To some extent the disagreements here are illusory, as Hobbes defines war in terms of the absence of settled peace where almost all other writers define war in terms of actual or threatened violence and define peace in terms of the absence of actual war. But, juridically considered, the disagreement is real, since Hobbes insists that, in time of war, force and fraud are the cardinal virtues and thus insists that we are foolish to expect anything better from foreign states, and from those who are not under the sway of some sovereign power. ROUSSEAU's account of the state of nature is notable for its complexity and subtlety, and for the fact that it makes the state of nature an anthropological notion rather than a purely juridical one. So Rousseau insists that the 'real' state of nature was much more remote from our present condition than Hobbes or Locke supposed. Human beings as they came from the hand of nature were not equipped with speech, with reason, with a sense of time, with any morality; they were utterly solitary – mothers and babies went about together, but the family was unknown. What Hobbes and Locke called the state of nature was already a social and developed state. The Hobbesian war of all against all could only break out among creatures who had the gift of speech, self-consciousness and morality – only then could they be competitive and resentful.

The rise of a historical and sociological interest in political development made the concept of the state of nature unfashionable. HUME denied that man had ever lived in the state of nature as envisaged by Hobbes – not a powerful blow against Hobbes, who was perfectly ready to employ it as a hypothetical condition to show the logic of political authority rather than to account for its actual genesis, but one which suggested that other ways of making the same point were intellectually more compelling. Certainly writers such as BENTHAM and his utilitarian successors were hostile to the idea of a state of nature, both because they thought it confused historical and moral questions and because they associated it with the contractarian and natural law theories of government which

507

they attacked in the name of utility. The rise of a scientific and positivist anthropology and sociology could only discredit the concept further. It is a matter for some surprise that the concept has come to life again in recent years. John RAWLS's *Theory of Justice* revived it along with contractarian ways of thinking about justice, and Rawls's critic, Robert Nozick, employs it to some effect in *Anarchy, State and Utopia* when asking the traditional question: 'if we had no sovereign, would we be compelled to create one?' These avowedly hypothetical questions revive 'state of nature theory' by disembarrassing it of any historical connotations; in so doing, they escape the objections of Hume and other critics who observe that men became human *in* society rather than out of it, while borrowing from disciplines such as economics and games theory whose similarities to much that we find in Grotius; Hobbes and Locke are too obvious to need stressing.   AR

Reading

Hobbes, T.: *Leviathan* (1651), ed. C. B. Macpherson. Harmondsworth: Penguin, 1968.

Hume, D.: Of the original contract, (1748). In *Essays Moral, Political and Literary*, ed. E. Miller. Indianapolis: Liberty Classics, 1985.

Nozick, R.: *Anarchy, State and Utopia*. Oxford: Blackwell, 1974.

Rawls, J.: *A Theory of Justice*. Cambridge, Mass.: Harvard University Press, 1971; Oxford: Oxford University Press, 1972.

Rousseau, J.-J.: A discourse on the origins of inequality (1755). In *The Social Contract and Discourses*, trans. G.D.H. Cole. London: Dent, 1973.

Stirner, Max (pseudonym of Johann Caspar Schmidt) (1806–1856) German philosopher. Stirner espoused a thoroughgoing form of egoism in *The Ego and his Own* (1844), a book which influenced MARX and the individualist school of ANARCHISM, as well as later thinkers on the right. See YOUNG HEGELIANS.

Suarez, Francisco (1548–1617) Spanish philosopher and theologian. The leading political philosopher of the Catholic Counter-Reformation, Suarez's philosophy of law and politics is laid out in *A Treatise on the Laws and God the Lawgiver* (1612), based on his lectures at the University of Coimbra, where he held the

chair in theology. In addition, he analysed the issue of sovereignty and resistance to tyranny in *A Defence of the Catholic and Apostolic Faith against the Errors of the Anglican Sect* (1612). Here he famously argued that the English people, as a corporate body and led by their constituted authorities, had the right to resist the heretical king, James I, in his attempt to impose the oath of allegiance.

Suarez's political philosophy is a response to two practical problems: the need for a justification of the Counter-Reformation struggle against militant Protestantism (see REFORMATION POLITICAL THOUGHT) and the need for a theory of the emerging sovereign states (especially of Spain, the first modern state and global *imperium*), their relations, and their subordination to the universal jurisdiction of the pope. In constructing his solution he drew upon the two great schools of Scholastic political philosophy, Thomism (*via antiqua*, from St Thomas AQUINAS) (see THOMIST POLITICAL THOUGHT) and Ockhamism (*via moderna*, from WILLIAM OF OCKHAM). Ockhamism, with its emphasis on the individual, subjective rights and popular sovereignty or CONCILIARISM, flourished in the fifteenth and early sixteenth centuries. However, in the early sixteenth century, Francisco de VITORIA revived Aquinas's theory of absolute monarchy and of natural law as an objective and rational standard of right, with no mention of subjective rights. This view triumphed at the Council of Trent in mid-century where counter-Reformation orthodoxy was hammered out.

Although Ockhamism was now discredited, mainly because of its use by Protestant thinkers, Suarez did not reject it completely in presenting his position in neo-Thomist terms. It was too well entrenched in Catholicism, especially in Portugal and the Spanish Netherlands; the concept of subjective rights, as Suarez pointed out, made juridical sense of early modern commercial activity without threatening the Thomistic primacy of positive duties; in addition, Catholics themselves required a right to resist Protestant monarchs.

Suarez sought therefore to integrate subjective rights in a subordinate manner into a natural law framework, where the positive duties of distributive justice would remain primary, and natural law would not be reduced solely to the negative duty of abstaining from the rights of others (as in fact it did in the hands of Hugo GROTIUS and Thomas HOBBES). This syncretic political theory failed in Protestant Europe but it informed, and continues to inform, political theory and practice in Iberian Europe and especially in Latin America.

Suarez's theory is a law-based or 'juridical' theory and, in opposition to Luther, natural law is the foundation for all human laws and relationships (see LAW). Ockhamists hold that natural law is right and binding because it is God's will – thus stressing His freedom; while, for Thomists, it is right and binding because it is God's intellect – thus stressing His reason. Suarez combined the two by saying that the content of natural law, and so any genuine law, is rational and relates to God's intellect, yet the obligation of natural law is dependent on it being the will of God, the lawmaker.

Second, rather than rendering INTER-NATIONAL LAW as directly a part of natural law, Suarez treated it as a kind of positive or human law, based on custom and only indirectly related to natural law, thus opening a space for the emerging discipline of international law. Hence, although war and slavery, like private property, are not necessary precepts of natural law, they are customary practices of states, and are natural and just since they do not contradict natural law.

The third and most important feature of Suarez's theory is his account of SOVEREIGNTY. Sovereignty is the power to make and enforce laws, with penalties of death, for the common good and in conformity with natural law. This power resides in the monarch of a state, who is absolute and above the law, but under the indirect, coercive and universal jurisdiction of the pope. His power comes from the people in the sense that God invests it in the community, considered as a corporate or mystical body, which then consents to alienate, and not merely delegate, it to the monarch. By denying that the people individually ever possess political power Suarez undercut the revolutionary implications of Ockhamist popular sovereignty that were brought out by, for example, the Calvinist George Buchanan, in *The Right of the Kingdom in Scotland* (1579).

Further, since the community alienates political power to the ruler, it can never reclaim and exercise political power, in the form of a rebellion, if the ruler abuses his power. In *A Defence*, however, Suarez argues that there are two cases in which it is lawful to resist a tyrant, and this in virtue of the community's natural and subjective right to preserve and defend itself against destruction. The first is a tyrant who usurps power without consent and threatens to destroy the community. Here, even part of the community has the right to resist. Second, if a consent-based sovereign becomes tyrannical and sets about destroying the community, the community as a body has the natural right to defend itself, under the natural leadership and careful deliberation of the constituted representatives of the kingdom. This view, applied by Suarez to England under James I, had become anachronistic even by the time of Locke.   JT

Reading

Buchanan, G.: *De jure regni apud Scotos (The Right of the Kingdom in Scotland)*. Amsterdam and New York: Da Capo, 1969.

Copleston, F.: *A History of Philosophy*, vol. III, pt 2: *The Revival of Platonism to Suarez*. Garden City, NY: Doubleday, 1963.

Fernandez-Santamaria, J.A.: *The State, War and Peace: Spanish Political Thought in the Renaissance 1516–1559*. Cambridge: Cambridge University Press, 1977.

Hamilton, B.: *Political Thought in Sixteenth-Century Spain*. Oxford: Oxford University Press, 1963.

Skinner, Q.: *The Foundations of Modern Political Thought*, vol. II: *The Reformation*. Cambridge: Cambridge University Press, 1978.

Suarez, F.: *Defensio fidei Catholicae et Apostolicae adversus Anglicanae sectae errores (A Defence of the Catholic and Apostolic Faith against the Errors of the Anglican Sect)*. 2 vols. Naples, 1872.

———: *Tractatus de legibus ac Deo legislatore (A Treatise on the Laws and God the Lawgiver)*. 2 vols. Naples, 1872.

†———: *Selections from Three Works*, Latin-English edn of major parts of *A Defence* and *On the Laws*, trans. G.L. Williams. In *The Classics of International Law*, ed. J.B. Scott. Oxford: Clarendon Press, 1944.

Tuck, R.: *Natural Rights Theories: Their Origin and Development*. Cambridge: Cambridge University Press, 1979.

†Wilenius, R.: *The Social and Political Theory of Francisco Suarez*. Helsinki: Societas Philosophica Fennica, 1963.

Sumner, William Graham (1840–1910) American sociologist. Influenced by Spencer, Sumner was a strong defender of economic individualism (see SOCIAL DARWINISM). As a sociologist, his major work was *Folkways* (1907).

Swift, Jonathan (1667–1745) Satirist, pamphleteer and poet. Swift was born (and died) in Dublin, was educated at Trinity College, Dublin, and ultimately became Dean of Dublin's Saint Patrick's Cathedral, but was English in his own eyes. Like much of his later work, Swift's first major publication, *The Contests and Dissensions in Athens and Rome* (1701), transcends its topical party-political context. *A Tale of a Tub*, *The Battel of the Books*, and *The Mechanical Operation of the Spirit* (published together in 1704) are satires on abuses in learning and in religion (following the *Hudibras* tradition of Restoration anti-puritan burlesque). Until 1710 Swift moved among prominent Whigs (such as Somers, Halifax, Addison and Steele, to whose *Tatler* he contributed essays, poems and suggestions), but his deep reservations about Whig policies of religious toleration found expression in *A Letter Concerning the Sacramental Test* (1709), the ironical *Argument against Abolishing Christianity* (1711), and *The Sentiments of a Church-of-England Man* (1711). Swift's defection to Harley's Tory ministry in 1710 was principled rather than expedient; in the *Examiner* papers (1710–11), *The Conduct of the Allies* (1711), and *The Publick Spirit of the Whigs* (1714) he spoke for the government, castigated Marlborough and the previous ministry, and prepared the nation for the Peace of Utrecht (1713). The *Journal to Stella* (1710–13) (addressed to Swift's dearest friend, Esther Johnson) describes this rich period. Harley's ministry fell in 1714, and Swift next involved himself in public affairs in the 1720s, defending Irish interests. His *Drapier's Letters* (1724; 1735), named after the plain-speaking draper who is their supposed author, successfully called for a boycott of the debased coinage which was to have been introduced into Ireland by William Wood under Walpole's patent. Swift's partly-deserved reputation as an Irish patriot stems from these and other Irish tracts, in particular the chilling *Modest Proposal* (1729) which soberly recommends marketing redundant Irish babies for the tables of the rich as a logical extension of England's 'devouring' of Ireland. *Gulliver's Travels* (1726) satirizes a wide range of political institutions and moral assumptions, particularly colonialism, narrow-minded nationalism, sectarianism, hubristic scientific inquiry, and propagandist adulteration of language.

Some commentators have drawn attention to the libertarian elements in Swift's politics, as he did himself in 'Verses on the death of Dr Swift' (1731, published 1739) and the epitaph that he wrote for himself ('imitare si poteris Strenuum pro virili Libertatis Vindicatorem'). Others consider this a sentimental emphasis that neglects Swift's radical authoritarianism, and the uncompromising attitudes of his satire. DE

Reading

†Ehrenpreis, I.: *Swift: The Man, His Works, and The Age*. 3 vols. London: Methuen, 1962–83.

†Lock, F.P.: *Swift's Tory Politics*. London: Duckworth, 1983.

†Rawson, C.J. ed.: *The Character of Swift's Satire: a Revised Focus*. Newark, Toronto and London: Associated University Presses, 1983.

Ross, A. and Woolley, D. eds: *Jonathan Swift*. Oxford: Oxford University Press, 1984.

Swift, J.: *The Prose Writings of Jonathan Swift*, ed. H. Davis *et al*. 16 vols. Oxford: Blackwell, 1939–74.

———: *Poems*, ed. H. Williams, 2nd edn. 3 vols. Oxford: Oxford University Press, 1958.

———: *Correspondence*, ed. H. Williams. 5 vols. Oxford: Oxford University Press, 1963–5.

syndicalism A theory that developed from the experiences of the French trade union movement. The term derived from the French word *syndicat* or trade union and is sometimes used to denote trade unionism in a general sense. More often it refers to a socialist theory holding that struggles by the working classes against capitalism should be fought by trade unions or other exclusively working-class organizations through direct action, such as strikes and general strikes, rather than through political or state activity. In its more militant forms it is sometimes called anarcho-syndicalism.

The anti-political nature of syndicalism was initially inspired by the collapse of the Fédération Nationale des Syndicats in 1894 after repeated attempts to support resolutions favouring a general strike were defeated by the political forces of Jules Guesde's Marxist Parti Ouvrier. The Confédération Générale du Travail was founded as a result in that same year. Together with the recently-founded national Fédération des Bourses du Travail (labour-run employment agencies) it spearheaded the development of syndicalism. The continued harassment of the Bourses and the brutal repression of strikes by a government that included a socialist minister, Millerand, strengthened syndicalism's anti-statist view. Furthermore, despite its highly centralized and sophisticated political and administrative system, France had a relatively underdeveloped economy permeated by a craft-and-artisan outlook; syndicalists therefore felt that, despite Marx's writings to the contrary, a centralized economy was not inevitable. Instead it was thought that if the free union of workers concentrated on economic activity and ignored politics, syndicalism would remain rooted in local traditions and decentralized self-government.

Syndicalism emerged under roughly similar conditions in other Mediterranean countries. In Italy it was organized under the Unione Sindicale and remained popular until it was co-opted and absorbed by the fascists. In Spain the Confederación Nacional de Trabajo (founded in 1911) attracted over a million members in the early days of the republic. It remained strong during the Spanish civil war but disappeared in 1939 after Franco's victory. In other, more industrialized, countries syndicalism did not thrive. In the United States the Industrial Workers of the World, founded in 1905, had a peak membership of 60,000. Though it fought a number of successful localized general strikes, its membership came disproportionately from non-English speaking workers or from non-urban sources such as miners and lumber workers in the west. On the other hand, the IWW did have some support among dockers, both in America and elsewhere (especially in Australia during the first world war).

The IWW and other syndicalist groups have often been associated with violence and sabotage, yet the theory of syndicalism is somewhat more moderate than the public image. Fernand

Pelloutier, head of the federation of French Bourses and one of the chief architects of syndicalism, argued in 1902 that there was 'no advantage to blood-stained revolutions of which the bourgeoisie were the sole beneficiaries'.

Instead Pelloutier conceived the revolution as a great refusal, a mass turning of backs on the established powers in the form of a general strike. Georges SOREL, who had little connection with official syndicalism but whose work *Reflections on Violence* (1908) is perhaps the most refined treatment of syndicalist theory, elaborated the theory of the general strike and asserted that it had a 'completely different meaning' from that of previous revolutions. Proletarian violence supposedly has built-in limits to brutality because syndicalists refused to use the power of the state for their own purposes. Hence for Sorel 'violence' simply meant rebellion against existing institutions while 'force' meant repression by existing institutions. In the coming proletarian revolution no state mechanism will be necessary because the aggressively anti-intellectual stance of the workers forecloses the use of utopian blueprints; reality does not have to be forced to conform to a preconceived plan. The revolution would not, in any case, need such blueprints because the socialist society already existed in the Bourses du Travail, in the trades unions, and in the workshops.

The practice was at times more violent than Sorel's writings indicated, and there were brutal confrontations between workers and established powers in many countries. The failure of the British general strike in 1926, though not led by syndicalists, tarnished the image of syndicalist tactics. Furthermore the anti-statist position of syndicalism was eventually defeated by the forces of the Third International and the politicization of European socialist movements.   JLS

Reading

Brissenden, P.F.: *The Launching of the Industrial Workers of the World* (1913). New York: Haskell, 1971.

Julliard, J.: *Fernand Pelloutier et les origines du syndicalisme d'action directe.* Paris: Éditions du Seuil, 1971.

Pelloutier, F.: *Histoire des Bourses du travail* (1884),

preface Georges Sorel. Paris: Gordon & Breach, 1971.

Ridley, F.F.: *Revolutionary Syndicalism in France: the direct action of its time*. Cambridge: Cambridge University Press, 1970.

Roberts, D.L.: *The Syndicalist Tradition in Italian Fascism*. Chapel Hill: University of North Carolina Press, 1979.

Sorel, G.: *Reflections on Violence*, trans. T.E. Hulme and J. Roth. New York and London: Macmillan, 1950.

Stearns, P.: *Revolutionary Syndicalism and French Labor*. New Brunswick, NJ: Rutgers University Press, 1971.

T

Tawney, Richard Henry (1880–1962) British social philosopher and economic historian. Born in India, and educated at Rugby and Balliol College, Oxford, Tawney's Christian social moralism and a prevailing concern with the 'social question' first led him into educational social work at Toynbee Hall in London's East End. However, soon convinced that social reconstruction was more important than charitable social relief, he increasingly turned his attention towards education, economic and social research, and politics. Thus began his lifelong association with adult education through the Workers' Educational Association; with the Labour and trade union movements (he wrote many policy documents for the Labour Party, and represented the union side on the Sankey Commission on the Coal Industry); and with the London School of Economics, where he held the chair of economic history. On his eightieth birthday *The Times* wrote: 'No man alive has put more people into his spiritual and intellectual debt than has Richard Henry Tawney . . . '.

In part, such a claim rested on Tawney's own personal qualities and moral stature. However, it rested even more on his contribution to social thought in Britain during the first half of the twentieth century. In a series of influential books he set out to identify the moral disorder of British capitalist society (*The Acquisitive Society*, 1921), to explore aspects of the historical genesis of this kind of society (most notably, in his *Religion and the Rise of Capitalism*, 1926), and to outline the basis for an alternative, socialist, form of human social organization (in *Equality*, 1931). These pivotal works were supplemented by essays, speeches, and papers on education, social reform, Christian social thinking, and socialism. Some of this material is collected in *The Attack, and other papers* (1953) and *The Radical Tradition* (1964). Taken together, Tawney's work arguably represents the most influential and authentic statement of early twentieth-century British SOCIALISM.

It was a socialism that addressed itself to general human values and their social expression, a reflection of Tawney's Christian humanism. It was, therefore, not a socialism of class power, economic determination, or historical inevitability. If Tawney's historical studies of the development of capitalism gave his work affinities with Marxism, both his indictment of capitalism and his presentation of the socialist project rested on distinctive foundations. In the notes for his *Commonplace Book*, written in the years just before the first world war, Tawney had recorded that society was 'sick through the absence of a moral ideal'. It was this moral sickness that provided the theme for *The Acquisitive Society*, with its analysis of a society in which industry and property had become detached from any principles of function and purpose (these are key Tawney words) and so inhabited a realm of moral lawlessness in which acquisition and 'industrialism' were unconstrained. The disorders of capitalist society, reflected in an economic life that is 'in a perpetual state of morbid irritation', were to be seen as inevitable consequences of its moral vacuum. Against such a society, Tawney advanced a doctrine of functional property and common social purpose.

In his historical work, Tawney was concerned to explore how a capitalist economy had come to acquire its autonomy from a general moral order, to demonstrate that this was a historically contingent development, which had an alternative that preceded it and, potentially, an alternative which could succeed it. Such an alternative required that human beings should choose their social values and then will that these be achieved. In his educational work, Tawney sought to promote the active citizenship that would make this project possible.

In *The Acquisitive Society* the moral disorder of capitalism was presented as the source of the industrial disorder and social malaise of such societies. A similar line of connection is argued in *Equality*. Here a moral doctrine of equal worth is advanced as a basic value (which means that the argument rests on different foundations from liberal arguments about distributional justice), and the implications and consequences of the social application of this value are explored. What it implied was not an arithmetical EQUALITY, or identity of treatment, but 'a general diffusion of the means of civilization' that would enlarge liberties, promote self-development, and 'narrow the space between valley and peak' in society. The social organization of equality was implied by a view of equal human worth, but such a social organization would in turn create the conditions for a common culture. Thus a common culture 'cannot be created merely by desiring it. It must rest upon practical foundations of social organization.' Tawney's socialist politics were therefore designed to lay down these practical foundations.

This directs attention to the central, durable preoccupation of Tawney's social thought. In an English tradition that includes Arnold, RUSKIN and MORRIS, Tawney explored the idea of a common culture. A concern for social cohesion and solidarity underpins the whole of his thought. Under capitalism, social unity was lacking because there was, and could be, no moral unity directed towards a common purpose. The case for socialism rested, finally, upon its ability to create a remoralized and integrated society of active citizens pursuing common ends. The mark of such a society would be the character and quality of the social relationships that it nourished, a society of 'fellowship' (another key word in Tawney's socialist vocabulary) in which citizens were

within co-operative reach of each other and so able to sustain and develop a genuine COMMUNITY.

Critics of Tawney have pointed to his lack of analytical rigour. For example, they have identified the problem of defining common ends for a society, especially in a way that is reconcilable with democratic PLURALISM, as well as some of the difficulties in making 'equal worth' or 'function' into operational principles of social organization. There are also doubts about the ability of Tawney's egalitarianism to deliver the kind of cohesive social energy that he describes. What is not in doubt, though, is the sustained force, for over half a century, of Tawney's argument that the organization of society is essentially a collective moral project, 'a common enterprise which is the concern of all'.

AWW

Reading
†Reisman, D.: *State and Welfare: Tawney, Galbraith and Adam Smith*. London: Macmillan, 1982.

Tawney, R.H.: *The Acquisitive Society*. London: Bell, 1921.

———: *Equality*. London: Allen & Unwin, 1931.

———: *The Attack, and other papers*. London: Allen & Unwin, 1953.

———: *The Radical Tradition*. London: Allen & Unwin, 1964.

†Terrill, R.: *R.H. Tawney and His Times*. London: Deutsch, 1974.

Winter, J.M. and Joslin, D.M. eds: *R. H. Tawney's Commonplace Book*. Cambridge: Cambridge University Press, 1972.

†Wright, A.: Tawneyism revisited: equality, welfare and socialism. In *Fabian Essays in Socialist Thought*, ed. B. Pimlott. London: Heinemann, 1984.

terrorism A form of political violence, directed at government but often involving ordinary citizens, whose aim is to create a climate of fear in which the aims of the terrorists will be granted by the government in question. The term is sometimes extended to apply to acts perpetrated by governments themselves in order to instil a sense of fear in their subjects. Both the definitional question, and the substantive political issues raised by terrorism, correspond to those posed by VIOLENCE generally.

DLM

Reading

Laqueur, W.: *Terrorism*. London: Weidenfeld & Nicolson, 1977.

Wilkinson, P.: *Terrorism and the Liberal State*, 2nd edn. London: Macmillan, 1986.

Thelwall, John (1764–1834) British radical pamphleteer and lecturer. An advocate of manhood suffrage as leader of the London Corresponding Society in the 1790s. See RADICALS, BRITISH.

Thomist political thought A collective term for those theories of society and social ethics inspired by the writings of St Thomas AQUINAS in the thirteenth century, in particular the *Summa theologiae, De regimine principum* and his commentaries on Aristotle's *Nicomachean Ethics* and *Politics*. The main representative of this tradition since the late nineteenth century has been political Neo-Thomism, which claims to follow a 'perennial philosophy' 'in the spirit of the angelic doctor'. Political Neo-Thomism developed within Roman Catholic thought as an attempt to respond to the political and social problems of emerging industrial societies. Although it has had a wide range of adherents from all parts of the political spectrum, its chief influence can be seen in the official pronouncements of Pope and Curia. This influence has markedly declined since the Second Vatican Council (1962–5), which was ambiguous in its attitude to Thomism.

Theoretical contents

Neo-Thomist political thought takes its view of human nature as the basis of its doctrine of the state and of its social ethics. Essential to this view is the belief that man is created in the image of God. From this it is held to follow that it is appropriate to man that he should live in organized society with the goal of ethical and intellectual perfection. Reaching such perfection would be equivalent to living the Good Life, at which all people are taken to aim. This is a Christianization of ARISTOTLE's doctrine that in all their actions, human beings are at root striving for happiness (*eudaimonia*). According to Aquinas and most of his followers, this striving takes place in the course of pursuing three fundamental natural inclinations: the preservation of the self, the preservation of the species, and life according to reason. This third impulsion includes desiring both to know the truth about God, and to live a life in society in pursuance of both individual and the common good. This makes up the core of Natural Law as this tradition sees it. Civil law, although it cannot be deduced directly from Natural Law, loses its binding character if it violates the tenets of the latter. Its purpose is to make the demands of Natural Law specific for the society concerned (see LAW).

Thus, for political Neo-Thomism, the function of civil law and the power of the state is to make life in society possible, by guaranteeing political order and distributing to each 'what is truly his'. This preserves peace and makes it possible to aim for the common good. Furthering the common good is the responsibility of everyone in the society, but especially of those legitimately charged with representing others' political and ethical interests: laws may be made either by the whole community or by any institution counting as its legal representative. The common good itself embraces not only God, as Man's highest goal, but also appropriate aspects of the society's culture, and the material and economic conditions needed to enable the society's members to pursue the Good Life to the best of their abilities. Hence social and state institutions, as well as national and international political activity, are to be treated as means to an end, not as ends in themselves. The end they serve is Man as a person and his ultimate perfection – the 'person principle'. This principle, the 'solidarity principle' and the 'subsidiarity principle', respectively maintain human dignity, equality and freedom.

The 'solidarity principle' states that political activity should be based on the assumption that the Good Life requires a mutual commitment between individual and society. From this it is taken to follow that private property, especially productive property, should not only benefit the individual owner but also serve the common good. This does not radically challenge the social rootedness of private property but, in practical terms, political Neo-Thomism would make state intervention into its distribution and use unavoidable. Not least, the principle of 'subsidiarity' takes it that each individual and each section of society should be enabled as far as possible to fulfil the tasks specifically appropriate to them. What they can perform, they should, and no other body should do it for them. On the state level, some Neo-Thomist authors therefore favour a form of federalism. All insist that society may not deprive the individual of the ability to actualize his capacities, and indeed should provide the opportunity to develop them. The state should provide help to self-help, by protecting the rights of the smaller components of society, in particular the family, thus making self-determination possible.

History

Neo-Thomist political thought gained its effectiveness within the official church notably from Leo XIII's encyclical *Aeterni Patris* (1879) and the condemnation of Modernism. Neo-Thomism was at one time formally enshrined in CANON LAW, and the teaching of Aquinas was used more frequently, and less eclectically, in papal encyclicals on social matters and in other types of papal address (e.g. *Rerum Novarum*, 1891; *Quadragesimo Anno*, 1931; Pius XII's radio address on the fiftieth anniversary of *Rerum Novarum* in 1941; and *Humani Generis*, 1950). Neo-Thomist political thought also formed an integral part of the *Cursus Thomisticus*, formerly the central component of theological education in Catholic universities and seminaries. Neo-Thomism's influential position was sharply diminished by the revision of theological education after the Second Vatican Council.

Originally, the attempt to construct a systematic Neo-Thomist political theory was mainly the work of Thomas Meyer (1821–1913) and Victor Cathrein (1845–1931). Their ideas were later extended, particularly in the German-speaking world, but less as a result of work in medieval studies than in reaction to developments in sociology, law and economics, as well as to political circumstances around the time of the second world war. Writers such as Eberhard Welty (1902–65), Johannes Messner (1891–1984) and Oswald von Nell-Breuning (1890–) added elements which made political Neo-Thomism in some respects not far distant from a type of Christian socialism. But at this time it was especially the 'open Thomism' propounded by Jacques Maritain (1882–1973) which attracted followers in France, England and America. His attempt to evolve a 'Christian philosophy' contained a theory of a 'new form of civilization' and a 'New Christendom' which was based on a 'theocentric integral humanism' and which cannot unambiguously be classed with mainstream Neo-Thomism. Maritain urged the founding of a new, 'social' society to succeed bourgeois capitalism. This was to aim at bringing about a freedom which entailed a fulfilment analogous to that enjoyed by those united with God in the 'beatific vision'. Such a society was to be pluralistic and democratic, to guarantee personal liberty and the right to work, and to embrace Christians and non-Christians in brotherly friendship.

After the second world war the motto 'The Third Way' was used by Neo-Thomist groups espousing a political theory which was intended to be neither neo-Marxist nor neo-socialist but pluralist and democratic, with the notion of an order based on Natural Law as its central ingredient. This direction is pursued by, among others, Arthur Fridolin Utz (1908–) of the Fribourg Neo-Thomist school, which is closer to the Thomism of the Schools than Maritain's theories were. Some basic principles of Neo-Thomism also survived, though mostly without explicit reference to Aquinas, in the social encyclicals of Pope John XXIII (*Mater et Magistra*, 1961; *Pacem in Terris*, 1963); of Pope Paul VI (*Populorum Progressio*, 1967); and of Pope John Paul II (*Laborem Exercens*, 1981), as well as in the Second Vatican Council promulgation *Gaudium et Spes* (1965).

Neo-Thomist political thought also influenced the theological basis of the Catholic social movements which developed in Britain, Europe and the Americas around the beginning of the twentieth century. In Britain its influence was felt not only through the Catholic Social Guild following in the steps of Charles Plater (1875–1921), but also in the aims of the Distributist League, founded in 1926. Figures associated with Distributism such as G. K. Chesterton (1874–1936) and Vincent McNabb (1868–1943) displayed attitudes characteristic of political Neo-Thomism, for example in urging rejection of the moral and practical shoddiness of industrialism from the standpoint of an ethically-grounded politics.

Nonetheless, in so far as political Neo-Thomism derives the goal and rationale of society from a view of Nature as unchanging Creation, it can hardly avoid an essentialism which treats history as merely accidental to man's social and rational nature. This somewhat formal point of view means that political Neo-Thomism is in danger of becoming a collection of very open statements whose binding application to concrete cases is problematic.   MHW

Reading

Gilby, T.: *Between Community and Society: a Philosophy and Theology of the State.* London, New York and Toronto: Longmans Green, 1953.

Maritain, J.: *Humanisme intégral.* Paris: Aubier, 1936.

————: *La Personne et le bien commun.* Paris: Desclée et Brouwer, 1947.

————: *Man and the State.* Chicago: University of Chicago Press, 1951.

Nell-Breuning, O. von : *Gerechtigkeit und Freiheit: Grundzüge katholischer Soziallehre.* Vienna: Europa, 1980.

Utz, A.F. *et al.* eds: *Bibliographie der Sozialethik.* Freiburg/Br.: Herder, 1959–80.

————: *Die katholische Sozialdoktrin in ihrer geschichtlichen Entfaltung: eine Sammlung päpstlicher Dokumente vom 15. Jahrhundert bis in die Gegenwart (Originaltexte mit Übersetzung).* Aachen: Hanstein, 1976.

Welty, E.: *A Handbook of Christian Social Ethics,* trans. G. Kirstein. Edinburgh and London: Nelson, 1960–4.

Thoreau, Henry David (1817–1862) American radical. Born at Concord, Massachusetts, Thoreau is associated with the New England Transcendentalists, mostly closely with Emerson. The eclectic Thoreau incorporated into his writings Greek and Latin classics, oriental scriptures, American Indian lore, and his observations as a surveyor and naturalist of the region. Thoreau was not a systematic thinker, and his published writings often reflect their origin as journal entries and lectures.

The unifying element of Thoreau's thought is radical individualism. He expressed it variously: romantically in terms of the spontaneity and uniqueness of natural phenomena; politically in terms of consent to government; and in terms of conscience and material self-sufficiency. Thoreau's individualism propelled him in two directions.

One direction was apolitical. *Walden* (1854), written after Thoreau's two-year experiment in living at Walden Pond, is an account of solitary immersion in nature and literary creation. It is a personal declaration of independence from the rules and institutions of a philistine society. Individualism means self-sufficiency, quietism, and detachment.

Thoreau's radical individualism also led in the direction of 'action from principle', political engagement, and resistance to authority. In 'Civil Disobedience' (1849) Thoreau prescribes noncomplicity in the evils of slavery and a determination to stand aloof from responsibility for 'the smooth working of their machinery' (see CIVIL DISOBEDIENCE). His claim that 'the only obligation I have a right to assume is to do at any time what I think right' has a basis both in conscience and in the principle of CONSENT; Thoreau speaks as both man and democratic citizen. Together with Thoreau's other reform papers, the essay contributes to the literature on the origin and limits of obligation. It raises larger questions about what societies we can be said to have joined and what constitutes membership in a political community. It also contributes to discussions of how much withdrawal to private life, and how much conscientious objection, democracy ought to tolerate.

In Thoreau's political vision the two stances – quietist withdrawal and action from principle – are reconciled. Thoreau sees detachment less as an ideal than as a powerful form of social criticism. He represents self-perfection as a way of 'casting one's whole influence' that goes beyond voting or collective political action and that spurs reform. He imagines liberal democracy not as a commercial or legalistic society but as an arena for the self-affirmation of heroic individualists.   NLR

Reading

Cavell, S.: *The Senses of Walden.* New York: Viking, 1972.

Harding, W. and Meyer, M.: *The New Thoreau Handbook.* New York: SUNY Press, 1980.

†Rosenblum, N.L.: Thoreau's militant conscience. *Political Theory* 9 (1981) 81–110.

Thoreau, H.D.: *Walden*. Princeton, NJ: Princeton University Press, 1971.

———: *Reform Papers*. Princeton, NJ: Princeton University Press, 1973. [Includes 'Civil Disobedience'.]

Tocqueville, Alexis de (1805–1859) French political theorist, sociologist and historian. Tocqueville was born into a royalist aristocratic family. His father, who had narrowly escaped execution by the Jacobins, served as a prefect under the Restoration Monarchy and Alexis himself, unsurprisingly, entered government service in 1827. The July Revolution of 1830 found him torn between sentiment and reason; given his family loyalties, he was loath to swear allegiance to the new Orleanist monarchy, but believed a Bourbon restoration to be impossible. In this dilemma he seized on the idea of visiting the United States accompanied by his friend, Gustave de Beaumont. The ostensible purpose of the journey, from spring 1831 into 1832, was to study the American penal system, and the two friends jointly published *Du système pénitentiaire aux États-Unis et de son application en France* in 1833. They both, however, had other and wider purposes, Beaumont's resulting in his novel *Marie* and Tocqueville's in his monumental *De la démocratie en Amérique* which appeared in two parts in 1835 and 1840. This quickly won him national and international renown. It was soon translated and published in America, England and Germany; and, after the appearance of the second part, he was elected to membership of the *Académie française*.

Tocqueville left government service soon after his return from America, turning to politics later in the decade. In 1839 he was elected as deputy for his home district of Valogner in Normandy and remained in the Chamber until 1848. Although active as a deputy he achieved no political prominence, partly because he was no orator, but partly also because he held to a political position between the Guizot administration and the opposition, which he saw as independent but others saw as ambiguous. He played a larger role in the politics of the Second Republic. After the February Revolution of 1848 he was elected to the Constituent Assembly, serving on the commission which drew up the republican constitution. He was elected to the new Legislative Assembly in 1849, became its vice-president and was briefly, from June to October 1849, minister for foreign affairs. His political career ended with Louis Napoleon's coup d'état, to which he was bitterly and vociferously opposed. The rest of his life he devoted to a plan he had long been pondering, a history of the Revolution and Empire which would investigate the ideological and social currents underlying the political narrative. In the event, he completed only a study of the eighteenth-century background to the Revolution, published in 1856 as *L'Ancien régime et la révolution*.

Despite the apparently different concerns and methods of Tocqueville's two major works, despite the gap in time between them, and despite the vicissitudes of his political life, there was a continuity in his ideas and a clear link between those ideas and his political endeavours. His studies both of America and of French history attempted to discuss and describe the emergence and effects of what he termed DEMOCRACY. However, these studies had, for him, a sharp practical edge; they were intended to point to what was politically necessary if liberty, threatened as he saw it by the emergence of democracy, was to be preserved. Both his intellectual and his political life were given coherence by this belief in the unity of theory and practice and by his ardent desire to use his theory to safeguard what was to him 'a *sacred* thing', liberty.

What then did he understand by democracy? What dangers did it pose in the modern world? And what action was needed to counter these dangers?

He gave two meanings to the term 'democracy'. In a political context, he used it to refer to a representative system based on an extended franchise; but, more commonly and more significantly, he was referring to social democracy, by which he meant a society in which equality was widely accepted as a primary social value. In this latter context, his analysis of democracy examined how such a commitment to equality might affect general social attitudes. He summed up these effects in the term 'INDIVIDUALISM', an idea to which, unlike most liberal thinkers, he gave a pejorative flavour. He pointed to two major aspects of this individualist character of democratic society – a faith in individual reason as the sole basis of opinion and belief, and a self-centred, self-interested concentration on personal ends.

Rebellion against intellectual authority and an assertion of the powers of individual reason he took to be the natural democratic stance. At the philosophic level this had been exhibited in the Cartesian revolution. At the level of social-attitudes he saw the same position as central to American mores, which embraced a Cartesian philosophy in a society where Descartes was unknown. In democratic America, he perceived unargued general assumptions that all ideas, however eminent those urging them or however sanctified by tradition, should be put to the test of individual reason, and that everyone had the capacity to impose such tests. These assumptions resulted in a peculiarly democratic cast of character, the belief in intellectual equality leading to a high notion of individual worth and dignity. They led also to a peculiar cast of thought, an attraction to general, abstract and comprehensive explanations of human affairs which, demanding little individual knowledge or judgment, were available to all.

The other aspect of democratic individualism was a pervasive egoism, a widespread tendency to withdraw from public concerns and to concentrate on the material welfare of the family as the final purpose in life. This egoism manifested itself partly in heightened personal ambition and competitiveness. In a society where the race for power and possession was open (or thought to be open) to all, and failure could not be ascribed to disadvantages of birth, the contest was inevitably bitterly fought. The ideological outcome was approval of equality of opportunity, but resentment of the success of others since this seemed to demonstrate inequality of ability. The egoism was manifested also in a narrow materialism. This essentially middle-class passion for material security (as Tocqueville saw it) was natural in a society in which few were so poor as to abandon hopes of material success and few so securely rich that they could forget the threat of poverty. Materialism and melancholy were, however, inextricably linked; the thirst for possession could never

be wholly quenched, since any achievement was followed by further and more extensive desires.

What were the political implications of these individualist attitudes? At the most general level, Tocqueville believed that they could constitute a threat to individual liberty, since they could encourage subservience to public opinion and the extension and centralization of state power.

Democratic ideology stressed the intellectual independence of the individual. Nevertheless, every society needed some intellectual authority, some source of unity, and democratic society found it in public opinion, the 'tyranny of the majority'. This conformity to generally-held attitudes and standards was partly the result of the imposition of social sanctions. When Tocqueville asked the question – natural to a Frenchman – why there were no atheists to be found in America, the answer was generally that professed atheists would not get jobs or customers. But there were, he thought, deeper psychological roots. Every individual assumed himself to be the intellectual peer of everyone else, but, when faced with the opinion of the majority of his equals, he felt powerless. If everyone was to count as one, and no one could claim a unique purchase on truth, the majority must be right. In this way, conformist norms were internalized and the individual himself came to believe that a dissenting position must be a wrong one. Whatever the political uses made of it, this conformist attitude was in itself a curtailment of individual autonomy.

A more direct threat to liberty lay in the likelihood that individualist attitudes would lead to the extension of the power of central government. The democratic attack upon privileges, the feudal liberties of individuals, groups and corporations, was inevitably conducted through the state and resulted in the disappearance of centres of power independent of central government. The general desire for equal, uniform treatment, and the consequent impatience with regional differences, led similarly to centralization, a 'democratic instinct' according to Tocqueville. The egoistic character of the society could further this process. Addiction to private benefits and apathy towards public responsibilities could lead to a willingness to leave politics to the politicians, at

519

any rate so long as they assured stability and order. Above all, the atomization of society that could follow from individualist attitudes might create a situation in which the state was the sole originator of social organization and initiator of collective action.

The possible consequence was 'a new kind of despotism'. It would be new because it would involve not tyranny and oppression, but an intrusive benevolence welcomed by individuals too afraid of public opinion to object, too engrossed in private concerns to participate in public activity, too aware of the economic value of order to threaten disorder. Such a system would weaken not only liberty but the will to liberty.

These were the political dangers of social democracy, but they were dangers that could be countered. Tocqueville has been pictured as a thinker concerned to sketch an inevitable future, and certainly he believed the trend towards social democracy, whose lineaments he had glimpsed in America, to be an inescapable part of the European future. Nevertheless, he was always a vigorous opponent of theories of historical inevitability, and the purpose of his analysis of social democracy was not just to uncover the constraints on political action which the new society would impose but to determine the alternative political possibilities it offered. Against the possibility of a new kind of despotism he balanced the possibility of a new system of democratic liberty.

All Tocqueville's institutional recommendations were geared towards the realization of this latter possibility. In part these recommendations were based on older liberal concerns with constructing checks on government; but they were also directed towards the sustenance of the will to liberty. This awareness of the contribution which the institutional framework could make to civic education is what distinguishes Tocqueville most clearly from earlier liberal thought (see LIBERALISM).

Foremost among Tocqueville's proffered cures for the possible ills of social democracy was political democracy. He saw many weaknesses in representative democracy at the level of central government: it encouraged inconsistency in policy over time, it provided weak political leadership and above all it could

add a formal political weight to the power of public opinion. As against this, it had considerable educational value: it drew men into political life, promoted awareness and discussion of public issues and nurtured a habit of involvement which counteracted the disposition to political apathy. Although democracy at the central level might be a necessary condition of democratic liberty, it was certainly not a sufficient one. He was even more vigorous in his advocacy of administrative devolution and local self-government. He saw many administrative advantages of such a system over the centralized administration of France, but again his emphasis was on the opportunity local self-government gave for a more extended participation in political life.

The same hopes informed his defence of intermediate voluntary associations and his pleas for freedom of association. A substitute was needed for the pluralist dispersion of power in aristocratic society and this could be found in a vigorous system of voluntary associations. They could act as counter-weights to state power; they could crystallize and publicize opinions and interests which would otherwise go unheard; they could stimulate collective self-help rather than reliance on state initiatives; above all, they could act as civic schools by drawing people into co-operative ventures, breaking down their social isolation and making them aware of wider social responsibilities. Free political parties were the most important form of voluntary association; and a free press was the most important pre-condition of an effective system of associations.

'A liberal of a new kind' Tocqueville called himself. The claim has justice. His respect for individual liberty was not, of course, new. But his awareness of new threats to it, and the political imagination he showed in suggesting counters to these threats, justify the claim.   JL

Reading
†Brogan, H.: *Tocqueville*. London: Fontana, 1973.
Drescher, S.: *Tocqueville and England*. Cambridge, Mass.: Harvard University Press, 1964.
———: *Dilemmas of Democracy: Tocqueville and Modernization*. Pittsburgh: Pittsburgh University Press, 1965.
Herr, R.: *Tocqueville and the Old Regime*. Princeton, NJ: Princeton University Press, 1962.

†Lively, J.: *The Social and Political Thought of Alexis de Tocqueville*. Oxford: Clarendon Press, 1962.

Poggi, G.: *Images of Society: essays on the sociological theories of Tocqueville, Marx and Durkheim*. London: Oxford University Press, 1972.

Tocqueville, A. de: *Democracy in America*, trans. G. Lawrence, ed. J.P. Mayer and M. Lerner. New York: Harper, 1966; London: Fontana, 1968.

———: *L'Ancien régime*, trans. M.W. Patterson. Oxford: Blackwell, 1947.

†Zetterbaum, M.: *Tocqueville and the Problem of Democracy*. Stanford, Calif.: Stanford University Press, 1967.

toleration The deliberate choice not to prohibit, hinder or interfere with conduct of which one disapproves, where one has both the requisite power and knowledge. Toleration is predicable of individuals, institutions and societies. Disapproval may be either moral or non-moral (dislike). When an action or practice is morally disapproved, its toleration is usually thought to be especially problematic or even paradoxical: toleration may seem to require that it is right to allow that which is wrong. Where the power to interfere with disapproved conduct is absent a disposition to tolerate may still be distinguishable from mere acquiescence. However, non-interference which is simply the result of ignorance concerning the occurrence of disapproved conduct is not toleration.

There is some unavoidable vagueness about how intrusive or restrictive interference with disapproved conduct may be while remaining consistent with toleration. At one extreme, the mere attempt to dissuade an agent by rational argument from engaging in disapproved conduct is fully consistent with tolerating the agent's engagement in that conduct. At the other extreme, physical coercion of an agent or the legal prohibition of an action clearly are not. The extent to which the imposition of costs such as informal social ostracism, taxation of disapproved conduct and other forms of disincentive short of coercion or prohibition are consistent with toleration is often a matter of circumstance and context. Obviously the more such disincentives incline towards prohibition or coercion the less they are consistent with toleration. Toleration is often a matter of degree, requiring fine judgments which allow room for some disagreement.

It is arguable whether refusal to interfere with disapproved conduct only because of the narrowly prudential or self-interested costs of interference should be properly understood as toleration, since it does not issue from any commitment to the value of toleration as such. At root, this dispute concerns whether toleration should be understood as a morally neutral descriptive concept or as a moral ideal. Both uses are to some extent sanctioned by ordinary language and political discourse. In political theory toleration understood as a moral ideal has usually been of most interest, especially within the tradition of LIBERALISM. In practical political life, however, narrowly prudential and self-interested arguments for toleration have often been the most effective. Within both CONSERVATISM and SOCIALISM, in so far as toleration has a place, it is generally understood in these terms.

Toleration contrasts with a range of negatives including intolerance, indulgence and indifference. Intolerance is the deliberate attempt to eliminate disapproved conduct by coercive means, usually vigorously, perhaps even ruthlessly (persecution). Indulgence, on the other hand, may be viewed as an excess of toleration. Indifference contrasts with toleration because here the conduct permitted is neither approved nor disapproved, and whereas indifference suggests mere passivity toleration implies active restraint. From the perspective of those who value it, toleration can be seen as a mean between intolerance, the refusal to tolerate what should be tolerated, and indulgence, the toleration of that which should not be tolerated, without succumbing to indifference, the refusal to judge that which should be judged. Much dispute about toleration has concerned its proper scope and limits. This, in turn, has usually been related to differing accounts of the moral basis or justification of toleration. Thus, for example, narrowly prudential or self-interested justifications set the limits of toleration at what, in the given circumstances, prudence or self-interest requires. Accounts of toleration that try to justify it in terms of a moral theory or principle, however, are more interesting.

Among the most influential moral arguments advanced in support of toleration are those that invoke the principles of utility, neutrality and respect for persons. Utilitarian justifications of toleration are not always easily distinguishable from prudential or self-interested arguments since UTILITARIANISM is inclined to understand morality just as a kind of collective prudence. Utilitarian defences of toleration claim that its benefits in terms of the maximization of happiness, welfare or whatever interpretation of utility is preferred, will in general outweigh the harms similarly construed. The limits of toleration should be set at the point where its benefits cease to outweigh its harms. As with all utilitarian justifications, however, this defence of toleration is unavoidably conditional upon the truth of a large number of disputable and historically and culturally variable empirical claims. For this reason utilitarianism provides a rather precarious and uncertain justification of toleration, heavily dependent upon contingent social circumstances. Although some utilitarians, notably J. S. MILL, have been among the most passionate advocates of toleration, others, such as Mill's contemporary J. F. Stephen, have been conspicuously intolerant. Indeed utilitarians will have most difficulty in justifying toleration where it is most needed; that is in a community with an intensely intolerant majority.

The principles of neutrality and respect for persons have both been strongly favoured by liberals. The principle of neutrality has been particularly prominent in recent liberal theorizing about the proper role of the state. This principle requires that the state should be in some sense neutral between the various conceptions of the good held and acted upon by its citizens. The state should neither prescribe nor proscribe any particular moral or religious view and should be equally tolerant of different ways of life. Various interpretations of this principle have been suggested, but it has proved difficult to formulate it in a way which is determinate about both the limits and requirements of toleration. More seriously, the principle of neutrality seems less an argument for toleration than a mere restatement of its desirability. Often underlying the principle of neutrality is some form of moral scepticism or relativism, but it is not clear that either of these doctrines necessarily supports toleration. For example,

the view that one way of life is as good as another, though quite compatible with a policy of toleration, is also consistent with the intolerant imposition of one way of life on everyone.

The principle of respect for persons does, however, offer a reason why it may be wrong to interfere with the free choices of another person. This principle, which has its roots in the moral philosophy of KANT, maintains that persons' moral choices express their nature as autonomous and rational agents. Respect for persons as autonomous and rational agents, therefore, requires toleration of their self-chosen actions. The limits of toleration are established by the principle itself since choices that do not exhibit respect for persons should not be tolerated. A serious problem with this principle is its vagueness. Concepts such as autonomy and RATIONALITY are crucial to the principle, yet they admit of many different interpretations and if they are understood very narrowly the scope for toleration may be severely restricted. For example, feminist arguments that pornography is degrading to women often invoke a version of the principle of respect for persons to deny that pornography should be tolerated. However, despite these difficulties, some version of the principle of respect for persons seems the most promising line of justification among currently favoured alternatives.

Historically the idea of toleration was associated primarily with religious practices and beliefs and emerged, as an idea of major significance, in the Europe of the Reformation, divided by fierce religious controversies and struggles. Many political theorists of the sixteenth and seventeenth centuries developed arguments for religious toleration; these included BODIN, ALTHUSIUS, MILTON and SPINOZA. But probably the most famous argument is LOCKE's *Letter Concerning Toleration* (1689). Among Locke's principal arguments was the claim that religious belief, because it requires conscientious assent, cannot be subjected to effective external coercion; also the contention that the proper function of the state was to maintain public order and security and that therefore religious intolerance was justified only when necessary to achieve that end. Gradually, the scope of the idea of toleration broadened to include other areas of civil and moral controversy. The ENLIGHTEN-MENT and the theory and practice of the US Constitution were important influences behind J. S. Mill's *On Liberty* (1859), perhaps the most sustained and eloquent plea for toleration yet written. In this work Mill argued that wide-spread toleration is essential to both social and scientific progress and the moral and spiritual development of the individual.

Toleration has never been short of critics or detractors. While the objections have shown some variety they have usually rested, in the last resort, on the claim that to tolerate morally disapproved conduct is effectively to condone it. Often there has been a genuine fear that the consequences of toleration will be moral chaos and social disintegration. The main areas of debate in this century have concerned religious belief, sexual practices, political opposition, race and, most recently, gender.   JPH

Reading

†Horton, J. and Mendus, S. eds: *Aspects of Toleration: Philosophical Studies*. London: Methuen, 1985.

†Kamen, H.: *The Rise of Toleration*. London: Weidenfield & Nicolson, 1967.

†King, P.: *Toleration*. London: Allen & Unwin, 1976.

Locke, J.: *A Letter Concerning Toleration*, ed. R. Kilbansky, trans. J.W. Gough. Oxford: Clarendon Press, 1968.

Mill, J.S.: *On Liberty*, ed. G. Himmelfarb. Harmondsworth: Penguin, 1974.

Milton, J.: *Areopagitica* (1644). In *John Milton: Selected Prose*, ed. C. Patrides. Harmondsworth: Penguin, 1974.

Wolff, R.P., Marcuse, H. and Moore, B.: *A Critique of Pure Tolerance*. London: Cape, 1969.

Tolstoy, Leo (Lev Nikolayevich) (1828–1910) Russian writer and public figure. From an aristocratic background, Tolstoy briefly attended the University of Kazan; in the 1850s he took part in military action in the Caucasus and the Crimea, and the same decade witnessed his first (autobiographical) published works. The 1860s saw the composition of *War and Peace*, the 1870s of *Anna Karenina*; late in that decade an inner crisis led to a radical reformulation of his attitudes to religion, his work and his public role. His modest country house at Yasnaya Polyana (south of Moscow) became a

focus for numerous disciples; this exacerbated family tensions that led him to leave home in the autumn of 1910, and he died ten days later at Astapovo railway station.

Tolstoy is, of course, best known as the author of the novels *War and Peace* (1868–9), *Anna Karenina* (1875–7) and *Resurrection* (1899), as well as of a large number of short stories and some plays. But he became almost equally famous world wide, particularly in the last years of his life, as a man of ideas. He was immensely prolific, not only in belles-lettres: half his ninety volumes of collected works consists of diaries and correspondence. It is hard if not impossible to distinguish between the 'literary' Tolstoy and Tolstoy the publicist, the historian, the educator, the moralist, the theoretician of art, the agricultural and social reformer, the founder of a religion; nor would he have wished it otherwise, intending as he did (however frustratedly) that all his activity should be part of a coherent and morally justifiable pattern. Populism and aristocratism met in his nature: he had little tolerance either for the bourgeoisie or for intellectuals.

Tolstoy's publicistic and didactic role long antedates the 'conversion' he underwent at around fifty, though it increased, indeed took over his life, thereafter. Readers of *War and Peace* were in the main disconcerted to find the novel used as a vehicle for, and illustration of, a theory of history that is explicitly set out at various points and occupies its whole closing section; almost as obtrusive is the theorizing on rural topics in *Anna Karenina*. The historical theory seeks to devalue the role and the scope for free action of supposed 'great men'; within the peasantry, by contrast, lies an unforced comprehension of the way things really happen and of how life should properly be lived. For Tolstoy corruption lurked everywhere in the urban, moneyed, and educated world; supposed experts in all walks of life were charlatans; justice was a mask for fraud and violence; the state a savage organ of oppression in the interests of the rich. Ultimately he was denouncing such evils with a virulence even few Marxists could match – yet for him neither constructive political activity nor revolutionary violence provided a better way. This could only arise from individual regeneration on the basis of instinctively-experienced religious sensibility, allied with the simple virtues of honest toil.

Though Tolstoy claimed he was 'not a Tolstoyan' (much as the older Marx sometimes distanced himself from 'Marxism') he energetically propagated his own version of Christianity, stripped down to the point of being a new religion. Discarding everything mystical, ritualistic, obscurantist, and hierarchical in church teaching, he extracted from the Gospels what he took to be their ethical core ('resist not evil'; 'judge not, that ye be not judged'). He sympathized with, and assisted, the Dukhobor sectarians. His success was far from negligible – there are still Tolstoyans today, though communes founded to realize his teachings failed to flourish – and his doctrine of nonviolent resistance exercised a direct influence on the young GANDHI, with whom he corresponded.

Tolstoy cannot be called a political thinker in the accepted sense: yet all his historical, religious, aesthetic, and publicistic ideas have a political dimension or socio-political implications. His talent was rather for attacking current evils – war, patriotism, the state, capital punishment, modern science, wealth, idleness, meat-eating, alcohol, and much else – than for realistically delineating the way towards, or features of, a better political and social order. This looks like ANARCHISM, and is often so considered, though Tolstoy himself would have resisted the description; there is also something patriarchal and primitivistic about his peasant-based vision of the good society. Characteristically his positive messages were rousing but imprecise: ' . . . you must not do what the Tsar, Governor, police-officers, Duma or some political party demand of you, but what is natural to you as a man, what is demanded of you by that Power which sent you into the world . . .' (*What's To Be Done?*, 1902). His chief positive ideal was that of 'brotherliness': N. Fyodorov, the utopian philosopher, was one of the rare major influences upon him here. Even more pervasive was the influence of ROUSSEAU, all aspects of whose achievement were in varying ways important to him, and who early fired his educational activities in his peasant school at Yasnaya Polyana.

Tolstoy's publicistic articles often seem overbearing, destructive, naive, or plain cranky; yet they seldom lack authority, crispness of argument, and a striking freshness of perception (the 'defamiliarization' so memorably employed in his fiction). He made a virtue of simply-expressed arguments from first principles, eschewing appeals to authority. To no work are these comments more applicable than to the book-length essay *What is Art?* (1898), in which most of his main ideological concerns come together. The 'infectious' power of the arts renders them of supreme importance in constructing human brotherhood; yet 'false art' – exploitative, unnatural, impure, untruthful, pretentious – is everywhere: even his own works do not escape his condemnation. Yet, as always with Tolstoy, even at his most provocative or prophetic his appeal is to good sense, to utility, and to lived experience; this strange figure seems at home not with the Russian intelligentsia, not with the nineteenth century of which he was an intellectual luminary, but with the later part of the eighteenth – with the age of Rousseau, Diderot, and Voltaire.   RRM-G

Reading

†Berlin, I.: *The Hedgehog and the Fox: an essay on Tolstoy's view of history.* London: Weidenfeld & Nicolson, 1967.

†Gifford, H.: *Tolstoy.* Oxford: Oxford University Press, 1982.

—— ed.: *Leo Tolstoy.* Penguin Critical Anthologies. Harmondsworth: Penguin, 1971.

†Jones, M.E. ed: *New Essays on Tolstoy.* Cambridge: Cambridge University Press, 1978. [Note particularly essays by Lampert, Greenwood and Seeley.]

Maude, A. ed.: *Tolstoy on Art.* Boston: Small, Maynard, 1924. [Includes the approved English edn of *What is Art?*]

Shklovsky, V.: *Lev Tolstoy.* Moscow: Progress Publishers, 1978.

Tolstoy, L.: *Tolstoy Centenary Edition,* trans. L. and A. Maude. 21 vols. Oxford: Oxford University Press, 1928–37.

——: *Recollections and Essays,* trans. and intro. A. Maude. Oxford: Oxford University Press, 1937. [Includes *Thou Shalt not Kill, Bethink Yourselves!, A Great Iniquity, What's To Be Done?, I Cannot Be Silent, Gandhi Letters.*]

Walicki, A.: *A History of Russian Thought,* ch. 15. Oxford: Clarendon Press, 1980.

totalitarianism   A modern concept, although

it has been used to refer to ancient as well as modern regimes. The first edition of the *Encyclopedia of the Social Sciences* (1933) did not include the term, and the *Oxford English Dictionary* takes its first citation from the *Contemporary Review* of April 1928. The word had enough popular currency by the second world war to crop up in films such as Gabriel Pascal's screen version of Shaw's *Major Barbara*, and in *Above Suspicion*, where Joan Crawford refers to a Nazi torture procedure as a 'totalitarian manicure'.

Early usage following the war suggested an attempt to improve on traditional classificatory schemes based on terms like dictatorship, DESPOTISM and tyranny. The primary aim was to offer a generic term for regimes of the left and right that were thought to have much more in common than might be indicated by the traditional ideological polarization of COMMUNISM and FASCISM. 'Totalistic' features of the Stalinist state were assimilated to similar features of the Nazi state in a fashion that permitted the criticism of erstwhile wartime enemies to be applied to erstwhile wartime allies who had become enemies in the new cold war. Karl POPPER employed a radical critique of Plato, Hegel and Marx to indict what he called 'utopian social engineering' in modern 'totalitarian' regimes in Germany and Russia – a procedure reproduced in recent times by André Glucksman, Bernard Henri-Lévy and other European 'new philosophers' disappointed with Marxism's twentieth-century incarnations in the Soviet Union and elsewhere. Popper, in fact, set the tone from the outset for the ideological use of the idea of totalitarianism, which would become a significant weapon in the West's arsenal of political rhetoric.

Although they were hardly immune to ideology, social scientists nevertheless took up the term and tried to endow it with significance as a value-neutral indicator of regime attributes. In contrast to Hannah ARENDT's pathbreaking analysis, which focused on 'total terror' as the essence of totalitarianism, students of comparative government such as Friedrich and Brzezinski gave the term a phenomenological definition, embracing features such as a totalist ideology, a single party

state, a secret police hegemony and a governmental monopoly over the economic, cultural and information structures of society. Running through these several features was the idea of totalitarianism as a form of regime that, in the description of Eckstein and Apter, 'annihilates all boundaries between the state and the groupings of society, even the state and individual personality' (p. 434). By the early 1970s, cross-polity survey research had uncritically absorbed the term as a standard indicator of comparison.

The term came under increasing conceptual criticism during this period (see Barber, for example), but continued to be employed as a standard tool by comparativists. Perhaps more importantly, it continued to be a weapon of conceptual-ideological warfare. In 1976, Jean-François Revel published *The Totalitarian Temptation*, combining arguments drawn from earlier work on the psychology of 'totalism', with a passionate indictment of Stalinism. The decoupling of Marxist totalitarian regimes of the left from their fascist cousins continued in Jeanne Kirkpatrick's celebrated *Commentary* essay 'Dictatorships and double standards' in which she asserted that 'authoritarian' regimes (on the right) which were allies of the West were distinct from (better than) 'totalitarian' regimes (on the left), mainly because authoritarian systems were putatively susceptible to incremental democratization – a disposition for which their enmity to communism served as the predominant piece of evidence.

The Reagan administration, which Kirkpatrick was eventually to serve, abandoned use of the term totalitarian to describe tyrannical allies, but extended it to include a variety of vaguely leftist adversaries – for example, the Sandinista regime in Nicaragua, which in 1984 was labelled a 'communist totalitarian state'. Ironically therefore, what began as a description of fascism, and gained respectability as a bridge concept to link rightist and leftist forms of modern centralist authoritarianism, has ended up as a description of communism. The evolution of the concept would thus seem to reveal more about the history of postwar ideology than about the study of comparative political regimes.

This is evident from the conceptual confusion that continues to cloud the term. Even the more impartial theorists of the notion disagree fundamentally about its relationship to ideas such as DEMOCRACY, modernity and POLITICS. Wolfe, Moore and Friedrich have, for example, insisted that totalitarianism is to be contrasted with democratic forms of government; but Talmon and others insist with equal vigour that totalitarianism is itself a particularly virulent form of democracy, equating it with the politics of mass man or mass society, and suggesting that 'most of the requisites of mass democracy are also requisites of totalitarianism' (Eckstein and Apter, p. 437).

Similarly, it has been asserted both that totalitarianism refers to a form of regime unique to modern industrial society (Eckstein and Apter) and that it is a form whose 'basic conception . . . arose prior to industrialism and independently of industrialism' (Moore, p. 74). There has also been disagreement over whether the term refers to a form of government and is therefore pre-eminently political, or to a form of society and is therefore a socio-economic idea.

In the absence of agreement on these issues, it is difficult to determine whether totalitarianism belongs to the debate between liberals (limited state advocates) and democrats (welfare state supporters) about the proper scope of state activity; or to the debate between democrats and authoritarians about the legitimacy of power – about the problem of popular sovereignty.

The confusing history of the idea of totalitarianism would seem to suggest that it is not merely an essentially contested concept on the model of liberty or democracy, or a value-laden normative idea in the fashion of all significant political ideas, but a term the primary meanings and uses of which are exclusively ideological. Having been employed to describe regimes as diverse as those of Nazi Germany, Stalinist Russia, Plato's Republic, the Ch'in Dynasty, fascist Italy, Sandinista Nicaragua, India during the Mauryu Dynasty, the Roman Empire under Diocletian, Geneva under Calvin, Japan under the Meiji, ancient Sparta, and the United States not only in the 1960s but also in the 1840s, the term would appear to lack any useful social scientific meaning. It remains, however, an invaluable clue to the character of cold war ideology and thus to the sociology of knowledge in the postwar era.   BRB

Reading

Arendt, H.: *The Origins of Totalitarianism*, 2nd edn. New York: Meridian, 1958.

Barber, B.R.: Conceptual foundations of totalitarianism. In *Totalitarianism in Perspective*, ed. C.J. Friedrich, M. Curtis and B.R. Barber. New York: Praeger, 1969.

Eckstein, H. and Apter, D. eds: *Comparative Politics*. New York: Free Press of Glencoe, 1963.

†Friedrich, C.J. and Brzezinski, Z.: *Totalitarian Dictatorship and Autocracy*. New York: Praeger, 1967.

Kirkpatrick, J.: Dictatorships and double standards. In *Commentary* 68.5 (1979) 34–45.

Moore, B., Jr: *Political Power and Social Theory*. Cambridge, Mass.: Harvard University Press, 1958.

Popper, K.: *The Open Society and its Enemies*. London: Routledge, 1945.

Revel, J.-F.: *The Totalitarian Temptation*. London: Secker & Warburg, 1976.

†Talmon, J.L.: *The Origins of Totalitarian Democracy*. New York: Praeger, 1961.

Wolfe, B.: *Communist Totalitarianism*. Boston: Beacon, 1956.

tradition In its literal sense, tradition covers everything in our culture that has been handed down, transmitted, from the past. In that encompassing sense, about the only thing not traditional in culture is the manifestly new or the obviously transitory. In common use, though, tradition is reserved for customs, ceremonies, beliefs, and institutions which are not only old but to which we assign a special value in the present. Generally, this is a moral or religious value, but it may be political or educational. In any event, a tradition properly so called is an element of culture that, however old it may be, is valued in the present for functional or ritual reasons.

Tradition acquired most of its current interest in the early nineteenth century. This was the time when the consequences of the two great revolutions, democratic and industrial, appeared to entail the erosion, if not the outright destruction, of many of the oldest parts of the western cultural and social heritage: most notably perhaps extended family, local community, parish, guild, handicraft, and also aristocracy and monarchy. A pregnant distinction emerged in the West between the 'traditional' and the 'modern'. In letters, arts, philosophy, and politics we find vociferous and often influential critics of revolution and reform, indeed of modernity as a category. These were the 'traditionalists' and, by the 1830s, the newly designated 'conservatives' in politics and in cultural matters.

Preoccupation with tradition and the historical past had previously been limited for the most part to antiquarians and sentimentalists. In the nineteenth century, chiefly as part of the whole reaction to natural law individualism, concern with tradition became virtually a staple of the emerging social sciences, especially anthropology, sociology, comparative philology, and folklore. The detailed study of important traditions in the present was seen as the opening of a window to the past.

The word 'tradition' helped to form one of the important typologies of western social thought in the nineteenth and twentieth centuries. Traditional vs. modern took on very clear typological meaning, reaching from politics to the arts. Moreover the particular passage from the first to the second in Western Europe at the end of the eighteenth century was enlarged into a paradigm designed to fit the world, past and present. Thus MAINE's 'status vs. contract', TOCQUEVILLE's 'traditional vs. democratic', MARX's 'feudal vs. bourgeois', Weber's 'traditional vs. rational', and DURKHEIM's 'mechanical vs. organic' may all be seen as rooted conceptually in the West's 'great transformation'.

A dynamics is also involved: the implication that development occurs naturally or normally from the traditional to the modern, and that it is the responsibility of enlightened statesmanship to facilitate this development by every means possible. COMTE, Marx, and Lester Ward all believed implicitly that an irreversible law operated to bring about the conversion everywhere of the traditional society into the modern, variously identified as capitalist, socialist, technological, democratic, individualist, and so on. Insensibly the distinction between traditional and modern acquired an invidious character; what was traditional in the world was inferior and needed help. Most western economists came to assume that modernization was the automatic aspiration and policy-goal of

'traditional' peoples all over the world; western aid to Third World countries has been deeply anchored in this highly ethnocentric typology, nowhere more prominently today than in the World Bank. (See also PROGRESS.)   RN

Reading

Lerner, D.: *The Passing of Traditional Society*. Glencoe, Ill.: Free Press of Glencoe, 1958.

Nisbet, R.: *The Social Bond*. New York: Knopf, 1970.

†Shils, E.: *Tradition*. Chicago: University of Chicago Press, 1981.

Tocqueville, A. de: *Democracy in America*, trans. G. Lawrence, ed. J.P. Mayer and M. Lerner. New York: Harper, 1966; London: Fontana, 1968.

Trotsky, Leon (adopted name of Lev Davidovich Bronstein) (1879–1940) Russian Marxist political thinker and revolutionary. After turning to MARXISM at an early age, Trotsky became involved in revolutionary activities and in 1905 emerged as the most conspicuous leader of the St Petersburg Soviet. Arrested and exiled to Siberia, he escaped and spent the decade before 1917 in Europe. Returning after the February Revolution, Trotsky joined forces with LENIN and the Bolsheviks and together with the former became the leader of the October insurrection and the architect of the revolution that followed. As commissar of foreign affairs he conducted the peace negotiations with the Germans at Brest-Litovsk, and as commissar of war he created and led triumphantly the Red Army during the Civil War. But following Lenin's death in 1924, he found himself isolated and outmanoeuvred in the party and thereafter his downfall was as rapid and spectacular as had been his previous rise to power. In 1929 Trotsky was banished from the Soviet Union and, after wandering from one temporary refuge to another, he finally settled in Mexico in 1937. There in 1940, and probably on the direct instruction of Stalin, he was assassinated.

Trotsky is one of the most dramatic and fascinating figures in twentieth-century revolutionary history. A brilliant orator and organizer, with a flair for the theatrical, he was a charismatic leader during crucial events, though he was largely inept at routine party and political work, and his abrasive, often arrogant,

527

manner, together with an aloof attitude toward lesser men, left him without a political following or base, and vulnerable to the manipulative skills of others. But he was courageous in defeat as well, remaining active and outspoken to the end, and during the 1930s he gathered around himself, and became the voice for, those outside the Soviet Union who, loyal to the ideals of 1917, saw in Stalinism the 'degeneration' of the revolution. But the Trotskyist movement was ineffective and Trotsky's last years were mainly devoted to salvaging what little remained of a once heroic era: if his voice was heard, it was largely as a voice in the wilderness.

Whatever the verdict on his political career and historical role, Trotsky deserves to be remembered as much, if not more, for his political and social ideas in general – he wrote voluminously throughout his life – and for his analysis, in particular, of the phenomenon of socialist revolution in a backward society. Already in 1906 he had formulated a conception of the Russian revolution which rejected the then prevalent view amongst his fellow Marxists that a society such as Russia had first to pass through capitalist development and a bourgeois revolution before contemplating the next, socialist, stage. His conception, which was almost entirely original and became known as the 'theory of the permanent revolution', was based on what he later called the 'law of uneven and combined development'. Societies such as Russia, he argued, while remaining for the most part backward and undeveloped, had nevertheless been penetrated by western influences, they had adopted certain of the most advanced methods of economic production and relations, and these pockets or islands of development had in turn brought into being large urban centres, a substantial proletariat, a westernized intellectual elite and radical forms of political opposition and activism. Concurrently, since industrialization had been imposed from above by the state, the bourgeoisie remained weak and liberalism ineffective. The consequent contradictions in this society – backwardness parallel to, but also in conflict with, modernity – created growing tension and instability and soon pitted the new radical forces against the old regime in a direct confrontation which could only be resolved through a virtually

sudden leap into the post-capitalist socialist era. But Trotsky was only too well aware that the large peasant population, interested at best only in the acquisition of land, would not follow the workers on their radical path. He postulated the outbreak of a general revolutionary conflagration in Europe and concluded that if this were to take place, a workers' government in Russia would be able to rely on support from outside to carry out further economic change and overcome the reactionary tendencies amongst the peasantry. In this way, he believed, 'unevenness of development' would culminate in 'combined development', i.e. the conjoining of two historical stages of social and economic development.

The events of 1917 confirmed, in Trotsky's view, the fundamental validity of his theoretical analysis – to which Lenin himself, originally sceptical, subsequently gave some credit. But the European revolution did not, of course, materialize and thereafter Trotsky was more and more inclined to blame Stalin's doctrine of 'socialism in one country' for that failure, since the aim of the doctrine was to abandon both world revolution and an international socialist orientation, giving priority instead to exclusively internal Soviet objectives (see SOVIET COMMUNISM). In numerous writings during the 1930s Trotsky analysed Stalinism, alternatively and sometimes concurrently, as 'Bonapartism', 'Thermidor', bureaucratic collectivism, or as simply a 'betrayal', or even the aberration of a deranged mind. None of this was very convincing, as Trotsky's confused, sometimes contradictory, categories of analysis testify; and he hardly knew what to make of the fact that Stalin was in the meantime carrying out a total transformation of Soviet society – though he contributed as much as anyone to the unmasking and exposure of the unprecedented dimensions of Stalin's horrors, or 'crimes' as he called them.

The difficulty of Trotsky's position – both theoretical and political – lay in his continued support for the achievements of the October Revolution, despite Stalin; and, most significantly, in his refusal to acknowledge any possible relationship between what had emerged under Stalin and the original Leninist-Bolshevik conception of party and politics, claiming to the end that the two were unrelated. Ironically, it was Trotsky himself who had initially (as far back as 1903) denounced Bolshevism as a formula for a 'dictatorship *over* the proletariat', and Lenin personally as a Robespierre-like conspirator plotting to undermine the democratic socialist movement in Russia. In fact, these early writings, which had led to a complete break with Lenin in the period 1903–17, are to this day the best analysis of the relationship between backwardness and Bolshevism, or of what would now be described as the structural phenomenon whereby the paucity of social institutions gives rise to the autonomous domination of politics and the state over society. Following his reconciliation with Lenin in 1917, Trotsky never again raised what he had so forthrightly perceived and analysed long before. In view of his political constraints in the 1920s and 1930s this may be understandable; but in the process he had failed to grasp the extent to which his theory of permanent revolution had become dependent on Bolshevism and thereby, perhaps, an unwitting accessory to Stalinism.

Nevertheless, Trotsky's analysis of the sociology and politics of backwardness, of the manifold possibilities that a particular historical evolution offered, and of the dynamics of revolutionary change, transformed significantly the relevance of Marxism in the twentieth century: from a theory originally intended for understanding the future of European capitalism to one far more pertinent to non-European, 'undeveloped' societies, as subsequent history was partly at least to demonstrate. A new kind of COLLECTIVISM had come into being under the banner of Marxism in the pre-capitalist world, though it had little to do with the kind of society that Trotsky had envisaged. He was more successful than anyone in explaining its historical logic, even if his own personal fate best symbolizes the limits of his political thought as well as the limited character of that collectivism.   BK

Reading

†Day, R.: *Leon Trotsky and the Politics of Economic Isolation*. Cambridge: Cambridge University Press, 1973.

†Deutscher, I.: *The Prophet Armed, The Prophet Unarmed, The Prophet Outcast*. 3 vols. London: Oxford University Press, 1954, 1959, 1963.

Howe, I.: *The Basic Writings of Trotsky*. London: Secker & Warburg, 1964.

†Knei-Paz, B.: *The Social and Political Thought of Leon Trotsky*. Oxford: Oxford University Press, 1978.

†Kolakowski, L.: *Main Currents in Marxism*, vol. III. Oxford: Oxford University Press, 1978.

Trotsky, L.: *Terrorism and Communism* (1920), trans. M. Shachtman. Ann Arbor: University of Michigan Press, 1961.

———: *The History of the Russian Revolution* (1932–3), trans. M. Eastman. London: Gollancz, 1965.

———: *The Permanent Revolution* and *Results and Prospects*, trans. J.G. Wright; rev. B. Pearce. London: New Park, 1962.

———: *My Life*, trans. M. Eastman. Harmondsworth: Penguin, 1975.

———: *The Revolution Betrayed*, trans. M. Eastman. London: Faber & Faber, 1937.

Trotskyism A variant of MARXISM, deriving largely from the writings of TROTSKY and especially from his later writings critical of Stalinism in the Soviet Union. It retains the original Marxist commitment to a workers' revolution, but refuses to see the Soviet Union or the regimes of Eastern Europe as authentic embodiments of socialism. Some Trotskyists remain faithful to Trotsky's original description of the Soviet Union as a degenerate workers' state; others characterize the regime more radically as one of STATE CAPITALISM.   DLM

Tucker, Benjamin R. (1854–1939) American anarchist. A publisher and journalist, Tucker became the foremost exponent in his period of individualist ANARCHISM.

Turgot, Anne-Robert-Jacques (1727–1781) French economist. Turgot was influenced by the general ideas of the FRENCH ENLIGHTENMENT and especially by the economic doctrines of PHYSIOCRACY. From the latter stemmed his commitment to an economic policy of LAISSEZ-FAIRE, which he tried to implement (unsuccessfully) during his brief period as comptroller-general to Louis XVI. His best-known work is *Reflections on the Formation and Distribution of Riches* (1766).   DLM

tyranny See DESPOTISM.

U

utilitarianism The name of that tradition in ethical theory that, either directly or indirectly, assesses the rightness of acts, policies, decisions, and choices by their tendency to promote the happiness of those affected by them. It is associated with the names of Jeremy BENTHAM and John Stuart MILL, more recently with those of Henry SIDGWICK and G. E. Moore, and, more recently still, with those of J. J. C. Smart and R. M. Hare. Since the days of Bentham and Mill, it has never ceased to occupy a central place in moral theorizing; and today, as a result of the widespread growth of applied ethics, in every area of which it underpins one of the contending positions, it has come to have significant impact upon the moral thinking of many laymen.

Bentham held that acts are right if they tend to promote happiness and wrong if they tend to produce the reverse of happiness, and that happiness is to be understood as pleasure and unhappiness as pain or the absence of pleasure. Pleasures and pains were to be assessed or weighed by means of a felicific calculus (for example, by their intensity, duration, and propinquity) that enabled units or values of pleasures and pains to be assigned and to be summed. This calculus was person-neutral, capable of being applied to the different pleasures of different people, as well as intensity-sensitive, capable of capturing the different levels of pleasures of different people. Extent, or the total number of persons affected by the act, was an important part of the calculus. Rightness was determined, therefore, by summing the units or values of the different pleasures and pains produced in the different people affected by the act: an act was right if it

produced a net balance of pleasure over pain. The overall aim was to maximize pleasure, that is, to produce the greatest net balance of pleasure over pain for the collectivity of those affected. The formula 'the greatest happiness of the greatest number' came to express this aim, and the circle of social, political, and legal reformers that had gathered around Bentham carried this formula for change into society (see PHILOSOPHIC RADICALISM).

In spite of some reservations, John Stuart Mill accepted Bentham's general position, including Bentham's hedonism and his view that our actions are motivated entirely by pleasure and pain. Mill wanted, however, to distinguish qualities, as well as quantities, of pleasures and to speak of higher and lower pleasures; and this poses difficulties. For it is unclear whether a distinction between qualities of pleasures can be sustained (along the lines that pleasure is pleasure, though what causes it can vary) and whether such a distinction lends itself to a calculus that enables units or values to be assigned to pleasures and so for pleasures to be summed and compared, interpersonally.

The classical utilitarianism of Bentham and Mill is a form of act-utilitarianism (doubts have occasionally been expressed about this interpretation of Mill), and this type of utilitarianism, according to which an act is right if its consequences are at least as good as those of any alternative, is today contrasted with other types, such as rule-utilitarianism and utilitarian generalization (and, also, motive-utilitarianism). According to rule-utilitarianism, an act is right if it conforms to a rule the general following of which would have (or has) good consequences. The point of this type of theory, which exists in many forms, is to de-emphasize the role of acts' consequences and to emphasize the role of (the consequences of) conformity to rules in determining acts' rightness. According to utilitarian generalization, an act is right if it is of a kind which would have (or has) good consequences if acts of that kind were performed universally (or generally). The point of this type of theory is to make an act's rightness a function not of its actual consequences, but of its consequences in the hypothetical situation in which an act of that kind is being universally (or generally) performed. Whether utilitarian generalization is a version of rule-utilitarianism and whether rule-utilitarianism collapses into act-utilitarianism are themselves matters of debate (see Lyons).

Thus, the term 'utilitarianism' refers not to a single theory but to a cluster of theories that are variations on a theme. This theme involves four components:

(1) a consequence component, according to which rightness is tied in some way to the production of good consequences;
(2) a value component, according to which the goodness or badness of consequences is to be evaluated by means of some standard of intrinsic goodness;
(3) a range component, according to which it is, say, acts' consequences as affecting everyone and not merely the agent that are relevant to determining rightness;
(4) a principle of utility, according to which one should seek to maximize that which the standard of goodness identifies as intrinsically good.

The act-utilitarian position that acts are right or wrong solely in virtue of the goodness or badness of their consequences possesses the four components. Its consequence component is consequentialism, or the view that consequences alone make acts right or wrong. Consequentialism itself is widely discussed and criticized, quite apart from any general difficulties there may be about telling where an act's consequences begin and end and about specifying the place, for example, of circumstances in a consequentialist account of rightness. On the one hand, there are those issues that arise in connection with consequentialism independently of its inclusion within act-utilitarianism. Earlier, these focused upon the defence of consequentialism against rival accounts of what makes right acts right and against the charges that consequentialism betokens a corrupt mind (it excludes no class of act as wrong independently of its consequences) and that it places one at the mercy of evil persons (who need only make the consequences of the alternatives worse than the consequences of the act they wish one to perform). Increasingly, however, these issues have centred around the much contested charge that consequentialism severs one from many of one's projects, commitments, and relationships and so from one's integrity, since one may not concern oneself more with one's own projects than with someone else's unless consequences so dictate (see Williams, in Smart and Williams).

On the other hand, there are those issues that arise in connection with act-utilitarianism as a result of its inclusion of consequentialism. At one time, these mostly pertained to the nature, place, and weight of moral and social rules within act-utilitarianism; today, they mostly pertain to the nature, place, and weight of individual moral RIGHTS within utilitarianisms generally. In consequentialism, what matters is consequences, not where consequences fall or who has what pleasures, and person-neutral accounts of rightness have been charged with failing to take seriously the separateness of persons, i.e. with failing to give due regard to people as autonomous persons in their own right, with their own individuality, projects and concerns, and inherent worth. How convincing this charge is against utilitarians is hotly disputed; but its prevalence has fostered the development of schemes of individual moral rights for the protection of persons (see Dworkin).

All act-utilitarianisms (and all utilitarianisms whatever) must contain a standard of intrinsic goodness, in order to evaluate the goodness of acts' consequences. Very broadly, a distinction can be drawn between hedonistic and non-hedonistic or ideal standards, though further distinctions exist within each camp. Hedonism may encompass only physical pleasure; or it may, as with Bentham, include such (admittedly slippery) things as benefit and advantage. Both

Mill and Sidgwick adopted pleasure-standards, though with differences: whereas Mill distinguished between qualities of pleasures, Sidgwick introduced a principle of justice in addition to and independent of his pleasure-standard, in order to evidence in his theory a concern with the distribution as well as the maximization of pleasure. Differences also exist in the ideal camp. W. T. Stace formulated his standard of goodness in terms of happiness, which includes but is not exhausted by pleasure, whereas Hastings Rashdall and G. E. Moore held that a number of things, in addition to pleasure and/or happiness, are good in themselves (e.g. experiences of beauty). Both camps agree on the identity of those things that are intrinsically good, viz. certain states of mind or consciousness, collectively referred to as 'pleasure', 'happiness', etc.

Recently, there has been a movement away from a mental-state view of value and utility to an interest-satisfaction view, where 'interests' is a generic term covering a multiplicity of desires or preferences. The question of which desires we are to maximize the satisfaction of – present, future, rational – then becomes paramount, and those who follow this line, because of problems with present and future desires, focus in the end upon rational or informed ones. A detailed value theory, in which rational desires are fleshed out, becomes necessary and must itself be defended. Whether on the mental-state view or the rational desire account of value and utility, interpersonal comparisons of, say, happiness or desire-satisfaction must be possible; and it remains a much disputed question of whether they are, though utilitarians and economists have begun to do fresh and important work on the issue.

The range component in act-utilitarianism covers all persons affected by the act, and it covers them equally, to the degree that they are affected. Are animals included? Bentham thought that they were, because he held that they could feel pain; but it is not obvious, if one shifts to a desire-satisfaction account of value, that animals can have rational desires. Nor is this clear in the cases of babies, the severely mentally-enfeebled, and the comatose (who do not meet Bentham's standard either). Part of the problem, as is clear from abortion controversies, is to decide who or what one is going to count as a person; for this, criteria of personhood need to be argued and defended.

Some standard of intrinsic goodness is necessary to the application of the principle of utility, since an abstract formulation, such as 'Always maximize net utility', does not tell one what to maximize. A standard of goodness makes possible a concrete, applicable formulation, such as 'Always maximize net desire-satisfaction'. The principle of utility is a maximizing principle, enjoining its adherents to maximize in the world whatever their standard of goodness has identified as intrinsically good; and, in the case of act-utilitarianism, the principle is applied directly to acts.

This last point causes difficulties: the direct application of the principle on an act-by-act basis can (a) produce clashes with 'ordinary moral convictions' (utility may be maximized in a particular case through, for example, harming someone) and (b) fail to maximize utility overall even though utility is maximized on each occasion (a person who desires to be a miler may find that, when it is time to train, he always desires to be doing something else more, so that, though he always maximizes desire-satisfaction on the particular occasions, he never satisfies his overall desire to be a miler). To meet these and other difficulties, R. M. Hare and other utilitarians have moved to a two-level account of moral thinking, which is a kind of rule-utilitarianism at the intuitive or first level, with moral rules and rights a part of the picture, and a kind of act-utilitarianism at the critical or second level. The crucial part of Hare's two-level theory is that one uses act-utilitarianism at the critical level in order to select those guides at the intuitive level by which to conduct one's life; and the guides chosen will be those whose general acceptance will maximize utility. Thus, given that these guides have been selected with an eye to the situations we are likely to find ourselves in, action in accordance with them is likely to give us the best chance of doing the right thing, i.e., of performing that act whose overall consequences are at least as good as those of any alternative. Hare's theory is only indirectly consequentialist, in that it bars any extensive appeal to acts' consequences at the intuitive level; and this effectively removes clashes with 'common opinion'. Since the theory does not apply the principle of utility on an act-by-act basis at the intuitive level, it avoids the other problems that stem from such an application.

RGF

Reading

Bentham, J.: *An Introduction to the Principles of Morals and Legislation* (1789), ed. J. Harrison. Oxford: Blackwell, 1948.

Brandt, R.B.: *A Theory of the Good and the Right.* Oxford: Clarendon Press, 1979.

Dworkin, R.: *Taking Rights Seriously*, rev. edn. London: Duckworth, 1979.

Hare, R.M.: *Moral Thinking.* Oxford: Clarendon Press, 1981.

Lyons, D.: *Forms and Limits of Utilitarianism.* Oxford: Oxford University Press, 1965.

Mill, J.S.: *Utilitarianism* (1861). In *The Collected Works of J.S. Mill*, vol. X. Toronto: University of Toronto Press, 1969. Indianapolis: Bobbs-Merrill, 1957.

Moore, G.E.: *Principia Ethica* (1903). Cambridge: Cambridge University Press, 1959.

———: *Ethics* (1912). Oxford: Oxford University Press, 1961.

Rashdall, H.: *Theory of Good and Evil.* 2 vols. Oxford: Clarendon Press, 1924.

Regan, D.H.: *Utilitarianism and Co-operation.* Oxford: Clarendon Press, 1980.

Sidgwick, H.: *The Methods of Ethics* (1874), 7th edn. London: Macmillan, 1907.

Smart, J.J.C. and Williams, B. eds: *Utilitarianism: For and Against.* Cambridge: Cambridge University Press, 1973. [Includes J.J.C. Smart: An outline of a system of utilitarian ethics; and B. Williams: A critique of utilitarianism.]

Stace, W.T.: *The Concept of Morals.* New York: Macmillan, 1937.

utopianism   *Utopia* was the title of Sir Thomas MORE's famous book (1516): his neologism, 'utopia', connotes a place which is both *good* and which is *nowhere*, playing on the similarity between the Greek words for 'good' (*eu*) and 'not' (*ou*). Since 1516, the term has been used to denote an ideal society or, pejoratively, an impossible society – or both. Utopias have often been discounted or despised simply because they are not grounded in contemporary reality. However, utopias perform two important functions in political thinking: first, they explicitly criticize existing political and social arrangements from a radical, rather than a reformist, perspective; and, second, they offer new ideals and illustrate how these might be realized in a different society. Most utopian thinkers seek to promote the well-being and happiness of individuals and to detail the social institutions and forms of personal life which will accomplish these; this places them outside mainstream political theory, with its emphasis on the political and its frequent neglect of the personal.

It is not always easy to recognize utopian thinking. The unmistakable utopias are those which depict an ideal society in a literary form: novels about future or past perfect societies, or ideal 'elsewheres'. But there are also non-literary works with utopian content: the ideal codes of law drawn up by Enlightenment thinkers such as Morelly, and detailed proposals for community experiments such as those of OWEN. Some political thinkers have utopian leanings, recognizable in their advocacy of a particular ideal, such as the communal ownership of property, from which stem a number of important consequences for social and political organization. But utopianism is not merely the advocacy of an ideal – if it were, all political thinkers would be utopians in some respect. It consists in the application of the ideal, or ideals, to every aspect of social life, with revolutionary consequences for the reorganization of society. Utopianism is clearly not an ideology (despite the 'ism') because many different kinds of utopia, of the right and left, and outside these categories, have been imagined. It *is* a unique method of reflecting on politics and society, which seeks the perfect, best, or happiest form of society, untrammelled by commitments to existing institutions.

Among the best-known and exemplary utopias are: PLATO's *Republic*, an ideal state ruled by philosopher-kings ('Guardians'), who live communally, without private property, and spend their time contemplating goodness and truth, which they realize through their decrees; More's *Utopia*, an island community organized on the basis of collective living, communal ownership, material security, and the obligation to work; BACON's *New Atlantis* (1627), a society run by scientists on enlightened, scientific principles; Campanella's *City of the Sun* (1602), a city built on a pattern of concentric circles, whose citizens are dedicated to knowledge and pious living; various sensual or legalistic utopias by the Enlightenment thinkers Mably, Morelly, Bretonne, and DIDEROT; the proposals for utopian communities of early socialists such as Owen, FOURIER and Cabet; Edward Bellamy's *Looking Backward* (1888), which describes a technological and socialist United States in the year AD 2000, and William MORRIS's *News From Nowhere* (1891), an idyllic, rural, craft society run on Marxist principles.

The number of accredited utopias runs into many thousands (see Sargent), so that it is impossible to generalize about the content of utopias. However, there are some recurrent themes and structures worthy of note. A great many utopias propose some form of socialized property or common ownership, and dwell on the harmful effects of possession and private property (see COMMUNISM). Most such utopias are egalitarian in principle, if not in every detail. This repeated advocacy of common or collective ownership constitutes an oblique or direct criticism of the writers' own societies in which private ownership (whether of land or capital) was the dominant social institution and therefore appeared as the primary cause of social evils. (A divergent current of nineteenth-century utopianism appeared in the United States, where many writers imagined 'improved capitalist' utopias – capitalism without capitalists! – see Negley and Patrick). A second theme is reliance on some kind of benevolently dictatorial implementation of the utopian ideal: in More's *Utopia*, the great ruler Utopus had laid down ideal laws 900 years previously, which still preserved peace and well-being for Utopia's inhabitants. The enlightened despot was naturally a popular choice of political instrument in pre-nineteenth-century (i.e. pre-democratic) utopias. Other utopias invoke rule by elites – an enlightened class of philosophers or scientists or industrialists, for example. Nineteenth- and twentieth-century utopias more often incorporate ideally democratic institutions, but the appeal of rule by a superior elite persists, for example in the utopias of H. G. Wells. It is this faith in intelligence and/or technical expertise which inspired anti-utopias such as Huxley's *Brave New World* (1932). The utopias reliant on elite rule are,

inevitably, societies in which social distinctions and some kind of class system are found, which reflects the utopian thinker's disbelief in the possibility of human equality. Plato's three-class Republic was the first of this genre of utopia, and a model for later utopians. There are, then, broad divisions between what might today be called 'socialist' and 'non-socialist' utopias and between egalitarian and elitist utopias. But there are egalitarian utopias which retain private ownership and utopias with elite rule but communalized property. This suggests that, for utopian authors, the distribution and ownership of resources and the form of government are conceptually distinct and not interdependent, as Marx would maintain.

The inspiration for any utopian enterprise lies in a dissatisfaction with existing society. The perception of injustice, or human misery, leads the thinker to imagine a form of organization which eradicates the putative causes of these evils. At this point, two strategies are open to the utopian theorist, depending on which of two hypotheses is made. If social evils are the result of the inherent badness of human nature, the remedy is to provide institutions which curb anti-social tendencies more strictly. But if social problems are considered to be the product of bad institutions, which distort or frustrate our natural inclinations, the remedy is to devise more liberal and humane institutions and to encourage individual development and amelioration. Utopians who make the first, pessimistic hypothesis are led to devise efficient institutions for social control and to stipulate severe penalties for deviance. Those who take the second line concentrate mostly on education for personal and moral development, and try to minimize social controls. The latter have been described as 'perfectibilists': that is, thinkers who believe that human nature is not immitigably bad, or marred by original sin, but is capable of improvement, or even perfection. For them, the problem is merely to devise social institutions which promote and hasten this improvement. Many eighteenth-century utopians fall into this group, as do the utopian socialists Fourier, Owen and SAINT-SIMON, anarchists like GODWIN, BAKUNIN and KRO-POTKIN, a few Marxists, and today's feminist utopians. For the anarchists, the logical conclusion of their premiss that human beings are naturally good was to abolish political institutions entirely, and to rely on 'natural morality' to maintain social order and preserve individual freedom. Others, such as Owen, believed it possible to formulate laws which would be attuned to human desires, rather than thwarting them. The analysis of human development and fulfilment offered by such thinkers adds a fruitful dimension rarely found in mainstream political theory. However, utopianism has this in common with other political theorizing: it is based on a conception of human nature and human good which dictates the form of political organization to be preferred. There is a rational progression from the conception of human beings to a particular conception of society.

As has been suggested, the distinctive quality of utopian thinking is that it embraces not only political but also economic, social, and private life (including matters of love, marriage, and childrearing). What is interesting in the present context is that so many utopians diminish the role and importance of politics (that is, politics viewed as the resolution of conflict, and policy debate) or eliminate politics altogether from their ideal societies. There are, of course, many utopias which describe ideal governmental institutions – philosopher-kings, exemplary parliaments, immutable codes of law – but many others reflect the supposition that a society with perfect social and economic institutions would operate harmoniously, without authoritative intervention or political dialogue. The reasons for this supposition are fourfold. First, some imaginary societies are placed in isolation from other societies (on islands, behind impenetrable mountains, etc.) so that no problems of external relations arise, while others are envisaged as embracing the whole world, with the same result. A primary function of government – some would say, its originating function – the conduct of foreign relations, is thus eliminated. Second, the 'apolitical' utopias are based on the premiss that there is one, discoverable Good and only one route to the Good Life, that which the utopian theorist has discovered and incorporated in the utopia. A set of laws or institutions reflecting these social and moral truths would therefore be beyond dispute or

question and would be universally accepted by the inhabitants of utopia. Thus, the necessity of politics (democratic or otherwise) as a policy-making device disappears. Third, social cohesion and the harmonious co-existence of individuals is achieved through the perfection of institutions and/or the moral development of utopian inhabitants. Therefore politics as a method of resolving conflicts of interest becomes redundant. Acceptance of this last conclusion, in particular, requires an unusual degree of faith in human nature; the assumption that co-operative, peaceful co-existence with our fellows is really possible makes utopian theories of this kind suspect, especially to traditional political theorists, who often have a Hobbesian view of human nature. A final reason for the unimportance of politics in utopia is that the perfect society is, by definition, a permanent one; any change would necessarily make it less perfect. There is thus no need for a political system to cope with change. This air of stasis also opens utopian thinking to criticism: it is argued – rightly – that society without change and history, at least in the long term, is unimaginable. This criticism is perhaps unjust to many utopians, who certainly did not wish, as Lapouge has charged, to 'incarcerate time'. Their endeavour was to describe an ideal society for the present; they could hardly be expected to predict its future history as well! Some utopians explicitly accept that even the ideal society will be transformed as history progresses.

It is noteworthy that, even after democracy became widely accepted as the best form of government, many utopians still preferred government by experts, or even no government at all. This may seem to reinforce the charge that utopianism is 'apolitical'. It can be argued in reply that utopians have expanded, rather than abolished, politics. It is only from a restricted perspective, which views politics as either adversarial democracy or coercive authoritarianism, and perceives it strictly in terms of formal institutions, that utopians can be regarded as dangerously or culpably non-political.

The treatment of politics and government in both political and apolitical utopias has been severely criticized by modern thinkers such as

POPPER, HAYEK, OAKESHOTT, and Talmon, who object to the 'closed' and contrived nature of utopian society. They argue that utopian thinking is a particular instance of totalitarian thinking, and should be repudiated by liberal democrats. The basic similarity between totalitarianism and utopianism is said to be that both promote a single, indisputable truth which must be inflicted on everyone, including non-believers; in a totalitarian or a utopian society, arguments about means are impermissible, let alone debates about ends. For Popper, Plato was the first enemy of the 'open society' (alias the liberal-democratic society), with his notion of an elite governing body imposing political 'truths' to which it alone had access. Marx, he says, is tarred with the same brush, as are all other utopians. Hayek objects to the 'constructivist rationalism' of utopians, who are planners writ large, arguing that human good can only emerge through spontaneous development. Oakeshott takes a similar view, believing that societies maintain themselves by an accretion of traditions, not by rational reconstruction or revolution. Popper's advocacy of piecemeal progress, the antithesis of 'social engineering', reflects similar convictions about the virtues of spontaneity and the non-manipulable nature of society and human happiness. The utopian mode of thinking can be defended in various ways against these critics: for example, by showing that the rationalist approach and commitment to a single truth has virtues which the empiricist, piecemeal, 'open', *laissez-faire* approach advocated by Popper and others lacks. It can also be shown that anti-totalitarian and anti-utopian thinkers deceive themselves in their presentation of liberal-democratic society as paradigmatically open. Most telling, perhaps, against Popper's tirade is the fact that most utopian thinkers have not proposed to enforce their schemes by revolution or coercion: education, small-scale experiment, or even democratic choice have been most favoured as the routes to utopia.

Implicit in the criticisms of Popper and others is the fear of MARXISM as the most menacing form of totalitarianism in the contemporary world. Marxism is branded as a utopian theory in the worst sense, realizable only through totalitarian practice. But is Marxism utopian? MARX himself attacked the utopian socialists. The practical ground for his attack was that they diverted the working class from concerted action against capitalism by fragmenting it into sects (e.g. the Saint-Simonians) or promoting the embourgeoisement of the workers, as Owen did. Marx's theoretical case against the utopians was that they were rationalist thinkers of the superseded Enlightenment genre, who attempted to impose intellectual constructs on the world, oblivious of concrete reality and the dialectic of history. They had no conception of class conflict and foolishly dreamed of uniting all classes – which Marx considered impossible. They also lacked a theory of history, Marx argued (despite his own debt to Saint-Simon's historical analysis). Marx therefore distinguished his own theory from utopian socialism, calling it 'scientific socialism' and eschewing utopian programmes. This left his followers sadly bereft of a model of the organization of communist society. Marx's enemies consider him utopian, whereas most Marxists deny this. However, the German philosopher Bloch argued that Marxism contains a cold (scientific, methodological) current and also a warm (utopian, humane) current, the latter being detectable in Marx's early writings about unalienated labour and human development. On the most obvious criteria, Marx is not a utopian, but Marxist thinkers such as Bloch and MARCUSE have developed his theory in utopian directions.

An influential theory about utopianism was offered by MANNHEIM in *Ideology and Utopia* (1929). He defined utopian ideas as ideas 'incongruent with reality' which, if translated into action, would tend to overthrow the existing social order. Ideology consists of ideas, also incongruent with reality, which tend to uphold the existing system. Clearly, on this definition, utopian ideas, once realized, will swiftly become ideological. This has happened, in different contexts, to liberal and Marxist ideas. Mannheim bemoaned the loss of the 'utopian mentality', which resulted from the assimilation of the workers within liberal democracy, in his view. He regretted the contemporary absence of the inspirational dimension of human thought and activity which utopianism represents.

Utopian thought, in Mannheim's view, was often grounded in social movements. Many commentators on utopianism also consider it impossible to separate utopian theories from the many social experiments attempted in the past, which reached their culmination in the USA in the nineteenth century. Yet a utopian theory is the product of an individual thinker, as is any other theory. A certain climate of opinion may cause individuals to think of certain kinds of utopia, but utopian theories are usually produced independently of movements, and are then taken up by some group as the basis for social experiment or political action. Some members of experimental communities have written about their experiences, as did Noyes, founder of the Oneida community (1848–81), but this is no longer utopianism, but a chronicle of experience.

Utopianizing is, therefore, primarily an intellectual and theoretical activity. This raises the question of how utopian theories fit into the main corpus of political thought. In terms of their form, they are certainly distinctive: other theorists do not write about imaginary societies, but abstract elements of existing society for elaboration, justification, or criticism. In terms of content, however, many utopians have ideas similar to those of other theorists. Socialism has, evidently, been presented both as utopia and as orthodox theory. It is the structure of utopian thought that makes it interestingly different from other theory, in three respects. First, the utopian attempt to picture a society in its entirety brings into focus a whole wealth of social detail not usually treated by other theorists. It is important to show the coherence of society and the causal networks between political, social, and personal life, as utopians do. Second, the explicit desire of utopians to achieve the best possible society, measured in terms of human happiness, makes their theory more ambitious and wide-ranging than conventional theory. Third, the process of imagining an ideal community, which necessarily rests on a negation of the non-ideal aspects of existing societies, gives utopian theory a certain distance from reality which makes it a sharper critical tool than much orthodox political theory. For

these reasons, utopianism should be taken seriously within the discipline of political thought.

Given the value of utopian thinking, why are there fewer utopias in this century than in the past? Several reasons suggest themselves. Mannheim may be right in thinking that the achievement of political rights by workers has stifled the passion for utopias. However, many past utopias were neither written nor read by unenfranchised, under-privileged groups, but rather by intellectuals. A more likely explanation is that, with the increasing specialization of the social sciences within universities, it has become unacceptable to present political and social philosophy in fictional or speculative form. Political arguments are expected to appear as rigorously argued theses, immediately accessible on a rational level to scholars and students, and confined within the bounds of the discipline. This rules out the detailed descriptions of daily life and the wider speculations on the meaning of life, death and happiness which appear in many utopias. 'Deviant' forms of political theorizing are, quite simply, neglected and debarred from the arena of political and academic debate. Likewise, the utopian 'method' of thinking is dismissed because it makes claims which, being outside the scope of current experience, are not empirically verifiable.

A more general reason for the lack of utopias may be that the various horrors of the twentieth century have produced a pessimistic outlook that cannot entertain perfectibilism or idealism where human beings are concerned. The major imaginative output in the utopian mode in this century has consisted of works such as Zamyatin's *We* (1920), Huxley's *Brave New World* (1932), and Orwell's *1984* (1949). These are sometimes called *dystopias*, that is, images of the worst possible society, but they are better entitled 'anti-utopias', works which attack the utopian genre by adopting but subverting its conventions. Fictionally, they do what Popper and others do academically.

However, there are signs that utopianism is alive and well. The radical politics of the 1960s produced a new interest in utopian thinking. On the academic level, many new commentaries on utopianism have been produced. America has a

537

thriving society for the study of utopian thought and, increasingly, international conferences are held on the subject. More importantly, the utopian mode has been used as a vehicle for new, radical ideas. There are ecological utopias such as Callenbach's *Ecotopia*. Also, a number of fictional utopias have emerged from the feminist movement, the best known being Leguin's *The Dispossessed* (1974) and Piercy's *Woman on the Edge of Time* (1976). It is significant that feminist writers have used utopian devices to express feminist ideals – for example, the ideals of conciliation and caring – which do not readily find acceptance in orthodox, 'masculine' political theory. Feminists also believe that 'the personal *is* the political', and so need the wider scope afforded by utopianism to express their conception of society fully. Such thinkers use the utopian mode for reasons similar to those which caused More to invent it: because certain radical hypotheses and aspirations will be flatly rejected if stated in conventional form (since they threaten powerful interest groups), because fictions gain a wider audience than political polemics, and conversion is the goal, and finally because certain truths are most powerfully expressed symbolically or by illustration. These constitute the advantages which utopian thought has over conventional political theory, and the reasons for hoping that utopias will continue to be written.   BG

Reading

Davis, J.C.: *Utopia and the Ideal Society*. Cambridge: Cambridge University Press, 1981.

†Goodwin, B. and Taylor, K.: *The Politics of Utopia*. London: Hutchinson, 1982.

†Kateb, G.: *Utopia and its Enemies*. New York: Collier-Macmillan, 1963.

Lapouge, A.: *Utopie et civilisations*. Paris: Flammarion, 1978.

†Manuel, F.E. and Manuel, F.P.: *Utopian Thought in the Western World*. Oxford: Blackwell, 1979.

Mannheim, K.: *Ideology and Utopia*, trans. L. Wirth and E. Shils. London: Routledge, 1936.

Morton, J.L.: *The English Utopia*. London: Lawrence & Wishart, 1969.

Negley, G.R. and Patrick, J.M.: *The Quest for Utopia*. New York: Doubleday, 1952.

Sargent, L.T.: *British and American Utopian Literature 1516–1975*. Boston: Hall, 1979.

Servier, J.: *Histoire de l'Utopie*. Paris: Gallimard, 1967.

V

Vattel, Emmerich de (1714–1767) Swiss jurist. His major work, *The Law of Nations* (1758), was an influential exposition of the principles of INTERNATIONAL LAW.

Vico, Giambattista (1668–1744) Italian philosopher, historian and jurist. Vico lived and died, in comparative international obscurity, in Naples, where he held the chair of rhetoric at the university from 1699 to 1741. International interest in his work came in the nineteenth and twentieth centuries, through the powerful advocacy first of the French historian Michelet and then of the Italian philosopher CROCE.

Of his more important early works, *On the Study Methods of our Time* (1709) reveals an interest in the education of the legislator and in the nature of political wisdom, but *On the Ancient Wisdom of the Italians* (1710) is primarily concerned with a non-Cartesian theory of knowledge. A more systematic interest in political theory is first expressed in *On the Coherence of the Jurist* (1721), but is later developed differently within the context of a science of the principles of humanity, which is the subject of his masterpiece, *The New Science*. This exists in three different editions (1725, 1730, and 1744) between the first two of which, in particular, there are major differences in form.

The central features of Vico's political thought are consequences of two different theses. First, that nations share a common developmental nature which changes as certain fundamental concepts, primarily those of truth and of justice, emerge and develop in the course of human interaction within society. Second, that the form of a state and of its government

must conform to the nature of the people governed. From these theses, it follows that the forms of a state and its government will change in accordance with the development of these fundamental concepts.

Vico develops these claims in producing a theory, the 'ideal eternal history', about a necessary process of cultural, social, and political development and decay which, in certain circumstances, would occur in the history of any actual nation. In the first phase or 'era' of this process, a wholly poetic or imaginative social and physical world is seen, in a totally mythical way, as different aspects of God or of the gods. Possession belongs immediately to God but mediately to those who claim to interpret His wishes, make sacrifices to placate Him and bring His law to the people. Making certain assumptions about the natural development of families, Vico concludes that the form of state appropriate to this phase is that of a theocratic despotism in which all rights of possession devolve upon the father of the family, in whose person are united all three sacerdotal functions, and thence to his nearest kin.

In the second era, the form of the state is determined by the desire of the fathers' descendants to retain the vast private possessions which they have inherited, the justification for which lies in their claim to semi-divine status, i.e., to be born of unions of mortals and gods. To explain this form of state Vico makes two further assumptions. First, that a class distinction will have arisen within the original family states through the admission into them of external vagrants who lack semi-divine status and, therefore, any civil rights. Second, that stimulated by an awakening sense of natural justice and developing rational doubts about the alleged semi-divine status of the ruling aristocrats, or 'heroes', the serfs proceed to wage a long war to improve their legal and civil status. Eventually, to retain their privileges, the heroes are forced to surrender some of their sovereignty to a supreme senate, membership of which is open only to themselves, in order that they can hold by force what they can no longer retain solely on grounds of ancestry.

In the third, 'fully human', era, reason is presumed to have developed to the extent that the true nature of things is understood and, in particular, that in the case of man this implies equality of civil status. This determines the form of the state, and government will be either by democracy or by a monarchy which supports this principle. Vico has little confidence in the capacity of this form of state to maintain itself and concludes the sequence with a final era, the 'barbarism of reflection', in which the habits of mind necessary for social cohesion succumb to man's essential self-interest, and civil anarchy both terminates the sequence and gives rise to the conditions for its recurrence.

One consequence of Vico's theory is that it enables him to reject theories which base POLITICAL OBLIGATION as such upon either force or contract, these being seen only as features of particular eras in his sequence. Vico's whole sequence presupposes the principle that political obligation rests upon what is seen as fitting or just, the content of which depends upon the mental development, or 'common sense', of the period. In this sense the theory is more liberal than its rivals, even though it entails the consequence, which Vico expressly accepts, that in some periods rule by tyrants will be justified.

Two difficulties should, however, be mentioned. First, the theory presupposes the necessary development of the concepts of truth and civil equity. Vico himself produces both *a priori* and *a posteriori* arguments to support this claim but it is not clear how the latter can ground the alleged necessity, while the former are weakened by the fact that Vico's theory allows the possibility that his own definitions of truth and equity may themselves reflect nothing more than a manifestation of local belief.

Second, if Vico believes that the rational era cannot sustain itself in the face of human self-interest, to which he ascribes the role of efficient cause of change throughout the sequence, it is not clear why such self-interest should not undermine the earlier developments of reason upon which the whole direction of the sequence depends, since the capacities of reason to develop or to sustain itself despite the influence of self-interest must be logically the same. This suggests that Vico is mistaken in thinking that his theory entails the inevitability of anarchy and recurrence rather than the development of different forms of rationality and different social and political forms.   LP

Reading
†Croce, B.: *The Philosophy of Giambattista Vico*, trans. R.G. Collingwood. London: Howard Latimer, 1913.

Tagliacozzo, G. ed.: *Vico: Past and Present*. Atlantic Highlands, NJ: Humanities, 1981.

—— and Verene, D.P. eds: *Giambattista Vico's Science of Humanity*. Baltimore: The Johns Hopkins University Press, 1976.

†Vaughan, C.E.: *Studies in the History of Political Philosophy Before and After Rousseau*, vol. I, 504–53. New York: Russell & Russell, 1960.

Vico, G.: *The Autobiography of Giambattista Vico*, trans. M.H. Fisch and T.G. Bergin. Ithaca, NY: Cornell University Press, 1962.

——: *On the Study Methods of our Time*, trans. E. Gianturco. Indianapolis: Bobbs-Merrill, 1965.

——: *Selected Writings*, trans. L. Pompa. Cambridge: Cambridge University Press, 1982.

——: *The New Science*, 3rd edn, trans. T.G. Bergin and M.H. Fisch. Ithaca, NY: Cornell University Press, 1984.

violence   In its most basic sense, violence means inflicting damage on people, by killing, maiming or hurting them. Its meaning may be extended to cover the threat of such damage, and to psychological as well as physical harm. Violence may also be defined so as to include destruction of property. Some political writers have stretched the concept of violence to embrace oppressive political, social, or economic systems that damage people living under them.

In political theory, the concern is with the use of organized violence by the state, or with violent rebellion against the state. The police are normally responsible for quelling internal dissent and the armed forces for confronting external enemies. Violence against the state includes riots, street fighting, assassination, guerrilla warfare, civil war, and revolution. Political attitudes to both types of violence are therefore influenced by attitudes to the state, or to particular types of state.

In the mainstream of western political thought violence is viewed as an unfortunate but sometimes necessary means to secure political ends. A minimum of violence by the state can be justified to maintain social order, but only within the context of law and in a regime resting on majority support. Violent rebellion may also be justified, but only against a tyranny. Wars are to be avoided when possible through diplomacy, trade and international law, but are legitimate in defence of national safety or to uphold certain principles. (See JUST WAR.)

Some political ideologies do however see violent action as positively good. FASCISM has glorified war, both because it is a means to extend the greatness of the state and because it can inspire heroism, self-sacrifice and comradeliness. Some ideologies of the left have also extolled violent rebellion, on the grounds that violence is psychologically liberating, promotes courage and pride, and inspires others to rebel. These ideas are to be found in one of the main theoretical treatises on violent rebellion, Georges SOREL's book *Reflections on Violence*, first published in 1908, which extols violent insurrection by the working class in the form of a general strike to bring down decadent bourgeois society (see also SYNDICALISM).

Violent revolution has also been idealized by movements striving for national liberation. Frantz FANON, writing in the context of the war against the French in Algeria in the early 1960s, is the best known exponent of the purifying and liberating effect of violent revolt against colonialism.

It is possible to distinguish between instrumental and expressive forms of violence. Instrumental violence is rationally designed to achieve specific ends by inflicting unacceptable damage or by its deterrent effect. Violence viewed as a form of individual or collective self-expression is an end in itself, and may be judged in terms of the heroism involved rather than by its specific results.

It may be politically relevant to distinguish between spontaneous and planned acts of violence, between the kind of violence which develops out of mass protests and violence that may be organized by a particular group, and to grade the seriousness of the damage involved and the nature of the targets. A confrontation between police and pickets in a strike, for example, does not have the same political implications as an attempt to blow up the key members of a government. But both may be labelled political violence.

One important theoretical question is how violence is related to POWER. Most theorists see violence as one element in the exercise of power. But Hannah ARENDT has argued that violence is the antithesis of power, since power flows from mass co-operative action, whilst violence depends not on numbers but on technology, which can magnify destruction.

Definitions of violence are often designed to justify one form of violence and to condemn others. Organized violence by the state is sometimes described as force in contrast to acts of political violence against the state. This distinction implies for many who use it that force is legitimate and violence is not, but Sorel who drew the same distinction reached opposite conclusions. To describe an entire political and social system as violent, as Fanon does when condemning the violence of colonialism, often implies that violent revolt against it is justified.

A definition which uses the same word, violence, for destructive action by agents of the state or by its opponents also has political implications, yet it adds clarity to focus on the act rather than the agent and then to make moral judgments about whether the act is justifiable. A definition which focuses solely on physical violence may seem to underestimate the harm done by some social systems and to exaggerate the importance of violence used as a means of protest. Nevertheless, the narrower definition is clearer, and other concepts are available to describe the psychological and social harm people suffer.   AFC

Reading

Arendt, H.: *On Violence*. Harmondsworth: Penguin, 1969.

Fanon, F.: *The Wretched of the Earth* (1961), trans. C. Farrington. London: MacGibbon & Kee, 1965.

†Macfarlane, L.: *Violence and the State*. London: Nelson, 1974.

Sorel, G.: *Reflections on Violence*, trans. T.E. Hulme and J. Roth. London and New York: Macmillan, 1950.

†Walter, E.V.: *Terror and Resistance: a Study of Political Violence*. Oxford: Oxford University Press, 1969.

Vitoria, Francisco de (Franciscus de Victoria) (1483?–1546) Spanish theologian, early theorist of international law. Born in the town of Vitoria in the Basque province of Alava, Francisco early in life entered the Dominican order. Distinguishing himself intellectually, he was sent in 1506 to study in Paris, where he also taught in the Dominican college. In 1521 or 1522, upon receiving his licentiate in theology from the Sorbonne, he was appointed senior lecturer in theology at the Dominican college in Valladolid, at that time the favourite residence of the Spanish royal court and the seat of the councils for the Indies. In 1526 Vitoria was chosen to fill the *prima* chair of theology at Salamanca; this was the principal theology chair in Spain's most distinguished university at the time. Vitoria remained there until his death. His main duty was to lecture on Thomas Aquinas and Peter Lombard; yet he went beyond this role, applying scholastic theology to contemporary issues in public lectures. Among these were his seminal contributions to INTERNATIONAL LAW, *De Indis* (On the Indians) and *De jure belli* (On the Law of War), both prepared in 1532 and both applying the inherited JUST WAR tradition to the question of the military rights of the Spaniards regarding the Indians of the New World. Vitoria's influence reached the Emperor Charles V, who consulted him four times (twice in 1539 and twice again in 1541) on matters of state. Among Vitoria's students were Domingo de Soto and Francisco SUAREZ, both of whom also distinguished themselves as theorists of just war tradition and international law.

The importance of Vitoria's work lies both in what he said and in the methodology he employed. As to the latter, Vitoria systematized the somewhat diffuse inheritance of medieval just war tradition by applying it concretely to the question of military rights in the New World. At the same time, since the Indians were not Christians, Vitoria had to recast this tradition entirely on a natural-law base. Later theorists built on both contributions. The line from medieval just war theory to modern international law as described by GROTIUS and later writers passes importantly through Vitoria.

As to the substance of Vitoria's position, he rejected religious grounds as a 'just cause' for war, insisting that only reasons rooted in natural rights could be just; he argued that sovereigns ought to seek the counsel of others before going to war in order to exercise responsibly 'right authority'; and, noting that often the justice of a conflict is obscure, he called for scrupulous observance of proportionality and the rights of noncombatants by belligerents. The first and last of these later became central features of the international law of war; the second is a peculiarly democratic insight from a man who lived all his life in an age of monarchs. JTJ

Reading
†Johnson, J.T.: *Ideology, Reason, and the Limitation of War*, ch. 3. Princeton, NJ and London: Princeton University Press, 1975.

Scott, J.B.: *The Spanish Origin of International Law*. Oxford: Clarendon Press; London: Humphrey Milford, 1934.

Victoria, Franciscus de : *De Indis et De jure belli reflectiones*, ed. E. Nys. Washington: Carnegie Institution, 1917.

Voltaire, François-Marie Arouet (1694–1778) French philosopher. Voltaire held up England to France, and the world, as a 'mirror of liberty'. But unlike MONTESQUIEU, who praised England in much the same words, Voltaire did not believe that the French should imitate in any way the English constitutional system. Voltaire's political ideas were 'English' only in the sense that they were derived from a reading of Francis BACON and John LOCKE. Inspired by Bacon, Voltaire produced what was seen by his critics as a sophisticated version of the seventeenth-century Bourbon *thèse royale*: the thesis that good, just and progressive government could only be achieved by a strong centralized modern monarchy, unimpeded by relics of medieval obstruction and vested interests. In Voltaire's eyes the chief of those 'relics' in France were the church, the nobility and the sovereign courts of magistrates called *parlements*, which Voltaire often pointed out had nothing in common with what was known as 'parliament', the elected legislative assembly of England. Whereas Montesquieu saw the *parlements* and the church as barriers to royal despotism Voltaire saw them as chief agencies of oppression in France. It was the magistrates and the clergy, not the royal government, who tortured and executed religious dissenters, burned books, and persecuted writers like himself.

Humiliated by the French nobility in a clash he had as a young man with Rohan-Chabot, Voltaire was a lifelong antagonist of any form of aristocratic interest, and an unashamed champion of the bourgeoisie. His hostility to the church was, by comparison, more moderate; and even though he mocked established religion, he was never an atheist, but rather a Deist – and indeed a protector of Jesuits when the Society of Jesus was suppressed. His experience at the court of Frederick II of Prussia, where he hoped to enact the role of philosopher to an enlightened monarch, ended in fiasco; he found that the king desired not advice but flattery. Yet Voltaire remained a royalist, and continued to urge the king of France to suppress the *parlements* in the 1770s, when liberal opinion in France generally took the side of the magistrates.

In the later years of his life, when he lived either in or on the borders of Geneva, Voltaire became an active champion of democratic movements in that city. He did not favour democratic government for France any more than he favoured republican government as a general rule, but in a small Swiss city-state, with a long tradition of popular government, Voltaire believed that democracy was the best possible system. He supported in turn the claims of the middle-class citizens against the patrician rulers of Geneva, and the claims of the lower-class inhabitants against the domination of the middle-class citizens. In this context Voltaire produced a fair amount of 'left-wing' and egalitarian pamphleteering, which needs to be understood as conveying a message to the Genevese, not to the French. It would be a mistake to treat it as evidence of Voltaire's becoming a republican and democrat in his attitude to the government of his own country.

Voltaire's most notable contribution to the political thinking of his time was that of an exponent of TOLERATION and of the rights of man. He was not an original philosopher, but was content to depend on Locke for the theoretical basis of his argument, despite the contradiction between Locke's Whiggish politics and the *étatisme* of Voltaire's other English master, Bacon. But what Voltaire lacked in originality and consistency he more than made up for in eloquence, vitality and style. He was perhaps the most widely read and influential writer of his time. Shortly before his death at the age of eighty-three he was 'crowned' emperor of the empire of letters at the Paris Opera House by his admirers; Voltaire had always thought of this as a greater and more universal kingdom than any political one. (See also FRENCH ENLIGHTENMENT.)   MC

Reading

†Gay, P.: *Voltaire's Politics*. Princeton, NJ: Princeton University Press, 1959.

†Mason, H.: *Voltaire*. London: Granada, 1981.

Voltaire, F.-M.: *Philosophical Dictionary* (1764), ed. and trans. T. Besterman. Harmondsworth: Penguin, 1965.

———: *Candide* (1759), trans. J. Butt. Harmondsworth: Penguin, 1970.

†Wade, I.O.: *The Intellectual Development of Voltaire*. Princeton, NJ: Princeton University Press, 1969.

W

Webb, Beatrice (1858–1943) and Sidney (1859–1947) British social reformers. Prominent members of the Fabian Society, the Webbs were known especially for their collaborative research in economic and social history. See FABIANISM.

Weber, Max (1864–1920) German political economist and theoretical sociologist. After early studies in the history of commercial law, Weber established himself as one of the leading figures in a new generation of historical political economists in the Germany of the 1890s. A personal breakdown in 1898 led to his withdrawal from academic teaching, but did little to impair the flow of his writing, the range of which was enormous. Its unifying focus was a concern with the mutual relationship between legal, political and cultural formations on the one hand, and economic activity on the other. His concern with these issues became increasingly theoretical, involving a systematization of the major categories of social and political life, both universally and as definitive of the specific character of modern western civilization. Weber was also actively and often controversially involved in the political issues of Wilhelmine Germany, from a progressive national-liberal standpoint, an involvement which gave particular point to his concern with the distinction between social science and political practice, and the place of value judgments in the former. It was only comparatively late in his life that he came to think of his work as 'sociology', and it is as one of the 'founding fathers' of sociology that he is now known. His work is, however, too complex to allow of any simple classification, whether in terms of disciplinary boundaries or of any particular school of thought.

Weber made his initial reputation in Germany with a study of the impact of capitalist organization on the agricultural estates east of the Elbe, and its implications for the continued dominance of the Junkers over Germany's political life. It is for a much wider study, however, of the origins of capitalism itself, that he is best known (*The Protestant Ethic and the Spirit of Capitalism*, 1904–5). The argument of this work is that the profit-maximizing behaviour so characteristic of the bourgeoisie, which could be explained under fully developed capitalist conditions by its sheer necessity for survival in the face of competition, could not be so explained under the earlier phases of capitalist development. It was the product of an autonomous impulse to accumulate far beyond the needs of personal consumption, an impulse which was historically unique. Weber traced its source to the 'worldly asceticism' of reformed Christianity, with its twin imperatives to methodical work as the chief duty of life, and to the limited enjoyment of its product. The unintended consequence of this ethic, which was enforced by the social and psychological pressures on the believer to prove (but not earn) his salvation, was the accumulation of wealth for investment.

Early critics of Weber's thesis misunderstood it as a purely cultural explanation for capitalism, as if a 'Siberian Baptist or a Calvinist inhabitant of the Sahara' must inevitably become a successful entrepreneur. Weber was, in fact, well aware both of the material preconditions for capitalist development, and of the social interests that are needed to support the dissemination of new ideas. The crucial question about his thesis is whether the employment of wage labour that made unlimited accumulation possible in principle, also made it inevitable in practice; whether, that is, the Protestant ethic should be seen as providing a necessary *motivation* for capitalist accumulation, or rather a *legitimation* for it in the face of prevalent values favouring conspicuous consumption on the part of a leisured class. The issue is probably impossible to resolve conclusively, since all later examples of capitalist take-off have been influenced by the impact of the original one. The theoretical importance of Weber's work, however, lies in the challenge it offers to reductionist attempts to treat ideas as simply the reflection of material interests, rather than as mutually interacting with them, or to provide an account of social change without reference to the motivation of the social agents involved, even though the consequences may not be what they intend.

The Protestant Ethic and the Spirit of Capitalism was only the first of a number of works on the economic ethic of the major world religions; the purpose of these was not, as has been claimed, to prove the capitalist spirit thesis by showing its absence elsewhere, but rather to elucidate the distinctive character of modern western rationalism. While instrumental RATIONALITY, according to Weber, was a universal characteristic of social action, only in the modern West had the goal-maximizing *calculation* of the most efficient means to given ends become generalized. And while other cultures had attempted to make the world intelligible through the development of elaborate theodicies, or to create internally consistent systems of ethics or law, the distinctive features of western rationalism were the scientific assumption that all things could be comprehended by reason, together with the attitude of practical mastery which sought to subject the world to human control (the achievement ethic). In Weber's mature work capitalism was shown to be simply one expression, rather than the unique locus, of this 'rationalization' process. To understand the history of modernization was to see it as a complex and interrelated set of changes from 'traditional' to 'rational' formations in all spheres of social life.

In the political sphere 'rationality' for Weber constituted a distinctive legitimating principle of AUTHORITY, which also determined the forms of law and administration. In traditional societies LEGITIMACY resided in the person of the lord or monarch through hereditary succession; the manner of rule was highly personalized and limited by customary norms and obligations. By contrast with 'traditional' authority, the 'rational' principle of legitimacy rested in impersonal rules, which divorced the office from the person of its incumbent, and freed it from the limitations of family or household. So too the criteria of valid law lay not in its substantive content but in the procedural correctness of its institution, so that the process of law-making itself became freed from the constraint of traditional norms. Finally, 'rationalized' administration was carried out as a continuous activity by trained professionals selected according to merit, rather than on an *ad hoc* basis by personal retainers of the political chief. In all these respects 'rationalization' marked a transformation in the scope and adaptability of political and administrative systems.

Weber's analysis of 'rationalization' revealed it also as a process with negative aspects. In his view the procedural norm of instrumental rationality tended to become divorced from the ends to which it was supposedly subordinate, and become a dominant social value in itself, while the organizational forms intended to expand human powers achieved a formidable power in their own right. Herein lay the irrationality of rational organization. Weber believed that social hierarchy was inevitable, and that its analysis lay in the relationship to be found between the analytically distinct dimensions of status, property and political or organizational power. Different societies could be distinguished by the predominance of one dimension over the others. If in early capitalism this was property, in advanced capitalism it was organizational power. It was the imperatives of the latter that determined the subordination of the worker at the workplace, not those of property, and such subordination would therefore continue under a system of social ownership. A central feature of Weber's critique of socialism was that the attempt to replace the 'anarchy' of the market and achieve greater equality through social planning would entail an enormous expansion of bureaucratic power, and hence of unfreedom and economic stagnation. The retention of the market and of private ownership were necessary in his view to secure competition between a plurality of social powers, and so guarantee freedom for the individual.

One important practical question for Weber was thus how to restrict the expansion of BUREAUCRACY. Another was how to subject bureaucratic administration to political control. This question was central to his theory of competitive leadership democracy. In Weberian political sociology, alongside the 'traditional' and 'rational' principles of legitimacy was a third principle, the 'charismatic'. This indicated an authority deriving from the person of the leader himself and the compelling power of his message, rather than from tradition or the rules governing a particular office. It was a specifically innovative, non-routinized force in social life. Crucial therefore to asserting control over bureaucratic administration and securing innovation in face of its conservative tendencies, was to ensure scope for the charismatic principle in the political process. Weber believed this could be provided by the circumstances of mass electoral politics. He observed how elections under universal suffrage were becoming a form of plebiscite for or against the party leaders, and were increasing their scope for determining policy over the heads of the individual parliamentary representatives and the party following. It was precisely for the premium it put on the qualities of political leaders and the initiative it accorded them, Weber believed, that mass democracy could be justified, not from any principle of popular sovereignty, which he regarded as fictional.

Underlying Weber's conception of democracy as a procedure for producing political leadership lay a basic philosophical assumption that political principles or values could not be grounded in reason or in the historical process, but were matters of subjective commitment and assertion. This post-Nietzschean perspective had important consequences for a number of different areas of his thought. It produced a theory of LIBERALISM in which the central place

was occupied, not by a doctrine of natural rights, but by institutions or procedures capable of giving expression to a plurality of competing values in society, and securing an accommodation between them. At the methodological level the perspective entailed a radical disjunction between the purely subjective domain of value judgments and the objective procedures and conclusions of empirical science. The Weberian ideal for social science was one of value-freedom. However, he also recognized that the direction of research and concept formation in the social sciences was dependent upon its relevance to social values, and that these were subject to historical change. It is a matter of dispute how far this criterion of value-relevance undermines the goal of value-freedom, or the thoroughgoing distinction Weber sought to draw between social science and political practice.

On all the issues considered above Weber's positions can be contrasted with those of MARXISM. His work is often characterized as a 'bourgeois riposte' to MARX. In fact on the occasions when Weber explicitly challenged Marxism, he usually criticized the cruder versions current in his time, and it is possible to identify considerable areas of compatibility between the work of the two writers. Weber was no mere 'methodological individualist', but like Marx sought an integration of structure, culture and social interests in historical explanation; his ideal-type method was not all that different from Marx's method of abstraction, and contained the same insistence on historical specificity; like Marx, he made social power and class relations central to his understanding of society. However, at root there remained basic differences in their characterizations of capitalism and in their assessments of its centrality to social theory, which represented differences between a socialist and a liberal perspective. These also reflected differences of period and place. If Marx's model of capitalism derived from Britain in the heyday of liberal capitalism, Weber's model of bureaucracy was drawn from Germany in the period when capitalism was taking increasingly organized and monopolistic forms. Weber's personal academic trajectory from the study of capitalism itself to the themes of rationalization and bureaucratic organization, and from political economy to sociology, can be seen to have reflected a more general shift in the preoccupations of social science, in response to the principal historical changes of the period.   DB

Reading

†Beetham, D.: *Max Weber and the Theory of Modern Politics*, 2nd edn. Cambridge: Polity, 1985.

Löwith, D.: *Max Weber and Karl Marx*. London: Allen & Unwin, 1982.

Mommsen, W.J.: *The Age of Bureaucracy*. Oxford: Blackwell, 1974.

†————: *Max Weber and German Politics 1890–1920*. Chicago: University of Chicago Press, 1985.

†Roth, G. and Schluchter, W.: *Max Weber's Vision of History*. Berkeley: University of California Press, 1979.

Weber, M.: *Max Weber: a Biography*, trans. H. Zohn. New York: Wiley, 1975.

Weber, M.: *Economy and Society*. New York: Bedminster, 1968.

————: *The Methodology of the Social Sciences*. New York: Free Press, 1949.

————: *The Protestant Ethic and the Spirit of Capitalism*. London: Allen & Unwin, 1930.

————: *Selections in Translation*, ed. W.G. Runciman, trans. E. Matthews. Cambridge: Cambridge University Press, 1978.

Weil, Simone (1909–1943) French social and religious thinker. In spite of her early death, Simone Weil has had a considerable influence on post-war philosophy, religion and political thought. Born and educated in Paris, she was strongly influenced by her teacher, the philosopher Alain (Émile Chartier, 1868–1951), from whom she absorbed a distinctive philosophical perspective derived from Descartes, SPINOZA, ROUSSEAU and KANT. She completed her studies at the École Normale Supérieure, but after a brief spell of teaching turned away from an academic career. She was anxious to understand and share the conditions of the manual worker, and in 1934 spent nine months working in various factories performing unskilled tasks. She was profoundly influenced by this experience in which she felt that she had 'received for ever the mark of a slave'. During this period she wrote a number of essays on contemporary European politics and on the conditions of factory work, the most important of which was *Réflexions sur les causes de la liberté et de l'oppression sociale* (Reflections on the Causes of Liberty and Social Oppression) (1955).

At the outbreak of the second world war, she and her family, of Jewish origin, moved first to Marseilles in 1940 and eventually to the United States in 1942. In November 1942 her wish to be as close as possible to those who were suffering in Europe was granted, and she joined the Free French in London for whom she wrote her best known work *L'Enracinement* (The Need for Roots) (1949), addressing the problems to be faced by the French in attempting to recover their spiritual roots in the post-war period. Her health was already poor from numerous self-imposed deprivations and illnesses, and it declined further in London where she refused to eat more than her compatriots in France were receiving at the time as rations. She died in August 1943 in a sanatorium in Kent. After the war more than fifteen volumes of various writings were published in France, and most were translated into English.

Simone Weil's writings fall into two periods, although there is considerable continuity between them. The first might be labelled 'rationalist' and is distinguished by important analyses of the condition of the manual worker in society, and critiques of Marxism and the concept of technological progress. The second period, after 1937, might be called 'mystical', though she did not at any time give up her commitment to rational understanding. In this later phase she developed in a striking manner the important insights into ancient philosophy and Christianity which have given her a considerable reputation as a Christian mystic, though one who, true to her convictions, refused baptism. In her social thought she emphasized the spiritual value of physical labour, offered a vision of a post-capitalist society which did not separate physical from mental labour, and developed a political theory based on duties instead of rights, duties which provided for the deepest spiritual needs.   FR

Reading

†Pétrement, S.: *Simone Weil: A Life*, trans. R. Rosenthal. Oxford: Mowbray, 1977.

†Rosen, F.: Marxism, mysticism and liberty: the influence of Simone Weil on Albert Camus. *Political Theory* 7 (1979) 301–19.

Weil, S.: *L'Enracinement. Prélude à une déclaration des*

devoirs envers l'être humain. Paris: Gallimard, 1950; *The Need for Roots*, trans. A. Wills, London: Routledge & Kegan Paul, 1952.

————: *La Condition ouvrière.* Paris: Gallimard, 1951.

————: *Oppression et liberté.* Paris: Gallimard, 1955; *Oppression and Liberty*, trans. A. Wills and J. Petrie. London: Routledge & Kegan Paul, 1958.

————: *Écrits historiques et politiques.* Paris: Gallimard, 1960.

welfare state The term describes collectively a range of social policies that aim to provide basic services such as health and education according to need, and normally free of charge, through state funding. It is sometimes extended more loosely to areas such as social security in which individuals are legally required to make substantial contributions in order to receive the benefit. The term came into use during the 1940s at a time when (in Britain especially) the role of government in this field was expanding rapidly.

The existence of some form of welfare state is now accepted across most of the political spectrum, and radically challenged only by libertarians, for whom it represents a violation of the rights of those who are taxed to provide its funding (see LIBERTARIANISM). The major point of debate is whether it should be regarded as a safety-net, establishing a minimum level of welfare beneath which no one is allowed to fall, or as an agency of redistribution from rich to poor, fostering greater social equality. These alternatives broadly mirror the division between traditional LIBERALISM and SOCIAL DEMOCRACY.

DLM

Reading
Timms, N. ed.: *Social Welfare: Why and How?* London: Routledge & Kegan Paul, 1980.

William of Ockham (*c.*1280/5–1349) Born in Surrey, Ockham entered the Franciscan order, and then studied in Oxford where as an apprentice Bachelor of Theology he commented (*c.*1317–19) on *The Sentences* of Peter Lombard to obtain his doctorate. This, however, he never achieved for in 1323 fifty-six extracts from his writings were taken by the recent chancellor of Oxford, John Lutterell, and presented for censure before the pope who

was then resident in Avignon. Ockham was summoned to defend his views; he was censured but not excommunicated. In 1328 he defected to the court of the Holy Roman Emperor, Louis of Bavaria, along with the Minister General of the Franciscans, Michael of Cesena. He spent the rest of his life as a political polemicist writing against papal pretensions to a plenitude of power in affairs spiritual and temporal.

His career can be divided into two parts: his philosophical, logical, and theological period at Oxford, and the period after 1328 when he was a political publicist writing to vindicate his Order and his imperial protector against the papacy.

His conception of logic was central to his outlook as a means of ordering knowledge and ascertaining the degrees of certainty which men can attain. He argued that there is a distinction to be made between the individual nature of all being and the universal nature of our concepts on the one hand, and the terms we use to constitute proper knowledge on the other. He has thus been classified as a *nominalist*, although this is much debated. His concern was to account for universals in a world of individuals. He identified God's own nature and His freedom as creator with God's law, the *lex evangelica*, which he further called a *lex libertatis*, a law of liberty.

Ockham argued that the function of temporal rulers was to chastise and punish wrongdoers and to defend the church from them. The church has exclusively spiritual power and is subject to the lay ruler with regard to the church's temporalities. Temporal and spiritual powers do not correspond to two distinct orders of nature and grace; rather the reality of temporal and spiritual power exists because of the individuals who constitute the respective temporal and spiritual orders. In each, as in all of creation, only the individual is real. In Christian society the spiritual and temporal powers embrace the same individuals who are both baptised members of the church *and* subjects of temporal rulers as citizens. Divine law governs the church and human laws regulate kingdoms.

According to Ockham, Christ, like St Francis and his followers, only used what was necessary to sustain life, and such use rather than ownership or possession of necessities was a natural right given to all men to keep themselves alive. This natural right came before all legal rights of possession. Ockham was not simply defending Franciscan poverty; he also argued against papal encroachment on the sphere of imperial autonomy when he sought to explain how ownership and possession resulted from the Fall. He accepted a *de facto* imperfection of fallen nature which was then expressed in human positive law. This was contrasted with the ideal of spiritual perfection exemplified in natural (divine) law. In his *Dialogus* he is more specific about the scope of papal power, circumscribed by evangelical law conferred on Peter by Christ: the church administers sacraments, ordains priests, instructs the faithful and the like. Right reason and the natural law rule the church; similarly right reason and natural law permit the existence of less than perfect temporal kingdoms. The ideal therefore circumscribes the activities of the church, and the state is left to be authoritative and autonomous in its own sphere. Within the temporal sphere, legitimacy is assured when the consent of those governed is obtained and the common good is pursued.

Sovereignty derives from the people, who have the natural power to make laws and institute rulers. But because the temporal sphere is imperfect, secular sovereignty may be legitimate even when tyrannical. Once conferred voluntarily by the people, legitimate authority can only be retracted in extreme circumstances – when the ruler commits egregious sins or crimes. Ockham sees the political realm as largely incapable of achieving its ideals; he therefore grants legitimate power to a sovereign secular government even when the people have been deprived of their power by wrongdoing, by transference, by purchase, donation, hereditary succession, by just war, i.e. by the legitimacy conferred by the *ius fori*, a result of a compact or a human ordinance such as custom. And once established by human positive law, Ockham says, the state must be accepted by those over whom it exercises its power. He has, in the political sphere, virtually nullified the power of the people to give their initial consent to a sovereign by asserting that, once installed, the ruler assumes all authority so long as his jurisdiction remains useful and advantageous to the common good. There is no social contract based on a revocable grant of popular representation except in the most extreme cases of scandal or criminality when the people's allegiance may be revoked.

This view results from Ockham's theological argument that all human sovereignty over men and things is a result of the Fall. *Dominium* was not granted eternally to all men according to right reason, but instead the power to own and rule was due to a contingent circumstance of Adam's sin, without which it would not have occurred. Before the Fall, Adam and Eve had a perfect, miraculous, non-proprietary power over all things and they ruled things with reason rather than by coercion. They simply used things as they needed them. There was no common *ownership* either before or after the Fall. After their sin they acquired the *power* to appropriate and divide things. Positive law *thereafter* regulates appropriation and division, ownership, and possession. Original *dominium* as enjoyed by Adam and Eve came from God: lordship and possession was an expression of human institution and will. Temporal authority accompanied property ownership and was a consequence of the Fall, and thus temporal sovereignty is regulated by positive as opposed to natural law. This is why temporal authorities are independent of ecclesiastical sanction. The development of the legitimacy of temporal power was a development common to all men, infidel and Christian, which God sanctioned, and it had nothing to do with the institutional church, nor with a supernatural gift.

Ockham's logic, theology, and his political writings were enormously influential during the fourteenth and fifteenth centuries. His assessment of papal power was widely read during the period of the Great Schism and the fifteenth-century reforming church councils. (See also MEDIEVAL POLITICAL THOUGHT.)   JC

Reading

†Leff, G.: *William of Ockham: the metamorphosis of scholastic discourse*. Manchester: Manchester University Press, 1975.

†McGrade, A.S.: *The Political Thought of William of Ockham*. Cambridge: Cambridge University Press, 1974.

————: Ockham and the birth of individual rights. In *Authority and Power*, ed. B. Tierney and P. Linehan. Cambridge: Cambridge University Press, 1980.

William of Ockham: *Opera Politica*, ed. J.G. Sikes and H.S. Offler. 3 vols. Manchester: Manchester University Press, 1940–74.

Winstanley, Gerrard (*c.*1609–1660) British radical pamphleteer. Leader of the Digger movement during the English Civil War, his best-known work was *The Laws of Freedom in a Platform* (1652). See LEVELLERS.

Wollstonecraft, Mary (1759–1797) British writer on political and social themes, novelist, reviewer and essayist. Mary Wollstonecraft has long been regarded as the intellectual pioneer of modern FEMINISM. Her most famous work, *A Vindication of the Rights of Woman* (1792), was unrivalled in its influence among sexual egalitarians until the appearance of J. S. MILL's *The Subjection of Women* (1869). Her difficult, quixotic personal life (as revealed by her husband, William GODWIN, in a posthumous *Memoir*), simultaneously shocked and fascinated her contemporaries – and has inspired dozens of biographies since. In the two centuries following her death, the woman and her work have acquired a symbolic significance unmatched by any other British feminist of her own or succeeding generations.

Yet despite this, or perhaps because of it, the actual substance of Wollstonecraft's political and social thought remains curiously under-explored. The arguments of the *Vindication* itself – complex, fragmented, in part derivative and yet strikingly innovative – have rarely been accorded more than summary treatment; her other works (which include two novels, a reply to Burke's *Reflections on the Revolution in France*, and a history of the French Revolution) have attracted little serious attention. Histories of political thought mention her, if at all, only as a minor figure within the tradition variously described as Lockeian liberalism, natural rights radicalism, or 'possessive individualism'; her feminism likewise is usually regarded simply as an application of the egalitarian perspectives of classical liberalism to the position of women. Historians of feminism have, for the most part, uncritically adopted this assessment, while adding to it the (Marxist, or quasi-Marxist) view of eighteenth-century liberalism as the ideology of a rising bourgeoisie: the image of Wollstonecraft which emerges is that of a middle-class reformer concerned to secure for her sex equal access to those privileges sought by the men of her class.

It is an assessment which singularly fails to illuminate either the style of political and social radicalism from which feminism emerged (see RADICALS, BRITISH) or the specific character of feminist discourse itself. The central preoccupation of *A Vindication of the Rights of Woman* is not with the position of middle-class women as subordinate members of a newly ascendant class, nor even (despite its title) with the entire sex's lack of legal, political, or economic rights. Rather, like most of Wollstonecraft's works, it is a highly complex study of womanhood itself; an intricate exploration of what she describes as the 'distinction of sex' and its implications for women's social and subjective experience. Above all, written at a time when woman's nature and capacities were identified almost wholly with her sexual functions, the *Vindication* is a bitter polemic against the imprisonment of female selfhood within feminine sexuality. The subjugation of brain to body, soul to sensuality, Wollstonecraft argues, enslaves and corrupts women – and, through them, society as a whole. Against this predominant definition of the eternal Eve she offers her alternative vision of the naturally genderless spirit – the rational, moral essence of every individual – whose liberation from artificially-induced sensualism will raise womankind from subjection to full, independent subjecthood – to a 'character as human being', in her words, 'regardless of the distinction of sex'.

This was not Wollstonecraft's project alone, but rather one of the defining features of the early feminist tradition as a whole. Formal equality with men, although certainly a key aim, was generally viewed as ancillary to the radical transformation of womanhood itself; a 'revolution in female manners', in Wollstonecraft's words, which would revolutionize the entire subjective dimension of male/female relations.

Viewing Wollstonecraft's feminist project in this light also brings her relationship to co-existing intellectual traditions into much sharper focus. As a political ideologue, Wollstonecraft espoused that visionary, world-regenerating brand of democratic radicalism (deeply influenced by ROUSSEAU) which reached a highpoint in the Godwinian-Jacobin circle to which she belonged. One of the least explored features of this style of radicalism was its preoccupation with the establishment of a right order in sexual relations as the key to the creation of a just social order (an aspiration which flowed into ROMANTICISM and later into utopian socialism). Wollstonecraft's views on women were clearly part of this wider sexual agenda shared by most of the leading radicals of her day: an agenda which, in the wake of counter-revolutionary panic in Britain, became the target of fierce conservative attack. Wollstonecraft in particular became the object of so much vilification that even in the 1880s many feminists were reluctant to claim her as a political ancestor, or if they did so it was by aligning her with the now highly respectable tradition of liberal politics while carefully ignoring those features of her radicalism which fell outside that political compass. Current studies, however, under the influence of the contemporary women's movement, are gradually re-encountering and re-claiming Wollstonecraft's feminist radicalism both in its own context and in relation to the preoccupations of late twentieth-century feminism.   BGT

Reading

Eisenstein, Z.: *The Radical Future of Liberal Feminism*, ch. 5. London: Longman, 1981.

Poovey, M.: *The Proper Lady and the Woman Writer*. London: University of Chicago Press, 1984.

†Taylor, B.: *Eve and the New Jerusalem: Socialism and Feminism in the Nineteenth Century*, ch. 1. London: Virago, 1983.

†Todd, J.: *Mary Wollstonecraft: an Annotated Bibliography*. London: Garland, 1976.

Wardle, R.: *Mary Wollstonecraft: a Critical Biography*. Lincoln: University of Kansas Press, 1966.

Wollstonecraft, M.: *A Vindication of the Rights of Woman*, ed. M. Kramnick. Harmondsworth: Penguin, 1982.

Y

Young Hegelians Disciples of the German philosopher G. W. F. HEGEL, characterized and brought together by their stress on the radical theological and political implications of Hegel's thought. These they saw as exposing the 'contradictions' and mystification on which established religion and the Prussian monarchy (and other monarchies) rested. This brought them into conflict with Old or Right Hegelians who followed the Master's view that the real was rational, that Protestant Christianity embodied the truths of philosophy in pictorial form and that the Prussian monarchy and civil service approximated to the rational state, with an undivided sovereign will and a bureaucracy acting impartially in the public interest. Increasingly anti-theological, republican, democratic and even revolutionary, the Young Hegelians stood for human emancipation, substituting individual consciousness, or the universal consciousness of the human species, for Hegel's objective spirit. They preached self-determination, and the overcoming of alienation and of divisiveness and particularity in social life. They thus implicitly stressed Kantian and Fichtian themes in Hegel's work, especially KANT's elevation of autonomy and universality, without subordinating these to the systematic and 'external' structures that Hegel thought necessary to make freedom rational.

Leading members of the group were David Friedrich Strauss (1808–74), Ludwig FEUER-BACH (1804–72), Bruno Bauer (1809–82) and his brother Edgar (1820–86), Arnold Ruge (1803–80), Max STIRNER (real name Johann Caspar Schmidt, 1806–56) and Moses Hess (1812–75). Between 1839 and 1842 the young Karl MARX and, separately, Friedrich ENGELS were associated with members of this group and were strongly influenced by them. By 1844 Marx and Engels had become sharply critical of the Young Hegelians for their elevation of theoretical criticism and of consciousness, and their neglect of social and material realities; in 1845/6 they denounced them in *The German Ideology*. The failure of the 1848 Revolution and the decline of Hegelian philosophical influence in the Germany of the 1850s and 1860s spelt an end to the Young Hegelians as a movement. They went their separate ways and are now studied chiefly for their role in the intellectual evolution of MARXISM. Ludwig Feuerbach, whose reputation long overshadowed those of the other Young Hegelians, became less and less Hegelian in the 1840s; he remains, however, an important figure in the critique of religion and the history of theology. Moses Hess has attracted independent interest as Germany's first communist, preceding Marx in that role, and as the author of *Rome and Jerusalem* (1862), an important text in the making of modern Zionism. Another writer loosely attached to the group was the Polish nobleman August von Cieszkowski (1814–94) who came to Berlin in 1832 and whose *Prolegomena zur Historiosophie* (1838) attracted interest then, and again recently, by carrying Young Hegelian positions beyond philosophy to a demand that practical action, 'spontaneous, willed and free', be applied to change the world.

Intimations of the scandal to be caused by the Young Hegelians and of the potentially radical implications of the Hegelian method were first given by the publication, anonymously, in 1830, of Ludwig Feuerbach's

Thoughts on Death and Immortality. Here Feuerbach denied, on Hegelian grounds, the possibility of personal survival after death. He argued that the doctrine represented a confused realization of the infinity and immortality of the human species, which alone was capable of adopting the standpoint of the infinite spirit. The scandal grew greater and the split between Hegel's disciples became open with the publication of D. F. Strauss's *Life of Jesus* in 1835/6. It flatly denied the historicity of the supernatural acts and attributes ascribed to Jesus in the New Testament. The story of Jesus was that of a human life around which the Early Church wove a series of myths – projections of human longings and experiences that contain spiritual not literal truth – a view Strauss also ascribed to Hegel. The concept of incarnation correctly recognises that Man – in the sense of humanity, encompassing all human beings – has divine characteristics. The book produced a controversy in which the Hegelian School fell into fairly clear divisions. These Strauss himself designated, on the model of the French parliament, as Left, Centre and Right – with himself on the Left.

In Berlin, Bruno Bauer argued that the Gospels reflected the historical conditions of the Early Church in the Roman Empire and, at a deeper level, the inability to sustain a conception of individual human self-consciousness in those conditions except by conceiving it as a divine power separated from man. Religion was thus a form of ALIENATION, particularly of self-alienation in which the universal self could only be conceived as existing outside Man. This line of thought reached its culmination and made its maximum popular impact with the publication of Ludwig Feuerbach's *Essence of Christianity* (1841), which systematically worked out and proclaimed the real content of religion: a celebration of the divine potentialities and attributes of the human species, capable of love, reason and will but fallen into servitude through its alienation of these qualities from itself and its projection of them into another, divine, being. What is given to God is stolen from Man – what religion celebrates, theology takes away and gives to another.

While the thought of the Young Hegelians in the 1830s was largely confined to the discussion of religion, it indicated ever more clearly their rejection of any Hegelian reconciliation with external systems and necessities and their insistence that man's destiny was to take all his capacities and powers back into himself, that every human being was capable of full and active citizenship. In German conditions the Young Hegelians saw themselves as heirs of the FRENCH ENLIGHTENMENT and of the heroes of the French Revolution, calling for a free and democratic Europe, secular and scientific. They were exposing superstition and heteronomy, showing that rationality required that science and education, human mastery over natural and social conditions, replace religion and political dependence and alienation. It is not surprising, given the censorship and police controls of the time, that the Young Hegelians were largely journalists and free intellectuals, dismissed from university posts or failing to gain them, while the Old Hegelians – though often liberal – accommodated themselves to the system and held important academic posts within it.

Nevertheless, the line between Old and Young Hegelian was not always as sharp as might be expected. Bruno Bauer was appointed to a lectureship in theology in the University of Berlin as a Right Hegelian philosopher of religion and dismissed when he became an atheist. Arnold Ruge, who formed the Hegelian review *Hallische Jahrbücher für deutsche Wissenschaft und Kunst* in 1838, opened the journal to all Hegelian tendencies, though he moved quickly to the Left. The journal got into trouble with the censorship in 1842, to become the more decidedly Left Hegelian *Deutsche Jahrbücher*. But it was with the (short-lived) relaxation of censorship in 1840, on the accession of the anti-Hegelian Christian-Romantic Frederick William IV, that the Young Hegelians and the *Hallische Jahrbücher*, now their organ, turned more frankly to politics, elevating Critical Critique and exposing alienation not only in religion but in the monarch, the Christian state and, as Moses Hess came to argue, in money.

Cieszkowski, in his *Prolegomena*, had argued that the end of history is the rational freedom and eventual divinity of mankind; Moses Hess in *The European Triarchy* (1841) called for an alliance between France, Prussia and England to topple Austrian and Russian reaction and to make possible a completely free Europe. Ruge began to criticize Hegel's political philosophy. Bruno and Edgar Bauer devoted themselves to the study of the French Revolution, to the emancipation of mankind from theological thinking in politics as well as in religion, to the emancipation of the Jews and to the 'spiritualization' of the masses. Only Max Stirner remained a maverick extremist, attacking all attempts to 'determine' man and proclaiming an amoral egoism as the true emancipation. His *The Ego and his Own* (1844) – the main butt of Marx's and Engels's criticism in *The German Ideology* – has had more influence on the European Right and on Fascism than on the Left, though he has also been admired, in part for his educational writings, by radical libertarian anarchists.

Renewed government measures against the radical press in 1842–3 scattered the Young Hegelians in and outside Germany and exacerbated their confusion about practical measures. Some remained radical democrats while others, like Hess, Marx and Engels, became active and committed communists. The years 1848–9 spelt failure for them all; many moved to the right. Today, politically, they are only of historical interest; philosophically, they helped to bring out, and establish in the subsequent literature, the tension between Hegel's system and his dialectical critical method.   EK

Reading

Hook, S.: *From Hegel to Marx: studies in the intellectual development of Karl Marx*, 2nd edn with a new intro. New York and Toronto: University of Michigan Press, 1962.

†Kamenka, E.: *The Philosophy of Ludwig Feuerbach*. London: Routledge & Kegan Paul, 1970.

———: *The Ethical Foundations of Marxism*, rev. edn. London: Routledge & Kegan Paul, 1972.

†McLellan, D.: *The Young Hegelians and Karl Marx*. New York: Praeger, 1969.

†Stepelevich, L.S. ed.: *The Young Hegelians: an anthology*. Cambridge: Cambridge University Press, 1983.

Stirner, M.: *The Ego and his Own*, trans. S.T. Byington, ed. J. Carroll. London: Cape, 1971.

Index

The Editors and Publishers are grateful to Mary Norris who compiled the index.
Page references to major entries on a subject are in bold type.